Social Psychology

TENTH EDITION

SAUL KASSIN
JOHN JAY COLLEGE OF CRIMINAL JUSTICE

STEVEN FEIN
WILLIAMS COLLEGE

HAZEL ROSE MARKUS
STANFORD UNIVERSITY

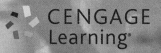
CENGAGE
Learning®

Australia • Brazil • Mexico • Singapore
United Kingdom • United States

CENGAGE Learning®

***Social Psychology*, Tenth Edition**
Saul Kassin, Steven Fein, and
Hazel Rose Markus

Product Director: Jon Goodspeed

Product Manager: Melissa Gena

Content Developer: Tangelique Williams-Grayer

Product Assistant: Kimiya Hojjat

Marketing Manager: Melissa Larmon

Content Project Manager: Michelle Clark

Art Director: Vernon Boes

Manufacturing Planner: Karen Hunt

Production Service: Graphic World Inc

Text and Photo Researcher: Lumina Datamatics

Copy Editor: Graphic World Inc

Illustrator: Graphic World Inc

Text Designer: Marsha Cohen

Cover Designer: Irene Morris

Cover Image: Jorge Lizana Photo /
Getty Images

Compositor: Graphic World Inc

For product information and technology assistance, contact us at
Cengage Learning Customer & Sales Support, 1-800-354-9706.

For permission to use material from this text or product,
submit all requests online at **www.cengage.com/permissions**.
Further permissions questions can be e-mailed to
permissionrequestcengage.com.

Library of Congress Control Number: 2015959689

Student Edition:
ISBN: 978-1-305-58022-0

Loose-leaf Edition:
ISBN: 978-1-305-86313-2

Cengage Learning
20 Channel Center Street
Boston, MA 02210
USA

Cengage Learning is a leading provider of customized learning solutions with employees residing in nearly 40 different countries and sales in more than 125 countries around the world. Find your local representative at **www.cengage.com**.

Cengage Learning products are represented in Canada by Nelson Education, Ltd.

To learn more about Cengage Learning Solutions, visit **www.cengage.com**.

Purchase any of our products at your local college store or at our preferred online store **www.cengagebrain.com**.

Printed in the United States of America
Print Number: 02   Print Year: 2017

We dedicate this book to our children: Briana, Marc, Andrew, Malin, Jordan, Elle, Alina, Hannah, and Krysia.

Brief Contents

Contents

Part 2   Social Perception

3. The Social Self | 52

4. Perceiving Persons | 104

5. Stereotypes, Prejudice, and Discrimination | 154

Part 3   Social Influence

6. Attitudes | 208

Putting Common Sense to the Test | 210

Part 4   Social Relations

9. Attraction and Close Relationships | 350

10. Helping Others | 408

11. Aggression | 452

Part 5   Applying Social Psychology

12.   Law | 504

14. Health and Well-Being | 600

The opening years of the twenty-first century have proved to be an exciting and tumultuous time—more so, it seems, than any in recent memory. On the one hand, thanks to the rise of Facebook, Twitter, Skype, YouTube, Instagram, Snapchat, and other social media, all of which are available on mobile apps, wherever we are, it has never been easier to be "social"—to talk to others or share opinions, pictures, music, and footage of live events as they occur with people from all corners of the world. On the other hand, deep social and political divisions; religious and ethnic conflicts all over the world; economic disparities; and an ever-present threat of terrorism surround us. As Charles Dickens (1859) said in *A Tale of Two Cities*, "It was the best of times, it was the worst of times."

Encircled by its place in science and world events, social psychology—its theories, research methods, and basic findings—has never been more relevant or more important. We used to think of social psychology as a discipline that is slow to change. As in other sciences, we thought, knowledge builds in small increments, one brick at a time. Social psychology has no "critical" experiments, no single study can "prove" a theory, and no single theory can fully explain the complexities of human social behavior. While all this remains true, the process of revising this textbook always seems to show us how complex, dynamic, and responsive our field can be. As the world around us rapidly changes, so too does social psychology. Whether the topic is world news, politics, business, health, education, law, travel, sports, or entertainment, social psychology has weighed in.

Despite the promise that it has fulfilled and brings to the future, social psychology has recently been rocked by scandal and controversy. Three events in particular have weighed on the field. First, in 2011, a social psychologist in the Netherlands was found to have falsified data that were published in some fifty articles. That case was followed by two other instances of fraud and a paper that survived peer review at *JPSP* purporting to prove ESP. Second, after an exhaustive multiyear effort to replicate 100 published studies, a group of social psychologists reported in *Science*, in 2015, that more than half of the findings they sought to replicate failed when retested. This finding was heavily reported in the news media, as seen in *The New York Times* article, "Many Psychology Findings Not as Strong as Claimed, Study Says." Third, a "political" controversy has erupted over the question of whether social psychology research is inherently biased by a liberal ideology. This debate—in terms of how ideology can influence what researchers choose to study and how they interpret the results—continues unabated as we revise this book.

It is clear that social psychology is undergoing a process of self-examination. This has led the field to adopt new, more rigorous methods, statistical practices, and safeguards, and it has led us to raise the bar in the standards we use to decide which new findings to report. What has not changed in this reassessment is the enthusiasm with which we present classic and contemporary social psychology in each and every page of this textbook.

Goals for This Edition

In the competitive college textbook business, it is a rare and special milestone to publish a tenth edition and span thirty years in print. Being the brainchild and inspiration of Sharon Brehm, our first lead author, the inaugural edition of this book was published in 1990—before any of us had access to the Internet or a cell phone and before e-books were an option. In countless ways, the world was a simpler and far different place. Yet human nature—our fundamental need to belong, and to be accepted; our deeply rooted and profound vulnerability to social influence, to satisfy these needs; and the range of settings in which social psychology is on display—has remained very much the same. The continuity of social psychology over time, its contributions to the field of psychology as a whole, and its acceptance within other professions and popular culture, has never been so clear.

We had three main goals for this revision.

1. Our first goal was to present the most important and exciting perspectives in the field as a whole. To communicate the breadth and depth of social psychology, we have self-consciously expanded our coverage to include not only the classics but also the most recent developments in the field—developments that capture new thinking about social neuroscience, evolutionary theory, nonconscious and implicit processes, effects of social media and technology, and cultural influences.

2. In light of questions that have surfaced concerning replicability, our second goal was to try to vet brand new findings in an effort to ensure that the discipline we present will prove accurate over time. No method of vetting is perfect. But as a departure from past practice, we have chosen to exclude any research presented at professional conferences or reported in the news that has not been published in a peer-reviewed journal. For articles newly published, we sought to determine if the findings were consistent with other research.

3. Finally, we want this book to serve as a good teacher outside the classroom. While speaking the student's language, we always want to connect social psychology to current events in politics, sports, business, law, music, travel, entertainment, the use of social networking sites, and other life domains. We will say more about this later in the preface, in the section, "Connections With Current Events."

What's New in This Edition

As in the past, we have tried both to capture the essence of social psychology from its inception as well as to reflect the shifts within the field over time and culture. It is our hope that the reader will feel the pulse of our field *today* in each and every page.

■ The Content

Comprehensive, Up-to-Date Scholarship Like its predecessors, the tenth edition offers a broad, balanced, mainstream look at social psychology. Thus, it includes detailed descriptions of classic studies from social psychology's historical warehouse as well as the latest research findings from hundreds of new references. In particular, we draw your attention to the following topics, which are either new to this edition or have received expanded coverage:

- The social brain and body (Chapter 1)
- The challenges of doing research across cultures (Chapter 2)
- Ethics and consent in online research (Chapter 2)
- Facebook as a venue for social comparison (Chapter 3)
- Social class as a cultural influence (Chapter 3)
- Attributing mind to machines (Chapter 4)
- Perceptions of moral character (Chapter 4)
- Racial tensions sparked by police shootings and ensuing protests (Chapter 5)
- New research and discussion of dehumanization (Chapter 5)
- Ethical dissonance (Chapter 6)
- Engaged followership model of obedience (Chapter 7)
- Collective intelligence: Are some groups smarter than others? (Chapter 8)
- Uses of technology to train real decision-making groups (Chapter 8)
- New research on online dating (Chapter 9)
- Mate selection and conspicuous consumption (Chapter 9)
- Neuroscience of empathy (Chapter 10)
- Social influences on helping in philanthropy (Chapter 10)
- Evolutionary psychology approaches to aggression (Chapter 11)
- Effects of genes, hormones, and brain functioning on aggression (Chapter 11)
- Alibis as eyewitnesses to innocence (Chapter 12)
- Pleading guilty in the shadow of trial (Chapter 12)
- Cybervetting in personnel selection (Chapter 13)
- Cultural influences on leadership (Chapter 13)
- The link between social class and health (Chapter 14)
- Cultural differences in social support seeking (Chapter 14)

As this nonexhaustive list shows, this tenth edition contains new—and newsy—material. In particular, you may notice that we have zeroed in on new developments in *social neuroscience, evolutionary theory, implicit and nonconscious processes, effects of social media and technology,* and *cultural perspectives*—including social class and racial and ethnic groups within cultures. As to this latter point, as social psychology is now a truly international discipline, this book routinely cites new research conducted throughout North and South America, Europe, Asia, Australia, and other parts of the world. We believe that the study of human diversity—from the perspectives of researchers who themselves are a diverse lot—can help students become better informed about social relations as well as about ethics and values.

Connections With Current Events To cover social psychology is one thing; to *use* its principles to explain events in the real world is quite another. Fifteen years ago, the events of 9/11 changed the world. In different ways not fully discernible, so did the severe economic recession—and slow recovery—in the United States and Europe; the rise of China as an economic power; the changes that have swept through the Middle East, as seen in the sudden rise of ISIS; the increasing threat of violence, as seen in mass shootings in the United States and terrorism in Paris and throughout the world; the racial tensions between police and citizens, which has spawned the "Black Lives Matter" movement; and the ease with which people can now meet, interact, and share services—as seen in the global rise of Uber and Airbnb—through online social networking sites on mobile devices. More than ever, connecting basic theory to real life is the best way to heighten student interest. Over the years, teachers and students have told us how much they value the "newsy" features of our book.

The tenth edition, like its predecessors, is committed to making social psychology *relevant.* Almost every page includes a passage, a quote, a figure, a table, a photo, or a cartoon that refers to people, places, events, music, social trends, and issues that are prominent in contemporary culture. The reader will find stories about the events in Ferguson, Missouri, and elsewhere; Edward Snowden, and his disclosures about mass surveillance; ongoing political debates over same-sex marriage and immigration; cases in the news—such as the South Africa trial of Olympian Oskar Pistorius; and the role of Facebook and other social media in bringing people together—for good purposes and bad.

As in past editions, you will also find in the margins various quotations, song lyrics, public opinion poll results, "factoids," and links to relevant websites. These high-interest items are designed to further illustrate the connectedness of social psychology to a world that extends beyond the borders of a college campus.

Social Psychology and Common Sense Several years ago, we introduced a feature that we remain excited about. Building on a discussion in Chapter 1 about the links (and lack thereof) between social psychology and common sense, each substantive chapter opens with *Putting Common Sense to the Test,* a set of true–false questions designed to assess the student's intuitive beliefs about material later contained in that chapter. Some examples: "Sometimes the harder you try to control a thought, feeling, or behavior, the less likely you are to succeed," "People often come to like what they suffer for," and "Opposites attract." The answers to these questions are revealed in a marginal box after the topic is presented in the text and then explained at the end of each chapter. We think that students will find this exercise engaging. It will also enable them, as they read, to check their intuitive beliefs against the findings of social psychology and to notice the discrepancies that exist.

■ The Organization

Of all the challenges faced by teachers and textbooks, perhaps the greatest is to put information together in a way that is both accurate and easy to understand. A strong organizational framework helps in meeting this challenge. There is nothing worse for a student than having to wade through a "laundry list" of names, dates, and studies whose interconnections remain a profound mystery. A strong structure thus facilitates the development of conceptual understanding.

But the tail should not wag the dog. Since organizational structure is a means to an end, not an end in itself, we want to keep it simple and unobtrusive. Look through the Table of Contents, and you will see that we present social psychology in five major parts—a heuristic structure that teachers and students have found sensible and easy to follow through nine editions. The book opens with two *Introduction* chapters on the history, subject matter, and research methods of social psychology (Part I). As before, we then move to an intraindividual focus on *Social Perception* (Part II), shift outward to *Social Influence* (Part III) and *Social Relations* (Part IV), and then conclude with *Applying Social Psychology* (Part V). We realize that some instructors like to reshuffle the deck to develop a chapter order that better fits their own approach. There is no problem in doing this. Each chapter stands on its own and does not require that others be read first.

The Presentation

Even when the content of a textbook is accurate and up to date, and even when its organization is sound, there is still the matter of presentation. As the "teacher outside the classroom," a good textbook should facilitate learning. Thus, every chapter contains the following pedagogical features:

- An abstract, chapter outline, and common-sense quiz (beginning with Chapter 3).

- Key terms highlighted in the text, defined in the margin, listed at the end of the chapter, and reprinted in an alphabetized glossary at the end of the book.

- Bar graphs, line graphs, tables, sketches, photographs, flow charts, and cartoons that illustrate, extend, enhance, and enliven material in the text. Some of these depict historic images; others, more contemporary, are new to the tenth edition and often "newsy."

- At the end of each chapter, a numbered list of "Top 10 Key Points" designed to provide students with a shorthand summary the major takeaway messages.

MindTap for Kassin, Fein, and Markus's *Social Psychology*

MindTap is a personalized teaching experience with relevant assignments that guide students to analyze, apply, and improve thinking, allowing you to measure skills and outcomes with ease.

- **Personalized Teaching:** Becomes yours with a Learning Path that is built with key student objectives. Control what students see and when they see it. Use it as-is or match to your syllabus exactly—hide, rearrange, add and create your own content.

- **Guide Students:** A unique learning path of relevant readings, multimedia, and activities that move students up the learning taxonomy from basic knowledge and comprehension to analysis and application.

- **Promote Better Outcomes:** Empower instructors and motivate students with analytics and reports that provide a snapshot of class progress, time in course, engagement and completion rates.

In addition to the benefits of the platform, MindTap for Kassin, Fein, and Markus's *Social Psychology* features:

- Videos and animations, all based on key social psychology topics and concepts.

- Chapter-opening assignments, including choose-your-own-activity style exercises, videos, animations, and polling questions which all integrate supporting social psychology research.

■ Supplements

Instructor's Resource Manual In each chapter of the Online Instructor's Resource Manual ISBN: 9781305968004, we provide:

- **Learning Objectives.** A listing of what students should be able to do after reading.

- **A Detailed Overview.** A comprehensive review, with key points highlighted and key terms listed.

- **Lecture/discussion ideas.** Many ways to introduce and discuss topics with students, including video suggestions and extended examples.

- **Class activity ideas.** Helpful prompts, including hand-out suggestions, for in-class activities. Each idea includes a "What if this bombs?" section for when executing an idea does not go as expected.

- **Multimedia resources.** An annotated list of related videos, websites, YouTube clips, computer programs, and video clip suggestions from the Research in Action collection from Cengage Learning.

- **Handouts.** Helpful handouts for students that correlate with suggested activities and homework.

- **MindTap Instructor's Resource Center.** Descriptions of assets and tools to integrate into your course in MindTap.

Cognero Cengage Learning Testing Powered by Cognero is a flexible, online system that allows you to author, edit, and manage test bank content from multiple Cengage Learning solutions, create multiple test versions in an instant, and deliver tests from your Learning Management System (LMS), your classroom, or wherever you want.
ISBN: 9781305856950

PowerPoint, online, features lecture outlines and key images from the text.
ISBN: 9781305967755

Acknowledgments

Textbooks are the product of a team effort—more today than ever before. We are grateful to Cengage Learning for its commitment to quality as the first priority. First, we want to thank Tangelique Williams-Grayer, our content developer. We also want to express our gratitude to Roman Barnes, our photo researcher, who has helped to make this book so photographically interesting. Finally, we want to thank all those whose considerable talents and countless hours of hard work can be seen on every page: Cassie Carey, Senior Project Manager, Graphic World; Michelle Clark, Senior Content Production Manager; and Kimiya Hojjat, Product Assistant. We also thank Publisher Jon-David Hague and Product Manager, Melissa Gena.

Over years, several colleagues have guided us through their feedback on prior editions. Every one of these teachers and scholars has helped to make this a better book. For their invaluable insights, comments, and suggestions, we thank the following reviewers of our more recent editions:

William Adler, *Collin County College*

Craig Anderson, *Iowa State University*

Dan Batson, *University of Kansas*

Lorraine Benuto, *University of Nevada, Las Vegas*

Bryan Bonner, *The University of Utah*

Rebecca Carey, *Stanford University*

Kimberly Coffman, *Florida International University*

John Dovidio, *Yale University*

Jean Egan, *Asnuntuck Community College*

Rebecca Francis, *West Virginia State University*

Rowell Huesmann, *University of Michigan*

Steven Karau, *Southern Illinois University*

John Levine, *University of Pittsburgh*

Mike Mangan, *University of New Hampshire, Durham*

Margo Monteith, *Purdue University*

Richard Moreland, *University of Pittsburgh*

Paul Paulus, *University of Texas at Arlington*

William Pedersen, *California State University, Long Beach*

Michele Reich, *Drexel University*

Todd Shackelford, *Oakland University*

Nicole Shelton, *Princeton University*

Jennifer Shibley, *Columbia College, Chicago*

Charles Stangor, *University of Maryland*

Nicole M. Stephens, *Northwestern University, Kellogg School of Management*

Arlene Stillwell, *SUNY College at Potsdam*

Eric Stocks, *University of Texas at Tyler*

Courtney von Hippel, *University of Queensland*

William von Hippel, *University of Queensland*

Gregory Walton, *Stanford University*

Kipling Williams, *Purdue University*

Elizabeth Williford, *Belhaven University*

Saul Kassin
Steven Fein
Hazel Rose Markus

SAUL KASSIN is Distinguished Professor of Psychology at John Jay College of Criminal Justice, in New York, and Massachusetts Professor of Psychology at Williams College in Williamstown, Massachusetts. Born and raised in Brooklyn, he received his Ph.D. from the University of Connecticut followed by fellowships at the University of Kansas and U.S. Supreme Court and a visiting professorship at Stanford University. In addition to authoring textbooks, he has co-authored and edited *Confessions in the Courtroom*, *The Psychology of Evidence and Trial Procedure*, and *The American Jury on Trial*. Interested in using social psychology to prevent wrongful convictions, Kassin pioneered the scientific study of police interrogations and false confessions several years ago, an interest that continues to this day. Kassin is past president of the American Psychology-Law Society and recipient of its Lifetime Contribution Award. He is also a Fellow of APS and APA. He has testified as an expert witness in state, military, and federal courts and has appeared as a media consultant in documentaries and on national news programs.

STEVEN FEIN is Professor of Psychology at Williams College, Williamstown, Massachusetts. Born and raised in Bayonne, New Jersey, he received his A.B. from Princeton University and his Ph.D. in social psychology from the University of Michigan. He has been teaching at Williams College since 1991, with time spent teaching at Stanford University in 1999. His edited books include *Emotion: Interdisciplinary Perspectives*, *Readings in Social Psychology: The Art and Science of Research*, and *Motivated Social Perception: The Ontario Symposium*. He has served on the executive committee of the Society of Personality and Social Psychology and as the social and personality psychology representative at the American Psychological Association. His research interests concern stereotyping and prejudice, suspicion and attributional processes, social influence, and self-affirmation theory.

HAZEL ROSE MARKUS is the Davis-Brack Professor in the Behavioral Sciences at Stanford University. She co-directs Stanford SPARQ (Social Psychological Answers to Real-world Questions) and also the Research Institute of the Stanford Center for Comparative Studies in Race and Ethnicity. Before moving to Stanford in 1994, she was a professor at the University of Michigan, where she received her Ph.D. Her work focuses on how the self-system, including current conceptions of self and possible selves, structures and lends meaning to experience. Born in England to English parents and raised in San Diego, California, she has been persistently fascinated by how nation of origin, region of the country, gender, ethnicity, race, religion, and social class shape self and identity. With her colleague Shinobu Kitayama at the University of Michigan, she has pioneered the experimental study of how culture and self influence one another. Markus was elected to the American Academy of Arts and Sciences in 1994, is a Fellow of APS, APA, and Division 8, and received the 2008 APA award for Distinguished Scientific Contribution. Some of her recent co-edited and co-authored books include *Culture and Emotion: Empirical Studies of Mutual Influence*, *Engaging Cultural Differences: The Multicultural Challenge in Liberal Democracies*, *Just Schools: Pursuing Equal Education in Societies of Difference*, and *Doing Race: 21 Essays for the 21st Century*, and *Clash! How to Thrive in a Multicultural World*.

Social Psychology

What Is Social Psychology?

This chapter introduces you to the study of social psychology. We begin by defining social psychology and identifying how it is distinct from but related to some other areas of study, both outside and within psychology. Next, we review the history of the field. We conclude by looking forward, with a discussion of the important themes and perspectives that are propelling social psychology today and in the years to come.

What Is Social Psychology? | 6

A Brief History of Social Psychology | 12

Social Psychology Today: What Is Trending Now? | 16

Review

We're certainly not one of the largest animals. But compared to the rest of the animal world, the size of the human brain, relative to the size of our bodies, is massive. Why is this? The most obvious explanation is that we're smarter, that we've mastered our environments to a degree no other animal has. But recent evidence suggests that the relatively huge size of the human brain—and particularly of the neocortex, at its outermost layer—may be due to something more specific, and rather surprising: We have such large brains in order to socialize (Dunbar, 2014; Spunt et al., 2015).

The remarkable success of our species can be traced to humans' ability to work together in groups, to infer others' intentions, to coordinate with extended networks of other people. Our brains needed to be able to handle the incredibly complex challenges associated with these tasks. Long ago Aristotle famously observed, "Man is by nature a social animal." Even Aristotle couldn't have imagined the degree to which that is true, that the social nature of humans seems to be written into our very DNA. Indeed, recent studies of brain activity have found that when the brain is basically at rest, not engaging in any active task, its default pattern of activity seems to involve social thinking, such as thinking about other people's thoughts and goals. Social neuroscientist Matthew Lieberman puts it, "Evolution has made a bet that the best thing for our brains to do in any spare moment is to get ready for what comes next in social terms" (E. E. Smith, 2013).

The social nature of the human animal is what this book, and the field of social psychology, is all about. The ways in which we are social animals are countless, and they can be obvious or incredibly subtle. We work, play, and live together. We hurt and help each other. We define happiness and success for each other. We forge our individual identities not alone but in the context of other people. We visit family, make friends, have parties, build networks, go on dates, pledge an enduring commitment, decide to have children. We watch others, speculate about them, and predict who will wind up with whom, whether in real life or in popular culture as we keep up with the Kardashians or watch *The Bachelorette*. Many of us text or tweet each other about everything we're up to, or we spend lots of time on social networking sites, interacting with countless peers from around the world, adding hundreds or even thousands of "friends" to our social networks. Our moods can fluctuate with the number of virtual friends who "like" our latest posted photo. Even being ignored by a stranger we don't really care about can be as painful as the experience of real physical pain (Eisenberger, 2015).

You've probably seen or at least heard about the movie *It's a Wonderful Life*. When the hero, George Bailey, is about to kill himself, the would-be angel Clarence doesn't save him by showing him how much personal happiness he'd miss if he ended his life. Instead, he shows George how much his life has touched the lives of others and how many people would be hurt if he was not a part of their world. It was these social relationships that saved George's life, just as they define our own.

Precisely because we need and care so much about social interactions and

> *"We take our bearings, daily, from others. To be sane is, to a great extent, to be sociable."*
>
> – John Updike

A woman eyes her many suitors on a summer 2015 episode of *The Bachelorette,* as viewers wondered which man the featured bachelorette might choose for possible marriage. The enormous popularity of shows like this illustrates part of the appeal of social psychology—people are fascinated with how we relate to one another.

Rick Rowell/Disney ABC Television Group/Getty Images

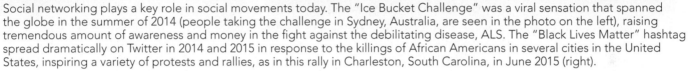

Social networking plays a key role in social movements today. The "Ice Bucket Challenge" was a viral sensation that spanned the globe in the summer of 2014 (people taking the challenge in Sydney, Australia, are seen in the photo on the left), raising tremendous amount of awareness and money in the fight against the debilitating disease, ALS. The "Black Lives Matter" hashtag spread dramatically on Twitter in 2014 and 2015 in response to the killings of African Americans in several cities in the United States, inspiring a variety of protests and rallies, as in this rally in Charleston, South Carolina, in June 2015 (right).

relationships, the social contexts in which we find ourselves can influence us profoundly. You can find many examples of this kind of influence in your own life. Have you ever laughed at a joke you didn't get just because those around you were laughing? Do you present yourself in one way with one group of people and in quite a different way with another group? The power of the social context can also be much more subtle than in these examples, as when others' unspoken and inaccurate expectations about you may have real and enduring impact on your own behavior and sense of who you are.

The relevance of social psychology is evident in everyday life, of course, such as when two people become attracted to each other or when a group tries to co-ordinate its efforts on a project. Dramatic events can heighten its significance all the more, as is evident in people's behavior during and after war, terrorist attacks, or natural disasters. In these traumatic times, a spotlight shines on how people help or exploit each other, and we witness some of the worst and best that human relations have to offer. These events invariably call attention to the kinds of questions that social psychologists study—questions about hatred and violence, about intergroup conflict and suspicion, as well as about heroism, cooperation, and the capacity for understanding across cultural, ethnic, racial, religious, and geographic divides. We are reminded of the need for a better understanding of social psychological issues as we see footage of death and destruction in the Middle East or Congo or are confronted with the reality of an all-too-violent world as nearby as our own neighborhoods and campuses. We also appreciate the majesty and power of social connections as we recognize the courage of a firefighter, read about the charity of a donor, or see the glow in the eyes of a new parent. These are all—the bad and the good, the mundane and the extraordinary—part of the fascinating landscape of social psychology.

Not only will you learn interesting and relevant research findings throughout the book, you also will learn *how* social psychologists have discovered this evidence. It is an exciting process and one that we are enthusiastic about sharing with you. The purpose of this first chapter is to provide you with a broad overview of the field of social psychology. By the time you finish it, you should be ready and (we hope) eager for what lies ahead.

What Is Social Psychology?

We begin by defining social psychology and mapping out its relationship to sociology and some other disciplines within the field of psychology.

■ Defining Social Psychology

Social psychology is the scientific study of how individuals think, feel, and behave in a social context. Let's look at each part of this definition.

Scientific Study   There are many approaches to understanding how people think, feel, and behave. We can learn about human behavior from novels, films, history, and philosophy, to name just a few possibilities. What makes social psychology different from these artistic and humanistic endeavors is that social psychology is a science. It applies the *scientific method* of systematic observation, description, and measurement to the study of the human condition. How, and why, social psychologists do this is the focus of Chapter 2.

Our social relationships and interactions are extremely important to us. Most people seek out and are profoundly affected by other people. This social nature of the human animal is what social psychology is all about.

How Individuals Think, Feel, and Behave   Social psychology concerns an amazingly diverse set of topics. People's private, even nonconscious beliefs and attitudes; their most passionate emotions; their heroic, cowardly, or merely mundane public behaviors—these all fall within the broad scope of social psychology. In this way, social psychology differs from other social sciences such as economics and political science. Research on attitudes offers a good illustration. Whereas economists and political scientists may be interested in people's economic and political attitudes, respectively, social psychologists investigate a wide variety of attitudes and contexts, such as individuals' attitudes toward particular groups of people or how their attitudes are affected by their peers or their mood. In doing so, social psychologists strive to establish general principles of attitude formation and change that apply in a variety of situations rather than exclusively to particular domains.

Note the word *individuals* in our definition of social psychology. This word points to another important way in which social psychology differs from some other social sciences. Sociology, for instance, typically classifies people in terms of their nationality, race, socioeconomic class, and other *group factors*. In contrast, social psychology typically focuses on the psychology of the *individual*. Even

social psychology   The scientific study of how individuals think, feel, and behave in a social context.

when social psychologists study groups of people, they usually emphasize the behavior of the individual in the group context.

A Social Context   Here is where the "social" in social psychology comes into play and how social psychology is distinguished from other branches of psychology. As a whole, the discipline of psychology is an immense, sprawling enterprise, concerned with everything from the actions of neurotransmitters in the brain to the actions of dancers in a crowded club. What makes social psychology unique is its emphasis on the social nature of individuals.

However, the "socialness" of social psychology varies. Social psychologists sometimes examine nonsocial factors that affect people's thoughts, emotions, motives, and actions. For example, they may study whether hot weather causes people to behave more aggressively (Anderson, 2012; Ranson, 2014). What is social about this is the behavior: people hurting each other. In addition, social psychologists sometimes study people's thoughts or feelings about nonsocial things, such as people's attitudes toward Nike versus Adidas basketball shoes. How can attitudes toward basketball shoes be of interest to social psychologists? One way is if these attitudes are influenced by something social, such as whether LeBron James's endorsement of Nike makes people prefer that brand. Both examples— determining whether heat causes an increase in aggression or whether LeBron James causes an increase in sales of Nike shoes—are *social* psychological pursuits because the thoughts, feelings, or behaviors either (a) *concern other people* or (b) *are influenced by other people*.

The "social context" referred to in the definition of social psychology does not have to be real or present. Even the implied or imagined presence of others can have important effects on individuals (Allport, 1985). For example, if people imagine receiving positive or negative reactions from others, their self-esteem can be affected significantly (Libby et al., 2011; Smart Richman & Leary, 2009). If students imagine having contact with a stranger from another country, their attitudes toward people from that country and their experiences visiting that country can become more positive (Vezzali et al., 2015). And if college students imagine living a day in the life of a professor, they are likely to perform better later on an analytic test; if they imagine instead being a cheerleader, however, they perform worse (Galinsky et al., 2008)!

■ Social Psychological Questions and Applications

For those of us fascinated by social behavior, social psychology is a dream come true. Just look at Table 1.1 and consider a small sample of the questions you'll explore in this textbook. As you can see, the social nature of the human animal is what social psychology is all about. Learning about social psychology is learning about ourselves and our social worlds. And because social psychology is scientific rather than anecdotal, it provides insights that would be impossible to gain through intuition or experience alone.

A well-liked celebrity such as Oprah Winfrey can influence the attitudes and behaviors of millions of people. When Oprah recommends a book, for example, sales of the book are likely to skyrocket.

Danny Moloshok/Landov

▲ **TABLE 1.1**

Examples of Social Psychological Questions

Social Perception: What Affects the Way We Perceive Ourselves and Others?

- Why do people sometimes sabotage their own performance, making it more likely that they will fail? (Chapter 3)
- How do people in East Asia often differ from North Americans in the way they explain people's behavior? (Chapter 4)
- Where do stereotypes come from, and why are they so resistant to change? (Chapter 5)

Social Influence: How Do We Influence Each Other?

- Why do we often like what we suffer for? (Chapter 6)
- How do salespeople sometimes trick us into buying things we never really wanted? (Chapter 7)
- Why do people often perform worse in groups than they would have alone? (Chapter 8)

Social Interaction: What Causes Us to Like, Love, Help, and Hurt Others?

- How similar or different are the sexes in what they look for in an intimate relationship? (Chapter 9)
- When is a bystander more or less likely to help you in an emergency? (Chapter 10)
- Does exposure to TV violence or to pornography trigger aggressive behavior? (Chapter 11)

Applying Social Psychology: How Does Social Psychology Help Us Understand Questions About Law, Business, and Health?

- Can interrogators really get people to confess to serious crimes they did not commit? (Chapter 12)
- How can business leaders most effectively motivate their employees? (Chapter 13)
- How does stress affect one's health, and what are the most effective ways of coping with stressful experiences? (Chapter 14)

© Cengage Learning®

The value of social psychology's perspective on human behavior is widely recognized. Courses in social psychology are often required or encouraged for students interested in careers in medicine, business, law, education, and journalism, as well as in psychology and sociology. Although many graduates of social psychology programs hold faculty appointments in colleges or universities, others work in medical centers, law firms, government agencies, the military, and a variety of business settings involving management, investment banking, marketing, advertising, human resources, negotiating, and social networking.

The number and importance of these applications continue to grow. Judges are drawing on social psychological research to render landmark decisions, and lawyers are depending on it to select juries and to support or refute evidence. Businesses are using cross-cultural social psychological research to operate in the global marketplace, and they are consulting research on group dynamics to foster the best conditions for their work forces. Health care professionals are increasingly aware of the role of social psychological factors in the prevention and treatment of disease. Indeed, we can think of no other field of study that offers expertise that is more clearly relevant to so many different career paths.

■ The Power of the Social Context: An Example of a Social Psychology Experiment

The social nature of people runs so deep that even very subtle clues about our social connection with others can have a profound effect on our lives. Think about your first weeks of high school or college. If you're like most students, there probably were times when you felt insecure and wondered if you fit in there. For some groups of students, however, these fears are especially frequent and strong. Students from underrepresented racial or ethnic minority groups, or women entering programs specializing in science, technology, engineering, or mathematics (STEM), are especially vulnerable to such doubts. Social psychological research has found that these concerns can interfere with the academic performance.

Gregory Walton and his colleagues (2015) are among the social psychologists who have studied this issue. For example, they wondered if they could improve the academic success of women at a prestigious engineering school who were taking courses in majors in which the very large majority of students were men. Women in these majors often report that they feel unwelcome and disrespected. To try to counter these concerns, the researchers conducted an experiment in which they provided some students early in their first semester at the engineering school with a brief bit of information suggesting how typical it is that most students—regardless of their gender—go through periods of social stress, disrespect, and feeling that they don't belong during their freshman year, and that these struggles tend to go away soon after their first year. After reading this information the students completed a pair of brief writing activities based on this information.

Walton and his colleagues wanted to assess how these students would do by the end of their first year compared to other students who did not receive any information about social belonging concerns. The results can be seen in ● Figure 1.1. The bars in this graph illustrate the students' first-year GPAs, as measured on a scale from 0 to 100. The first pair of bars on the left show the GPAs of men and women who did not receive the belongingness intervention. As the difference in height of these two bars indicates, the GPAs of the women were far below that of the men. Compare this to the pair of bars on the right. These are the GPAs of the men and women who received the brief information designed to counter concerns about belonging. With this brief intervention, the women earned GPAs as high as the men. The large gender difference was eliminated, therefore, by just a small amount of social information received early in their first year. This study illustrates the power of the social context—or more accurately, of the *perceived* social context—on a critically important real-world outcome. You'll learn more about this and related research by Walton and others in Chapter 5.

■ Social Psychology and Related Fields: Distinctions and Intersections

Social psychology is sometimes confused with certain other fields of study. Before we go on, we should clarify how social psychology is distinct from these other fields, and we will also illustrate that interesting and significant questions can be addressed through interactions between social psychology and these other fields (see Table 1.2 on page 10).

Social Psychology and Sociology Sociologists and social psychologists share an interest in many issues, such as violence, prejudice, cultural differences, and marriage. As noted, however, sociology tends to focus on the group level, whereas social psychology tends to focus on the individual level. For example, sociologists might track the racial attitudes of the middle class in the United States, whereas social psychologists might examine some of the specific factors that make individuals more or less likely to behave in a racist way toward members of some group.

According to social psychological research described in this chapter and elsewhere in the book, how socially connected students feel with their fellow students can have a significant effect on their academic success.

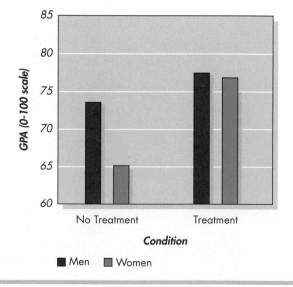

● FIGURE 1.1

Social Belonging and GPA

Some students early in their first semester at an engineering school were given information designed to reduce their doubts about fitting in and belonging at their school, and other students were not given this information. The bars on the left represent the average first-year grades of the men (red) and women (green) who did not receive the information about belonging. Women's average first-year grades were far worse than the men's in this no-treatment condition. The bars on the right illustrate that the women's underperformance was completely eliminated if they received the information designed to reduce their uncertainty about belonging. Adapted from Walton et al., 2015.

▲ **TABLE 1.2**

Distinctions Between Social Psychology and Related Fields: The Case of Research on Prejudice

To see the differences between social psychology and related fields, consider an example of how researchers in each field might conduct a study of prejudice.

Field of Study	Example of How a Researcher in the Field Might Study Prejudice
Sociology	Measure how prejudice varies as a function of social or economic class
Clinical psychology	Test various therapies for people with antisocial personalities who exhibit great degrees of prejudice
Personality psychology	Develop a questionnaire to identify men who are very high or low in degree of prejudice toward women
Cognitive psychology	Manipulate exposure to a member of some category of people and measure the thoughts and concepts that are automatically activated (*A study of prejudice in this field would, by definition, be at the intersection of cognitive and social psychology.*)
Social psychology	Manipulate various kinds of contact between individuals of different groups and examine the effect of these manipulations on the degree of prejudice exhibited

© Cengage Learning®

In addition, although there are many exceptions, social psychologists are more likely than sociologists to conduct experiments in which they manipulate some variable and determine the effects of this manipulation using precise, quantifiable measures.

Despite these differences, sociology and social psychology are clearly related. Indeed, many sociologists and social psychologists share the same training and publish in the same journals. When these two fields intersect, the result can be a more complete understanding of important issues. For example, interdisciplinary research on stereotyping and prejudice has examined the dynamic roles of both societal and immediate factors, such as how particular social systems or institutional norms and beliefs affect individuals' attitudes and behaviors (Foels & Pratto, 2015; Koenig & Eagly, 2014; Rosenthal & Levy, 2013; D. Sanchez et al., 2014).

Social Psychology and Related Areas of Psychology   Tell people not very familiar with psychology that you are taking a social psychology class, and they may say things like "Are you going to start psychoanalyzing me?" or "Great, maybe you can tell me why everyone in my family is so messed up." The assumption underlying these reactions, of course, is that you are studying clinical, or abnormal, psychology. If you base your impressions of psychology primarily by how it's portrayed in popular culture, you're likely to miss how incredibly broad and diverse the field is. Although these various areas of psychology are related to each other, each has a very different focus.

Clinical psychologists, for example, seek to understand and treat people with psychological difficulties or disorders. Social psychologists do not focus on disorders; rather, they focus on the more typical ways in which individuals think, feel, behave, and influence each other. Personality psychology is another area that is often confused with social psychology. However, personality psychology seeks to understand stable differences between individuals, whereas social psychology seeks to understand how social factors affect most individuals *regardless of* their different personalities. In other words, a personality psychologist may ask, "Is this person outgoing and friendly almost all the time, in just about any setting?" A social psychologist may ask, "Are people in general more likely to seek out friends when they are made anxious by a situation than when they are made to feel relaxed?"

Cognitive psychologists study mental processes such as thinking, learning, remembering, and reasoning. Social psychologists are often interested in these same processes, but they are concerned with these processes more specifically in a social context.

These examples show the contrast between the fields, but, in fact, social psychological theory and research often intersect with these other areas quite a bit. For example, both clinical and social psychology may address how people cope with anxiety, emotion, or pressure in social situations, or how being bullied or stereotyped by others can affect individuals' physical and mental health (Cheung et al., 2015; M. Knowles et al., 2015; Rosenthal et al., 2015; Young-Jones et al., 2015).

Personality and social psychology are especially closely linked because they complement each other so well. For example, some social psychologists examine how receiving negative feedback or experiencing conflict (social factors) can have different effects on people as a function of their self-esteem (a personality factor), or whether people who are high in empathy (a personality factor) are especially likely to go out of their way to help other people (a social factor) (Krizan & Johar, 2015; Morelli et al., 2015).

Cognitive and social psychology are also closely connected. The last few decades have seen an explosion of interest in the intersection of cognitive and social psychology. The study of *social cognition* is discussed in more detail later in this chapter, and it is a focus throughout this text, especially in Part II on Social Perception.

Social Psychology and Other Fields of Study Social psychologists today are doing research that spans across traditional boundaries between fields more than ever. The intersections of social psychology with disciplines such as neuroscience, biology, economics, political science, public health, environmental studies, law, and medicine are increasingly important to contemporary social psychology. We will discuss a bit more about some of these intersections later in this chapter, but you should see these connections throughout this book, most especially in Part V on Applying Social Psychology.

Do provocative, sexualized images of women in advertising, such as on the billboard seen here, make people more sexist or prone to treat women in more objectified ways? Do they affect women's self-esteem or body issues? These are among the questions that social psychology addresses.

■ Social Psychology and Common Sense

After reading about a theory or finding of social psychology, you may sometimes think, "Of course. I knew that all along. Everyone knows that." This "knew-it-all-along" phenomenon often causes people to question how social psychology is different from common sense, or traditional folk wisdom. After all, would any of the following social psychological findings be surprising to you?

- Beauty and brains don't mix. Physically attractive people tend to be seen as less smart than physically unattractive people.

- People will like an activity more if you offer them a large reward for doing it, causing them to associate the activity with the positive reinforcement.

- People think that they're more unique than they really are. They tend to underestimate the extent to which others share the same opinions or interests.

- Playing contact sports or violent video games releases aggression and makes people less likely to vent their anger in violent ways.

In a minute, we will have more to say about each of these statements.

Common sense may seem to explain many social psychological findings after the fact. The problem is distinguishing commonsense fact from commonsense myth. After all, for many commonsense notions, there is an equally sensible-sounding notion that says the opposite. Is it "Birds of a feather flock together" or "Opposites attract"? Is it "Two heads are better than one" or "Too many cooks spoil the broth"? Which are correct? We have no reliable way to answer such questions through common sense or intuition alone.

Social psychology, unlike common sense, uses the scientific method to put its theories to the test. How it does so will be discussed in greater detail in the next chapter. But before we leave this section, one word of caution: Those four "findings" listed above? *They are all false.* Although there may be sensible reasons to believe each of the statements to be true, research indicates otherwise. Therein lies another problem with relying on common sense: Despite offering very compelling predictions and explanations, it is sometimes wildly inaccurate. And even when it is not completely wrong, common sense can be misleading in its simplicity. Often there is no simple answer to a question such as "Does absence make the heart grow fonder?" In reality, the answer is more complex than common sense would suggest, and social psychological research reveals how such an answer depends on a variety of factors.

To emphasize these points and to encourage you to think critically about social psychological issues *before* as well as after learning about them, this textbook contains a feature called "Putting Common Sense to the Test." Beginning with Chapter 3, each chapter opens with a few statements about social psychological issues that will be covered in that chapter. Some of the statements are true, and some are false. As you read each statement, make a prediction about whether it is true or false and think about why this is your prediction. Marginal notes throughout the chapter will tell you whether the statements are true or false. In reading the chapter, check not only whether your prediction was correct but also whether your reasons for the prediction were accurate. If your intuition wasn't quite on the mark, think about what the right answer is and how the evidence supports that answer. There are few better ways of learning and remembering than through this kind of critical thinking.

A Brief History of Social Psychology

People have probably been asking social psychological questions for as long as humans could think about each other. Certainly early philosophers such as Plato offered keen insights into many social psychological issues. But no systematic and scientific study of social psychological issues developed until the end of the nineteenth century. The field of social psychology is therefore a relatively young one. Recent years have marked a tremendous interest in social psychology and an injection of many new scholars into the field. As social psychology is now in its second century, it is instructive to look back to see how the field today has been shaped by the people and events of its first century.

"Psychology has a long past, but only a short history."
— Herman Ebbinghaus, *Summary of Psychology*

■ The Birth and Infancy of Social Psychology: 1880s–1920s

Like most such honors, the title "founder of social psychology" has many potential recipients, and not everyone agrees on who should prevail. Over the years, most have pointed to the American psychologist Norman Triplett, who is credited with having published the first research article in social psychology at the end of the nineteenth century (1897–1898). Triplett's work was noteworthy because after observing that bicyclists tended to race faster when racing in the presence of others than when simply racing against a clock, he designed an experiment to study this phenomenon in a controlled, precise way. This scientific approach to studying the effects of the social context on individuals' behavior can be seen as marking the birth of social psychology.

A case can also be made for the French agricultural engineer Max Ringelmann. Ringelmann's research was conducted in the 1880s but wasn't published until 1913. In an interesting coincidence, Ringelmann also studied the effects of the presence of others on the performance of individuals. In contrast to Triplett, however, Ringelmann noted that individuals often performed worse on simple tasks such as pulling rope when they performed the tasks with other people. The issues addressed by these two early researchers continue to be of vital interest, as will be seen later in Chapter 8.

Some scholars (Haines & Vaughan, 1979; Stroebe, 2012) suggest a handful of other possible examples of the first social psychology studies, including research that Triplett himself cited. These studies also were conducted in the 1880s and 1890s, which seems to have been a particularly fertile time for social psychology to begin to spring roots.

Despite their place in the history of social psychology, these late-nineteenth-century studies did not truly establish social psychology as a distinct field of study. Credit for this creation goes to the writers of the first three textbooks in social psychology: the English psychologist William McDougall (1908) and two Americans, Edward Ross (1908) and Floyd Allport (1924). Allport's book in particular, with its focus on the interaction of individuals and their social context and its emphasis on the use of experimentation and the scientific method, helped establish social psychology as the discipline it is today. These authors announced the arrival of a new approach to the social aspects of human behavior. Social psychology was born.

Tolga Akmen/Anadolu Agency/Getty Images

A Call to Action: 1930s–1950s

What one person would you guess has had the strongest influence on the field of social psychology? Various social psychologists, as well as psychologists outside of social psychology, might be mentioned in response to this question. But someone who was not a psychologist at all may have had the most dramatic impact on the field: Adolf Hitler.

Hitler's rise to power and the horrendous consequences that followed caused people around the world to become desperate for answers to social psychological questions about what causes violence, prejudice, genocide, conformity and obedience, and a host of other social problems and behaviors. In addition, many social psychologists living in Europe in the 1930s fled to the United States and helped establish a critical mass of social psychologists who would give shape to the rapidly maturing field. The years just before, during, and soon after World War II marked an explosion of interest in social psychology.

Racers from around the world compete in the Tour de France in July 2014. Would these cyclists have raced faster or slower if they were racing individually against the clock rather than racing simultaneously with their competitors? More generally, how does the presence of others affect an individual's performance? The earliest social psychology experiments ever done sought to answer questions such as these. Chapter 8 on group processes brings you up to date on the latest research in this area.

In 1936, Gordon Allport (younger brother of Floyd, author of the 1924 textbook) and a number of other social psychologists formed the Society for the Psychological Study of Social Issues. The name of the society illustrates these psychologists' concern for making important, practical contributions to society. Also in 1936, a social psychologist named Muzafer Sherif published groundbreaking experimental research on social influence. As a youth in Turkey, Sherif had witnessed groups of Greek soldiers brutally killing his friends. After immigrating to the United States, Sherif drew on this experience and began to conduct research on the powerful influences groups can exert on their individual members. Sherif's research was crucial for the development of social psychology because it demonstrated that it is possible to study complex and important social issues in a rigorous, scientific manner.

Another great contributor to social psychology, Kurt Lewin, fled the Nazi onslaught in Germany and immigrated to the United States in the early 1930s. Lewin was a bold and creative theorist whose concepts have had lasting effects on the field (e.g., Lewin, 1935, 1947). One of the fundamental principles of social psychology that Lewin helped establish was that behavior is a function of the interaction between the person and the environment. This position, which later became known as the **interactionist perspective** (Blass, 1991; Snyder, 2013), emphasized the dynamic interplay of internal and external factors, and it marked a sharp contrast from other major psychological paradigms during his lifetime: psychoanalysis, with its emphasis on internal motives and fantasies; and behaviorism, with its focus on external rewards and punishments.

What determines whether people are likely to volunteer to help others, such as dedicating one's time and energy to work with others to construct a house for those in need? Built on the legacy of Kurt Lewin, applied social psychology contributes to the solution of numerous social problems.

Lewin also profoundly influenced the field by advocating for social psychological theories to be applied to important, practical issues. Lewin researched a number of practical issues, such as how to persuade Americans at home during the war to conserve materials to help the war effort, how to promote more economical and nutritious eating habits, and what kinds of leaders elicit the best work from group members. Built on Lewin's legacy, applied social psychology flourishes today in areas such as advertising, business, education, environmental protection, health, law, politics, public policy, religion, and sports. Throughout this text, we draw on the findings of applied social psychology to illustrate the implications of social psychological principles for our daily lives. In Part V, three prominent areas of applied social psychology are discussed in detail: law, business, and health. One of Lewin's statements can be seen as a call to action for the entire field: "No research without action, no action without research."

During World War II, many social psychologists answered Lewin's call as they worked for their government to investigate how to protect soldiers from the propaganda of the enemy, how to persuade citizens to support the war effort, how to select officers for various positions, and other practical issues. During and after the war, social psychologists sought to understand the prejudice, aggression, and conformity the war had brought to light. The 1950s saw many major contributions

interactionist perspective An emphasis on how both an individual's personality and environmental characteristics influence behavior.

to the field of social psychology. For example, Gordon Allport (1954) published *The Nature of Prejudice*, a groundbreaking book that continues to inspire research on stereotyping and prejudice more than six decades later. Solomon Asch's (1951) demonstration of how willing people are to conform to an obviously wrong majority amazes students even today. Leon Festinger (1954, 1957) introduced two important theories—one concerning how people try to learn about themselves by comparing themselves to other people, and one about how people's attitudes can be changed by their own behavior—that remain among the most influential theories in the field. These are just a sample of a long list of landmark contributions made during the 1950s. With this remarkable burst of activity and impact, social psychology was clearly, and irrevocably, on the map.

■ Confidence and Crisis: 1960s–Mid-1970s

In spectacular fashion, Stanley Milgram's research in the early and middle 1960s linked the post–World War II era with the coming era of social revolution. Milgram's research was inspired by the destructive obedience demonstrated by Nazi officers and ordinary citizens in World War II, but it also looked ahead to the civil disobedience that was beginning to challenge institutions in many parts of the world. Milgram's experiments, which demonstrated individuals' vulnerability to the destructive commands of authority, became the most famous research in the history of social psychology. This research is discussed in detail in Chapter 7.

With its foundation firmly in place, social psychology entered a period of expansion and enthusiasm. The sheer range of its investigations was staggering. Social psychologists considered how people thought and felt about themselves and others. They demonstrated why people fail to help others in distress. They examined aggression, physical attractiveness, and stress. For the field as a whole, it was a time of great productivity.

Ironically, it was also a time of crisis and heated debate. Many of the strong disagreements during this period can be understood as a reaction to the dominant research method of the day: the laboratory experiment. Critics of this method asserted that certain practices were unethical, that experimenters' expectations influenced their participants' behavior, and that the theories being tested in the laboratory were historically and culturally limited (Gergen, 1973; Kelman, 1967; Rosenthal, 1976). Those who favored laboratory experimentation, on the other hand, contended that their procedures were ethical, their results were valid, and their theoretical principles were widely applicable (McGuire, 1967). For a while, social psychology seemed split in two.

■ An Era of Pluralism: Mid-1970s–2000s

Fortunately, both sides won. As we will see in the next chapter, more rigorous ethical standards for research were instituted, more stringent procedures to guard against bias were adopted, and more attention was paid to possible cross-cultural differences in behavior. Laboratory experiments continued to dominate, but often with more precise methods. Laboratory experiments did, however, get some company. A pluralistic approach emerged as a wider range of research techniques and questions became established.

Courtesy of the National Archives and Records Administration

This World War II poster featuring Rosie the Riveter was part of the U.S. government's campaign to encourage women to take jobs in traditionally male-dominated occupations, such as welding. When the war was over and the men who had served in the military returned to the workforce, new advertisements were designed to encourage women to leave these jobs and concentrate on raising families.

Social psychologists are becoming increasingly interested in cross-cultural research, which helps us break out of our culture-bound perspective. Many of our behaviors differ across cultures. In some cultures, for example, people are expected to negotiate about the price of the products they buy, as in this market in Tunisia. In other cultures, such bargaining would be highly unusual and cause confusion and distress.

Pluralism in social psychology extends far beyond its methods. There are also important variations in what aspects of human behavior are emphasized. For example, social psychologists became more and more interested in processes relevant to (as well as to adapt methods from) cognitive psychology. A new subfield was born called **social cognition**, the study of how we perceive, remember, and interpret information about ourselves and others. Social cognition research continues to thrive today and examines issues important to virtually every major area in social psychology.

Another source of pluralism in social psychology is its development of international and multicultural perspectives. Although individuals from many countries helped establish the field, social psychology achieved its greatest professional recognition in the United States and Canada. At one point, it was estimated that 75% to 90% of social psychologists lived in North America (Smith & Bond, 1993; Triandis, 1994). However, this aspect of social psychology began to change rapidly in the 1990s, reflecting not only the different geographic and cultural backgrounds of its researchers and participants but also the recognition that many social psychological phenomena once assumed to be universal may actually vary dramatically as a function of culture. You can find evidence of this new appreciation of the role of culture in every chapter of this book.

Social Psychology Today: What Is Trending Now?

social cognition The study of how people perceive, remember, and interpret information about themselves and others.

The field today continues to grow in the number and diversity of researchers and research topics, areas of the world in which research is conducted, and industries that hire social psychologists and apply their work.

Throughout this text, we emphasize the most current, cutting-edge research in the field, along with the classic findings of the past. In the remainder of the chapter, we focus on a few of the exciting themes and perspectives emerging today.

Integration of Emotion, Motivation, and Cognition

In the earlier days of social cognition research in the 1970s and 1980s, the dominant perspective was called "cold" because it emphasized the role of cognition and de-emphasized the role of emotion and motivation in explaining social psychological issues. This was contrasted with a "hot" perspective, focusing on emotion and motivation as determinants of our thoughts and actions. Today there is growing interest in integrating both "hot" and "cold" perspectives, as researchers study how individuals' emotions and motivations influence their thoughts and actions, and vice versa. For example, researchers examine how motivations we aren't even consciously aware of (such as being motivated to treat others fairly, or being motivated to feel superior to others) can bias how we interact with or interpret information about another person (Dunning, 2015; Higgins & Scholer, 2015; Moskowitz, 2014; Spencer et al., 2005).

One issue illustrating the integration of "hot" and "cold" variables concerns the conflict between wanting to be *right* and wanting to *feel good* about oneself, and how these different motivations influence how we process information. On the one hand, we want to be accurate in our judgments about ourselves and others. On the other hand, we don't want to be accurate if it means we will learn something bad about ourselves or those closest to us. These goals can pull our cognitive processes in very different directions. How we perform the required mental gymnastics is an ongoing concern for social psychologists (Balcetis et al., 2014; Hardin & Larsen, 2014; Stroessner & Dweck, 2015; Wojcik & Ditto, 2014).

Another theme running through many chapters of this book is the growing interest in distinguishing between automatic and controllable processes and in understanding the relationship between them. How much do we have control over our thoughts and actions, and how vulnerable are we to influences beyond our awareness or control? Are we sometimes influenced by stereotypes even if we don't want to believe them? Can we train ourselves to regulate ourselves against automatic impulses? These are among the questions that social psychologists are studying today (Bargh et al., 2012; Monteith et al., 2013; J. W. Sherman et al., 2014).

Our desire to be accurate in our judgments can sometimes interfere with our desire to feel good about ourselves.

Genetic and Evolutionary Perspectives

Recent advances in **behavioral genetics**—a subfield of psychology that examines the effects of genes on behavior—has triggered new research to investigate such matters as the extent to which political attitudes are at least partially inherited and the roles that genes play in individuals' sexual orientation or identity (Bell & Kandler, 2015; Burri et al., 2015; Sanders et al., 2015). The role of genes in an ever-growing array of social behaviors is being better understood as breakthroughs continue to drive interdisciplinary research involving genetics.

Evolutionary psychology, which uses the principles of evolution to understand human behavior, is another growing area that is sparking new research in social psychology. According to this perspective, to understand a social psychological

"On the one hand, eliminating the middleman would result in lower costs, increased sales, and greater consumer satisfaction; on the other hand, we're the middleman."

behavioral genetics A subfield of psychology that examines the role of genetic factors in behavior.

evolutionary psychology A subfield of psychology that uses the principles of evolution to understand human social behavior.

issue such as jealousy, we should ask how tendencies and reactions underlying jealousy today may have evolved from the natural-selection pressures our ancestors faced. Evolutionary psychological theories can then be used to explain and predict gender differences in attraction, the situational factors most likely to trigger jealousy, and so on (Brase et al., 2014; Perilloux & Kurzban, 2015; Shackelford & Hansen, 2015). This perspective is discussed in many places throughout the textbook, especially in Part IV on Social Relations.

■ Cultural Perspectives

Because of the fantastic advances in communication technologies in recent years and the globalization of the world's economies, it is faster, easier, and more necessary than ever before for people from vastly different cultures to interact with one another. Thus, our need and desire to understand how we are similar to and different from one another are greater than ever as well. Social psychology is currently experiencing tremendous growth in research designed to give us a better understanding and appreciation of the role of culture in all aspects of social psychology.

What is meant by "culture" is not easy to pin down, as many researchers think of culture in very different ways. Broadly speaking, **culture** may be considered to be a system of enduring meanings, beliefs, values, assumptions, institutions, and practices shared by a large group of people and transmitted from one generation to the next. Whatever the specific definition, it is clear that how individuals perceive and derive meaning from their world are influenced profoundly by the beliefs, norms, and practices of the people and institutions around them.

Increasing numbers of social psychologists are evaluating the universal generality or cultural specificity of their theories and findings by conducting **cross-cultural research**, in which they examine similarities and differences across a variety of cultures. More and more social psychologists are also conducting **multicultural research**, in which they examine racial and ethnic groups within cultures.

These developments are already profoundly influencing our view of human behavior. For example, cross-cultural research has revealed important distinctions between the collectivist cultures (which value interdependence and social harmony) typically found in Africa, Asia, and Latin America and the individualist cultures (which value independence and self-reliance) more commonly found in North America and Europe. The implications of these differences can be seen throughout the textbook.

Consider, for instance, a recent experiment by Alyssa Fu and Hazel Markus (2014) in which Asian-American and European-American high school students worked on a task that involved trying to make words out of scrambled letters. The researchers designed the task to be extremely difficult, and they told each student that he or she did worse than average for the school. Fu and Markus then gave the students a chance to work on this task a second time. How much effort would they put into this task after having experienced the initial failure?

Before they were given the second task, half of the students were asked to describe their mother in a few sentences, whereas the other students were asked to describe themselves. The researchers predicted that subtly getting the students to think about their moms would be particularly motivating for Asian-American students, but not for the European-American students. Why? As will be discussed in Chapter 3, social psychological research has shown that Asian Americans are more likely than European Americans to have an *interdependent* model of self, one in which motivation and action stem in large part from the influences of close others, especially of one's mother. Although European Americans also certainly are influenced by close others such as their mother, they tend to have a relatively

culture A system of enduring meanings, beliefs, values, assumptions, institutions, and practices shared by a large group of people and transmitted from one generation to the next.

cross-cultural research Research designed to compare and contrast people of different cultures.

multicultural research Research designed to examine racial and ethnic groups within cultures.

independent model of self, one emphasizing personal preferences and goals. On the basis of this cultural difference, Fu and Markus reasoned that thinking about their moms would be more motivating for Asian-American than for European-American students as they were about to try the task a second time. (As one example of this kind of reaction, see the quote by Amy Chua in the margin.)

As can be seen in ● Figure 1.2, the results supported this prediction. When made to think about themselves, European-American students worked on the task slightly more than the Asian-American students, but this difference was not significant. When made to think about their mothers, in contrast, the Asian-American students worked harder than the European-American students. More generally, results such as these demonstrate that recognizing cultural differences can be vital in understanding what motivates individuals most effectively.

In this text, we describe studies conducted in dozens of countries, representing every populated continent on earth. As our knowledge expands, we should be able to see much more clearly both the behavioral differences among cultures and the similarities we all share. But it is important to note that even within a particular society, people are often treated differently as a function of social categories such as gender, race, physical appearance, and economic class. They may be raised differently by their parents, confronted with different expectations by teachers, exposed to different types of advertising and marketing, and offered different kinds of jobs. In a sense, then, even people within the same town or region may develop and live in distinct subcultures, and these differences can have profound effects on people's lives.

Some social psychology textbooks devote a separate chapter to culture or to culture and gender. We chose not to do so. Because we believe that cultural influences are inherent in *all* aspects of social psychology, we chose instead to integrate discussions of the role of culture and gender in every chapter of the textbook.

● **FIGURE 1.2**

Motivated by Mom? A Cultural Difference

Asian-American and European-American high-school students attempted a difficult letter-unscrambling task after having previously done poorly on it. The students worked equally hard on the task if they first were asked to think about themselves (the two bars on the right), but the Asian-American students worked harder than the European-American if they were first asked to think about their mothers (the two bars on the left). Based on Fu & Markus, 2014.

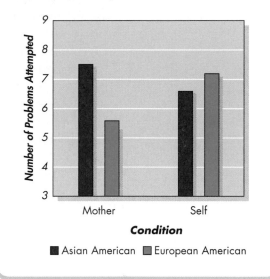

Behavioral Economics, Political and Moral Issues, and Other Interdisciplinary Approaches

A rapidly growing number of social psychologists today are asking questions and using methodologies that cross traditional academic boundaries. We've already discussed intersections of social psychology with neuroscience, evolutionary theory, and cultural psychology. Other topics are beginning to trend in increasing numbers.

For example, one relatively new area of study that has received a great deal of attention is known as **behavioral economics**. This subfield focuses on how psychology—particularly social and cognitive psychology—relates to economic decision making. Behavioral economics research has revealed that the traditional economic models were inadequate because they failed to account for the powerful—and often seemingly irrational—role that psychological factors have on people's economic behavior. For example, Jiang Jiang and others (2015) conducted a series of experiments with high school students in China in which some students were made to either experience a rejection by a peer while playing a simple game or to recall a time when they were rejected by peers. Compared to other

"[My daughter Lulu] had looked at a question and had drawn a blank. Lulu said, 'Then I heard your annoying voice in my head, saying, 'Keep thinking! I know you can do this'—and the answer just came to me.'"

— Amy Chua, about her influence on her daughter. *Time,* 1/20/2011.

behavioral economics An interdisciplinary subfield that focuses on how psychology—particularly social and cognitive psychology—relates to economic decision making.

students who were not made to experience or recall a peer rejection, those who did became materialistic, such as by answering the question, "What makes me happy?" by emphasizing material things such as new clothes and money. This is but one example of how subtle social psychological factors seemingly unrelated to an economic-related judgment can exert significant influence in ways that would not be predicted by economic analyses alone. The rise of behavioral economics has come with an increasing number of social psychologists hired by business schools and in the business world more generally.

Social psychologists are also increasingly involved in research intersecting other areas such as politics and moral philosophy. Jonathan Haidt (2012, 2017) is one prominent example of a social psychologist who recently has bridged both of these areas with social psychology, addressing questions such as whether we can better understand the political divide between liberals and conservatives by recognizing the different conceptions of morality that underlie political attitudes. The surge of interest in questions like this has brought together an exciting and productive mix of social psychology, political science, philosophy, and neuroscience.

Similarly, social psychologists are collaborating in greater numbers with researchers in environmental studies, public health, and related areas to address issues as varied as how to get people to conserve energy, adopt healthier habits, and avoid skin cancer, or to study how even simple alterations to the physical surroundings around primary schools, such as providing some green space, can improve students' education (Dadvand et al., 2015; Hamilton & Lobel, 2015; R. G. Jones, 2015; Wilson & Albarracín, 2015).

■ The Social Brain and Body

"You carry [your friends and family] with you in your heart, your mind, your stomach, because you do not just live in a world but a world lives in you."

— Frederick Buechner

We are, of course, biological organisms, and it is clear that our brains and bodies influence, and are influenced by, our social experiences. This interaction between the physical and the social is the focus of more research than ever before in the field, and examples can be found throughout the textbook, such as in studies demonstrating how being the target of racial discrimination can affect individuals' physical health, and research examining the role of hormones and neurotransmitters in human aggression (de Almeida et al., 2015; Dover et al., 2015; Gibbons et al., 2014.

A particularly exciting recent development is the emergence of the subfield of **social neuroscience**—the study of the relationship between neural and social processes. This intersection of social psychology and neuroscience is addressing a rapidly growing number of fascinating issues, such as how playing violent video games can affect brain activity and subsequent acts of aggression, or how different patterns of activity in parts of the brain relate to how people are likely to perceive themselves or members of a different racial group (Amodio, 2014; Beer, 2015; Engelhardt et al., 2011).

Another interdisciplinary area of research attracting increasing interest among social psychologists today is known as **embodied cognition**, which focuses on the close links between our minds and the positioning, experiences, and actions of our bodies. According to this perspective, people's perceptions and judgments reflect and can influence their bodily experiences. For example, recent studies have found that participants who were touching something rough (rough sandpaper) judged an interaction between two people as more rough and unfriendly than if they were touching something smooth, and that participants made to sit in an upright position experienced higher self-esteem and lower fear in response to a

social neuroscience The study of the relationship between neural and social processes.

embodied cognition An interdisciplinary subfield that examines the close links between our minds and the positioning, experiences, and actions of our bodies.

stressful situation than did those sitting in a more slumped position (Meier et al., 2012; Nair et al., 2015; Schaefer et al., 2014).

We began this chapter discussing how the evolution of the human brain seems to have been linked closely to the social nature of our species. Research continues to find new evidence for how deeply rooted and basic this social nature is. Consider just a few examples from very recent studies:

- Having close friends and staying in contact with family members is associated with health benefits such as protecting against heart disease, infection, diabetes, and cancer, and with living longer and more actively (Cacioppo et al., 2015). One analysis reports that having a friend one sees on most days may affect one's well-being as much as making an extra $100,000 a year does (Lieberman, 2013)!

- Experiencing a social rejection or loss is so painful that it produces activity in the same parts of the brain as when we feel physical pain. Being treated well and fairly by other people, on the other hand, activates parts of the brain associated with physical rewards such as desirable food and drink (Eisenberger, 2015).

- There is something medically very real about a "broken heart." For example, a person is more than 20 times more likely than usual to suffer a heart attack within one day of the death of a loved one, and the effects of "broken heart syndrome" can endure for months (Mostofsky et al., 2012; Neil et al., 2015).

New Technologies and the Online World

The new wave of research on what we have called the social brain has been possible only through advances in technology. Researchers today can see images of the brain at work through noninvasive procedures, enabling social psychologists to address questions they never could have attempted before. Social psychologists are now using techniques such as *positron emission tomography (PET)*, *event-related potential (ERP)*, *transcranial magnetic stimulation (TMS)*, and *functional magnetic resonance imaging (fMRI)* to study the interplay of the brain and discrete

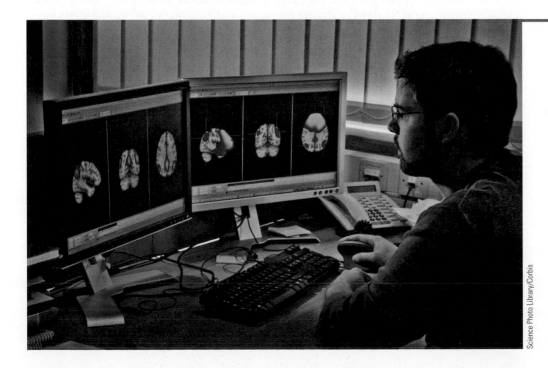

Advances in technology enable social psychologists to extend their research in exciting new directions, such as by using functional magnetic resonance imaging (fMRI) and Magnetoencephalograpy (MEG) to study activity in the brain in response to various thoughts or stimuli.

Science Photo Library/Corbis

Joe Raedle/Getty Images News/Getty Images

Together, and apart. Even when interacting in a group, many of us today are also pulled away by our individual phones, electronic games, laptops, tablets, and so on. How new technologies and living so much of our lives online affect human interaction is becoming increasingly important to social psychology.

thoughts, feelings, and behaviors. Social psychology research today benefits from other technological advances as well, such as new and better techniques to measure hormone levels and to code people's everyday speech quickly into quantifiable units. Some researchers are using virtual reality technology to examine a number of social psychological questions. The University of California at Santa Barbara's Research Center for Virtual Environments and Stanford University's Virtual Human Interaction Lab are among the new labs conducting fascinating high-tech research on issues such as conformity, group dynamics, aggression, altruism, social support, and eyewitness testimony (e.g., Bailey & Bailenson, 2015; Blascovich, 2014). Because participants in these experiments are immersed in a virtual reality that the experimenters create for them, the researchers can test questions that would be impractical, impossible, or unethical without this technology.

Awesome is an overused word, but it surely describes the revolution that is taking place in how we access information and communicate with each other. The waves of this revolution have carried social psychology research along with it. Social psychologists around the world can now not only communicate and collaborate much more easily but can also gain access to research participants from populations that would otherwise never have been available. These developments have sparked the field's internationalization, perhaps its most exciting course in its second century.

Online communication not only facilitates research but is also itself becoming a provocative topic of study. As more people interact with each other through social networking sites, online dating services, and communications services such as Skype or FaceTime, there is growing interest in studying how attraction, prejudice, group dynamics, and a host of other social psychological phenomena unfold online versus offline. Other important, and potentially troubling, questions raised by our increasingly online lives are the subject of new research, such as: What factors contribute to or protect against cyberbullying? Can too much time on social networking sites lead to depression or loneliness? Does the habit of frequent texting or checking to see who has commented on one's most recent shared photo lead to attentional and social problems?

We would be presumptuous, and probably naive, to try to predict how new communication and new technologies will influence the ways that people will interact in the coming years, but it probably is safe to predict that their influence will be great. As more people fall in love online, or fall into social isolation, or react with violence to the loss of individual privacy, social psychology will explore these issues. We expect that some of the students reading this textbook today will be among those explorers in the years to come.

Review

Top 10 Key Points in Chapter 1

1. Social psychology is the scientific study of how individuals think, feel, and behave in a social context.

2. Women in one study achieved greater academic success at an engineering school if they received information early in their first year designed to reduce their concerns about fitting in and belonging in their male-dominated majors.

3. Early research by Triplett and Ringelmann established an enduring topic in social psychology: how the presence of others affects an individual's performance.

4. Social psychology began to flourish as the world needed explanations for the tragic questions and challenges that World War II raised.

5. Stanley Milgram's experiments in the 1960s demonstrated individuals' vulnerability to the destructive commands of authority.

6. Individuals sometimes are faced with a conflict between two motivations that can affect cognitive processes: wanting to be right and wanting to feel good about oneself.

7. A great deal of recent social psychological research has explored the automatic versus controllable nature of a number of processes, such as stereotyping.

8. Subfields that have been growing rapidly in recent years include: behavioral genetics, which examines the effects of genes on behavior; evolutionary psychology, which applies the principles of evolution to understand contemporary human behavior; behavioral economics, which studies how psychology relates to economic decision making; and social neuroscience, which involves the study of the relationship between neural and social processes.

9. Increasing numbers of social psychologists are evaluating the universal generality or cultural specificity of their theories and findings through cross-cultural research.

10. Online communication has fostered collaboration among researchers around the world, enabled researchers to study participants from diverse populations, and inspired researchers to investigate whether various social psychological phenomena are similar or different online versus offline.

Key Terms

behavioral economics (19)

behavioral genetics (17)

cross-cultural research (18)

culture (18)

embodied cognition (20)

evolutionary psychology (17)

interactionist perspective (14)

multicultural research (18)

social cognition (16)

social neuroscience (20)

social psychology (6)

Doing Social Psychology Research

This chapter examines how social psychologists do their research. We begin by asking, "Why should you learn about research methods?" We answer this question by discussing how learning about research methods can benefit you both in this course and beyond. Then we consider how researchers come up with and develop ideas and begin the research process. Next, we provide an overview of the research designs that social psychologists use to test their ideas. Finally, we turn to important questions about ethics and values, including new controversies and practices, in social psychology.

2

Courtesy of Alina P. Fein

You're starting a new semester or quarter at school, and you're just beginning to settle into a new schedule and routine. You're looking forward to your new courses. In general, it's an exciting time. But there's one major catch: As you spend more and more time with your new classmates and new responsibilities, you're leaving someone behind. It could be a boyfriend or girlfriend, a spouse, or a close friend—someone who is not involved in what you are doing now. You may now live far apart from each other or your new commitments in school may be keeping you apart from each other much more than you'd like. The romantic in you says, "Together forever." Or at least, "No problem." But the realist in you worries a bit. Will your love or friendship be the same? Can it survive the long distance, or the new demands on your time, or the new people in your respective environments? Your friends or family may have advice to offer in this situation. Some might smile and reassure you: "Don't worry. Remember what they say, 'Absence makes the heart grow fonder.' This will only strengthen your relationship." Others might call you aside and whisper, "Don't listen to them. Everybody knows, 'Out of sight, out of mind.' You'd better be careful."

Taking your mind off this problem, you begin to work on a class project. You have the option of working alone or as part of a group. Which should you do? You consult the wisdom of common sense. Maybe you should work in a group. After all, everyone knows that "two heads are better than one." As some members of your group begin to miss meetings and shirk responsibilities, though, you remember that "too many cooks spoil the broth." Will you regret having been so quick to decide to join this group? After all, haven't you been taught to "look before you leap"? Then again, if you had waited and missed the chance to join the group, you might have regretted your inaction, recalling that "he who hesitates is lost."

Questions about the course of relationships, the efficiency of working in groups, and the regret from action versus inaction are social psychological questions. And because we all are interested in predicting and understanding people's behaviors and their thoughts and feelings about each other, we all have our own opinions and intuitions about social psychological matters. If the discipline of social psychology were built on the personal experiences, observations, and intuitions of everyone who is interested in social psychological questions, it would be full of interesting theories and ideas, but it would also be a morass of contradictions, ambiguities, and relativism. Instead, social psychology is built on the scientific method.

Scientific? It's easy to see how chemistry is scientific. When you mix two specific compounds in the lab, you can predict exactly what will happen. The compounds will act the same way every time you mix them if the general conditions in the lab are the same. But what happens when you mix together two chemists, or any two people, in a social context? Sometimes you get great chemistry between them; other times you get apathy or even repulsion. How, then, can social behavior, which seems so variable, be studied scientifically?

"The most exciting phrase to hear in science, the one that heralds new discoveries, is not 'Eureka!' (I found it!) but 'That's funny. . . .'"

—Isaac Asimov

To many of us in the field, that's the great excitement and challenge of social psychology—the fact that it *is* so dynamic and diverse. Furthermore, in spite of these characteristics, social psychology can, and should, be studied according to scientific principles. Social psychologists develop specific, quantifiable hypotheses that can be tested empirically. If these hypotheses are wrong, they can be proven wrong. In addition, social scientists report the details of how they conduct their tests so that others can try to replicate their findings. They integrate evidence from across time and place. And slowly but steadily they build a consistent and ever more precise understanding of human nature. How social psychologists investigate social psychological questions scientifically is the focus of this chapter. Before we explain the methodology they use, we first explain why it's important and interesting for you to learn about these matters.

Why Should You Learn About Research Methods?

One important benefit for learning about research methods is that it can make you a better, more sophisticated consumer of information. Training in research methods in psychology can improve your reasoning about real-life events and problems (Bensley et al., 2010; Daniel & Braasch, 2013; Lehman et al., 1988; VanderStoep & Shaughnessy, 1997). We are constantly bombarded with "facts" from the media, from sales pitches, and from other people. Much of this information turns out to be wrong or, at best, oversimplified and misleading. We are told about the health benefits of eating certain kinds of food, the college entrance exam score benefits of certain preparation courses, or the social status benefits of driving a certain kind of car or wearing a certain kind of shoe. To each of these pronouncements, we should say, "Prove it." What is the evidence? What alternative explanations might there be?

For example, a commercial tells us that most doctors prefer a particular brand of aspirin. So should we buy this brand? Think about what it was compared with. Perhaps the doctors didn't prefer that brand of aspirin more than other (and cheaper) brands of aspirin but rather were asked to compare that brand of aspirin with several nonaspirin products for a particular problem. In that event, the doctors may have preferred *any* brand of aspirin more than nonaspirin products for that need. Thinking like a scientist while reading this text will foster a healthy sense of doubt about claims such as these. You will be in a better position to critically evaluate the information to which you're exposed and separate fact from fiction.

Victor Fraile/Corbis News/Corbis

We are bombarded with information in our everyday lives, such as in the countless advertisements designed to persuade us to buy particular products or adopt particular opinions or attitudes. Learning the methods used in social psychology research can help students become more sophisticated consumers of this information.

More immediately, learning about research methods should help you better understand the research findings reported in the rest of this book, which will in turn help you on tests and in subsequent courses. If you simply read a list of social psychological findings without knowing and understanding the evidence that researchers have produced to support the findings, you may discover later that the task of remembering which were the actual findings and which merely sound plausible can be difficult. Being able to understand, and therefore remember, the research evidence on which social psychological principles are based should provide you with a deeper comprehension of the material.

Developing Ideas: Beginning the Research Process

The research process involves coming up with ideas, refining them, testing them, and interpreting the meaning of the results obtained. This section describes the first stage of research—coming up with ideas. It also discusses the roles of hypotheses and theories and of basic and applied research.

■ Getting Ideas and Finding Out What's Been Done

Every social psychology study begins with a question. And the questions come from everywhere. As discussed in Chapter 1, one of the first social psychology experiments published was triggered by the question "Why do bicyclists race faster in the presence of other bicyclists?" (Triplett, 1897–1898). Or consider a much more recent example—social psychologist Dylan Selterman has been conducting fascinating studies examining the connection between people's dreams about romantic partners and their actual patterns of emotions and behaviors in personal relationships (Selterman et al., 2012, 2014). Where did this idea come from? It was inspired in part by the dreams some of his ex-girlfriends told him about!

Questions can come from a variety of sources, from something tragic, such as a controversial interracial shooting of an unarmed man; to something perplexing, such as why men are less likely to ask for help than are women; to something amusing, such as the lyrics of a country song suggesting that other patrons in a bar seem more attractive as closing time approaches (Correll et al., 2014; Pennebaker et al., 1979; Rosette et al., 2015).

Ideas also come from reading about research that has already been done. The most important research not only answers some pressing questions but raises new questions, inspiring additional research. The most reliable way to get ideas for new research, therefore, is to read about research already published. Even if you already have an idea, you'll need to search the social psychological literature to find out what's been published already. How do you find these published studies? Textbooks such as this one offer a good starting point. You also can find information about many research findings by searching the Internet, of course, but general searches online, such as through Google, can be wildly variable in the relevance, quality, and accuracy of the information presented. Instead, scholars in the field rely on electronic databases of published research, typically available via college or university library systems. Some of these databases, such as PsycINFO, are specific to the psychology literature; others are more general. These databases allow one to instantly search massive numbers of published articles and books.

■ Hypotheses and Theories

An initial idea for research may be so vague that it amounts to little more than a hunch or an educated guess. Some ideas vanish with the break of day. But others can be shaped into a **hypothesis**—an explicit, testable prediction about the conditions under which an event will occur. Based on observation, existing theory, or previous research findings, one might test a hypothesis such as "Teenage boys are more likely to be aggressive toward others if they have just played a violent video game for an hour than if they played a nonviolent video game for an hour." This is a specific prediction, and it can be tested empirically. Formulating a hypothesis is a critical step toward planning and conducting research. It allows us to move from the realm of common sense to the rigors of the scientific method.

As hypotheses proliferate and data are collected to test the hypotheses, a more advanced step in the research process may take place: the proposal of a **theory**—an organized set of principles used to explain observed phenomena. Social psychologists aspire to do more than collect a list of findings. The goal

"Education is not the filling of a pail, but the lighting of a fire."
—William Butler Yeats

"The currency of science is not truth, but doubt."
—Dennis Overbye

hypothesis A testable prediction about the conditions under which an event will occur.

theory An organized set of principles used to explain observed phenomena.

is to explain these findings, to articulate the connections between the variables that are studied, and to thereby predict and more completely understand our social worlds. All else being equal, the best theories are efficient and precise; encompass all of the relevant information; and lead to new hypotheses, further research, and better understanding. Good social psychological theories inspire subsequent research designed to test various aspects of the theories and the specific hypotheses that are derived from them. Whether it truly is accurate or not, a theory has little worth if it cannot be tested.

A theory may make an important contribution to the field even if it turns out to be wrong. The research it inspires may prove more valuable than the theory itself, as the results shed light on new truths that might not have been discovered without the directions suggested by the theory. Indeed, the best theorists want their ideas to be debated and even doubted, to inspire others in the field to put their ideas to the test. The goal is for these theories to evolve, to become more and more accurate and complete.

"Give people facts and you feed their minds for an hour. Awaken curiosity and they feed their own minds for a lifetime."
—Ian Russell

■ Basic and Applied Research

Is testing a theory the purpose of research in social psychology? For some researchers, yes. **Basic research** seeks to increase our understanding of human behavior and is often designed to test a specific hypothesis from a specific theory. **Applied research** focuses more specifically on making applications to the world and contributing to the solution of social problems.

Despite their differences, basic and applied research are closely connected in social psychology. Some researchers switch back and forth between the two—today basic, tomorrow applied. Some studies test a theory and examine a real-world phenomenon simultaneously. For instance, Carol Dweck and others have tested theories about the effects of people's beliefs about human abilities while addressing important problems such as students dropping out of school or the underrepresentation of women in math and science (Good et al., 2012; Paunesku et al., 2015). As a pioneer in both basic and applied approaches, Kurt Lewin (1951) set the tone when he encouraged basic researchers to be concerned with complex social problems and urged applied researchers to recognize that "there is nothing so practical as a good theory."

"Close cooperation between theoretical and applied psychology can be accomplished . . . if the theorist does not look toward applied problems with highbrow aversion or with a fear of social problems, and if the applied psychologist realizes that there is nothing so practical as a good theory."
—Kurt Lewin

Refining Ideas: Defining and Measuring Social Psychological Variables

To test their hypotheses, researchers always must decide how they will define and measure the variables in which they are interested. This is sometimes a straightforward process. For example, if you are interested in comparing how quickly people run a 100-meter dash when alone and when racing against another person, you're all set if you have a stopwatch and runners who can race alone or in pairs. Many other times, however, the process is less straightforward. For example, imagine you are interested in studying the effects of mood on altruistic (helpful) behavior. Sounds simple, right? But wait. You need to step back and ask yourself, "What do I mean by mood? How would I measure or manipulate it? What do I mean by altruistic behavior?" You will need to define these concepts, and there may be countless ways to do this. Which ones should you pick?

basic research   Research whose goal is to increase the understanding of human behavior, often by testing hypotheses based on a theory.

applied research   Research whose goal is to make applications to the world and contribute to the solution of social problems.

From this picture, we can guess that the boy sitting by himself on the playground is lonely, but how do researchers precisely define and measure conceptual variables such as loneliness? Researchers may use any of a number of approaches, such as asking people how they feel and observing their behavior.

From the Abstract to the Specific: Conceptual Variables and Operational Definitions

When a researcher first develops a hypothesis, the variables typically are in an abstract, general form. These are *conceptual variables*. Examples of conceptual variables include prejudice, conformity, attraction, love, group pressure, and social anxiety. In order to test specific hypotheses, we must then transform these conceptual variables into variables that can be manipulated or measured in a study. The specific way in which a conceptual variable is manipulated or measured is called the **operational definition** of the variable. Part of the challenge and fun of designing research in social psychology is taking an abstract conceptual variable such as love or group pressure and deciding how to operationally define it so as to manipulate or measure it.

Imagine, for example, wanting to conduct a study on the effects of alcohol intoxication on aggression. One of the conceptual variables might be whether or not participants are intoxicated. There are several ways of measuring this variable, most of which are relatively straightforward. For instance, one researcher might operationally define intoxication as when a participant has a blood alcohol level of .10 or more, whereas another might define it as when a participant says that he or she feels drunk. A second conceptual variable in this study would be aggression. Measuring aggression in experiments is particularly difficult because of ethical and practical issues—researchers can't let participants in their studies attack each other. Researchers interested in measuring aggression are thus often forced to measure relatively unusual behaviors, such as administering shocks, blasts of noise, or even hot sauce to another person as part of a specific task.

Often there is no single best way to transform a variable from the abstract (conceptual) to the specific (operational). A great deal of trial and error may be involved. However, sometimes there are systematic, statistical ways of checking how valid various manipulations and measures are, and researchers spend a great deal of time fine-tuning their operational definitions to best capture the conceptual variables they wish to study.

operational definition The specific procedures for manipulating or measuring a conceptual variable.

"Clemson here, how may I disappoint you?"

This person would probably score low on the Rosenberg Self-Esteem Scale.

Researchers evaluate the manipulation and measurement of variables in terms of their **construct validity**. Construct validity refers to the extent to which (1) the manipulations in an experiment really manipulate the conceptual variables they were designed to manipulate, and (2) the measures used in a study (experimental or otherwise) really measure the conceptual variables they were designed to measure.

■ Measuring Variables: Using Self-Reports, Observations, and Technology

Social psychologists measure variables in many ways, but most can be placed into one of two categories: self-reports and observations. We discuss each of these methods in the next sections, along with how advances in technology are enabling social psychologists to measure variables in new ways.

The challenge of measuring variables. This may not be the most precise way to measure height, but it's pretty charming.

Self-Reports   Collecting *self-reports*—in which participants disclose their thoughts, feelings, desires, and actions—is a widely used measurement technique in social psychology. Self-reports can consist of individual questions or sets of questions that together measure a single conceptual variable. For example, one popular self-report measure, the Rosenberg Self-Esteem Scale, consists of a set of questions that measures individuals' overall self-esteem. Respondents are asked the extent to which they agree with statements such as "I feel that I have a number of good qualities," and "All in all, I am inclined to feel that I'm a failure." This scale, first developed by Morris Rosenberg in the 1960s, continues to be used today in a wide variety of settings in countries around the world because many researchers consider it to have good construct validity (Alessandri et al., 2015; Galanou et al., 2014; Westaway et al., 2015).

Self-reports give the researcher access to an individual's beliefs and perceptions. But self-reports are not always accurate and can be misleading. For example, the desire to look good to ourselves and others can influence how we respond. This is evident in the results of research using the **bogus pipeline technique**—a procedure in which participants are led to believe that their responses will be verified by an infallible lie detector. When participants believe their lies will be detected, they report facts about themselves more accurately and endorse socially unacceptable opinions more frequently. The bogus pipeline is, in fact, bogus; no such infallible device exists. But belief in its powers discourages people from lying (Brunell & Fisher, 2014; Grover & Miller, 2012; Jones & Sigall, 1971).

Self-reports are also affected by the way that questions are asked, such as how they are worded or in what order or context they are asked (Betts & Hartley, 2012; Schwarz & Oyserman, 2011). For instance, although "global warming" and "climate change" mean the same thing to most Americans, Jonathon Schuldt and others (2015) found that Republican (but not Democratic) respondents to a survey in the United States were much less likely to indicate that they believe in the issue if it was referred to as "global warming" rather than "climate change." In another study, a large majority (88%) of participants indicated that they thought condoms were effective in stopping AIDS when condoms were said to have a "95 percent success rate." However, when condoms were said to have a "5 percent

construct validity   The extent to which the measures used in a study measure the variables they were designed to measure and the manipulations in an experiment manipulate the variables they were designed to manipulate.

bogus pipeline technique   A procedure in which research participants are (falsely) led to believe that their responses will be verified by an infallible lie detector.

● FIGURE 2.1

"Black" vs. "African American": What's in a Name?

Although most Americans think of "Black" and "African American" as the same thing when identifying the race of someone, a 2015 experiment found that white American participants estimated someone's salary as significantly lower (graph on top), and had more negative reactions to a suspected criminal (graph on bottom), if the individual was identified as Black rather than African American. Based on Hall et al., 2015.

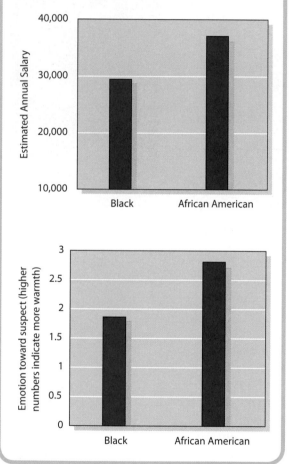

failure rate" (which is merely another way of saying the same thing), less than half (42%) of the participants indicated that they thought condoms were effective (Linville et al., 1992). More recently, Erika Hall and others (2015) found in one study that that white Americans estimated a man's salary as significantly lower, and in another study felt more negatively toward a criminal suspect, if the man was identified as "Black" rather than "African American" (see ● Figure 2.1). There are theoretical explanations that can account for the seemingly irrational results reported in these studies, but the point here is that subtle factors can have significant effects on the attitudes and opinions that people report.

Indeed, even the exact same question can elicit very different responses depending on the context in which the question occurs. For example, all individuals contacted in one survey were asked how important the issue of skin cancer was in their lives, but this question was asked either before or after a series of questions about other health concerns. Even though the wording of the question was identical, respondents rated skin cancer as significantly more important if the question was asked first than if it came after the other health questions (Rimal & Real, 2005). In another example of the impact of previous questions, Kimberly Rios Morrison and Adrienne Chung (2011) found that white college students indicated significantly less support for multiculturalism if they had earlier marked their race/ethnicity as "white" on a questionnaire than if the questionnaire used the term "European American" instead.

Another reason self-reports can be inaccurate is that they often ask participants to report on thoughts or behaviors from the past, and people's memories are very prone to error, particularly if how they feel *now* about things is different from how they felt in the past. To minimize this problem, psychologists have developed ways to reduce the time that elapses between an actual experience and the person's report of it. For example, some use *interval-contingent* self-reports, in which respondents report their experiences at regular intervals, usually once a day. Researchers may also collect *signal-contingent* self-reports. Here, respondents report their experiences as soon as possible after being signaled to do so, usually by means of a text message or a special app. Finally, some researchers collect *event-contingent* self-reports, in which respondents report on a designated set of events as soon as possible after such events have occurred.

Observations Self-reports are but one tool social psychologists use to measure variables. Researchers also observe people's actions. Sometimes these observations are very simple, as when a researcher notes which of two items a person selects. At other times, however, the observations are more elaborate, as when judging whether someone is acting warmly or coldly toward another person, and require that interrater reliability be established. **Interrater reliability** refers to the level of agreement among multiple observers of the same behavior. Only when different observers agree can the data be trusted.

The advantage of observational methods is that they avoid our sometimes-faulty recollections and distorted interpretations of our own behavior. Actions can speak louder than words. Of course, if individuals know they are being observed, their behaviors, like their self-reports, may be biased by the desire to present

interrater reliability The degree to which different observers agree on their observations.

themselves in a favorable light. Therefore, researchers sometimes make observations much more subtly. For example, in experiments concerning interracial interactions, researchers may record participants' eye contact and seating distance to demonstrate biases that would not be revealed using more overt measures (Goff, Steele, & Davies, 2008; Todd et al., 2011).

Technology Social psychologists use more than merely their eyes and ears to observe their subjects, of course. Various kinds of technology are used to measure cognitive and physiological responses such as reaction time or heart rate, levels of particular hormones, and sexual arousal. Eye-tracking technology is used to measure exactly where and for how long participants look at particular parts of a stimulus, such as a face or a video of an interaction.

Most recently, social psychologists have begun opening a window into the live human brain—fortunately, without having to lift a scalpel. Brain-imaging technologies take and combine thousands of images of the brain in action. These images can show researchers what parts of the brain seem to "light up"—or show increased activity—in response to a particular stimulus or situation. For example, although participants in a study may show no signs of intergroup bias on their self-reports or through easily observable behavior in the lab, their patterns of brain activity may reveal very different emotional reactions to a picture of someone on the basis of their perceived group membership (Amodio, 2014; Cikara & Van Bavel, 2014).

Observational research can reveal some fascinating—and sometimes disturbing!—insights into social behavior.

Matthew Diffee/The New Yorker Collection/The Cartoon Bank

"Just as we suspected—they're beginning to form a boy band."

Testing Ideas: Research Designs

Social psychologists use a variety of methods to test their research hypotheses and theories. Although methods vary, the field generally emphasizes objective, systematic, and quantifiable approaches. Social psychologists do not simply seek out evidence that supports their ideas; rather, they test their ideas in ways that could very clearly prove them wrong. We can divide these types of tests into three categories: descriptive, correlational, and experimental.

■ Descriptive Research: Discovering Trends and Tendencies

One obvious way of testing ideas about people is simply to record how frequently or how typically people think, feel, or behave in particular ways. The goal of *descriptive research* in social psychology is, as the term implies, to describe people and their thoughts, feelings, and behaviors. This method can test questions such as: Do most people support capital punishment? What percentage of people who encounter a person lying on the sidewalk would offer to help that person? What do men and women say are the things most likely to make them jealous of their partner? Particular methods of doing descriptive research include observing people, studying records of past events and behaviors, and surveying people. We discuss each of these methods in this section.

"You can observe a lot just by watching."

—Yogi Berra

AP Images/Christopher Szagola

Are professional basketball players more likely to miss a free throw if they were awarded the shot because of an obviously bad call by the referee? A 2010 study reported here attempted to answer that question.

Observational Studies   We just discussed using observations as a way to measure and assess variables. Many social psychologists use these methods to test ideas involving descriptive research. For example, some researchers have gotten an unfiltered look at the frequency and severity of bullying among adolescents by spending time in playgrounds and school-yards carefully watching and taking notes on the children's interactions, sometimes using hidden cameras and microphones (with the schools' and parents' consent) (Frey et al., 2009; Hawkins et al., 2001).

One particularly interesting study involved National Basketball Association (NBA) basketball games. Graeme Haynes and Thomas Gilovich (2010) wanted to see how often professional players missed free-throw attempts in cases when they were awarded the shots because of an obviously bad foul call against the other team. The researchers were testing the idea that when players benefit from an obviously bad call by the referee, they subtly, even unknowingly, may be troubled by the sense that they were awarded something they didn't deserve, leading them to be more likely to miss their free-throw attempt.

The researchers couldn't run an experiment in which they induced refs into making bad calls during actual games, so they did the next best thing: they watched tapes of NBA games. A lot of them. One hundred and two games, to be precise. Obviously bad foul calls were identified, and whether the subsequent free-throw shooter made or missed his ensuing shots was noted.

Consistent with the adage used by some athletes, "The ball don't lie," the results indicated that justice was indeed served, specifically on the first of the two free throws players took after the bad call. As can be seen in ● Figure 2.2, the percentage of shots made on the first shot after the bad call was significantly lower than normal. This effect disappeared, however, by the time of the second shot.

Archival Studies   Archival research involves examining existing records of past events and behaviors, such as newspaper articles, medical records, diaries, sports statistics, personal ads, crime statistics, or hits on a website. A major advantage of archival measures is that because the researchers are observing behavior secondhand, they can be sure that they did not influence the behavior by their presence. A limitation of this approach is that available records are not always complete or sufficiently detailed, and they may have been collected in a nonsystematic manner.

Archival measures are particularly valuable for examining cultural and historical trends. In Chapter 11 on Aggression, for example, we report a number of trends concerning how the rates of violent crimes have changed in recent years. These data come from archival records, such as the records of police stations, the Federal Bureau of Investigation (FBI), and the United Nations. Recent examples of archival research include studies that analyzed the content of TV commercials or the wording of job advertisements to examine if they were biased as a function of gender stereotypes (Gaucher et al., 2011; Kay & Furnham, 2013).

Surveys   It seems that nobody in politics today sneezes without first conducting an opinion poll. Surveys have become increasingly popular in recent years, and they are conducted on everything from politics to attitudes about social issues to the percentages of people who think the best cure for hiccups is to drink a glass of water or hold your breath. (OK, we'll tell you: According to a May 2012 poll on Yahoo.com with almost 60,000 responses, 52% say drink water, 37% say hold your breath—and 12% say have someone scare you.) Conducting surveys involves asking people questions about their attitudes, beliefs, and behaviors. Surveys can be conducted in person, over the phone, by mail, or via the Internet. Many social psychological questions can be addressed only with surveys because they involve variables that are impossible or unethical to observe directly or manipulate, such as people's sexual behaviors or their optimism about the future.

Although anyone can conduct a survey (and sometimes it seems that everyone does), there is a science to designing, conducting, and interpreting the results of surveys properly and to avoid the kinds of problems we described earlier in this chapter about how wording and question order can bias self-reports.

One of the most important issues that survey researchers face is how to select the people who will take part in the survey. The researchers first must identify the *population* in which they are interested. Is this survey supposed to tell us about the attitudes of North Americans in general, shoppers at Wal-Mart, or students in an Introduction to Social Psychology course at University X, for example? From this general population, the researchers select a subset, or *sample,* of individuals. For a survey to be accurate, the sample must be similar to, or representative of, the population on important characteristics such as age, sex, race, income, education, and cultural background. The best way to achieve this representativeness is to use **random sampling**, a method of selection in which everyone in a population has an equal chance of being selected for the sample. Survey researchers use randomizing procedures, such as randomly distributed numbers generated by computers, to decide how to select individuals for their samples.

To see the importance of random sampling, consider a pair of U.S. presidential elections (Rosnow & Rosenthal, 1993). Just before the 1936 election, a magazine called the *Literary Digest* predicted that Alfred Landon, the Republican governor of Kansas, would win by 14 percentage points over Franklin Roosevelt. The *Digest* based its prediction on a survey of more than 2 million Americans. In fact, though, Landon *lost* the election by 24 percentage points. The magazine, which had been in financial trouble before the election, declared bankruptcy soon after.

Twenty years later, the Gallup survey's prediction of Dwight Eisenhower's victory was almost perfect—it was off by less than 2%. The size of its sample? Only about 8,000. How could the 1936 survey, with its much larger sample of 2 million people, be so wrong and the 1956 survey be so right? The answer is that the 1936 sample was not randomly selected. The *Digest* contacted people through sources such as phone books and club membership lists. In 1936, many people could not afford to have phones or belong to clubs. The people in the sample, therefore, tended to be wealthier than much of the population, and wealthier people preferred Landon. In 1956, by contrast, Gallup pollsters randomly selected election districts throughout the country and then randomly selected households within those districts. Today,

● **FIGURE 2.2**

Observing Basketball: The Ball Don't Lie

This graph compares the free-throw success rates for (a) the average NBA player that season (left bar), the season average for the players included in the study (second bar), (c) the first shots after a bad call (third bar), and (d) the second shots after a bad call (right-most bar). As you can see, players shot much worse immediately after benefiting from a bad call. From Haynes & Gilovich, 2010.

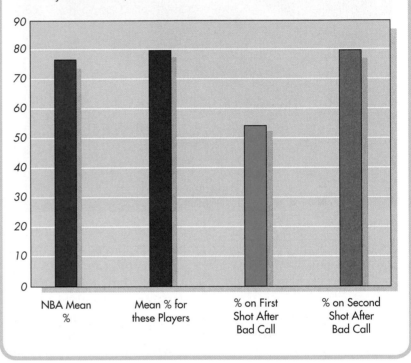

random sampling   A method of selecting participants for a study so that everyone in a population has an equal chance of being in the study.

In the 1948 U.S. presidential election, pollsters nationwide predicted that Thomas Dewey would defeat Harry Truman by a wide margin. As Truman basked in his victory, pollsters realized that their predictions were based on nonrandom samples of voters. Random sampling would have led to much more accurate predictions.

because of improved sampling procedures, surveys conducted on little more than 1,000 Americans can be used to make accurate predictions about the entire U.S. population.

■ Correlational Research: Looking for Associations

Although there is much to learn from descriptive research, social psychologists typically want to know more. Most research hypotheses in social psychology concern the relationship between variables. For example, is there a relationship between people's gender and their willingness to ask for help from others or between how physically attractive people are and how much money they make?

One way to test such hypotheses is with correlational research. Like descriptive research, **correlational research** can be conducted using observational, archival, or survey methods. Unlike descriptive research, however, correlational approaches measure the *relationship* between different variables. The extent to which variables relate to each other, or *correlate*, can suggest how similar or distinct two different measures are (for example, how related are people's self-esteem and popularity) and how well one variable can be used to predict another (for example, how well we can predict academic success in college from college entrance exam scores). It is important to note that researchers doing correlational research typically do not manipulate the variables they study; they simply measure them.

One interesting correlational study was conducted recently by a team of researchers who got access to 826 million tweets (!) made available to them by Twitter. The researchers looked at the relationship between the language that people in more than 1,300 counties in the United States used on Twitter and measures of health (from public records) in those counties. They found, for example, that communities in which people tended to tweet using angry language also tended to have greater rates of heart-disease mortality (Eichstaedt et al., 2015).

Correlation Coefficient When researchers examine the relationship between variables that vary in quantity (such as height or degree of self-esteem), they can measure the strength and direction of the relationship between the variables and calculate a statistic called a **correlation coefficient**. Correlation coefficients can range from +1.0 to −1.0. The absolute value of the number (the number itself, without the positive or negative sign) indicates how strongly the two variables are associated. The larger the absolute value of the number, the stronger the association between the two variables, and thus the better either of the variables is as a predictor of the other. Whether the coefficient is positive or negative indicates the direction of the relationship. A positive correlation coefficient indicates that as one variable increases, so does the other.

For example, college entrance exam scores correlate positively with grades. The positive direction of this relationship indicates higher entrance exam scores are associated with higher grades and lower entrance exam scores are associated with lower grades. This correlation is not perfect; some people with high entrance

correlational research Research designed to measure the association between variables that are not manipulated by the researcher.

correlation coefficient A statistical measure of the strength and direction of the association between two variables.

exam scores have poor grades and vice versa. Therefore, the correlation is less than +1.0, but it is greater than 0 because there is some association between the two. A negative coefficient indicates that the two variables go in opposite directions: As one goes up, the other tends to go down. For example, number of classes missed and GPA are likely to be negatively correlated. And a correlation close to 0 indicates that there is no consistent relationship at all. These three types of patterns are illustrated in ● Figure 2.3. Because few variables are perfectly related to each other, most correlation coefficients do not approach +1.0 or −1.0 but have more moderate values, such as +.39 or −.57.

Some correlational studies involve a variable that does not vary in quantity, such as race, gender, political affiliation, or whether one's favorite food is Italian, Mexican, or Thai. In this case, researchers cannot compute a typical correlation coefficient but instead use different kinds of statistical analysis. The same point applies, though, as the researchers can determine if there is a relationship between the two variables.

Advantages and Disadvantages of Correlational Research

Correlational research has many advantages. It can study the associations of naturally occurring variables that cannot be manipulated or induced—such as ethnicity, age, and income. It can examine phenomena that would be difficult or unethical to create for research purposes, such as love, hate, and abuse. And it offers researchers a great deal of freedom in where variables are measured. Participants can be brought into a laboratory specially constructed for research purposes or they can be approached in a real-world setting (often called "the field") such as a shopping mall or airport.

Despite these advantages, however, correlational research has one very serious disadvantage. And here it is in bold letters: **Correlation is not causation.**

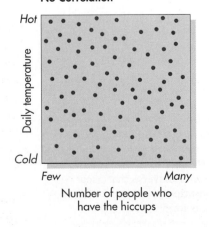

Moodboard/Corbis

Similarity is correlated with attraction—the more similar two people are (such as in their attitudes and personalities), the more attractive they are likely to find each other. But a correlation cannot identify the cause of this attraction. Chapter 9 discusses correlational and experimental research on the role of similarity in the attraction process.

● FIGURE 2.3

Correlations: Positive, Negative, and None

Correlations reveal a systematic association between two variables. Positive correlations indicate that variables are in sync: Increases in one variable are associated with increases in the other; decreases, with decreases. Negative correlations indicate that variables go in opposite directions: Increases in one variable are associated with decreases in the other. When two variables are not systematically associated, there is no correlation.

© Cengage Learning®

Positive Correlation

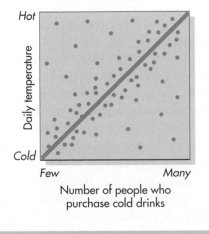

Daily temperature — Hot / Cold

Number of people who purchase cold drinks — Few / Many

Negative Correlation

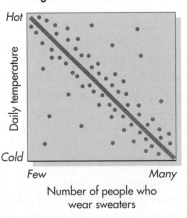

Daily temperature — Hot / Cold

Number of people who wear sweaters — Few / Many

No Correlation

Daily temperature — Hot / Cold

Number of people who have the hiccups — Few / Many

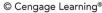

● FIGURE 2.4

Explaining Correlations: Three Possibilities

A positive correlation between how much children play violent video games and how aggressively they behave could potentially be explained in each of the following ways:

1. Playing violent video games causes aggressive behavior.
2. Children who behave aggressively like to play a lot of violent video games.
3. Children who have family troubles, such as parents who are not very involved in the children's development, tend both to play a lot of violent video games and to behave aggressively.

© Cengage Learning®

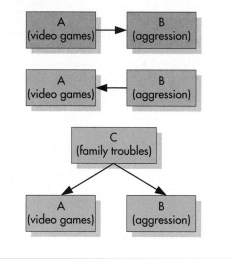

In other words, a correlation cannot demonstrate a cause-and-effect relationship. Instead of revealing a specific causal pathway from one variable, A, to another variable, B, a correlation between variables A and B contains within it three possible causal effects: A could cause B; B could cause A; or a third variable, C, could cause both A and B. For example, imagine learning that the number of hours per night one sleeps is negatively correlated with the number of colds one gets. This means that as the amount of sleep increases, colds decrease in frequency; conversely as sleep decreases, colds become more frequent. One reasonable explanation for this relationship is that lack of sleep (variable A) causes people to become more vulnerable to colds (variable B). Another reasonable explanation, however, is that people who have colds can't sleep well, and so colds (variable B) cause lack of sleep (variable A). A third reasonable explanation is that some other variable (C) causes both lack of sleep and greater frequency of colds. This third variable could be stress. Indeed, stress has many effects on people, as will be discussed in Chapter 14 on Health. ● Figure 2.4 describes another correlation that can be explained in many ways—the correlation between playing violent video games and aggression.

We can guarantee you this: There will be many, many times in your life when you'll encounter reports in the media that suggest cause-and-effect relationships based on correlational research. Even the most respectable news sources are guilty of this repeatedly. If you look for it, you can find numerous examples on a weekly basis. One of the great benefits of learning and gaining experience with the material in this chapter is that you can see the flaws in media reports such as these and become less likely to be taken in by them. Correlation is not causation.

Do we learn nothing, then, from correlations? To say that would be to take caution too far. Correlations tell researchers about the strength and direction of relationships between variables, thus helping them understand these variables better and allowing them to use one variable to predict the other. Correlations can be extremely useful in developing new hypotheses to guide future research. And by gathering large sets of correlations and using complicated statistical techniques to crunch the data, we can develop highly accurate predictions of future events.

▇ Experiments: Looking for Cause and Effect

Social psychologists often do want to examine cause-and-effect relationships. Although it is informative to know, for example, that playing a lot of violent video games is correlated with violent behavior in real life, the inevitable next question is whether playing these video games *causes* an increase in violent behavior. If we want to examine cause-and-effect relationships, we need to conduct an **experiment**. Experiments are the most popular method of testing ideas in social psychology, and they can range from the very simple to the incredibly elaborate. All of them, however, share two essential characteristics.

1. The researcher has *control* over the experimental procedures, manipulating the variables of interest while ensuring uniformity elsewhere. In other words, all participants in the research are treated in exactly the same manner—except for the specific differences the experimenter wants to create.

experiment   A form of research that can demonstrate causal relationships because (1) the experimenter has control over the events that occur and (2) participants are randomly assigned to conditions.

2. Participants in the study are *randomly* assigned to the different manipulations (called "conditions") included in the experiment. If there are two conditions, who goes where may be determined by simply flipping a coin. If there are many conditions, a computer program may be used. But however it's done, **random assignment** means that participants are not assigned to a condition on the basis of their personal or behavioral characteristics. Through random assignment, the experimenter attempts to ensure a level playing field. *On average, the participants randomly assigned to one condition are no different from those assigned to another condition.* Differences that appear between conditions after an experimental manipulation can therefore be attributed to the impact of that manipulation and not to any preexisting differences between participants.

Because of experimenter control and random assignment of participants, an experiment is a powerful technique for examining cause and effect. Both characteristics serve the same goal: to eliminate the influence of any factors other than the experimental manipulation. By ruling out alternative explanations for research results, we become more confident that we understand just what has, in fact, caused a certain outcome to occur. Table 2.1 summarizes the distinctions between correlational and experimental research.

▲ **TABLE 2.1**

Correlations Versus Experiments

	Correlational Research	Experimental Research
What does it involve?	Measuring variables and the degree of association between them	Random assignment to conditions and control over the events that occur; determining the effects of manipulations of the independent variable(s) on changes in the dependent variable(s)
What is the biggest advantage of using this method?	Enables researchers to study naturally occurring variables, including variables that would be too difficult or unethical to manipulate	Enables researchers to determine cause-and-effect relationships—that is, whether the independent variable can cause a change in the dependent variable

© Cengage Learning®

Random Sampling Versus Random Assignment You may recall that we mentioned random sampling earlier, in connection with surveys. It's important to remember the differences between random *sampling* and random *assignment*. Random sampling concerns how individuals are selected to be in a study. It is important for generalizing the results obtained from a sample to a broader population, and it is therefore very important for survey research. Random assignment concerns not who is selected to be in the study but rather how participants in the study are assigned to different conditions, as explained above. Random assignment is essential to experiments because it is necessary for determining cause-and-effect relationships; without it, there is always the possibility that any differences found between the conditions in a study were caused by preexisting differences among participants. Random sampling, in contrast, is not necessary for establishing causality. For that reason, and because random sampling is difficult and expensive, very few experiments use random sampling. We consider the implications of this fact later in the chapter.

Laboratory and Field Experiments Most experiments in social psychology are conducted in a *laboratory* setting, usually located in a college or university, so that the environment can be controlled and the participants carefully studied. Social psychology labs do not necessarily look like stereotypical laboratories with liquid bubbling in beakers or expensive equipment everywhere (although many social psychology labs are indeed very high-tech). They can resemble ordinary classrooms or even game rooms. The key point here is that the laboratory setting enables researchers to have control over the setting, measure participants' behaviors precisely, and keep conditions identical for participants.

random assignment A method of assigning participants to the various conditions of an experiment so that each participant in the experiment has an equal chance of being in any of the conditions.

Gideon Mendel/Corbis News/Corbis

In field research, people are observed in real-world settings. Field researchers may observe children in a schoolyard, for example, to study any of a variety of social psychological issues, such as friendship patterns, group dynamics, conformity, helping, aggression, and cultural differences.

Field research is conducted in real-world settings outside the laboratory. Researchers interested in studying helping behavior, for example, might conduct an experiment in a public park. The advantage of field experiments is that people are more likely to act naturally in a natural setting than in a laboratory in which they know they are being studied. The disadvantage of field settings is that the experimenter often has less control and cannot ensure that the participants in the various conditions of the experiment will be exposed to the same things.

Because of the important role that experiments play in social psychology, let's take a closer look at the elements of experiments by focusing on one example.

A Social Psychology Experiment on Presidential Debates   While watching a debate between candidates for the presidency of the United States, one of the authors of this textbook wondered if the applause, laughter, and jeering of people in the audience at the debate might affect the judgments of the millions of potential voters watching on television. This led to a series of experiments, including one in which college students watched a tape of a 1984 presidential debate between Ronald Reagan and Walter Mondale (Fein et al., 2007). During that debate Reagan fired off a pair of one-liners that elicited a great deal of laughter and applause from the audience. Political analysts have wondered whether those one-liners may have won the debate, and possibly the election, for Reagan. The one-liners comprised only seconds of a long debate concerning the most important issues of the day. Could these few seconds have made such a difference?

To study this issue, we had students watch 40 minutes of the debate under one of three conditions. One-third of the students saw the debate as it was, without any editing. One-third of the students saw the debate with the two one-liners and the ensuing audience reaction edited out. By comparing these two conditions, we could see whether the presence versus absence of this pair of jokes could make a large difference in people's impressions of Reagan from the debate. However, there was also a third condition. One-third of the students saw the debate with the one-liners intact but the audience reaction edited out. That is, Reagan told his jokes, but there appeared to be no audience response, and the debate continued uninterrupted.

After watching the debate, the students judged the performance of the candidates on a scale ranging from 0 *(terrible)* to 100 *(excellent)*. As you can see from the first two bars in ● Figure 2.5, the students who saw the entire unedited tape did not rate Reagan much more positively than did the students who saw the debate without the one-liners. This suggests that Reagan's jokes did not have much impact on these viewers' perceptions of him. But look at the third bar in the figure. It illustrates that the students who saw the version of the debate with the one-liners kept in but the audience reaction edited out rated Reagan much less positively than did either of the other groups. What could explain their negativity toward Reagan's debate performance? Perhaps when Reagan's jokes appeared to elicit no reaction, the students unknowingly used the lack of reaction as an indication that Reagan's attempts at wit were inept, and this conclusion caused them to see Reagan in a much less positive light.

What is interesting about these results from a social psychological standpoint is that the students' judgments were influenced more by other people's *reactions* to what Reagan said (that is, whether or not the audience appeared to laugh) than by the *content* of what he said (that is, whether or not the one-liners were edited out of the tape). And it is important to note that these "other people" were not in the room with the students; they were simply sounds on a videotape recorded many years before. Findings such as this demonstrate that the "social context" can be very subtle and yet can have very powerful effects on our thoughts, feelings, and behaviors.

Independent and Dependent Variables Now that we've looked at an experiment, let's focus on some of the specific elements. In an experiment, researchers manipulate one or more **independent variables** and examine the effect of these manipulations on one or more **dependent variables**. In the experiment we've just described, there was only one independent variable: the variations of the debate video, with each participant randomly assigned to one of the three versions. The dependent variable was the ratings of Reagan's performance. It was the dependent variable because the researchers were interested in seeing if the ratings would *depend* on (that is, be influenced by) the manipulation of the independent variable (that is, by which version of the debate they watched).

Subject Variables Some experiments include variables that are neither dependent nor truly independent. The gender, ethnicity, and prior political leanings of the participants may vary, for example, and researchers may be interested in examining some of these differences. These variables cannot be manipulated and randomly assigned, so they are not true independent variables, and they are not influenced by the independent variables, so they are not dependent variables. Variables such as these are called **subject variables** because they characterize preexisting differences among the subjects, or participants, in the experiment. If a study includes subject variables but no true, randomly assigned independent variable, it is not a true experiment. But experiments often include subject variables along with independent variables so that researchers can test whether the independent variables have the same or different effects on different kinds of participants. In our presidential debate experiment, for example, we could have examined if the results might have varied not only as a function of our manipulated variable (the version of the debate) but also as a function of the participant's gender. (In fact, we did look at this, and gender did not make a difference.)

Statistical Significance and Replications In the presidential debate experiment, the average rating of Reagan in the unedited condition was 66 on a 0–100 point scale, and it was 49 in the condition in which the audience reaction was removed. Is the difference between 66 and 49 large enough to be meaningful, or could this difference simply be due to chance (that is, just random variation, like flipping a coin 10 times and getting heads 6 times and tails 4)? The answer is that you can't tell just by looking at these numbers alone. Results obtained in an experiment are examined with statistical analyses that allow the researcher to determine how likely it is that the results could have occurred by random chance. The standard convention is that

● **FIGURE 2.5**

Influence of Others' Reactions

This graph shows the results of research in which participants saw different versions of a tape of a 1984 presidential debate between Ronald Reagan and Walter Mondale. During the debate, Reagan had delivered a pair of witty one-liners that elicited a positive audience reaction. Participants who saw an unedited version of the tape and participants who saw a version with the jokes and the audience reaction edited out judged Reagan's performance similarly. Participants who saw a version with the jokes left in but the audience reaction edited out (suggesting that the audience didn't find the jokes funny) rated Reagan much more negatively. Adapted from Fein, Goethals, & Kugler, 2007.

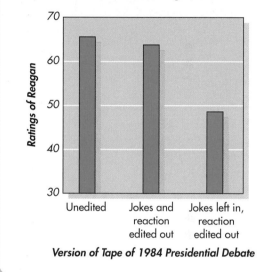

Version of Tape of 1984 Presidential Debate

independent variable In an experiment, a factor that experimenters manipulate to see if it affects the dependent variable.

dependent variable In an experiment, a factor that experimenters measure to see if it is affected by the independent variable.

subject variable A variable that characterizes preexisting differences among the participants in a study.

if the results could have occurred by chance 5 or fewer times in 100 possible outcomes, then the result is *statistically significant* and should be taken seriously.

The fact that results are statistically significant does not mean, however, that they are absolutely certain. In essence, statistical significance is an attractive betting proposition. The odds are quite good (at least 95 out of 100) that the effects obtained in the study were due to the experimental manipulation of the independent variable. But there is still the possibility (as high as 5 out of 100) that the findings occurred by chance. This is one reason why it is important to try to *replicate* the results of an experiment—to repeat the experiment and see if similar results are found. If similar results are found, the probability that these results could have occurred by chance both times is less than 1 out of 400. Statistical significance is relevant not only for the results of experiments but also for many other kinds of data as well, such as correlations. A correlation between two variables may be statistically significant or not, depending on the strength of the correlation and the number of participants or observations in the data.

When the results of some research are reported in the media or an advertisement, it's not always clear from the reporting whether the results are statistically significant, so it is important to be very cautious when learning about them. You can be sure, however, that whenever we report in this textbook that there is a difference between conditions of an experiment or that two variables are correlated, these results are statistically significant.

Very recently there has been a growing emphasis in psychology (and some other disciplines, such as medicine) on the importance of both replicating research findings and using statistical techniques that serve as alternatives to the focus on statistical significance (Trafimow & Marks, 2015). In the coming years these alternatives will no doubt become more popular. We will return to this issue in the final section of this chapter.

Internal Validity: Did the Independent Variable Cause the Effect?

When an experiment is properly conducted, its results are said to have **internal validity**: There is reasonable certainty that the independent variable did, in fact, cause the effects obtained on the dependent variable (Cook & Campbell, 1979). As noted earlier, both experimenter control and random assignment seek to rule out alternative explanations of the research results, thereby strengthening the internal validity of the research. If some other factor varies consistently along with the manipulation, this other factor is called a **confound**. A confound is a serious threat to internal validity and, therefore, makes the issue of cause and effect in the experiment uncertain. For example, if the students in the presidential debate study who watched the unedited version of the debate did so in one room, and the students who watched the edited versions did so in a different room, then this would be a confound. It would be impossible to know if it was the manipulation of the version of the debate or if it was some difference between the rooms (such as the temperature, the art on the wall, etc.) that caused the effect on ratings of Reagan's performance. Fortunately, the experimenters knew to avoid this problem.

Experiments often include *control groups* for purposes of internal validity. Typically, a control group consists of participants who experience all of the procedures except the experimental treatment. In the debate study, for example, the participants in the condition in which the video of the debate was unedited was the control group, which provided a baseline against which to compare the judgments of participants who watched the other versions.

Outside the laboratory, creating control groups in natural settings that examine real-life events raises many practical and ethical problems. For example,

internal validity The degree to which there can be reasonable certainty that the independent variables in an experiment caused the effects obtained on the dependent variables.

confound A factor other than the independent variable that varies between the conditions of an experiment, thereby calling into question what caused any effects on the dependent variable.

researchers testing new medical treatments for deadly diseases face a terrible dilemma. Individuals randomly assigned to the control group are excluded for the duration of the study from what could turn out to be a life-saving new intervention. Yet without such a comparison, it is extremely difficult to determine which new treatments are effective and which are useless.

In assessing internal validity, researchers need to consider their own role as well. Unwittingly, they can sometimes sabotage their own research. For example, imagine you are a researcher and you know which participants are in which conditions of your experiment. You will no doubt have expectations (and possibly even strong hopes) about how your participants will respond differently between conditions. Because of these expectations, and without realizing it, you may treat the participants a little differently between conditions. It turns out that even very subtle differences in an experimenter's behavior can influence participants' behavior (Rosenthal, 1976). Therefore, because of these **experimenter expectancy effects**, the results you find in your experiment may be produced by your own actions rather than by the independent variable.

The best way to protect an experiment from these effects is to keep experimenters uninformed about assignments to conditions. This often is called being "blind to the conditions" in a study. If the experimenters do not know the condition to which a participant has been assigned, they cannot treat participants differently as a function of their condition. Of course, there may be times when keeping experimenters uninformed is impossible or impractical. In such cases, the opportunity for experimenter expectancy effects to occur can be reduced at least somewhat by minimizing the interaction between experimenters and participants. For example, rather than receiving instructions directly from an experimenter, participants can be asked to read the instructions on paper or a computer screen.

External Validity: Do the Results Generalize?　In addition to guarding internal validity, researchers are concerned about **external validity**, the extent to which the results obtained under one set of circumstances would also occur in a different set of circumstances (Berkowitz & Donnerstein, 1982). When an experiment has external validity, its findings can be assumed to generalize to other people and to other situations. Both the participants in the experiment and the setting in which it takes place affect external validity.

To help increase external validity, social psychologists would love to conduct their experiments with huge samples of participants that are representative of the general population. Usually, however, they must rely on convenience samples drawn from populations that are readily available to them, which explains why so much of social psychological research is conducted on college students. There are very practical reasons for the use of convenience samples. Representative samples are fine for surveys that require short answers to a short list of questions. But what about complex, time-consuming experiments? The costs and logistical problems associated with this would be staggering. Advocates of convenience samples contend that the more basic the principle, the less it matters who participates in the research. For example, people from different cultures, regions, and ages might differ in the *form* of aggression they typically exhibit when angry, but the situational factors that cause people to be *more likely to* aggress—in whatever way that aggression is expressed—may be similar for most individuals across time and place. Yet in spite of these arguments, having the most diverse, representative samples of research participants as possible is ideal. The growing interest in cross-cultural research in the field is certainly one step in the right direction.

experimenter expectancy effects　The effects produced when an experimenter's expectations about the results of an experiment affect his or her behavior toward a participant and thereby influence the participant's responses.

external validity　The degree to which there can be reasonable confidence that the results of a study would be obtained for other people and in other situations.

Blue Jean Images/Collage/Corbis

Many individuals earn money at home by participating in online research projects through a service provided by Amazon called Mechanical Turk. Online services like this now allow social psychologists to reach out to vastly more diverse samples of people from around the world to participate in their studies.

Another promising development is the rapidly increasing use of online data collection, which allows for far more diverse sets of participants. There are numerous challenges associated with this approach as well, however, such as having less control over what participants are seeing or doing as they participate in the study from afar. Fortunately, recent research testing the data collected via one of the most popular online services, called Mechanical Turk, suggests that the data are at least as reliable as data collected through traditional methods and offer a much greater diversity of participants, although some reasons for caution have been noted as well (Bates & Lanza, 2013; Goodman et al., 2013; Gosling & Mason, 2015).

The external validity of an experiment may also depend in part on how realistic the study is for the participants. But what is meant by realistic is not as straightforward as one might think. Two types of realism can be distinguished: mundane versus experimental (Aronson & Carlsmith, 1968). **Mundane realism** refers to the extent to which the research setting resembles the real-world setting of interest. In order to study interpersonal attraction, Theodore Newcomb (1961) set up an entire college dormitory—a striking example of mundane realism. Advocates of mundane realism contend that if research procedures are more realistic, research findings are more likely to reveal what really goes on. In contrast, **experimental realism** refers to the degree to which the experimental setting and procedures are real and involving to the participant, regardless of whether they resemble real life or not. According to those who favor experimental realism, if the experimental situation is compelling and real to the participants while they are participating in the study, their behavior in the lab—even if the lab is in the basement of the psychology building—will be as natural and spontaneous as their behavior in the real world. The majority of social psychologists who conduct experiments emphasize experimental realism.

mundane realism The degree to which the experimental situation resembles places and events in the real world.

experimental realism The degree to which experimental procedures are involving to participants and lead them to behave naturally and spontaneously.

deception In the context of research, a method that provides false information to participants.

confederate Accomplice of an experimenter who, in dealing with the real participants in an experiment, acts as if he or she is also a participant.

Deception in Experiments Researchers who strive to create a highly involving experience for participants often rely on **deception**, providing participants with false information about experimental procedures. Toward this end, social psychologists sometimes employ **confederates**, people who act as though they are participants in the experiment but are really working for the experimenter. For example, in Solomon Asch's (1956) classic research on conformity, research participants made judgments about the lengths of lines while in the midst of a number of confederates—who were pretending to be ordinary participants—who at various times all gave wrong answers. The researchers wanted to see if the real participants would conform to the confederates and give the obviously wrong answer that the confederates had given. Although it was a very odd setting, the situation was a very real one to the participants (and therefore was high in experimental realism), and many of the participants clearly struggled with the decision about whether or not to conform.

Deception not only strengthens experimental realism but also provides other benefits: It allows the experimenter to create situations in the laboratory that would be difficult to find in a natural setting, such as a regulated, safe environment in which to study a potentially harmful behavior such as aggression or discrimination. Some research has shown that participants are rarely bothered by deception and often particularly enjoy studies that use it (Smith & Richardson, 1983). Nevertheless, the use of deception creates some serious ethical concerns, leading to debate about whether and how it should be used (Hegtvedt, 2014; Kimmel, 2012). Fortunately, as we will see a bit later in the chapter, procedures have been put in place to try to ensure the ethical integrity of research today.

■ Meta-Analysis: Combining Results Across Studies

We have seen that social psychologists conduct descriptive, correlational, and experimental studies to test their hypotheses. Another way to test hypotheses in social psychology is to use a set of statistical procedures to examine, in a new way, relevant research that has already been conducted. This technique is called **meta-analysis**. By "meta-analyzing" the results of a number of studies that have been conducted in different places and by different researchers, researchers can measure precisely how strong and reliable particular effects are. For example, studies published concerning the effects of alcohol on aggression may sometimes contradict each other. Sometimes alcohol increases aggression; sometimes it doesn't. By combining the data from all the studies that are relevant to this hypothesis and conducting a meta-analysis, a researcher can determine what effect alcohol typically has, how strong that effect typically is, and perhaps under what specific conditions that effect is most likely to occur. This technique is being used with increasing frequency in social psychology today, and we report the results of many meta-analyses in this textbook.

Robert Harding/Corbis

The setting in which children attend school can vary dramatically across cultures. Here students sit outside in a class in Malawi, Africa. Recognizing cultural variation has become increasingly important in social psychology today, and social psychologists are conducting their research across a wider range of cultures and contexts than ever before.

■ Culture and Research Methods

Throughout this book you will see examples of social psychological research that examines differences and similarities across cultures. One of the advantages of this approach is that it provides better tests of the external validity of research that has been conducted in any one setting. By examining whether the results of an experiment generalize to a very different culture, social psychologists can begin to answer questions about the universality or cultural specificity of their research. It is important to keep in mind that when a finding in one culture does not generalize well to another culture, this should not be seen simply as a failure to replicate but instead may be an opportunity to learn about potentially interesting and important cultural differences.

meta-analysis   A set of statistical procedures used to review a body of evidence by combining the results of individual studies to measure the overall reliability and strength of particular effects.

▲ **TABLE 2.2**

Lost in Translation

- "Drop your trousers here for best results." (a dry cleaner in Thailand)
- "You are invited to take advantage of the chambermaid." (a hotel in Japan)
- "Ladies are requested not to have children in the bar." (a cocktail lounge in Mexico)
- "Take one of our horse-driven city tours—we guarantee no miscarriages." (a tourist agency in the former Czechoslovakia)
- "We take your bags and send them in all directions." (an airline in Denmark)

Source: Triandis (1994).

Cultural investigations present special challenges to researchers. For example, cultural differences have been found in how affected people are by the context of questions as they complete a survey, or about the assumptions respondents make about what the researchers have in mind for a given question (Schwarz et al., 2010; Uskul et al., 2013). It also can be difficult for researchers to translate materials from one language into another. Although it is relatively easy to create literal translations, it can be surprisingly challenging to create translations that have the same meaning to people from various cultures. Table 2.2 presents examples—from signs displayed around the world—of what can go wrong when simple sentences are poorly translated.

An even more subtle point about language is that multilingual people may think or act differently as a function of what language is being used in a particular setting. A study by Nairán Ramírez-Esparza and others (2008) illustrates this point. They found that how agreeable a sample of bilingual Mexican American participants appeared to be—either on a self-report questionnaire or in their behavior in an interview—varied significantly as a function of whether the study was conducted in Spanish or in English.

Ethics and Values in Social Psychology

Regardless of where research is conducted and what method is used, ethical issues must always be considered. Researchers in all fields have a moral and legal responsibility to abide by ethical principles. In social psychology the use of deception has caused some concern about ethics, as we indicated earlier. In addition, several studies have provoked fierce debate about whether the procedures used in the studies went beyond the bounds of ethical acceptability. The most famous of these controversial studies was designed by Stanley Milgram in the early 1960s. Milgram (1963) designed a series of studies to address the question "Would people obey orders to harm an innocent person?" To test this question, he put volunteers into a situation in which an experimenter commanded them to administer painful electric shocks to someone they thought was another volunteer participant. (In fact, the other person was a confederate who was not actually receiving any shocks.) The experiment had extremely high experimental realism—many of the participants experienced a great deal of anxiety and stress as they debated whether they should disobey the experimenter or continue to inflict pain on another person. The details and results of this experiment will be discussed in Chapter 7 on Conformity, but suffice it to say that the results of the study made people realize how prevalent and powerful obedience can be.

Milgram's research was inspired by the obedience displayed by Nazi officers in World War II. No one disputes the importance of his research question. What has been debated, however, is whether the significance of the research topic justified exposing participants to possibly harmful psychological consequences. Even though no one in Milgram's studies actually received the electric shocks, the participants were quite stressed during the study because they *thought* they were harming another person, until the experimenter finally told them the truth at the conclusion of the experiment. Under today's provisions for the protection of human participants, Milgram's classic experiments probably could not be conducted in their original form. (In an interesting twist, even though conducting an experiment like Milgram's might be impossible now, in popular culture today individuals endure far greater stress and even humiliation in numerous unscripted TV shows for the entertainment of viewers at home.)

Several studies in the history of social psychology have sparked ethical debate or controversy, including a famous study in which Philip Zimbardo and others simulated a prison environment in the basement of Stanford University's psychology department building to study how ordinary people can be affected in extraordinary ways by the roles they are assigned in a prison environment (Haney et al., 1973). This study is discussed in detail in Chapter 12 on Law. Although the controversial studies such as Milgram's and Zimbardo's have received the most public attention, today virtually every social psychology study is evaluated for its ethics by other people before the study can be conducted. In the following sections, we describe current policies and procedures as well as continuing and new concerns about ethics and values in social psychological research.

> One reason for the use of deception in an experiment is so that the participants will act more naturally when they are not aware of what is being studied. In these cases, it is especially important for the researchers to provide a full and thorough debriefing.

■ Institutional Review Boards and Informed Consent

In 1974, the agency then called the U.S. Department of Health, Education, and Welfare established regulations designed to protect human participants in research. These regulations created institutional review boards (IRBs) at all institutions seeking federal funding for research involving human participants. IRBs became a key safeguard for research, taking on the responsibility of reviewing research proposals to ensure that the welfare of participants is adequately protected.

Besides submitting their research to IRBs, researchers must also abide by their profession's code of ethics. The American Psychological Association (APA), for example, requires psychologists to follow its *Ethical Principles of Psychologists and Code of Conduct* (2002, 2010), which considers a wide range of ethical issues, including those related to research procedures and practices. The APA code stipulates that researchers are obligated to guard the rights and welfare of all those who participate in their studies.

One extremely important practice is to obtain **informed consent**. Through informed consent individuals are asked whether they wish to participate in the research project and must be given enough information to make an informed decision. Participants must also know that they are free to withdraw from participation in the research at any point. The APA code also recognizes that research "involving only anonymous questionnaires, naturalistic observations, or certain kinds of archival research" may not require informed consent.

Mike Twohy/The New Yorker Collection/The Cartoon Bank

"What if these guys in white coats who bring us food are, like, studying us and we're part of some kind of big experiment?"

informed consent   An individual's deliberate, voluntary decision to participate in research, based on the researcher's description of what will be required during such participation.

debriefing   A disclosure, made to participants after research procedures are completed, in which the researcher explains the purpose of the research, attempts to resolve any negative feelings, and emphasizes the scientific contribution made by the participants' involvement.

■ Debriefing

Just as participants should receive informed consent before they begin their participation in a study, they should receive a **debriefing** at the end of it, especially if deception was used. Debriefing is a process of disclosure in which researchers fully inform their participants about the nature of the research in which they have participated. During a debriefing, the researcher goes over all procedures, explaining exactly what happened and why. The researcher discusses the purpose of the research, reveals any deceptions, and makes every effort to help the participant feel good about having participated. A skillful debriefing takes time and requires close attention to the individual participant. Indeed, we have known students who became so fascinated by what they learned during a debriefing that it sparked their interest in social psychology, and eventually they became social psychologists themselves!

■ Ethics and Consent Online

Along with the tremendous benefits of our ever-expanding online worlds has come troubling losses of privacy. This loss of privacy has opened the window for corporations, marketers, and researchers to peek in to record your actions in ways that raise new questions about ethics. A firestorm of controversy erupted in the summer of 2014, for instance, when scientists working with Facebook published a paper in which they revealed having conducted an experiment on nearly 700,000 Facebook users—without their knowledge—by manipulating their news feeds and recording how the manipulation affected users' subsequent status updates. As the opening line of a *New York Times* article about the controversy put it, "To Facebook, we are all lab rats" (Goel, 2014).

Technically, every Facebook user gives consent to being "lab rats" to Facebook scientists when he or she agrees to its terms of service, but in reality we all know that very few people pay attention to all that fine print when they begin to use a new app or service. Other Internet giants like Google routinely manipulate and measure what their users are doing, although typically the (stated) purpose is to improve the user experience or make a site or app more popular. Questions about ethics and informed consent in the online world will no doubt continue to be asked and wrestled with in the coming years.

■ Values and Science: Ongoing Debates and New Controversies

Ethical principles are based on moral values. These values set standards for and impose limits on the conduct of research, but do values affect science in other ways as well? Although many people hold science to a standard of complete objectivity, science can probably never be completely unbiased and objective because it is a human enterprise. Scientists choose what to study and how to study it; their choices are affected by personal values as well as by professional rewards. Indeed, some think that values *should* fuel scientific research and that scientists would be not only naive but also irresponsible to try to keep values out of the picture. Most social psychologists, however, strive to use the scientific methods described in this chapter to free themselves of their preconceptions and, thereby, to see reality more clearly and objectively, even if never perfectly.

One value on which the entire field agrees is that researchers must conduct and report their research with complete honesty. It is therefore both shocking and deeply disturbing when a case of academic fraud is revealed. One such example rocked the field toward the end of 2011, when a Dutch social psychologist was caught—and soon confessed to—having committed a massive amount of dishonesty, involving the fabrication of data published in dozens of studies for about a decade (Bartlett, 2011). The news of this scandal, together with the announcements of several other cases of fraud or suspected fraud in the next few years, caused some social psychologists to question the field's practices. Also around this time, social psychologist Jonathan Haidt made news criticizing the lack of diversity of political ideologies represented by social psychologists today and suggesting that this could bias research (Tierney, 2011). This too triggered a good deal of criticism and controversy.

With all this in the air, a wave of suggestions for how the field should better protect itself against intentional or unintentional bias or dishonesty has emerged. These suggestions include using more advanced and precise statistical methods to better and more fairly test researchers' ideas, demanding researchers to be more open for public scrutiny of their materials and data, instituting much more emphasis on replicating each other's research, making public commitments to articulating predictions and planning data analyses *before* the data are collected—and for journals to agree to publish the results no matter how the data turn out, and so on (Cumming, 2014; Finkel, Eastwick, & Reis, 2015; Klein, Ratliff, et al., 2014; Nosek, Alter, et al., 2015).

It is important to note that these concerns are by no means specific to social psychology. High-profile cases of fraud, for example, span across all fields, including physics, medicine, history, literature, and journalism (Coscarelli, 2012; Deer, 2011; Rayner, 2010; Sovacool, 2008). For example, a political science article that reported a remarkably effective way of changing people's attitudes about equal rights for gays received a great deal of national attention in late 2014 and early 2015. In May 2015 evidence came to light that the results apparently were totally fabricated (Bartlett, 2015). The fraud was discovered in large part because other researchers were attempting to replicate this research—providing an important lesson about the value of replication for advancing science and correcting erroneous or fraudulent findings.

It is also important to note that the strong reaction by the social psychology community to these issues is a testament to how much it cares about its integrity and will work diligently to reassert and protect it in the years to come. The new practices and directions that researchers are taking to ensure integrity and accuracy are exciting and energizing, particularly for the next generation of young social psychologists who are beginning to take the reins of the field as it continues to grow rapidly in its findings, scope, and importance.

Your introduction to the field of social psychology is now complete. In these first two chapters, you have gone step by step through a definition of social psychology, a review of its history and discussion of its future, an overview of its research methods, and a consideration of ethics and values. As you study the material presented in the coming chapters, the three of us who wrote this book invite you to share our enthusiasm. You can look forward to information that overturns commonsense assumptions, to lively debate and heated controversy, and to a better understanding of yourself and other people. Welcome to the world according to social psychology. We hope you enjoy it!

"[Objectivity in science] is willingness (even the eagerness in truly honorable practitioners) to abandon a favored notion when testable evidence disconfirms key expectations."

—Stephen Jay Gould

Review

Top 10 Key Points in Chapter 2

1. Theories in social psychology attempt to explain and predict social psychological phenomena. The best theories are precise, explain all the relevant information, and generate research that can support or disconfirm them. They should be revised and improved as a result of the research they inspire.

2. The goal of basic research is to increase understanding of human behavior; the goal of applied research is to make applications to the world and contribute to the solution of social problems.

3. Researchers often must transform abstract, conceptual variables into specific operational definitions that indicate exactly how the variables are to be manipulated or measured. The construct validity of a study is the extent to which the variables were operationalized well.

4. Researchers use self-reports, observations, and technology to measure variables.

5. Correlational research examines the association between variables. Correlation does not indicate causation; the fact that two variables are correlated does not necessarily mean that one causes the other.

6. Experiments require (1) control by the experimenter over events in the study and (2) random assignment of participants to conditions. Experiments examine the effects of one or more independent variables on one or more dependent variables.

7. Experimental findings have internal validity to the extent that changes in the dependent variable can be attributed to the independent variables. Research results have external validity to the extent that they can be generalized to other people and other situations.

8. Meta-analysis uses statistical techniques to integrate the quantitative results of different studies.

9. Established by the federal government, Institutional Review Boards are responsible for reviewing research proposals to ensure that the welfare of participants is adequately protected.

10. Recent controversies in social psychology have led to a variety of suggestions for how the field should better protect itself against intentional or unintentional bias or dishonesty, including more openness to scrutiny, use of different statistical analyses, and greater emphasis on replication.

Key Terms

applied research (29)

basic research (29)

bogus pipeline technique (31)

confederate (44)

confound (42)

construct validity (31)

correlation coefficient (36)

correlational research (36)

debriefing (47)

deception (44)

dependent variable (41)

experiment (38)

experimental realism (44)

experimenter expectancy effects (43)

external validity (43)

hypothesis (28)

independent variable (41)

informed consent (47)

internal validity (42)

interrater reliability (32)

meta-analysis (45)

mundane realism (44)

operational definition (30)

random assignment (39)

random sampling (35)

subject variable (41)

theory (28)

The Social Self

This chapter examines three interrelated aspects of the "social self." First, it considers the self-concept and the question of how people come to understand who they are, their own actions, emotions, and motivations. Second, it considers self-esteem, the affective component, and the question of how people evaluate themselves and defend against threats to their self-esteem. Third, it considers self-presentation, a behavioral manifestation of the self, and the question of how people present themselves to others. As we will see, the self is complex and multifaceted.

AP Images/Hassan Ammar

Can you imagine living a meaningful or coherent life without a clear sense of who you are? In *The Man Who Mistook His Wife for a Hat,* neurologist Oliver Sacks (1985) described such a person—a patient named William Thompson. According to Sacks, Thompson suffered from an organic brain disorder that impairs a person's memory of recent events. Unable to recall anything for more than a few seconds, Thompson was always disoriented and lacked a sense of inner continuity. The effect on his behavior was startling. Trying to grasp a constantly vanishing identity, Thompson would construct one tale after another to account for who he was, where he was, and what he was doing. From one moment to the next, he would improvise new identities—a grocery store clerk, a minister, or a medical patient, to name just a few. In social settings, Thompson's behavior was especially intriguing. As Sacks (1985) observed,

> The presence of others, other people, excite and rattle him, force him into an endless, frenzied, social chatter, a veritable delirium of identity-making and -seeking; the presence of plants, a quiet garden, the nonhuman order, making no social demands upon him, allow this identity-delirium to relax, to subside. (p. 110)

Thompson's plight is unusual, but it highlights two important points—one about the private "inner" self, the other about the "outer" self we show to others. First, the capacity for self-reflection is necessary for people to feel as if they understand their own motives and emotions and the causes of their behavior. Unable to ponder his own actions, Thompson appeared vacant and without feeling—"desouled," as Sacks put it. Second, the self is heavily influenced by social factors. Thompson himself seemed compelled to put on a face for others and to improvise characters for the company he kept. We all do, to some extent. We may not create a kaleidoscope of multiple identities as Thompson did, but the way we manage ourselves is influenced by the people around us.

This chapter examines the ABCs of the self: A for *affect,* B for *behavior,* and C for *cognition.* First, we ask a cognitive question: How do people come to know themselves, develop a self-concept, and maintain a stable sense of identity? Second, we explore an affective, or emotional, question: How do people evaluate themselves, enhance their self-images, and defend against threats to their self-esteem? Third, we confront a behavioral question: How do people regulate their own actions and present themselves to others according to interpersonal demands? As we'll see, the self is a topic that has attracted unprecedented interest among social psychologists (Leary & Tangney, 2003; Sedikides & Spencer, 2007; Swann & Bosson, 2010; Vohs & Finkel, 2006).

Putting COMMON SENSE to the Test

Circle Your Answer

T   F   Humans are the only animals who recognize themselves in the mirror.

T   F   Smiling can make you feel happier.

T   F   Sometimes the harder you try to control a thought, feeling, or behavior, the less likely you are to succeed.

T   F   People often sabotage their own performance in order to protect their self-esteem.

T   F   It's more adaptive to alter one's behavior than to stay consistent from one social situation to the next.

The Self-Concept

Have you ever been at a noisy gathering—holding a drink in one hand and a spring roll in the other, struggling to have a conversation over music, vibrating phones, and the chatter of voices—and yet managed to hear someone at the other end of the room say your name? If so, then you have experienced the "cocktail party effect"—the tendency of people to pick a personally relevant stimulus, like a name, out of a complex and noisy environment (Cherry, 1953; Conway, Cowan, & Bunting, 2001). Even infants who are too young to walk or talk exhibit the tendency to respond to their own name (Newman, 2005). To the cognitive psychologist, this phenomenon shows that human beings are selective in their attention. To the social psychologist, it also shows that the self is a brightly lit object of our own attention.

The term **self-concept** refers to the sum total of beliefs that people have about themselves. But what specifically does the self-concept consist of? According to Hazel Markus (1977), the self-concept is made up of cognitive molecules she called **self-schemas**: beliefs about oneself that guide the processing of self-relevant information. Self-schemas are to an individual's total self-concept what hypotheses are to a theory or what books are to a library. You can think of yourself as masculine or feminine, as independent or dependent, as liberal or conservative, as introverted or extroverted. Indeed, any specific attribute may have relevance to the self-concept for some people but not for others. The self-schema for body weight is a good example. Men and women who regard themselves as overweight or underweight, or for whom body image is a conspicuous aspect of the self-concept, are considered *schematic* with respect to weight. For body-weight schematics, a wide range of otherwise mundane events—maybe a trip to the supermarket, the sight of a fashion model, dinner at a restaurant, a day at the beach, or watching a friend diet—may trigger thoughts about the self. In contrast, those who do not regard their own weight as extreme or as an important part of their lives are *aschematic* on that attribute (Markus et al., 1987).

It is important to realize that people are multifaceted and that our self-concept may consist of a multitude of self-schemas. As we will see shortly, people who identify with two cultures may have a "double consciousness" about who they are and hold different self-schemas that fit within each culture. African Americans, for example, have one self-schema that fits generally within mainstream American culture and another tied more specifically to African American culture (Brannon, Markus, & Taylor, 2015).

Rudiments of the Self-Concept

Clearly the self is a special object of our attention. Whether you are mentally focused on a memory, a tweet, a foul odor, the song in your head, your growling stomach, or this sentence, consciousness is like a "spotlight." It can shine on only one object at a point in time, but it can also shift rapidly from one object to another and process information outside of awareness. In this spotlight, the self is front and center. But is the self so special that it is uniquely represented in the neural circuitry of the brain? And is the self a uniquely human concept, or do other animals also distinguish the self from everything else?

Is the Self Specially Represented in the Brain? As illustrated by the story of William Thompson that opened this chapter, our sense of identity is biologically

self-concept The sum total of an individual's beliefs about his or her own personal attributes.

self-schema A belief people hold about themselves that guides the processing of self-relevant information.

rooted. In *The Synaptic Self: How Our Brains Become Who We Are*, neuroscientist Joseph LeDoux (2002) argues that the synaptic connections in the brain provide the biological base for memory, which makes possible the sense of continuity that is needed for a normal identity. In *The Self Illusion: How the Social Brain Creates Identity*, developmental psychologist Bruce Hood (2012) notes that our sense of self emerges in childhood through our social interactions—and that it is a mere illusion, "a powerful deception generated by our brains for our own benefit." In *The Lost Self: Pathologies of the Brain and Identity*, Todd Feinberg and Julian Keenan (2005) describe how the self can be transformed or completely destroyed by severe head injuries, brain tumors, diseases, and exposure to toxic substances that damage the brain and nervous system.

Social neuroscientists have started to explore these possibilities. Using PET scans, fMRI, and other imaging techniques that capture the brain in action, these researchers are finding that certain areas become more active when laboratory participants see a picture of themselves rather than a picture of another person (Platek et al., 2008), when they viewed self-relevant words such as their own name or street address rather than other-relevant words (Moran et al., 2009), and when they take a first-person perspective while playing a video game as opposed to a third-person perspective (David et al., 2006). As we will see throughout this chapter, the self is a frame of reference that powerfully influences our thoughts, feelings, and behaviors. Not all aspects of the self are housed in a single structure of the brain. However, the bulk of research does seem to suggest that various self-based processes can be traced to activities occurring in certain areas (Qin, Duncan, & Northoff, 2013; Heatherton, 2011).

Do Nonhuman Animals Show Self-Recognition?   When you stand in front of a mirror, you recognize the image as a reflection of yourself. But what about dogs, cats, and other animals—how can we possibly know what nonhumans think about mirrors? In a series of studies, Gordon Gallup (1977) placed different species of animals in a room with a large mirror. At first, they greeted their own images by vocalizing, gesturing, and making other social responses. After several days, only great apes (chimpanzees, gorillas, and orangutans)—but not other animals—seemed capable of self-recognition, using the mirror to pick food out of their teeth, groom themselves, blow bubbles, and make faces for their own entertainment. From all appearances, the apes recognized themselves.

In other studies, Gallup anesthetized the animals, then painted an odorless red dye on their brows and returned them to the mirror. Upon seeing the red spot, only the apes spontaneously reached for their own brows—proof that they perceived the image as their own (Povinelli et al., 1997; Keenan et al., 2003). Among the apes, this form of self-recognition emerges in young adolescence and is stable across the life span, at least until old age (de Veer et al., 2003). By using a similar red dye test (without anesthetizing the infants), developmental psychologists have found that most humans begin to recognize themselves in the mirror between the ages of 18 and 24 months (Lewis & Brooks-Gunn, 1979).

Many researchers believe that self-recognition among great apes and human infants is the first clear expression of the concept "me." Recent research suggests that certain intelligent non-primates can also recognize themselves. In one study, researchers at a New York aquarium found that two bottlenose dolphins marked with black ink often stopped to examine themselves in a mirror (Reiss & Marino, 2001). In a second study, researchers found that three Asian elephants placed in

Researchers found that elephants placed in front of the jumbo-size mirror pictured here used the mirror to inspect themselves. This observation suggests that elephants join human beings, great apes, and bottlenose dolphins as animal species that exhibit self-recognition (Plotnik et al., 2006).

Joshua Plotnik/PA Photos/Landov

front of a jumbo-sized mirror used the mirror to inspect themselves—as when they moved their trunks to see the insides of their mouths, a part of the body they usually cannot see (Plotnik et al., 2006). In contrast, testing of thirty-four giant pandas of varying ages showed that they did *not* recognize their own images in the mirror (Ma et al., 2015).

It's important not to assume from this research that the mirror test is a pure measure of self-recognition or that it emerges at the same age throughout the world. Tanya Broesch and others (2011) tested children between the ages of 33 and 72 months in a number of countries. In line with past research, 88% of American children and 77% of Canadian children "passed" the test. Yet elsewhere it was only 58% in Saint Lucia, 52% in Peru, and 51% in Grenada; only two children passed in Kenya and none did so in Fiji. Based on their observations, the researchers speculated that the children in these non-Western countries did not lack self-recognition. They knew it was their image in the mirror but—having been raised for compliance and trained not to ask questions—they did not dare touch or remove the mark. Whatever the interpretation, this cross-cultural research raises questions as to whether the mirror test can be used to measure the self-concept (Broesch et al., 2011).

Humans are the only animals who recognize themselves in the mirror.

What Makes the Self a Social Concept? The ability to see yourself as a distinct entity in the world may be a necessary first step in the evolution and development of a self-concept. The second step involves social factors. Sociologist Charles Horton Cooley (1902) introduced the term *looking-glass self* to suggest that other people serve as a mirror in which we see ourselves. Expanding on this idea, George Herbert Mead (1934) added that we often come to know ourselves by imagining what significant others think of us and then incorporating these perceptions into our self-concepts.

Picking up where the classic sociologists left off, Susan Andersen and Serena Chen (2002) theorized that the self is "relational"—that we draw our sense of who we are from our past and current relationships with the significant others in our lives. It is interesting that when Gallup tested his apes, those that had been raised in isolation—without exposure to peers—did not recognize themselves in the mirror. Only after such exposure did they begin to show signs of self-recognition. Among human beings, our self-concepts match our *perceptions* of what others think of us. Illustrating our capacity for "meta-insight," research also shows that people can distinguish between how they perceive themselves—for example, how smart, funny, or outgoing—and how others see them (Carlson et al., 2011). In fact, it seems that we can tell when our perceptions of what others think of us are more or less correct (Carlson & Furr, 2013).

In recent years, social psychologists have broken new ground in the effort to understand the social self. People are not born thinking of themselves as smart, lazy, reckless, likable, shy, or outgoing. So where do their self-concepts come from? In the coming pages, the following sources are considered: introspection, perceptions of our own behavior, other people, autobiographical memories, and the cultures in which we live.

Introspection

Let's start at the beginning: How do people achieve insight into their own beliefs, attitudes, emotions, desires, personalities, and motivations? Although common sense makes this question seem ludicrous, many social psychologists have sought to answer the question of how, and how well, people gain self-knowledge (Vazire & Wilson, 2012).

Think about this: Don't you know what you think because *you* think it? And don't you know how you feel because *you* feel it? Look through popular books on how to achieve self-insight, and you'll find the unambiguous answers to these questions to be yes. Whether the prescribed technique is yoga, meditation, psychotherapy, religion, dream analysis, or hypnosis, the advice is basically the same: Self-knowledge is derived from introspection, a looking inward at one's own thoughts and feelings.

If the how-to books are correct, it stands to reason that no one can know you as well as you know yourself. Thus, people tend to assume that for others to know you at all, they would need information about your private thoughts, feelings, and other inner states—not just your behavior. But is this really the case? Most social psychologists are not sure that this faith in introspection is justified. Some forty years ago, Richard Nisbett and Timothy Wilson (1977) conducted a series of experiments in which they found that research participants often could not accurately explain the causes or correlates of their own behavior. This observation forced researchers to confront a thorny question: Does introspection provide a direct pipeline to self-knowledge?

In *Strangers to Ourselves*, Wilson (2002) argued that it does not. In fact, he finds that introspection can sometimes lead us astray on the road to self-knowledge. In a series of studies, he found that the attitudes people reported having about different objects corresponded closely to their behavior toward those objects. The more participants said they enjoyed a task, the more time they spent on it; the more attractive they found a scenic landscape, the more pleasure was revealed in their facial expressions; the happier they said they were with a current dating partner, the longer the relationship with that partner ultimately lasted. Yet after participants were told to analyze the reasons for how they felt, the attitudes that they reported no longer corresponded to their behavior. There are two problems. The first, as described by Wilson, is that human beings are mentally busy processing information, which is why we so often fail to understand our own thoughts, feelings, and behaviors. Apparently, it is possible to think too much and be too analytical, only to get confused.

In *Self-Insight: Roadblocks and Detours on the Path to Knowing Thyself*, David Dunning (2005) points to a second type of problem in self-assessment: that people overestimate the positives. Most people, most of the time, think they are better than average, even though it is statistically impossible for this to happen. As we will see in our later discussion of self-enhancement, people from all walks of life tend to overrate their own skills, their prospects for success, the accuracy of their opinions, and the impressions they form of others—possibly with dire consequences for their health and well-being. We will also see, however, that many people have insight into their own positive—and sometimes negative—biases. In a study that demonstrates the point, Kathryn Bollich and others (2015) found that most people who harbor biased self-perceptions (for example, about how warm, dependable, stable, and funny they are relative to how they are rated by their own peers) accurately describe themselves as biased when prompted.

When it comes to self-insight, people do have difficulty projecting forward and predicting how they would feel in response to future emotional events—a process known as **affective forecasting**. Imagine that you have a favorite candidate in an upcoming political campaign. Can you anticipate how happy you would be one month after the election if this candidate were to win? How unhappy would you be if he or she were to lose? Closer to home, how happy would you be six months after winning a million-dollar lottery? Or how unhappy would you be if you were injured in an automobile accident?

In a series of studies, Timothy Wilson and Daniel Gilbert (2003) asked research participants to predict how they would feel after various positive and negative life events and compared their predictions to how others experiencing those events said they actually felt. Consistently, they and others have found that people overestimate the strength and duration of their emotional reactions, a phenomenon they call the *impact bias* (Wilson & Gilbert, 2013). In one study, junior professors predicted that receiving tenure would increase their happiness levels for several years, yet professors who actually received tenure were no happier several years later than those not granted tenure. In a second study, voters predicted they would be happier a month after an election if their candidate won than if he or she lost. In actuality, supporters of the winning and losing candidates did not differ in their happiness levels one month after the election.

There are two possible reasons for the impact bias in affective forecasting. First, when it comes to negative life events—such as an injury, illness, or big financial loss—people do not fully appreciate the extent to which our psychological coping mechanisms help us to cushion the blow. In the face of adversity, human beings can be remarkably resilient—and not as devastated as we fear we will be (Gilbert et al., 1998). In fact, people are even more likely to overlook the coping mechanisms that *others* use. The result is a self–other difference by which we tend to predict that others will suffer even longer than we will (Igou, 2008). A second reason for overestimates is that when we introspect about the emotional impact on us of a future event—say, the breakup of a close relationship—we become so focused on that single event that we neglect to take into account the effects of

Robert Mankoff/The New Yorker Collection/The Cartoon Bank

"Look, babe. At this point, you've reinvented yourself so many times you're back to who you were at the start."

In some ways, our sense of self is malleable and subject to change.

affective forecasting   The process of predicting how one would feel in response to future emotional events.

other life experiences. To become more accurate in our predictions, then, we need to force ourselves to think more broadly, about *all* the events that impact us. In one study, college students were asked to predict their emotional reactions to their school football team's winning or losing an important game. As usual, they tended to overestimate how long it would take them to recover from the victory or defeat. This bias disappeared, however, when the students first completed a "prospective diary" in which they estimated the amount of future time they will spend on everyday activities like going to class, talking to friends, studying, and eating meals (Wilson & Ross, 2000).

■ Self-Perception

Regardless of what we can learn from introspection, Daryl Bem (1972) proposed that people can learn about themselves the same way outside observers do—by watching their own behavior. Bem's **self-perception theory** is simple yet profound. To the extent that internal states are weak or difficult to interpret, people infer what they think or how they feel by observing their own behavior and the situation in which that behavior takes place. Have you ever listened to yourself arguing with someone in an e-mail exchange, only to realize with amazement how angry you were? Have you ever devoured a sandwich in record time, only then to conclude that you must have been incredibly hungry? In each case, you made an inference about yourself by watching your own actions.

There are limits to self-perception, of course. According to Bem, people do not infer their own internal states from behavior that occurred in the presence of compelling situational pressures such as reward or punishment. If you argued vehemently or wolfed down a sandwich because you were paid to do so, you probably would not assume that you were angry or hungry. In other words, people learn about themselves through self-perception only when the situation alone seems insufficient to have caused their behavior.

Over the years, a good deal of research has supported self-perception theory. When people are gently coaxed into saying or doing something and when they are not otherwise certain about how they feel, they often come to view themselves in ways that are consistent with their public statements and behaviors (Chaiken & Baldwin, 1981; Kelly & Rodriguez, 2006; Schlenker & Trudeau, 1990). In one study, participants induced to describe themselves in flattering terms scored higher on a later test of self-esteem than did those who were led to describe themselves more modestly (Jones et al., 1981; Rhodewalt & Agustsdottir, 1986). In another study, people who were maneuvered by leading questions into describing themselves as introverted or extroverted—whether or not they really were—often came to define themselves as such later on (Fazio & Zanna, 1981; Swann & Ely, 1984). British author E. M. Forster long ago anticipated the theory when he asked, "How can I tell what I think 'til I see what I say?"

Self-perception theory may have even more reach than Bem had anticipated. Bem argued that people sometimes learn about themselves by observing their *own* freely chosen behavior. But might you also infer something about yourself by observing the behavior of *someone else* with whom you completely identify? In a series of studies, Noah Goldstein and Robert Cialdini (2007) demonstrated this phenomenon, which they call *vicarious self-perception*. In one experiment, for example, they asked college students to listen to an interview with a fellow student who had agreed afterward to spend a few extra minutes helping out on a project on homelessness. Before listening to the interview, all participants were fitted with an EEG recording device on their foreheads that allegedly measured

self-perception theory The theory that when internal cues are difficult to interpret, people gain self-insight by observing their own behavior.

brain activity as they viewed a series of images and words. By random assignment, some participants but not others were then told that their brain-wave patterns closely resembled that of the person whose interview they would soon hear—a level of resemblance, they were told, that signaled genetic similarity and relationship closeness. Would participants in this similarity feedback condition draw inferences about themselves by observing the behavior of a fellow student? Yes. In a post-interview questionnaire, these participants (compared to those in the no-feedback control group) rated themselves as more sensitive and as more self-sacrificing if the student whose helpfulness they observed was said to be similar, biologically. What's more, when the session was over, 93% of those in the similarity condition agreed to spend some extra time themselves helping the experimenter— compared to only 61% in the no-feedback control group.

Introspection and self-perception theory make different predictions about the extent to which people can know themselves. If self-knowledge derives from private introspection, then clearly you know yourself better than anyone else can. If self-knowledge derives solely from observations of behavior, then it should be possible for others to know us as well as we know ourselves. Assuming that self-knowledge is gained from both sources, then the truth lies somewhere in the middle. But wait. Is it ever possible for others to know us *better* than we know ourselves?

Simine Vazire (2010) asked this very question and came up with a surprising answer. Vazire proposed a Self–Other Knowledge Asymmetry (SOKA) model in which she predicts that we know ourselves better than others do when it comes to traits that are "internal" and hard to observe (such as how optimistic, anxious, or easily upset a person is) and that there is no self-other difference when it comes to traits that are "external" and easy to observe (such as how quiet, sociable, or messy a person is). She also predicts that others may actually know us *better* than we know ourselves when it comes to observable traits that can be so touchy for self-esteem purposes that we have motivated "blind spots" (such as how smart, creative, or rude a person is). In these latter instances, Vazire predicts, others can be more objective than we are about ourselves.

To test these predictions, Vazire asked college students to rate themselves—and then had their friends rate the participants—on a number of personality traits. Three types of traits were studied: (1) high in observability (talkativeness, dominance, and leadership), (2) low in observability and not evaluative (self-esteem and anxiety), and (3) low in observability and highly evaluative (intelligent and creative). To determine accuracy, Vazire then measured how participants fared on objective measures of these traits using various laboratory exercises and paper-and-pencil tests. The results provided strong support for the SOKA model. ● Figure 3.1 shows that self- and friend-ratings were equally accurate for highly observable traits, that self-ratings

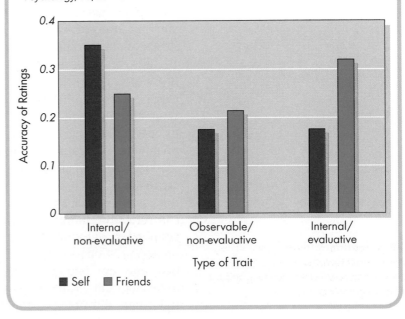

●   **FIGURE 3.1**

The Self–Other Knowledge Asymmetry (SOKA) Model

Participants rated themselves and were rated by friends on personality traits for which they took various objective tests. As shown, self-ratings were more accurate for internal/nonevaluative traits (left) and self- and friend-ratings were equally accurate for observable/nonevaluative traits (center). Interestingly, however, friend-ratings were more accurate for internal/evaluative traits. Supporting SOKA, this pattern shows that "know thyself" requires a combination of information and objectivity.

Based on Vazire, S. (2010). Who knows what about a person? The self–other knowledge asymmetry (SOKA) model. *Journal of Personality and Social Psychology, 98*, 281–300.

"I don't sing because I am happy.
I am happy because I sing."

As suggested by self-perception theory, we sometimes infer how we feel by observing our own behavior.

Edward Frascino/The New Yorker Collection/Cartoon Bank.com

were more accurate for internal non-evaluative traits, but that friend-ratings were more accurate for internal evaluative traits. Clearly, to know thyself requires a combination of information and objectivity (Vazire & Carlson, 2011).

Self-Perceptions of Emotion Draw the corners of your mouth back and up and tense your eye muscles. Okay, relax. Now raise your eyebrows, open your eyes wide, and let your mouth drop open slightly. Relax. Now pull your brows down and together and clench your teeth. Relax. If you followed these directions, you would have appeared to others to be feeling first happy, then fearful, and finally angry. The question is, how would you have appeared to yourself?

Social psychologists who study emotion have asked precisely that question. Viewed within the framework of self-perception theory, the **facial feedback hypothesis** states that changes in facial expression can trigger corresponding changes in the subjective experience of emotion. In the first test of this hypothesis, James Laird (1974) told participants that they were taking part in an experiment on activity of the facial muscles. After attaching electrodes to their faces, he showed them a series of cartoons. Before each one, the participants were instructed to contract certain facial muscles in ways that created either a smile or a frown. As Laird predicted, participants rated what they saw as funnier when they were smiling than when they were frowning. Suggesting that this effect is universal, researchers recently replicated these findings in Ghana, West Africa (Dzokoto et al., 2014).

In one particularly interesting field study that illustrates how our emotional state can be influenced by naturally occurring changes in facial expression, researchers from Italy stopped a random sample of men and women on a beach and asked them in a questionnaire to report on how angry and aggressive they were feeling. Some of the beach goers faced the bright sun while answering the question, causing "sun-induced frowning" on their faces. Others were questioned with their back to the sun or while wearing sunglasses. As predicted by the facial feedback hypothesis, and even though participants themselves said that their mood was not affected by the sunlight, those who frowned at the sun reported higher levels of anger than all others (Marzoli et al., 2013).

It is clear that facial feedback can evoke and magnify certain emotional states. It's important to note, however, that the face is not *necessary* to the subjective experience of emotion. When neuropsychologists recently tested a young woman who suffered from bilateral facial paralysis, they found that despite her inability to outwardly *show* emotion, she reported *feeling* various emotions in response to positive and negative visual images (Keillor et al., 2003).

How does facial feedback work? With 80 muscles in the human face that can create over 7,000 expressions, can we actually vary our own emotions by contracting certain muscles and wearing different expressions? Research suggests that we can, though it is not clear what the results mean. Laird argues that facial expressions affect emotion through a process of self-perception: "If I'm smiling, I must be happy." Consistent with this hypothesis, Chris Kleinke and others (1998) asked people to emulate either happy or angry facial expressions depicted in a series of photographs. Half the participants saw themselves in a mirror during the task; the others did not. Did these manipulations affect mood states? Yes. Compared

facial feedback hypothesis The hypothesis that changes in facial expression can lead to corresponding changes in emotion.

to participants in a no-expression control group, those who put on happy faces felt better, and those who put on angry faces felt worse. As predicted by self-perception theory, the differences were particularly pronounced among participants who saw themselves in a mirror.

Other researchers believe that facial movements spark emotion by producing physiological changes in the brain. For example, Robert Zajonc (1993) argues that smiling causes facial muscles to increase the flow of air-cooled blood to the brain, a process that produces a pleasant state by lowering brain temperature. Conversely, frowning decreases blood flow, producing an unpleasant state by raising temperature. To demonstrate, Zajonc and his colleagues (1989) conducted a study in which they asked participants to repeat certain vowels 20 times each, including the sounds *ah*, *e*, *u*, and the German vowel *ü*. In the meantime, temperature changes in the forehead were measured and participants reported on how they felt. As it turned out, *ah* and *e* (sounds that cause people to mimic smiling) lowered forehead temperature and elevated mood, whereas *u* and *ü* (sounds that cause us to mimic frowning) increased temperature and dampened mood. In short, people need not infer how they feel. Rather, facial expressions evoke physiological changes that produce an emotional experience.

Other expressive behaviors, such as body posture, can also provide us with sensory feedback and influence the way we feel. When people feel proud, they stand erect with their shoulders raised, chest expanded, and head held high (*expansion*). When dejected, however, we slump over with shoulders drooping and head bowed (*contraction*). Clearly, your emotional state is revealed in the way you carry yourself. But is it also possible that the way you carry yourself affects your emotional state? Can people lift their spirits by expansion or lower their spirits by contraction? Yes. Sabine Stepper and Fritz Strack (1993) arranged for people to sit in either a slumped or an upright position by varying the height of the table they had to write on. Those forced to sit upright reported feeling more pride after succeeding at a task than did those placed in a slumped position.

Smiling can make you feel happier.

TRUE

Self-Perceptions of Motivation   Without quite realizing it, the American author Mark Twain was a self-perception theorist. In *The Adventures of Tom Sawyer,* written in the late 1800s, he quipped, "There are wealthy gentlemen in England who drive four-horse passenger coaches 20 or 30 miles on a daily line, in the summer, because the privilege costs them considerable money; but if they were offered wages for the service that would turn it into work then they would resign." Twain's hypothesis—that reward for an enjoyable activity can undermine interest in that activity—seems to contradict both our intuition and the results of psychological research. After all, aren't we all motivated by reward, as B. F. Skinner and other behaviorists have declared? The answer depends on how *motivation* is defined.

A keen observer of human behavior, Twain anticipated a key distinction between intrinsic and extrinsic motivation. *Intrinsic motivation* originates in factors within a person. People are said to be intrinsically motivated when they engage in an activity for the sake of their own interest, the challenge, or sheer enjoyment. Eating a good meal; listening to music; spending time with friends, or on Facebook; or getting engrossed in a book, a Netflix movie, a sports event, or a video game—these are the kinds of activities that you might find intrinsically motivating. In contrast, *extrinsic motivation* originates in factors outside the person. People are said to be extrinsically motivated when they engage in an activity as a means to an end, for tangible benefit. It might be to acquire money, grades, or some other kind of recognition; to fulfill an obligation; or to avoid a penalty or

Time Life Pictures/Getty Images

Nineteenth century American author Mark Twain understood the effects of reward on intrinsic motivation.

punishment. Clearly, people strive for reward. But what happens to the intrinsic motivation once that reward is no longer available?

From the standpoint of self-perception theory, Twain's hypothesis makes sense. When someone is offered a reward for something they already like to do—whether it's listening to music, playing a game, or eating a tasty food—that behavior becomes *overjustified*, or overrewarded, which means that it can be attributed to extrinsic as well as intrinsic motives. By creating ambiguity about a person's motivation, can the **overjustification effect** have unintended consequences? When athletes are paid millions of dollars to play their sport, does the money overwhelm their love of the game, making play feel like work? Once paid, do people begin to wonder if the activity was ever worth pursuing in its own right?

Research has shown that when people start getting rewarded for a task they already enjoy, they sometimes lose interest in it over time. In a classic demonstration of this phenomenon, Mark Lepper and his colleagues (1973) gave preschool children an opportunity to play with colorful felt-tipped markers—an opportunity most could not resist. By observing how much time the children spent on the activity, the researchers were able to measure their intrinsic motivation. Two weeks later, the children were divided into three groups, all about equal in terms of initial levels of intrinsic motivation. In one, the children were simply asked to draw some pictures with the markers. In the second, they were told that if they used the markers, they would receive a "Good Player Award," a certificate with a gold star and a red ribbon. In a third group, the children were not offered a reward for drawing pictures, but—like those in the second group—they received a reward when they were done.

About a week later, the teachers placed the markers and paper on a table in the classroom while the experimenters observed through a one-way mirror. Since no rewards were offered on this occasion, the amount of free time the children spent playing with the markers reflected their intrinsic motivation. As predicted, those who had expected and received a reward for their efforts were no longer as interested in the markers as they had been. Children who had not received a reward were not adversely affected, nor were those who had received the unexpected reward. Having played with the markers without the promise of tangible benefit, these children remained intrinsically motivated (see ● Figure 3.2).

The paradox that reward can undermine rather than enhance intrinsic motivation has been observed in many settings and with both children and adults (Deci & Ryan, 1985; Tang & Hall, 1995). Accept money for a leisure activity, and before you know it, what used to be "play" comes to feel more like "work." In the long run, this can have unintended negative effects on the quality of your performance.

In a series of studies, Teresa Amabile (1996) and others had participants write poems, draw or paint pictures, make paper collages, and generate creative solutions to business dilemmas. Consistently, they found that people are more creative when they feel interested and challenged by the work itself than when they feel pressured to make money, fulfill obligations, meet deadlines, win competitions, or impress others. When Amabile had art experts rate the works of professional

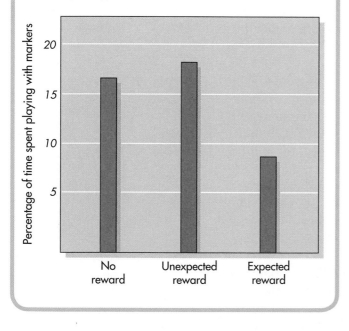

● **FIGURE 3.2**

Paradoxical Effects of Reward on Intrinsic Motivation

In this study, an expected reward undermined children's intrinsic motivation to play with felt-tipped markers. Children who received an unexpected reward or no reward did not lose interest.
Based on Lepper, M. R., Greene, D., and Nisbett, R. E. (1973). Undermining children's intrinsic interest with extrinsic reward: A test of the 'overjustification' hypothesis. *Journal of Personality and Social Psychology, 28*, 129–137.

overjustification effect The tendency for intrinsic motivation to diminish for activities that have become associated with reward or other extrinsic factors.

artists, she found that their commissioned work (art they were contracted for) was judged as lower in quality than their noncommissioned work. People are likely to be more creative when they are intrinsically motivated in relation to the task, not compelled by outside forces.

Looking back over this research, Beth Hennessey (2015) notes that "[i]f I were secretary of education," she would focus on ways to enhance *intrinsic* motivation in the classroom—as opposed to the use of grades, testing standards, competition, and other *extrinsic* means of motivating students.

But wait. If extrinsic benefits serve to undermine intrinsic motivation, should teachers and parents *not* offer rewards to their children? Are the employee incentive programs that are so often used to motivate workers in the business world doomed to fail, as some (Kohn, 1993) have suggested? This turns out to be a complex question that depends on how the reward is perceived and by whom. If a reward is presented in the form of verbal praise that is perceived to be sincere or as a special "bonus" for superior performance, then it can *enhance* intrinsic motivation by providing positive feedback about competence—as when people win competitions, scholarships, or a pat on the back from people they respect (Cameron & Pierce, 1994; Cameron et al., 2005; Eisenberger & Cameron, 1996; Henderlong & Lepper, 2002).

The notion that intrinsic motivation is undermined by some types of reward but not others was observed even among 20-month-old babies. In a clever study, Felix Warneken and Michael Tomasello (2006) brought babies into a lab, where the experimenter accidentally dropped a pen or crumpled paper onto the floor and appeared unable to reach it. The child could help by picking up the object and handing it to the experimenter. Most of the babies helped in this situation. In a treatment phase, the researchers responded to the assistance by giving the child a toy cube ("For this you get a cube"), verbal praise ("Thank you, that's really nice!"), or nothing at all. Would these same children continue to help? Results showed that in a later test phase, when presented with a number of helping opportunities, those in the no-response condition continued to help 89% of the time and that this tendency remained high at 81% in the verbal praise condition. Yet among children who had earlier received a reward, helping in the test phase dropped to 53% when that reward was no longer available (see also Warneken & Tomasello, 2014).

Individual differences in people's motivational orientation toward work must also be considered. For intrinsically oriented people who say, "What matters most to me is enjoying what I do" and "I seldom think about salary and promotions," reward may be unnecessary and may even be detrimental (Amabile et al., 1994). Yet for people who are laser-focused on the achievement of certain goals—whether at school, at work, or in sports—inducements such as grades, scores, bonuses, awards, trophies, and the sheer thrill of competition, as in team sports, tend to boost intrinsic motivation (Durik & Harackiewicz, 2007; Harackiewicz & Elliot, 1993).

◼ Influences of Other People

As noted earlier, Cooley's (1902) theory of the looking-glass self emphasized that other people help us define ourselves. In this section, we will see the importance of this proposition to our self-concepts.

Social Comparison Theory Suppose a stranger were to ask, "Who are you?" If you had only a minute or two to answer, would you mention your religion or your ethnic background? What about your hometown? Would you describe your talents and your interests or your likes and dislikes? When asked this question, people tend to describe themselves in ways that set them apart from others in their immediate vicinity (McGuire & McGuire, 1988). Among children, boys are more likely to cite their gender when they grow up in families that are predominantly female; girls do the same when living in families that are predominantly male (McGuire et al., 1979). Similarly, on the college campus, "nontraditional" older students are more likely to cite their age than are traditional younger students (Kite, 1992). Regardless of whether the unique attribute is gender, age, height, or eye color, this pattern is basically the same. The implication is intriguing: Change someone's social surroundings, and you can change that person's spontaneous self-description.

This reliance on distinguishing features in self-description indicates that the self is "relative," a social construct, and that each of us defines ourselves in part by using family members, friends, acquaintances, and others as a benchmark (Mussweiler & Rüter, 2003; Mussweiler & Strack, 2000). Importantly, the self is also "malleable" according to our need to fit in with those around us. In an article entitled "Reaching Out by Changing What's Within," Stephanie Richman and her colleagues (2015) reported on a series of studies showing that when college students are induced to suffer through a social exclusion experience—being left out of an online three-person game—they go on to modify their self-concept descriptions (for example, on such traits as warm, adventurous, creative, enthusiastic, thoughtful, and funny) in ways that make them more similar to a fellow student who looms as a potential friend.

Enter Leon Festinger's (1954) **social comparison theory**. Festinger argued that when people are uncertain of their abilities or opinions—that is, when objective information is not readily available—they evaluate themselves through comparisons with similar others. The theory seems reasonable, but is it valid? Over the years, social psychologists have put social comparison theory to the test, focusing on two key questions: (1) *When* do people turn to others for comparative information? (2) Of all the people who inhabit the Earth, *with whom* do we choose to compare ourselves? (Suls & Wheeler, 2000).

As Festinger proposed, the answer to the "when" question appears to be that people engage in social comparison in states of uncertainty, when more objective means of self-evaluation are not available. It's not clear whether Festinger understated the importance of social comparison processes. Some research suggests that people judge themselves in relation to others even when more objective standards really are available (Klein, 1997). Yet other research supports Festinger's theory that people are less influenced by social comparisons when objective information is available—for example, through our personal histories of success and failure (Steyn & Mynhardt, 2008).

The "with whom" question has also been the subject of many studies. The answer seems to be that when we evaluate our own taste in music, value on the job market, or athletic ability, we look to others who are similar to us in relevant ways (Goethals & Darley, 1977; Wheeler et al., 1982). If you are curious about your flair for writing, for example, you're more likely to compare yourself with other college students than with high schoolers or best-selling authors. There are exceptions to this rule, of course. Later in this chapter, we will see that people often cope with personal inadequacies by focusing on others who are less able or less fortunate than themselves.

social comparison theory The theory that people evaluate their own abilities and opinions by comparing themselves to others.

Facebook as a Venue for Social Comparison Currently, *Facebook*—the most heavily populated social networking site—has 1.5 billion active users worldwide

(Facebook, 2015). On computers, tablets, and mobile phones, more than a billion people a day log into their Facebook accounts, Twitter, LinkedIn, Pinterest, Tumblr, and other sites. Two types of usage can be distinguished: active usage, where people post information about themselves and communicate with others; and passive usage, in which people consume information from other people's Facebook pages without making direct contact (Deters & Mehl, 2013; Verduyn et al., 2015).

Now that social networking sites enable us to access countless numbers of people, what effect do all the social comparison opportunities available to us have on our self-concepts, our self-evaluations, and our overall well-being? Does looking at other people's Facebook pages make you feel better about yourself, or worse, or does it depend on whose pages you visit and how they present themselves? At first, research was reported in the news suggesting a phenomenon that was being called "Facebook Depression"—the more time people spent on Facebook, the more unhappy they were (Feinstein et al., 2013; Kalpidou, Costin, & Morris, 2011; O'Keeffe & Clarke-Pearson, 2011). Immediately, social psychologists were quick to warn that this *correlation* should not be interpreted to mean that Facebook usage *causes* depression.

There are two reasons why Facebook usage may undermine a person's well-being. First, as predicted by Festinger's social comparison theory, recent studies have shown that the link between Facebook usage and self-evaluation depends on whom we compare ourselves to. After college-age adults were randomly assigned to engage in upward—as opposed to downward—social comparisons, with others who are highly active and successful, they came to rate themselves less favorably (Vogel et al., 2014). A second possible reason for this negative effect is that people on Facebook, as in life more generally, tend to portray themselves in overly flattering ways—which increases the likelihood that the social comparisons we make are not personally favorable. For that reason, research shows that the more Facebook time that people passively scroll through other people's pages—rather than directly interacting with others—the worse they felt about themselves (Verduyn et al., 2015).

Two-Factor Theory of Emotion People seek social comparison information to evaluate their abilities and opinions. Do they also turn to others to determine something as subjective as their own emotions? In classic experiments on affiliation, Stanley Schachter (1959) found that when people were frightened into thinking they would receive painful electric shocks, most sought the company of others who were in the same predicament. Nervous and uncertain about how they should be feeling, participants wanted to affiliate with similar others, presumably for the purpose of comparison. Yet when they were not fearful and expected only mild shocks or when the "others" were not taking part in the same experiment, participants preferred to be alone. As Schachter put it, "Misery doesn't just love any kind of company; it loves only miserable company" (p. 24).

Intrigued by the possibilities, Schachter and his research team took the next step. Could it be, they wondered, that when people are uncertain about how they feel, their emotional state is actually determined by the reactions of others around them? In answer to this question, the researchers proposed that two factors are necessary to feel a specific emotion. First, the person must experience the symptoms of physiological arousal—such as a racing heart, perspiration, rapid breathing, and tightening of the stomach. Second, the person must make a *cognitive interpretation* that explains the source of the arousal. And that is where the people around us come in: Their reactions help us interpret our own arousal.

To test this provocative **two-factor theory of emotion**, Schachter and Singer (1962) injected male volunteers with epinephrine, a drug that heightens physiological arousal. Although one group was forewarned about the drug's effects, a second group was not. Members of a third group were injected with a harmless placebo. Before the drug (which was described as a vitamin supplement) actually took effect, participants were left alone with a male confederate introduced as another participant who had received the same injection. In some sessions, the confederate behaved in a euphoric manner. For 20 minutes, he bounced around happily, doodling on scratch paper, sinking jump shots into the wastebasket, flying paper airplanes across the room, and playing with a Hula-Hoop. In other sessions, the confederate displayed anger, making fun of a questionnaire they were filling out and, in a fit of rage, ripping it up and hurling it into the wastebasket.

Think for a moment about these various combinations of situations. As the drug takes effect, participants in the *drug-informed* group will begin to feel their hearts pound, their hands shake, and their faces flush. Having been told to expect these symptoms, however, they need not search for an explanation. Participants in the *placebo* group will not become aroused in the first place, so they will have no symptoms to explain. But now consider the plight of those in the *drug-uninformed* group, who suddenly become aroused without knowing why. Trying to identify the sensations, these participants, according to the theory, should take their cues from someone else in the same predicament—namely, the confederate.

In general, the experimental results supported Schachter and Singer's line of reasoning. Drug-uninformed participants reported feeling relatively happy or angry depending on the confederate's performance. In many instances, they even exhibited similar kinds of behavior. One participant, for example, "threw open the window and, laughing, hurled paper basketballs at passersby." In the drug-informed and placebo groups, however, participants were, as expected, less influenced by these social cues.

Schachter and Singer's two-factor theory attracted controversy when some studies corroborated their findings but others did not. In one experiment, for example, participants who were injected with epinephrine and not forewarned about the symptoms later exhibited more fear in response to a scary film, but they were not more angry or amused while seeing films that tend to elicit these other emotions (Mezzacappa et al., 1999). It now appears that one limited but important conclusion can safely be drawn: When people are unclear about their own emotional states, they sometimes interpret how they feel by watching others (Reisenzein, 1983). The "sometimes" part of the conclusion is important. For other people to influence your emotion your level of physiological arousal cannot be too intense or else it will be experienced as aversive, regardless of the situation (Maslach, 1979; Zimbardo et al., 1993). Also, research shows that other people must be present as a possible explanation for arousal *before* its onset. Once people are aroused, they turn for an explanation to events that preceded the change in their physiological state (Schachter & Singer, 1979; Sinclair et al., 1994).

In subsequent chapters, we will see that the two-factor theory of emotion has far-reaching implications for passionate love, anger and aggression, and other affective experiences.

two-factor theory of emotion
The theory that the experience of emotion is based on two factors: physiological arousal and a cognitive interpretation of that arousal.

■ Autobiographical Memories

Philosopher James Mill once said, "The phenomenon of the Self and that of Memory are merely two sides of the same fact." If the story of patient William Thompson at the start of this chapter is any indication, Mill was right. Without autobiographical memories—recollections of the sequences of events that have touched your life (Bernsten & Rubin, 2012; Fivush & Haden, 2003; Rubin, 1996)—you would have no coherent self-concept. After all, who would you be if you could not remember your parents or childhood friends, your successes and failures, the places you lived, the schools you attended, the books you read, and the teams you played for? Clearly, memories shape the self-concept. In this section, we'll see that the self-concept shapes our personal memories as well (Conway & Pleydell-Pearce, 2000).

When people are prompted to recall their own experiences, they typically report more events from the recent past than from the distant past. There are, however, two consistent exceptions to this simple recency rule. The first is that older adults tend to retrieve a large number of personal memories from their adolescence and early adult years—a "reminiscence bump" found across many cultures that may occur because these are busy and formative years in one's life (Conway et al., 2005; Fitzgerald, 1988; Jansari & Parkin, 1996). A second exception is that people tend to remember transitional "firsts." Reflect for a moment on your own college career. What events pop to mind—and when did they occur? Did you come up with the day you arrived on campus or the first time you met your closest friend? What about notable classes, parties, or sports events? When David Pillemer and his colleagues (1996) asked college juniors and seniors to recount the most memorable experiences of their first year, 32% of all recollections were from the transitional month of September. When college graduates were given the same task, they too cited a disproportionate number of events from the opening two months of their first year, followed by the next major transitional period, the last month of their senior year. Among students, these busy transitional periods are important regardless of whether their schools follow a semester calendar or some other academic schedule (Kurbat et al., 1998).

Obviously, not all experiences leave the same impression. Ask people old enough to remember November 22, 1963, and to this day they probably can tell you exactly where they were, who they were with, what they were thinking, and what was happening the moment they heard the news that President John F. Kennedy had been shot. Ask anyone old enough to remember the terrorist attacks of September 11, 2001, and they too could probably recount exquisite levels of detail about the event and their personal relation to it. Roger Brown and James Kulik (1977) coined the term *flashbulb memories* to describe these enduring, detailed, high-resolution recollections and speculated that humans are biologically equipped for survival purposes to "print" dramatic events in memory. These flashbulb memories are not necessarily accurate or even consistent over time. Still, these recollections "feel" special and serve as prominent landmarks in the biographies that we tell about ourselves (Conway, 1995; Luminet & Curci, 2009).

By linking the present to the past and providing us with a sense of inner continuity over time, autobiographical memory is a vital part of—and can be shaped by—our life story and sense of identity. The links between our sense of self and autobiographical memory are subtle, complex, and often not straightforward (Prebble et al., 2013).

One complicating factor is that people tend to distort the past in ways that inflate their own sense of importance and achievement. In one study, Harry Bahrick and others (1996) had college students try to recall all of their high school grades and then checked their reports against the actual transcripts. Overall, the majority of grades were recalled correctly. But most of the errors in memory were grade

"The nice thing about having memories is that you can choose."
—William Trevor

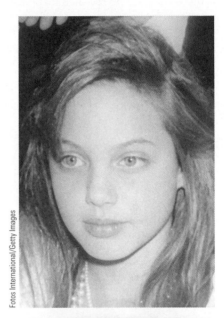
Fotos International/Getty Images

Lorenzo Ciniglio/Sygma/Corbis

Although adults recall more events from the recent than distant past, people are filled with memories from late adolescence and early adulthood. These formative years are nicely captured by high school photos, such as those of American actresses Angelina Jolie (top) and Jennifer Aniston (bottom).

● **FIGURE 3.3**

Distortions in Memory of High School Grades

College students were asked to recall their high school grades, which were then checked against their actual transcripts. These comparisons revealed that most errors in memory were grade inflations. Lower grades were recalled with the least accuracy (and the most inflation). It appears that people sometimes revise their own past to suit their current self-image.

Based on Bahrick et al., "Accuracy and distortion in memory for high school grades," *Psychological Science* vol 7 (pp. 265–271).

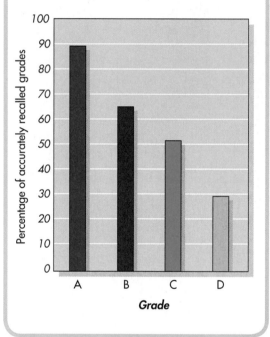

inflations—and most of these were made when the actual grades were *low* (see ● Figure 3.3).

In a second study, Burcu Demiray and Steve Janssen (2015) asked hundreds of adults, 18 to 80 years old, to report the seven most important events from their lives and to rate these memories for how good, important, emotional, vivid, and close they were. The results showed that respondents felt psychologically "closer" to memories that were positive rather than negative. Suggesting that this bias serves an adaptive purpose, the results also showed that this tendency that was particularly evident in people who evaluate themselves favorably. These findings bring to mind George Herbert Mead's (1934) suggestion that our visions of the past are like pure "escape fancies . . . in which we rebuild the world according to our hearts' desires" (pp. 348–349). Or, as Anthony Greenwald (1980) put it: "The past is remembered as if it were a drama in which the self was the leading player" (p. 604).

Our autobiographies are so interconnected with our sense of who were are that as our self-concept changes, so does our visual perspective on the past. Think about an important way in which you have changed. Once you were a kid, now you are in college or working. Or maybe you were a smoker and stopped, or obese and lost weight. Or maybe you underwent a religious conversion, or had cancer and survived it—and now you feel "reborn." Theorizing that our current self-concept colors how we see our past selves, Lisa Libby and Richard Eibach (2002) asked college students to write about one aspect of themselves that had changed a lot and another that had not changed since high school. Analyzing the words used to describe these recollections, these researchers found that participants used more third-person pronouns to describe past actions that no longer fit their current selves—and they rated themselves as more detached from these actions.

Finally, it is interesting to note that just as the *contents* of our autobiographical memories are intertwined with our sense of who we are, the *process* of remembering can prove to be a positive emotional experience. Have you ever lost yourself in a daydream, thinking back to a childhood vacation, a graduation, the time you spent at a sports camp, or the day you met a good friend? *Nostalgia*—defined as a sentimental longing for the past—is common and universal. Research shows that people often become nostalgic during distressing life events such as a breakup or divorce, a long distance move, feelings of loneliness, or serious illness (Wildschut et al., 2006). Research also shows that the effect of making people nostalgic is not merely inform or reinforce the self-concept but to boost their self-esteem and positive mood states, instill a sense that life is meaningful and worth living, and increase optimism about the future (Baldwin et al., 2015; Baldwin & Landau, 2014; Cheung et al., 2013; Routledge et al., 2011).

■ Culture and the Self-Concept

The self-concept is also heavily influenced by cultural factors. In America, it is said that "the squeaky wheel gets the grease"; in Japan, it is said that "the nail that stands out gets pounded down." Thus, American parents try to raise their children to be independent, self-reliant, and assertive (a "cut above the rest"), whereas Japanese children are raised to fit into their groups and community.

Differences in Cultural Orientation   The preceding example illustrates two contrasting cultural orientations. One values *individualism* and the virtues of independence, autonomy, and self-reliance. The other orientation values *collectivism* and the virtues of interdependence, cooperation, and social harmony. Under the banner of individualism, one's personal goals take priority over group allegiances. In collectivist cultures, by contrast, a person is first and foremost a loyal member of a family, team, company, church, and state, motivated to be part of a group—not different, better, or worse (Triandis, 1994). In what countries are these orientations the most extreme? In a worldwide study of 116,000 employees of IBM, Geert Hofstede (1980) found that the most fiercely individualistic people were from the United States, Australia, Great Britain, Canada, and the Netherlands—in that order. The most collectivist people were from Venezuela, Colombia, Pakistan, Peru, Taiwan, and China.

Individualism and collectivism are not opposites on a continuum; the similarities and differences between countries do not fit a simple pattern. Daphna Oyserman and others (2002) conducted a meta-analysis of thousands of respondents in 83 studies. Within the United States, they found that African Americans were the most individualistic subgroup and that Asian Americans and Latino Americans were the most collectivistic. Comparing nations, they found that collectivist orientations varied within Asia, as the Chinese were more collectivistic than Japanese and Korean respondents.

On average, all humans are 99.5% similar to other humans. What is it about cultures, therefore, that creates such different orientations among people? In *Clash!: How to Thrive in a Multicultural World*, Hazel Rose Markus and Alan Conner (2013) describe the conflicts that often arise between groups all over the world—East vs. West, rich vs. poor, urban vs. rural, coastal vs. heartland, and whites vs. people of color, to name a few. They note that national boundaries are not the only source of cultural differences, that each of us combines a special mix of biology and cultures to make us who we are. According to Markus and Conner, culture is made up of four I's—*ideas*, *institutions*, and social *interactions* that shape how *individuals* think, feel, and act. In turn, how individuals act influences their ideas, institutions, and social interactions. This dynamic *culture cycle* is depicted in ● Figure 3.4.

Cultural Influences on the Self   Individualism and collectivism are so deeply ingrained in a culture that they mold our very self-conceptions and identities. According to Hazel Markus and Shinobu Kitayama (1991), most North Americans and Europeans have an *independent* view of the self. In this view, the self is an entity that is distinct, autonomous, self-contained, and endowed with unique dispositions. Yet in much of Asia, Africa, and Latin America, people hold an

● **FIGURE 3.4**

The Culture Cycle

The culture cycle shows that individuals are shaped by their interactions with others, by formal institutions, and by commonly shared ideas of what is a good and right way to be a person. In turn, through their actions and behaviors, individuals shape these aspects of their own world.

Based on Markus, H.R., & Conner, A. (2013). Clash!: 8 cultural conflicts that make us who we are. New York, NY: Hudson Street Press.

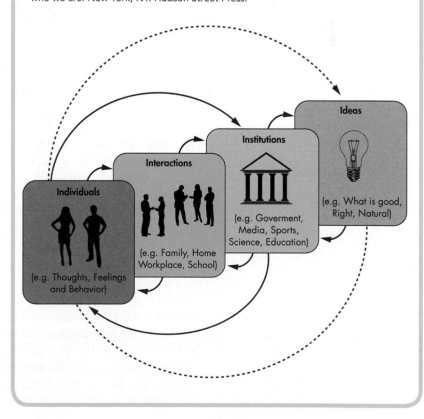

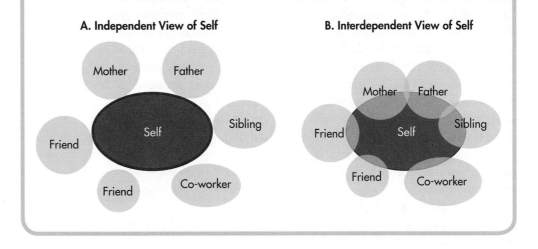

● FIGURE 3.5

Cultural Conceptions of Self

As depicted here, different cultures foster different conceptions of the self. Many Westerners have an *independent view* of the self as an entity that is distinct, autonomous, and self-contained. Yet many Asians, Africans, and Latin Americans hold an *interdependent view* of the self that encompasses others in a larger social network. Based on Marcus, H. R. and Kitayama, S. (1991). Culture and the self: Implications for cognition, emotion, and motivation. *Psychological Review, 98,* 224–253.

A. Independent View of Self

Mother Father Sibling Self Friend Friend Co-worker

B. Interdependent View of Self

Mother Father Sibling Friend Self Friend Co-worker

interdependent view of the self. Here, the self is part of a larger network that includes one's family, co-workers, and others with whom one is socially connected. People with an independent view say that "the only person you can count on is yourself" and "I enjoy being unique and different from others." In contrast, those with an interdependent view are more likely to agree that "I'm partly to blame if one of my family members or co-workers fails" and "My happiness depends on the happiness of those around me" (Rhee et al., 1995; Triandis et al., 1998). These contrasting orientations—one focused on the personal self, the other on a collective self—are depicted in ● Figure 3.5.

Research of various sorts confirms the close link between cultural orientation and conceptions of the self. In one study, David Trafimow and others (1991) had North American and Chinese college students complete 20 sentences beginning with "I am. . . ." Americans were more likely to fill in the blank with trait descriptions ("I am shy"), whereas the Chinese were more likely to identify themselves by group affiliations ("I am a college student"). Consistent with this finding, a second study has shown that when Chinese participants—but not Americans—think about themselves areas of the brain are activated that are also activated when they think about their mothers (Zhu et al., 2007b). A third study has shown that when it comes to making career decisions, Chinese students with interdependent selves are more likely to seek advice from others and compromise than are American students with independent selves (Guan et al., 2015).

Our cultural orientations can color the way people perceive, evaluate, and present themselves in relation to others. In this regard, Markus and Kitayama (1991) identified two interesting differences between East and West: The first is that people in individualistic cultures strive for personal achievement, whereas those living in collectivist cultures derive more satisfaction from the status of a valued group. Thus, whereas North Americans tend to overestimate their own contributions to a team effort, seize credit for success, and blame others for failure, people from collectivist cultures tend to underestimate their own role and present themselves in more modest, self-effacing terms in relation to other members of the group (Heine et al., 2000).

A second consequence of these differing conceptions of the self is that American college students see themselves as less similar to other people than do Asian students. This difference reinforces the idea that individuals with independent self-conceptions believe they are unique. In fact, our cultural orientations toward conformity or independence may lead us to favor similarity or uniqueness *in all things*. In a study that illustrates the point, Heejung Kim and Hazel Markus (1999) showed abstract figures to subjects from the United States and Korea. Each figure contained nine parts. Most of the parts were identical in shape, position, and direction. One or more were different. Look at ● Figure 3.6. Which of the nine subfigures within each group do you like most? The American subjects liked the subfigures that were unique or in the minority, while Korean subjects preferred those that "fit in" as part of the group. In another study, these same researchers approached pedestrians of American and East Asian heritage at San Francisco's airport to fill out a questionnaire. Afterward, as a gift, they offered the participants a choice of one pen from a handful of pens, three or four of which had the same color barrel, green or orange. The result: 74% of the Americans chose a uniquely colored pen, and 76% of the East Asians selected a commonly colored pen! It seems that culturally ingrained orientations to conformity and independence leave a mark on us, leading us to form preferences for things that "fit in" or "stand out."

Are people from disparate cultures locked into thinking about the self in either personal or collective terms, or are both aspects present in everyone, to be expressed according to the situation? Reconsider the study noted earlier, where American students described themselves more in terms of personal traits and Chinese students cited more group affiliations. In a follow-up to that study, Trafimow and others (1997) tested students from Hong Kong, all of whom spoke English as a second language. One half of the students were given the "Who am I?" test in Chinese, and the other half took the test in English. Did this variation influence the results? Yes. Students who took the test in English focused more on personal traits, whereas those who took the test in Chinese focused more on group affiliations. It appears that each of us have both personal and collective aspects of the self to draw on—and that the part that comes to mind depends on the situation we are in.

The more closely social psychologists examine cultures and their impact on how people think, the more complex is the picture that emerges. Clearly, research documents the extent to which self-conceptions are influenced by the individualist and collectivist impulses within a culture. But there are other core differences as well. Kaiping Peng and Richard Nisbett (1999) note that people in East Asian cultures think in dialectical terms about contradictory characteristics—accepting, for example, that apparent opposites (such as black and white, friend and enemy, and strong and weak) can coexist within a single person either at the same time or as a result of changes over time. Grounded in Eastern traditions, **dialecticism** is a system of thought characterized by the acceptance of such contradictions

● **FIGURE 3.6**

What's Your Preference: Similarity or Uniqueness?

Which subfigure within each set do you prefer? Kim and Markus (1999) found that Americans tend to like subfigures that "stand out" as unique or in the minority, while Koreans tend to like subfigures that "fit in" with the surrounding group.

From Kim, H. and Marcus, H. R., "Deviance or uniqueness, harmony or conformity? A cultural analysis," *Journal of Personality and Social Psychology* vol 77 (pp. 785–800). Copyright © 1999 by the American Psychological Association. Reprinted by permission.

dialecticism   An Eastern system of thought that accepts the coexistence of contradictory characteristics within a single person.

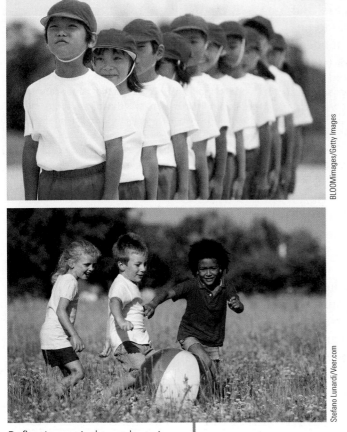

BLOOMimages/Getty Images

Stefano Lunardi/Veer.com

Reflecting an independent view of the self, children in Japan are taught to fit into the community. Reflecting a more independent view of the self, children in the United States are encouraged to express their individuality.

through compromise, as implied by the Chinese proverb "Beware of your friends, not your enemies." This thought style contrasts sharply with the American and European perspective, grounded in Western logic, by which people differentiate seeming opposites on the assumption that if one is right, the other must be wrong.

Wondering if a dialectical style of thought has implications for the self, Tammy English and Serena Chen (2007) conducted a series of studies in which they questioned American college students who were of European or Asian descent about what kind of person they are in such different everyday situations as a classroom, a cafeteria, a party, or the gym. Overall, they found that compared to European Americans who portray their "true selves" as stable across the board, Asian Americans vary their self-concepts more to suit different relationship situations—though they are consistent within these situations. Other research too has shown that East Asians are more willing than Americans to see and accept contradictory aspects of themselves (Spencer-Rodgers et al., 2009)—as seen in their willingness to accept both positive and negative aspects of themselves at the same time (Boucher et al., 2009).

The study of cultural aspects of the self is also expanded by social psychologists interested in Latin American cultures, where social and emotional relationships are a very important part of the collectivist orientation. According to Renee Holloway and others (2009), Latino cultures prize the concept of *simpatico*, which emphasizes expressive displays of personable charm, graciousness, and hospitality. Does this cultural value become part of the Latino self-concept? Clearly, no two individuals are the same. But when these researchers presented Latino and white Americans with the "Who am I?" task described earlier, they found that the Latino participants on average were more likely to describe themselves using simpatico-related terms such as likable, friendly, sympathetic, amiable, and gracious. Similarly, Nairán Ramírez-Esparza and colleagues (2012) found that Mexican participants were more likely to describe their own personality using words about relationships (e.g., parents, house, love, friends) and empathy (e.g., affectionate, honest, noble, tolerant).

Finally, it is important to realize that cultures themselves change over time, from one generation to another. Patricia Greenfield (2013) looked at the frequency of word usage from the year 1800 until 2000. She found that accompanying a shift from a more rural to urban population, there was also a shift in cultural values. As the occurrence of words such as "duty," "obliged," "give," "obedience," "authority," "belong," and "benevolence" decreased over time, the words "decision," "choose," "unique," "individual," "self," and "acquisition" increased over time.

Generational changes within a culture can also be seen within smaller frames of time. Americans who were children in the 1940s and 1950s, a generation known as "baby boomers," grew up in a very different culture than those who grew up in the 1960s and 1970s, a group commonly referred to as "GenX'ers," and those who grew up in the 1980s and 1990s—a group known as "Millennials." Analyzing questionnaire data collected from 9.2 million American high school seniors and college students from 1966 to 2009, Jean Twenge and her colleagues (2012) found that compared to boomers, subsequent generations were more focused on

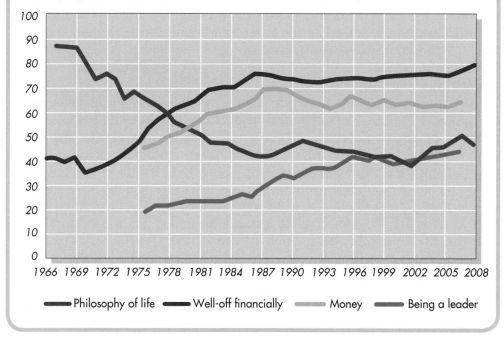

● FIGURE 3.7

Generational Differences in American Cultural Orientation

Over the years, surveys have been administered to millions of Americans who grew up in the 1940s–1950s ("baby boomers"), 1960s–1970s ("GenX'ers"), and 1980s–1990s ("Millennials"). From the responses of high school and college students from 1966 to 2009, it seems that compared to boomers, later generations were more focused on money, fame, and self-image, and less concerned with affiliation, community, and civic engagement. These changes suggest that American culture is more individualistic today than it was a half century ago.

Based on Twenge, J. M., Campbell, W. K., & Freeman, E. C. (2012). Generational differences in young adults' life goals, concern for others, and civic orientation, 1966–009, *Journal of Personality and Social Psychology, 102,* 1045–062.

money, fame, and self-image and less concerned with affiliation, community, and civic engagement (see ● Figure 3.7). This change in values—often described as a shift from "Generation We" to "Generation Me"—suggests that American culture is more individualistic today than it was a half century ago.

Social Class as a Cultural Influence   In all cultures of the world, individuals differ in their wealth, material possessions, education, and level of prestige. In a continuum that ranges from people who live in poverty up through multibillionaires, the term *social class* is used to categorize people within a culture who have in common a *low-*, *working-*, *middle-*, or *upper-*class socioeconomic status.

Social class is another cultural factor that can influence the self-concept. In Western countries, people with more income, education, and status tend to have many opportunities to exhibit individualism by expressing their desires, their autonomy, and the pursuit of personal goals. They have more control over the lives, greater personal choice, and more independence and self-focus. In contrast, people with less income, education, and status are more constrained in terms of what they can and cannot do. Navigating a low-income world means having to rely more on others and fitting-in, fostering "hard *inter*dependence" (Fiske & Markus, 2012; Kraus et al., 2012; Stephens et al., 2014). Recent studies confirm that the characteristics of the self that are associated with social class. In one study, for example, working-class men were more likely than middle-class men to see themselves in terms of their relationships to others (Markus & Conner, 2013). In a second study, people classified as low in social class were less likely to agree with statements of entitlement such as "I honestly feel I'm just more deserving than others" and with statements indicating narcissism such as "I like to look at myself in the mirror" (Piff, 2015).

Self-Esteem

How do you feel about yourself? Are you generally satisfied with the way you look, your personality, academic and athletic abilities, your accomplishments, and your friendships? Are you optimistic about your future? When it comes to the self, people are not cool, objective, dispassionate observers. Rather, we are judgmental, motivated, emotional, and highly protective of our **self-esteem**—an evaluative component of the self.

The word *esteem* comes from the Latin *aestimare*, which means "to estimate or appraise." The term *self-esteem* thus refers to our positive and negative evaluations of ourselves (Coopersmith, 1967). Some individuals have a higher self-esteem than others do—an attribute that can have a profound impact on the way they think about, feel about, and present themselves. It's important to keep in mind that although some of us have higher self-esteem than others, a feeling of self-worth is not a single trait etched permanently in stone. Rather, it is a state of mind that fluctuates up and down in response to success, failure, social relations, and other life experiences (Heatherton & Polivy, 1991).

With the self-concept made up of many self-schemas, people typically view parts of the self differently: Some parts they judge more favorably or see more clearly or as more important than other parts (Pelham, 1995). In fact, just as individuals differ according to how high or low their self-esteem is, they also differ in the extent to which their self-esteem is stable or unstable. As a general rule, self-esteem stays roughly the same from childhood through old age—people who are high or low in self-esteem remain in that relative position throughout life (Trzesniewski et al., 2003).

Although an individual's self-esteem relative to others remains stable, the average level of self-esteem in a population varies over the course of a lifetime. Longitudinal studies that track individuals over time, and cross-sectional studies that compare at one point in time people from different age groups, show that self-esteem declines from childhood to adolescence, gradually increases during the transition to adulthood, continues to rise as adults get older, and declines in old age (Erol & Orth, 2011; Orth et al., 2010). Research with college students shows that average levels of self-esteem vary even over the course of a college career. Think for a moment about the whole college experience. What changes in self-esteem might you predict? In a longitudinal study, 295 male and female students had their self-esteem tested six times over a four-year period. ● Figure 3.8 shows that average levels dropped sharply during the very first semester, rebounded by the end of the first year, and then gradually increased from that point on (Chung et al., 2014).

▦ The Need for Self-Esteem

self-esteem An affective component of the self, consisting of a person's positive and negative self-evaluations.

You, me, and just about everyone else on the planet seem to have a need for self-esteem, wanting to see ourselves in a positive light. As a result of who we are

● FIGURE 3.8

Self-Esteem Over the Course of a College Career

In this longitudinal study of college students who were repeatedly tested, self-esteem dropped sharply during their first semester but then recovered and increased into their senior year.
Chung et al., 2014 Chung, J. M., Robins, R. W., Trzesniewski, K. H., Noftle, E. E., Roberts, B. W., & Widaman, K. F. (2014). Continuity and change in self-esteem during emerging adulthood. *Journal of Personality and Social Psychology, 106*, 469-483.

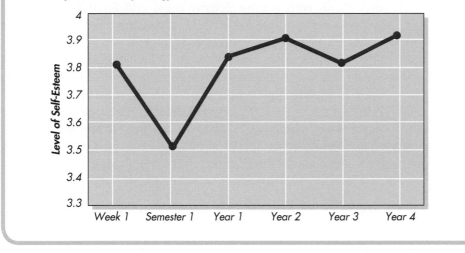

and the culture we live in, each of us may value different attributes and pursue this need in different ways. Some people derive a sense of worth from their appearance; others value physical strength, professional accomplishments, wealth, people skills, or group affiliations. Whatever the source, it is clear that the pursuit of self-worth is an aspect of human motivation that runs deep. But let's step back for a moment and ask, why? Why do we seem to need self-esteem the way we need food, air, sleep, and water?

At present, there are two social psychological answers to this question. **Sociometer Theory**, proposed by Mark Leary and Roy Baumeister (2000), maintains that people are inherently social animals and that the desire for self-esteem is driven by a more primitive need to connect with others and gain their approval. As a result of this social connection for survival, people may have evolved a "sociometer"—a mechanism that enables us to detect acceptance and rejection and then translate these perceptions into high and low self-esteem. In this way, self-esteem serves as a rough indicator of how we're doing in the eyes of others. The threat of social rejection thus lowers self-esteem, which activates the need to regain approval and acceptance. In an experiment aimed at identifying a "neural sociometer," participants underwent fMRI while viewing positive and negative feedback words that a confederate ostensibly used to describe them (words such as *interesting* and *boring)*. Participants also rated their self-esteem in response to each feedback word. Results showed that increased activity in rejection-related brain regions was associated with lowered self-esteem (Eisenberger et al., 2011).

There is a second particularly important answer to this question. Jeff Greenberg, Sheldon Solomon, and Thomas Pyszczynski (1997) proposed **Terror Management Theory** to help explain our relentless need for self-esteem. According to this provocative and influential theory, we humans are biologically programmed for life and

Sociometer Theory The theory that self-esteem is a gauge that monitors our social interactions and sends us signals as to whether our behavior is acceptable to others.

Terror Management Theory The theory that humans cope with the fear of their own death by constructing worldviews that help to preserve their self-esteem.

self-preservation. Yet we are conscious of—and terrified by—the inevitability of our own death. To cope with this paralyzing, deeply rooted fear, we construct and accept cultural worldviews about how, why, and by whom the Earth was created; religious explanations of the purpose of our existence; and a sense of history filled with heroes, villains, and momentous events. These worldviews provide meaning and purpose and a buffer against anxiety. In a series of experiments, these investigators found that people react to graphic scenes of death or to the thought of their own death with intense defensiveness and anxiety. When people are given positive feedback on a test, however, which boosts their self-esteem, that reaction is muted. Other research has since confirmed this type of result (Schmeichel et al., 2009). As we'll see in later chapters, Terror Management Theory has been used to explain how people cope with traumas such as the terrorist attack of 9/11 (Pyszczynski et al., 2002) and why people all over the world seek solace in religion, strong leaders, and cultural institutions (Pyszczynski et al., 2015).

As for the need for self-esteem, Pyszczynski and his colleagues (2004) put it this way:

> Self-esteem is a protective shield designed to control the potential for terror that results from awareness of the horrifying possibility that we humans are merely transient animals groping to survive in a meaningless universe, designed only to die and decay. From this perspective, each individual human's name and identity, family and social identifications, goals and aspirations, occupation and title, and humanly created adornments are draped over an animal that, in the cosmic scheme of things, may be no more significant or enduring than any individual potato, pineapple, or porcupine. (p. 436)

Confirming folk wisdom, a good deal of research shows that high and low self-esteem can color our outlook on life. People with positive self-images tend to be happy, healthy, productive, and successful. They also tend to be confident, bringing to new challenges a winning attitude that leads them to persist longer at difficult tasks, sleep better at night, maintain their independence in the face of peer pressure, and suffer from fewer ulcers. In contrast, people with negative self-images tend to be more depressed, pessimistic about the future, and prone to failure. Lacking confidence, they bring to new tasks a losing attitude that traps them in a vicious, self-defeating cycle. Expecting to fail and fearing the worst, they become anxious, exert less effort, and "tune out" on important challenges.

Does high self-esteem ensure good life outcomes? This seemingly simple question is the subject of debate. On the one hand, based on their review of the research, Roy Baumeister and others (2003) conclude that although high self-esteem leads people to feel good, take on new challenges, and persist in the face of failure, the correlational evidence does not clearly support the strong conclusion that boosting self-esteem *causes* people to perform well in school or at work, to be socially popular, or to behave in ways that foster physical health. What's more, Jennifer Crocker and Lora Park (2004) argue that the process of pursuing self-esteem itself can be costly. They point to research showing that in trying hard to boost and maintain their self-esteem, people often become anxious, avoid activities that risk failure, neglect the needs of others, and suffer from stress-related health problems. Self-esteem has its benefits, they concede, but striving for it can also be costly.

Challenging the conclusion that self-esteem is not worth striving for, William Swann and others (2007) note that although a person's overall, or *global*, sense of self-worth may not be predictive of positive life outcomes, people with particular domains of self-esteem benefit in more circumscribed ways. In other words, research suggests that individuals with high self-esteem—specifically for public speaking, mathematics, or social situations—outperform those who have less self-confidence in the domains of public speaking, math, and social situations, respectively. In addition to facilitating success in various life domains, research suggests that self-esteem is associated with a reduced risk for physical and mental health problems, substance abuse, and antisocial behavior (Orth et al., 2012; Swann et al., 2007).

■ Are There Gender and Race Differences?

Just as individuals differ in their self-esteem, so too do social and cultural groups. If you were to administer a self-esteem test to thousands of people all over the world, would you find that some segments of the population score higher than others? Would you expect to see differences in the averages of men and women, blacks and whites, or inhabitants of different cultures? Believing that self-esteem promotes health, happiness, and success and concerned that some groups are disadvantaged in this regard, researchers have indeed made these types of comparisons.

Are there gender differences in self-esteem? Over the years, a lot has been written in the popular press about the inflated but fragile "male ego," the low self-regard among adolescent girls and young women, and the resulting gender-related "confidence gap" (Orenstein, 1994). Does the research support this assumption? To find out, Kristin Kling and others (1999) statistically combined the results of 216 studies involving 97,000 respondents and then analyzed the surveys of 48,000 American students conducted by the National Center for Education Statistics. The result: Among adolescents and adults, males outscored females on various general measures of self-esteem. Contrary to popular belief, however, the difference was small, particularly among older adults. In fact, male–female differences are specific to different aspects of self-esteem. In a meta-analysis of 115 studies involving 32,486 individuals, Brittany Gentile and her colleagues (2009) found, for example, that men have higher self-esteem with regard to their physical appearance and athletic abilities, while women have higher self-esteem when it comes to matters of ethics and personal morality.

Researchers have also wondered if low self-esteem is a problem for members of stigmatized minority groups who historically have been victims of prejudice and discrimination. Does membership in a minority group, such as African Americans, deflate one's sense of self-worth? Based on the combined results of studies involving more than half a million respondents, Bernadette Gray-Little and Adam Hafdahl (2000) reported that black American children, adolescents, and adults consistently score higher—not lower—than their white counterparts on measures of self-esteem.

In a meta-analysis of hundreds of studies that compared all age groups and different American minorities, Jean Twenge and Jennifer Crocker (2002) confirmed the African American advantage in self-esteem relative to whites but found that Hispanic, Asian, and Native American minorities have lower self-esteem scores. This self-esteem advantage is not easy to interpret. Surprised by the high African American scores, some researchers have suggested that perhaps African Americans—more than other minorities—are able to preserve their self-esteem in the face of adversity by attributing negative outcomes to the forces of discrimination and using this adversity to build a sense of group pride. In this regard, Twenge and Crocker found that self-esteem scores of black Americans, relative to those of whites, have risen over time from the pre–civil rights days of the 1950s to the present.

■ Self-Discrepancy Theory

What determines how people feel about themselves? According to E. Tory Higgins (1989), our self-esteem is defined by the match or mismatch between how we see ourselves and how we want to see ourselves. To demonstrate, try the following exercise. On a blank sheet of paper, write down 10 traits that describe the kind of person you think you *actually* are (smart? easygoing? sexy? excitable?). Next, list 10 traits that describe the kind of person you think you *ought* to be, characteristics that would enable you to meet your sense of duty, obligation, and responsibility. Then make a list of traits that describe the kind of person you *would like* to be, an *ideal* that embodies your hopes, wishes, and dreams. If you follow these instructions, you should have three lists: your actual self, your ought self, and your ideal self.

Research has shown that these lists can be used to predict your self-esteem and your emotional well-being. The first list is your self-concept. The others represent your personal standards, or *self-guides*. To the extent that you fall short of these standards, you will experience lowered self-esteem, negative emotion, and, in extreme cases, a serious affective disorder. The specific consequence depends on which self-guide you fail to achieve. If there's a discrepancy between your actual and ought selves, you will feel guilty, ashamed, and resentful. You might even suffer from excessive fears and anxiety-related disorders. If the mismatch is between your actual and ideal selves, you'll feel disappointed, frustrated, unfulfilled, and sad. In the worst-case scenario you might even become depressed (Boldero & Francis, 2000; Higgins, 1999; Strauman, 1992). Each and every one of us must cope with some degree of self-discrepancy. In fact, recent research shows that people's self-discrepancies—and the associated depression and anxiety—tend to remain stable over time, at least when retested over the course of three years (Watson et al., in press).

Our self-discrepancies may even set into motion a self-perpetuating process. Participating in a study of body images, college women with high rather than low discrepancies between their actual and ideal selves were more likely to compare themselves with thin models in TV commercials, which further increased their body dissatisfaction and depression (Bessenoff, 2006). Nobody's perfect. Yet we do not all suffer from the emotional consequences. The reason, according to Higgins, is that self-esteem depends on a number of factors. One is simply the amount of discrepancy. The more of it there is, the worse we feel. Another factor is the importance of the discrepancy to the self. The more important the domain in which we fall short, again, the worse we feel. A third factor is how much we focus on our self-discrepancies. The more focused we are, the greater the harm. This last observation raises an important question: What causes us to be more or less focused on our personal shortcomings? For an answer, we turn to self-awareness theory.

■ The Self-Awareness "Trap"

If you review your daily routine—your classes, work, errands, sports, leisure activities, social interactions, and meals—you will probably be surprised at how little time you actually spend thinking about yourself. In a study that illustrates this point, more than 100 people, ranging in age from 19 to 63, were equipped for a week with electronic beepers that sounded every two hours or so between 7:30 a.m. and 10:30 p.m. Each time the beepers went off, participants interrupted whatever they were doing, wrote down what they were thinking at that moment, and filled out a brief questionnaire. Out of 4,700 recorded thoughts, only 8 % were about the self. For the most part, attention was focused on work and other activities. In fact, when participants were thinking about themselves, they reported feeling relatively unhappy and wished they were doing something else (Csikszentmihalyi & Figurski, 1982).

State of Self-Awareness   The finding that people may be unhappy while they think about themselves is interesting, but what does it mean? Does self-reflection bring out our personal shortcomings the way staring into a mirror draws our gaze to every blemish on the face? Is self-awareness an unpleasant mental state from which we need to retreat?

Many years ago, Robert Wicklund and his colleagues theorized that the answer is yes (Duval & Wicklund, 1972; Silvia & Duval, 2001; Wicklund, 1975). According to their **self-awareness theory**, most people are not usually self-focused, but certain situations predictably force us to turn inward and become the objects of our own attention. When we talk about ourselves, glance into a mirror, stand before an audience or in front of a camera, watch ourselves on videotape, or behave in a socially conspicuous manner, we enter into a state of heightened self-awareness that leads us naturally to compare our behavior to some high standard. Even a brightly lit room can make us feel self-aware and acutely "concerned about what other people think of me" (Steidle & Werth, 2014).

As you might expect, comparing oneself to some high standard often results in a negative discrepancy and a temporary reduction in self-esteem as we discover that we fall short. Thus, research participants who are seated in front of a mirror tend to react more negatively to their self-discrepancies, often slipping into a negative mood state (Hass & Eisenstadt, 1990; Phillips & Silvia, 2005). Interestingly, Japanese people—whose culture already leads them to be highly concerned about their public "face"—are unaffected by the added presence of a mirror (Heine et al., 2008).

The real-life consequences of self-awareness can be substantial. The more self-focused people are in general, the more likely they are to find themselves in a bad mood (Flory et al., 2000) or depressed (Pyszczynski & Greenberg, 1987). People who are self-absorbed are also more likely to suffer from alcoholism, anxiety, and other clinical disorders (Mor & Winquist, 2002) and have self-destructive, suicide-related thoughts when they fail to meet their own standards (Chatard & Selimbegovic, 2011).

Is there a solution? Self-awareness theory suggests two basic ways of coping with such discomfort: (1) "shape up" by behaving in ways that help to reduce our self-discrepancies or (2) "ship out" by withdrawing from self-awareness. According to Charles Carver and Michael Scheier (1981), the solution chosen depends on whether people think they can reduce their self-discrepancy and whether they're pleased with the progress they make once they try (Duval et al., 1992). If so, they tend to match their behavior to personal or societal standards; if not, they will tune out, look for distractions, and turn attention away from the self. This process is depicted in ● Figure 3.9.

In general, research supports the prediction that when people are self-focused, they are more likely to behave in ways that are consistent with their own personal values or with socially accepted ideals. It's why one team of researchers, after using bright lights to induce a state of self-awareness, has concluded that

"I have the true feeling of myself only when I am unbearably unhappy."

—Franz Kafka

self-awareness theory   The theory that self-focused attention leads people to notice self-discrepancies, thereby motivating either an escape from self-awareness or a change in behavior.

● **FIGURE 3.9**

The Causes and Effects of Self-Awareness

Self-awareness pressures people to reduce self-discrepancies either by matching their behavior to personal or societal standards or by withdrawing from self-awareness.

© Cengage Learning®

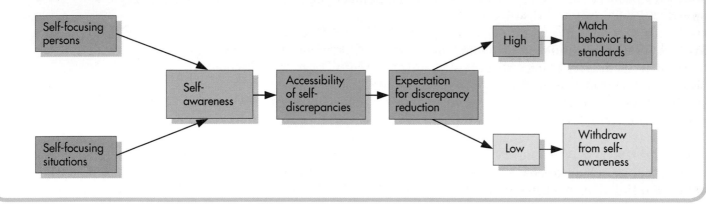

"[g]ood lamps are the best police" (Zhong et al., 2010). Two interesting field studies illustrate this point. In one, Halloween trick-or-treaters—children with masks, costumes, and painted faces—were greeted at a researcher's door and left alone to help themselves from a bowl of candy. Although the children were asked to take only one piece, 34% violated the request. When a full-length mirror was placed behind the candy bowl, however, that number dropped to 12%. Apparently, the mirror forced the children to become self-focused, leading them to behave in a way that was consistent with public standards of desirable conduct (Beaman et al., 1979). In a second study, in England, customers at a lunch counter were trusted to pay for their coffee, tea, and milk by depositing money into an unsupervised "honesty box." Hanging on the wall behind the counter was a poster that featured a picture of flowers or a pair of eyes. By calculating the ratio of money deposited to drinks consumed, researchers observed that people paid nearly three times more money in the presence of the eyes (Bateson et al., 2006).

Self-awareness theory states that if a successful reduction of self-discrepancy seems unlikely, individuals will take a second route: escape from self-awareness. Baumeister (1991) theorized that drug abuse, sexual masochism, spiritual ecstasy, binge eating, and suicide all serve this escapist function. Even television can serve as a form of escape. Sophia Moskalenko and Steven Heine (2003) brought college students into a laboratory and tested their actual–ideal self-discrepancies twice. Half watched a brief TV show on nature before the second test. In a second study, students were sent home with the questionnaire and instructed to fill it out either before or after watching TV. In both cases, those who watched TV had lower self-discrepancies on the second measure. In yet a third study, students who were told they had done poorly on an IQ test spent more time watching TV while waiting in the lab than those who were told they had succeeded. Perhaps TV and other forms of entertainment enable people to "watch their troubles away."

One troubling health implication concerns the use of alcohol. According to Jay Hull, people often drown their sorrows in a bottle as a way to escape the negative implications of self-awareness. To test this hypothesis, Hull and Richard Young (1983) administered what was supposed to be an IQ test to male participants and gave false feedback suggesting that they had either succeeded or failed. Supposedly as part of a separate study, those participants were then asked to taste and rate different wines. As they did so, experimenters kept track of how much they drank during a 15-minute tasting period. As predicted, participants who were prone to self-awareness drank more wine after failure than after success, presumably to dodge the blow to their self-esteem. Among participants not prone to self-awareness, there was no difference in alcohol consumption. These results come as no surprise. Indeed, many of us expect alcohol to grant this form of relief (Leigh & Stacy, 1993) and help us manage our emotional highs and lows (Cooper et al., 1995).

Claude Steele and Robert Josephs (1990) proposed that alcoholic intoxication offers more than just a means of tuning out on the self. Alcohol can cause us to lose touch with who we are and to shed our inhibitions (Giancola et al., 2010). It can also evoke in us a state of "drunken self-inflation." In one study, for example, participants rated their ac-

---

▲ TABLE 3.1

How Self-Conscious Are You?

These sample items appear in the Self-Consciousness Scale. How many of these statements indicating private or public self-consciousness would you use to describe yourself?

Items That Measure Private Self-Consciousness

- I'm always trying to figure myself out.
- I'm constantly examining my motives.
- I'm often the subject of my fantasies.
- I'm alert to changes in my mood.
- I'm aware of the way my mind works when I work on a problem.

Items That Measure Public Self-Consciousness

- I'm concerned about what other people think of me.
- I'm self-conscious about the way I look.
- I'm concerned about the way I present myself.
- I usually worry about making a good impression.
- One of the last things I do before leaving my house is look in the mirror.

From Fenigstein, A., Scheier, M. F., & Buss A. H. (1975). Public and private self-consciousness: Assessment and theory. *Journal of Consulting and Clinical Psychology, 43*, 522–527.

---

tual and ideal selves on various traits—some important to self-esteem, others not important. After drinking either an 80-proof vodka cocktail or a harmless placebo, they re-rated themselves on the same traits. As measured by the perceived discrepancy between actual and ideal selves, those participants who were drinking expressed inflated views of themselves on traits they considered important (Banaji & Steele, 1989).

Trait of Self-Consciousness   Just as *situations* evoke a state of self-awareness, some *individuals* are generally more self-focused than others. Research has revealed an important distinction between **private self-consciousness**—the tendency to introspect about our inner thoughts and feelings—and **public self-consciousness**—the tendency to focus on our outer public image (Buss, 1980; Fenigstein et al., 1975; Fenigstein, 2009). Table 3.1 presents a sample of items used to measure these traits.

Private and public self-consciousness are distinct traits. People who score high on a test of private self-consciousness tend to fill in incomplete sentences with first-person pronouns. They also make self-descriptive statements and recognize self-relevant words more quickly than other words (Mueller, 1982; Eichstaedt & Silvia, 2003). In contrast, those who score high on a measure of public self-consciousness are sensitive to the way they are viewed from an outsider's perspective. Thus, when people were asked to draw a capital letter E on their foreheads, 43% of those with high levels of public self-consciousness, compared with only 6% of those with low levels, oriented the E so that it was backward from their own standpoint but correct for an observer (Hass, 1984). People who are high in public self-consciousness are also particularly sensitive to the extent to which others share their opinions (Fenigstein & Abrams, 1993).

The distinction between private and public self-awareness has implications for how to reduce self-discrepancies. According to Higgins (1989), people are motivated to meet either their own standards or the standards held for them by

private self-consciousness   A personality characteristic of individuals who are introspective, often attending to their own inner states.

public self-consciousness   A personality characteristic of individuals who focus on themselves as social objects, as seen by others.

● **FIGURE 3.10**

Revolving Images of Self

According to self-awareness theory, people try to meet either their own standards or standards held for them by others—depending, perhaps, on whether they are in a state of private or public self-consciousness. As Scheier and Carver (1983, p. 123) put it, there are "two sides of the self: one for you and one for me." Snyder et al., 1983.

significant others. If you're privately self-conscious, you listen to an inner voice and try to reduce discrepancies relative to your own standards; if you're publicly self-conscious, however, you try to match your behavior to socially accepted norms. As illustrated in ● Figure 3.10, there may be "two sides of the self: one for you and one for me" (Scheier & Carver, 1983, p. 123).

God: Like a Camera in the Sky? Across nations, cultures, and religions, more than 90% of the people on Earth believe in God or some other omnipotent force. In most religions, people believe that God watches, evaluates, rewards, and punishes people for their moral and immoral behavior (Atran & Norenzayan, 2004).

For people of faith, thinking about God should trigger a state of self-focus—in the way that cameras, microphones, and other forms of surveillance do. As we saw, self-awareness theory predicts that self-focus should heighten a concern for our personal standards of good behavior. Does thinking about God have this effect? In a series of experiments, Will Gervais and Ara Norenzayan (2012) administered a religiosity scale to sort people into groups of high believers and low believers. All participants were then randomly assigned to complete a word task that required them to think about God, the presence of others, or something neutral. One study showed that high believers who were primed to think about God—but not low believers—became more self-aware, as if they were being observed by other people. A second study showed that thinking about God, as opposed to something neutral, led high believers to answer various questions in ways that were socially desirable—claiming, for example, that they are always good listeners and that they were never irritated by people who ask for favors (see ● Figure 3.11). For individuals of faith, note Gervais and Norenzayan, God is "like a camera in the sky."

As you might expect from this finding, other research has shown that thoughts of God can lead people of faith to behave more prosocially toward others. In one study, reported in an article entitled "God Is Watching You," participants were given 10 $1 coins to keep or donate to an anonymous stranger. Before engaging in this "economic decision-making task," participants were asked to unscramble sentences containing words that were neutral or religious *(God, divine, spirit, prophet, sacred).* How much of the $10 did the participants then leave for the stranger? Those who had worked with neutral words left an average of $1.84; those primed with God-related words left more than twice that amount, an average of $4.44 (Shariff & Norenzayan, 2007). Reasoning that thoughts of an all-knowing God should reduce people's sense of anonymity, and increase their sense of accountability, other researchers have found that reminders of God increase resistance to temptation—as measured, for example, by the number of bite-sized chocolate chip cookies participants ate in a taste-testing experiment (Laurin et al., 2012).

■ Self-Regulation and Its Limits

To this point, we have seen that self-focused attention can motivate us to control our behavior and strive toward personal or social ideals. Achieving these goals—which enables us to reduce the self-discrepancies that haunt us—means that we must constantly engage in **self-regulation**—the processes by which we seek to control or alter our thoughts, feelings, behaviors, and urges in order to live an acceptable social life. From lifting ourselves out of bed in the early morning to dieting, running the extra mile, limiting how much we drink at a party, practicing safe

self-regulation The process by which people control their thoughts, feelings, or behavior in order to achieve a personal or social goal.

sex, smiling politely at people we really don't like, and working when we have more fun things to do, the exercise of self-control is something we are taught as children and do all the time (Baumeister & Vohs, 2004; Bridgett et al., 2015; Carver & Scheier, 1998; Forgas et al., 2009; Heatherton, 2011).

Conflicts between our desires and the need for self-control are constant. When a sample of 205 adults wore Blackberry beepers for a week and reported their current states on cue, they indicated 7,827 episodes of *desire*—including, in order, biological desires to eat, sleep, and drink, followed by desires for media use, leisure activities, social contact, grooming and hygiene, sex, work, and sports activities. In nearly half of all instances, the desire was described as posing a conflict with other of the participants' motivations, goals, and values (Hofmann et al., 2012).

Although the need is constant, Mark Muraven and Roy Baumeister (2000) theorized that self-control is a limited inner resource that can temporarily be depleted by usage. There are two components to their theory. The first is that all self-control efforts draw from a single common reservoir. The second is that exercising self-control is like flexing a muscle: Once used, it becomes fatigued and loses strength, making it more difficult to re-exert self-control—at least for a while, until the resource is replenished. Deny yourself the ice cream or donut that tickles your sweet tooth, and you'll find it more difficult to hold your temper when provoked. Try to conceal your stage fright as you stand before an audience, and you'll find it harder to resist the urge to watch TV when you should be studying.

Research has supported this provocative hypothesis. Muraven and Baumeister (1998) had participants watch a brief clip from an upsetting film that shows scenes of sick and dying animals exposed to radioactive waste. Some of the participants were instructed to stifle their emotional responses to the clip, including their facial expressions; others were told to amplify or exaggerate their facial responses; a third group received no special instructions. Both before and after the movie, self-control was measured by the length of time participants were able to squeeze a handgrip exerciser without letting go. As predicted, those who had to inhibit or amplify their emotions during the film—but not those in the third group—lost their strength it the handgrip task from the first time they tried it to the second (see ● Figure 3.12). In laboratory experiments and in everyday life, other studies have since confirmed the point: After people exert self-control in one task, their capacity for self-regulation is weakened—causing them to talk too much, disclose too much, or brag too much in a later social situation (Hagger et al., 2010; Hofmann et al., 2012).

It appears that we can control ourselves only so much before self-regulation fatigue sets in, causing us to "lose it." What might this mean, then, for people who constantly regulate their behavior? To find out, Kathleen Vohs and Todd Heatherton (2000) showed a brief and dull documentary to individual female college students, half of whom were chronic dieters. Placed in the viewing room—either within arm's reach (high temptation) or 10 feet away (low temptation)—was a bowl filled with Skittles, M&Ms, Doritos, and salted peanuts that participants were free to sample. After watching the movie, they were taken to

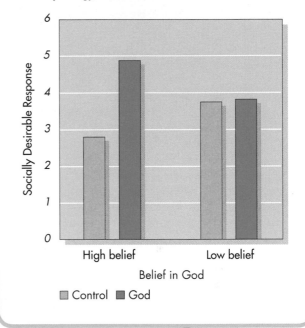

● FIGURE 3.11

Does Thinking About God Produce Self-Awareness Effects?

Participants classified as high or low believers completed a word task that led them to think about God or something neutral. Afterward, they answered questions about themselves. Consistent with self-awareness theory, thinking about God—as opposed to something neutral—led High Believers (but not Lows) to answer the questions in ways that were more socially desirable.
Based on Gervais, W. M., & Norenzayan, A. (2012). Like a camera in the sky? Thinking about God increases public self-awareness and socially desirable responding. *Journal of Experimental Social Psychology, 48,* 298–302.

● **FIGURE 3.12**

Self-Control as a Limited Inner Resource

Participants were shown an upsetting film and told to amplify or suppress their emotional responses to it (a third group received no self-control instruction). Before and afterward, self-control was measured by persistence at squeezing a handgrip exerciser. As shown, the two groups that had to control their emotions during the film—but not those in the third group—later lost their willpower on the handgrip. Muraven, M., & Baumeister, R. F. (1998). Self-control as a limited resource: Regulatory depletion patterns. *Journal of Personality and Social Psychology, 74,* 774–789.

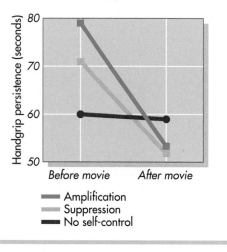

— Amplification
— Suppression
— No self-control

● **FIGURE 3.13**

Does the Belief in Willpower Predict Self-Regulation?

Tracking college students over time, researchers found that students who endorsed a non-limited belief in willpower, compared to those who endorsed a limited belief, were less likely to procrastinate when work demands were high. Job, V., Walton, G. M., Bernecker, K., & Dweck, C. S. (2015). Implicit theories about willpower predict self-regulation and grades in everyday life. *Journal of Personality and Social Psychology, 108,* 637–647

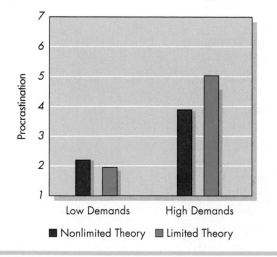

■ Nonlimited Theory   ■ Limited Theory

another room for an ice-cream taste test and told they could eat as much as they wanted. How much ice cream did they consume? The researchers predicted that dieters seated within reach of the bowl would have to fight the hardest to avoid snacking—an act of self-control that would cost them later. The prediction was confirmed. As measured by the amount of ice cream consumed in the taste test, dieters in the high-temptation condition ate more ice cream than did all nondieters and dieters in the low-temptation situation. What's more, a second study showed that dieters who had to fight the urge in the high-temptation situation were later less persistent and quicker to give up on a set of impossible cognitive problems they were asked to solve.

Additional research has focused on the question of whether the resource limits of self-regulation are absolute and set in stone, or whether they can be overcome by various psychological factors—such as the exercise of *willpower*. Supporting the first hypothesis, some studies suggest that self-regulation fatigue invariably sets in because exerting self-control is physically taxing, as measured by the extent to which it consumes glucose, a vital source of bodily energy. Across a range of experiments, Matthew Gailliot and others (2007) had participants engage in an act of self-control—such as suppressing a word, thought, or emotion—before and after which blood samples were taken. Consistently, acts of self-control—relative to similar acts not requiring self-control—were followed by reduced blood glucose levels and a lessened capacity. What's more, these researchers were able to counteract these adverse effects by feeding participants sugared lemonade between tasks, which restored glucose to the bloodstream.

In contrast, other research indicates that psychological factors can counteract self-regulation fatigue. In one program of research, for example, Veronika Job and others (2010, 2015) theorized that people who hold a nonlimited theory of willpower (as described by the statement, "After a strenuous mental activity, you feel energized for further challenging activities") are more likely to maintain the ability to self-regulate after exertion than those who believe that self-control is limited and difficult to overcome ("After a strenuous mental activity, your energy is depleted and you must rest to get it refueled again"). In longitudinal studies that tracked college students over a semester, these researchers found that students who endorsed a nonlimited belief in willpower relative to those who endorsed a limited belief were better able to self-regulate during the difficult week before final exams: They ate fewer unhealthy foods, did less impulsive shopping, and spent more time studying. But does having a nonlimited theory of willpower create problems in everyday life when self-regulation demands are particularly high? Not necessarily. Among students who took a heavier-than-normal course load, and in other ways had a highly demanding semester, those who endorsed a nonlimited theory procrastinated less and ultimately scored higher grades (see ● Figure 3.13).

◾ Ironic Mental Processes

There's another possible downside to self-control that is often seen in sports when athletes become so self-focused under pressure that they stiffen up and "choke." Although many athletes rise to the occasion, the pages of sports history are filled with stories of basketball players who lose their shooting touch in the final minute of a championship game, of golfers who cannot sink a routine putt to win a tournament, and of tennis players who lose their serve, double-faulting when it matters most. "Choking" in these ways seems to be a paradoxical type of failure caused by trying too hard and thinking too much. When you learn a new motor activity like how to throw a curve ball or land a jump, you must think through the mechanics in a slow and cautious manner. As you get better, however, your movements become automatic, so you do not have to think about timing, breathing, the position of your head and limbs, or the distribution of your weight. You relax and just do it. Unless trained to perform while self-focused, athletes under pressure often try their hardest not to fail, become self-conscious, and think too much—all of which disrupts the fluid and natural flow of their performance (Baumeister, 1984; Beilock & Carr, 2001; Gray, 2004).

The paradoxical effects of attempted self-control are evident in other situations, too. Studying what he calls *ironic processes,* Daniel Wegner (1994) has found that, at times, the harder you try to inhibit a thought, feeling, or behavior, the less likely you are to succeed. Try not to think about a white bear for the next 30 seconds, he finds, and that very image intrudes upon consciousness with remarkable frequency. Instruct the members of a jury to disregard inadmissible evidence, and the censored material is sure to pop to mind as they deliberate. Try not to worry about how long it's taking to fall asleep, and you'll stay awake. Try not to laugh in class, think about the chocolate cake in the fridge, or scratch the itch on your nose—well, you get the idea.

According to Wegner, every conscious effort at maintaining control is met by a concern about failing to do so. This concern automatically triggers an "ironic operating process" as the person, trying hard *not* to fail, searches his or her mind for the unwanted thought. The ironic process will not necessarily prevail, says Wegner. Sometimes we can put the imaginary white bear out of mind. But if the person is cognitively busy, tired, distracted, hurried, or under stress, then the ironic process, because it "just happens," will prevail over the intentional process, which requires conscious attention and effort. As Wegner (1997) put it, "Any attempt at mental control contains the seeds of its own undoing" (p. 148).

"The highest possible stage in moral culture is when we recognize that we ought to control our thoughts."

—Charles Darwin

Why do some athletes choke under pressure and others rise to the occasion? Heading into the 2006 Winter Olympics in Turin, Italy, American downhill racer Bode Miller, a daredevil from New Hampshire, was favored to win several gold medals. Yet after slipping, falling, and missing gates, he failed to win a single medal, gold or otherwise (left). In contrast, American beach volleyball players Misty May-Treanor and Kerri Walsh Jennings were the twice-reigning gold medalists when they entered the 2012 Summer Olympics in London. Despite the pressure to defend their title, they turned in a series of clutch performances and won gold for the third straight Olympics (right).

● **FIGURE 3.14**

Ironic Effects of Mental Control

In this study, participants tried to hold a pendulum motionless over a grid. As illustrated in the tracings shown here, they were better at the task when simply instructed to keep the pendulum steady (a) than when specifically told to prevent horizontal movement (c). Among participants who were mentally distracted during the task, this ironic effect was even greater (b and d).

Wegner et al., 1998. © Cengage Learning

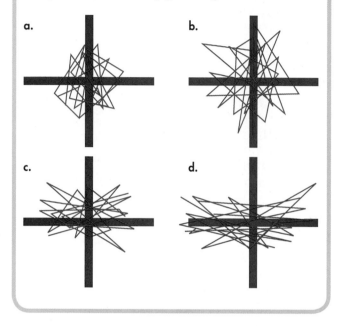

a.   b.

c.   d.

Sometimes the harder you try to control a thought, feeling, or behavior, the less likely you are to succeed.

TRUE

Ironic processes have been observed in a wide range of behaviors. In an intriguing study of this effect on motor behavior, Wegner and others (1998) had participants hold a pendulum (a crystalline pendant suspended from a nylon fishing line) over the center of two intersecting axes on a glass grid, which formed a +. Some participants were instructed simply to keep the pendulum steady; others were pointedly told not to allow it to swing back and forth along the horizontal axis. Try this yourself and you'll see that it's not easy to prevent all movement. In this experiment, however, the pendulum was more likely to swing horizontally when this direction was specifically forbidden. To further examine the role of mental distraction, the researchers had some participants count backward from a thousand by sevens while trying to control the pendulum. In this situation, the ironic effect was even greater. Among those who tried to prevent horizontal movement but could not concentrate fully on the task, the pendulum swayed freely back and forth in the forbidden direction (see ● Figure 3.14).

Applying this logic to keeping secrets, other researchers have found that instructing word-game players to conceal hidden clues from a fellow player increased rather than decreased their tendency to leak that information (Lane et al., 2006). It may seem both comic and tragic, but at times our efforts at self-control backfire, thwarting even the best of intentions.

■ Mechanisms of Self-Enhancement

We have seen that self-awareness can lower self-esteem by focusing attention on self-discrepancies. We have seen that people often avoid focusing on themselves and turn away from unpleasant truths but that such avoidance is not always possible. And we have seen that efforts at self-regulation often fail and sometimes even backfire. How, then, does the average person cope with his or her faults, inadequacies, and uncertain future?

The Better-Than-Average Effect   At least in Western cultures, most people most of the time think highly of themselves. Consistently, and across a broad range of life domains, people see positive traits as more self-descriptive than negative traits, rate themselves more highly than they do others, rate themselves more highly than they are rated *by* others, exaggerate their control over life events, and predict that they have a bright future (Dunning et al., 2004; Sedikides & Gregg, 2008; Taylor, 1989).

The list of self-enhancement biases is long and impressive. Research shows that people overrate their effectiveness as speakers to an audience (Keysar & Henly, 2002); overestimate their own contributions to a group and how much they would be missed if absent (Savitsky et al., 2003); selectively recall positive feedback while neglecting the negative (Green et al., 2008); believe that they will achieve more in the future than they had in the past (Johnson, 2009); recognize themselves in self-portraits that were digitally morphed with 10% of another face that is highly attractive (Eply & Whitchurch, 2008); and credit themselves but not others for future but yet unrealized potential (Williams et al., 2012). Relative to others across a wide range of domains, it seems that people in general believe they are better, more honorable, more capable, and more compassionate. This pattern is known as the "better-than-average" effect.

What is particularly interesting is that people are more likely to see themselves as better than average when it comes to personal traits that are important. Jonathon Brown (2012) presented participants with a list of characteristics and, for each one, he asked them to rate how important it is, how well it describes the self, and how well it describes most other people. He found that the effect is greater for traits that were rated as high in importance (such as *honest, kind, responsible,* and *intelligent)* than for traits of lesser importance (such as *conscientious, agreeable, imaginative,* and *outgoing).*

Implicit Egotism   It is clear and perhaps not surprising that people tilt positive when asked explicitly to evaluate themselves relative to others. But research suggests that people also exhibit **implicit egotism**, or implicit self-esteem—an unconscious and subtle expression of self-esteem. Implicit egotism is illustrated in studies showing that people are *quicker* to associate "self" words with positive traits than with negative traits. Particularly interesting in this regard is the finding that people evaluate the letters contained within their own names more favorably than other letters of the alphabet (Hoorens & Nuttin, 1993). This name-letter effect is also found in people's preferences for their own birthday numbers (Jones et al., 2004).

In an article entitled "Why Susie Sells Seashells by the Seashore," Brett Pelham and his colleagues (2002) theorized that the positive associations people form with the sight and sound of their own name may draw them toward other people, places, and entities that share this most personal aspect of "self." In a thought-provoking series of studies, these researchers examined several important life choices that we make and found that people exhibit a small but statistically detectable tendency to gravitate toward things that contain the letters of their own name. For example, men and women are more likely than would be predicted by chance to live in places (Mike in Michigan, George in Georgia), attend schools (Kari from the University of Kansas, Preston from Penn State University), and choose careers (Dennis and Denise as dentists) whose names resemble their own. Marriage records found on genealogical websites also indicate that people are disproportionately likely to marry others with first or last names that resemble their own (Jones et al., 2004). Even more impressive, perhaps, is that people with high self-esteem are more likely to seek out romantic partners who are similar to themselves (Brown & Brown, 2015). In subtle but remarkable ways, it seems that we unconsciously seek out reflections of the self in other people and in our surroundings (Pelham et al., 2005).

Uri Simonsohn (2011) is not so sure. Although impressed with evidence for implicit egotism in the laboratory, Simonsohn re-analyzed the real-life data and concluded that too often the links resulted from a statistical fluke. Consider the finding that people are more likely than expected to marry others whose names resemble their own. A close look at these numbers reveals that the name effect may result from an "ethnic bias" so that people often marry others who share the same Hispanic, Asian, or other group's last name. As for women named Georgia from that state, birth records show that more babies born in Georgia are named after the state of Georgia. In turn, Pelham and Carvallo (2011) point to ways in which Simonsohn's criticism is overstated. To sum up: It's clear that people prefer the letters of their own name and the number of their own birthday. What is less clear is whether these preferences influence the highest stakes decisions we make with regard to a marriage partner, or career, or a place to live.

implicit egotism A nonconscious form of self-enhancement.

Research on implicit egotism shows that, consciously or unconsciously, people hold themselves in high regard. We can't all be perfect, however, nor can we all be better than average. So what supports this common illusion? In this section, we examine four methods that people use to rationalize or otherwise enhance their self-esteem: self-serving beliefs, self-handicapping, basking in reflected glory, and downward social comparisons.

"We don't see things as they are, we see them as we are."

—Anaïs Nín

Self-Serving Beliefs How well did you do on the SAT? When James Shepperd (1993b) asked college students about their performance on this infamous college entrance test, he uncovered two interesting patterns. First, the students overestimated their actual scores by an average of 17 points. This inflationary distortion was most pronounced among those with relatively low scores, and it persisted somewhat even when students knew that the experimenter would check their academic files. Second, a majority of students whose SAT scores were low described their scores as inaccurate and the test in general as invalid. In fact, the SATs for the group as a whole were predictive of their grade point averages. It's not that people are delusional. But as memories fade, which occurs with the passage of time, the potential for self-enhancing recollections of test scores is increased (Willard & Gramzow, 2008).

When students receive exam grades, those who do well take credit for the success; those who do poorly complain about the instructor or test questions. When researchers have articles accepted for publication, they credit the quality of their work; when articles are rejected, they blame the editors and reviewers. When gamblers win a bet, they marvel at how skilled they are; when they lose, they blame fluke events that transformed near-victory into defeat. Whether people have high or low self-esteem, explain their own outcomes publicly or in private, and try to be honest or to make a good impression, there is bias. Across a range of cultures, people tend to take credit for success and distance themselves from failure (Mezulis et al., 2004; Schlenker et al., 1990)—all while seeing themselves as objective, not biased (Pronin et al., 2004).

Most of us are also unrealistically optimistic about the future. College students who were asked to predict their own futures compared with that of the average peer believed that they would graduate higher in their class, get a better job, have a happier marriage, and bear a gifted child. They also believed that they were less likely to get fired or divorced, have a car accident, become depressed, be victimized by crime, or suffer a heart attack (Weinstein, 1980). A number of later studies have shown that in matters of sports, politics, health and illness, romantic relationships, economics, and social issues, people exhibit an optimistic bias— essentially, an instance of wishful thinking—about their own future, judging desirable events as more likely to occur than undesirable events (Krizan & Windschitl, 2007; Shepperd et al., 2013).

Perhaps one reason that people are eternally optimistic is that they harbor illusions of control, overestimating the extent to which they can influence personal outcomes that are not, in fact, within their power to control (Stefan & David, 2013). In a series of classic experiments on the illusion of control, Ellen Langer (1975) found that college students bet more money in a chance game of high-card when their opponent seemed nervous rather than confident and were more reluctant to sell a lottery ticket if they had chosen the number themselves than if it was assigned to them. Emily Pronin and others (2006) then tested the related hypothesis that imagining an event before it occurs can lead people to think they had influenced it. In one study, participants watched a trained confederate shoot hoops on a basketball court. Before each shot, they were instructed to visualize his success ("the shooter releases the ball and it swooshes through the net") or an irrelevant event ("the shooter's arm curls to lift a dumbbell"). After the confederate's successful shooting spree, spectators rated the extent of their influence over his performance. As if linking thoughts to outcomes, they exhibited an illusion of mental causation, taking more credit when they had visualized the shooter's success than when they had not.

Self-Handicapping   "My dog ate my homework." "I had a flat tire." "My alarm didn't go off." "My phone battery died." "I had a bad headache." "The referee blew the call." On occasion, people make excuses for past performance. Sometimes we come up with excuses in anticipation of *future performance*. When people are afraid that they might fail in an important situation, they use illness, shyness, anxiety, pain, trauma, and other complaints as excuses for the possibility of failure (Snyder & Higgins, 1988). The reason people self-handicap is simple: By admitting to a limited physical or mental weakness, they can shield themselves from what could be the most shattering implication of failure—a lack of ability.

One form of excuse-making that many of us can relate to is procrastination —a purposive delay in starting or completing a task that is due at a particular time (Ferrari et al., 1995). Some people procrastinate chronically, whereas others do so only in certain situations. The phenomenon itself is found in a number of cultures—including Spain, Peru, Venezuela, England, Australia, and the United States, where nearly 15% of men and women identify themselves as chronic procrastinators (Ferrari et al., 2007). There are many reasons why someone might put off what needs to get done—whether it's studying for a test, shopping for Christmas, or preparing for the April 15 tax deadline. According to Joseph Ferrari (1998), one "benefit" of procrastinating is that it helps to provide an excuse for possible failure.

Making excuses is one way to cope with the threatening implications of failure. Sometimes, however, this strategy is taken one step further, as when people actually sabotage their own performance. It seems like the ultimate paradox, but there are times when we purposely set ourselves up for failure in order to preserve our precious self-esteem. As first described by Stephen Berglas and Edward Jones (1978), **self-handicapping** refers to actions people take to handicap their own performance in order to build an excuse for anticipated failure. To demonstrate, Berglas and Jones recruited college students for an experiment supposedly concerning the effects of drugs on intellectual performance. All the participants worked on a 20-item test of analogies and were told that they had done well, after which they expected to work on a second, similar test. For one group, the problems in the first test were relatively easy, leading participants to expect more success in the second test; for a second group, the problems were insoluble, leaving participants confused about their initial success and worried about possible failure. Before seeing or taking the second test, participants were given a choice of two drugs: Actavil, which was supposed to improve performance, and Pandocrin, which was supposed to impair it.

Although no drugs were actually administered, most participants who were confident about the upcoming test selected the Actavil. In contrast, most males (but not females) who feared the outcome of the second test chose the Pandocrin. By handicapping themselves, these men set up a convenient excuse for failure—an excuse, we should add, that may have been intended more for the experimenter's benefit than for the benefit of the participants themselves. A follow-up study showed that although self-handicapping occurs when the experimenter witnesses the participants' drug choice, it is reduced when the experimenter is not present while that choice is being made (Kolditz & Arkin, 1982).

self-handicapping Behaviors designed to sabotage one's own performance in order to provide a subsequent excuse for failure.

Some people use self-handicapping as a defense more than others do—and in different ways (Rhodewalt, 1990). For example, some men self-handicap by taking drugs (Higgins & Harris, 1988) or neglecting to practice (Hirt et al., 1991), whereas women tend to report stress and physical symptoms (Smith et al., 1983). Another tactic is to set one's goals too high, as perfectionists like to do, which sets up failure that is not interpreted to reflect a lack of ability (Hewitt et al., 2003). Yet another paradoxical tactic used to reduce performance pressure is for people to play down their own ability, lower expectations, and publicly predict that they will fail—a self-presentation strategy called *sandbagging* (Gibson & Sachau, 2000). People also differ in their reasons for self-handicapping. Dianne Tice (1991) found that people who are low in self-esteem use self-handicapping to set up a defensive, face-saving excuse in case they fail, whereas those who are high in self-esteem use it as an opportunity to claim extra credit if they succeed.

> People often sabotage their own performance in order to protect their self-esteem.
>
> **TRUE**

Whatever the tactics and whatever the goal, self-handicapping seems like an ingenious strategy: With the odds seemingly stacked against us, withholding effort, procrastinating, or otherwise pulling back can help to insulate the self from failure and enhance the self in the case of success. But this strategy is not without a real cost. Sabotaging ourselves—by not practicing or by drinking too much, faking illness, or setting goals too high—objectively increases the risk of failure, even in important life domains. Indeed, research shows that self-handicapping is maladaptive when used in school and ultimately limits students' academic achievement and potential (Urdan & Midgley, 2001; Schwinger et al., 2014).

Basking in Reflected Glory   To some extent, your self-esteem is influenced by individuals and groups with whom you identify. According to Robert Cialdini and his colleagues (1976), people often **bask in reflected glory (BIRG)** by showing off their connections to successful others. Cialdini's team first observed BIRGing on the university campuses of Arizona State, Louisiana State, Notre Dame, Michigan, Pittsburgh, Ohio State, and Southern California. On the Monday mornings after football games, they counted the number of school sweatshirts worn on campus and found that more of them were worn if the team had won its game on the previous Saturday. In fact, the larger the margin of victory was, the more school shirts they counted.

When Vietnam veterans returned home without victory more than 40 years ago, they were neglected, even scorned, by the American public. It seems that the tendency to bask in reflected glory is matched by an equally powerful need to cut off reflected failure.

Tom Williams/CQ Roll Call/Getty Images

To evaluate the effects of self-esteem on BIRGing, Cialdini gave students a general-knowledge test and rigged the results so half would succeed and half would fail. The students were then asked to describe in their own words the outcome of a recent football game. In these descriptions, students who thought they had just failed a test were more likely than those who thought they had succeeded to share in their team's victory by exclaiming that "we won" and to distance themselves from defeat by lamenting how "*they* lost." In another study, participants coming off a recent failure were quick to point out that they had the same birth date as someone known to be successful—thus BIRGing by a merely coincidental association (Cialdini & De Nicholas, 1989).

bask in reflected glory (BIRG)   To increase self-esteem by associating with others who are successful.

If self-esteem is influenced by our links to others, how do we cope with friends, family members, teammates, and co-workers of low status? Again, consider sports fans, an interesting breed. They loudly cheer their team in victory, but they often turn and jeer their team in defeat. This behavior seems fickle, but it is consistent with the notion that people derive part of their self-esteem from associations with others. In one study, participants took part in a problem-solving team that then succeeded, failed, or received no feedback about its performance. Participants were later offered a chance to take home a team badge. In the success and no-feedback groups, 68% and 50%, respectively, took badges; in the failure group, only 9% did (Snyder et al., 1986). For diehard sports fans—male and female alike—the tendency to bask in reflected glory is matched by an equally powerful tendency to CORF—that is, to cut off reflected failure (Ware & Kowalski, 2012).

Downward Social Comparisons   Earlier, we discussed Festinger's (1954) theory that people evaluate themselves by comparison with similar others. But contemplate the implications. If the people around us achieve more than we do, what does that do to our self-esteem? Perhaps adults who shy away from class reunions in order to avoid having to compare themselves with former classmates are acting out an answer to that question. More to the point, perhaps the "Facebook Depression" link described earlier in this chapter provides a statistical answer to the question (Feinstein et al., 2013; Verduyn et al., 2015; Vogel et al., 2014).

Long ago, Festinger fully realized that people don't always seek out objective information and that social comparisons are sometimes made in self-defense. When a person's self-esteem is at stake, he or she often benefits from making **downward social comparisons** with others who are less successful, less happy, or less fortunate (Wills, 1981; Wood, 1989). Research shows that people who suffer some form of setback or failure adjust their social comparisons in a downward direction (Gibbons et al., 2002) and that these comparisons have an uplifting effect on their mood and on their outlook for the future (Aspinwall & Taylor, 1993; Gibbons & McCoy, 1991).

Although Festinger never addressed the issue, Anne Wilson and Michael Ross (2000) note that in addition to making social comparisons between ourselves and similar others, we make *temporal* comparisons between our past and present selves. In one study, these investigators had college students describe themselves; in another, they analyzed the autobiographical accounts of celebrities appearing in popular magazines. In both cases, they counted the number of times the self-descriptions contained references to past selves, to future selves, and to others. The result was that people made more comparisons to their own past selves than to others, and most of these temporal comparisons were favorable. Other research has confirmed the basic point. Keenly aware of how "I'm better today than when I was in the past," people use downward temporal comparisons the way they use downward social comparisons as a means of self-enhancement (Zell & Alicke, 2009).

"I had to stop watching the news—it was making my own problems seem insignificant."

Whether people make upward or downward social comparisons can have striking health implications. When victimized by tragic life events (perhaps a crime, an accident, a disease, or the death of a loved one), people like to *affiliate* with others in the same predicament who have adjusted well, role models who

downward social comparison The defensive tendency to compare ourselves with others who are worse off than we are.

offer hope and guidance. But they tend to *compare* themselves with others who are worse off, a form of downward social comparison (Taylor & Lobel, 1989).

Clearly it helps to know that life could be worse, which is why most cancer patients tend to compare themselves with others in the same predicament but who are adjusting less well than they are. In a study of 312 women who had early-stage breast cancer and were in peer support groups, Laura Bogart and Vicki Helgeson (2000) had the patients report every week for seven weeks on instances in which they talked to, heard about, or thought about another patient. They found that 53% of all the social comparisons made were downward, to others who were worse off; only 12% were upward, to others who were better off (the rest were "lateral" comparisons to similar or dissimilar others). In fact, the more often patients made these social comparisons, the better they felt. Downward social comparison is also associated with an ability to cope with the kinds of life regrets that sometimes haunt people as they get older. Adult development researchers have observed that aging adults often experience intense feelings of regret over decisions made, contacts lost, opportunities passed up, and the like—and these regrets can compromise the quality of their lives. Isabelle Bauer and others (2008) asked adults ranging from 18 to 83 years old to disclose their biggest regret and then indicate whether their same-age peers had regrets that were more or less severe. Among the older adults in the sample, those who tended to see others as having more severe regrets than their own felt better than those who saw others as less regretful.

■ Are Positive Illusions Adaptive?

Psychologists used to maintain that an accurate perception of reality is vital to mental health. In recent years, however, this view has been challenged by research on the mechanisms of self-enhancement. Consistently, as we have seen, people preserve their self-esteem through biased beliefs, self-handicapping, BIRGing, and downward comparisons. The result: Most people see themselves as better than average. Are these strategies a sign of health and well-being or are they symptoms of disorder?

When Shelley Taylor and Jonathon Brown (1988) first reviewed the research, they found that individuals who are depressed or low in self-esteem actually have more realistic views of themselves than do most others who are better adjusted. Their self-appraisals are more likely to match appraisals of them made by neutral observers, they make fewer self-serving attributions to account for success and failure, they are less likely to exaggerate their control over uncontrollable events, and they make more balanced predictions about their future. Based on these results, Taylor and Brown reached the provocative conclusion that positive illusions promote happiness, the desire to care for others, and the ability to engage in productive work—hallmark attributes of mental health: "These illusions help make each individual's world a warmer and more active and beneficent place in which to live" (p. 205). People with high self-esteem appear to be better adjusted in personality tests and in interviews rated by friends, strangers, and mental health professionals (Taylor et al., 2003).

Drawing on evolutionary theory, William von Hippel and Robert Trivers (2011) offered a new and provocative perspective on the adaptive advantages of self-deception. Over the years, evolutionary psychologists have noted that deceit is a communication skill that animals use to curry favor, attract a mate, and influence others to share food, shelter, and other resources. Just as humans have evolved ways to deceive others, we have also evolved ways to detect deception in others. The more skilled we are in these interactions, the more we flourish. The problem is that when people lie, they become nervous, try to suppress the nervousness, and work hard to make the lie sound believable—especially when talking to others who know them. Here's the hitch: If deceivers can convince themselves that their deception is true, they will not be as nervous, not have to suppress, not have to work so hard, and, therefore, be more successful. As *Seinfeld* character George Costanza advised Jerry, who was scheduled to take a lie-detector test, "It's not a lie if *you* believe it."

When it comes to the illusion of control, unrealistic optimism, and the other self-enhancement biases that enable people to see themselves as better than average, von Hippel and Trivers (2011) extend their argument: By deceiving ourselves in ways that create positive illusions, we are able to display greater confidence in public than we may actually feel, making us more successful in our social relations. Perhaps this explains the research finding that people tend to overestimate the self-esteem of other people—independent of how well we know them (Kilianski, 2008).

Not everyone agrees with the notion that it is adaptive in the long run to wear rose-colored glasses. Roy Baumeister and Steven Scher (1988) warned that positive illusions can give rise to chronic patterns of self-defeating behavior, as when people escape from self-awareness through alcohol and other drugs, self-handicap themselves into failure and underachievement, deny health-related problems until it's too late for treatment, and rely on the illusion of control to protect them from the inescapable odds of the gambling casino. Others have noted that people sometimes need to be self-critical in order to improve. In a study on success and failure feedback, Heine and others (2001) found that whereas North American college students persisted less on a task after an initial failure than after success, Japanese students persisted more in this situation. Sometimes we have to face up to our shortcomings in order to correct them.

From an interpersonal standpoint, C. Randall Colvin and others (1995) found that people with inflated rather than realistic views of themselves were rated less favorably on certain dimensions by their own friends. In their studies, self-enhancing men were seen as boastful, condescending, hostile, and less considerate; self-enhancing women were seen as more hostile, more defensive and sensitive to criticism, more likely to overreact to minor setbacks, and less well liked. People with inflated self-images may make a good first impression on others, but they are liked less and less as time wears on (Paulhus, 1998).

Realism or illusion—which orientation is more adaptive? As social psychologists debate the short-term and long-term effects of positive illusions and their evolutionary advantages, it seems that there is no simple answer. For now, the picture that has emerged is this: People who harbor positive illusions of themselves are likely to enjoy the benefits and achievements of high self-esteem and social influence. But these same individuals may pay a price in other ways, as in their relations with others. Do positive illusions motivate personal achievement but alienate us socially from others? Is it adaptive to see oneself in slightly inflated terms but maladaptive to take a view that is too biased? It will be interesting to see how this thorny debate is resolved in the years to come.

Culture and Self-Esteem

Earlier we saw that inhabitants of individualistic cultures tend to view themselves as distinct and autonomous, whereas those in collectivist cultures view the self as part of an interdependent social network. Do these different orientations have implications for self-esteem? This turns out to be a tricky question.

Steven Heine and his colleagues (1999) argued that cultures have differing effects on the pursuit of self-esteem. Comparing the distribution of self-esteem test scores in Canada and Japan, they found that while most Canadians' scores clustered in the high-end range, a majority of Japanese respondents scored in the center of that same range. In other studies, they also observed that Japanese respondents can sometimes be quite self-critical, talking about themselves in negative, self-effacing terms.

Do Japanese people have a less positive self-esteem compared to Americans? Or do Japanese respondents have a positive self-esteem but feel compelled to present themselves modestly *to others* (as a function of the collectivist need to "fit in" rather than "stand out")? To answer this question, some researchers have used less direct, subtle tests that measure implicit self-esteem—a person's unconscious tendency to positively evaluate people and objects that reflect upon themselves (Falk & Heine, 2015). In a timed word-association study, researchers found that despite their lower scores on overt self-esteem tests, Asian Americans—just like their European American counterparts—are quicker to associate themselves with positive words like *happy* and *sunshine* than with negative words such as *vomit* and *poison* (Greenwald & Farnham, 2000; Kitayama & Uchida, 2003). In keeping with the Eastern dialectical perspective described earlier, other implicit self-esteem research has shown that although East Asians, like most Westerners, are quick to associate the self with positive traits, they are more likely to associate the self with contradictory negative traits as well (Boucher et al., 2009).

Drawing on these results, Constantine Sedikides and colleagues (2003) maintained that people from individualist and collectivist cultures are similarly motivated to think highly of themselves—that the burning need for positive self-regard is universal, or "pancultural." The observed differences, they argue, stem from the fact that cultures influence *how* we seek to fulfill that need: Individualists present themselves as unique and self-confident, while collectivists present themselves as modest, equal members of a group. From this perspective, people are tactical in their self-enhancements, exhibiting self-praise or humility depending on what is desirable within their cultural surroundings (J. D. Brown, 2003; Lalwani et al., 2006; Sedikides et al., 2005). As for what is desirable—when Japanese and American students evaluated a fictitious person from his or her high or low responses on a self-esteem questionnaire, Americans showed a stronger preference for the high self-esteem person (Brown, 2010).

Heine and his colleagues agree only in part with this interpretation of the research. They too argue that all people have a need for positive self-regard, wanting to become "good selves" within their own culture. They note, however, that in the effort to achieve this goal, individualists tend to use self-enhancement tactics to stand out, confirm, and express themselves, whereas East Asians and other collectivists tend to maintain face in order to fit in, improve the self, and adjust to the standards set by their groups. To sum up: Although the underlying need for positive self-regard is universal, the specific drive toward self-enhancement is culturally ingrained (Heine, 2005; Heine & Hamamura, 2007).

Self-Presentation

The human quest for self-knowledge and esteem tells us about the inner self. The portrait is not complete, however, until we paint in the outermost layer, the behavioral expression of the social self. Most people are acutely concerned about the image they present to others. The fashion industry, tattoos, piercings, and cosmetic surgeries designed to reshape everything from eyelids and noses to butts and breasts, and the endless search for miracle drugs that grow hair, remove hair, whiten teeth, freshen breath, and smooth out wrinkles all exploit our preoccupation with physical appearance. In a similar manner, we are concerned about the impressions we convey through our public behavior both in person and on Facebook and other social networking sites.

Thomas Gilovich and others (2000) found that people are so self-conscious in public settings that they are often subject to the *spotlight effect*, a tendency to believe that the social spotlight shines more brightly on them than it really does. In one set of studies, participants were asked to wear a T-shirt with a flattering or embarrassing image into a room full of strangers, after which they estimated how many of those strangers would be able to identify the image. Demonstrating that people self-consciously feel as if all eyes are upon them, the T-shirted participants overestimated by 23% to 40% the number of observers who had noticed and could recall what they were wearing. Follow-up studies have similarly shown that when people commit a public social blunder, they later overestimate the negative impact of their behavior on those who had observed them (Savitsky et al., 2001).

In *As You Like It,* William Shakespeare wrote, "All the world's a stage, and all the men and women merely players." This insight was first put into social science terms by sociologist Erving Goffman (1959), who argued that life is like a theater and that each of us acts out certain *lines,* as if from a script. Most important, said Goffman, is that each of us assumes a certain *face,* or social identity, that others politely help us maintain. This "dramaturgical" perspective on social behavior—in which society is seen as an elaborately scripted play in which individuals enact different roles, as if performing in a reality TV show—has a long tradition in social psychology (Sandstrom et al., 2009; Sullivan et al., 2014).

Inspired by Goffman's theory, social psychologists study **self-presentation**—the process by which we try to shape what other people think of us and what we think of ourselves (Schlenker, 2003). An act of self-presentation may take many different forms. It may be conscious or unconscious, accurate or misleading, or intended for an external audience or for ourselves. In *The Manipulation of Online Self-Presentation: Create, Edit, Re-edit and Present,* Alison Attrill (2015) describes how this process plays out on social networking sites, where people determine how to present their selves to a vast online public. In this section, we look at the goals of self-presentation and the ways that people try to achieve these goals.

When Ellen DeGeneres hosted the Academy Awards in 2014, she invited stars from the audience to join in this famous celebrity selfie. As you try to recognize as many stars as you can, note that people in general, whether posing for pictures or not, are acutely aware of the image they present to others.

■ Strategic Self-Presentation

There are basically two types of self-presentation, each serving a different motive. *Strategic self-presentation* consists of our efforts to shape others' impressions in specific ways in order to gain influence, power, sympathy, or approval. Prominent examples of strategic self-presentation are everywhere: in personal ads, in online message boards, in political campaign promises, in defendants' appeals to the jury. The specific goals vary and include the desire to be seen as likable, competent, moral, dangerous, or helpless. Whatever the goal may be, people find it less effortful

self-presentation Strategies people use to shape what others think of them.

▲ **TABLE 3.2**

Strategic Self-Presentation in the Employment Interview

In studies of the influence tactics that job applicants report using in employment interviews, the following uses of ingratiation and self-promotion were commonly reported.

Ingratiation

● I complimented the interviewer or organization.
● I discussed interests I shared in common with the recruiter.
● I indicated my interest in the position and the company.
● I indicated my enthusiasm for working for this organization. I smiled a lot or used other friendly nonverbal behaviors.

Self-Promotion

● I played up the value of positive events that I took credit for.
● I described my skills and abilities in an attractive way.
● I took charge during the interview to get my main points across.
● I took credit for positive events even if I was not solely responsible.
● I made positive events I was responsible for appear better than they actually were.

Higgins & Judge, 2004; Stevens & Kristof, 1995. © Cengage Learning

to present themselves in ways that are accurate rather than contrived (Vohs et al., 2005).

To illustrate this point, Beth Pontari and Barry Schlenker (2000) instructed research participants who tested as introverted or extroverted to present themselves to a job interviewer in a way that was consistent or inconsistent with their true personality. Without distraction, all participants successfully presented themselves as introverted or extroverted, depending on the task they were given. But could they present themselves as needed if, during the interview, they also had to keep an eight-digit number in mind for a memorization test? In this situation, cognitively busy participants self-presented successfully when asked to convey their true personalities but not when asked to portray themselves in a way that was out of character.

The specific identities that people try to present may vary from one person and situation to another. However, two strategic self-presentation goals are very common. The first is *ingratiation,* a term used to describe acts that are motivated by the desire to "get along" with others and be liked. The other is *self-promotion,* a term used to describe acts that are motivated by a desire to "get ahead" and gain respect for one's competence (Arkin, 1981; Jones & Pittman, 1982). As shown in Table 3.2, observations of employment interviews reveal that ingratiation and self-promotion are the most common self-presentation tactics that Western job applicants use (Stevens & Kristof, 1995) and that these tactics lead recruiters to form positive impressions (Higgins & Judge, 2004). Of course, as you might expect, research shows that job applicants will present themselves in very different ways depending on the ideals of their culture (Sandal et al., 2014).

On the surface, it seems easy to achieve these goals. When people want to be liked, they put their best foot forward, smile a lot, nod their heads, express agreement, and, if necessary, use favors, compliments, and flattery. When people want to be admired for their competence, they try to impress others by talking about themselves and immodestly showing off their status, knowledge, and exploits. In both cases, there are trade-offs. As the term brown-nosing graphically suggests, ingratiation tactics need to be subtle or else they will backfire (Jones, 1964). People also do not like those who relentlessly trumpet and brag about their own achievements (Godfrey et al., 1986) or who exhibit a "slimy" pattern of being friendly to superiors but not to subordinates (Vonk, 1998).

Self-presentation may give rise to other problems as well. Suggesting that "Self-Presentation Can Be Hazardous to Your Health," Mark Leary and others (1994) reviewed evidence suggesting that the need to project a favorable public image can lure us into unsafe patterns of behavior. For example, self-presentation concerns can increase the risk of AIDS (as when men are too embarrassed to buy condoms and talk openly with their sex partners), skin cancer (as when people bake under the sun for an attractive tan), eating disorders (as when women over-diet to stay thin), drug abuse (as when teenagers smoke, drink, and use drugs to impress their peers), and accidental injury (as when young men drive recklessly to look fearless to others).

Self-Verification

In contrast to strategic self-presentation is a second motive, *self-verification:* the desire to have others perceive us as we truly perceive ourselves. According to William Swann (1987), people are highly motivated in their social encounters to confirm or verify their existing self-concept in the eyes of others. Swann and his colleagues have gathered a great deal of evidence for this hypothesis and have found, for example, that people selectively elicit, recall, and accept personality feedback that confirms their self-conceptions. In fact, people sometimes bend over backward to correct others whose impressions are positive but mistaken. In one study, participants interacted with a confederate who later said that they seemed dominant or submissive. When the comment was consistent with the participant's self-concept, it was accepted at face value. Yet when it was inconsistent, participants went out of their way to prove the confederate wrong: Those who perceived themselves as dominant but were labeled submissive later behaved more assertively than usual; those who viewed themselves as submissive but were labeled dominant subsequently became even more docile (Swann & Hill, 1982).

Self-verification seems desirable, but do people who harbor a negative self-concept want others to share that impression? Nobody is perfect, and everyone has some faults. But do we really want to verify these faults in the eyes of others? Do those of us who feel painfully shy, socially awkward, or insecure about an ability want others to see these weaknesses? Or would we prefer to present ourselves in public as bold, graceful, or competent? What happens when the desire for self-verification clashes with the need for flattery and self-enhancement?

Seeking to answer this question, Swann and his colleagues (1992) asked each student participant in a laboratory study to fill out a self-concept questionnaire and then choose an interaction partner from two other participants—one who supposedly had evaluated them favorably and a second who had supposedly evaluated them unfavorably. The result? Although participants with a positive self-concept chose partners who viewed them in a positive light, a majority of those with a negative self-concept preferred partners who confirmed their admitted shortcomings. In a later study, 64% of participants with low self-esteem (compared with only 25% with high self-esteem) sought clinical feedback about their weaknesses rather than strengths when given a choice (Giesler et al., 1996). Research also suggests that people prefer to interact with others who verify their group memberships, a key aspect of the collective self (Chen et al., 2009). Indeed, the desire for self-verification appears to be universal, observed in both individualist and collectivist cultures (Seih et al., 2013).

If people seek self-verification from laboratory partners, it stands to reason that they would want the same from their close relationships. In a study of married couples, husbands and wives separately answered questions about their self-concepts, their spouse, and their commitment to the marriage. As predicted, people who had a positive self-concept expressed more commitment to partners who appraised them favorably, whereas those with a negative self-concept felt more committed to partners who appraised them unfavorably (Swann et al., 1992).

Peter C. Vey/The New Yorker Collection/Cartoon Bank.com

"I don't want to be defined by who I am."

People often distinguish between their public and private self. However, research on self-verification suggests that this cartoon is wrong—that people do want to be defined by who they are.

▲ **TABLE 3.3**

Self-Monitoring Scale

Are you a high or low self-monitor? For each statement, answer *True* or *False*. When you are done, give yourself one point if you answered *T* to items 4, 5, 6, 8, 10, 12, 17, and 18. Then give yourself one point if you answered *F* to items 1, 2, 3, 7, 9, 11, 13, 14, 15, and 16. Count your total number of points. This total represents your Self-Monitoring Score. Among North American college students, the average score is about 10 or 11.

1. I find it hard to imitate the behavior of other people.
2. At parties and social gatherings, I do not attempt to do or say things that others will like.
3. I can only argue for ideas that I already believe.
4. I can make impromptu speeches even on topics about which I have almost no information.
5. I guess I put on a show to impress or entertain others.
6. I would probably make a good actor.
7. In a group of people I am rarely the center of attention.
8. In different situations and with different people, I often act like very different persons.
9. I am not particularly good at making other people like me.
10. I'm not always the person I appear to be.
11. I would not change my opinions (or the way I do things) in order to please someone or win their favor.
12. I have considered being an entertainer.
13. I have never been good at games like charades or improvisational acting.
14. I have trouble changing my behavior to suit different people and different situations.
15. At a party I let others keep the jokes and stories going.
16. I feel a bit awkward in company and do not show up quite as well as I should.
17. I can look anyone in the eye and tell a lie with a straight face (if for a right end).
18. I may deceive people by being friendly when I really dislike them.

From Snyder, M., and Gangstad, S., "On the nature of self-monitoring: Matters of assessment, matters of validity," *Journal of Personality and Social Psychology* vol 51 (pp. 125–139). Copyright © 1986 by the American Psychological Association. Reprinted by permission.

self-monitoring The tendency to change behavior in response to the self-presentation concerns of the situation.

On important aspects of the self-concept, research shows that people would rather reflect on and learn more about their positive qualities than negative ones. Still, it appears that the desire for self-verification is powerful and can even, at times, trump the need for self-enhancement. We all want to make a good impression, but we also want others in our lives to have an accurate impression (Swann & Bosson, 2010). Studying online social networking sites, Mitja Back and others (2010) found strong support for this proposition. These researchers studied 236 Facebook users in the United States and Germany and found that the impressions conveyed by their posted profiles correlated highly with a combination of objective personality tests, self-reports, and reports from a sample of well-acquainted friends.

■ Self-Monitoring

Although self-presentation is a way of life for all of us, it differs considerably among individuals. Some people are generally more conscious of their public image than others. Also, some people are more likely to engage in strategic self-presentation, whereas others seem to prefer self-verification. According to Mark Snyder (1987), these differences are related to a personality trait he called **self-monitoring**: the tendency to regulate one's own behavior to meet the demands of social situations.

Individuals who are high in self-monitoring appear to have a repertoire of selves from which to draw. Sensitive to strategic self-presentation concerns, they are poised, ready, and able to modify their behavior as they move from one setting to another. As measured by the Self-Monitoring Scale (Snyder, 1974; Snyder & Gangestad, 1986), they are likely to agree with such statements as "I would probably make a good actor" and "In different situations and with different people, I often act like very different persons." In contrast, low self-monitors are self-verifiers by nature, appearing less concerned about the social acceptability of their behavior. Like character actors always cast in the same role, they express themselves in a consistent manner from one situation to the next, exhibiting what they regard as their true and honest self. On the Self-Monitoring Scale, low self-monitors say, "I can only argue for ideas which I already believe" and "I have never been good at games like charades or improvisational acting" (see Table 3.3).

Social psychologists disagree on whether the Self-Monitoring Scale measures one global trait or a combination of two or more specific traits. They also disagree about whether high and low self-monitors represent two discrete types of people or just varying points along a continuum—a position supported by a recent analysis of test scores (Wilmott, 2015). Either way, the test scores do appear to predict important social behaviors (Gangestad & Snyder, 2000).

Concerned with public image, high self-monitors go out of their way to learn about others with whom they might interact and about the rules for appropriate conduct. Then, once they have the situation sized up, they modify their behavior accordingly. If a situation calls for conformity, high self-monitors conform; if the same situation calls for autonomy, they refuse to conform. By contrast, low self-monitors maintain a relatively consistent posture across a range of situations (Snyder & Monson, 1975). Unconsciously adapting to social situations, high self-monitors are likely to mimic the demeanor of others in subtle ways that facilitate smooth social interactions (Cheng & Chartrand, 2003). They are also more likely to switch dialects according to their local surroundings, facilitating "linguistic adaptation" (Blank et al., 2012). Consistent with the finding that high self-monitors are more concerned than lows about what *other people* think, research conducted in work settings shows that high self-monitors receive higher performance ratings and more promotions and that they are more likely to emerge as leaders (Day et al., 2002).

> It's more adaptive to alter one's behavior than to stay consistent from one social situation to the next.
>
>

Throughout this textbook, we see that because so much of our behavior is influenced by social norms, self-monitoring is relevant to many aspects of social psychology. There are also interesting developmental implications. A survey of 18- to 73-year-olds revealed that self-monitoring scores tend to drop with age, presumably because people become more settled and secure about who they are as they get older (Reifman et al., 1989). For now, however, ponder this question: Is it better to be a high or low self-monitor? Is one orientation inherently more adaptive than the other?

The existing research does not enable us to make this kind of value judgment. Consider high self-monitors. Quite accurately, they regard themselves as *pragmatic*, flexible, and adaptive and as able to cope with the diversity of life's roles. But they could also be described as fickle or phony opportunists, more concerned with appearances than with reality and willing to change colors like a chameleon just to fit in. Now think about low self-monitors. They describe themselves as *principled* and forthright; they are without pretense, always speaking their minds so others know where they stand. Of course, they could also be viewed as stubborn, insensitive to their surroundings, and unwilling to compromise in order to get along. Concerning the relative value of these two orientations, then, it is safe to conclude that neither high nor low self-monitoring is necessarily undesirable—unless carried to the extreme. Goffman (1955) made the same point many years ago, when he wrote:

> Too little perceptiveness, too little savoir faire, too little pride and considerateness, and the person ceases to be someone who can be trusted to take a hint about himself or give a hint that will save others embarrassment. . . . Too much savoir faire or too much considerateness and he becomes someone who is too socialized, who leaves others with the feeling that they do not know how they really stand with him, nor what they should do to make an effective long-term adjustment. (p. 227)

Reflections: The Multifaceted Self

Throughout human history, writers, poets, philosophers, and personality theorists have portrayed the self as an enduring aspect of personality, as an invisible "inner core" that is stable over time and slow to change. The struggle to find your "true self" is based on this portrait. Indeed, when people older than 85 years were asked to reflect on their lives, almost all said that despite having changed in certain ways, they had remained essentially the same person (Troll & Skaff, 1997). In recent years, however, social psychologists have focused on change. In doing so, they have discovered that at least part of the self is malleable—molded by life experiences and varying from one situation to the next, online and offline, in public and in private, and depending on cultural context. From this perspective, the self has many different faces.

When you look into the mirror, what do you see: one self or many? Do you see a person whose self-concept is enduring or one whose identity seems to change from time to time? Do you see a person whose strengths and weaknesses are evaluated with an objective eye or one who is insulated from unpleasant truths by mechanisms of self-defense? Do you see a person who has an inner, hidden self that is different from the face shown to others?

Based on the material presented in this chapter, the answers seem always to be the same: The self has all these characteristics. Long before social psychology was born, William James (1890) remarked that the self is not simple but multifaceted. Based on current theories and research, we can now appreciate just how right James was. Sure, there's an aspect of the self-concept that we can come to know only by introspection and that is stable over time. But there's also an aspect that changes with the company we keep and the information we get from others. When it comes to self-esteem, there are times when we are self-focused enough to be acutely aware of our shortcomings. Yet there are also times when we guard ourselves through self-serving cognitions, self-handicapping, BIRGing, and downward social comparisons. Then there is the matter of self-presentation. It's clear that each of us has a private self that consists of our inner thoughts, feelings, and memories. But it is equally clear that we also have an outer self, portrayed by the roles we play and the masks we wear in public. As you read through the later pages of this text, you will see that the cognitive, affective, and behavioral components of the self are not separate and distinct but interrelated. They are also of great significance for the rest of social psychology.

Review

Top 10 Key Points in Chapter 3

1. People are especially attentive to information of relevance to the self and are self-conscious, as if under a "spotlight," in the presence of other people.

2. Your self-concept represents the sum total of beliefs you have about the kind of person you are—your traits, abilities, motivation, and so on.

3. Often people learn about themselves not by introspection but by observing their own behavior and comparing themselves to other people.

4. While most Westerners have an independent view of themselves as distinct and autonomous, people in many Asian cultures and elsewhere hold an interdependent view of the self as part of a larger social network.

5. All over the world, people have a strong need for high self-esteem and want to see themselves in a positive light.

6. When people enter a state of self-awareness—which happens in front of an audience, for example, or looking in a mirror—they become their own worst critics and experience a temporary drop in self-esteem.

7. In striving to meet our personal ideals, we often engage in self-regulation—trying to control our own thoughts, urges, and behaviors—which can be physically taxing.

8. Despite our shortcomings and self-critical tendencies, most people think highly of themselves thanks to various adaptive means of self-enhancement (for example, by taking credit for success but denying blame for failure or comparing to others who are less well off).

9. Through the processes of self-presentation, people put on a public face that may or may not be consistent with their private self in an effort to get others to see them in a positive light.

10. In public, individuals differ in their level of self-monitoring—some people modify what they do to suit the social situation; others behave more consistently regardless of the situation.

Answers to Putting Common Sense to the Test

The Self-Concept

Humans are the only animals who recognize themselves in the mirror.

F **False.** *Studies have shown that the great apes (chimpanzees, gorillas, and orangutans) are also capable of self-recognition.*

Smiling can make you feel happier.

T **True.** *Consistent with the facial feedback hypothesis, facial expressions can trigger or amplify the subjective experience of emotion.*

Self-Esteem

Sometimes the harder you try to control a thought, feeling, or behavior, the less likely you are to succeed.

T **True.** *Research on ironic processes in mental control have revealed that trying to inhibit a thought, feeling, or behavior often backfires.*

People often sabotage their own performance in order to protect their self-esteem.

T **True.** *Studies have shown that people often handicap their own performance in order to build an excuse for anticipated failure.*

Self-Presentation

It's more adaptive to alter one's behavior than to stay consistent from one social situation to the next.

F **False.** *High and low self-monitors differ in the extent to which they alter their behavior to suit the situation they are in, but neither style is inherently more adaptive.*

Key Terms

affective forecasting (59)

bask in reflected glory (BIRG) (92)

dialecticism (73)

downward social comparisons (93)

facial feedback hypothesis (62)

implicit egotism (89)

overjustification effect (64)

private self-consciousness (83)

public self-consciousness (83)

self-awareness theory (81)

self-concept (55)

self-esteem (76)

self-handicapping (91)

self-monitoring (100)

self-perception theory (60)

self-presentation (97)

self-regulation (84)

self-schema (55)

social comparison theory (66)

Sociometer Theory (77)

Terror Management Theory (77)

two-factor theory of emotion (68)

Perceiving Persons

This chapter examines how people come to know (or think that they know) other persons. First, we introduce the elements of social perception—those aspects of persons, situations, and behavior that guide initial observations. Next, we examine how people make explanations, or attributions, for the behavior of others and how they form integrated impressions based on initial perceptions and attributions. We then consider various confirmation biases, the subtle ways that initial impressions resist change by leading people to distort later information, setting in motion a self-fulfilling prophecy.

Patrik Giardino/Crave/Corbis

Oscar Pistorius is a South African sprinter. Although both his legs

were amputated below the knee when he was a baby, he went on with artificial limbs to become a Paralympic record-setting gold medalist. In summer of 2012, he became the first amputee to compete in the summer Olympic games. Pistorius was a national hero and an inspiration to disabled people all over the world.

Then on Valentine's Day of 2013, Pistorius shot and killed his girlfriend, Reeva Steenkamp, in his home. He said he thought she was an intruder hiding in the locked bathroom when he fired four shots through the door. Pistorius was arrested, charged, and tried for murder. The prosecutor noted that he and Steenkamp had argued that day, that neighbors heard a woman screaming before the gunshots, and that the story of an intruder made no sense. Pistorius was emotional at trial, often breaking down in tears. Ultimately, the judge convicted Pistorius of "culpable homicide" by finding that he had not committed premeditated murder but rather that his killing of Steenkamp was unintentional. Pistorius was then sentenced to only five years in prison. While the prosecutor appealed the verdict, and over objections from Steenkamp's parents, Pistorius was granted a release on parole. Then in November 2015, the South Africa Supreme Court overturned the original verdict and convicted Pistorius of murder.

The world was riveted to the Pistorius trial. Is it possible that a hero, so admired, had shot his girlfriend on purpose, in a moment of passion, or was it an accident for which a good person had suffered enough and deserved mercy? When Pistorius broke down and cried at trial, repeatedly, did his tears betray genuine heartfelt emotion or an attempt to manipulate the judge and public opinion? What information did the judge use to determine his state of mind that night? Who is Oscar Pistorius—a hero, a villain, or both?

More than a year later, on July 17, 2014, a Malaysia Airlines plane carrying 298 passengers from Amsterdam to Kuala Lumpur was shot down over eastern Ukraine. No one survived. Ukrainian officials blamed Russian-backed separatists who were in the area; Russia blamed the Ukraine. Even after incriminating tape recordings and physical evidence retrieved from the crash site suggested that the plane was shot down by a Russian surface-to-air missile, President Vladimir Putin adamantly denied direct or indirect involvement—not only in downing the plane but even in supporting the separatist uprising. As a European Union investigation into the crash proceeded, the world wondered: Did Putin know what had happened? Was he telling the truth or lying about Russia's lack of involvement? Did the people of the world, and the media, react on the basis of evidence or national bias?

Recent events involving Oscar Pistorius, Vladimir Putin, and Tom Brady illustrate the kinds of questions that social perceivers often ask in trying to understand other people.

On January 18, 2015, the Indianapolis Colts and New England Patriots met in Foxborough, Massachusetts, to play the AFC Championship game. The winner would go on to play in the NFL Super Bowl. The Patriots led 17–7 after the first half when a columnist for Indiana television station tweeted: "Breaking: A league source tells me the NFL is investigating the possibility the Patriots deflated footballs. More to come." Although the Patriots went on to win the game by a one-sided margin of 45–7, the scandal that broke, that the Patriots had deflated their footballs, making it easier for the quarterback to grip and pass was referred to as "Deflategate" and investigated by the NFL.

For two weeks leading up to the Super Bowl, sports fans and the news media were laser-focused. The balls used by the Patriots—but not those used by the Colts—were lighter at half time than at the start of the game. The Patriots went on to win the Super Bowl and become NFL Champions. After completing its investigation, the NFL concluded that the balls were deflated and that Brady probably knew about it. The NFL suspended Brady for four games the following year. Reactions to the results were quick and mixed. The Patriots appealed the suspension and in September of 2015 a federal judge threw it out. In response, the NFL appealed. To this day, questions linger: Were the balls intentionally deflated? If so, who did it and why? Did quarterback Tom Brady ask for it, or know about it? Throughout the ordeal, Brady denied "knowledge of wrongdoing." Was his denial believable? What did Patriots fans think? What about fans of opposing teams?

Whatever the topic—crime, world politics, sports, business, entertainment, or personal events closer to home—we are all engaged and interested participants in **social perception**, the processes by which people come to understand one another. This chapter is divided into four sections. First we look at the "raw data" of social perception: persons, situations, and behaviors. Second, we examine how people explain and analyze behavior. Third, we consider how people integrate their various observations into a coherent impression of other persons. Fourth, we discuss some of the subtle ways that our impressions create a distorted picture of reality, often setting in motion a self-fulfilling prophecy. As you read this chapter, you'll notice that we consider the various processes from a perceiver's vantage point. Keep in mind, however, that in the events of life, you are both a *perceiver* and a *target* of others' perceptions.

Putting COMMON SENSE to the Test

Circle Your Answer

T   F   The impressions we form of others are influenced by superficial aspects of their appearance.

T   F   Adaptively, people are skilled at knowing when someone is lying rather than telling the truth.

T   F   Like social psychologists, people are sensitive to situational causes when explaining the behavior of others.

T   F   People are slow to change their first impressions on the basis of new information.

T   F   The notion that we can create a "self-fulfilling prophecy" by getting others to behave in ways we expect is a myth.

T   F   People are more accurate at judging the personalities of friends and acquaintances than of strangers

---

Observation: The Elements of Social Perception

As our opening examples suggest, understanding other people may not be easy, but it is an essential and adaptive part of everyday life. How do we do it? What kinds of information do we use? We cannot actually "see" someone's mental or emotional state or his or her motives or intentions any more than a detective can see a crime that has already been committed. So like a detective who tries to reconstruct a crime by turning up witnesses, fingerprints, blood samples, and

social perception A general term for the processes by which people come to understand one another.

other evidence, the social perceiver comes to know others by relying on indirect clues—the elements of social perception. These clues arise from an interplay of three sources: persons, situations, and behavior.

■ A Person's Physical Appearance

Have you ever met someone for the first time, or visited their Facebook page for the first time, and formed a quick impression based only on a quick "snapshot" of information? As children, we were told that we should not judge a book by its cover, that things are not always what they seem, that surface appearances are deceiving, and that all that glitters is not gold. Yet as adults we can't seem to help ourselves.

To illustrate the rapid-fire nature of the process, Janine Willis and Alexander Todorov (2006) showed college students photographs of unfamiliar faces for one-tenth of a second, half a second, or a full second. Whether the students judged the faces for how attractive, likable, competent, trustworthy, or aggressive they were, their ratings—even after the briefest exposure—were quick and highly correlated with judgments that other observers made without time limits (see Table 4.1). Additional research has shown that people evaluate quickly, spontaneously, and unconsciously whether a face indicates that a person is dominant or submissive, and trustworthy or untrustworthy (Stewart et al., 2012). This tendency to infer personal characteristics from the face is not only quick but early to develop. For example, young children as young as 3 and 4 years show this adult-like tendency to judge whether a person is "mean" or "nice" based on a brief exposure to the face (Cogsdill et al., 2014). There's no doubt about it: If you flip through the pages of a magazine, or browse *Snapchat*, *Instagram*, or *Pinterest*, you will see for yourself that sometimes it takes a mere fraction of a second for you to form impressions of a stranger from his or her face.

If first impressions are quick to form, then on what are they based? In 500 B.C.E., the mathematician Pythagoras looked into the eyes of prospective students to see if they were gifted. At about the same time, Hippocrates, the founder of modern medicine, used facial features to make diagnoses of life and death. In the nineteenth century, Viennese physician Franz Gall introduced a carnival-like science called phrenology and claimed that he could assess a person's character by the shape of his or her skull. And in 1954, psychologist William Sheldon concluded from flawed studies of adult men that there is a strong link between physique and personality.

People may not measure each other by bumps on the head, as phrenologists used to do, but our first impressions are influenced in subtle ways by a person's height, weight, skin color, hair color, tattoos, piercings, eyeglasses, and other aspects of physical appearance. As social perceivers, we also form impressions of people that are often accurate based on a host of indirect telltale cues. In *Snoop: What Your Stuff Says About You*, Sam Gosling (2008) describes research he has conducted showing that people's personalities can be revealed

▲ **TABLE 4.1**

First Impressions in a Fraction of a Second

Participants rated unfamiliar faces based on pictures they saw for one-tenth of a second, half a second, or a full second. Would their impressions stay the same or change with unlimited time? As measured by the correlations of these ratings with those made by observers who had no exposure time limits, the results showed that ratings were highly correlated even at the briefest exposure times. Giving participants more time did not increase these correlations.

Traits Being Judged	0.10 sec	0.50 sec	1 sec
Trustworthy	.73	.66	.74
Competent	.52	.67	.59
Likable	.59	.57	.63
Aggressive	.52	.56	.59
Attractive	.69	.57	.66

Willis & Todorov, 2006.

in the knick-knacks found in their offices and dormitory rooms, the identity claims they make on Facebook pages, the books that line their shelves, and the types of music that inhabit their iPods.

Other superficial cues can also lead us to form quick impressions. In one study, fictional characters with "old-generation" names such as Harry, Walter, Dorothy, and Edith were judged to be less popular and less intelligent than those with younger-generation names such as Kevin, Michael, Lisa, and Michelle (Young et al., 1993). In a second study, both men and women were seen as more feminine when they spoke in high-pitched voices than in lower-pitched voices (Ko et al., 2006). In a third study, cleverly entitled "I like you but I don't know why," people rated computer-generated faces more positively when these faces—unbeknownst to them—were created to resemble a boyfriend or girlfriend in a satisfying relationship (Günaydin et al., 2012). In a fourth study, people formed impressions of strangers they had never met—seeing them as introverted or extroverted, calm or anxious, and agreeable or disagreeable—on the basis of the cartoon-like avatars these strangers had created to represent themselves online (see ● Figure 4.1) (Fong & Mar, 2015).

The human face in particular attracts more than its share of attention (Todorov et al., 2015). Since the time of ancient Greece, people have attended to physiognomy—the art of reading character from faces. Although we may not realize it, this tendency persists today. For example, Ran Hassin and Yaacov Trope (2000) found that people pre-judge others in photographs as kind-hearted rather than mean-spirited based on such features as a full, round face, curly hair, long eyelashes, large eyes, a short nose, full lips, and an upturned mouth. Interestingly, these researchers also found that just as people read traits *from* faces, at times they read traits *into* faces based on prior information. In one study, for example, participants who were told that a man was kind—compared to those told he was mean—later judged his face to be fuller, rounder, and more attractive.

In social perception studies of the human face, researchers have found that adults who have baby-faced features—large, round eyes; high eyebrows; round cheeks; a large forehead; smooth skin; and a rounded chin—tend to be seen as warm, kind, naive, weak, honest, and submissive. In contrast, adults who have mature features—small eyes, low brows and a small forehead, wrinkled skin, and an angular chin—are seen as stronger, more dominant, and more competent (Berry & Zebrowitz-McArthur, 1986). In small claims court, judges are more likely to favor baby-faced defendants who are accused of intentional wrongdoing but rule against them when accused of negligence. In the work setting, baby-faced job applicants are more likely to be recommended for employment as day-care teachers, whereas mature-faced adults are considered to be better suited for work as bankers. Recent research even shows that this link between baby-faced appearance and personal characteristics is seen not only in Western cultures but also among the Tsimané people living in a Bolivian rainforest (Zebrowitz et al., 2012). Leslie Zebrowitz and Joann Montepare (2005) thus conclude that baby-facedness "profoundly affects human behavior in the blink of an eye" (p. 1565).

● **FIGURE 4.1**

Sample avatars used in a study showing that people form impressions of unknown others—for example, as introverted or extroverted—on the basis of what they "see" in their online visual representations (Fong & Mar, 2015).

© Cengage Learning®

Julio Cesar Aguilar/AFP/Getty Images

What is your first impression of this person? Posing during an International Tattoo Exposition in Mexico, in 2013, Maria Jose Cristerna, also known as Vampire Woman, set the Guinness World Record for the most changes made to her body.

What accounts for these findings? And why, in general, are people so quick to judge others by appearances? One explanation is that human beings are programmed by evolution to respond gently to babyish features so that real babies are treated with tender loving care. Many years ago, animal behaviorist Konrad Lorenz noted that babyish features in many animal species seem to trigger a special nurturing response to cuteness. Recently, this old idea derived new support from a brain-imaging study showing that a frontal brain region associated with love and other positive emotions is activated when people are exposed, even fleetingly, to pictures of babies' faces but not to pictures of the faces of other adults (Kringelbach et al., 2008).

Our reflex-like response to babies is understandable. But why would we respond in the same way to baby-faced adults? Leslie Zebrowitz believes that we associate babyish features with helplessness traits and then overgeneralize this expectation to baby-faced adults. Consistent with this point, she and her colleagues found in a brain-imaging study that the region of the brain activated by pictures of babies' faces was also activated by pictures of baby-faced men (Zebrowitz et al., 2009).

Other researchers also believe that people as social perceivers overgeneralize in making snap judgments. Alexander Todorov and others (2008) find that people are quick to perceive unfamiliar faces as more or less trustworthy—a judgment we must often make—and that we do so by focusing on features that resemble the expressions of happiness and anger (a trustworthy face has a U-shaped mouth and raised eyebrows; in an untrustworthy face, the mouth curls down and the eyebrows form a V). In other words, faces are seen as trustworthy if they look happy, an emotion that signals a person who is safe to approach, and untrustworthy if they look angry, an emotion that signals danger to be avoided. Facial expressions may be temporary, but they too can influence our perceptions. When people smile, their faces look lighter and brighter than when they frown (Song et al., 2012).

> "Our faces, together with our language, are social tools that help us navigate the social encounters that define our "selves" and fashion our lives."
>
> —Alan J. Fridlund

The impressions we form of others are influenced by superficial aspects of their appearance.

TRUE

■ Perceptions of Situations

In addition to the beliefs we hold about persons, we also have preset notions about certain types of situations—"scripts" that enable us to anticipate the goals, behaviors, and outcomes likely to occur in a particular setting (Abelson, 1981; Read, 1987). Based on past experience, people can easily imagine the sequences of events likely to unfold in a typical greeting or at a shopping mall, the dinner table, or a tennis match. The more experience you have in a given situation, the more detail your scripts will contain.

In *Do's and Taboos Around the World*, Roger Axtell (1993) described scripts that are culture specific. In Bolivia, he notes, dinner guests are expected to fully clean their plates to prove that they enjoyed the meal. Eat in an Indian home, however, and you'll see that many native guests will leave some food on the plate to show the host that they had enough to eat. Social scripts of this nature can influence perceptions and behavior. As we'll see in Chapter 11 on aggression, in places that foster a culture of *honor*, men are expected to defend against all insult, women are expected to remain modest and loyal, and indications of female infidelity can trigger domestic violence (Vandello & Cohen, 2003). According to Angela Leung and Dov Cohen (2011), similar socials scripts can be found in other cultures, where a greater value is placed on *face* (the notion that people are expected to show deference to others of higher status and humility in public situations) and *dignity* (the notion that everyone at birth has intrinsic and equal value).

Behavioral scripts can be quite elaborate. Studying the "first date" script, John Pryor and Thomas Merluzzi (1985) asked U.S. college students to list the sequence of events that take place in this situation. From these lists, a picture of a typical American first date emerged. Sixteen steps were identified, including (1) male arrives; (2) female greets male at door; (3) female introduces date to parents or roommate; (4) male and female discuss plans and make small talk; (5) they go to a movie; (6) they get something to eat or drink; (7) male takes female home; (8) if interested, he remarks about a future date; (9) they kiss; (10) they say good night. Sound familiar? Pryor and Merluzzi then randomized their list of events and asked participants to arrange them into the appropriate order. They found that those with extensive dating experience were able to organize the statements more quickly than those who had less dating experience. For people who are familiar with a script, the events fall into place like pieces of a puzzle. In fact, almost 30 years later, despite changes in gender and dating norms, research shows that this basic script has remained essentially the same (Eaton & Rose, 2011; Morr Serewicz & Gale, 2008).

Knowledge of social settings provides an important context for understanding other people's verbal and nonverbal behavior. For example, this knowledge leads us to expect someone to be polite during a job interview, playful at a picnic, and rowdy at a NASCAR rally. Often our expectations for how situations affect us can influence the way we interpret other people's facial expressions. In one study, participants looked at photographs of human faces that had ambiguous expressions. When told that the person in the photo was being threatened by a vicious dog, they saw the facial expression as fearful; when told that the individual had just won money, participants interpreted the same expression as a sign of happiness (Trope, 1986). In other studies, scowling faces were seen as afraid when the surrounding situation was described as dangerous or as determined when said to be in a medal race on an Olympic rowing team (Carroll & Russell, 1996). Context effects on the perception of joy, anger, fear, pride, disgust, surprise, and other emotions in a facial expression—and even whether someone is audibly laughing or crying—are quick and automatic (Aviezer et al., 2008; Barrett et al., 2011; Lavan et al., 2015). ● Figure 4.2 illustrates this point.

■ Behavioral Evidence

An essential first step in social perception is recognizing what someone is doing at a given moment. Identifying actions from movement is surprisingly easy. Even when actors dressed in black move about in a dark room with point lights attached only to the joints of their bodies, people quickly and easily recognize such complex acts as walking, running, jumping, and falling (Johansson et al., 1980). This ability is found in people of all cultures (Barrett et al., 2005), and it enables us to recognize specific individuals, such as friends, strictly by their movements (Loula et al., 2005).

More interesting, perhaps, is that we derive *meaning* from our observations by dividing the continuous stream of human behavior into discrete "units." By having participants observe someone on videotape and press a button whenever they detect a "meaningful action," Darren Newtson and others (1987) found that some perceivers break the behavior stream into a large number of fine units, whereas others break it into a small number of

● **FIGURE 4.2**

Judging Emotions in Context

Look at the face of tennis star Serena Williams (left). How is she feeling—angry, perhaps, or in agony? Now look at her in a fuller context (right). You can see that Williams was actually euphoric, clenching her fist in victory at the 2008 U.S. Open.

Timothy A Cla·y/AFP/Getty Images

gross units. While watching a baseball game, for example, you might press the button after each pitch, after each batter, after every inning, or only after runs are scored. The manner in which people divide a stream of behavior can influence their perceptions. Research participants who were told to break an event into fine units rather than gross units attended more closely, detected more meaningful actions, and remembered more details about the actor's behavior than did participants who were told to break events into gross units (Lassiter et al., 1988).

Mind Perception In a developing area of research, social psychologists are now interested in **mind perception**, the process by which people attribute humanlike mental states to various animate and inanimate objects, including other people. Studies show that people who identify someone's actions in high-level terms rather than low-level terms (for example, by describing the act of "painting a house" as "trying to make a house look new," not just "applying brush strokes") are also more likely to attribute humanizing thoughts, feelings, intentions, consciousness, and other states of mind to that actor (Kozak et al., 2006).

Although people do not tend to attribute mental states to inanimate objects, in general the more humanlike a target object is, the more likely we are to attribute to it qualities of "mind." In a series of studies, Carey Morewedge and others (2007) found that whether people are asked to rate different animals in nature (such as a sloth, turtle, housefly, deer, wolf, and hummingbird); cartoon robots or human beings whose motion was presented in slow, medium, and fast speeds; or a purple blob oozing down a city street at the same, slower, or faster pace than the people around it, the result is always the same: People see inner qualities of mind in target objects that superficially resemble humans in their speed of movement.

"What kinds of things have minds?" To answer this question, Heather Gray and others (2007) conducted an online survey in which they presented more than 2,000 respondents with an array of human and nonhuman characters such as a 7-week-old fetus, a 5-month-old infant, an adult man, a man in a vegetative state, a dead woman, a frog, the family dog, a chimpanzee, God, and a sociable robot. They then asked respondents to rate the extent to which each character possessed various mental capacities such as pleasure, pain, fear, pride, embarrassment, memory, self-control, and morality. Once statistically combined, the results showed that people perceive minds along two dimensions: agency (a target's ability to plan and execute behavior) and experience (the capacity to feel pleasure, pain, and other sensations). Overall, the more "mind" respondents attributed to a character, the more they liked it, valued it, wanted to make it happy, and wanted to rescue it from destruction.

The perception of mind is an important aspect in how we perceive, connect with, and behave toward one another; that we sometimes see human mindlike qualities in nonhuman beings, and in certain inanimate objects; and that people are more likely to ascribe mind to others with whom they share a social connection than to distant others (Waytz et al., 2010). In a series of studies, for example, Adam Waytz and Nicholas Epley (2012) found that research participants who were asked to reflect on someone in their lives to whom they are close—say, a good friend, significant other, or family member—were then less likely to attribute humanizing mental qualities to other people.

What about the gadgets we tuck into our hip pockets? Does an iPhone have qualities of mind? In 2012, Apple introduced a series of television commercials

mind perception The process by which people attribute humanlike mental states to various animate and inanimate objects, including other people.

for the iPhone that are focused on Siri, the virtual assistant that is programmed to answer questions. In one commercial, actor John Malkovich asks Siri about the meaning of life. She advises him to be nice to people, avoid eating fat, and read a good book every now and then. "And try to live together in peace and harmony with people of all creeds and nations." Malkovich thanks Siri for the advice: "I enjoyed this chat immensely. You are very eloquent." "That's nice of you to say," Siri responds.

If people see mind in machines, what about autonomous vehicles, like Google's experimental self-driving car? Waytz and others (2014) put subjects into a simulated autonomous vehicle and found that they saw the car as smart and trustworthy—and as able to feel, anticipate, and plan.

As technology becomes more and more sophisticated, with robots programmed with artificial intelligence, will people come to see a humanlike mind in machines? For example, what about autonomous vehicles—self-driving cars of the near future, equipped with special cameras, maps, and collision avoidance software—that will control their own steering and speed? This technology is currently being developed and tested. In a fascinating study, Waytz, Heafner, and Epley (2014) brought 100 people into a driving simulator to "drive" a normal car; an autonomous vehicle that controlled steering and speed; or an autonomous vehicle enhanced by a name (Iris), gender (female), and voice (captured by human audio files). Those placed in the enhanced autonomous vehicle were more likely to see their car as *smart* and to sense that it could *feel, anticipate,* and *plan* a route. They were also more likely to *trust* the vehicle.

The Silent Language of Nonverbal Behavior   Behavioral cues are used not only to identify a person's physical actions but also to determine his or her inner states. Knowing how someone is feeling can be tricky because people often try to conceal their true emotions from others. Have you ever had to suppress your rage at someone, mask your disappointment after failure, feign surprise, make excuses, or pretend to like something just to be polite? Sometimes people come right out and tell us how they feel. But sometimes they do not tell us, they are themselves not sure, or they actively try to hide their true feelings. For these reasons, we often tune in to the silent language of **nonverbal behavior**.

What kinds of nonverbal cues do people use in judging how someone else is feeling? In *The Expression of the Emotions in Man and Animals,* naturalist Charles Darwin (1872)—whose theory of evolution transformed our understanding of human history—proposed that the face expresses emotion in ways that are both innate and understood by people all over the world. Contemporary research supports this notion. Many studies have shown that when presented with photographs similar to those on page 114, people can reliably identify at least six "primary" emotions: happiness, sadness, anger, fear, surprise, and disgust. In one study, participants from 10 different countries—Estonia, Germany, Greece, Hong Kong, Italy, Japan, Scotland, Sumatra, Turkey, and the United States— exhibited high levels of agreement in their recognition of these emotions (Ekman et al., 1987).

From one end of the world to the other, it's clear that a smile is a smile and a frown is a frown and that just about everyone knows what they mean, even when the expressions are "put on" by actors and are not genuinely felt. But do the results fully support the claim that basic emotions are "universally" recognized from the face, or is the link culturally specific? To answer this question, Hillary Elfenbein and Nalini Ambady (2002) meta-analyzed 97 studies involving a total

nonverbal behavior   Behavior that reveals a person's feelings without words, through facial expressions, body language, and vocal cues.

Can you tell how these individuals are feeling? If you are like most people, regardless of culture, you will have little trouble recognizing the emotions portrayed.

of 22,148 social perceivers from 42 different countries. As shown in ● Figure 4.3, they found support for both points of view. On the one hand, people all over the world are able to recognize the primary emotions from photographs of facial expressions. On the other hand, people are 9% more accurate at judging faces from their own national, ethnic, or regional groups than from members of less familiar groups—indicating that we enjoy an "in-group advantage" when it comes to knowing how those who are closest to us are feeling.

In a study that illustrates the point, Elfenbein and Ambady (2003) showed pictures of American faces to groups with varying degrees of exposure to Americans. As predicted, more life exposure was associated with greater accuracy, from a low of 60% among Chinese participants living in China up to 83% among Chinese living in the United States and 93% among non–Chinese Americans. When it comes to recognizing emotions in the face, it appears that familiarity breeds accuracy.

Darwin believed that the ability to recognize emotion in others has survival value for all members of a species. This hypothesis suggests that it is more important to identify some emotions than others. For example, it may be more adaptive to be wary of someone who is angry, and hence prone to lash out in violence, than of someone who is happy, a nonthreatening emotion. Indeed, studies have shown that angry faces arouse us and cause us to frown even when presented subliminally and without our awareness (Dimberg et al., 2000). Illustrating what Christine and Ranald Hansen (1988) called the "anger superiority effect," researchers have found that people are quicker to spot—and slower to look away from—angry faces in a crowd than faces with neutral, non-threatening emotions (Fox et al., 2002; Horstmann & Bauland, 2006).

It is interesting that people are not always quicker to spot the threatening face of anger in a crowd than, say, a face of happiness. Our tendencies are more complicated in two ways. First, what we search for may be conditioned by our current motivational state. In a visual search task resembling "Where's Waldo?" research participants who were induced to fear social rejection and loneliness were quicker to spot faces in diverse crowds that wore welcoming smiles than other expressions (DeWall et al., 2009). Second, while static angry faces do not necessarily capture our attention, presentations of faces *in motion*, which is more realistic, may well have this effect. Studies that compared happy and angry faces in a crowd that were dynamic rather than static confirm this hypothesis. When shown neutral faces in a crowd that gradually turn positive or negative in their expression, people are quicker to spot those faces that turn angry (Ceccarini & Caudek, 2013).

Disgust is another basic emotion that has adaptive significance. When confronted with an offensive stimulus such as a foul odor, spoiled food, feces, rotting flesh, or the sight of mutilation, people react with an aversion that shows in the way they wrinkle the nose, raise the upper lip, and gape. This visceral reaction is often accompanied by nausea; in the case of bad food, this can facilitate gagging and vomiting (Rozin & Fallon, 1987). In nature, food poisoning is a real threat, so it is adaptive for us to recognize disgust in the face of others. To illustrate, Bruno Wicker and others (2003) had 14 men watch video clips of people smelling pleasant, disgusting, or neutral odors. Afterward, these same men were exposed to the odors themselves. If you've ever inhaled the sweet, floury

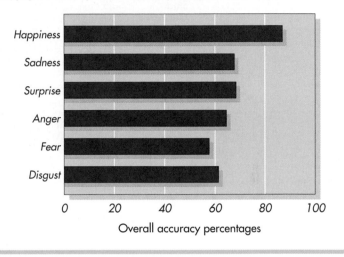

● **FIGURE 4.3**

How Good Are People at Identifying Emotions in the Face?

A meta-analysis of emotion recognition studies involving 22,148 participants from 42 countries confirmed that people all over the world can recognize the six basic emotions from posed facial expressions.

Based on Elfenbein, H.A., and Ambady, N. (2002). How good are people at identifying emotions in the face? *Psychological Bulletin* vol 128 (pp. 203–235). Copyright © 2002 by the American Psychological Association.

aroma of a bakery or inserted your nose into a carton of soured milk, you'll appreciate the different reactions that would appear on your face. Using fMRI, researchers monitored activity in the participants' brains throughout the experiment. They found that a structure in the brain known as the *insula* was activated not only when participants sniffed the disgusting odor but also when they watched *others* sniffing it. This result suggests that people more than recognize the face of disgust; they experience it at a neural level.

The social value of the human face is evident when we communicate by texting, Twitter, or e-mail. When e-mail first became popular, the written word was often misinterpreted, especially when the writer tried to be funny or sarcastic, because we lacked the nonverbal cues that normally animate and clarify live interactions. To fill in this gap, e-mailers created smiley faces and other "emoticons" (emotion icons) from standard keyboard characters. A sampling of routinely used emoticons, which are meant to be viewed with one's head tilted 90 degrees to the left, are shown in ● Figure 4.4. To simplify the task, Gmail, Hotmail, AOL, Yahoo!, and other e-mail providers now offer a choice of still and animated emoticon faces to communicate an assortment of emotions and other mental states.

Other nonverbal cues can also influence social perception, enabling us to make quick and sometimes accurate judgments of others based on *thin slices* of expressive behavior (Ambady & Rosenthal, 1993). But wait. Can you really tell how much eye contact a person gives to people, or how often they smile, or nod, or gesture, from only a 5-second sample of behavior? Wouldn't it help to have more time? To answer these questions, Nora Murphy and others (2015) conducted several studies in which they taped college students, medical interns, and job applicants engaged in various social interactions. After fully coding their nonverbal behaviors, they took thin slices to determine if these small samples accurately

Some Common E-mail "Emoticons"

In order to clarify meaning of their written words, e-mailers often add smiles, winks, and other face-like symbols, or emoticons, to their electronic messages. One set of emoticons is shown here; you may be familiar with others.
Based on "Smileys" © 1996 O'Reilly & Associates, Inc. All rights reserved.
www.oreilly.com

Wink	Smirk	Said smiling	Said frowning	Sardonic incredulity
'-)	:-,	:-)	:-(	;-)

Disgusted	Kiss, kiss	Clowning around	Said late at night	Said tongue-in-cheek
:-I	:-X	:*)	I-(	:-J

captured the whole. The answer was yes. You can tell how much eye contact a person tends to give in a conversation—or how much smiling, nodding, and gesturing—from a mere 30, 60, and 90 seconds of observation.

Sometimes the impressions people form from thin slices of behavior are quite accurate. In one study, people accurately judged the intelligence of strangers, as measured by actual IQ test scores, based only on hearing them read short sentences (Borkenau et al., 2004). In a second study, people rated 8- to 12-year-old children on personality characteristics based on mere thin slices of behavior; these ratings too matched the personality assessments of these children made by their own parents (Tackett et al., 2015). In a third study, people watched brief video clips from interviews of maximum security inmates. Even with only 5 seconds of exposure, their ratings significantly correlated with clinical diagnoses of the inmates' personality disorders (Fowler et al., 2009). Taking these findings as a whole, it's no wonder that Nalini Ambady (2010) described the quick judgments we often make as "intuitive" and "efficient." "Thin slicing is not an exotic gift," notes Malcolm Gladwell (2005), author of the best seller *Blink*. "It is a central part of what it means to be human" (p. 43).

Eye contact, or gaze, is a particularly powerful form of nonverbal communication. As social beings, people are highly attentive to eyes, often following the gaze of others. Look up, down, left, or right, and someone observing you will likely follow the direction of your eyes (Langton et al., 2000). Even 1-year-old infants tend to follow gaze, looking toward or pointing at the object of an adult researcher's attention (Brooks & Meltzoff, 2002). Clearly, each of us is drawn like a magnet to the gaze of others. Controlled laboratory studies of this "eye contact effect" show that people who look us straight in the eye quickly draw and hold our attention, increase arousal, and activate key social areas of the brain—and that this sensitivity is present at birth (Senju & Johnson, 2009) and even when the other person's gazing eyes are hidden behind dark sunglasses (Myllyneva & Hietanen, 2015).

Eyes have been called the "windows of the soul." In many cultures, people assume that someone who avoids eye contact is evasive, cold, fearful, shy, or indifferent; that frequent gazing signals intimacy, sincerity, self-confidence, and respect; and that the person who stares is tense, angry, and unfriendly. If you've ever conversed with someone who kept looking away, as if uninterested, then you would understand why people might form negative impressions from "gaze disengagement" (Mason et al., 2005). Sometimes eye contact is interpreted in light of a preexisting relationship. If two people are friendly, frequent eye contact elicits a positive impression. If a relationship is not so friendly, that same eye contact is seen in negative terms. Hence, it is said that if two people lock eyes for more than a few seconds, they will either make love or kill each other (Kleinke, 1986).

Before concluding our discussion of nonverbal behavior, it is important to note Axtell's (1993) advice, useful for travel to other countries, that there is a great deal of cultural variation. In Bulgaria, nodding your head means "no," and shaking your head sideways means "yes." In Germany and Brazil, the American "okay" sign (forming a circle with your thumb and forefinger) is an obscene gesture. Personal-space habits also vary across cultures. Japanese people like to maintain a comfortable distance while interacting. But in Puerto Rico and much of Latin America, people stand very close and backing off is considered an insult. Also beware of what you do with your eyes. In Latin America, locking eyes is a must, yet in Japan, too much eye contact shows a lack of respect. If you're in the habit of stroking your cheek, you should know that in Italy, Greece, and Spain it means that you find the person you're talking to attractive. And don't ever touch someone's head in predominantly Buddhist countries, especially Thailand. The head is sacred there. Even a smile does not convey a universal impression: While smiling tends to make you look smart in Germany and China, it can have the opposite effect in Iran (Krys et al., 2014).

After the 9/11 terrorist attacks in 2001, the Transportation Security Administration has trained its agents to observe the facial expressions and demeanor of airport passengers in an effort to detect signs of malintent. Thus far, there is little evidence that the judgments they make by this type of observations are accurate.

Different cultures also have different rules for the common greeting. In Finland, you should give a firm handshake; in France, you should loosen the grip; in Zambia, you should use your left hand to support the right; and in Bolivia, you should extend your arm if your hand is dirty. In Japan, people bow; in Thailand, they put both hands together in a praying position on the chest; and in Fiji, they smile and raise their eyebrows. In certain parts of Latin America, it is common for people to hug, embrace, and kiss upon meeting. And in most Arab countries, men greet one another by saying *salaam alaykum*, then shaking hands, saying *kaifhalak*, and kissing on the cheek.

Detecting Truth and Deception

Social perception can be tricky because people often try to hide or stretch the truth about themselves. Poker players bluff to win money, witnesses lie to protect themselves, public officials make campaign promises they know they can't keep, and acquaintances pass compliments to each other to be polite. On occasion, everyone tells something less than "the truth, the whole truth, and nothing but the truth." Can social perceivers tell the difference? Can *you* tell when someone is lying?

Sigmund Freud, the founder of psychoanalysis, once said that "no mortal can keep a secret. If his lips are silent, he chatters with his fingertips; betrayal oozes out of him at every pore" (1905, p. 94). Paul Ekman and Wallace Friesen (1974) later revised

"I'm not pretending to be asleep—I'm pretending to be sexually satisfied."

People often stretch or conceal the truth, which can make social perception a tricky endeavor.

Research on lying and its detection has shown that there is no one behavioral cue, like Pinocchio's growing wooden nose, that can be used to signal deception.

Freud's observation by pointing out that some pores "ooze" more than others. Ekman and Friesen proposed that some channels of communication are difficult for deceivers to control, whereas others are relatively easy. To test this hypothesis, they showed a series of films—some pleasant, others disgusting—to a group of female nurses. While watching, the nurses were instructed either to report their honest impressions of these films or to conceal their true feelings. Through the use of hidden cameras, these participants were videotaped. Others, acting as observers, then viewed the tapes and judged whether the participants had been truthful or deceptive. The results showed that judgment accuracy rates were influenced by which types of nonverbal cues the observers were exposed to. Observers who watched tapes that focused on the body were better at detecting deception than were those who saw tapes focused on the face. The face can communicate emotion but is relatively easy for deceivers to control, unlike nervous movements of the hands and feet. Clearly, there is nothing like the wooden Pinocchio's nose to reveal whether someone is lying or telling the truth.

This study was the first of hundreds that have been conducted to this day. In all this research, one group of participants makes truthful or deceptive statements, while another group reads the transcripts, listens to audiotapes or watches videotapes, and then tries to judge the statements. Consistently, in laboratories all over the world, results show that people are only about 54% accurate in judging truth and deception, in part because they too often accept what others say at face value (Bond & DePaulo, 2006; Vrij, 2008). In fact, research shows that professionals who are specially trained and who make these kinds of judgments for a living—such as police detectives, judges, psychiatrists, customs inspectors, and those who administer lie-detector tests for the CIA, the FBI, and the military—are also highly prone to error (Ekman & O'Sullivan, 1991; Meissner & Kassin, 2002; Vrij, 2008; see Table 4.2).

What seems to be the problem? One hypothesis is that there is a mismatch between the behavioral cues that actually signal deception and those we use to detect deception (Zuckerman et al., 1981; DePaulo et al., 2003). Think about it. There are four channels of communication that provide potentially relevant information: the spoken word, the face, the body, and the voice. Yet when people have a reason to lie, the words they choose cannot be trusted, and they are generally able to control both the face and body (the voice is the most telling channel; when people lie, they tend to hesitate, then speed up and raise the pitch of their voice). In a survey of approximately 2,500 adults in 58 countries, an international team of researchers found that more than 70% believed that liars tend to avert their eyes—a cue that is not supported by any research. Similarly, most survey

▲ **TABLE 4.2**

Can the "Experts" Distinguish Truth and Deception?

Lie-detection experts with experience at making judgments of truth and deception were shown brief videotapes of 10 women telling the truth or lying about their feelings. Considering that there was a 50–50 chance of guessing correctly, the accuracy rates were remarkably low. Only a sample of U.S. Secret Service agents posted a better-than-chance performance.

Observer Groups	Accuracy Rates (%)
College students	52.82
CIA, FBI, and military	55.67
Police investigators	55.79
Trial judges	56.73
Psychiatrists	57.61
U.S. Secret Service agents	64.12

From Ekman, P., & O'Sullivan, M. (1991). Who can catch a liar? *American Psychologist, 46*, 913–20. Copyright © 1991 by the American Psychological Association. Reprinted by permission.

respondents believed that people squirm, stutter, fidget, and touch themselves when they lie—also cues that are not supported by the research (Global Deception Research Team, 2006).

Perhaps people rely on the wrong cues to deception, but a recent analysis of this same literature shows that the problem should be somewhat differently stated: It's not that people make truth and lie judgments on the basis of the *wrong* cues, but rather the problem is that none of the behavioral cues people look for are very telling (Hartwig & Bond, 2011). In a recent meta-analysis of 144 samples containing 9,380 speakers, providing a total of 26,866 messages, and spanning more than forty years, Hartwig and Bond (2014) found that the low level of detectability of deception did not differ much regardless of whether the speaker was a college student or nonstudent; whether or not the speaker was highly motivated to evade detection; or whether the truths and lies told were accompanied by high or low levels of emotion.

Throughout history, people have assumed that the way to spot a liar is to watch for outward signs of stress or anxiousness in his or her behavior. Yet in important real-life situations—for example, at a high-stakes poker table, the security screening area of an airport, or a police interrogation room—innocent truth tellers are also likely to exhibit signs of stress. For this reason, researchers today are seeking a different approach. Most notably, Aldert Vrij, Anders Granhag, and their colleagues have theorized that lying is harder to do and requires more thinking than telling the truth (Vrij et al., 2010; Vrij & Granhag, 2012). Therefore, they argue, we should both induce and focus on behavioral cues that betray cognitive *effort*.

Joe Giron/Corbis Entertainment/Corbis

This realization has led researchers to create more challenging types of interviews that could outsmart liars, force them to think harder, and struggle more, and thereby expose their deception. In one study, for example, they asked truth tellers and liars to recount their stories in reverse chronological order. This task was more effortful for the deceivers to do, which made the interviewers better able to distinguish between truths and lies (Vrij et al., 2008). In a second study, truth tellers and liars were urged to maintain eye contact with their interviewer. This added burden taxed those who were lying more it did those who were telling the truth, which enabled observers to better distinguish between the two groups (Vrij et al., 2010).

Sweden's Martin Jacobson won $10 million as the 2014 Champion of the World Series of Poker. As with all great players, Jacobson wears the proverbial "poker face" while playing so as not to betray how he feels about his hand.

In the wake of the September 11 terrorist attacks and heightened worldwide concerns about security at airports, train stations, and other public places, the ability to distinguish truths and lies is essential, potentially a matter of life and death. Yet research shows that social perceivers are misguided. Too easily seduced by the silver tongue, the smiling face, and the restless body, we often fail to notice the quivering voice or the verbal content of what is said. Too focused on how stressed a person seems while speaking—an emotional state that afflicts not only guilty liars but innocent truth tellers who stand falsely accused—we fail to notice how much effort it takes someone to recite their story or answer a question. With social psychologists in hot pursuit of ways to improve upon human lie-detection skills—for example, by preventing individuals from thinking too much before making their judgments (Reinhard et al., 2013) or, by contrast, having individuals come together in groups to discuss and make these judgments (Klein & Epley, 2015)—stay tuned for further developments in years to come.

Adaptively, people are skilled at knowing when someone is lying rather than telling the truth.

FALSE

Attribution: From Elements to Dispositions

To interact effectively with others, we need to know how they feel and when they can be trusted. But to understand people well enough to predict their future behavior, we also try to identify their inner *dispositions*—stable characteristics such as personality traits, attitudes, and abilities. Since we cannot actually see dispositions, we infer them indirectly from what a person says and does. In this section, we look at the processes that lead us to make these inferences.

■ Attribution Theories

Do you ever think about the influence you have on other people? What about the roles of heredity, childhood experiences, and social forces? Do you wonder why some people succeed while others fail? Individuals differ in the extent to which they feel a need to explain the events of human behavior (Weary & Edwards, 1994). Although there are vast differences among us, people in general tend to ask "why?" when confronting events that are important; harmful, immoral, or otherwise negative; or unexpected (Chakroff & Young, 2015; Weiner, 1985)—and when understanding these events has personal relevance (Malle & Knobe, 1997).

"It's not you, Frank, it's me—I don't like you."

People make personal and situational attributions all the time in an effort to make sense of their social world. But what kind of attribution is being made here?

To make sense of our social world, we try to understand the causes of other people's behavior. But what kinds of explanations do we make, and how do we go about making them? In a classic book entitled *The Psychology of Interpersonal Relations*, Fritz Heider (1958) took the first step toward answering these questions. To Heider, we are all scientists of a sort. Motivated to understand others well enough to manage our social lives, we observe, analyze, and explain their behavior. The explanations we come up with are called *attributions*, and the theory that describes the process is called **attribution theory**. The questions posed at the beginning of the chapter regarding the behaviors of Vladimir Putin, Oscar Pistorius, and Tom Brady are all questions of attribution.

Ask people to explain why their fellow human beings behave as they do—why they succeed or fail, laugh or cry, work or play, or help or hurt others—and you'll see that they come up with complex explanations focused on whether the behavior they observe is intentional or unintentional—and whether it reflects on the actor's desire, belief, and personality (Malle & Holbrook, 2012). Interested in how people answer these kinds of *why* questions, Heider found it particularly useful to group the causal attributions people give into two categories: *personal* and *situational*. In the Oscar Pistorius shooting incident, everyone wanted to know what caused him to pick up his gun in the middle of the night and spray four bullets into the bathroom door. The prosecution pointed the finger of blame at Pistorius, an intensely driven young man overheard yelling at his girlfriend (a **personal attribution**). Yet others speculated that his actions were provoked by what he thought to be the sound of an intruder inside his house and a state of confusion that ensued (a **situational attribution**).

The task for the attribution theorist is not to determine the true *causes* of such an event but rather to understand people's *perceptions* of causality. Heider's

attribution theory A group of theories that describe how people explain the causes of behavior.

personal attribution Attribution to internal characteristics of an actor, such as ability, personality, mood, or effort.

situational attribution Attribution to factors external to an actor, such as the task, other people, or luck.

Robert Mankoff/The New Yorker Collection/Cartoon Bank.com

insights provided an initial spark for a number of formal models that together came to be known as attribution theory (Weiner, 2008). For now, we describe two of these theories.

Jones's Correspondent Inference Theory

According to Edward Jones and Keith Davis (1965), each of us tries to understand other people by observing and analyzing their behavior. Jones and Davis's *correspondent inference theory* predicts that people try to infer from an action whether the act corresponds to an enduring personal trait of the actor. Is the person who commits an act of aggression a beast? Is the person who donates money to charity an altruist? To answer these kinds of questions, people make inferences on the basis of three factors.

The first factor is a person's degree of *choice*. Behavior that is freely chosen is more informative about a person than behavior that is coerced by the situation. In one study, participants read a speech, presumably written by a college student, which either favored or opposed Fidel Castro, then the former communist leader of Cuba. Some participants were told that the student had freely chosen this position and others were told that the student had been assigned the position by a professor. When asked to judge the student's true attitude, participants were more likely to assume a correspondence between the essay (behavior) and the student's attitude (disposition) when the student had had a choice than when he or she had been assigned to the role (Jones & Harris, 1967; see ● Figure 4.5). Keep this study in mind. It supports correspondent inference theory, but as we'll see later, it also demonstrates one of the most tenacious biases of social perception.

A second factor that leads us to make dispositional inferences is the *expectedness* of behavior. As previously noted, an action tells us more about a person when it departs from the norm than when it is typical, part of a social role, or otherwise expected under the circumstances (Jones et al., 1961). Thus, people think they know more about a student who wears three-piece suits to class or a citizen who openly refuses to pay taxes than about a student who wears blue jeans to class or a citizen who dutifully files tax returns on April 15.

Third, social perceivers take into account the intended *effects* or consequences of someone's behavior. Acts that produce many desirable outcomes do not reveal a person's specific motives as clearly as acts that produce only a single desirable outcome (Newtson, 1974). For example, you are likely to be uncertain about exactly why a person stays on a job that is enjoyable, high paying, and in an attractive location—three highly desirable outcomes, each sufficient to explain the behavior. In contrast, you may feel more certain about why a person stays on a job that is tedious and low paying but is in an attractive location—only one desirable outcome.

● **FIGURE 4.5**

What Does This Speechwriter Really Believe?

As predicted by correspondent inference theory, participants who read a student's speech (behavior) were more likely to assume that it reflected the student's true attitude (disposition) when the position taken was freely chosen (left) rather than assigned (right). But also note the evidence for the fundamental attribution error. Even participants who thought the student had been assigned a position inferred the student's attitude from the speech.

Based on Jones, E. E., & Harris, V. A. (1967). The attribution of attitudes. *Journal of Experimental Social Psychology*, 3, 1–24. Copyright © 1967 Elsevier.

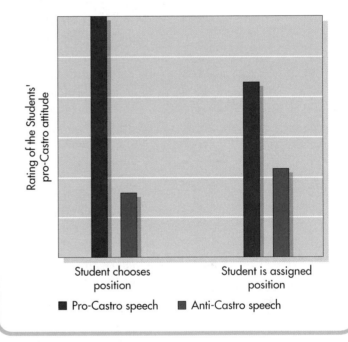

Kelley's Covariation Theory Correspondent inference theory seeks to describe how perceivers try to discern an individual's personal characteristics from a slice of behavioral evidence. However, behavior can be attributed not only to personal factors but to situational factors as well. How is this distinction made? In the opening chapter, we noted that the causes of human behavior can be derived only through experiments. That is, one has to make more than a single observation and compare behavior in two or more settings in which everything stays the same except for the independent variables. Like Heider, Harold Kelley (1967) theorized that people are much like scientists in this regard. They may not observe others in a controlled laboratory, but they too search for clues, make comparisons, and think in terms of "experiments."

According to Kelley, people make attributions by using the **covariation principle**: In order for something to be the cause of a behavior, it must be present when the behavior occurs and absent when it does not. Three kinds of covariation information in particular are useful: consensus, distinctiveness, and consistency. To illustrate these concepts, imagine you are standing on a street corner one hot, steamy evening minding your own business, when all of a sudden a stranger comes out of an air-conditioned movie theater and blurts out, "Great flick!" Looking up, you don't recognize the movie title, so you wonder what to make of this "recommendation." Was the behavior (the rave review) caused by something about the person (the stranger), the stimulus (the film), or the circumstances (say, the comfortable theater)? If you are possibly interested in a night at the movies, how would you proceed to explain what happened? What kinds of information would you want to obtain?

Thinking like a scientist, you might seek out *consensus information* to see how different persons react to the same stimulus. In other words, what do other moviegoers think about this film? If others also rave about it, then this stranger's behavior is high in consensus and is attributed to the stimulus. If others are critical of this film, however, then the behavior is low in consensus and is attributed to the person.

Still thinking like a scientist, you might also want *distinctiveness information* to see how the same person reacts to different stimuli. In other words, what does this moviegoer think of other films? If the stranger is generally critical of other films, then the target behavior is high in distinctiveness and is attributed to the stimulus. If the stranger raves about everything he or she sees, however, then the behavior is low in distinctiveness and is attributed to the person.

Finally, you might want to seek *consistency information* to see what happens to the behavior at another time when the person and the stimulus both remain the same. How does this moviegoer feel about this film on other occasions? If the stranger raves about the film on video as well as in the theater, regardless of surroundings, then the behavior is high in consistency. If the stranger does not always enjoy the film, the behavior is low in consistency. According to Kelley, behavior that is consistent is attributed to the stimulus when consensus and distinctiveness are also high and to the person when they are low. In contrast, behavior that is low in consistency is attributed to transient circumstances, such as the temperature of the movie theater.

Does Kelley's attribution theory describe the kinds of information you seek when you try to determine what causes people to behave as they do? Often it does. Research shows that when people are asked to make attributions for various events, they tend to follow the logic of covariation so long as it is socially safe to do so (Fosterling, 1992; McArthur, 1972; Quayle & Naidoo, 2012). However, this research also shows that individuals have their own attributional styles, so

covariation principle A principle of attribution theory that holds that people attribute behavior to factors that are present when a behavior occurs and are absent when it does not.

people often disagree about what caused a particular behavior (Robins et al., 2004). There are two ways that social perceivers differ. First, we vary in the extent to which we believe that human behaviors are caused by personal traits that are fixed ("Everyone is a certain kind of person; there is not much that can be done to really change that") or by characteristics that are malleable ("People can change even their most basic qualities") (Dweck, 2012). Second, some of us are more likely than others to process new information in ways that are colored by self-serving motives (von Hippel et al., 2005).

■ Attribution Biases

Daniel Kahneman won a Nobel Prize in Economics for work on the psychology of judgment and decision making. In his recent book, *Thinking, Fast and Slow*, Kahneman (2011) summarizes a lifetime of research showing that the human mind operates by two different systems of thought. System 1 is quick, easy, and automatic—using a process that one might call "intuitive." Determining which of two objects is more distant, detecting anger in a face, adding 2 1 2, and understanding a simple sentence are the kinds of automatic activities engaged by this system. In contrast, System 2 is slow, controlled, and requires attention and effort—using a process that feels more reasoned. Looking for a specific face in a crowd, parking in a narrow space, counting the number of letters on a page, figuring out how a magic trick works, and filling out taxes are the kinds of activities that require your focused and undivided attention. According to Kahneman, Systems 1 and 2 are both active when people are awake. System 1 runs automatically and guides us until it runs into difficulty, as when something unexpected happens. At that point the more effortful System 2 is activated.

When the theories of attribution were first proposed, they were represented by elaborate flow charts, formulas, and diagrams, leading many social psychologists to wonder: Do people really analyze behavior in the way that one might expect of scientists, or computers? Do people have the time, the motivation, or the cognitive capacity for such elaborate, mindful, System 1 processes? The answer is sometimes yes, sometimes no. As social perceivers, we are limited in our ability to process all relevant information, or we lack the kinds of training needed to employ fully the principles of attribution theory. More important, we often don't bother to think carefully about the attributions we make. With so much to explain and not enough time in a day, people take mental shortcuts, cross their fingers, hope for the best, and get on with life. The problem is that speed brings bias and perhaps even a loss of accuracy. In this section, we examine some of these shortcuts and their consequences.

Cognitive Heuristics   According to Kahneman, Tversky, and others, people often make attributions and other types of social judgments using "cognitive heuristics"—information-processing rules of thumb that enable us to think in ways that are quick and easy but that often lead to error (Gigerenzer et al., 2011; Gilovich et al., 2002; Kahneman et al., 1982; Nisbett & Ross, 1980).

One rule of thumb that has particularly troublesome effects on attribution is the **availability heuristic**, a tendency to estimate the odds that an event will occur by how easily instances of it pop to mind. To demonstrate, Tversky and Kahneman (1973) asked research participants: Which is more common, words that start with the letter *r* or words that contain *r* as the third letter? In actuality, the English language has many more words with *r* as the third letter than as the first. Yet most people guessed that more words begin with *r*. Why? Because it's

availability heuristic The tendency to estimate the likelihood that an event will occur by how easily instances of it come to mind.

▲ **TABLE 4.3**

The False-Consensus Effect

In this study, participants who did and participants who did not rate various personality traits as descriptive of themselves estimated the percentage of other people who had these traits. As shown below, participants' estimates of the population consensus were biased by their own self-perceptions.

Traits	Self Yes (%)	Self No (%)
Alert	75	65
Discontented	48	33
Loud	46	43
Meticulous	52	41
Sly	36	28
Smug	41	33

Krueger (2000).

"A single death is a tragedy; a million is a statistic."

—Joseph Stalin

false-consensus effect The tendency for people to overestimate the extent to which others share their opinions, attributes, and behaviors.

base-rate fallacy The finding that people are relatively insensitive to consensus information presented in the form of numerical base rates.

easier to bring to mind words in which *r* appears first. Apparently, our estimates of likelihood are heavily influenced by events that are readily available in memory (MacLeod & Campbell, 1992).

Research shows that the availability heuristic can lead us astray in two ways. First, it gives rise to the **false-consensus effect**, a tendency for people to overestimate the extent to which others share their opinions, attributes, and behaviors. This bias is pervasive. Regardless of whether people are asked to predict how others feel about military spending, abortion, gun control, Campbell's soup, certain types of music, favorite celebrities, or norms for appropriate behavior, they exaggerate the percentage of others who behave similarly or share their views (Bui, 2012; Krueger, 1998; Ross et al., 1977). To illustrate the effect, Joachim Krueger (2000) asked participants in a study to indicate whether or not they had certain personality traits. Then they were asked to estimate the percentage of people in general who have these same traits. As shown in Table 4.3, participants' beliefs about other people's personalities were biased by their own self-perceptions. In part, the false-consensus bias is a by-product of the availability heuristic. We tend to associate with others who are like us in important ways, so we are more likely to notice and recall instances of similar rather than dissimilar behavior.

A second consequence of the availability heuristic is that social perceptions are influenced more by one vivid life story than by hard statistical facts. Have you ever wondered why so many people buy lottery tickets despite the astonishingly low odds or why so many travelers are afraid to fly even though they are more likely to perish in a car accident? These behaviors are symptomatic of the **base-rate fallacy**—the fact that people are relatively insensitive to numerical base rates, or probabilities; they are influenced more by graphic, dramatic events such as the sight of a multimillion-dollar lottery winner celebrating on TV or a photograph of bodies being pulled from the wreckage of a plane crash.

The base-rate fallacy can lead to various misperceptions of risk. For that reason, people overestimate the number of those who die in shootings, fires, floods, and terrorist bombings and underestimate the death toll caused by heart attacks, strokes, diabetes, and other mundane events. Perceptions of risk seem more relevant now than in the past by newly acquired fears of terrorism, or economic collapse, and research shows that such perceptions are affected more by fear, anxiety, and other emotions than by cold and objective probabilities (Loewenstein et al., 2001; Pachur et al., 2012; Slovic, 2000). At times the effect of strong emotion can be capricious and downright irrational. For example, consistent with the fact that people tend to fear things that sound unfamiliar, participants in one study rated fictional food additives as more hazardous to health when the names were hard to pronounce—such as Hnegripitrom, than when they were easier to pronounce—such as Magnalroxate (Song & Schwarz, 2009).

Every day, we are besieged by both types of information: We read about the jobless and unemployment rates, and we watch personal interviews with people who were recently laid off; we read the casualty figures of war, and we witness the agony of a parent who has lost a child in combat. Logically, statistics that summarize the experiences of large numbers of people are more informative than a single and perhaps atypical case, but perceivers are not influenced by numbers.

As long as the personal anecdote is seen as relevant (Schwarz et al., 1991) and the source as credible (Hinsz et al., 1988), and particularly to the extent that it involves someone we know (Hills & Pachur, 2012), it seems that one vivid image is worth a thousand numbers.

Counterfactual Thinking   Interestingly, people can also be influenced by how easy it is to imagine events that did *not* occur. As thoughtful and curious beings, we are often not content to accept what happens to us or to others without wondering, at least in private, "What if . . . ?"

According to Kahneman and Miller (1986), people's emotional reactions to events are often colored by **counterfactual thinking**, a tendency to imagine alternative outcomes that might have occurred but did not. There are different types of counterfactual thoughts. If we imagine a result that is better than the actual result, then we're likely to experience disappointment, regret, and frustration. If the imagined result is worse, then we react with emotions that range from relief and satisfaction to elation. Thus, the psychological impact of positive and negative events depends on the way we think about "what might have been" (Roese, 1997; Roese & Olson, 1995).

What domains of life trigger the most counterfactual thinking—and the regret that may follow? Summarizing past research, Neal Roese and Amy Summerville (2005) found that people's top three regrets center, in order, on education ("I should have stayed in school"), career ("If only I had applied for that job"), and romance ("If only I had asked her out")—all domains that present us with opportunities that we may or may not realize. Of course, counterfactual thinking does not necessarily lead people into a sense of regret. In fact, Laura Kray and others (2010) note that reflecting on "what might have been" can sometimes help us to define ourselves as well as the meaning in our lives. Think about it. What would you be like today if you had chosen to attend a different school, or if you had not met your best friend? These researchers found that participants who were asked to reflect on these counterfactual "what if" questions later saw their college choices and friendships as more meaningful than those who did not stop to ask these questions. Perhaps by thinking about what might have been, people can more fully appreciate what they have.

Some individuals think in counterfactual terms more than others do. As you might expect, for example, people who strongly believe in free will—the idea that we can control our own fate by the choices we make—are more likely to wonder "what if" than those who believe that their fate is predetermined or unpredictable (Alquist et al., 2015). Also, some types of experiences lead people to engage in counterfactual thought more than others. Research shows that we are more likely to think about what might have been, often with feelings of regret, after negative outcomes that result from actions we take rather than from actions we don't take (Byrne & McEleney 2000). Consider an experience that may sound familiar: You take a multiple-choice test, and after reviewing an item you struggled over, you want to change the answer. What do you do? Research has shown that most changes in test answers are from incorrect to correct. Yet most college students harbor the "first instinct fallacy" that it is best to stick with one's original answer. Why? Justin Kruger and his colleagues (2005) found that this myth arises from counterfactual thinking: that students are more likely to react with regret and frustration ("If only I had . . .") after changing a correct answer than after failing to change an incorrect answer.

Country singer Lee Brice wrote a song about counterfactual thinking. In *A Woman Like You*, his girlfriend asks, "Honey, what would you do if you'd never met me?" Here's part of his response:

I'd do a lot more offshore fishin'
I'd probably eat more drive-thru chicken
Take a few strokes off my golf game
If I'd have never known your name
I'd still be driving that old green Nova
I probably never would have heard of yoga
Be a better football fan
But if I was a single man
Alone and out there on the loose
Well I'd be looking for a woman like you.

Rick Diamond/Getty Images Entertainment/Getty Images

counterfactual thinking   The tendency to imagine alternative events or outcomes that might have occurred but did not.

Entering the 2012 Summer Olympics in London, U.S. gymnast McKayla Maroney was the best female vaulter in the world. She went on to win a silver medal. In what fast became an iconic image, here she is during the podium ceremony. Thinking about what might have been, Maroney, clearly, was focused on not winning gold.

Ronald Martinez/Getty Images

"During the 1996 Olympics, Nike ran a counterfactual (and controversial) ad: 'You don't win silver, you lose gold.'"

fundamental attribution error
The tendency to focus on the role of personal causes and underestimate the impact of situations on other people's behavior.

According to Victoria Medvec and Kenneth Savitsky (1997), certain situations—such as being on the *verge* of a better or worse outcome, just above or below some cutoff point—also make it especially easy to conjure up images of what might have been. The implications are intriguing. Imagine, for example, that you are an Olympic athlete and have just won a silver medal—a remarkable feat. Now imagine that you have just won the bronze medal. Which situation would make you feel better? Rationally speaking, you should feel more pride and satisfaction with a silver medal. But what if your achievement had prompted you to engage in counterfactual thinking? What alternative would haunt your mind if you had finished in second place? Where would your focus be if you had placed third? Is it possible that the athlete who is better off objectively will feel worse?

To examine this question, Medvec and others (1995) videotaped 41 athletes in the 1992 summer Olympic Games at the moment they realized that they had won a silver or a bronze medal and again, later, during the medal ceremony. Then they showed these tapes, without sound, to people who did not know the order of finish. These participants were asked to observe the medalists and rate their emotional states on a scale ranging from "agony" to "ecstasy." The intriguing result, as you might expect, was that the bronze medalists, on average, seemed happier than the silver medalists. Was there any more direct evidence of counterfactual thinking? In a second study, participants who watched interviews with many of these same athletes rated the silver medalists as more negatively focused on finishing second rather than first and the bronze medalists as more positively focused on finishing third rather than fourth. For these world-class athletes, feelings of satisfaction were based more on their thoughts of what might have been than on the reality of what was.

The Fundamental Attribution Error By the time you finish reading this textbook, you will have learned the cardinal lesson of social psychology: People are profoundly influenced by the *situational* contexts of their behavior—or, as Samuel Sommers (2011) put it, *Situations Matter*. This point is not as obvious as it may seem. For instance, parents are often surprised to hear that their impossibly mischievous child is a perfect angel in the classroom. And students are often surprised to observe that their favorite professor, so eloquent in the lecture hall, may stumble over words in less formal gatherings. These reactions are symptomatic of a well-documented aspect of social perception. When people explain the behavior of others, they tend to overestimate the role of personal factors and overlook the impact of situations. Because this bias is so pervasive (and sometimes so misleading) it has been called the **fundamental attribution error** (Ross, 1977).

Evidence of the fundamental attribution error was first reported in the Jones and Harris (1967) study described earlier, in which participants read an essay presumably written by a student. In that study, participants were more likely to infer the student's true attitude when the position taken had been freely chosen than when they thought that the student had been assigned to it. But look again at Figure 4.5, and you'll notice that even when participants thought that the student had no choice but to assert a position, they still used the speech to infer his or her attitude. This finding has been repeated many times. Whether the essay topic is nuclear power, abortion, drug laws, or the death penalty, the results are essentially the same (Jones, 1990).

People fall prey to the fundamental attribution error even when they are fully aware of the situation's impact on behavior. In one experiment, the participants were themselves assigned to take a position, whereupon they swapped essays and rated each other. Remarkably, they still jumped to conclusions about each other's attitudes (Miller et al., 1981). In another experiment, participants inferred attitudes from a speech even when they were the ones who had assigned the position to be taken (Gilbert & Jones, 1986).

A fascinating study by Lee Ross and his colleagues (1977) demonstrates the fundamental attribution error in a familiar setting, the TV quiz show. By a flip of the coin, participants in this study were randomly assigned to play the role of either the questioner or the contestant in a quiz game while spectators looked on. In front of the contestant and spectators, the experimenter instructed each questioner to write 10 challenging questions from his or her own store of general knowledge. If you are a trivia buff, you can imagine how esoteric such questions can be: Who was the founder of eBay? What team won the NHL Stanley Cup in 1976? It is no wonder that contestants correctly answered only about 40% of the questions asked. When the game was over, all participants rated the questioner's and contestant's general knowledge on a scale of 0 to 100.

Picture the events that transpired. The questioners appeared more knowledgeable than the contestants. After all, they knew all the answers. But a moment's reflection should remind us that the situation put the questioner at a distinct advantage (there were no differences between the two groups on an objective test of general knowledge). Did participants take the questioner's advantage into account, or did they assume that the questioners actually had greater knowledge? The results were startling. Spectators rated the questioners as above average in their general knowledge and the contestants as below average. The contestants even rated themselves as inferior to their partners. Like the spectators, they too were fooled by the loaded situation (see ● Figure 4.6).

What's going on here? Why do social perceivers consistently make assumptions about persons and fail to appreciate the impact of situations? According to Daniel Gilbert and Patrick Malone (1995), the problem stems in part from *how* we make attributions. Attribution theorists used to assume that people survey all the evidence and then decide on whether to make a personal or a situational attribution. Instead, it appears that social perception is a two-step process: First, we identify the behavior and make a quick personal attribution; then we correct or adjust that inference to account for situational influences. At least for those raised in a Western culture, the first step is simple and automatic, like a reflex; the second requires attention, thought, and effort.

Several research findings support this hypothesis. First, without realizing it, people often form impressions of others based on a quick glimpse at a face or fleeting sample of behavior (Kressel & Uleman, 2015; Uleman et al., 2012). Second, perceivers are *more* likely

● **FIGURE 4.6**

Fundamental Attribution Error and the TV Quiz Show

Even though the simulated quiz show situation placed questioners in an obvious position of advantage over contestants, observers rated the questioners as more knowledgeable (right). Questioners did not overrate their general knowledge (left), but contestants rated themselves as inferior (middle) and observers rated them as inferior as well. These results illustrate the fundamental attribution error.

Based on Ross, L., Amabile, T.M., & Steinmetz, J.L. (1977). Social roles, social control, and biases in social-perception processes. *Journal of Personality and Social Psychology, 35*, 485–494.

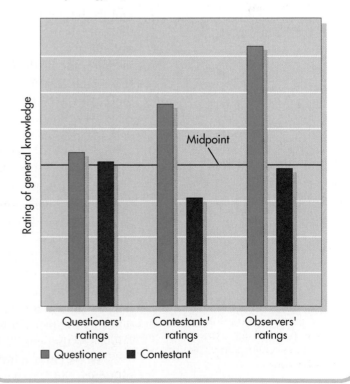

■ Questioner   ■ Contestant

Roth Stock/Everett Collection

How knowledgeable is this man? Alex Trebek has hosted the TV quiz show *Jeopardy!* since 1984. As host, Trebek reads questions to contestants and then reveals the correct answers. In light of the quiz show study by Ross and others (1977), which illustrates the fundamental attribution error, viewers probably see Trebek as highly knowledgeable, despite knowing that the answers he recites are provided to him as part of his job.

to commit the fundamental attribution error when they are cognitively busy, or distracted, as they observe the target person than when they pay full attention (Gilbert et al., 1992; Trope & Alfieri, 1997). Since the two-step model predicts that personal attributions are automatic but that the later adjustment for situational factors requires conscious thought, it makes sense to suggest that when attention is divided, when the attribution is made hastily, or when perceivers lack motivation, the second step suffers more than the first. As Gilbert and his colleagues (1988) put it, "The first step is a snap, but the second one's a doozy" (p. 738).

Why is the first step such a snap, and why does it seem so natural for people to assume a link between acts and personal dispositions? One possible reason is based on Heider's (1958) insight that people see others' dispositions in behavior because of a perceptual bias, something like an optical illusion. When you listen to a speech or watch a show, the actor is the conspicuous *figure* of your attention; the situation fades into the *background* ("out of sight, out of mind"). According to Heider, people attribute events to factors that are perceptually conspicuous, or *salient*. To test this hypothesis, Shelley Taylor and Susan Fiske (1975) varied the seating arrangements of observers who watched as two actors engaged in a carefully staged conversation. In each session, the participants were seated so that they faced actor A, actor B, or both actors. When later questioned about their observations, most participants rated the actor they faced as the more dominant member of the pair, the one who set the tone and direction.

■ Culture and Attribution

In the fifth century B.C.E., Herodotus, a Greek historian, argued that Greeks and Egyptians thought differently because the Greeks wrote from left to right and the Egyptians from right to left. Many years later, inspired by anthropologist Edward Sapir, Benjamin Lee Whorf (1956) theorized that the language people speak—the words, the rules, and so on—can influence the way they conceptualize the world. To illustrate, he pointed to cultural variations in the use of words to represent reality. He noted that the Hanunoo of the Philippines have 92 different terms for rice, in contrast to the crude distinction North Americans make between "white rice" and "brown rice." Similarly, while English speakers have one word for snow, Eskimos have several words, which, Whorf argued, enables them to make distinctions that others may miss between "falling snow, snow on the ground, snow packed hard like ice, slushy snow, wind-driven flying snow—whatever the situation may be" (p. 216).

As a result of many years of research, it is now clear that language and culture can influence the way people think about time, space, objects, and other aspects of the physical world around them. Consider our perceptions of color. The rainbow is a continuum of light varying smoothly between the shortest and longest wavelengths of the visible spectrum. Yet when we look at it, we see distinct classes of color that correspond to "red," "orange," "yellow," "green," "blue," and so on. Languages differ in the parts of the color spectrum that are named. In Papua, New Guinea, where Berinmo speakers distinguish between green and brown (they single out a form of "khaki" as the color of dead leaves), an object reflecting light at 450 nanometers would be called green. Yet many English speakers, who distinguish between colors that cross the blue-green part of the spectrum, might see that same object as blue (Özgen, 2004).

Just as culture influences the way we perceive the physical world, it can also influence the way we view individuals and their place in the social world around them. Hence, although attribution researchers used to assume that people all over the world explained human behavior in the same ways, it is now clear that cultures shape in subtle but profound ways the kinds of attributions we make about people, their behavior, and social situations (Nisbett, 2003).

Culture and the Fundamental Attribution Error Consider the contrasting orientations between Western "individualist" cultures (whose members tend to believe that persons are autonomous, motivated by internal forces, and responsible for their own actions) and non-Western "collectivist" cultures (whose members take a more holistic view that emphasizes the relationship between persons and their surroundings). Do these differing worldviews influence the attributions we make? Is the fundamental attribution error is a uniquely Western phenomenon?

To answer these questions, Joan Miller (1984) asked Americans and Asian Indians of varying ages to describe the causes of positive and negative behaviors they had observed in their lives. Among young children, there were no cultural differences. With increasing age, however, the American participants made more personal attributions, while the Indians made more situational attributions (see ● Figure 4.7). Testing this hypothesis in different ways, other studies as well have revealed that people form habits of thought, learning to make attributions according to culturally formed beliefs about the causes of human behavior (Miller et al., 2011; Miyamoto & Kitayama, 2002; Na & Kitayama, 2011).

> Like social psychologists, people are sensitive to situational causes when explaining the behavior of others.
>
> **FALSE**

● **FIGURE 4.7**

Fundamental Attribution Error: A Western Bias?

American and Asian Indian participants of varying ages described the causes of negative actions they had observed. Among young children, there were no cultural differences. With increasing age, however, Americans made more personal attributions and Indian participants made more situational attributions. Explanations for positive behaviors followed a similar pattern. This finding suggests that the fundamental error is a Western phenomenon.

Based on Miller, J. G. (1984). Culture and the development of everyday social explanation. *Journal of Personality and Social Psychology, 46,* 961–978. Copyright © 1984 by the American Psychological Association.

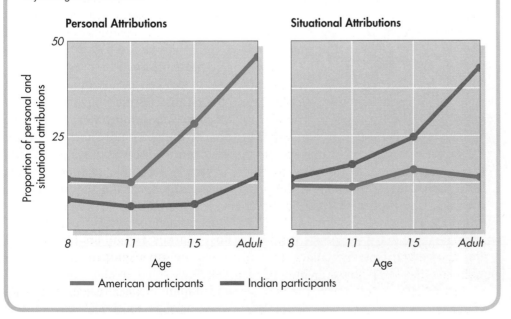

In all cultures of the world, individual members vary in their wealth, material possessions, education, and prestige. These differences in social class can be seen as yet another cultural influence on attributions. People in upper social classes, relative to those less fortunate, have more choices to make, more opportunities, and greater control over the lives (Fiske & Markus, 2012; Kraus et al., 2012). Consistent with these differences, recent research shows that people in the upper social classes are more likely than those in the lower classes to see behavior in general as caused by internal personal traits (Varnum et al., 2012).

Focal Objects and Backgrounds Ara Norenzayan and Richard Nisbett (2000) note that cultural differences in attribution are founded on varying folk theories about human causality. Western cultures, they note, emphasize the individual person and his or her attributes, whereas East Asian cultures focus on the background or field that surrounds that person. To test this hypothesis, they showed American and Japanese college students underwater scenes featuring a cast of small fish, small animals, plants, rocks, and coral and one or more large, fast-moving *focal* fish, the stars of the show. Moments later, when asked to recount what they had seen, both groups recalled details about the focal fish to a nearly equal extent, but the Japanese reported far more details about the supporting cast in the background. Other researchers have also observed cultural differences in the extent to which people notice, track, think about, and remember the details of focal objects versus their contexts (Kitayama et al., 2003; Masuda & Nisbett, 2006; Savani & Markus, 2012).

Cultural differences in terms of what people focus on can be seen in natural settings outside the psychology laboratory. For example, Takahiko Masuda and others (2008) found that the art created in Western countries—whether the artists were professionals or schoolchildren—tends to highlight individual people and objects, whereas art created in East Asia dedicates more space to backgrounds and scenery (see ● Figure 4.8). Today, this difference in emphasis can be seen on the Internet. Comparative analyses show Western websites tend to present a small number of central details on a page, while East Asian websites contain more information overall, including more peripheral details (Wang et al., 2012). Similarly, while the *focal face* tends to dominate Facebook profile pictures posted in Western countries, more *background* space appears in Facebook profile pictures in East Asian cultures (Huang & Park, 2013).

Moving from visual representations into the world of sports, Hazel Rose Markus and others (2006) compared the way Olympic performances were described in the United States and Japan. These researchers analyzed newspaper and TV coverage in

● FIGURE 4.8

East Asian and Western Art

As demonstrated by these pieces of thirteenth-century art, East Asian art tends to have higher horizons and smaller people-to-scenery ratios (left). By contrast, Western art tends to occupy more space focusing on people (right).

RMN-Grand Palais/Art Resource, NY

Icon of Santa Marina and stories of his life, 13th century Byzantine art. Church of the Holy Cross, Pedhoulas, Nicosia, Cyprus. / De Agostini Picture Library / A. Dagli Orti / Bridgeman Images

these countries and discovered that although everyone attributed victory and defeat to the athletes, American media were more likely to focus on an athlete's unique personal attributes such as speed, strength, health, and determination): "I just stayed focused," said Misty Hyman, American gold medalist swimmer. "It was time to show the world what I could do." In contrast, Japanese media were also more likely and more fully to report on an athlete's background and the role of others such as parents, coaches, and competitors. Woman's marathon gold medalist Naoko Takahashi explained her own success this way: "Here is the best coach in the world, the best manager in the world, and all of the people who support me—all of these things were getting together and became a gold medal."

Increasingly, the world is becoming a global village characterized by more and more racial and ethnic diversity within countries. Many people who migrate from one country to another become *bicultural* in their identity, retaining some ancestral manners of thought while adopting some of the lifestyles and values of their new homeland. How might these bicultural individuals make attributions for human behavior? Is it possible that they view people through one cultural frame or the other, depending on which one is brought to mind? It's interesting that when shown a picture of one fish swimming ahead of a group, and asked why, Americans see the lone fish as *leading* the others (a personal attribution), while Chinese see the same fish as being *chased* by the others (a situational attribution). But what about bicultural social perceivers? In a study of China-born students attending college in California, researchers presented images symbolizing one of the two cultures (such as the U.S. and Chinese flags), administered the fish test, and found that compared to students exposed to the American images, those who saw the Chinese images made more situational attributions, seeing the lone fish as being chased rather than as leading. Apparently, it is possible for us to hold differing cultural worldviews at the same time and to perceive others through either lens, depending on which culture is brought to mind (Hong et al., 2000; Oyserman & Lee, 2008).

◼ Motivational Biases

As objective as we try to be, our social perceptions are sometimes colored by personal hopes, needs, wishes, and preferences. This tendency shows itself in the officiating controversies of the Olympics every four years, in other competitive sports, and in talent contests such as *American Idol, The Voice,* and *The X Factor*.

Wishful Seeing   To illustrate wishful seeing in action, look at the object in ● Figure 4.9. What do you see? In a series of studies, Emily Balcetis and David Dunning (2006) showed stimuli like this one to college students who thought that they were participating in a taste-testing experiment. The students were told that they would be randomly assigned to taste either freshly squeezed orange juice or a greenish, foul-smelling "organic" drink—depending on whether a letter or a number was flashed on a laptop computer. For those told that a letter would assign them to the orange juice condition, 72% saw the letter *B*. For those told that a number would assign them to the orange juice, 61% saw the number *13*. In another study, research participants in a laboratory were quicker to identify rapidly presented food words on a computer screen when they were hungry than when they had recently eaten (Radel & Clement-Guillotin, 2012). In some very basic ways, people have a tendency to see what they want to see (Dunning & Balcetis, 2013).

● **FIGURE 4.9**

Motivated Visual Perception: How People See What They Want to See

Look at the image below. What do you see, the letter *B* or the number *13*? The stimulus itself is ambiguous and can plausibly be seen either way. Research participants who thought they were in a taste-testing experiment were told that they would be assigned to taste orange juice or a foul-smelling green drink depending on whether a letter or a number was flashed on a laptop computer. For those told that a *letter* would yield orange juice, 72% saw the image as *B*. For those told that a *number* would yield orange juice, 61% saw a *13*. This difference shows that sometimes people see what they *want* to see.

From Balcetis, E., & Dunning, D. (2006). See what you want to see: Motivational influences on visual perception. *Journal of Personality and Social Psychology, 91*, 612–625. Copyright © 2006 by the American Psychological Association. Reprinted by permission.

In a particularly ingenious program of research on "wishful seeing," Balcetis and Dunning (2010) wondered if people would judge objects that they want to be physically closer than more neutral objects. In one study, college students who were thirsty (fed pretzels without water) compared to those who were quenched (drank as much water as they wanted) estimated that a bottle of water across a table was 3 inches closer to them. In a second study, students estimated their distance in a room from a $100 bill as 8 inches closer when they thought they could win it than when it had no potential value. In a third study, participants took part in a beanbag toss in which they tried to hit a target on the floor that was 13 feet away. When the target was said to be worth $25 compared to when it had $0 value, participants underthrew the beanbag by an average of 9 inches—suggesting that they perceived the target to be closer than it was.

Need for Self-Esteem   Motivations can bias our social perceptions in other ways as well. In Chapter 3, we saw that people have a strong need for self-esteem, a motive that can lead us to make favorable, self-serving, and one-sided attributions for our own behavior. Research with students, teachers, parents, workers, athletes, and others shows that people tend to take more credit for success than they do blame for failure. This self-serving bias in attribution holds even when people outperform a competitor who is incompetent (Zell et al., 2015)! Similarly, other research shows that people seek more information about their strengths than about weaknesses, overestimate their contributions to group efforts, exaggerate their control, and predict an optimistic and rosy future. This positivity bias in attributions is ubiquitous. Based on a meta-analysis of 266 studies involving thousands of participants, Amy Mezulis and others (2004) found that except in some Asian cultures, "the self-serving bias is pervasive in the general population" (p. 711).

According to Dunning (2005), the need for self-esteem can bias social perceptions in other subtle ways too, even when we don't realize that the self is implicated. For example, do you consider yourself to be a "people person," or are you more of a "task-oriented" type? And which of the two styles do you think makes for great leadership? It turns out that students who describe themselves as people-oriented see social skills as necessary for good leadership, whereas those who are more task-focused see a task orientation as better for leadership. Hence, people tend to judge favorably others who are similar to themselves rather than different on key characteristics (McElwee et al., 2001).

Sometimes *ideological motives* can color our attributions for the behavior of others. In the United States, it is common for political conservatives to blame poverty, crime, and other social problems on an "underclass" of people who are uneducated, immoral, lazy, or self-indulgent; in contrast, liberals often attribute these same problems to social and economic institutions that favor powerful groups over others. Do conservatives and liberals think differently about the causes of human behavior, or do the attributions they make depend on whether the particular behavior they're trying to explain fits with their ideology? Linda Skitka and others (2002) had college students who identified themselves as conservative or liberal make attributions for various events. They found that even though participants in general made personal attributions, as Westerners reflexively tend to do, they corrected for situational factors when ideologically motivated to do so. To explain why a prisoner was paroled, conservatives were more likely to believe that the facility was overcrowded (a situational attribution) than that the prisoner had reformed (a personal attribution); to explain why a man lost his job, liberals were more likely to blame the company's finances (a situational attribution) than the worker's poor performance (a personal attribution).

Belief in a Just World   At times, personal defensive motives lead us to blame others for their misfortunes. Consider the following classic experiment. Participants thought they were taking part in an emotion-perception study. One person, actually a confederate, was selected randomly to take a memory test while the others looked on. Each time the confederate made a mistake, she was jolted by a painful electric shock (actually, there was no shock; what participants saw was a staged videotape). Since participants knew that only the luck of the draw had kept them off the "hot seat," you might think they would react with sympathy and compassion. Not so. In fact, they belittled the hapless confederate (Lerner & Simmons, 1966).

Melvin Lerner (1980) argues that the tendency to be critical of victims stems from our deep-seated **belief in a just world**. According to Lerner, people need to view the world as a just place in which we "get what we deserve" and "deserve what we get"—a world where hard work and clean living always pay off and where laziness and a sinful lifestyle are punished. To believe otherwise is to concede that we, too, are vulnerable to the cruel twists and turns of fate. A good deal of research supports this theory (Hafer & Bègue, 2005). Research also suggests that the belief in a just world can help victims cope and serves as a buffer against stress. But how might this belief system influence perceptions of *others?* If people cannot help or compensate the victims of misfortune, they turn on them. Thus, it is often assumed that poor people are lazy, that crime victims are careless, that battered wives provoke their abusive husbands, and that gay men and women with AIDS are promiscuous. As you might expect, cross-nation comparisons reveal that people in poorer countries are less likely than those in more affluent countries to believe in a just world (Furnham, 2003). Similarly, as you might expect, political ideology can skew the belief in a just world. In a study of whether U.S. citizens believe in the ideal that America is a land of opportunity in which upward social mobility enables poor children to become successful adults, politically liberal respondents believe that there is less social mobility relative to conservative respondents (Chambers et al., 2015).

The tendency to disparage victims may seem like a symptom of the fundamental attribution error: too much focus on the person and not enough on the situation. But the conditions that trigger this tendency suggest there is more to it. Over the years, studies have shown that accident victims are held more responsible for their fate when the damages from the accident are severe rather than mild (Walster, 1966), when the victim's situation is similar to the perceiver's (Shaver, 1970), when the perceiver is generally anxious about threats to the self (Thornton, 1992), and when the perceiver identifies with the victim (Aguiar et al., 2008). Apparently, the more threatened we feel by an apparent injustice, the greater is the need to protect ourselves from the dreadful implication that it could happen to us—an implication that we defend by disparaging the victim. Ironically, recent research shows that people may also satisfy their belief in a just world by *enhancing* members of disadvantaged groups—for example, by inferring that poor people are happy and that obese people are sociable, both attributes that restore justice by compensation (Kay & Jost, 2003; Kay et al., 2005).

In a laboratory experiment that reveals part of this process at work, participants watched a TV news story about a boy who was robbed and beaten. Some were told that the boy's assailants were captured, tried, and sent to prison. Others were told that the assailants fled the country, never to be brought to trial—a story that strains one's belief in a just world. Afterward, participants were asked to name as quickly as they could the colors in which various words in a list were typed (for

Bernard Schoenbaum/The New Yorker Collection/Cartoon Bank.com

"And see that you place the blame where it will do the most good."

Attributions of blame are often biased by self-serving motivations.

belief in a just world The belief that individuals get what they deserve in life, an orientation that leads people to disparage victims.

example, the word *chair* may have been written in blue, *floor* in yellow, and *wide* in red). When the words themselves were neutral, all participants—regardless of which story they had seen—were equally fast at naming the colors. But when the words pertained to justice (words such as *fair* and *unequal*), those who had seen the justice-threatened version of the story were more distracted by the words and hence slower to name the colors. In fact, the more distracted they were, the more they derogated the victim. With their cherished belief in a just world threatened, these participants became highly sensitive to the concept of "justice" and quick to disparage the innocent victim (Hafer, 2000).

Integration: From Dispositions to Impressions

When behavior is attributed to situational factors, we do not make strong inferences about the actor. However, personal attributions often lead us to infer that a person has a certain disposition—that the leader of a failing business is incompetent, for example, or that the enemy who extends an olive branch wants peace. Human beings are not one-dimensional, however, and one trait does not constitute a full person. To have a complete picture of someone, social perceivers must assemble the various bits and pieces into a unified impression.

■ Information Integration: The Arithmetic

Once personal attributions are made, how are they combined into a single coherent picture of a person? How do we approach the process of **impression formation**? Do we simply add up all of a person's traits and calculate a mental average, or do we combine the information in more complicated ways? Anyone who has written or received letters of recommendation will surely appreciate the practical implications. Suppose you're told that an applicant is friendly and intelligent, two highly favorable qualities. Would you be more or less impressed if you then learned that this applicant was also prudent and even-tempered, two moderately favorable qualities? If you are more impressed, then you are intuitively following a *summation* model of impression formation: The more positive traits there are, the better. If you are less impressed, then you are using an *averaging* model: The higher the average value of all the various traits, the better.

To quantify the formation of impressions, Norman Anderson (1968) had participants rate the desirability of 555 traits on a 7-point scale. By calculating the average ratings, he obtained a *scale value* for each trait (*sincere* had the highest scale value; *liar* had the lowest). In an earlier study, Anderson (1965) used similar values and compared the summation and averaging models. Specifically, he asked a group of participants to rate how much they liked a person described by two traits with extremely high scale values (*H, H*). A second group received a list of four traits that included two that were high and two that were moderately high in their scale values (*H, H, M1, M1*). In a third group, participants received two extremely low, negative traits (*L, L*). In a fourth group, they received four traits, including two that were low and two that were moderately low (*L, L, M2, M2*). What effect did the moderate traits have on impressions? As predicted by an averaging model, the moderate traits diluted from rather than added to the impact of the highly positive and negative traits. The practical advice for those who write letters of recommendation is clear: Applicants are better off if their letters include only the most glowing comments and omit favorable remarks that are somewhat more guarded in nature.

After extensive amounts of research, it appears that although people do tend to combine traits by averaging, the process is more complicated. Consistent with

impression formation The process of integrating information about a person to form a coherent impression.

Anderson's (1981) **information integration theory**, impressions formed of others are based on a combination, or integration, of (1) personal dispositions and the current state of the perceiver and (2) a *weighted* average, not a simple average, of the target person's characteristics (Kashima & Kerekes, 1994). Let's look more closely at these two sets of factors.

■ Deviations From the Arithmetic

Like other aspects of our social perceptions and attributions, impression formation does not follow the rules of cold logic. Weighted averaging may describe the way most people combine different traits, but the whole process begins with a warm-blooded human perceiver, not a computer. Thus, certain deviations from the "arithmetic" are inevitable.

Perceiver Characteristics   To begin with, each of us differs in terms of the kinds of impressions we form of others. Some people seem to measure others with an intellectual yardstick; others look for physical beauty, a warm smile, a good sense of humor, or a firm handshake. Whatever the attribute, each of us is more likely to notice certain traits than others (Bargh et al., 1988; Higgins et al., 1982). Thus, when people are asked to describe a group of target individuals, there's typically more overlap between the various descriptions provided by the same perceiver than there is between those provided for the same target (Dornbusch et al., 1965; Park, 1986). Part of the reason for differences among perceivers is that we tend to use ourselves as a standard, or frame of reference, when evaluating others. Compared with the inert couch potato, for example, the high-energy athlete is more likely to see others as less active.

A perceiver's current mood state can also influence the impressions formed of others (Forgas, 2000). In a classic experiment, Joseph Forgas and Gordon Bower (1987) told research participants that they had performed very well or poorly on a test of social adjustment. This positive feedback not only altered their moods but affected their view of other people. When presented with behavioral information about various characters, participants spent more time attending to positive facts and formed more favorable impressions when they were happy than when they were sad. Follow-up research has shown that people who are induced into a happy mood are also more optimistic, more lenient, and less critical in the attributions they make for others who succeed or fail (Forgas & Locke, 2005). In a positive mood, we are also more likely to interpret another person's smile as genuine and heartfelt (Forgas & East, 2008a), more trusting and gullible in judging someone who is lying (Forgas & Rebekah, 2008), and more likely to form a quick impression of someone based on the first information we receive (Forgas, 2011).

Embodiment Effects   Current mood is one aspect of our temporary state that can influence how we perceive other people. More and more, social psychologists are also finding that human thought is "embodied"—that the way we view ourselves and others is affected by the physical position, orientation, sensations, and movements of our bodies (Lakoff & Johnson, 1999; Niedenthal et al., 2005).

A number of studies illustrate *embodiment effects* in social perception. Consider the physical sensations of warmth and cold. The language we use tells us that people equate physical and social temperature—as when we describe someone as having a "warm personality" or "giving the cold shoulder." In fact, research has shown that warm–cold is one of the most powerful dimensions in terms of the way we judge others. As we will see shortly, once we see a person as warm versus cold we assume that this person is also trustworthy, friendly,

information integration theory
The theory that impressions are based on (1) perceiver dispositions and (2) a weighted average of a target person's traits.

caring, and helpful. Of course, warmth is also a physical sensation that because of early life experiences we tend to associate with shelter, safety, and nourishment. Would feeling warm, physically, influence our social perceptions? In one study, Lawrence Williams and John Bargh (2008) asked research participants to hold a cup of hot or iced coffee just before they read about and evaluated a fictitious target person. Compared to those who held the iced coffee, those who held the hot drink described the target as warmer, more generous, and more caring. In a second study, participants who were seated in a warm room, compared to those in a colder room, reported feeling interpersonally closer to the experimenter (Ijzerman & Semin, 2009).

These results may seem far-fetched, but other studies have also demonstrated embodiment effects in social perception. In one study, participants made harsher moral judgments about the behavior of other people when they were given a bitter herbal mix rather than a sweet berry punch or water to drink during the experiment (Eskine et al., 2011). In a second study, participants on a computer judged people in photographs to be more trustworthy when they were induced to pull the palm of their hand up against the underside of the desk (a motion that we associate with approach) than when they were induced to press that same palm down against the top of the desk (a motion we associate with avoidance) (Slepian et al., 2012). These embodiment effects may be rooted in the brain. Social neuroscience research shows that physical warmth and social closeness activate neural activity in the same region: The structure that regulates body temperature may also regulate feelings of social warmth (Inagaki & Eisenberger, 2013).

Priming Effects   The combined effects of stable perceiver differences, fluctuating moods, and bodily sensations point to an important conclusion: To some extent, impression formation is in the eye of the beholder. The characteristics we tend to see in other people also change from time to time, depending on recent experiences. Have you ever noticed that once a seldom-used word slips into a conversation or appears on a blog, it is often repeated over and over again? If so, then you have observed **priming**, the tendency for frequently or recently used concepts to come to mind easily and influence the way we interpret new information.

The effect of priming on person impressions was first demonstrated by E. Tory Higgins and others (1977). Research participants were presented with a list of trait words, ostensibly as part of an experiment on memory. In fact, the task was designed as a priming device to plant certain ideas in their minds. Some participants read words that evoked a positive image: *brave, independent, adventurous*. Others read words that evoked a more negative image: *reckless, foolish, careless*. Later, in what they thought to be an unrelated experiment, participants read about a man named Donald who climbed mountains, drove in a demolition derby, and tried to cross the Atlantic Ocean in a sailboat. As predicted, their impressions of Donald were shaped by the trait words they had earlier memorized. Those exposed to positive words later formed more favorable impressions of him than those exposed to negative words. All participants read exactly the same description, yet they formed different impressions depending on what concept was already on their minds to be used as a basis for comparison (Mussweiler & Damisch, 2008). In fact, priming seems to work best when the prime words are presented so rapidly that people are not even aware of the exposure (Bargh & Pietromonaco, 1982).

Our motivations and even our social behaviors are also subject to the automatic effects of priming without awareness. In one provocative study, John Bargh and Tanya Chartrand (1999) gave participants a "word search" puzzle that contained

priming   The tendency for recently used or perceived words or ideas to come to mind easily and influence the interpretation of new information.

either neutral words or words associated with achievement motivation (*strive, win, master, compete, succeed*). Afterward, the participants were left alone and given 3 minutes to write down as many words as they could form from a set of Scrabble letter tiles. When the 3-minute limit was up, they were signaled over an intercom to stop. Did these participants, who were driven to obtain a high score, stop on cue or continue to write? Through the use of hidden cameras, the experimenters observed that 57% of those primed with achievement-related words continued to write after the stop signal, compared to only 22% in the control group.

Looking at priming effects on social behavior, Bargh, Chen, and Burrows (1996) gave people 30 sets of words presented in scrambled order ("he it hides finds instantly") and told them to use some of the words in each set to form grammatical sentences. After explaining the test, which would take 5 minutes, the experimenter told participants to locate him down the hall when they were finished so he could administer a second task. So far so good. But when participants found the experimenter, he was in the hallway immersed in conversation, and he stayed in that conversation for 10 full minutes without acknowledging their presence. What's a person to do, wait patiently or interrupt? The participants didn't know it, but some had worked on a scrambled word test that contained many "politeness" words (*yield, respect, considerate, courteous*), whereas others had been exposed to words related to rudeness (*disturb, intrude, bold, bluntly*). Would these test words secretly prime participants, a few minutes later, to behave in one way or the other? Yes. Compared with those given the neutral words to unscramble, participants primed for rudeness were more likely—and those primed for politeness were less likely—to break in and interrupt the experimenter (see ● Figure 4.10).

What accounts for this effect of priming, not only on our social perceptions but also on our behavior? The link between perception and behavior is automatic; it happens like a mindless reflex. Present scrambled words that prime the "elderly" stereotype (*old, bingo*) and research participants walk out of the experiment more slowly as if mimicking an elderly person (Dijksterhuis & Bargh, 2001). But why? Joseph Cesario and others (2006) suggest that the automatic priming of behavior is an adaptive social mechanism that helps us to prepare for upcoming encounters with a primed target if we are so motivated. After measuring participants' attitudes toward the elderly, these researchers predicted and found that those who liked old people walked more slowly after priming (as if synchronizing with a slow friend), while those who disliked old people walked more quickly (as if fleeing from such an interaction).

Target Characteristics   Just as not all social perceivers are created equal, neither are all traits created equal. In recent years, personality researchers have discovered, across cultures, that individuals can reliably be distinguished from one another along five broad traits, or factors: extroversion, emotional stability, openness to experience, agreeableness, and conscientiousness (De Raad, 2000; McCrae

● **FIGURE 4.10**

The Priming of Social Behavior Without Awareness

Would waiting participants interrupt the busy experimenter? Compared with those who had previously been given neutral words to unscramble (center), participants given politeness words were less likely to cut in (left), and those given rudeness words were more likely to cut in (right). These results show that priming can influence not only our social judgments but our behavior as well.

Based on Bargh, J. A., Chen, M., & Burrows, L. (1996). Automaticity of social behavior: Direct effects of trait construct and stereotype activation on action. *Journal of Personality and Social Psychology, 71,* 230–244. Copyright © 1996 by the American Psychological Association.

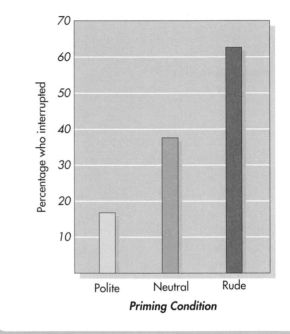

& Costa, 2003; Wiggins, 1996). Some of these factors are easier to judge than others. Based on a review of 32 studies, David Kenny and others (1994) found that social perceivers are most likely to agree in their judgments of a target's extroversion: that is, the extent to which he or she is sociable, friendly, fun-loving, outgoing, and adventurous. It seems that this characteristic is easy to spot, and different perceivers often agree on it even when rating a target person whom they are seeing for the first time.

The valence of a trait—whether it is considered good or bad—also influences its impact on our final impressions. Over the years, research has shown that people exhibit a *trait negativity bias*, the tendency for negative information to weigh more heavily on our impressions than positive information (Rozin & Royzman, 2001; Skowronski & Carlston, 1989). This means that we form more extreme impressions of a person who is said to be dishonest than of one who is said to be honest. When you think about it, this makes sense. We tend to view others favorably, so we are quick to take notice and pay careful attention when this expectation is violated (Pratto & John, 1991). For that reason, one bad trait may be enough to tarnish a person's reputation, regardless of other qualities. In light of this research, Baumeister and others (2001) have concluded that bad is stronger than good in a "disappointingly relentless pattern" (p. 362).

Our positive expectations of others are so strong that the absence of a favorable evaluation may lead us to assume the worst. If you've ever read or written letters of recommendation, you will understand this next study. In evaluating people—whether it's for school or a job or membership in a social group—it is customary to comment on two characteristics of that person—warmth and competence. What if you're reading a letter that raves about how competent an applicant is but says nothing about how nice he or she is as a person? Or what if a letter comments on how nice the applicant is but says nothing about competence? No negative information is stated, but is it implied by omission? Yes. In a series of studies, Nicolas Kervyn and others (2012) found that when research participants read brief but praiseworthy evaluations of a person that focused only on competence ("seems like a very smart, hardworking, and competent person") or only on warmth ("seems like a very nice, sociable, and outgoing person"), they drew negative inferences about the dimension that was omitted. Illustrating the expression, "Damned by faint praise," Kervyn et al. referred to this result as the innuendo effect.

When you think about it, it's probably adaptive for us to stay alert for negative, potentially threatening information. Recent research suggests that people are quicker to sense their exposure to subliminally presented negative words such as *bomb*, *thief*, *shark*, and *cancer* than to positive words such as *baby*, *sweet*, *friend*, and *beach* (Dijksterhuis & Aarts, 2003). This sensitivity to negative information is found in infants less than a year old (Vaish et al., 2008). It can also be "seen" in the brain (N. K. Smith et al., 2003). In one study, Tiffany Ito and others (1998) exposed research participants to slides that depicted images that were positive (a red Ferrari, people enjoying a roller coaster), negative (a mutilated face, a handgun pointed at the camera), or neutral (a plate, a hair dryer). Using electrodes attached to participants' scalps, these researchers recorded electrical activity in different areas of the brain during the presentation. Sure enough, certain types of activity were more pronounced when participants saw negative images than when they saw stimuli that were positive or neutral. It appears, as these researchers commented, that "negative information weighs more heavily on the brain" (p. 887).

The impact of trait information on our impressions of other people depends not only on characteristics of the perceiver and target but on context as well. Think, for example, about a time when you met a person for the first time who was in the company of someone you like or dislike, or find attractive or unattractive. Would your impression of the target person be colored by this relationship? In studies of "stigma by association," John Pryor and his colleagues (2012) found that the answer is yes. Even when a target person's relationship to the positive or negative other comes about by chance, not as a matter of choice, our first impressions are influenced by it. Two other contextual factors are also particularly important: (1) implicit theories of personality and (2) the order in which we receive information about one trait relative to other traits.

Implicit Personality Theories   Whether we realize it or not, each of us harbors an *implicit personality theory*—a network of assumptions about the relationships among various types of people, traits, and behaviors. Knowing that someone has one trait leads us to infer that he or she has other traits as well (Bruner & Tagiuri, 1954; Schneider, 1973; Sedikides & Anderson, 1994). For example, you might assume that a person who is unpredictable may also be dangerous or that someone who speaks slowly is also slow-witted. You might also assume that certain traits and behaviors are linked together (Reeder, 1993; Reeder & Brewer, 1979)—that a celebrity with a sweet and beloved persona, for example, could not possibly have skeletons in the closet.

Solomon Asch (1946) was the first to discover that the presence of one trait often implies the presence of other traits. Asch told one group of research participants that an individual was "intelligent, skillful, industrious, warm, determined, practical and cautious." Another group read an identical list of traits, except that the word *warm* was replaced by *cold*. Only the one term was changed, but the two groups formed very different impressions. Participants inferred that the warm person was also happier and more generous, good-natured, and humorous than the cold person. Yet when two other words were varied (*polite* and *blunt*), the differences were less pronounced. Why? Asch concluded that *warm* and *cold* are **central traits**, meaning that they imply the presence of certain other traits and exert a powerful influence on final impressions. In fact, when college students in different classes were told ahead of time that a guest lecturer was a warm or cold person, their impressions after the lecture were consistent with these beliefs, even though he gave the same lecture to everyone (Kelley 1950; Widmeyer & Loy 1988).

Is there something magical about the traits warm and cold? To learn more about the structure of implicit personality theories, Seymour Rosenberg and his colleagues (1968) handed research participants 60 cards, each with a trait word written on it, and asked them to sort the cards into piles that represented specific people, perhaps friends, co-workers, acquaintances, or celebrities. The traits were then statistically correlated to determine how often they appeared together in the same pile. The results were plotted to display the psychological distance between the various characteristics. The "map" shown in ● Figure 4.11 shows that the traits—positive and negative alike—were best captured by two dimensions: social and intellectual. Based on their review of many years of research, Susan Fiske, Amy Cuddy, and Peter Glick (2007) conclude that people differentiate each other first in terms of their warmth (*warm* is seen in such traits as friendly, helpful, and sincere), and second in terms of their competence (*competent* is seen in such traits as smart, skillful, and determined)—and that these are "universal dimensions of social cognition."

central traits   Traits that exert a powerful influence on overall impressions.

● **FIGURE 4.11**

Universal Dimensions of Social Cognition

Rosenberg and others (1968) asked people to sort 60 cards, each with a trait word on it, into piles that depicted specific individuals. Through a statistical procedure used to plot how frequently the various traits appeared together, an implicit personality theory "map" emerged. This map shows that both positive and negative traits can be ordered along two dimensions: social (warmth) and intellectual (competent). Since this study, other research has confirmed that warmth and competence are universal dimensions by which people perceive each other.

From Rosenberg, S., Nelson, C., & Vivekananthan, P. S. (1968). A multidimensional approach to the structure of personality impressions. *Journal of Personality and Social Psychology, 9,* 283–294. Copyright © 1968 by the American Psychological Association. Reprinted by permission.

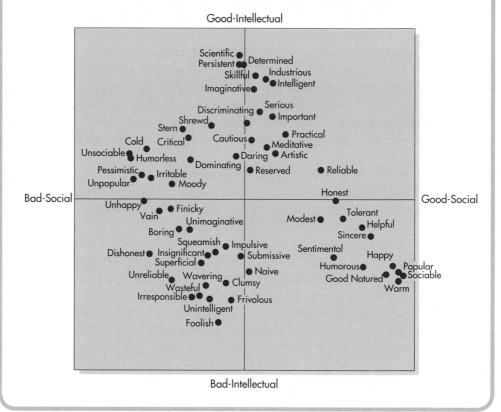

■ Perceptions of Moral Character

In addition to focusing on warmth and competence, social perceivers all over the world also form strong impressions of how *moral* people are. When you think about it, accurate perceptions of moral character are essential for social living so that we can identify whether someone we meet, and may need to rely on in the future, is moral and good—and therefore can be trusted.

Geoffrey Goodwin (2015) argues that morality is not just a third facet of social perception, but rather that it is the most important factor in the impressions we form of others. Noting that people sometimes conflate warm and moral, Goodwin and others (2014) conducted a series of studies in which they found that distinctly "moral" traits (such as *courageous, fair, principled, just, honest, trustworthy,* and *loyal*) proved more important than distinctly "warm" traits (such as *warm, sociable, happy, agreeable, enthusiastic, easygoing, fun,* and *playful*) at predicting the positive and negative impressions that people form of others. This result was the same regardless of whether participants judged real people from their own lives, U.S. presidents, fictitious individuals described in the laboratory, or deceased men and women whose *New York Times* obituaries they were given to read.

There is a growing consensus among researchers that the perception of morality plays a special role in the impressions we form of others (Brambilla & Leach, 2014). In fact, research shows that people make moral judgments about others instantly and intuitively— without intention, thought, or awareness (Haidt, 2001; Van Berkum et al., 2009). If perceptions of moral character are so basic and so adaptive, it would stand to reason that different social perceivers, despite their otherwise unique perspectives, would agree on what constitutes moral character. Does research support this hypothesis? Yes. To measure agreement rates among different social perceivers, Erik Helzer and others (2014) developed a "Moral Character Questionnaire" in which people were asked to rate the extent to which various brief statements accurately described the self, a friend, an acquaintance, and a family member. Each of the statements described a facet of moral character—such as *fairness* ("treats everyone in a similar way"), *honesty* ("tells the truth), *compassion* ("takes time out to help others"), *self-control* ("is good at resisting temptation"), *moral concern* ("thinks about how to be a good person"), and *general morality* ("is an ethical person"). The results showed that there were high levels of agreement both in participants' self-ratings, their ratings of others, and others' ratings of the participants themselves.

The Primacy Effect   The order in which a trait is discovered can also influence its impact. It is often said that first impressions are critical, and social psychologists are quick to agree. Studies show that information often has greater impact when presented early in a sequence rather than late, a common phenomenon known as the **primacy effect**.

In another of Asch's (1946) classic experiments, one group of participants learned that a person was "intelligent, industrious, impulsive, critical, stubborn, and envious." A second group received exactly the same list but in reverse order. Rationally speaking, the two groups should have felt the same way about the person. But instead, participants who heard the first list in which the more positive traits came first formed more favorable impressions than did those who heard the second list. Similar findings were obtained among participants who watched a videotape of a woman taking an SAT-like test. In all cases, she correctly answered 15 out of 30 multiple-choice questions. But participants who observed a pattern of initial success followed by failure perceived the woman as more intelligent than did those who observed the opposite pattern of failure followed by success (Jones et al., 1968). There are exceptions, but as a general rule, people tend to be more heavily influenced by the "early returns."

What accounts for this primacy effect? There are two basic explanations. The first is that once perceivers think they have formed an accurate impression of someone, they tend to pay less attention to subsequent information. Thus, when research participants read a series of statements about a person, the amount of time they spent reading each of the items declined steadily with each succeeding statement (Belmore, 1987).

Does this mean that we are doomed to a life of primacy? Not at all. If you are mentally tired or unstimulated, your attention may wane. But if you are sufficiently motivated to avoid tuning out and are not pressured to form a quick first impression, then primacy effects are diminished (Anderson & Hubert, 1963; Kruglanski & Freund, 1983). In one study, college students "leaped to conclusions" about a target person on the basis of preliminary information when they were mentally fatigued from having just taken a two-hour exam but not when they

primacy effect   The tendency for information presented early in a sequence to have more impact on impressions than information presented later.

were fresh, alert, and motivated to pay attention (Webster et al., 1996). In addition, Arie Kruglanski and Donna Webster (1996) found that some people are more likely than others to "seize" upon and "freeze" their first impressions. Apparently, individuals differ in their **need for closure**, the desire to reduce ambiguity. People who are low in this regard are open-minded, deliberate, and perhaps even reluctant to draw firm conclusions about others. In contrast, those who are high in the need for closure tend to be impulsive and impatient and to form quick and lasting judgments of others.

More unsettling is the second reason for primacy, known as the *change-of-meaning hypothesis*. Once people have formed an impression, they start to interpret inconsistent information in light of that impression. Asch's research shows just how malleable the meaning of a trait can be. When people are told that a kind person is *calm*, they assume that he or she is gentle, peaceful, and serene. When a cruel person is said to be *calm*, however, the same word is interpreted to mean cool, shrewd, and calculating. There are many examples to illustrate the point. Based on your first impression, the word *proud* can mean self-respecting or conceited, *critical* can mean astute or picky, and *impulsive* can mean spontaneous or reckless.

It is remarkable just how creative we are in our efforts to transform a bundle of contradictions into a coherent, integrated impression. For example, the person who is said to be "good" but also "a thief" can be viewed as a Robin Hood–like character (Burnstein & Schul, 1982). Asch and Henri Zukier (1984) presented people with inconsistent trait pairs and found that they used different strategies to reconcile the conflicts. For example, a brilliant-foolish person may be seen as "very bright on abstract matters, but silly about day-to-day practical tasks," a sociable-lonely person has "many superficial ties but is unable to form deep relations," and a cheerful-gloomy person may simply be someone who is "moody."

Confirmation Biases: From Impressions to Reality

It is a striking feature of human nature but too often true: Once people make up their minds about something—even if they don't have all the necessary information—they become more and more unlikely to change their minds when confronted with new evidence. People can be quite intellectually stubborn. Political leaders often refuse to withdraw support for government programs that don't work, and scientists often steadfastly defend their pet theories in the face of contradictory research data. These instances are easy to explain. Politicians and scientists have personal stakes in their opinions, as votes, pride, funding, and reputation may be at risk. But what about people who more innocently fail to revise their opinions, often to their own detriment? What about the baseball manager who clings to old strategies that don't work or the trial lawyer who consistently selects juries according to false stereotypes? Why are they often slow to face the facts? As we will see, people are subject to various **confirmation biases**—tendencies to interpret, seek, and create information in ways that verify existing beliefs.

■ Perseverance of Beliefs

Imagine you are looking at a slide that is completely out of focus. Gradually, it becomes focused enough so that the image is less blurry. At this point, the experimenter wants to know if you can recognize the picture. The response you're likely to make is interesting. Participants in experiments of this type have more trouble

need for closure The desire to reduce cognitive uncertainty, which heightens the importance of first impressions.

confirmation bias The tendency to seek, interpret, and create information that verifies existing beliefs.

making an identification if they watch the gradual focusing procedure than if they simply view the final, blurry image. In the mechanics of the perceptual process, people apparently form early impressions that interfere with their subsequent ability to "see straight" once presented with improved evidence (Bruner & Potter, 1964). As we will see in this section, social perception is subject to the same kind of interference, which is another reason why first impressions often stick like glue even after we are forced to confront information that discredits them.

Consider what happens when you're led to expect something that does not materialize. In one study, John Darley and Paget Gross (1983) asked participants to evaluate the academic potential of a 9-year-old girl named Hannah. One group was led to believe that Hannah came from an affluent community in which both parents were well-educated professionals (high expectations). A second group thought that she was from a run-down urban neighborhood and that both parents were uneducated blue-collar workers (low expectations). As shown in ● Figure 4.12, participants in the first group were slightly more optimistic in their ratings of Hannah's potential than were those in the second group. In each of these groups, however, half the participants then watched a videotape of Hannah taking an achievement test. Her performance on the tape seemed average. She correctly answered some difficult questions but missed others that were relatively easy. Look again at Figure 4.12 and you'll see that even though all participants saw the same tape, Hannah now received much lower ratings of ability from those who thought she was poor and higher ratings from those who thought she was affluent. Apparently, presenting an identical body of mixed evidence did not extinguish the biasing effects of beliefs; it *fueled* these effects.

Events that are ambiguous enough to support contrasting interpretations are like inkblots: We see or hear in them what we expect to see or hear. Illustrating the point, one group of researchers had people rate from photographs the extent to which pairs of adults and children resembled each other. Interestingly, the participants did not see more resemblance in parents and offspring than in random pairs of adults and children. Yet when told that certain pairs were related, they did "see" a resemblance, even when the relatedness information was false (Bressan & Martello, 2002). In a second study, participants listened to noisy, more or less "degraded" tape recordings of two people talking—not unlike what you hear in 9-1-1 dispatch recordings. Some participants were told that the interviewee was a crime suspect; others were told that he was a job applicant. When the speech recordings were degraded, participants were more likely to "hear" incriminating statements when they thought that the interviewee was a suspect than an applicant (Lange et al., 2011). In a third study, participants acting as mock jurors were asked to determine if the handwriting in a bank robbery note was similar to a handwriting sample taken from a suspect who had confessed or denied involvement in the crime. Consistent with expectations, participants who believed the suspect had confessed were more likely to see the two handwritings as a match—even though they were not (Kukucka & Kassin, 2014; for a discussion of the implications of "forensic confirmation biases," see Kassin, Dror, & Kukucka, 2013).

AF archive/Alamy

"Please your majesty," said the knave, "I didn't write it and they can't prove I did; there's no name signed at the end." "If you didn't sign it," said the King, "that only makes the matter worse. You must have meant some mischief, or else you'd have signed your name like an honest man."

This exchange, taken from Lewis Carroll's *Alice's Adventures in Wonderland,* illustrates the power of existing impressions.

Mixed Evidence: Does It Extinguish or Fuel First Impressions?

Participants evaluated the potential of a schoolgirl. Without seeing her test performance, those with high expectations rated her slightly higher than did those with low expectations. Among the participants who watched a tape of the girl taking a test, the expectations effect was even greater.

Based on Darley, J. M., & Gross, P. H. (1983). A hypothesis-confirming bias in labeling effects. *Journal of Personality and Social Psychology, 44*, 20–33. Copyright © 1983 by the American Psychological Association.

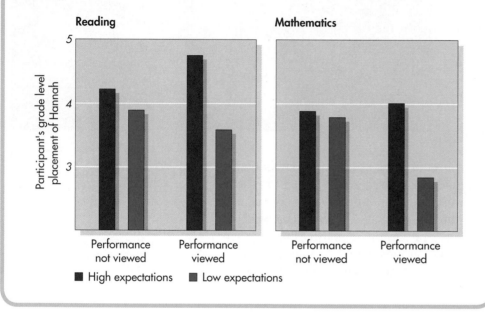

What about information that plainly disconfirms our beliefs? What then happens to our first impressions? Craig Anderson and his colleagues (1980) addressed this question by supplying participants with false information. After they had time to think about it, they were told that it was untrue. In one experiment, half the participants read case studies suggesting that people who take risks make better firefighters than do those who are cautious. The others read cases suggesting the opposite conclusion. Next, participants were asked to come up with a theory for the suggested correlation. The possibilities are easy to imagine: "He who hesitates is lost" supports risk-taking, whereas "You have to look before you leap" supports caution. Finally, participants were led to believe that the session was over and were told that the information they had received was false, manufactured for the sake of the experiment. Participants, however, did not abandon their theories about firefighters. Instead, they exhibited **belief perseverance**, a tendency to retain to one's initial beliefs even after they had been discredited.

In a brilliant illustration, Tobias Greitemeyer (2014) wondered what happens when a scientific journal retracts an article it has already published because of proof that data were fabricated and could not be trusted. To answer this question, he presented college students with a summary of a research paper "indicating" that people who experience an elevated physical height (as in riding an escalator up) are more likely to offer help to a stranger than those who experience a lowered physical height (as in riding an escalator down). Students who read this summary, compared to those who did not, were later more likely to believe the result when asked for their beliefs about the link between physical height and helping. In a third group, however, the students read after the summary that the data supporting this hypothesis had been fabricated. Did this disclosure and retraction fully erase the effect? No. Students who read the summary and retraction persevered in their belief in the result.

Why do beliefs often outlive the evidence on which they are supposed to be based? The reason is that once people form a belief, they conjure up explanations that make sense—and those explanations help to perpetuate the belief even after it has been discredited! This is what happened to the students in Greitemeyer's (2014) study. In fact, research shows that once people form an opinion, that opinion becomes strengthened just by *thinking* about the topic. And therein lies a possible solution. By asking people to consider why an *alternative* theory might be true, we can reduce or eliminate the belief perseverance effects to which they are vulnerable (Anderson & Sechler, 1986).

> People are slow to change their first impressions on the basis of new information.
> **TRUE**

belief perseverance The tendency to maintain beliefs even after they have been discredited.

■ Confirmatory Hypothesis Testing

Social perceivers are not passive recipients of information. Like detectives, we ask questions and actively search for clues. But do we seek information objectively or are we inclined to confirm the suspicions we already hold?

Mark Snyder and William Swann (1978) addressed this question by having pairs of participants who were strangers to one another take part in a getting-acquainted interview. In each pair, one participant was supposed to interview the other. But first, that participant was falsely led to believe that his or her partner was either introverted or extroverted (actually, participants were assigned to these conditions on a random basis) and was then told to select questions from a prepared list. Those who thought they were talking to an introvert chose mostly introvert-oriented questions ("Have you ever felt left out of some social group?"), whereas those who thought they were talking to an extrovert asked extrovert-oriented questions ("How do you liven up a party?"). Expecting a certain kind of person, participants unwittingly sought evidence that would confirm their expectations. By asking loaded questions, in fact, the interviewers actually gathered support for their beliefs. Thus, neutral observers who later listened to the tapes were also left with the mistaken impression that the interviewees really were as introverted or extroverted as the interviewers had assumed.

This last part of the study is powerful but in hindsight not all that surprising. Imagine yourself on the receiving end of an interview. Asked about what you do to liven up parties, you would probably talk about organizing group games, playing dance music, and telling jokes. On the other hand, if you were asked about difficult social situations, you might talk about being nervous before oral presentations or about what it feels like to be the new kid on the block. In other words, simply by going along with the questions that are asked, you supply evidence confirming the interviewer's beliefs. Thus, perceivers set in motion a vicious cycle: Thinking someone has a certain trait, they engage in a one-sided search for information. In doing so, they create a reality that ultimately supports their beliefs (Zuckerman et al., 1995).

Sadly, the fact that people can be blinded by their existing beliefs is a pervasive phenomenon with consequences. In one study, research participants reviewed a mock police file on a crime investigation into a home invasion and shooting case. The file contained weak circumstantial evidence pointing to a possible suspect. At that point, some participants but not others were asked to form and state an initial hypothesis as to the likely offender. As predicted, those who did went on to search for additional evidence and then interpret that evidence in ways that confirmed their hypothesis. In these ways, a weak suspect became the *prime* suspect (O'Brien, 2009). In a second study, researchers presented psychiatrists and medical students with an experimental patient file and found that 13% of psychiatrists and 25% of students who had made a preliminary diagnosis exhibited confirmation biases in searching for new information—and those who did were less likely than others to make the correct diagnosis and prescribed treatment (Mendel et al., 2011).

Let's stop for a moment and contemplate what all this research means for the broader question of why we often seem to resist changing our negative but mistaken impressions of others more than our positive but mistaken impressions. Jerker Denrell (2005) argued that even when we form a negative first impression of someone on the basis of all available evidence and even when we interpret that evidence accurately, our impression may be misleading. The reason is *biased*

"It is a capital mistake to theorize before you have all the evidence. It biases the judgment."

—Arthur Conan Doyle

"Of course, this could also be confirmation bias from me wanting you to get sick."

Paul Noth/New Yorker Cartoon/The Cartoon Bank

experience sampling. Meet someone who seems likable and you may interact with that person again. Then if he or she turns out to be twisted, dishonest, or self-centered, you'll be in a position to observe these traits and revise your impression. But if you meet someone you don't like, you will try to avoid that person in the future, cutting yourself off from new information and limiting the opportunity to revise your opinion. Attraction breeds interaction, which is why our negative first impressions in particular tend to persist.

■ The Self-Fulfilling Prophecy

In 1948, sociologist Robert Merton told a story about Cartwright Millingville, president of the Last National Bank during the Great Depression of the 1930s. The bank was solvent, yet a rumor began to spread that it was floundering. Within hours, hundreds of depositors were lined up to withdraw their savings before no money was left to withdraw. The rumor was false, but the bank eventually failed. Using stories such as this, Merton proposed what seemed like an outrageous hypothesis: that a perceiver's expectation can actually lead to its own fulfillment, a **self-fulfilling prophecy**.

Merton's hypothesis lay dormant within psychology until Robert Rosenthal and Lenore Jacobson (1968) published the results of a study in a book entitled *Pygmalion in the Classroom*. Noticing that teachers had higher expectations for better students, they wondered if teacher expectations *influenced* student performance rather than the other way around. To address the question, they told teachers in a San Francisco elementary school that certain pupils were on the verge of an intellectual growth spurt. The results of an IQ test were cited, but in fact, the pupils had been randomly selected. Eight months later, when real tests were administered, the "late bloomers" exhibited an increase in their IQ scores compared with children assigned to a control group. They were also evaluated more favorably by their classroom teachers.

When the Pygmalion study was first published, it was greeted with chagrin. If positive teacher expectations boost student performance, can negative expectations have the opposite effect? What about the social implications? Could it be that affluent children are destined for success and disadvantaged children are doomed to failure because educators hold different expectations for them? Many researchers were critical of the study and skeptical about the results. Unfortunately, these findings could be swept under the rug. In a review of additional studies, Rosenthal (1985) found that teachers' expectations significantly predicted students' performance 36% of the time. Fortunately, teachers are less and less able to make these accurate predictions as children graduate from one grade to the next (A. Smith et al., 1999).

How might teacher expectations be transformed into reality? There are two points of view. According to Rosenthal (2002), the process involves covert communication. The teacher forms an initial impression of students early in the school year based, perhaps, on their background or reputation, physical appearance, initial classroom performance, and standardized test scores. The teacher then alters his or her behavior in ways that are consistent with that impression. If initial

self-fulfilling prophecy The process by which one's expectations about a person eventually lead that person to behave in ways that confirm those expectations.

expectations are high rather than low, the teacher gives the student more praise, more attention, more challenging homework, and better feedback. In turn, the student adjusts his or her own behavior. If the signals are positive, the student may become energized, work hard, and succeed. If negative, there may be a loss of interest and self-confidence. The cycle is thus complete, and the expectations are confirmed.

While recognizing that this effect can occur, Lee Jussim (2012) has questioned whether teachers in real life are prone in the first place to form erroneous impressions of their students. It's true that in many naturalistic studies, in real classrooms, the expectations teachers have at the start of a school year are ultimately confirmed by their students—a result that is consistent with the notion that the teachers had a hand in producing that outcome. But that same result is also consistent with a more innocent possibility—that perhaps the expectations that teachers form of their students are *accurate*. In other words, sometimes teachers can accurately *predict* how their students will perform in the future without necessarily *influencing* that performance (Alvidrez & Weinstein, 1999).

Jussim admits that there are times when teachers stereotype a student and without realizing it behave in ways that create a self-fulfilling prophecy. But his review of the research literature suggests that evidence for *bias* is not nearly as strong as it appears on the surface. Addressing this question in a longitudinal study of mothers and their children, Stephanie Madon and others (2003) found that underage adolescents are more likely to consume alcohol when their mothers had previously expected them to. Statistical analyses revealed that this prophecy was fulfilled in part because the mothers *influence* their sons and daughters, as Rosenthal's work would suggest, but also in part because the mothers are able to *predict* their own children's behavior, as Jussim's model would suggest. In fact, a follow-up study suggests that the link between a mother's expectations and her adolescent's later alcohol consumption did not strengthen or weaken over time, remaining stable as the child moved from the seventh grade through the twelfth (Madon et al., 2006).

It is clear that self-fulfilling prophecies are at work, to a greater or lesser degree, not only in schools but also in a wide range of organizations, including the military (Kierein & Gold, 2000; McNatt, 2000). In a study of 1,000 men assigned to 29 platoons in the Israel Defense Forces, Dov Eden (1990) led some platoon leaders but not others to expect that groups of trainees they were about to receive had great potential (in fact, these groups were of average ability). After 10 weeks, the trainees assigned to the high-expectation platoons scored higher than the others on written exams and on the ability to operate a weapon. The process may also be found in the criminal justice system when police interrogate suspects. To illustrate, Kassin and others (2003) had some college students but not others commit a mock crime, stealing $100 from a laboratory. All suspects were then questioned by interrogators who were led to believe that their suspect was probably guilty or innocent. Interrogators who presumed guilt asked more incriminating questions, were more coercive, and tried harder to get the suspect to confess. In turn, this more aggressive style made the suspects sound defensive and led observers who later listened to the tapes to judge them guilty, even when they were innocent.

On a more personal level, the self-fulfilling prophecy is a process that can have particularly sad and ironic effects on people who are insecure about their social relationships. Studying what they have called the rejection prophecy, Danu

Stinson, Jessica Cameron, and others have found that (1) people who are insecure are fearful of rejection, which makes them tense and awkward in the social situations; (2) their resulting behavior is off-putting to others, which (3) increases the likelihood of rejection and reinforces their initial insecurity (Stinson et al., 2009, Cameron et al., 2010). Fortunately, there is a way to break this vicious cycle. In a three-phased study that spanned 8 weeks, Stinson and others (2011) found that participants who were provided with an early opportunity to affirm the self—by writing about values that were important to them—became more secure over time and more relaxed in their social interactions.

The self-fulfilling prophecy is a powerful phenomenon (Darley & Fazio, 1980; Harris & Rosenthal, 1985). But how does it work? As social perceivers, how do we transform our expectations of others into reality? Research suggests a three-step process. First, a perceiver forms an impression of a target person, which may be based on interactions with the target or on other information. Second, the perceiver behaves in a manner that is consistent with that first impression. Third, the target person unwittingly adjusts his or her behavior to the perceiver's actions. The net result is behavioral confirmation of the first impression (see ● Figure 4.13).

Now let's straighten out this picture. It would be a sad commentary on human nature if each of us were so easily molded by others' perceptions into appearing brilliant or stupid, introverted or extroverted, competitive or cooperative, warm or cold. The effects are well established, but there are limits. By viewing the self-fulfilling prophecy as a three-step process, social psychologists can identify the links in the chain that can be broken to prevent the vicious cycle.

Consider the first step, the link between one's expectations and one's behavior toward the target person. In the typical study, perceivers try to get to know the target on only a casual basis and are not necessarily driven to form an accurate impression. But when perceivers are highly motivated to seek the truth

● **FIGURE 4.13**

The Self-Fulfilling Prophecy as a Three-Step Process

How do people transform their expectations into reality? (1) A perceiver has expectations of a target person; (2) the perceiver then behaves in a manner consistent with those expectations; and (3) the target unwittingly adjusts his or her behavior according to the perceiver's actions.

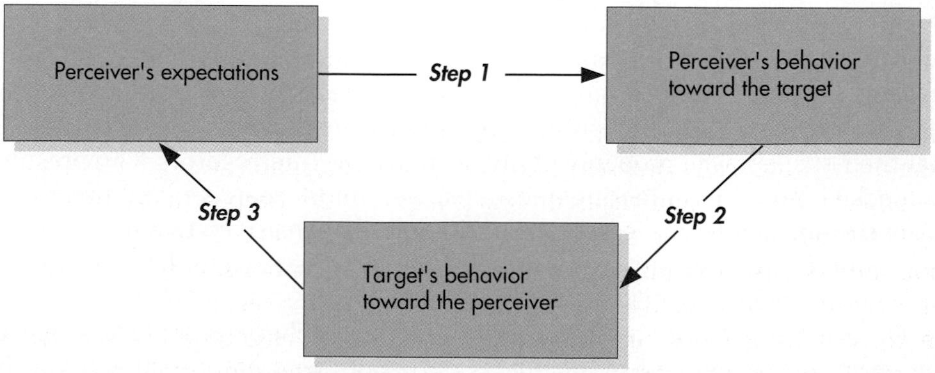

© Cengage Learning®

(as when they need to consider the target as a possible teammate or opponent), they become more objective and often do not confirm prior expectations (Harris & Perkins, 1995; Hilton & Darley, 1991).

The link between expectations and behavior depends in other ways as well on a perceiver's goals and motivations in the interaction (Snyder & Stukas, 1999). In one study, John Copeland (1994) put either the perceiver or the target into a position of relative power. In all cases, the perceiver interacted with a target person who was said to be introverted or extroverted. In half the pairs, the perceiver was given the power to accept or reject the target as a teammate for a money-winning game. In the other half, it was the target who was empowered to choose a teammate. The two participants interacted, the interaction was recorded, and neutral observers listened to the tapes and rated the target person. Did perceivers cause the targets to behave as introverted or extroverted, depending on initial expectations? Yes and no. Illustrating what Copeland called "prophecies of power," the results showed that high-power perceivers triggered the self-fulfilling prophecy, as in past research, but that low-power perceivers did not. In the low-power situation, the perceivers spent less time getting to know the target person and more time trying to be liked.

Now consider the second step, the link between a perceiver's behavior and the target's response. In the designs of much of the past research (as in much of life), target persons were not aware of the false impressions held by others. Thus, it is unlikely that Rosenthal and Jacobson's (1968) "late bloomers" knew of their teachers' high expectations or that Snyder and Swann's (1978) "introverts" and "extroverts" knew of their interviewers' misconceptions. But what if they had known? How would *you* react if you found yourself being cast in a particular light? When it happened to participants in one experiment, they managed to overcome the effect by behaving in ways that forced the perceivers to abandon their expectations (Hilton & Darley, 1985).

As you may recall from the discussion of self-verification in Chapter 3, this result is most likely to occur when the expectations of perceivers clash with a target person's own self-concept. When targets who viewed themselves as extroverted were interviewed by perceivers who believed they were introverted (and vice versa), what changed as a result of the interaction were the perceivers' beliefs, not the targets' behavior (Swann & Ely, 1984). Social perception is a two-way street; the persons we judge have their own prophecies to fulfill.

> The notion that we can create a "self-fulfilling prophecy" by getting others to behave in ways we expect is a myth.
> **FALSE**

Social Perception: The Bottom Line

Trying to understand people—whether they are world leaders, crime suspects, professional athletes, celebrities, trial lawyers, or loved ones closer to home—is no easy task. As you reflect on the material in this chapter, you will notice that there are two radically different views of social perception. One suggests that the process is quick and relatively automatic. At the drop of a hat, without much thought, effort, or awareness, people make rapid-fire snap judgments about others based on physical appearance, preconceptions, cognitive heuristics, or just a hint of behavioral evidence. According to a second view, however, the process is far more mindful. People observe others carefully and reserve judgment until their analysis of the target person, behavior, and situation is complete. As suggested by theories of attribution and information integration, the process is eminently logical. In light of recent research, it is now safe to conclude that both accounts of social perception are correct. Sometimes our judgments are made instantly; at other times, they are based on a more painstaking analysis of behavior. Either way, we often steer our interactions with others along a path that is narrowed by first impressions, a process that can set in motion a self-fulfilling prophecy. The various aspects of social perception, as described in this chapter, are summarized in ● Figure 4.14.

At this point, we must confront an important question: How *accurate* are our impressions of each other? For years, this question has proved provocative but hard to answer (Cronbach, 1955; Jussim, 2012; Kenny, 1994; Stern et al., 2013; West & Kenny, 2011). Granted, people often depart from the ideals of logic and exhibit occasional bias in their social perceptions. In this chapter alone, we have seen that perceivers typically focus on the wrong cues to judge if someone is lying; use cognitive heuristics without regard for numerical base rates; overlook the situational influences on behavior; disparage victims whose misfortunes threaten their sense of justice; form premature first impressions; and then interpret, seek, and create evidence in ways that support these impressions.

To make matters worse, we often have little awareness of our limitations, leading us to feel *overconfident* in our judgments. In a series of studies, David Dunning and his colleagues (1990) asked college students to predict how a target person would react in various situations. Some made predictions about a fellow student whom they had just met and interviewed, and others made predictions about their roommates. In both cases, participants reported their confidence in each prediction, and accuracy was determined by the responses of the target persons themselves. The result: Regardless of whether they judged a stranger or a roommate, students consistently overestimated the accuracy of their predictions. In fact, Kruger and Dunning (1999) found that people who scored low on tests of spelling, logic, grammar, and humor appreciation were later the most likely to overestimate their own performance. These results

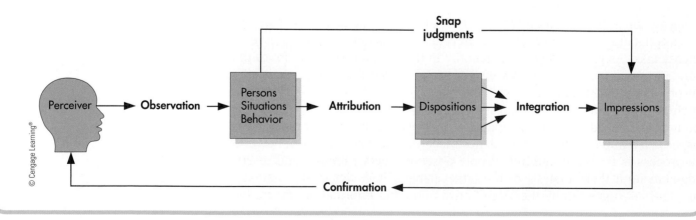

● **FIGURE 4.14**

The Processes of Social Perception

Summarizing Chapter 4, this diagram depicts the processes of social perception. As shown, it begins with the observation of persons, situations, and behavior. Sometimes we make snap judgments from these cues. At other times, we form impressions only after making attributions and integrating these attributions. Either way, our impressions are subject to confirmation biases and the risk of self-fulfilling prophecy.

suggest that poor performers may be doubly cursed: They don't know what they don't know (Dunning et al., 2003)—and they don't know they are biased (Ehrlinger et al., 2005).

Standing back from the material presented in this chapter, you may find that the list of our shortcomings, punctuated by the problem of overconfidence, is long and depressing. How can this list be reconciled with the triumphs of civilization? To put it another way: "If we're so dumb, how come we made it to the moon?" (Nisbett & Ross, 1980, p. 249). Yes, it is true that people fall prey to the biases identified by social psychologists and probably even to some that have not yet been noticed. It is also true that we often get fooled by con artists, misjudge our partners in marriage, vote for the wrong leaders, and hire the wrong job applicants, and that our biases can have real and harmful consequences—sometimes giving rise, as we'll see in Chapter 5, to stereotypes, prejudice, and discrimination. Despite our imperfections, however, there are reasons to be guardedly optimistic about our competence as social perceivers:

1. The more experience people have with each other, the more accurate they are. For example, although people have a limited ability to assess the personality or emotional states of strangers they meet in a laboratory, they are generally better at judging their own friends and acquaintances (Kenny & Acitelli, 2001; Levesque, 1997; Malloy & Albright, 1990; Sternglanz & DePaulo, 2004).
2. Although we are not good at making global judgments of others (that is, at knowing what people are like across a range of settings), we are able to make more limited specific predictions of how others will behave in our own presence. You may well misjudge the personality of a roommate or co-worker, but to the extent that you can predict your roommate's actions at home or your co-worker's actions on the job, the mistakes may not matter (Swann, 1984).
3. People can form more accurate impressions of others when they are motivated by concerns for accuracy and open-mindedness (Biesanz & Human, 2010). Some of the studies described in this chapter have shown that people show less bias when the accuracy of their social perceptions are personally important—as when participants are asked to judge a prospective teammate's ability to facilitate success in a future task (Fiske & Neuberg, 1990) or a future dating partner's social competence (Goodwin et al., 2002).
4. Not everyone suffers from high levels of error and bias. Some individuals are more accurate than others in their social perceptions—for example, individuals who are psychologically well adjusted (Human & Biesanz, 2011).

To summarize, research on the accuracy of social perceptions offers a valuable lesson: To the extent that we observe others with whom we've had time to interact, make judgments that are reasonably specific, are motivated to form an accurate impression, and are reasonably well adjusted, the problems that plague us can be minimized. Indeed, just being aware of the biases described in this chapter may well be a necessary first step toward a better understanding of others and our perceptions of them.

> People are more accurate at judging the personalities of friends and acquaintances than of strangers.
>
> **TRUE**

Review

Top 10 Key Points in Chapter 4

1. People often make snap judgments about other people based on superficial cues such as physical appearance and nonverbal demeanor.

2. Although we often form accurate impressions based on other people's behavior, research shows that we are not accurate at knowing when someone else is telling the truth or lying.

3. Although we often form first impressions of others quickly, sometimes we are more analytical, observing behavior and making personal or situational attributions for it according to the logic of attribution theory.

4. At least in Western cultures, however, people commit the fundamental attribution error when observing others, overestimating the role of a person's dispositions and underestimating the impact of the situation they are in.

5. In forming impressions of other people, three sets of traits loom as particularly important: how competent the person is, how warm, and how moral.

6. Although we tend to form impressions of others by mentally averaging their various traits, a number of biases come into play—for example, some traits are more central to the overall impressions we form than others.

7. Once we form an impression of someone, we become slow to change that impression when faced with new information that is nonsupportive or even contradictory.

8. Once we form an impression, we engage in confirmation biases, tending to seek new information in ways that are likely to confirm what we already believe.

9. Beginning with classic research on the effects of teacher expectations on student performance, research also shows that our perceptions of others can influence our behavior, and in turn their behavior, resulting in a self-fulfilling prophecy.

10. Research promotes two radically different views of social perception. At times we are quick and instinctive social perceivers and at times we are careful and analytic; at times we are accurate, and at times we are biased and in error.

Putting Common Sense to the Test

Observation: The Elements of Social Perception

The impressions we form of others are influenced by superficial aspects of their appearance.

T **True.** *Research shows that first impressions are influenced by height, weight, clothing, facial characteristics, and other aspects of appearance.*

Adaptively, people are skilled at knowing when someone is lying rather than telling the truth.

F **False.** *People frequently make mistakes in their judgments of truth and deception, too often accepting what others say at face value.*

Attribution: From Elements to Dispositions

Like social psychologists, people are sensitive to situational causes when explaining the behavior of others.

F **False.** *In explaining the behavior of others, people overestimate the importance of personal factors and overlook the impact of situations, a bias known as the fundamental attribution error.*

Confirmation Biases: From Impressions to Reality

People are slow to change their first impressions on the basis of new information.

T **True.** *Studies have shown that once people form an impression of someone, they become resistant to change even when faced with contradictory new evidence.*

The notion that we can create a "self-fulfilling prophecy" by getting others to behave in ways we expect is a myth.

(F) **False.** *In the laboratory and in the classroom, a perceiver's expectation can actually lead to its own fulfillment.*

Social Perception: The Bottom Line

People are more accurate at judging the personalities of friends and acquaintances than of strangers.

(T) **True.** *People often form erroneous impressions of strangers but tend to be more accurate in their judgments of friends and acquaintances.*

Key Terms

attribution theory (120)
availability heuristic (123)
base-rate fallacy (124)
belief in a just world (133)
belief perseverance (144)
central traits (139)
confirmation bias (142)
counterfactual thinking (125)

covariation principle (122)
false-consensus effect (124)
fundamental attribution error (126)
impression formation (134)
information integration theory (135)
mind perception (112)

need for closure (142)
nonverbal behavior (113)
personal attribution (120)
primacy effect (141)
priming (136)
self-fulfilling prophecy (146)
situational attribution (120)
social perception (107)

Stereotypes, Prejudice, and Discrimination

This chapter focuses on stereotyping, prejudice, and discrimination. We begin by examining the nature of the problem—how aspects of stereotyping, prejudice, and discrimination have changed dramatically in recent years, as well as how persistent they can be. Next, we examine a variety of causes underlying these problems. We conclude with a number of ways to reduce stereotypes, prejudice, and discrimination.

Getty Images

1965 or 2015? Although there certainly has been great progress in civil rights and interracial relations in a half century, these two photos of African American men being arrested during protests about institutional racism in 1965 (left) and 2015 (right) illustrate the tragic persistence of some deep-rooted problems.

Heavily-armed police

Heavily-armed police and National Guard forces are called in as racial tensions erupt into protests and riots in multiple American communities in response to a series of killings of unarmed African American men by the police. A white man opens fire on worshipers in an historic African-American church in South Carolina, killing nine; investigators report that the shooter told them he wanted to start a race war. Supreme Court justices are split five to four in a ruling about the legality of practices that result in housing discrimination.

If you're familiar with twentieth-century American history, this should sound like the volatile 1960s, as battles over Civil Rights boiled over in many parts of the nation. But what we've just described occurred a full half century later, at the end of 2014 and in the first half of 2015. The sins of the past seemed to be repeating, demonstrating that although much has changed, much also remains the same.

The problems are by no means limited to black–white relations, or to the United States. Around the same time period, violence and hatred directed toward Jews throughout Europe and Australia were on the rise (see ● Figure 5.1). Laws against pro-LGBT (lesbian, gay, bisexual, and transgender) "propaganda" were passed in Russia. Anti-Muslim sentiment increased in many parts of the West, while anti-West sentiment continued to flourish among large numbers of radical Muslims. The prime minister of India decried the continuing (though officially banned) practice of parents selectively aborting girls. As billionaire Donald Trump announced his candidacy for president of the United States, he denounced Mexican immigrants as criminals and rapists and leaped to the top of the polls (Ahmed, 2015; Fletcher, 2014; Gjelten, 2015; Luke, 2015; Mahr, 2015).

Putting COMMON SENSE to the Test

Circle Your Answer

T F Children do not tend to show biases based on race; it is only after they become adolescents that they learn to respond to people differently based on race.

T F Interracial interactions tend to go better and to reduce the perceptions of racism if a colorblind mentality is used, which denies or minimizes any acknowledgment of racial differences.

T F An African American student is likely to perform worse on an athletic task if the task is described as one reflecting sports intelligence than if it is described as reflecting natural athletic ability.

T F Being reminded of one's own mortality makes people put things into greater perspective, thereby tending to reduce ingroup–outgroup distinctions and hostilities.

T F People's very quick judgments are not influenced by a stereotype unless they actually believe the stereotype to be true.

Faced with these headlines, it's easy to lose sight of the fact that progress, in some cases tremendous progress, has been made. The United States had elected, and then re-elected, its first African American president. The Supreme Court ruled that same-sex marriage was now legal throughout the United States. Today more people than ever rush to defend the targets and denounce the perpetrators of prejudice and discrimination. The march toward progress is real, but its rhythm is frustratingly unsteady, at its best a "two-steps forward and one-step back" motion.

To better understand and improve our diverse world, to help the march toward progress accelerate in the right direction, it is critically important to understand the complexity and causes of stereotypes, prejudice, and discrimination. That is the primary goal of this chapter. We begin by taking a close look at the nature of the problem of intergroup bias in contemporary life. Later in the chapter we address some of the key causes and important consequences of intergroup biases, and we close by discussing some of the most promising directions in efforts to reduce these problems.

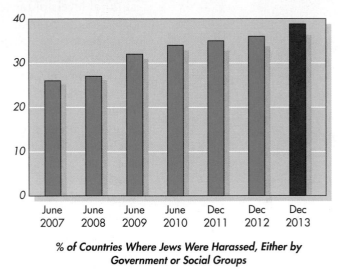

● **FIGURE 5.1**

Harassment of Jews Reaches Seven-Year High

This is one of many indicators of the increase in prejudice and discrimination against Jews in recent years. These numbers are higher than for any other religious group, and are especially high in Europe, where Jews faced harassment by the government or social groups in 76% of the countries. Pew Research Center (2015a).

% of Countries Where Jews Were Harassed, Either by Government or Social Groups

The Nature of the Problem: Persistence and Change

In this section, we discuss some of the progress that has been made concerning stereotypes, prejudice, and discrimination, along with the persistence of more subtle forms of these biases. To provide a focus and to reflect the topics that have most dominated the research literature, we will concentrate in this section primarily on racism and sexism in particular—even though many of the points hold true across a wide variety of targets of stereotypes, prejudice, and discrimination.

Defining Our Terms

Given the complexity of these issues, defining concepts such as prejudice or racism is no simple matter. Debates persist about how best to define the terms—how broad or specific they should be, whether they should focus on individual or institutional levels, and so on. For example, one way to define **racism** is as prejudice and discrimination based on a person's racial background. It is important to realize, however, that racism exists at several different levels.

At the individual level, as this definition reflects, any of us can be racist toward anyone else. At the institutional and cultural levels, in contrast, some people

racism Prejudice and discrimination based on a person's racial background, or institutional and cultural practices that promote the domination of one racial group over another.

are privileged while others are disadvantaged. Aspects of various institutions and the culture more generally may perpetuate this inequality, even if unintentionally. For example, institutions may unwittingly perpetuate racism by tending to accept or hire individuals similar or connected to the people who already are in the institution, and popular culture may signal what kinds of people are most and least valued. Therefore, another way to define racism is as institutional and cultural practices that promote the domination of one racial group over another (Jones, 1997b). The incidents described at the beginning of this chapter sparked much discussion about *systemic* racism, which concerns these institutional and cultural levels of racial discrimination. Similarly, **sexism** may be defined as prejudice and discrimination based on a person's gender or as institutional and cultural practices that promote the domination of one gender (typically men) over another (typically women).

For the purposes of this chapter, we define **stereotypes** as beliefs or associations that link whole groups of people with certain traits or characteristics. **Prejudice** consists of negative feelings about others because of their connection to a social group. Whereas stereotypes concern associations or beliefs and prejudice concerns feelings, **discrimination** concerns behaviors—specifically, negative behaviors directed against persons because of their membership in a particular group. Stereotypes, prejudice, and discrimination can operate somewhat independently, but they often influence and reinforce each other.

■ Racism: Current Forms and Challenges

A close examination of legislation, opinion polls, sociological data, and social psychological research indicates that racial prejudice and discrimination have been decreasing in the United States and in many other countries over the last 70 years, although elements of it may once again be on the rise, particularly in Western Europe. In a classic study of ethnic stereotypes published in 1933, Daniel Katz and Kenneth Braly found that white college students viewed the average white American as smart, industrious, and ambitious, and they saw the average African American as superstitious, ignorant, lazy, and happy-go-lucky. In multiple follow-up surveys with demographically similar samples of white students conducted from 1951 through 2001, these negative images of blacks largely faded and were replaced by more favorable images (Dovidio et al., 1996; Madon et al., 2001). For example, 75% of white participants chose "lazy" as a trait to describe black Americans in 1933, whereas only 5% did so 60 years later. Similarly, public opinion polls have indicated that racial prejudice in the United States has dropped sharply since World War II. ● Figure 5.2 depicts one dramatic example of this trend, concerning attitudes toward inter-racial marriage (Newport, 2015).

The election of Barack Obama as the first African American president of the United States in 2008 was a significant sign of racial progress, as was his re-election in 2012. As Obama pointed out when he was inaugurated, his own father would not have been served in many restaurants in the nation's capital 60 years before, and now that father's son was being sworn in to the highest office in the land. That amount of progress in a person's lifetime is staggering. However, when those of us who study stereotypes, prejudice, and discrimination saw story after story in the popular media at the time of Obama's election heralding the dawn of a "postracial America," we knew how naive and wrong such notions were.

While serving as president, for example, Obama—along his wife, Michelle—was the target with shocking regularity of hateful racial epithets and blatant stereotypes hurled by politicians, police officials, journalists, political cartoonists,

sexism Prejudice and discrimination based on a person's gender, or institutional and cultural practices that promote the domination of one gender over another.

stereotype A belief or association that links a whole group of people with certain traits or characteristics.

prejudice Negative feelings toward persons based on their membership in certain groups.

discrimination Behavior directed against persons because of their membership in a particular group.

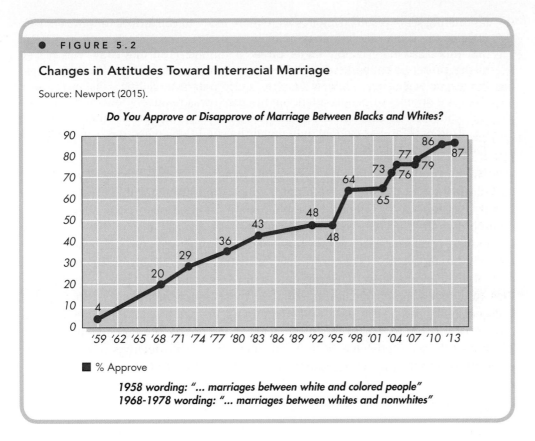

● FIGURE 5.2

Changes in Attitudes Toward Interracial Marriage

Source: Newport (2015).

Do You Approve or Disapprove of Marriage Between Blacks and Whites?

■ % Approve

1958 wording: "... marriages between white and colored people"
1968-1978 wording: "... marriages between whites and nonwhites"

celebrities, and ordinary citizens. During this time the spate of killings of unarmed African American men by police in several cities led to investigations that revealed persistent systemic racial discrimination. Data from archival analyses, surveys, and even experiments in which other variables are held constant continue to show how African American and Hispanic individuals suffer in comparison to white Americans in housing, employment, salaries, incarceration rates, and a host of other important quality-of-life variables (Gabrielson et al., 2014; Horwitz, 2015; Pager & Shepherd, 2008; Reskin, 2012).

In sum, then, there are legitimate reasons both to celebrate racial progress and to acknowledge that racism remains a fact of life and is by no means limited merely to the actions of some fringe individuals or groups. And as we will see in the following section, it exists in ways that escape the recognition of most people.

Modern, Aversive, and Implicit Racism Consider two stories from the world of sports:

1. As the first half ended during a high school basketball game near Pittsburgh, fans of a predominately white high school ran onto the court in full body banana suits, surrounded the players from the predominately African American opposing team, and "allegedly began making monkey noises and hurling racial epithets" at the players (C. Smith, 2012). A few months later in Poland and Croatia, black members of the Dutch and Italian national soccer teams were the targets of racial abuse—including being on the receiving end of monkey chants and a flung banana—during the Euro 2012 championships. Indeed, the 2012 tournament, and the World Cup tournament in 2014 were marred by a variety of incidents of racist taunting by players and fans from multiple European and South American nations (Barnes, 2014; Brown, 2012; Cue, 2012).

2. Christopher Parsons and others (2009) analyzed every pitch from four Major League Baseball seasons—more than 3.5 million pitches in all—and found a

fascinating set of results. Umpires were more likely to call strikes for pitchers who were of the same race/ethnicity as they were. Even more interesting is the fact that this bias emerged only under three conditions: (1) if the game was played in the subset of ballparks that did not have a computerized monitoring system the league was using to review umpires' performance in calling balls and strikes; (2) if the number of people attending the game was relatively low; and (3) if the call would not be the final ball or strike for the player at bat. In other words, the racial/ethnic bias was evident only under the conditions when there would be the least accountability or public outcry.

The first of these examples—concerning racist taunting—illustrates what some call old-fashioned racism. It is blatant, explicit, and unmistakable. The second—concerning the bias in umpiring—is what some call **modern racism**, a subtle form of prejudice that tends to surface when it is safe, socially acceptable, or easy to rationalize. Modern racism is far more subtle and most likely to be present under the cloud of ambiguity. Like germs lurking beneath a seemingly clean countertop, stereotypes, prejudice, and discrimination in contemporary life live under the surface to a much, much greater extent than most people realize. And like germs, their existence can have a profound effect on us, despite how hidden they may be.

According to theories of modern racism, many people are racially ambivalent. They want to see themselves as fair, but they still harbor feelings of anxiety and discomfort about other racial groups (Hass et al., 1992). There are several specific theories of modern racism, but they all emphasize contradictions and tensions that lead to subtle, often unconscious forms of prejudice and discrimination (Gawronski et al., 2012; Levy et al., 2013; Nier & Gaertner, 2012). For example, Samuel Gaertner and John Dovidio (1986; Hodson et al., 2010) proposed the related concept of **aversive racism**, which concerns the ambivalence between individuals' sincerely fair-minded attitudes and beliefs, on the one hand, and their largely unconscious and unrecognized prejudicial feelings and beliefs, on the other hand. In addition, some scholars today use the term *microaggression* to characterize the everyday, typically subtle but hurtful forms of discrimination that are experienced quite frequently by members of targeted groups (Forrest-Bank et al., 2015).

modern racism A form of prejudice that surfaces in subtle ways when it is safe, socially acceptable, and easy to rationalize.

aversive racism Racism that concerns the ambivalence between fair-minded attitudes and beliefs, on the one hand, and unconscious and unrecognized prejudicial feelings and beliefs, on the other hand.

An opponent tries to prevent Barcelona's Samuel Eto from leaving the game after he was targeted by racist taunts from Spanish League fans.

AP Images/Manu Fernande

In these forms of racism, prejudice and discrimination surface in very subtle ways, often clouded by ambiguity. For example, several studies have found that white participants playing the role of jurors may be more likely to convict a black than a white defendant for a crime when the evidence is rather ambiguous, and thus one can justify either a guilty or not-guilty verdict for reasons having nothing to do with race. If, on the other hand, race seems to be an important aspect of the case, then this bias may be eliminated or even reversed (Bucolo & Cohn, 2010; Fein et al., 1997; Sommers & Ellsworth, 2009).

These modern, ambivalent forms of racism are often evident in the "but some of my best friends are . . ." excuse. That is, people establish their *moral credentials* of not being racist by demonstrating—to others or even to themselves—that they have good friends from the racial or ethnic group in question or they have behaved in ways that were quite fair to members of this group (Cascio & Plant, 2015; Merritt et al., 2010). Having such good behavior to their credit gives people the license to take actions that might otherwise put them at risk for seeming prejudiced. Indeed, Anna Merritt and others (2012) found that people sometimes go out of their way to try to establish such credits, such as by rating an African American job candidate more positively, if they anticipate being in a situation later in which they might be judged as racist.

In just about any setting, examples of subtle but impactful discrimination can be found. Here is just a sample from recent research: In the workplace, businesses were less likely to contact job candidates based on their resumes if the name of the candidate was stereotypically African American than European American; in the classroom, students expected lower competence from a professor with a stereotypically African American rather than European American name, and professors were less likely to reply to e-mail requests about research opportunities if the name of the sender seemed African American than European American; in the marketplace, car salespeople charged black customers higher prices than white customers for the same cars, and iPods sold on the Internet received lower offers when the ads showed the iPods being held by black hands rather than by white hands (Bavishi et al., 2010; Brewster & Lynn, 2014; Doleac & Stein, 2013; Eberhardt et al., 2006; E. B. King et al., 2006; Milkman et al., 2015; Morgan et al., 2013).

Let's take a closer look at one recent finding along these lines. Jason Okonofua and Jennifer Eberhardt (2015) gave schoolteachers information about an incident in which a middle-school child misbehaved (such as by sleeping in class and then not listening to the teacher when the teacher wakes him up). The teachers rated how troubled they would be by the behavior if they were the teacher and how severe the discipline of the child should be. Then they read about a second incident of misbehavior by this same child. The teachers then made the same judgments a second time.

For half of the teachers, the name of the boy was, according to previous research, stereotypically black (Darnell or DeShawn), and for the others it was stereotypically white (Jake or Greg). The researchers found no bias in teachers' judgments after the first infraction. That is, they reported being equally troubled and recommended equal punishments whether the boy seemed to be black or white. This would suggest no implicit racism here, right? But after the second infraction, a different story emerges. The teachers reported being more troubled, and recommended more severe discipline, after the second round of misbehavior if he apparently was black than white (see ● Figure 5.3).

All these examples suggest two key points. First, although these biases are often very difficult to see, they are present in abundance, across a multitude

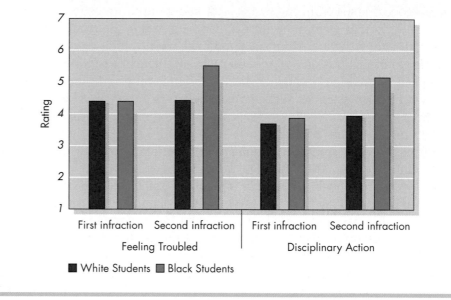

● FIGURE 5.3

Two Strikes: Race and Teachers' Reactions to Children's Misbehavior

Teachers read about an instance in which a middle-school child misbehaved in class. The teachers reported being no more troubled by, nor did they suggest more severe discipline, in response to the misbehavior if they were led to believe the child was black than white. However, after the child misbehaved a second time, a significant racial bias emerged, with teachers being more troubled and recommending more severe discipline if the child was black than white.

Based on Okonofua & Eberhardt (2015)

of settings, ranging from the everyday to the profound. On the more profound side of things, consider a pair of findings in the legal system. Jennifer Eberhardt and others (2006) examined more than 600 death-penalty-eligible trials from Philadelphia and found that in cases involving a white victim and a black male defendant, the more the defendant's physical appearance was stereotypically black, the more likely he would be sentenced to death. Jill Viglione and others (2011) found in a sample of more than 12,000 adult black women imprisoned in North Carolina that black women with lighter skin color received on average about 12% less prison time than black women with darker skin (see ● Figure 5.4).

The second key point is that in each of the cases described in the previous several paragraphs, it would be impossible to be sure that racism was behind any one person's specific behavior. After all, there may be many reasons why any one person might receive a job offer or not, or a severe punishment or not. There's just too much ambiguity or subtlety. This is even more true when looking at our own behaviors than when looking at those of others, as we tend to think that we're less biased than others (Scopelliti, 2015). But by looking at trends and by running experiments with careful controls, the underlying bias can be revealed.

Measuring Implicit Racism The modern forms of racism sometime operate consciously but more frequently operate outside people's conscious awareness. Scholars call racism that operates unconsciously and unintentionally **implicit racism**. This raises a question: How can we measure how implicitly biased someone is? Because of

implicit racism Racism that operates unconsciously and unintentionally.

● **FIGURE 5.4**

Facial Features and Prison Sentences

According to a study by Jill Viglione and others (2011) of more than 12,000 adult black women imprisoned in North Carolina, the chances are good that if the two women depicted here were each found guilty of a crime, the woman on the left (whose face would be considered more "stereotypically black") would receive a longer prison sentence than the woman on the right.

its implicit nature, it can't be assessed by simply asking people to answer some questions about their attitudes. Rather, much more subtle, indirect measures typically are used. By far the most well known of these measures is the Implicit Association Test (IAT), first developed and tested by Anthony Greenwald and others (1998). The IAT measures the extent to which two concepts are associated. It measures implicit racism toward African Americans, for instance, by comparing how quickly participants associate African American cues (such as a black face) with negative or positive concepts compared to how quickly they associate European American cues with these same concepts. If someone is consistently slower identifying something good after seeing a black face than a white face, for example, this would indicate a degree of implicit racism.

Other IATs focus on associations concerning older versus younger people, men versus women, and so on. The IAT is discussed in more detail in Chapter 6 on Attitudes. It has sparked an explosion of research, with many hundreds of scientific publications already, along with some controversy about its validity and uses. The IAT has been so popular that between October 1998 and October 2015 more than 17 *million* IATs were completed by visitors to the IAT website (Nosek, 2015).

Implicit racial bias as measured by the IAT has been found between groups around the world and even among children as young as 3 and 4 years old (Baron & Banaji, 2006; Dunham et al., 2008, 2013, 2015; Newheiser & Olson, 2012). One interesting point is that compared to 6-year-olds, 10-year-olds begin to show less bias on explicit measures, and adults exhibit even less than the 10-year-olds; however, levels of implicit racism as measured by the IAT remain consistent across children and adults.

Implicit racism correlates with a variety of attitudes and behaviors. For example, higher implicit racism by white participants in several studies predicted negative,

Children do not tend to show biases based on race; it is only after they become adolescents that they learn to respond to people differently based on race.

FALSE

unfriendly nonverbal behaviors in interracial interactions, such as physical distancing or lack of eye contact—actions that can make the other person feel disliked and that can lead to, for instance, poor performance in a job interview (Greenwald et al., 2009). A particularly disturbing, and growing, set of findings concerns the link between doctors' and other health care providers' implicit racism and their treatment of patients from racial and ethnic minority groups (Blair et al., 2015; Penner et al., 2013; Schaa et al., 2015). For example, Janice Sabin and Anthony Greenwald (2012) found that doctors with stronger pro-white bias on the IAT were more likely to recommend prescribing pain-relieving medication after surgery for white patients, and less likely to do so for black patients, compared to physicians with less of a pro-white IAT score.

Interracial Interactions The divides between racial and ethnic groups tend to be more vast and may promote stronger feelings of hostility, fear, and distrust than the divides based on other social categories, such as those based on gender, appearance, and age. This can make interracial interaction particularly challenging and fraught with emotion and tension. When engaging in interracial interactions, whites may be concerned about a number of things, including not wanting to be, or to appear to be, racist. They may therefore try to regulate their behaviors, be on the lookout for signs of distrust or dislike from their interaction partners, and so on. Because of these concerns, what should ideally be a smooth-flowing normal interaction can become awkward and even exhausting. This, in turn, can affect their partner's perceptions of them, possibly leading to the ironic outcome of well-intentioned individuals appearing to be racist precisely because they were trying not to be. Because of these concerns, engaging in interracial interactions can be so stressful as to leave the individuals cognitively exhausted, less able immediately after the interaction to complete mental tasks (Shelton & Richeson, 2015).

According to Jacquie Vorauer (2003; Vorauer & Sasaki, 2014), individuals engaging in intergroup interactions often activate *metastereotypes*, or thoughts about the outgroup's stereotypes about them, and worry about being seen as consistent with these stereotypes. Indeed, this kind of concern about interracial interactions can lead to unhealthy cardiovascular reactions associated with feelings of threat (Mendes et al., 2002; Trawalter et al., 2012). It should not be surprising, then, that people sometimes try to avoid interracial interaction for fear of appearing racist or being treated in a racist way, and this avoidant behavior can have the ironic effect of making things all the worse. Ashby Plant and David Butz (2006), for example, found that when nonblack participants with this avoidant concern interacted with a black confederate, they had shorter and less pleasant interactions. Philip Goff, Claude Steele, and Paul Davies (2008) found that white male students sat farther away from black students than white students in an interaction—but only if they thought they would be engaged in a conversation about a racially sensitive topic.

In a clever demonstration of the kind of anxiety whites sometimes feel about race, Michael Norton and others (2006) paired white participants with either a white or black confederate in a game (similar to the children's board game *Guess Who?*) that required the participants to ask the confederate questions so they could guess which of a series of photographs the confederate had been given. As can be seen in ● Figure 5.5, participants were significantly less likely to ask about the race of the person in the photograph when playing the game with

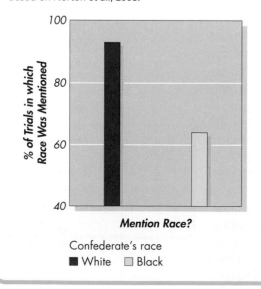

● **FIGURE 5.5**

Colorblind?

When white participants played a face-matching game in which they had to ask questions of a confederate to guess which of a series of photographs the confederate had, they were much less likely to ask about the race of the people in the photographs if they were interacting with a black confederate than a white confederate, even though this hurt their performance in the game.

Based on Norton et al., 2006.

a black confederate than a white confederate, even though this hurt their ability to win the game. It seemed that the white participants would rather lose the game than run the risk of appearing racist by paying any attention to the race of the people in the photographs.

An interesting follow-up to this study examined the performance of children in this task (Apfelbaum et al., 2008). On a race-neutral version of the game, older children (10 and 11 years old), not surprisingly, outperformed younger children (8 and 9 years old). However, when race was a relevant category, the older children were much more likely to avoid asking about race, presumably because they were more aware of the sensitivities surrounding race. The result of this was that in the race-relevant version of the game, the younger children significantly outperformed the older children!

White adults in an interracial interaction often try to adopt a "colorblind" mentality and demeanor, acting—or trying to act—as if race is so unimportant to them that they don't even notice and certainly don't care about their interaction partner's race. Often this attempt is sincere and with the best of intentions, but a growing body of research findings indicates that this approach often backfires and makes members of racial minority groups more, rather than less, uncomfortable. A multicultural approach that acknowledges and positively values racial and ethnic differences is often more effective in promoting better intergroup attitudes and behaviors (Plaut et al., 2015; Rattan & Ambady, 2013). Lisa Rosenthal and Sheri Levy (2013) similarly find that thinking in a more *polycultural* way—that is, focusing on the ways that racial and ethnic groups have interacted and influenced each other's cultures throughout history—can be very effective in promoting positive intergroup relations.

> Interracial interactions tend to go better and to reduce the perceptions of racism if a colorblind mentality is used, which denies or minimizes any acknowledgment of racial differences.
>
> **FALSE**

Anxieties and challenges associated with intergroup interactions are not limited to those between whites and blacks, of course. Research has demonstrated that feelings of threat and anxiety affect interactions involving a large number of groups, such as gay and lesbian individuals, overweight people, and a variety of other social categories (Blair et al., 2003; Everly et al., 2012; Madera & Hebl, 2012; Newheiser et al., 2015; Stephan, 2014).

■ Sexism: Ambivalence, Objectification, and Double Standards

As with racism, old-fashioned blatant displays of sexism are less socially accepted than in years past, although they continue to exist at a frequency and with an intensity that would surprise many. As with racism, researchers have been documenting and studying modern and implicit forms of sexism that tend to escape the notice of most people but that can exert powerful discriminatory effects (Girvan et al., 2015; Swim & Hyers, 2009).

There are some ways that sexism is different, however. Gender stereotypes are distinct from virtually all other stereotypes in that they often are *prescriptive* rather than merely *descriptive*. In other words, they indicate what many people in a given culture believe men and women *should* be like, not merely what people think they actually *are* like. Few people, for example, think that gays *should* be artistic and sensitive or that old people *should* be forgetful and conservative, but many think that women *should* be nurturing and that men *should* be unemotional. Therefore, women who exhibit traits that are valued in society but that defy gender stereotypes, such as by being ambitious or assertive, often are viewed in especially harsh terms, contributing to the double standards that are a hallmark of sexism

(Brescoll et al., 2010; Prentice & Carranza, 2002; Rudman et al., 2012; Rudman, Fetterolf, & Sanchez, 2013).

Another way that sexism is unique concerns the degree to which the ingroup and outgroup members interact. Men and women are intimately familiar with each other. Girls and boys often grow up together, women and men often live together. In contrast to the effects of contact in reducing many other intergroup biases, however, all this contact between women and men often does little to reduce sexist beliefs, attitudes, and behaviors.

Ambivalent Sexism It may surprise you to learn that, overall, stereotypes of women tend to be more positive than those of men (Eagly et al., 1994). However, the positive traits associated with women are less valued in important domains such as the business world than the positive traits associated with men.

These contradictions are reflected in Peter Glick and Susan Fiske's (2001, 2012) concept of **ambivalent sexism**. Ambivalent sexism consists of two elements: *hostile sexism,* characterized by negative, resentful feelings about women's abilities, value, and challenge to men's power (e.g., "Women seek special favors under the guise of equality"), and *benevolent sexism,* characterized by affectionate, chivalrous feelings founded on the potentially patronizing belief that women need and deserve protection (e.g., "Women should be cherished and protected by men"). Benevolent sexism, on the surface, does not strike many women or men as terribly troubling, but the two forms of sexism are positively correlated. Benevolent sexism is associated in particular with negative reactions toward women who defy traditional gender roles and stereotypes.

Both types of sexism are associated with supporting gender inequality in a variety of ways, and both predict many kinds of discriminatory behaviors and negative consequences (Durán et al., 2011; Masser et al., 2010; Rudman & Fetterolf, 2014). For example, Allison Skinner and others (2015) found that, depending on the context, hostile and benevolent sexism each predicted more negative judgments of the driver in an accident if the driver was said to be a woman rather than a man. Kristen Salomon and colleagues (2015) found that being the target of either type of sexism triggered negative cardiovascular responses in the women in their study.

Glick, Fiske, and others (2000) conducted an ambitious study of 15,000 men and women in 19 nations across 6 continents and found that ambivalent sexism was prevalent around the world. Among their most intriguing findings was that people from countries with the greatest degree of economic and political inequality between the sexes tended to exhibit the most hostile and benevolent sexism.

Objectification Women are all too often treated in objectifying ways. That is, they are viewed or treated more as mere bodies or objects and less as fully functioning human beings. The advertising industry specifically, and the popular media more generally, are filled with imagery of women represented as sexual objects or just parts of a body (Kilbourne, 2003). For example, Julie Stankiewicz and Francine Rosselli (2008) examined almost 2,000 advertisements depicting women from 58 popular magazines in the United States and found that half of them featured women as sex objects. Women also experience being treated and seen as objects in numerous interactions in their real lives. In one study involving in-depth interviews with 600 women in and around Paris, France, an astonishing 100% reporting having been sexually harassed while using public transportation (Palet, 2015)!

Although men are objectified in the media as well (and this is a growing trend), and are sometimes objectified in real interactions, it is still the case that

ambivalent sexism A form of sexism characterized by attitudes about women that reflect both negative, resentful beliefs and feelings and affectionate and chivalrous but potentially patronizing beliefs and feelings.

women experience this much more frequently, and a good deal of research documents a variety of negative effects of this objectification on women, including on their mental and physical health, their academic performance, and their social interactions (Calogero et al., 2011; Fredrickson et al., 1998; Saguy et al., 2010; Tiggemann & Williams, 2012).

Sex Discrimination: Double Standards and Pervasive Stereotypes Many years ago, Philip Goldberg (1968) asked students at a small women's college to evaluate the content and writing style of some articles. When the material was supposedly written by John McKay rather than Joan McKay it received higher ratings, a result that led Goldberg to wonder if even women were prejudiced against women. Certain other studies showed that people often devalue the performance of women who take on tasks usually reserved for men (Lott, 1985) and attribute women's achievements to luck rather than ability (Deaux & Emswiller, 1974; Nieva & Gutek, 1981). These studies generated a lot of attention, but it now appears that this kind of devaluation of women is not commonly found in similar studies. More than 100 studies modeled after Goldberg's indicate that people are not generally biased by gender in the evaluation of performance (Swim & Sanna, 1996; Top, 1991). More recently, two different sets of studies involved having professors from science-related fields evaluate the materials of candidates for research or faculty positions in their fields, and these studies found completely contradictory results: One found a bias in favor candidates if they were said to be male (Moss-Racusin et al., 2012), and the other found a bias in favor candidates if they were said to be female (Williams & Ceci, 2015). The point here is that in studies involving the evaluation of materials that are identical except for the gender of the person who supposedly produced the materials, the findings have been inconsistent.

After surviving being shot in the head by the Taliban for defying their ban against girls attending school in Pakistan, Malala Yousafzai has worked tirelessly in her quest to help girls around the world receive education. She became the youngest person to win the Nobel Peace Price in 2014.

The Asahi Shimbun/Getty Images

What is quite clear, however, is that sex discrimination continues to exist in numerous other ways and instances. As with forms of modern and implicit racism, subtle but impactful examples of sexism abound. For example, Juan Madera and others (2015) looked at real letters of recommendation that professors wrote for candidates for academic jobs. A quick look at these letters probably would not reveal any obvious differences based on the gender of the candidates. A more thorough analysis, however, indicated that both male and female professors tended to include more pieces of information raising slight doubts (e.g., "she has a somewhat challenging personality," "she might make a good colleague") for female than for male candidates. Moreover, these seemingly minor doubts made a significant difference in the evaluations of people reading these letters.

Sexism today is by no means limited to subtle biases. In many parts of the world blatant sexism not only is still quite evident, but it is the law of the land. A law in Morocco that enables rapists to escape prosecution by marrying their victim came under fire when a 16-year-old girl committed suicide after a court ordered her to marry the man who raped her (Hirsch, 2012). Malala Yousafzai, a Pakistani teenage girl, was shot in the head in 2012 by the Taliban when she defied their bans against girls attending school. She survived the attack, became an inspiring activist dedicated to female education, and in October 2014 became the youngest person to win a Nobel Peace Prize.

Other examples are far less extreme but still important. Look at ● Figure 5.6 and Table 5.1, for instance, and you'll notice some striking sex differences in occupational choice. How many female airline pilots have you met lately? What about male dental hygienists? (It's interesting to note that 98% of the dental hygienists in the United States in 2011 were women, but only 22% of the dentists were.) The question is, of course, what explains these differences? Decades of social science research point to sexist attitudes and discrimination as a key part of the equation. Sex discrimination during the early school years may pave the way for diverging career paths in adulthood. Then, when equally qualified men and women compete for a job, gender considerations enter in once again, as business professionals and others favor men for so-called masculine jobs (such as a manager for a machinery company) and women for so-called feminine jobs (such as a receptionist) (Barbulescu & Bidwell, 2013; Caleo & Heilman, 2014; Koch et al., 2015).

● **FIGURE 5.6**

Percentage of Women in Specific Occupations in the United States, 2011

Recent labor statistics reveal that men and women occupy very different positions in the U.S. workforce.
U.S. Bureau of Labor Statistics, 2012.

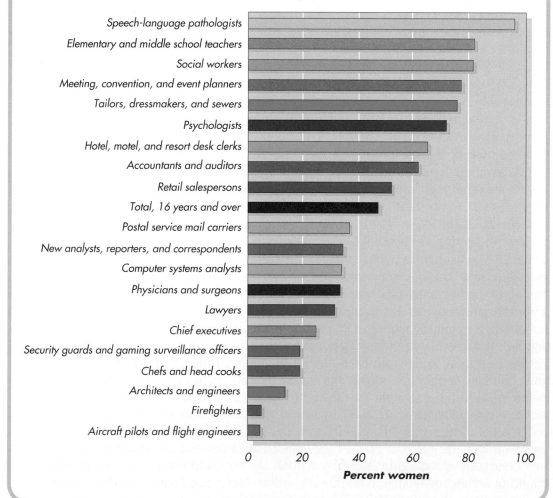

▲ **TABLE 5.1**

Women in Work Settings in Selected Countries Around the World

These international labor statistics show the percentage of workers in each category who are women in each of several countries. These data show some of the differences between nations, as well as some similarities concerning which types of jobs women are more or less likely to occupy around the world.

Country	Total Workforce	Clerks	Craft and Trade Workers	Legislators, Senior Officials, Managers	Sales and Service Workers
Australia	45%	67%	5%	37%	68%
Canada	47%	77%	8%	37%	63%
Columbia	39%	58%	19%	46%	61%
Costa Rica	37%	57%	14%	27%	54%
Egypt	21%	29%	3%	11%	10%
Iran	18%	24%	23%	13%	11%
Israel	46%	74%	5%	30%	60%
Italy	39%	59%	14%	33%	57%
Republic of Korea	42%	52%	15%	9%	63%
Mexico	37%	61%	24%	31%	54%
Morocco	27%	25%	19%	12%	6%
Netherlands	45%	69%	5%	28%	69%
United Kingdom	46%	78%	8%	34%	76%

Data from International Labour Office, 2008.

Even when women and men have comparable jobs, the odds are good that the women will be paid less than their male counterparts and will be confronted with a so-called glass ceiling that makes it harder for women to rise to the highest positions of power in a business or organization (Evers & Sieverding, 2014; Gorman & Kmec, 2009). A 2011 study by Anthony Lo Sasso and others found that the starting salaries of new female physicians trained in New York State averaged almost $17,000 less than that of their male counterparts! (This difference could not be accounted for by things such as different areas of specialization, work hours, or setting.) Reshma Jasi and others (2013) found a similar result with a different sample of newly hired physicians.

Women vying for jobs, career advancement, and political office often face a virtually impossible dilemma: They are seen as more competent if they present themselves with stereotypically masculine rather than feminine traits, yet when they do this, they are also perceived as less socially skilled and attractive—a perception that may ultimately cost them the position or career advancement they were seeking (Phelan et al., 2008; Rudman et al., 2012; Schneider & Bos, 2014).

For both women and men, being in a job that is traditionally seen as more typical of the other gender can be especially challenging. Consistent with this idea are the results of a study by Victoria Brescoll and others (2010). These researchers found that men and women were judged more harshly for a mistake made on a job traditionally held by the other sex than for the same kind of mistake on a job in

According to a 2011 national survey by Gallup, 40% of Americans would prefer to have a boy compared to 28% preferring a girl, if they could have only one child (the rest indicated no preference). These percentages are almost identical to those from a similar survey in 1941.

which their gender was the majority. In another study Brescoll and others (2012) found that men were perceived as less masculine if they worked for a female supervisor in a traditionally masculine occupation. Laurie Rudman, Kris Mescher, and Corinne Moss-Racusin (2013) found in a series of experiments that women liked men described as caring about issues of gender equality and women's rights, but both these women and other men judged these supportive men in more feminized ways compared to men who were less supportive of women, perceiving them to be relatively weak and questioning their sexuality. Examples like these show that defying traditional gender roles can still be daunting.

■ Beyond Racism and Sexism: Age, Weight, Sexuality, and Other Targets

We have focused in this section on racism and sexism not only because of their historic significance but also because they have been dominant in social psychological research. It is important to note that other forms of bias and discrimination are, of course, quite important and are the subject of contemporary social psychological research. In fact, social psychologists today are studying a wider variety of types of stereotypes, prejudices, and discrimination than ever. It is probably no coincidence, for example, that as our population ages and people tend to live longer, more researchers are studying ageism—prejudice and discrimination targeting the elderly (Nelson, 2011; North & Fiske, 2015). Other forms of discrimination that are getting recent attention include those targeting people's physical disabilities or disfigurements, mental health, political ideology, economic class, being unmarried, or religion (or the lack of religious beliefs) (DePaulo, 2011; Gervais, 2013; Madera & Hebl, 2013; West et al., 2014).

Russ Espinoza and Cynthia Willis-Esqueda (2015), for example, studied biases based on individuals' socioeconomic status. They gave almost 600 individuals who were called for jury duty information about a case and asked them to make a verdict and, if they thought the defendant was guilty, recommend a sentence. European American participants who thought the defendant was guilty were significantly more likely to recommend the death penalty if the defendant was described as having little education or money than if he was highly educated and had a good deal of money.

When former Olympic champion Bruce Jenner announced to the world in 2015 that he was transitioning to a female identity with the name Caitlyn, the response was much more understanding and supportive than could have been expected just a few years before.

AP Images/Chris Pizzello

Although it is much less socially acceptable to display obvious prejudice and discrimination of many kinds today, some forms of these biases appear to be considered more acceptable by many people. Among these are prejudice based on weight and based on sexuality. Although what is considered ideal body types can vary dramatically across times and cultures, it is clear that in some cultures today, jokes, negative attitudes, and insensitive behaviors directed toward those who are perceived to be overweight can be pervasive and hurtful (Brochu & Esses, 2011; Hebl et al., 2009; Ruggs et al., 2015; Schafer & Ferraro, 2011). Lisa Rosenthal and others (2015), for example, found that fifth and sixth grade children who experienced weight-based bullying were more likely to show negative health outcomes two years later, even after statistically controlling for any physical and mental health differences that existed at the beginning of the study.

Prejudice and discrimination based on sexuality have gone through some dramatic changes very recently. When the former Olympic champion Bruce Jenner revealed to the public in 2015 that he was transitioning to a female identity, with the name Caitlyn, the support that Caitlyn received from the general public was enormous (although certainly not universal) and probably would have been unthinkable just a few years before. Americans' attitudes toward same-sex marriage also have shifted dramatically in just a few years (see ● Figure 5.7).

On the other hand, acts of overt and blatant prejudice, discrimination, and violence toward members of the LGBT community continue to occur in disturbing numbers, and discriminatory attitudes and even laws remain in many parts of the world. In addition to these overt examples, there are many more ways in which these prejudices and discrimination can operate more subtly. For example, András Tilcsik (2011) sent pairs of resumes in response to almost 1,800 job postings in seven states across the United States. The resumes in each pair were virtually identical except that in one of them, the job candidate indicated having volunteered time for a gay campus organization. Would these (fictitious) job applicants get invited to interview for the jobs? Even though the job-relevant skills and experiences were identical, the applicant with the experience in the gay campus organization was about 40% less likely to be invited for an interview than the other applicant.

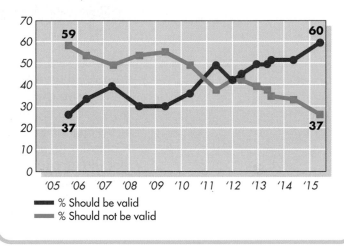

● **FIGURE 5.7**

Changes in Attitudes Toward Same-Sex Marriage

Opinion polls from 2005 to 2015 have shown that responses to the question, "Do you think marriages between same-sex couples should or should not be recognized by law as valid, with the same rights as traditional marriages?" have become much more favorable in recent years, showing a complete reversal in percentages.
Based on Gallup (2015)

Being Stigmatized

We are *all* targets of other people's stereotypes and prejudices. These may be based on how we look, how we talk, how we dress, where we come from, and so on. None of us is immune from having our work evaluated in a biased way, our motives questioned, or our attempts at making new friends rejected because of stereotypes and prejudices. But for the targets of some stereotypes and prejudices, these concerns are relentless and profound. For them, there seem to be few safe havens. Social psychologists often refer to these targets as **stigmatized**—individuals who are targets of negative stereotypes, perceived as deviant, and devalued in society because they are members of a particular social group or because they have a particular characteristic (Major & Crocker, 1993). What are some of the effects of being stigmatized by stereotypes and prejudice?

In *Color-Blind*, writer Ellis Cose (1997), who is African American, tells a story about how he was treated in a job interview 20 years earlier. He was an award-winning newspaper reporter at the time and was hoping to land a job with a national magazine. The editor he met with was pleasant and gracious, but he said that the magazine didn't have many black readers. "All the editor saw was a young black guy, and since *Esquire* was not in need of a young black guy, they were not in need of me. . . . He had been so busy focusing on my race that he was incapable of seeing me or my work" (p. 150). Then, a few years later, and in light of affirmative action policies, Cose was asked if he was interested in a position in a firm as corporate director of equal opportunity. "I was stunned, for the question made no sense. I was an expert neither on personnel nor on equal

stigmatized Being persistently stereotyped, perceived as deviant, and devalued in society because of membership in a particular social group or because of a particular characteristic.

employment law; I was, however, black, which seemed to be the most important qualification" (p. 156).

The targets of stigmatizing stereotypes frequently wonder whether and to what extent others' impressions of them are distorted through the warped lens of social categorization. On some occasions these suspicions can actually serve a self-protective function. For example, in a study by Jennifer Crocker and her colleagues (1991), black students who received negative interpersonal feedback from a white student suffered less of a blow to their self-esteem if they could easily attribute the white student's negative reaction to racism than if they could not. On the other hand, the self-esteem of black students was actually *reduced* by positive feedback from a white student if they could suspect that this feedback may have been due to their race.

Although attributing negative feedback to discrimination can protect one's overall self-esteem, it can also make people feel as if they have less personal control over their lives and thus feel worse about themselves, especially when they have reason to think that the discrimination against them could persist over time. Indeed, a recent meta-analysis by Michael Schmitt and others (2014) of hundreds of correlational and experimental studies involving nearly 150,000 participants supports this point, that perceiving that one has been discriminated against and that the discrimination is likely to be experienced frequently is associated with negative effects on one's self-esteem, depression, anxiety, and life satisfaction. Even simply anticipating interacting with someone who one thinks is prejudiced can trigger cardiovascular stress responses (Sawyer et al., 2012). It is understandable, therefore, that when people who have a stigmatized status that they can hide during an interaction with someone, such as a history of mental illness, they often prefer to do so, but even the act of hiding it during the interaction can itself be stressful and lead to negative effects and outcomes (Newheiser & Barreto, 2014; Newheiser et al., 2015).

More generally, there has been a surge of research findings in recent years concerning how stigmatized targets are at increased risk for serious and long-term physical and psychological problems, including increased blood pressure, depression, breast cancer rates, diabetes, stroke, respiratory problems, chronic pain, substance abuse, and impaired relationships (e.g., Earnshaw et al., 2015; Lukachko et al., 2014; Murphy et al., 2015; Taylor, 2015).

■ Stereotype Threat: A Threat in the Air

One of the more tragic effects of stereotyping in contemporary life is its effects on the intellectual performance and identity of its targets. An enormous wave of research on this issue was generated when social psychologist Claude Steele began writing about this problem in the 1990s. Steele proposed that in situations where a negative stereotype can apply to certain groups, members of these groups can fear being seen "through the lens of diminishing stereotypes and low expectations" (1999, p. 44). Steele (1997) called this predicament **stereotype threat**, for it hangs like "a threat in the air" when the individual is in the stereotype-relevant situation. The predicament can be particularly threatening for individuals whose identity and self-esteem are invested in domains where the stereotype is relevant. Steele argued that stereotype threat plays a crucial role in influencing the intellectual performance and identity of stereotyped group members. Steele and his colleagues (2002) later broadened the scope of their analysis to include *social identity threats* more generally. These threats are not necessarily tied to specific stereotypes but instead reflect a more general devaluing of a person's social group.

stereotype threat The experience of concern about being evaluated based on negative stereotypes about one's group.

According to Steele's theory, stereotype threat can hamper achievement in academic domains in two ways. First, reactions to the "threat in the air" can directly interfere with performance—for example, by increasing anxiety and triggering distracting thoughts. Second, if this stereotype threat is chronic in the academic domain, it can cause individuals to *disidentify* from that domain—to dismiss the domain as no longer relevant to their self-esteem and identity.

To illustrate, imagine a black student and a white student who enter high school equally qualified in academic performance. Imagine that while taking a particularly difficult test at the beginning of the school year, each student struggles on the first few problems. Both students may begin to worry about failing, but the black student may have a whole set of additional worries about appearing to confirm a negative stereotype. Even if the black student doesn't believe the stereotype at all, the threat of being reduced to a stereotype in the eyes of those around her can trigger anxiety and distraction, impairing her performance. And if she experiences this threat in school often—perhaps because she stands out as one of only a few black students in the school or because she is treated by others in a particular way—the situation may become too threatening to her self-esteem. To buffer herself against the threat, she may disidentify with school. If she does this, her academic performance will become less relevant to her identity and self-esteem, and she will therefore work less hard and perform worse.

The Original Experiments Steele and others conducted a series of experiments in which they manipulated factors likely to increase or decrease stereotype threat as students took academic tests. For example, Steele and Joshua Aronson (1995) had black and white students from a highly selective university take a very difficult standardized verbal test. To some participants, it was introduced as a test of intellectual ability; to others, it was introduced as a problem-solving task unrelated to ability. Steele and Aronson reasoned that because of the difficulty of the test, *all* the students would struggle with it. If the test was said to be related to intellectual ability, however, the black students would feel the threat of a negative stereotype in addition to the stress of struggling with the test. In contrast, if the test was described simply as a research task and not a real test of intelligence, then negative stereotypes would be less applicable and the stereotype threat would be reduced. In that case, black students would be less impaired while taking the test. As shown in ● Figure 5.8, the results supported these predictions.

Thus, a seemingly minor change in the setting—a few words about the meaning of a test—had a powerful effect on the black students' performance. In a second study, the researchers used an even more subtle manipulation of stereotype threat: whether or not the students were asked to report their race just before taking the test. Making them think about race for a few seconds just before taking the test impaired the performance of black students but had no effect on white students. Think about the implications of such findings

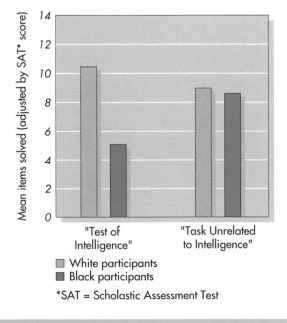

● **FIGURE 5.8**

Stereotype Threat and Academic Performance

Black students did worse on a difficult verbal test than white students (even after the students' scores were adjusted based on their performance on standardized college entrance verbal examinations) if they had been told the test was of intellectual ability (left). In contrast, there was no difference in adjusted scores between black and white students on the same test if they had been told the test was unrelated to ability (right). Source: Based on Steele & Aronson, 1995.

White participants
Black participants

*SAT = Scholastic Assessment Test

for important real-world contexts. (After years of conducting this research, social psychologists were finally able to convince the College Board and Educational Testing Service in 2012 to agree to discontinue the practice of asking students demographic questions immediately before they begin some high-stakes testing such as Advanced Placement exams.)

Because negative stereotypes concerning women's advanced math skills are prevalent, women may often experience stereotype threat in settings relevant to these skills. Reducing stereotype threat in these settings, therefore, should reduce the underperformance that women tend to exhibit in these areas. To test this idea, Steven Spencer and others (1999) recruited male and female students who were good at math and felt that math was important to their identities. The researchers gave these students a very difficult standardized math test, one on which all of them would perform poorly. Before taking the test, some students were told that the test generally showed no gender differences, thereby implying that the negative stereotype of women's ability in math was *not* relevant to this particular test. Other students were told that the test *did* generally show gender differences. As Steele's theory predicted, women performed worse than men when they were told that the test typically produced gender differences, but they performed as well as men when they were told that the test typically did not produce gender differences.

The Prevalence and Diversity of Threats Since these original studies, research inspired by the theory of stereotype threat grew at a stunningly fast pace. The evidence for underperformance due to stereotype threat is quite strong and broad (Inzlicht & Schmader, 2012; Schmader et al., 2015). It has been found both in the laboratory and in real-world settings, including schools and businesses. The examples of these threats run far and wide. For instance, many white athletes feel stereotype threat whenever they step onto a court or playing field where they constitute the minority. Will the white athlete feel the added weight of this threat while struggling against the other athletes in a game? To address this question, Jeff Stone and others (1999) had black and white students play miniature golf. When the experimenters characterized the game as diagnostic of "natural athletic ability," the white students did worse. But when they characterized it as diagnostic of "sports intelligence," the black students did worse.

It should be pointed out that a person can be affected by stereotype threat even if he or she does not believe in the negative stereotype. Just knowing about the stereotype seems to be enough, particularly if the individual identifies strongly with the targeted group and cares about performing well. This last point is particularly poignant—the performance of people who have had success at something and who care the most may be most affected by stereotype threat effects. (An interesting side note: The first experiment to show that students who most identify with and care about success in school may be the most vulnerable to stereotype threat effects was conducted in an inner-city Los Angeles high school by a Stanford University undergraduate student named Mikel Jollet, working with Claude Steele. Jollet soon after formed and became lead singer and songwriter of the very successful alt-rock group, The Airborne Toxic Event.)

Here is a small sample of groups whose performance in various domains was hurt by stereotype threat, as demonstrated in experiments around the world:

- Low-socioeconomic-status students in France and the United States on a verbal test when the test was said to be diagnostic of intellectual ability (Croizet & Claire, 1998)

- European American men on a math test when compared with Asians (Aronson et al., 1999)

> An African American student is likely to perform worse on an athletic task if the task is described as one reflecting sports intelligence than if it is described as reflecting natural athletic ability.
>
> **TRUE**

- Older adults on memory or other cognitive tests when presented, even subliminally (that is, without their conscious awareness), with negative stereotypes about the elderly (Krendl et al., 2015; Lamont et al., 2015)

- First-generation students taking a biology class (Harackiewicz et al., 2014)

- Women on a math test in a co-ed rather than an all-female setting (Ben-Zeev et al., 2005; Sekaquaptewa & Thompson, 2003)

Three scholars who have done research on stereotype threat reunite backstage after an Airborne Toxic Event concert. Can you guess which one became the rock star?

- Women playing chess on the computer when they were told that their opponent was male (Maass et al., 2008)

- White participants taking an IAT when they thought the test was diagnostic of racism (Frantz et al., 2004)

- Individuals with a history of mental illness on a test of reasoning ability when asked about their illness before taking the test (Quinn et al., 2004)

- Women performing soccer drills when the task was described as one in which men tend to outperform women (Heidrich & Chiviacowsky, 2015)

- Student athletes primed to think about their identity as athletes before taking a difficult math test (Yopyk & Prentice, 2005)

- Overweight individuals primed to think about weight-related stereotypes (Major et al., 2014; Seacat & Mickelson, 2009)

- Women driving after being reminded of demeaning stereotypes about female drivers (causing women in a driving simulator to crash into jaywalkers!) (Yeung & von Hippel, 2008)

It is important to note that in each of these cases, the underperformance is significantly or completely eliminated when the stereotype threat is reduced. We will discuss how this occurs in the final section of the chapter (see, for example, Table 5.4).

Causes of Stereotype Threat Effects Stereotype threat exerts its effects in multiple ways (Forbes & Leitner, 2014; Rydell et al., 2014; Schmader et al., 2015). Stereotype threat has been shown to do each of the following to people: trigger physiological arousal and stress; drain cognitive resources; cause a loss of focus to the task at hand because of attempts to suppress thoughts about the relevant stereotype; impair working memory; activate negative thoughts, worry, feelings of dejection, and concerns about trying to avoid failure rather than trying to achieve success; elicit neural activity biased toward negative, stereotype-confirming feedback. Think about trying to do your best on a difficult test that is important to you while all of these things are happening to you—you'd get some sense of how stereotype threat can undermine people's performance and ambitions.

Even though stereotype threat effects are widespread, the growing body of research on this subject also gives us reason to hope. Social psychologists have been uncovering ways that people can be better protected against these threats. We will focus on these promising ways in the final section of this chapter. Before we get to the solutions to stereotype threat and the other problems we have been discussing thus far in this chapter, we turn next to the social psychological causes at the root of these problems.

Causes of the Problem: Intergroup, Motivational, Cognitive, and Cultural Factors

One of the reasons that stereotypes, prejudice, and discrimination persist is because they are caused by multiple factors. There are many sources fueling these problems, and they operate both independently and in tandem. Some stem from the ways that humans cognitively process and remember information. Others can be traced to motivations and goals that drive us to see or react to our social worlds in particular ways. Still others concern how groups of people are represented or valued in one's culture. In this section we turn to look at some of the most important of these causes.

■ Social Categories and Intergroup Conflict

At the root of stereotyping, prejudice, and discrimination is the fact that we divide our social world into groups. As perceivers, we routinely sort each other into groups on the basis of gender, race, age, and other common attributes in a process called **social categorization**. In some ways, social categorization is natural and adaptive. It allows us to form impressions quickly and use experience to guide new interactions. With so many things to pay attention to in our social worlds, we can save time and effort by using people's group memberships to make inferences about them. The time and energy saved through social categorization does come at a cost, however. Categorizing people leads us to overestimate the differences between groups and to underestimate the differences within groups (Krueger & DiDonato, 2008; Wyer et al., 2002).

Indeed, even basic perception is affected by categorization. For example, studies have shown that people see racially ambiguous faces as darker, and they trigger more negative implicit association, if the faces are labeled racially black than white (Levin & Banaji, 2006; Willadsen-Jensen & Ito, 2015). In addition, prejudice can heighten this kind of bias. Markus Kemmelmeier and Lysette Chavez (2014) found that white Americans perceived Barack Obama's face as darker if they were relatively high in racism. Even young children show these kinds of effects: Yarrow Dunham and others (2013) found that children were more likely to categorize a racially ambiguous face as black than white if it is expressing anger.

Each of us is a member of multiple social categories, but some categorizations—particularly involving race, gender, and age—are more likely to quickly dominate our perceptions than others (Amodio et al., 2014; Kaul et al., 2014; Ito, 2011). The distinctions between some of these social categories may be seen as more rigid, even more biologically rooted, than they actually are. Many people assume, for example, that there is a clear genetic basis for classifying people by race. The fact is, however, that numerous biologists, anthropologists, and psychologists note that there is more genetic variation *within* races than *between* them and emphasize that race is more of a social conception than a genetic reality (Marks, 2011; Markus, 2008; Plaks et al., 2012). Indeed, how societies make distinctions between races

"In the 2010 census of the population of the United States, more than 21.7 million Americans did not believe the government's traditional categories of race fit them."

—Yen (2012)

social categorization The classification of persons into groups on the basis of common attributes.

can change dramatically as a function of historical contexts. For instance, it was fairly common for Americans in the early part of the twentieth century to consider Irish Americans as a racial group distinct from whites, but today such thinking is quite rare. As people today increasingly identify themselves in multiracial ways, or in ways that defy the traditional binary distinction between men and women, a greater recognition of the role of factors beyond biology in social categorization becomes all the more relevant. Along these lines, Diana Sanchez and others (2015) found that after a brief interaction with a racially ambiguous other student, white students became less likely to see race as a fixed, biological entity, an effect that endured when the students' attitudes were assessed again two weeks later.

Whether individuals think of various social categories as fixed and biologically rooted or not can be important (Andreychik & Gill, 2015; Cimpian & Salomon, 2014; D. Sanchez & Garcia, 2009). For example, Melissa Williams and Jennifer Eberhardt (2008) found that people who tend to think of race as a stable, biologically determined entity are less likely to interact with racial outgroup members and are more likely to accept racial inequalities than are people who see race as more socially determined. Other research has found that biracial individuals are more vulnerable to some effects of stereotypes if they think of race as stable and biological (D. Sanchez & Garcia, 2009; Shih et al., 2007).

Just as race is a blurrier category than many people realize, so too are nationalities. A series of studies by Thierry Devos and others demonstrated how various ethnic minority groups such as Latino Americans, Asian Americans, and African Americans are not seen as truly American, but some situational factors—such as presenting individuals with examples of positive stereotypic traits of one of these groups—can reduce this tendency (Devos et al., 2010; Huynh et al., 2011; Rydell et al., 2010). As immigration battles intensify throughout much of the world, a variety of social, historical, economic, and political factors all play a role in who is categorized as "foreign."

Diana Sanchez and Julie Garcia (2012) reported a number of ways in which racial categorization is also affected by people's social and economic status. For example, perceivers are more likely to categorize others as racially black if they are of lower socioeconomic status, if they are incarcerated, or if they are unemployed. These same factors may have similar effects on how people categorize themselves racially.

Ingroups Versus Outgroups Although categorizing humans is much like categorizing objects, there is a key difference. When it comes to *social* categorization, perceivers themselves are members or nonmembers of the categories they use. Groups that we identify with—our country, religion, political party, even our hometown sports team—are called **ingroups**, whereas groups other than our own are called **outgroups**. We see people in fundamentally different ways if we consider them to be part of our ingroup or as part of an outgroup.

One consequence is that we exaggerate the differences between our ingroup and other outgroups, and this exaggeration of differences helps to form and reinforce stereotypes. Another consequence is a phenomenon known as the **outgroup homogeneity effect**, whereby perceivers assume that there is a greater similarity among members of outgroups than among members of one's own group. In other words, there may be many and subtle differences among "us," but "they" are all alike (Linville & Jones, 1980). It is easy to think of real-life examples. People from China, Korea, Taiwan, and Japan see themselves as quite distinct from one another, of course, but to many Westerners they are seen simply as Asian. English majors see themselves as dissimilar to

"The percentage of babies classified by the U.S. Census as 'multiracial' has risen from 1% in 1970 to 10% in 2013."
—Pew Research Center, 2015b

ingroups Groups with which an individual feels a sense of membership, belonging, and identity.

outgroups Groups with which an individual does not feel a sense of membership, belonging, or identity.

outgroup homogeneity effect The tendency to assume that there is greater similarity among members of outgroups than among members of ingroups.

Whether people are likely to immediately categorize this person by her race, gender, or occupation depends on a combination of cognitive, cultural, and motivational factors.

Kris Timken/Blend Images/Corbis

history majors, but science majors often lump them together as "humanities types." Californians proclaim their tremendous cultural, ethnic, and economic diversity, whereas outsiders talk of the "typical Californian." To people outside the group, outgroup members even *look* alike: People are less accurate in distinguishing and recognizing the faces of members of racial outgroups than of ingroups (Horry et al., 2015; McDonnell et al., 2014; Meissner et al., 2013).

Why do people tend to perceive outgroups as homogeneous? One reason is that people tend to have less personal contact and familiarity with individual members of outgroups. Indeed, the more familiar people are with an outgroup, the less likely they are to perceive it as homogeneous. Second, people often do not encounter a representative sample of outgroup members. A student from one school who encounters students from a rival school only when they cruise into town for a Saturday football game, screaming at the top of their lungs, sees only the most avid rival fans acting in their most rowdy, competitive ways—hardly a diverse lot.

Lack of familiarity and lack of diversity of experiences with outgroup members are two reasons why "*they* all look alike," but there's more to the story than that. Research using brain imaging or cognitive methods has found that as soon as we categorize an unfamiliar person as a member of our ingroup or an outgroup, we immediately process information about them differently at even the most basic levels. For example, student participants in experiments by Kurt Hugenberg and Olivier Corneille (2009) were exposed to unfamiliar faces of people who were the same race as the participants. These faces were categorized as ingroup members (from the same university as the participants) or outgroup members (from a rival university). The students processed faces more holistically (that is, they integrated the features of the faces into a global representation of the overall face) when they had been categorized as being from their ingroup than they did when they had been categorized as members of the outgroup. Jay Van Bavel, William Cunningham, and their colleagues (2008; 2011; Van Bavel et al., 2014) have found related results in a series of studies, revealing greater activation in particular areas of perceivers' brains, such as the fusiform face area and the orbitofrontal cortex, upon exposure to unfamiliar faces labeled as ingroup members than outgroup members (see ● Figure 5.9). The effects of ingroup/outgroup labeling can even override the effects of racial biases on these measures.

Dehumanizing Outgroups   Perceivers may not only process outgroup faces more superficially but also sometimes process them more like objects and lower-order animals than like fellow humans. Dehumanization has played a role in atrocities throughout history, such as in the Nazi propaganda that characterized the Jews in Germany as disease-spreading rats and blacks as half-apes. The continued presence of some of this kind of imagery in contemporary life is chilling, as in the examples discussed in the introduction of this chapter of black athletes in numerous countries being taunted with monkey chants. When former rock star Ted Nugent called Barack Obama "a chimpanzee" and "sub-human mongrel" in a 2014 interview (Haraldsson, 2014), this marked only one of countless examples of white Americans using such imagery to describe Obama.

These blatant examples are shockingly plentiful deep into the second decade of the twenty-first century, but they are more the exception than the rule. What may be much more common, however, is how people often implicitly dehumanize members of particular outgroups. Just as measures like the IAT are used to capture implicit racism, similar measures have been used to assess automatic, implicit dehumanization. Using these techniques, researchers around the world have found strong evidence for automatic dehumanization of various outgroups (Haslam, 2015; Kteily et al., 2015). Studies have shown, for example, that many individuals (even as young as 6 years old) automatically but nonconsciously associate black men, people of low socioeconomic status, and people from various countries with animals such as apes, rats, and dogs (Costello & Hodson, 2014; Goff, Eberhardt et al., 2008; Loughnan et al., 2014; Wilde et al., 2014). Indeed, this tendency may be so deeply rooted that we can see it play out in the brain. Lasana Harris and others have found that when people perceive or think about members of particular stigmatized outgroups, their patterns of brain activity suggest that they are responding to these outgroup members more as they would to objects than to fully human individuals who are capable of their own agency and mental states (Harris & Fiske, 2011; Lee & Harris, 2014).

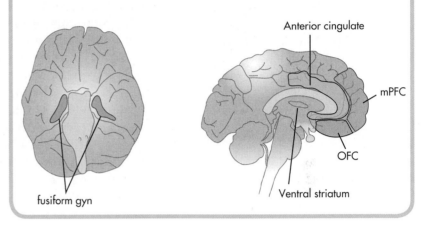

● **FIGURE 5.9**

The Neuroscience of Ingroups and Outgroups

Highlighted in color in these anatomical images of the brain are some key brain regions associated with making ingroup/outgroup distinctions and related intergroup evaluations. "OFC" is the orbitofrontal cortex, and "mPFC" is the medial prefrontal cortex. Greater activity in the OFC, for example, has been associated with stronger preference for ingroup faces.
Based on Cikara & Van Bavel, 2014

These implicit processes of dehumanization may be subtle, but the consequences can be profound. Phillip Goff and his colleagues (2014) found that police officers who more strongly associated black men with apes were more likely to use force against black children. Laurie Rudman and Kris Mescher (2012) found that men who automatically associated women with animals or objects showed stronger inclination to sexually harass or rape women. Luca Andrighetto and others (2014) found that Italian students who tended to associate Japanese and Haitians in dehumanizing ways (as machines or animals, respectively) were less willing than other students to help them after natural disasters in Japan and Haiti.

Fundamental Motives Between Groups The roots of dividing into ingroups and outgroups run quite deep in our evolutionary history, as early humans' survival depended on forming relatively small groups of similar others. A fundamental motive to protect one's ingroup and be suspicious of outgroups is therefore likely to have evolved. Consistent with this idea are the results of experiments that demonstrate that when people's basic motivations of self-protection are activated—such as in response to a threatening situation, economic scarcity, a scary movie, concerns about the flu, or even being in a completely dark room— people are more prone to exhibit prejudice toward outgroups or to be especially hesitant to see possible outgroup members as part of one's ingroup (Makhanova et al., 2015; Maner et al., 2012; Schaller & Neuberg, 2012).

The flip side to the distrust of outgroups is the positive feelings we have toward being part of an ingroup. The feeling of connection and solidarity we have with our own groups enhances our sense of control and meaning, and it is associated with numerous psychological as well as physical health benefits (Greenaway et al., 2015; Paéz et al., 2015). William Swann and Michael Buhrmester (2015) use the term *identity fusion* to describe the sense of "oneness" that people may feel with a group. This feeling can motivate helpful behavior toward the group, even at the risk of personal sacrifice. In general, when we are feeling threatened or uncertain, we become especially motivated to reaffirm our identification and closeness with an ingroup, which can make us feel more safe and secure (Cikara & Van Bavel, 2014; Hogg, 2014; Knapton et al., 2015).

From time to time our fundamental motivation for self-protection and preservation runs smack into the ultimate obstacle: thoughts about death and mortality. According to *Terror Management Theory*, which was discussed in Chapter 3, people cope with the fear of their own death by constructing worldviews that help preserve their self-esteem and important values. According to this perspective, favoring ingroups over outgroups is one important way that people preserve their cultural worldviews and, by doing so, try to attain a kind of immortality. This theory has been supported by numerous studies that demonstrate that when individuals are made to think about mortality—such as by presenting them with images of cemeteries or making them think about decomposing bodies—they become more likely to exhibit various ingroup biases, including through stereotypes and prejudice toward a variety of outgroups (Greenberg & Arndt, 2012; Greenberg et al., 2009). Male students in an experiment by Russell Webster and Donald Saucier (2011), for example, expressed significantly more discrimination toward gay men if they had just written about what they thought would happen to them when they die than if they had written about the pain of going to the dentist.

> Being reminded of one's own mortality makes people put things into greater perspective, thereby tending to reduce ingroup–outgroup distinctions and hostilities.
>
> **FALSE**

Motives Concerning Intergroup Dominance and Status Some people are especially motivated to preserve inequities between groups of people in society. For example, people with a **social dominance orientation** have a desire to see their ingroups as dominant over other groups and tend to support cultural values that contribute to the oppression of other groups. Individuals with this orientation tend to endorse sentiments such as "If certain groups stayed in their place, we would have fewer problems" and to disagree with statements such as "Group equality should be our ideal." Research in numerous countries throughout the world has found that ingroup identification and outgroup derogation and dehumanization can be especially strong among people with a social dominance orientation (Kteily et al., 2015; Levin et al., 2013; Prati et al., 2015; Pratto et al., 2013).

Social dominance orientations promote self-interest. But some ideologies support a social structure that may actually oppose one's self-interest, depending on the status of one's groups. John Jost and his colleagues (Jost et al., 2015; van der Toorn et al., 2015) have focused on what they call **system justification theory**, which proposes that people are motivated (at least in part) to defend and justify the existing social, political, and economic conditions. System-justifying beliefs protect the status quo. Groups with power, of course, may promote the status quo to preserve their own advantaged position. But although some disadvantaged groups might be able to improve their circumstances if they were to challenge an economic or political system, members of disadvantaged groups with a system justification orientation think that the system is fair and just, and they may admire and even show outgroup favoritism to outgroups that thrive in this system.

social dominance orientation A desire to see one's ingroup as dominant over other groups and a willingness to adopt cultural values that facilitate oppression over other groups.

system justification theory A theory that proposes that people are motivated (at least in part) to defend and justify the existing social, political, and economic conditions.

Stereotype Content Model   According to the **stereotype content model** (Kervyn et al., 2015; North & Fiske, 2014), many group stereotypes vary along two dimensions: warmth and competence. Groups may be considered high on both dimensions, low on both, or high on one dimension but low on the other. For example, the elderly may be stereotyped as high on warmth but low on competence.

The stereotype content model proposes that stereotypes about the competence of a group are influenced by the relative *status* of that group in society—higher relative status is associated with higher competence. Stereotypes about the warmth of a group are influenced by perceived *competition* with the group—greater perceived competition is associated with lower warmth. For example, groups that are of low status but that remain compliant and do not try to upset the status quo are likely to be stereotyped as low in competence but high in warmth. On the other hand, a wave of immigrants who enter a country with low status but are seen as competing for jobs and resources may be perceived as low in both competence and warmth. For groups that are seen as high on one dimension but low on the other, there may be a perceived trade-off between competence and warmth. A woman climbing up the corporate ladder by demonstrating strong competence, for example, may be seen as much less warm. If she tries to demonstrate warmth, however, she may be seen as less competent.

Robbers Cave: A Field Study in Intergroup Conflict   Robbers Cave State Park in Oklahoma was the unlikely setting for one of the most classic field experiments in social psychology. In the summer of 1954, a small group of 11-year-old boys—all white middle-class youngsters, all strangers to one another—arrived at a 200-acre camp located in a densely wooded area of the park. The boys spent the first week or so hiking, swimming, boating, and camping out. After a while, they gave themselves a group name and printed it on their caps and T-shirts. At first, the boys thought they were the only ones at the camp. Soon, however, they discovered that there was a second group and that tournaments had been arranged between the two groups.

What these boys didn't know was that they were participants in an elaborate study conducted by Muzafer Sherif and his colleagues (1961). Parents had given permission for their sons to take part in an experiment for a study of competitiveness and cooperation. The two groups were brought in separately, and only after each had formed its own culture was the other's presence revealed. When the "Rattlers" and the "Eagles" finally met, they did so under tense circumstances, competing against each other in football, a treasure hunt, tug of war, and other events. For each event, the winning team was awarded points; the tournament winner was promised a trophy, medals, and other prizes. Almost overnight, the groups turned into hostile antagonists, and their rivalry escalated into a full-scale war. Group flags were burned, cabins were ransacked, and a food fight that resembled a riot exploded in the mess hall. Keep in mind that the participants in this study were well-adjusted boys. Yet as Sherif (1966) noted, a naive observer would have thought the boys were "wicked, disturbed, and vicious" (p. 85).

Creating a monster through competition was easy. Restoring the peace, however, was not. First the experimenters tried saying nice things to the Rattlers about the Eagles and vice versa, but the propaganda campaign did not work. Then the two groups were brought together under noncompetitive circumstances,

stereotype content model   A model proposing that the relative status and competition between groups influence group stereotypes along the dimensions of competence and warmth.

but that didn't help either. What did eventually work was the introduction of **superordinate goals**, mutual goals that could be achieved only through cooperation between the groups. For example, the experimenters arranged for the camp truck to break down, and both groups were needed to pull it up a steep hill. This strategy worked like a charm. By the end of camp, the two groups were so friendly that they insisted on traveling home on the same bus. In just three weeks, the Rattlers and Eagles experienced the kinds of changes that often take generations to unfold: They formed close-knit groups, went to war, and made peace.

The events of Robbers Cave mimicked the kinds of conflict that plague people all over the world. The simplest explanation for this conflict is competition. Assign strangers to groups, throw the groups into contention, stir the pot, and soon there's conflict. Similarly, the intergroup benefits of reducing the focus on competition by activating superordinate goals are also evident around the world. When the disparate and contentious groups of a country or university find themselves pulling together in conflict or competition with another country or college, for example, the prejudices and discrimination that kept the groups apart often are cast aside in the pursuit of a common goal.

Realistic Conflict Theory The view that direct competition for valuable but limited resources breeds hostility between groups is called **realistic conflict theory** (Levine & Campbell, 1972). As a simple matter of economics, one group may fare better in the struggle for land, jobs, or power than another group. The losing group becomes frustrated and resentful, the winning group feels threatened and protective—and, before long, conflict heats to a rapid boil. It is likely that a good deal of prejudice in the world is driven by the realities of competition (Duckitt & Mphuthing, 1998; Filindra & Pearson-Merkowitz, 2013; Stephan et al., 2005; Zárate et al., 2004). For example, Marcel Coenders and others (2008) found that support for discrimination against ethnic minority groups tended to increase in the Netherlands when the unemployment level had recently risen. David Butz and Kuma Yogeeswaran (2011) found that students in the United States indicated more prejudice against Asian Americans if they had just read information about serious economic problems and growing competition for scarce resources.

But there is much more to prejudice than real competition. "Realistic" competition for resources may in fact be imagined—a perception in the mind of an individual who is not engaged in any real conflict. In addition, people may become resentful of other groups not because of their conviction that their own security or resources are threatened by these groups but because of their sense of **relative deprivation**, the belief that they fare poorly compared with others. What matters to the proverbial Smiths is not the size of their house per se but whether it is larger than the Jones's house next door (Moscatelli et al., 2014; H. J. Smith & Pettigrew, 2015).

Social Identity Theory

People all over the world believe that their own nation, culture, language, and religion are better and more deserving than others. Part of the reason for that is even more basic than real or perceived competition for finite resources. Rather, it stems from something more subtle and psychological.

superordinate goal A shared goal that can be achieved only through cooperation among individuals or groups.

realistic conflict theory The theory that hostility between groups is caused by direct competition for limited resources.

relative deprivation Feelings of discontent aroused by the belief that one fares poorly compared with others.

A classic study of high school boys in Bristol, England, conducted by Henri Tajfel and his colleagues (1971) begins to reveal this point. The boys in this study were shown a series of dotted slides, and their task was to estimate the number of dots on each. The slides were presented in rapid-fire succession so the dots could not be counted. Later, the experimenter told the participants that some people are chronic "overestimators" and that others are "underestimators." As part of a second, entirely separate task, participants were divided into two groups—one that was said to consist of overestimators and the other of underestimators. (In fact, they were divided randomly.) Participants were then told to allocate points to other participants that could be cashed in for money.

Joe Raedle/Getty Images

American fans bask in the glory of their team's success at a World Cup soccer game.

This procedure was designed to create *minimal groups* in which people are categorized on the basis of trivial, minimally important similarities. Tajfel's overestimators and underestimators were not long-term rivals, did not have a history of antagonism, were not frustrated, did not compete for a limited resource, and were not even acquainted with each other. Still, participants consistently allocated more points to members of their own group than to members of the other group. This pattern of discrimination, called **ingroup favoritism**, has been found repeatedly in studies in many countries and using a variety of different measures (Capozza & Brown, 2000; Pinter & Greenwald, 2011; Scheepers et al., 2006).

To explain ingroup favoritism, Tajfel (1982) and John Turner (1987) proposed **social identity theory**. According to this theory, which is illustrated in ● Figure 5.10, each of us strives to enhance our self-esteem, which has two components: (1) a *personal* identity and (2) various collective or *social* identities that are based on the groups to which we belong. In other words, people can boost their self-esteem through their own personal achievements or through affiliation with successful groups. What's nice about the need for social identity is that it leads us to derive pride from our connections with others even if we don't receive any direct benefits from these others. What's sad, however, is that we often feel the need to belittle "them" in order to feel secure about "us." Religious fervor, racial and ethnic conceit, and aggressive nationalism may all fulfill this more negative side of our social identity. Even gossiping can play this role; Jennifer Bosson and others (2006; Weaver & Bosson, 2011) found that when people shared negative attitudes about a third party, they felt closer to each other.

Shadenfreude is an intimidating-looking word for a familiar feeling—the experience of pleasure at other people's misfortunes, particularly for celebrities or others we don't feel empathy for. Mina Cikara (2015; Cikara et al., 2014) has found that people who identify strongly with their social groups frequently experience this pleasure toward outgroup misfortunes, along with a lack of empathy.

Two basic predictions arose from social identity theory: (1) Threats to one's self-esteem heighten the need for ingroup favoritism, and (2) expressions of

ingroup favoritism The tendency to discriminate in favor of ingroups over outgroups.

social identity theory The theory that people favor ingroups over outgroups in order to enhance their self-esteem.

● **FIGURE 5.10**

Social Identity Theory

According to social identity theory people strive to enhance self-esteem, which has two components: a personal identity and various social identities that derive from the groups to which we belong. Thus, people may boost their self-esteem by viewing their ingroups more favorably than outgroups.

© Cengage Learning

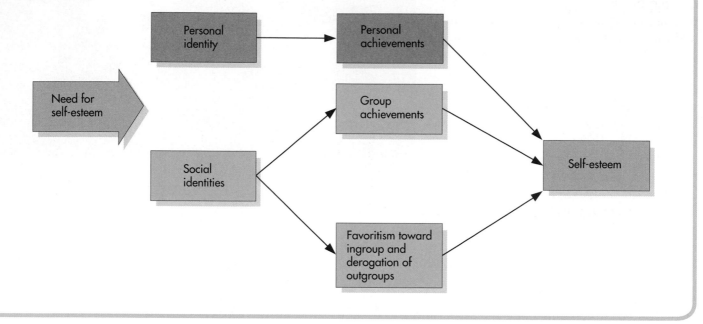

ingroup favoritism enhance one's self-esteem. Research generally supports these predictions (Fiske & Tablante, 2015; Mackie & Smith, 2015).

Steven Fein and Steven Spencer (1997) proposed that threats to one's self-esteem can lead individuals to use available negative stereotypes to derogate members of stereotyped groups, and that by derogating others they can feel better about themselves. In one study, for example, Fein and Spencer gave participants positive or negative feedback about their performance on a test of social and verbal skills—feedback that temporarily bolstered or threatened their self-esteem. These participants then took part in what was supposedly a second experiment in which they evaluated a job applicant. All participants received a photograph of a young woman, her résumé, and a videotape of a job interview. Half the participants were given information that suggested that the woman (named Julie Goldberg) was Jewish. The other half was given information that suggested that the woman (named Maria D'Agostino) was not Jewish. On the campus where the study was held, there was a popular negative stereotype of the "Jewish American Princess" that often targeted upper-middle-class Jewish women from the New York area.

As predicted, there were two important results (see ● Figure 5.11). First, among participants whose self-esteem had been lowered by negative feedback, they rated the woman more negatively if she seemed to be Jewish than if she did not, even though the videotaped job interview and credentials of the two women were the same. Second, participants who had received negative feedback and were given an opportunity to belittle the Jewish woman later exhibited a post-experiment increase in self-esteem—the more negatively they evaluated the Jewish woman, the better

● FIGURE 5.11

Self-Esteem and Prejudice

Participants in a study by Fein and Spencer received positive or negative feedback and then evaluated a female job applicant who was believed to be either Jewish or not Jewish. This study had two key results: (1) Participants whose self-esteem had been lowered by negative feedback evaluated the woman more negatively if they thought she was Jewish than if they thought she was not (left); and (2) negative-feedback participants given the opportunity to belittle the Jewish woman showed a post-experiment increase in self-esteem (right).
Fein and Spencer, 1997.

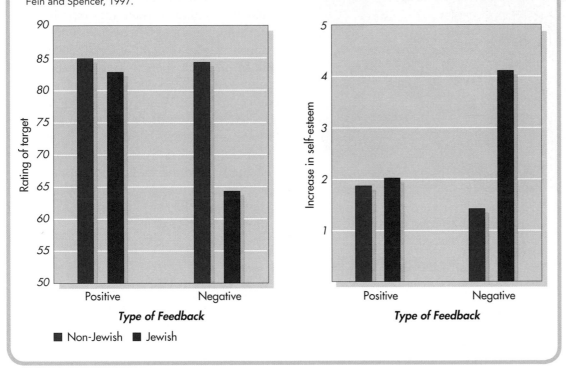

■ Non-Jewish   ■ Jewish

these participants felt about themselves. In sum, the results of this experiment suggest that a blow to one's self-image evokes prejudice and the expression of prejudice helps restore self-image.

Intergroup discrimination is achieved not only through negative reactions and behaviors toward outgroups but also through being especially favorable and helpful toward one's ingroups. In their aptly titled paper, "With Malice Toward None and Charity For Some," Anthony Greenwald and Thomas Pettigrew (2014) propose that this is the more common type of intergroup bias, at least in the United States today. Malice toward outgroups tends to be frowned upon, whereas providing important advantages to one's ingroups may be more subtle and acceptable.

■ Culture and Social Identity

Individuals' social identities are clearly important to people across cultures. Collectivists are more likely than individualists to value their connectedness and interdependence with the people and groups around them, and their personal identities are tied closely with their social identities. Collectivists do show some biases favoring their ingroups—indeed, being oriented strongly toward one's ingroup can be highly valued in their cultures—and may draw sharper distinctions

Being part of a small, close-knit group can be an important, rewarding part of one's personal identity.

between ingroup and outgroup members than individualists do (Chen et al., 2002; Gudykunst & Bond, 1997; Owe et al., 2013; Ruffle & Sosis, 2006). Along these lines, in a study of nearly 45,000 individuals from 36 countries André van Hoorn (2015) found that collectivists tend to have a narrower circle of people they trust than do individualists.

However, a number of researchers have found that people from collectivist cultures are less likely to enhance their ingroups in order to boost their own self-esteem (Heine, 2005; Lehman et al., 2004; Snibbe et al., 2003; Yuki, 2003). In addition, people from the collectivist cultures of East Asia tend to have higher tolerance for what Westerners would consider contradictions (such as that something can be both good and bad at the same time), and this may explain why East Asianers are more likely to see their ingroups as having both positive and negative qualities compared to Westerners, who tend to emphasize the positive aspects of their ingroups much more exclusively (Spencer-Rogers et al., 2012).

Culture and Socialization

The list of familiar stereotypes is quite long. Athletes are dumb, math majors are geeks, Americans are loud, Italians are emotional, Californians are laid back, white men can't jump, car salesmen can't be trusted. And on and on it goes. Dividing people into social categories, including ingroups and outgroups, certainly is a key factor in the formation of stereotypes and prejudices. But with so many well-known stereotypes and prejudices, many of which are shared around the world, it is clear that we are somehow taught these stereotypes from our culture. We turn now to examine those processes.

Socialization refers to the processes by which people learn the norms, rules, and information of a culture or group. We learn a tremendous amount of information (often without even realizing it) by absorbing what we see around us in our culture, groups, and families. These lessons include what various stereotypes are, how valued or devalued various groups are, and which prejudices are acceptable to have.

Consider the story of something that happened to one of the authors of this book. When he was about 8 years old, his two best friends one day turned on him and derisively called him a "Jew ball." They had never thought of him as different from them or categorized him as Jewish before, and yet on this day, suddenly Jewishness was relevant—and negative to them. But why *then*, and how did they come up with "Jew ball"?! Only much later did it become clear that they had misheard their father say "Jew boy." Trying to model their father's values, they used an approximation of this expression against their friend, and thereafter they saw him in a different way. The biased lens through which the father saw people was passed down to the next generation.

Although it certainly isn't always the case, the stereotypes and prejudices of a parent can shape the stereotypes and prejudices of a child, often in implicit ways (Castelli et al., 2009). More generally, and more pervasively, the stereotypes and prejudices exhibited by peers, the popular media, and one's culture are part of the air each of us breathes as we develop, and these influences can be profound. These effects typically are gradual, as they develop over the course of a lifetime of exposure. But they can also be immediate, as demonstrated in a recent set of studies by Greg Willard and others (2015). White students who were exposed to a fellow white student's negative nonverbal behavior toward a black student became more likely to exhibit a variety of negative racial attitudes and behaviors than if they saw the same behavior targeting a white student or if they saw positive nonverbal behavior toward a black student. Willard and his colleagues characterized this effect as a contagion of racial bias, as if the students "caught" the disease from exposure to the subtly prejudiced behavior of a fellow student.

To narrow our discussion we will focus in this section on gender stereotypes and sexism, but it is important to recognize that these processes are relevant to all kinds and targets of stereotypes, prejudice, and discrimination.

Gender Stereotypes: Blue for Boys, Pink for Girls
Our traditional story begins with what are often the first words uttered when a baby is born: "It's a boy!" or "It's a girl!" In many hospitals, the newborn boy is immediately given a blue hat and the newborn girl a pink hat. The infant receives a gender-appropriate name and is showered with gender-appropriate gifts. Over the next few years, the typical boy is supplied with toy trucks, baseballs, pretend tools, toy guns, and chemistry sets; the typical girl is furnished with dolls, stuffed animals, pretend makeup kits, kitchen and tea sets, and dress-up clothes. As they enter school, many expect the boy to earn money by mowing lawns and to enjoy violent superhero movies, while they expect the girl to earn money by babysitting and to enjoy sweet stories about friendship or love.

These distinctions persist in college, as more male students major in economics and the sciences and more female students major in the arts, languages, and humanities. In the workforce, more men become doctors, construction workers, auto mechanics, airplane pilots, investment bankers, and engineers. In contrast, more women become secretaries, schoolteachers, nurses, flight attendants, bank tellers, and housewives. Back on the home front, the life cycle begins again when a couple has their first baby and hear the words, "It's a girl!" or "It's a boy!"

The Blues and the Pinks. Even a very quick look at a toy store illustrates dramatic differences in how boys and girls are socialized. For example, boys are encouraged to play active, loud, and violent games (left), whereas girls are encouraged to engage in quieter, nurturing role play (right).

UrbanZone / Alamy

Spencer Grant/Art Directors & Trip / Alamy

The traditional pinks and blues are not as distinct today as they used to be. Many gender barriers of the past have broken down, and the colors have somewhat blended together. Indeed, there has been a dramatic increase in awareness of gender as something other than a binary category and that the gender one is assigned to at birth does not always reflect the gender identity of the individual later in life. In addition, people are more likely to defy and confront gender-based stereotyping and discrimination today than in years past. Nevertheless, the stereotypes—and, as we discussed earlier, sexism—persist.

What do people say when asked to describe the typical man and woman? Around the world males are said to be more adventurous, assertive, aggressive, independent, and task-oriented; females are thought to be more sensitive, gentle, dependent, agreeable, emotional, and people-oriented. Young children distinguish men from women well before their first birthday, often identify themselves and others as boys or girls by 3 years of age, form gender-stereotypic beliefs and preferences about stories, toys, and other objects soon after that, and then use their stereotypes in judging others and favoring their own gender in intergroup situations (Golombok & Hines, 2002; Knobloch et al., 2005; Löckenhoff et al., 2014; Martin & Ruble, 2010; Wood & Eagly, 2010).

Gerianne Alexander (2003) proposed that children's preferences about sex-based toys, although partly due to gender socialization, also have neurobiological and evolutionary roots. She based this conclusion from data about children exposed prenatally to atypical levels of sex hormones and from data about sex differences in toy preferences among nonhuman primates. For example, one intriguing study reported that vervet monkeys showed sex differences in toy preferences similar to those seen in human children (Alexander & Hines, 2002).

Although biological and evolutionary factors may play a role in some of these preferences, it is clear that children have ample opportunity to learn gender stereotypes and roles from their parents and other role models (Montañés et al., 2012; Tenenbaum & Leaper, 2002). Beliefs about males and females are so deeply ingrained that they influence the behavior of adults literally the moment a baby is born. In one fascinating study, the first-time parents of 15 girls and 15 boys were interviewed within 24 hours of the babies' births. There were no differences between the male and female newborns in height, weight, or other aspects of physical appearance. Yet the parents of girls rated their babies as softer, smaller, and more finely featured. The fathers of boys saw their sons as stronger, larger, more alert, and better coordinated (Rubin et al., 1974). Could it be there really were differences that only the parents were able to discern? Doubtful. In another study, Emily Mondschein and others (2000) found that mothers of 11-month-olds underestimated their infants' crawling ability if they were girls but overestimated it if they were boys.

As they develop, boys and girls receive many divergent messages in many different settings. Barbara Morrongiello and Tess Dawber (2000) conducted a study that reflects this point. They showed mothers videotapes of children engaging in somewhat risky activities on a playground and asked them to stop the tape and indicate whatever they would ordinarily say to their own child in the situation shown. Mothers of daughters intervened more frequently and more quickly than did mothers of sons. As shown in Table 5.2, mothers of daughters were more likely to caution the child about getting hurt, whereas mothers of sons were more likely to encourage the child's risky playing. In a more recent study by Morrongiello and others (2010), mothers and fathers were more likely to react to a toddler's risk-taking behavior with anger and a focus on discipline if it was a boy, and with safety and the sense that the child could learn not to engage in such behavior if it was a girl.

Social Role Theory As children develop, they begin to look at the larger culture around them and see who occupies what roles in society as well as how these roles are valued. According to Alice Eagly's (Eagly & Wood, 2012; Koenig & Eagly, 2014) **social role theory**, although the perception of sex differences may be based on some real differences, it is magnified by the unequal social roles men and women occupy.

The process involves three steps. First, through a combination of biological and social factors, a division of labor between the sexes has emerged over time, both at home and in the work setting. Men are more likely to work in construction or business; women are more likely to care for children and to take lower-paying jobs. Second, since people behave in ways that fit the roles they play, men are more likely than women to wield physical, social, and economic power. Third, these behavioral differences provide a continuing basis for social perception, leading us to perceive men as dominant and women as domestic "by nature," when in fact the differences may reflect the roles they play. In short, sex stereotypes are shaped by—and often confused with—the unequal distribution of men and women into different social roles. According to this theory, perceived differences between men and women are based on real behavioral differences that are mistakenly assumed to arise from gender rather than from social roles. Social role theory and socialization processes more generally can, of course, be extended beyond gender stereotypes and sexism. Seeing what groups of people tend to occupy what roles in society can fuel numerous stereotypes and prejudices.

Media Effects More than ever, children, adolescents, and adults seem to be immersed in popular culture transmitted via the mass media. Watching TV shows on our phones or iPads while on the stationary bike at the gym, checking out the latest viral videos or celebrity Instagram posts while taking a break at work or the coffee shop, seeing advertisements popping up on our computer screens like weeds, glancing at the tabloid cover shots of the latest starlet hounded by relentless paparazzi—there often seems no escape. Through the ever-present media, we are fed a steady diet of images of people. These images have the potential to perpetuate stereotypes and discrimination.

Fortunately, the days when the media portrayed women and people of color in almost exclusively stereotypical, powerless roles are gone. Still, research in numerous countries around the world examining such varied content as music videos, commercials and print ads, TV programs, and children's books reveals that stereotyping does persist (Kay & Furnham, 2013; Kirsch & Murnen, 2015; Michelle, 2012; Wallis, 2011).

More to the point is the fact that media depictions can influence viewers, often without the viewers realizing it. Studies have shown, for example, that female college students who had just watched a set of commercials in which the female characters were portrayed in stereotypical fashion tended to express lower self-confidence, less independence, and fewer career aspirations, and even performed more poorly on a math test, than did those who viewed stereotype-irrelevant or

▲ **TABLE 5.2**

What Mothers Would Say

Mothers of young boys or girls watched a videotape of another child engaging in somewhat risky behavior on a playground. The mothers were instructed to stop the videotape whenever they would say something to the child if the child were theirs and to indicate what they would say. Mothers of daughters stopped the tape much more often than mothers of sons to express caution ("Be careful!"), worry about injury ("You could fall!"), and directives to stop ("Stop that this instant!"). In contrast, mothers of sons were more likely to indicate encouragement ("Good job! Let me see you go higher!").

Context of Statement	Frequency of Statement by	
	Mothers of Girls	Mothers of Boys
Caution	3.9	0.7
Worry about injury	9.2	0.2
Directive to stop	9.3	0.6
Encouragement	0.5	3.0

Adapted from Morrongiello & Dawber, 2000.

social role theory The theory that small gender differences are magnified in perception by the contrasting social roles occupied by men and women.

counter-stereotypical ads (Davies et al., 2002; Geis et al., 1984; Jennings et al., 1980; Ward & Friedman, 2006). These effects are by no means limited to gender. Playing violent video games or listening to particular types of music, for example, can heighten aggression and discrimination against outgroup members (Greite-meyer, 2014; LaMarre et al., 2012).

Media images of impossibly thin or proportioned female models are implicated in the near-epidemic incidence of eating disorders and debilitating anxiety over physical appearance, particularly among young European American women (Henderson-King et al., 2001; Moradi et al., 2005; Ward & Friedman, 2006). The media's impact may be especially negative among individuals who already have concerns about their appearance or are particularly concerned with other people's opinions (Henderson-King & Henderson-King, 1997; McCabe et al., 2010). Men's body images are also affected by the media (Ricciardelli & McCabe, 2011; Sebag-Montefiore, 2015). Indeed, graphic images of muscular and lean male models have become increasingly prevalent of late. More and more cases come to light every year of boys and young men copying star athletes by taking steroids and other drugs that can make them look more like their role models but that can seriously threaten their health (Martin & Govender, 2011; McCreary, 2011; Melki et al., 2015).

Bill Aron/PhotoEdit

Mike Margol/PhotoEdit

Although images of attractive people sell magazines and many consumers enjoy looking at them, they do raise the question of whether exposure to so many of these kinds of images also produce negative consequences. For example, does repeated exposure to such images perpetuate stereotypes or cause some people to engage in dangerous behaviors to try to achieve what are often impossible and unhealthy standards of masculinity and femininity?

■ How Stereotypes Distort Perceptions and Resist Change

Once stereotypes and prejudices are in place due to the factors we've been discussing, why are they often so resistant to change? Although some stereotypes may be accurate, some certainly are false, and many are at least over-simplifications (Jussim, 2012; Madon et al., 1998; McCrae et al., 2013; Scherer et al., 2015). Why, then, do inaccurate stereotypes persist despite evidence that should discredit them? In this section we turn to some of the mechanisms that help perpetuate stereotypes.

Confirmation Biases and Self-Fulfilling Prophecies Imagine learning that a mother yelled at a 16-year-old girl, a lawyer behaved aggressively, and a Boy Scout grabbed the arm of an elderly woman crossing the street. Now imagine that a construction worker yelled at a 16-year-old girl, a homeless man behaved aggressively, and an ex-con grabbed the arm of an elderly woman crossing the street. Do very different images of these actions come to mind? This is a fundamental effect of stereotyping: Stereotypes of groups influence people's perceptions and interpretations of the behaviors of group members. This is especially likely when a target of a stereotype behaves in an ambiguous way; perceivers reduce the ambiguity by interpreting the behavior as consistent with the stereotype (Dunning & Sherman, 1997; Kunda et al., 1997).

The effect of stereotypes on individuals' perceptions is a type of confirmation bias, which, as we saw in Chapter 4, involves people's tendencies to interpret, seek, and create information that seems to confirm their expectations. In one classic study, for example, black and white sixth-grade boys saw pictures and descriptions of ambiguously aggressive behaviors (such as one child bumping into another). Both the black and the white boys judged the behaviors as more mean and threatening if the behaviors were performed by black boys than if they were done by white boys, thereby seeming to confirm racial stereotypes (Sagar & Schofield, 1980).

Stereotypes can be reinforced also through the **illusory correlation**, a tendency for people to overestimate the link between variables that are only slightly or not at all correlated (Hamilton & Rose, 1980; Kutzner & Fiedler, 2015; Sherman et al., 2009; Van Rooy et al., 2013). One kind of illusory correlation occurs when people overestimate the association between variables that are relatively rare. For example, if people read about a variety of criminal acts, most of which are committed by members of a majority group and some of which are committed by members of a particular minority group, they may overestimate the association between minority group status (a relatively rare group) and criminal behavior (a relatively rare behavior). This tendency can create or perpetuate negative stereotypes. Illusory correlations may also be produced through people's tendency to overestimate the association between variables they already expect to go together. For example, if perceivers who hold stereotypes about women being poor drivers witness 100 men and 100 women driving, and 10% of each group get into an accident, they may overestimate the number of women and underestimate the number of men who had accidents. In other words, they see an association between gender and accidents that is not supported by the data.

Stereotypes typically are held not just by individuals but by many people within a culture, and they are often perpetuated through repeated communications. In a classic demonstration, Gordon Allport and Leo Postman (1947) showed participants a picture of a subway train filled with passengers. In the picture were a black man dressed in a suit and a white man holding a razor. One participant viewed the scene briefly and then described it to a second participant who had not seen it. The second participant communicated the description to a third participant and so on, through six rounds of communication. The result: In more than half the sessions, the final participant's report indicated that the black man, not the white man, held the razor.

In a more recent demonstration of a similar point, Yoshihisa Kashima and others (2013) had Australian students read a story about an Australian Rules Football player. The students were put in groups of four. One person read the story, and after a delay of a few minutes transmitted the story to the next student, and so on down the four-person chain. The students were supposed to relay the story as accurately as possible. Some of the information in the story was consistent with stereotypes about Australian Rules Football players (e.g., "On the way, Gary and his mate drank several beers in the car"), and some of it was inconsistent with the stereotype (e.g., "He switched on some classical music"). Although the first student in the chain was likely to communicate both stereotype-consistent and stereotype-inconsistent information, as the story went from person to person the stereotype-inconsistent information was progressively screened out (see ● Figure 5.12). By the time the third person told the story to the final person in the chain, the football player seemed more clearly stereotypical than he had seemed in the original story.

Confirmation biases are bad enough. But even more disturbing are situations in which stereotyped group members are led to actually behave in stereotype-confirming ways. In other words, stereotypes can create self-fulfilling prophecies

● **FIGURE 5.12**

Stereotype Confirmation via Communication

Australian students read a story about an Australian Rules Football player who behaved in ways both consistent and inconsistent with stereotypes about such players. Each student who read the story then had to orally tell another student as much as he or she could remember about the story, who then in turn told a third student, who in turn told a fourth. Although the first student told both stereotype-consistent and -inconsistent details, by the time of the final telling of the story, more of the stereotype-inconsistent details dropped out, making the player sound much more stereotypic than he was.
Kashima et al., 2013

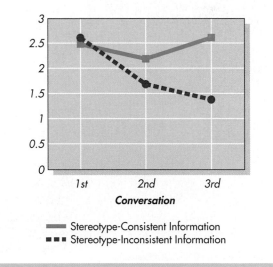

Stereotype-Consistent Information
■■■ Stereotype-Inconsistent Information

illusory correlation An overestimate of the association between variables that are only slightly or not at all correlated.

(Madon et al., 2011; Rosenthal, 2002). As noted in Chapter 4, a self-fulfilling prophecy occurs when a perceiver's false expectations about a person cause the person to behave in ways that confirm those expectations. Stereotypes can trigger such behavioral confirmation. Consider a classic experiment by Carl Word and others (1974) involving a situation of great importance in people's lives: the job interview. White participants, without realizing it, sat farther away, made more speech errors, and held shorter interviews when interviewing black applicants than they did when interviewing white applicants. This colder interpersonal style, in turn, caused the black applicants to behave in a nervous and awkward manner. In short, the whites' racial stereotypes and prejudice actually hurt the interview performance of the black candidates. Since the black candidates' interview performance tended to be objectively worse than that of the white candidates, it seemed to confirm the interviewers' negative stereotypes—but this poor performance was caused by the interviewers, not the interviewees.

> "Not everyone's life is what they make it. Some people's life is what other people make it."
> —A character in Alice Walker's short story "You Can't Keep a Good Woman Down"

Attributions and Subtyping People also maintain their stereotypes through how they explain the behaviors of others. Chapter 4 discusses how perceivers make attributions, or explanations, about the causes of other people's behaviors and how these attributions can sometimes be flawed. One key finding discussed in that chapter is that people often don't take into account the context that someone was in when they try to explain his or her behavior. This can help perpetuate negative stereotypes by, for example, people failing to recognize how a poor performance by a member of a stereotyped group may be due to the effects of these stereotypes rather than a lack of actual ability.

On the other hand, when people see others acting in ways that seem to contradict a stereotype, they may be *more* likely to think about situational factors in order to explain the surprising behavior. Rather than accept a stereotype-disconfirming behavior at face value, such as a woman defeating a man in an athletic contest, perceivers imagine the situational factors that might explain away this apparent exception to the rule, such as random luck, ulterior motives, or other special circumstances. In this way, perceivers can more easily maintain their stereotypes of these groups (Espinoza et al., 2014; Sekaquaptewa et al., 2003; Sherman et al., 2005).

People who believe that women are not tough and athletic may maintain this stereotype even in the face of examples like these women who defy it. One way they do this is by subtyping such individuals as exceptions who don't truly represent the general category of women.

If we encounter someone's behavior that clearly contradicts our stereotypes and we can't easily explain it away as due to some situational factor, we may unwittingly pull out another trick to preserve our stereotypes: We consider the action or the person a mere exception to the rule. Confronted with a woman who does not seem modest and nurturing, for example, people can either develop a more diversified image of females or toss the mismatch into a special *subtype*—say, "cutthroat women" or "divas." To the extent that people create this subtype, their existing image of women in general may remain relatively intact (Riek et al., 2013; Schneider & Bos, 2014; Wilder et al., 1996).

■ Automatic Stereotype Activation

Part of the power of stereotypes is they can bias our perceptions and responses even if we don't personally agree with them. In other words, we don't have to believe a stereotype for it to trigger illusory correlations and self-fulfilling prophecies or to influence how we think, feel, and behave toward group members. Sometimes just being aware of stereotypes in one's culture is enough to cause these effects. Moreover, stereotypes can be activated without our awareness.

In a very influential line of research, Patricia Devine (1989) distinguished between automatic and controlled processes in stereotyping. She argued that people have become highly aware of the content of many stereotypes through socialization from their culture. Because of this high awareness people may automatically activate stereotypes whenever they are exposed to members of groups for which popular stereotypes exist. Thus, just as after hearing *bacon and* many of us are automatically primed to think *eggs*, when we think of a stereotyped group we are also primed to think of concepts relevant to the stereotype.

To demonstrate this point Devine exposed white participants in one study to **subliminal presentations** on a computer monitor. Subliminally presented information is presented so quickly that perceivers do not even realize that they have been exposed to it. In Devine's study these presentations consisted of words relevant to stereotypes about black people, such as *Africa, ghetto, welfare,* and *basketball.* Because the words were presented subliminally, the participants were not consciously aware that they had seen these words. Those who were subliminally primed with many of these words activated the African American stereotype and saw another person's behavior in a more negative, hostile light. Especially noteworthy is the fact that these effects occurred *even among participants who did not consciously believe in the stereotypes in question.*

> People's very quick judgments are not influenced by a stereotype unless they actually believe the stereotype to be true.
>
> **FALSE**

Devine's theory sparked an explosion of interest in these issues. The conclusions from the ensuing research is that stereotypes can be activated implicitly and automatically, influencing subsequent thoughts, feelings, and behaviors even among perceivers who are relatively low in prejudice. But it also is clear that several factors can make such activation more or less likely to happen. For example, some stereotypes are much more prevalent than others in a particular culture, and with more exposure to a stereotype comes a greater likelihood of automatic activation. Another factor is how prejudiced the perceiver is. Although stereotypes can be activated automatically even among perceivers very low in prejudice, the threshold for what triggers stereotype activation may be lower for those relatively high in prejudice (Lepore & Brown, 2002; Wittenbrink et al., 1997).

Motivation can also play an important role. For example, when people's self-esteem is threatened, they may become motivated to stereotype others so that they will feel better about themselves, and this can make them more likely to activate stereotypes automatically (Spencer et al., 1998). What about being motivated to control oneself from activating or applying stereotypes? Is this effective? People who are motivated for intrinsic reasons (that is, they really don't want to *be* prejudiced, rather than just not wanting to *be seen by others* as prejudiced) tend to be somewhat more successful at this kind of self-regulation. We will return to this issue in more detail later in the chapter.

■ The Shooter Bias

The issue of automatic activation of stereotypes and its effects can be seen in concrete terms by focusing on one particular type of tragedy that has occurred far

subliminal presentation A method of presenting stimuli so faintly or rapidly that people do not have any conscious awareness of having been exposed to them.

too often: the shooting of an unarmed African American man by the police. The opening of this chapter mentioned protests stemming from a series of incidents in late 2014 and 2015 in which police shot or killed unarmed African American men in response to what the police said was threatening behavior. One such incident that occurred more than a decade before inspired a wave of social psychological research relevant to this issue. In New York City on February 4, 1999, a West African immigrant named Amadou Diallo was spotted by four white police officers who thought he was acting suspiciously and that he matched the general description of a suspected rapist they were searching for. As they approached him, Diallo reached into his pocket and began pulling out his wallet. One of the officers yelled, "Gun!" The police fired at Diallo 41 times, hitting him with 19 of the bullets. Diallo lay dead in the vestibule; he did not have a weapon.

Protesters held rallies in the days that followed, chanting "41 shots" and holding up wallets. Others defended the police officers, noting how difficult it is to make life-or-death decisions in the blink of an eye. The officers were found not guilty of any criminal charges. A central question, of course, was whether stereotypes associated with the color of Diallo's skin made the officers more likely to misperceive the wallet as a gun. Although none of us can ever know whether this was the case in the Diallo tragedy, it is possible to apply social psychology research to answer the more general question of whether an unarmed man is more likely to be misperceived as holding a gun if he is black than if he is white.

Keith Payne (2001) was the first to publish a study directly inspired by this question. The participants in his study were undergraduate students, not police officers, but their task was to try to make the kind of decision the police had to make: very quickly identify an object as a weapon or not. Pictures of these objects (such as guns or tools) were presented on a computer screen, immediately preceded by a quick presentation of a black or a white male face. The pictures were presented for fractions of a second. Payne found that the participants were more likely to mistake a harmless object for a weapon if it was preceded by a black face than if the object was preceded by a white face. In other words, a quick glimpse of a black male face primed the participants to see a threatening object more than seeing a white male face did.

Joshua Correll and others (2002) designed a video game for their experiment in which they had participants decide whether or not to "shoot" a target person who appeared on their computer screen (see ● Figure 5.13). Some of these targets were white men and others were black men. Some of them held guns and others held harmless objects (such as a black cell phone or a wallet). If the target held a gun, the participants were supposed to hit a "shoot" key as quickly as possible. If he held a harmless object, they were to hit a "don't shoot" key as quickly as they could.

As in the Payne study, these participants showed a bias consistent with racial stereotypes. If the target held a gun, they were quicker to press the "shoot" key if he was black than if he was white. If the target held a harmless object, they took longer to press the "don't shoot" key if he was black than if he was white. In addition, participants were more likely to mistakenly "shoot" an unarmed target if he was black than if he was white.

Since these first experiments, a large number of others followed to examine the processes involved more closely. For example, Debbie Ma and Joshua Correll (2011) found that this racial bias in decisions to shoot was significantly stronger if the targets looked more stereotypic of their respective races (as rated by samples of participants) than if they did not. In a study examining a different stereotype, Christian Unkelbach and others (2008) found that Australian participants were

● **FIGURE 5.13**

Shoot or Not?

These are examples of scenes from the video game that Joshua Correll and his colleagues created to investigate whether perceivers, playing the role of police officers, would be biased by the target's race when trying to determine very quickly whether they should shoot him because he is holding a weapon or refrain from shooting because he is holding a harmless object.
Correll et al., 2002.

more likely to shoot at targets wearing Muslim headgear than bareheaded targets who did not appear Muslim.

Taken together the results of these studies suggest that when the decision must be made very quickly, members of some groups are more likely to be mistakenly perceived as holding a gun than members of other groups. It is important to note, though, that the participants in the initial studies were not police officers; they were undergraduate students or individuals from a community sample. Police officers receive extensive training in these kinds of tasks. But as the quote in the margin by social psychologist Anthony Greenwald indicates, the police may not be trained to avoid activating racial stereotypes, and given the prevalence and power of these stereotypes in our society, there is good reason to suspect that they would be influenced by them in split-second decisions.

Fortunately, several researchers have conducted these experiments with police officers as participants (Correll et al., 2007b; Peruche & Plant, 2006). In some of this research, police officers have shown a similar bias to mistakenly "shoot" a black than white target, and in some they have shown little or no racial bias in the decision to shoot. Even in the studies in which the officers' *decisions* were not as racially biased, however, racial bas was evident in the officers' *response times*, indicating that they were quicker to decide to shoot armed black than white targets and slower to decide to not shoot unarmed black than white targets. In addition, several studies have also found that for both civilians and police officers, training designed specifically to curtail these biases can be effective, at least to some degree.

Reviewing all these studies, Joshua Correll and others (2014) concluded that stereotypes certainly can alter perceptions about the presence of weapons and the decision to shoot. In addition, even though police officers are able to avoid these biases under testing conditions, when officers must make these decisions under conditions of fatigue, high stress, and distraction—the conditions officers often face when having to make real shoot-or-not decisions—their ability to overcome stereotype-based biases are compromised, thus increasing the likelihood of the mistakes seen in the tragic incidents that sparked all this research.

"Police receive training to make them more sensitive to weapons, but they don't get training to undo unconscious race stereotypes or biases."

—Anthony Greenwald

David Sipress/The New Yorker Collection 2000/Cartoonbank.com.

You look like this sketch of someone who is thinking about committing a crime.

If individuals are racially biased in these perceptions and decisions, does that mean that they have racist attitudes and beliefs? The evidence thus far suggests that this may not be the case. For example, Correll and others (2002) found that the the racial bias in the decision to shoot was not related to participants' levels of racial prejudice. In addition, these researchers also found that African American participants showed the same bias against black targets as white participants did, again suggesting that racial prejudice is not necessarily reflected in this bias. Consistent with much of the research we've reported in this chapter, *awareness* of the stereotype was a necessary factor, but believing it to be true was not. Indeed, Correll and others (2007a) found that by manipulating the accessibility of stereotypes that associate blacks with danger in perceivers' minds (such as by having them first read newspaper articles about black or white criminals), they could strengthen or weaken this bias.

Reducing the Problem: Social Psychological Solutions

We have discussed the persistence of stereotypes, prejudice, and discrimination today, as well as numerous factors at the root of these problems. In this final section, we focus on some of the approaches that have been suggested for combating stereotypes, prejudice, and discrimination.

Intergroup Contact

One of the many enduring ideas in Gordon Allport's (1954) classic book, *The Nature of Prejudice,* was the **contact hypothesis**, which states that under certain conditions, direct contact between members of rival groups will reduce intergroup prejudice. Around the time of the publication of this book, the U.S. Supreme Court ruled in the historic 1954 case of *Brown v. Board of Education of Topeka* that racially separate schools were inherently unequal and violated the U.S. Constitution. In part, the decision was informed by empirical evidence supplied by 32 eminent social scientists on the harmful effects of segregation on both race relations and the self-esteem and academic achievement of black students (Allport et al., 1953). The Supreme Court's decision propelled the nation into a large-scale social experiment. What would be the effect?

Despite the Court's ruling, desegregation proceeded slowly. There were stalling tactics, lawsuits, and vocal and even violent opposition. Many schools remained untouched until the early 1970s. Then, as the dust began to settle, research brought the grave realization that contact between black and white schoolchildren was not having the intended effect on intergroup attitudes. Walter Stephan (1986) reviewed studies conducted during and after desegregation and found that although 13% of the studies reported a decrease in prejudice among whites, 34% reported no change, and 53% reported an *increase*. These findings forced social psychologists to challenge the wisdom of their testimony to the Supreme Court and to reexamine the contact hypothesis that had guided that advice in the first place.

"'see that man over there?'
'Yes'
'Well, I hate him'
'But you don't know him.'
'That's why I hate him.'
—Gordon Allport

contact hypothesis The theory that direct contact between hostile groups will reduce intergroup prejudice under certain conditions.

(Left) Students at Central High School in Little Rock, Arkansas, in September 1957 shout insults at 16-year-old Elizabeth Eckford as she walks toward the school entrance. National Guardsmen blocked the entrance and would not let her enter. (Right) Jackie Robinson and Branch Rickey discuss Robinson's contract with the Brooklyn Dodgers. In 1947, Robinson became the first African American to cross "the color line" and play Major League Baseball, thereby beginning the integration of major American sports.

Is the original contact hypothesis wrong? No. Although desegregation did not immediately produce the desired changes, it's important to realize that the ideal conditions for successful intergroup contact did not exist in the public schools that desegregated. Nobody ever said that deeply rooted prejudices could be erased just by throwing groups together. According to the contact hypothesis, four conditions are ideal for contact to succeed. These conditions are summarized in Table 5.3.

Thomas Pettigrew and Linda Tropp have extensively reviewed the research relevant to the contact hypothesis, and their conclusions have been very encouraging (Pettigrew et al., 2011; Tropp, 2013; Tropp & Page-Gould, 2015). In a series of meta-analyses involving more than 500 studies and a quarter of a million participants in 38 nations Pettigrew and Tropp (2000, 2006, 2008) found reliable support for the benefits of intergroup contact in reducing prejudice, particularly when the contact satisfies at least some of the conditions in Table 5.3. These researchers propose that contact reduces prejudice by (1) enhancing knowledge about the outgroup; (2) reducing anxiety about intergroup contact; and (3) increasing empathy and perspective taking.

One of the most successful demonstrations of desegregation took place on the baseball diamond. On April 15, 1947, Jackie Robinson played for baseball's Brooklyn Dodgers and became the first black man to break "the color barrier" in a major American sport. Robinson's opportunity came through Dodgers owner Branch Rickey, who felt that integrating baseball was both moral and good for the game (Pratkanis & Turner, 1994). Rickey knew all about the contact hypothesis and was assured by a social scientist friend that a team could furnish the conditions needed for it to work: equal status among teammates, personal interactions, dedication to a common goal, and a positive climate from the owner, managers, and coaches. The rest is history. Rickey signed Robinson and tried to create the situation necessary for success. Although Robinson did face a great deal of racism, he endured, and baseball was integrated. At the end of his first year, Jackie Robinson was named rookie of the year, and in 1962 he was elected to the

▲ **TABLE 5.3**

The Contact Hypothesis: Conditions

Four conditions are deemed ideal for intergroup contact to serve as a treatment for racism.

1. *Equal status.* The contact should occur in circumstances that give the two groups equal status.

2. *Personal Interaction.* The contact should involve one-on-one interactions among individual members of the two groups.

3. *Cooperative activities.* Members of the two groups should join together in an effort to achieve superordinate goals.

4. *Social norms.* The social norms, defined in part by relevant authorities, should favor intergroup contact.

© Cengage Learning

Baseball Hall of Fame. At his induction ceremony, Robinson asked three people to stand beside him: his mother, his wife, and his friend Branch Rickey.

Another potential cause for optimism, although perhaps tinged with some regret, is the finding by Nicole Shelton and Jennifer Richeson (2005) that both whites and blacks would like to have more contact with each other but believe that the other group does not want to have contact with them! This may be a case in which education about the problem can be an important tool in correcting it.

■ Intergroup Friendships and Extended Contact

Developing friendships across groups is one of the best ways to experience many of the optimal conditions for contact that are listed in Table 5.3. Friendships typically involve equal status, meaningful one-on-one interactions that extend across time and settings, and cooperation toward shared goals. It therefore makes sense that one of the most encouraging lines of research on improving intergroup relations has focused on cross-group friendships. A recent meta-analysis by Kristin Davies and others (2011) on 135 studies supports the idea that cross-group friendships are associated with more positive attitudes and behaviors toward outgroup members.

"A friendship is bonding capital, but when that friendship is multi-racial, it is also bridging capital."
—Emerson et al., 2002, p. 70.

The evidence for this comes not only from correlational studies, such as surveys that show the strong association between cross-group friendships and less intergroup anxiety and prejudice, but also from experiments in which the researchers create such friendships among some of their participants. A series of creative experiments along these lines by Elizabeth Page-Gould, Rodolfo Mendoza-Denton, and their colleagues has found strong evidence for the causal role that such friendships can play in reducing intergroup prejudice (Mendoza-Denton & Page-Gould, 2008; Page-Gould et al., 2008; 2010).

Of course there's often even greater contact—psychologically as well as physically—between romantic partners than friends, and some research has examined whether cross-group dating is associated with more positive intergroup attitudes. For example, a longitudinal study of dating in college by Shana Levin and others (2007) revealed that white, Asian American, and Latino students who dated outside their group more during college showed less ingroup bias and intergroup anxiety at the end of college than students who did not date outside their own racial group.

Even people who do not have a friend from an outgroup can benefit from having ingroup friends who do. A number of studies have found evidence for what is known as the *extended contact effect,* or the *indirect contact effect*—knowing that an ingroup friend has a good and close relationship with a member of an outgroup can produce positive intergroup benefits in ways similar to direct contact. Why would this happen? Several causes are involved, such as reducing ignorance and anxiety about outgroup members and providing individuals with positive

Although Charleston High School in Mississippi has been integrated for decades, it was not until 2008 that the school board allowed a racially integrated senior prom, although some at the school organized a "white prom" as an alternative. Pictured here are two of the students who attended the prom standing in front of a poster for the movie *Prom Night in Mississippi*, an award-winning documentary about this story. Some integrated schools in the United States still hold racially separate proms.

examples of outgroup members (Cameron et al., 2011; Dovidio et al., 2011; Eller et al., 2011; Wright et al., 2008).

The Jigsaw Classroom

As the third condition in Table 5.3 indicates, cooperation and shared goals are ideal for intergroup contact to be successful. Yet the typical classroom is filled with competition—exactly the wrong ingredient. Picture the scene. The teacher stands in front of the class and asks a question. Many children wave their hands, each straining to catch the teacher's eye. Then, as soon as one student is called on, the others groan in frustration. In the competition for the teacher's approval, they are losers—hardly a scenario suited to positive intergroup contact. To combat this problem in the classroom, Elliot Aronson and his colleagues (1978) developed a cooperative learning method called the **jigsaw classroom**. In newly desegregated public schools in Texas and California, they assigned fifth graders to small racially and academically mixed groups. The material to be learned within each group was divided into subtopics, much the way a jigsaw puzzle is broken into pieces. Each student was responsible for learning one piece of the puzzle, after which all members took turns teaching their material to one another. In this system, everyone—regardless of race, ability, or self-confidence—needs everyone else if the group as a whole is to succeed.

The method produced impressive results (Aronson, 2004, 2011). Compared with children in traditional classes, those in jigsaw classrooms grew to like each other more, liked school more, were less prejudiced, and had higher self-esteem. What's more, academic test scores improved for minority students and remained the same for white students.

Shared Identities

One important consequence of the jigsaw classroom technique is that individuals became more likely to classify outgroup members as part of their own ingroup. Instead of seeing racial or ethnic "others" within the classroom, the students now see fellow classmates. Students feel that they are all in the same boat together. More generally, intergroup contact that emphasizes shared goals and fates can effectively reduce prejudice and discrimination—specifically by changing how group members categorize each other (Bettencourt et al., 2007; Van Bavel & Cunningham, 2009).

The Common Ingroup Identity Model developed by Samuel Gaertner and John Dovidio (2010; 2012) proposes that if members of different groups recategorize themselves as members of a more inclusive superordinate group, intergroup attitudes and relations can improve. By recognizing their shared categorization, just as the Rattlers and Eagles did when they changed from competitors to collaborators in Robbers Cave State Park, "they" become "we," and a common ingroup identity can be forged. Researchers have induced a common ingroup identity among participants in their studies in a variety of ways, such as by having different groups share a common label, dispersing them around a table so that they are not separated according to group, or having them wear similar t-shirts. For example, Blake Riek and others (2010) put Democrats and Republicans together into two-person groups. When their different political party memberships were highlighted, the participants rated the other group more negatively. When their shared identity as Americans was highlighted, however, such as by having them wear shirts with the American flag printed on the front and calling their group the America Group, their intergroup ratings were significantly more positive.

jigsaw classroom A cooperative learning method used to reduce racial prejudice through interaction in group efforts.

It is worth noting that at least in some contexts, individuals from minority groups or groups that have less power in a society tend to not feel as positively as majority group members do about recategorizing their groups into one common ingroup. A group with smaller numbers or less power may feel overwhelmed and a sense of lost identity if they merge completely with a larger or more powerful group. Instead, members of these groups sometimes prefer or benefit more from dual-identity categorizations, in which their distinctiveness as a member of their specific group is preserved but in which they recognize their connection and potential for cooperation with the majority or more powerful group (Dovidio et al., 2012). A key point remains, though, that seeing connections between the groups and ways in which their identities are shared is essential.

■ Trust, Belonging, and Reducing Stereotype Threat

Claude Steele's theory of stereotype threat discussed earlier in the chapter received a great deal of attention because it not only helped explain causes underlying some profound social problems—such as the underperformance or reduced interests of large groups of people in various academic and career pursuits—but also offered encouragement rather than pessimism. It illustrated that making even small changes in the situational factors that give rise to stereotype threat can reduce the tremendous weight of negative stereotypes, allowing the targets of stereotypes to perform to their potential.

Dozens and dozens of experiments on stereotype threat were published soon after the theory was introduced in the mid-1990s, and in virtually each of them the negative effects of stereotype threat were reduced significantly or eliminated completely in some conditions of the study. Often this was achieved with seemingly very minor—but important—changes in the setting. Table 5.4 lists a sample of these ways.

A theme running through many of the successful interventions against stereotype threat effects is that the individuals feel a sense of trust and safety in the situation. That is, in this particular setting they feel that they are not the target of others' low expectations and they do not have to be concerned with unfairness or other obstacles that would otherwise distract, worry, or discourage them. The importance of establishing this trust is evident in the results of an experiment by Geoffrey Cohen and others (1999). Students in this study performed a writing task and then received criticism of their writing from a reviewer who presumably was white. Compared to white students, black students tended to respond less constructively and were more likely to dismiss the criticism as biased against them. These negative reactions to the criticism were eliminated, however, if the reviewer who gave the criticism added two elements: (1) he made it clear that he had high standards, and (2) he assured the students that he was confident that they had the capacity to achieve those standards. This combination of factors made the students trust the criticism and gave them the sense that they had a fair shot at succeeding at the task.

▲ **TABLE 5.4**

Combating Stereotype Threat Effects

Researchers have reduced or eliminated the negative effects of stereotype threat in particular settings in a variety of ways. Here is a sample of these successful interventions.

- Describing the task as not indicative of individuals' intellectual capabilities (Steele & Aronson, 1995)

- Informing individuals that their group typically does not perform worse than other groups on the task (Spencer et al., 1999)

- Giving individuals reason to attribute their anxiety while taking a test to irrelevant factors (Ben-Zeev et al., 2005)

- Getting individuals to think of intelligence as not a fixed trait but instead as something that is malleable and can be improved (Good et al., 2003)

- Exposing individuals to a member of their group who is said to be an expert in the domain in question (Stout et al., 2011)

- Having individuals think about values and interests that are very important to them that are not under threat (Taylor & Walton, 2011; C. von Hippel et al., 2011)

- Highlighting other aspects of individuals' identities that are associated with positive performance on the task at hand (Shih et al., 2012; Yopyk & Prentice, 2005)

- Excluding the presence of members of outgroups (Sekaquaptewa & Thompson, 2003)

© Cengage Learning

In addition to causing distrust, one of the most powerful ways in which stereotype threat undermines students is that it reduces their sense of *belonging.* That is, targeted students are likely to feel that *people like me do not belong here,* such as in a particular major, school, career, or some other domain (Cook et al., 2012; Walton & Cohen, 2007). Geoffrey Cohen, Gregory Walton, and their colleagues have applied social psychological techniques to create interventions outside the lab that have had truly remarkable success with students in a number of schools (Walton, 2014). For example, Walton and Cohen (2011) gave some first-semester African American students at a predominately European American college information designed to reduce feelings of uncertainty about their sense of belonging at the university. They read that it is quite typical of most students—regardless of their gender, race, or ethnicity—to go through periods of social stress and uncertainty during their freshman year, and that these struggles tend to go away soon after their first year. Walton and Cohen found that giving this information to African American students during their first semester at school raised their grade-point averages significantly higher relative to other African American students who were not given this information. Especially impressive was that this effect lasted through their entire college experience. As discussed in Chapter 1 of this book, Walton and others (2015) used a similar type of intervention that dramatically improved the performance of female students in majors dominated by male students at an engineering school. (You can see this effect illustrated in ● Figure 1.1 on p. 9 of Chapter 1.)

Nilanjana Dasgupta and others (2015) also conducted a recent study with female engineers. They reasoned that women's uncertainty about belonging in engineering is heightened by typically being so outnumbered by men. To examine this issue, the researchers had female engineers work on engineering problems in small groups that were either mostly female, mostly male, or equally male and female. The results indicated that women who were in the majority were more motivated and interested in the group task, demonstrated more confidence, and gave more helpful input than women who were in the minority or even women who were in groups with equal numbers of males and females (● see Figure 5.14 for an illustration of one of these findings).

■ Exerting Self-Control

A key point in this chapter is that people often stereotype and show prejudice toward others even when they would rather not, sometimes by merely being aware of the stereotype. Can we learn to control and rise above these impulses?

One of the challenges is that trying to suppress stereotyping or to control prejudiced actions can take mental effort, and people often don't have the time, energy, or awareness to dedicate to this effort (Ito et al., 2015). Eric Wesselmann and colleagues (2012), for example, found that after watching a

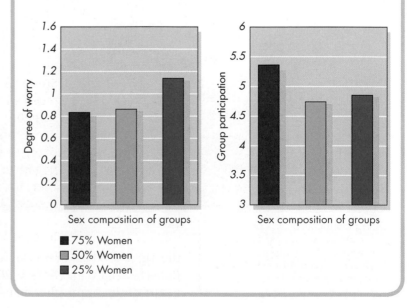

● **FIGURE 5.14**

Safety in Numbers

Female engineers worked on engineering problems in small groups that were either mostly (75%) female, equally male and female, or mostly (75%) male. Women in the male-majority groups felt significantly more worried about working on the group task than did the women in the female-majority groups (left). Women in the female-majority groups actively participated on the task much more than did women in the other two groups (right).

From Dasgupta et al., 2015

Degree of worry

Group participation

Sex composition of groups

Sex composition of groups

■ 75% Women
　50% Women
■ 25% Women

video of a young man's behavior, participants judged him to be more threatening if they had been led to believe that he had been suffering from mental health problems than from dental pain. Interestingly, this effect occurred only when participants had to make their judgments quickly, suggesting that they relied on their stereotypes more when they didn't have time to try to overcome their biases.

Some factors make people less likely to have sufficient cognitive resources for successful control. For example, older people have a harder time suppressing stereotypes than younger people, which may explain in part why older people often appear more prejudiced than younger people (von Hippel & Henry, 2011). Some research suggests that being low in blood sugar, such as from being hungry, can weaken people's ability to control stereotyping and prejudice, and that a sugar-heavy drink can correct this problem (Gailliot, 2013; Gailliot et al., 2009). However, some researchers are more skeptical about these blood-sugar findings (Lange & Eggert, 2014; Molden et al., 2012), and so more research will certainly be done to clarify the issue. What is more clear is that being intoxicated makes people have a difficult time suppressing thoughts or inhibiting impulses (for example, consider the dreaded drunk dialing or texting). It may come as little surprise, therefore, that intoxication impairs people's ability to control stereotype activation and application (Bartholow et al., 2012; Loersch et al., 2015; Parrott & Lisco, 2015).

Being physically tired or being affected by strong emotion or arousal can sap perceivers of the cognitive resources necessary to avoid stereotyping. In an intriguing demonstration of this, Galen Bodenhausen (1990) ran an experiment with two types of people: "morning people" (who are most alert early in the morning) and "night people" (who peak much later, in the evening). By random assignment, participants took part in an experiment that was scheduled at either 9 p.m. or 8 p.m. The result? Morning people were more likely to use stereotypes when tested at night; night owls were more likely to do so early in the morning. More recently, Sonia Ghumman and Christopher Barnes (2013) found that the more sleepy the students in their study were, the more stereotyping and prejudice they exhibited. (Sleep also plays a role in a particularly unusual recent finding reported by Xiaoqing Hu and others (2015), in which participants who had received training to reduce implicit racial and gender bias showed longer reductions in these biases if they were exposed to cues associated with that training while they slept!)

Just as a good night's sleep might improve people's cognitive control, so too might the right kind of brain stimulation. That is the implication of recent work by Roberta Sellaro and others (2015). Through noninvasive methods they stimulated a part of the brain (the medial prefrontal cortex) that is thought to be associated

Being intoxicated robs people of cognitive resources, making them less able to inhibit impulses and control expressions of stereotyping and prejudice.

Martin Thomas Photography/Alamy

with cognitive control. As the researchers predicted, this led to a reduction in participants' implicit biases toward outgroup members.

In addition to people's *ability* to control prejudice, another issue is what *motivates* people to do so. Researchers have distinguished between two kinds of motivation to control prejudiced responses and behaviors. One kind is *externally* driven—not wanting to *appear* to others to be prejudiced. A second type is *internally* driven—not wanting to *be* prejudiced, regardless of whether or not others would find out (Dunton & Fazio, 1997; Plant & Devine, 1998, 2009). Internally motivated individuals are likely to be more successful at controlling stereotyping and prejudice, even on implicit measures, but even they are vulnerable to the strong power of automatic stereotyping and implicit biases.

According to the *self-regulation of prejudiced responses model* proposed by Margo Monteith and others (2002; Monteith & Mark, 2009), internally motivated individuals in particular may learn to control their prejudices more effectively over time. According to this model, people who are truly motivated to be fair and unprejudiced are often confronted with the sad reality that they have failed to live up to that goal. These realizations lead to unpleasant emotions such as guilt. As individuals experience such feelings of guilt repeatedly, they begin to develop expertise at recognizing the situations and stimuli that tend to trigger these failures, and therefore they can exert more control over them. In so doing, they begin to interrupt what had been automatic stereotype activation.

A great example of this process is reflected in the quotes of a student in one of Monteith's studies (Monteith et al., 2010). The student described how close he once came to describing a classmate in a racist way, and how terrible he felt about it. "I don't know why I was going to say it. It was kind of scary how it had been programmed into my head by those people around me." Later, this participant indicated how often he is reminded of that experience: "When I see people say stuff like that I think about it a lot. . . . It kind of quiets me down and makes me think about what I'm doing and makes me think about what I'm thinking, what I'm saying. It makes me feel that I should be more careful about what I say" (pp. 193–194).

Just as people who are internally motivated to control prejudice tend to become more successful at self-regulation than people who are motivated for external reasons, antiprejudice messages that are designed to appeal more to people's internal motivations may be more effective than messages that seem more externally focused. To study this issue, Lisa Legault and others (2011) developed a pair of prejudice-reduction brochures. One of these brochures was designed to appeal to internal motivations. This brochure emphasized the personal as well as societal benefits of tolerance and diversity. For example, one line read, "When we let go of prejudice, the rich diversity of society is ours to enjoy." The other brochure appealed to external motivations, emphasizing the obligations that compel individuals and organizations to act in nonprejudiced ways. For example, an excerpt from this brochure included, "Teachers and students caught displaying racist attitudes and behavior can face serious consequences, such as termination and expulsion."

Students at a Canadian university were randomly assigned to read either of the two brochures, or they received no brochure at all. Later these students completed a measure of their prejudice toward black people (no black students were included in the study). The researchers found that these students exhibited significantly less prejudice if they received the brochure that appealed to internal motivations to control prejudice than if they received no brochure. On the other hand, the students who received the brochure appealing to external factors exhibited significantly *more* prejudice than

● **FIGURE 5.15**

Productive and Counterproductive Antiprejudice Messages

Compared to students who did not receive any brochure, those who read an antiprejudice brochure that emphasized internally driven motivations to not be prejudiced (such as why one would benefit by promoting diversity) later exhibited significantly less prejudice toward black people. In contrast, students who received the brochure that appealed to external factors (such as how one could get in trouble if caught doing or saying something racist) exhibited significantly more prejudice.

From Legault et al., 2012

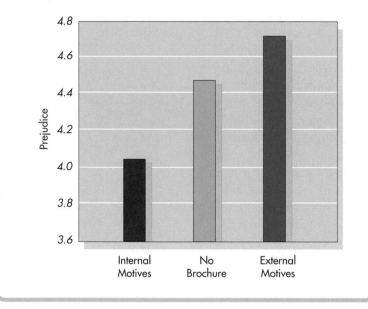

the students who received no brochure (see ● Figure 5.15). The brochure that emphasized the external rather than internal reasons to control prejudice likely came across to the students as very controlling and made students rebel against it somewhat. People don't like to be told how they must think and not think, and so antiprejudice messages that are perceived in that way can be counterproductive.

■ Changing Cognitions, Cultures, and Motivations

We have just discussed some of the challenges involved in trying *not* to think about stereotypes or act in a prejudiced way. There are several ways of thinking that can be more productive. Social–cognitive factors that research has shown can reduce stereotyping and prejudice include:

- Being exposed to and thinking about examples of group members that are inconsistent with the stereotype (Columb & Plant, 2011).

- Learning about the variability that exists among the people in a group (Brauer & Er-rafiy, 2011; Brauer et al., 2012).

- Being induced to take the perspective of a person from a stereotyped group (Maister et al., 2015; Peck et al., 2013; Todd et al., 2012).

- Being encouraged to pay attention to or confront instances of discrimination (Becker & Swim, 2011; Dickter & Newton, 2013; Gulker et al., 2013).

- Believing that prejudice can be learned and unlearned and is therefore malleable rather than a fixed, unchanging reality (Carr et al., 2012; Neel & Shapiro, 2012).

- Learning that race is more ambiguous and socially determined than simply a genetic, fixed category (Williams & Eberhardt, 2008).

- Taking multicultural views that recognize but also value group differences, that reveal new ways of thinking, and that acknowledge how different groups have influenced each other throughout history, as opposed to pretending to not notice distinctions between groups (Apfelbaum et al., 2008; Holoien & Shelton, 2012; Plaut et al., 2009; Rattan & Ambady, 2012; Rosenthal & Levy, 2013; Tadmor et al., 2012).

- Thinking of multiculturalism as an approach that is inclusive of everyone, *including* the majority group (Plaut et al., 2011).

How can these types of thinking be promoted? One important factor no doubt is education. More generally, it is at the cultural level that much potential for positive change can be found. Exposure to images and individuals that reflect the diversity within social groups, for example, can help weaken stereotypes and combat their automatic activation. These images might also change people's tendency to see groups as relatively fixed entities and help them see groups as dynamic entities with less rigid borders.

Motivations, norms, and values can and often do change over time. Here again popular culture is a key player. People—especially younger people—look to images in popular culture as well as to their peers and role models for information about what attitudes and behaviors are in fashion or out of date. Popular culture has played an important role in many of these changes. For example, many people cite celebrities such as Ellen DeGeneres or television shows like *Modern Family* for helping to change their attitudes toward gay rights (Lang, 2015). Similarly, seeing antiprejudice campaigns that promote ideas like "Black Lives Matter" or "It Gets Better" go viral around the world in response to violence against targeted groups no doubt affects many people's attitudes.

We also look to our peers to get a sense of the local norms around us, including norms about stereotypes and prejudice (e.g., Fein et al., 2003; Nelson, 2015; Pryor et al., 2013). In a particular high school, a senior might feel comfortable calling a friend a "fag" and mean little by it and think nothing of it. Yet several months later as a first-semester college student, this student might realize how wrong that is and feel guilty for ever having done so. If this lesson is learned, it's more likely to have been learned by watching and interacting with one's peers than from having been lectured to about diversity and sensitivity by a campus speaker. Learning these norms can motivate us to adopt them. Legislating against hate speech, unequal treatment, and hostile environments can also be an important weapon, of course. Although they can create resistance and backlashes, laws and policies that require behavior change can—if done right, with no suggestion of compromise and with important leaders clearly behind them—cause hearts and minds to follow (Aronson, 1992). Laura Barron and Mikki Hebl (2013), for example, recently found across a series of studies that laws that make employment discrimination against gays illegal (which many states in the United States do not currently have) do make a significant and positive difference in individuals' attitudes and behaviors.

Elizabeth Levy Paluck (2011) has conducted some fascinating field studies showing the power of peer and cultural influences. In one study, students in several high schools were trained to be "peer leaders" who would confront expressions of intergroup prejudice. These students not only engaged in more antiprejudice behaviors, but these behaviors spread to their friends. Paluck (2009) also examined the role of the media in promoting positive norms in an unusual year-long field experiment in Rwanda, which has been the site of terrible war, genocide, and intergroup conflict, particularly between the Hutus and Tutsis. She had Rwandans listen to a radio soap opera (radio being the most important form of mass media there) over the course of a year. She randomly assigned half to listen to a soap opera about conflicts that paralleled real conflicts in the country but that were solved in ways that modeled intergroup cooperation and communication, nonviolence, and opposition to prejudice. The other half of the participants listened to a soap opera about health issues. At the end of the year, those Rwandans who listened to the soap opera promoting positive intergroup norms had significantly more positive feelings about intergroup cooperation, trust, and interactions.

Yasuyoshi Chiba/AFP/Getty Images

After a series of racist incidents, fans denounce racism at the World Cup in Brazil, in September 2014.

Studies like these show that a source for much positive change stems from what is at the very core of social psychology: the social nature of the human animal. Some of our baser instincts, such as intergroup competition that breeds intergroup biases, may always be present, but we also can learn from each other the thoughts, values, and goals that make us less vulnerable to perpetuating or being the targets of stereotypes, prejudice, and discrimination.

Review

Top 10 Key Points in Chapter 5

1. Prejudice and discrimination operate not only on an individual level, in which anyone can be both a perpetrator and a target, but also on institutional and cultural levels, which involve practices that promote the domination of one group over another.

2. Many stories in the news as well as data from numerous studies provide compelling evidence that racism, sexism, and other forms of prejudice and discrimination persist, but also that progress has been made.

3. Stereotypes, prejudice, and discrimination today often operate implicitly, without conscious intent or awareness on the part of perceivers, but with significant consequences.

4. Ambivalent sexism reflects both hostile sexism, characterized by negative and resentful feelings toward women, and benevolent sexism, characterized by affectionate, chivalrous, but potentially patronizing feelings toward women.

5. There are some striking sex differences in occupational choices and in the treatment individuals experience in the workplace.

6. Stereotype threat can impair the performance and affect the identity of members of stereotyped or devalued groups. Slight changes in a setting can reduce stereotype threat and its negative effects significantly.

7. People tend to exaggerate the differences between ingroups and outgroups, treat ingroup members more favorably (especially when feeling threatened or uncertain), and see outgroup members as more homogenous and often in dehumanizing ways.

8. We learn information relevant to stereotypes, prejudice, and discrimination without even realizing it by absorbing what we see around us in our culture, groups, and families.

9. A fundamental effect of stereotyping is that it influences people's perceptions and interpretations of the behaviors of group members, causing them to perceive confirmation of their stereotype-based expectancies.

10. Among the factors that have been found to be successful to reduce stereotyping, prejudice, and discrimination are: having intergroup contact (especially if the ideal conditions for contact are met), perceiving connections and a shared identity with people from other groups, adopting a multicultural rather than colorblind perspective, and being intrinsically (rather than extrinsically) motivated to reduce prejudiced responses.

Putting Common Sense to the Test

The Nature of the Problem: Persistence and Change

Children do not tend to show biases based on race; it is only after they become adolescents that they learn to respond to people differently based on race.

(F) **False.** *Children learn about social categories quite early and use stereotypes when they are very young. Children show biases in favor of their racial ingroup on both explicit and implicit measures.*

Interracial interactions tend to go better and to reduce the perceptions of racism if a colorblind mentality is used, which denies or minimizes any acknowledgment of racial differences.

(F) **False.** *Research has shown that this approach often backfires and makes members of racial minority groups more, rather than less, uncomfortable; a multicultural approach that acknowledges and positively values racial and ethnic differences is often more effective.*

An African American student is likely to perform worse on an athletic task if the task is described as one reflecting sports intelligence than if it is described as reflecting natural athletic ability.

(T) **True.** *Research suggests that African American students are likely to experience stereotype threat and therefore underperform if the task is described as one that is diagnostic of their sports intelligence. White students tend to show the opposite effect: Their performance is worse if the task is described as reflecting natural athletic ability.*

Causes of the Problem: Intergroup, Motivational, Cognitive, and Cultural Factors

Being reminded of one's own mortality makes people put things into greater perspective, thereby tending to reduce ingroup–outgroup distinctions and hostilities.

(F) **False.** *Research has shown that when people feel threatened by thoughts of their own mortality, they tend to seek greater affiliation with their ingroups and exhibit greater prejudice against outgroups, in part to reaffirm their sense of place and purpose in the world.*

People's very quick judgments are not influenced by a stereotype unless they actually believe the stereotype to be true.

(F) **False.** *Even very brief exposure to a member of a stereotyped group can activate the stereotype about the group, even if the person does not believe the stereotype.*

Key Terms

ambivalent sexism (166)
aversive racism (160)
contact hypothesis (196)
discrimination (158)
illusory correlation (191)
implicit racism (162)
ingroup favoritism (183)
ingroups (177)
jigsaw classroom (199)
modern racism (160)

outgroup homogeneity effect (177)
outgroups (177)
prejudice (158)
racism (157)
realistic conflict theory (182)
relative deprivation (182)
sexism (158)
social categorization (176)
social dominance orientation (180)

social identity theory (183)
social role theory (189)
stereotype content model (181)
stereotypes (158)
stereotype threat (172)
stigmatized (171)
subliminal presentation (193)
superordinate goal (182)
system justification theory (180)

Attitudes

This chapter examines social influences on attitudes. We define attitudes and then discuss how they are measured and when they are related to behavior. Then we consider two methods of changing attitudes. First, we look at source, message, and audience factors that win persuasion through the media of communication. Second, we consider theories and research showing that people often change their attitudes as a consequence of their own actions.

ISIS. Taxes. Same-sex marriage. The death penalty. Gun control. Israelis and Palestinians. Abortion. Climate change. Immigration. Anyone who has followed recent events in the United States—or anywhere else in the world, for that matter—knows how passionately people feel about the issues of the day. Attitudes and the mechanisms of attitude change, or persuasion, are a vital part of human social life. This chapter addresses three sets of questions: (1) What is an attitude, how can it be measured, and what is its link to behavior? (2) What kinds of persuasive messages lead people to change their attitudes? (3) Why do we often change our attitudes as a result of our own actions?

The Study of Attitudes

Are you a Democrat, Republican, or Independent? Should marijuana be legalized? Would you rather listen to alternative rock, country-western, or hip-hop? Do you prefer drinking Coke or Pepsi, water, or fruit juice? Do you have an iPhone or an Android? Should terrorism be contained by war or conciliation?

As these questions suggest, each of us has positive and negative reactions to various persons, objects, and ideas. These reactions are called **attitudes**. Skim the chapters in this book, and you'll see just how pervasive attitudes are. You'll see, for example, that self-esteem is an attitude we hold about ourselves, that attraction is a positive attitude toward another person, and that prejudice is a negative attitude often directed against certain groups. Indeed, the study of attitudes—what they are, where they come from, how they can be measured, what causes them to change, and how they interact with behavior—is central to the whole field of social psychology (Bohner & Dickel, 2011; Crano & Prislin, 2014; Perloff, 2010; Maio & Haddock, 2015).

An attitude is a positive, negative, or mixed evaluation of an object that is expressed at some level of intensity—nothing more, nothing less. *Like, love, dislike, hate, admire,* and *detest* are the kinds of words that people use to describe their attitudes. It's important to realize that attitudes cannot simply be represented along a single continuum ranging from wholly positive to wholly negative—as you might expect if attitudes were like the volume button on a remote control unit or the lever on a thermostat that raises or lowers temperature. Rather, as depicted in ● Figure 6.1, our attitudes can vary in strength along both positive and negative dimensions. In other words, we can react to something with positive affect, with negative affect, with ambivalence (mixed emotions), or with apathy and indifference (Cacioppo et al., 1997). Some people more than others are troubled by this type of inconsistency (Newby-Clark et al., 2002). In fact, at times people have both positive and negative reactions to the same attitude object without feeling conflict because they are conscious of one reaction but not the other. Someone who is welcoming toward racial minorities but harbors unconscious prejudice is a case in point (Wilson et al., 2000).

Each and every one of us routinely forms positive and negative evaluations of the people, places, objects, and ideas we encounter. We like some things but not

---

Putting COMMON SENSE to the Test

Circle Your Answer

T F Researchers can tell if someone has a positive or negative attitude by measuring physiological arousal.

T F In reacting to persuasive communications, people are influenced more by superficial images than by logical arguments.

T F People are most easily persuaded by commercial messages that are presented without their awareness.

T F The more money you pay people to tell a lie, the more they will come to believe it.

T F People often come to like what they suffer for.

---

attitude A positive, negative, or mixed reaction to a person, object, or idea.

others. This attitude formation process is often quick, automatic, and "implicit"—much like a reflex action (Bargh et al., 1996; De Houwer, 2014; Ferguson, 2007).

You might assume that a person's attitude represents a unique relation between that person and a specific attitude object. There are two ways, however, in which our attitudes reveal a lot about us as individuals. First, people differ in terms of their tendency in general to like or dislike things. Consider an array of very different and unrelated attitude objects: How do you feel about bicycles? What about crossword puzzles, camping, Japan, taxes, politics, architecture, chess, statistics, Hulu, Netflix, religion, and bottled water? Curious as to whether people have tendencies in general to like or dislike things, which they called *dispositional attitudes*, Justin Hepler and Dolores Albarracín (2013) found that when they asked research participants to rate how much they liked or disliked a long list of unrelated things, some individuals on average tended to report positive attitudes; others on average were negative (also see Eschleman et al., 2015).

A second way in which our attitudes reveal something about us as individuals is that people differ not only in terms of whether they tend to like or dislike things but in the extent to which how quickly and how strongly they react. Think about yourself. Do you form opinions easily? Do you tend to have strong likes and dislikes? Or do you tend to react in more guarded, less effusive ways? Individuals who describe themselves as high rather than low in the need for evaluation are more likely to view their daily experiences in highly judgmental terms and they are more opinionated—positive and negative—on a whole range of social, moral, and political issues (Bizer et al., 2004; Jarvis & Petty, 1996).

Before we examine the elusive science of attitude measurement, let's stop for a moment and ponder this question: Why do human beings bother to form and have attitudes? Does forming a positive or negative judgment of people, objects, and ideas serve any useful purpose? Over the years, researchers have found that attitudes serve important functions—such as enabling us to judge quickly and without much thought whether something we first encounter is good or bad, helpful or hurtful, and to be sought or avoided (Maio & Olson, 2000). The downside is that having preexisting attitudes can lead us to be closed-minded, bias how we interpret new information, and make us more resistant to change. For example, Russell Fazio and others (2000) found that people who were focused on their positive or negative attitudes toward computerized faces, compared to those who were not, were later slower to notice when the faces were "morphed" and no longer the same.

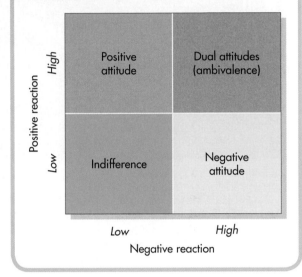

● **FIGURE 6.1**

Four Possible Reactions to Attitude Objects

As shown, people evaluate objects along both positive and negative dimensions. As a result, our attitudes can be positive, negative, ambivalent, or indifferent.
Cacioppo et al., 1997.

How Attitudes Are Measured

In 1928, Louis Thurstone published an article entitled "Attitudes Can Be Measured." What Thurstone failed to fully anticipate, however, is that attitude measurement is tricky business. At one point, several years ago, over 500 different methods were available to determine an individual's attitudes (Fishbein & Ajzen, 1972).

Self-Report Measures   The easiest way to assess a person's attitude about something is to ask. All over the world, public opinions are recorded on a range of issues in politics, the economy, health care, foreign affairs, science and technology,

AP Images/Thibault Camus

As in this January 7, 2014 unity rally in Paris, where 3 million gathered to pay respect for the victims of a terrorist attack on the Charlie Hebdo magazine, people can be very passionate about the attitudes they hold. Their message here: "Not Afraid." On November 13, 2015, not quite two years later, Paris was once again rocked by a cluster of heinous terrorist attacks.

To view new public opinion poll results online, you can visit: http://www. harrisinteractive.com/, http://www. gallup.com/home.aspx, and http:// www.pewresearch.org/.

attitude scale   A multiple-item questionnaire designed to measure a person's attitude toward some object.
bogus pipeline   A phony lie-detector device that is sometimes used to get respondents to give truthful answers to sensitive questions.

sports, entertainment, religion, and lifestyles. Simply by asking people, public opinion surveys conducted by Harris, Gallup, Pew Research Center, and other polling organizations have recently revealed that 33% of Americans will never consider buying or leasing a self-driving car; 82% believe that childhood vaccinations should be mandatory; 74% would delete themselves from Internet search results if they could; 70% do not "feel engaged or inspired at their jobs;" and 88% trust online reviews of products and services as much as personal recommendations. Still other surveys have shown that Americans prefer to watch football over baseball and like to eat chocolate ice cream more than vanilla and other flavors; that more than half say they surf the Internet while watching TV; that one in five adults has a tattoo; and that Christmas is America's favorite holiday, followed by Thanksgiving and Halloween.

Self-report measures are direct and straightforward. But attitudes are sometimes too complex to be measured by a single question. As you may recall from Chapter 2, one problem recognized by public opinion pollsters is that responses to attitude questions can be influenced by their wording, the order and context in which they are asked, and other extraneous factors (Sudman et al., 2010; Tourangeau et al., 2000). In one survey, the National Opinion Research Center asked hundreds of Americans if the U.S. government spent too little money on "assistance to the poor" and 65% said yes. Yet when the same question was asked using the word "welfare" instead, only 20% said the government spent too little (Schneiderman, 2008). In a second survey, researchers asked more than 2,000 registered voters about their belief in the phenomenon of "global warming" or "climate change." Democrats uniformly endorsed the proposition at a high rate, but the number of Republicans who did so increased from 44% when asked about global warming to 60% when asked about climate change (Schuldt et al., 2011).

Recognizing the shortcomings of single-question measures, survey researchers have developed more sophisticated methods (Fowler, 2014). Often single questions are replaced by multiple-item questionnaires known as **attitude scales** (Robinson et al., 1991; 1998). Attitude scales come in different forms, perhaps the most popular being the Likert Scale, named after its inventor, Rensis Likert (1932). In this technique, respondents are presented with a list of statements about an attitude object and are asked to indicate on a multiple-point scale how strongly they agree or disagree with each statement. Each respondent's total attitude score is derived by summing responses to all the items. However, regardless of whether attitudes are measured by one question or a full-blown scale, the results should be taken with caution. All self-report measures assume that people honestly express their true opinions. Sometimes this assumption is reasonable and correct, but often it is not. Wanting to make a good impression, people are often reluctant to admit to their failures, vices, weaknesses, unpopular opinions, and prejudices.

One approach to this problem is to increase the accuracy of self-report measures. To get respondents to answer attitude questions more truthfully, researchers have sometimes used the **bogus pipeline**, an elaborate mechanical device that supposedly records our true feelings physiologically, like a lie-detector test. Not wanting to get caught in a lie, respondents tend to answer attitude questions more honestly, and with less positive spin, when they think that any deception would be exposed by the bogus pipeline (Jones & Sigall, 1971; Roese & Jamieson, 1993). In one study, people were more likely to admit to drinking too much, using cocaine, having frequent oral sex, and not exercising enough when the bogus pipeline was used than when it was not (Tourangeau et al., 1997). In another study, adolescents were more likely to admit to smoking when the bogus pipeline was used than when it was not (Adams et al., 2008).

Covert Measures A second general approach to the self-report problem is to collect indirect, covert measures of attitudes that cannot be controlled. One possibility in this regard is to use observable behavior such as facial expressions, tone of voice, and body language. In one study, Gary Wells and Richard Petty (1980) secretly videotaped college students as they listened to a speech and noticed that when the speaker took a position that the students agreed with (that tuition costs should be lowered), most made vertical head movements. But when the speaker took a contrary position (that tuition costs should be raised), head movements were in a horizontal direction. Without realizing it, the students had signaled their attitudes by nodding and shaking their heads.

Although behavior provides clues, it is far from perfect as a measure of attitudes. Sometimes we nod our heads because we agree; at other times, we nod to be polite. The problem is that people monitor their overt behavior just as they monitor self-reports. But what about internal physiological reactions that are difficult if not impossible to control? Does the body betray how we feel? In the past, researchers tried to divine attitudes from involuntary physical reactions such as perspiration, heart rate, and pupil dilation. The result, however, was always the same: Measures of arousal reveal the intensity of one's attitude toward an object but not whether that attitude itself is positive or negative. On the physiological record, love and hate look very much the same (Petty & Cacioppo, 1983).

Although physiological arousal measures cannot distinguish between positive and negative attitudes, some interesting alternatives have been discovered. One is the **facial electromyograph (EMG)**. As shown in ● Figure 6.2, certain muscles in the face contract when we are happy and different facial muscles contract when we are sad. Some of the muscular changes cannot be seen with the naked eye, however, so the facial EMG is used. To determine whether the EMG can be used to measure the affect associated with attitudes, John Cacioppo and Richard Petty (1981) recorded facial muscle activity of college students as they listened to a message with which they agreed or disagreed. The agreeable message increased activity in the cheek muscles—the facial pattern that is characteristic of happiness. The disagreeable

"What I drink and what I tell the pollsters I drink are two different things."

Pollsters and attitude researchers are well aware that self-reports cannot always be trusted, especially on sensitive topics.

● **FIGURE 6.2**

The Facial EMG: A Covert Measure of Attitudes?

The facial EMG makes it possible to detect differences between positive and negative attitudes. Notice the major facial muscles and recording sites for electrodes. When people hear a message with which they agree rather than disagree, there is a relative increase in EMG activity in the depressor and zygomatic muscles but a relative decrease in corrugator and frontalis muscles. These changes cannot be seen with the naked eye.

From Cacioppo, J. T. and Petty, R. E., "Electromyograms as measures of extent and affectivity of information processing," *American Psychologist* vol 36 (pp. 441–456). Copyright © 1981 by the American Psychological Association. Reprinted by permission.

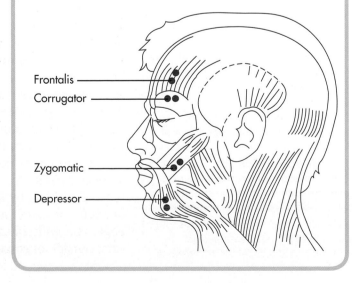

Frontalis

Corrugator

Zygomatic

Depressor

message sparked activity in the forehead and brow area—the facial patterns that are associated with sadness and distress. Outside observers who later watched the participants were unable to see these subtle changes. Apparently, the muscles in the human face reveal smiles, frowns, feelings of disgust, and other reactions to attitude objects that might otherwise be hidden from view (Cacioppo et al., 1986; Tassinary & Cacioppo, 1992).

From a social neuroscience perspective, electrical activity in the brain may also assist in the measure of attitudes. In 1929, Hans Burger invented a machine that could detect, amplify, and record "waves" of electrical activity in the brain using electrodes pasted to the surface of the scalp. The instrument is called an *electroencephalograph,* or EEG, and the information it provides takes the form of line tracings called *brain waves.* Based on an earlier discovery that certain patterns of electrical brain activity are triggered by exposure to stimuli that are novel or unexpected, Cacioppo and others (1993) had participants list 10 items they liked and 10 they did not like within various object categories (fruits, sports, movies, universities, etc.). Later, these participants were brought into the laboratory, wired to an EEG, and presented with a list of category words that depicted objects they liked and disliked. The result: Brain-wave patterns that are normally triggered by inconsistency increased more when a disliked stimulus appeared after a string of positive items or when a liked stimulus was shown after a string of negative items than when either stimulus evoked the same attitude as the items that preceded it.

Today, social psychologists are also starting to use new forms of brain imaging in the measurement of attitudes. In one study, researchers used fMRI to record brain activity in participants as they read names of famous—and infamous—figures such as John F. Kennedy, Bill Cosby, and Adolf Hitler. When the names were read, they observed in participants greater activity in the amygdala, a brain structure associated with emotion, regardless of whether or not participants were asked to evaluate the famous figures (Cunningham et al., 2003). In a study focused on political attitudes, other researchers used fMRI to record brain activity in opinionated men during the 2004 presidential election as they listened to positive and negative statements about their preferred candidate. Although brain areas associated with cognitive reasoning were unaffected during these presentations, activity increased in areas typically associated with emotion (Westen et al., 2006). These studies suggest that people react automatically to positive and negative attitude objects and that these attitudes may be measurable by electrical activity in the brain.

The Implicit Association Test (IAT) When it comes to covert measurement, one particularly interesting development is based on the notion that each of us has all sorts of **implicit attitudes** that we cannot self-report in questionnaires because we are not even aware of having these attitudes (Fazio & Olson, 2003). To measure these unconscious attitudes, a number of indirect methods have been developed (De Houwer et al., 2009; Nosek et al., 2011; Payne & Lundberg, 2014). The most popular is the **Implicit Association Test (IAT)** created by Anthony Greenwald, Mahzarin Banaji, Brian Nosek, and others. As we saw in Chapter 5, the IAT measures the sheer speed—in fractions of a second—with which people associate pairs of concepts (Greenwald et al., 1998). To see how it works, visit the IAT website by logging onto Project Implicit at https://implicit.harvard.edu/implicit/ or installing a free IAT app onto your Android or iPhone. On the first page, you will read that "Project Implicit investigates thoughts and feelings that exist outside of conscious awareness or conscious control."

Researchers can tell if someone has a positive or negative attitude by measuring physiological arousal.

FALSE

facial electromyograph (EMG) An electronic instrument that records facial muscle activity associated with emotions and attitudes.

implicit attitude An attitude, such as prejudice, that one is not aware of having.

Implicit Association Test (IAT) A covert measure of unconscious attitudes derived from the speed at which people respond to pairings of concepts—such as black or white with good or bad.

To take a test that measures your implicit racial attitudes, you go through a series of stages. First, you are asked to categorize black or white faces as quickly as you can, for example, by pressing a left-hand key in response to a black face and a right-hand key for a white face. Next, you are asked to categorize a set of words, for example, by pressing a left-hand key for positive words *(love, laughter, friend)* and a right-hand key for negative words *(war, failure, evil)*. Once you become familiar with the categorization task, the test combines faces and words. You may be asked, for example, to press the left-hand key if you see a black face or positive word and a right-hand key for a white face or negative word. Then, in the fourth stage, the opposite pairings are presented—black or negative, white or positive. Black and white faces are then interspersed in a quick sequence of trials, each time paired with a positive or negative word. In rapid-fire succession, you have to press one key or another in response to stimulus pairs such as *black-wonderful, black-failure, white-love, black-laughter, white-evil, white-awful, black-war,* and *white-joy*. As you work through the list, you may find that some pairings are harder and take longer to respond to than others. In general, people are quicker to respond when liked faces are paired with positive words and disliked faces are paired with negative words than the other way around. Using the IAT, your implicit attitudes about African Americans can thus be detected by the speed it takes you to respond to *black-bad/white-good* pairings relative to *black-good/white-bad* pairings. The test takes only 10–15 minutes to complete. When you're done, you receive the results of your test and an explanation of what it means (see ● Figure 6.3).

● **FIGURE 6.3**

The Implicit Association Test

Through a sequence of tasks, the IAT measures implicit racial attitudes toward, for example, African Americans, by measuring how quickly people respond to *black-bad/white-good* word pairings relative to *black-good/white-bad* pairings. Most white Americans are quicker to respond to the first type of pairings than to the second, which suggests that they do not as readily connect *black-good* and *white-bad*.

From Kassin, S. *Essentials of psychology.* Copyright © 2004. Reprinted by permission of Pearson Education, Inc., Upper Saddle River, NJ.

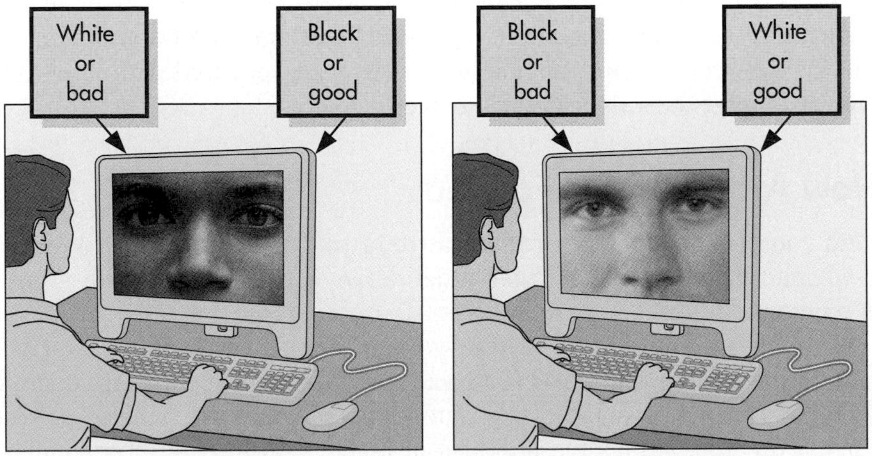

From 1998 to the present, visitors to the IAT website completed millions of tests. In questionnaires, interviews, public opinion polls, and Internet surveys, people don't tend to express stereotypes, prejudices, or other unpopular attitudes. Yet on the IAT, respondents have exhibited a marked implicit preference for self over other, white over black, young over old, straight over gay, able over disabled, thin over obese, and the stereotype that links males with careers and females with family (Greenwald et al., 2003; Nosek et al., 2002). Because more and more researchers are using these kinds of indirect measures, social psychologists who study attitudes find themselves in the midst of a debate over what IAT scores mean, how the implicit attitudes revealed in the IAT are formed and then changed, how well these attitudes predict or influence societally important behaviors, and how they differ from the more explicit attitudes that we consciously hold and report (Blanton et al., 2009; Gawronski & Bodenhausen, 2006; Greenwald et al., 2015; Oswald et al., 2015; Petty et al., 2009).

Do implicit attitudes matter? Do millisecond differences in response times on a computerized test really predict behavior in real-world settings of consequence? And what does it mean when one's implicit and explicit attitudes clash? The importance of these questions cannot be overstated. If the IAT reveals unconscious prejudices that people do not self-report, should individuals be scrutinized in the laboratory for hidden motives underlying potentially unlawful behaviors—as when a police officer shoots a black suspect, fearing that he or she is armed; as when an employer hires a male applicant over a female applicant, citing his credentials as opposed to an act of discrimination; or as when a jury chooses to convict a Latino defendant on the basis of ambiguous evidence?

Eager to use the IAT for predicting social behaviors of consequence, some researchers have speculated about the relevance of implicit attitudes in the domains of law (Lane et al, 2007) and politics (Gawronski et al., 2015). But is their speculation justified? Some researchers are critical of claims concerning the predictive validity of the IAT, citing the need for more and stronger behavioral evidence (Blanton et al., 2009; Oswald et al., 2015). Based on a meta-analysis of 122 IAT studies involving 15,000 participants, Greenwald and others (2009) conceded that people's implicit attitudes are generally less predictive of behavior than their explicit attitudes. They also found, however, that IAT measures are better when it comes to socially sensitive topics for which people often conceal or distort their self-reports. In a poignant illustration of this point, one research team administered to a large group of psychiatric patients an IAT that measured their implicit associations between self and suicide. Over the next six months, patients appearing in the emergency room because of a suicide attempt had a stronger implicit association between self and suicide than those who appeared with other types of psychiatric emergencies (Nock et al., 2010).

■ How Attitudes Are Formed

How did you become liberal or conservative in your political values? Why do you favor or oppose same-sex marriage? What draws you toward or away from organized religion?

Are Attitudes Inherited? One hypothesis, first advanced by Abraham Tesser (1993), is that strong likes and dislikes are rooted in our genetic makeup. Research shows that on some issues the attitudes of identical twins are more similar than those of fraternal twins and that twins raised apart are as similar to each other as those who are raised in the same home. This pattern of evidence suggests that people may be predisposed to hold certain attitudes. Indeed, Tesser found that when asked about attitudes for which there seems to be a predisposition (such as attitudes toward sexual promiscuity, religion, and the death penalty), research participants were quicker to respond and less likely to alter their views toward social norms.

Tesser speculated that individuals are disposed to hold certain strong attitudes as a result of inborn physical, sensory, and cognitive skills, temperament, and personality traits. Other twin studies, too, as well as complex comparisons within extended families, have supported the notion that people differ in their attitudes toward a range of social and political issues in part because of genetically rooted differences in their biological makeup (Hatemi et al., 2010; Olson et al., 2001). There are different ways in which a person's inborn tendencies may influence social and political attitudes. In one study, for example, researchers brought 40 adults with strong political views into the lab for testing and found that those who physiologically were highly reactive to sudden noise and other unpleasant stimuli were more likely to favor capital punishment, the right to bear arms, defense spending, and other policies seen as protective against domestic and foreign threats (Oxley et al., 2008).

Are Attitudes Learned?   Whatever dispositions nature provides to us, our most cherished attitudes often form as a result of our exposure to attitude objects; our history of rewards and punishments; the attitudes that our parents, friends, and enemies express; the social and cultural context in which we live; and other types of experiences. In a classic naturalistic study, Theodore Newcomb (1943) surveyed the political attitudes of students at Bennington College in Vermont. At the time, Bennington was a women's college that drew its students from conservative and mostly affluent families. Once there, however, the students encountered professors and older peers who held more liberal views. Newcomb found that as the women moved from their first year to graduation, they became progressively more liberal.

Chances are, these identical twins have more in common than being truck driving partners. Research suggests that people may also be genetically predisposed to hold certain attitudes.

(In the 1936 presidential election, 62% of first-year Bennington students preferred the Republican Landon to the Democrat Roosevelt, compared to only 43% of sophomores and 15% of juniors and seniors.) This link between cultural environment and attitudes is particularly evident in the current political landscape of America—a "house divided" into red states and blue states by geography, culture, and ideology (Seyle & Newman, 2006).

Clearly, attitudes are formed through basic processes of learning. For example, a number of studies have shown that people can form strong positive and negative attitudes toward neutral objects that somehow are linked to emotionally charged stimuli. At the start of the twentieth century, Russian physiologist Ivan Pavlov (1927) discovered that dogs would naturally and reflexively salivate in response to food in the mouth. He then discovered that by repeatedly ringing a bell—a neutral stimulus—before the food was placed in the mouth, the dog would eventually start to salivate at the sound of the bell itself. This process by which organisms learn to associate a once neutral stimulus with an inherently positive or negative response is a basic and powerful form of learning. In fact, Pavlov found that once a dog was conditioned to salivate to one tone, it went to "generalize" by responding to other sounds that were similar but not identical.

It is now clear that this form of learning can help to explain the development of social attitudes. In a classic first study, college students were presented with a list of adjectives that indicate nationality (*German, Swedish, Dutch, Italian, French,* and *Greek*), each of which was repeatedly presented with words that were known to have very pleasant (*happy, gift, sacred*) or unpleasant (*bitter, ugly, failure*) connotations. When the participants later evaluated the nationalities by name, they were more positive in their ratings of those that had been paired with pleasant words than with unpleasant words (Staats & Staats, 1958). And as discovered by Pavlov nearly a hundred years ago, research shows that when an attitude is changed toward one object, attitudes toward similar and related objects are often changed as well (Glaser et al., 2015).

More recent studies of **evaluative conditioning** have shown that implicit and explicit attitudes toward neutral objects can form by their association with positive and negative stimuli, even in people who are not conscious of this association (Hofmann et al., 2010; Olson & Fazio, 2001; Sweldens et al., 2014; Walther et al., 2011). That's why political leaders all over the world wrap themselves in a national flag to derive a benefit from positive associations, while advertisers strategically pair their products with sexy models, uplifting music, celebrities, nostalgic images, and other positive emotional symbols. In a series of laboratory studies, researchers found that people came to prefer brands of a consumer product that were paired with humorous ads more than those that were associated with non-humorous ads (Strick et al., 2009).

■ The Link Between Attitudes and Behavior

People take for granted the notion that attitudes influence behavior. We assume that voters' opinions of opposing candidates predict the decisions they will make on Election Day, that consumer preference for one product over competing products will influence the purchases they make, and that feelings of prejudice will trigger bad acts of discrimination. Yet as sensible as these assumptions seem, the link between attitudes and behavior has proved far from perfect.

Sociologist Richard LaPiere (1934) was the first to notice that attitudes and behavior don't always go hand in hand. In the 1930s, during the height of the Great Depression, LaPiere took a young Chinese American couple on a three-month,

evaluative conditioning The process by which we form an attitude toward a neutral stimulus because of its association with a positive or negative person, place, or thing.

10,000-mile car trip, visiting 250 restaurants, campgrounds, and hotels across the United States. Although prejudice against Asians was widespread at the time, the couple was refused service only once. Yet when LaPiere wrote back to the places they had visited and asked if they would accept Chinese patrons, more than 90% of those who returned an answer said they would not. Self-reported attitudes did not correspond with behavior.

This study was provocative but seriously flawed. LaPiere measured attitudes several months after his trip, and during that time the attitudes may have changed. He also did not know whether those who responded to his letter were the same people who had greeted the couple in person. It was even possible that the Chinese couple were served wherever they went because they were accompanied by LaPiere—or because businesses were desperate during hard economic times.

Despite these limitations, LaPiere's study was the first of many to reveal a lack of correspondence between attitudes and behavior. In 1969, Allan Wicker reviewed the applicable research and concluded that attitudes and behavior are correlated only weakly, if at all. Sobered by this conclusion, researchers were puzzled: Could it be that the votes we cast do *not* follow from our political opinions, that consumers' purchases are *not* based on their attitudes toward a product, or that discrimination is *not* related to underlying prejudice? Is the study of attitudes useless to those interested in human social behavior? Not at all. During subsequent years, researchers went on to identify the conditions under which attitudes and behavior are correlated. Thus, when Stephen Kraus (1995) meta-analyzed all of this research, he concluded that "attitudes significantly and substantially predict future behavior" (p. 58). In fact, he calculated that there would have to be 60,983 new studies reporting a zero correlation before this conclusion would have to be revised. Based on a meta-analysis of 41 additional studies, Laura Glasman and Dolores Albarracín (2006) went on to identify some of the conditions under which attitudes most clearly predict future behavior.

Attitudes in Context One important condition is the level of *correspondence,* or similarity, between attitude measures and behavior. Perhaps the reason that LaPiere (1934) did not find a correlation between self-reported prejudice and discrimination was that he had asked proprietors about Asians in general but then observed their actions toward only one couple. To predict a single act of discrimination, he should have measured people's more specific attitudes toward a young, well-dressed, attractive Chinese couple accompanied by an American professor.

Icek Ajzen and Martin Fishbein (1977) analyzed more than 100 studies and found that attitudes correlate with behavior only when attitude measures closely match the behavior in question. Illustrating the point, Andrew Davidson and James Jaccard (1979) tried to use attitudes to predict whether women would use birth control pills within the next two years. Attitudes were measured in a series of questions ranging from very general ("How do you feel about birth control?") to very specific ("How do you feel about using birth control pills during the next two years?"). The more specific the initial attitude question was, the better it predicted the behavior. Other researchers as well have replicated this finding (Kraus, 1995).

The link between our feelings and our actions should also be placed within a broader context. Attitudes are one determinant of social behavior, but there are other determinants as well. This limitation formed the basis for Fishbein's (1980) theory of reasoned action, which Ajzen (1991) later expanded into his **theory of planned behavior**. According to these theories, our attitudes influence our behavior through a process of deliberate decision making, and their impact is limited in four respects (see ● Figure 6.4).

theory of planned behavior The theory that attitudes toward a specific behavior combine with subjective norms and perceived control to influence a person's actions.

● **FIGURE 6.4**

Theory of Planned Behavior

According to the theory of planned behavior, attitudes toward a specific behavior combine with subjective norms and perceived behavior control to influence a person's intentions. These intentions, in turn, guide but do not completely determine behavior. This theory places the link between attitudes and behavior within a broader context.

From Ajzen, *Organizational Behavior and the Human Decision Process*, vol 50, pp. 179–211. Copyright © 1991 Elsevier. Reprinted with permission.

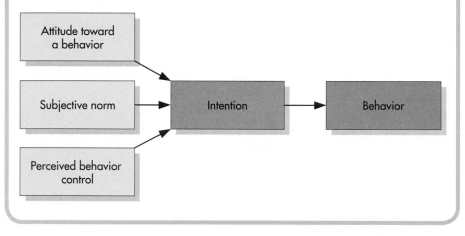

First, as just described, behavior is influenced less by general attitudes than by attitudes toward a specific behavior. Second, behavior is influenced not only by attitudes but by *subjective norms*—our beliefs about what others think we should do. As we'll see in Chapter 7, social pressures to conform often lead us to behave in ways that are at odds with our inner convictions. Third, according to Ajzen, attitudes give rise to behavior only when we perceive the behavior to be within our *control*. To the extent that people lack confidence in their ability to engage in some behavior, they are unlikely to form an intention to do so. Fourth, although attitudes (along with subjective norms and perceived control) contribute to an *intention* to behave in a particular manner, people often do not or cannot follow through on their intentions.

A good deal of research now supports the theories of reasoned action and planned behavior (Ajzen & Fishbein, 2005). Indeed, this general approach, which places the link between attitudes and behaviors within a broader context, has successfully been used to predict a wide range of practical behaviors—such as using condoms, obeying speed limits, washing hands and other food safety habits, donating blood, complying with medical regimens, and reducing risky sexual behaviors (Albarracín et al., 2001; Conner et al., 2013; Elliott et al., 2003; Milton & Mullan, 2012; Rich et al., 2015; Tyson et al., 2014).

Strength of the Attitude According to the theories of reasoned action and planned behavior, specific attitudes combine with social factors to produce behavior. Sometimes attitudes have more influence on behavior than do the other factors; sometimes they have less influence. In large part, it depends on the importance, or *strength*, of the attitude. Each of us has some views that are nearer and dearer to the heart than others. Computer jocks become attached to PCs or to Macs, religious fundamentalists care deeply about issues pertaining to life and death, and political activists have fiery passions for one political party or policy over others. In each case, the attitude is held with great confidence and is difficult to change (Petty & Krosnick, 1995).

Why are some attitudes stronger than others? David Boninger and others (1995) identified three psychological factors that consistently seem to distinguish between our strongest and weakest attitudes. These investigators asked people to reflect on their views toward defense spending, gun control, the legalization of marijuana, abortion rights, and other issues. They found that the attitudes people held most passionately were those that concerned issues that (1) directly affected their own self-interests; (2) related to deeply held philosophical, political, and religious values; and (3) were of concern to their close friends, family, and social ingroups. This last, highly social, point is important. Research shows that when people are surrounded by others who are like-minded, the attitudes they hold are stronger and more resistant to change (Visser & Mirabile, 2004).

Several factors indicate the strength of an attitude and its link to behavior. One is that people tend to behave in ways that are consistent with their attitudes when they are well informed. For example, college students were asked which of two candidates they preferred in an upcoming local election for mayor. Those who knew the factual campaign issues were later the most likely to actually vote for their favored candidate (Davidson et al., 1985). In another study, college students were questioned about their views on various environmental issues and later were asked to take action—to sign petitions, participate in a recycling project, and so on. Again, the more informed the students were, the more consistent their attitudes about the environment were with their behavior (Kallgren & Wood, 1986).

The strength of an attitude is indicated not only by the *amount* of information on which it is based but also by *how* that information was acquired. Research shows that attitudes are more stable and more predictive of behavior when they are born of direct personal experience than when based on indirect, secondhand information. In a series of experiments, for example, Russell Fazio and Mark Zanna (1981) introduced two groups of participants to a set of puzzles. One group worked on sample puzzles; the other group merely watched someone else work on them. All participants were then asked to rate their interest in the puzzles (attitude) and were given an opportunity to spend time on them (behavior). As it turned out, attitudes and behaviors were more consistent among participants who had previously sampled the puzzles.

Third, an attitude can be strengthened, ironically, by an attack against it from a persuasive message. According to Zakary Tormala and Richard Petty (2002), people hold attitudes with varying degrees of certainty, and they become more confident in their positions after they successfully resist changing that attitude in response to a persuasive communication. In one study, researchers confronted university students with an unpopular proposal to add senior comprehensive exams as a graduation requirement. Each student read a pro-exam argument that was described as strong or weak, after which they were asked to write down counterarguments and indicate their attitude toward the policy. The result: Students who continued to oppose the policy despite reading what they thought to be a strong argument became even more certain of their opinion.

Additional studies have shown that this effect depends on how satisfied people are with their own resistance. When people resist a strong message and believe that they have done so in a compelling way, they become more certain of their attitude and more likely to form a behavioral intention that is consistent with it. When people resist a persuasive message "by the skin of their teeth," however, and see their own counterarguments as weak, they become less certain of their initial attitude and more vulnerable to subsequent attack (Tormala et al., 2006). Even if a person's belief in his or her own thoughtful response is incorrect, it can influence the strength of the attitude in question (Barden & Petty, 2008).

A fourth key factor is that strong attitudes are highly accessible to awareness, which means that they are quickly and easily brought to mind (Fazio, 1990). To return to our earlier examples, computer jocks think often about their computer preferences, and political activists think often about their allegiances to political parties. It turns out that many attitudes—not just those we feel strongly about—easily pop to mind by the mere sight or even just the mention of an attitude object (Bargh et al., 1992). When this happens, the attitude can trigger behavior in a quick, spontaneous way or by leading us to think carefully about how we feel and how to respond (Fazio & Towles-Schwen, 1999).

Attitudes in a Cultural Context   Bo Kyung Park and colleagues (2013) tell this story: "In the hallways of a local library in Korea, it is not unusual to see individuals in front of a vending machine, wavering between two beverage options for a while, eventually making a choice by doing 'eeny, meeny, miny, moe.' Thus a vending machine in the library has the unique option, 'Random.' If you press this option, the machine will give you Coke or Sprite randomly! Such an idea may sound hilarious or absurd to North Americans. However, this vending machine anecdote nicely illustrates a cultural difference regarding preference and choice" (pp. 106-107).

In Western cultures that value independence, it is common to see our attitudes as a part of who we are, embodying our values, tastes, preferences, and personalities. Making choices is an exercise of our attitudes and preferences. From that perspective, it is natural to expect that our likes and dislikes will remain relatively consistent over time and predictive of behavior. In many East Asian cultures, however, where independence, choice, and personal preference are less highly valued, a person's attitude may well not show this level of consistency. Indeed, Hila Riemer and colleagues (2014) have observed that whereas Western views of attitudes are often person-centric in these ways, in other parts of the world attitudes depend more on contextual factors such as social norms, others' expectations, roles, and obligations.

To the extent that norms can change over time and across situations, people in non-Western cultures may well exhibit less consistency in their attitudes. Research by Wilken and others (2011) supports this hypothesis. In one study, American and Japanese participants were asked to report on their favorite musical artists, TV shows, restaurants, and other preferences—and to estimate how long these preferences have lasted. Overall, the Japanese participants reported liking their favorites for a shorter period of time than Americans did. In a second study, participants evaluated how trendy various items were, such as the iPod, Harry Potter books, and the Wii. When questioned about those same items one year later, American participants stayed relatively consistent in their evaluations; Japanese participants reported significant changes in their attitudes.

If attitudes in Western cultures are consistent parts of a person, which we carry with us over time and across situations, it stands to reason that our attitudes and behavior would be highly correlated. But does it also stand to reason that attitudes would be less predictive of behavior in non-Western cultures, where context matters as well? In one study, North American and Indian participants rated how much they liked everyday items like watches, shoes, and shirts. Later when they had to choose one item from a set of four, Indians were less likely than Americans to choose the watch, shoes, or shirts they said they liked the best (Savani et al., 2008). For Indian participants, their choices presumably depended on factors other than personal preferences. Is the link between attitudes and behavior stronger in some cultures than others? It is possible. At this point, however, more research is needed to test this specific proposition.

To sum up: Research on the link between people's attitudes and behavior leads to an important conclusion. Our evaluations of an object do not always determine our actions because other factors must be taken into account. However, when attitudes are strong and specific to a behavior, at least in Western cultures, the effects are beyond dispute. Under these conditions, voting is influenced by political opinions, consumer purchasing is affected by product attitudes, and racial discrimination is rooted in feelings of prejudice. Attitudes can be important determinants of behavior. The question is, *how can attitudes be changed?*

Persuasion by Communication

On a day-to-day basis, we are all involved in the process of changing attitudes. On TV, on Facebook pages and blogs, in pop-up ads, magazines, and billboards, advertisers flood us with ad campaigns designed to sell cars, soft drinks, credit cards, sneakers, prescription drugs, airlines, new movies, and travel destinations. Likewise, politicians make speeches, run commercials, pass out bumper stickers, and kiss babies to win votes. Attitude change is sought whenever parents socialize their children, scientists advance theories and seek funding, religious groups seek converts, financial analysts recommend stocks, or trial lawyers argue cases to a jury. Some appeals work; others do not. Some are soft and subtle; others are hard and blatant. Some serve the public interest, whereas others serve commercial interests. The point is, there is nothing inherently evil or virtuous about changing attitudes—a process known as **persuasion**. We do it all the time.

If you wanted to change someone's attitude on an issue, you'd probably try to do it by making a persuasive *communication*. Appeals made in person, over the Internet, or through the mass media rely on the spoken word, the written word, and the image or video that is worth a thousand words. What determines whether an appeal succeeds or fails? To understand why certain approaches are effective whereas others are not, social psychologists have long sought to understand *how* and *why* persuasive communications work. For that, we need a road map of the persuasion process.

■ Two Routes to Persuasion

It's a familiar scene in American politics: Every four years, two or more presidential candidates launch extensive—and expensive—campaigns for office. In a way, if you've seen one election, you've seen them all. The names and dates may change, but over and over again, opposing candidates accuse each other of ducking substantive issues and turning the election into a high stakes, money driven, mud-slinging popularity contest.

True or not, these criticisms show that politicians are keenly aware that they can win votes through two different methods. They can stick to policy, issues, and rational argumentation using the power of words or they can base their appeals on other grounds. Interestingly, these "other grounds" can well determine who wins an election. In *The Political Brain*, Drew Westen (2007) presents a wealth of research evidence indicating that in the marketplace of politics, emotions trump reason. Based on a combination of laboratory experiments and public opinion polls, other political psychologists agree (Brader, 2006; Neuman et al., 2007). Outside the realm of politics too, influence can be quick and automatic. In *Split-Second Persuasion*, Kevin Dutton (2010) described how Buddhist monks, magicians, advertisers, con artists, hostage negotiators, and other "super-persuaders" use simplicity, empathy, an air of self-confidence, and other disarming tactics to effect instant persuasion.

To account for the two alternative approaches to persuasion, Richard Petty and John Cacioppo (1986) proposed a dual-process model of persuasion. This model assumes that we do not always process communications the same way. When people think hard and critically about the contents of a message, they are said to take a **central route to persuasion** and are influenced by the strength and quality of the arguments. When people do not think hard or critically about the contents of a message but focus instead on other cues, they take a **peripheral route to persuasion**. As we'll see, the route taken depends on whether one is

persuasion The process by which attitudes are changed.

central route to persuasion The process by which a person thinks carefully about a communication and is influenced by the strength of its arguments.

peripheral route to persuasion The process by which a person does not think carefully about a communication and is influenced instead by superficial cues.

In U.S. presidential politics, candidates try to win votes by addressing the issues, as in debates and speeches delivered from a podium (the central route) or through the use of banners, balloons, music, and other theatrics (the peripheral route).

willing and able to scrutinize the information contained in the message itself. Over the years, this model has provided an important framework for understanding the factors that elicit persuasion (Petty & Wegener, 1998).

The Central Route In the first systematic attempt to study persuasion, Carl Hovland and colleagues (1949, 1953) started the Yale Communication and Attitude Change Program. They proposed that for a persuasive message to have influence, the recipients of that message must learn its contents and be motivated to accept it. According to this view, people can be persuaded only by an argument they attend to, comprehend, and retain in memory for later use. Regardless of whether the message takes the form of a live personal appeal, a newspaper editorial, a Sunday sermon, a TV commercial, or a pop-up window on a website, these basic requirements remain the same.

A few years later, William McGuire (1969) reiterated the information-processing steps necessary for persuasion and like the Yale group before him distinguished between the learning, or *reception,* of a message, a necessary first step, and its later *acceptance.* In fact, McGuire (1968) used this distinction to explain the surprising finding that a recipient's self-esteem and intelligence are unrelated to persuasion. In McGuire's analysis, these characteristics have opposite effects on reception and acceptance. People who are smart or high in self-esteem are better able to learn a message, but are less likely to accept its call for a change in attitude. People who are less smart or low in self-esteem are more willing to accept the message, but they may have trouble learning its contents. Overall, then, neither group is generally more vulnerable to persuasion than the other—a prediction that is supported by a good deal of research (Rhodes & Wood, 1992).

Anthony Greenwald (1968) and others then argued that persuasion requires a third, intermediate step: **elaboration**. To illustrate, imagine you are offered a job and your prospective employer tries to convince you over lunch to accept. You listen closely, learn the terms of the offer, and understand what it means. But if it's a really important interview, your head will spin with questions as you weigh all the pros and cons and contemplate the implications: What would it cost to move? Is there potential for advancement? Am I better off staying where I am? When confronted with personally significant messages, we don't listen merely

elaboration The process of thinking about and scrutinizing the arguments contained in a persuasive communication.

to collect information; we think about that information. When this happens, the message is effective to the extent that it leads us to focus on favorable rather than unfavorable thoughts.

These theories of attitude change all share the assumption that the recipients of persuasive appeals are attentive, active, critical, and thoughtful of every word spoken. This assumption is correct—some of the time. When it is and when people consider a message carefully, their reaction to it depends on the strength of its contents. In these instances, messages have greater impact when they are easily learned rather than difficult, when they are memorable rather than forgettable, and when they stimulate a good deal of favorable rather than unfavorable elaboration. Ultimately, strong arguments are persuasive and weak arguments are not.

On the central route to persuasion, the process is eminently rational. It's important to note, however, that thinking hard and carefully about a persuasive message does not guarantee that the process is objective or that it necessarily promotes truth seeking. At times, each of us prefers to hold a particular attitude and become biased in the way we process information (Petty & Wegener, 1998). Among college students who were politically conservative or liberal, the tendency to agree with a social welfare plan was influenced more—rapidly, strongly, and persistently—by whether it was said to have the support of Democrats or Republicans than by the logical merits of the policy itself (Cohen, 2003; Smith et al., 2012). Similarly, college students were less likely to be persuaded by a proposed tuition hike to fund campus improvements when the increase would take effect in one year, thus raising the personal stakes, than by a proposal to raise tuition in eight years (Darke & Chaiken, 2005).

There is one additional complicating factor to consider. Several years ago, Petty and his colleagues (2002) proposed the *self-validation hypothesis* that people not only "elaborate" on a persuasive communication with positive or negative attitude-relevant thoughts; they also seek to assess the validity of these thoughts. Those thoughts that we hold with high confidence will have a strong impact on our attitudes, as predicted by the Dual-Process Model of persuasion; but those we hold with low confidence will not have a strong impact on our attitudes. This means that various aspects of a persuasive communication—such as whether the source is a knowledgeable expert, and whether the position he or she advocates is one with which we agree or disagree—can affect the confidence we have in our own thoughts and, in turn, our attitudes (see Briñol & Petty, 2009).

The Peripheral Route   "The receptive ability of the masses is very limited, their understanding small; on the other hand, they have a great power of forgetting." The author of this cynical assessment of human nature was Adolf Hitler (1933, p. 77). Believing that human beings are incompetent processors of information, Hitler relied in his propaganda on the use of slogans, uniforms, swastika-covered flags, a special salute, and other symbols. For Hitler, "meetings were not just occasions to make speeches; they were carefully planned theatrical productions in which settings, lighting, background music, and the timing of entrances were devised to maximize the emotional fervor of an audience" (Qualter, 1962, p. 112).

Do these ploys work? Can the masses be so handily manipulated into persuasion? History shows that they can. Audiences are not always thoughtful. Sometimes people do not follow the central route to persuasion but instead take a shortcut through the peripheral route. Rather than try to learn about a message and think through the issues, they respond with little effort on the basis of superficial peripheral cues.

On the peripheral route to persuasion, people will often evaluate a communication by using simple-minded heuristics, or rules of thumb (Chaiken, 1987; Chen & Chaiken, 1999). If a communicator has a good reputation, speaks fluently, or writes well, we tend to assume that his or her message must be correct. And when a speaker has a reputation for being honest, people think less critically about the contents of his or her communication (Priester & Petty, 1995). Likewise, we assume that a message must be correct if it contains a long litany of arguments or statistics or an impressive list of supporting experts, if it's familiar, if it elicits cheers from an audience, or if the speaker seems to argue against his or her own interests. In some cases, people will change their attitudes simply because they know that an argument has majority support (Giner-Sorolla & Chaiken, 1997).

On the mindless peripheral route, people are also influenced by a host of factors that are not relevant to attitudes—such as cues from their own body movements. Increasingly, social psychologists are coming to appreciate the extent to which human thought is embodied—that the way we think and feel about things is influenced by the physical position, orientation, and movements of our bodies (Lakoff & Johnson, 1999; Niedenthal et al., 2005).

Several studies illustrate *attitude embodiment effects.* In one study, participants were coaxed into nodding their heads up and down (as if saying yes) or shaking their heads from side to side (as if saying no) while listening via headphones to an editorial, presumably to test whether the headphones could endure the physical activity. Those coaxed into nodding later agreed more with the arguments than those coaxed into shaking their heads from side to side (Wells & Petty, 1980). In other studies, participants viewed graphic symbols or word-like stimuli (*surtel, primet*) while using an exercise bar to either stretch their arms out (which mimics what we do to push something away) or flex their arms in (which we do to bring something closer). Participants later judged these stimuli to be more pleasant when they were associated with the flexing of the arm than when they were associated with the stretching-out motion (Cacioppo et al., 1993; Priester et al., 1996). Even our attitudes toward consumer products can be influenced by bodily sensations. In one study, for example, participants evaluated the appearance of vases, flowers, and other products placed at a distance as more appealing when they stood on a soft, comfortable carpet than on a hard tile floor (Meyers-Levy et al., 2010).

Route Selection Thanks to Petty and Cacioppo's (1986) two-track distinction between the central and peripheral routes, it is easy to understand why the persuasion process seems so logical on some occasions yet so illogical on others—why voters may select candidates according to issues or images, why juries may base their verdicts on evidence or a defendant's appearance, and why consumers may base their purchases on marketing reports or on product images. The process that is engaged depends on whether the recipients of a persuasive message have the *ability* and the *motivation* to take the central route or whether they rely on peripheral cues instead.

To understand the conditions that lead people to process information on one route or the other, it's helpful to view persuasive communication as the outcome of three factors: a *source* (who), a *message* (says what and in what context), and an *audience* (to whom). Each of these factors steers a recipient's approach to the communication. If a source speaks clearly, if the message is important, if there is a bright, captive, and involved audience that cares deeply about the issue and has time to absorb the information, then audience members will be willing and able to take the effortful central route. But if the source speaks at a rate too fast to comprehend, if the message is trivial or too complex to process, or if audience

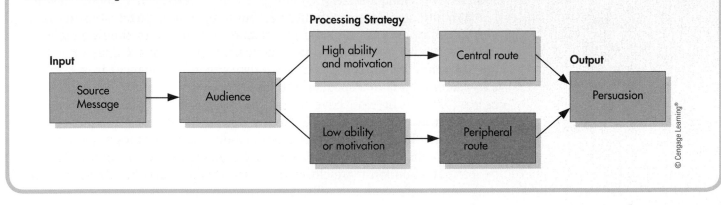

● **FIGURE 6.5**

Two Routes to Persuasion

Based on aspects of the source, message, and audience, recipients of a communication take either a central or peripheral route to persuasion. On the central route, people are influenced by strong arguments and evidence. On the peripheral route, persuasion is based more on heuristics and other superficial cues. This two-process model helps explain how persuasion can seem logical on some occasions and illogical on others.

members are distracted, pressed for time, or uninterested, then the less strenuous peripheral route is taken.

● Figure 6.5 presents a road map of persuasive communication. In the next three sections, we will follow this map from the input factors (source, message, and audience) through the central or peripheral processing routes to reach the final destination: persuasion.

> In reacting to persuasive communications, people are influenced more by superficial images than by logical arguments.
>
> **FALSE**

▉ The Source

Golfer Tiger Woods is a living legend, one of the most gifted athletes of our time. Until recently, he was also paid more millions of dollars per year than just about anyone else—to endorse Nike, American Express, and other products. Woods was considered a highly effective spokesman until 2009 when various extramarital affairs were exposed, causing the breakup of his marriage and the demise of his championship caliber golf game. He has struggled since that time and is no longer the top-ranked golfer in the world or the most highly sought spokesperson. What does the story of Tiger Woods tells us about source effects in persuasion? More specifically, what makes some communicators in general more effective than others? As we'll see, there are two key attributes: credibility and likability.

Credibility   Imagine you are waiting in line in a supermarket and you catch a glimpse of this large boldfaced headline: "Doctors Discover Cure for AIDS!" As your eye wanders across the front page, you discover that you are reading a supermarket tabloid that features aliens from another planet. What would you think? In contrast, imagine that you are reading through scientific periodicals in a library when you come across a similar article, but this time it appears in the *New England Journal of Medicine.* Now what would you think?

Chances are, you'd react with more excitement to the medical journal than to the tabloid, even though both sources report the same news item. In a study conducted during the Cold War era of the 1950s, American participants read a speech that advocated for the development of nuclear submarines. The speech elicited more agreement when it was attributed to an eminent American physicist than when the source was said to be the Soviet government–controlled newspaper (Hovland & Weiss, 1951). Likewise, when participants read a lecture favoring more lenient treatment of juvenile offenders, they changed their attitudes more when they thought the speaker was a judge than when they believed the speaker was a convicted drug dealer (Kelman & Hovland, 1953). Recent research confirms that high-credibility sources are generally more persuasive than low-credibility sources (Pornpitakpan, 2004).

Why are some sources more credible than others? Why were the medical journal, the physicist, and the judge more credible than the tabloid, government-controlled newspaper, and drug dealer? For communicators to be seen as credible, they must have two characteristics: competence and trustworthiness. *Competence* refers to a speaker's ability. People who are knowledgeable, smart, or well spoken or who have impressive credentials are persuasive by virtue of their expertise (Hass, 1981). Experts can have a disarming effect on us. We assume they know what they're talking about. So when they speak, we listen. And when they take a position, often we yield. Indeed, research shows that people pay attention more closely to experts than to nonexperts and scrutinize their arguments more carefully (Tobin & Raymundo, 2009).

The impact of experts on our attention, confidence, and attitudes, is not simple or uniform. The effect depends on how we feel about the attitude they advocate—say, on politically charged issues such as gun control, immigration policy, or climate change. As suggested by the self-validation hypothesis described earlier, a highly credible source who argues for a position we tend to favor (yay!) bolsters our confidence and existing attitude—more than someone less credible would. In this case, there is less need to scrutinize the expert than the supportive but questionable nonexpert. But a highly credible source who advocates for a position we oppose (yikes!) poses a real threat to our confidence and existing attitude—more than someone less credible. In this instance, we need to scrutinize the expert more than the nonexpert. Research is consistent with this nuanced hypothesis: People scrutinize nonexperts more than experts when they advocate a position we agree with, but they scrutinize nonexperts more when they advocate a position we oppose (Clark et al., 2012; Clark & Evans, 2014; Clark & Wegner, 2013).

Expertise is only one aspect of credibility. To have credibility, however, sources must also be *trustworthy*—that is, they must be seen as willing to report their knowledge truthfully and without compromise. What determines whether we trust a communicator? To some extent, we make these judgments on the basis of stereotypes. In 2014, in an update to a survey conducted many times over the years, the Gallup Organization asked 1,000 Americans to rate how honest people are from various occupational categories. As shown in Table 6.1, nurses topped the list as the most trusted occupational group. Car salesmen, members of Congress, and advertisers were the least trusted.

▲ **TABLE 6.1**

Who Do You Trust?

Please tell me how you would rate the honesty and ethical standards of people in these different fields—very high, high, average, low, or very low?

Occupation	% Very high/High
Nurses	80
Medical doctors	65
Pharmacists	65
Police officers	48
Clergy	46
Bankers	23
Lawyers	21
Business executives	17
Advertising practitioners	10
Car salespeople	8
Members of Congress	7

In December of 2014, a Gallup poll was conducted to determine the level of honesty attributed to people from various occupational groups. Indicated alongside are the percentages of respondents who rated each group as "high" or "very high" in honesty.

At an October 2014 press conference at Tsinghua University in Beijing, Facebook co-founder Mark Zuckerberg stunned the crowd by speaking and answering questions in Mandarin. In his effort to bring Facebook to China, "Zuck" may have enhanced his persuasive appeal by appearing more similar and, hence, more likeable.

In judging the credibility of a source, common sense arms us with a simple rule of caution: Beware of people who have something to gain from successful persuasion. If a speaker has been paid off, has an ax to grind, or is simply telling us what we want to hear, we suspect some degree of bias. This rule sheds light on a classic dilemma in advertising concerning the value of celebrity spokespersons: The more products a celebrity endorses, the less trustworthy he or she appears to consumers (Tripp et al., 1994). In the courtroom, the same rule of caution can be used to evaluate witnesses. In one study, research participants served as jurors in a mock trial involving a man who claimed that his exposure to an industrial chemical at work had caused him to contract cancer. Testifying in support of this claim was a biochemist paid either $4,800 or $75 for his expert testimony. You might think that jurors would be more impressed by the scientist who commanded the higher fee. Yet while he was highly paid, the expert was perceived to be a "hired gun" and was as a result less believable and less persuasive (Cooper & Neuhaus, 2000).

The self-interest rule has other interesting implications. One is that people are impressed by others who take unpopular stands or argue against their own interests. When research participants read a political speech accusing a large corporation of polluting a local river, those who thought the speechmaker was a pro-environment candidate addressing a staunch environmentalist group perceived him to be biased, whereas those who thought he was a pro-business candidate talking to company supporters assumed he was sincere (Eagly et al., 1978).

Trust is also established by speakers who do not purposely try to change our views. Thus, people are influenced more when they think that they are accidentally overhearing a communication than when they receive a sales pitch clearly intended for their ears (Walster & Festinger, 1962). That's why advertisers sometimes use the "overheard communicator" trick, in which the source appears to tell a buddy about a new product that works. As if eavesdropping on a personal conversation, viewers assume that what one friend says to another can be trusted. The self-interest rule also has great relevance in law, which is why people are far more likely to believe a crime suspect's admissions of guilt than his or her denials (Kassin, 2012).

Likability More than anything else, the celebrity star power of Tiger Woods was based on his athletic prowess, his popularity, and his winning smile. Before the revelations that ended Woods' marriage and derailed his game, he was seen as a likable person. But does that quality necessarily enhance someone's impact as a communicator? Yes. In his classic bestseller, *How to Win Friends and Influence People*, Dale Carnegie (1936) said that being liked and being persuasive go hand in hand. The question is, what makes a communicator likable? As we'll see in Chapter 9, two factors that spark attraction are *similarity* and *physical attractiveness*.

A study by Diane Mackie and others (1990) illustrates the persuasive power of similarity. Students enrolled at the University of California, Santa Barbara, read a strong or a weak speech that argued against continued use of the SATs in college admissions. Half the participants were led to believe that the speech was written by a fellow UCSB student; the other half thought the author was a student from the University of New Hampshire. Very few participants were persuaded by the weak arguments. In contrast, many of those who read the strong message did change their attitudes, but only when they believed it was given by a fellow UCSB student.

Just as source similarity can spark persuasion, dissimilarity can have the opposite inhibiting effect. In a study of people's taste in music, Clayton Hilmert and others (2006) introduced participants to a confederate who seemed to like the same or different kinds of music, such as rock, pop, country, or classical. Others did not meet a confederate. When later asked to rate a particular song, participants were positively influenced by the similar confederate's opinion and negatively influenced by the dissimilar confederate's opinion. In fact, although the effect is more potent when the points of similarity seem relevant to the attitude in question (Berscheid, 1966), the participants in this study were also more or less persuaded by a confederate whose similarities or differences were wholly

When he was just out of high school, basketball star LeBron James (left) signed a multimillion dollar contract with Nike. Also paid millions, music star Taylor Swift is surrounded by kittens in this TV commercial for Diet Coke (top right) and Oscar-winning actor Bradley Cooper is the new, and first-ever, face of Haagen-Dazs ice cream (bottom right). Can celebrities sell products? Targeting the peripheral route to persuasion, the advertising industry seems to think so.

unrelated to music—for example, when the confederate had similar or different interests in shopping, world politics, museums, foods, or social media websites.

The effect of source similarity on persuasion has obvious implications for those who wish to exert influence. We're all similar to one another in some respects. We might agree in politics, share a common friend, have similar tastes in food, or enjoy spending summers on the same beach. If aware of the social benefits of similarity and the social costs of dissimilarity, the astute communicator can use common bonds to enhance his or her impact on an audience.

Advertising practices presuppose that beauty is also persuasive. After all, online, magazine, and TV ads routinely feature supermodels who are young, tall, and slender supermodels (for women) or muscular (for men) and who sport hard bodies, glowing complexions, and radiant smiles. Sure, these models can turn heads, you may think, but can they change minds? In a study that addressed this question, Shelly Chaiken (1979) had male and female college students approach others on campus. They introduced themselves as members of an organization that wanted the university to stop serving meat during breakfast and lunch. In each case, these student assistants gave reasons for the position and then asked respondents to sign a petition. The result: Attractive sources were able to get 41% of respondents to sign the petition, whereas those who were less attractive succeeded only 32% of the time. Additional research has shown that attractive male and female salespersons elicit more positive attitudes and purchasing intentions from customers than less attractive salespersons, even when they are up front about their desire to make a sale (Reinhard et al., 2006).

When What You Say Is More Important Than Who You Are   To this point, it must seem as if the source of a persuasive communication is more important than the communication itself. Is this true? Certainly there are enough real-life examples—as when books used to skyrocket to the top of the best-seller list because Oprah Winfrey recommended them. The advertising industry has long debated the value of high-priced celebrity endorsements. David Ogilvy (1985), who was called "the king of advertising," used to say that celebrities are not effective because viewers know they've been bought and paid for. Ogilvy was not alone in his skepticism. Still, many advertisers scramble furiously to sign famous entertainers and athletes. From Tiger Woods to Tina Fey, Rihanna, LeBron James, Peyton Manning, Taylor Swift, Scarlett Johansson, Bono, Danica Patrick, Beyonce Knowles, Katy Perry, Jay Z, and Bradley Cooper, TV commercials regularly feature a parade of stars. The bigger the star, they say, the more valuable the testimonial.

Compared with the contents of a message, does the source really make the big difference that advertisers pay for? Are we so impressed by the expert, so enamored of the physical talent, and so drawn to the charming face that we embrace whatever they have to say? And are we so scornful of ordinary or unattractive people that their presentations fall on deaf ears? In light of what is known about the central and peripheral routes to persuasion, the answer to these questions is "it depends."

First, a recipient's level of involvement plays an important role. When a message has personal relevance to your life, you pay attention to the source and think critically about the message, the arguments, and the implications. When

Versace/Advertising Archives

Advertisers are so convinced that beauty sells products that they pay millions of dollars for supermodels to appear in their ads. Shown here, supermodel Kate Moss appears in an ad for Italian fashion house Versace.

● **FIGURE 6.6**

Source Versus Message: The Role of Audience Involvement

People who were high or low in their personal involvement heard a strong or weak message from an expert or nonexpert. For high-involvement participants (left), persuasion was based on the strength of arguments, not on source expertise. For low-involvement participants (right), persuasion was based more on the source than on the arguments. Source characteristics have more impact on those who don't care enough to take the central route. Reprinted by permission from Richard E. Petty.

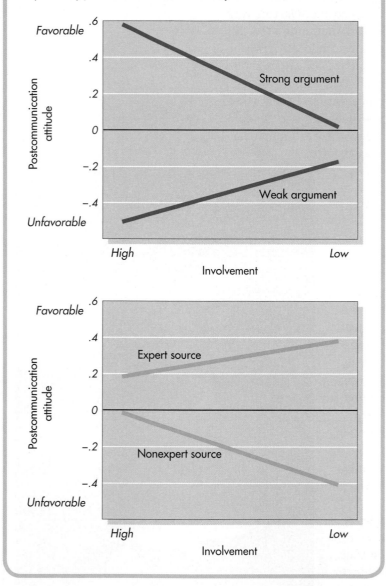

a message does not have personal relevance, however, you may take the source at face value and spend little time scrutinizing the information. In a classic study, Richard Petty and others (1981) had students listen to a speaker who proposed that all seniors should be required to take comprehensive exams in order to graduate. Three aspects of the communication situation were varied. First, participants were led to believe that the speaker was either an education professor at Princeton University or a high school student. Second, participants heard either well-reasoned arguments and hard evidence or a weak message based only on anecdotes and personal opinion. Third, participants were told either that the proposed exams might be used the following year (Uh oh, that means me!) or that they would not take effect for another 10 years (Who cares, I'll be long gone by then!).

As predicted, personal involvement determined the relative impact of the expertise of the source and the quality of speech. Among participants who would not be affected by the proposed change, attitudes were based largely on the speaker's credibility: The professor was persuasive; the high school student was not. Among participants who thought that the proposed change would affect them directly, attitudes were based on the quality of the speaker's proposal. Strong arguments were persuasive; weak arguments were not. As depicted in ● Figure 6.6, people followed the source rather than the message under low levels of involvement, illustrating the peripheral route to persuasion. But message factors did outweigh source characteristics under high levels of involvement, when participants cared enough to take the central route to persuasion. Likewise, research has shown that the tilt toward likable and attractive communicators is reduced when recipients take the central route (Chaiken, 1980).

There is a second limit to source effects. It is often said that time heals all wounds. Well, time may also heal the effects of a bad reputation. Hovland and Weiss (1951) varied communicator credibility (for example, the physicist versus the Soviet-controlled newspaper) and found that the change had a large and immediate effect on persuasion. But when they measured attitudes again four weeks later, the effect had vanished. Over time, the attitude change produced by the high-credibility source had decreased and the change caused by the low-credibility source had increased. This finding of a delayed persuasive impact of a low-credibility communicator is called the **sleeper effect**.

To explain this unforeseen result, the Hovland research group proposed the *discounting cue hypothesis*. According to this hypothesis, people immediately

sleeper effect A delayed increase in the persuasive impact of a noncredible source.

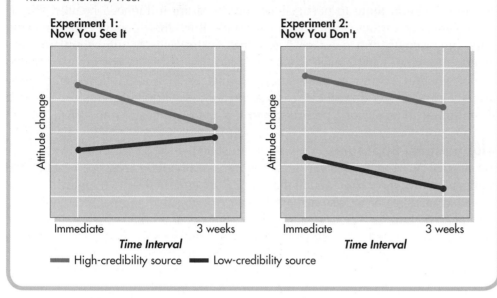

● FIGURE 6.7

The Sleeper Effect

In Experiment 1, participants changed their immediate attitudes more in response to a message from a high-credibility source than from a low-credibility source. When attitudes were measured again after three weeks, the high-credibility source had lost impact and the low-credibility source had gained impact—the sleeper effect. In Experiment 2, the sleeper effect disappeared when participants were reminded of the source.
Kelman & Hovland, 1953.

Experiment 1:
Now You See It

Experiment 2:
Now You Don't

Attitude change

Immediate   3 weeks
Time Interval

Immediate   3 weeks
Time Interval

━━ High-credibility source   ━━ Low-credibility source

discount the arguments made by noncredible communicators, but over time, they dissociate what was said from who said it. In other words, we tend to remember the message but forget the source (Pratkanis et al., 1988). To examine the role of memory in this process, Kelman and Hovland (1953) reminded a group of participants of the source's identity before reassessing their attitudes. If the sleeper effect was caused by forgetting, they reasoned, then it could be eliminated through reinstatement of the link between the source and the message. As shown in ● Figure 6.7, they were right. When attitudes were measured after three weeks, participants who were not reminded of the source showed the usual sleeper effect. Yet those who did receive a source reminder did not. For these latter participants, the effects of high and low credibility endured. Recent studies by cognitive psychologists have confirmed that over time, people "forget" the connection between information and its source (Underwood & Pezdek, 1998).

The sleeper effect generated a good deal of controversy. There was never a doubt that credible communicators lose some impact over time. But researchers had a harder time finding evidence for delayed persuasion by noncredible sources. Exasperated at one point by their own failures to obtain this result, Paulette Gillig and Anthony Greenwald (1974) wondered, "Is it time to lay the sleeper effect to rest?" As it turned out, the answer was no. More recent research showed that the sleeper effect is reliable provided that participants do not learn who the source is until *after* they have received the original message (Greenwald et al., 1986; Kumkale & Albarracín, 2004).

To appreciate the importance of timing, imagine that you're searching for music online when you come across what appears to be a review of a new CD. Before you begin reading, however, you notice in the fine print that this so-called

"The truth is always the strongest argument."
—Sophocles

review is really an advertisement. Aware that you can't always trust what you read, you skim the ad and reject it. Now imagine the same situation, except that you read the entire ad before realizing what it is. Again you reject it. But notice the difference. This time, you have read the message with an open mind. You may still reject it, but after a few weeks, the information will have sunk in to influence your evaluation of the music. This scenario illustrates the sleeper effect.

◼ The Message

On the peripheral route to persuasion, audiences are influenced heavily, maybe too heavily, by various source characteristics. But when people care about an issue, the strength of a message determines its impact. On the central route to persuasion, what matters most is whether a scientist's theory is supported by the data or whether a company has a sound product. Keep in mind, however, that the target of a persuasive appeal comes to know a message only through the medium of communication—*what* a person has to say and *how* that person says it.

Informational Strategies Communicators often struggle with how to structure and present an argument to maximize its impact. Should a message be long and crammed with facts or short and to the point? Is it better to present a highly partisan, one-sided message or to take a more balanced, two-sided approach? How should arguments be ordered—from strongest to weakest or the other way around? These are the kinds of questions often studied by persuasion researchers—including those interested in marketing, advertising, and consumer behavior.

Often the most effective strategy to use will depend on whether members of the audience process the message on the central or the peripheral route. Consider the length of a communication. When people process a message lazily, with their eyes and ears half-closed, they often fall back on a simple heuristic: The longer a message, the more valid it must be. In this case, a large number of words gives the superficial appearance of factual support regardless of the quality of the arguments (Petty & Cacioppo, 1984; Wood et al., 1985). Thus, as David Ogilvy (1985) concluded from his years of advertising experience, "The more facts you tell, the more you sell" (p. 88).

When people process a communication carefully, however, length is a two-edged sword. If a message is long because it contains lots of supporting information, then longer does mean better. The more supportive arguments you can offer or the more sources you can find to speak on your behalf, the more persuasive your appeal will be (Harkins & Petty, 1981). But if the added arguments are weak or if the new sources are redundant, then an alert audience will not be fooled by length alone. When adding to the length of a message dilutes its quality, an appeal might well *lose* impact (Friedrich et al., 1996; Harkins & Petty, 1987).

When two opposing sides try to persuade the same audience, order of presentation becomes a relevant factor as well. During the summer of 2012, before the November presidential election, the Republicans held their national convention a few days before the incumbent Democrats held theirs. These events were watched on television by millions of voters. Do you think the order in which they were scheduled gave one party an advantage? If you believe that information that is presented first has more impact, you'd predict *a primacy effect* (advantage to the Republicans). If you believe that the information presented last has the edge, you'd predict a *recency effect* (advantage to the Democrats).

There are good reasons for both predictions. On the one hand, first impressions are important. On the other hand, memory fades over time, and often people recall only the last argument they hear before making a decision. In light of these contrasting predictions, Norman Miller and Donald Campbell (1959) searched for the "missing link" that would determine the relative effects of primacy and recency. They discovered that the missing link is *time*. In a study of jury simulations, they had people (1) read a summary of the plaintiff's case; (2) read a summary of the defendant's case; and (3) make a decision. The researchers varied how much time separated the two messages and then how much time elapsed between the second message and the decisions. When participants read the second message right after the first and then waited a whole week before reporting their opinion, a primacy effect prevailed and the side that came first was favored. Both messages faded equally from memory, so only the greater impact of first impressions was left. When participants made a decision immediately after the second message but a full week after the first, however, there was a recency effect. The second argument was fresher in memory, thus favoring the side that went last. Using these results as a guideline, let's revisit our original question: What is the impact on Election Day of how national conventions are scheduled? Think for a moment about the placement and timing of these events. The answer appears in Table 6.2.

"It is a superb vision of America, all right, but I can't remember which candidate projected it."

Research on the sleeper effect shows that people often remember the message but forget the source.

Message Discrepancy   Persuasion is a process of changing attitudes. This objective is not easy to achieve. As a general rule, people are motivated to defend their opinions and attitudes, which they do, in part, through selective exposure to information that supports their views (Hart et al., 2009). Given an opportunity to advocate for attitude change, communicators confront what is perhaps the most critical strategic question: How extreme a position should they take? How *discrepant* should a message be from the audience's existing position in order to have the greatest impact? Common sense suggests two opposite answers. One approach is to take an extreme position in the hope that the more change you advocate, the more you will get. Another approach is to exercise caution and not push for too much change so that the audience will not reject the message outright. Which approach seems more effective? Imagine trying to convert your politically conservative friends into liberals or the other way around. Would you stake out a radical position in order to move them toward the center or would you preach moderation so as not to be cast aside?

Research shows that communicators should adopt the second, more cautious approach. To be sure, some discrepancy is needed to produce a change in attitude. But the relationship to persuasion can be pictured as an upside-down U with the most change being produced at moderate amounts of discrepancy (Bochner & Insko, 1966). A study by Kari Edwards and Edward Smith (1996) helps explain why taking a more extreme position is counterproductive. These investigators first measured people's attitudes on a number of hot social issues—for example, whether lesbian and gay couples

▲ **TABLE 6.2**

Effects of Presentation Order and Timing on Persuasion

A study by Miller and Campbell (1959) demonstrated the effect of presentation order and the timing of opposing arguments on persuasion. As applied to our example, the Democratic and Republican conventions resemble the fourth row of this table. From these results, it seems that the scheduling of such events is fair, promoting neither primacy nor recency.

	Conditions			Results		
1. **Message 1**	**Message 2**	One week	Decision			**Primacy**
2. **Message 1**	One week	**Message 2**	Decision			**Recency**
3. **Message 1**	**Message 2**	Decision				None
4. **Message 1**	One week	**Message 2**	One week	Decision		None

should adopt children, whether employers should give preference in hiring to minorities, and whether the death penalty should be abolished. Several weeks later, they asked the same people to read, think about, and rate arguments that were either consistent or inconsistent with their own prior attitudes. The result: When given arguments to read that preached attitudes that were discrepant from their own, the participants spent more time scrutinizing the material and judged the arguments to be weak. Clearly, people tend to refute and reject persuasive messages they don't agree with. In fact, the more personally important an issue is to us, the more stubborn and resistant to change we become (Zuwerink & Devine, 1996).

Fear Appeals   Many trial lawyers say that to win cases they have to appeal to jurors through the heart rather than through the mind. The evidence is important, they admit, but what matters most is whether the jury reacts to their client with anger, disgust, sympathy, or sadness. Of course, very few messages are entirely based on rational argument or on emotion.

Fear is a particularly primitive and powerful emotion, serving as an early warning system that signals danger. Neuroscience research shows that fear is aroused instantly in response to pain, stimulation from noxious substances, or threat, enabling us to respond quickly without having to stop to think about it (LeDoux, 1996). The use of fear-based appeals to change attitudes is common. Certain religious cults have used scare tactics to indoctrinate new members. So do public health organizations that graphically portray the damage done to those who smoke cigarettes, eat too much junk food, drink too much alcohol, text while driving, or have unprotected sex.

Negative campaigning in American politics is prevalent, though the effects on voters are not clear (Lau & Rovner, 2009). From the large number of attack ads that flood the political scene, it would certainly seem that candidates, their consultants, and Super PACS strongly believe in the power of attacking their opponents by arousing fear about the consequences of voting for them. Presidential campaign ads are more negative than ever. Yet the most hard-hitting and controversial ever was a TV commercial that aired just once, on September 7, 1964. In an ad to reelect Democratic president Lyndon Johnson, who was running against Republican Barry Goldwater, a young girl pictured in a field counted to 10 as she picked the petals off a daisy. As she reached 9, an adult voice broke in to count down from 10 to 0, followed by a blinding nuclear explosion and this message: "Vote for President Johnson on November 3. The stakes are too high for you to stay home."

The effects of fear arousal in politics are evident. Guided by Terror Management Theory (Greenberg et al., 1997; Pyszczynski et al., 2004; see Chapter 3) and the prediction that a deeply rooted fear of death motivates people to rally around their leaders as a way to ward off anxiety, Mark Landau and others (2004) found that college students expressed more support for then-President George W. Bush and his policies when they were reminded of their own mortality or subliminally exposed to images of 9/11 than when they were not. This result is not limited to the laboratory. Analyzing patterns of government-issued terror warnings and Gallup polls, Robb Willer (2004) found that increased terror alerts were predictably followed by increases in presidential approval ratings.

Is fear similarly effective for commercial purposes? What about using fear to promote health and safety? If you're interested in public service advertising, visit the website of the Ad Council, the organization that created Smokey Bear ("Only you can prevent forest fires") and the crash test dummies ("Don't be a dummy— buckle up"). In recent years, the Ad Council has run campaigns on a range of issues such as the dangers of using of steroids, flu prevention, AIDS prevention, cyber bullying, and the online sexploitation of youth. To get people to change behavior in these domains, is it better to arouse a little nervousness or a full-blown

Public health organizations often use fear, or scare tactics, to change health-related attitudes and behavior. In 2014, a public service ad was aired on the dangers of texting while driving. In what starts out as a fun car ride with friends, this driver takes her eye of the road to text. All of a sudden her car is T-boned by a truck, hurls over and over in slow motion, and lands with a silent thud. In a spot aimed at teenagers, the theme is: "*U drive. U text. U pay.*"

anxiety attack? To answer this question, social psychologists over the years have compared communications that vary in the levels of fear they arouse. In the first such study, Irving Janis and Seymour Feshbach (1953) found that high levels of fear did not generate increased agreement with a persuasive communication. Since then, however, research has shown that appeals that arouse high levels of fear can be highly effective (de Hoog et al., 2007).

Fear arousal increases the incentive to change for those who do not actively resist it, but its ultimate impact depends on the strength of the arguments and on whether the message also contains clear and reassuring advice on how to cope with the threatened danger (Keller, 1999; Leventhal, 1970; Rogers, 1983). This last point is important. Without specific instructions on how to cope, people feel helpless, and they panic and tune out the message. In one study, for example, participants with a chronic fear of cancer were less likely than others to detect the logical errors in a message that called for regular cancer checkups (Jepson & Chaiken, 1990). When clear instructions are included, however, high dosages of fear can be effective. In the past, research had shown that antismoking films elicit more negative attitudes toward cigarettes when they show gory lung-cancer operations than when they show charts filled with dry statistics (Leventhal et al., 1967) and that films about driving safety are more effective when they show bloody accident victims than when they show plastic crash test dummies (Rogers & Mewborn, 1976). In a meta-analysis of 105 studies, however, Natascha de Hoog and others (2007) found that communications that arouse fear do not have to be gruesome to be effective.

In a highly controversial appeal to fear, a TV commercial that aired only once during the 1964 presidential campaign, pictured this young girl in an open field, a blinding nuclear explosion, and the message: "Vote for President Johnson on November 3. The stakes are too high for you to stay home."

The more personally vulnerable people feel about a threatened outcome, the more attentive they are to the message and the more likely they are to follow its recommendations.

Positive Emotions   It's interesting that just as fear helps induce a change in attitude, so does positive emotion. In one study, people were more likely to agree with a series of controversial arguments when they snacked on peanuts and soda than when they did not eat (Janis et al., 1965). In another study, participants liked a television commercial more when it was embedded within a program that was upbeat rather than sad (Mathur & Chattopadhyay, 1991). Research shows that people are "soft touches" when they're in a good mood. Depending on the situation, food, drinks, a soft reclining chair, warm and tender memories, a success experience, breathtaking scenery, laughter, and good music can lull us into a positive emotional state and ripe for persuasion (Schwarz et al., 1991).

According to Alice Isen (1984), people see the world through rose-colored glasses when they are in a good mood. Filled with high spirits, we become more sociable, more generous, and generally more positive in our outlook. We also make decisions more quickly and with relatively little thought. The result: Positive feelings activate the peripheral route to persuasion, facilitating change and allowing superficial cues to take on added importance (Petty et al., 1993; Worth & Mackie, 1987).

What is it about feeling good that leads us to take shortcuts to persuasion rather than the more effortful central route? There are three possible explanations. One is that a positive emotional state is cognitively distracting, causing the mind to wander and impairing our ability to think critically about the persuasive arguments (Mackie & Worth, 1989; Mackie et al., 1992). A second explanation is that when people are in a good mood, they assume that all is well, let down their guard, and become somewhat lazy processors of information (Schwarz, 1990). A third explanation is that when people are happy, they become motivated to savor the moment and maintain their happy mood rather than spoiling it by thinking critically about new information (Wegener & Petty, 1994).

This last notion raises an interesting question: What if happy people are presented with a positive and uplifting persuasive message? Would they still appear cognitively distracted, or lazy, or would they pay close attention in order to prolong the rosy glow? To find out, Duane Wegener and others (1995) showed some college students a funny segment from *The Late Show with David Letterman.* Others, less fortunate, watched a somber scene from an HBO movie called *You Don't Have to Die.* The students were then asked to read and evaluate either an uplifting article they agreed with about a new plan to cut tuition or a distressing article they disagreed with about a new plan to raise tuition. In half the cases, the article they read contained strong arguments; in the other cases, the arguments were weak. Did the students read the material carefully enough to distinguish between the strong and weak arguments? Those in the somber condition clearly did. Among those in the happy condition, however, the response depended on whether they expected the message to be one they wanted to hear. When the happy students read about a tuition increase, they tuned out and were equally persuaded by the strong and weak arguments. When they read about the proposal to cut tuition, however, they were persuaded more when the arguments were strong than when they were weak. Because they were in a good mood and were receiving an agreeable message that would not spoil it, these happy students took the effortful central route to persuasion.

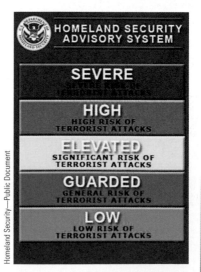

Suggesting that a fear of death leads people to rally around their leaders, public opinion polls have shown that as terror threat levels increase, so do presidential approval ratings.

Subliminal Messages In 1957, Vance Packard published *The Hidden Persuaders,* an exposé of Madison Avenue. As the book climbed the best-seller list, it awakened in the public a fear of being manipulated by forces they could not see or hear. What had Packard uncovered? In the 1950s, amid growing fears of communism and the birth of rock 'n' roll, a number of advertisers were said to have used *subliminal advertising,* the presentation of commercial messages outside of conscious awareness. It all started in a drive-in movie theater in New Jersey, where the words "Drink Coke" and "Eat popcorn" were secretly flashed on the screen during intermissions for a third of a millisecond. Although the audience never noticed the message, Coke sales were said to have increased 18% and popcorn sales 58% over a six-week period (Brean, 1958).

This incident was followed by several others. A Seattle radio station presented subaudible anti-TV messages during its programs ("TV is a bore"), and department stores played music tapes over public address systems that contained subaudible warnings about theft ("If you steal, you'll get caught"). Later, in books entitled *Subliminal Seduction* (1973) and *The Age of Manipulation* (1989), William Bryan Key charged that advertisers routinely sneak faint sexual images in visual ads to heighten the appeal of their products. Several years ago, concerns were also raised about subliminal messages in rock music. In one case, the families of two boys who committed suicide blamed the British rock group Judas Priest for subliminal lyrics ("Do it") that promoted Satanism and suicide (*National Law Journal,* 1990). Although the families lost their case, it's clear that many people believe in the power of hidden persuaders.

At the time the story about the New Jersey theater broke, research on the topic was so sketchy and the public so outraged by the sinister implications that the matter was quickly dropped. But soon there was renewed interest in subliminal influences and new research developments. In one recent field study, for example, researchers played traditional German or French music on alternating days for two weeks at a supermarket display of wines. Keeping track of sales, the researchers found that of the total number of wines bought, 83% were German on German-music days and 65% were French on French-music days. Yet when asked the reasons for their choices, customers did not cite the music as a factor, suggesting that they were not aware of the effect it had on them (North et al., 1999).

American Association of Advertising Agencies

PEOPLE HAVE BEEN TRYING TO FIND THE BREASTS IN THESE ICE CUBES SINCE 1957.

The advertising industry is sometimes charged with sneaking seductive little pictures into ads.

Supposedly, these pictures can get you to buy a product without your even seeing them.

Consider the photograph above. According to some people, there's a pair of female breasts hidden in the patterns of light refracted by the ice cubes.

Well, if you really searched you probably *could* see the breasts. For that matter, you could also see Millard Fillmore, a stuffed pork chop and a 1946 Dodge.

The point is that so-called "subliminal advertising" simply doesn't exist. Overactive imaginations, however, most certainly do.

So if anyone claims to see breasts in that drink up there, they aren't in the ice cubes.

They're in the eye of the beholder.

ADVERTISING
ANOTHER WORD FOR FREEDOM OF CHOICE.
American Association of Advertising Agencies

For years, advertisers have defended against the charge that they embed suggestive and sexual images in print ads. This piece by the American Association of Advertising Agencies defends against this claim.

Current uses of subliminal influence are varied. In what is now a multimillion-dollar industry, companies today sell self-help tapes, DVDs, and MP3 downloads that play New Age music or nature images and sounds—and also contain fleeting messages or "affirmations" that promise to help you relax, lose weight, make

● FIGURE 6.8

Subliminal Influence

Thirsty and nonthirsty research participants were subliminally exposed to neutral or thirst-related words. Afterward they participated in a beverage taste test in which the amount they drank was measured. You can see that the subliminal thirst cues had little impact on nonthirsty participants but that they did increase consumption among those who were thirsty. Apparently, subliminal cues can influence our behavior when we are otherwise predisposed.
Strahan et al., 2002.

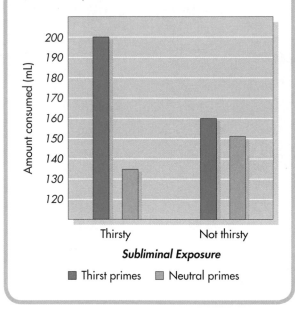

friends, raise self-esteem, make money, improve athletic performance, and even improve your sex life. Can subliminal messages reflexively trigger behavior without our awareness? In 1982, Timothy Moore reviewed the existing research and concluded that "what you see is what you get"—nothing, "complete scams." Moore was right. The original story about the Coke-and-popcorn messages at the New Jersey theater was later exposed as a publicity stunt and hoax (Pratkanis, 1992). To further complicate matters, controlled experiments using subliminal self-help CDs that promise to raise self-esteem, improve memory, or lose weight show that these products offer no therapeutic benefits (Greenwald et al., 1991; Merikle & Skanes, 1992).

If there is no solid evidence of subliminal influence, why, you may wonder, does research demonstrate perception without awareness in studies of priming (described elsewhere in this book) but not in studies of subliminal persuasion? If you think about it, the two sets of claims are different. In the laboratory, subliminal exposures have a short-term effect on simple judgments and actions. But in claims of subliminal persuasion, the exposure is presumed to have long-term effects on eating, drinking, consumer purchases, voter sentiment, or even the most profound of violent acts, suicide. Psychologists agree that people can process information at an unconscious level, but they're quick to caution that this processing is "analytically limited" (Greenwald, 1992).

Perhaps people *perceive* subliminal cues but are not *persuaded* into action unless they are motivated to do so. To test this hypothesis, Erin Strahan and others (2002) brought thirsty college students into the laboratory for a marketing study and provided drinking water to some but not to others. Then, as part of a test administered by computer, they subliminally exposed these students to neutral words (*pirate, won*) or to thirst-related words (*thirst, dry*). Did the subliminal "thirsty" message later lead the students, like automatons, to drink more in a taste test of Kool-Aid beverages? Yes and no. ● Figure 6.8 shows that the subliminal thirst primes had little impact on students whose thirst had just been quenched, but they quite clearly increased consumption among those who were thirsty and had been deprived of water. For a subliminal message to influence behavior, it has to strike "while the iron is hot."

Other researchers have since extended this interesting effect in important ways. In one study, participants who were subliminally presented with the name of a specific soft drink, Lipton Ice, were later more likely to report that they would select that particular brand over others—provided they were thirsty (Karremans et al., 2006). In a second study, participants were subliminally presented with a logo for one brand of dextrose (a sugar pill) or another, after which they worked on a cognitive task that required intense concentration. The results showed that when given an opportunity to enhance their concentration, participants were more likely to select and consume the subliminally advertised brand than the other brand—provided they were mentally tired and in need of a boost (Bermeitinger et al., 2009).

People are most easily persuaded by commercial messages that are presented without their awareness.

FALSE

■ The Audience

Although source and message factors are important, the astute communicator must also take his or her audience into account. Presentation strategies that succeed with some people fail with others. Audiences on the central route to persuasion, for example, bear little resemblance to those found strolling along the peripheral route. In this section, we'll see that the impact of a message is influenced by two additional factors: the recipient's personality and his or her expectations.

Right from the start, social psychologists tried to identify types of people who were more or less vulnerable to persuasion. But it turned out that very few individuals are *consistently* easy or difficult to persuade. Based on this insight, the search for individual and group differences is now guided by an "interactionist" perspective. Assuming that each of us can be persuaded more in some settings than in others, researchers look for an appropriate match between characteristics of the message and the audience. So, what kinds of messages turn *you* on?

▲ **TABLE 6.3**

Need for Cognition Scale: Sample Items

Are you high or low in the need for cognition? These statements are taken from the NC Scale. If you agree with items 1, 3, and 5 and disagree with items 2, 4, and 6, you would probably be regarded as high in NC.

1. I really enjoy a task that involves coming up with new solutions to problems.

2. Thinking is not my idea of fun.

3. The notion of thinking abstractly is appealing to me.

4. I like tasks that require little thought once I've learned them.

5. I usually end up deliberating about issues even when they do not affect me personally.

6. It's enough for me that something gets the job done; I don't care how or why it works.

From Cacioppo, J. T., and Petty, R. E., "The need for cognition," *Journal of Personality and Social Psychology* vol 42 (pp. 116–131). Copyright © 1982 by the American Psychological Association. Reprinted by permission.

The Need for Cognition   Earlier, we saw that people tend to process information more carefully when they are highly involved. Involvement can be determined by the importance and self-relevance of a message. According to Cacioppo and Petty (1982), however, there are also individual differences in the extent to which people become involved and take the central route to persuasion. Specifically, they have found that individuals differ in the extent to which they enjoy and participate in effortful cognitive activities, or, as they call it, the **need for cognition (NC)**. People who are high rather than low in their need for cognition like to work on hard problems, search for clues, make fine distinctions, and analyze situations. These differences can be identified by the items contained in the Need for Cognition Scale, some of which appear in Table 6.3.

The need for cognition has interesting implications for changing attitudes. If people are prone to approach or avoid effortful cognitive activities, then a communicator could prepare messages unique to a particular audience. In theory, the high-NC audience should receive information-oriented appeals and the low-NC audience should be treated to appeals that rely on the use of peripheral cues. The theory is fine, but does it work? Can a message be customized to fit the information-processing style of its recipients?

In a test of this hypothesis, participants read an editorial that consisted of either a strong or a weak set of arguments. As predicted, the higher their NC scores were, the more the participants thought about the material, the better they later recalled it, and the more persuaded they were by the strength of its arguments (Cacioppo et al., 1983). In contrast, people who are low in the need for cognition are persuaded by cues found along the peripheral route, such as a speaker's reputation and physical appearance, the overt reactions of others in the audience, and a positive mood state (Cacioppo et al., 1996). At times, they are mindlessly influenced by a reputable source even when his or her arguments are weak (Kaufman et al., 1999).

Self-Monitoring   Just as people high in the need for cognition crave information, other personality traits are associated with an attraction to other kinds of messages. Consider the trait of *self-monitoring*. As described in Chapter 3, high

need for cognition (NC)   A personality variable that distinguishes people on the basis of how much they enjoy effortful cognitive activities.

self-monitors regulate their behavior from one situation to another out of concern for public self-presentation. Low self-monitors are less image conscious and behave according to their own beliefs, values, and preferences. In the context of persuasion, high self-monitors may be particularly responsive to messages that promise desirable social images. Whether the product is beer, soft drinks, blue jeans, or cars, or smart phones, this technique is common in advertising, where often the image is the message.

To test the self-monitoring hypothesis, Mark Snyder and Kenneth DeBono (1985) showed image- or information-oriented print ads to high and low self-monitors. In an ad for Irish Mocha Mint coffee, for example, a man and woman were depicted as relaxing in a candlelit room over a steamy cup of coffee. The image-oriented version promised to "Make a chilly night become a cozy evening," while the informational version offered "a delicious blend of three great flavors—coffee, chocolate, and mint." As predicted, high self-monitors were willing to pay more for products after reading imagery ads; low self-monitors were influenced more by information-oriented appeals. Smidt and DeBono (2011) found a similar result for energy drinks. They found that high self-monitors rated the drinks more favorably when they had an image-oriented name; low self-monitors preferred the drinks more when they had a self-descriptive name. Imagery can even influence the way that high self-monitors evaluate a product, independent of its quality. DeBono and others (2003) presented people with one of two perfume samples packaged in more or less attractive bottles. Whereas low self-monitors preferred the more pleasant-scented fragrance, high self-monitors preferred whatever scent came from the more attractive bottles.

Regulatory Fit Setting aside your political views, do you find yourself drawn to some *types* of speeches, arguments, editorials, and television commercials more than others? Joseph Cesario and others (2004) proposed that people are more likely to be influenced by messages that fit their frame of mind and "feel right." In particular, they noted that in an effort to regulate their own emotion state, some individuals are promotion-oriented (drawn to the pursuit of success, achievement, and their ideals), whereas others are more prevention-oriented (protective of what they have, fearful of failure, and vigilant about avoiding loss). Do these differing outlooks on life make people more responsive to some types of persuasive messages than others? To find out, these researchers presented two versions of an article advocating for a new after-school children's program. They found that promotion-motivated participants were more persuaded by the article when the arguments in it were framed in promotional terms ("because it will *advance* children's education and *support* more children to *succeed*"), while prevention-motivated participants were persuaded more when the very same arguments were framed in more defensive terms ("because it will *secure* children's education and *prevent* more children from *failing*").

In a follow-up study, Cesario and Higgins (2008) found that audience members are also influenced when a speaker's nonverbal style fits their motivational orientations. Watching a high school teacher deliver the same communication about a new after-school program, promotion-motivated participants were more receptive when the speaker exhibited an "eager" delivery style (fast, animated, and forward leaning, with hand gestures projecting outward), whereas prevention-oriented participants were more receptive when he displayed a cautious style (slow, precise, and backward leaning, with hand gestures pushing in). In studies conducted in France, in the context of messages that advertised healthful diet, Lucia Bosone and others (2015) also found that persuasion is maximized when there is a regulatory fit between audience members and a role model whose approach is either positive ("always very healthy thanks to a balanced diet") or negative (always sick because of an unbalanced diet").

There are plenty of other ways that you may be more comfortable with some types of messages than others. We saw earlier that some of us are high in the need for cognition, enjoying effortful forms of reasoning and problem solving. Some of us are also high in the *need for affect*, seeking out and enjoying feelings of strong emotion. In matters of persuasion, these traits lead people to be more receptive to messages that are presented in primarily cognitive or emotional terms (Haddock et al., 2008).

Forewarning and Resistance   When our attitudes or values come under attack, we can succumb to the challenge and change the attitude or we can resist it and maintain the attitude. There are different means of resistance. In a series of studies, Julia Jacks and Kimberly Cameron (2003) asked people to describe and rate the ways that they manage to resist persuasion in their attitudes on abortion or the death penalty. They identified seven strategies, the most common being attitude bolstering ("I think about all the reasons I believe the way I do") and the least common being source derogation ("I look for faults in the person who challenges my belief"). These means of resistance are listed in Table 6.4.

What leads people to invoke these mechanisms of resistance? Does it help to be forewarned that your attitude is about to come under attack? Perhaps the toughest audience to persuade is the one that knows you're coming. When people are aware that someone is trying to change their attitude, they become more likely to resist. All they need is some time to collect their thoughts and come up with a good defense. Jonathan Freedman and David Sears (1965) first discovered this when they told high school seniors to expect a speech on why teenagers should not be allowed to drive (an unpopular position, as you can imagine). The students were warned either 2 or 10 minutes before the talk began or not at all. Those who were the victims of a sneak attack were the most likely to succumb to the speaker's position. Those who had a full 10 minutes' warning were the least likely to agree. To be forewarned is to be forearmed. But why?

At least two processes are at work here. To understand them, let's take a closer look at what forewarning does. Participants in the Freedman and Sears (1965) study were put on notice in two ways: (1) They were informed of the position the speaker would take, and (2) they were told that the speaker intended to change their opinion. Psychologically, these two aspects of forewarning have different effects. The first effect is purely cognitive. Knowing in advance what position a speaker will take enables us to come up with counterarguments and, as a result, to become more resistant to change. To explain this effect, William McGuire (1964) drew an analogy: Protecting a person's attitudes from persuasion, he said, is like inoculating the human body against disease. In medicine, injecting a small dose of infection into a patient stimulates the body

▲ **TABLE 6.4**

Strategies for Resisting Persuasion

Strategy	Example
Attitude bolstering	"I reassure myself of facts that support the validity of my belief."
Counterarguing	"I would talk to myself and play devil's advocate."
Social validation	"I also rely on others with the same opinion to be there for me."
Negative affect	"I tend to get angry when someone tries to change my beliefs."
Assertions of confidence	"I doubt anybody could change my viewpoint."
Selective exposure	"Most of the time I just ignore them."
Source derogation	"I look for faults in the person presenting the challenging belief."

Based on the results of Jacks and Cameron (2003). © Cengage Learning®

to build up a resistance to it. According to this **inoculation hypothesis**, an attitude can be immunized the same way. As with flu shots and other vaccines, our defenses can be reinforced by exposure to weak doses of the opposing position before we actually encounter the full presentation. Studies of negative political ads show that inoculation can be used to combat the kinds of attack messages that sometimes win elections (Pfau et al., 1990).

Simply knowing that someone is trying to persuade us also sparks a motivational reaction as we brace ourselves to resist the attempt regardless of what position is taken. As a TV viewer, you have no doubt heard the phrase "And now, we pause for a message from our sponsor." What does this warning tell us? Not knowing yet who the sponsor is, even the grouchiest among us is in no position to object. Yet imagine how you would feel if an experimenter said to you, "In just a few minutes, you will hear a message prepared according to well-established principles of persuasion and designed to induce you to change your attitudes." If you are like the participants who actually heard this warning, you might be tempted to reply, "Oh yeah? Try me!" Indeed, participants rejected that message without counterargument and without much advance notice (Hass & Grady, 1975).

When people think that someone is trying to change their attitude or otherwise manipulate them, a red flag goes up. That red flag is called **psychological reactance**. According to Jack Brehm's theory of psychological reactance, all of us want the freedom to think, feel, and act as we (not others) choose. When we sense that a cherished freedom is being threatened, we become motivated to maintain it. And when we sense that a freedom is slipping away, we try to restore it (Brehm & Brehm, 1981). One possible result is that when a communicator comes on too strongly, we may react with *negative attitude change* by moving in the direction that is the opposite of the one being advocated— even, ironically, when the speaker's position agrees with our own (Heller et al., 1973). Sometimes, the motive to protect our freedom to think as we choose trumps our desire to hold a specific opinion. Reactance can trigger resistance to persuasion in two ways. Once aroused, the reactant target of attempted persuasion may simply shut down in a reflex-like response or disagree in a more thoughtful manner by questioning the credibility of the source and counterarguing the message (Silvia, 2006).

It's important to realize that forewarning does not always increase resistance to persuasion because the effects are not that simple. Based on a meta-analysis of 48 experiments, Wendy Wood and Jeffrey Quinn (2003) found that when people are forewarned about an impending persuasive appeal on a topic that is personally not that important, they start to agree before they even receive the message so as not to appear vulnerable to influence. Yet when people are forewarned about a persuasive appeal on a topic of personal importance, they feel threatened and think up counterarguments to bolster their attitude. This cognitive response strengthens their resistance to change once that appeal is delivered. It takes mental effort to resist a persuasive appeal. When people know that someone will try to influence them, they conserve their energy and generate the necessary counterarguments (Janssen et al., 2010).

■ Culture and Persuasion

A communication is persuasive to the extent that the source is favorable and the message, however it is presented, meets the psychological needs of its audience. In this regard, cultural factors also play a subtle but important role.

"To do just the opposite is also a form of imitation."

—Lichtenberg

inoculation hypothesis The idea that exposure to weak versions of a persuasive argument increases later resistance to that argument.

psychological reactance The theory that people react against threats to their freedom by asserting themselves and perceiving the threatened freedom as more attractive.

In earlier chapters, we saw that cultures differ in the extent to which people are oriented toward individualism or collectivism. In light of these differences, Sang-Pil Han and Sharon Shavitt (1994) compared the contents of magazine advertisements in the United States, an individualistic country, and Korea, a country with a more collectivistic orientation. They found that American advertising campaigns were focused more on personal benefits, individuality, competition, and self-improvement ("She's got a style all her own"; "Make your way through the crowd"), and that Korean ads appealed more to the integrity, achievement, and well-being of one's ingroups ("An exhilarating way to provide for your family"; "Celebrating a half-century of partnership"). Clearly, there are different ways to appeal to the members of these two cultures.

In a second study, Han and Shavitt created two sets of ads for various products. One set portrayed individuals ("Treat yourself to a breath-freshening experience"), and the other set featured groups ("Share this breath-freshening experience"). Both sets were presented to American and Korean participants. The result: Americans were persuaded more by individualistic ads, and Koreans preferred collectivistic ads. Similar differences are found in the way celebrity endorsements are used in the two cultures. In the United States, celebrities tend to portray themselves using or talking directly about a product; in Korean commercials that appeal to belongingness, family, and traditional values, celebrities are more likely to play the role of someone else without being singled out (Choi et al., 2005).

As people from all over the world come into contact with each other through travel, satellite television, international trade agreements, and the Internet, cultural values begin to change. Just as humans develop as they get older, cultures sometimes change over time from one generation to the next. Recent and substantial modernization efforts in China—home to roughly one out of every five people on the planet—illustrate the point. There is so much recent change that Zhang and Shavitt (2003) sought to compare the contents of television commercials, which are primarily directed at the traditional mass market, with advertisements in new magazines that specifically target 18- to 35-year-old, educated, high-income citizens who constitute China's "X-generation." Based on their analysis of 463 ads, they found that although traditional and collectivist values predominated on mainstream TV, magazine ads were characterized by more modern and individualistic impulses. To be persuasive, a message should appeal to the culturally shared values of its audience.

In a series of print ads, Apple Computer featured Albert Einstein and other creative geniuses throughout history who dared to "think different." In a marketing campaign that paid tribute to individualism, Apple saluted "The crazy ones. The misfits. The rebels. The troublemakers. The round pegs in the square holes. The ones who see things differently."

Persuasion by Our Own Actions

Anyone who has ever acted on stage knows how easy it is to become so absorbed in a role that the experience seems real. Feigned laughter can make an actor feel happy, and crocodile tears can turn into sadness. Even in the high stakes of real life, the effect can be dramatic. In 1974, Patty Hearst, a sheltered college student from a wealthy California family, was kidnapped. By the time she was arrested months later, she was a gun-toting revolutionary who called herself Tania. How could someone be so totally converted? In Hearst's own words, "I had thought I was humoring [my captors] by parroting their clichés and buzzwords without believing in them . . . In trying to convince them I convinced myself" (Hearst, 1982).

■ Role Playing: All the World's a Stage

The Patty Hearst case illustrates the powerful effects of *role playing.* Of course, you don't have to be kidnapped or terrorized to know how it feels to be coaxed into behavior that is at odds with your sense of who you are. People frequently engage in attitude-discrepant behavior as part of a job, for example, or to fit into a group. As commonplace as this seems, it raises a profound question. When we play along, saying and doing things that are privately discrepant from our own attitudes, do we begin to change those attitudes as a result? How we feel can determine the way we act. Is it also possible that the way we act can determine how we feel?

Many years ago, Irving Janis (1968) theorized that attitude change would persist more when it is inspired by our own behavior than when it stems from a passive exposure to a persuasive communication. Janis conducted a study in which one group of participants listened to a speech that challenged their positions on a topic and others were handed an outline and asked to give the speech themselves. As predicted, participants changed their attitudes more after giving the speech than after listening to it (Janis & King, 1954). According to Janis, role playing works to change attitudes because it forces people to learn the message.

Posing as a revolutionary named Tania, Patty Hearst was converted by the role her captors forced her to play. "In trying to convince them I convinced myself," she said.

People tend to remember arguments they come up with on their own better than they remember arguments provided to them by other people (Slamecka & Graff, 1978). In fact, attitude change is more enduring even when people who read a persuasive message merely *expect* that they will later have to communicate it to others (Boninger et al., 1990).

But there's more to role playing than improved memory. The effects of enacting a role can be staggering, in part because it is so easy to confuse what we do or what we say with how we really feel. Think about the times you've dished out compliments you didn't mean or flashed a smile at someone you didn't like or nodded your head in response to a statement you disagreed with. We often shade what we say just to please a particular listener. What's fascinating is not that we make adjustments to suit others but that this role playing has such powerful effects on our own private attitudes. For example, participants in one study read about a man and then described him to someone else, who supposedly liked or disliked him. As you might expect, they described the man in more positive terms when their listener was favorably disposed. In the process, however, they also convinced themselves. At least to some extent, "saying is believing" (Higgins & Rholes, 1978).

Recent research into this process of *self-generated persuasion* has shown that more attitude change is produced by having people generate arguments themselves than listen passively to others making the same arguments. Often in life, people hold attitudes they wish they could change—as when we wish we could like a job more than we do, or our favorite junk foods less. In these instances, people may try to talk themselves deliberately into something they do not already believe (Maio & Thomas, 2007). This research raises an interesting question: What produces more change in attitude, formulating arguments in order to convince *yourself* of something, or trying to convince *someone else*? The answer is, it depends. In a series of experiments, researchers found that when college students were instructed to advocate for a policy that was largely consistent with their own attitudes (that their university's tuition should be lowered), more self-persuasion occurred when their intended audience was another student. Not knowing how their target felt about the issue, these students tried harder to generate good arguments and moved themselves in the process. However, when instructed to advocate for a position that they opposed (that tuition should be raised), more self-persuasion occurred among students who had sought to convince themselves as opposed to another student. Knowing full well that self-persuasion on the issue would be particularly challenging, these students tried harder and generated better arguments (Briñol et al., 2012).

The kind of self-persuasion that occurs when people advocate for something, as when they play a role, is a fascinating process. Consider the implications. We know that attitudes influence behavior, as when people help those whom they like and hurt those whom they dislike. But research on role playing emphasizes the flip side of the coin—that behavior can change attitudes. Perhaps we come to like people because we have helped them and dislike people whom we have hurt. To change a person's inner feelings, then, maybe we should begin by focusing on their behavior. Why do people experience changes of attitude in response to changes in their own behavior? One answer to this question is provided by the theory of cognitive dissonance.

■ Cognitive Dissonance Theory: The Classic Version

Many social psychologists believe that people are strongly motivated by a desire for cognitive consistency—a state of mind in which one's beliefs, attitudes, and behaviors are compatible with each other (Abelson et al., 1968). Cognitive consistency theories seem to presuppose that people are generally logical. However, Leon Festinger (1957) turned this assumption on its head. Struck by the irrationalities of human behavior, Festinger proposed **cognitive dissonance theory**, which states that a powerful motive to maintain cognitive consistency can give rise to irrational, sometimes maladaptive behavior.

According to Festinger, all of us hold many cognitions about ourselves and the world around us. These cognitions include everything we know about our own beliefs, attitudes, and behavior. Although generally our cognitions coexist peacefully, at times they clash. Consider some examples. You say you're on a diet, yet you just dove headfirst into a tub of chocolate fudge brownie ice cream. Or you waited in line for hours to get into a concert, and then the band proved to be disappointing. Or you baked for hours under the hot summer sun while listening to your iPod even though you knew the health risks. Each of these scenarios harbors inconsistency and conflict: You've already committed yourself to a course of action, yet you realize that the action is inconsistent with your attitude.

Under certain conditions, discrepancies such as these can evoke an unpleasant state of tension known as cognitive dissonance. But discrepancy doesn't

"If you don't like something, change it. If you can't change it, change your attitude."

—Maya Angelou

cognitive dissonance theory
Theory holding that inconsistent cognitions arouses psychological tension that people become motivated to reduce.

▲ **TABLE 6.5**

Ways to Reduce Dissonance

"I need to be on a diet, yet I just dove head first into a tub of chocolate fudge brownie ice cream." If this were you, how would you reduce dissonance aroused by the discrepancy between your attitude and your behavior?

Techniques	Examples
Change your attitude.	"I don't really need to be on a diet."
Change your perception of the behavior.	"I hardly ate any ice cream."
Add consonant cognitions.	"Chocolate ice cream is very nutritious."
Minimize the importance of the conflict.	"I don't care if I'm overweight—life is short!"
Reduce perceived choice.	"I had no choice; the ice cream was served for this special occasion."

© Cengage Learning®

always produce dissonance. If you broke a diet for a Thanksgiving dinner with family, your indiscretion would not lead you to experience dissonance. Or if you mistakenly thought the ice cream you ate was low in calories only to find out the truth later, then, again, you would not experience much dissonance. As we'll see, what really hurts is the knowledge that you committed yourself to an attitude-discrepant behavior freely and with some knowledge of the consequences. When that happens, dissonance is aroused, and you become motivated to reduce it. As shown in Table 6.5, there are many possible ways to reduce dissonance—such as rationalizing that others in one's ingroup are also hypocrites (McKimmie et al., 2009), denying personal responsibility for the behavior (Gosling et al., 2006), and trivializing the issue in question (Starzyk et al., 2009). Of course, sometimes the easiest way to reduce dissonance is to change your attitude to bring it in line with your behavior.

Right from the start, cognitive dissonance theory captured the imagination of social psychology. Festinger's basic proposition is simple, yet its implications are far-reaching. In this section, we examine three research areas that demonstrate the breadth of what dissonance theory has to say about attitude change.

Justifying Attitude-Discrepant Behavior: When Doing Is Believing

Imagine for a moment that you are a participant in the classic study by Leon Festinger and J. Merrill Carlsmith (1959). As soon as you arrive, you are greeted by an experimenter who says that he is interested in various measures of performance. Wondering what that means, you all too quickly find out. The experimenter hands you a wooden board containing 48 square pegs in square holes and asks you to turn each peg a quarter turn to the left, then a quarter turn back to the right, then back to the left, then back again to the right. The routine seems endless. After 30 minutes, the experimenter comes to your rescue. Or does he? Just when you think things are looking up, he hands you another board, another assignment. For the next half-hour, you are to take 12 spools of thread off the board, put them back, take them off, and put them back again. By now, you're just about ready to tear your hair out. As you think back over better times, even the first task begins to look good.

Finally, you're done. After one of the longest hours of your life, the experimenter lets you in on a secret: There's more to this experiment than meets the eye. You were in the control group. To test the effects of motivation on performance, other participants are being told that the experiment will be fun and exciting. You don't realize it, but you are now being set up for the critical part of the study. Would you be willing to tell the next participant that the experiment is enjoyable? As you hem and haw, the experimenter offers to pay for your services. Some participants are offered $1; others are offered $20. In either case, you agree to help out. Before you know it, you find yourself in the waiting

"It's a crazy idea, but it just might work."

One way to reduce dissonance is to minimize the importance of the conflict.

Permission, Cartoon Features Syndicate.

Reprinted from the Wall Street Journal. Permission, Cartoon Features Syndicate room trying to dupe an unsuspecting fellow student (who is really a confederate).

By means of this elaborate staged presentation, participants were goaded into an attitude-discrepant behavior, an action that was inconsistent with their private attitudes. They knew how dull the experiment really was, yet they raved about it. Did this conflict arouse cognitive dissonance? It depends on how much the participants were paid. Suppose you were one of the lucky ones offered $20 for your assistance. By today's standards, that payment would be worth $80—surely a sufficient justification for telling a little white lie, right? Feeling well compensated, these participants experienced little if any dissonance. But wait. Suppose you were paid only $1. Surely your integrity is worth more than that, don't you think? In this instance, you have **insufficient justification** for going along, so you need a way to cope. According to Festinger (1957), unless you can deny your actions (which is not usually possible), you'll feel pressured to change your attitude about the task. If you can convince yourself that the experiment wasn't that bad, then saying it was interesting is all right.

The results were as Festinger and Carlsmith had predicted. When the experiment was presumably over, participants were asked how they felt about the peg-board tasks. Those in the control group who did not mislead a confederate openly admitted that the tasks were boring. So did those in the $20 condition, who had ample justification for what they did. However, participants who were paid only $1 rated the experiment as somewhat enjoyable. Having engaged in an attitude-discrepant act without sufficient justification, these participants reduced cognitive dissonance by changing their attitude. The results can be seen in ● Figure 6.9.

Two aspects of this classic study are noteworthy. First, it showed the phenomenon of self-persuasion: When people behave in ways that contradict their attitudes, they sometimes go on to change those attitudes without any exposure to a persuasive communication. Demonstrating the power of this phenomenon, Michael Leippe and Donna Eisenstadt (1994) found that white college students who were coaxed into writing essays in favor of new scholarship funds only for black students later reported more favorable attitudes in general toward African Americans. The second major contribution of Festinger and Carlsmith's results is that they contradicted the time-honored belief that big rewards produce greater change. In fact, the more money participants were offered for their inconsistent behavior, the more justified they felt and the less likely they were to change their attitudes.

Just as a small reward provides insufficient justification for attitude-discrepant behavior, mild punishment is **insufficient deterrence** for attitude-discrepant non-behavior. Think about it. What happens when people refrain from doing something they really want to do? Do they devalue the activity and convince themselves that they never really wanted to do it in the first place? In one study, children were prohibited from playing with an attractive toy by being threatened with a mild or a severe punishment. All participants refrained. As cognitive dissonance theory predicts, however, only those faced with the mild punishment—an insufficient

● **FIGURE 6.9**

The Dissonance Classic

Participants in a boring experiment (attitude) were asked to say that it was enjoyable (behavior) to a fellow student. Those in one group were paid $1 to lie; those in a second group were offered $20. Members of a third group, who did not have to lie, admitted that the task was boring. So did the participants paid $20, which was ample justification for telling a lie. Participants paid only $1, however, rated the task as more enjoyable. Behaving in an attitude-discrepant manner without justification, these latter participants reduced dissonance by changing their attitude.

Based on Festinger, L. and Carlsmith, J. M., "Cognitive Consequences and Forced Compliance," *Journal of Abnormal and Social Psychology* vol 58 (pp. 203–210). Copyright © 1959 by the American Psychological Association. Reprinted by permission.

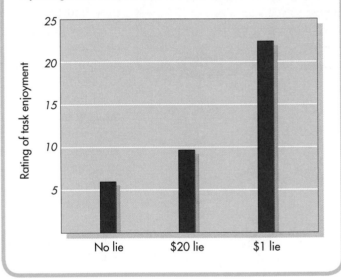

insufficient justification A condition in which people freely perform an attitude-discrepant behavior without receiving a large reward.

insufficient deterrence A condition in which people refrain from engaging in a desirable activity, even when only mild punishment is threatened.

deterrent—later showed disdain for the forbidden toy. Those who confronted the threat of severe punishment did not (Aronson & Carlsmith, 1963). Once again, cognitive dissonance theory turned common sense on its head: The less severe the threatened punishment, the greater the attitude change produced.

Justifying Effort: Coming to Like What We Suffer For Have you ever spent tons of money or tried really hard to achieve something, only to discover later that it wasn't worth all the effort? This kind of inconsistency between effort and outcome can arouse cognitive dissonance and motivate a change of heart toward the unsatisfying outcome. The hypothesis is simple but profound: We alter our attitudes to justify our suffering.

In a classic test of this hypothesis, Elliot Aronson and Judson Mills (1959) invited female students to take part in a series of group discussions about sex. But there was a hitch. Because sex is a sensitive topic, participants were told that they would have to pass an "embarrassment test" before joining the group. The test consisted of reading sexual material aloud in front of a male experimenter. One group of participants experienced what amounted to a *severe* initiation in which they had to recite obscene words and lurid passages taken from paperback novels. A second group underwent a *mild* initiation in which they read a list of more ordinary words pertaining to sex. A third group was admitted to the discussions without an initiation test.

Moments later, all participants were given headphones and permitted to eavesdrop on the group they would soon be joining. Actually, what they heard was a tape-recorded discussion about "secondary sex behavior in the lower animals." It was dreadfully boring. When it was over, participants were asked to rate how much they liked the group members and their discussion. Keep in mind what dissonance theory predicts: The more time or money or effort you choose to invest in something, the more anxious you will feel if the outcome proves disappointing. One way to cope with this inconsistency is to alter your attitudes. That's exactly what happened. Participants who had endured a severe initiation rated the discussion group more favorably than did those who had endured little or no initiation.

Social embarrassment is not the only kind of "effort" we feel we need to justify to ourselves. As a general rule, the more you pay for something—whether you pay in physical exertion, pain, time, or money—the more you will come to like it. This principle has provocative implications for hazing practices in fraternities and sororities, on sports teams, and in the military. Research even suggests that the harder psychotherapy patients have to work at their own treatment, the more likely they are to feel better when that treatment is over (Axsom, 1989; Axsom & Cooper, 1985).

Justifying Difficult Decisions: When Good Choices Get Even Better Whenever we make difficult decisions—whether to marry, what school to attend, where to live, or what job to accept—we feel dissonance. By definition, a decision is difficult when the alternative courses of action are about equally desirable. Marriage offers comfort and stability; staying single enables us to seek out exciting new relationships. One job might pay more money; the other may offer more interesting work. Once people make tough

> The more money you pay people to tell a lie, the more they will come to believe it.
>
> **FALSE**

This frat better be worth it!

Cognitive dissonance theory would predict that this character, if he survives, will come to like the "frat" - a lot.

decisions like these, they are at risk because as negative aspects of the chosen alternatives and positive aspects of the unchosen alternatives are at odds with their decisions. According to dissonance theory, people rationalize whatever they decide by exaggerating the positive features of the chosen alternative and the negative features of the unchosen alternative.

In an early test of this hypothesis, Jack Brehm (1956) asked female participants to evaluate various consumer products, presumably as part of a marketing research project. After rating a toaster, a coffee pot, a radio, a stopwatch, and other products, participants were told that they could take one home as a gift. In the high-dissonance condition, they were offered a difficult choice between two items they found equally attractive. In the low-dissonance group, they were offered an easier choice between a desirable and an undesirable item. After receiving the gift, participants read a few research reports and then reevaluated all the products. The results provided strong support for dissonance theory. In the low-dissonance group, the participants' post-decision ratings were about the same as their pre-decision ratings. But in the high-dissonance condition, ratings increased for the chosen item and decreased for the item that was not chosen. Participants torn between two equivalent alternatives coped by reassuring themselves that they had made the right choice.

This phenomenon appears in a wide range of settings. For example, Robert Knox and James Inskter (1968) took dissonance theory to the racetrack and found that bettors who had already placed $2 bets on a horse were more optimistic about winning than were those still standing in line. This type of optimism may even begin to set in once a thoughtful decision is made, even before the bet is placed (Brownstein et al., 2004). Similarly, Dennis Regan and Martin Kilduff (1988) visited several polling stations on Election Day and found that voters were more likely to think that their candidates would win when they were interviewed after submitting their ballots than when they were interviewed before they submitted them. Since bets and votes cannot be taken back, people who had committed to a decision were motivated to reduce post-decision dissonance. So they convinced themselves that the decision they made was right.

■ Cognitive Dissonance Theory: A New Look

Following in Festinger's bold footsteps, generations of social psychologists have studied and refined the basic theory (Cooper, 2007; Harmon-Jones & Mills, 1999). Nobody disputes the fact that when people are gently coaxed into performing an attitude-discrepant behavior, they often go on to change their attitudes. In fact, people will feel discomfort and change their attitudes when they disagree with others in a group (Matz & Wood, 2005) or even when they observe inconsistent behavior from others with whom they identify—a process of vicarious dissonance (Cooper & Hogg, 2007).

Researchers have also examined possible perceptual consequences of cognitive dissonance. In one study, Emily Balcetis and David Dunning (2007) took college students to the crowded center of campus and asked them to put on—and

> People often come to like what they suffer for.
>
> **TRUE**

William Manning/Terra/Corbis

Suggesting that people need to justify difficult irrevocable decisions to quell the dissonance they arouse, researchers found that gamblers who had already bet on a horse rated themselves as more certain of winning than those who were still waiting to place a bet.

walk around in—a costume consisting of a grass skirt, a coconut bra, a flower lei around the neck, and a plastic fruit basket on the head. Embarrassing as it was to appear this way in public, all the participants walked across campus in this costume. In a high-choice condition, they were led to believe that they could decline in favor of a different task (insufficient justification). In a low-choice condition, they were told that no alternative tasks were available (sufficient justification). How bad was it? Afterward, all the students were asked to estimate the distance they had walked from one point to the other. Needing to justify their embarrassing antics, those in the high-choice condition underestimated how far they had walked relative to those in the low-choice condition. Apparently, the motivation to reduce dissonance can alter our visual representations of the natural environment.

Through systematic research, it became evident early on that Festinger's (1957) original theory was not to be the last word. People do change their attitudes to justify attitude-discrepant behavior, effort, and difficult decisions. But for dissonance to be aroused, certain specific conditions must be present. Thanks to Joel Cooper and Russell Fazio's (1984) "new look" at dissonance theory, we now have a pretty good idea of what those conditions are.

According to Cooper and Fazio, four steps are necessary for both the arousal and reduction of dissonance. First, the attitude-discrepant behavior must produce unwanted *negative consequences.* Recall the initial Festinger and Carlsmith (1959) study. Not only did participants say something they knew to be false but they also deceived a fellow student into taking part in a painfully boring experiment. Had these participants lied without causing hardship, they would *not* have changed their attitudes to justify the action (Cooper et al., 1974). To borrow an expression from schoolyard basketball, "no harm, no foul." In fact, negative consequences can arouse dissonance even when people's actions are consistent with their attitudes, as when college students who wrote against fee hikes were led to believe that their essays had backfired, prompting a university committee to favor an increase (Scher & Cooper, 1989).

The second necessary step in the process is a feeling of *personal responsibility* for the unpleasant outcomes of behavior. Personal responsibility consists of two factors. The first is the freedom of *choice.* When people believe they had no choice but to act as they did, there is no dissonance and no attitude change (Linder et al., 1967). Had Festinger and Carlsmith coerced participants into raving about the boring experiment, the participants would not have felt the need to further justify what they did by changing their attitudes. But the experimental situation led participants to think that their actions were voluntary and that the choice was theirs. Participants were pressured without realizing it and believed that they did not have to comply with the experimenter's request.

For people to feel personally responsible, they must also believe that the potential negative consequences of their actions were *foreseeable* at the time (Goethals et al., 1979). When the outcome could not realistically have been anticipated, then there is no dissonance and no attitude change. Had Festinger and Carlsmith's participants lied in private and found out only later that their statements had been tape-recorded for subsequent use, then, again, they would not have felt the need to further justify their behavior.

The third necessary step in the process is physiological *arousal.* Right from the start, Festinger viewed cognitive dissonance as a state of discomfort and tension that people seek to reduce—much like hunger, thirst, and other basic drives. Research has shown that this emphasis was well placed. In a study by Robert Croyle and Joel Cooper (1983), participants wrote essays that supported or contradicted their own attitudes. Some were ordered to do so, but others were led to believe that the choice was theirs. During the session, electrodes were attached to each participant's fingertips to record levels of physiological arousal. As predicted by cognitive dissonance theory, those who freely wrote attitude-discrepant essays were the most aroused, an observation made by other researchers as well (Elkin & Leippe, 1986). In fact, participants who write attitude-discrepant essays in a "free-choice" situation report feeling high levels of discomfort—which subside once they change their attitudes (Elliot & Devine, 1994).

The fourth step in the dissonance process is closely related to the third. It isn't enough to feel generally aroused. A person must also make an *attribution* for that arousal to his or her own behavior. Suppose you just lied to a friend or studied for an exam that was canceled or made a tough decision that you might soon regret. Suppose further that although you are upset, you believe that your discomfort is caused by some external factor, not by your dissonance-producing behavior. Under these circumstances, will you exhibit attitude change as a symptom of cognitive dissonance? Probably not. When participants were led to attribute their dissonance-related arousal to a drug they had supposedly taken (Zanna & Cooper, 1974), to the anticipation of painful electric shocks (Pittman, 1975), or to a pair of prism goggles that they had to wear (Losch & Cacioppo, 1990), attitude change did not occur. ● Figure 6.10 summarizes these four steps in the production and reduction of dissonance.

To this day, social psychologists continue to debate the "classic" and "new look" theories of cognitive dissonance. On the one hand, research has shown that attitude-discrepant actions do not always produce dissonance, in part because not everyone cares about being cognitively consistent (Cialdini et al., 1995) and in part because a change in attitude often seems to require the production of negative consequences (Johnson et al., 1995). On the other hand, some researchers have found that mere inconsistency can trigger cognitive dissonance, even without negative consequences. For example, Eddie Harmon-Jones and others (1996) had people drink a Kool-Aid beverage that was mixed with sugar or vinegar. They either told the participants (no choice) or asked them (high choice) to state in writing that they liked the beverage and then toss these notes, which were not really needed, into the wastebasket. Afterward, they rated how much they really liked the drink. You may have noticed that this experiment parallels the Festinger and Carlsmith study with one key exception: For participants in the high-choice situation who consumed vinegar and said they liked it, the lie—although it

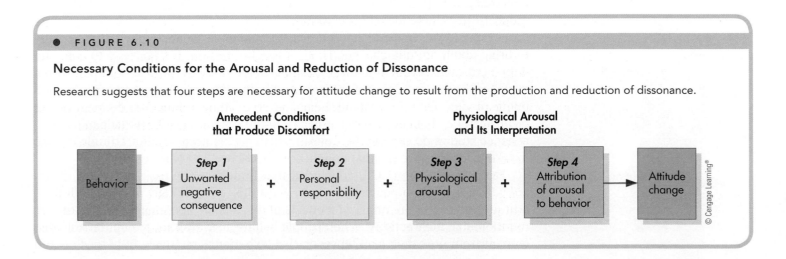

● FIGURE 6.10

Necessary Conditions for the Arousal and Reduction of Dissonance

Research suggests that four steps are necessary for attitude change to result from the production and reduction of dissonance.

Antecedent Conditions that Produce Discomfort   **Physiological Arousal and Its Interpretation**

Behavior → **Step 1** Unwanted negative consequence + **Step 2** Personal responsibility + **Step 3** Physiological arousal + **Step 4** Attribution of arousal to behavior → Attitude change

© Cengage Learning®

contradicted their true attitudes—did not cause harm to anyone. Did they experience dissonance that they would have to reduce by overrating the vinegar Kool-Aid? Yes. Compared with participants who lied about the vinegar in the no-choice situation, those in the high-choice situation rated its taste as more pleasant. The lie was harmless, but the feeling of inconsistency still forced a change in attitude.

■ Alternative Routes to Self-Persuasion

It is important to distinguish between the empirical facts uncovered by dissonance researchers and the theory that is used to explain them. The facts themselves are clear: Under certain conditions, people who behave in attitude-discrepant ways go on to change their attitudes. Whether this phenomenon reflects a human need to reduce dissonance, however, is a matter of some controversy. Over the years, three other explanations have been proposed.

Self-Perception Theory Daryl Bem's (1965) *self-perception theory*, described in Chapter 3, posed the first serious challenge to dissonance theory. Noting that we don't always have firsthand knowledge of our own attitudes, Bem proposed that we infer how we feel by observing ourselves and the circumstances of our own behavior. This sort of self-persuasion is not fueled by the need to reduce tension or justify our actions. Instead, it is a cool, calm, and rational process in which people interpret ambiguous feelings by observing their own behavior. But can Bem's theory replace dissonance theory as an explanation of self-persuasion?

Bem confronted this question head-on. What if neutral observers who are not motivated by the need to reduce dissonance were to read a step-by-step description of a dissonance study and predict the results? This approach to the problem was ingenious. Bem reasoned that observers can have the same behavioral information as the participants themselves but not experience the same personal conflict. If observers generate the same results as real participants, it shows that dissonance arousal is not necessary for the resulting changes in attitudes.

To test his hypothesis, Bem (1967) described the Festinger and Carlsmith study to observers and had them guess participants' attitudes. Some were told about the $1 condition, some were told about the $20 condition, and others read about the control group procedure. The results closely paralleled the original study. As observers saw it, participants who said the task was interesting for $20 didn't mean it; they just went along for the money. But those who made the claim for only $1 must have been sincere. Why else would they have gone along? As far as Bem was concerned, the participants themselves reasoned the same way. No conflict, no arousal—just inference by observation.

So should we conclude that self-perception, not dissonance, is what's necessary to bring about attitude change? That's a tough question. It's not easy to come up with a critical experiment to distinguish between the two theories. Both predict the same results, but for different reasons. And both offer unique support for their own points of view. On the one hand, Bem's observer studies show that dissonance-like results can be obtained without arousal. On the other hand, the participants of dissonance studies *do* experience arousal, which seems necessary for attitude change to take place. Can we say that one theory is right and the other wrong?

Fazio and others (1977) concluded that both theories are right but in different situations. When people behave in ways that are strikingly at odds with their attitudes, they feel the unnerving effects of dissonance and change their attitudes to rationalize their actions. When people behave in ways that are not terribly discrepant from how they feel, however, they experience relatively little tension and form their attitudes as a matter of inference. In short, highly discrepant behavior produces attitude change through dissonance, whereas slightly discrepant behavior produces change through self-perception.

Impression-Management Theory   Another alternative to a dissonance view of self-persuasion is *impression-management theory,* which says that what matters is not a motive to be consistent but a motive to *appear* consistent. Nobody wants to be called fickle or be seen by others as a hypocrite. So we calibrate our attitudes and behaviors publicly in order to present ourselves to others in a particular light (Baumeister, 1982; Tedeschi et al., 1971). Or perhaps we are motivated not by a desire merely to appear consistent but by a desire to avoid being held responsible for the bad consequences of our actions (Schlenker, 1982). Either way this theory places the emphasis on our concern for self-presentation. According to this view, participants in the Festinger and Carlsmith study mostly did not want the experimenter to think they had sold out for a paltry sum of money.

If the impression-management approach is correct, then cognitive dissonance does not produce attitude change at all—only reported change. In other words, if research participants were to state their attitudes anonymously or if they were to think that the experimenter could determine their true feelings through covert measures, then dissonance-like effects should vanish. Sometimes the effects do vanish, but other times they do not. In general, studies have shown that although self-persuasion can be motivated by impression management, it can also occur in situations that do not clearly arouse self-presentation concerns (Baumeister & Tice, 1984).

Self-Esteem Theories   A third competing explanation relates self-persuasion to the self. According to Elliot Aronson, acts that arouse dissonance do so because they threaten the self-concept, making the person feel guilty, dishonest, or hypocritical, and motivating a change in attitude or future behavior (Aronson, 1999; Stone, Wiegand, Cooper, & Aronson et al., 1997). This being the case, perhaps Festinger and Carlsmith's participants needed to change their attitudes toward the boring task in order to repair damage to the self, not to resolve cognitive inconsistency.

If cognitive dissonance is aroused only by behavior that lowers self-esteem, then people with already low expectations of themselves should not be affected: "If a person conceives of himself as a 'schnook,' he will expect to behave like a schnook" (Aronson, 1969, p. 24). In fact, Jeff Stone (2003) found that when college students were coaxed into writing an essay in favor of a tuition increase (a position that contradicted their attitude) and into thinking about their own standards of behavior, those who had high self-esteem changed their attitude to meet their behavior, as dissonance theory would predict, more than those who had low self-esteem.

Claude Steele (1988) took this notion two steps further. First, he suggested that a dissonance-producing situation—engaging in attitude-discrepant behavior, exerting wasted effort, or making a tough decision—sets in motion a process of *self-affirmation* that serves to revalidate the integrity of the self-concept. Second, this revalidation can be achieved in many ways, not just by resolving dissonance. Self-affirmation theory makes a unique prediction: If the active ingredient in dissonance situations is a threat to the self, then people who have an opportunity to affirm the self in other ways will not suffer from the effects of dissonance. Give Festinger and Carlsmith's $1 participants a chance to donate money, help a victim in distress, or solve a problem, and their self-concepts should bounce back without further need to justify their actions.

Research provides support for this hypothesis. For example, Steele and others (1993) gave people positive or negative feedback about a personality test they had taken. Next, they had them rate 10 popular music CDs and then offered them a choice of keeping either their fifth- or sixth-ranked CD. Soon after making the decision, participants were asked to rate the CDs again. As predicted by dissonance theory, most inflated their ratings of the chosen CD relative to the unchosen one. The key word, however, is *most*. The ratings of the participants who had received positive feedback did not change. Why not? According to Steele, it was because they had just enjoyed a self-affirming experience that was enough to overcome the need to reduce dissonance.

Steele's research suggests that there are many possible ways for people to repair a dissonance-damaged self. But if these efforts at indirect self-affirmation fail, would cognitive dissonance return and create pressure to make a change in attitude? Yes. In one study, college students were asked (high-choice) or told (low-choice) to deliver an attitude-discrepant speech advocating that a popular campus tradition (running nude on the evening of the first snowfall) be banned. For those in the basic high-choice condition, cognitive dissonance was aroused, creating pressure on them to change their attitude favoring the ban. Students in another high-choice group who were subsequently given an opportunity to self-affirm by expressing some cherished values felt less discomfort and exhibited less attitude change. For them, self-affirmation provided the necessary relief. However, among students in a fourth group (also high in choice) who self-affirmed but then received negative feedback about the values they expressed, cognitive dissonance returned, creating pressure to change their attitude toward the ban. In essence, cognitive dissonance and its impact on attitudes reemerged from the failed attempt at self-affirmation (Galinsky et al., 2000).

To summarize, cognitive dissonance theory states that people come to change their attitudes to justify attitude-discrepant behaviors, efforts, and decisions. Self-perception theory argues that the change occurs because people infer how they feel by observing their own behavior. Impression-management theory claims that the attitude change is spurred by concerns about self-presentation. And self-affirmation theory says that the change is motivated by threats to the self-concept (see ● Figure 6.11). To this day, new theories are being proposed—for example,

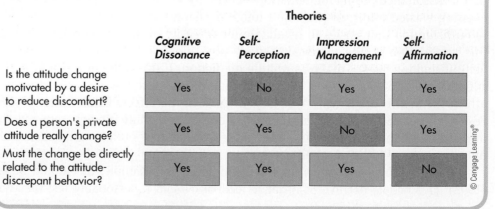

● FIGURE 6.11

Theories of Self-Persuasion: Critical Comparisons

Here we compare the major theories of self-persuasion. Each alternative challenges a different aspect of dissonance theory. Self-perception theory assumes that attitude change is a matter of inference, not motivation. Impression-management theory maintains that the change is more apparent than real, reported for the sake of public self-presentation. Self-affirmation theory contends that the motivating force is a concern for the self and that attitude change will not occur when the self-concept is affirmed in other ways.

	Theories			
	Cognitive Dissonance	Self-Perception	Impression Management	Self-Affirmation
Is the attitude change motivated by a desire to reduce discomfort?	Yes	No	Yes	Yes
Does a person's private attitude really change?	Yes	Yes	No	Yes
Must the change be directly related to the attitude-discrepant behavior?	Yes	Yes	Yes	No

© Cengage Learning®

the notion that feelings of dissonance are aroused not by inconsistency but by the fact that the conflict impedes our ability to know whether to approach or avoid and how to act (Harmon-Jones et al., 2015).

◼ Ethical Dissonance

In recent years, in domains as far and wide as business, law, sports, health and education, many social psychologists have become interested in *behavioral ethics*, the study of how individuals behave when facing temptations to cheat, steal, plagiarize, commit fraud, lie, or otherwise behave unethically. From standing in a supermarket express line with too many groceries to overstating business expenses in tax forms, our day-to-day lives provide more examples than any of us would care to admit (Bazerman & Gino, 2012).

Within this new field, researchers have addressed two types of problems. The first focuses on the unintentional lapses in ethics that can occur when otherwise good people do not pay attention and are not sufficiently vigilant, causing "blind spots" in ethical judgment (Bazerman & Tenbrunsel, 2011). Research shows that such lapses are most likely to occur when people are fatigued—which is why participants in a series of laboratory experiments were more likely to lie and cheat when tested in the afternoon than in the morning (Kouchaki & Smith, 2014) and when they are overly focused on the temptation of what is to be gained (Pittarello et al., 2015).

The second approach to the study of ethical behavior focuses on acts of intentional wrongdoing that people knowingly commit in order to serve their own interests. From a strictly economic standpoint, individuals are thought to engage in unethical acts when the tangible benefits (monetary and other rewards) exceed the tangible costs (exposure and punishment). In the laboratory, research shows that when payment is based on self-reported performance and cheating cannot be detected, participants tend to inflate their claims in order to increase the amount of money they receive. In one study, participants inflated by 15% the number of arithmetic problems they solved (Mazar et al., 2008). In a second study, they lied about random rolls of dice on 40% of occasions (Shalvi et al., 2015). People are particularly prone to cheat for money after seeing a peer confederate they identify with cheat and get away with it (Gino et al., 2009).

Although people can be induced into unethical behavior by the perception of benefits relative to costs, a growing body of research has shown that human nature is complicated by the fact that most people feel badly about their unethical acts even when they do not fear exposure (Hilbig & Hessler, 2013). To put it another way, behaving in ways that violate our own moral code threatens our self-esteem and arouses an inner state of turmoil that Rachel Barkan and her colleagues (2012) have called *ethical dissonance*. Following in Festinger's footsteps, these researchers and others have suggested that when temptation lures us into the possibility of an unethical behavior, our moral self-concept is threatened both *before* and *after* we do it. To help attenuate this threat, we use various self-serving justifications to cope with both the *anticipation* and the *experience* of ethical dissonance. These processes are illustrated in ● Figure 6.12.

Social psychologists have begun to explore some of the pre-violation and post-violation types of justifications that enable unethical behavior by helping violators to do wrong but feel moral. Reviewing this research, Shaul Shalvi and others (2015) describe a number of ways in which people reduce their ethical dissonance—for example, citing social norms to suggest that "everyone is doing it"; blaming others or circumstances; rationalizing the good that comes from the misdeed; confessing, apologizing, and offering compensation; and distancing

● FIGURE 6.12

Ordinary people often behave badly but still feel moral. How is this discrepancy possible? As shown, temptation may lead us to misbehave, which threatens our moral self-concept both beforehand (when ethical dissonance is anticipated) and afterward (when ethical dissonance is experienced). Once tempted, *pre-violation justifications* excuse what we are about to do. Afterward, *post-violation justifications* compensate for what we did. In these ways, people manage to behave immorally yet maintain a moral self-concept.
Shalvi et al., 2015.

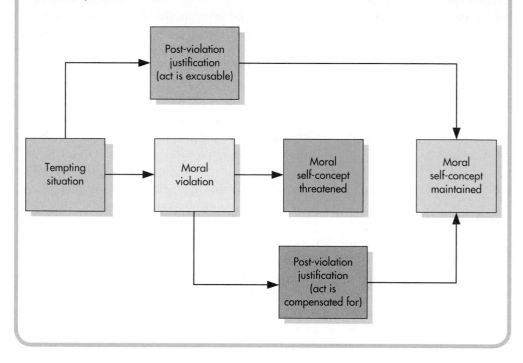

themselves from the misdeed by asserting stricter ethical standards for the future and judging other transgressors more harshly.

One particularly interesting form of self-justification, which "enables" people to behave unethically, is called *moral licensing,* a tendency to justify an anticipated misdeed by citing good things that we have done. In an article entitled "Moral self-licensing: When being good frees us to be bad," Anna Merritt and her colleagues (2010) reviewed research suggesting that past good deeds can liberate individuals to engage in unethical behaviors that they would otherwise avoid for fear of feeling or appearing immoral. In one study, participants were randomly assigned to write stories that describe their own positive or negative traits. Afterward, they were asked if they would make a small donation to a charity of their choice. Those who wrote positively about themselves later donated $1.07—only a fifth of the $5.30 donated by those who wrote negative (Sachdeva et al., 2009). In a second study, participants were assigned to shop from an online store that carried a predominance of green, environment-friendly products or conventional products equal in price. Moments later, those who shopped at the green store were more likely to lie to the experimenter to increase the money they earned (Mazar & Zhong, 2010). Overall, more than 90 studies have shown that moral licensing operates like something moral balancing scale. When people feel as if they have established moral credentials, they anticipate less ethical dissonance about engaging in an unethical behavior and become more likely to do so (Blanken et al., 2015).

Cultural Influences on Cognitive Dissonance

Over the years, social psychologists have presumed that the cognitive dissonance effects uncovered in 50 years of research and described in this chapter are universal and characteristic of human nature. More and more, however, it appears that cultural context may influence both the arousal and reduction of cognitive dissonance.

In Western cultures, individuals are expected to make decisions that are consistent with their personal attitudes and to make those decisions free from outside influences. In East Asian cultures, however, individuals are also expected to make decisions that benefit their ingroup members and to take the well-being of others into account in making those decisions. In light of these differences, Etsuko Hoshino-Browne and colleagues (2005) compared the reactions of Canadian and Japanese research participants in a post-decision dissonance experiment in which they rank-ordered items on a menu by choosing their top 10 dishes. Then they ranked the list again: Half made the choices for themselves, and the others were asked to imagine a close friend whose tastes they knew and choose on behalf of that friend. Did participants show the classic post-decision justification effect, becoming more positive in their ratings of the chosen items relative to nonchosen items? Yes and no. When they made decisions for themselves, only the Canadian participants exhibited a significant justification effect. When Japanese participants made decisions for a friend, however, they exhibited the stronger effect (see ● Figure 6.13). Similar results have been found in other studies (Kitayama et al., 2004).

To sum up: Cognitive dissonance is both universal and dependent on culture. At times everyone feels and tries to reduce dissonance, but cultures influence the conditions under which these processes occur.

● FIGURE 6.13

Cognitive Dissonance as Both Universal and Culturally Dependent

Researchers compared Canadian and Japanese research participants in a post-decision dissonance study in which they rank ordered items on a menu, chose their top dishes, then ranked the list again. Half made the choices for themselves; the others were asked to imagine a close friend. When deciding for themselves, only the Canadians exhibited a significant justification effect; when deciding for a friend, however, Japanese participants exhibited the stronger effect. Hoshino-Browne et al., 2005.

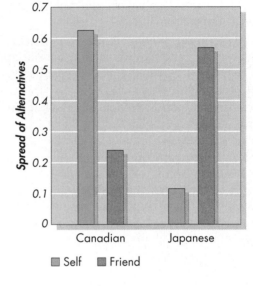

Changing Attitudes

Attitudes and attitude change are an important part of social life. In this chapter, we have seen that persuasion can be achieved in different ways. The most common approach is through communication from *others*. Faced with newspaper editorials, junk mail, books, TV commercials, blogs, websites, and other messages, we take one of two routes to persuasion. On the central route, attitude change is based on the merits of the source and his or her communication. On the peripheral route, it is based on superficial cues. Either way, the change in attitude often precipitates a change in behavior.

A second, less obvious means of persuasion originates within *ourselves*. When people behave in ways that run afoul of their true convictions, they often go on to change their attitudes. Once again, there are many routes to change, not just one. Cognitive dissonance, self-perception, impression management, and self-esteem concerns are among the possible avenues. From attitudes to behavior and back again, the processes of persuasion are complex and interwoven.

Review

Top 10 Key Points in Chapter 6

1. An attitude is an evaluative—positive or negative—reaction to a person, place, issue, or object.

2. Researchers typically measure attitudes through self-report, as in public opinion surveys, or by covert measures of a person's behavior—most notably, by using the Implicit Association Test (IAT).

3. Research shows individuals may be genetically predisposed to hold certain attitudes but that our attitudes are also shaped by personal experiences, observations, and associations.

4. The most common approach to changing attitudes—as seen in marketing, politics, advertising, and religion—is through the presentation of a persuasive communication.

5. There are two pathways by which people are persuaded by a communication: (1) on the "central route," people think critically about the strength and quality of arguments, or (2) on the "peripheral route," people are influenced by surface cues like a speaker's appearance or reputation.

6. Research shows that people are more likely to change their attitudes in response to a speaker who is likeable and credible; by arguments that are well developed and not too extreme; when motivated by fear; or when relaxed by positive emotions.

7. To be effective, persuasive messages should present arguments that appeal to the individual and cultural values of audience members.

8. According to Cognitive Dissonance Theory, people often come to change their attitudes in order to justify their own actions—as when they lie for profit, waste effort on something that proves disappointing; or make a difficult decision they start to regret.

9. For more than fifty years now, social psychologists have debated how and why cognitive dissonance leads people to change their attitudes—for example, whether the change represents a logical inference or a motivation to protect one's self-esteem.

10. It now appears that people all over the world will try to reduce dissonance when it arises but that the conditions that trigger it are influenced by cultural factors.

Putting Common Sense to the Test

The Study of Attitudes

Researchers can tell if someone has a positive or negative attitude by measuring physiological arousal.

Ⓕ **False.** *Measures of arousal can reveal how intensely someone feels, but not whether the person's attitude is positive or negative.*

Persuasion by Communication

In reacting to persuasive communications, people are influenced more by superficial images than by logical arguments.

Ⓕ **False.** *As indicated by the dual-process model of persuasion, people can be influenced by images or arguments, depending on their ability and motivation to think critically about the information.*

People are most easily persuaded by commercial messages that are presented without their awareness.

Ⓕ **False.** *There is no research evidence to support the presumed effects of subliminal ads.*

Persuasion by Our Own Actions

The more money you pay people to tell a lie, the more they will come to believe it.

Ⓕ **False.** *Cognitive dissonance studies show that people believe the lies they are underpaid to tell as a way to justify their own actions.*

People often come to like what they suffer for.

Ⓣ **True.** *Studies show that the more people work or suffer for something, the more they come to like it as away to justify their effort.*

Key Terms

attitude (210)

attitude scale (212)

bogus pipeline (212)

central route to persuasion (223)

cognitive dissonance
   theory (247)

elaboration (224)

evaluative conditioning (218)

facial electromyograph
   (EMG) (214)

Implicit Association Test
   (IAT) (214)

implicit attitude (214)

inoculation hypothesis (244)

insufficient deterrence (249)

insufficient justification (249)

need for cognition (NC) (241)

peripheral route to
   persuasion (223)

persuasion (223)

psychological reactance (244)

sleeper effect (232)

theory of planned
   behavior (219)

Conformity

This chapter opens by examining ways in which social influences are "automatic." We then look at three processes. First, we consider the reasons why people exhibit conformity to group norms. Second, we describe the strategies used to elicit compliance with direct requests. Third, we analyze the causes and effects of obedience to the commands of authority. The chapter concludes with a discussion of the continuum of social influence.

Richard McManus/Getty Images

On a Thursday evening in the summer of 2009, a couple of hundred ordinary people who were strangers to one another showed up in San Francisco's Union Square. At precisely 6 p.m., on cue, the impromptu group belted out the Beatles' song "With a Little Help from My Friends." Earlier that week, in England, feathers flew outside of the well-known Yorkshire Museum and Gardens when 500 happy Facebook users appeared, pillows in hand, for a massive pillow fight. In both cases, participants had received instructions on the Internet, gathered at a set time and place, did a silly but harmless thing, and dispersed. Illustrating the viral power of mobile apps and the Internet to serve as a vehicle for social influence, other "flash mobs" have formed in cities all over the world. In one particularly striking event, at New Hampshire's Portsmouth High School 2015 graduation ceremony, the valedictorian concluded his speech by saying, "All you have to do is shake it off." At that point, Taylor Swift's pop hit "Shake It Off" started to play over the loudspeaker and all 230 graduates got up and danced.

Sometimes the social influences that move us are not entertaining and funny but potentially hazardous to our health. Consider the unusual events that occurred a while back in a Tennessee high school. It started when a teacher noticed a gas-like smell in her classroom and then came down with a headache, nausea, shortness of breath, and dizziness. Word spread. Others soon reported the same symptoms, and the school was evacuated. Eighty students and several staff members were taken to a local emergency room. Nothing showed up in blood tests, urine tests, or other medical procedures, nor were gases, pesticides, or other toxins detected. What the investigation did turn up was that students who reported feeling ill that day were more likely than others to have seen or heard about someone with symptoms. Reporting in the *New England Journal of Medicine*, researchers concluded that the problem stemmed from "mass psychogenic illness"—a profound, almost contagious form of social influence (Jones et al., 2000).

Thomas Coex/Getty Images

Online videos that go viral and spread like a contagious disease have the power to attract millions across the internet. In 2015, Google announced that Psy's 2012 YouTube music video, "Gangnam Style," officially broke the 2,147,483,647-view barrier, an all-time record.

"We are discreet sheep; we wait to see how the drove is going and then go with the drove."

—Mark Twain

In *Outbreak! The Encyclopedia of Extraordinary Social Behavior*, Hilary Evans and Robert Bartholomew (2009) note that these types of incidents have occurred throughout human history, causing people to break out in rashes, vomit, bark, twirl, faint, strip naked, or laugh uncontrollably. The behaviors may vary. A few years ago, in Le Roy High School in Western New York, 6 girls—a number that grew to 18—developed a number of mysterious motor tics, uncontrollably writhing, shaking, twitching, head jerking, arms swinging, grimacing, and stuttering (Dominus, 2012).

Flash mobs and mass psychogenic illnesses reveal the awesome power of social influence. The effects that people have on each other can also be seen in mundane human events. Thus, sports fans spread the "wave" around massive stadiums, sing in unison, or chant "de-fense" in a spectacular show of unison. TV producers insert canned laughter into sitcoms to increase viewer responsiveness. Politicians trumpet inflated results from their own public opinion polls to attract voters. Bartenders, waiters, waitresses, and street musicians stuff dollar bills into their tip jars as a way to get others to follow suit. And online videos that go viral spread like a wildfire, capturing millions across the Internet. As they say, "Monkey see, monkey do."

You don't need to be a social psychologist to know that people have an impact on each other's behavior. The trickier question is, how and with what effect? The term *social influence* refers to the ways that people are affected by the real and imagined pressures of others (Cialdini & Goldstein, 2004; Kiesler & Kiesler, 1969). The kinds of influences brought to bear on an individual come in different shapes and sizes. In this chapter, we look at social influences that are mindless and automatic. Then we consider three forms of influence that vary in the degree of pressure exerted on an individual—*conformity, compliance,* and *obedience.* As depicted in Figure 7.1, conformity, compliance, and obedience are not distinct, qualitatively different "types" of influence. In all three cases, the influence may emanate from a person, a group, or an institution. In all instances, the behavior in question may be constructive (helping oneself or others), destructive (hurting oneself or others), or neutral. It is useful to note, once again, that social influence varies as points along a continuum according to the degree of pressure exerted on the individual. It is also useful to note that we do not always succumb under pressure. People may conform or maintain their independence from others, they may comply with direct requests or react with assertiveness, or they may obey the commands of authority or oppose powerful others in an act of defiance. In this chapter, we examine the factors that lead human beings to yield to or resist social influence.

> **Putting COMMON SENSE to the Test**
>
> **Circle Your Answer**
>
> **T F** When all members of a group give an incorrect response to an easy question, most people most of the time conform to that response.
>
> **T F** An effective way to get someone to do you a favor is to make a first request that is so large the person is sure to reject it.
>
> **T F** In experiments on obedience, most participants who were ordered to administer severe shocks to an innocent person refused to do so.
>
> **T F** As the number of people in a group increases, so does the group's impact on an individual.
>
> **T F** Conformity rates vary across different cultures and from one generation to the next.

Social Influence as "Automatic"

Before we consider the explicit forms of social influence depicted in ● Figure 7.1, whereby individuals choose whether or not to "go along," it's important to note that as social animals humans are vulnerable to a host of subtle, almost reflex-like influences. Without realizing it, we often crack open an involuntary yawn when we see others yawning, laugh aloud when we hear others laughing, and grimace when we see others in pain. In an early demonstration, Stanley Milgram and

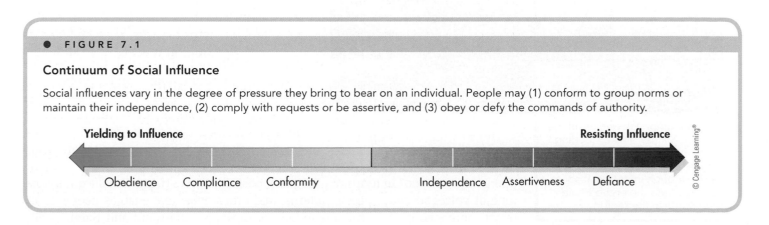

● **FIGURE 7.1**

Continuum of Social Influence

Social influences vary in the degree of pressure they bring to bear on an individual. People may (1) conform to group norms or maintain their independence, (2) comply with requests or be assertive, and (3) obey or defy the commands of authority.

Yielding to Influence   Resisting Influence

Obedience   Compliance   Conformity   Independence   Assertiveness   Defiance

© Cengage Learning®

others (1969) had research confederates stop on a busy street in New York City, look up, and gawk at the sixth-floor window of a nearby building. Films shot from behind the window indicated that about 80% of passersby stopped and gazed up when they saw the confederates.

Rudimentary forms of automatic imitation have been observed in various animal species, such as pigeons, monkeys, hamsters, and fish (Heyes, 2011; Zentall, 2012). There is even evidence to suggest that "cultures" are transmitted through imitation in groups of whales, as when humpback whales off the coast of Maine use lobtail feeding, a technique in which they slam their tail flukes onto the water, then dive and exhale, forming clouds of bubbles that envelop schools of prey fish to be gulped. This complex behavior was first observed in 1980. By 1989 it was measurably adopted by 50% of the whale population in that area (Rendell & Whitehead, 2001). Even more recently, researchers using a "network-based diffusion analysis" found that up to 87% of whales that adopted this technique learned it by exposure from other humpbacks (Allen et al., 2013). Similar observations in other species have led animal scientists to suggest that many nonhuman animals form and transmit cultures in this manner to succeeding generations (Laland & Galef, 2009).

Do humans similarly imitate one another automatically, without thought, effort, or conflict? It appears that we do. Controlled studies of human infants have shown that some time shortly after birth, babies not only look at faces but (to the delight of parents all over the world) often they mimic simple gestures such as moving the head, pursing the lips, and sticking out the tongue (Meltzoff & Moore, 1977; Ray & Heyes, 2010). Studying 162 infants from 6 to 20 months old, Susan Jones (2007) found that imitation developed at different rates for different behaviors. Using parents as models, she found, for example, that infants mimicked opening the mouth wide, tapping their fingers on a table, and waving bye-bye before they mimicked clapping hands, flexing their fingers, or putting their hands on the head.

You may not realize it, but we humans unwittingly mimic each other all the time. You might not know you're doing it, but when you are in a conversation with someone, chances are you are subtly mirroring them as you speak: nodding when they do, sitting back, leaning forward, scratching your face, or crossing your legs. To demonstrate, Tanya Chartrand and John Bargh (1999) set up participants to work on a task with a partner, a confederate who exhibited the habit of rubbing his face or shaking his foot. Hidden cameras recording the interaction revealed that without realizing it, participants mimicked these motor behaviors, rubbing their face or shaking a foot to match their partner's behavior. Chartrand and Bargh dubbed this phenomenon the "chameleon effect," after the reptile that changes colors according to its physical environment (see ● Figure 7.2).

Among humpback whales off the coast of Maine, "lobtail feeding" (a complex behavior that traps prey fish) was first observed in 1981. Through imitation, it soon spread across the entire whale population in the region.

iStock/Getty Images Plus/Getty Images

There are two possible reasons for this nonconscious form of imitation. Chartrand and Bargh theorized that such mimicry serves an important *social* function, that being "in sync" in terms of their pace, posture, mannerisms, facial expressions, tone of voice, accents, speech patterns, and other behaviors enables people to interact more smoothly with one another. Accordingly, Chartrand and Bargh (1999) turned the tables in a second study in which they instructed their confederate to match in subtle ways the mannerisms of some participants but not others. Sure enough, participants who had been mimicked liked the confederate more than those who had not.

Two additional sets of findings further demonstrate the social benefits of mimicry. First, research shows that people mimic others more when they are highly motivated to affiliate—say, because they are similar to these others or are feeling excluded—than when they are not (Chartrand & Lakin, 2013; Chartrand & van Baaren, 2009; Lakin et al., 2008). Second, research shows that when participants interact with others who exhibit negative, antisocial behaviors—say, in their tone of voice—mimicry backfires and causes the participants to be perceived unfavorably (Smith-Genthôs et al., 2015).

Social mimicry is so powerful that it can influence us even when the mimicker is not a real person. In a study entitled "digital chameleons," Jeremy Bailenson and Nick Yee (2005) immersed college students, one at a time, in a virtual reality environment in which they found themselves seated at a table across from an avatar, a human-like person that looked something like a three-dimensional cartoon character. This avatar proceeded to argue that students should be required to carry identification cards at all times for security purposes. In half the sessions, his back-and-forth head movements perfectly mimicked the participant's head movements at a four-second delay. In the other half, he repeated the head movements of an earlier recorded participant. Very few of the students who were mimicked were aware of it. Yet when later asked about the experience, they rated the avatar as more likable and were persuaded by its speech more if it imitated their head movements than the previous participant.

The human impulse to mimic others may have adaptive social value, but these types of effects can also be found in *nonsocial* situations. In one study, Roland Neumann and Fritz Strack (2000) had people listen to an abstract philosophical speech that was recited on tape in a happy, sad, or neutral voice.

Afterward, participants rated their own mood as more positive when they heard the happy voice and as more negative when they heard the sad voice. Even though the speakers and participants never interacted, the speaker's emotional state was infectious, an automatic effect that can be described as a form of "mood contagion." The same can be true about the way we mimic the language we hear in other people's expressions and speech styles. To illustrate, Molly Ireland and James Pennebaker (2010) found that college students answering essay questions or working from excerpts of fictional writing tended in subtle ways to match the language style of the target material to which they were exposed—for example, in terms of their use of personal pronouns (such as *I, you*), conjunctions (such as *but, while*), and quantifiers (such as *many, few*).

It is also important to realize that mimicry is a dynamic process, as when two people who are walking together or dancing become more and more coordinated over time. To demonstrate, Michael Richardson and others (2005) sat pairs of

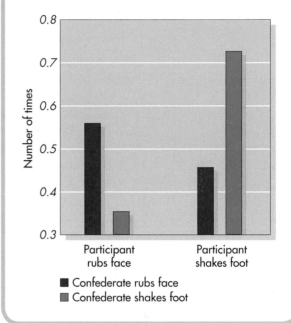

● **FIGURE 7.2**

The Chameleon Effect

Based on the study by Chartrand and Bargh (1999), this graph shows the number of times per minute participants rubbed their face or shook their foot when they were with a confederate who was rubbing or shaking his foot.

Adapted from Kassin, S., *Psychology* 3rd ed. Copyright © 1997.

■ Confederate rubs face
■ Confederate shakes foot

Often we are not aware of the influence other people have on our behavior.

college students side by side to work on visual problems while swinging a hand-held pendulum as "a distraction task." The students did not need to be synchronized in their swinging tempo to get along or solve the problems. Yet when each could see the other's pendulum, even without speaking, their tempos gradually converged over time—like two hearts beating as one.

Conformity

It is hard to find behaviors that are not in some way affected by exposure to the actions of others. When social psychologists talk of **conformity**, they specifically refer to the tendency of people to change their perceptions, opinions, and behavior in ways that are consistent with group norms.

Using this definition, would you call yourself a conformist or a nonconformist? How often do you feel inclined to follow what others are saying or doing? At first, you may deny the tendency to conform and, instead, declare your individuality and uniqueness. But think about it. When was the last time you attended a formal wedding dressed in blue jeans or remained seated during the national anthem at a sports event? When was the last time you tweeted an unpopular contrarian position for others to see? People find it difficult to breach social norms. In an early demonstration of this point, research assistants were recruited to ask subway passengers to give up their seats—a conspicuous violation of the norm of acceptable conduct. Many of the assistants could not carry out their assignment. In fact, some of those who tried it became so anxious that they pretended to be ill just to make their request appear justified (Milgram & Sabini, 1978).

With conformity being so widespread and seemingly so natural to human nature, it is interesting and ironic that research participants in North America who are coaxed into following a group norm will often not admit to being influenced. Instead, they try to reinterpret the task and rationalize their behavior as a way to see themselves in as independent (Hornsey & Jetten, 2004). But there is a second reason why people do not see themselves as conformist. In a series of studies, Emily Pronin and others (2007) found that people perceive others to be more conforming than themselves in all sorts of domains—from why they bought an iPad to why they hold a popular opinion. Part of the reason for this asymmetry is that people judge others by their overt behavior and the degree to which it matches what others do, but they tend to judge themselves by focusing inward and introspecting about their thought processes, which blinds them to their own conformity.

People understandably have mixed feelings about conformity. On the one hand, some degree of it is essential if individuals are to maintain communities and coexist peacefully, as when people assume their rightful place in a waiting line. Yet at other times, conformity can have harmful consequences, as when people drink too heavily at parties, cheat on taxes, or tell offensive jokes because they believe others are doing the same. For the social psychologist, the goal is to understand the conditions that promote conformity or independence and the reasons for these behaviors.

■ The Early Classics

In 1936, Muzafer Sherif published a classic laboratory study of how norms develop in small groups. His method was ingenious. Male students, who believed they

conformity The tendency to change our perceptions, opinions, or behavior in ways that are consistent with group norms.

were participating in a visual perception experiment, sat in a totally darkened room. Fifteen feet in front of them, a small dot of light appeared for two seconds, after which participants were asked to estimate how far it had moved. This procedure was repeated several times. Although participants didn't realize it, the dot of light always remained motionless. The movement they thought they saw was merely an optical illusion known as the *autokinetic effect:* In darkness, a stationary point of light appears to move, sometimes erratically, in various directions.

At first, participants sat alone and reported their judgments to the experimenter. After several trials, Sherif found that they settled in on their own stable perceptions of movement, with most estimates ranging from 1 to 10 inches (although one participant gave an estimate of 80 feet!). Over the next three days, people returned to participate openly in three-person groups. As before, lights were flashed and the participants, one by one, announced their estimates. As shown in ● Figure 7.3, initial estimates varied considerably, but participants later converged on a common perception. Eventually, each group established its own set of norms.

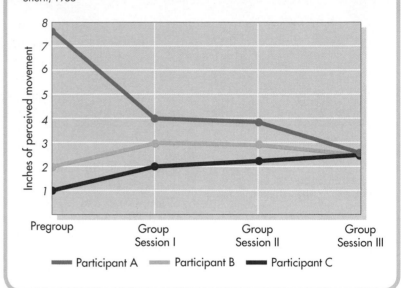

● **FIGURE 7.3**

A Classic Case of Suggestibility

This graph, taken from Sherif's study, shows how three participants' estimates of the apparent movement of light gradually converged. Before they came together, their perceptions varied considerably. Once in groups, however, participants conformed to the norm that had developed.
Sherif, 1936

Some 15 years after Sherif's demonstration, Solomon Asch (1951) constructed a very different task for testing how people's beliefs affect the beliefs of others. To appreciate what Asch did, imagine yourself in the following situation. You sign up for a psychology experiment, and when you arrive, you find six other students waiting around a table. Soon after you take an empty seat, the experimenter explains that he is interested in the ability to make visual discriminations. As an example, he asks you and the others to indicate which of three comparison lines is identical in length to a standard line.

That seems easy enough. The experimenter then says that after each set of lines is shown, you and the others should take turns announcing your judgments out loud in the order of your seating position. Beginning on his left, the experimenter asks the first person for his judgment. Seeing that you are in the next-to-last position, you patiently await your turn. The opening moments pass uneventfully. The task and discriminations are clear and everyone agrees on the answers. On the third set of lines, however, the first participant selects what is quite clearly the wrong line. Huh? What happened? Did he suddenly lose his mind, his eyesight, or both? Before you have the chance to figure this one out, the next four participants choose the same wrong line. Now what? Feeling as if you have entered the twilight zone, you wonder if you misunderstood the task. And you wonder what the others will think if you have the nerve to disagree. It's your turn now. You rub your eyes and take another look. What do you see? More to the point, what do you do?

● Figure 7.4 gives you a sense of the bind in which Asch's participants found themselves—caught between the need to be right and a desire to be liked (Insko et al., 1982; Ross et al., 1976). As you may suspect by now, the other "participants" were actually confederates and had been trained to make incorrect judgments on 12 out of 18 presentations. There seems little doubt that the real participants

After two uneventful rounds in Asch's study, the participant (seated second from the right) faces a dilemma. The answer he wants to give in the third test of visual discrimination differs from that of the first five confederates, who are all in agreement. Should he give his own answers or conform to theirs?

Archives of the History of American Psychology/University of Akron

knew the correct answers. In a control group, where they made judgments in isolation, they made almost no errors. Yet Asch's participants went along with the incorrect majority 37% of the time—far more often than most of us would ever predict. Not everyone conformed, of course. About 25% refused to agree on any of the incorrect group judgments. Yet 50% went along on at least half of the critical presentations, and remaining participants conformed on an occasional basis. Similarly high levels of conformity were observed when Asch's study was repeated years later and in recent studies involving other cognitive tasks. For example, recent research demonstrates strong conformity effects on memory—as when an eyewitness is influenced by the report of a co-witness (Gabbert et al., 2003; Horry et al., 2012). Asch-like conformity effects are also found in the perceptual judgments of 3- and 4-year-old children (Corriveau et al., 2009; Corriveau & Harris, 2010).

Let's compare Sherif's and Asch's classic studies of social influence. Obviously, both demonstrate that our visual perceptions can be heavily influenced by others. But how similar are they, really? Did Sherif's and Asch's participants exhibit the same kind of conformity and for the same reasons or was the resemblance in their behavior more apparent than real?

From the start, it was clear that these studies differed in some important ways. In Sherif's situation, participants were quite literally "in the dark," so they naturally turned to others for guidance. When physical reality is ambiguous and we are uncertain of our own judgments, as in the autokinetic situation, others can serve as a valuable source of information (Festinger, 1954). In contrast, Asch's participants found themselves in a much more awkward position. Their task was relatively simple, and they could see with their own eyes which answers were correct. Still, they often followed the incorrect majority. In interviews, many of Asch's participants reported afterward that they went along with the group even though they were not convinced that the group was right. Many who did not conform said they felt "conspicuous" and "crazy," like a "misfit" (Asch, 1956, p. 31).

Worldwide, 3.05 billion people, accounting for over 42% of Earth's population, have access to the Internet (Internet World Stats, 2015). This being the case, you may wonder: Do the social forces that influence people in the face-to-face encounters studied by Sherif and Asch also operate in virtual groups whose other members are nameless, faceless, and anonymous? The answer is yes. McKenna and Bargh (1998) observed behavior in various online blogs in which people with common interests posted and responded to messages on a whole range of topics, from obesity and sexual orientation to money and the stock market. The social nature of the medium in this virtual

● **FIGURE 7.4**

Line Judgment Task Used in Asch's Conformity Studies

Which comparison line—A, B, or C—is the same in length as the standard line? What would you say if you found yourself in the presence of a unanimous majority that answered A or C? The participants in Asch's experiments conformed to the majority about a third of the time.
Asch, 1955

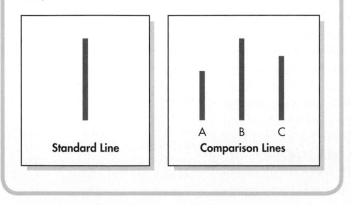

situation was "remote." Still, these researchers found that in newsgroups that brought together people with "hidden identities" (such as gays and lesbians who had concealed their sexuality), members were highly responsive to social feedback. Those who posted messages that were met with approval rather than disapproval later became more active participants of the newsgroup. When it comes to social support and rejection, even remote virtual groups have the power to shape our behavior (Bargh & McKenna, 2004; Kassner et al., 2012; Williams et al., 2000).

> When all members of a group give an incorrect response to an easy question, most people most of the time conform to that response.
> **FALSE**

■ Why Do People Conform?

The Sherif and Asch studies demonstrate that people conform for two very different reasons: one informational, the other normative (Cialdini & Goldstein, 2004; Crutchfield, 1955; Deutsch & Gerard, 1955).

A Need to Be Right   Through **informational influence**, people conform because they want to make good and accurate judgments of reality and assume that when others agree on something, they must be right. In Sherif's autokinetic task, as in other difficult or ambiguous tasks, it's natural to assume that four eyes are better than two. Hence, research shows that eyewitnesses trying to recall a crime or some other event will alter their recollections and even create false memories in response to what they hear other witnesses report (Gabbert et al., 2003).

When people are in a state of uncertainty, following the collective wisdom of others may prove to be an effective strategy. In the popular TV game show *Who Wants to Be a Millionaire?* contestants who were stumped on a question were able to invoke one of two human forms of assistance: (1) calling a friend or relative who served as a designated "expert"; or (2) polling the studio audience, which casted votes by computer for instant feedback. Overall, the "experts" were useful, as they offered the correct answer 65% of the time. Illustrating the wisdom of crowds, however, the studio audiences were even more useful, picking the right answer 91% of the time (Surowiecki, 2005). These days, relying on the collective wisdom of large numbers of other people is something we do all the time. When you look to buy merchandise on Amazon.com, you will see average customer satisfaction ratings from 1 to 5 stars and product reviews; similar ratings can be found on Zagat, Yelp, and OpenTable for restaurants; Expedia.com and TripAdvisor for hotels; Rotten Tomatoes for movies, and, well you get the idea.

A Fear of Ostracism   In contrast to the informational value of conformity, **normative influence** leads people to conform because they fear the consequence of rejection that follows deviance. It's easy to see why. Early on, research showed that individuals who stray from a group's norm tend to be disliked, rejected, ridiculed, and outright dismissed (Schachter, 1951). Although some people are more resilient than others, these forms of interpersonal rejection can be hard to take (Smart Richman & Leary, 2009).

In a series of controlled experiments, people who were socially *ostracized*—for example, by being neglected, ignored, and excluded in a live or online chatroom conversation—react with various types of emotional distress, feeling alone, hurt, angry, and lacking in self-esteem (Williams et al., 2002; Gerber & Wheeler, 2009). Even being left out of a three-way text-messaging conversation on a cell phone can have this effect on us (Smith & Williams, 2004). Kipling Williams and Steve Nida (2011) note that the research on this point is clear: Some people become so distressed when they are ignored or excluded from a group, even one that is newly and briefly formed, that they begin to feel numb, sad, angry, or some combination of these emotions. Over

informational influence   Influence that produces conformity when a person believes others are correct in their judgments.

normative influence   Influence that produces conformity when a person fears the negative social consequences of appearing deviant.

time, ostracism becomes a form of social death, making it difficult to cope.

Why does being ostracized hurt so much? Why, for example, have some teenage victims of cyber bullying, reacted with such devastation that they committed suicide? Increasingly, social psychologists are coming to appreciate the extent to which human beings, over the course of evolution, have needed each other in order to survive and to flourish. According to Geoff MacDonald and Mark Leary (2005), our need to belong is so primitive that rejection can inflict a social pain that feels just like physical pain. You can sense the connection in the way people describe their emotional reactions to social loss using such words as "hurt," "brokenhearted," and "crushed." Social neuroscience research lends provocative support to this linkage. In brain-imaging studies, for example, young people who were left out by other players in a three-person Internet ball-tossing game called "Cyberball" exhibited elevated neural activity in a part of the brain that is normally associated with physical pain (Eisenberger et al., 2003). In some instances, people who are excluded report feeling a heightened sensitivity to pain; in other cases, the experience leads them to feel numb (Bernstein & Claypool, 2012).

"How much do we have to leave to avoid a social-media incident?"

Emily Flake/Conde Nast Collection

A good deal of conformity is driven by a fear of public disapproval.

If there is a silver lining, it is that social pain can have positive motivating effects. Once feeling rejected, people seek to re-affiliate with others, which should increase their sensitivity to social perception cues that signal opportunities for inclusion. In a study that tested this hypothesis, Michael Bernstein and others (2008) found that research participants who were led to feel socially rejected or excluded became more accurate in their ability to distinguish between true smiles, which betray happiness and an openness to interaction, and "masking" smiles, which do not express a genuine emotion. Even young children are highly sensitive to cues that signal ostracism. In one study, 4- and 5-year-old children were shown a cartoon video in which a character repeatedly approached a group at play and was either accepted into the group or excluded. Shortly afterward, all the children were asked to "draw a picture of you and your friend." Interestingly, those who saw the social rejection version of the cartoon drew pictures that placed themselves and their friend closer together and that adults rated as more affiliative (Song et al., 2015).

On final point about being ostracized is important: The effect depends on the source of exclusion and the cultural context. In a fascinating series of studies designed to address this question, Ayse Uskul and Harriet Over (2014) compared farmers and herders in the Eastern Black Sea region of Turkey—two groups that shared the same geographical space, national identity, language, and religion. The farmers, who grow tea and other products, show a high level of interdependence *within* their social network, having to rely heavily on family and neighbors. In contrast, the herders, who sell cattle and dairy products, tend to be more individualistic and independent, moving between neighboring towns and interacting with strangers and others *outside* their immediate social circle. In one study, participants were asked to visualize themselves as the character in a vignette who was socially excluded either by a close other person or by a stranger. They were then asked to rate in various ways how they would feel about themselves. Two important results consistently emerged. First, both groups were more distressed about being excluded by close others than by strangers. Second, the herders felt worse about being excluded by strangers than the farmers did. As a cultural subgroup that relies on strangers to make a living, herders did not make the same ingroup-outgroup distinction that the farmers did. In this domain of social influence, as in others, cultural context plays an important role.

Distinguishing Types of Conformity   In group settings, both informational and normative influences are typically at work. Consider the Asch experiment. Even though many of his participants said they had conformed just to avoid being different, others said that they came to agree with their group's erroneous judgments. Is that possible? At the time, Asch had to rely on what his participants reported in interviews. Thanks to recent developments in social neuroscience, however, researchers can now peer into the socially active brain. In an ingenious medical school study that illustrates the point, Gregory Berns and others (2005) put 32 adults into a visual-spatial perception experiment in which they were asked to "mentally rotate" two geometric objects to determine if they were the same or different (see ● Figure 7.5). As in the original Asch study, participants were accompanied by four confederates who unanimously made incorrect judgments on certain trials. Unlike in the original study, however, participants were placed in an fMRI scanner while engaged in the task. There were two noteworthy results. First, participants conformed to 41% of the group's incorrect judgments. Second, these conforming judgments were accompanied by heightened activity in a part of the brain that controls spatial awareness—not in areas associated with conscious decision making. These results suggest that the group altered perceptions, not just behavior.

The distinction between the two types of social influence—informational and normative—is important, not just for understanding why people conform but because the two sources of influence produce different types of conformity: private and public (Allen, 1965; Kelman, 1961). Like beauty, conformity may be skin deep or it may penetrate beneath the surface. **Private conformity**, also called true acceptance or conversion, describes instances in which others cause us to change not only our overt behavior but our minds as well. To conform at this level is to be truly persuaded that others in a group are correct. In contrast, **public conformity** (sometimes called *compliance*, a term used later in this chapter to describe a different form of influence) refers to a more superficial change in behavior. People often respond to normative pressures by

● **FIGURE 7.5**

Conformity Effects on Perception

In this study, participants tried to determine if pairs of geometric objects were the same or different after observing the responses of four unanimous confederates. Participants followed the incorrect group 41% of the time. Suggesting that the group had altered perceptions, not just behavior, fMRI results showed that these conforming judgments were accompanied by increased activity in a part of the brain that controls spatial awareness. Berns et al., 2005

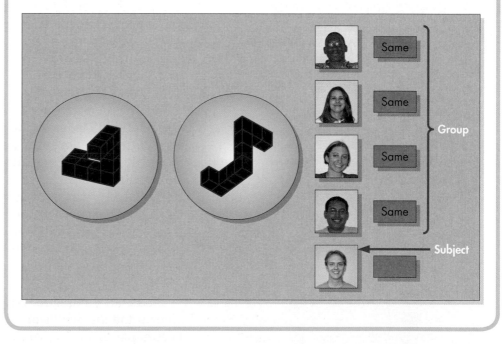

private conformity   The change of beliefs that occurs when a person privately accepts the position taken by others.

public conformity   A superficial change in overt behavior without a corresponding change of opinion that is produced by real or imagined group pressure.

pretending to agree even when privately they do not. This often happens when we want to curry favor with others. The politician who tells voters whatever they want to hear is a case in point.

How, you might be wondering, can social psychologists ever tell the difference between the private and public conformist? After all, both exhibit the same change in their observable behavior. The difference is that compared with someone who merely acquiesces in public, the individual who is truly persuaded maintains that change long after the group is out of the picture. When this distinction is applied to Sherif's and Asch's research, the results come out as expected. At the end of his study, Sherif (1936) retested participants alone and found that their estimates continued to reflect the norm previously established in their group—even among those who were retested a full year after the experiment (Rohrer et al., 1954). Similar results were recently reported in a study in which college students rated the attractiveness of various faces, were shown the average higher or lower results from other students, and then re-rated the same faces—one, three, or seven days or three months later. In this situation, the conformity effect lasted three to seven days (Huang et al., 2014). Yet in contrast to these results, Asch (1956) himself had reported that when he had participants write their answers privately, so that others in the group could not see, their level of conformity dropped sharply (Deutsch & Gerard, 1955; Mouton et al., 1956).

In a study that showed both processes at work, Robert S. Baron and others (1996) had people in groups of three (one participant, two confederates) act as eyewitnesses: First, they would see a picture of a person, then they would try to pick that person out of a lineup. In some groups, the task was difficult, like Sherif's, since participants saw each picture only once for half a second. For other groups, the task was easier, like Asch's, in that they saw each picture twice for a total of 10 seconds. How often did participants conform when the confederates made the wrong identification? It depended on how motivated they were. When the experimenter downplayed the task as only a "pilot study," the conformity rates were 35% when the task was difficult and 33% when it was easy. But when participants were offered a financial incentive to do well, conformity went up to 51% when the task was difficult and down to 16% when it was easy (see ● Figure 7.6). With pride and money on the line, the Sherif-like participants conformed more and the Asch-like participants conformed less.

Table 7.1 summarizes the comparison of Sherif's and Asch's studies and the depths of social influence that they demonstrate. Looking at this table, you can see that the difficulty of the task is crucial. When reality cannot easily be validated by physical evidence, as in the autokinetic situation, people turn to others for information and conform because they are truly persuaded by that information. When reality is clear, however, the cost of dissent becomes the major issue. As Asch found, it can be difficult to depart too much from others even when you know that they—not you—are wrong. So you play along. Privately you don't change your mind. But you nod your head in agreement anyway.

● FIGURE 7.6

Distinguishing Types of Conformity

People made judgments under conditions in which they had a high or low level of motivation. Regardless of whether the judgment task was difficult or easy, there were moderate levels of conformity when participants had low motivation (left). But when they were highly motivated (right), participants conformed more when the task was difficult (as in Sherif's study) and less when it was easy (as in Asch's study).

From Baron, R. et al., (1996). *Journal of Personality and Social Psychology* vol 71 (pp. 915–927).

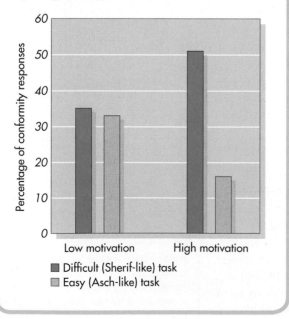

> ▲ **TABLE 7.1**
>
> **Two Types of Conformity**
>
> A comparison of Sherif's and Asch's studies suggests different kinds of conformity for different reasons. Sherif used an ambiguous task, so others provided a source of information and influenced the participants' true opinions. Asch used a task that required simple judgments of a clear stimulus, so most participants exhibited occasional public conformity in response to normative pressure but privately did not accept the group's judgments.
>
> | Experimental Task | Primary Effect of Group | Depth of Conformity Produced |
> | --- | --- | --- |
> | Sherif's ambiguous autokinetic effect | Informational influence | Private acceptance |
> | Asch's simple-line judgments | Normative influence | Public conformity |
>
> © Cengage Learning®

Majority Influence

Realizing that people often succumb to pressure from peers is only a first step in understanding the process of social influence. The next step is to identify the situational and personal factors that make us more or less likely to conform. We know that people tend to conform when the social pressure is intense and that they are insecure about how to behave. But what creates these feelings of pressure and insecurity? Here, we look at four factors: the size of the group, a focus on norms, the presence of an ally, and gender.

Group Size: The Power in Numbers   Common sense would suggest that as the number of other people in a majority increases, so should their impact. Actually, it is not that simple. Asch (1956) varied the size of groups, using 1, 2, 3, 4, 8, or 15 confederates, and he found that conformity increased with group size—but only up to a point. Once there were 3 or 4 confederates, the amount of *additional* influence exerted by the rest was negligible. Other researchers have obtained similar results (Gerard et al., 1968).

Beyond the presence of three or four others, additions to a group are subject to the law of "diminishing returns" (Knowles, 1983; Mullen, 1983). As we will see later, Bibb Latané (1981) likens the influence of people on an individual to the way lightbulbs illuminate a surface. When a second bulb is added to a room, the effect is dramatic. When the tenth bulb is added, however, its impact is barely felt, if at all. Economists say the same about the perception of money. An additional dollar seems greater to the person who has only three dollars than it does to the person who has 300.

Another possible explanation is that as more and more people express the same opinion, an individual is likely to suspect that they are acting either in "collusion" or as "spineless sheep." According to David Wilder (1977), what matters is not the actual number of others in a group but one's perception of how many distinct others who are thinking independently the group includes. Indeed, Wilder found that people were more influenced by two groups of two than by one four-person group and by two groups of three than by one six-person group. Conformity increased even more when people were exposed to three two-person groups. When faced with a majority opinion, we do more than just count the number of warm bodies—we try to assess the number of independent minds.

A Focus on Norms   The size of a majority may influence the amount of pressure that is felt, but social norms give rise to conformity only when we know the norms and focus on them. This may sound like an obvious point, yet we often misperceive what is normative, particularly when others are too afraid or too embarrassed to publicly present their true thoughts, feelings, and behaviors.

One common example of this "pluralistic ignorance" concerns perceptions of alcohol usage. In a number of college-wide surveys, Deborah Prentice and Dale Miller (1996) found that most students overestimated how comfortable their peers were with the level of drinking on campus. Those who most over-estimated how others felt about drinking at the start of the school year eventually conformed to this misperception in their own attitudes and behavior. In contrast, students who took part in discussion sessions that were designed to correct these misperceptions actually consumed less alcohol six months later. These findings are important. Additional research has shown that both male and female students tend to overestimate how frequently their same-sex peers use various substances and the quantities they consume. Whether the substance in question is alcohol, tobacco, or marijuana, the more normative students perceive peer usage to be, the more they consume (Henry et al., 2011). More generally, across a range of situations and intervention purposes, changing people's perceptions of norms can be used to change their behavior (Miller & Prentice, 2016).

Knowing how others are behaving in a situation is necessary for conformity, but these norms will influence us only when they are brought to our awareness, or "activated." Robert Cialdini (2003) and his colleagues have demonstrated this point in studies on littering. In one study, researchers had confederates pass out handbills to amusement park visitors and varied the amount of litter that appeared in one section of the park (an indication of how others behave in that set-ting). The result: The more litter there was, the more likely visitors were to toss their handbills to the ground (Cialdini et al., 1990).

A second study showed that passersby were most influenced by the prior behavior of others when their attention was drawn to the existing norm. In this instance, people were observed in a parking garage that was either clean or cluttered with cigarette butts, candy wrappers, paper cups, and trash. In half of the cases, the norm that was already in place—clean or cluttered—was brought to participants' attention by a confederate who threw paper to the ground as he walked by. In the other half, the confederate passed by without incident. As participants reached their cars, they found a "Please Drive Safely" handbill tucked under the windshield wiper. Did they toss the paper to the ground or take it with them? The results showed that people were most likely to conform (by littering more when the garage was cluttered than when it was clean) when the confederate had littered—an act that drew attention to the norm (Cialdini et al., 1991).

An Ally in Dissent: Getting by With a Little Help   In Asch's initial experi-ment, unwitting participants found themselves pitted against unanimous majori-ties. But what if they had an ally, a partner in dissent? Asch investigated this issue and found that the presence of a single confederate who agreed with the partici-pant reduced conformity by almost 80%. This finding, however, does not tell us why the presence of an ally was so effective. Was it because he or she *agreed with the participant* or because he or she *disagreed with the majority*? In other words, were the views of the participants strengthened because a dissenting confederate offered validating information or because dissent per se reduced normative pressures?

A series of experiments explored these two possibilities. In one, Vernon Allen and John Levine (1969) led participants to believe that they were working together with four confederates. Three of these others consistently agreed on the wrong judgment. The fourth then followed the majority, agreed with the participant, or made a third judgment, which was also incorrect. This last variation was the most interesting: Even when the confederate did not validate their own judgment, participants conformed less often to the majority. In another experiment, Allen and Levine (1971) varied the competence of the ally. Some participants received support from an average person. In contrast, others found themselves supported by someone who wore very thick glasses and complained that he could not see the visual displays. Not a very reassuring ally, right? Wrong. Even though participants derived less comfort from this supporter than from one who seemed more competent at the task, his presence still reduced their level of conformity.

Two important conclusions follow from this research. First, it is substantially more difficult for people to stand alone for their convictions than to be part of even a tiny minority. Second, *any* dissent—whether it validates an individual's opinion or not—can break the spell cast by a unanimous majority and reduce the normative pressures to conform. In an interesting possible illustration of how uncommon it is for individuals to single-handedly oppose a majority, researchers examined voting patterns on the U.S. Supreme Court from 1953 to 2001. Table 7.2 shows that out of 4,178 decisions in which all nine justices voted, the 8-to-1 split was the least frequent, occurring in only 10% of all decisions (Granberg & Bartels, 2005).

Gender Differences   Are there gender differences in conformity? Based on Asch's initial studies, social psychologists used to think that women, once considered the "weaker" sex, conform more than men. In light of all the research, however, it appears that two additional factors have to be considered. First, sex differences depend on how comfortable people are with the experimental task. In a classic study, Frank Sistrunk and John McDavid (1971) had male and female participants answer questions on stereotypically masculine, feminine, and gender-neutral topics. Along with each question, participants were told the percentage of others who agreed or disagreed. Although females conformed to the contrived majority more on masculine items, males conformed more on feminine items. There were no sex differences on the neutral questions. This finding suggests that one's familiarity with the issue at hand, not gender, is what affects conformity (Eagly & Carli, 1981).

A second factor is the type of social situation people face. As a general rule, gender differences are weak and unreliable. But there is an important exception: In face-to-face encounters, where people must disagree with each other openly, small differences do emerge. In fact, when participants think

▲ **TABLE 7.2**

On Being a Lone Dissenter: Voting Patterns on the U.S. Supreme Court

Out of 4,178 U.S. Supreme Court decisions handed down from 1953 to 2001, the 8-to-1 breakdown involving a lone dissenter was the least common type of vote. This historical observation is consistent with conformity research showing the power of the majority over an individual who lacks an ally

Vote Breakdowns	Frequency
9 to 0	35%
8 to 1	10%
7 to 2	14%
6 to 3	20%
5 to 4	21%

Granberg & Bartels, 2005

they are being observed, women conform more and men conform less than they do in a more private situation. Why does being "in public" create such a divergence in behavior? Alice Eagly (1987) argues that in front of others, people worry about how they come across and feel pressured to behave in ways that are viewed as acceptable according to traditional gender-role constraints. At least in public, men feel pressured to behave with fierce independence and autonomy, whereas women are expected to play a gentler, more harmonious role.

From an evolutionary perspective, Vladas Griskevicius and others (2006) suggest that people are most likely to behave in gender-stereotyped ways when motivated to attract someone of the opposite sex. Consistent with the stereotypic notion that women tend to like men who distinguish themselves as independent and dominant, whereas men prefer women who are agreeable and cooperative, their research shows that women conform more—and that men conform less—when primed to think about themselves in a romantic situation. But here's the interesting part: When Matthew Hornsey and others (2015) asked people in a series of experiments to indicate their personal preferences for a romantic partner, both men and women alike were attracted to others who are *non*conformists. This pairing of results begs the question: Why did female participants in the first study present themselves as conformist to attract a male partner when men in the second set of studies consistently expressed a preference for *non*conformist women? Although more research is needed, these studies seem to suggest that women harbor the belief that men like conformist women—a belief, grounded in the past, that may well turn out to be a myth.

The Guardian/Handout/Getty Images News/Getty Images

This image, from the 2014 documentary *CitizenFour*, shows ex-CIA employee Edward Snowden, on the days when he leaked classified information from the U.S. National Security Agency (NSA). The information disclosed a massive surveillance program, which spied on U.S. citizens without a warrant. Although his disclosures proved accurate and sparked reform, the U.S. government charged Snowden with the crime of espionage, causing him to flee. He was granted temporary asylum in Russia, where he now lives. Engaging in one of the most profound acts of dissent in modern history, Snowden has been variously called a hero, a whistleblower, a patriot, and a traitor.

■ Minority Influence

In a book entitled *Dissent in Dangerous Times*, Austin Sarat (2005) noted that while the freedom to dissent is highly valued in the American national psyche, individual dissenters are often vilified for their beliefs—especially in today's post-9/11 war on terrorism.

The fact is, it has never been easy for individuals to express unpopular views and enlist support for these views from others. Philosopher Bertrand Russell once said, "Conventional people are roused to frenzy by departure from convention, largely because they regard such departure as criticism of themselves." He may have been right. Although people who assert their beliefs against the majority are generally seen as competent and honest, they are also disliked and roundly rejected (Bassili & Provencal, 1988; Levine, 1989). It's no wonder that most people think twice before expressing unpopular positions. In a series of survey studies of what he called the "minority slowness effect," John Bassili (2003) asked people about their attitudes on social policy issues such as affirmative action or about their likes and dislikes for various celebrities, sports, foods, places, and activities. Consistently, and regardless of the topic, respondents who held minority opinions were slower to answer the questions than those in the majority.

Resisting the pressure to conform and maintaining one's independence may be socially difficult, but it is not impossible. History's most famous heroes, villains, and creative minds are living proof: Joan of Arc, Jesus Christ, Galileo, Charles Darwin, Mahatma Gandhi, and Nelson Mandela, to name just a few, were dissenters of their time who continue to capture the imagination. Then there is human behavior in the laboratory. Social psychologists have been so intrigued by Asch's initial finding that participants conformed 37% of the time that textbooks such as this one routinely refer to "Asch's conformity study." Yet the overlooked flip side of the coin is that Asch's participants refused to acquiesce 63% of the time—thus also indicating the power of independence, truth telling, and a concern for social harmony (Friend et al., 1990; Hodges & Geyer, 2006; Jetten & Hornsey, 2011).

Twelve Angry Men, a classic film starring Henry Fonda, illustrates how a lone dissenter can resist the pressure to conform and convince others to follow. Almost as soon as the door of the jury room closes, the jury in this film takes a show-of-hands vote. The result is an 11-to-1 majority in favor of conviction with Fonda the lone holdout. Through 90 minutes of heated deliberation, Fonda works relentlessly to plant a seed of doubt in the minds of his peers. In the end, the jury reaches a unanimous verdict: *not* guilty.

Sometimes art imitates life; sometimes it does not. In this instance, Henry Fonda's heroics are highly atypical. When it comes to jury decision making, as we'll see in Chapter 12, the majority usually wins. Yet in trial juries, as in other small groups, there are occasional exceptions where minorities prevail—as when someone from the majority faction defects. Thanks to Serge Moscovici and others, we now know quite a bit about **minority influence** and the strategies that astute nonconformists use to act as agents of social change (Gardikiotis, 2011; Maass & Clark, 1984; Moscovici et al., 1985; Mugny & Perez, 1991).

Moscovici's Theory   According to Moscovici, majorities are powerful by virtue of their sheer *numbers,* whereas nonconformists derive power from the *style* of their behavior. It is not just what nonconformists say that matters but how they say it. To exert influence, says Moscovici, those in the minority must be forceful, persistent, and unwavering in support of their position. Yet at the same time, they must appear flexible and open-minded. Confronted with a consistent but even-handed dissenter, members of the majority will sit up, take notice, and rethink their own positions.

Why should a consistent behavioral style prove effective? One possible reason is that unwavering repetition draws attention from those in the mainstream, which is a necessary first step to social influence. Another possibility is that consistency signals that the dissenter is unlikely to yield, which leads those in the majority to feel pressured to seek compromise. A third possible reason is that when confronted with someone who has the self-confidence and dedication to take an unpopular stand without backing down, people assume that he or she must have a point. Of course, it helps to be seen as part of "us" rather than "them." Research shows that dissenters have more influence when people identify with them and perceive them to be similar in ways that are relevant and desirable (Turner, 1991; Wood et al., 1996).

Based on a meta-analysis of 97 experiments investigating minority influence, Wendy Wood and her colleagues (1994) concluded that there is strong support for the consistency hypothesis. In one classic study, for example, Moscovici and others (1969) turned Asch's procedure on its head by confronting people with a *minority* of confederates who made incorrect judgments. In groups of six, participants took part in what was supposed to be a study of color perception. They viewed a series of slides that all were blue but varied in intensity. For each slide, the participants took turns naming the color. The task was simple, but two confederates announced that the slides were green. When the confederates were *consistent*—that

minority influence   The process by which dissenters produce change within a group.

is, when both made incorrect green judgments for all slides—they had a surprising degree of influence. About a third of all participants incorrectly reported seeing at least one green slide, and 8% of all responses were incorrect. Subsequent research confirmed that the perception of consistency increases minority influence (Clark, 2001; Crano, 2000).

Noting that social dissent can also breed hostility, Edwin Hollander (1958) recommended a different approach. Hollander warned that people who seek positions of leadership or challenge a group without first becoming accepted full-fledged members of that group run the risk that their opinions will fall on deaf ears. As an alternative to Moscovici's consistency strategy, Hollander suggested that to influence a majority, people should first conform in order to establish their credentials as competent insiders. By becoming members of the mainstream, they accumulate **idiosyncrasy credits**, or "brownie points." Once they have accumulated enough goodwill within the group, a certain amount of their deviance will then be tolerated. Several studies have shown that this "first conform, then dissent" strategy, like the "consistent dissent" approach, can be effective (Bray et al., 1982; Lortie-Lussier, 1987; Rijnbout & McKimmie, 2012).

Processes and Outcomes of Minority Influence Regardless of which strategy is used, minority influence is a force to be reckoned with. But does it work just like conformity, or is there something different about the way minorities and majorities effect change? Some theorists have proposed that a *single process* accounts for both directions of social influence—that minority influence is like a "chip off the old block" (Latané & Wolf, 1981; Tanford & Penrod, 1984). Others have taken a *dual-process* approach (Moscovici, 1980; Nemeth, 1986). In this second view, majorities and minorities exert influence in different ways and for different reasons. Majorities, because they have power and control, elicit *public* conformity by bringing stressful normative pressures to bear on the individual. But minorities, because they are seen as seriously committed to their views, produce a deeper and more lasting form of *private* conformity, or *conversion,* by leading others to become curious and rethink their original positions.

To evaluate these single- and dual-process theories, researchers have compared the effects of majority and minority viewpoints on participants who are otherwise neutral on an issue in dispute. On the basis of this research, two conclusions can be drawn. First, the relative impact of majorities and minorities depends on whether the judgment that is being made is objective or subjective, a matter of fact or opinion. In a study conducted in Italy, Anne Maass and others (1996) found that majorities have greater influence on factual questions, for which only one answer is correct ("What percentage of its raw oil does Italy import from Venezuela?"), but that minorities exert equal impact on opinion questions, for which there is a range of acceptable responses ("What percentage of its raw oil *should* Italy import from Venezuela?"). People feel freer to stray from the mainstream on matters of opinion, when there is no right or wrong answer.

The second conclusion is that the relative effects of majority and minority points of view depend on how and when conformity is measured. To be sure, majorities have a decisive upper hand on direct or public measures of conformity. After all, people are reluctant to oppose a group norm in a conspicuous manner. But on more indirect or private measures of conformity, on attitude issues that are related but not focal to the point of conflict, or after the passage of time—all of which softens the extent to which majority

idiosyncrasy credits Interpersonal "credits" that a person earns by following group norms.

participants would appear deviant—minorities exert a strong impact (Clark & Maass, 1990; Crano & Seyranian, 2009; Moscovici & Personnaz, 1991). As Moscovici cogently argued, each of us is changed in a meaningful but subtle way by minority opinion.

In *Rogues, Rebels and Dissent: Just Because Everyone Agrees, Doesn't Mean They're Right,* Charlan Nemeth (2016) reviews more than 30 years of research indicating that dissenters in a group serve an invaluable purpose—regardless of whether their views are correct. Dissenters may feel like a nuisance, she notes, and an unnecessary source of conflict, forcing others to defend a position that everyone else agrees with. Yet research shows that dissent sparks innovation (De Dreu & De Vries, 2001).

Simply by their willingness to stay firmly independent, minorities can force other group members to think more carefully, more openly, in new and different ways, and more creatively about a problem, enhancing the quality of a group's output. In one study, participants exposed to a minority viewpoint on how to solve anagram problems later found more novel solutions themselves (Nemeth & Kwan, 1987). In a second study, those exposed to a consistent minority viewpoint on how best to recall information later recalled more words from a list they were trying to memorize (Nemeth et al., 1990). In a third study, interacting groups with one dissenting confederate produced more original analyses of complex business problems (Van Dyne & Saavedra, 1996). Importantly, Nemeth and her colleagues (2001) found that to have influence over a group, lone individuals must exhibit "authentic dissent," not merely play "devil's advocate," a tactic that actually bolsters a majority's position.

■ Culture and Conformity

We humans are a heterogeneous and diverse lot. As a matter of *geography,* some of us live in large, heavily populated cities whereas others live in small towns, affluent suburbs, rural farming or fishing communities, jungles, expansive deserts, high-altitude mountains, tropical islands, and vast arctic plains. Excluding dialects, more than 6,500 different *languages* are spoken. There are also hundreds of *religions* that people identify with—the most common being Christianity (32%), Islam (23%), Hinduism (14%), and Buddhism (8%), with Judaism (0.20%) and others claiming fewer adherents. Roughly 15% of the world's population is not affiliated with a religion (Adherents.com, 2015).

Linked together by historical time and geographical space, each culture has its own ideology, music, fashions, foods, laws, customs, and manners of expression. As many tourists and exchange students traveling abroad have come to learn, sometimes the hard way, the social norms that influence human conduct can vary in significant ways from one part of the world to another.

In *Do's and Taboos Around the World,* R. E. Axtell (1993) warns world travelers about some of these differences. Dine in an Indian home, he notes, and you should leave food on the plate to show the host that the portions were generous and you had enough to eat. Yet as a dinner guest in Bolivia, you would show your appreciation by cleaning your plate. Shop in an outdoor market in Iraq, and you should expect to negotiate the price of everything you buy. Plan an appointment in Brazil, and the person you're scheduled to meet is likely to be late; it's nothing personal. In North America, it is common to sit casually opposite someone with your legs outstretched. Yet in Nepal, as in many Muslim countries, it is an insult to point the bottoms of your feet at

Cultures differ in their unique, often colorful norms. In Nigeria it's common to ask guests to wear color-coordinated outfits, called *aso ebi*, at social events, such as this wedding in Lagos (top left). In Mumbai, India, a man smears a woman's face with brightly colored powders in the festival of Holi, which marks the beginning of spring (top right). In Spain, revelers in Pamplona hold up their bandanas before the festival of San Fermín, during which six bulls run through the crowded streets in the center of town (bottom left).

individualism   A cultural orientation in which independence, autonomy, and self-reliance take priority over group allegiances.

collectivism   A cultural orientation in which interdependence, cooperation, and social harmony take priority over personal goals.

someone. Even the way we space ourselves from each other is influenced by culture. Americans, Canadians, British, and northern Europeans keep a polite distance between themselves and others and feel "crowded" by the touchier, nose-to-nose style of the French, Greeks, Arabs, Mexicans, and people of South America. In the affairs of day-to-day living, each culture operates by its own rules of conduct.

Just as cultures differ in their social norms, so too they differ in the extent to which people are expected to adhere to those norms. As we saw in Chapter 3, there are different cultural orientations toward persons and their relationships to groups. Some cultures primarily value **individualism** and the virtues of independence, autonomy, and self-reliance, whereas others value **collectivism** and the virtues of interdependence, cooperation, and social harmony. Under a banner of individualism, personal goals take priority over group allegiances. Yet in collectivistic cultures, the person is first and foremost a loyal member of a family, city, team, company, church, and state.

What determines whether a culture becomes individualistic or collectivistic? Speculating on the origins of these orientations, Harry Triandis (1995) suggested that there are three key factors. The first is the *complexity* of a society. As people come to live in more complex industrialized societies (compared, for example, with a simpler life of food gathering among desert nomads), there are more groups to identify with, which means less loyalty to any one group and a greater focus on personal rather than collective goals. Second is the *affluence* of a society. As people prosper, they gain financial independence from others, a condition that promotes social independence as well as mobility and a focus on personal rather than collective goals. The third factor is *heterogeneity*. Societies that are homogeneous or "tight" (where members share the same language, religion, and social customs) tend to be rigid and intolerant of those who veer from the norm. Societies that are culturally diverse or "loose" (where two or more cultures co-exist) tend to be more permissive of dissent, thus allowing for more individual expression. According to Edward Sampson (2000), cultural orientations may also be rooted in religious ideologies, as in the link between Christianity and individualism.

Early research across nations showed that autonomy and independence were most highly valued in the United States, Australia, Great Britain, Canada, and the Netherlands, in that order. In contrast, other cultures value social harmony and "fitting in" for the sake of community, the most collectivist people being from Venezuela, Colombia, Pakistan, Peru, Taiwan, and China (Hofstede, 1980). Although research shows that the differences are even more complicated, that individuals differ even within cultures, and that cultures change over time, it is clear that nations on average vary in their orientations on the dimension of individualism (Schimmack et al., 2005). The difference can be measured in books and other written materials—by the contents of the stories told (Imada, 2012) and the use of the first-person singular pronouns, "I" and "me" (Hamamura & Xu, 2015; Twenge et al., 2013).

Do cultural orientations influence conformity? Among the Bantu of Zimbabwe, an African people in which deviance is scorned, 51% of participants who were placed in an Asch-like study conformed—more than the number typically seen in the United States (Whittaker & Meade, 1967). When John Berry (1979) compared participants from 17 cultures, he found that conformity rates ranged from a low of 18% among Inuit hunters of Baffin Island to a high of 60% among village-dwelling Temne farmers of West Africa. Additional analyses have shown that conformity rates are generally higher in cultures that are collectivistic rather than individualistic in orientation (Bond & Smith, 1996). Hence, many anthropologists—interested in human culture and its influence over individuals—study the processes of conformity and independence (Spradley et al., 2015).

Wenn Ltd/Alamy

Say what you think
Love who you love
'Cause you just get
So many trips 'round the sun…
Follow your arrow
Wherever it points.

Country musician Kacey Musgraves performs her hit song, *Follow Your Arrow*. Read the lyrics above and you will see that the song expresses a cultural value of "individualism."

Compliance

In conformity situations, people follow implicit or explicit group norms. But another common form of social influence occurs when others make *direct requests* of us in the hope that we will comply. Situations that call for **compliance** take many forms. These include a friend's plea for help, sheepishly prefaced by the question "Can you do me a favor?" They also include the pop-up ads on the Internet designed to lure you into a commercial site and the salesperson's pitch for business prefaced by the dangerous words "Have I got a deal for you!" Sometimes, the request is up front and direct; what you see is what you get. At other times, it is part of a subtle and more elaborate manipulation.

How do people get others to comply with self-serving requests? How do police interrogators get crime suspects to confess? How do political parties and charitable organizations draw millions of dollars in contributions from voters? How do *you* exert influence over others? Do you use threats, promises, politeness, deceit, or reason? Do you hint, coax, sulk, negotiate, trick, throw tantrums, or pull rank whenever you can? To a large extent, the compliance strategies we use depend on how well we know the person we target, our status within a relationship, our personality, our culture, and the nature of the request.

By observing the masters of influence—advertisers, fund-raisers, politicians, and business leaders—social psychologists have learned a great deal about the

compliance Changes in behavior that are elicited by direct requests.

subtle but effective strategies that are commonly used. What they have discovered is that people often get others to comply with their requests by setting subtle psychological traps. Once caught in these traps, the unwary victim finds it difficult to escape. Anthony Pratkanis (2007) identified 107 methods of social influence that have been researched and published. These tactics go by various colorful names, including *the lure*, the *1-in-5 prize technique*, the *dump-and-chase technique*, the *disrupt-then-reframe* technique, and the *driving toward a goal* technique. In the coming pages, some of the best known approaches will be described.

■ Mindlessness and Compliance

Sometimes people can be disarmed by the simple phrasing of a request, regardless of its merit. Consider, for example, requests that sound reasonable but offer no real basis for compliance. Ellen Langer and her colleagues (1978) have found that words alone can sometimes trick us into submission. In their research, an experimenter approached people who were using a library copying machine and asked to cut in. Three different versions of the request were used. In one, participants were simply asked, "Excuse me. I have five pages. May I use the Xerox machine?" In a second version, the request was justified by the added phrase "because I'm in a rush." As you would expect, more participants stepped aside when the request was justified (94%) than when it was not (60%). A third version of the request, however, suggests that the actual reason offered had little to do with the increase in compliance. In this case, participants heard the following: "Excuse me. I have five pages. May I use the Xerox machine because I have to make some copies?" Huh? Read this request closely and you'll see that it really offered no reason at all. Yet 93% in this condition complied! It was as if the appearance of a reason, triggered by the word *because,* was all that was needed. In fact, Langer (1989) finds that the mind is often on "automatic pilot"—we respond *mindlessly* to words without fully processing the information they are supposed to convey. At least for requests that are small, "sweet little nothings" may be enough to win compliance.

Langer's research shows that sometimes we process oral requests lazily, without critical thought. In these instances, words alone, if they sound good, can be used to elicit compliance. Consider, for example, words that evoke the concept of freedom. In a series of experiments, researchers found that merely by inserting the phrase "*But you are free* to accept or refuse this request" into a plea, they were able to increase the numbers of people who agreed to donate money, give someone a cigarette, fill out a survey, and buy pancakes. This technique increased compliance consistently in face-to-face requests, on the street and in shopping malls, by mail, over the phone, and on the internet (Guéguen et al., 2013). In a meta-analysis of 42 attempts involving more than 22,000 participants, mostly in France, Christopher Carpenter (2013) concluded that the technique of evoking freedom through words is consistently effective.

It is interesting that although a state of mindlessness can make us vulnerable to compliance, it can also have the opposite effect. For example, many city dwellers will automatically walk past panhandlers on the street looking for a handout. Perhaps the way to increase compliance in such situations is to disrupt this mindless refusal response by making a request that is so unusual that it piques the target person's interest. To test the effect of this *pique technique*, researchers had a confederate approach people on the street and make a request that was either typical ("Can you spare a quarter?") or atypical ("Can you spare 17 cents?"). The result: Atypical pleas elicited more comments

Con artists prosper from the tendency for people to respond mindlessly to requests that sound reasonable but offer no real basis for compliance.

Robert Mankoff/Conde Nast Collection

and questions from those who were targeted—and produced a 60% increase in the number of people who gave money (Santos et al., 1994). In another study, researchers who went door to door selling holiday cards gained more compliance when they disrupted the mindless process and reframed the sales pitch. They sold more cards when they said the price was "three hundred pennies—that's three dollars, it's a bargain" than when they simply asked for three dollars (Davis & Knowles, 1999).

■ The Norm of Reciprocity

One of us recently used Lyft for the first time. Lyft is a peer-to-peer ridesharing company whose service connects drivers in the area to prospective passengers via a mobile app. Founded in 2013, in San Francisco, Lyft is a taxi service that competes with Uber. After arriving at the GPS-set destination and completing credit card payment for the ride, this author received from Lyft a request to rate the driver on a 5-point scale (to help ensure customer satisfaction, average driver ratings can be found on the Lyft app). That was easy. He was a 5. The car was clean and comfortable; the ride was quick; the conversation was interesting. The next day, this author was notified that the driver had rated *him* a 5. Not only does the company seek passenger ratings of drivers but also driver ratings of passengers! The author/passenger being a social psychologist, he could not resist wondering: Had he "earned the 5 rating, or was it "payback" for his prior high rating of the driver?

A simple, unstated, but powerful rule of social behavior known as the *norm of reciprocity* dictates that we treat others as they have treated us (Gouldner, 1960). On the negative side, this norm can be used to sanction retaliation against those who cause us harm—as captured in the expression "an eye for an eye." On the positive side, reciprocity can lead us to feel obligated to repay others for acts of kindness. Thus, whenever we receive gifts, invitations, compliments, and free samples, we usually go out of our way to return the favor.

The norm of reciprocity contributes to the predictability and fairness of social interaction. But it can also be used to exploit us. Dennis Regan (1971) examined this possibility in the following laboratory study. Individuals were brought together with a confederate who was trained to act in a likable or unlikable manner for an experiment on "aesthetics." In one condition, the confederate did the participant an unsolicited favor. He left during a break and returned with two bottles of Coca-Cola, one for himself and the other for the participant. In a second condition, he returned from the break empty-handed. In a third condition, participants were treated to a Coke, but by the experimenter, not the confederate. The confederate then told participants in all conditions that he was selling raffle tickets at 25 cents apiece and asked if they would be willing to buy any. On average, participants bought more raffle tickets when the confederate had earlier brought them a soft drink than when he had not. The norm of reciprocity was so strong that they returned the favor even when the confederate was not otherwise a likable character. In fact, participants in this condition spent an average of 43 cents on raffle tickets. At a time when soft drinks cost less than a quarter, the confederate made a handsome quick profit on his investment!

It's clear that the norm of reciprocity can be used to trap us, unwittingly, into acts of compliance. For example, research conducted in restaurants shows that waiters and waitresses can increase their tip percentages by writing, "Thank you" on the back of the customer's check, by drawing a happy face on it, or by placing candy on the check tray (Rind & Strohmetz, 2001; Strohmetz et al., 2002). But does receiving a favor make us feel indebted forever or is there a time limit to the social obligation that is so quietly unleashed? In an experiment designed to answer this question, Jerry Burger and others (1997) used Regan's soft drink favor and had the confederate try to "cash in" with a request either immediately or one week later. The

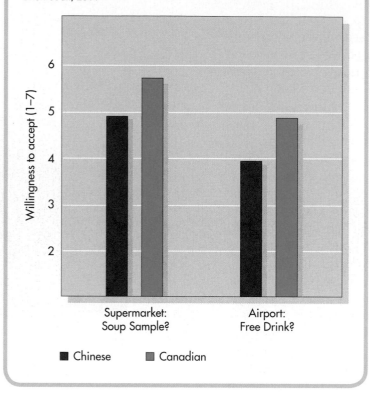

● **FIGURE 7.7**

People from China and Canada rated the likelihood that they would accept a free sample of soup in a supermarket (left) or a free drink from a casual friend at an airport (right). Feeling a greater burden to reciprocate, Chinese participants in both cases said they were less likely to accept the gift.
Shen et al., 2011

result: Compliance levels increased in the immediate condition but not after a full week had passed. People may feel compelled to reciprocate, but that feeling—at least for small acts of kindness—is relatively short-lived.

Some people are more likely than others to trigger and exploit the reciprocity norm. According to Martin Greenberg and David Westcott (1983), individuals who use reciprocity to elicit compliance are called "creditors" because they always try to keep others in their debt so they can cash in when necessary. On a questionnaire that measures *reciprocation ideology,* people are identified as creditors if they endorse such statements as "If someone does you a favor, it's good to repay that person with a greater favor." On the receiving end, some people try more than others not to accept favors that might later set them up to be exploited. On a scale that measures *reciprocation wariness,* people are said to be wary if they express the suspicion, for example, that "asking for another's help gives them power over your life" (Eisenberger et al., 1987).

Cultures may also differ in terms of their reciprocation wariness—with interesting consequences for social behavior. Imagine that you bump into a casual friend at the airport, stop for a drink, and the friend offers to pay for it. Would you let the friend pay? Or, suppose a sales clerk in a supermarket offered you a free sample of soup to taste. Would you accept the offer? Theorizing that the norm of reciprocity operates with particular force in collectivist cultures that foster interdependence, Hao Shen and others (2011) conducted a series of studies in which they posed these kinds of questions to Chinese college students from Hong Kong and to European American students from Canada. As you can see in ● Figure 7.7, the students from China were consistently less willing to accept the favor. Additional questioning revealed that these participants were more likely to see the gift giver's motives as self-serving and to feel uncomfortably indebted by the situation.

Setting Traps: Sequential Request Strategies

People who raise money or sell for a living know that it often takes more than a single plea to win over a potential donor or customer. Social psychologists share this knowledge and have studied several compliance techniques that are based on making two or more related requests. *Click!* The first request sets the trap. *Snap!* The second captures the prey. In a classic and important book entitled *Influence: Science and Practice,* Robert Cialdini (2009) described a number of sequential request tactics in vivid detail. Other social psychologists have continued in this tradition (Dolinski, 2016; Kenrick et al., 2012). The best known of these methods are presented in the following pages.

The Foot in the Door Folk wisdom has it that one way to get a person to comply with a sizable request is to start small. First devised by traveling salespeople peddling vacuum cleaners, hairbrushes, cosmetics, magazine subscriptions, and encyclopedias, the trick is to somehow get your "foot in the door." The expression need not be taken literally, of course. The point of the **foot-in-the-door technique**

foot-in-the-door technique A two-step compliance technique in which an influencer sets the stage for the real request by first getting a person to comply with a much smaller request.

is to break the ice with a small initial request that the customer can't easily refuse. Once that first commitment is elicited, the chances are increased that another, larger request will succeed.

Jonathan Freedman and Scott Fraser (1966) tested the impact of this technique in a series of field experiments. In one, an experimenter pretending to be employed by a consumer organization telephoned a large number of female homemakers in Palo Alto, California, and asked if they would be willing to answer some questions about the household products they use. Those who consented were then asked a few quick and innocuous questions and thanked for their assistance. Three days later, the experimenter called back and made a considerable, almost outrageous, request. He asked the women if they would allow a handful of men into their homes for two hours to rummage through their drawers and cupboards so they could take an inventory of their household products.

The foot-in-the-door technique proved to be very effective. When the participants were confronted with only the very intrusive request, 22% consented. Yet the rate of agreement among those who had been surveyed earlier more than doubled, to 53%. This basic result has now been repeated over and over again. People are more likely to donate time, money, food, blood, the use of their home, and other resources once they have been induced to go along with a small initial request. Although the effect is not always as dramatic as that obtained by Freedman and Fraser, it does appear in a wide variety of circumstances, and it increases compliance rates, on average, by about 13% (Burger, 1999).

The practical implications of the foot-in-the-door technique are obvious. But why does it work? Over the years, several explanations have been suggested. One that seems plausible is based on self-perception theory—that people infer their attitudes by observing their own behavior. This explanation suggests that a two-step process is at work. First, by observing your own behavior in the initial situation, you come to see yourself as the kind of person who is generally cooperative when approached with a request. Second, when confronted with the more burdensome request, you seek to respond in ways that maintain this new self-image. By this logic, the foot-in-the-door technique should succeed only when you attribute an initial act of compliance to your own personal characteristics.

Based on a review of dozens of studies, Jerry Burger (1999) concluded that the research generally supports the self-perception account. Thus, if the first request is too trivial or if participants are paid for the first act of compliance, they won't later come to view themselves as inherently cooperative. Under these conditions, the technique *does not* work. Likewise, the effect occurs only when people are motivated to be consistent with their self-images. If participants are unhappy with what the initial behavior implies about them, if they are too young to appreciate the implications, or if they don't care about behaving in ways that are personally consistent, then again the technique does not work. Other processes may be at work, but it appears that the foot opens the door by altering self-perceptions, leading people who agree to the small initial request—without any compensation—to see themselves as helpful (Burger & Caldwell, 2003). In fact, this process can still occur even when a person tries to comply with the initial small request but fails. In a series of studies, Dariusz Dolinski (2000) found that when people were asked if they could find directions to a bogus street address or decipher an unreadable message—small favors that they could not satisfy—they too become more compliant with the next request.

Knowing that a foot in the door increases compliance rates is both exciting and troubling—exciting for the owner of the foot, troubling for the owner of the door. As Cialdini (2009) put it, "You can use small commitments to manipulate a person's self-image; you can use them to turn citizens into 'public servants,' prospects into 'customers,' prisoners into 'collaborators.' And once you've got a man's self-image where you want it, he should comply *naturally* with a whole range of your requests that are consistent with this view of himself" (p. 74).

Lowballing   Another two-step trap, arguably the most unscrupulous of all compliance techniques, is also based on the "start small" idea. Imagine yourself in the following situation. You're at a local car dealership. After some negotiation, the salesperson offers a great price on the car of your choice. You cast aside other considerations and shake hands on the deal and as the salesperson goes off to "write it up," you begin to feel the thrill of owning a new car. Absorbed in fantasy, you are suddenly interrupted by the return of the salesperson. "I'm sorry," he says. "The manager would not approve the sale. We have to raise the price by another $450. I'm afraid that's the best we can do." As the victim of an all-too-common trick known as **lowballing**, you are now faced with a tough decision. On the one hand, you really like the car; and the more you think about it, the better it looks. On the other hand, you don't want to pay more than you bargained for and you have an uneasy feeling in the pit of your stomach that you're being duped. What do you do?

Salespeople who use this tactic are betting that you'll make the purchase despite the added cost. If the way research participants behave is any indication, they are often right. In one study, experimenters phoned introductory psychology students and asked if they would be willing to participate in a study for extra credit. Some were told up front that the session would begin at the uncivilized hour of 7 a.m. Knowing that, only 31% volunteered. But other participants were lowballed. Only *after* they agreed to participate did the experimenter inform them of the 7 a.m. starting time. Would that be okay? Whether or not it was, the procedure achieved its objective—the signup rate rose to 56% (Cialdini et al., 1978).

Disturbing as it may be, lowballing is an interesting technique. Surely, once the lowball offer has been thrown, many recipients suspect that they were misled. Yet they go along. Why? The reason appears to hinge on the psychology of commitment (Kiesler, 1971). Once people make a particular decision, they justify it to themselves by thinking of all its positive aspects. As they get increasingly committed to a course of action, they grow more resistant to changing their mind, even if the initial reasons for the action have been changed or withdrawn entirely. In the car dealership scenario, you might very well have decided to purchase the car because of the price. But then you would have thought about its sleek appearance, the scent of the leather interior, the iPod dock, and the brand-new satellite radio. By the time you learned that the price would be more than you'd bargained for, it would be too late—you would already have been hooked.

Lowballing also produces another form of commitment. When people do not suspect duplicity, they feel a nagging sense of unfulfilled obligation to the person with whom they negotiated. Even though the salesperson was unable to complete the original deal, you might feel obligated to buy anyway, having already agreed to make the purchase. This commitment to the other person may account for why lowballing works better when the second request is made by the same person than by someone else (Burger & Petty, 1981). It may also explain why people are most vulnerable to the lowball when they make their commitment in public rather than in private (Burger & Cornelius, 2003).

The Door in the Face   Although shifting from an initial small request to a larger one can be effective, as in the foot-in-the-door and lowball techniques, oddly enough the opposite is also true. Cialdini (2009) described the time he was approached by a Boy Scout and asked to buy two five-dollar tickets to an upcoming circus. Having

lowballing   A two-step compliance technique in which the influencer secures agreement with a request but then increases the size of that request by revealing hidden costs.

better things to do with his time and money, he declined. Then the boy asked if he would be interested in buying chocolate bars at a dollar apiece. Even though he does not particularly like chocolate, Cialdini—an expert on social influence—bought two of them. After a moment's reflection, he realized what had happened. Whether the Boy Scout planned it that way or not, Cialdini had fallen for what is known as the **door-in-the-face technique**.

The technique is as simple as it sounds. An individual makes an initial request that is so large it is sure to be rejected and then comes back with a second more reasonable request. Will the second request fare better after the first one has been declined? Plagued by the sight of uneaten chocolate bars, Cialdini and others (1975) tested the effectiveness of the door-in-the-face technique. They stopped college students on campus and asked if they would volunteer to work without pay at a counseling center for juvenile delinquents. The time commitment would be forbidding: roughly two hours a week for the next two years! Not surprisingly, everyone who was approached politely slammed the proverbial door in the experimenter's face. But then the experimenter followed up with a more modest proposal, asking the students if they would be willing to take a group of kids on a two-hour trip to the zoo. The strategy worked like a charm. Only 17% of the students confronted with only the second request agreed. But of those who initially declined the first request, 50% said yes to the zoo trip. Importantly, the door-in-the-face technique does not elicit mere empty promises. Most research participants who comply subsequently do what they've agreed to do (Cialdini & Ascani, 1976).

Why is the door-in-the-face technique such an effective trap? One possibility involves the principle of *perceptual contrast:* To the person exposed to a very large initial request, the second request "seems smaller." Two dollars' worth of candy bars is not bad compared with ten dollars for circus tickets. Likewise, taking a group of kids to the zoo seems trivial compared with two years of volunteer work. As intuitively sensible as this explanation seems, Cialdini and others (1975) concluded that perceptual contrast is only partly responsible for the effect. When participants only heard the large request without actually having to reject it, their rate of compliance with the second request (25%) was only slightly larger than the 17% rate of compliance exhibited by those who heard only the small request.

A more compelling explanation for the effect involves the notion of *reciprocal concessions.* A close cousin of the reciprocity norm, this refers to the pressure to respond to changes in a bargaining position. When an individual backs down from a large request to a smaller one, we view that move as a concession that we should match by our own compliance. Thus, the door-in-the-face technique does not work if the second request is made by a different person (Cialdini et al., 1975). Nor does it work if the first request is so extreme that it comes across as an insincere "first offer" (Schwarzwald et al., 1979). On an emotional level, refusing to help on one request may also trigger feelings of guilt, which we can reduce by complying with the second, smaller request (O'Keefe & Figge, 1997; Millar, 2002).

That's Not All, Folks! If the notion of reciprocal concessions is correct, then a person shouldn't actually have to refuse the initial offer in order for the shift to a smaller request to work. Indeed, another familiar sales strategy manages to use concession without first eliciting refusal. In this strategy, a product is offered at a particular price, but then, before the buyer has a chance to respond, the seller adds, "And that's not all!" At that point, either the original price is reduced or a bonus is offered to sweeten the pot. The seller, of course, intends all along to make the so-called concession.

> An effective way to get someone to do you a favor is to make a first request that is so large the person is sure to reject it.
>
> **TRUE**

door-in-the-face technique A two-step compliance technique in which an influencer prefaces the real request with one that is so large that it is rejected.

This ploy, called the **that's-not-all technique**, seems transparent, right? Surely no one falls for it, right? Burger (1986) was not so sure. He predicted that people are more likely to make a purchase when a deal seems to have improved than when the same deal is offered right from the start. To test this hypothesis, Burger set up a booth at a campus fair and sold cupcakes. Some customers who approached the table were told that the cupcakes cost 75 cents each. Others were told that they cost a dollar, but then, before they could respond, the price was reduced to 75 cents. Rationally speaking, Burger's manipulation did not affect the ultimate price, so it should not have affected sales. But it did. When customers were led to believe that the final price represented a reduction, sales increased from 44% to 73%.

At this point, let's step back and look at the various compliance tactics described in this section. All of them are based on a two-step process that involves a shift from a request of one size to another. What differs is whether the small or large request comes first and how the transition between steps is made (see Table 7.3). Moreover, all these strategies work in subtle ways by manipulating a target person's self-image, commitment to the product, feelings of obligation to the seller, or perceptions of the real request. It is even possible to increase compliance by first asking "How are you feeling?" (Howard, 1990) or "I hope I'm not disturbing you, am I?" (Meineri & Guéguen, 2011), or by claiming some coincidental similarity like having the same first name or birthday (Burger et al., 2004). When you consider these various traps, you have to wonder whether it's ever possible to escape.

◼ Assertiveness: When People Say No

Cialdini (2009) opened his book with a confession: "I can admit it freely now. All my life I've been a patsy." As a past victim of compliance traps, he is not alone.

▲ **TABLE 7.3**

Sequential Request Strategies

Various compliance techniques are based on a sequence of two related requests. *Click!* The first request sets the trap. *Snap!* The second captures the prey. Research has shown that the four sequential request strategies summarized in this table are all effective.

Request Shifts	Technique	Description
From small to large	Foot-in-the-door	Begin with a very small request, secure agreement, then make a separate, larger request.
	Lowballing	Secure agreement with a request and then increase the size of that request by revealing hidden costs.
From large to small	Door-in-the-face	Begin with a very large request that will be rejected; then follow that up with a more modest request.
	That's-not-all	Begin with a somewhat inflated request, then immediately decrease the apparent size of that request by offering a discount or bonus.

© Cengage Learning®

Many people find it difficult to assert themselves in social situations. Faced with an unreasonable request from a friend, spouse, or stranger, they become anxious at the mere thought of putting a foot down and refusing to comply. There are times when it is uncomfortable for anyone to say no. However, just as we can maintain our autonomy in the face of conformity pressures, we can also refuse direct requests—even clever ones. The trap may be set, but you don't have to get caught.

According to Cialdini, being able to resist compliance pressures rests, first and foremost, on being vigilant. If a stranger hands you a gift and then launches into a sales pitch, you should recognize the tactic for what it is and not feel indebted by the norm of reciprocity. And if you strike a deal with a salesperson who later reneges on the terms, you should be aware that you're being lowballed and react accordingly. That is exactly what happened to one of the authors of this book. After a Saturday afternoon of careful negotiation at a local car dealer, he and his wife finally came to terms on a price. Minutes later, however, the salesman returned with the news that the manager would not approve the deal. The cost of a power moonroof, which was supposed to be included, would have to be added on. Familiar with the research, the author turned to his wife and exclaimed, "It's a trick; they're lowballing us!" She then became furious, went straight to the manager, and made such a scene in front of other customers that he backed down and honored the original deal.

"Knowledge is power, and if you know when a clever technique is being used on you, then it becomes easier to ignore."

—Burke Leon

What happened in this instance? Why did recognizing the attempted manipulation spark such anger and resistance? As this story illustrates, compliance techniques work smoothly only if hidden from view. The problem is, these techniques are not only attempts to influence us; they are deceptive. Flattery, gifts, and other ploys often win compliance, but not if perceived as insincere (Jones, 1964) or if the target has a high level of reciprocity wariness (Eisenberger et al., 1987). Likewise, sequential request traps are powerful only to the extent that they are subtle and cannot be seen for what they are (Schwarzwald et al., 1979). People don't like to be hustled. In fact, feeling manipulated typically leads us to react with anger, psychological reactance, and stubborn noncompliance—unless the request is a command and the requester is a figure of authority.

Obedience

Allen Funt, the creator and producer of the original TV program *Candid Camera* (a forerunner of the show *Punk'd*), spent as much time observing human behavior in the real world as most psychologists do. When asked what he learned from all his people watching, Funt replied, "The worst thing, and I see it over and over, is how easily people can be led by any kind of authority figure, or even the most minimal signs of authority." He cited the time he put up a road sign that read "Delaware Closed Today." The reaction? "Motorists didn't question it. Instead they asked, 'Is Jersey open?'" (Zimbardo, 1985, p. 47).

Funt was right about the way we react to authority. Taught from birth that it's important to respect legitimate forms of leadership, people think twice before defying parents, teachers, employers, coaches, and government officials. The problem is that mere symbols of authority—titles, uniforms, badges, or the trappings of success, even without the necessary credentials—can sometimes turn ordinary people into docile servants. Leonard Bickman (1974) demonstrated this phenomenon in a series of studies in which a male research assistant stopped passersby on the street and ordered them to do something unusual. Sometimes he pointed to a paper bag on the ground and said, "Pick up this bag for me!" At other times, he pointed to an individual standing beside a parked car and said, "This fellow is overparked at the meter but doesn't have any change. Give him a dime!" Would anyone really take this guy seriously? When he was dressed in street clothes, only a third of the people stopped followed his orders. But when he wore a security guard's uniform, nearly 9 out of every 10 people obeyed! Even when the uniformed assistant turned the corner and walked away after issuing his command, the vast majority of passersby followed his orders. Clearly, uniforms signify the power of authority (Bushman, 1988).

Blind **obedience** may seem funny, but if people are willing to take orders from a total stranger, how far will they go when it really matters? As the pages of history attest, the implications are sobering. In World War II, Nazi officials participated in the deaths of millions of Jews, as well as of Poles, Russians, gypsies, and homosexuals. Yet when tried for these crimes, all of them raised the same defense: "I was following orders."

Surely, you may be thinking, the Holocaust was a historical anomaly that says more about the Nazis as a group of bigoted, hateful, and pathologically frustrated individuals than about the situations that lead people in general to commit acts of destructive obedience. In *Hitler's Willing Executioners,* historian Daniel Goldhagen (1996) argued on the basis of past records that many German officials were willing participants in the Holocaust—not mere ordinary people forced to follow orders. Citing historical records, others have similarly argued that Nazi killers knew, believed in, and celebrated their mission (Cesarani, 2004; Haslam & Reicher, 2007; Vetlesen, 2005).

Yet two lines of evidence suggest that laying blame on this subgroup of German people is too simple as an explanation of what happened. First, interviews with Nazi war criminals and doctors who worked in concentration camps suggested, at least to some, the provocative and disturbing conclusion that these people were "utterly ordinary" (Arendt, 1963; Lifton, 1986; Von Lang & Sibyll, 1983). Second, the monstrous events of World War II do not stand alone in modern history. Even today, various crimes of obedience—which may include torture, suicide bombings, and public beheadings—are being committed in ruthless regimes, militaries, and terrorist organizations throughout the world (Haritos-Fatouros, 2002; Kelman & Hamilton, 1989; Victoroff & Kruglanski, 2009).

As seen in recent Wall Street scandals, crimes of obedience are also found in the corporate world, where business leaders and their subordinates "morally disengage" from fraud and other unethical actions by denying personal responsibility, minimizing consequences, and dehumanizing victims (Beu & Buckley, 2004; Moore et al., 2012). On extraordinary but rare occasions, obedience is carried to its ultimate limit. In 1978, 900 members of the People's Temple cult obeyed a command from Reverend Jim Jones to kill themselves by drinking poison. In 1997, Marshall Applewhite, leader of the Heaven's Gate cult in California, killed himself and convinced 37 followers to do the same. Fanatic cult members had committed mass suicide before, and they will likely do so again (Galanter, 1999).

Taken to the extreme, blind obedience can have devastating results. Nazi officials killed millions during World War II, and many said they did it "because I was just following orders."

"Far more, and far more hideous, crimes have been committed in the name of obedience than have ever been committed in the name of rebellion."

—C. P. Snow

obedience Behavior change produced by the commands of authority.

■ Milgram's Research: Forces of Destructive Obedience

During the time that Adolf Eichmann was being tried in Jerusalem for his Nazi war crimes, Stanley Milgram began a dramatic series of 18 experiments. The first was published in the *Journal of Abnormal and Social Psychology* in 1963; the rest were reported later in his 1974 book, *Obedience to Authority*. Milgram did not realize it at the time—and neither did his research participants—but they were about to make history in one of the most famous psychology research programs ever conducted.

For many years, the ethics of this research has been the focus of much debate. Those who say it was not ethical point to the potential psychological harm to which Milgram's participants were exposed. In contrast, those who believe that these experiments met appropriate ethical standards emphasize the profound contribution it has made to our understanding of human nature and an important social problem. They conclude that on balance, the danger that destructive obedience poses for all humankind justified Milgram's unorthodox methods. Consider both sides of the debate, which were summarized in Chapter 2, and make your own judgment. Now, however, take a more personal look. Imagine yourself as one of the approximately 1,000 participants who found themselves in a situation much like the following.

The experience begins when you arrive at a Yale University laboratory and meet two men. One is the experimenter, a stern young man dressed in a gray lab coat and carrying a clipboard. The other is a middle-aged gentleman named Mr. Wallace, an accountant who is slightly overweight and average in appearance. You exchange quick introductions, and then the experimenter explains that you and your co-participant will take part in a study on the effects of punishment on learning. After lots have been drawn, it is determined that you will serve as the teacher and that Mr. Wallace will be the learner. So far, so good.

Soon, however, the situation takes on a more ominous tone. You find out that your job is to test the learner's memory and administer electric shocks of increasing intensity whenever he makes a mistake. You are then escorted into another room, where the experimenter straps Mr. Wallace into a chair, rolls up his sleeves, attaches electrodes to his arms, and applies "electrode paste" to prevent blisters and burns. Mr. Wallace is concerned but the experimenter responds by reassuring him that although the shocks will be painful, the procedure will not cause "permanent tissue damage." In the meantime, you can personally vouch for how painful the shocks are because the experimenter stings you with one that is supposed to be mild. The experimenter then takes you back to the main room, where you

From the film Obedience by Stanley Milgram copyright 1965 and distributed by The Penn. State University Audio Visual Services

This is the shock generator Milgram used (left). It still exists and can be seen in the Archives of the History of American Psychology at the University of Akron. Participants in Milgram's studies believed they were shocking Mr. Wallace, the man being strapped into his chair (right).

are seated in front of a "shock generator," a machine with 30 switches that range from 15 volts, labeled "slight shock," to 450 volts, labeled "XXX."

Your role in this experiment is straightforward. First you read a list of word pairs to Mr. Wallace through a microphone. Then you test his memory with a series of multiple-choice questions. The learner answers each question by pressing one of four switches that light up signals on the shock generator. If his answer is correct, you move on to the next question. If it is incorrect, you announce the correct answer and shock him. When you press the appropriate shock switch, a red light flashes above it, relay switches click inside the machine, and you hear a loud buzzing sound go off in the learner's room. After each wrong answer, you're told, the intensity of the shock should be increased by 15 volts.

You aren't aware, of course, that the experiment is rigged and that Mr. Wallace—who is actually a confederate—is never really shocked. As far as you know, he gets zapped each time you press one of the switches. As the session proceeds, the learner makes more and more errors, leading you to work your way up the shock scale. As you reach 75, 90, and 105 volts, you hear the learner grunt in pain. At 120 volts, he begins to shout. If you're still in it at 150 volts, you can hear the learner cry out, "Experimenter! That's all. Get me out of here. I refuse to go on!" Screams of agony and protest continue. At 300 volts, he says he absolutely refuses to continue. By the time you surpass 330 volts, the learner falls silent and fails to respond—not to be heard from again. Table 7.4 lists his responses in grim detail.

Somewhere along the line, you turn to the experimenter for guidance. "What should I do? Don't you think I should stop? Shouldn't we at least check on him?" You might even confront the experimenter head-on and refuse to continue. Yet in answer to your inquiries, the experimenter—firm in his tone and seemingly unaffected by the learner's distress—prods you along as follows:

- Please continue (or, please go on).
- The experiment requires that you continue.
- It is absolutely essential that you continue.
- You have no other choice; you must go on.

What do you do? In a situation that begins to feel more and more like a bad dream, do you follow your own conscience or obey the experimenter? Milgram described this procedure to psychiatrists, college students, and middle-class adults, and he

---

▲ **TABLE 7.4**

The Learner's Protests in the Milgram Experiment

As participants administered progressively more intense shocks, they heard the learner moan, groan, protest, and complain. All participants heard the same programmed set of responses. Eventually, the learner fell silent and ceased to respond.

75 volts	Ugh!
90 volts	Ugh!
105 volts	Ugh! (*louder*)
120 volts	Ugh! Hey, this really hurts!
135 volts	Ugh!!
150 volts	Ugh!!! Experimenter! That's all. Get me out of here. I told you I had heart trouble. My heart's starting to bother me now. Get me out of here, please. My heart's starting to bother me. I refuse to go on. Let me out.
165 volts	Ugh! Let me out! (*shouting*)
180 volts	Ugh! I can't stand the pain. Let me out of here! (*shouting*)
195 volts	Ugh! Let me out of here. Let me out of here. My heart's bothering me. Let me out of here! You have no right to keep me here! Let me out! Let me out of here! Let me out! Let me out of here! My heart's bothering me. Let me out! Let me out!
210 volts	Ugh!! Experimenter! Get me out of here. I've had enough. I won't be in the experiment any more.
225 volts	Ugh!
240 volts	Ugh!
255 volts	Ugh! Get me out of here.
270 volts	(*Agonized scream*) Let me out of here. Let me out of here. Let me out of here. Let me out. Do you hear? Let me out of here.
285 volts	(*Agonized scream*)
300 volts	(*Agonized scream*) I absolutely refuse to answer any more. Get me out of here. You can't hold me here. Get me out. Get me out of here.
315 volts	(*Intensely agonized scream*) I told you I refuse to answer. I'm no longer part of this experiment.
330 volts	(*Intense and prolonged agonized scream*) Let me out of here. Let me out of here. My heart's bothering me. Let me out, I tell you. (*Hysterically*) Let me out of here. Let me out of here. You have no right to hold me here. Let me out! Let me out! Let me out of here! Let me out! Let me out!

From Milgram, S., *Obedience to authority: An experimental view* (pp. 56–57). Copyright © 1974 by Stanley Milgram.

asked them to predict how they would behave. On average, these groups estimated that they would call it quits at the 135-volt level. Not a single person thought he or she would go all the way to 450 volts. When asked to predict the percentage of *other* people who would deliver the maximum shock, those interviewed gave similar estimates. The psychiatrists estimated that only one out of a thousand people would exhibit that kind of extreme obedience. They were wrong. In the study just described, involving 40 men from the New Haven area, participants exhibited an alarming degree of obedience, administering an average of 27 out of 30 possible shocks. In fact, 26 of the 40 participants—that's *65%*—delivered the ultimate punishment of 450 volts.

The Obedient Participant At first glance, you may see these results as a lesson in the psychology of cruelty and conclude that Milgram's participants were seriously disturbed. But research does not support such a simple explanation. To begin with, those in a "control group" who were not prodded along by an experimenter refused to continue early into the shock sequence. What's more, Milgram found that virtually all participants, including those who had administered severe shocks, were tormented by the experience. Many of them pleaded with the experimenter to let them stop. When he refused, they continued. But in the process, they trembled, stuttered, groaned, perspired, bit their lips, and dug their fingernails into their flesh. Some burst into fits of nervous laughter. On one occasion, said Milgram, "we observed a [participant's] seizure so violently convulsive that it was necessary to call a halt to the experiment" (1963, p. 375).

Was Milgram's 65% "baseline" level of obedience attributable to his unique sample of male participants? Not at all. Forty women who participated in a later study exhibited precisely the same level of obedience: 65% threw the 450-volt switch. Before you jump to the conclusion that something was amiss in New Haven, consider the fact that Milgram's basic finding has been obtained in several cultures and with children as well as college students and older adults (Blass, 2012). Obedience in the Milgram situation is so universal that it led one author to ask, "Are we all Nazis?" (Askenasy, 1978).

The answer, of course, is no. An individual's character makes a difference, and some people, depending on the situation, are far more obedient than others. In the aftermath of World War II, a group of social scientists—searching for the root causes of prejudice and bigotry—sought to identify individuals with an *authoritarian personality* and developed a questionnaire known as the F-Scale to measure it (Adorno et al., 1950; Stone et al., 1993). What they found is that people who get high scores on the F-Scale (F stands for "Fascist") are rigid, dogmatic, sexually repressed, ethnocentric, intolerant of dissent, and punitive. They are submissive toward figures of authority but aggressive toward subordinates. Indeed, people with high F scores are also more willing than low scorers to administer high-intensity shocks in Milgram's obedience situation (Elms & Milgram, 1966).

Although personality characteristics may make someone vulnerable or resistant to destructive obedience, it is clear that the situation in which people find themselves has a profound effect. By carefully altering particular aspects of his basic scenario, Milgram was able to identify factors that increase and decrease the 65% baseline rate of obedience in more than 20 variations of the basic experiment (see ● Figure 7.8). Three factors in particular are important: the authority figure, the proximity of the victim, and the experimental procedure (Blass, 1992; Miller, 1986).

The Authority What is perhaps most remarkable about Milgram's findings is that an experimenter in a white lab coat is *not* a powerful figure of authority. Unlike

● FIGURE 7.8

Factors That Influence Obedience

Milgram varied many factors in his research program. Without commands from an experimenter, fewer than 3% of the participants exhibited full obedience. Yet in the standard baseline condition, 65% of male and female participants followed the orders. To identify factors that might reduce this level, Milgram varied the location of the experiment, the status of the authority, the participant's proximity to the victim, and the presence of confederates who rebel. The effects of these variations are illustrated here.
Milgram, 1974

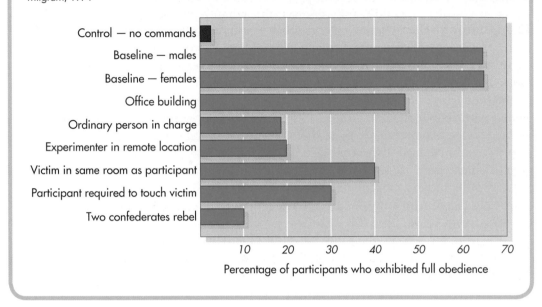

Percentage of participants who exhibited full obedience

military superiors, employers, coaches, or teachers, the experimenter in Milgram's research could not ultimately enforce his commands. Still, his physical presence and apparent legitimacy played major roles in drawing obedience. When Milgram diminished the experimenter's status by moving his lab from the distinguished surroundings of Yale University to a run-down urban office building in nearby Bridgeport, Connecticut, the rate of total obedience dropped to 48%. When the experimenter was replaced by an ordinary person—supposedly another participant—there was a sharp reduction to 20%. Similarly, Milgram found that when the experimenter was in charge but issued his commands by telephone, only 21% fully obeyed. (In fact, when the experimenter was not watching, many participants in this condition feigned obedience by pressing the 15-volt switch.) One conclusion, then, is clear. At least in the Milgram setting, destructive obedience requires the physical presence of a prestigious authority figure.

If an experimenter can exert such control over research participants, imagine the control wielded by truly powerful leaders—whether they are physically present or not. An intriguing field study examined the extent to which hospital nurses would obey unreasonable orders from a doctor. Using a fictitious name, a male physician called several female nurses on the phone and told them to administer a drug to a specific patient. His order violated hospital regulations: The drug was uncommon, the dosage was too large, and the effects could have been harmful. Yet out of the 22 nurses who were contacted, 21 had to be stopped as they prepared to obey the doctor's orders (Hofling et al., 1966).

The Victim   Situational characteristics of the victim are also important factors in destructive obedience. Milgram noted that Nazi war criminal Adolf Eichmann felt sick when he toured concentration camps but only had to shuffle papers from behind a desk to play his part in the Holocaust. Similarly the B-29 pilot who dropped the atom bomb on Hiroshima in World War II said of his mission, "I had no thoughts, except what I'm supposed to do" (Miller, 1986, p. 228). These events suggest that because Milgram's participants were physically separated from the learner, they were able to distance themselves emotionally from the consequences of their actions.

To test the impact of a victim's proximity on destructive obedience, Milgram seated the learner in one of his studies in the same room as the participant. Under these conditions, only 40% fully obeyed. But when participants were required to physically grasp the victim's hand and force it against his will onto a metal shock plate, full obedience dropped to 30%. These findings represent significant reductions from the 65% baseline. Still, 3 out of 10 participants were willing to use brute force in the name of obedience.

Milgram ran one last variation, never published, that was only recently discovered in Yale University's library, where Milgram's records have been archived for historical purposes. Located in a rundown office building in a nearby city, he called it the "Bring-a-Friend" condition. In this situation, 20 male participants were told to bring a friend, neighbor, family member, or coworker. When they arrived, the two participants drew straws to determine who would be the teacher and who the learner. Unbeknownst to the teacher, Milgram then coached the learner on how to play the role and react to the shocks according to script, at times pleading to the teacher by name. Would participants obey less in this version? Yes. Compared to a Wallace-as-victim condition run in the same location, where the full obedience rate was 50%, the obedience rate in the friend condition was only 15%. Following in the footsteps of some German citizens who defied the Nazi regime by protecting friends they were ordered to report, Milgram's participants were indeed capable of resistance when they had a prior relationship with the victim (Rochat & Blass, 2014).

The Procedure   Finally, there is the carefully scripted situation created by Milgram. Looking at the dilemma that confronted Milgram's participants, Burger (2014) points to four critical aspects of the experimental procedure that contributed to the surprising results. First, participants were led to feel relieved of personal *responsibility* for the victim's welfare. The experimenter said up front that he was accountable. Burger notes that in a partial replication of Milgram that he more recently conducted, a "Milgram-lite" version to be described later, only 12% of participants who exhibited full obedience gave any indication during their sessions that they bore any sense of responsibility. In fact, when participants are led to believe that they were responsible, their levels of obedience drop considerably (Tilker, 1970).

The ramifications of felt responsibility are immense. In the military, on Wall Street, in corporations and other organizations, individuals often occupy positions in a hierarchical chain of command. Eichmann was a mid-level bureaucrat who received orders from Hitler and transmitted them to others for implementation. Caught between individuals who make policy and those who carry it out, how personally responsible do those in the middle feel? Wesley Kilham and Leon Mann (1974) examined this issue in an obedience study that cast participants in one of two roles: the *transmitter* (who took orders from the experimenter and passed them on) and the *executant* (who actually pressed the shock levers). As they predicted, transmitters were more obedient (54%) than executants (28%).

The second feature of Milgram's scenario that promoted obedience is the use of gradual escalation in small increments. Participants began the session by delivering mild shocks and then only gradually escalated to voltage levels of high intensity. After all, what's another 15 volts compared with the current level? By the time they realized the frightening implications of what they were doing—for example, choosing to align with the experimenter once the learner protested at 150 volts—it had become more difficult to stop (Gilbert, 1981; Packer, 2008). This sequence is much like the foot-in-the-door technique. In Milgram's words, people become "integrated into a situation that carries its own momentum. The subject's problem . . . is how to become disengaged from a situation which is moving in an altogether ugly direction" (1974, p. 73). We should point out that obedience by momentum is not unique to Milgram's research paradigm. As reported by Amnesty International, many countries still torture political prisoners, and those who are recruited for the dirty work are trained, in part, through an escalating series of commitments (Haritos-Fatouros, 2002).

According to Burger (2014), the third feature of Milgram's situation that made it difficult for participants to resist is that participants found themselves in a novel situation, unimaginable, like no other they have been in before. As such, they did not know what the norms were, how others have reacted, or how they were supposed to respond. That is why, in a variation of Milgram's research in which two confederates posed as co-participants who refused to continue, the full obedience rate plummeted to 10% (see Figure 7.8).

The fourth aspect of the procedure that promoted obedience is that the task was quickly paced. At the outset, Milgram's experimenter instructed participants to work at a "brisk pace." Indeed, as one can plainly see in a film that Milgram had produced of his sessions, those who hesitated were immediately prompted to proceed. All this gave participants no time to ponder, consider their values and their options, think about possible consequences, or make careful decisions.

Milgram in the Twenty-First Century

When Stanley Milgram published the results of his first experiment in 1963, at the age of 28, a *New York Times* headline read: "Sixty-Five Percent in Test Blindly Obey Order to Inflict Pain." Milgram had pierced the public consciousness and was poised to become an important and controversial figure in psychology—and beyond. In a biography, Thomas Blass (2004) tells of how Milgram became interested in obedience and the impact his studies have had on social scientists, legal scholars, the U.S. military, and popular culture around the world (Milgram's book has been translated into 11 languages). Now, in an age filled with threats of global conflict, extremism, terrorism, economic hardship, breaches to cybersecurity and privacy, and new forms of lethal weaponry, obedience to authority is an issue of such importance that social psychologists all over the world continue to ponder its ramifications (Benjamin & Simpson, 2009; Blass, 2009; Jetten & Mols, 2014; Reicher et al., 2014). Milgram himself died in 1984 at the age of 51.

Today, a grainy black-and-white film that Milgram produced in 1965 in which a number of sessions were recorded from a hidden camera stands as visual proof of this phenomenon. It is clear from looking at this film that this experiment was conducted in another era, a pre-computer, pre-digital era in which research participants called the young experimenter "sir." Would these results be repeated today? Would *you* obey the commands of Milgram's experimenter?

In an effort to answer this question, Dutch researchers Wim Meeus and Quinten Raaijmakers (1995) created a different but analogous situation. They

---

In experiments on obedience, most participants who were ordered to administer severe shocks to an innocent person refused to do so.

FALSE

constructed a moral dilemma much like Milgram's. Rather than order participants to inflict physical pain on someone, however, they ordered them to cause psychological harm. When participants arrived at a university laboratory, they met a confederate supposedly there to take a test as part of a job interview. If the confederate passed the test, he'd get the job; if he failed, he would not. As part of a study of performance under stress, the experimenter told participants to distract the test-taking applicant by making an escalating series of harassing remarks. On cue, the applicant pleaded with participants to stop, became angry, faltered, and eventually fell into a state of despair and failed. As in Milgram's research, the question was straightforward: How many participants would obey orders through the entire set of 15 stress remarks, despite the apparent harm caused to a real-life job applicant? In a control group that lacked a prodding experimenter, no one persisted. But when the experimenter ordered them to go on, 92% exhibited complete obedience despite seeing the task as unfair and distasteful. It appears that obedience is a powerful aspect of human nature brought about by the docile manner in which people relate to figures of authority—even today.

In a more recent—and even more direct—attempt to revisit Milgram, Burger (2009) conducted a "partial replication" for which he paid $50 to 70 men and women, a diverse group that ranged from 20 to 81 years old, and used the same procedure. In the original experiment, the learner first protested and asked to stop at 150 volts, at which point nearly all participants paused and indicated a reluctance to continue. Some outright refused at this point. Of those participants who did continue, however, most went all the way. On the basis of this finding, Burger followed the Milgram protocol up to 150 volts in order to estimate the number of participants who would have pulled the switch at 450 volts. He also added a condition in which a defiant confederate posing as another participant refused to continue. In light of post-Milgram changes in standards for research ethics, he took additional precautions; he excluded from the study individuals he feared would experience too much stress and then informed and reminded participants three times that they could withdraw from the study at any time without penalty.

Despite all that has changed in 45 years, the obedience rate was not appreciably lower (see ● Figure 7.9). In the experiment that Burger modeled, 83% of Milgram's participants had continued past 150 volts. In Burger's more recent study, 70% did the same (it can be estimated, therefore, that 55% would have exhibited full 450-volt obedience in the original experiment). Two additional results proved interesting: (1) Just as Milgram had found, there were no differences between men and women, and (2) the obedience rate declined only slightly, to 63%, among participants who saw a defiant confederate refuse to continue.

● **FIGURE 7.9**

Obedience in the Twenty-First Century

In the version of the experiment that Burger modeled, 83% of Milgram's original participants continued past 150 volts. Forty-five years later, Burger saw a slight drop to 70%. Note too that the obedience rate dropped only slightly, to 63%, among participants who saw a defiant confederate refuse to continue. These results show that obedience to authority may have declined a bit over the years, but it has by no means extinguished.
Burger, 2009

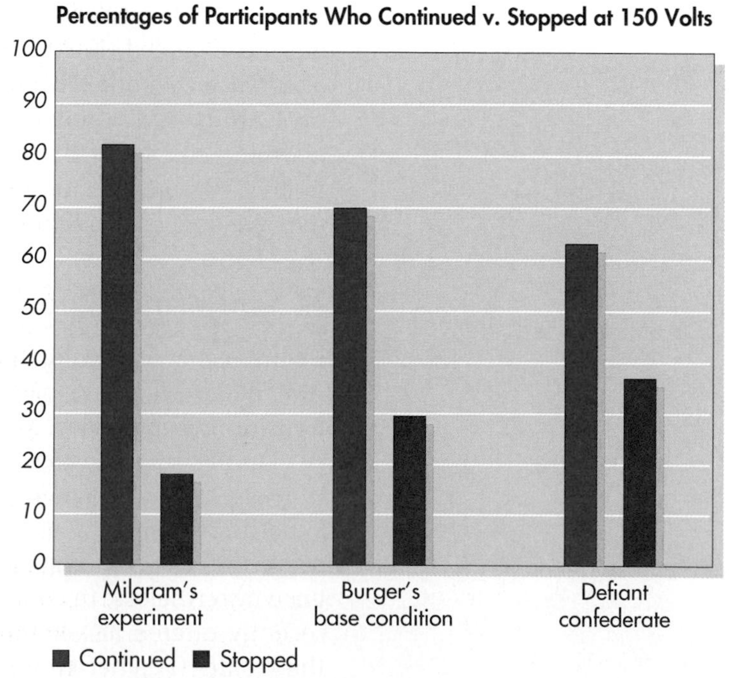

Percentages of Participants Who Continued v. Stopped at 150 Volts

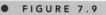

■ Continued   ■ Stopped

Obedience to authority is a timeless phenomenon. In 2004, then 18-year-old Louise Ogburn, working in a McDonald's in Kentucky, was accused of stealing money by a prank phone caller and taken into her manager's office. Posing as police, the caller ordered several of the girl's coworkers to have her strip naked. For four hours, she was searched, spanked, and forced into humiliating positions on command. All but one coworker obeyed the prank caller—and the girl obeyed the coworkers. Remarkably, seventy similar incidents were reported elsewhere. As seen here, Ms. Ogburn sued McDonald's and was awarded $6 million (left). Perhaps even more astonishing, Juan Rivera of Illinois spent 20 years in prison for a crime he did not commit after he was badgered into the ultimate act of obedience—a false confession to murder. In March of 2015, Rivera and his attorneys announced that he was awarded $20 million in a settlement against prosecutors and police who coerced this confession (right).

This recent replication has drawn a good deal of interest. Alan Elms (2009), a graduate student of Milgram's in the 1960s, is cautious about comparing Burger's "obedience lite" procedure to Milgram's but eager to see it revitalize the research program Milgram had initiated. Arthur Miller (2009), author of *The Obedience Experiments,* voices the same cautious excitement. Blass (2009), author of the Milgram biography, *The Man Who Shocked the World,* sees Burger's experiment as an important milestone that demonstrates the stability and resilience of obedience in human social behavior. In contrast, Jean Twenge (2009), author of *Generation Me*—a 2006 book on how Americans have become more self-centered and wholly focused on personal rights—is skeptical of that conclusion that nothing has changed. Making precise comparisons, Twenge notes that relative to an obedience rate of 83% among Milgram's male participants, only 67% of Burger's men exhibited 150-volt obedience, a decline that is statistically comparable to the alarming change in U.S. obesity rates during that same period of time. Although impressed with the power of Milgram's situation, Twenge is hopeful that destructive obedience is less prevalent today, in the twenty-first century, than in the past.

■ Lingering Questions

Before leaving the Milgram studies, let's consider two important questions: Why exactly did Milgram's participants follow orders, and what are the moral implications of their behavior?

On the why question, Milgram had theorized that participants were swept up in a situational momentum he had created, leading them to exhibit *obedience.* What they displayed was not a "blind obedience," as some commentators have suggested; the personal conflict they experienced was palpable—but it was obedience nevertheless. In contrast, Alex Haslam, Stephen Reicher, and their colleagues recently offered an alternative account—an *engaged followership* explanation of the results (Reicher et al., 2012; Haslam et al., 2014). These researchers theorize that participants shocked the learner because they identified with the scientific enterprise and wanted to both help the experimenter and make a contribution.

From this perspective, their behavior indicated their engagement in the science, not obedience to authority. In support of this account, they noted that Milgram's second prod, which appealed to science ("The *experiment* requires that you continue") was followed by more shock to the learner than his fourth prod, which took the form of a strong command ("You have *no other choice*, you must go on").

To test this hypothesis in a single new experiment, Haslam et al. (2014) created an online procedure in which they asked participants to engage in a task that involved denigrating certain groups of people in a way that became increasingly unpleasant—much like climbing a shock scale. In this case, they randomly varied which prod came first and found, as predicted, that 64% of participants completed the study after receiving Prod 2, the science prod, compared to only 44% who received Prod 4, the obedience prod. This is an interesting result. But for two reasons it represents only a weak test of the obedience hypothesis. First, "You have no choice" is exactly the kind of command phrase that arouses psychological reactance and leads people in general to refuse in order to protect their threatened freedom (see Chapter 6). Second, the participants completed this task via computer without the physical presence of an authority figure, which Milgram had shown to be necessary. Obedience or engaged followership? It will be interesting to see what future studies will be conducted to distinguish these possible explanations.

Then there is the moral question: By providing a situational explanation for the evils of Nazi Germany or modern-day terrorism, do social psychologists unwittingly excuse the perpetrators? Does focusing on situational forces let them off the hook of responsibility? Since many of Milgram's participants were disobedient, indicating that they were free to choose resistance, one would hope not. Andrew Monroe and Glenn Reeder (2014) note that observers integrate information about the participant, his or her behavior, and the situation, in a manner that accounts for the subtle nature of the participant's motives in light of the dilemma, "as caught between wanting to help the learner and wanting to placate the experimenter" (p. 550).

In a series of studies, Miller and others (1999) found that after people were asked to come up with explanations for acts of wrongdoing, they tended to be more forgiving of those who committed the acts and they were seen as more forgiving by others. This appearance of forgiveness was certainly not Milgram's intent, nor is it the intent of other researchers today who seek to understand human cruelty, even while continuing to condemn it. Miller and his colleagues were thus quick to caution, "To explain is not to forgive" (p. 265).

◼ Defiance: When People Rebel

History books will call it the "Arab Spring." On December 17, 2010, a young, unemployed, frustrated Tunisian man by the name of Mohamed Bouazizi set fire to himself in protest after police confiscated the fruits and vegetables he was selling on the street because he lacked a permit. Almost immediately, men and women took to the streets in protest. Despite the government's determination to suppress dissent, the crowds grew in size, marching, holding rallies, and demanding the resignation of the prime minister. On January 14, 2011, the government was overthrown and set off protests in other countries throughout the Middle East. It's no wonder the regimes in power sought to censor and block the social media (Howard & Hussain, 2011).

Reading Milgram's research, it is easy to despair in light of the impressive forces that compel people toward blind obedience. But there's also good news. Just as social influence processes can breed subservience to authority, social influence processes can also breed rebellion and defiance. The Arab Spring is a modern-day example. A similar phenomenon was seen during World War II. In *Resistance of the Heart,* historian Nathan Stoltzfus (1996) described a civil protest in

In Hong Kong, in September of 2014, thousands of pro-democracy protesters waved phones activated with LED lights in a show of unison and instantly sent powerful images across the world. The power of this social-media facilitated demonstration led the government of China to block the photo-sharing service Instagram.

Corbis News/Corbis

Berlin in which the non-Jewish wives of 2,000 newly captured Jews congregated outside the prison. The women were there initially to seek information about their husbands. Soon they were filling the streets, chanting and refusing to leave. After eight straight days of protest, the defiant women prevailed. Fearing the negative impact on public opinion, the Nazis backed down and released the men.

In addition to the role of social networking media, recent studies indicate that for better or for worse, *synchrony* of behavior—for example, walking in step with others, clapping, singing, chanting, or raising arms in unison—can have a unifying effect on people, increasing the tendency to follow what others are doing. In one study, pairs of participants were seated in rocking chairs, side by side, and asked to rock in unison. Other pairs also rocked, but they could not see each other and were not in rhythm. Those in the synchrony condition were later more "in synch" when working jointly to move a steel ball through a wooden maze (Valdesolo et al., 2010). Other studies have shown that acting in unison with others can also increase our tendency to feel socially connected, cooperate for the common good, and even comply with a request to aggress against another person (Wiltermuth, 2012; Wiltermuth & Heath, 2010).

Are the actions of a whole group harder to control than the behavior of a single individual? Consider the following study. Pretending to be part of a marketing research firm, William Gamson and others (1982) recruited people to participate in a supposed discussion of "community standards." Scheduled in groups of nine, participants were told that their discussions would be videotaped for a large oil company that was suing the manager of a local service station who had spoken out against higher gas prices. After receiving a summary of the case, most participants sided with the station manager. But there was a hitch. The oil company wanted evidence to win its case, said the experimenter posing as the discussion coordinator. He told each of the group members to get in front of the camera and express the company's viewpoint. Then he told them to sign an affidavit giving the company permission to edit the tapes for use in court.

"A little rebellion now and then is a good thing."

—Thomas Jefferson

You can see how the obedience script was supposed to unfold. Actually, only 1 of 33 groups even came close to following the script. In all others, people were incensed by the coordinator's behavior and refused to continue. Some groups were so outraged that they planned to take action. One group even threatened to blow the whistle on the firm by calling the local newspapers. Faced with one emotionally charged mutiny after another, the researchers had to discontinue the experiment.

Why did this study produce such active, often passionate revolt when Milgram's revealed such utterly passive obedience? Could it reflect a change in values from the 1960s, when Milgram's studies were run? Many college students believe that people would conform less today than in the past, but an analysis of obedience studies has revealed that there is no correlation between the year a study was conducted and the level of obedience that it produced (Blass, 1999)— right up through Burger's (2009) recent effort. So what accounts for the contrasting results? One key difference is that people in Milgram's studies took part alone and those in Gamson's were in groups. Perhaps Michael Walzer was right: "Disobedience, when it is not criminally but morally, religiously, or politically motivated, is always a *collective act*" (quoted in Brown, 1986, p. 17).

Our earlier discussion of conformity indicated that the mere presence of one ally in an otherwise unanimous majority gives individuals the courage to dissent. The same may hold true for obedience. Notably, Milgram typically did not have more than one participant present in the same session. But in one experiment, he did use two confederates who posed as co-teachers along with the real participant. In these sessions, one confederate refused to continue at 150 volts and the second refused at 210 volts. These models of disobedience had a profound influence on participants' willingness to defy the experimenter: In their presence, only 10% delivered the maximum level of shock (see Figure 7.8).

We should add that the presence of a group is not a guaranteed safeguard against destructive obedience. Groups can trigger aggression, as we'll see in Chapter 11. For example, the followers of Jim Jones were together when they collectively followed his command to die. And lynch mobs are just that—groups, not individuals. Clearly, there is power in sheer numbers. That power can be destructive, but it can also be used for constructive purposes. Indeed, the presence and support of others often provide the extra ounce of courage that people need to resist orders they find offensive.

The Continuum of Social Influence

As we have seen, social influence on behavior ranges from the implicit pressure of group norms to the traps set by direct requests to the powerful commands of authority. In each case, people choose whether to react with conformity or independence, with compliance or assertiveness, and with obedience or defiance. From all the research, it is tempting to conclude that the more pressure brought to bear on people, the greater the influence. Is it possible, however, that more produces less? In a series of studies, Lucian Conway and Mark Schaller (2005) cast participants into a corporate decision-making task in which they were asked to choose between two business options after watching others make the same decision. Consistently, the participants followed the group more when its members had formed their opinions freely than when they were compelled by a leader. It appears that strong-arm tactics that force people to change their behavior may backfire when it comes to changing opinions.

At this point, let's step back and ask two important questions. First, although different kinds of pressure influence us for different reasons, is it possible to predict all effects with a single overarching principle? Second, what does all the theory and research on social influence say about human nature?

Social Impact Theory

In 1981, Bibb Latané proposed that a common bond among the different processes involved in social influence leads people toward or away from such influence. Specifically, Latané proposed **social impact theory**, which states that social influence of any kind—the total impact of others on a target person—is a function of the others' strength, immediacy, and number. According to Latané, social forces act on individuals in the same way that physical forces act upon objects. Consider, for example, how overhead lights illuminate a surface. The total amount of light cast on a surface depends on the strength of the bulbs, their distance from the surface, and their number. As illustrated in the left portion of Figure 7.10, the same factors apply to social impact.

The *strength* of a source is determined by his or her status, ability, or relationship to a target. The stronger the source, the greater the influence. When people view the other members of a group as competent, they are more likely to conform in their judgments. When it comes to compliance, sources enhance their strength by making targets feel obligated to reciprocate a small favor. And to elicit obedience, authority figures gain strength by wearing uniforms or flaunting their prestigious affiliations.

"I invited a few friends over who think you should see a psychiatrist."

According to social impact theory, this "intervention" should prove persuasive.

Frank Cotham/The New Yorker Collection/The Cartoon Bank

Immediacy refers to a source's proximity in time and space to the target. The closer the source, the greater its impact. Milgram's research offers the best example. Obedience rates were higher when the experimenter issued commands in person rather than from a remote location, and when the victim suffered in close proximity to the participant, he acted as a contrary source of influence and obedience levels dropped. Consistent with this hypothesis, Latané and others (1995) asked individuals to name up to seven people in their lives and to indicate how far away those people lived and how many memorable interactions they'd had with them. In three studies, the correlation was the same: The closer others are, geographically, the more impact they have on us.

Finally, the theory predicts that as the *number* of sources increases, so does their influence—at least up to a point. You may recall that when Asch (1956) increased the number of live confederates in his line-judgment studies from one to four, conformity levels rose, yet further increases had only a negligible additional effect.

Social impact theory also predicts that people sometimes resist social pressure. According to Latané, this resistance is most likely to occur when social impact is *divided* among many strong and distant *targets*, as seen in the right part of ● Figure 7.10. There should be less impact on a target who is strong and far from the source than on one who is weak and close to the source, and there should be less impact on a target who is accompanied by other target persons than on one who stands alone. Thus, we have seen that conformity is reduced by the presence of an ally and that obedience rates drop when people are in the company of rebellious peers.

Over the years, social impact theory has been challenged, defended, and refined on various grounds (Jackson, 1986; Mullen, 1985; Sedikides & Jackson,

social impact theory The theory that social influence depends on the strength, immediacy, and number of source persons relative to target persons.

1990). On the one hand, critics say that it does not enable us to *explain* the processes that give rise to social influence or answer *why* questions. On the other hand, the theory enables us to predict the emergence of social influence and determine *when* it will occur. Whether the topic is conformity, compliance, or obedience, this theory provides a stage for interesting new research in the years to come.

A number of social psychologists have recently argued that social impact is a fluid, dynamic, ever-changing process (Vallacher et al., 2002). Fifteen years before the Arab Spring became a reality, Latané and L'Herrou (1996) refined the theory in that vein. By having large groups of participants network through e-mail and by controlling their lines of communication, they found that the individuals within the network formed "clusters." Over time, neighbors (participants who were in direct e-mail contact with each other) became more similar to each other than did those who were more distant (not in direct e-mail contact) within the network. Referring to the geometry of social space, Latané and L'Herrou note that in the real world, immediacy cannot be defined strictly in terms of physical distance. Speculating on the role of technology, they noted that social impact theory has to account for the type of events that unfolded in the Middle East, in 2011, and that fact that remote social media may diminish the importance of physical proximity.

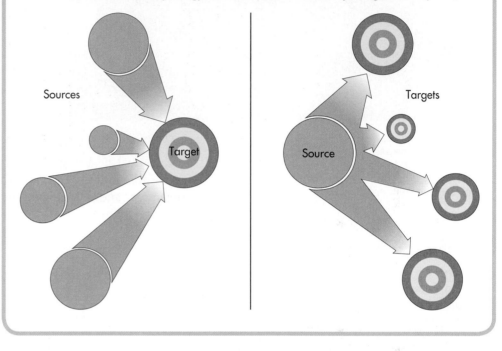

● FIGURE 7.10

Social Impact: Source Factors and Target Factors

According to social impact theory, the total influence of other people, or "sources," on a target individual depends on three source factors: their strength (size of source circles), immediacy (distance from the target), and number (number of the source circles). Similarly, the total influence is diffused, or reduced, by the strength (size of target circles), immediacy (distance from source circle), and number of target persons.

From Latane, B. (1981). "The Psychology of Social Impact," *American Psychologist*, vol 36 (p. 344).

As the number of people in a group increases, so does the group's impact on an individual.

FALSE

◼ Perspectives on Human Nature

From the material presented in this chapter, what general conclusions might you draw about human nature? Granted, social influence is more likely to occur in some situations than in others. But are people generally malleable or unyielding? Is there a tilt toward accepting influence or toward putting up resistance?

There is no single universal answer to these questions. As we saw earlier, some cultures value autonomy and independence; others place greater emphasis on conformity to one's group. Even within a given culture, values may change over time. To demonstrate the point, ask yourself: If you were a parent, what traits would you like your child to have? When this question was put to American mothers in 1924, they chose "obedience" and "loyalty," key characteristics of conformity. Yet when mothers were asked the same question in 1978, they cited "independence" and "tolerance of others," key characteristics of autonomy.

According to social impact theory, a marine sergeant will exert influence to the extent that he is strong (in a position of power), immediate (physically close), and numerous (backed by others in the institution) relative to his trainees.

Similar trends were found in surveys conducted not only in the United States but also in West Germany, Italy, England, and Japan (Alwin, 1990; Remley 1988) and in laboratory experiments, where conformity rates are somewhat lower today than in the past (Bond & Smith, 1996).

Is it possible that today's children, tomorrow's adults, will exhibit more resistance to the various forms of social influence? If so, what effects will this trend have on society as a whole? And what will be the future effects of Facebook, Twitter, and other social media? Cast in a positive light, conformity, compliance, and obedience are good and necessary human responses. They promote group solidarity and agreement—qualities that keep groups from being torn apart by dissension. Cast in a negative light, a lack of independence, assertiveness, and defiance are undesirable behaviors that lend themselves to narrow-mindedness, cowardice, and destructive obedience, often with terrible costs. For each of us and for society as a whole, the trick is to strike a balance.

Conformity rates vary across different cultures and from one generation to the next.

TRUE

Review

Top 10 Key Points in Chapter 7

1. Sometimes people are influenced by others without awareness—as when we mimic each other's nonverbal behaviors and gestures without realizing it.

2. Sherif's (1936) classic study showed that sometimes we conform to other people's judgments and behaviors because we are uncertain of what is correct and use others for informational guidance.

3. Asch's (1951) classic study showed that sometimes we conform to other people's judgments and behaviors even when they are clearly incorrect because we do not want to deviate and risk rejection.

4. Conformity is increased by the size of a unanimous majority, up to a point, though the presence of a single dissenting ally empowers people to resist the pressure to conform.

5. By staking out a consistent and unwavering position, dissenting individuals inside a group can exert "minority influence" and enhance the quality of a group's decision making.

6. Just as cultures differ in terms of their social norms, they differ in adherence to those norms—people from collectivist cultures conform more than do people from individualistic cultures.

7. At times, people are likely to comply with direct requests—for example, when taken by surprise, when the request sounds reasonable, and when they feel indebted to the requestor.

8. Over the years, social psychologists have studied two-step request approaches that lead people to gain compliance—for example, by using the foot-in-the-door and door-in-the-face techniques.

9. In Milgram's classic, controversial, and profound research, 65% of subjects fully obeyed an experimenter's command to administer increasingly painful electric shocks to a confederate.

10. Even today, Milgram's experiments continue to generate controversy and inform important aspects of human nature and the question of how to minimize destructive acts of obedience in real life settings.

Putting Common Sense to the Test

Conformity

When all members of a group give an incorrect response to an easy question, most people most of the time conform to that response.

(F) **False.** *In Asch's classic conformity experiments, respondents conformed only about a third of the time.*

Compliance

An effective way to get someone to do you a favor is to make a first request that is so large the person is sure to reject it.

(T) **True.** *This approach, known as the door-in-the-face technique, increases compliance by making the person feel bound to make a concession.*

Obedience

In experiments on obedience, most participants who were ordered to administer severe shocks to an innocent person refused to do so.

(F) **False.** *In Milgram's classic research, 65% of all participants obeyed the experimenter and administered the maximum possible shock.*

The Continuum of Social Influence

As the number of people in a group increases, so does the group's impact on an individual.

(F) **False.** *Increasing group size boosts the impact on an individual only up to a point, beyond which further increases have very little added effect.*

Conformity rates vary across different cultures and from one generation to the next.

(T) **True.** *Research shows that conformity rates are higher in cultures that are collectivistic rather than individualistic in orientation and that values change over time even within cultures.*

Key Terms

collectivism (282)
compliance (283)
conformity (268)
door-in-the-face technique (289)
foot-in-the-door technique (286)
idiosyncrasy credits (280)

individualism (282)
informational influence (271)
lowballing (288)
minority influence (279)
normative influence (271)
obedience (292)

private conformity (273)
public conformity (273)
social impact theory (304)
that's-not-all technique (290)

Group Processes

This chapter examines social influence in a group context. First, we focus on the fundamentals of groups, in which we discuss issues such as why people are drawn to groups and how groups develop. We then turn to how the behavior of individuals is affected by the presence of others. Then we focus on group performance and discuss why the whole (the group decision or performance) so often is different from the sum of its parts (the attitudes and abilities of the group members). In the final section, on conflict, we examine how groups intensify or reconcile their differences.

Carin Perilloux

Fundamentals of Groups | 311

Individuals in Groups: The Presence of Others | 316

Group Performance: Problems and Solutions | 325

Conflict: Cooperation and Competition Within and Between Groups | 339

Review

NASA team members celebrate in July 2015 the extraordinary feat of its space vehicle, *New Horizons,* flying close up to Pluto and sending back remarkable photos.

Bill Ingalls/NASA/Getty Images News/Getty Images

Putting COMMON SENSE to the Test

Circle Your Answer

T   F   People will cheer louder when they cheer as part of a group than when they cheer alone.

T   F   People brainstorming as a group come up with a greater number of better ideas than the same number of people working individually.

T   F   Group members' attitudes about a course of action usually become more moderate after group discussion.

T   F   People and groups tend to do worse when they have "do your best" goals than when they have very specific, ambitious goals.

T   F   Large groups are more likely than small groups to exploit a scarce resource that the members collectively depend on.

T   F   When people or groups negotiate with each other, the best solution is one in which both parties compromise and split the resources 50–50.

It was a road trip like no other. On July 15, 2015, a vehicle reached a destination that had been a long time coming, and sent photos back home. When members of the U.S. National Aeronautics and Space Administration (NASA) received the photos, celebrations erupted. Their spacecraft, *New Horizons*, had finally approached Pluto, which, depending on your classification scheme, is either the farthest planet in our solar system or the most beloved dwarf planet in the Kuiper belt. Either way, it's far, far away, and this was an incredible achievement. The historic scientific and engineering feat necessary to complete this nearly 10-year, 3-*billion*-mile journey to the far reaches of our solar system required not only the tireless work of a very large group of people, but also precise coordination among all its members. This is what groups can do at their best.

While impressive, it may not seem surprising that this super-intelligent, hardworking group of people at NASA could pull this off. After all, they really are *rocket scientists*. But history, and social psychology, teach us that groups of even super-smart people can make really bad decisions, and there is something about the dynamics of groups that can make this happen. For example, two of the biggest tragedies in NASA's history, the explosions of the space shuttles *Challenger* and *Columbia*, in 1986 and 2003, respectively, occurred in no small part because of bad group processes—involving factors such as poor communication, biased sampling of information, and pressure toward conformity. This, unfortunately, is also what groups can do.

In short, people are often at their best—and their worst—in groups. It is through groups that individuals form communities, pool resources, and share successes. But it is also through groups that ideas stagnate in endless discussion, selfish impulses flourish in the anonymity of a crowd, and prejudices turn into genocide and war. Clearly, it is important that we understand how groups work and how individuals influence, and are influenced by, groups. In this chapter, we first introduce the fundamentals of what groups are and how they develop, then we examine groups on several levels: At the individual level, we explore how individuals are influenced by groups; at the group level, we explore how groups perform; and at the intergroup level, we explore how groups interact with each other in cooperation and competition.

The research we report in this chapter reveals a fascinating fact: *Groups can be quite different from the sum of their parts.* When you think about that statement, it suggests something almost mystical or magical about groups. How can a group be better—or worse—than its individual members? The math may not seem to add up, but the theory and research discussed in this chapter will help answer this question.

"You think because you understand 'one,' you must understand 'two' because one and one make two. But you must also understand 'and.'"
—Ancient Sufi saying

Fundamentals of Groups

We begin our exploration of groups by asking the basic questions: What is a group? Why do people join groups? We then focus on three important aspects of groups: roles, norms, and cohesiveness.

■ What Is a Group? Why Join a Group?

What Is a Group?   The question might seem quite simple, but if you step back and think about it, the answer is less obvious. For example, many students are members of a variety of groups on social media. Are these really groups? You may be part of a large social psychology class: Is this a group identity that is meaningful to you?

A **group** may be characterized as a set of individuals who have direct interactions with each other over a period of time and share a common fate, identity, or set of goals. A group can also consist of people who have joint membership in a social category based on sex, race, or other attributes; this characteristic is especially relevant for the issues discussed in Chapter 5 on Stereotypes, Prejudice, and Discrimination.

Groups vary in the extent to which they are seen as distinct *entities,* such as whether they have rigid boundaries that make them distinct from other groups. In other words, some groups seem more "groupy" (or in the unfortunate choice of word used by researchers on this issue: "entitative") than others (Brewer, 2015; Hamilton et al., 2011). On the very low end of this dimension would be people attending a concert or working out near each other in a gym. These typically are not considered real groups. Such assemblages are sometimes called *collectives*—people engaging in a common activity but having little direct interaction with each other (Milgram & Toch, 1969). Much more integrated groups include tight-knit clubs, sports teams, or work teams—groups that engage in very purposeful activities with a lot of interaction over time and clear boundaries of who is in and not in the group. People tend to identify more strongly with these more integrated, coherent groups and to get more satisfaction from them (Crawford & Salaman, 2012).

Culture can also shape the nature of what makes a group a group. People in Western cultures are more likely to define and identify with groups based on what

group   A set of individuals who interact over time and have shared fate, goals, or identity.

Sarah Sudhoff/Redux

People join a group for any of several reasons, such as to affiliate with others, obtain social status, and interact with individual group members.

members *do,* whereas in Eastern cultures how group members *relate* to each other may be more important (Yuki, 2003).

As we will discuss later in this chapter, more groups today defy our traditional view of what is a group. Particularly in the worlds of business and technology, groups often consist of people who are dispersed widely across time and space and communicate exclusively through technology, and the dynamics of these groups may be extremely different from those of traditional groups. For example, these newer, more dispersed types of groups tend to have more shifting boundaries and membership, and they tend to be more self-managed or have shared leadership (Hackman & Katz, 2010). Understanding these unique dynamics and determining how to help these groups reach their potential is one of the more exciting challenges in contemporary social psychological research on groups.

Why Join a Group? The complexity and ambitions of human life require that we work in groups. Much of what we hope to produce and accomplish can be done only through collective action. Lone individuals cannot play symphonies or football games, build cities or industries, or run governments or universities.

At a more fundamental level, humans may have an innate need to belong to groups stemming from evolutionary pressures that increased people's chances of survival and reproduction if they lived in groups rather than in isolation. Indeed, according to the *social brain hypothesis,* the unusually large size of humans' brains evolved because of our unusually complex social worlds. As we wrote in the first paragraph of Chapter 1: We have such large brains in order to socialize (Dunbar, 2014; Spunt et al., 2015; van Vugt & Kameda, 2014).

For humans, attraction to group life serves not only to protect against threat and uncertainty in a physical sense but also to gain a greater sense of personal and social identity. According to *social identity theory,* which was discussed in Chapter 5, an important part of people's feelings of self-worth comes from their identification with particular groups, and so people care a great deal about being part of groups and about how their groups are valued (Ellemers & Haslam, 2012; Greenaway et al., 2015; Hogg, 2014; Jetten et al., 2015). Beyond feelings of self-worth, our groups often give us meaning and purpose and, according to some scholars, perhaps even a symbolic sense of immortality as our most cherished groups live on beyond our lifetimes (Schimel & Greenberg, 2013). These cherished aspects of group membership are at the root of why being rejected by a group is one of life's most painful experiences (Eisenberger, 2015).

■ Key Features of Groups: Roles, Norms, and Cohesiveness

Once an individual has joined a group, a process of adjustment takes place as the individual is socialized to how things work in the group. This socialization process may be formal and explicit, such as through an initiation or orientation program, mentoring or supervision, or documentation, or it may be implicit, as newcomers observe how established members behave in the group. Effectively socializing new members can produce short-term and long-term benefits for the group as a whole (Levine & Choi, 2010; Moreland & Levine, 2002). One thing that newcomers can do to more quickly get older members to accept them and utilize their knowledge is to use more group-focused language (such as using "we" and "us" rather than "I" and "you") with group members (Kane & Rink, 2015).

Two of the things that are especially important for newcomers to learn—and for more established members of the group to continue to understand or revise—are the roles they are expected to play in the group, and what the norms of the group are. Newcomers also learn how cohesive the group is. We focus on each of these three features of groups—roles, norms, and cohesiveness—in the following sections.

Roles People's *roles* in a group—their set of expected behaviors—can be formal or informal. Formal roles are designated by titles: teacher or student in a class, vice president or account executive in a corporation. Informal roles are less obvious but still powerful. Robert Bales (1958) distinguished between two fundamental types of roles: an *instrumental* role to help the group achieve its tasks and an *expressive* role to provide emotional support and maintain morale. The same person can fill both roles, but often they are assumed by different individuals, and which of these roles is emphasized in groups may fluctuate over time, depending on the needs of the group.

One problem that can seriously harm the performance of groups is when there is a mismatch between members' skills and what roles they occupy in the group. It is far too common in groups for members to be assigned or take on group roles in a way that is less than thoughtful and systematic. Members may be assigned roles simply based on who is available at a given point in time rather than who is best suited for the role. Groups function much better when members are assigned roles that best match their talents and personalities, and social psychologists are among the consultants often hired to help groups do this better (Woolley et al., 2007).

Group members sometimes are uncertain about exactly what their group roles are supposed to be. They may also find themselves in roles that conflict with other roles they have to play, either within the group (such as needing to be demanding while also being the source of emotional support) or between groups (such as between work and family). Role uncertainty, instability, and conflict are all associated with poorer job performance, as well a variety of other problems, including workplace bullying or other interpersonal conflicts, emotional exhaustion and burnout, and high turnover in the group (Bowling et al., 2015; Dishon-Berkovits, 2014; Kauppila, 2014; Tubre & Collins, 2000; Wilson & Baumann, 2015).

Sometimes an opposite problem of role uncertainty or conflict develops: Group members can become so absorbed in their role that they lose themselves—and their personal beliefs and sense of morality—in their group role. Interrogators of a prisoner or suspect may get so lost in their role that they fail to recognize the ethical lines they are crossing. One of the most disturbing studies in the history of social psychology examined this kind of issue, in what came to be known as The Stanford Prison Experiment (Haney et al., 1973). Participants in this study were randomly assigned to play the roles of prisoners or guards in a simulated prison. The guards in particular got so into their roles as protectors of the "prison" and enforcer of the rules that they soon became cruel and sadistic.

"The individuals which took the greatest pleasure in society would best escape various dangers, whilst those that cared least for their comrades, and lived solitary, would perish in greater numbers."
—Charles Darwin *The Descent of Man*

Tom Cheney /The New Yorker Collection/The Cartoon Bank

"I've had to be both hunter and gatherer."

When roles in a group are not distributed properly, group performance suffers.

Even the social psychologist in charge of the study was so focused on his role as "prison warden" that he ignored his ethical responsibilities as a researcher. This fascinating but troubling study is discussed in detail in Chapter 12 on Law.

Norms In addition to roles for its members, groups also establish *norms,* rules of conduct for members. Like roles, norms may be either formal or informal. Fraternities and sororities, for example, usually have written rules for the behavior expected from their members. Informal norms are more subtle. What do I wear? How hard can I push for what I want? Who pays for this or that? What kind of language, joking, or socializing is typical? These norms provide individuals with a sense of what it means to be a good group member. Figuring out the unwritten rules of the group can take time and cause anxiety.

Groups often exert strong conformity pressures on individuals who deviate from group norms and perceive or treat these members very harshly, in part because deviations from group norms can threaten group members' sense of uniformity and social identity with the group (Hutchison et al., 2013; Packer, 2014). One way that low-status or new group members may try to establish a stronger position in the group is to be especially punishing of members who break group norms—especially if high-status group members would witness their harsh reaction to norm violators (Jetten et al., 2010). On the other hand, group members who are highly identified with the group and care about its collective success may be willing to deviate from a group norm if they think that the norm is likely to harm the group (Jetten & Hornsey, 2014; Packer et al., 2014).

How tolerant groups are to violations of norms can be, itself, a kind of norm. Some groups, for example, pride themselves on how heterogeneous and free-thinking its members are. Others strongly value uniformity. Paul Hutchison and others (2011) designed an experiment to see if they could manipulate this sense of how uniform the group members are supposed to be. They asked some British students questions about their university that were designed to highlight the uniformity of the students' backgrounds and attitudes at their school. For example, they were asked what percentage of the students preferred popular music over classical music, and what percentage liked to watch movies. Because the large majority of the students would prefer popular music and would like movies, questions like these would prime the students to see their similarities. The researchers asked other students questions induced to make them see their school as full of diverse backgrounds and attitudes. They were asked to estimate the percentages of students who most preferred dance, rock, hip-hop, pop, or classical music, and what percentages most preferred movies featuring science fiction, love stories, comedy, martial arts, and so on. These questions would highlight the wide variety of opinions and tastes that were accepted at their university.

The students then read about a student who expressed an attitude about a war that was either typical or atypical of the students there. How would the participants react to this student? Participants in general rated the student with the typical attitude toward the war positively. If the student expressed an atypical attitude, however, they disliked him more if they were induced to see their university as very uniform than if they were induced to see their university as diverse and heterogeneous (see ● Figure 8.1). In other words, a deviation from a group norm was met with more tolerance if the

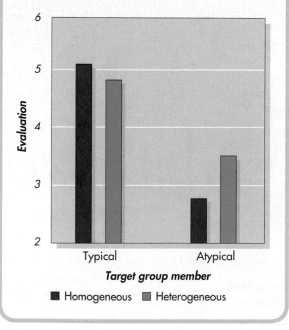

● **FIGURE 8.1**

Tolerance for Deviating From the Norm

Students evaluated a fellow student who expressed an attitude that was either typical or atypical for their university. In general, the student expressing the typical attitude was evaluated more positively than the atypical student. But if the students had first been primed to see their university as heterogeneous, they were less negative toward the atypical student than were the students who had been primed to see their university as homogenous.
Hutchison et al., 2011.

■ Homogeneous   ■ Heterogeneous

participants saw the group as more variable than if they saw their group as typically sharing similar background and values. Indeed, when a group develops a strong norm of encouraging diverse viewpoints, it can cause members to conform to the norm of not conforming!

Culture and Norms   Cultures vary in how much they tolerate behavior that deviates from the norm. Anthropologist Pertii Pelto (1968) first described the difference between "tight" and "loose" cultures. He proposed that *tight* cultures have strong norms and little tolerance for behavior that deviates from the norm, while *loose* cultures have relatively weaker norms and greater tolerance for deviant behavior. Michele Gelfand and others (2011, 2012) demonstrate that greater ecological and historical threats (such as resource scarcity or natural disasters), higher population density, and more restrictive governments and religious institutions encourage the formation of tight societies. Loose societies, in contrast, are more likely to thrive in environments that have fewer historical and ecological threats and are characterized by situations that have few constraints on individuals, allowing individuals to behave according to their own discretion. Analyzing the similarity between people's values, norms, and behavior across 65 countries, Uz (2015) identified Egypt, Indonesia, and Morocco as the tightest countries and Belgium, Luxembourg, and France as the loosest countries (see Table 8.1). However, one does not have to travel to another country to experience differences in tightness and looseness. For example, within the United States, Harrington and Gelfand (2014) found that the southern states of Mississippi, Alabama, and Arkansas had the highest tightness rankings, while the western states of California, Oregon, and Washington had the highest looseness rankings.

> ▲ **TABLE 8.1**
>
> **Tightness–Looseness of Various Countries**
>
> Cultures considered "tight" have strong and homogenous norms, values, and behaviors, and there is much less tolerance for deviance from norms. The numbers next to the countries listed in this table are an index according to one recent analysis of how tight–loose these countries are, with higher numbers indicating greater looseness.
>
> | Country | Index | Country | Index |
> |---|---|---|---|
> | Argentina | 75 | Luxembourg | 114 |
> | Bangladesh | 7 | Mexico | 75 |
> | Belgium | 120 | Morocco | 0 |
> | Canada | 84 | Netherlands | 79 |
> | Egypt | 4 | Nigeria | 18 |
> | France | 100 | Philippines | 32 |
> | Greece | 58 | Poland | 43 |
> | India | 44 | Russian Fed. | 57 |
> | Indonesia | 3 | Saudi Arabia | 22 |
> | Ireland | 71 | South Africa | 68 |
> | Japan | 43 | Spain | 84 |
> | Jordan | 5 | USA | 58 |
>
> Based on Uz, 2015

Cohesiveness   Groups whose members share similar attitudes and closely follow the groups' norms are more likely than other groups to be cohesive. **Group cohesiveness** refers to the forces exerted on a group that push its members closer together (Cartwright & Zander, 1960; Festinger, 1950). Members of cohesive groups tend to feel commitment to the group task, feel positively toward the other group members, feel group pride, and engage in many—and often intense—interactions in the group (Dion, 2000; Rosh et al., 2012).

An interesting question is whether cohesiveness makes groups perform better. It may seem obvious that it should. Indeed, groups often strive to achieve cohesiveness, and if they feel that they are not very cohesive, they may take steps to improve it, such as ordering everyone to go through bonding exercises or hang out together at a rustic retreat. In fact, however, the relationship between cohesiveness and performance is not a simple one. The causal relationship works both ways: On the one hand, when a group is cohesive, group performance often improves; on the other hand, when a group performs well, it often becomes more cohesive. Many team athletes recognize that winning creates team chemistry even more than team chemistry creates winning.

Whatever the cause and effect, several longitudinal studies and meta-analyses of hundreds of studies have provided evidence showing that group cohesion is associated with better performance, but other variables tend to be important in

group cohesiveness   The extent to which forces push group members closer together, such as through feelings of intimacy, unity, and commitment to group goals.

20th Century Fox Film Corp/Everett Collection

A scene from the classic cult movie, *Office Space,* depicts frustrated employees from a work group that is anything but cohesive.

predicting when and to what extent this relationship emerges, such as how large the group is, whether the cohesiveness is primarily about the group's attraction to the task (*task cohesion*) or to each other (*interpersonal cohesion*), and what type of task the group performs (Castaño et al., 2013; Mathieu et al., 2015; Picazo et al., 2015). As we will see a bit later in the chapter, group cohesiveness can also lead to conformity and narrow-mindedness that can cause major problems for groups.

Culture and Cohesiveness

Group cohesiveness can be affected in different ways as a function of cultural differences. For example, cohesiveness in collectivist cultures may be associated more with social harmony, cooperation, and interpersonal relations than in individualist cultures, where recognizing members' unique skills, perspectives, and job-focused efforts may be more essential for group cohesiveness (Lai et al., 2013). Cultural differences exist also in norms about how leaders are expected to behave in groups, and this has consequences for group cohesiveness. Respect and obedience to leaders are more important to people from collectivist cultures than those in individualist cultures. Consistent with this point, Hein Wendt and others (2009) found in a study of over 150,000 individuals from 615 organizations across 80 countries that having a directive, controlling leader was associated with greater group cohesiveness in collectivist societies than in individualist cultures.

The extent to which groups are comfortable with conflict and heated debate among their members also varies across culture. This was demonstrated in a study by Roger Nibler and Karen Harris (2003) involving five-person groups of strangers and friends in China and the United States. Each group had to decide how to rank 15 items to be taken aboard a lifeboat from a ship that was about to sink. This task tends to trigger a fair amount of initial disagreement among group members before a consensus can be reached. With the Chinese groups and the groups of American strangers, these kinds of disagreements tended to be perceived as troubling and interfered with group performance. To the groups of American friends, in contrast, these disagreements were more likely to be seen as simply part of a freewheeling debate, and the sense of freedom to exchange opinions and disagree with one another tended to improve rather than hurt performance on this task. More recently, Daan Bisseling and Filipe Sobral (2011), using surveys and interviews of 366 members of companies from the Netherlands and Brazil, found that intragroup conflict was associated with reduced satisfaction and job performance among employees in the more collectivistic culture of Brazil, but not among the more individualistic Dutch workers.

Individuals in Groups: The Presence of Others

When we engage in activities in groups, we are in the presence (either physically or virtually) of others. It's an obvious point, but some of its consequences are profound and surprising. In this section we focus on three important effects that the presence of others can have on individuals: social facilitation, social loafing, and deindividuation.

■ Social Facilitation: When Others Arouse Us

Social psychologists have long been fascinated by how the presence of others affects behavior. In Chapter 1, we reported that Norman Triplett's article, "The Dynamogenic Factors in Pacemaking and Competition" (1897–1898), is often cited as the earliest publication in the field. Triplett began his research by studying the official bicycle records from the Racing Board of the League of American Wheelmen for the 1897 season. He noticed that cyclists who competed against others performed better than those who cycled alone against the clock. After dismissing various theories of the day (our favorite is "brain worry"), he proposed his own hypothesis: The presence of another rider releases the competitive instinct, which increases nervous energy and enhances performance. To test this proposition, Triplett got 40 children to wind up fishing reels, alternating between performing alone and working in parallel. Triplett reported that children were more likely to perform better when they worked side by side than when they worked alone. (In a contemporary twist on this classic, Michael Strube (2005) used modern statistical techniques to reanalyze Triplett's original data and found that the results were quite weak and not as straightforward as Triplett's report suggested.)

Later research following Triplett's studies proved mixed. Sometimes the presence of others (side by side or with an audience out front) enhanced performance; at other times, performance declined. It seemed that Triplett's promising lead had turned into a blind alley, and social psychologists had largely abandoned this research by World War II. But years later, Robert Zajonc (1965; 1980) saw a way to reconcile the contradictory results by integrating research from experimental psychology with social psychological research. Zajonc offered an elegant solution: The presence of others increases arousal, which can affect performance in different ways, depending on the task at hand. Let's see how this works.

The Zajonc Solution   Zajonc proposed a three-step process:

1. The presence of others creates general physiological *arousal*, which energizes behavior. Based on experimental psychology research and principles of evolution, Zajonc argued that all animals, including humans, tend to become aroused when in the presence of *conspecifics*—that is, members of their own species.
2. Increased arousal enhances an individual's tendency to perform the *dominant response*. The dominant response is the reaction elicited most quickly and easily by a given stimulus.
3. The quality of an individual's performance varies according to the type of *task*. On an easy task (one that is simple or well learned), the dominant response is usually correct or successful. But on a difficult task (one that is complex or unfamiliar), the dominant response is often incorrect or unsuccessful.

Putting these three steps together (see ● Figure 8.2) yields the following scenarios. Suppose you are playing the

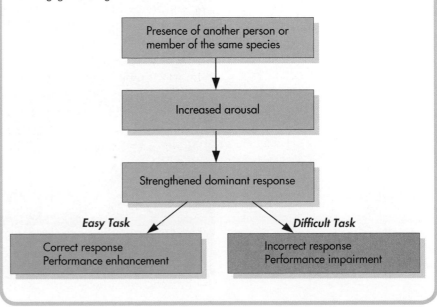

● **FIGURE 8.2**

Social Facilitation: The Zajonc Solution

According to Zajonc, the presence of others increases arousal, which strengthens the dominant response to a stimulus. On an easy task, the dominant response is usually correct, and thus the presence of others enhances performance. On a difficult task, the dominant response is often incorrect, and thus the presence of others impairs performance.

© Cengage Learning®

Presence of another person or member of the same species

↓

Increased arousal

↓

Strengthened dominant response

Easy Task ↙   ↘ *Difficult Task*

Correct response
Performance enhancement

Incorrect response
Performance impairment

violin. If you're an excellent player and are performing a well-learned, familiar arrangement, having other people around should enhance your performance; the presence of others will increase your arousal, which will enhance your dominant response. Because this arrangement is so well learned, your dominant response will be to perform it well. However, if you are just learning to play the violin and you are unfamiliar with this arrangement, the presence of others is the last thing you'll want. The increase in arousal should enhance the dominant response, which in this case would be *unsuccessful* violin playing.

Taken as a package, these two effects of the presence of others—helping performance on easy tasks but hurting performance on difficult tasks—are known as **social facilitation**. Unfortunately this term has been a prime source of confusion for countless students. The trick is to remember that the presence of others facilitates the dominant response, not necessarily the task itself. This facilitation of the dominant response does, in effect, facilitate easy tasks, but it makes difficult tasks even more difficult.

Zajonc proposed that social facilitation is universal, occurring not only in human activities but also among other animals, even insects. Have you ever wondered, for instance, how well a cockroach performs in front of other cockroaches? Neither did we—that is, we didn't until we first learned of Zajonc's creative research on the topic. Zajonc and his colleagues (1969) had cockroaches placed in a brightly lit start box connected to a darkened goal box. When the track was a simple one, with a straight runway between the start box and the goal box, cockroaches running in pairs ran more quickly toward the goal box than did those running alone. But in a more complex maze that required a right turn to reach the goal box, solitary cockroaches outraced pairs. In a particularly creative follow-up experiment, Zajonc and his colleagues found that cockroaches completed the easy maze faster, and the difficult maze slower, if they raced in front of a crowd of spectator cockroaches than if they raced with no audience. How did the researchers get cockroaches to participate as spectators? The researchers placed cockroaches in plexiglass "audience boxes" along either side of the maze, and this "audience" produced social facilitation.

social facilitation A process whereby the presence of others enhances performance on easy tasks but impairs performance on difficult tasks.

U.S. swimmer Michael Phelps surges to the lead on the way to one of his record-setting gold medals at the 2012 Olympics in London. Through social facilitation, some of the best athletes benefit from the presence of an audience and high pressure when performing well-learned routines.

Francois Xavier Marit/AFP/Getty Images

Social Facilitation Research Today Zajonc's formulation revived interest in the issues raised by Triplett's early research, and suddenly the inconsistent findings that had been reported began to make sense. The results of a meta-analysis of 241 studies were consistent with much of Zajonc's account (Bond & Titus, 1983). And despite its long history, research today continues to demonstrate new examples of social facilitation and to test its scope and limitations. Rui-feng Yu and Xin Wu (2015), for example, found that the presence of an observer slowed down participants' screening of baggage in an X-ray security scan when the task was complex but sped up the performance when the task was simple. Social facilitation effects have been demonstrated in settings where individuals are taking driving tests (a word of advice: Don't take your road test with another test-taker present in the car!), gambling electronically, and being given neuropsychological tests, and the effects have been found even when the "others" present were merely a photograph of a favorite TV character or a computer display of a "virtual" person (Eastvold et al., 2012; Gardner & Knowles, 2008; Park & Catrambone, 2007; Rockloff et al., 2012; Rosenbloom et al., 2007).

It is in part because of the effects of social facilitation that firefighters, police officers, military personnel, and others must train so much to be ready to make split-second decisions under highly arousing situations. They may seem to practice scenarios to the point of overtraining, but it is only through such repetition that their dominant response can be assured to typically be the correct one. When they are in the midst of a raging fire or military firefight, it is often impossible for them to think carefully, and so it's all the more essential that their dominant response be a good one (Gladwell, 2005).

"God, this is going to be all over YouTube."

Fear of being evaluated by others can sometimes hurt performance.

Alternative Explanations for Social Facilitation Social facilitation effects have been replicated across many domains, but not all of Zajonc's theory has received universal support. Zajonc proposed that the **mere presence** of others is sufficient to produce social facilitation. Some have argued, however, that a better explanation is the **evaluation apprehension theory**, which proposes that performance will be enhanced or impaired only in the presence of others who are in a position to evaluate that performance (Geen, 1991; Henchy & Glass, 1968). In other words, it's not simply because others are around that I'm so aroused and therefore inept as I try to learn to snowboard on a crowded mountain. Rather, it's because I worry that the others are watching and probably laughing at me, possibly uploading a video of my performance to YouTube. These concerns increase my dominant response, which, unfortunately, is falling.

Another account of social facilitation, **distraction–conflict theory**, points out that being distracted while we're working on a task creates attentional conflict (Baron, 1986; Sanders, 1981). We're torn between focusing on the task and glancing at the distracting stimulus. When we are conflicted about where to pay attention, our arousal increases.

So is one of these theories right and the others wrong? Probably not. It seems likely that all three of the basic elements described by these theories (mere presence, evaluation, and attention) can contribute to the impact others have on our own performance (Uziel, 2007). But as we are about to see in the next section, there is even more to the story of how individuals are affected by the presence of others.

mere presence The proposition that the mere presence of others is sufficient to produce social facilitation effects.

evaluation apprehension theory A theory that the presence of others will produce social facilitation effects only when those others are seen as potential evaluators.

distraction–conflict theory A theory that the presence of others will produce social facilitation effects only when those others distract from the task and create attentional conflict.

● FIGURE 8.3

Social Loafing: When Many Produce Less

Social loafing is a group-produced reduction in individual output on simple tasks. In this study, college students were told to cheer or clap as loudly as they could. The noise produced by each of them decreased as the size of the group increased.

Based on Latané et al., 1979.

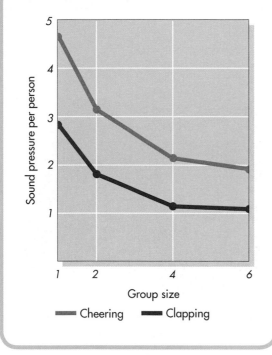

People will cheer louder when they cheer as part of a group than when they cheer alone.

FALSE

social loafing A group-produced reduction in individual output on tasks where contributions are pooled.

Social Loafing: When Others Relax Us

In the tasks relevant to social facilitation effects, an individual's behavior can be identified and evaluated. But on some tasks, efforts are pooled so that the specific performance of any one individual cannot be determined. It just so happens that research on these kinds of collective endeavors can also be traced back to Triplett's era of the late nineteenth century. In Chapter 1 we mentioned the French agricultural engineer Max Ringelmann as another contender for having conducted the first social psychology research. In research conducted during the 1880s, Ringelmann discovered that people's output declined when they worked together rather than alone on simple tasks like pulling a rope or pushing a cart (Kravitz & Martin, 1986; Ringelmann, 1913).

Why did individual output decline? One explanation is that the individuals exerted less effort when they acted collectively, but another explanation is that the individuals simply demonstrated poor coordination when working together—some pulled while others relaxed and vice versa. How can you distinguish lack of effort from poor coordination in a task like this? Nearly 100 years after Ringelmann's research, Alan Ingham and his colleagues (1974) answered this question by using a rope-pulling machine and blindfolding participants. In one condition, participants were led to *think* that they were pulling with a bunch of other participants, and in another condition the participants were informed that they were pulling alone (which, in fact, they were). The researchers told the participants to pull as hard as they could. Ingham and colleagues were able to measure exactly how hard each individual participant pulled, and they observed that the participants pulled almost 20% harder when they thought they were pulling alone than when they thought they were pulling with others.

Bibb Latané and his colleagues (1979) found that group-produced reductions in individual output, which they called **social loafing**, are common in other types of tasks as well. For example, imagine being asked as part of a psychology experiment to cheer or clap as loudly as you can. Common sense might lead you to think that you would cheer and clap louder when doing this together with others in a group than when performing alone because you would be less embarrassed and inhibited if others were doing the same thing as you. But Latané and his colleagues found that when performing collectively, students tended to loaf—they exerted less effort. The noise generated by each individual decreased as the size of the group increased (see ● Figure 8.3). This social loafing occurred even among cheerleaders, who are supposed to be experts at cheering and clapping with others!

Social loafing is not restricted to simple motor tasks. Sharing responsibility with others reduces the amount of effort that people put into more complex motor tasks, such playing team sports; cognitive tasks, such as completing memory, math, or verbal tests; and important, enduring real-world behaviors, such as working collaboratively on collective farms or team projects (Hoigaard & Ommundsen, 2007; Liden et al., 2004; Miles & Greenberg, 1993; Plaks & Higgins, 2000; Tan & Tan, 2008; Weldon et al., 2000). When others are there to pick up the slack, people slack off.

Most college students are quite familiar with having to work on group projects, and many have seen the pitfalls of social loafing in these settings. Praveen Aggarwal and Connie O'Brien (2008) studied several hundred college students to assess what factors can reduce the incidence of social loafing, and they offer these three strategies: (1) limit the scope of the project—projects that are very large and complex should be broken into smaller components; (2) keep the groups small; and (3) use peer evaluations. Curt Dommeyer (2012)'s research suggests also that making each group member a "manager" of different segments of the task can also help reduce loafing.

Businesses have taken note of social loafing and have applied these research findings in an effort to reduce it in the workplace. For example, one form of social loafing at the workplace has come to be known as *cyberloafing*, which involves personal non-work use of online technology, such as online shopping, watching videos, or messaging friends; cyberloafing can be a huge drain on workers' productivity (Askew et al., 2014; Glassman et al., 2015; Karaoğlan et al., 2015). One result is that workers' actions on the job are coming under increasing surveillance as the number of computer keystrokes they make per hour or the content of their calls, e-mails, or Internet browsing can be recorded electronically.

Collective Effort Model   Several researchers have constructed theoretical accounts to explain the findings about when social loafing is more or less likely to occur. The most influential of these is the **collective effort model** (Karau & Williams, 2001). This model asserts that individuals will try hard on a collective task when they think their efforts will help them achieve outcomes they personally value. If the outcome is important to individual members of the group *and* if they believe they can help achieve the desired outcome, they are less likely to socially loaf. In fact, in these cases they may even engage in *social compensation* by increasing their efforts on collective tasks to try to compensate for the anticipated social loafing or poor performance of other group members. The next time you work on a group project, such as a paper that you and several other students are supposed to write together, consider the factors that increase and decrease social loafing. You might want to try to change aspects of the situation so that all group members are motivated to do their share of the work.

Sam Gross /The New Yorker Collection/The Cartoon Bank

"We just haven't been flapping them hard enough."

Individuals often don't try as hard in groups as they do alone. If they can be convinced that their efforts will pay off, however, their output can soar.

Culture and Social Loafing

Steven Karau and Kipling Williams (1993) conducted a meta-analysis of 78 studies and found social loafing to be a reliable phenomenon that is evident across numerous tasks and in countries around the world. Despite its prevalence around the world, some group and cultural differences in tendencies to socially loaf have been found.

Karau and Williams's meta-analysis found that social loafing was less prevalent among women than among men and less prevalent among people from East Asian, collectivist cultures (such as those in China, Japan, and Taiwan) than among people from Western, individualist cultures (such as those in Canada and the United States). With their tendencies to be more aware of their connections and mutual reliance on others, women and people from collectivist cultures may be relatively more concerned about the possible negative interpersonal impact of social loafing. If someone in the group does violate a norm of hard work, however, people from collectivist cultures may take more offense. That is the implication of research by Tsang-Kai Hung and others (2009), who found that workers in Taiwan who perceived co-workers as socially loafing were likely to be motivated to seek revenge toward their co-workers.

In an interesting twist, Ying-yi Hong and others (2008) hypothesized that there are times when people from collectivist cultures may be especially likely to socially loaf. Because people from collectivist cultures tend to be concerned with behaving consistently with group norms, they may be tempted to socially loaf if they are working in a group that has established a group norm of low productivity and effort.

collective effort model   The theory that individuals will exert effort on a collective task to the degree that they think their individual efforts will be important, relevant, and meaningful for achieving outcomes that they value.

Here, Chinese farmers cooperate on a task in which individual contributions cannot be identified. Social loafing on such tasks occurs less often in Eastern cultures than in Western ones.

AStock/Collage/Corbis

The researchers found support for this idea in a set of studies with Chinese students. When these students engaged in a task with a group of co-workers who were not being productive, the participants reduced their own efforts if they thought their effort would be evident to their co-workers. Not wanting to publicly deviate from the group norm, these students conformed to the norm of working less hard.

Deindividuation

Being in the presence of others can lead to the relatively common effects of social facilitation and social loafing. But occasionally the presence of others can lead to extreme actions. A group of sports fans excited at their home team's victory spills out of the arena onto the street, and soon a riot develops, complete with small fires, overturned cars, and looting. A conflict between two people late at night in a loud dance club suddenly turns to a raucous brawl, with bottles flying and punches thrown involving dozens of people. What turns an unruly crowd into a violent mob? No doubt there are many factors, including imitation of aggressive models, intense frustration, and alcohol consumption. These factors are discussed in Chapter 11 on Aggression. But there's also **deindividuation**, the loss of a person's sense of individuality and the reduction of normal constraints against deviant behavior. Most investigators believe that deindividuation is a collective phenomenon that occurs primarily in the presence of others (Diener et al., 1976; Festinger et al., 1952).

Philip Zimbardo (1969) observed that *arousal, anonymity,* and reduced feelings of individual *responsibility* together contribute to deindividuation. These elements certainly seem to be in play in the destructive behavior that groups of sports fans often exhibit after a big win or loss. For example, immediately after the University of Connecticut's men's basketball team won the national championship tournament in April 2014, thousands of rowdy fans gathered on and around UConn's campus, and the celebration took a destructive turn as some students set fires, flipped cars, and threw a light post through the window of a college building (Ward, 2014). The losing team that night was the University of Kentucky; when Kentucky won the championship two years before, similar rioting and destruction broke out there. It's important to note that the fans in these incidents were not frustrated and angry at a bitter loss;

"The sentiments and ideas of all the persons in the gathering take one and the same direction, and their conscious personality vanishes."

—Gustave Le Bon (1895)

deindividuation The loss of a person's sense of individuality and the reduction of normal constraints against deviant behavior.

they were happy! So why would they—and the fans of many teams around the world after a big victory—act out destructively? All three elements that Zimbardo specified were present here: The fans were very *aroused* by their team's victory, the thousands of celebrating fans provided the individuals with relative *anonymity,* and these factors, quite possibly along with alcohol consumed during the game, contributed to reduced feelings of individual *responsibility.*

According to Steven Prentice-Dunn and Ronald Rogers (1982; 1983), two types of environmental cues—accountability cues and attentional cues—make deviant behaviors such as this rioting more likely to occur. *Accountability cues* affect the individual's cost–reward calculations. When accountability is low, those who commit deviant acts are less likely to be caught and punished, and people may deliberately choose to engage in gratifying but usually inhibited behaviors. Being in a large crowd or wearing a mask are two examples of instances when accountability may be low, and these factors are associated with more extreme and destructive behaviors.

Attentional cues focus a person's attention away from the self. In this state, the individual attends less to internal standards of conduct, reacts more to the immediate situation, and is less sensitive to long-term consequences of behavior (Diener, 1980). Behavior slips out from the bonds of cognitive control, and people act on impulse. When you are at a party with very loud music and flashing lights, you may be swept up with the pulsating crowd and feel your individual identity slipping away.

One context ripe for deindividuation is online behavior. If you've ever been part of an online community where people can post comments anonymously (such as through the popular app, Yik Yak), there is a good chance that you've witnessed some of the nasty effects of deindividuation. Many well-intentioned sites or discussions or even the comments sections linked to online newspaper stories, videos, or celebrity gossip blogs soon devolve into a torrent of crude, hostile, and prejudiced venting and taunting that would never happen without the cloak of anonymity.

Trick or Treat: Field Experiments on Halloween   One particularly creative set of field experiments by Edward Diener and Arthur Beaman and their colleagues (Beaman et al., 1979; Diener et al., 1976) demonstrated how accountability and

University of Kentucky fans turn over a car as they celebrate Kentucky's win over archrival Louisville in men's basketball in March 2012. Two years later, when Kentucky lost to UConn in April 2014, similar scenes played out on UConn's campus. In the midst of crowds like these, people may feel deindividuated, which can lead to deviant behavior.

AP Images/Christian Randolph

● FIGURE 8.4

Trick or Treat(s)

Children trick-or-treating on Halloween were part of a field experiment. Some were alone and some were in groups with other trick-or-treaters. The experimenter who greeted them allowed a random half of the children to remain anonymous but asked the other half to indicate their names and where they lived. The experimenter instructed each child to take only one piece of candy, after which she left the children alone. The bars in this graph represent the percentage of children who took more than the one piece of candy. Consistent with predictions based on deindividuation, the children who were in a group and were anonymous were most likely to cheat by taking extra candy.

Based on Diener et al., 1976.

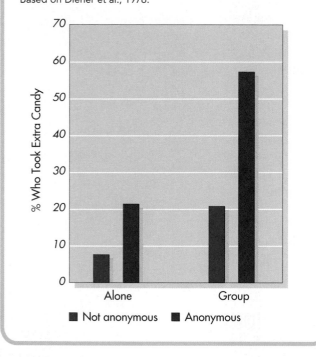

attentional cues can affect behavior on a night when many otherwise well-behaved individuals act in antisocial ways: Halloween. When you think about it, Halloween is a perfect time to study deindividuation: Children often wear costumes with masks, travel in large groups at night, and are highly aroused. In one study, the researchers unobtrusively observed more than 1,300 children who came trick-or-treating to 27 homes spread around Seattle. At each of these homes, a researcher met and greeted the children, who were either alone or in groups. In one condition, the researcher asked the children their names and where they lived; in another condition, the researcher did not ask them any questions about their identities. When asked to identify themselves, the children should have become more self-aware and more accountable for their actions. Children who were not asked to reveal their identities and were in a group should have felt relatively deindividuated, safe, and anonymous in their costumes.

The children were then invited to take *one* item from a bowl full of candy and were left alone with the bowl. Hidden observers watched to see how many pieces of candy each child took. What did the observers see? As ● Figure 8.4 illustrates, children who were in a group were more likely to break the rule and take extra candy than were children who were alone. Add anonymity to the presence of a group, and children were even more likely to do so. In other words, the children were most likely to take extra candy when they were the most deindividuated: when they were in a group and had not been asked to identify themselves. In another experiment, the researchers placed a mirror behind the candy bowl in some conditions. As noted in Chapter 3, the presence of a mirror tends to increase people's self-awareness. Children who had been asked their names, especially older children, were much less likely to steal candy if there was a mirror present than if there wasn't. Older children are more likely to have internal standards against stealing, and making these children self-aware made them more likely to act according to those standards.

Moving From Personal to Social Identity   The loss of personal identity does not always produce antisocial behavior. In a study conducted by Robert Johnson and Leslie Downing (1979), female undergraduates donned garments resembling either robes associated with the Ku Klux Klan (a very racist hate group) or nurses' uniforms. Half of the participants were individually identified throughout the study; the others were not. All of the participants were then given the opportunity to increase or decrease the intensity of electric shocks delivered to a supposed other participant (actually, a confederate in the experiment) who had previously behaved in an obnoxious manner. Participants wearing Ku Klux Klan costumes increased shock levels in both the identified and anonymous conditions. However, among those in nurse's apparel, anonymous participants *decreased* shock intensity four times more frequently than did identified participants!

These findings support the **social identity model of deindividuation effects (SIDE)**, which proposes that whether deindividuation affects people for better or

social identity model of deindividuation effects (SIDE)   A model of group behavior that explains deindividuation effects as the result of a shift from personal identity to social identity.

for worse reflects the characteristics and norms of the group immediately surrounding the individual as well as the group's power to act according to these norms. As personal identity and internal controls are submerged, social identity emerges and conformity to the group increases. If a group defines itself in terms of prejudice and hatred against another group, for example, deindividuation can ignite an explosion of violence. If a group defines itself in terms of helping others, in contrast, deindividuation may promote prosocial, selfless actions. The consequences of losing your personal identity, therefore, depend on what you lose it to (Chen & Wu, 2015; Spears & Postmes, 2015).

Group Performance: Problems and Solutions

Social facilitation, social loafing, and deindividuation can all affect individuals whether they are working in real groups or are merely part of a collective or crowd. In this section, we examine processes that are specific to groups, where interaction among members is more direct and meaningful. We focus on how well groups perform, and in doing so, we address a fundamental question: Aren't two (or more) heads better than one? Although eight people typically can outproduce a lone individual, do eight people working together in a group typically outperform the sum of eight people working individually? You may be surprised to learn how often and in what ways groups perform worse than their potential would suggest. We also discuss when and how groups are more likely to perform well.

■ Losses and Gains in Groups

When a group performs worse than its potential, it experiences what Ivan Steiner (1972) called **process loss**. Process loss refers to the reduction of group productivity due to problems in the dynamics of a group. According to Steiner, some types of group tasks are more vulnerable to process loss than others.

Gordon Wiltsie/Getty Images

Just as the strength of a chain depends on its weakest link, the group product of a conjunctive task is determined by the individual with the poorest performance. In mountain climbing, for example, if one person slips or falls, the whole team is endangered.

For instance, on an *additive* task, the group product is the *sum* of all the members' contributions. Donating to a charity is an additive task, as is making noise at a pep rally. Of course, for these tasks, the more the merrier in terms of overall output. A group will make more noise at the rally than an individual. However, as we have seen, people often indulge in social loafing during additive tasks, which creates process loss. In other words, each member's contribution may be less than it would be if that person worked alone. As a result the group performs less than its potential.

On a *conjunctive* task, the group product is determined by the individual with the *poorest* performance. Mountain-climbing teams or an offensive line trying to protect the quarterback on a pass play in football may be engaged in such a task; the "weakest link" will determine their success or failure. Because of this vulnerability to the poor performance of a single group member, group performance on conjunctive tasks tends to be worse than the performance of a single average individual.

On a *disjunctive* task, the group product is (or can be) determined by the performance of the individual with the *best* performance. Trying to solve a problem or develop a strategy may be a disjunctive task: What the group needs is a single successful idea or answer, regardless of the number of failures. In principle, groups

process loss The reduction in group performance due to obstacles created by group processes, such as problems of coordination and motivation.

have an edge on individuals in the performance of disjunctive tasks. The more people involved, the more likely it is that someone will make a breakthrough. In practice, however, group processes can interfere with coming up with ideas and getting them accepted, resulting in process loss. For example, groups may not realize which group members have the best ideas or are most expert. Unless the best solution for a particular problem is easily and clearly identifiable once it has been suggested, the group may fail to implement it; as a result, the group will perform worse than its best members (Soll & Larrick, 2009; Stasser et al., 1995; Straus et al., 2009). Have you ever had the experience of *knowing* you had the right idea but being unable to convince others in your group until it was too late? If so, then you have experienced firsthand the problem of process loss on a disjunctive task. A bit later in this chapter, we will discuss strategies that help groups recognize and utilize expertise.

On some kinds of tasks, groups can even show **process gain**, in which they outperform even the best members. Groups often perform better than the best individuals on tasks in which (1) the correct answer is clearly evident to everyone in the group once it is presented, and (2) the work on the task can be divided up so that various subgroups work on different aspects of the task (Carey & Laughlin, 2012). In the business world, process gain tends to be called *synergy,* and it is the ideal that business and organizational groups strive for (Mercier et al., 2015; Meslec & Curşeu, 2013; Schulz-Hardt & Mojzisch, 2012).

> *"A committee should consist of three men, two of whom are absent."*
>
> —Herbert Beerbohm Tree

■ Brainstorming

During the 1950s, advertising executive Alex Osborn developed a technique called **brainstorming** that was designed to enhance the creativity and productivity of problem-solving groups. The ground rules for brainstorming call for a freewheeling, creative approach:

- Express all ideas that come to mind even if they sound crazy.
- The more ideas, the better.
- Don't worry whether the ideas are good or bad, and don't criticize anyone's ideas; they can be evaluated later.
- All ideas belong to the group, so members should feel free to build on each other's work.

Alex Osborn (1953) claimed that by using these procedures, groups could generate more and better ideas than could individuals working alone. The idea caught on. Brainstorming was soon a popular exercise in business, government, and education. In fact, it remains very popular today. But when the research caught up with the hype, it turned out that Osborn's faith in the group process was unfounded. In fact, "nominal groups" (several individuals working alone) produce a greater number of better ideas than do real groups in which members interact with each other. Brainstorming can indeed be effective, but people brainstorming individually produce more and higher-quality ideas than the same number of people brainstorming together. One meta-analysis concluded that brainstorming groups are only about half as productive as an equal number of individuals working alone (Mullen et al., 1991). Rather than being inspired by each other and building on each other's ideas, people brainstorming in a group underperform (Paulus et al., 2015; Stroebe et al., 2010).

The top half of Table 8.2 presents several explanations for why group brainstorming is ineffective. Recall our discussion of social loafing from earlier in the

process gain The increase in group performance so that the group outperforms the individuals who make up the group.

brainstorming A technique that attempts to increase the production of creative ideas by encouraging group members to speak freely without criticizing their own or others' contributions.

Small groups engaging in brainstorming. Despite its popularity, interactive group brainstorming suffers from several group dynamics problems. Fortunately, researchers have determined some ways to improve brainstorming.

chapter, for example. As you can see in Table 8.2, social loafing is one factor that contributes to process loss in group brainstorming. The first obstacle listed in the table, production blocking, seems to be especially problematic for groups.

Despite the research evidence, brainstorming is still a popular device in many organizations. People who participate in interactive brainstorming groups typically think that it works wonderfully and evaluate their performance more favorably than do individuals in nominal groups. They also enjoy themselves more, and group brainstorming can increase group cohesiveness (Henningsen & Henningsen, 2013). But they are working under the illusion that group brainstorming is much more effective than it really is.

Fortunately, after the initial shock at how poor group brainstorming really is, researchers have demonstrated a number of strategies that improve productivity while also preserving the enjoyment that group brainstorming can produce. For example, alternating types of brainstorming sessions (such as by having members brainstorm alone and then together, or first together and then alone) has proven very effective. Other strategies that improve group performance include training people in effective brainstorming, giving the group a subset of categories to begin the brainstorming process, using a trained facilitator during brainstorming sessions, and giving groups more time (rather than rush them with a tight deadline) (Baruah & Paulus, 2011; Henningsen & Henningsen, 2013; Oxley et al., 1996; Paulus et al., 2006, 2015).

Using technology to allow groups to engage in what is called electronic brainstorming can help groups brainstorm more effectively. By allowing all group members to enter ideas from their own laptops, phones, or other devices and have the ideas appear on a central screen, electronic brainstorming combines the freedom of working alone and not having to wait their turns with the stimulation of seeing others' ideas. The bottom half of Table 8.2 presents some of the factors that make this type of brainstorming effective. A meta-analysis of research on electronic brainstorming reported encouraging results (DeRosa et al., 2007). Groups using electronic brainstorming tend to perform much better than other brainstorming groups, although the evidence is mixed concerning whether electronic

People brainstorming as a group come up with a greater number of better ideas than the same number of people working individually. **FALSE**

▲ **TABLE 8.2**

Brainstorming in Groups: Problems and Solutions

Factors That Reduce the Effectiveness of Group Brainstorming

- *Production blocking.* Having to wait their turn to speak, people may forget their ideas, don't generate additional ideas until they can speak, or simply lose interest.

- *Free riding.* As others contribute ideas, individuals see their own contributions as less needed or less likely to have much impact. They therefore try less hard and engage in social loafing.

- *Evaluation apprehension.* People may be hesitant to suggest unusual ideas for fear of looking foolish and being criticized.

- *Performance matching.* Group members work only as hard as they see others work. Once the other three factors above have reduced the performance of a brainstorming group, performance matching can help maintain this relatively inferior performance.

Why Electronic Brainstorming Is Effective

- Production blocking is reduced because members can type in ideas whenever they come to mind.

- Free riding is reduced by having the computer keep track of each member's amount of input.

- Evaluation apprehension is reduced because group members contribute their ideas anonymously.

- Performance matching is reduced because group members spend less time focusing on the performance of others as they type in their own ideas. In addition, performance matching is less of a problem because the initial performance of groups that brainstorm electronically is likely to be high.

- Group members can benefit by seeing the ideas of others, which can inspire new ideas that they might not otherwise have considered.

© Cengage Learning®

brainstorming groups outperform nominal groups (Dornburg et al., 2009). One interesting finding is that when the group size gets relatively large, electronic brainstorming seems to be especially effective (Paulus et al., 2013).

■ Group Polarization

Imagine that you're asked to recommend whether someone should behave in a risky or a cautious manner, such as whether a business should risk trying to expand or whether an employee in a stable but boring job should quit and take a more creative job in a new but unproven tech company. Imagine after you process the relevant information and come to an initial opinion on this, you and a group of other people who have also arrived at initial opinions come together and discuss the case. What will be the result of the group discussion of the various opinions?

Common sense suggests two alternative predictions. Perhaps the most reasonable prediction is that there will be a compromise as group members move toward the average of all the individuals' attitudes. But common sense also suggests another prediction. Many people familiar with committees agree that forming a committee is a good way *not* to get something done. We think that as lone individuals we are willing to take risks and implement new ideas, but we recognize that groups tend to be cautious and slow moving. Wary of leading the group toward a risky decision, people often become more cautious in their views as they discuss them with other group members. So another prediction here would be that the people in your group would become more cautious in what they advocate.

So which prediction is the correct one: movement toward the average attitude or movement toward caution? It turns out that neither commonsense notion is correct. Rather, group discussion tends to enhance or exaggerate the initial leanings of the group. Thus, if most group members initially lean toward a risky position on a particular issue, the group members on average will move toward an even riskier position after the discussion. But if group members in general initially lean toward a cautious position, the group discussion leads to greater caution. This effect is called **group polarization**: the exaggeration through group discussion of initial tendencies in the thinking of group members (Moscovici & Zavalloni, 1969; Myers & Lamm, 1976).

Group polarization is not restricted to decisions involving risk versus caution. Any group decision can be influenced by group polarization, from serious decisions such as how to allocate scarce medical resources or how much to pay CEOs, to more mundane decisions such as what theme a sorority should use at its next party (Chandrashekaran et al., 1996; Furnham et al., 2000; Zhu, 2014).

What causes group polarization? According to *persuasive arguments theory,* the greater the number and persuasiveness of the arguments to which group members are exposed, the more extreme their attitudes become. If most group members favor a cautious decision, for example, most of the arguments discussed will favor

group polarization The exaggeration of initial tendencies in the thinking of group members through group discussion.

caution, giving the members more and more reasons to think caution is the correct approach (Pavitt, 1994; Vinokur & Burnstein, 1974). Another set of explanations is based on how people *compare* themselves to fellow group members as well as to outgroup members. In the case of group discussions, as individuals learn that most of the other group members lean in one direction on some issue, they may adopt a more extreme attitude in this same direction. In other words, people who are members of a group that believes that X is good may be willing to state to the group that twice X is even better. By advocating for twice X, individuals can distinguish themselves in the group in a manner that is approved by the group. In addition, groups may become more extreme as a way to differentiate themselves from other groups (Lamm & Myers, 1978; McGarty et al., 1992; Suhay, 2015).

Each of these accounts spotlights particular processes, but taken together they all seem to contribute to the emergence of group polarization. Now that you know about group polarization, you should be able to see evidence of it often as you observe the groups around you. It seems that political groups today have become more and more polarized, moving to extremes rather than toward moderation and compromise. On a smaller level, observe how the culture of a team may evolve over the course of a season or follow the attitudes of a group as it prepares for a debate against another group and you're likely to see group polarization develop through the processes we've just described.

> **Group members' attitudes about a course of action usually become more moderate after group discussion.**
>
> **FALSE**

Groupthink

The processes involved in group polarization may set the stage for an even greater and more dangerous bias in group decision making. This bias can be seen in examples of very smart people collectively making very dumb decisions. For example, several days before the U.S. space shuttle *Columbia* disintegrated as it reentered the Earth's atmosphere on its way home on February 1, 2003, a team of engineers at NASA reviewed a video of foam breaking off the shuttle during launch and hitting the area near the left wing. The group speculated about whether the impact could have damaged the heat-shielding tiles located there. One engineer, Rodney Rocha, made more than half a dozen requests of NASA managers to go outside the agency

Christian Kober/JAI/ Passage/Corbis

Scholars have identified groupthink as underlying poor group decision making in a number of contexts, including decisions involving war, the economy, and even proceeding with a climb of Mount Everest in dangerous conditions.

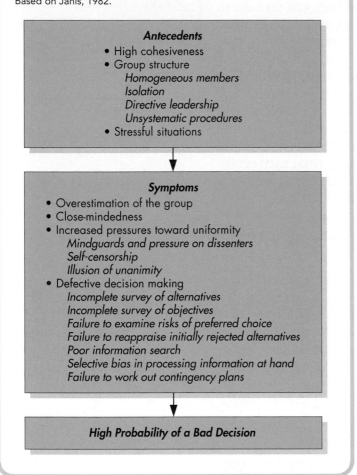

● **FIGURE 8.5**

Charting the Course of Groupthink

Irving Janis depicted groupthink as a kind of social disease, complete with antecedents and symptoms, that increases the chance of making a bad decision.
Based on Janis, 1982.

Antecedents
- High cohesiveness
- Group structure
  Homogeneous members
  Isolation
  Directive leadership
  Unsystematic procedures
- Stressful situations

Symptoms
- Overestimation of the group
- Close-mindedness
- Increased pressures toward uniformity
  Mindguards and pressure on dissenters
  Self-censorship
  Illusion of unanimity
- Defective decision making
  Incomplete survey of alternatives
  Incomplete survey of objectives
  Failure to examine risks of preferred choice
  Failure to reappraise initially rejected alternatives
  Poor information search
  Selective bias in processing information at hand
  Failure to work out contingency plans

High Probability of a Bad Decision

and seek images from spy satellite photos or powerful telescopes that could provide a better look at the possible damage to the *Columbia* while it was in space. These requests were ignored or rejected. One manager said that he refused to be a "Chicken Little." The flight director e-mailed his rejection of the engineer's request with these chilling words: "I consider it to be a dead issue" (Glanz & Schwartz, 2003). The engineer's concerns about the tiles turned out to be justified, and all seven crew members on *Columbia* died in the ensuing tragedy.

Or consider one of the greatest fiascoes in U.S. history: the decision to invade Cuba in 1961. When John Kennedy became president of the United States, he assembled one of the most impressive, most highly educated groups of advisers in the history of American government. But this group devised a plan—inherited from the previous administration—to launch a small invasion of Cuba at the Bay of Pigs in order to spark a people's revolt that would overthrow Fidel Castro's government. Despite the intelligence of Kennedy and his group of advisers, their plan was hopelessly flawed. For example, once the invaders landed at the Bay of Pigs, they expected to be supported by anti-Castro forces camped in the mountains nearby. But had Kennedy and his advisers consulted a proper map, they might have noticed that the invaders were to land 80 miles away from these mountains and were separated from them by a huge swamp. This was just one of a number of baffling mistakes the planners made. Ultimately the invasion failed miserably. The invaders were quickly killed or captured, the world was outraged at the United States, and Cuba allied itself more closely with the Soviet Union—exactly the opposite of what Kennedy had intended. The United States was humiliated. After the fiasco, Kennedy himself wondered, "How could we have been so stupid?" (Janis, 1982).

According to Irving Janis (1982), the answer to this question lies in a particular kind of flawed group dynamic that he called **groupthink**, an excessive tendency to seek concurrence (that is, agreement or uniformity) among group members. Groupthink emerges when the need for agreement takes priority over the motivation to obtain accurate information and make appropriate decisions. ● Figure 8.5 outlines the factors that contribute to groupthink, along with its symptoms and consequences.

Janis believed that three characteristics contribute to the development of groupthink:

1. Because *highly cohesive groups* are more likely to reject members with deviant opinions, Janis thought they would be more susceptible to groupthink.
2. *Group structure* is also important. Groups that are composed of people from similar backgrounds, isolated from other people, directed by a strong leader, and lacking in systematic procedures for making and reviewing decisions should be particularly likely to fall prey to groupthink.
3. *Stressful situations* can provoke groupthink. Under stress, urgency can overrule accuracy and the reassuring support of other group members becomes highly desirable.

groupthink A group decision-making style characterized by an excessive tendency among group members to seek concurrence.

The idea that high cohesiveness contributes to groupthink got a lot of attention when Janis introduced the model because, as we indicated earlier, cohesiveness is something that most people view as something that groups should strive for and value. However, even though high cohesiveness in a group might feel great and make for smooth and easy interactions among group members, it can foster emphasis on preserving each other's feelings rather than an objective examination of the facts or an honest discussion of differences of opinion. Such a concern with agreement over accuracy is a hallmark of groupthink. Working collectively, individuals may be focused more on mutually reinforcing each other's judgments than arriving at the most accurate decisions.

In Janis's formulation, groupthink is a kind of social disease, and infected groups display the behavioral symptoms indicated in the middle of ● Figure 8.5. For example, NASA's refusal to ask for outside help in obtaining images of the *Columbia* shuttle in space clearly illustrated the symptom of *closed-mindedness.* Another symptom, *pressures toward uniformity,* was evident in these examples. During the planning of the Bay of Pigs invasion, the president's brother, Robert Kennedy, served as a "mindguard" and warned dissenting members to keep quiet. An alarming example of this occurred during the debate about whether to go ahead with the launch of the space shuttle *Challenger* in 1986, 17 years before the *Columbia* disaster. When a vice president for engineering called for a delay in the launching of the *Challenger* because of fear that the unusually cold weather could cause the O-ring seals in the rocket boosters to fail, a manager pressured him to change his vote by telling him to "take off your engineer hat and put on your management hat." Pressured to abandon one role and adopt the other, he changed his vote, and the tragic fate of the *Challenger* and its crew may have been sealed at that moment, as an O-ring seal did fail and the shuttle exploded 73 seconds into the flight. In the end, this vice president's decision helped foster an *illusion of unanimity* because top-level managers at NASA were unaware of all the dissent voiced by the engineers that morning.

More recently, scholars have proposed that groupthink was behind poor group decision making in a number of contexts, including in the decisions to go to war in Iraq, torture prisoners of war, and climb Mount Everest in dangerous conditions, as well as in the economic decisions that contributed to the global financial disaster in 2008 (Ben-Hur et al., 2012; Burnette et al., 2011; Houghton, 2008; Post, 2011).

When alternatives are not considered, the behavioral symptoms of groupthink can result in the defective decision making outlined in Figure 8.5.

Preventing Groupthink   To guard against groupthink, Janis urged groups to make an active effort to process information more carefully and accurately. He recommended that decision-making groups use the following strategies:

- To avoid isolation, groups should consult widely with outsiders.

- To reduce group pressures to conform, leaders should explicitly encourage criticism and not take a strong stand early in the group discussion.

- To establish a strong norm of critical review, subgroups should separately discuss the same issue, a member should be assigned to play devil's advocate and question all decisions and ideas, and a "second chance" meeting should be held to reconsider the group decision before taking action.

President Kennedy appeared to arrive at similar conclusions after the Bay of Pigs disaster. In the following year, 1962, the United States and the Soviet Union were at the brink of war after U.S. military intelligence discovered that Soviet missiles in Cuba were aimed at the United States. During this crisis, Kennedy stayed

"A committee is a cul-de-sac down which ideas are lured and then quietly strangled."

—Barnett Cocks

away from initial meetings about how to respond to the situation, he consulted with experts outside his inner circle of advisers, and he told his brother Robert to play "devil's advocate" and challenge all ideas—in sharp contrast to Robert's role of "mindguard" during the Bay of Pigs planning sessions. Unlike the Bay of Pigs invasion, the Cuban missile crisis ended exactly as Kennedy had hoped: The Soviet Union withdrew its missiles from Cuba, and a war was avoided.

"On second thought, don't correct me if I'm wrong."

A controlling leader who discourages disagreement can promote groupthink, leading to bad decisions.

"Nor is the people's judgment always true: The most may err as grossly as the few."

—John Dryden

Research on Groupthink: Myth or Reality? Groupthink is a rather distinctive theory in social psychology. On the one hand, its impact has been unusually broad: It is discussed in a variety of disciplines outside psychology including business, political science, and communication, and it has spawned numerous workshops, websites, and training videos. Yet on the other hand, the empirical support for the model is much less impressive than its fame would suggest. This may be partly due to the difficulty of experimentally testing such a broad set of variables in high-pressure group settings. In addition, many researchers disagree with Janis about the specific conditions that make groups vulnerable to groupthink (Baron, 2005; Hackman & Katz, 2010; Turner & Pratkanis, 1998). For example, group cohesiveness does not seem to be as much of a risk factor as Janis thought it was.

Some researchers do believe, however, that when multiple antecedents of groupthink are evident simultaneously, such as a strong and controlling leader and a great deal of stress, groups are indeed vulnerable to the kinds of faulty decision making that Janis described. For now, the bottom line may be that even if one is skeptical about the details of Janis's theory of groupthink, as many and perhaps most scholars are, it does seem clear that many of the factors that Janis specified as antecedents and symptoms of groupthink can contribute to very faulty group decision making, and groups would be wise to be on the lookout for these traps.

Perhaps most important, the steps that Janis advocated to avoid these traps should help most groups, regardless of the merits or problems with the theory of groupthink. Indeed, research has shown empirical support for the effectiveness of several strategies in curtailing groupthink tendencies. These include inserting someone in the group to play the role of a "reminder" who is responsible for informing the group about the dangers of biased decision making, making individual group members believe that they will be held personally responsible for the outcome of their group's decisions, increasing the diversity of group members, and creating a group norm that encourages critical thinking and discourages the search for concurrence (Ben-Hur et al., 2012; Postmes et al., 2001; Schultz et al., 1995; t'Hart, 1998).

■ Communicating Information and Utilizing Expertise

One of the biggest flaws in how groups perform is that they often fail to use all the information or skills that group members have. In this section we will explore some of the dynamics that cause this problem, as well as some factors that can help groups better communicate and use important information.

Information Sharing and Biased Sampling Imagine that the chief executives of a company meet to decide whether to launch a risky expansion of their business. All of them share much of the same information about the potential costs and benefits, and the weight of this evidence suggests the risk is worth it. But one of the executives is an expert on some technical aspects of the stock market and knows a reason why this move might have bad stock implications. Another executive has special knowledge of one of their primary competitors and knows that the competitor might make a countermove that could be devastating. A third executive has a better sense than the other executives that the morale among the company's personnel could be hurt by the expansion. If these unique pieces of information made it into the discussion, the weight of the evidence would tip the other way, toward not expanding the company yet. But too often group members fail to share their uniquely held information, and bad decisions result.

This example illustrates what Garold Stasser (1992; Stasser & Titus, 2003) termed **biased sampling**. Because of biased sampling, a group may fail to consider important information that is not common knowledge in the group. Inadequately informed, the group may make a bad decision. There are several reasons why groups tend to exhibit this bias. For example, commonly shared information is likely to be socially validated by the group, and this in turn causes it to be more easily remembered and trusted. The validation also makes group members more confident in discussing and reiterating these pieces of information (Levine & Smith, 2013). The results of meta-analyses of hundreds of studies involving many thousands of people make clear how important sufficient information sharing is for group performance, and how biased the information sharing in groups tends to be (Lu et al., 2012; Mesmer-Magnus & DeChurch, 2009).

Sometimes biased sampling can have tragic consequences. The commission that investigated the 1986 explosion of the space shuttle *Challenger* concluded that inadequate sharing of information contributed to the disaster. For example, some engineers had information indicating that it would be unsafe to launch the shuttle that morning because of the low temperature, but this information was not shared with everyone. The people who ultimately made the decision to launch therefore were not aware of all the information that was relevant for their decision. The commission concluded, "If the decision-makers had known all the facts, it is highly unlikely that they would have decided to launch" (Presidential Commission on the Space Shuttle Challenger Accident, 1986, p. 82). Lessons learned after that tragedy appeared to have been forgotten 17 years later: Inadequate sharing of vital information also appeared to have contributed to the *Columbia* disaster in 2003.

Part of the problem in the NASA disasters was that the *communication network*, which defines who can speak with whom based on a group's structure, made it difficult for information to be distributed to all of the decision makers. In many organizations, information is passed up a chain of command through layers of middle management and only some of this information makes it all the way up to the executives who make the final decisions. This was the case at NASA. The engineers who were most familiar with the physical details of the shuttle could not communicate directly with the NASA officials at the top of the chain of command. According to Rodney Rocha, who was one of the engineers who most emphatically warned about the possible damage to the *Columbia,* "Engineers were often told not to send messages much higher than their own rung in the ladder" (Glanz & Schwartz, 2003). Because warnings were suppressed as the flow of information moved up the chain of command, the people at the top did not know the extent of the concerns of those lower in the chain.

Fortunately, researchers have discovered several conditions under which biased sampling is less likely to occur. For example, leaders who encourage a lot of group participation and a thorough exchange and critical discussion of ideas are

The U.S. space shuttle *Challenger* explodes shortly after its launch on January 28, 1986, killing all seven crew members. Inadequate sharing of information and a flawed communication network were among the group dynamics problems that contributed to NASA's flawed, and ultimately fatal, decision to launch the shuttle that cold morning.

AP Images/Bruce Weaver

biased sampling The tendency for groups to spend more time discussing shared information (information already known by all or most group members) than unshared information (information known by only one or a few group members).

more likely to elicit unshared (as well as shared) information during group discussions than are leaders who are more controlling or who encourage group members to find common ground (Larson et al., 1998; Lee et al., 2010; van Ginkel & van Knippenberg, 2008, 2012).

J. Lukas Thürmer and others (2015) found that information sharing and group decisions were much better when group members had to make a plan of when and how they would review alternatives before settling on their ultimate decision. In one of their experiments, for example, three-person groups had to make a series of decisions, such as which job applicant should be hired. All of the group members were given a set of identical information relevant for their decision, but each member also received information unique to them that was crucial for the overall decision. If only commonly shared information was discussed, one of the job candidates would seem the best. But if *all* of the information, including the unshared information, was discussed, then the best decision would be to hire a different candidate. This *hidden-profile* technique is commonly used in studies of group decision making.

All of the groups in this study were given financial incentives to reach the best decisions, all knew that each group member had a slightly different (but all true) set of information, and all were encouraged to consider alternatives before reaching their final decision. The only difference between conditions was that half of the groups were given a specific plan about how and when to consider alternatives: "When we finally take the decision sheet to note our preferred alternative, then we will go over the advantages of the non-preferred alternatives again." Having a specific plan made a big difference. As can be seen in ● Figure 8.6, groups

● **FIGURE 8.6**

Improving Information Sharing

Small groups received sets of information to be used to make a series of group decisions. Some information was known to all group members, but each group member also had some unique information. If only commonly shared information was discussed, the group would make bad decisions. Groups that were given a specific plan about how and when to consider alternatives to the group decision discussed more of the unique information (left) and made better decisions (right) than did groups just given the more general goal of considering alternatives.

Based on Thürmer et al., 2015

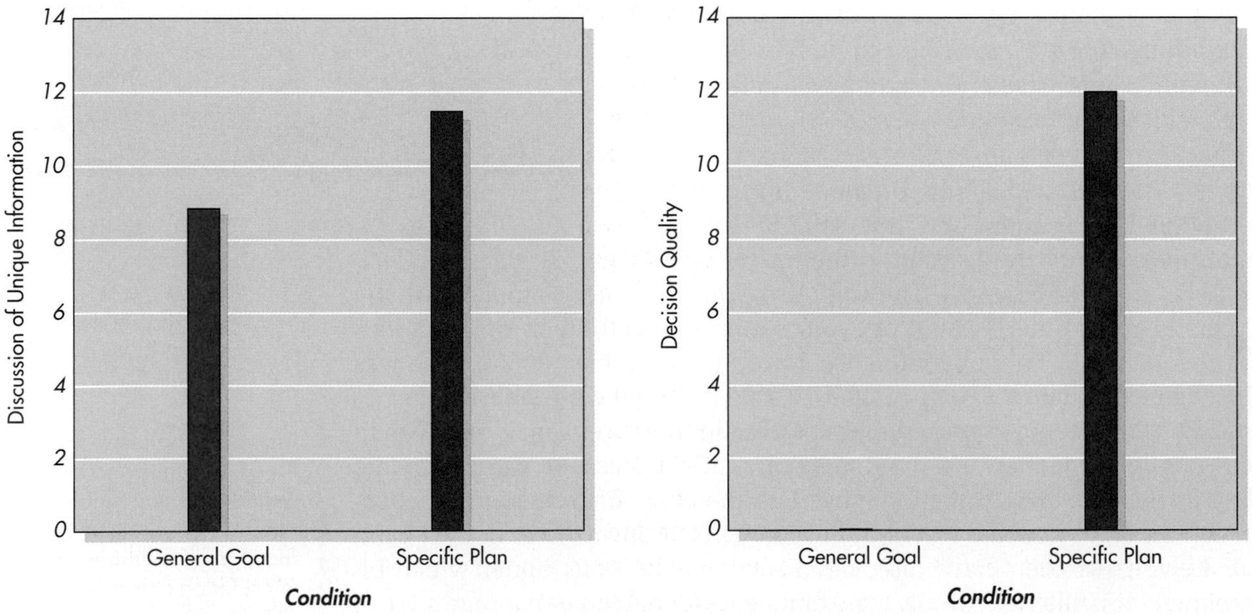

given this plan were more likely to discuss the unshared information and more likely to reach the correct decision.

Information Processing and Transactive Memory In general, groups are susceptible to the same information-processing biases as individuals, only more so. In reviewing the research on group information processing, Verlin Hinsz and others (1997) concluded, "If some bias, error, or tendency predisposes individuals to process information in a particular way, then groups exaggerate this tendency. However, if this bias, error, or tendency is unlikely among individuals processing the information (e.g., less than half the sample), then groups are even less likely to process information in this fashion" (pp. 49–50). Vivid examples, for example, often affect individuals' judgments more than do statistics covering a much larger sample of information. Hinsz and others (2008) have found that groups are even more susceptible to this bias than individuals are.

One key advantage of groups, though, is that they can divide a large body of information into smaller portions and delegate different members to remember these more manageable portions. Have you and a friend ever divided up a list of things to remember, such as which grocery items to remember to buy at the store or which sections of a textbook chapter each of you should be responsible for remembering before you study together? If so, you have tried to take advantage of a shared process known as **transactive memory**, which helps groups remember more information more efficiently than individuals (Heavey & Simsek, 2015; Liao et al., 2015; Wegner et al., 1991). This is one of the great benefits of working in groups. But process loss can occur in this domain as well. Social loafing may occur, for example, when group members don't do their share of the work while expecting others to pick up the slack. A particularly important problem is that groups may not distribute the tasks and roles among group members in a rational or efficient manner. They may, for example, fail to match individuals to tasks based on their skills, expertise, and preferences.

Groups that develop good transactive memory systems have enormous advantages over other groups (Heavey & Simsek, 2015; Huang et al., 2013; Seong et al., 2015). Effective transactive memory systems involve a few key elements. First, the group must develop a division of knowledge, and the group members must be able to communicate and remember this information in the group; everyone must know *who knows what*. Second, the group members must be able to trust each other's specialized knowledge. And third, the group members need to coordinate their efforts so that they can work together on a task smoothly and efficiently. Julija Mell and others (2014) found that having a central group member who is the expert at the "metaknowledge" of being able to identify which group members know which information or skills can also be a big advantage.

Conde Naste

"Thank you for neglecting your work long enough to listen to my thoughts on efficiency."

A clear example of process loss.

People and groups tend to do worse when they have "do your best" goals than when they have very specific, ambitious goals.

TRUE

transactive memory A shared system for remembering information that enables multiple people to remember information together more efficiently than they could do so alone.

■ Goals and Plans in Groups

You've probably worked in many groups for which the goal was simply to "do your best." Despite the popularity of such goals, the research clearly shows that they are not as effective as specific goals. As Edwin Locke and Gary Latham (2002) concluded from their review of 35 years' worth of studies, "When people are asked to do their best, they do not do so" (p. 706). People are indeed capable of better than their vaguely defined "best." Groups, like individuals, tend to perform better on a task when they have specific, challenging, and reachable goals, particularly if the group members are committed to the goals and believe they have the ability to

● FIGURE 8.7

Sticking to a Plan: Exercise and Weight Loss

Participants wanting to exercise more and lose weight worked either alone or with another person, and were either instructed to set specific plans for how to achieve their goal (including how they would respond in particular situations) or were not instructed to do so. Six months later, the participants who both set a specific plan and worked with a partner lost significantly more weight than did the participants in any of the other conditions.

Based on Prestwich et al., 2012

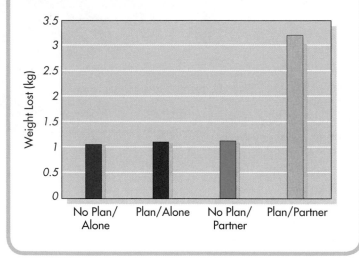

achieve them. In addition to having challenging and specific goals, groups are most likely to benefit when there are incentives in place for achieving these goals.

One benefit of groups over individuals is that group members can hold each other accountable and encourage each other to keep trying to achieve a goal. For example, Andrew Prestwich and others (2012) recruited a sample of British individuals who were interested in participating in a study on increasing their physical activity. Some of the participants were instructed to set specific plans for how to achieve their goal of increasing physical activity, including how they would respond in particular situations (*if we're in situation X, then we'll do Y*), and some were not asked to make these plans. In addition, some of these participants worked alone, and others worked with a partner. In a follow-up six months later, results indicated that participants who both had these plans and worked with a partner significantly increased their physical activity and lost significantly more weight than if they had no specific plans or if they had these plans but did not have a partner (see ● Figure 8.7).

If a group doesn't make a good, specific plan, it can fail to utilize the expertise that various group members have. In an experiment by Anita Williams Woolley and others (2008), some four-person groups had two members who were particularly expert at some of the skills needed to solve a complex task, and other groups included no experts. If the groups weren't instructed to make a specific plan of how to proceed before they began working on the task, the groups with experts did not do better than the group without; in fact, the group with experts did a bit worse! Without the specific planning, the individuals' expertise was not used properly. The other groups were required to discuss—before working on the task—who would be responsible for which type of evidence and plan how they would integrate the various types of evidence they were given. Only the groups that both had experts and went through this planning did well on the task.

▲ TABLE 8.3

Conditions for Team Effectiveness

Ruth Wageman and her colleagues (2009) reviewed the research on what makes teams most effective. Below is a list of some of the conditions they emphasize.

● Teams should be interdependent for some common purpose and have some stability of membership.

● The team's overall purpose should be challenging, clear, and consequential.

● Teams should be as small as possible and have clear norms that specify what behaviors are valued or are unacceptable.

● A reward system should provide positive consequences for excellent team performance.

● Technical assistance and training should be available to the team.

■ Training and Technology

We have discussed a variety of factors that can enhance group processes. Table 8.3 presents a set of the conditions that Ruth Wageman and her colleagues (2009) suggest are best for team effectiveness. These suggestions are consistent with the principles that we have addressed throughout this chapter, and they help illustrate the tremendous value that understanding the social psychology of groups can have in the business world or wherever group performance is essential. Social psychologists often are hired to train businesses and organizations to use these kinds of principles, and a great deal of research supports the value of training in improving group performance (Driskell & Salas, 2014; Salas et al., 2007, 2012).

Some of the obstacles that get in the way of good group discussion and decision making can be reduced through the use of interactive computer programs. Often referred to as **group support systems** (or *group decision support systems*), these programs help remove communication barriers and provide structure and incentives for group discussions and decisions. Compared to groups that use more conventional face-to-face modes of discussion, groups that use these systems often do a better job of sampling information, communicating, avoiding groupthink, and arriving at good decisions (Adla et al., 2011; Bergey & King, 2014; Bose, 2015; Lim & Guo, 2008; Tegarden et al., 2015). Table 8.4 lists some of the ways that computerized group support systems can help groups avoid groupthink.

▲ **TABLE 8.4**

How Computerized Group Support Systems Help Groups Avoid Groupthink

1. Allow group members to raise their concerns anonymously through the computer interface, enabling them to risk challenging group consensus without fear of direct attacks.

2. Reduce the directive role of the leader.

3. Enable group members to provide input simultaneously, so they don't have to wait for a chance to raise their ideas.

4. Allow the least assertive group members to state their ideas as easily as the most dominating.

5. Provide a systematic agenda of information gathering and decision making.

6. Keep the focus in the group meetings on the ideas themselves rather than on the people and relationships within the group.

Based on Miranda, 1994.

■ Virtual Teams

Teams consisting of people dispersed widely across the globe are a relatively recent and rapidly growing part of the business world. Recent estimates indicate that a majority of professional workers today spend time working in virtual teams, and the numbers are expected to continue to grow (Gilson et al., 2015; Mesmer-Magnus et al., 2011). Virtual teams, sometimes called dispersed teams, are "groups of people who work interdependently with shared purpose across space, time, and organization boundaries using technology to communicate and collaborate" (Kirkman et al., 2002, p. 67). Due to globalization and a variety of related factors, virtual teams will be increasingly important in businesses and organizations.

By using virtual teams dispersed across time and space, businesses and organizations can have much greater reach, diversity of perspectives and skills, and understanding of broader markets and groups of people than can traditional groups. But virtual groups can be especially vulnerable to some of the factors that harm traditional groups. Given the physical distances between members and how little interaction they may have with each other, virtual groups may have a harder time building cohesiveness, keeping membership stable, socializing new members, keeping roles clear, sharing information, and developing transactive memory systems that enable the members to recognize or recall who has what knowledge or expertise in the group. Special attention must be paid to virtual groups, therefore, to offset these problems. For example, directories should be available and updated to allow members to access information about who knows what across the virtual team. Frequent teleconferencing sessions and occasional short visits to allow dispersed group members to spend some time together can also help (Beyerlein et al., 2015; Hackman & Katz, 2010; Purvanova, 2014). The lack of cohesiveness in virtual groups can have some advantages, though, such as in helping these groups avoid some of the conformity pressures associated with groupthink-like problems.

group support systems
Specialized interactive computer programs that are used to guide group meetings, collaborative work, and decision-making processes.

■ Culture and Diversity

One outgrowth of the surging use of groups dispersed around the world is the creation of greater diversity among members of the groups. Even in face-to-face groups, though, groups are becoming increasingly diverse, most obviously in terms of gender, race, ethnicity, and cultural background.

How does diversity affect group performance? How can a group best use diversity to its advantage? The answers to such questions—and even the meaning of *diversity*—are likely to change as society changes in terms of its demographics and attitudes. In addition, diversity is not restricted to demographic differences among group members but can also mean differences in attitudes, personalities, skill levels, and so on. Thus, the issues surrounding diversity are particularly complex.

The evidence from empirical research concerning the effects of diversity on group performance is decidedly mixed (Hackman & Katz, 2010; Paulus & van der Zee, 2015). On the one hand, diversity often is associated with negative group dynamics. Miscommunications and misunderstandings are more likely to arise among heterogeneous group members, causing frustration and resentment and damaging group performance by weakening coordination, morale, and commitment to the group. Cliques and conflicts often form in diverse groups, causing some group members to feel alienated.

On the other hand, research has also demonstrated positive effects of diversity, such as on patterns of socialization, creativity, and the complexity and inclusiveness of group discussion (Antonio et al., 2004; Juvonen et al., 2006; Toosi, Sommers, & Ambady, 2012). Samuel Sommers (2006), for example, found that racially diverse juries exchanged a wider range of information, cited more facts about the case being decided, and made fewer errors in their deliberations than racially homogenous juries, at least when the defendant was black. Sommers and others (2008) also found that merely *anticipating* being in a racially mixed group made white individuals process information relevant to race more thoroughly.

As more organizations try to attract customers and investors from diverse cultures, diversity in personnel should offer more and more advantages. Cedric Herring (2009) analyzed data from over 1,000 work establishments in the United States from 1996 to 1997 and found that racial diversity was associated with greater profits and market share. Sangeeta Badal and James Harter (2014) found similar results regarding gender diversity. On the other hand, Andrea Garnero and others (2014) found that whether diversity predicted greater profits varied depending on what types of diversity (e.g., age vs. gender) and industries were studied.

Although the overall picture remains mixed, more promising is research focused on understanding specific factors that can help groups achieve the benefits of diversity while avoiding or reducing its problems (Hebl & Avery, 2013; Paulus & van der Zee, 2015). One set of recent findings is that multicultural groups perform better if their members or leaders have relatively high awareness of their own and others' cultural assumptions—what is sometimes called *cultural metacognition* (Chua et al., 2012; Moon, 2013; Mor et al., 2013). People exhibit cultural metacognition to the extent that they often think about and check the accuracy of their cultural knowledge, particularly in cross-cultural interactions. William Maddux and others (2014) similarly

Because groups have become increasingly diverse in many settings, it is more important than ever that groups learn how to utilize the great benefits and minimize the costs of diversity in group processes.

Jon Feingersh/Getty Images

found that students in an international business school program who most exhibited "multicultural engagement"—that is, they adapted to and learned about new cultures—were the most successful students on the job market following the program. These researchers also found that students and professionals who had experienced diversity by living abroad were more creative in tasks and more successful in their careers when they identified with both their home and abroad cultures (Tadmor, Galinsky, & Maddux, 2012).

In addition, culturally diverse groups whose members have a positive attitude toward learning new information tend to benefit from the diversity of their groups more than other groups (Nederveen Pieterse et al., 2013). Finally, diverse groups whose members are encouraged or trained to take each other's perspectives may outperform homogenous groups or diverse groups not given special instructions to promote perspective taking (Hoever et al., 2012; Lindsey et al., 2015).

■ Collective Intelligence: Are Some Groups Smarter Than Others?

We have seen throughout this chapter that groups consisting of very intelligent people, or even people who are expert at a task very relevant to what the group is working on, are far from immune to making really dumb decisions or falling short of their potential. But are some groups—as a collective working together— particularly smart and effective at, well, group stuff? Anita Williams Woolley and others (2010) tried to answer this kind of question. They had 699 people work in small groups on a wide variety of group tasks. Across these various group tasks, some groups did tend to outperform the other groups. The researchers considered these groups that tended to do well on a wide variety of group tasks as being high in "collective intelligence." What predicts which groups are like this? The average level of intelligence of the individual members of the group did not correlate much with the group's collective intelligence, nor did the maximum level of intelligence of any particular group member. Three factors did, however, predict collective intelligence of the groups: (1) the average social sensitivity of the group members, (2) the tendency to allow the various group members to take turns participating in the discussion (rather than having one or a few people dominate), and (3) a higher proportion of women (who tended to be higher than the men in social sensitivity).

Conflict: Cooperation and Competition Within and Between Groups

Many of the most crucial issues confronting our world today involve conflicts between groups or between individuals and their groups. The desire of some individuals to consume valuable resources conflicts with the need to protect the environment for the greater good. A nation's claim to important territory or the right to nuclear arms conflicts with another nation's national security. In this section, we describe some of the dilemmas groups often must confront and what factors influence whether individuals and groups act cooperatively or competitively in dealing with them. We also look at an important mechanism for resolving group conflicts: negotiation.

■ Mixed Motives and Social Dilemmas

Imagine that you have to choose between cooperating with others in your group versus pursuing your own self-interests, which can hurt the others. Examples of these mixed-motive situations are everywhere. An actor in a play may be motivated to try to "steal" a scene, a basketball player may be inclined to hog the ball, an executive may want to keep more of the company's profits, a family member may want to eat more than his fair share of the leftover birthday cake, and a citizen of the Earth may want to use more than her fair share of finite valuable resources.

In each case, the individual can gain something by pursuing his or her self-interests, but if everyone in the group pursues self-interests, all of the group members will ultimately be worse off than if they had cooperated with each other. Each option, therefore, has possible benefits as well as potential costs. When you are in a situation like this, you may feel torn between wanting to cooperate and wanting to compete, and these mixed motives create a difficult dilemma. The notion that the pursuit of self-interest can sometimes be self-destructive is the basis for what is called a **social dilemma**. In a social dilemma, what is good for one is bad for all. If everyone makes the most self-rewarding choice, everyone suffers the greatest loss. This section examines how people resolve the tension between their cooperative and competitive inclinations in social dilemmas.

The Prisoner's Dilemma   We begin with a crime story. Two partners in crime are picked up by the police for questioning. Although the police believe they have committed a major offense, there is only enough evidence to convict them on a minor charge. In order to get a conviction for the more serious crime, the police will have to convince one of the criminals to testify against the other. Separated during questioning, the criminals weigh their alternatives (see ● Figure 8.8). If neither confesses,

social dilemma   A situation in which a self-interested choice by everyone will create the worst outcome for everyone.

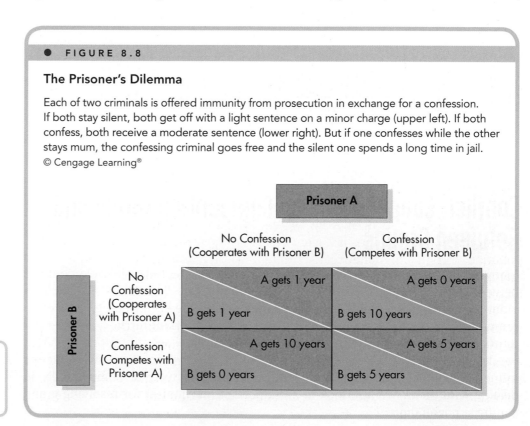

● **FIGURE 8.8**

The Prisoner's Dilemma

Each of two criminals is offered immunity from prosecution in exchange for a confession. If both stay silent, both get off with a light sentence on a minor charge (upper left). If both confess, both receive a moderate sentence (lower right). But if one confesses while the other stays mum, the confessing criminal goes free and the silent one spends a long time in jail.
© Cengage Learning®

they will both get light sentences on the minor charge. If both confess and plead guilty, they will both receive somewhat longer sentences. But if one confesses and the other stays silent, the confessing criminal will go free while the silent criminal will pay the maximum penalty.

This situation forms the basis for the research paradigm known as the **prisoner's dilemma**. In the two-person prisoner's dilemma, participants are given a series of choices that give them the option of cooperating or competing with each other, but either option has potential costs. Imagine that you're Prisoner A in ● Figure 8.8. You should see that no matter what Prisoner B does, you're better off if you compete with B and confess. (You'd get 0 years rather than 1 year if B cooperates with you by not confessing; you'd get 5 rather than 10 years if B also confesses.) But here's the dilemma: If you *both* confess, each of you gets 5 years. If *neither* of you confesses, each of you gets only 1 year. In other words, each individual is better off selling out his or her partner, but if both individuals do this, they are worse off than if neither did. It's really a perplexing situation. What do you think you would do?

This kind of social dilemma is not limited to situations involving only two individuals at a time. Imagine, for example, being in a burning building or a sinking ship. Each individual might want to race for the exit or the lifeboats as quickly as possible and push others out of the way, but if everyone does that, more people will die in the panic. More lives will be saved if people leave in an orderly fashion. Soldiers engaged in combat may be better off individually if they take no chances and duck for cover, but if their comrades do the same thing, they all will be slaughtered by the enemy. Nations face such dilemmas as well. Two countries locked in an arms race would be better off if they stopped spending money and resources on weapons of mass destruction, but neither country wants to risk falling behind the other (Dawes, 1980).

Resource Dilemmas One particular category of social dilemmas that people face frequently and in vitally important contexts is called **resource dilemmas**, which concern how two or more people share a limited resource. As with prisoner's dilemmas, attempts to gain a personal advantage will backfire if the other party also makes the competitive choice. Resource dilemmas come in two basic types: (1) commons dilemmas and (2) public goods dilemmas.

In the *commons dilemma,* if people take as much as they want of a limited resource that does not replenish itself, nothing will be left for anyone. One popular example of this dilemma is known as the "tragedy of the commons" (Hardin, 1968). In earlier times, people would let their animals graze on the town's lush grassy commons. But if all the animals grazed to their hearts' content (and to their owners' benefit), the commons would be stripped, the animals' food supply would be diminished, and the owners' welfare would be threatened. Today, the tragedy of the commons is a clear danger on a global scale. Deforestation, air pollution, carbon emission, ocean dumping, massive irrigation, overfishing, commercial development of wilderness areas, overpopulation, and overconsumption all pit individual self-interest against the common good.

To teach his students about the tragedy of the commons, in June 2015 a social psychologist named Dylan Selterman gave his class a chance to earn extra credit points during their exam. Each student had to indicate whether they'd prefer 2 or 6 points of extra credit—the catch was that if more than 10% of the class chose 6 points, no one would get *any* extra credit. In the end, about 20% chose the 6 points, and therefore nobody earned any extra credit—and this is the typical result Selterman and others have found whenever they present this dilemma to their

Want to participate in an online prisoner's dilemma game? Simply search online with the phrase "Play Prisoner's Dilemma" and you should find several websites that offer a chance to do this.

prisoner's dilemma A type of dilemma in which one party must make either cooperative or competitive moves in relation to another party. The dilemma is typically designed so that the competitive move appears to be in one's self-interest, but if both sides make this move, they both suffer more than if they had both cooperated.

resource dilemmas Social dilemmas involving how two or more people will share a limited resource.

students. It's simply too tempting for too many individuals to try to maximize their own points, at the risk of the greater good. A student tweeted a picture of this exam question, and it went viral; as a result Selterman was soon on the national news explaining social dilemmas to the nation.

In *public goods dilemmas,* all of the individuals are supposed to *contribute* resources to a common pool. Examples of these public goods include the blood supply, public broadcasting, schools, libraries, roads, and parks. If no one gives, the service can't continue, and all will suffer. Again, self-interest conflicts with the public good.

Responding to Social Dilemmas: Groups and Individuals

Social dilemmas pose serious threats to people's quality of life and even to life itself. How do people try to solve them? What factors make them more or less cooperative when faced with these dilemmas?

Fear and greed are two critically important factors in determining reactions to these dilemmas—the fear of being exploited by others and the greedy desire to maximize one's own outcomes. Trust, therefore, is essential in promoting cooperation because it reduces the fear of being exploited. Similarly, a sense of belongingness and identity with the greater group also promotes cooperation, in part because this perspective can reduce fear and greed (Klapwijk & Van Lange, 2009; McLeish & Oxoby, 2011; Swann et al., 2012). In an interesting twist on this idea, Carsten De Dreu (2012) found that individuals who tend to feel that they can't depend on others were significantly more likely to cooperate on a social dilemma if they received a dose of oxytocin—a neurochemical that can increase people's feeling of bonding with another person and reduce their concerns of betrayal.

Cultural and individual differences also play a role. Some research has found that collectivists tend to cooperate more when dealing with friends or ingroup members but compete more aggressively when dealing with strangers or outgroup members; individualists' behavior does not vary as much as a function of who the other party is (De Dreu et al., 2007; Oyserman et al., 2002; Wong & Hong, 2005). Individuals' *social value orientation* also matters (Murphy & Ackermann, 2014). People with a *prosocial, cooperative* orientation seek to maximize joint gains or achieve equal outcomes. Those with an *individualist* orientation seek to maximize their own gain. And people with a *competitive* orientation seek to maximize their own gain relative to that of others.

These are just a few of the variables that help determine competition or cooperation in social dilemmas. Take a look at the factors listed in Table 8.5. Each of these has been shown to facilitate the best solutions to social dilemmas.

Groups tend to be more competitive than individuals in mixed-motive situations (Insko et al., 2013; Kugler & Bornstein, 2013; Pinter & Wildschut, 2012). One reason for this is that it can be harder to establish trust between groups than between individuals. Another reason is that members of a group feel that they are more anonymous than if they act alone, freeing them to act in a self-interested or aggressive manner. This is one reason why large groups are more likely to exploit scarce resources than small ones are (Balliet & Van Lange, 2013; Nosenzo et al., 2015; Pruitt, 2012). Unfortunately, social dilemmas often do involve very large

> *"If a free society cannot help the many who are poor, it cannot save the few who are rich."*
>
> —John F. Kennedy

Pollution from an oil refinery in Edmonton, Canada, glows in the dusk. A clean environment is a public resource that is vital for all of us, but protecting it often runs into conflict with the economic self-interest of individuals or groups.

Dan Riedlhuber/Reuters/Corbis

Large groups are more likely than small groups to exploit a scarce resource that the members collectively depend on.

TRUE

groups—a city, a state, a nation, the whole world. In these circumstances, the structural arrangements listed toward the bottom of Table 8.5 may be most appropriate for trying to reduce exploitation.

■ Negotiation

Social dilemmas are but one type of conflict between individuals or groups that often must be resolved through negotiation. Successful negotiation can reduce many conflicts, but it is important to ask this question: What *is* a successful negotiation? You might think a 50–50 compromise is an ideal outcome for two negotiating parties. Here, the negotiators start at extreme positions and gradually work toward a mutually acceptable midpoint. In many situations, however, *both* sides can do better than this. The reason for this is that most negotiations are not simply fixed-sum situations in which each side can gain something only if the other side loses it (Bazerman & Neale, 1992). Instead, both sides often have the opportunity to reach an **integrative agreement**, in which both parties obtain outcomes that are superior to a 50–50 split.

Carolita Johnson /The New Yorker Collection/The Cartoon Bank

"I'm running late—some people were waiting for my table so I had to take my sweet time."

People with a competitive social value orientation may go out of their way to prevent others from using a resource, even if in doing so, they hurt themselves in the long run as well.

▲ **TABLE 8.5**

Solving Social Dilemmas

Behavior in a social dilemma is influenced by both psychological factors and structural arrangements. The characteristics listed here contribute to the successful solution of social dilemmas.

Psychological Factors

Individual Differences

- Having a prosocial, cooperative orientation
- Trusting others

Situational Factors

- Being in a good mood
- Having had successful experience managing resources and working cooperatively
- Being exposed to unselfish models
- Having reason to expect others to cooperate

Group Dynamics

- Acting as an individual rather than in a group
- Being in a small group rather than in a large group
- Sharing a social identity or superordinate goals

Structural Arrangements

- Creating a payoff structure that rewards cooperative behavior and/or punishes selfish behavior
- Removing resources from the public domain and handing them over to private ownership
- Establishing an authority to control the resources

© Cengage Learning®

integrative agreement A negotiated resolution to a conflict in which all parties obtain outcomes that are superior to what they would have obtained from an equal division of the contested resources.

A good way to understand this is to consider the tale of the two sisters and the orange (Follett, 1942). One sister wanted the juice to drink; the other wanted the peel for a cake. So they sliced the orange in half and each one took her portion. These sisters suffered from an advanced case of what is known as the *fixed-pie syndrome,* the belief that whatever one of them won, the other one lost. In fact, however, each of them could have had the whole thing: all of the juice for one, all of the peel for the other. An integrative agreement was well within their grasp, but they failed to see it. Unfortunately, research indicates that this happens all too often. Negotiators frequently agree to settlements that are worse for both sides (Chambers & De Dreu, 2014; L. Thompson, 2015).

It is often difficult for participants in a dispute to listen carefully to each other and reach some reasonable understanding of each other's perspective. But communication in which both sides disclose their goals and needs is critically important in allowing each side to see opportunities for joint benefits. This may seem obvious, and yet people in negotiations, just like the two sisters with the orange, very often fail to communicate their goals and needs. They may hold back information because of lack of trust in the other side, or because they think their goals are more clear to the other party than they actually are. If communication is improved, however, the outcomes can improve dramatically. Outcomes often improve also in response to a number of other factors, such as training in conflict-resolution techniques, using computerized negotiation support systems, establishing trust, and getting the parties to take a less egocentric perspective or to think about higher-order motives than just their preferred outcomes (Eden & Ackermann, 2014; Kong et al., 2014; Trötschel et al., 2011; Wilson & Thompson, 2014; Zerres et al., 2013).

Negotiating with car dealers is a form of negotiation that many of us engage in from time to time. Want some tips? Try the Tips & Advice section on the Edmunds website at http://www.edmunds.com.

When people or groups negotiate with each other, the best solution is one in which both parties compromise and split the resources 50–50.

FALSE

Representatives of nations from around the world meet in Geneva to try to negotiate agreements about nuclear policies. Negotiations across cultures and between groups with a history of conflict pose special challenges. They highlight the usefulness of social psychological research that has specified factors that make negotiations more or less likely to succeed.

Culture and Negotiation

As the world becomes smaller because of advances in technology, the globalization of business and the economy, and global threats concerning the environment and terrorism, the ability to negotiate effectively across cultures becomes increasingly important. Understanding cultural differences relevant to negotiation is therefore vital. Table 8.6 lists some common assumptions made by negotiators from Western, individualistic cultures that are not always shared by representatives from other cultures.

Consider, for example, our statement that good communication is a key ingredient in successful negotiation. Communication across cultures can present special challenges (Liu & Wilson, 2011; Thompson et al., 2010). Whereas an individualistic perspective emphasizes direct communication and confrontation, a collectivistic perspective emphasizes more indirect communication and a desire to avoid direct conflict. Whereas individualistic negotiators may emphasize rationality, collectivistic negotiators have a greater tolerance of contradiction and emotionality—although collectivists prefer emotionality that is not confrontational. Negotiators from individualistic cultures are more likely to respond with a direct "no" to a proposal than are collectivists; negotiators from collectivistic cultures are more likely to refer to social roles and relationships than are individualists.

AP Images/Pool/Anja Niedringhaus

▲ **TABLE 8.6**

Cultural Assumptions About Negotiating

People from different cultures make different assumptions about the negotiation process. This table summarizes some assumptions commonly made by U.S. and other Western negotiators. It also presents some alternative assumptions that negotiators from other cultures might hold. As you can see, such different assumptions could make it very difficult to reach a successful agreement.

Assumptions of Negotiators From the United States and Other Western Countries	Assumptions of Negotiators From Non-Western Cultures
Negotiation is a business, not a social activity.	The first step in negotiating is to develop a trusting relationship between the individual negotiators.
Points should be made with rational, analytical arguments without contradiction.	Arguments may be more holistic, and emotionality and contradiction may be tolerated.
Communication is direct and verbal.	Some of the most important communication is nonverbal or indirect.
Written contracts are binding; oral commitments are not.	Written contracts are less meaningful than oral communications because the nonverbal context clarifies people's intentions.
Current information and ideas are more valid than historical or traditional opinions and information.	History and tradition are more valid than current information and ideas. Information must be understood in its greater context.
Time is very important; punctuality is expected; deadlines should be set and adhered to.	Building a relationship takes time and is more important than punctuality; setting deadlines is an effort to humiliate the other party.

© Cengage Learning®

According to Yunxia Zhu and others (2007a), relationship building is an important part of the negotiation process among Chinese. Negotiators from individualistic cultures may need to be uncharacteristically patient with processes that may seem irrelevant to the task at hand because they are important in creating *guanxi,* a Chinese term for relationship. The initial sessions in negotiations with Chinese take on particular importance because they can set the tone for establishing *guanxi.*

Another difference concerns the timing of concessions. Individualists tend to prefer to make compromises and concessions toward the end of a negotiation, whereas collectivists may prefer to begin with generous concessions and gradually reduce their concessions later. Yet another factor concerns "saving face"—feeling that others continue to respect you and that you have maintained honor. Although saving face in a negotiation is important across cultures, it may be of more central importance in collectivist cultures (Oetzel et al., 2008; Rodriguez Mosquera et al., 2008; Tjosvold et al., 2004). Michele Gelfand and others (2015), for example, illustrate the contrasting values of rationality and honor across cultures with culture-specific quotations: "Separate the people from the problem" is advice given to negotiators in the West and emphasizes being objective and rational, whereas the Arabic proverbs "I'd rather you

● FIGURE 8.9

Culture and Negotiation: Rational vs. Honor Focus

Participants in the United States and in Egypt engaged in hour-long negotiations, and the transcripts from these negotiations were analyzed to measure the frequency with which words associated with more traditionally Western objective, rational perspectives were used as well as words concerning honor that are more associated with Arabic thinking. The more that rational-related words were used during the negotiation, the better the negotiation outcomes were in the United States but the worse they were in Egypt. The more that honor-related words were used, the better the outcomes were in Egypt.
Based on Gelfand et al., 2015

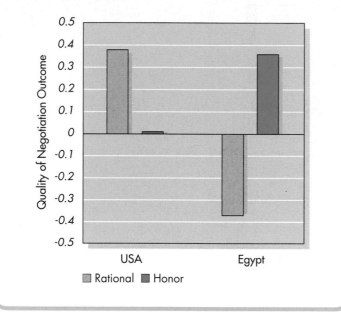

respect me than feed me" or "Dignity before bread" reflect the role of maximizing honor rather than profit in cultures such as in Egypt. To study this cultural difference Gelfand and her colleagues had participants in the United States and in Egypt engage in hour-long negotiations. The researchers transcribed the audio from these negotiations and measured the frequency of words that emphasized "a distinctively Western form of logical reasoning," such as "rational," "logic," "deduce," "cause," and "solution," as well as words that concerned honor, such as "honest," "reputation," "appear," and "forbid."

The results revealed not only the expected cultural difference in how frequently these types of words were used, but also in the relationship between using these expressions and the success of the negotiation. The more that words reflecting a rational model were used, the better the negotiation outcomes (e.g., the more likely they would reach integrative agreements) were in the United States, but the *worse* the outcomes were in Egypt. On the other hand, the more that words reflecting honor were used, the better the negotiation outcomes were in Egypt; there was no relationship between use of honor words and negotiation outcomes in the United States (see ● Figure 8.9).

Emotional responses may hurt negotiations between members of different cultures if they are deemed inappropriate in one of the cultures. Expressions of pride are more likely to be received positively in individualist cultures, whereas expressions of shame are more likely to be received positively in collectivist cultures (Rodriguez Mosquera et al., 2004). Shirli Kopelman and Ashleigh Shelby Rosette (2008) conducted an experiment that illustrates cultural differences in sensitivity to particular emotions. Business students from Hong Kong and Israel participated in a negotiation exercise in which an American female business manager offered them a take-it-or-leave-it proposal by video. For half the students, the manager made the offer displaying positive emotion—she spoke in a friendly tone, smiled and nodded often, and appeared cordial. For the other half, the manager displayed negative emotion—she spoke in a more angry tone and appeared intimidating and irritated.

As the researchers had predicted, the students from Hong Kong responded very differently as a function of the emotion displayed. As can be seen in ● Figure 8.10, they were much more likely to accept the offer if it was made with a display of positive than negative emotions. Students from Israel, where direct and confrontational negotiations are more commonplace (and perhaps where an American woman would be seen less as an outgroup), were relatively unaffected by the emotional display of the negotiator when deciding whether or not to accept the offer.

Understanding these kinds of cultural differences is essential for ensuring the best resolutions of conflicts and negotiations. Consistent with this point,

Kevin Groves and others (2015) were able to measure the "cultural intelligence" of the business school students in their study, and they found that students with higher cultural intelligence outperformed other students in cross-cultural negotiations. Fortunately, education may help even those who are less culturally intelligent. Sujin Lee and others (2013) had participants from East Asian and North American cultures negotiate with each other. Some of the participants learned information about the kinds of cross-cultural differences discussed in this section of the textbook and were encouraged to think about the other culture's perspective during the negotiation. Other participants did not receive this cultural information and were instead encouraged to think about the other person's alternatives in the negotiation. The participants who received the cross-cultural perspective-taking procedure achieved much better negotiation outcomes than did the other participants.

Wendi Adair and Jeanne Brett (2005) describe negotiation as a kind of dance. The partners move with each other according to various rhythms, and the dance will work only if they can synchronize their movements and work together. Negotiations across cultures can be challenging because the participants have different ways of performing these dances. As Adair and Brett put it, "Just as it will take time for a Cuban, who is accustomed to the rapid, staircase movements of Latin social dancing, and an American—accustomed to smooth walking dances like the waltz—to get in sync, it will take time for cross-cultural negotiators to synchronize their movements" (p. 46). It is in the best interest of negotiators, therefore, to learn each other's perspectives so they can work together more effectively and fluently without stepping on each other's toes.

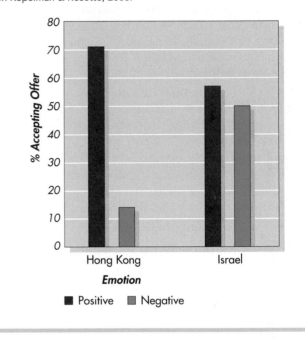

● **FIGURE 8.10**

Emotions During Negotiation: Cross-Cultural Differences

Business students from Hong Kong and Israel participated in a negotiation exercise in which they received a take-it-or-leave-it proposal from an American business manager. The manager displayed either warm, positive emotion or angry, negative emotion while making the offer. Students from Hong Kong were much less likely to accept the offer if it was made with negative emotion rather than with positive emotion. The Israeli students' decisions were not strongly affected by the emotions displayed.
Based on Kopelman & Rosette, 2008.

Finding Common Ground

Groups inevitably fall into conflict with each other, as do people within groups. Although each conflict may be unique, all efforts to find a constructive solution to conflict require some common ground to build upon. Recognition of a *superordinate identity* is one way to establish common ground between groups in conflict. When group members perceive that they have a shared identity across group boundaries, the attractiveness of outgroup members increases, and interactions between the groups often become more peaceful. Those who would make peace, rather than stoke conflict, realize that it is in their own self-interest to find common ground and to understand that the cloak of humanity is large enough to cover a multitude of lesser differences.

Review

Top 10 Key Points in Chapter 8

1. People join a group for a variety of reasons, not only to perform tasks that can't be accomplished alone but also to enhance self-esteem, social identity, and a greater sense of purpose; indeed, attraction to groups seems to be an evolved psychological mechanism.

2. When members' roles are clear, assigned appropriately, and don't come in conflict with other roles, and when members understand the group's norms, greater satisfaction and group performance result.

3. Cohesiveness is related to group performance, but the causal direction of this relationship could go either way; moreover, cultures differ in what is most important for group cohesiveness.

4. When individual contributions are identifiable, the presence of others enhances performance on easy tasks but impairs performance on difficult tasks. When group members pool their efforts together, individuals often exert less effort and engage in social loafing.

5. Contrary to popular belief, group brainstorming typically is less effective than the same number of individuals brainstorming alone. Fortunately, researchers have identified a number of techniques, such as electronic brainstorming, that can greatly improve group brainstorming.

6. Group decisions can be harmed by group polarization, in which opinions become more extreme in the direction that most members were initially favoring, and groupthink, in which members seek concurrence rather than a thorough and candid analysis of all the information and alternative courses of action.

7. Information may not be communicated adequately because of problems in the group's communication network and by the tendency for groups to pay more attention to information that is already known by all or most group members than to important information that is known by only one or a few group members

8. Setting specific and ambitious goals and plans and doing so with one or more partners improves performance more than vague "do your best" goals.

9. In a social dilemma, personal benefit conflicts with the overall good, and groups tend to be more competitive than individuals in dealing with these dilemmas.

10. Many negotiations have the potential to result in integrative agreements in which outcomes exceed a 50–50 split, but negotiators often fail to achieve such outcomes. Communication, trust, and an understanding of the other party's perspective and cultural norms and values are key ingredients of successful negotiation.

Putting Common Sense to the Test

Individuals in Groups: The Presence of Others

People will cheer louder when they cheer as part of a group than when they cheer alone.

Ⓕ **False.** *People tend to put less effort into collective tasks, such as group cheering, than into tasks where their individual performance can be identified and evaluated.*

Group Performance: Problems and Solutions

People brainstorming as a group come up with a greater number of better ideas than the same number of people working individually.

Ⓕ **False.** *Groups in which members interact face to face produce fewer creative ideas when brainstorming than the same number of people brainstorming alone.*

Group members' attitudes about a course of action usually become more moderate after group discussion.

Ⓕ **False.** *Group discussion often causes attitudes to become more extreme as the initial tendencies of the group are exaggerated.*

People and groups tend to do worse when they have "do your best" goals than when they have very specific, ambitious goals.

Ⓣ **True.** *People and groups that have vague "do your best goals" don't tend to do their best. They can do better if they set specific, ambitious but reachable goals.*

Conflict: Cooperation and Competition Within and Between Groups

Large groups are more likely than small groups to exploit a scarce resource that the members collectively depend on.

Ⓣ **True.** *Large groups are more likely to behave selfishly when faced with resource dilemmas, in part because people in large groups feel less identifiable and more anonymous.*

When people or groups negotiate with each other, the best solution is one in which both parties compromise and split the resources 50–50.

Ⓕ **False.** *Both sides often can do better than a 50-50 split, as what each side most wants or needs may be different; however, many negotiators fail to recognize this opportunity.*

Key Terms

biased sampling (333)

brainstorming (326)

collective effort model (321)

deindividuation (322)

distraction–conflict theory (319)

evaluation apprehension theory (319)

group (311)

group cohesiveness (315)

group polarization (328)

group support systems (337)

groupthink (330)

integrative agreement (343)

mere presence (319)

prisoner's dilemma (341)

process gain (326)

process loss (325)

resource dilemmas (341)

social dilemma (340)

social facilitation (318)

social identity model of deindividuation effects (SIDE) (324)

social loafing (320)

transactive memory (335)

Attraction and Close Relationships

This chapter examines how people form relationships with each other. First, we describe the fundamental human need for being with others, why people affiliate, and the problem of loneliness. Then we consider various personal and situational factors that influence our initial attraction to specific others. Third, we examine different types of close relationships—what makes them rewarding, how they differ, the types of love they arouse, and the factors that keep them together or break them apart.

Need to Belong: A Fundamental Human Motive | 352

Review

No topic fascinates the people of this planet more than interpersonal attraction.

Needing to belong, we humans are obsessed about friendships, hookups, romantic relationships, dating, love, sex, reproduction, sexual orientation, marriage, and divorce. Playwrights, poets, and musicians write with eloquence and emotion about love desired, won, and lost. In recent years, television all over the world has been filled with relationship-centered reality TV shows such as *The Bachelor, The Bachelorette, Wife Swap, Bachelor Pad, Blind Date, The Dating Game, Here Come the Newlyweds,* and *Cheaters.* More and more, people are meeting up in person, through friends, at work, in bars, and online—on Facebook, in mobile apps such as Tinder, and in dating service websites such as Match.com, eHarmony, and OkCupid. Both in our hearts and in our minds, the relationships we seek and enjoy with other people are more important than anything else.

At one time or another, each of us has been startled by our reaction to someone we have met. In general, why are human beings drawn to each other? Why are we so attracted to some people and yet indifferent to or repelled by others? What determines how our intimate relationships evolve over time? What does it mean to love someone, and what problems are likely to arise along the way? As these questions reveal, the processes of attraction among people—from the first spark through the flames of an intimate connection and the possibility of a cooling off—seem like a wild card in the deck of human behavior. This chapter unravels some of the mysteries.

Need to Belong: A Fundamental Human Motive

Although born helpless, human infants are equipped with reflexes that orient them toward people. They are uniquely responsive to human faces, they turn their head toward voices, and they are able to mimic certain facial gestures on cue. Then, a few weeks later the baby flashes a first smile, surely the warmest sign of all. Much to the delight of parents all over the world, the newborn seems an inherently social animal. But wait. If you reflect on the amount of time that you spend talking to, being with, flirting with, confiding in, pining for, or worrying about other people, you'll realize that we are all social animals. It seems that people need people.

According to Roy Baumeister and Mark Leary (1995), the need to belong is a basic human motive, "a pervasive drive to form and maintain at least a minimum quantity of lasting, positive, and significant interpersonal relationships" (p. 497). This general proposition is supported by everyday observation and a great deal of research. All over the world, people feel joy when they form new social attachments and react with anxiety and grief when these bonds are broken—as when separated from a loved one by distance, divorce, or death. The need to belong runs deep, which is why people get very distressed when they are neglected by others, rejected, excluded,

---

Putting COMMON SENSE to the Test

Circle Your Answer

T F People seek out the company of others, even strangers, in times of stress.

T F Infants do not discriminate between faces considered attractive and unattractive in their culture.

T F People who are physically attractive are happier and have higher self-esteem than those who are unattractive.

T F When it comes to romantic relationships, opposites attract.

T F Men are more likely than women to interpret friendly gestures by the opposite sex in sexual terms.

T F After the honeymoon period, there is an overall decline in levels of marital satisfaction.

stigmatized, or ostracized, all forms of "social death" (Leary, 2001; Smart Richman & Leary, 2009; Williams & Nida, 2011).

We care deeply about what others think of us, which is why we spend so much time and money to make ourselves presentable and attractive. In fact, some people are so worried about how they appear to others that they suffer from various symptoms of *social anxiety disorder* characterized by intense feelings of discomfort in situations that invite public scrutiny (Leary & Kowalski, 1995). One very familiar example is public-speaking anxiety, or "stage fright"—a performer's worst nightmare. If you've ever had to make a presentation only to feel weak in the knees and hear your voice quiver, you have experienced a hint of this disorder. When sufferers are asked what there is to fear, the most common responses are shaking and showing other signs of anxiety, going blank, saying something foolish, and being unable to continue (Stein et al., 1996). For people with high levels of social anxiety, the problem is also evoked by other social situations, such as eating at a public lunch counter, signing a check in front of a store clerk, and, for males, urinating in a crowded men's room. In extreme cases, the reaction can become so debilitating that the person just stays at home (Beidel & Turner, 1998; Crozier & Alden, 2005).

Our need to belong is a fundamental human motive. People who have a network of close social ties—in the form of lovers, friends, family members, and co-workers—have higher self-esteem and greater satisfaction with life compared to those who live more isolated lives (Denissen et al., 2008; Leary & Baumeister, 2000). People who are socially connected rather than isolated are also physically healthier and less likely to die a premature death (Cacioppo et al., 2015; Holt-Lunstad et al., 2015; House et al., 1988). Recent research shows that people can even draw the motivation to achieve success from their connections with others (Walton et al., 2012).

With regard to social networks, does it help to have a presence on Facebook and other online social media sites—which enable people to stay in touch, even if not in person? This medium is new but already it is sweeping through Western culture. In the United States, more than 90% of high school and college students have posted a profile on a social media site complete with a list of network "friends." ● Figure 9.1 shows that in 2006, the average network size among college students was 137; in 2007, it climbed to 185; in

All over the world, for both men and women, the need to belong is a powerful human motive.

ImagesBazaar/Getty Images

● FIGURE 9.1

Social Media Networks: How Many Friends Do You Have?

In the United States, the trend is clear: Since 2006, college students have exhibited a sharp increase in the number of network "friends" they have. Most of this growth comes from an increase in distant and superficial relationships.
Manago et al., 2012.

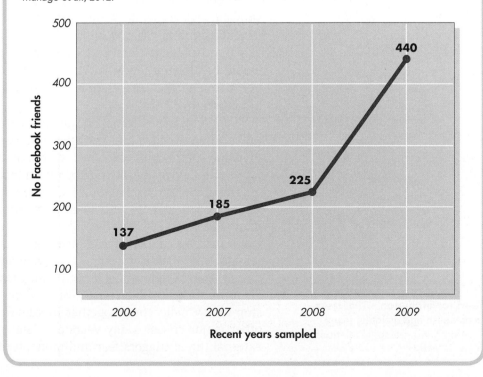

"At this point, my privacy needs are interfering with my intimacy goals."

People are motivated to establish and maintain an optimum level of social contact.

2008, to 225. By 2009, the average had soared to 440. According to Statista (2015), five years later, that average number—on Facebook alone—had reached 521 (ages 12 to 17) and 649 (ages 18 to 24). It comes as no surprise that as Facebook friends lists have grown, most of that growth has come from an increase in distant and superficial relations. Importantly, it seems that the larger your online social network is, the more people there are to view your status updates and the more socially connected you are likely to feel (Manago et al., 2012).

■ The Thrill of Affiliation

As social beings, humans are drawn to each other like magnets to metal. We work together, play together, live together, and often make lifetime commitments to grow old together. This social motivation begins with the **need for affiliation**, defined as a desire to establish social contact with others (McAdams, 1989). Individuals differ in the strength of their need for affiliation. Everyone is highly motivated to establish and maintain an *optimum* balance of social contact—sometimes craving the company of others, sometimes wanting to be alone—the way a body is set to maintain a certain temperature level. In an interesting experiment, Bibb Latané and Carol Werner (1978) found that even laboratory rats were more likely to approach others of their species after a period of isolation and were less likely to approach others after prolonged contact. These researchers suggested that rats, like many other animals, have a built-in "sociostat" (social thermostat) to regulate their affiliative tendencies.

Is there evidence of a similar mechanism in humans? Shawn O'Connor and Lorne Rosenblood (1996) recruited college students to carry portable beepers for four days. Whenever the beepers went off (on average, every hour), the students wrote down whether at the time they were *actually* alone or in the company of other people and whether they *wanted* to be alone or with others. The results showed that students were in the state they desired two-thirds of the time. In fact, the situation they desired on one occasion (saying they wanted to be alone at 4 p.m.) predicted their actual situation the next time they were signaled (they would be alone at 5 p.m.). Whether it was solitude or social contact that the students sought, they successfully managed to regulate their own personal needs for affiliation.

People may well differ in the strength of their affiliative needs, but there are times when we all want to be with other people. Recall the scenes in recent championship sports cities whenever the home team won the final championship game. From one city to the next, jubilant fans stayed long after the game had ended, milling about and exchanging high-fives, slaps on the back, and hugs and kisses. In each of these cities, it's clear that people wanted to celebrate together rather than alone.

Affiliating can satisfy us for other reasons too, as others provide energy, attention, stimulation, information, and emotional support (Hill, 1987). What conditions lead people to seek out others? One condition that strongly arouses our need for affiliation is stress. Have you ever noticed the way neighbors who never stop to say hello come together in snowstorms, hurricanes, power failures, and other major crises? Many years ago, Stanley Schachter (1959) theorized that an external threat triggers fear and motivates us to affiliate, particularly with others

need for affiliation The desire to establish and maintain many rewarding interpersonal relationships.

who face a similar threat. In a laboratory experiment that demonstrated the point, Schachter found that people who were expecting to receive painful electric shocks chose to wait with other nervous participants rather than alone. So far, so good. But when Irving Sarnoff and Philip Zimbardo (1961) led college students to expect that they would be engaging in an embarrassing behavior—sucking on large bottle nipples and pacifiers—their desire to be with others fell off. It seemed puzzling. Why do people in fearful misery love company while those in embarrassed misery seek solitude?

Yacov Rofé (1984) proposed a simple answer: *utility.* Rofé argued that stress sparks the desire to affiliate only when being with others is seen as useful in reducing the negative impact of the stressful situation. Schachter's participants had reason to believe that affiliation would be useful. They would have an opportunity to compare their emotional reactions with those of others to determine whether they really needed to be fearful. For those in the Sarnoff and Zimbardo study, however, affiliation had less to offer. When we face embarrassment, being with others is more likely to increase our stress than reduce it.

Fabian Bimmer/Reuters/Corbis

When Germany defeated Brazil on the way to winning the World Cup Soccer championship in 2014, people poured into the streets to be with and celebrate with one another.

Let's return to Schachter's initial study. What specific benefit do people get from being in the presence of others in times of stress? Research suggests that people facing an imminent threat seek each other out in order to gain *cognitive clarity* about the danger they are in. In one experiment, Kulik and others (1994) found that research participants anticipating the painful task of soaking a hand in ice-cold water preferred to wait with someone who had already completed the task rather than with someone who had not. They also asked more questions of these experienced peers than participants who did not know that the water would be painful. Under stress, we adaptively become motivated to affiliate with others who can help us cope with an impending threat. Summarizing his own work, Schachter (1959) noted that misery loves miserable company. Based on their more recent studies, Gump and Kulik (1997) further amended this assertion: "Misery loves the company of those in the same miserable situation" (p. 317).

Stress is not the only state of mind that inspires people to affiliate. John Cacioppo and others (2015) have noted that being alone—*and feeling lonely*—motivates people of all ages to connect with others in order to satisfy a "reaffiliation motive." Charleen Case and others (2015) theorized that individuals who *lack power* and influence also feel a need to seek out other people. In one study, they found that participants who were primed to imagine lacking power displayed more interest in joining a campus service aimed at fostering new friendships. In a second study, people assigned to a position of low power sought more physical proximity to a partner. Consistent with Rofé's (1984) utility explanation for why people affiliate, it now appears that stress, loneliness, and a lack of power are among the states of mind that inspire social affiliation.

> **People seek out the company of others, even strangers, in times of stress.**
>
> **TRUE**

■ The Agony of Loneliness

People need other people—to celebrate with, share news with, commiserate with, talk to, and learn from. But some people are painfully shy, socially awkward, inhibited, and reluctant to approach others. Shyness itself is a common characteristic. Roughly 49% of all Americans describe themselves as shy, as do 31% in Israel, 40% in Germany, 55% in Taiwan, and 57% in Japan (Henderson & Zimbardo, 1998). People who are shy find it difficult to approach strangers, make small talk, telephone someone for a date, participate in small groups, or mingle at parties. Often reject others, perhaps because they fear being rejected themselves. For people whose shyness is extreme, the result is a pattern of risk avoidance that can set them up for unpleasant and unrewarding interactions (Crozier, 2001; Hofmann & DiBartolo, 2014).

Shyness can arise from different sources. In some cases, it may stem from an inborn personality trait. Jerome Kagan (1994) and others have found that some infants are highly sensitive to stimulation, inhibited, and cautious shortly after birth. In other cases, shyness develops as a learned reaction to failed interactions. In other words, interpersonal problems of the past can ignite social anxieties about the future (Leary & Kowalski, 1995). Not all shy infants grow up to become inhibited adults. But longitudinal research indicates that there is some continuity, that this aspect of our personalities may be predictable from our temperament and behavior as young children. Toddlers observed to be inhibited, shy, and fearful at age 3, for example, are more likely than toddlers who were more outgoing to be socially isolated at age 21 (Caspi, 2000). The differences can be seen in the adult brain. Using fMRI, researchers have recently observed that people who are shy, compared to those who are bold, exhibit greater activity in the amygdala—a region of the brain responsible for fear processing—when exposed to pictures of strangers (Beaton et al., 2008; Schwartz et al., 2003).

Whatever the source, shyness is a real problem, and it has painful consequences. Studies show that shy people evaluate themselves negatively, expect to fail in their social encounters, and blame themselves when they do. As a result, many shy people go into self-imposed isolation, which often makes them feel lonely. In part, the problem stems from a paralyzing fear of rejection, which inhibits people from making friendly or romantic overtures to those they are interested in. If you ever wanted to approach someone you liked but stopped yourself, you know that this situation often triggers an approach–avoidance conflict, pulling you between the desire for contact and a fear of being rejected. What's worse, research shows that people who fear rejection think that their friendly or romantic interest is transparent to others, which leads them to back off (Vorauer et al., 2003).

Loneliness is a sad and heart-wrenching emotional state. To be lonely is to feel deprived of human social connections, which occurs whenever we have less contact with others than we want (Cacioppo & Patrick, 2008; Peplau & Perlman, 1982). Based on their review of research, Stephanie Cacioppo and others (2015) have noted that there are three facets or dimensions of loneliness—intimate, relational, and collective (see ● Figure 9.2). *Intimate loneliness* is felt when someone wants but does not have a spouse, significant other, or best friends to rely on for emotional support, especially during personal crises. Somewhat outside our circle of personal space, *relational loneliness* is felt when someone wants but lacks friendships from school and work and family connections, the 15 or 50 people

"Loneliness and the feeling of being unwanted is the most terrible poverty."

—Mother Teresa

● **FIGURE 9.2**

Loneliness is a heart-wrenching emotional state in which one feels deprived of human social connections. As depicted in this image, research suggests that there are three facets of loneliness—intimate, relational, and collective.

(Cacioppo et al., 2015.)

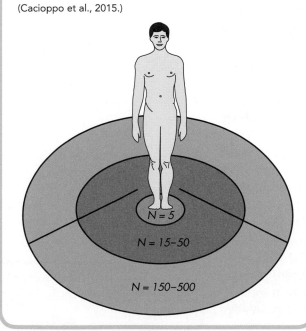

N = 5

N = 15–50

N = 150–500

loneliness A feeling of deprivation about existing social relations.

whom we see regularly and rely on for occasional help, child care, resources, contacts, and advice. Representing the outermost layer of our social network, *collective loneliness* comes from remote relationships and the social identities we derive from, say, from alumni of the schools we have attended and clubs we join on the basis of common needs or interests. The more voluntary associations we have, the lower one's collective loneliness.

From childhood through adolescence, adulthood, and old age, most people feel lonely at some point in life—either briefly, which motivates a need for reaffiliation, or for a prolonged and unhealthy period of time, which triggers a range of physical and mental health problems, including depression, alcoholism, and anxiety (Hawkley et al., 2009; Heinrich & Gullone, 2006; Cacioppo et al., 2015).

Francesco Jodice, Hikikomori, film, 22', 2004, film still

In Japan, some number of young adults suffer from hikikomori, an extreme form of social withdrawal, which in English means "pulling away." Not attending school or working, these individuals live isolated at home, often in a single room.

It's important to realize that although loneliness is a universal phenomenon, and perhaps rooted in an individual's temperament, it can take shape in different ways from one culture to the next. In Japan, for example, a significant number of young adults today are afflicted by *hikikomori*, a form of social withdrawal. Hikikomori, which translates to "pulling away" in English, is characterized by a full withdrawal from intimate relationships outside of the family (Teo, 2010). Those afflicted with hikikomori do not attend school or have jobs and they spend much of their time isolated at home, often in a single room. They do not seem to suffer from depression or other well-known psychological disorders. However, some research suggests the young adults who enter these episodes share histories of parental rejection, family disruption, and peer bullying and rejection (Krieg & Dickie, 2013). Ironically, it appears that people in collectivist cultures are at a high risk for loneliness, relative to Westerners, perhaps reflecting the greater urgency placed on relationships in these cultures (Lykes & Kemmelmeier, 2014).

On the individualization question of who is lonely, research in Western cultures suggests a simple answer: *Anyone* can feel lonely at anytime and anywhere—which is why it has been said, "Loneliness does not discriminate" (Cacioppo et al., 2015). Feeling lonely (which is not the same as being alone) is most likely to strike during times of life transition or disruption—as in the first year at college, after a romantic breakup, or when a loved one moves far away. Surveys show that people who are unattached are lonelier than those with romantic partners, but that those who are widowed, divorced, and separated are lonelier than people who have never been married. Despite the stereotypic image of the lonely old man passing slow time on a park bench, adolescents and adults with numerous social media friends and contacts are not immune. From 3% to 22% of people report having endured a prolonged bout of loneliness (Peplau & Perlman, 1982; Qualter et al., 2015). Happily, despite social commentaries on how detached people have become (for example, club membership rates are lower than they used to be), a comparison of multiple recent surveys of American high school and college students have indicated that loneliness rates have steadily declined from 1978 to 2012 (Clark et al., 2015).

How do people cope with this distressing state? When college students were asked what behavioral strategies they use to combat loneliness, 96% said they often or sometimes try harder to be friendly to other people, 94% take their mind off the problem by reading or watching TV, and 93% try extra hard to succeed at another aspect of life. Others said that they distract themselves by running, shopping, washing the car, doing yoga, or staying busy at other activities. Still others seek new ways to meet people, try to improve their appearance, or talk to a friend, relative, or therapist about the problem. Although fewer in number, some people are so desperate that they use alcohol or drugs to wash away feelings of loneliness (Rook & Peplau, 1982).

The Initial Attraction

Affiliation is a necessary first step in the formation of a social relationship. But each of us is more drawn to some people than to others. If you've ever had a crush on someone, felt the tingly excitement of a first encounter, lusted after a celebrity, or enjoyed the first moments of a new friendship, then you know the meaning of the term *attraction*.

In many ways, the subject of attraction, liking, loving, lusting, and forming new relationships does not seem to conform to logic. For example, research using the online dating site OkCupid shows that women who look right into the camera or sport cleavage do quite well but that men are more successful when they look away, don't smile—and hold animals! When researchers looked at commonalities in couples who had met on this site, they discovered that their answers tended beyond coincidence to match on certain odd questions, such as "Do you like horror movies?" and "Wouldn't it be fun to chuck it all and go live on a sailboat?" (Ansari & Klinenberg, 2015). In light of these discoveries, writer Dan Slater's (2013) chose a fitting title for his book, *Love in the Time of Algorithms: What Technology Does to Meeting and Mating*.

Cyberstock/Alamy

Tinder is a GPS-based dating app that enables people to connect with others in their geographic vicinity. Facebook photos come up—men or women, depending on one's sexual preference. Then based on a snapshot of information, users swipe right for faces they like and swipe left to move on to the next option. The attraction impulse is instantaneous. "On Tinder, there are no questionnaires to fill out. No discussion of your favorite hiking trail, star sign or sexual proclivities. You simply log in through Facebook, pick a few photos that best describe 'you' and start swiping" (Bilton, 2014). Approximately one billion "swipes" per day are recorded.

When you meet someone for the first time, what qualities do *you* look for? Does familiarity breed fondness or contempt? Do birds of a feather flock together or do opposites attract? Is beauty the object of your desire or do you believe that outward appearances are deceiving? And what is it about a situation or the circumstances of an initial meeting that draws you in for more? According to one classic perspective, people are attracted to those with whom they can have a relationship that is rewarding (Byrne & Clore, 1970; Lott & Lott, 1974). The rewards may be direct, as when people provide us with attention, support, money, status, information, and other valuable resources. Or the rewards may be indirect, as when it feels good to be with someone who is beautiful, smart, or funny, or who happens to be in our presence when times are good. In an important extension of this perspective, R. Matthew Montoya and Robert Horton (2014) have suggested that each of us is attracted to others we see as being both able and willing to fulfill our various relationship needs.

A second powerful perspective on attraction has also emerged in recent years—that of evolutionary psychology, the subdiscipline that uses principles of evolution to understand human social behavior. According to this view, human beings all over the world exhibit patterns of attraction and mate selection that favor the conception, birth, and survival of their offspring. This approach has a great deal to say about differences in this regard between men and women (Buss, 2011; Schaller et al., 2006).

Recognizing the role of rewards and the call of our evolutionary past provides broad perspectives for understanding human attraction. But there's more to the story—much more. Over the years, social psychologists have identified many important determinants of attraction and the development of intimate relationships (Berscheid & Regan, 2004; Fugère et al., 2014; Miller, 2012; Regan, 2011). Most research used to be focused on heterosexuals, so we often do not know how well specific findings apply to the lesbian, gay, bisexual, and transgender (LGBT) population. At the same time, it is important to realize that many of the basic processes described in this chapter relate to the development of all close relationships—regardless of whether the individuals involved are gay, lesbian, or straight (Herek, 2006; Kurdek, 2005; Peplau & Fingerhut, 2007).

Finally, it is important to realize that the way that people meet is a process that has transformed in an explosive way as a result of online dating services such as Match.com, eHarmony, OkCupid, and Plenty of Fish, not to mention the mobile phone dating apps such as Tinder, Zoosk, and Badoo. Match.com was first launched in 1995, so online dating is still a relatively new phenomenon. In a national survey, 4,002 adults were asked how they met their current partners. Among those who met between 2007 and 2009, the most recent time frame fully sampled, 22% of heterosexual couples had met on the Internet. The numbers were far higher for same-sex couples, nearly 70% of whom had met online (Rosenfeld & Thomas, 2012).

Why are online dating platforms so popular? Does meeting in cyberspace rather than in-person alter the attraction process? In a critical analysis of this phenomenon, Eli Finkel and others (2012) note that online dating promises three benefits: (1) exposure and access to large numbers of profiles of potential romantic partners, (2) a means of communicating through e-mail, instant messaging, and live chat via webcams; and (3) a matching "algorithm" that brings together users who are likely to be attracted to one another. Thus far, note Finkel et al. (2012), there is no published research to support the claim that online dating produces romantic outcomes better than more traditional processes described in this chapter. Stay tuned. There is sure to be a surge of research on this topic in the years ahead.

Re: Online dating, did you know that . . .
49.25 million people in the U.S. have tried online dating—52% male, 48% female. In a single recent year, 17% of U.S. couples who married met on a dating site.
—Statistic Brain (http://www.statisticbrain.com/online-dating-statistics)

Familiarity: Being There

In 1932, sociologist James Bossard examined 5,000 marriage licenses in Philadelphia. He found that 17% of couples had lived within one city block of each other, that 31% lived within four blocks, and that 80% lived in the same city. When you think about it, this result is simple but striking: The vast majority of potential partners live far away. Yet disproportionate numbers tend to live within a small radius of space from us. It seems so obvious that people tend to overlook it: People are most likely to become attracted to someone they have seen and become familiar with. So let's begin with two basic and necessary factors in the attraction process: proximity and exposure.

The Proximity Effect   It hardly sounds romantic, but the single best predictor of whether two people will get together is—or used to be—physical proximity or nearness. Today, of course, we often interact at a distance by instant messaging, texting, e-mailing, and the phone. These days it's common for people to find friends, lovers,

"Sometimes I think you married me because I lived next door!"

● FIGURE 9.3

Becoming Friends by Chance

First-year college students were randomly assigned to specific seats for a semester-long class. Illustrating the proximity effect on attraction, those who happened to be seated nearby or in the same row were more likely to rate each other as friends one year later.

Back et al. (2008).

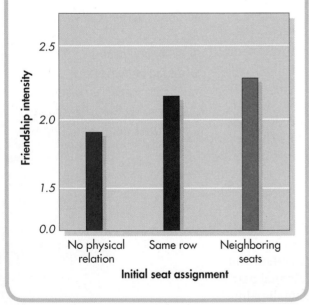

and sexual partners from a distance. Yet some of our most important social interactions still occur among people who find themselves living or working in the same place at the same time (Latané et al., 1995).

To begin with, where we live influences the friends we make. Many years ago, Leon Festinger and his colleagues (1950) studied friendship patterns in married-student college housing and found that people were more likely to become friends with residents of nearby apartments than with those who lived farther away. More recent research has also shown that college students—who live in off-campus apartments, dormitories, fraternities and sorority houses—tend to date those who live either nearby (Hays, 1985) or in the same type of housing as they do (Whitbeck & Hoyt, 1994). In a field experiment on how people can become friends by chance, researchers randomly assigned first-year college students in a psychology class to their seats for the semester. ● Figure 9.3 shows that those who happened to be seated nearby or even in the same row were more likely to rate each other as friends one year later (Back et al., 2008).

The Mere Exposure Effect   Proximity does not necessarily spark attraction, but to the extent that it increases frequency of contact, it's a good first step. Folk wisdom often suggests a dim view of familiarity, as in the saying that it "breeds contempt." But in a series of experiments, Robert Zajonc (1968) found that the more often people saw a novel stimulus—whether it was a foreign word, a geometric form, or a human face—the more they came to like it. This phenomenon, which Zajonc called the **mere exposure effect**, has since been observed in more than 200 experiments (Bornstein, 1989).

People do not have to be aware of their prior exposures for this effect to occur. In a typical study, participants are shown pictures of several stimuli, each for 1 to 5 milliseconds, which is too quick to register in awareness much less enable you to realize that some stimuli are presented more often than others. After the presentation, participants are shown each of the stimuli *for real* and asked two questions: Do you like it, and have you ever seen it before? Perhaps you can predict the result. The more frequently the stimulus is presented, the more people like it. Yet when asked if they've ever seen the liked stimulus before, they say no. These results demonstrate that the mere exposure effect can influence us without our awareness (Kuntz-Wilson & Zajonc, 1980). In fact, the effect is stronger under these conditions (Bornstein & D'Agostino, 1992; Zajonc, 2001).

To appreciate the implications in a naturalistic situation, imagine yourself in a psychology class that is held in a large lecture hall. Three times a week, you trudge over to class, shake the cobwebs out of your head, and try your best to be alert. The room holds several hundred students. You come in and look down the tiered seats to the front where your instructor stands. During the semester, you're vaguely aware of another student who sits up front, but you never talk to her, and you probably would not recognize her if you saw her somewhere else. Then, at the end of the semester, you attend a special session where you are shown

mere exposure effect   The phenomenon whereby the more often people are exposed to a stimulus, the more positively they evaluate that stimulus.

photographs of four women and asked some questions about them. Only then do you learn that you have participated in a study of the mere exposure effect.

Now view the same events from the perspective of Richard Moreland and Scott Beach (1992). These researchers selected four women who looked like typical students to be confederates in this study. One had a very easy job: She had her picture taken. But the other three also attended the class—5, 10, or 15 times. Did frequency of exposure spark attraction among the real students in this situation? Yes it did. In questionnaires they completed after viewing pictures of all four women, students rated each woman on various traits (such as popularity, honesty, intelligence, and physical attractiveness) and recorded their beliefs about how much they would like her, enjoy spending time with her, and want to work with her on a mutual project. The results lined up like ducks in a row: The more classes a woman attended, the more attracted the students were to her.

In a controlled test of the familiarity hypothesis, Harry Reis and his colleagues (2011) recruited 110 same-sex pairs of college students who did not know each other to chat freely by e-mail, using anonymous screen names—once, twice, four times, six times, or eight times in a week. ● Figure 9.4 shows that when participants were asked to rate how much they liked their partner, ratings increased the more interactions they had. When asked if they would like to learn each other's identities so they could stay in contact, the percentages who said yes also increased with their number of interactions. Although they may be exceptions, the general rule is clear: familiarity breeds attraction.

Ponder this clever implication, that familiarity can even influence self-evaluations. Imagine that you had a portrait photograph of yourself edited into two pictures: one that depicted your actual appearance and the other a mirror-image copy (which you can get by horizontally flipping the image using Photoshop and other photo editing software). Which image would you prefer? Which do you think a friend would prefer? Theodore Mita and others (1977) tried this interesting experiment with female college students and found that most preferred their own mirror images, while their friends liked the actual photos. In both cases, the preference was for the view of the face that was most familiar.

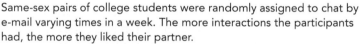

● FIGURE 9.4

Virtual Familiarity Breeds Liking

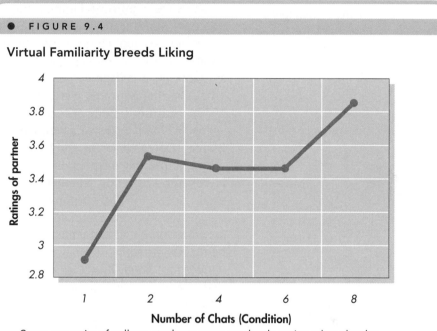

Same-sex pairs of college students were randomly assigned to chat by e-mail varying times in a week. The more interactions the participants had, the more they liked their partner.

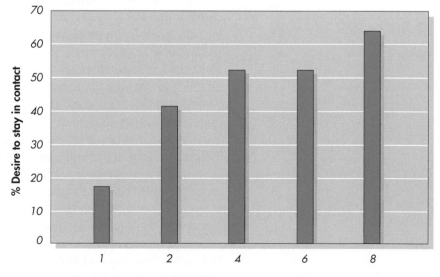

When participants were asked if they wanted to stay in contact after the experiment, the percentage who said yes also increased with the number of interactions they had.

Reis et al. (2011).

■ Physical Attractiveness: Getting Drawn In

What do you look for in a friend or romantic partner: Intelligence? Kindness? An appetite for risk? A sense of humor? How important, really, is a person's looks? As children, we were taught that "beauty is only skin deep" and that we should not "judge a book by its cover" Yet as adults, we react more favorably to others who are physically attractive than to those who are not. Over the years, studies have shown that in the affairs of our social and economic world, physical beauty is a force to be reckoned with (Langlois et al., 2000; Patzer, 2006; Swami & Furnham, 2008).

"Beauty is a greater recommendation than any letter of introduction."
—Aristotle

The human bias for beauty is pervasive. In an early demonstration, fifth-grade teachers were given background information about a boy or girl, accompanied by a photograph. All teachers received identical information, yet those who saw an attractive child saw that child as smarter and more likely to do well in school (Clifford & Walster, 1973). In a second study, male and female research assistants approached students on a college campus and tried to get them to sign a petition. The more attractive the assistants were, the more signatures they were able to get (Chaiken, 1979). In a third study, Texas judges set lower bail and imposed smaller fines on suspects who were rated as attractive rather than unattractive on the basis of photographs (Downs & Lyons, 1991). In a fourth study, members of elite sorority houses who glimpsed at pictures of prospective members were influenced by physical attractiveness in rating whether the young women would prove acceptable (Krendl et al., 2011). Finally, economists in the United States, Canada, and England, have discovered from employment statistics that in many occupational groups physically attractive men and women earn more pay than peers who are comparable except for being less attractive (Hamermesh & Biddle, 1994; Mobius & Rosenblat, 2006). There is no doubt about it: Across a range of settings, in matters of justice and law, social living, and economics, people fare better if they are attractive than if they are not (Hamermesh, 2013; Rhode, 2010).

It all seems so shallow, so superficial. Yet this bias for beauty begins literally in the eye of the beholder. Research shows that beautiful faces capture our attention (Lindell & Lindell, 2014; Maner et al., 2003). In one study, participants looked at Facebook profiles of unfamiliar men and women who varied in facial attractiveness. Using an eye tracking device, researchers found that the participants spent more time looking at attractive versus nonattractive faces relative to advertisements (Seidman & Miller, 2013). In a second study, participants were seated at a computer to complete a visual task on the right or left side of the screen. During the task, faces were flashed on the opposite side of the screen. Although participants tried to stay focused, the appearance of beautiful faces, as opposed to ordinary faces, distracted them and slowed down their ability to execute the task (Liu & Chen, 2012).

The fact that beauty captures attention can help to explain an odd phenomenon. Imagine looking at photographs of several individuals in a group and rating each on a 1–7 point scale for how attractive they are. Or, imagine you were asked to look at the same pictures but rate the group as a whole. Would the average of your individual ratings (let's say they were, 3, 3, 5, 7, 2, 2, 3, 2, 6, 7) equal your overall rating of the group (in this case, the average would be 4)? What do you think? In a series of clever experiments conducted both over the Internet and in the laboratory, Yvette van Osch and her colleagues (2015) sought to answer this question. Time and again, the results supported what they call the *group attractiveness effect*: The perceived physical attractiveness of a group as a whole is greater than the average attractiveness of its individual members. These researchers next tried to figure out why this occurs. Using an eye-tracking device, the results proved revealing. Participants unwittingly spent more time looking at the most attractive members, which skewed upward their perceptions of the group as a whole.

Before we go on to accept the notion that people look at and prefer others who are physically attractive, let's stop for a moment and consider a fundamental question: What constitutes beauty? Is it an objective and measurable human characteristic like height, weight, or hair color? Or is beauty a subjective quality, existing in the eye of the beholder? There are advocates on both sides.

What Is Beauty?   No one would argue that there is a universal "gold standard" for beauty. However, some researchers do believe that certain faces are inherently more attractive, on average, than others. There are three sources of evidence for this proposition.

First, when people are asked to rate unfamiliar faces on a 7- or 10-point scale, there is typically a high level of agreement among children and adults, men and women, and people from the same or different cultures (Langlois et al., 2000). For example, Michael Cunningham and others (1995) asked Asian and Latino students and black and white American students to rate the appearance of women from all these groups. Overall, some faces were rated more attractive than others, leading these investigators to argue that people everywhere share an image of what is beautiful. It is interesting that people also tend to rate others similarly regardless of their attractiveness. By analyzing the ratings of pictures that people post of themselves on a rate-and-date website called HOTorNOT.com, Leonard Lee and others (2008) found that members tend to evaluate specific others similarly regardless of how high or low their own ratings were on the site.

People also tend to agree about what constitutes an attractive body. For example, men tend to be drawn to the "hourglass" figure often seen in women of average weight whose waists are a third narrower than their hips, a shape that is thought to be associated with reproductive fertility. In general, women with a 0.7 WHR (a waist-to-hip ratio where the waist circumference is 70% of the hip circumference) are rated as more attractive. In fact, when shown photographs of women before and after they had microfat grafting surgery (where fat tissue is taken from the waist and implanted on the buttocks, which lowers the WHR), people rated the postoperative photographs as more attractive—independent of any changes in body weight (Singh & Randall, 2007). The preference is found not only among European men but in diverse groups in Africa, Indonesia, Samoa, New Zealand, and elsewhere in the world (Singh et al., 2010). In contrast, women like men with a waist-to-hip ratio that forms a tapering V-shaped physique, signaling more muscle than fat (Singh, 1995). If marriage statistics are any indication, women also seem

Perceptions of facial beauty are largely consistent across cultures. Those regarded as good-looking in one culture also tend to be judged as attractive by people from other cultures. From left to right, the individuals pictured here are from Venezuela, Hawaii, Kenya, and the United States (the American is the actress Marilyn Monroe).

to prefer men with height. Comparisons made in Europe indicate that married men are a full inch taller, on average, than unmarried men (Pawlowski et al., 2000).

Second, a number of researchers have identified physical features of the human face that are reliably associated with ratings of attractiveness, such as smooth skin, a pleasant expression, and youthfulness (Rhodes, 2006). Particularly intriguing are studies showing that people like faces in which the eyes, nose, lips, and other features are not too different from the average. Judith Langlois and Lori Roggman (1990) showed college students both actual yearbook photos and computerized facial composites that "averaged" features from 4, 8, 16, or 32 of the photos. Consistently, they found that the students preferred the averaged composites to the individual faces and that the more faces used to form the composite, the more highly it was rated. Other studies have since confirmed this result (Jones et al., 2007; Langlois et al., 1994; Rhodes et al., 1999).

It seems odd that "averaged" faces are judged attractive when, after all, the faces we find most beautiful are anything but average. What accounts for these findings? Langlois and others (1994) believe that people like averaged faces because they are more prototypically face-like and have features that are less distinctive, so they seem more familiar to us. Consistent with this notion, research shows that just as people are more attracted to averaged human faces than to individual faces, they also prefer averaged dogs, birds, fish, wristwatches, and cars (Halberstadt & Rhodes, 2003).

Computerized averaging studies also show that people are drawn to faces that are symmetrical, where the paired features of the right and left sides line up and mirror each other (Grammer & Thornhill, 1994; Mealey et al., 1999). Why do we prefer symmetrical faces? Although support is mixed, evolutionary psychologists have speculated that our pursuit of symmetry is adaptive because symmetry is naturally associated with biological health, fitness, and fertility, qualities that are highly desirable in a mate (Perrett, 2010; Rhodes et al., 2001; Shackelford & Larsen, 1999). Perhaps for that reason, people throughout the world try to enhance their appeal by wearing or painting symmetrical designs on their faces and bodies—designs that others find attractive (Cárdenas & Harris, 2006).

A third source of evidence for the view that beauty is an objective quality is that babies who are too young to have learned their culture's standards of beauty show a nonverbal preference for faces considered attractive by adults. Picture the scene in an infant laboratory: A baby, lying on its back in a crib, is shown a series of faces previously rated by college students. The first face appears and a clock starts ticking as the baby looks at it. As soon as the baby looks away, the clock stops and the next face is presented. The result: Young infants spend more time tracking and looking at attractive faces than at unattractive ones, regardless of whether the faces are young or old, male or female, or black-skinned or white (Game et al., 2003; Langlois et al., 1991). "These kids don't read *Vogue* or watch TV" notes Langlois, "yet they make the same judgments as adults" (Cowley, 1996, p. 66).

In contrast to this strong objective perspective, other social psychologists believe that physical attractiveness is subjective, and they point for evidence to the influences of culture, time, and the circumstances of our perception. When Johannes Hönekopp (2006) had large numbers of people rate the same faces, he found that although some faces were seen as more attractive than others, individuals differed a great deal in their private preferences. To some extent, beauty really is in the eye of the beholder.

One source of evidence for our variability in taste, first noted by Charles Darwin (1872), is that people from different cultures enhance their beauty in very different ways through face painting, makeup, plastic surgery, scarring, tattoos, hairstyling, the molding of bones, the filing of teeth, braces, and the piercing of ears and other body parts—all contributing to the "enigma of beauty" (Newman, 2000). In dramatic ways, what people find attractive in one part of the world may be seen as repulsive in another part of the world (Landau, 1989).

Ideals also vary when it comes to bodies. Looking at preferences for female body size in 545 cultures, Judith Anderson and others (1992) found that heavy women are judged more attractive than slender women in places where food is frequently in short supply. In one study, for example, Douglas Yu and Glenn Shepard (1998) found that Matsigenka men living in the Andes Mountains of southeastern Peru see female forms with "tubular" shapes—as opposed to hourglass shapes—as healthier, more attractive, and more desirable in a mate.

Differences in preference have also been found among racial groups within a given culture. Michelle Hebl and Todd Heatherton (1998) asked black and white female college students from the United States to rate thin, average, and over-weight women from a set of magazine photographs. The result: The white students saw the heavy women as the least attractive, but black students did not similarly discriminate. Follow-up studies showed the same difference in perceptions of black and white men (Hebl & Turchin, 2005). Why the difference? Based on the fact that white Americans are, on average, thinner than black Americans, one possible explanation is that people in general prefer a body type that is more typical of their group. Another possibility is that white Americans identify more with the "mainstream" weight-obsessed culture as portrayed in TV shows, magazine ads, and other media.

Standards of beauty also change over time, from one generation to the next. Many years ago, Brett Silverstein and others (1986) examined the measurements of female models appearing in women's magazines from the years 1901 to 1981, and they found that "curvaceousness" (as measured by the bust-to-waist ratio) varied over time, with a boyish, slender look becoming particularly desirable in recent years. More recently, researchers took body measurements from all *Playboy* centerfolds, beginning with the first issue, in 1953, which featured Marilyn Monroe, through the last issue of 2001, with Eva Herzigova. The result: Over time, models became thinner and had lower bust-to-waist ratios—away from the ample "hourglass" to a more slender, athletic, sticklike shape (Voracek & Fisher, 2002).

Still other evidence for the subjective nature of beauty comes from various research laboratories. Time and again, social psychologists have found that our perceptions of someone's beauty can be inflated or deflated by various circumstances. Research shows, for example, that people often see others as more physically attractive if they have nonphysical qualities that make them likable (Kniffin & Wilson, 2004)—especially when they are romantically involved (Solomon & Vazire, 2014). This link is illustrated in the student evaluations of professors posted on RateMyProfessors.com, a popular website. An analysis

Computer-generated images that average the features of different faces are seen as more attractive than the individual faces on which they were based. In fact, up to a point, the more faces are represented in a composite, the more attractive it is. Shown here are sets of male and female composites that combine 2, 4, and 32 faces. Which do you prefer? (Langlois & Roggman, 1990.)

2-Face Composite

2-Face Composite

4-Face Composite

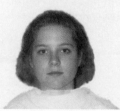
4-Face Composite

32-Face Composite

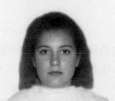
32-Face Composite

Courtesy of Dr. Judith Langlois; University of Texas, Austin

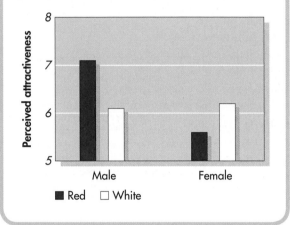

Romantic Red: The Color of Attraction?

In this experiment, college students rated pictures of women that were set against a solid red or white background. Perhaps illustrating a learned association between the color red and romance, male students—but not their female counterparts—rated the pictured women as more attractive in the red background condition.

From Elliot, A. J., & Niesta, D., "Romantic red: Red enhances men's attraction to women," *Journal of Personality and Social Psychology* vol 95 (p. 1154). Copyright © 2008 by the American Psychological Association. Reprinted by permission.

Infants do not discriminate between faces considered attractive and unattractive in their culture.

FALSE

"There is no known culture in which people do not paint, pierce, tattoo, reshape or simply adorn their bodies."

—Enid Schildkrout, anthropologist

of actual ratings on this site revealed that both male and female professors who were rated highly for their teaching were also more likely to be described as "hot" (Riniolo et al., 2006). Of particular interest in this regard is that the more in love people are with their partners, the less attractive they find others of the opposite sex (Johnson & Rusbult, 1989; Simpson et al., 1990).

When it comes to men's attraction to women, one particularly interesting context factor concerns color. The color red is routinely associated with sex. In many species of primates, females display red swelling on their genitals, chest, or face as they near ovulation. In human rituals that date back thousands of years, girls painted red ochre on their face and body at the emergence of puberty and fertility. Today, women use red lipstick and rouge to enhance their appeal, red hearts symbolize Valentine's Day, red lingerie is worn to entice, and red-light districts signal the availability of sex through prostitution.

Are men so conditioned by the color red that its presence boosts their perceptions of attractiveness? In a study of the "red–sex link," Andrew Elliot and Daniela Niesta (2008) had male and female research participants rate female photos that were set against a solid red or white background. Everyone saw the same photos, yet the attractiveness ratings were highest among the men in the red background condition (see ● Figure 9.5). In other studies, men continued to rate women as more attractive—and as more sexually desirable (but not generally more likable)—in the presence of red compared to women who were surrounded by gray, blue, or green. What is the process by which female red sparks male attraction? Follow-up research provides an answer: Women in red are perceived to be sexually receptive (Pazda et al., 2012).

There may be an empirical truth to this perception. Naturalistic research has shown that women on dating websites who say they are looking for casual sex are more likely to wear red in their profile pictures than women seeking other types of relationships (Elliot & Pazda, 2012). Even in the mundane psychology laboratory, female participants were more likely to choose to wear a red shirt, as opposed to a comparable blue or green shirt, when they expected to meet an attractive man relative to an unattractive man or a woman (Elliot et al., 2013). The receptivity signaled by the color red is what men find attractive—increasing the odds that they will respond to a personal ad, pick up a female hitchhiker, and leave a larger tip. This same receptivity, however, is what led female participants in recent studies to malign women clad in red versus other colors by rating her as more promiscuous and more likely to cheat on a relationship (see Pazda et al., 2014).

Why Are We Blinded by Beauty?   Regardless of how beauty is defined, it's clear that people seen as physically attractive are at a social advantage. Perhaps that's why billions of dollars a year are spent on diets, fitness activities, shaving, waxing, hair coloring, makeup, perfumes, tattoos, body piercings, and cosmetic surgery designed to plump up sunken skin, peel and scrape wrinkles from the face, vacuum out fat deposits, lift faces, reshape noses, tuck in tummies, and enlarge or reduce breasts.

What creates the bias for beauty, and why are we drawn like magnets to people who are physically attractive? One possibility is that it is inherently rewarding to be in the company of people who are aesthetically appealing—that we derive pleasure from beautiful men and women the same way that we enjoy a breathtaking landscape or a magnificent work of art. In an fMRI study of men, for example, researchers found that areas of the brain known to respond to rewards such as food, money, and drugs such as cocaine are also activated by facial beauty (Aharon et al., 2001). Or perhaps the rewards are more extrinsic. Perhaps, for example, we expect the glitter of another's beauty to rub off on us. When average-looking men and women are seen alongside someone else of the same sex, they are rated as more attractive when the other person is good-looking and as less attractive when he or she is plain-looking (Geiselman et al., 1984).

A second reason for the bias toward beauty is that people tend to associate physical attractiveness with other desirable qualities, an assumption known as the **what-is-beautiful-is-good stereotype** (Dion et al., 1972). Think about children's fairy tales, where Snow White and Cinderella are portrayed as beautiful *and* kind, while the witch and stepsisters are said to be both ugly *and* cruel. This link between beauty and goodness can be seen in Hollywood movies. Stephen Smith and others (1999) asked people to watch and rate the main characters who appeared in the 100 top-grossing movies between 1940 and 1990. They found that the more attractive the characters were, the more frequently they were portrayed as virtuous, romantically active, and successful. This link can also be seen in Disney movies geared to children. Doris Bazzini and others (2010) asked people to rate human characters in 21 Disney films and found a significant link between perceptions of attractiveness and goodness. It appears that the entertainment industry unwittingly helps to perpetuate our tendency to judge people by their physical appearance.

The stereotyped link between beauty and goodness can also be seen in the human brain. In an experiment using fMRI, Takashi Tsukiura and Roberto Capeza (2011) scanned the brains of participants while they evaluated faces for physical attractiveness and actions for goodness. Both types of judgments increased activity in one region of the brain and decreased activity in another. Within each of these regions, the activations sparked by the two types of judgments were similar.

Studies have shown that good-looking people are judged to be smart, successful, happy, well-adjusted, sociable, confident, and assertive—but also vain (Eagly et al., 1991). Is this physical attractiveness stereotype accurate? Only to a limited extent. Research shows that good-looking people do have more friends, better social skills, and a more active sex life—and they are more successful at attracting a mate (Rhodes et al., 2005). But beauty is *not* related to objective measures of important traits such as intelligence, personality, adjustment, or self-esteem. In these domains, popular perception appears to exaggerate the reality (Feingold, 1992b). It also seems that the specific nature of the stereotype depends on cultural conceptions of what is "good." When Ladd Wheeler and Youngmee Kim (1997) asked people in Korea to rate photos of various men and women, they found that people seen as physically attractive were also assumed to have "integrity" and "a concern for others"—traits that are highly valued in this collectivist culture. In contrast to what is considered desirable in more individualistic cultures, attractive people in Korea were not assumed to be dominant or assertive. What is beautiful is good, but what is good is (in part) culturally defined.

The Art archives/Alamy

This painting depicts a Greek myth in which Pygmalion, the king of Cyprus, sculpted his ideal woman in an ivory statue he called Galatea, illustrating the power of a self-fulfilling prophecy. Pygmalion fell in love with his creation, caressed it, adorned it with jewelry, and eventually brought it to life.

what-is-beautiful-is-good stereotype The belief that physically attractive individuals also possess desirable personality characteristics.

If the physical attractiveness stereotype is true only in part, why does it endure? One possibility is that each of us creates support for the bias via the type of *self-fulfilling prophecy* model described in Chapter 4. In a classic study of interpersonal attraction, Mark Snyder and others (1977) brought together unacquainted pairs of male and female college students. All the students were given biographical sketches of their partners. Each man also received a photograph of a physically attractive or unattractive woman, supposedly his partner. At that point, the students rated each other on several dimensions and had a phone-like conversation over headphones, conversations that were taped and later heard by uninvolved participants. The results were provocative. Men who thought they were interacting with a woman who was attractive (1) formed more positive impressions of her personality and (2) were friendlier in their conversational behavior. And now for the clincher: (3) the female students whose partners had seen the attractive picture were later rated by listeners to the conversation as warmer, more confident, and more animated. Fulfilling the prophecies of their own expectations, men who expected an attractive partner actually created one. These findings call to mind the Greek myth of Pygmalion, who fell in love with a statue he had carved and thus brought it to life.

The Benefits and Costs of Beauty There's no doubt about it, good-looking people have a significant edge. As a result, they are more popular, more socially skilled, more sexually experienced, and more likely to attract a mate. In light of these advantages, it's remarkable that physical attractiveness is not a sure ticket to health, happiness, or high self-esteem (Diener et al., 1995; Feingold, 1992b; Langlois et al., 2000). The life of Marilyn Monroe is a case in point. A celebrity of the 1950s and 1960s, Monroe was considered the most ravishing woman of her time and one of the hottest actresses in Hollywood. Yet she was terribly vulnerable and insecure. Why?

One possible problem is that highly attractive people can't always tell if the attention and praise they receive from others is due to their talent or just their good looks. A study by Brenda Major and others (1984) illustrates the point. Male and female participants who saw themselves as attractive or unattractive wrote essays that were later positively evaluated by an unknown member of the opposite sex. Half the participants were told that their evaluator would be watching them through a one-way mirror as they wrote the essay; the other half were led to believe that they could not be seen. In actuality, there was no evaluator, and all participants received identical, very positive evaluations of their work. Participants were then asked why their essay was so favorably reviewed. The result: Those who saw themselves as unattractive felt better about the quality of their work after getting a glowing evaluation from someone who had seen them. Yet those who saw themselves as attractive and thought they had been seen attributed the glowing feedback to their looks, not to the quality of their work. For people who are highly attractive, positive feedback is sometimes hard to interpret (see ● Figure 9.6).

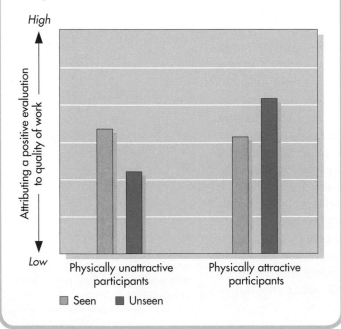

● **FIGURE 9.6**

When Being Seen Leads to Disbelief

People who believed they were physically unattractive were more likely to cite the quality of their work as the reason for receiving a positive evaluation when they thought they were seen by the evaluator. However, people who believed they were attractive were less likely to credit the quality of their work when they thought they were seen.

From Major, B., and Konar, E., "An investigation of sex differences in pay expectations and their possible causes," *Academy of Management Journal* vol 27 (pp. 777–791). Copyright © 1984 by Academy of Management.

This distrust may be well founded. In one study, many men and women openly admitted that if a prospective date was highly attractive, they would lie to present themselves well (Rowatt et al., 1999).

Another burden of physical attractiveness as a social asset is the pressure to maintain one's appearance. In today's American society, such pressure is particularly strong when it comes to the body. This focus on the human form can produce a healthy emphasis on nutrition and exercise. But it can also have unhealthy effects, as when men pop steroids to build muscle and women over-diet to lose weight. Among young women in particular, an obsession with thinness can give rise to serious eating disorders such as *bulimia nervosa* (food binges followed by purging) and *anorexia nervosa* (self-imposed starvation, which can prove fatal). Although estimates vary, studies have indicated that less than 1% of women suffer from anorexia, that 2% to 3% have bulimia, and that these rates are higher among female college students than nonstudents (Fairburn & Brownell, 2002; Smolak & Thompson, 2009).

Women are more likely than men to experience what Janet Polivy and others (1986) once called the "modern mania for slenderness." This ideal is projected in the mass media. Studies have shown that young women who see magazine ads or TV commercials that feature ultra-thin models become more dissatisfied with their own bodies than those who view neutral materials (Posavac et al., 1998). Trying to measure up to the multimillion-dollar supermodels can prove frustrating. What's worse, the cultural ideal for thinness may get set in childhood. Several years ago, Kevin Norton and others (1996) projected the life-size dimensions of the original Ken and Barbie dolls that are popular all over the world. They found that both were unnaturally thin compared with the average young adult. In fact, the estimated odds that any young woman would have Barbie's original shape are approximately 1 in 100,000.

In sum, being beautiful may be a mixed blessing. There are some real benefits that cannot be denied, but there may be some costs as well. This trade-off makes you wonder about the long-term effects. Some years ago, Ellen Berscheid and others (1972) compared the physical attractiveness levels of college students (based on yearbook pictures) to their adjustment when they reached middle age. There was little relationship between their appearance in youth and their later happiness. Those who were especially good-looking in college were more likely to be married, but they were not more satisfied with marriage or more content with life. Beauty may confer advantage, but it is not destiny.

> People who are physically attractive are happier and have higher self-esteem than those who are unattractive.
>
> **FALSE**

■ First Encounters: Getting Acquainted

Speed dating is a fascinating platform for men and women who are looking for a romantic relationship. In speed-dating events, individuals pay to have between 10 and 25 very brief "dates" lasting no more than four minutes. After rotating like clockwork from one partner to another, participants—who wear nametags—let the event hosts know which partners, if any, they'd be interested in seeing again. If two participants double-match, the host provides each with the other's contact information so they can schedule a real date (Finkel & Eastwick, 2008).

For a first encounter, does speed dating provide people with enough information? Is four minutes enough time for you to determine if you are romantically attracted to someone? To be sure, you get an up-close-and-personal look at a person's physical appearance. But then what other information would you want? Proximity boosts the odds that we will meet someone, familiarity puts us at ease, and beauty draws us in like magnets to a first encounter. But what determines whether sparks will fly in the early getting-acquainted stages of a relationship? In this section, we consider three characteristics of others who can influence our attraction: similarity, reciprocity, and being hard to get.

Liking Others Who Are Similar   The problem with proverbial wisdom is that it often contradicts itself. Common sense tells us that "birds of a feather flock together." Yet we also hear that "opposites attract." So which is it? Before answering this question, imagine meeting someone in person, or through a mobile dating app, and striking up a conversation about school, sports, restaurants, movies, where you live, where you've traveled, or your favorite band—and you realize that the two of you have a lot in common. Now imagine the opposite experience of chatting with someone new who is very different in his or her background, interests, values, and outlook on life. Which of the two strangers would you want to meet, the one who is similar or the one who is different?

Over the years, research has consistently shown that people tend to associate with others who are similar to themselves (Montoya et al., 2008; Montoya & Horton, 2013). Of course, in a very brief first-time meeting, which happens in speed dating, where participants get a sum total of four minutes to interact (not enough time to get to know each other), it's the mere *perception* of similarity that draws people together (Tidwell et al., 2013). The vast array of online dating sites illustrates the presumed importance of similarity. In addition to the generic services for all people of all ages, demographic groups, and sexual orientations, a number of specialty services are specifically designed to bring together people of like backgrounds and minds—hence, ConservativeMatch.com, LiberalHearts.com, JDate.com, ChristianCafe.com, Muslima.com, and HappyBuddhist.com.

Four types of similarity are most relevant. The first is demographic. On a whole range of demographic variables—such as age, education, race, religion, height, level of intelligence, and socioeconomic status—people who go together as friends, dates, lovers, or partners in marriage tend to resemble each other more than randomly paired couples (Warren, 1966). These correlations cannot be used to prove that similarity causes attraction. A more compelling case could be made, however, by first measuring people's demographic characteristics and then determining whether these people, when they met others, liked those who were similar to them more than those who were dissimilar. This is what Theodore Newcomb did more than 50 years ago. In an elaborate study, Newcomb (1961) set up an experimental college dormitory and found that students who had similar backgrounds grew to like each other more than those who were dissimilar did.

Speed dating is a recent phenomenon that can be found all over the world. In London, pictured here, men and women gather for quick pairings in a round-robin series of "dates."

Caroline Cortizo/Alamy

Is demographic similarity still a factor even today, with all the choices we have in our diverse and multicultural society? Yes. Commenting on the persistently magnetic appeal of similarity, sociologist John Macionis (2014) notes that "Cupid's arrow is aimed by society more than we like to think." One unfortunate result, as described in Chapter 5, is that by associating with similar others, people form social niches that are homogeneous and divided along the lines of race, ethnic background, age, religion, level of education, and occupation (McPherson et al., 2001).

People can also be similar in other ways, as when they share the same opinions, interests, and values. For example, what about *attitude* similarity and attraction? Here, the time course is slower because people have to get to know each other first. In Newcomb's study, the link between actual similarity and liking increased gradually over the school year. Laboratory experiments have confirmed the point. For example, Donn Byrne (1971) had people give their opinions on a whole range of issues and then presented them with an attitude survey that had supposedly been filled out by another person (the responses were rigged). In study after study, he found that participants liked this other person better when they perceived his or her attitudes as being more similar to theirs (Byrne, 1997).

The link between attitudes and attraction is evident among newly married couples. In a comprehensive study, Shanhong Luo and Eva Klohnen (2005) tested 291 newlywed couples and found that people tended to marry others who shared their political attitudes, religiosity, and values but who did not necessarily start out having similar personalities. Yet once in the relationship, similarities in personality became relevant: The more similar they were, the happier was the marriage. Clearly, birds of a feather both flock together and stay together. But wait. Does this necessarily mean that similarity breeds attraction, or might attraction breed similarity? In all likelihood, both mechanisms are at work. Luo and Klohnen compared couples who had been together for varying lengths of time before marriage and found that similarity was unrelated to the length of the relationship. Yet another study of dating couples showed that when partners who are close discover that they disagree on important moral issues, they bring their views on these issues into alignment and become more similar from that point on (Davis & Rusbult, 2001).

According to Milton Rosenbaum (1986), attraction researchers have overplayed the role of attitudinal similarity. Similarity does not spark attraction, he said. Rather, dissimilarity triggers repulsion: the desire to avoid someone. Rosenbaum argued that people expect most others to be similar, which is why others who are different grab our attention. Taking this hypothesis one step further, Lykken and Tellegen (1993) argued that in mate selection, *all* forms of interpersonal similarity are irrelevant. After a person discards the 50% of the population who are least similar, they claim, a random selection process takes over.

So which is it: Are we turned on by others who are similar in their attitudes, or are we turned off by those who are different? As depicted in ● Figure 9.7, Byrne and his colleagues proposed a two-step model that takes both reactions

William Haefeli/Conde Nast Collection

"I'd like to meet the algorithm that thought we'd be a good match."

into account. First, they said, we avoid associating with others who are dissimilar; then, among those who remain, we are drawn to those who are most similar (Byrne et al., 1986; Smeaton et al., 1989). Our reactions may also be influenced by expectations. People expect similarity from ingroup members, like fellow Democrats or Republicans or fellow straights or gays. In a several studies, Fang Chen and Douglas Kenrick (2002) found that research participants were particularly attracted to outgroup members who expressed similar attitudes, and they were most repulsed by ingroup members who expressed dissimilar attitudes.

In addition to demographics and attitudes, a third source of similarity and difference is also at work, at least in romantic relationships. Have you ever noticed

● FIGURE 9.7

A Two-Stage Model of the Attraction Process

Proposed by Byrne and his colleagues (1986), the two-stage model of attraction holds that first we avoid dissimilar others, and then we approach similar others.

Byrne, D., Clore, G. L., & Smeaton, G. (1986). The attraction hypothesis: Do similar attitudes affect anything? *Journal of Personality and Social Psychology* 51, 1167–1170.

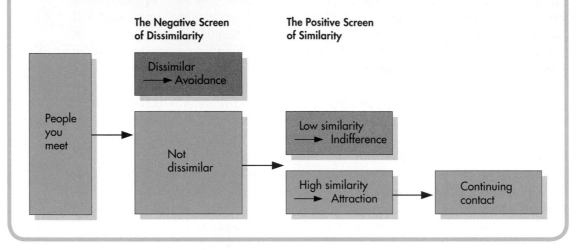

the way people react to couples in which one partner is a knockout and the other is not? Typically, we are startled by "mismatches" of this sort, as if expecting people to pair off with others who are similarly attractive—not more, not less. This reaction has a basis in reality. Early on, laboratory studies showed that both men and women yearn for partners who are highly attractive. Thus, when incoming first-year students at the University of Minnesota were randomly coupled for a dance, their desire for a second date was influenced more by their partner's physical attractiveness than by any other variable (Walster et al., 1966). In real-life situations, however, where one can be accepted or rejected by a prospective partner, people tend to shy away from making romantic overtures with others who seem "out of reach" (Berscheid et al., 1971; van Straaten et al., 2009).

Correlational studies of couples who are dating, living together, or married support this "**matching hypothesis**" the idea that people tend to become involved romantically with others who are equivalent in their physical attractiveness (Feingold, 1988). Activity in a successful online dating site provides interesting new support. Based on activity logs, "popularity" was calculated for each user on the site. Sure enough, analysis of their interactions indicated popularity-based matching: Men and women tended to contact and be contacted by others whose relative popularity on the site was similar to their own (Taylor et al., 2011).

A fourth type of similarity can trigger attraction among strangers: a similarity in subjective experience. Imagine that a professor says something in class that strikes you as funny. You glance at the student next to you, who glances back and the two of you burst out laughing, as if bonded by a private joke. Whenever two people who are at a common event laugh, cry, jump to their feet, cheer, shake their heads, slap high-fives, or roll their eyes at the same time, they feel as if they have shared a subjective experience. Elizabeth Pinel and others (Pinel et al., 2006; Pinel & Long 2012) called this experience "I-sharing" and theorized that people who I-share, even if they are otherwise dissimilar, feel a profound sense of connection to one another—like "kindred spirits." In a series of experiments,

matching hypothesis The proposition that people are attracted to others who are similar in physical attractiveness.

participants were asked to imagine being with a similar or dissimilar stranger with whom they did or did not react in the same way to an external event. Consistently, the participants liked the I-sharers more than everyone else, even when they had different backgrounds. The implications are intriguing: "A fundamentalist Christian and an atheist can find themselves enjoying the same sunset; a staunch Republican and an equally staunch Democrat can share a laugh. When two objectively different people I-share in these and other ways, their disliking for one another might lessen, if only for a moment" (Pinel et al., 2006, p. 245).

Before concluding that similarity is the key to attraction, what about the old adage that opposites attract? Many years ago, sociologists proposed the *complementarity hypothesis*, which holds that people seek others whose needs "oppose" their own—that people who need to dominate, for example, are naturally drawn to those who are submissive (Winch et al., 1954). Is there any support for this view? Surprisingly, the answer is no. Of course, most human beings are romantically attracted to others of the opposite sex. But when it comes to fitting mutual needs and personality traits the way keys fit locks, research shows that complementarity does not make for compatible attraction (Gonzaga et al., 2007; Luo & Klohnen, 2005; O'Leary & Smith, 1991). In an interview with the *Washington Post*, Gian Gonzaga—a researcher for eHarmony, the online dating service that matches people according to similarities—debunked the complementarity hypothesis, noting that while opposites may seem exotic at first glance, over time the differences become difficult to negotiate (McCarthy, 2009).

Isabelle Selby

Brian was from Dallas; Kate was from Seattle. Both went to New York for school and then met on *Match.com*. After some exchanges, they met for a first date on the Staten Island Ferry, in the shadow of the Statue of Liberty. Now they are married and have a young son. According to Match.com (2015), the site has thus far helped to create 517,000 relationships and 92,000 marriages.

Liking Others Who Like Us   Many years ago, Fritz Heider (1958) theorized that people prefer relationships that are psychologically "balanced" and that a state of imbalance causes distress. In groups of three or more individuals, a balanced social constellation exists when we like someone whose relationships with others parallel our own. Thus, we want to like the friends of our friends and the enemies of our enemies (Aronson & Cope, 1968). If you've ever had a good friend who dated someone you detested, then you know how awkward and unpleasant an unbalanced relationship can be. The fact is, we don't expect our friends and enemies to get along (Chapdelaine et al., 1994).

Between two people, a state of balance exists when a relationship is characterized by **reciprocity**: a mutual exchange between what we give and what we receive. Liking is mutual, which is why we tend to like others who indicate that they like us. In one experiment, Rebecca Curtis and Kim Miller (1986) brought pairs of students into the laboratory, arranged for them to talk, and then "revealed" to one member in each pair that he or she was liked by the partner or disliked. When the students were later reunited for conversation, those who thought that they were liked were, in turn, warmer, more agreeable, and more self-disclosing. Feeling liked is important. When groups of men and women were asked to reflect on how they fell in love or developed friendships with specific people, many spontaneously said they had been turned on initially by the realization that they were liked (Aron et al., 1989).

But does reciprocity mean simply that the more people like us, the more we will like them back? In a classic experiment, Elliot Aronson and Darwyn Linder (1965)

When it comes to romantic relationships, opposites attract.

FALSE

reciprocity   A mutual exchange between what we give and receive— for example, liking those who like us.

had female college students meet in pairs several times. In each pair, one student was a research participant; her partner was a confederate. After each meeting, the participant overheard a follow-up conversation between the experimenter and the confederate in which she was discussed and evaluated. Over time, the confederate's evaluation of the participant either was consistent or underwent a change—from negative to positive (gain) or from positive to negative (loss). Put yourself in the participant's shoes. All else being equal, in which condition would you like your partner most? In this study, participants liked the partner more when her evaluation changed from negative to positive than when it was positive all along. As long as the "conversion" is gradual and believable, people like others more when their affection takes time to earn than when it comes easily. Within a heterosexual speed-dating situation, Paul Eastwick and others (2007) confirmed the conversion point: People are drawn to members of the opposite sex who like them—but only when these others are selective in their liking and, hence, discriminating.

Pursuing Those Who Are Hard to Get The Aronson and Linder (1965) finding suggests that we like others who are socially selective. This seems to support the popular notion that you can spark romantic interest by playing hard to get. Several years ago, Ellen Fein and Sherri Schneider (1996) wrote a book for women titled *The Rules: Time-Tested Secrets for Capturing the Heart of Mr. Right.* What were the rules? Here's one: "Don't call him and rarely return his calls." Here's another: "Let him take the lead." In all cases, the theme was that men are charmed by women who are hard to get. It's an interesting hypothesis.

Despite intuition, researchers found that the **hard-to-get effect** is harder to get than originally anticipated (Walster et al., 1973). One problem is that we are turned *off* by those who reject us because they are committed to someone else or have no interest in us (Wright & Contrada, 1986). Another problem is that we tend to prefer people who are moderately selective compared with those who are nonselective (they have poor taste or low standards) or too selective (they are snobs). In a study that well illustrates the point, researchers arranged for male and female college students to have four-minute speed dates with 10 or so other students of the opposite sex, after which they all rated each other and indicated on a website if they were interested in meeting again. Analyses of the ratings showed that participants liked dates who selectively desired them more than others, but they did not like nondiscriminating dates who had indicated a desire for several of the men they encountered (Eastwick & Finkel, 2008).

Individuals differ a great deal in terms of how selective they are in the search for a romantic partner. In a research article titled "Settling for Less Out of Fear of Being Single," Stephanie Spielmann and others (2013) theorized that people who fear being single—both because they desire an intimate connection and because of the social stigma attached to being alone in a largely coupled world (DePaulo & Morris, 2005; Greitemeyer, 2009; Sharp & Ganong, 2011)—set lower standards, are less selective, and tolerate lesser relationships. To test this hypothesis, they created a questionnaire called the Fear of Being Single Scale in which respondents are asked to rate their level agreement with statements such as "It scares me to think that there might not be someone out there for me" and "As I get older, it will get harder and harder to find someone."

In one study, Spielmann and colleagues administered this new test to 214 single, straight men and women and then asked these participants to rate their romantic interest in ostensibly real profiles from an Internet dating site. The profiles contained a photo that depicted an opposite-sex person who was high or low in facial attractiveness and a personal statement that conveyed an attitude that was

hard-to-get effect The tendency to prefer people who are highly selective in their social choices over those who are more readily available.

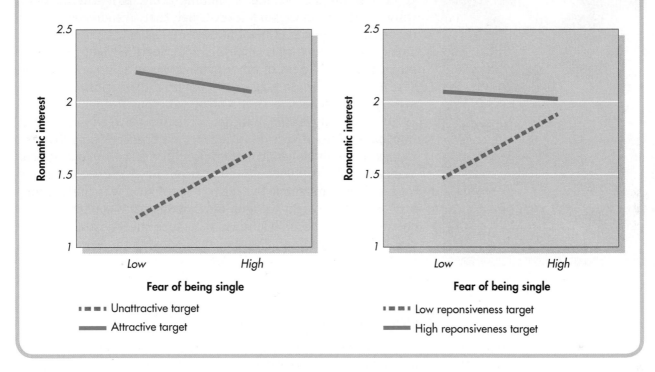

● FIGURE 9.8

Settling for Less For Fear of Being Single?

In this study, 214 single and straight men and women completed the Fear of Being Single Scale and then rated their romantic interest in bogus profiles from an online dating site. The profiles depicted someone who was more or less attractive and more or less responsive. As you can see, everyone preferred the more desirable profiles. But participants who feared being single also expressed an interest in profiles that were not attractive or responsive (Spielmann et al., 2013).

highly responsive ("When I'm dating someone, I really care about putting in the effort . . . that means paying attention to my girlfriend [boyfriend] and getting to know who she really is as a person") or not responsive ("I love what I do, so I need someone who respects that and is willing to take a back seat when necessary . . . I'd like to keep conversations light and not too serious"). Look at ● Figure 9.8 and you'll see that while everyone expressed romantic interest in highly attractive and responsive profiles, participants with high scores on the Fear of Being Single Scale *also* expressed an interest in profiles that were not attractive or responsive. These results confirm the hypothesis that the fear of being single leads people to settle for less desirable partners. Indicating this lack of discrimination in a high stakes setting, a follow-up study of men and women registered for a speed-dating event showed that those with a high fear of being single stated a desire to date more of the participants they had only briefly met.

Finally, on the question of how we respond to people who are hard to get, suppose that someone you are interested in is hard to get for reasons beyond their control. What if a desired relationship is opposed or forbidden by parents, as in the story of Romeo and Juliet? What about a relationship threatened by catastrophe, as in the love story portrayed in the 1997 hit movie *Titanic*, involving Leonardo DiCaprio and Kate Winslet—or a relationship threatened by parents over differences in religion, or social class, as in the 2004 movie *The Notebook*, starring Ryan Gosling and Rachel McAdams? What about distance, a lack of time,

Imageshop/Getty Images

Consistent with reactance theory, studies conducted in bars like this have shown that men and women who are not in committed relationships see each other as more attractive as the night wears on.

or renewed interest from a partner's old flame? Chapter 6 describes the theory of psychological reactance, the proposition that people are highly motivated to protect their freedom to choose and behave as they please. When a valued freedom is threatened (not getting the object of one's affection), people reassert themselves, often by wanting that which is unavailable too much—like the proverbial forbidden fruit (Brehm & Brehm, 1981).

Consider what happens when you think that your chance to get a date for the evening is slipping away. Is it true, to quote country-western musician Mickey Gilley, that "the girls all get prettier at closing time"? To find out, researchers entered some bars in Texas and asked patrons three times during the night to rate the physical attractiveness of other patrons of the same and opposite sex. As Gilley's lyrics suggested, people of the opposite sex were seen as more attractive as the night wore on (Pennebaker et al., 1979). The study is cute, but the correlation between time and attraction can be interpreted in other ways (perhaps attractiveness ratings rise with blood-alcohol levels!). In a follow-up study, Scott Madey and others (1996) also had patrons in a bar make attractiveness ratings throughout the night. They found that these ratings increased as the night wore on only among patrons who were not committed to a relationship. As reactance theory would predict, closing time posed a threat—which sparked desire—only to those on the lookout for a late-night date.

■ Mate Selection: The Evolution of Desire

Before moving on to the topic of close relationships, let's stop and consider this question: When it comes to the search for a short-term or long-term mate, are men and women similarly motivated? If not, what are the differences? Later in this chapter, we'll see that most men appear to be more sex-driven than most women, wanting more frequent and more casual sex, more partners, and more variety, all of which leads some researchers in the area to conclude that "men desire sex more than women" (Baumeister et al., 2001, p. 270).

Mate Selection Preferences Why do these sex differences exist, and what do they mean? In *The Evolution of Desire,* David Buss (2003) argues that the answer can be derived from evolutionary psychology. According to this perspective, human beings all over the world exhibit mate-selection patterns that favor the conception, birth, and survival of their offspring—and women and men, by necessity, employ different strategies to achieve that common goal (Buss & Schmitt, 1993; Gangestad & Simpson, 2000; Trivers, 1972).

According to Buss, women must be highly selective because they are biologically limited in the number of children they can bear and raise in a lifetime. A woman must, therefore, protect her children and so searches for a mate who possesses (or has the potential to possess) economic resources and is willing to commit those resources to support her offspring. The result is that women should be attracted to men who are older and financially secure or who have ambition, intelligence, stability, and other traits predictive of future success.

In contrast, men can father an unlimited number of children and can ensure their reproductive success by inseminating many women. Men are restricted, however, by their ability to attract fertile partners and by their lack of certainty as to whether the babies born are actually their own. With these motives springing from evolution, men seek out women who are young and physically attractive (having smooth skin, full lips, lustrous hair, good muscle tone, and other youthful features)—attributes that signal health and reproductive fertility. To minimize their paternal uncertainty, men should also favor chastity, pursuing women they think will be sexually faithful rather than promiscuous.

In an initial test of this theory, Buss (1989) and a team of researchers surveyed 10,047 men and women in 37 cultures in North and South America, Asia, Africa, Eastern and Western Europe, and the Pacific. All respondents were asked to rank-order and rate the importance of various attributes in choosing a mate. The results were consistent with predictions. Both men and women gave equally high ratings to certain attributes, such as "having a pleasant disposition." In the vast majority of countries, however, "good looks" and "no previous experience in sexual intercourse" were valued more by men, whereas "good financial prospect" and "ambitious and industrious" were more important to women.

Other studies have added support for the evolutionary approach. Analyses of personal ads appearing in magazines and newspapers revealed that in the dating marketplace the "deal" is that women offer beauty, while men offer wealth (Feingold, 1992a; Sprecher et al., 1994). As Buss had suggested, this "deal" is not limited to men and women of the United States. In a field experiment using an online dating site in China, researchers randomly assigned income levels to the front pages of 360 contrived profiles and then recorded "visits" to the full profiles. Records showed that although men uniformly visited profiles across all levels of income, women visited male profiles with higher income levels at higher rates. This "income attraction" effect was so large that male profiles with the highest income level received 10 times more visits than the lowest (Ong & Wang, 2015).

Joel Sartore/National Geographic Creative

This young man spies through his sunglasses at women on the beach. From an evolutionary perspective, his attraction is biologically (though not consciously) driven by the search for a fertile reproductive partner.

Some researchers have suggested that these gendered preferences are not mere luxuries but are actually necessities in the mating marketplace. In Buss's (1989) study, men were more likely to prefer good looks, and women were more likely to prefer good financial prospects, but both sexes saw other characteristics—such as being funny, dependable, and kind—as more important. But what happens in real life, where mate seekers who can't have it all must prioritize their desires? Studying "the necessities and luxuries in mate preferences," Norman Li and others (2002) asked participants to design an ideal marriage partner by purchasing different characteristics using "mate dollars." In some cases, they were granted a large budget to work with; in other cases, the budget was limited. In the large-budget condition, men spent somewhat more play money on physical attractiveness, and women spent somewhat more on social status, but both were just as interested in a partner who was kind, lively, and creative. In the low-budget condition, however, men spent even more of their play money on physical attractiveness, and women spent even more on social status. When mate seekers can't have it all and must therefore focus on what's most important, they prioritize their choices in the ways predicted by evolutionary theory.

Also consistent with the evolutionary perspective is a universal tendency for men to seek younger women (who are most likely to be fertile) and for women to desire older men (who are most likely to have financial resources). Buss (1989) found this age-preference discrepancy in all cultures he studied, with men on average wanting to marry women who were 2.7 years younger and women wanting

"Men seek to propagate widely, whereas women seek to propagate wisely."

—Robert Hinde

men who were 3.4 years older. Based on their analysis of personal ads, Douglas Kenrick and Richard Keefe (1992) found that men in their twenties are equally interested in younger women and slightly older women still of fertile age. But men in their thirties seek out women who are 5 years younger, whereas men in their fifties prefer women 10 to 20 years younger. In contrast, girls and women of all ages are attracted to men who are older than they are. These patterns can also be seen in marriage statistics taken from different cultures and generations. There is one interesting exception: Teenage boys say they are most attracted to women who are slightly *older* than they are, women in their fertile twenties (Kenrick et al., 1996).

One might think that the mate preferences predicted by evolutionary theory would be limited to fertile men and women of youth. Not so. Recently, 600 Yahoo! personal ads were analyzed from four age groups: 20–34, 40–54, 60–74, and 75+ years. At all ages, men were more likely than women to offer information about their educational, employment, and income status. They were also more likely to seek indications of physical attractiveness. The older they were, the more the men wanted increasingly younger women. In contrast, women of all ages were more likely to seek out status information and men who were older (at least until the women were 75, at which point they sought men younger than themselves). Apparently, in the United States, the mate preferences predicted by evolutionary theory persist throughout the life span (Alterovitz & Mendelsohn, 2009). In the words of one investigator, it appears that the search for a heterosexual mate features "men as success objects and women as sex objects" (Davis, 1990).

Conspicuous Consumption If women are drawn to men who have wealth or the ability to obtain it, then it stands to reason that men would flaunt their resources the way the male peacock displays his brilliantly colored tail. Showy displays of wealth are seen in cultures all over the world—from Iceland to Japan, Polynesia, and the Amazon jungle—leading evolutionary psychologists to speculate that *conspicuous consumption* may have evolved as a sexually selected mating signal (Miller, 2009; Saad, 2007). To see if it works, Jill Sundie and colleagues (2011) briefly described to female participants a 32-year-old MBA graduate who made a good living as a financial analyst; who liked to bike, go to movies, and listen to music; and who just purchased a new car— either an expensive Porsche or a Honda Civic. Sure enough participants saw him as a more desirable date when he was said to have bought the flashier car.

If men flaunt their resources to attract women, then it stands to reason that the more competitive the reproductive landscape is for men, the more likely they are to spend money in conspicuous ways. Historically, the ratio of men to women in a population can vary over time and from one city to another. An abundance of women relative to men is associated with lower marriage rates and lower paternal investment; a relative abundance of men is associated with higher marriage rates and more paternal investment. To test "the financial consequences of too many men," Vladas Griskevicius and others (2012) presented male college students with one of two versions of a reputable local newspaper article concerning the ratio of men to women on their campus. One version indicated that the sex ratio was fast becoming female-biased (more women than men); a second version indicated that the sex ratio was male-biased (more men than women). Afterward, all participants were asked to rate how much money in dollars was appropriate to spend on a Valentine's Day gift, a dinner date, and an engagement ring. Across the board, the results strongly

Evolutionary psychologists predict that if women are drawn to men with resources, then men should flaunt their wealth through conspicuous consumption, a sexually selected mating signal. This iconic eggshell-blue gift box from Tiffany & Company, adorned with a strand of pearls, is an iconic Western image of conspicuous consumption.

supported the prediction that the perception of competition among men would lead them to spend more money on mating-related expenditures.

Expressions of Love   Chances are, common sense arms you to predict the male–female differences found in research on the evolution of desire. But what about romantic expressions of love and affection? Male and female stereotypes would suggest that whereas men are more likely to chase sex, women seek love. It comes as no surprise, therefore, that when Valentine's Day cards were analyzed for content, female authors were more likely than men to express love (Gonzalez & Koestner, 2006).

Saying "I love you" is a bold step for people seeking a mate because the words signal a marked shift in satisfaction and has implications for devotion, sacrifice, and commitment. Who normally professes their love first in a heterosexual relationship—the man or the woman? Have you ever been in love? If so, who broke the ice in *your* relationship? Interested in gender and expressions of love, Joshua Ackerman and his colleagues (2011) stopped pedestrians on a street corner and asked them to indicate which partner in general says it first. The result was consistent with expectations: 64% chose women. When asked who "gets serious" first, 84% chose women. Next, however, these researchers asked male and female college students who once had a past romantic relationship to recall who actually said "I love you" first. The result: 62% reported that the man said it first. In a third study, heterosexual couples from an online community sample were asked to report on their own relationship. Not all partners agreed on the answer—which is interesting. Among those who did agree, however, 70% reported that the man said it first (see ● Figure 9.9).

Does an evolutionary perspective shed light on why men would say "I love you" before women do? Do men and women react similarly to this heartfelt

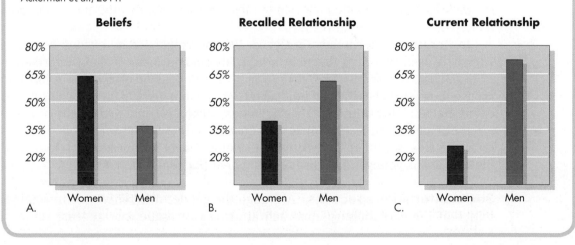

● **FIGURE 9.9**

Who's the First to Say "I Love You"?

In one study, people were asked for their beliefs about which partner in a heterosexual relationship—the man or the woman—is more likely to say "I love you" first. In a second study, men and women who had a past romantic relationship were asked to recall who said "I love you" first. In a third study, both partners in heterosexual couples were asked to report on their own relationship. Contrary to our stereotypic belief (left), it appears that men are more likely to confess their love first (center and right).
Ackerman et al., 2011.

expression? Ackerman et al. (2011) predicted that timing matters—specifically, in relation to the onset of sexual activity. In an online study, they recruited male and female Craigslist posters who had received an "I love you" for the first and asked a number of questions about the experience—including whether the expression of love had come before or after sexual intercourse and how happy they were by the disclosure. Prior to sexual activity, men reported feeling happier and more positive about the expression of love than women did. After sexual activity, however, women reacted with somewhat more positive emotion. What does it all mean? As interpreted through the lens of an evolutionary perspective: "A presex confession may signal interest in advancing a relationship to include sexual activity, whereas a postsex confession may instead more accurately signal a desire for long-term commitment" (p. 1090).

Jealousy Particularly supportive of evolutionary theory is research on *jealousy*, "the dangerous passion"—a negative emotional state that arises from a perceived threat to one's relationship. Although jealousy is a common and normal human reaction, men and women may be aroused by different triggering events. According to the theory, a man should be most upset by *sexual* infidelity because a wife's extramarital affair increases the risk that the children he supports are not his own. In contrast, a woman should feel threatened more by *emotional* infidelity because a husband who falls in love with another woman might leave and withdraw his financial support (Buss, 2000). Male or female, jealousy reactions are intensified among people who believe that there is a scarcity of potential mates, as opposed to an abundance, in the population (Arnocky et al., 2014).

A number of studies support the hypothesis with regard to gender differences. In one, male and female college students were asked whether they would be more upset if their romantic partner were to form a deep emotional attachment or have sex with another person. Which situation would *you* find more distressing? The results revealed a striking gender difference: 60% of the men said they would be more upset by a partner's sexual infidelity, but 83% of the women felt that emotional infidelity was worse (Buss et al., 1992). This difference seems to reveal itself whenever men and women are asked which type of infidelity is more upsetting (Schützwohl, 2004; Shackelford et al., 2004). This gender difference also appeared when newly married husbands and wives were interviewed about how they would react if they suspected their partner of cheating. The men said they would use more "mate-retention" tactics (concealing or threatening the wife; taking action against the male rival) when their wives were young and attractive; women said they would use more mate-retention tactics (being watchful; enhancing their appearance) when married to men who strove for status and made more money (Buss & Shackelford, 1997).

In one study, researchers analyzed 398 individuals from various countries who had been clinically diagnosed with "morbid jealousy." Using information from published case histories, they found that whereas men were more likely to accuse their partners of sexual infidelity, women were more likely to be upset over emotional infidelity. Although only a few case histories contained details concerning the feared rival, jealous men were more likely to report that their rival had greater status and/or resources; jealous women were more likely to report that their rival was younger and/or more attractive (Easton et al., 2007).

Sociocultural Perspectives Although the gender differences are intriguing, critics of the evolutionary approach are quick to argue that at least some of the results can be interpreted in terms that are "psychological" rather than "evolutionary." One common argument is that women trade youth and beauty for money not for reproductive purposes but rather because they often lack *direct* access to economic power. With this hypothesis in mind, Steven Gangestad (1993) examined women's access to wealth in each of the countries in Buss's cross-cultural study. He found that the more economic power women had, the more important male physical attractiveness was to them. Similarly, Marcel Zentner and Klaudia Mitura (2012) looked at 37 countries that varied measurably in the extent to which men and women are equitable in their economic participation and opportunity, educational attainment, health and survival, and political empowerment. They found that greater gender parity was associated with less gender differentiation in mating preferences. Together, these results suggest that it may be the generally low status of women relative to men that leads them to care less about the physical attributes of a potential mate.

Another argument concerns the finding that men are more fearful of a mate's sexual infidelity (which threatens paternal certainty) and that women worry more about emotional infidelity (which threatens future support). The predicted difference is consistent, but what does it mean? There are two criticisms. First, in contrast to the explanation evolutionary theory provides, some researchers have found that men get more upset over sexual infidelity not because of uncertain paternity but because they reasonably assume that a married woman who has a sexual affair is also likely to have intimate feelings for her extramarital partner. In other words, the man's concern, like the woman's, may be over the threats of loss, not about fatherhood issues (DeSteno & Salovey 1996; Harris & Christenfeld, 1996). Second, although men and women react differently when asked to imagine a partner's sexual or emotional infidelity, they are equally more upset by emotional infidelity when asked to recall actual experiences from a past relationship (Harris, 2002). At present, researchers continue to debate what the observed gender differences in romantic jealousy mean and the evolutionary model that is used to explain them (Harris, 2005; Sagarin, 2005).

A third argument is that the self-report differences typically found between the sexes are small compared to the similarities. This is an important point. In Buss's original cross-cultural study, both men and women gave their highest ratings to such attributes as kindness, dependability, a good sense of humor, and a pleasant disposition (physical attractiveness and financial prospects did not top the lists). In fact, research shows that women desire physical attractiveness as much as men do when asked about what they want in a short-term casual sex partner (Li & Kenrick, 2006; Regan & Berscheid, 1997).

Also limiting is the question of whether the *stated* preferences reported in the Buss (1989) surveys match the *actual* preferences when people find themselves face to face with real flesh-and-blood partners. In a recent study, Paul Eastwick and Eli Finkel (2008) recruited men and women for a speed-dating event. Beforehand, they asked participants about their preferences for an ideal partner. Replicating the usual effect, men were more likely to cite "physically attractive," and women were more likely to cite "earning prospects." Yet the romantic attraction ratings of partners during and after speed dating revealed that the differences among male and female participants about what traits were important had disappeared. In theory, men and women enacted the different roles cast by evolution; yet in practice, their attraction to

A. Abbas/Magnum Photos

The Bari tribeswomen of Venezuela are sexually promiscuous. The Bari believe that a baby can have multiple fathers, so being promiscuous enables a woman to secure child support from many men. This exception to the evolutionary norm illustrates that human behavior is flexible and that people can develop mating strategies to suit their cultural environment.

each other was based on similar characteristics. These results can be seen in ● Figure 9.10.

Finally, some have argued that the sex differences often observed are neither predictable nor universal. Human societies are flexible in terms of the ways people adapt to their environments, and there are revealing exceptions to the rules that are thought to govern human play on the evolutionary field. For example, David Geary (2000) points out that while human fathers spend less time doing child care than mothers do, they are unique among mammals—including baboons and chimpanzees, our evolutionary cousins—in the amount of care they give to their offspring. Geary speculates that human men care for their children in part because they enjoy more paternal certainty than do other male primates.

Consider, too, the puzzling observation that women of the Bari tribe in Venezuela are highly promiscuous. From an evolutionary standpoint, this behavior does not seem adaptive since women who "sleep around" may scare off potential mates fearful of wasting resources on children who are not their own. So why is female promiscuity the norm in this culture? In *Cultures of Multiple Fathers,* anthropologists Stephen Beckerman, Paul Valentine, and others note that the Bari and other aboriginal people in lowland South America believe that a baby can have multiple fathers and that all men who have sex with a pregnant woman make a biological contribution to her yet-to-be-born child (some groups believe that more than one father, or at least more than one insemination, are *required* to form a fetus). Thus, by taking many lovers a woman increases the number of men who will provide for her child. It appears that this strategy works. A multifathered Bari child is 16% more likely than a single-fathered child to survive to the age of 15 (Beckerman & Valentine, 2002).

Summing Up The evolutionary perspective offers social psychologists an important and provocative perspective on relationships. The approach draws the criticism that the results are weak, limited, or explainable by nonevolutionary means (Eastwick et al., 2014; Harris, 2003; Hazan & Diamond, 2000; Pedersen et al., 2002). However, it also continues to generate new and interesting ideas. Currently, scientists in this area are studying a range of issues—such as the possible links between facial appearance and health and fertility (Weeden & Sabini, 2005); the flexibility or "plasticity" of sexual orientation in men and women (Lippa, 2006; Overbeek et al., 2013); the potentially deadly link between sexual jealousy and violence (Buss, 2000); the reason some men refuse to make child support payments (Shackelford et al., 2005); the use of oral sex as a mate retention tactic (Pham et al., 2015; Sela et al., 2015); women's ability to detect and prefer men who are intelligent (Prokosch et al., 2009); and the conditions under which men and women misperceive each other's sexual interest (Perilloux et al., 2012).

Close Relationships

Being attracted to people can be exhilarating or frustrating, depending on how the initial encounters develop. How important is a good relationship to you? Several years ago, researchers asked 300 students to weigh the importance of having a satisfying romantic relationship against the importance of other life goals (such as getting a good education, having a successful career, or contributing to a better society) and found that 73% said they would sacrifice most other goals before giving up a good relationship (Hammersla & Frease-McMahan, 1990).

● FIGURE 9.10

Evolutionary Mate Preferences: In Theory and in Practice

Before they engaged in speed dating, male and female participants stated their preferences for an ideal partner. Consistent with the evolutionary perspective, males were more likely to cite "physically attractive," and females were more likely to cite "earning prospects" (left). In ratings of actual speed-dating partners, however, male and female participants did not differ in their preferences for these characteristics (right).

Finkel, E. J., & Eastwick, P. W., "Speed-dating," *Current Directions in Psychological Science* vol 17 (pp. 193–197). Copyright © 2008 by Sage Publcations, Inc. Reprinted by permission.

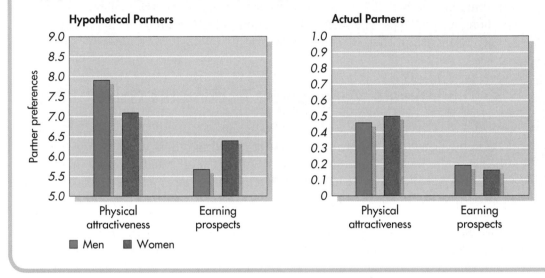

Intimate relationships often involve three basic components: (1) feelings of attachment, affection, and love; (2) fulfillment of psychological needs; and (3) interdependence between partners, each of whom has a meaningful influence on the other. Although people have many significant relationships in their lives that contain one or more of these components, social psychologists have concentrated much of their research on friends, dating partners, lovers, and married couples (Hendrick & Hendrick, 2000; Miller, 2012; Regan, 2011; Simpson & Campbell, 2013; Sprecher et al., 2008).

Not all intimate relationships contain all three ingredients. A summer romance is emotionally intense, but in the fall, both partners resume their separate lives. An "empty shell" marriage revolves around coordinated daily activities, but emotional attachment is weak and psychological needs go unmet. Clearly, relationships come in different shapes and sizes. Some are sexual; others are not. Some involve partners of the same sex; others, partners of the opposite sex. Some partners commit to a future together; others drop by for a brief stay. Feelings run the gamut from joyful to painful and from loving to hateful, with emotional intensity ranging all the way from mild to megawatt.

How do we advance from our first encounters to the intimate relationships that warm our lives? Do we proceed gradually over time, in stages, step by step, or by leaps and bounds? According to one perspective, relationships progress in order through a series of stages. For example, Bernard Murstein's (1986) *stimulus–value–role (SVR) theory* says there are three: (1) the stimulus stage, in which attraction is sparked by external attributes such as physical appearance; (2) the value stage, where attachment is based on similarity of values and beliefs; and (3) the role stage, where commitment is based on the enactment of such roles as husband and wife. All three factors are important throughout a relationship, but each one is said to be first and foremost during only one stage.

intimate relationship A close relationship between two adults involving emotional attachment, fulfillment of psychological needs, or interdependence.

In evaluating any stage theory, the critical issue is *sequence*. Does the value stage always precede the role stage or might a couple work out roles before exploring whether their values are compatible? Most researchers do not believe that intimate relationships progress through a fixed sequence of stages. What, then, accounts for how they change? One common answer is *rewards*. Love, like attraction, depends on the experience of positive emotions in the presence of a partner. Step by step, as the rewards pile up, love develops. Or, as rewards diminish, love erodes. In reward theories, quantity counts. But some would disagree. Think about your own relationships. Are your feelings for someone you love simply a more intense version of your feelings for someone you like? Is the love of a close friend the same as the love of a romantic partner? If not, then you appreciate that there are qualitative differences among relationships. The next section examines the reward-based approach to building a relationship. Then we consider differences among various types of relationships.

The Intimate Marketplace: Tracking the Gains and Losses

Earlier, we saw that people are initially attracted to others who provide them with direct or indirect rewards. But is "What's in it for me?" still important in a relationship that has blossomed and grown? Can an economic approach predict the future and longevity of a close relationship?

Social Exchange Theory **Social exchange theory** is an economic model of human behavior according to which people are motivated by a desire to maximize profit and minimize loss in their social relationships just as they are in business (Homans, 1961; Thibaut & Kelley, 1959). The basic premise is simple: Relationships that provide more rewards and fewer costs will be more satisfying and endure longer. Between intimates, the rewards include love, companionship, consolation in times of distress, and sexual gratification if the relationship is of this nature. The costs include the work it takes to maintain a relationship, work though conflict, compromise, and sacrifice opportunities elsewhere.

The development of an intimate relationship is clearly associated with the overall level of rewards and costs. Research has shown that dating couples who experience greater increases in rewards as their relationship progresses are more likely to stay together than are those who experience small increases or declines (Berg & McQuinn, 1986). People do not worry about costs during the honeymoon phase of a relationship (Hays, 1985). After a few months, however, both rewards and costs start to contribute to levels of satisfaction, both in married couples (Margolin & Wampold, 1981) and in gay and lesbian couples who are living together (Kurdek, 1991a).

Rewards and costs do not arise in a psychological vacuum. All people bring to a relationship certain expectations about the balance sheet to which they are entitled. John Thibaut and Harold Kelley (1959) coined the term *comparison level (CL)* to refer to this average expected outcome in relationships. A person with a high CL expects his or her relationships to be rewarding; someone with a low CL does not. Situations that meet or exceed a person's expectations are more satisfying than those that fall short. Even a bad relationship can look pretty good to someone who has a low CL.

According to Thibaut and Kelley, a second kind of expectation is also important. They coined the term *comparison level for alternatives (CLalt)* to refer to people's expectations about what they would receive in an alternative situation. If

William Hamilton/The New Yorker Collection/The Cartoon Bank

"I've done the numbers, and I will marry you."

social exchange theory A perspective that views people as motivated to maximize benefits and minimize costs in their relationships with others.

the rewards available elsewhere are believed to be high, a person will be less committed to staying in the present relationship (Drigotas & Rusbult, 1992). If people perceive that they have few acceptable alternatives (a low CLalt), they will tend to remain, even in an unsatisfying relationship that fails to meet expectations (CL).

Of course, just as these alternatives can influence our commitment, a sense of commitment can influence our perceptions of the alternatives. If you've ever been in love, you probably were not cold, calculating, and altogether objective in your perceptions of the alternatives. In close and intimate relationships, we tend to act like lovers, not like scientists, and harbor positive illusions. Research shows that people who are in love tend to see their partners and relationships through rose-colored glasses (Collins & Feeney 2000; Sanderson & Evans, 2001; Solomon & Vazire, 2014). People in love also tend to see other prospective partners as less appealing (Johnson & Rusbult, 1989; Simpson et al., 1990)—a motivated perception that enables those in a committed relationship to resist temptation (Lydon, 2010). This positive perspective on one's own partner relative to others is generally conducive to a happy and stable relationship (Murray et al., 1996; Murray & Holmes, 1999)

"Love looks not with the eyes, but with the mind; And therefore is wing'd Cupid painted blind."
—William Shakespeare, *A Midsummer Night's Dream*

A third element in the social exchange is investment. An *investment* is something a person puts into a relationship that he or she cannot recover if the relationship ends. If you don't like the way an intimate relationship is working out, you can pack your clothes, grab your laptop, and drive away. But what about all the time you put into trying to make the relationship last? What about all the romantic and career opportunities you sacrificed along the way? As you might expect, investments increase commitment. Because of those things we can't take with us, we're more likely to stay (Rusbult & Buunk, 1993).

Over the years, research has shown that the building blocks of the social exchange framework—as depicted in ● Figure 9.11 and as incorporated into Caryl

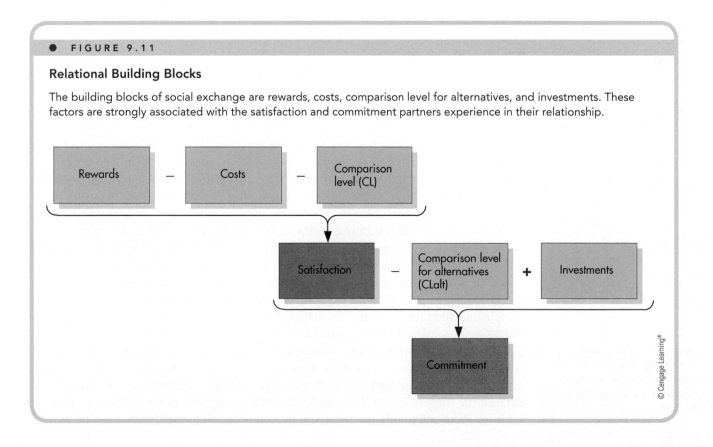

● FIGURE 9.11

Relational Building Blocks

The building blocks of social exchange are rewards, costs, comparison level for alternatives, and investments. These factors are strongly associated with the satisfaction and commitment partners experience in their relationship.

© Cengage Learning®

Rusbult et al.'s (1998) investment model—can be used to determine the level of commitment partners bring to a relationship (Le & Agnew, 2003; Rusbult et al., 2012). This model is important because commitment levels predict how long relationships will last. In studies of dating and married couples, research shows that the best-adjusted ones are those in which each partner is committed and sees the other as mutually committed (Drigotas et al., 1999).

Particularly important for the durability of a relationship, people who are highly committed are more likely to forgive and forget when their partners betray the relationship norm by flirting, lying, forgetting an anniversary, revealing a private and embarrassing story in public, or having an affair (Finkel et al., 2002). Unfortunately, there are times when commitment can be a trap. A study of battered women showed that the investment model can be used to predict whether battered women will remain in an abusive relationship (Rhatigan & Axsom, 2006).

Equity Theory **Equity theory** provides a special version of how social exchange operates in interpersonal interactions (Adams, 1965; Messick & Cook, 1983; Walster et al., 1978). According to this theory, an equitable relationship is a matter of social justice (Hatfield et al., 2008). All over the world, people are most content when the ratio between what they get out of a relationship (benefits) and what they put into it (contributions) is similar for both partners. Thus, the basic equity formula is

$$\frac{\text{Your Benefits}}{\text{Your Contributions}} = \frac{\text{Your Partner's Benefits}}{\text{Your Partner's Contributions}}$$

Equity is different from equality. According to equity theory, the balance is what counts. So if one partner benefits more from a relationship but also makes a greater contribution, then the situation is equitable. In an inequitable relationship, the balance is disturbed: One partner (called the *overbenefited*) receives more benefits than he or she deserves on the basis of contributions made, while the other partner (aptly called the *underbenefited*) receives fewer benefits than deserved.

Both overbenefit and underbenefit are unstable and often unhappy states. As you might expect, underbenefited partners feel angry and resentful because they are giving more than their partner for the benefits they receive, whereas overbenefited partners feel guilty because they are profiting unfairly. Both kinds of inequity are associated with negative emotions in dating couples (Walster et al., 1978), married couples (Schafer & Keith, 1981; Guerrero et al., 2008), and friendships among elderly widows (Rook, 1987). When it comes to satisfaction with a relationship, as you might expect, it is more unpleasant to feel underbenefited than overbenefited. People prefer to receive too much in life rather than too little, even if they feel bad about it (Grote & Clark, 2001; Hatfield et al., 1982; Sprecher, 2001).

If equity is so important, then any partner in a close relationship may at times feel a need to restore the balance sheet when he or she is feeling inferior as if he or she is falling short, or insecure. According to Sandra Murray and John Holmes (2008), people in relationships naturally and unconsciously maintain something of a "trust-insurance system" by which they keep a tally of costs and benefits in order to detect and then repair possible imbalances.

Murray and others (2009) went on to demonstrate the process in a series of studies of newlyweds. In one of these studies, more than 200 married couples, averaging 27 years of age, were recruited from local city clerk's offices when they applied for their marriage license. Each couple had been married for less than six months. All participants were given a personal digital assistant for keeping a daily

equity theory The theory that people are most satisfied with a relationship when the ratio between benefits and contributions is similar for both partners.

diary by answering specific questions—about their feelings, behaviors, and doubts about the marriage—each night before going to bed. By tracking and statistically correlating each partner's answers over time, the researchers observed three steps of the trust-insurance system in action: (1) On days after participants anxiously felt that they were not good enough for their partner, they were more likely to make sacrifices—for example, by doing the dishes, making lunch, or picking up after the partner; (2) these restorative actions were accompanied by lowered feelings of inferiority that same day; and (3) on the next day, the partners who benefited from these actions expressed fewer doubts about their marriage. Murray and her colleagues went on to propose an equilibrium model of relationship maintenance, which states that people are motivated to preserve important relationships, that declines in satisfaction and commitment motivate threat-mitigating tactics (for example, accommodating the partner rather than retaliating), and that these tactics serve to restore levels of satisfaction and commitment (Murray & Holmes, 2011; Murray et al., 2015).

■ Types of Relationships

Social exchange models focus on quantity: The more (rewards, equity), the better (satisfaction, endurance). But is reward always necessary? What about qualitative differences among our relationships? Does more reward turn casual acquaintances into friends, and friends into lovers, or are these types of relationships different from each other?

Exchange and Communal Relationships According to Margaret Clark and others, people operate by a reward-based model when they are in **exchange relationships**, which are characterized by an immediate tit-for-tat repayment of benefits. In these situations, people want costs to be quickly offset by compensation, leaving the balance at zero. But not all relationships fit this mold. Clark maintains that in **communal relationships**, partners respond to each other's needs and well-being over time and in different ways, without regard for whether they have given or received a benefit (Clark, 1984; Clark & Mills, 1979).

Exchange relationships typically exist between strangers and casual acquaintances and in certain long-term arrangements such as business partnerships. In contrast, strong communal relationships are usually limited to close friends, romantic partners, and family members (Clark & Mills, 1993). Based on fieldwork in West Africa, Alan Fiske (1992) is convinced that this distinction applies to human interactions all over the world. But the cynics among us wonder: Are communal relationships truly free of social exchange considerations? Can people really give without any desire to receive, or do partners in a communal relationship follow a more subtle version of social exchange, assuming that the benefits will balance out in the long run? Clark and Judson Mills (1993) believe that true communal relationships do exist—that once a communal norm has been adopted in a relationship, regardless of how it started, the motivation to respond to the other's needs becomes automatic.

Secure and Insecure Attachment Styles Another approach to understanding close relationships is provided by Phillip Shaver, Cindy Hazan, and others who have theorized that just as infants display different kinds of attachment toward their parents, adults also exhibit specific learned **attachment styles** in their romantic relationships (Cassidy & Shaver, 1999; Mikulincer & Shaver, 2007; Rholes & Simpson, 2004).

exchange relationship A relationship in which the participants expect and desire strict reciprocity in their interactions.

communal relationship A relationship in which the participants expect and desire mutual responsiveness to each other's needs.

attachment style The way a person typically interacts with significant others.

For many years, child development psychologists had noticed that infants form intense, exclusive bonds with their primary caretakers. This first relationship is highly charged with emotion, and it emerges with regularity from one culture to the next. By observing the way babies react to both separations from and reunions with the primary caretaker, usually the mother, researchers also noticed that babies have different attachment styles. Those with *secure* attachments cry in distress when the mother leaves and then beam with sheer delight when she returns. Those with *insecure* attachments show one of two patterns. Some babies, described as anxious, cling and cry when the mother leaves but then greet her with anger or apathy upon her return. Others are generally more detached and *avoidant,* not reacting much on either occasion (Ainsworth et al., 1978).

How important is this first attachment? Does a secure and trusting bond in the first year of life set a foundation for close relationships later in life? John Bowlby (1988), a psychiatrist and influential theorist, has argued that there is a link—that infants form "internal working models" of attachment figures and that these models guide their relationships later in life. Research shows that infants classified as securely attached are later more positive in their outlook toward others (Cassidy et al., 1996). Other research has shown that adult relationship patterns are predictable from parent–child relations in adolescence (Nosko et al., 2011). Either way, whether adult attachment styles are rooted in infancy or traced from adolescence, the distinction among adults has proved to be a useful one (Dinero et al., 2008).

Read the descriptions of three attachment types in Table 9.1. Which fits you best? Hazan and Shaver (1987) presented this task initially in a "love quiz" that appeared in a Denver newspaper and then in a study of college students. As shown in Table 9.1, the distribution of responses was similar in the two samples and in a later nationwide sample of 8,000 adults (Mickelson et al., 1997). In addition, the researchers found that people who have a secure attachment style report having satisfying relationships that are happy, friendly, based on mutual trust, and enduring. Cognitively, they see people as good-hearted, and they believe in romantic love. In contrast, avoidant lovers fear intimacy and believe that romantic love is doomed to fade; and anxious lovers report a love life full of emotional highs and lows, obsessive preoccupation, a greater willingness than others to make long-term commitments, and extreme sexual attraction and jealousy.

To some extent, our attachment styles can be seen in our everyday behavior. For example, Jeffrey Simpson and others (1996) videotaped dating couples as they tried to resolve various conflicts and then showed the tapes to outside observers. They found that men classified from a questionnaire as having an insecure-avoidant attachment style were the least warm and supportive and that women with an insecure-anxious style were the most

TABLE 9.1

Attachment Styles

Question: Which of the following best describes your feelings?

Answers and Percentages	Newspaper Sample	University Sample
Secure	56	56
I find it relatively easy to get close to others and am comfortable depending on them and having them depend on me. I don't often worry about being abandoned or about someone getting too close to me.		
Avoidant	25	23
I am somewhat uncomfortable being close to others; I find it difficult to trust them completely and difficult to allow myself to depend on them. I am nervous when anyone gets too close, and often love partners want me to be more intimate than I feel comfortable being.		
Anxious	19	21
I find that others are reluctant to get as close as I would like. I often worry that my partner doesn't really love me or won't want to stay with me. I want to merge completely with another person, and this desire sometimes scares people away.		

From Hazan, C., and Shaver, P., "Romantic love conceptualized as an attachment process," *Journal of Personality and Social Psychology* vol 52 (pp. 511–524).

upset and negative in their behavior. There is also reason to believe that people's attachment styles influence their physiological reactions to relationship conflict. In one study, Sally Powers and her colleagues (2006) brought 124 college-age dating couples into the laboratory to discuss a heated conflict they'd been having. Before and after this "conflict negotiation task," the researchers took saliva samples from all participants to measure levels of cortisol, a stress hormone. The results showed that boyfriends and girlfriends who were insecurely attached exhibited more physiological stress in response to the conflict task than did those who were securely attached.

What about the future? Does the attachment style you endorse today foretell relational outcomes tomorrow? On this question, the evidence is mixed. People who are secure do tend to have more lasting relationships. But the prognosis for those classified as insecure is harder to predict, with the results less consistent. What's important to realize is that although styles of attachment are modestly stable over time—perhaps as holdovers from infancy and childhood—they are not fixed, or set in stone. Lee Kirkpatrick and Cindy Hazan (1994) tracked down participants from a study that had taken place four years earlier and found that 30% had different attachment styles. Adult development plays a key role in this regard. In a massive internet survey of 91,000 men and women, 18 to 64 years old, from 81 countries all over the world, William Chopik and Robin Edelstein (2014) discovered that there is a universal shift in attachment styles over the lifespan. Specifically, for both men and women and across genders and cultures, attachment anxiety was highest among young adults and declined thereafter; attachment avoidance was lowest among young adults but then peaked in middle age. In keeping with the central theme of social psychology—that we are profoundly shaped by the situations and roles we are in—research suggests that people may continuously revise their own attachment styles in response to new relationship experiences.

How Do I Love Thee? Counting the Ways

The poet Elizabeth Barrett Browning asked, "How do I love thee?" and then went on to "count the ways." And there are many. When college students were asked to list all kinds of love that came to mind, they produced 216 entries, such as friendship, parental, brotherly, sisterly, romantic, sexual, spiritual, obsessive, possessive, and puppy love (Fehr & Russell, 1991). Focusing on the ups and downs and vagaries of romantic love, anthropologist Helen Fisher (2015), Chief Scientific Advisor to Match.com, reports on the basis of a large national survey of 25,000 *Singles in America*, that over 54% of American singles believe in love at first sight; that 58% of men and 50% of women said that they have had a "friend with benefits" (FWB) relationship; that 28% have had a FWB friend turn into a long-term partnership; that 89% believe you can stay married to the same person forever; 36% said they wanted a prenuptial agreement; and 33% believe it's OK to leave a "satisfactory marriage" if you are no longer passionately in love.

Over the years, various schemes for classifying types of love have been proposed (Berscheid, 2010; Sternberg & Weis, 2006). From ancient writings, sociologist John Alan Lee (1988) identified three primary love styles: *eros* (erotic love), *ludus* (game-playing, uncommitted love), and *storge* (friendship love). As with primary colors, Lee theorized, these three styles can be blended together to form new secondary types of love, such as *mania* (demanding and possessive love), *pragma* (pragmatic love), and *agape* (other-oriented, altruistic love). On a scale designed to measure these "colors of love," men tend to score higher than women on *ludus,* and women score higher on *storge, mania,* and *pragma* (Hendrick & Hendrick, 1995).

Another popular taxonomy is derived from Robert Sternberg's (1986) **triangular theory of love**. According to Sternberg, there are eight basic subtypes of love (seven different forms and an eighth combination that results in the absence of love)—and all can be derived from the presence or absence of three components. The combination can thus be viewed as the vertices of a triangle (see ● Figure 9.12). The components—and sample items used to measure each one—are described below:

Intimacy. The emotional component, which involves liking and feelings of closeness. ("I have a comfortable relationship with ___.")

Passion: The motivational component, which contains drives that trigger attraction, romance, and sexual desire. ("Just seeing ___ is exciting for me.")

Commitment: The cognitive component, which reflects the decision to make a long-term commitment to a loved partner. ("I will always feel a strong responsibility for ___.")

Research provides some support for this tri-component model of love (Sternberg, 1999). In one study, Arthur Aron and Lori Westbay (1996) asked people to rate 68 prototypical features of love and found that all the various features fell into three categories: passion (*gazing at the other, euphoria, butterflies in the stomach*), intimacy (*feeling free to talk about anything, supportive, understanding*), and commitment (*devotion, putting the other first, long-lasting*). In a second study, Sternberg (1997) asked people to state what they see as important in different kinds of relationships and found that the results were consistent with the theory. For example, "ideal lover" scored high on all three components, "friend" scored high on intimacy and commitment but low on passion, and "sibling" scored high on commitment but low on intimacy and passion.

In light of theories involving infant attachment styles, colors, triangles, and other love classification schemes that have been proposed over the years, one wonders: How many types of love are there, really? It's hard to tell. But there are two basic types that are built into all models: *liking,* the type of feeling you would have for a platonic friend, and *loving,* the kind of feeling you would have for a romantic partner. According to Zick Rubin (1973), liking and loving are two distinct reactions to an intimate relationship. There is some question, however, about how sharp the difference is. Kenneth and Karen Dion (1976) questioned casual daters, exclusive daters, engaged couples, and married couples. Although casual daters reported more liking than loving, liking and loving did not differ for those in the more committed dating relationships. The two-pronged distinction Elaine Hatfield (1988) and her colleagues (Hatfield & Rapson, 1993) make between passionate and companionate love is even sharper. According to Hatfield, **passionate love** is an emotionally intense and *often erotic state* of absorption in another person, whereas **companionate love** is a slow-building, secure, trusting, and stable partnership, similar to what Rubin called liking.

Passionate Love

Passionate love is an intense, sometimes fast to develop, emotional, heart-thumping state of absorption in another person. From thrilling highs to agonizing lows, it is the bittersweet stuff of romance paperbacks, popular music, poems, and soap operas. What is passionate love, and where does it come from? According to Ellen Berscheid and Elaine Walster (later Hatfield) (1974), the key to understanding passionate love is to recognize that it is an emotion that can be

triangular theory of love A theory proposing that love has three basic components—intimacy, passion, and commitment—that can be combined to produce eight subtypes.

passionate love Romantic love characterized by high arousal, intense attraction, and fear of rejection.

companionate love A secure, trusting, stable partnership.

analyzed like any other emotion. Drawing on Schachter's (1964) two-factor theory of emotion (see Chapter 3), they theorized that passionate love is fueled by two ingredients: (1) a heightened state of physiological arousal and (2) the belief that this arousal was triggered by the beloved person.

Sometimes, the arousal–love connection is obvious, as when a person feels a surge of sexual desire at the sight of a romantic partner. At other times, however, the symptoms of arousal—such as a pounding heart, sweaty palms, and weak knees—can be hard to interpret. When you're in the company of an attractive person, these symptoms may be attributed or "misattributed" to passionate love. Dolf Zillmann (1984) calls the process **excitation transfer**. According to Zillmann, arousal triggered by one stimulus can be transferred or added to the arousal from a second stimulus. The combined arousal is then perceived as having been caused only by the second stimulus.

Donald Dutton and Arthur Aron (1974) first tested this provocative hypothesis in a field study that took place on two bridges above British Columbia's Capilano River. One was a narrow, wobbly suspension bridge (450 feet long and 5 feet wide, with a low handrail) that sways 230 feet above rocky rapids—a nightmare for anyone the least bit afraid of heights. The other bridge was wide, sturdy, and only 10 feet from the ground. Whenever an unaccompanied young man walked across one of these bridges, he was met by an attractive young woman who introduced herself as a research assistant, asked him to fill out a brief questionnaire, and gave her phone number in case he wanted more information about the project. As predicted, men who crossed the scary bridge were later more likely to call her than those who crossed the stable bridge. In a study of "love at first fright" that took place in two amusement parks, Cindy Meston and Penny Frohlich (2003) similarly found that men and women who were not with a romantic partner rated a photographed person of the opposite sex as more attractive right after they rode on a roller-coaster than they did before they began the ride. Perhaps terror can fan the hot flames of romance.

Or maybe not. Maybe it's just a relief to be with someone when we're in distress. To rule out the possibility that relief rather than arousal is what fuels attraction, Gregory White and his colleagues (1981) had to create arousal without distress. How? A little exercise can do it. Male participants ran in place for either

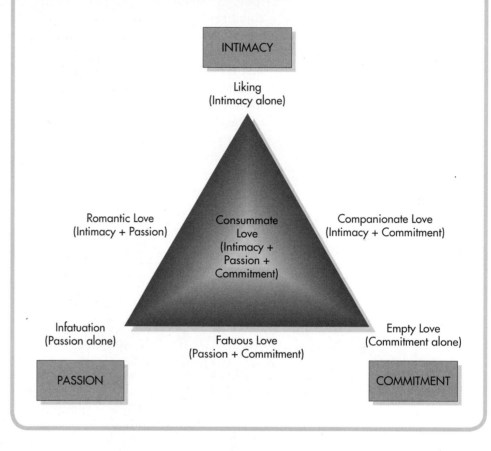

● **FIGURE 9.12**

Sternberg's Triangular Theory of Love

According to Sternberg, various combinations of passion, intimacy, and commitment give rise to seven different types of love. (Although it is not shown, the absence of all three components produces an eighth result, nonlove.)

From Sternberg, R., and Barnes, M. L. (eds.), *The Psychology of Love*, Yale University Press, 1986. Copyright © 1986 by Yale University Press. Reprinted by permission.

INTIMACY

Liking
(Intimacy alone)

Romantic Love
(Intimacy + Passion)

Consummate Love
(Intimacy + Passion + Commitment)

Companionate Love
(Intimacy + Commitment)

Infatuation
(Passion alone)

Fatuous Love
(Passion + Commitment)

Empty Love
(Commitment alone)

PASSION

COMMITMENT

excitation transfer The process whereby arousal caused by one stimulus is added to arousal from a second stimulus and the combined arousal is attributed to the second stimulus.

2 minutes or 15 seconds and then saw a videotape of a woman they expected to meet. The woman had been made up to look physically attractive or unattractive. After watching the video, participants rated her appearance. The result: Those who exercised for 2 minutes as opposed to only 15 seconds saw the physically attractive woman as even more attractive and the unattractive woman as less attractive. This study and others like it (Allen et al., 1989) showed that arousal—even without distress—intensifies emotional reactions, positive or negative.

The implication of this research—that our passions are at the mercy of bridges, roller-coasters, exercise, and anything else that causes the heart to race—is intriguing. It is certainly consistent with the common observation that people are vulnerable to falling in love when their lives are turbulent. But does the effect occur, as theorized, because people *mis*attribute their arousal to a person they have just met? Yes and no. Based on their review of 33 experiments, Craig Foster and others (1998) confirmed that the arousal–attraction effect does exist. They also found, however, that the effect occurs even when people know the actual source of their arousal—in other words, even without misattribution. According to these investigators, just being aroused, even if we know why, facilitates whatever is the most natural response. If the person we meet is good-looking and of the right sex, we become more attracted. If the person is not good-looking or is of the wrong sex, we become less attracted. No thought is required. The response is automatic.

Rich Lam/Getty Images News/Getty Images

In June of 2011, after the Vancouver Canucks hockey team lost the Stanley Cup, a riot broke out in the city. Many people were injured; many others were arrested. Illustrating the intense state of absorption that defines passionate love, this young couple was photographed amidst the chaos kissing in the street. *Sports Illustrated* called this iconic image "the most compelling sports image of the year."

It is now clear that passionate love is erotic and highly sexualized. In a book titled *Lust: What We Know About Human Sexual Desire,* Pamela Regan and Ellen Berscheid (1999) present compelling evidence for the proposition that intense sexual desire and excitement are a vital part of passionate love. In this regard, they note that "loving" is different from "being in love." To illustrate, Berscheid and Meyers (1996) asked college men and women to make three lists: people they loved, people they were in love with, and people they were sexually attracted to. As it turned out, only 2% of those in the "love" category also appeared in the sex list. Yet among those in the "in love" category, the overlap with sex was 85%. And when Regan and her colleagues (1998) asked people to list the characteristics of romantic love, two-thirds cited sexual desire—more than the number who put happiness, communication, loyalty, sharing, or commitment on the list.

Romantic ideals notwithstanding, many people doubt the staying power of passionate love. Does the fire within a relationship burn hot and bright over time, or is it just a passing infatuation? Comparisons of couples at different stages of their relationships and longitudinal studies that measure changes in the same couples over time have suggested that intense, sexual, passionate love does tend to diminish somewhat over time (Acker & Davis, 1992). Yet this decline is not clearly defined or inevitable. Bianca Acevedo and Arthur Aron (2009) meta-analyzed past survey research and asked couples who had been together for varying lengths of time questions about passionate love. They found that although the initial "obsessional" aspect of passionate love clearly diminishes in long-term relationships ("I sometimes find it difficult to concentrate on work because thoughts of my partner occupy my mind"), there is a "romantic" aspect that often endures ("I would rather be with my partner than anyone else"). Acevedo and others (2012) next studied men and women who were married an average of 21 years—and who reported long-term, intense, romantic love for their partner. They had these participants undergo fMRI while viewing facial images of their partner; a highly familiar acquaintance; a close friend; and a low-familiar person. The scans revealed activity in regions of the brain specific to their partner—namely, in dopamine-rich reward areas and areas that are typically activated by maternal attachment. More research is needed, but these results support the self-report data that for some people, the intense love of their long-term partner may last for long periods of time.

Companionate Love   In contrast to the intense, emotional, erotic, and sometimes obsessional nature of passionate love, companionate love is a form of affection that binds close friends as well as lovers. Companionate relationships rest on a foundation of mutual trust, caring, respect, friendship, and commitment—characteristics that John Harvey and Julie Omarzu (2000) see as necessary for "minding the close relationship."

Compared with the passionate form of love, companionate love is less intense but is in some respects deeper and more enduring. Susan Sprecher and Pamela Regan (1998) administered passionate and companionate love scales to heterosexual couples who had been together for varying amounts of time and found that the passionate love scores of both men and women initially rose over time but then peaked and declined somewhat during marriage. Companionate love scores, however, did not similarly decline. In fact, in couples that stay together, partners are likely to report that "I love you more today than yesterday" (Sprecher, 1999). Like the slow but steady tortoise in Aesop's fable, companionate love may seem to be outpaced by the flashier start of passionate love, but it can still cross the finish line well ahead.

"True love never grows old."

—Proverb

Companionate love is characterized by high levels of **self-disclosure**, a willingness to open up and share intimate facts and feelings. In a way, self-disclosure is to companionate love what arousal is to passionate love. Think for a moment about your most embarrassing moment, your most cherished ambitions, or your sex life. Would you bare your soul on these private matters to a complete stranger? What about a casual acquaintance, date, friend, or lover? Whether or not to self-disclose—what, when, how much, and to whom—is a decision that each of us makes based on a consideration of what we stand to gain and lose in a relationship (Omarzu, 2000).

The willingness to disclose intimate facts and feelings lies at the heart of our closest and most intimate relationships (Derlega et al., 1993). Research shows that the more emotionally involved people are in a close relationship, the more they self-disclose to each other. Nancy Collins and Lynn Miller (1994) note three possible reasons for this correlation: (1) We disclose to people we like; (2) we like people who disclose to us; and (3) we like people to whom we have disclosed. Thus, among pairs of college students brought together in a laboratory for brief getting-acquainted conversations, the more they self-disclosed, the better they felt about each other afterward (Vittengl & Holt, 2000). In a longitudinal study of adult dating couples, partners who reported

self-disclosure   Revelations about the self that a person makes to others.

"Just curious: when, exactly, were you planning to tell me that you're the product of a 3-D printer?"

Michael Maslin/Condé Nast Collection

Companionate relationships are characterized by increasing amounts of self-disclosure—hence, the failure to self-disclose something essential in a timely manner is met with surprise.

"As soon as you cannot keep anything from a woman, you love her."
—Paul Geraldy

higher levels of self-disclosure also expressed more satisfaction, commitment, and love (Sprecher & Hendrick, 2004). When it comes to sex, too, partners who self-disclose their likes and dislikes to each other are more satisfied sexually than those who are less open (MacNeil & Byers, 2009).

Over the years, researchers have observed three patterns of self-disclosure in social relationships. One is that partners reveal more to each other as their relationship grows over time. According to Irving Altman and Dalmas Taylor (1973), self-disclosure is a basic form of social exchange that unfolds as relationships develop. Their *social penetration theory* holds that relationships progress from superficial exchanges to more intimate ones. At first, people give relatively little of themselves to each other and receive little in return. If the initial encounters prove rewarding, however, the exchanges become both *broader* (covering more areas of their lives) and *deeper* (involving more sensitive areas). In short, social interaction grows from a narrow, shallow sliver to a wider, more penetrating wedge.

Recently, Tang and Wang (2012) conducted an online survey to explore the topics that 1,027 bloggers in Taiwan disclosed on their blogs and in the real world. Their results showed that bloggers self-disclose on a range of topics—including their attitudes, body, money, work, feelings, interests, and experiences. With regard to what is self-disclosed to three target audiences (online, best friend, and parents), bloggers expressed themselves to their best friends the most, followed by parents and online audiences, both in depth and in width. It appears that social penetration theory—proposed long before there was an Internet—provides a good description of self-disclosure, today, in online relationships.

A second observation is that patterns of self-disclosure change according to the state of a relationship. During a first encounter and in the budding stages of a new relationship, people tend to reciprocate another's self-disclosure with their own—at a comparable level of intimacy. If a new acquaintance opens up, it is polite to match that self-disclosure by revealing more of ourselves. Once a relationship is well established, however, strict reciprocity occurs less frequently (Altman, 1973; Derlega et al., 1976). Among couples in distress, two different self-disclosure patterns have been observed. For some, breadth and depth both decrease as partners withdraw and cease to communicate (Baxter, 1987). For others, the breadth of self-disclosure declines but depth increases as the partners express anger at each other (Tolstedt & Stokes, 1984). In this case, the social *de*penetration process resembles neither the sliver of a superficial affiliation nor the wedge of a close relationship but rather a long, thin dagger of discontent.

A third common observation is that individuals differ in the tendency to share private, intimate thoughts with others. For example, Kathryn Dindia and Mike Allen (1992) conducted a meta-analysis of 205 studies involving 23,702 white North Americans and found, on average, that women are more open than men—and that people in general are more self-disclosing to women than to men. This being the case, it comes as no surprise that women rate their same-sex friendships more highly than men rate theirs. At least in North America, male friends seem to bond more by taking part in common activities, whereas female friends engage more in a sharing of feelings (Duck & Wright, 1993). As Paul Wright (1982) put it, women tend to interact "face-to-face" but men go "side-by-side."

Culture, Attraction, and Close Relationships

In looking at attraction, desire, relationships, and love, one wonders: Are people all over the world similar or different? To what extent are these processes universal or different from one culture to another? In recent years, several social psychologists have raised these kinds of questions (Hatfield et al., 2007).

In his original cross-cultural study of mate selection, for example, Buss (1989) found that physical attractiveness is more important to men all over the world and that financial resources are more important to women—gender differences that appeared to be universal. Yet even Buss was struck by the powerful impact that culture had on mate preferences. In China, India, Indonesia, Iran, Taiwan, and the Palestinian territories of Israel, for example, people valued chastity in a mate. Yet in Finland, France, Norway, Sweden, the Netherlands, and West Germany, chastity was either unimportant or negatively valued.

When it comes to close relationships, research has shown that passionate love is a widespread and universal emotion. In surveys conducted throughout the world, William Jankowiak and Edward Fischer (1992) detected indications of passionate love in 147 out of 166 cultures as varied as Indonesia, China, Turkey, Nigeria, Trinidad, Morocco, Australia, and Micronesia. Drawing on this universality, some researchers have begun to explore the underlying neuroscience. For example, anthropologist Helen Fisher (2004) believes that romantic love is hardwired in the neurochemistry of the brain. In particular, Fisher argues that the neurotransmitter dopamine, which drives animals to seek rewards such as food and sex, is essential to the pleasure that is felt when these drives are satisfied. Hence, she argues, dopamine levels are associated with both the highs of romantic passion and the lows of rejection. Citing evidence from studies of humans and other animals, she also points to neurochemical parallels between romantic love and substance addiction.

Although most people in the world agree that sexual desire is what injects the passion into passionate love, not everyone sees it as necessary for marriage. Think about this question: If a man or woman had all other qualities you desired, would you marry this person if you were *not* in love? When American students were surveyed in 1967, 35% of men and 76% of women said yes. Twenty years later, only 14% of men and 20% of women said they would marry someone with whom they were not in love (Simpson et al., 1986). The shift among women may reflect the pragmatic point that marrying for love is an economic luxury that few women of the past could afford. As seen in the current popularity of prenuptial agreements, pragmatic considerations continue to influence marriage practices, even today.

The willingness to marry without love is also highly subject to cultural variation. In light of the different values that pervade individualist and collectivist cultures, the differences are not surprising. In many cultures, marriage is seen as a transaction between families that is influenced by social, economic, and religious considerations. Indeed, arranged marriages are still common in India, China, many Muslim countries, and sub-Saharan Africa. So, when Robert Levine and others (1995) asked college students from 11 countries about marrying without love, they found that the percentage who said they would do so ranged from 4% in the United States, 5% in Australia, and 8% in England, up to 49% in India, and 51% in Pakistan.

In cultures in which love is not a sufficient basis for marriage, other factors play a role. In India, a historically entrenched caste system divides its citizens and holds sway over love and marriage (Singh, 2009). Indeed, even though the government legalized intercaste marriage more than 50 years ago and is now offering

"To an American in love, his/her emotions tend to overshadow everything else . . . to a Chinese in love, his/her love occupies a place among other considerations."

—Hsu

This traditional Indian wedding was held in Pushkar, a town in the Indian state of Rajasthan. In a tradition that seems strange to most Americans, for whom being in love is essential, Indian marriages are often arranged.

Pep Roig/Alamy

incentives for intercaste couples to marry, an invisible separation remains between the upper and lower castes that lasts from birth to death—and "honor killings" of couples who dare to cross these traditional lines are not uncommon (Wax, 2008).

In China, where a cultural premium is placed on devotion, respect, and obedience of children to parents and other family elders, there is less emphasis on the Western "fairytale ideals" of love and romance (Higgins et al., 2002; Jackson et al., 2006). In surveys, young adults in China, more than in the United States, said they would be influenced in their mate selection decisions by parents and close friends—for example, that they would try to persuade their parents to accept a dating partner and stop dating that partner if their parents did not approve (Zhang & Kline, 2009). In a recent study, researchers asked participants from China and the United States what their minimum criteria were for choosing a spouse. Chinese participants set higher minimum requirements for reputational characteristics such as "high social status," "powerful," "wealthy," "high earning capacity," and "good family background," while Americans rated personal attributes such as "honest and trustworthy," "has a sense of humor," "intelligent," "exciting," and "highly educated" as more important (Chen et al., 2014).

The influence of culture on love is interesting. On the one hand, it could be argued that the rugged individualism found in many Western cultures would inhibit the tendency to become intimate and interdependent with others. On the other hand, individualism leads people to give priority in making marital decisions to their own feelings rather than to family concerns, social obligations, religious constraints, income, and the like (Dion & Dion, 1996). In an illustration of this point, Fred Rothbaum and Bill Yuk-Piu Tsang (1998) compared popular love songs in the United States and China. They found that the American lyrics focused more on the two lovers as isolated entities, independent of social context ("There is nobody here, it's just you and me, the way I want it to be").

■ Relationship Issues: The Male–Female Connection

Browse the offerings of any real or online bookstore and you'll see one title after another on the general topic of gender. There are books for men, books for women, books for gays and straights, books that preach the masculine ideal and books that tell us how to be more feminine, books that portray men and women as similar, and books that accentuate the differences. Is it true, to borrow John Gray's (1997) provocative book title, that *Men Are from Mars, Women Are from Venus?* Where does the LGBT community fit in? And what about the desire for sex—and control; is it aptly portrayed in the erotic romance novel by E. L. James, brought to life in the 2015 hit movie, *Fifty Shades of Grey?* If so, what are the implications when it comes to male–female relationships?

Sexuality   Before the turn of the twentieth century, Sigmund Freud shocked the scientific community by proposing psychoanalytic theory, which placed great emphasis on sex as a driving force in human behavior. At the time, Freud's closest associates rejected this focus on sexual motivation. But was he wrong? Sexual images and themes pop up, quite literally, in our dreams, in the jokes we tell, in the TV shows we watch, in the novels we read, in the music we hear, and in the sex scandals that swirl around public figures in the news. It's no wonder that advertisers use sex to sell everything from blue jeans to perfume, soft drinks, and cars.

Sex, a most private aspect of human relations, is difficult to study systematically. During the 1940s, biologist Alfred Kinsey and his colleagues (1948; 1953) conducted the first large-scale survey of sexual practices in the United States. Based on confidential interviews of more than 17,000 men and women, these researchers sought for the first time to describe what nobody would openly talk about: sexual activity. Many of his results were shocking; reported sexual activity was more frequent and more varied than anyone had expected. Kinsey's books were instant bestsellers. Certain aspects of his methodology were flawed, however. For example, participants were mostly young, white, urban, and middle-class—hardly a representative sample. He also asked leading questions to enable respondents to report on sexual activities—or make up stories (Jones, 1997a). Kinsey died in 1954, but his Institute for Sex Research at Indiana University remains to this day a major center for the study of human sexuality.

Since Kinsey's groundbreaking study, many sex surveys have been conducted, and they form part of the research history that has been chronicled, both seriously and with humor, in books with such titles as *Kiss and Tell: Surveying Sex in the Twentieth Century* (Ericksen & Steffen, 1999), and *Bonk: The Curious Coupling of Science and Sex* (Roach, 2008). The limits of self-reports—regardless of whether they are taken in face-to-face interviews, telephone surveys, or on the Internet—is that we can never know for sure how accurate the results are. Part of the problem is that respondents may not be honest in their disclosures. Another limiting factor is that people differ in their interpretations of survey questions.

Researchers have used an array of methods to measure sexual attitudes and behavior. Studies of everyday interactions reveal that men view the world in more sexualized terms than women do. In 1982, Antonia Abbey arranged for pairs of male and female college students to talk for five minutes while other students observed the sessions. When she later questioned the actors and observers, Abbey found that the males were more sexually attracted to the females than vice versa. The males also rated the female actors as being more seductive and more flirtatious than the women had rated themselves as being. Among men more than women, eye contact, a compliment, a friendly remark, a brush against the arm, and an innocent smile are often interpreted as sexual come-ons (Kowalski, 1993).

Despite all that has changed over the past quarter of a century, it appears that these gender differences in perceptions of sexual interest still exist (Levesque et al., 2006). A recent speed-dating study showed that while men *over*perceive sexual interest, women tended to *under*perceive sexual interest (Perilloux et al., 2012). Also, in a series of online questionnaire studies, female participants were asked how likely they would be to have sex with a man if they had engaged in each of 15 dating behaviors—such as holding his hand, complimenting his appearance, cooking dinner, staring deeply into his eyes, kissing him, and saying "I love you." Male participants were asked to estimate the sexual intention of women who engaged in those same behaviors. As in the past, men saw more sexual intent in various female behaviors than the women reported about themselves. Interestingly, other women perceived these behaviors in sexual terms—agreeing more the male participants than the female participants (Perilloux & Kurzban, 2015).

Pioneering sex researcher Alfred Kinsey.

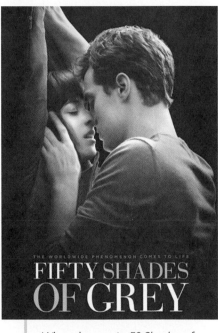

When the movie *50 Shades of Grey* opened in 2015, based on a novel by E. L. James, it attracted enormous attention. In depicting an explicit sexual relationship between a young college graduate, played by Dakota Johnson, and a wealthy businessman, played by Jamie Dornan, *50 Shades* featured unconventional and controversial sexual encounters involving bondage, dominance and submission, and elements of sadism and masochism (BDSM). Illustrating what biologist Alfred Kinsey discovered many years ago, human sexual activity is more varied than anyone had expected.

Gender differences are particularly common in self-report surveys, where in contrast to women, men report being more promiscuous, more likely to think about sex, more permissive, more likely to enjoy casual sex without emotional commitment, and more likely to fantasize about sex with multiple partners (Oliver & Hyde, 1993). When asked to select 10 private wishes from a list, for example, most men and women similarly wanted love, health, peace on earth, unlimited ability, and wealth. But more men than women also wanted "to have sex with anyone I choose" (Ehrlichman & Eichenstein, 1992). In a large-scale study of 16,000 respondents from 52 countries, David Schmitt (2003) found that most men desire more sex partners and more sexual variety than most women do, regardless of their relationship status or sexual orientation. Based on this study and others, Roy Baumeister and others (2001) concluded that "men desire sex more than women" (p. 270).

Sexual Orientation In recent years, policymakers, judges, religious leaders, scholars, and laypeople have openly debated the topic of same-sex marriage. On June 26, 2015, this debate culminated in the historic U.S. Supreme Court landmark ruling that the Constitution "requires a State to license a marriage between two people of the same sex and to recognize a marriage between two people of the same sex when their marriage was lawfully licensed and performed out-of-State" (*Obergefell v. Hodges*, 2015). In light of all that has changed, no discussion of human sexuality is complete without a consideration of differences in **sexual orientation**—defined as one's sexual preference for members of the same sex (homosexuality), the opposite sex (heterosexuality), or both sexes (bisexuality).

How common is homosexuality, and where does it come from? Throughout history and in all cultures, a vast majority of people have been heterosexual in their orientation. But how vast a majority is a subject of some debate. A 1970 survey funded by the Kinsey Institute revealed that 3.3% of American men sampled said that they had frequent or occasional homosexual sex (Fay et al., 1989). Between 1989 and 1992, the National Opinion Research Center reported that 2.8% of American men and 2.5% of women had exclusive homosexual activity. Together, large-scale surveys in the United States, Europe, Asia, and the Pacific have suggested that the exclusively homosexual population in the world is 3% or 4% among men and about half that number among women (Diamond, 1993).

Although an exclusive homosexual *orientation* is relatively rare among humans and other animals, homosexual *behaviors* are far more common. In *Biological Exuberance,* Bruce Bagemihl (1999) reports that sexual encounters among male–male and female–female pairs have been observed in more than 450 species, including giraffes, goats, birds, chimpanzees, and lizards. Among humans, the incidence of homosexual behavior varies from one generation and culture to the next, depending on prevailing attitudes. In *Same Sex, Different Cultures,* Gilbert Herdt (1998) notes that in parts of the world, stretching from Sumatra to Melanesia, it's common for adolescent males to engage in homosexual activities before being of age for marriage, even though homosexuality as a permanent trait is rare. It's important, then, to realize that sexual orientation cannot be viewed in black-or-white terms but should be seen along a continuum. In the center of that continuum, 1% of people describe themselves as actively bisexual.

To explain the roots of homosexuality, various theories have been proposed. The Greek philosopher Aristotle believed that it was inborn but strengthened by habit; post-Freud psychoanalysts argue that it stems from family dynamics, specifically a child's overattachment to a parent of the same or opposite sex; social learning theorists point to rewarding sexual experiences with same-sex peers in

---

Men are more likely than women to interpret friendly gestures by the opposite sex in sexual terms.

TRUE

In an ABC Primetime survey of 1,501 American adults, a number of gender differences were found (Langer et al., 2004):

	Men	Women
Think about sex every day	*70%*	*34%*
Have visited a sex website	*34%*	*10%*
Have fantasized about a threesome	*33%*	*9%*

---

sexual orientation A person's preference for members of the same sex (homosexuality), opposite sex (heterosexuality), or both sexes (bisexuality).

childhood. Yet there is little hard evidence to support these claims. In a particularly comprehensive study, Alan Bell and others (1981) interviewed 1,500 homosexual and heterosexual adults about their lives. There were no differences in past family backgrounds, absence of a male or female parent, relationship with parents, sexual abuse, age of onset of puberty, or high school dating patterns. Except for the fact that homosexual adults described themselves as less conforming as children, the two groups could not be distinguished by past experiences. Both groups felt strongly that their sexual orientation was set long before it was "official."

Increasingly, there is scientific evidence of a biological disposition. In a highly publicized study, neurobiologist Simon LeVay (1991) autopsied the brains of 19 homosexual men who had died of AIDS, 16 heterosexual men (some of whom had died of AIDS), and 6 heterosexual women. LeVay examined a tiny nucleus in the hypothalamus that is involved in regulating sexual behavior and is known to be larger in heterosexual men than in women. The specimens were numerically coded, so LeVay did not know whether a particular donor he was examining was male or female, straight or gay. The result: In the male homosexual brains he studied, the nucleus was half the size as in male heterosexual brains and comparable in size to those found in female heterosexual brains. This research is described in Levay's (1993) book *The Sexual Brain.*

It's important to recognize that this study revealed only a correlation between sexual orientation and the brain and cannot be used to draw conclusions about cause and effect. More convincing support for the biological roots of sexual orientation comes from twin studies suggesting that there is a genetic predisposition. Michael Bailey and Richard Pillard (1991) surveyed 167 gay men and their twins and adopted brothers. Overall, 52% of the identical twins were gay, compared to only 22% of fraternal twins and 11% of adoptive brothers. Two years later, Bailey and others (1993) conducted a companion study of lesbians with similar results.

The origins of sexual orientation are complex for two reasons. First, it's not clear that sexual orientation for men and women is similarly rooted. In Australia, Bailey and others (2000) had hundreds of pairs of twins rate their own sexuality on a 7-point scale that ranged from "exclusively heterosexual" to "exclusively homosexual." Overall, 92% of both men and women saw themselves as exclusively heterosexual. Among the others, however, more women than men said that they had bisexual tendencies and more men than women said they were exclusively homosexual. In a longitudinal investigation of 18- to 25-year-old women, Lisa Diamond (2003) found that more than a quarter of those who had initially identified themselves as lesbian or bisexual changed their orientation over the next five years—far more change than is ever reported among men.

Recent experiments in laboratory reinforce the point. In one study, Meredith Chivers and others (2004) recruited men and women who had identified themselves as heterosexual or homosexual in their orientation. In a private, dimly lit room, these participants watched a series of brief sex clips—some involving male couples, others involving female couples. While watching, the participants rated their subjective feelings of sexual attraction on a 10-point scale. At the same time, genital arousal was measured using devices that recorded penile erection (for males) and vaginal pulse (for females). Results showed that the women were genitally aroused by both male *and* female sex clips, regardless of whether they identified themselves as straight or lesbian in their orientation. Yet males exhibited more arousal in response to men *or* women, depending on their sexual orientation. In fact, although self-identified bisexual men reported an attraction to both sexes, most were genitally aroused by men or by women—but not both (Rieger et al., 2005). Although one study has since identified a group of men who are bisexual in their genital arousal (Rosenthal et al., 2012), a number of other findings too compel the conclusion that women are sexually more flexible than men, having more *erotic plasticity.* Simply put, women are more open and more likely to change sexual preferences over the course of a lifetime (Baumeister, 2000; Diamond, 2007; Peplau, 2003; Lippa, 2006).

A second complicating factor is that although there is strong evidence for a biological disposition, this does not necessarily mean that there's a "gay gene" (Hamer et al., 1999). Rather, Daryl Bem (1996; 2000) sees the development of sexual orientation as a *psycho*biological process. According to Bem, genes influence a person's temperament at birth, leading some infants and young children to be naturally more active, energetic, and aggressive than others. These differences in temperament draw some children to male playmates and "masculine" activities and others to female playmates and "feminine" activities. Bem refers to children who prefer same-sex playmates as gender conformists and to those who prefer opposite-sex playmates as gender nonconformists ("sissies" and "tomboys").

Activity preferences in childhood may be biologically rooted, but what happens next is the psychological part. According to Bem, gender-conforming children come to see members of the opposite sex as different, unfamiliar, arousing, and even exotic. Gender-nonconforming children, in contrast, come to see same-sex peers as different, unfamiliar, arousing, and exotic. Later, at puberty, as children become physically and sexually mature, they find that they are attracted to members of the same or opposite sex—depending on which is the more exotic. Bem describes his proposed chain of events as the "exotic becomes erotic" theory of sexual orientation.

At present, there is only sketchy support for this theory. It is true that genetic makeup can influence temperament and predispose a child to favor certain kinds of activities over others (Kagan, 1994). It is also true that gay men are likely to have been more feminine and lesbians to have been more masculine as children—differences seen not only in people's self-reported accounts from childhood (Bailey & Zucker, 1995) but also in their behavior, as memorialized in home videos (Rieger et al., 2008). It may even be true that people are genetically hardwired to engage in gender-nonconforming behavior as children (Bailey et al., 2000). But do peer preferences in childhood alter adult sexual orientation, as Bem suggests, because the exotic becomes erotic? Or is there a "gay gene" that fosters gender nonconformity in childhood as well as homosexuality in adolescence and adulthood? And can a single theory explain homosexuality in both men and women or are separate

When same-sex marriage became legal in California, in 2008, Ariel Owens and Joseph Barham were married in San Francisco (left). Little did they know, seven years later, the U.S. Supreme Court would declare same-sex marriage a constitutional right nationwide. Outside the Supreme Court, on June 26, 2015, gay rights supporters Pooja Mandagere and Natalie Thompson celebrate the historic announcement (right).

theories needed, as some have suggested (Peplau et al., 1998)? At present, more research is needed to answer these questions and tease apart the biological and psychological influences. Either way, one point looms large: People, especially men, do not seem to willfully choose their sexual orientation, nor can they easily change it.

Is there any reason to believe that the attraction process and the formation of intimate relationships are any different for same-sex couples? Not really. According to the U.S. Census Bureau, an estimated 650,000 same-sex couples were living together in the United States in 2010—up substantially from 10 years earlier. An estimated 132,000 reported that they were married. Recent research shows that gays and lesbians meet people in the same ways as straights, by seeking out others who are attractive and similar in their attitudes; that their satisfaction and commitment levels are affected by social exchange and equity concerns just as they are in heterosexual relationships; and that they report levels of liking and loving in their intimate relationships that are comparable to those in heterosexual couples. Same-sex couples differ from straight couples in two ways: They are more likely to retain friendships with former sex partners after breaking up, and they tend to divide chores more equally within a household (Kurdek, 2005; Peplau & Fingerhut, 2007).

Are the romantic relationships formed by same-sex partners as stable and long-lasting as those formed by couples of the opposite-sex? In light of the very recent acceptance and increased prevalence of same sex marriage in many U.S. states, sociologist Michael Rosenfeld (2014) analyzed a new nationally representative data set—the *How Couples Meet and Stay Together* surveys. By tracking 3,009 newly married or marriage-like couples for three years, including 471 of the same sex, Rosenfeld found that heterosexual couples overall had longer lasting relationships and a lower break-up rate (4.9%)—but that this difference vanished when only married couples were compared. The reason: The annual breakup rate was lower among same-sex couples who were married or had civil unions (2.6%) than among those who were not (12.8%). This study represents an important first step toward understanding the links between sexual orientation and long-term relationships. In light of the Supreme Court's (2015) ruling to legalize same-sex marriage, more research on gay and lesbian couples is sure to be conducted in the years to come.

The Marital Trajectory   Because we are social beings, having close relationships is important to us all—for our happiness, emotional well-being, physical health, and longevity. As noted at the start of this chapter, 73% of American college students surveyed said they would sacrifice most other life goals rather than give up a satisfying relationship (Hammersla & Frease-McMahan, 1990). Yet sadly, if they live in the United States or Canada, these students live in a society in which roughly 40% of first marriages are likely to end in divorce. With just one previously divorced partner, the odds of divorce are even greater. This discrepancy between the stability most people want and the disruption they may have to confront is dramatic. Couples argue, break up, separate, and divorce. How do marriages evolve over time, and why do some last while others dissolve?

Ellen Berscheid and Harry Reis (1998) say that for social psychologists who study intimate relationships, this is the most frequently asked and vexing question. Is there a typical developmental pattern? No and yes. No, it's clear that all marriages are different and cannot be squeezed into a single mold. But yes, certain patterns do emerge when survey results are combined from large numbers of married couples that have been studied over long periods of time. Lawrence

In 2001, the Netherlands became the first modern nation to grant same-sex marriages full legal status. Same-sex marriage has since become legal in Belgium (2003), Spain (2005), Canada (2005), South Africa (2006), Norway (2009), Sweden (2009), Portugal (2010), Iceland (2010), Argentina (2010), Denmark (2012), Brazil (2013), France (2013), Uruguay (2013), New Zealand (2013), Luxembourg (2014), United Kingdom (2014), Finland (2014), Ireland (2015), and the United States (2015).

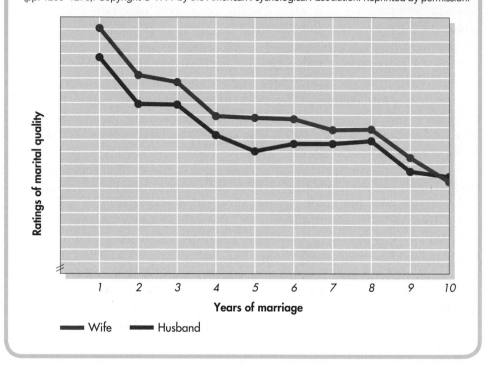

● **FIGURE 9.13**

Marital Satisfaction Over Time

In a longitudinal study that spanned 10 years, married couples rated the quality of their marriages. On average, these ratings were high, but they declined among both husbands and wives. As you can see, there were two steep drops, occurring during the first and eighth years of marriage.

From Kurdeck, L. A., "The nature and predictors of the trajectory of change in marital quality for husbands and wives over the first 10 years of marriage," *Developmental Psychology* vol 35 (pp. 1283–1296). Copyright © 1999 by the American Psychological Association. Reprinted by permission.

Kurdek (1999) reported on a longitudinal study of married couples in which he measured each spouse's satisfaction every year for 10 years (of the 522 couples he started with, 93 completed the study). ● Figure 9.13 shows that there was an overall decline in ratings of marital quality and that the ratings given by husbands and wives were very similar. There are two marked periods of decline. The first occurs during the first year of marriage. Newlyweds tend to idealize each other and to enjoy an initial state of marital bliss (Murray et al., 1996). However, this "honeymoon" is soon followed by a decline in satisfaction (Bradbury, 1998; Huston et al., 2001). After some stabilization, a second decline is observed at about the eighth year of marriage—a finding that is consistent with the popular belief in a "seven-year itch" (Kovacs, 1983).

This marital trajectory is interesting, but it represents a crude average of different types of marriages. There is no single mold, however, and one size does not fit all relationships. Realizing this limitation, researchers are actively seeking to plot more precise trend lines for specific marital situations. Thus far, for example, these studies have shown that in straight couples with a first child, the transition to parenthood hastens the sense of decline in both partners (Lawrence et al., 2008); that cohabiting gay and lesbian couples do not self-report the lowered satisfaction often seen in heterosexual couples (Kurdek, 2008); and that, despite the initial dip, marital satisfaction increases again in middle age for parents whose children grow up, leave home, and empty the nest (Gorchoff et al., 2008).

Do specific factors predict future outcomes? To address this question, Benjamin Karney and Thomas Bradbury (1995) reviewed 115 longitudinal studies of more than 45,000 married couples and found only that certain positively valued variables (education, employment, constructive behaviors, similarity in attitudes) are somewhat predictive of positive outcomes. They did find, however, that the steeper the initial decline in satisfaction, the more likely couples are to break up later. This decline is, in part, related to the stress of having and raising children, a stress that is common among newly married couples. Boredom is also predictive of a loss in marital satisfaction. In a longitudinal study of 123 married couples, husbands and wives who felt like they were in a rut at one point in time were significantly less satisfied nine years later (Tsapelas et al., 2009).

Is there anything a couple can do to avoid a rut and keep the honeymoon alive? Perhaps there is. Arthur Aron and his colleagues (2000) have theorized that after the exhilaration of a new relationship wears off, partners can combat boredom by engaging together in new and arousing activities. By means of questionnaires and a door-to-door survey, these researchers found that the more new experiences spouses said they'd had together, the more satisfied they were with their marriages. To test this hypothesis in a controlled experiment, they brought randomly selected couples into the laboratory, spread gymnasium mats across the floor, tied the partners together at a wrist and ankle, and had them crawl on their hands and knees, over a barrier, from one end of the room to the other—all while carrying a pillow between their bodies. Other couples were given the more mundane task of rolling a ball across the mat, one partner at a time. A third group received no assignment. Afterward, all participants were asked about their relationships. As predicted, the couples that had struggled and laughed their way through the novel and arousing activity reported more satisfaction with the quality of their relationships than did those in the mundane and no-task groups. It's possible that the benefit of shared participation in this study was short-lived. But maybe, just maybe, a steady and changing diet of exciting new experiences can help keep the flames of love burning.

> After the honeymoon period, there is an overall decline in levels of marital satisfaction.
>
> **TRUE**

Communication and Conflict Disagreements about children, money, sex and affection, jealousy, parents and in-laws, household chores, trust, independence, careers, and leisure time are constant issues that can stir conflict in all marriages (Lavner et al., 2014). Of particular relevance in turbulent economic times, research shows that financial pressures can put enormous amounts of strain on marital relations (Conger et al., 1999). Whatever the cause, all couples experience some degree of friction. The issue is not whether it occurs but how we respond to it. One source of conflict is the difficulty some people have talking about their disagreements. When relationships break up, communication problems are among the most common causes cited by straight and gay couples alike (Kurdek, 1991b; Sprecher, 1994). But what constitutes "bad communication"? Comparisons of happy and distressed couples have revealed a number of communication patterns that often occur in troubled relationships (Fincham, 2003).

One common pattern is called *negative affect reciprocity*—a tit-for-tat exchange of expressions of negative feelings. Generally speaking, expressions of negative affect within a couple trigger more in-kind responses than do expressions of positive affect. But negative affect reciprocity, especially in nonverbal behavior, is greater in couples that are unhappy, distressed, and locked into a duel. For couples in distress, smiles pass by unnoticed, but every glare, every disgusted look, provokes a sharp reflex-like response. The result, as observed in unhappy couples around the world, is an inability to break the vicious cycle and terminate unpleasant interactions (Gottman, 1998).

Men and women react differently to conflict. Most women report more intense emotions and are more expressive than most men (Grossman & Wood, 1993). She tells him to "warm up"; he urges her to "calm down." Thus, many unhappy marriages are also characterized by a *demand/withdraw interaction pattern*, in which the wife demands that the couple discuss the relationship problems, only to become frustrated when her husband withdraws from such discussions (Christensen & Heavey, 1993). This pattern is not unique to married couples. When dating partners were asked about how they typically deal with problems, the same demand/withdraw pattern was found (Vogel et al., 1999). According to John Gottman (1994), there is nothing wrong with either approach to dealing with conflict. The problem lies in the discrepancy—that healthy relationships are most likely when both partners have similar styles of dealing with conflict.

Whatever one's style, there are two basic approaches to reducing the negative effects of conflict. The first is so obvious that it is often overlooked: Increase rewarding behavior in other aspects of the relationship. According to Gottman and Levenson (1992), marital stability rests on a "fairly high balance of positive to negative behaviors" (p. 230). If there's conflict over one issue, partners can and should search for other ways to reward each other. As the balance of positives to negatives improves, so should overall levels of satisfaction, which can reduce conflict (Huston & Vangelisti, 1991). A second approach is to try to understand the other's point of view. Being sensitive to what the partner thinks and how he or she feels enhances the quality of the relationship (Honeycutt et al., 1993; Long & Andrews, 1990). What motivates individuals in the heat of battle to make that effort to understand? For starters, it helps if they agree that there is a communication problem.

The attributions that partners make for each other's behaviors and the willingness to forgive are correlated with the quality of their relationship (Bradbury & Fincham, 1992; Fincham et al., 2007; Harvey & Manusov, 2001). As you might expect, happy couples make *relationship-enhancing attributions:* They see the partner's undesirable behaviors as caused by factors that are situational ("a bad day"), temporary ("It'll pass"), and limited in scope ("That's just a sore spot"). Yet they perceive desirable behaviors as caused by factors that are inherent in the partner, permanent, and generalizable to other aspects of the relationship. In contrast, unhappy couples flip the attributional coin on its tail by making the opposite *distress-maintaining attributions.* Thus, whereas happy couples minimize the bad and maximize the good, distressed couples don't give an inch. In light of these differing attributional patterns, it would seem that over time happy couples would get happier and miserable couples more miserable. Do they? Yes. By tracking married couples longitudinally, researchers have found that husbands and wives who made distress-maintaining attributions early in marriage reported less satisfaction at a later point in time (Fincham et al., 2000; Karney & Bradbury, 2000).

Breaking Up When an intimate relationship ends, as in divorce, the effect can be traumatic (Fine & Harvey, 2006)—and so stressful that people who get divorced are later 23% more likely to die early from all causes of death (Sbarra et al., 2011). As part of a longitudinal study of adults in Germany, Richard Lucas (2005) zeroed in on 817 men and women who at some point were divorced. Every year for 18 years, the participants were interviewed and asked to rate how satisfied they were with life on a scale of 0 to 10. On average, the divorcees were more than a half point less satisfied than their married counterparts. But did time heal the wound? ● Figure 9.14 shows three interesting patterns: (1) Participants had become less and less satisfied even before divorce; (2) satisfaction levels rebounded somewhat immediately after divorce; and (3) satisfaction levels never returned to original baseline levels. In short, people may adapt but often they do not fully recover from the experience.

People's ability to cope with divorce depends on the nature of the loss. One vital factor is the closeness of a relationship, or the extent to which the line between self and other becomes so blurred that mine and yours are one and the same. Another factor is interdependence, the social glue that binds us together. Research shows that the more interdependent couples are (as measured by the amount of time they spend together, the activities they share, and the influence each partner has over the other) and the more invested they are in the relationship, the longer it will likely last (Berscheid et al., 1989; Rusbult & Buunk, 1993) and the more devastated they will become when it ends (Fine & Sacher, 1997; Simpson, 1987).

In trying to explain how people regulate the risks of involvement in close romantic relationships, Murray and her colleagues (2006) note that an ironic theme runs through much of the research: "The relationships that have the most potential to satisfy adult needs for interpersonal connection are the very relationships that activate the most anxiety about rejection" (p. 661). We are, to put it mildly, darned if we do and darned if we don't. The factors that contribute to the endurance of a relationship (closeness and interdependence) turn out to be the same factors that intensify the fear of rejection and make coping more difficult after a relationship ends. So, how do you balance making the psychological investment necessary for a lasting relationship against holding back enough for self-protection?

In the United States and other Western countries, various demographic markers indicate how problematic traditional forms of commitment have become: A high divorce rate, more single-parent families, more unmarried couples living together, and more never-married individuals. Yet the desire for long-term intimate relationships has never wavered or disappeared. On the contrary, people spend millions of dollars on online dating sites, gays and lesbians actively seek legal recognition of same-sex marriages, the vast majority of divorced individuals remarry, and stepfamilies forge a new sense of what it means to be a "family." It seems that we are in the midst of a great and compelling search as millions of men and women try to find ways to affiliate with, attract, get closer to, love, and commit themselves with permanence to other.

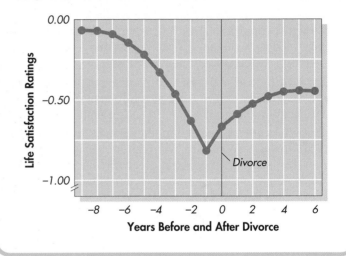

● FIGURE 9.14

Changes in Life Satisfaction Before and After Divorce

In this study, 817 men and women who were divorced at some point rated how satisfied they were with life on a scale of 0 to 10 every year for 18 years. Overall, divorcees were less satisfied than their married counterparts—a common result. On the question of whether time heals the wound, you can see that satisfaction levels dipped before divorce and rebounded afterward, but did not return to original levels. It appears that people adapt but do not fully recover from this experience. Lucas, 2005.

Review

Top 10 Key Points in Chapter 9

1. The need to belong is a fundamental human motive, a pervasive drive to form and maintain lasting relationships.

2. Although people differ in the strength of the affiliation needs, people who are painfully shy may suffer from loneliness, which is an unhealthy state.

3. Beauty being a social asset, attractive people are more popular, socially skilled, and sexually experienced—but they are not happier or higher in self-esteem.

4. Although beauty is partly in the eye of the beholder and influenced by culture and context, certain types of faces—for example, those that are symmetrical from left to right—are considered attractive across cultures and to infants as well as adults.

5. During the process of getting acquainted, people tend to like others who are similar in their backgrounds, attitudes, interests, values, and levels of physical attractiveness.

6. Evolutionary psychologists have found that whereas men seek out women who are young and attractive, attributes that signal health and fertility, women seek men who are older and have financial security or attributes predictive of future success.

7. As predicted by Equity Theory, people seek not only to maximize benefits and minimize losses in their relationships but to ensure that the ratio of benefits to costs are equivalent for both partners.

8. It is important to distinguish passionate love, an intense, emotional, often erotic state; and companionate love, which is less intense but deeper and more enduring.

9. Both biological and developmental theories explain the origins of a homosexual orientation, which exclusively characterizes 3-4% of men and 2% of women (the incidence of homosexual behaviors is higher).

10. Longitudinal studies of couples indicate that while there is an average decline in satisfaction over time, until relationships stabilize, marital satisfaction is influenced by many extraneous factors (such as children, economics, and patterns of conflict and communication).

Putting Common Sense to the Test

Need to Belong: A Fundamental Human Motive

People seek out the company of others, even strangers, in times of stress.

Ⓣ **True.** *Research has shown that external threat causes stress and leads people to affiliate with others who are facing or have faced a similar threat.*

The Initial Attraction

Infants do not discriminate between faces considered attractive and unattractive in their culture.

Ⓕ **False.** *Two-month-old infants spend more time gazing at attractive than unattractive faces, indicating that they do make the distinction.*

People who are physically attractive are happier and have higher self-esteem than those who are unattractive.

Ⓕ **False.** *Attractive people are at an advantage in their social lives, but they are not happier, better adjusted, or higher in self-esteem.*

When it comes to romantic relationships, opposites attract.

Ⓕ **False.** *Consistently, people are attracted to others who are similar—not opposite or complementary—on a whole range of dimensions.*

Close Relationships

Men are more likely than women to interpret friendly gestures by the opposite sex in sexual terms.

(T) **True.** *Experiments have shown that men are more likely than women to interpret friendly interactions with members of the opposite sex as sexual come-ons.*

After the honeymoon period, there is an overall decline in levels of marital satisfaction.

(T) **True.** *High marital satisfaction levels among newlyweds are often followed by a measurable decline during the first year and then, after a period of stabilization, by another decline at the eighth year—a pattern found among parents and nonparents alike.*

Key Terms

attachment style (387)

communal relationship (387)

companionate love (390)

equity theory (386)

exchange relationship (387)

excitation transfer (391)

hard-to-get effect (374)

intimate relationship (383)

loneliness (356)

matching hypothesis (372)

mere exposure effect (360)

need for affiliation (354)

passionate love (390)

reciprocity (373)

self-disclosure (393)

sexual orientation (398)

social exchange theory (384)

triangular theory of love (390)

what-is-beautiful-is-good stereotype (367)

Helping Others

This chapter describes the social psychology of giving and receiving help. We examine the evolutionary, motivational, situational, personal, and interpersonal factors that predict whether a potential helper will provide assistance to a person in need. In the concluding section, we discuss the helping connection, the role of social ties in promoting helpfulness to others.

It was their bravery

that compelled them to risk their lives, but it was their compassion that ultimately saved them. Six firefighters from New York City's Ladder Company 6 were among the many rescue workers who courageously climbed up the stairs of the World Trade Center on September 11, 2001. The jets that had flown into each of the Twin Towers of the skyscraper were hemorrhaging fuel, causing an inferno of unprecedented proportion. A massive stream of people trying to flee raced down the narrow stairs, passing the firefighters who were going up. Awed by their courage and resolve, people yelled encouragement and blessings to the firefighters as they passed them. Under the burden of more than 100 pounds of equipment, the men of Ladder Company 6 had reached the 27th floor of the North Tower when they heard the horrifying sound of the South Tower collapsing. Their captain ordered them to turn back, realizing that if the other tower could collapse, so could theirs.

On their way down, around the 14th or 15th floor, they encountered a frail woman named Josephine Harris. She had walked down almost 60 flights already, and she was exhausted. The firefighters helped her walk, but she was slowing them down dangerously. Their captain, John Jonas, was growing more anxious: "I could hear the clock ticking in the back of my head. I'm thinking, 'C'mon, c'mon. We've got to keep moving.'" But none of the six men considered leaving her behind, so they slowly walked down together. Josephine didn't think she could go on, but one of the firefighters asked her about her family and told her that her children and grandchildren wanted to see her again. She continued but finally collapsed as they got near the fourth floor. On the fourth floor, they tried to find a chair to carry her in. And then, the 110-story skyscraper collapsed all around them.

Other rescue workers who had passed this slow-moving group on the stairs were killed on the floors below them. Virtually everyone who was still above them was killed. And yet somehow this group survived, trapped in an inexplicable pocket of safety amid the unimaginable wreckage, along with two other firefighters, a fire department chief, and a Port Authority police officer. After a harrowing search for a way out, they eventually found a small ray of light—a literal ray of hope—and followed it to safety.

The firefighters later called Josephine Harris their guardian angel and thanked *her* for saving *their* lives. They realized that had they not encountered her, they would have gone down the stairs faster, and had she not kept walking despite exhaustion, they would have been a few floors above. Either way, they would have been killed. But Josephine Harris knew that she owed her life to these brave men who risked not seeing their own children again so that she could see hers.

There were many other heroes that day, including ordinary citizens whose acts of self-sacrifice to help others were not part of their job descriptions. Some of the help was dramatically heroic, like that of the passengers aboard hijacked United Airlines Flight 93. They decided to fight the terrorists on their flight and sacrifice their

Putting COMMON SENSE to the Test

Circle Your Answer

T   F   People are more likely to help someone in an emergency if the potential rewards seem high and the potential costs seem low.

T   F   In an emergency, a person who needs help has a much better chance of getting it if three other people are present than if only one other person is present.

T   F   People are much more likely to help someone when they're in a good mood.

T   F   People are much less likely to help someone when they're in a bad mood.

T   F   Attractive people have a better chance than unattractive people of getting help when they need it.

T   F   Women seek help more often than men do.

own lives in order to try to prevent the terrorists from killing many more people on the ground. And much of the help was behind the scenes, as in the cases of people who volunteered endless hours to do the grueling work of cleaning up the disaster area, helping the injured and the grieving, and donating money, clothes, and other resources.

When people read stories such as these, it is natural for them to wonder what they would have done: Would they have risked their lives to help others? What makes some people, at some times, act to help others? The wonderful acts of helping during the chaos of 9/11 are inspiring, to be sure. But there were also many stories that day of people who turned their backs on others, even on people who had just helped them.

Every day there are numerous unheralded acts of helping others and of failing to help others. A volunteer works tirelessly in a health clinic, a college student tutors a child, a congregation raises money for a charity, an older sister lets her little brother win at checkers. And yet every day someone ignores the screams outside his or her window, drives past motorists stranded on the side of a road, or tries to avoid making eye contact with a homeless person on the street.

Neville Elder/Corbis

Firefighter Mike Kehoe holds a photo taken of himself a few months before that became a famous symbol of heroism: He is seen in the photo walking up the stairs of one of the towers of the World Trade Center to help with the rescue efforts during the terrorist attacks on the morning of September 11, 2001, despite the enormous danger he knew he would be facing.

Every few months we see a story like that of Ismael Jimenez, an 18-year-old on a school trip in April 2014. The bus he and his classmates were on was hit by a truck and burst into flames. He busted open a window at the front of the bus and spent his last moments alive lifting children out of the bus rather than saving himself (Serna & Megerian, 2014). And we learn about someone like Jena Meaux, who in July 2015 jumped in front of a friend to protect her from a man's shooting rampage in a movie theater in Louisiana. Meaux was shot in the leg, apparently saving her friend's life (Schapiro, 2015).

And all too often we also learn stories like what happened on a beach in Panama City, Florida in March 2015. A group of men in broad daylight sexually assaulted a young woman passed out on the beach, which was filled with hundreds of others celebrating spring break. Many took video of the incident. Not a single person came to her aid or called the police. A sheriff described it as the "most disgusting, sickening thing" he's ever seen (Golgowski, 2015).

These stories are by no means limited to the United States. For example, consider these two incidents from China's Guangdong province. In June 2012 a toddler fell through an opening in a window ledge on the fourth floor of his apartment building and dangled by his neck on the metal grating of a ledge used to hold plants. One of the residents of the building heard the boy's screams, climbed through a window on the floor below, and inched his way up until he could help relieve the pressure on the child's neck and wait for rescue workers to arrive. The fate of another toddler from the same province several months before was far, far worse, however. An absolutely horrifying video from a surveillance camera captured the scene of a 2-year-old girl run over by a van on a narrow road. As the girl lay under the van, the driver stopped the car for a few seconds and then drove on, running her over again with a back tire. More than a dozen people walked or drove past the gravely injured girl for about seven minutes. A second vehicle—a truck—ran over her crushed body. Finally, a woman checked on her and pulled her away,

A 2-year-old girl named Wang Yue lies on a narrow road in Guangdong, China, in October 2011, after getting run over by a van. For several horrifying minutes more than a dozen people passed by the gravely injured girl without checking on her, including the man seen in this photo. While lying in the street she was run over by a second vehicle. She died just over a week later. As discussed in this chapter, this kind of inaction by bystanders is all too common.

AP Images/Kyodo

just before the girl's mother arrived. The girl died more than a week later (Blanchard, 2011).

There is no simple answer to the question of why some people help and others don't or why some situations lead to quick assistance and others to shocking displays of inaction. The determinants of helping behavior are complex and multifaceted. But social psychologists have learned a great deal about these determinants—and therefore about human nature. As you will see in the pages to come, some of their findings are quite surprising.

In this chapter, we examine several questions about helping: *Why* do people help? *When* do they help? *Who* is likely to help? *Whom* do they help? The concluding section concentrates on a major recurring theme—social connection—that underlies much of the theory and research on helping.

Evolutionary and Motivational Factors: Why Do People Help?

Although few individuals reach the heights of heroic helping, virtually everyone helps somebody sometime. People give their friends a ride to the airport; donate money, food, and clothing for disaster relief; babysit for a relative; work as a volunteer for charitable activities; pick up the mail for a neighbor who's out of town. The list of **prosocial behaviors**—actions intended to benefit others—is endless. But *why* do people help? We examine this question from a variety of perspectives, from principles of evolution to trying to change a rotten mood.

■ Evolutionary Factors in Helping

prosocial behaviors Actions intended to benefit others.

We begin with evolution. From an evolutionary perspective, what possible function can there be in helping others, especially at the risk of one's own life? Doesn't risking one's life for others fly in the face of evolutionary principles such as "survival of the fittest"?

The "Selfish Gene" In fact, as the title of the classic book, *The Selfish Gene*, by evolutionary biologist Richard Dawkins (1976, 2006) suggests, evolutionary perspectives emphasize not the survival of the fittest individuals but the survival of the individuals' *genes*. If a specific behavior enhances reproductive success, then the genetic underpinnings of that behavior are more likely to be passed on to subsequent generations. In this way, the behavior can eventually become part of the common inheritance of the species (Hamilton, 1964). The behavior of helping others could have served the function of preserving individuals' genes by promoting the survival of those who share their genetic makeup. By means of this indirect route to genetic survival, the tendency to help genetic relatives, called **kin selection**, could become an innate characteristic of humans. In fact, kin selection is evident in the behavior of many organisms. For example, just as humans often risk their lives to save close relatives, ground squirrels, capuchin monkeys, and many other mammals and birds emit an alarm to warn nearby relatives of a predator. The alarm helps their relatives but makes the individual who sounds the alarm more vulnerable to attack (Freeberg et al., 2014; Hollén & Radford, 2009; Schel et al., 2009).

Because kin selection serves the function of genetic survival, preferential helping of genetic relatives should be strongest when the biological stakes are particularly high. This appears to be the case (Burnstein et al., 1994; Stewart-Williams, 2007). For example, participants in a study by Carey Fitzgerald and Stephen Colarelli (2009) were asked how willing they would be to offer different kinds of help to a friend, a half-sibling, or a sibling. There were three levels of helping behavior: the lowest risk involved picking up items from a store for the person; the medium risk involved loaning the person $10,000; and the highest risk involved trying to rescue the person from a burning house.

As can be seen in ● Figure 10.1, for the lowest-risk helping scenario, participants rated themselves as likely to help a friend as a sibling. For the higher-risk scenarios, however, they were significantly more willing to help a sibling than a friend. Their willingness to help a half-sibling fell in between their willingness to help a friend and their willingness to help a sibling.

In a later study, Fitzgerald and others (2010) found that under low-risk scenarios participants were more likely to help romantic partners than siblings, and they were as willing to help romantic partners with whom they had no biological children as they were to help those with whom they did. Under high-risk situations, however, participants became more likely to help siblings and romantic partners with whom they had biological children, but less willing to help romantic partners with whom they had no children or had adopted

According to the National Philanthropic Trust, Americans gave $358.38 billion to charity in 2014. Individuals comprised 72% of the total giving.

kin selection Preferential helping of genetic relatives, which results in the greater likelihood that genes held in common will survive.

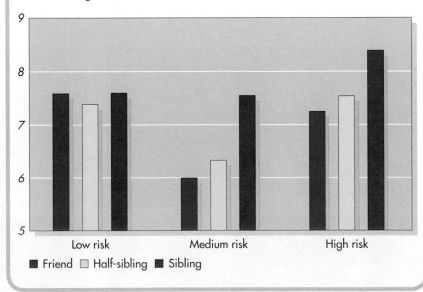

● **FIGURE 10.1**

Helping Kin When Risks Are High

Participants indicated how willing they would be to offer different types of help to a friend, a half-sibling, or a sibling. For the low-risk helping, participants were as willing to help a friend as they were to help a sibling. For high-risk helping, in contrast, they were more willing to help a sibling than a friend, with willingness to help a half-sibling coming in the middle. Based on Fitzgerald, 2009.

children. In other words, under high-risk scenarios, genetic relatedness became more important in decisions about helping.

Reciprocal Altruism Even though relatives may get preferential treatment, most people help out non-kin as well. What's the reproductive advantage of helping someone who isn't related to you? The most common answer is reciprocity. Through **reciprocal altruism**, helping someone else can be in your best interests because it increases the likelihood that you will be helped in return (Krebs, 1987; Trivers, 1985). If A helps B and B helps A, both A and B may increase their chances of survival and reproductive success. Over the course of evolution, therefore, individuals who engage in reciprocal altruism should survive and reproduce more than individuals who do not, thus enabling this kind of altruism to flourish.

Robert Trivers (1971) cited several examples of reciprocal altruism in animals. Many animals groom each other; for instance, monkeys groom other monkeys and cats groom other cats. Large fish (such as groupers) allow small fish (such as wrasses) to swim in their mouths without eating them; the small fish get food for themselves and at the same time remove parasites from the larger fish. Frans de Waal has observed thousands of interactions among chimpanzees and seen how chimps who share with other chimps at one feeding are repaid by the other chimps at another feeding; those who are selfish are rebuffed, sometimes violently, at a later feeding (de Waal, 1996, 2008, 2013). What's more, de Waal has observed more complicated forms of reciprocation. If Chimp A groomed Chimp B, for instance, B became much more likely to then share his or her food with A. Similar types of behaviors among capuchin monkeys have also been recorded (Tiddi et al., 2011).

It's interesting that these chimps and monkeys were able to negotiate this kind of reciprocity across acts: in grooming and food sharing. Chimpanzees have also been reported sharing plants and tools (Pruetz & Lindshield, 2012). It is as if these primates often operate under a norm of "You scratch my back, I'll scratch yours—or maybe I'll give you some of my apples." This more complicated reciprocation is not uncommon. For example, in a meta-analysis of studies involving 14 different primate species, Gabriele Schino (2007) found evidence that grooming is reciprocated with support in fights (against some other individual). You scratch my back and I'll have your back in a fight! A more charming type of reciprocation was reported by Barbara Tiddi and her colleagues (2010). They report that capuchin mothers allow other females to handle their infants (which young capuchin females apparently love to do) in exchange for being groomed by them.

"Scratch my back and I'll scratch yours."

—Proverb

reciprocal altruism Altruism that involves an individual helping another (despite some immediate risk or cost) and becoming more likely to receive help from the other in return.

Many animals groom each other, whether they are chimpanzees in Tanzania or young girls in the United States. According to evolutionary psychologists, such behavior often reflects reciprocal altruism.

Learning to cooperate, therefore, can be rewarding for both parties. One clever study that illustrates this was conducted by Frans de Waal and Michelle Berger (2000). They observed same-sex pairs of capuchin monkeys working cooperatively in a test chamber to obtain a tray of food. The two monkeys were separated from each other by a mesh partition. One monkey by itself could not pull the tray, but the two monkeys could accomplish the task if they cooperated. When successful, the monkey that wound up with the food consistently shared it with its helper. When they were rewarded in this way, the monkeys became even more likely to help each other on subsequent occasions.

Animals also go beyond direct reciprocity and sometimes show **indirect reciprocity**, through which an individual who has helped someone becomes more likely to be helped by someone else. In other words, A helps B, and C (who saw A's helpful behavior toward B) then helps A. Through indirect reciprocity cooperation among many members of a group can be established (Roberts, 2015). For it to flourish, individuals in the group are rewarded by others for being helpful and punished for being selfish. Consistent with this point, studies have shown that even monkeys and human infants show reliable preferences for individuals they've observed being helpful to others (Anderson et al., 2013; Hamlin, 2013, 2015; Rand & Nowak, 2013). And animals from reef fish to chimpanzees and humans have been shown to punish individuals they've seen failing to help others, often through social exclusion (dos Santos & Wedekind, 2015; Kurzban et al., 2015; Sasaki & Uchida, 2013).

Reciprocal altruism is not restricted to basic needs such as safety and food acquisition. Think of file sharing instead of food sharing. Swapping music and movies online through file-sharing services may be considered a form of reciprocal altruism, since an individual makes his or her own files available to others so that he or she can have access to theirs. (Of course, record companies and movie studios have other terms for these activities, such as *criminal* and *unethical*.) Strong norms often develop in these peer-to-peer networks. Individuals who download songs or videos from others but don't make their own files available are likely to be chastised emphatically.

The Evolution of Empathy

Helping, of course, can go beyond assisting kin or members of one's own group. Consider the story of Binti Jua, for example. At the end of 1996, *People* magazine honored her as one of the 25 "most intriguing people" of the year, and *Newsweek* named her "hero of the year." Earlier that year while caring for her own 17-month-old daughter, Binti came across a 3-year-old boy who had fallen almost 20 feet onto a cement floor and been knocked unconscious. She picked up the boy and gently held him, rocking him softly, and then turned him over to paramedics. What was most "intriguing" about Binti? The fact that she was a gorilla.

When the boy climbed over a fence and fell into the primate exhibit at the Brookfield Zoo, near Chicago, witnesses feared the worst. One paramedic said, "I didn't know if she was going to treat him like a doll or a toy." With her own daughter clinging to her back the entire time, Binti "protected the toddler as if he were her own," keeping other gorillas at bay and eventually placing him gently at the entrance where zookeepers and paramedics could get to him. "I could not believe how gentle she was," observed a zoo director (O'Neill et al., 1996, p. 72).

Was this an act of kindness and compassion, or did the gorilla just do what she had been trained to do—pick up and fetch things dropped into her cage? Cases

indirect reciprocity A kind of reciprocal altruism in which an individual who helps someone becomes more likely to receive help from someone else.

AP Images/WLS-TV

Binti Jua, a gorilla at the Brookfield Zoo, near Chicago, gently rocks a 3-year-old boy who had fallen 18 feet into the primate exhibit. The gorilla was acclaimed as a hero for her role in saving the boy. Did Binti Jua act out of kindness and empathy? Or did she simply do what she was taught—fetch objects that fall into her cage? This episode brings the altruism debate to life, even in the animal world.

empathy Understanding or vicariously experiencing another individual's perspective and feeling sympathy and compassion for that individual.

like this raise the more fundamental question of whether concepts such as morality and empathy can apply to nonhuman animals. Most people think of these as qualities that allow humans to resist and rise above our more selfish, violent, "animal" nature, but instead they may reflect the social nature of many mammals, and particularly primates. In order to live successfully in small groups, it was important for social animals to develop some sense of the proper way to behave in groups and an ability to recognize and respond to danger or suffering in other group members. Humans certainly have much more highly developed moral reasoning and capacity for empathy, but their moral roots can be traced down the evolutionary chain (de Waal, 2014).

We will see in several places throughout this chapter the critically important role that **empathy** plays in helping. Unfortunately, the exact definition of empathy is much debated; for example, Dan Batson (2009b) identified no fewer than eight distinct definitions of empathy that scholars use. Most researchers regard empathy as having both a cognitive component of understanding the emotional experience of another individual and an emotional experience that is consistent with what the other is feeling (Decety & Cowell, 2015; Eisenberg et al., 2015). A major cognitive component of empathy is *perspective taking:* using the power of imagination to try to see the world through someone else's eyes. A key emotional component of empathy is *empathic concern,* which involves other-oriented feelings, such as sympathy, compassion, and tenderness.

Although higher-order cognitive aspects of empathy are specific to humans, other animals show evidence of empathy in a variety of ways. Frans de Waal (2008, 2013), has cited numerous and startling examples of primates such as chimpanzees and bonobos seeming to show empathy. ● Figure 10.2 depicts a juvenile chimpanzee putting an arm around an adult male who had just been defeated in a fight. This kind of consoling behavior is not uncommon in chimpanzees, and it has been shown to reduce the recipient's arousal. de Waal also reports examples of chimpanzees who risked their lives trying to save companions from drowning, even though they themselves were unable to swim. Less dramatically, young chimps have been seen helping to push an old and arthritic group member up onto a climbing frame for a grooming session. The examples de Waal has collected suggest at least some degree of perspective taking and sympathy among nonhuman primates. Some research suggests that even rodents show evidence of being sensitive to the pain of other individuals of their species (Jensen et al., 2014).

Very young human infants show signs of being affected by the distress of others and, by their first birthday, begin to comfort victims of distress (Decety et al., 2011; Hamlin, 2013). In one particularly interesting study, Felix Warneken and Michael Tomasello (2006) placed 18-month-old human infants with an adult experimenter. At various points in time, the experimenter appeared to have trouble reaching a goal. For example, he accidentally dropped a marker on the floor and tried unsuccessfully to reach it, or he couldn't put some magazines into a cabinet because the doors were closed. Twenty-two of the 24 infants tested in the study helped the experimenter in at least one of the tasks, and many infants helped on several tasks. In doing so, the infants apparently understood that the experimenter needed help—that is, that he was having trouble completing a task by himself.

Two additional details are worth noting about the study. First, the experimenter never requested help from the infants, nor did he praise or reward the infants when they did help. Second, for every task he needed help with, the experimenter created a similar situation in which he did not seem to have a problem. For example, rather than accidentally drop the marker on the floor and try to reach it, the experimenter sometimes intentionally threw the marker on the floor and did not try to retrieve it. In these situations, the infants were not likely to take action such as picking up the marker. This suggested that when they did help the experimenter, the infants did so because they understood he was trying to achieve some goal.

The researchers also tested three young chimpanzees using a similar procedure. The chimpanzees also helped the human experimenter when they saw that he appeared to need help reaching his goal, although not across as many tasks or as reliably as the human infants did.

Neuroscience research supports the idea that the capacity for empathy is part of our biology. Seeing someone else experience positive or negative emotion triggers in an empathic perceiver's brain activation of neural structures associated with the actual experience of that emotion. This activation, in turn, predicts individuals' tendencies to actually engage in everyday helping behavior (Lamm et al., 2011; Morelli et al., 2014). In addition, the hormone oxytocin—which is well known as being involved in mother–infant attachment as well as in bonding between mating pairs—is implicated in empathy and prosocial behaviors (Uzefovsky et al., 2015; Weisman et al., 2015).

An important characteristic of mammals related to empathy is how much care their offspring require to survive. Caregivers must understand the emotional communications from their young and respond to their emotional needs. The gorilla Binti Jua very well may have been acting on maternal caregiving impulses as she gently held the little boy who had fallen into her area. The importance of caring for offspring may have played a critical role in the evolution of empathy (Batson, 2011; Decety & Svetlova, 2012). According to anthropologist Judith Burkart (2014), a key feature in human evolution was when our hominin ancestors began to raise their offspring cooperatively, with fathers, siblings, aunts, and others occasionally helping to support the helpless infant rather than just the mother. This set the foundation for what Burkart calls the "hyper-cooperation" that is characteristic of humans (Burkart et al., 2014).

● **FIGURE 10.2**

Consolation in Chimps

A juvenile chimpanzee puts an arm around an adult male who has just lost a fight. Frans de Waal has observed many such acts of consoling behavior among apes.
Frans B. M. de Waal, 2008

"Charity begins at home but shouldn't end there."
—Scottish proverb

■ Rewards of Helping: Helping Others to Help Oneself

People are more likely to help someone in an emergency if the potential rewards seem high and the potential costs seem low.

TRUE

The theorizing and research discussed above help solve the mystery of how altruism could have evolved despite it putting individuals at risk of injury or death. Working cooperatively and helping others can help the individual—or the individuals' genes— through kin selection, reciprocal altruism, protection against predators, and so on. In contemporary life, the rewards of helping others can be psychological as well as material. We all like the idea of being the hero, lifted onto the shoulders of our peers for coming to the rescue of someone in distress. The potential rewards of helping, however, can be offset with significant costs. In this section we discuss some of these rewards, and costs, of helping today.

Feeling Good   Imagine someone hands you $20 and gives you one rule: You have to spend it on yourself by the end of the day. Sweet, right? OK, imagine instead that your instruction is that you have to spend it on someone else. Nice, but not quite as sweet a deal for you, right? When Elizabeth Dunn and colleagues (2008) asked people which would make them happier, most people said they'd be happier spending the money on themselves. But in a clever set of studies across several cultures and age groups, the researchers actually gave people money with one of those two sets of instructions, and they found that people who spent the money on others were significantly happier than those who purchased something for themselves. This held true across a wide variety of age groups and cultures, even in places in which resources were very limited (Aknin et al., 2015; Dunn et al., 2014) (see ● Figure 10.3).

The simple but important point is: Helping often feels good. A growing body of research reveals a strong relationship between giving help and feeling better, including improvements in mental *and* physical health (Dillard et al., 2008; Omoto et al., 2009; Mojza et al., 2011; Piliavin & Siegl, 2008; Post, 2005). Social neuroscience research provides additional evidence for the rewarding feeling of helping. Numerous studies have shown that engaging in altruistic behavior—even though it costs the self—activates areas of the brain associated with receiving actual material rewards (Moll et al., 2006; Rilling & Sanfey, 2011).

In their **negative state relief model**, Robert Cialdini and his colleagues (1987) propose that because of this positive effect of helping, people who are feeling bad are inclined to help others in order to improve their mood. People who have experienced traumatic events, for example, show mental and physical health benefits from helping others (Frazier et al, 2013; Vollhardt & Staub, 2011; Wayment, 2004).

The relationship between helping and feeling good might be a psychological universal. Looking at 136 countries across the world, Lara Aknin and her colleagues (2013) found a positive correlation between donating money and happiness in the majority of the countries. They found that altogether, charitable giving had twice the association with happiness as income did. According to

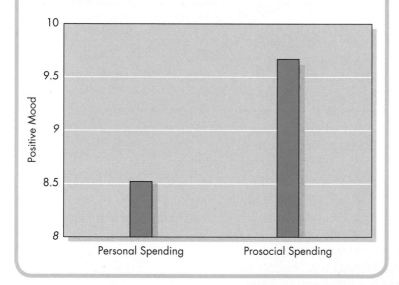

● **FIGURE 10.3**

The Joy of Giving

Adults living in villages on Vanuatu, a small island nation in the South Pacific, were given vouchers and randomly assigned to use the vouchers to purchase candy (a rare commodity in the village) for themselves or for someone else. The participants exhibited more positive mood if they purchased the candy for someone else than if they purchased it for themselves.
Based on Aknin et al., 2015

"Doing good is the only certainly happy action of a man's life."
— Sir Philip Sidney

negative state relief model   The proposition that people help others in order to counteract their own feelings of sadness.

their analysis, people who do not donate their money would have to be twice as rich to have the same predicted amount of happiness. Furthermore, when they asked participants in Canada, Uganda, and India (a diverse bunch) to think about a time they spent money on someone else, they were subsequently happier than those asked to think about a time they spent money on themselves.

Even when the costs of helping are high enough that it doesn't feel good immediately, it can pay off in the long run. When parents reluctantly sacrifice relaxing with a good book or movie at the end of a hard day in order to help their child finish some homework, they might not feel immediate joy from giving help, but in the long run, they can expect to reap the benefits of their behavior (Salovey et al., 1991).

A volunteer helps in the fight against the deadly Ebola virus in the West African nation, Sierra Leone, in September 2014. Volunteering one's time, energy, and skills to help others can be exhausting and even dangerous, but it can also be extremely rewarding.

The Cost of Helping or of Not Helping

Clearly helping has its rewards, but it has its costs as well. The firefighters in Ladder Company 6 who somehow survived the collapse of the North Tower of the World Trade Center while saving Josephine Harris were among the lucky ones. Many people were killed while helping others that day, such as Abraham Zelmanowitz, a computer programmer who refused to leave his quadriplegic friend who could not descend the stairs. And beyond 9/11, we often are moved by stories of the costs paid by those who offer help, such as Donald Liu, who in August 2012 saw two boys swept up by rip tides in Lake Michigan and swam in to save them, despite the protests from his own children about the dangerous conditions. The boys were saved, but the 50-year-old chief of pediatric surgery at the University of Chicago and father of three young children did not survive (Dizikes & Sobol, 2012).

"When you give to someone else, you get so much more."
—Former U.S. Secretary of State Colin Powell

Other helpers have done more sustained and deliberate helping, such as the people who helped hide runaway slaves in the nineteenth-century United States or the people who helped hide Jews during the Holocaust. Sharon Shepela and others (1999) call this type of thoughtful helping in the face of potentially enormous costs *courageous resistance.* And although giving help is often associated with positive affect and health, when the help involves constant and exhausting demands, which is often the case when taking long-term care of a very ill person, the effects on helpers' physical and mental health—as well as on their financial security—can be quite negative (Earle & Heymann, 2012; Fujino & Okamura, 2009; Miller, 2011; Mioshi et al., 2009).

Rescue workers risk their lives regularly despite the potential costs involved in their jobs.

Although some people sometimes help despite tremendous risk, most people often seem to conduct a cost–benefit analysis before deciding whether or not to help (Dovidio et al., 2006; Fischer et al., 2011; Fritzsche et al., 2000). To lower some of the costs of helping, some legislatures have created "Good Samaritan" laws that encourage

Liz Wallace and Mallory Holtman carry their opponent, Sara Tucholosky, around the bases in their college softball tournament game. After hitting the first home run of her career, Tucholosky injured her knee and could not run around the bases to complete the run, and her teammates and coaches were not allowed to help her and preserve the home run. Despite costing their own team a run, Wallace and Holtman volunteered to help her around the bases in an inspiring act of altruism.

"The charity that hastens to pro-claim its good deeds, ceases to be a charity, and is only pride and ostentation."

—William Hutton

egoistic Motivated by the desire to improve one's own welfare.

altruistic Motivated by the desire to improve another's welfare.

bystanders to intervene in emergencies by offering them legal protection, such as for doctors who volunteer medical care when they happen upon emergencies, or for people who otherwise would worry about criminal prosecution if they call the police to report a drug overdose (Albert, 2015; Arditi, 2015). Other kinds of Good Samaritan laws increase the costs of failing to help. Sometimes called "duty to rescue" laws, these laws require people to provide or summon aid in an emergency, so long as they do not endanger themselves in the process. In the United States, this kind of duty to rescue law is relatively rare, but they are more common in Europe and Canada.

■ Altruism or Egoism: The Great Debate

We have documented some of the ways that helping others can help the helper. This raises a classic question, however: Are our helpful behaviors always **egoistic**—motivated by selfish concerns? Or are humans ever truly **altruistic**—motivated by the desire to increase another's welfare? Many psychological theories assume an egoistic, self-interested bottom line. It is not difficult to imagine egoistic interpretations for almost any acts of helping, even the most seemingly altruistic ones. Tutoring the disadvantaged? It will look good on your résumé or college application. Anonymously helping the homeless? It reduces your guilt. Donating blood to people you'll never know? It makes you feel a bit more noble. Risking your life for a stranger? Such heroism may benefit your reputation and status. So is all helping at some level egoistic?

Daniel Batson (2009a, 2011) thinks not. As we will see in the following section, he believes that the motivation behind some helpful actions is truly altruistic and that empathy plays a critically important role in it.

The Empathy–Altruism Hypothesis Batson's model of altruism is based on his view of the consequences of empathy. According to Batson, if you perceive someone in need and imagine how *that person* feels, you are likely to experience other-oriented feelings of empathic concern (similar to what some call *compassion*—DeSteno, 2015), which in turn produce the altruistic motive to reduce the other person's distress. There are, however, instances in which people perceive someone in need and focus on their *own* feelings about this person or on how *they* would feel in that person's situation. Although many people (and some researchers) may think of this as empathy, Batson contrasts this with instances in which people's concern is with how the *other person* is feeling. It's when your focus is on the other person that true altruism is possible.

A story that may illustrate empathic concern occurred during a college softball tournament game between Central Washington and Western Oregon in April 2008. In the second inning, a short, "really tiny" senior named Sara Tucholsky shocked everyone by hitting the first home run of her career. In her excitement she missed touching first base, and when she turned to go back and touch it, she tore a ligament in her knee and crumpled to the ground in agony. There was no way she could run around the bases. Her coach talked with officials about what to do. They said that no one from her team could help her around the bases and that she would have to be replaced and the home run would not count. Then someone stepped in and asked, "Excuse me, would it be OK if we carried her around and she touched each bag?"

It was the star hitter from the opposing team, Mallory Holtman. Mallory and one of her teammates, Liz Wallace, carried Sara around the diamond, lowering her enough at each base to allow her to touch it so that she could preserve the one and only home run of her softball career. They did this despite the fact that it would cost their own team a run in a close and important game—a game they would ultimately lose by just two runs, thereby ending their season. According to Mallory, she didn't do it for any glory. Indeed, she couldn't understand why people made a fuss about it afterward. "Everyone else would have done it," she said (Hays, 2008). It is impossible to know from a story like this exactly what factors could have motivated the helping behavior, but clearly some degree of taking the other person's perspective and feeling sympathy for her were crucial elements behind Mallory Holtman's decision to help her fallen opponent.

The basic features of Batson's **empathy–altruism hypothesis** are outlined in ● Figure 10.4. The hard part, though, is this: How can we tell the difference between egoistic and altruistic motives? In both cases, people help someone else, but the helpers' reasons are different. Confronted with this puzzle, Batson came up with an elegant solution. When a person's motive is egoistic, helping should decline if it's easy for the individual to escape from the situation and therefore escape from his or her own feelings of distress. When a person's motive is altruistic, however, help will be given regardless of the ease of escape.

Based on this reasoning, Batson and others conducted dozens of experiments that support the empathy–altruism hypothesis. For example, Eric Stocks and his colleagues (2009) designed a clever experiment in which student participants learned about a fellow student named Katie whose parents and sister had recently been killed in a car accident, leaving her to care for her younger brother and sister. At the conclusion of the study the students were given an opportunity to help Katie, such as by volunteering to help her with transportation or to babysit her siblings while she took night classes. Would the students offer to help Katie?

> *"The great gift of human beings is that we have the power of empathy."*
>
> —Meryl Streep

empathy–altruism hypothesis
The proposition that empathic concern for a person in need produces an altruistic motive for helping.

● **FIGURE 10.4**

The Empathy-Altruism Hypothesis

According to the empathy-altruism hypothesis, taking the perspective of a person in need creates feelings of empathic concern, which produce the altruistic motive to reduce the other person's distress. When people do not take the other's perspective, they experience feelings of personal distress, which produce the egoistic motive to reduce their own discomfort.
Based on Batson, 1991.

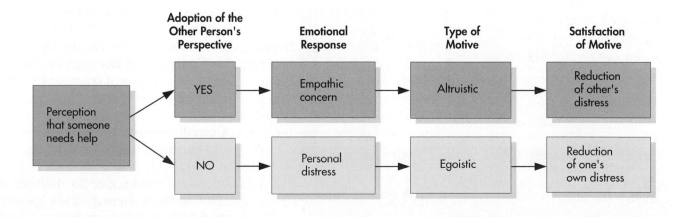

The researchers manipulated two variables before the students read about Katie's plight. One was a manipulation of empathy. Students in the *low-empathy* condition read that they should "try to remain as objective as possible about what has happened to the person described and how it has affected his or her life." Students in the *high-empathy* condition, in contrast, read that they should "try to imagine how the person described in the segment feels about what has happened and how it has affected his or her life." The researchers also manipulated whether or not the students would have an easy opportunity to not worry about the distress Katie was going through. Students were informed that they would be using a memory training technique that would either *enhance* or *eliminate* their memory of the information they would be learning (that is, the information about Katie).

The key question: Would students help Katie if they could simply forget about her, or would they want to help her anyway? If they would only help her if they could not easily forget her plight, this would suggest an egoistic motivation. But if they would help her even if they were confident they would not have to remember her suffering, this would suggest altruism. The results supported the empathy–altruism hypothesis. In the low–empathy condition, students' helping decisions seemed to be governed by egoistic concerns—they agreed to help Katie only if they thought they would remember her problems. In the high-empathy condition, however, they agreed to help her regardless of whether they thought they would remember her or not (see ● Figure 10.5).

It should be noted that too much empathy can be overwhelming if it is not properly controlled. Doctors, nurses, and clinicians are often better able to help their patients if they can maintain some emotional distance and objectivity from them, and too much empathy can be a risk factor for depression (Decety & Svetlova, 2012; Hunsaker et al., 2015; Salvers et al., 2015). In addition, it is important to recognize that many—and probably most—helpful acts are the products of other motives and processes we describe in this chapter. Indeed, as we will discuss next, the most effective way to increase consistent helping in many contexts may be to encourage both self-oriented and other-oriented concerns.

Convergence of Motivations: Volunteering People tend to engage in more long-term helping behavior, such as volunteerism, due to multiple motives. Some of these motives are associated with empathy, such as perspective

● FIGURE 10.5

Empathy and Helping: Not Taking the Easy Way Out

Students were induced to experience low or high empathy toward a suffering student named Katie. They were led to believe that they would remember or soon forget what they learned about Katie. The students were then given a chance to volunteer to help Katie. Students in the low-empathy condition tended to not offer their help if they thought they wouldn't remember Katie and her plight. Students in the high-empathy condition offered to help whether or not they thought they would forget her situation.

Based on Stocks et al., 2009.

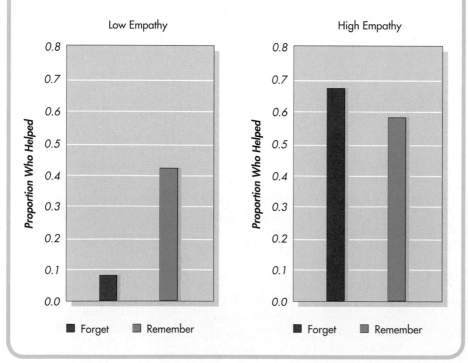

taking and empathic concern, whereas other motives are more egoistic, such as wanting to enhance one's résumé, relieve negative emotions, or conform to prosocial norms (Hur, 2006; Penner et al., 2005; Piferi et al., 2006; Reeder et al., 2001). Allen Omoto and others (2009) found that both other-focused motivation and self-focused motivation predicted volunteerism.

Table 10.1 lists five categories of motives that Allen Omoto and Mark Snyder (1995) determined were behind volunteers' decisions to help people with AIDS. One interesting finding was that people remained active volunteers longer if they had initially endorsed self-oriented motives, such as gaining understanding and developing personal skills, rather than other-oriented motives, such as humanitarian values and community concern. Why were the more egoistic goals associated with longer service? Snyder and Omoto (2008) observed that purely altruistic motives may not keep individuals motivated long enough to withstand the personal costs associated with some kinds of prolonged helping. As Mark Snyder noted, "The good, and perhaps romanticized, intentions related to humanitarian concern simply may not be strong enough to sustain volunteers faced with the tough realities and personal costs of working with [persons with AIDS]" (Snyder, 1993, p. 258). When helping demands more of us, self-interest may keep us going.

According to the empathy-altruism hypothesis, taking the perspective of someone in need is the first step toward altruism. When 13-year-old Avis Martin (left) lost her hair after receiving chemotherapy for leukemia, Sheriff Deputy Rick Johnson and several others showed their empathy and support for Avis by shaving their heads.

▲ **TABLE 10.1**

Motivations to Volunteer to Help People with AIDS

Within each category, three examples of specific statements representative of the general motive are presented.

Values	Community Concern
Because of my humanitarian obligation to help others	Because of my sense of obligation to the gay community
Because I enjoy helping other people	Because I consider myself an advocate for gay-related issues
Because I consider myself a loving and caring person	Because of my concern and worry about the gay community
Understanding	**Esteem Enhancement**
To learn more about how to prevent AIDS	To feel better about myself
To learn how to help people with AIDS	To escape other pressures and stress in my life
To deal with my personal fears and anxiety about AIDS	To feel less lonely
Personal Development	
To get to know people who are similar to myself	
To meet new people and make new friends	
To gain experience dealing with emotionally difficult topics	

From Omoto & Snyder (1995).

Almost 63 million Americans volunteered during 2014, according to the U.S. Bureau of Labor Statistics.

Interested in volunteering? One place to find information is Volunteermatch.org.

Egoistic motives, therefore, can be put to good use. This was evident in a set of studies by Eamonn Ferguson and others (2008). They conducted a longitudinal study of blood donation in the United Kingdom and found that having other-oriented beliefs about blood donation (for example, *society* benefits from blood donation) and having self-oriented beliefs (for example, *the donor* would benefit by donating blood) each predicted people's later actual blood donation, but having the self-oriented beliefs was the stronger predictor.

■ Helping as a Default?

We've discussed a number of reasons why people help others. Still, despite all these reasons, most people assume that our instincts are selfish and that we have to control and rise above those instincts in order to do the morally right thing and act altruistically. Does that idea ring true? Recent work by David Rand and his colleagues suggest common sense is wrong here. They point out that for most of us, being helpful and cooperative with others is the sensible way to act much of the time. We typically spend most of our time with people we can trust, and when we help others we're likely to receive help in turn. Therefore, our default inclination may prime us to be helpful, and only if we have time might we reconsider this in light of the potential costs. Consistent with this idea, Rand and his colleagues have found in a series of studies that when participants had to act really fast, they were more likely to cooperate with or help others than if they had time to think about the costs and benefits of their actions (Cone & Rand, 2014; Rand et al., 2015). Rand and Ziv Epstein (2014) also examined the testimony of people awarded medals by the Carnegie Hero Fund Commission for extreme acts of heroism. The statements of these heroes overwhelmingly emphasized intuitiveness rather than deliberativeness. In other words, they consistently described themselves as acting on instinct, without thinking.

Situational Influences: When Do People Help?

Thus far, we have focused on *why* people help others. We now turn to the question of *when* people help—and when they don't. We begin by discussing a remarkably creative and provocative set of research findings that make a surprising point: If you need help in an emergency, you may be better off if there is only one witness to your plight than if there are several. We then examine a wide range of other situational factors related to helping.

■ The Bystander Effect

On January 15, 2008, a man named Rage Ibrahim was convicted for sexually assaulting a woman in the hallway of an apartment building in St. Paul, Minnesota, the previous summer. Surveillance video from the hallway showed several residents, as many as 10, opening their apartment doors, looking at the man beating and raping the screaming woman, and closing their doors as they went back into their apartments. At one point three men approached them, but they left after Ibrahim got off the woman and shoved one of them in the back. Despite the woman's cries for someone to call the police, no one called 911 for more than an hour. A police commander who saw the video said, "It was horrifying. I can't describe how it sent chills up my back, watching this woman getting assaulted and people turning their backs and doing nothing" (Gottfried, 2007, 2008).

The sad truth is that this kind of story of bystanders failing to act, while chilling, is not as uncommon as most people imagine. Two of the stories in the opening to this chapter—the hit-and-run tragedy in China and the sexual assault on the beach in Florida—are additional examples of this problem. The most famous of these stories occurred more than 50 years ago. It has remained famous in large part because of the fascinating social psychology research it inspired.

The story begins at about 3:20 in the morning on March 13, 1964, in the New York City borough of Queens. Twenty-eight-year-old Kitty Genovese was returning home from her job as a bar manager. Suddenly, a man attacked her with a knife. She was stalked, stabbed, and sexually assaulted just 35 yards from her own apartment building. Lights went on and windows went up as she screamed, "Oh my God! He stabbed me! Please help me!" She broke free from her attacker twice, but only briefly. Newspaper reports at the time indicated that 38 of her neighbors witnessed her ordeal, but not one intervened. Finally, after nearly 45 minutes of terror, one man called the police. But before they got her to the hospital, Genovese was dead.

The murder of Kitty Genovese shocked the nation. Were her neighbors to blame? It seemed unlikely that all 38 of them could have been moral monsters. Most of the media attention focused on the decline of morals and values in contemporary society and on the anonymity and apathy seen in large cities. A few days after the incident, social psychologists John Darley and Bibb Latané discussed over dinner the events and the explanations being offered for it. They were not convinced that these explanations were sufficient to account for why Kitty Genovese didn't get the help she needed, and they wondered if other, more social psychological processes might have been at work. They speculated that because each witness to the attack could see that many other witnesses had turned on their lights and were looking out their windows, each witness may have assumed that others would, or should, take responsibility and call the police. To test their ideas, Darley and Latané (1968) set out to see if they could produce unresponsive bystanders under laboratory conditions. Let's take a look at one of their studies.

When a participant arrived, he or she was taken to one of a series of small rooms located along a corridor. Speaking over an intercom, the experimenter explained that he wanted participants to discuss personal problems college students often face. Participants were told that to protect confidentiality, the group discussion would take place over the intercom system and that the experimenter would not be listening. They were required to speak one at a time, taking turns. Some participants were assigned to talk with one other person, whereas other participants joined larger groups of three or six people.

Although one participant did mention in passing that he suffered from a seizure disorder that was sometimes triggered by study pressures, the opening moments of the conversation were uneventful. But soon, an unexpected problem developed. When the time came for this person to speak again, he stuttered badly, had a hard time speaking clearly, and sounded as if he were in very serious trouble:

> I could really—er—use some help so if somebody would—er—give me a little h-help—uh—er—er—er—er—c-could somebody—er—er—help—er—uh—uh—uh [choking sounds]. . . . I'm gonna die—er—er—I'm . . . gonna die—er—help—er—er—seizure—er [chokes, then quiet].

Confronted with this situation, what would *you* do? Would you interrupt the experiment, dash out of your cubicle, and try to find the experimenter? Or would you sit there—concerned, but unsure how to react?

As it turns out, participants' responses to this emergency were strongly influenced by the size of their group. Actually all participants were participating alone, but tape-recorded material led them to believe that others were present. All the participants who thought that only they knew about the emergency quickly

The murder of Kitty Genovese, pictured here, shocked the nation in 1964. How could 38 witnesses stand by and do nothing? Research conducted in the aftermath of this tragedy suggests that if there had been only one witness rather than almost 40, Kitty Genovese might have had a better chance of receiving help, and she might be alive today.

The New York Times/Redux

In an emergency, a person who needs help has a much better chance of getting it if three other people are present than if only one other person is present.

FALSE

bystander effect   The effect whereby the presence of others inhibits helping.

left the room to try to get help. In the larger groups, however, participants were less likely or were slower to intervene. Indeed, 38% of the participants in the six-person groups never left the room at all during the 6 minutes before the experimenter would finally terminate the study! This research led Latané and Darley to a chilling conclusion: The presence of others inhibits helping. This came to be known as the **bystander effect**.

Before the pioneering work of Latané and Darley, most people would have assumed just the opposite. Isn't there safety in numbers? Don't we feel more secure rushing in to help when others are around to lend their support? Latané and Darley overturned this commonsense assumption and provided a careful, step-by-step analysis of the decision-making process involved in emergency interventions. In the following sections, we examine each of five steps in this process. These steps, and the obstacles along the way, are summarized in ● Figure 10.6.

● **FIGURE 10.6**

The Five Steps to Helping in an Emergency

On the basis of their analysis of the decision-making process in emergency interventions, Latané and Darley (1970) outlined five steps that lead to providing assistance. But obstacles can interfere, and if a step is missed, the victim won't be helped.

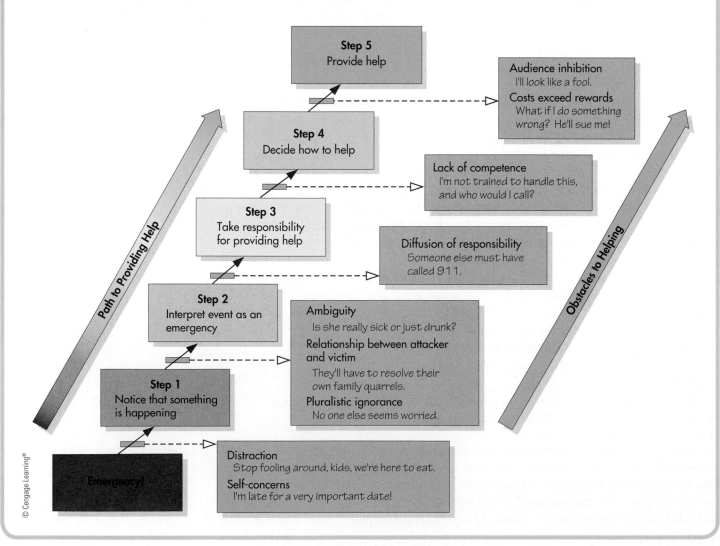

© Cengage Learning®

Noticing   Participants in the seizure study could not help but notice the emergency, but the presence of others can sometimes be distracting and divert attention away from noticing a victim's plight. People who live in big cities and noisy environments may become so used to seeing people lying on sidewalks or hearing screams that they begin to tune them out, becoming susceptible to what Stanley Milgram (1970) called *stimulus overload.*

Interpreting   Noticing is a necessary first step toward helping, but then people must interpret the meaning of what they notice. A shriek outside one's window may be a cry of terror or just friends horsing around; a person lying by a doorway could be heart-attack victim or a sleeping drunk. In general, the more ambiguous the situation is, the less likely it is that bystanders will intervene.

The first step toward providing help is to notice that someone needs assistance. Distracted by their own concerns or by the overwhelming stimuli of a big, bustling city, these people walking in midtown Manhattan may not even notice the homeless couple begging for spare change.

Perhaps the most powerful information available during an emergency is the behavior of other people. Startled by a sudden, unexpected, possibly dangerous event, each person looks quickly to see what others are doing. As everyone looks at everyone else for clues about how to behave, the entire group may be paralyzed by indecision. When this happens, the person needing help is a victim of **pluralistic ignorance**. In this state of ignorance, each individual believes that his or her own thoughts and feelings are different from everyone else's, when in fact, many of the other people are thinking or feeling the same way. Each bystander thinks that other people aren't acting because somehow they know there isn't an emergency. Actually, everyone is confused and hesitant, but taking cues from each other's inaction, each observer concludes that help is not required.

Latané and Darley (1968) put this phenomenon to the test in an experiment in which participants completed a questionnaire in a room in which they were either (a) alone; (b) with two confederates who remained passive and took no action; or (c) with two other naive participants just like them. As the participants were working on the questionnaire, smoke began to seep into the room through a vent. Was this an emergency? How do you think you would respond? Within 4 minutes, half of the participants who were working alone took some action, such as leaving the room to report the smoke to someone. Within 6 minutes—the maximum time allotted before the researchers terminated the experiment—three-quarters of these participants took action. Clearly, they interpreted the smoke as a potential emergency.

But what about the participants working in groups of three? Common sense suggests that the chances that *somebody* will take action should be greater when more people are present. But only 1 of the 24 participants in this condition took action within 4 minutes, and only 3 did so before the end of the study—even though, at that point, the smoke was so thick they had to fan it away from their faces to see the questionnaire they were working on! The rate of action was even lower when participants were in a room with two passive confederates; in this condition, only 1 in 10 participants reported the smoke. If the participants in either of the two group conditions had interpreted the smoke as a potential emergency, they would have acted, because their own lives would have been at stake. But instead they looked at the reactions of the others in the room, and because of their individual attempts not to look panicky or uncool, they defined the situation for each other as nothing to be worried about.

pluralistic ignorance   The state in which people in a group mistakenly think that their own individual thoughts, feelings, or behaviors are different from those of the others in the group.

Taking Responsibility Noticing a victim and recognizing an emergency are crucial steps, but by themselves, they don't ensure that a bystander will come to the rescue. The issue of responsibility remains. When help is needed, who is responsible for providing it? If a person knows that others are around, it's all too easy to fail to help because of the **diffusion of responsibility**: the belief that others will or should intervene. Presumably, each of those people who watched or listened to Kitty Genovese's murder thought that someone else would do something to stop the attack. The witnesses to the hit-and-run in China or to the sexual assault on the crowded beach in Florida (described at the beginning of the chapter) also knew that lots of other people could be the ones to get involved. But remember those helpful participants in the seizure study who thought that they alone heard the other person's cry for help? Diffusion of responsibility cannot occur if an individual believes that only he or she is aware of the victim's need.

Some research suggests that the presence of others can even be imaginary and still produce some diffusion of responsibility. Participants in studies in which they simply imagined being in a crowd as opposed to being alone, or in which they played a video game with multiple characters rather than with a single character, were subsequently less likely to help someone (Garcia et al., 2002; Stenico & Greitemeyer, 2014).

A very clever recent study by Maria Plötner and others (2015) tested diffusion of responsibility with 5-year-olds. During the study, children were doing some coloring when the adult experimenter had a little problem—she "accidentally" knocked over a cup containing colored water and it was beginning to spill all over her table and onto the floor. She groaned that she needed some paper towels as she feebly tried to hold back the water with her arms. There just happened to be a pile of paper towels between the children and the experimenter's table. So, did the children stop what they were doing and try to help?

The children in one condition of the study were alone with the experimenter. The children in another condition were with two 5-year-old confederates who were trained to be friendly but to keep coloring and not offer assistance during the spill. Replicating the bystander effect, the children who were in the presence of these passive bystanders were much less likely to help than were the children who were alone. But the researchers went a step further. Could the inaction among these children be due to something other than diffusion of responsibility, such as feeling shy around the other kids or just following the other children's behavior? To isolate the role of responsibility, Plötner and her colleagues cleverly added a third condition. In this condition, there again were two confederates, but in this case, the confederates were sitting behind a barrier that made it difficult or impossible for them to get to the paper towels (see ● Figure 10.7). In this condition, therefore, the responsibility was solely on the one child who could help. Would this child help? Indeed, the children in this condition—in which diffusion of responsibility was no longer plausible—were as likely to help as if they had been the only witness.

Deciding How to Help and Providing Help If a person has assumed the responsibility to help, he or she still must pass through the final two steps before taking action: deciding how to help and then deciding to provide help. Obstacles here include feeling a lack of competence in knowing how to help, or worrying that the potential costs of helping may too great to justify taking the risk. The presence of other witnesses can be obstacles in these two steps as well. People sometimes feel too socially awkward and embarrassed to act helpfully in a public setting. When observers do not act in an emergency because they fear making a bad impression on other observers, they are under the influence of **audience inhibition**.

diffusion of responsibility The belief that others will or should take the responsibility for providing assistance to a person in need.

audience inhibition Reluctance to help for fear of making a bad impression on observers.

● FIGURE 10.7

Bystander Effect and Diffusion of Responsibility Among Children

These photos recreate the experimental setup in the three conditions of a study to see if 5-year-olds would help an experimenter by bringing over paper towels to deal with a spill. When participants were alone with the experimenter (Photo A), they were much more likely to help the experimenter than if they were in the presence of two confederates (Photo B). However, if the two confederates were trapped behind a barrier and thus unable to help (Photo C), responsibility for helping could not be diffused, and the participants were as likely to help as if they were alone.

From Plötner et al., 2015

(a)　　　　　　　　　　(b)　　　　　　　　　　(c)

This is a very common obstacle to helping, but sometimes it can be especially tragic. Melanie Carlson (2008) reports about a gang rape of an unconscious 15-year-old girl by four perpetrators in the presence of six bystanders at a party in 2002. The district attorney said that the bystanders did not intervene for fear of being considered "wusses" or being "made fun of" (p. 3). When Carlson interviewed young men from a university in California about how they would respond in situations like the gang rape, many of them raised similar concerns, indicating that their masculinity would be threatened if they intervened. This kind of concern about being embarrassed in front of friends and breaking perceived norms that promote minding one's own business plays a role in a tremendous amount of bystander inaction, involving everything from sexual assault to bullying to abuse of animals (Arluke, 2012; Banyard, 2011).

The Bystander Effect Online　One relatively new application of the research on the bystander effect is in the world of electronic-based communication. Daniel Stalder (2008) reviewed studies on individuals' responses to e-mail or Internet-based requests for help. Even here, the bystander effect emerged, indicating that the virtual presence of others reduced the likelihood that any one individual would intervene. Abuse online, such as in the form of bullying via a social network site, or cries for attention and help from suicidal individuals may be met with the bystander effect. The diffusion of responsibility can be all the greater online because of the additional physical and psychological distance the online world creates. Indeed, in multiple cases of people announcing on Facebook or an online group that they were going to kill themselves, the posts elicited many instances of taunting and indifference from online bystanders (Murphy, 2012; Wells, 2011).

Avoiding the Bystander Effect　There are conditions in which the bystander effect is less likely to occur, or may even be reversed. Groups in which the members know or feel connected to each other are usually more helpful than groups of strangers (Fischer et al., 2011; Levine & Manning, 2013). When effective helping would require multiple helpers, such as in cases in which helping might be more dangerous if attempted alone, the presence of others can sometimes lead to more helping rather than less helping, presumably because the potential costs and benefits of helping would favor multiple helpers acting together (Fischer & Greitemeyer, 2013; Greitemeyer & Mügge, 2015). In addition, when people think they will be scorned by others for failing to help, the presence of an audience *increases* their helpful actions (Schwartz & Gottlieb, 1980). We return to this point a bit later, when we discuss the effects of social influence on helping.

Diffusion of responsibility can be defeated by a person's role. A group leader, even if he or she has only recently been assigned to that position, is more likely than other group members to act in an emergency (Baumeister et al., 1988). And some occupational roles increase the likelihood of intervention. Registered nurses, for example, do not diffuse responsibility when confronted by a possible physical injury (Cramer et al., 1988). Recall Donald Liu, whose brave attempt to rescue two boys in Lake Michigan was described earlier the chapter. Liu was a pediatric surgeon, whose job was all about saving children. The woman who shielded her friend from a gunman in a movie theater in Louisiana in July 2015, as described in the beginning of this chapter, was a schoolteacher. A mutual friend attributed her heroism to her training as a teacher (Schapiro, 2015).

The Legacy of the Bystander Effect Research As you can see in Figure 10.6, providing help in an emergency is a challenging process. At each step along the way, barriers and diversions can prevent a potential helper from becoming an actual one. Meta-analyses of the large body of studies inspired by Latané and Darley's work have found strong support for the bystander effect model (Fischer et al., 2011; Latané & Nida, 1981).

Bully

Victim

3 People Involved in Bullying

Bystander

NSR Publications

The legacy of the bystander intervention research lives on today as it is being applied to programs designed to encourage witnesses to destructive behaviors such as bullying and sexual assault to take action.

The power and relevance of Latané and Darley's analysis are evident in the fact that all these decades later news reports around the world continue to cite their work or mention Kitty Genovese when reporting the latest shocking incident of bystander nonintervention. Given its enduring legacy, it is interesting to note that some of the original details reported about the witnesses to the Kitty Genovese murder—accounts that have been repeated countless times over the years since then—may, in fact, be inaccurate. Rachel Manning and others (2008) published an article suggesting that some of the witnesses may have called the police well before the police finally arrived. These were in the days before "911" calls, and it is impossible to know whether or not these calls were made or what may have been said in them. Manning and her colleagues also question whether 38 was the correct number of witnesses and suggest that far fewer were likely to have actually seen the incident, although possibly even more than 38 heard it. As 2014 marked the 50th anniversary of the tragedy, a slew of books and newspaper articles on the topic were published to coincide with the anniversary, a testament to the enduring legacy of this story. Many of these books and articles included critiques of how the original newspaper reports got various details wrong. In October 2015 a new film called *The Witness* focused on Kitty Genovese's brother trying to get to the truth about the case.

To us, these questions are interesting but beside the main point. Whether fully accurate or not, these original reports were what inspired John Darley and Bibb Latané to pursue the line of research we have reported in this section, and that research has yielded valuable—and accurate—insight concerning the social psychology of bystander intervention, as have the numerous studies conducted by researchers inspired by this work.

Many of us who teach social psychology have stories of former students who witnessed an emergency and jumped in to help while consciously thinking of the lessons they'd learned in their social psychology classes about Darley and Latané's bystander intervention research. Some research supports this point, finding that teaching participants about the research makes them less vulnerable to these effects (Beaman et al., 1978). Indeed, one of the authors of this book remembers being at a lecture in a room filled with social psychologists when a loud crash suddenly emanated from an adjacent room. After a few seconds of delay, dozens of social psychologists burst out of their chairs, almost trampling each other as they rushed to see if there was an emergency. And the only ones who were not explicitly thinking "Darley and Latané" while doing so were the ones thinking "Latané and Darley."

The legacy of the bystander research has recently been reaffirmed all the more by an explosion of interest in applying and extending the work to a constantly growing list of prevention and training programs aimed at reducing aggression, bullying, sexual assault, workplace violence, and other antisocial and dangerous behaviors that are often witnessed by bystanders (Polanin et al., 2012; Quirk & Campbell, 2015; Saarento et al., 2015). This wave of research has found strong support for the applicability of the bystander research to understanding when and why bystanders are likely to fail to intervene in these situations, and researchers are beginning to find some positive results of training programs to reduce these effects. Numerous primary and secondary schools throughout the world have made "bystander" a buzzword as they try to educate and encourage students to intervene to reduce the prevalence and impacts of bullying.

Getting Help in a Crowd: What Should You Do?   So what do all these stories and experiments teach you about what to do if you need help in the presence of many people? Is there anything you can do to enhance the chances that someone will come to your aid? We can offer this advice: Counteract the ambiguity of the situation by making it very clear that you do need help, and reduce diffusion of responsibility by singling out particular individuals for help, such as with eye contact, pointing, or, ideally, with a direct request (Guéguen et al., 2015; Markey, 2000; Moriarty, 1975; Shotland & Stebbins, 1980).

■ Time Pressure

The presence of others can create obstacles at each step on the way toward helping in an emergency. Other factors, too, can affect multiple steps in this process. Our good intentions of helping those in need can sometimes conflict with other motivations. One such source of conflict is time pressure. When we are in a hurry or have a lot on our minds, we may be so preoccupied that we fail to notice others who need help, become less likely to accept responsibility for helping someone, or decide that the costs of helping are too high because of the precious time that will be lost. When we have other demands on us that seem very important, getting involved in someone else's problems may seem like a luxury we can't afford. John Darley and Daniel Batson (1973) examined the role of time pressure in an experiment that produced what may be the most ironic finding in the history of social psychology.

Their study was based on the parable of the Good Samaritan, from the Gospel of Luke. This parable tells the story of three different people—a priest, a Levite, and a Samaritan—each traveling on the road from Jerusalem to Jericho. Each encounters a man lying half-dead by the roadside. The priest and the Levite—both considered busy, important, and relatively holy people—pass by the man without stopping. The only one who helps is the Samaritan, a social and religious outcast of that time. A moral of the tale is that people with low status are sometimes more virtuous than those who enjoy high status and prestige. Why? Perhaps in part because high-status individuals tend to be busy people, preoccupied with their own concerns and rushing around to various engagements. Such characteristics may prevent them from noticing or deciding to help a victim in need of assistance.

Darley and Batson brought this ancient story to life. They asked seminary students to prepare to give a talk. Half of them were told that the talk was to be based on the parable of the Good Samaritan; the other half expected to discuss the jobs that seminary students like best. All participants were then instructed to walk over to a nearby building where the speech would be recorded. At this point, participants were told either that they were running ahead of schedule, that they were right on time, or that they were already a few minutes behind schedule. On the way to the other building, all participants passed a research confederate slumped in a doorway, coughing and groaning. Which of these future ministers stopped to lend a helping hand?

Perhaps surprisingly, the topic of the upcoming speech had little effect on helping. The pressure of time, however, made a real difference. Of those who thought they were ahead of schedule, 63% offered help—compared with 45% of those who believed they were on time and only 10% of those who had been told they were late. In describing the events that took place in their study, Darley and Batson noted that "on several occasions a seminary student going to give his talk on the parable of the Good Samaritan literally stepped over the victim as he hurried on his way!" The amazing result is that these seminary students unwittingly demonstrated the very point that the parable they were going to lecture about warns against.

■ Moods and Helping

We discussed earlier that helping someone can put people in a better mood, but can being in a good mood make people more likely to help someone? Are we less likely to help if we're in a bad mood? What's your prediction?

Good Moods and Doing Good Sunshine in Minneapolis and in France, and sweet scents in Albany, New York, give us some clues about the relationship between good mood and helping. Over the course of a year, pedestrians in Minneapolis, Minnesota, were stopped and asked to participate in a survey of social opinions. When Michael Cunningham (1979) tabulated their responses according to the weather conditions, he discovered that people answered more questions on sunny days than on cloudy ones. Cunningham also found that on sunny days restaurant customers gave more generous tips. More recently Nicolas Guégen and Jordy Stefan (2013) found that drivers in Brittany, France, were more likely to pick up hitchhikers (who were confederates of the study) on sunny than on similarly warm but cloudy days. Why should sunshine and helping go together? Probably it's the mood we're in, as a sunny day cheers us up and a cloudy day makes us feel, well, gray.

When the sun is not shining, many people head for the mall. One of the more powerful sensations you can count on experiencing while strolling through the mall comes when you pass a bakery or coffee shop, as the pleasant aroma of freshly baked chocolate chip cookies or freshly brewed French roast stops you in your tracks. Robert Baron (1997) believed that these pleasant scents put people in a good mood, and he wondered if this good mood would make them more likely to help someone in need. He tested this with passersby in a large shopping mall in Albany, New York. Each selected passerby was approached by a member of the research team and asked for change for a dollar. This interaction took place in a location containing either strong pleasant odors (such as near a bakery or a coffee-roasting café) or no discernible odor (such as near a clothing store).

As can be seen in ● Figure 10.8, the results were clear: People approached in a pleasant-smelling location were much more likely to help than people approached in a neutral-smelling location. In addition, people were in a better mood when they were in the pleasant-smelling environments. This effect on their mood appears to have caused their greater tendency to help. (Very similar results were found more recently by Nicolas Guéguen (2012) in a replication in a mall in Rennes, France.)

A variety of other studies, including under more controlled conditions, support the point that good moods increase helping (Batson, 2012). The next question is: Why? There seem to be several factors at work. Table 10.2 summarizes some of the reasons why feeling good often leads to doing good, and when this link between feeling good and doing good is weakened.

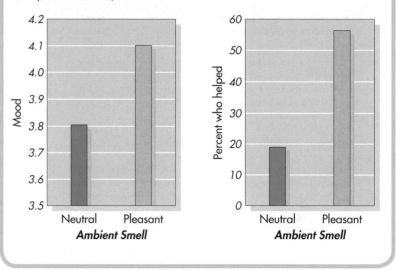

● FIGURE 10.8

Scents and Sensibilities

People approached by a researcher in a mall reported being in a better mood (left) and were more likely to comply to a request for change (right) if they were in an area of the mall with pleasant ambient odors than if they were in an area with no clear odors.
Adapted from Baron, 1997

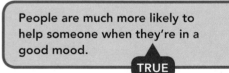

People are much more likely to help someone when they're in a good mood.   **TRUE**

Bad Moods and Doing Good   Since a good mood increases helping, does a bad mood decrease it? Not necessarily. Under many circumstances, negative feelings can elicit positive behavior toward others (Cryder et al., 2012; Vollhardt & Staub, 2011; Xu & Shankland, 2011; Zemack-Rugar et al., 2007).

Why might a bad mood promote prosocial behavior? As noted earlier, people know that helping makes them feel good. This point underlies the negative state relief model, which, as we discussed earlier, states that people may be motivated to try to repair a negative mood by helping others. If the likelihood of feeling better by helping is reduced, however, such as because the helping would be difficult and stressful, then helping becomes less likely (Kayser et al., 2010).

Although negative moods can often boost helping, it is not as strong and consistent a relationship as that between good moods and helping. As Table 10.3 indicates, there are several limits to this effect. For example, one important variable is whether people accept responsibility for their bad feelings. If we blame others for our feeling lousy, we're less likely to be generous in our behavior toward others. If, instead, we feel guilty for something bad that we have caused to happen, we are more likely to act prosocially (Rogers et al., 1982; Zemack-Rugar et al., 2007).

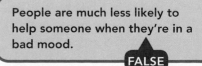

People are much less likely to help someone when they're in a bad mood.   **FALSE**

▲ **TABLE 10.2**

Good Moods Lead to Helping: Reasons and Limitations

Research shows that people in positive moods are more likely to help someone in need than are people in neutral moods. There are several explanations for this effect as well as some limiting conditions that can weaken or reverse the help-promoting effects of good moods.

Why Feeling Good Leads to Doing Good

- Desire to maintain one's good mood. When we are in a good mood, we are motivated to maintain that mood. Helping others makes us feel good, so it can help maintain a positive mood.

- Positive thoughts and expectations. Positive moods trigger positive thoughts, and if we have positive thoughts about others, we should like them more and should have positive expectations about interacting with others, and these factors should make us more likely to help them.

When Feeling Good Might Not Lead to Doing Good

- Costs of helping are high. If the anticipated costs of helping in a particular situation seem high, helping would put our good mood at risk. In this case, if we can avoid getting involved and thus maintain our good mood, we are less likely to help.

- Positive thoughts about other social activities that conflict with helping. If our good mood makes us want to go out and party with our friends, our motivation to engage in this social activity may prevent us from taking the time to notice or take responsibility for helping someone in need.

© Cengage Learning®

▲ **TABLE 10.3**

Bad Moods and Helping: When Does Feeling Bad Lead to Doing Good, and When Doesn't It?

Research shows that people in negative moods are often more likely to help someone in need than are people in neutral moods. However, there are several limitations to this effect. This table summarizes some of the factors that make it more or less likely for people to do good when they feel bad.

When Negative Moods Make Us More Likely to Help Others

- If we take responsibility for what caused our bad mood ("I feel guilty for what I did.")

- If we focus on other people ("Wow, those people have suffered so much.")

- If we think about our personal values that promote helping ("I really shouldn't act like such a jerk next time; I have to be nicer.")

When Negative Moods Make Us Less Likely to Help Others

- If we blame others for our bad mood ("I feel so angry at that jerk who put me in this situation.")

- If we become very self-focused ("I am so depressed.")

- If we think about our personal values that do not promote helping ("I have to wise up and start thinking about my own needs more.")

© Cengage Learning®

■ Prosocial Media Effects

The possible harmful effects of watching violent entertainment or playing violent video games has generated a great deal of public debate and research, as is discussed in Chapter 11 on Aggression. But what has garnered far less attention is whether popular media might have *positive* effects, including on promoting prosocial attitudes and behaviors. Douglas Gentile and others (2009) are among the researchers who have tested this question. They conducted an experiment to test the idea that playing video games featuring characters who help and support each other in nonviolent ways can make people more likely to behave in prosocial ways. They randomly assigned students to play a prosocial game (Super Mario Sunshine or Chibi-Robo!), a violent game (Ty2 or Crash Twinsanity), or a neutral game (Pure Pinball or Super Monkey Ball Deluxe) for 20 minutes. (We've never played any of these ourselves, but we must admit to being intrigued by the title, Super Monkey Ball Deluxe.) In the prosocial games, the player tries to get "happy points" by cleaning up a house or to help the people of an island that has been polluted by others.

After playing the game, the students then had the task of assigning a fellow student puzzles to complete. Some of the puzzles were easy, and others were difficult. The participants could help their fellow student earn more money by giving their partner the easier puzzles. As can be seen in the left side of ● Figure 10.9, participants who had played the prosocial game were more likely to help their partner by assigning easy puzzles than were the participants who had played the violent or neutral game. Muniba Saleem and others (2012) replicated this finding with children ranging in age from 9 to 14 (see right side of Figure 10.9).

● **FIGURE 10.9**

Super Mario Makes You Super Nice? Effects of Prosocial Video Games

College students or young children played a video game in which the characters acted either in helpful, cooperative ways (prosocial game), violent ways (violent game), or neither (neutral game). They later had the opportunity to help a partner's chances of earning money by assigning them easy puzzles in a task. Students (graph on left) and children (right) were significantly more likely to help their partner if they had played a prosocial video game than if they had played a neutral or violent game.

Adapted from Gentile et al., 2009; Saleem et al. 2012

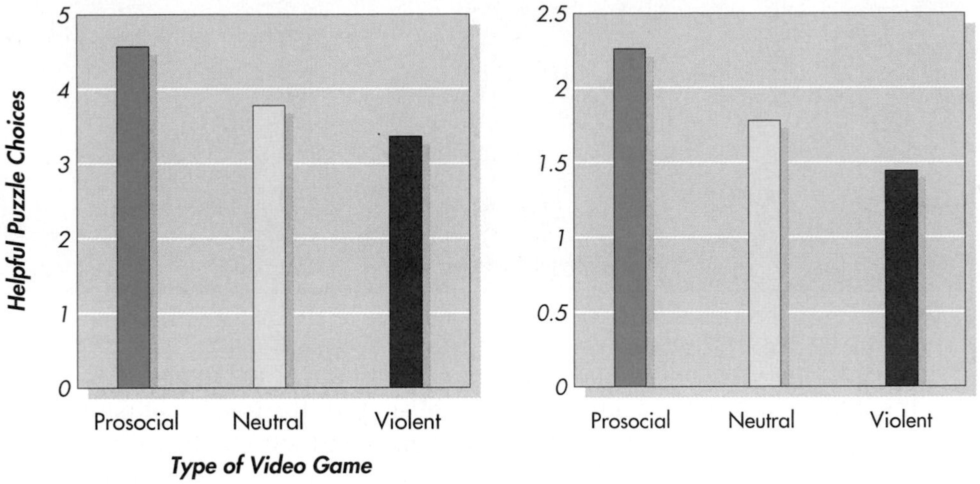

Longitudinal studies of children and adolescents in Japan and Singapore offer additional support for an association between prosocial game playing and subsequent helping behavior. Playing prosocial games at one point in time predicted increases several months or even two years later in empathy and in prosocial behavior. Playing violent video games, in contrast, predicted less subsequent helping behavior (Gentile et al., 2009; Prot et al., 2014).

Prosocial television can also have positive impact. A meta-analysis of 34 studies involving more than 5,000 children found a reliable positive effect of prosocial television on children's prosocial behavior, especially when specific acts of altruism were modeled on TV (Mares & Woodard, 2005).

■ Role Models and Social Influence

Role Models Prosocial examples in the media and in games present models for people to follow. Research has found that observing helpful models increases helping in a variety of situations (Hearold, 1986; Ng & van Dyne, 2005; Sechrist & Milford, 2007; Siu et al., 2006). Similarly, seeing models of selfish, greedy behavior can promote selfish, greedy behavior in turn (Gray et al., 2014).

Why do people who exemplify helping inspire us to help? Three reasons stand out. First, they provide an example of behavior for us to imitate directly. Second, when they are rewarded for their helpful behavior, people who model helping behavior teach us that helping is valued and rewarding, which strengthens our own inclination to be helpful. Third, the behavior of these models makes us think about and become more aware of the standards of conduct in our society.

Students in the Philippines take the Ice Bucket Challenge in 2014. Through publicly challenging friends and others around the world to film themselves dumping ice cold water on their heads to raise money and awareness in the fight against the neurological disease, ALS, this viral craze illustrated the power of social influence to motivate helping behavior.

Ezra Acayan/Corbis News/Corbis

Indeed, one especially important type of role model for many of us are our parents. Many studies from around the world support the point that parents' prosocial attitudes and tendencies have an influence on their children's corresponding attitudes and tendencies (Ottoni-Wilhelm et al., 2014; Mesurado et al., 2014; Newton et al., 2014; Waugh et al., 2015).

Social Influence   Have you ever agreed to chip in to buy a present for someone or to do a favor for someone only because your friends or co-workers were doing so and you didn't want to be the only one not contributing? If so you've experienced the act of doing something altruistic for reasons having nothing to do with altruism. Rather, your prosocial behavior was due to peer pressure and social influence. This cause of helping behavior doesn't get as much attention as the other factors we've been discussing in this chapter, but it does play an important role in determining when people help in a variety of situations. As we will discuss later in a section on Culture and Helping, this type of influence may be especially strong in collectivist cultures.

Charities and other fundraisers often are quite aware of and utilize the power of social influence to motivate donations, such as by encouraging people to match others' contributions and making public lists of who has contributed. "Pay it forward" schemes sometimes exert great social pressure on individuals to keep the chain going, such as when a long line of people at Starbucks or a drive-thru window pay for the person next in line and nobody wants to be the one to end the run. The stunning viral success of the Ice Bucket Challenge in 2014 to raise money and awareness to fight the neurological disease ALS was due in large part to people publicly naming their friends as the next people who should participate in the challenge.

Several recent studies support these points. Diane Reyniers and Richa Bhalla (2013), for example, gave participants in their study money in return for completing a survey, and then they invited the participants to donate some of this money to charity. If participants thought a fellow participant would know whether and how much they donated, they donated significantly more money than if they did this privately. Some researchers call this kind of peer-influenced behavior **reluctant altruism**.

reluctant altruism   Altruistic kinds of behavior that result from pressure from peers or other sources of direct social influence.

● **FIGURE 10.10**

Promoting Cooperation in the Field

This summary from a review of field studies on the effectiveness of interventions designed to promote cooperation highlights the effectiveness of interventions based on social influence factors, as opposed to interventions based on cost-benefit factors. Kraft-Todd et al., 2015

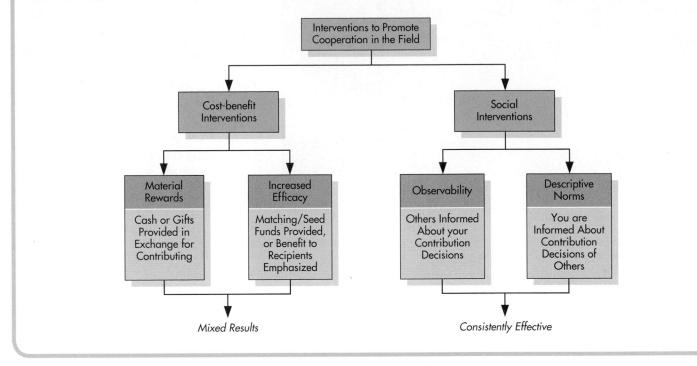

Another kind of social influence is illustrated in a creative recent study by Marco van Bommel and others (2014). Participants either alone or in the presence of confederates witnessed someone steal some money left unattended by the experimenter who had left the room. Replicating the classic bystander effect, the researchers found that participants were less likely to intervene in the presence of the witnesses than if they were alone. This effect was eliminated (and even reversed), however, if the participants knew there was a security camera recording the room. Not wanting to look unresponsive and callous on camera, and perhaps wanting to have their heroism documented on video, participants sprung to action.

Social influence factors therefore can be effective in eliciting prosocial behavior. This point is highlighted by the results of a recent analysis by Gordon Kraft-Todd and others (2015). They reviewed the research literature on the effectiveness of field experiments designed to promote cooperative behavior, such as involving conservation, charitable donations, and voting. As can be seen in ● Figure 10.10, those interventions based on the kinds of social influence factors we've been discussing here have been more consistently effective than those based on cost–benefit perspectives.

Personal Influences: Who Is Likely to Help?

We have established that situational factors such as the presence of bystanders, mood, and peer pressure, can overwhelm individual differences in influencing helping behaviors in many contexts. But individual differences can matter as well. We turn now to examine these individual differences.

Movie star Angelina Jolie has used her celebrity as well as her own time and energy to raise awareness and resources for impoverished and malnourished children around the world. In this photo she is at a refugee camp in Myanmar in July 2015.

Handout/Getty Images

Are Some People More Helpful Than Others?

Although situational factors can make anyone more or less likely to help in a given context, researchers have found that some people tend to be more helpful than others across multiple situations and over time (Dovidio et al., 2006; Hay & Cook, 2007; Laible, Carlo, et al., 2014; Rushton, 1981). For example, Nancy Eisenberg and others (2002) found that the degree to which preschool children exhibited spontaneous helping behavior predicted how helpful they would be in later childhood and early adulthood.

As with so many other individual differences, variation in helpfulness appears to be partly based on genetics. Genetically identical (monozygotic) twins are more similar to each other in their helpful behavioral tendencies and their helping-related emotions and reactions, such as empathy, than are fraternal (dizygotic) twins, who share only a portion of their genetic makeup. These findings suggest that there may be a heritable component to helpfulness (Ebstein et al., 2010; Fortuna & Knafo, 2014; Mikolajewski et al., 2014). Joan Chiao (2011) estimates that between 56% and 72% of prosocial behavior can be attributed to genetic effects.

What Is the Altruistic Personality?

Some people are more helpful than others, but can we predict who these people are by looking at their personalities more generally? If so, what are the various components of *the altruistic personality*?

Consider, for example, Oskar Schindler, the wealthy German businessman during the Nazi regime who became the hero of the book and movie *Schindler's List*. Schindler was a shady operator, cheating in business and marriage, partying with sadistic German military officers. From his overall personality, could anyone have predicted his altruistic actions of risking his own life to save over 4,000 Jews during the Holocaust? It is doubtful. What about more recent models of altruism? Consider these people: Bill Gates, a computer geek who cofounded Microsoft and became the richest man in the world; Bono, the extraverted Irish rock star; Dikembe Mutombo, a 7-foot, 2-inch former professional basketball player originally from the Congo; Mother Teresa, a Roman Catholic nun from Macedonia. Gates and his wife Melinda have pledged *billions* of dollars to charity, much of it to target health issues around the world. Bono has worked tirelessly to raise money and awareness about the plight of poor African nations. Mutombo raised millions of dollars for the construction of hospitals in the Congo. Mother Teresa devoted her life to the poor in India. These well-known figures seem *quite* different from each other in overall personality—except for their concern with helping others.

The quest to discover the altruistic personality has not been an easy one. Much of the research conducted over the years failed to find consistent, reliable

In 2014 alone Bill and Melinda Gates donated almost 2 billion dollars in Microsoft stock to charitable causes.

"The purpose of human life is to serve and to show compassion and the will to help others."
—Albert Schweitzer

personality characteristics that predict helping behavior across situations. Some researchers have changed the nature of the quest, however, focusing on personality variables that predict helping in some specific situations rather than across all situations; their studies have been more successful in identifying traits that predict such behavior (Carlo et al., 2005; Eberly-Lewis et al., 2015; Finkelstein, 2009; Penner, 2004). For example, in their sample of 564 Japanese undergraduates Ryo Oda and others (2014) found that conscientiousness was associated with altruism toward family members, agreeableness was associated with altruism toward friends and aquaintances, and openness was associated to altruism toward strangers.

Some research has found, however, that a few traits do tend to be related to helping behavior. People who tend to be very agreeable, and people who are relatively humble, are more likely to be helpful than people who are disagreeable or lack humility (Caprara et al., 2012; Courbalay et al., 2015; Hilbig et al., 2014; LaBouff et al., 2012). Individual differences in moral reasoning may be particularly important. Children and adults who exhibit internalized and advanced levels of moral reasoning tend to behave more altruistically than others. Such reasoning involves adhering to moral standards and taking into account the needs of others when making decisions about courses of action. In contrast, people whose reasoning is focused on their own needs or on the concrete personal consequences that their actions are likely to have tend not to engage in many helping behaviors (Eisenberg et al., 2014; Laible, Murphy, & Augustine, 2014; Ongley et al., 2014).

If you've been paying attention in this chapter, you shouldn't be too surprised at what trait has received the most attention in predicting helping behavior: empathy. We've already discussed empathy a couple of times in this chapter, and here it comes again, this time as a personality variable: Being able to take the perspective of others and experience empathy is clearly associated with helping and other prosocial behaviors in children and adults. The evidence on this point is strong and growing (Eisenberg et al., 2015; FeldmanHall et al., 2015; Hastings et al., 2014; Morelli et al., 2015). Some interesting additional support comes from social neuroscience. Sylvia Morelli and others (2015) found that empathy was associated with brain activation in individuals corresponding to the emotional experiences they saw other people were expressing in photos, and this activation in turn predicted the individuals' degree of everyday helping behavior. Abigail Marsh and

Rock star Bruce Springsteen (left) may not seem to have a lot in common with the Dalai Lama (seen in the photo on the right serving lunch at a soup kitchen in 2009) and many of the other people mentioned on the previous page as models of altruism, but like them, he donates a tremendous amount of time and money to helping others. At every stop on his concert tours in recent years, Springsteen has raised money for local causes, such as food banks, youth centers, and shelters.

A Virtual Emergency

Seen here is an image of what participants immersed in a virtual technology world encountered as they tried to escape a burning building: another person (allegedly the avatar of another participant) who was injured and trapped. Would they risk their own virtual lives to help him?

From Zanon et al., 2014

others (2015) recently found an intriguing neurological difference between people who volunteered to donate a kidney to a stranger and other people: The volunteers showed greater responsiveness in the right amygdala to others' fearful facial expressions, consistent with the idea that these individuals exhibited more empathic concern for the suffering of a stranger.

Another recent brain-imaging study went a step further by also utilizing virtual technology. In a particularly creative study by Marco Zanon and others (2014) participants were virtually immersed in a building on fire and had to evacuate to save their virtual selves. They came across another person who was injured, trapped, and calling for help—allegedly the avatar of a fellow participant in the study (but in reality it was programmed by the experimenters) (see ● Figure 10.11). Would the participants risk their own virtual lives to stop and help this trapped person, or would they look out for themselves and head straight for the exit? Remarkably, while all this was happening the participants were in an MRI scanner and their brain activity was recorded. Zanon and his colleagues found that participants who showed heightened activation in neural regions associated with perspective taking were the ones most likely to risk their virtual lives to try to help the trapped other person.

The importance of both empathy and moral reasoning is illuminated in a fascinating line of research by Elizabeth Midlarsky, Stephanie Fagin-Jones, and their colleagues (Fagin-Jones & Midlarsky, 2007; Midlarsky et al., 2005). They contrasted the personalities of "non-Jewish heroes of the Holocaust"—people who risked their lives to help Jews despite having no expectation of any extrinsic rewards—with bystanders who did not help during the Holocaust.

The researchers found that rescuers did indeed tend to differ from bystanders on a combination of several variables associated with prosocial behavior, particularly empathic concern and moral reasoning. Both of these qualities are reflected in the quote of one woman who sheltered 30 Jews in her home in Poland: "Helping to give shelter was the natural thing to do, the human thing. When I looked into those eyes, how could I not care? Of course I was afraid—always afraid—but there was no choice but to do the only decent thing" (Midlarsky et al., 2005, p. 908).

People differ in how empathic they tend to be, but a growing body of research suggests that empathy can be developed and taught. Emily van Berkhout and John Malouff (2015) conducted a meta-analysis of 19 studies of the impact of empathy training programs and found reliable support for their effectiveness. Moreover, Karina Schumann and others (2014) demonstrated that when people are made to recognize that empathy can be developed and strengthened, they are more willing to exert effort to empathize with others, in part to use these experiences as opportunities to improve this skill.

"True kindness presupposes the faculty of imagining as one's own the suffering and joy of others."
—André Gide

■ Culture and Helping

Does the propensity to help others vary across cultures? Given the many different types of helping there are, it's difficult to pin down a simple answer to this question. In the United States, for example, some evidence suggests people in the southern and northern central regions, or people in rural areas, tend to be more helpful than people in other regions or in urban areas, but this holds true for only some measures of helping and not others (Levine et al., 2008; Whitehead, 2014).

The role of religion in promoting prosocial behavior is also rather mixed. Individual differences in religiosity often do correlate with prosocial behavior, but much of this research finds a strong intergroup bias—religious people are especially likely to help members of their religious ingroup rather than an outgroup (Clobert et al., 2015; Saroglou, 2014). Indeed, religiosity has been found in some cases to correlate with higher levels of aggression toward outgroup members (Blogowska et al., 2013). Priming individuals with symbols or tenets of one's religion, however, may at least temporarily boost helping behavior. In a meta-analysis of 25 studies with over 4,000 participants, Azim Shariff and colleagues (2015) found that priming religion had a small but positive effect on prosocial behavior for people who were religious. There was no effect of religious priming for those who were not religious.

Priming individuals with Buddhist concepts may be particularly effective, including for outgroup members. Participants of both Buddhist and Christian backgrounds in one series of studies behaved in more prosocial and tolerant ways after being primed with words associated with Buddhism (e.g., Buddha, monk, reincarnation) than with words associated with Christianity (e.g., Jesus, Church, Bible) or with neutral words (Clobert et al., 2015). Some scholars believe that Buddhism is especially strong in emphasizing compassion and tolerance for contradiction, and these qualities encourage not only prosocial behavior but also greater acceptance of outgroups (Cheng, 2015). In a sample of college students in Thailand, Paul Yablo and Nigel Field (2007) found relatively high rates of self-reported altruistic behaviors, and the researchers attributed this to the fact that the Thai students were very likely to cite Thai-Buddhist values to explain why they would help in various situations.

Independent of religion, some people are motivated by a *world change orientation*—marked by their desire to make the world a better place. This motivation leads to greater helping behavior in situations that are framed as relevant to this goal, as opposed to situations framed as helping a particular individual (Oceja & Salgado, 2013). Similarly, individuals characterized as having values associated with *self-transcendence*—which emphasizes care for the welfare of other others, whether close or distant, and disengagement from selfish concerns—have been found to be more helpful (Daniel et al., 2015).

In one ambitious attempt to compare helping rates across cultures, Robert Levine and others (2001) conducted field studies of spontaneous helping in a major city in each of 23 large countries around the world. In a downtown area in each of these cities during normal business hours on clear summer days, experimenters measured the proportion of passersby who would help in the following scenarios: (1) picking up a pen that a stranger had apparently dropped accidentally, (2) helping a stranger with a heavy limp pick up a pile of magazines that the stranger had dropped, and (3) helping a blind person seeking help crossing the street. The results indicated that pedestrians in Brazil, Costa Rica, and Malawi exhibited the highest rates of helping, and pedestrians in Singapore, the United States, and Malaysia exhibited the lowest rates.

So what did this research reveal about cultural differences in propensity to help? One cultural variable that predicted helping was what is called *simpatía* in Spanish or *simpático* in Portuguese. Some researchers report that this is an important element of Spanish and Latin American cultures and involves a concern with the social well-being of others (Markus & Lin, 1999; Sanchez-Burks et al., 2000). The five cultures in the study conducted by Levine and colleagues that value *simpatía* did tend to show higher rates of helping than the non-*simpatía* cultures.

You may find it surprising to learn that collectivism was not a predictor of helping. The research on the relationship between individualism or collectivism and prosocial behavior, however, is quite mixed at this time. This inconsistency may stem in part from differences in the kinds of helping studied. Compared to individualists, collectivists may be more likely to help ingroup members but less likely to help outgroup members or to help in more abstract situations (Conway et al., 2001; Knafo et al., 2009; Schwartz, 1990). Consistent with this point, Markus Kemmelmeier and others (2006) found that people from the more individualistic states in the United States (primarily in the West and Midwest) tended to exhibit greater charitable giving and volunteering than people from the more collectivistic states. This was particularly true for donations and volunteering that were not specific to one's ingroup affiliations. The authors propose that when helping involves this more abstract kind of giving—as opposed to, for example, helping someone from within one's ingroup—individualism may be associated with greater helping.

According to the Charities Aid Foundation's (2014) analysis of several measures of helping from 135 countries around the world, the United States has the world's highest overall rates of helping from 2009 through 2013. This result stands in sharp contrast to the poor showing of the United States in Robert Levine's international field studies discussed above. This discrepancy reflects how different measures of helping can produce very different findings. Although one of the measures used in the Charities Aid Foundation report concerned helping a stranger, the others involved donating money and volunteering time. As can be seen in the list of the top 16 countries on this index presented in Table 10.4 there are many different types of countries and cultures represented among the most helpful. Some of the wealthiest countries are at the top of the list, for example, but some of the wealthiest are toward the bottom as well.

"In our increasingly interdependent world, we have seen the terrifying power of individuals to do great harm. Yet there is a more hopeful side of this interconnected age: private citizens have never had more power to advance the common good and secure a brighter future."
—Former U.S. President Bill Clinton

Speaking of wealth, do you think individuals who are wealthy help more or less than other people? There would be good reason to believe that having money, and the freedoms that go with it, would make people more comfortable offering help to others. Although there isn't a great deal of research on this yet, some recent studies suggest the opposite may be true. For example, participants in studies by Paul Piff and his associates (2010) completed various measures of prosociality, such as giving points to a partner, allocating money to charity, or completing the tasks that were most time-consuming when working with a partner. Across the studies, the researchers found that lower social class predicted more prosocial behavior. They proposed that people navigating lower-class and working-class worlds are more likely to need and rely on others to survive, and as a consequence, they are more likely to value helping others. Along these lines, other researchers have found that individuals in lower-class contexts have more empathic accuracy, such as in more accurately judging the emotions of others (Kraus, Cote, & Keltner, 2010).

Some research suggests that helping that is due to peer pressure or similar types of social influence might be especially common in collectivist cultures, where there are strong pressures to conform to norms. In a study looking at bystander intervention in bullying in Italy (a relatively individualistic culture) and Singapore (a relatively collectivistic culture), researchers asked participants to report how much they felt their peers expected them to intervene in bullying situations. While students in both countries were more likely to report intervening when they felt more pressure from peers, this relationship was stronger for students in Singapore (Pozzoli, Ang, & Gini, 2012). Another interesting cultural difference was reported by Deborah Cai and others (2012). They found that Chinese participants were more willing to give money to help someone who needed some money than were American participants, but American participants were more willing than the Chinese participants to spend time and talk with someone who needed that kind of social support.

▲ **TABLE 10.4**

Helping Around the World

These are the 16 countries scoring at the top of the World Giving Index from the years 2009 through 2013, a measure of rates of helping a stranger, donating money, and volunteering time.

World Giving Index 5-year ranking

1. United States of America	9. Qatar
2. Ireland	10. Hong Kong
3. New Zealand	11. Malta
4. Australia	12. Denmark
5. Canada	13. Thailand
6. United Kingdom	14. Turkmenistan
7. Netherlands	15. Liberia
8. Sri Lanka	16. Indonesia

—Based on Charities Aid Foundation (2015)

Interpersonal Influences: Whom Do People Help?

We have just seen how some people are more helpful than others, but now we turn to our final major question of the chapter: Are some people more likely to *receive* help than others? We also explore some of the interpersonal aspects of helping.

Perceived Characteristics of the Person in Need

Although many characteristics of a person in need might affect whether that individual is helped, researchers have paid special attention to two: the personal attractiveness of the person in need and whether or not the person seems responsible for being in the position of needing assistance.

Attractiveness In Chapter 9, we described the social advantages physically attractive individuals enjoy. The bias toward beauty also affects helping. Attractive people are more likely to be offered help and cooperation across a number of different settings, whether it be asking for directions on campus, playing a game that could be either competitive or cooperative, or requesting money in a health emergency

(Farrelly et al., 2007; West & Brown, 1975; Wilson, 1978). In addition to physical attractiveness, interpersonal attractiveness matters; people who seem particularly nice, sociable, or happy, for example, are more likely to receive help, even for acts as seemingly mindless as holding a door open for someone (Hauser et al., 2014; Siem et al., 2014; Stürmer et al., 2005).

Certainly one explanation for some of these findings is that people help attractive others in the hope of establishing some kind of relationship with an attractive person. Not many people would be shocked to learn, for example, that male motorists in France were more likely to stop their cars and offer a ride to female hitchhikers whose bust size was enhanced (by a bra worn by a confederate) or who were smiling (Guéguen, 2007; Guéguen & Fischer-Lokou, 2004). (For whatever it's worth, Guéguen and colleagues (Guéguen & Lamy, 2009; Guéguen & Stefan, 2015) have also reported that female hitchhikers wearing a blond wig were more likely to be helped by male motorists than those wearing brown or black wigs, and men were more likely to help an experimenter by taking her survey if she was wearing high heels than flat or short heels.)

What may be surprising, however, is that attractive people receive more help even when the helper does it anonymously, with no chance for any reward. One demonstration of this was a study by Peter Benson and his colleagues (1976) in a large metropolitan airport. Darting into a phone booth to make a call (these were the days long before cell phones), each of 604 travelers discovered some materials supposedly left behind accidentally by the previous caller (but actually planted by the experimenters): a packet containing a completed graduate school application form, a photograph of the applicant, and a stamped, addressed envelope. In some packets, the photo depicted a physically attractive individual; in others, the person was relatively unattractive. What was a busy traveler to do? When the researchers checked their mail, they found that people were more likely to send in the materials of the good-looking applicants than those of the less attractive applicants.

Attributions of Responsibility People are more likely to help someone in need if they think the person shouldn't be held responsible for his or her predicament. If they think that the person can be blamed for his or her situation, they are less likely to help. These effects can be seen on fairly mundane issues, such as requests to take notes for a fellow student (Barnes et al., 1979), or in life-and-death matters, such as intervening in an instance of domestic violence (Gracia et al., 2009) or helping someone very ill. This latter case was illustrated in research by Michelle Lobchuk and others (2008), who found that caregivers of people with lung cancer had more negative emotions and gave less supportive help if they believed the patient was largely responsible for his or her disease. Similarly, studies have found that medical and nursing staff at an emergency room and medical students show more anger and are less helpful to patients whose injuries they felt were more controllable and avoidable (Mackay & Barrowclough, 2005; Nazione & Silk, 2013). Jean Decety and others (2010) found that when participants learned about the pain of individuals with AIDS, they showed brain activity indicating greater sensitivity if they thought the individuals had contracted AIDS through a blood transfusion rather than drug use.

A Little Help for Our Friends, and Others Like Us

Not surprisingly, people are usually more helpful to those they know and care about than to strangers or superficial acquaintances, but the type of relationship people are in with each other can affect norms about helping (Clark & Mills, 2012; Stewart-Williams, 2008). People in an *exchange* relationship, such as

---

Attractive people have a better chance than unattractive people of getting help when they need it.

TRUE

acquaintances or business associates, give help with the expectation of receiving comparable benefits in return—"If I help you move your furniture, you'd better give me a ride to the airport." People in a *communal* relationship, such as close friends or romantic partners, feel responsibility for each other's needs and are more likely to help, and are less likely to be concerned with keeping track of rewards and costs, than people in an exchange relationship are.

Whether they are friends or strangers, we are more likely to help others who are similar to us. All kinds of similarity—from dress to attitudes to nationality—increase our willingness to help, and signs of dissimilarity decrease it (Batson et al., 2005; Dovidio, 1984). People also are much more likely to help fellow ingroup members than they are to help members of an outgroup (Bernhard et al., 2006; Kogut & Ritov, 2007; Levine & Cassidy, 2010; Stürmer et al., 2005). The results of a recent meta-analysis of 212 studies affirm the reliability of this intergroup bias and also suggest that it is based more on people being especially helpful to ingroup members rather than being especially negative to outgroup members (Balliet et al., 2014). Mark Levine and others (2005) demonstrated this point in a clever field experiment based on the bystander intervention research discussed earlier in the chapter. Participants were British university students who were supporters of a particular popular football (soccer) team. After completing some questions about their support of the team (which served to highlight their identification with it), the participants had to walk to another building on campus, allegedly to watch a video for the next part of the study. On the way they encountered a jogger (actually, a confederate) who fell and seemed to be in pain with an injured ankle. For some of the participants, this jogger happened to be wearing the shirt of the participants' favorite team. For others, the jogger was wearing either a shirt of a rival team or a neutral shirt with no team logo. Would the jogger's shirt affect whether participants would offer to help?

As you can see in ● Figure 10.12, the shirt did make a big difference. Participants were much more likely to offer help to a person wearing their favorite team's shirt—a fellow ingroup member—than they were to help a person wearing either a neutral or a rival shirt. In this study, wearing a rival team's shirt did not reduce the jogger's chances of getting help compared to wearing a neutral shirt; it was just that wearing a shirt that signified similar team affiliation led to increased helping.

Once again, empathy seems to play an important role here. Numerous scholars mention an "empathy gap" in intergroup relations—people consistently show greater empathy for the needs and suffering of ingroup members than outgroup members. This has been demonstrated in a variety of ways, including through brain imaging studies—we seem to literally feel the pain of a suffering ingroup member more than a suffering outgroup member (Cikara et al., 2014; Eres & Molenberghs, 2013; Gutsell & Inzlicht, 2012; Hackel et al., 2014).

How strongly connected people feel with an ingroup can influence how willing they are to help fellow group members. William Swann and Michael Buhrmester (2015) report that people who experience **identity fusion** with a group—that is, a strong sense of "oneness" and shared identity with a group and its individual members—are more likely to help group members, even to the point of risking or sacrificing their lives in the process. The groups to which people feel fused may even be relatively large and abstract. Buhrmester and Swann (2015) measured how fused a sample of Americans felt with their country. The researchers

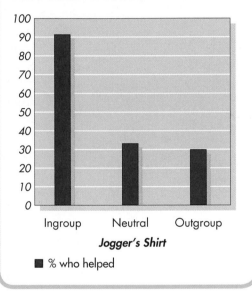

● **FIGURE 10.12**

Helping Ingroup Members

Participants who were fans of a particular British football (soccer) team came across a fallen jogger who seemed to be in pain. They were much more likely to offer the jogger help if he was wearing a shirt of the participants' favorite team than if he was wearing either a rival team's shirt or a neutral shirt.

Based on Levine et al., 2005.

Jogger's Shirt

■ % who helped

identity fusion A strong sense of "oneness" and shared identity with a group and its individual members.

couldn't have known this, of course, but a week later there was a terrorist bombing at the 2013 Boston Marathon. Two days after the bombing the researchers contacted the participants again and asked them what actions, if any, they had taken to help the victims of the bombing. The more fused the participants were with their country, the more likely they were to have taken actions to provide support for the victims.

Intergroup biases in helping can be reduced significantly if the members of the different groups can perceive themselves as members of a common group. Through fostering perceptions of shared identities and highlighting similarities between individuals across groups, an ingroup and an outgroup can begin to see each other as more similar than different, thereby promoting helping and other positive behaviors (Dovidio et al., 2010; Gaertner & Dovidio, 2012).

The effects of similarity and ingroup status on helping suggest that members of the same race should help each other more than they help members of different races. However, in a meta-analysis of more than 30 studies, Donald Saucier and others (2005) found no consistent overall relationship between racial similarity and helping. What accounts for these inconsistencies? First, although helping can be a compassionate response to another, it can also be seen as a sign of superiority over the person who needs help, and this can greatly complicate the decision about helping someone (Halabi et al., 2012; Nadler & Halabi, 2015; Täuber & van Zomeren, 2012; Vorauer & Sasaki, 2012). Given the possibility that helping someone can seem threatening or condescending, it may make it harder to predict when helping as a function of racial ingroup or outgroup will or won't occur. Second, public displays of racial prejudice risk social disapproval, and prejudiced individuals may bend over backward (in public, at least) to avoid revealing their attitudes. As discussed in Chapter 5, however, modern racism relies on more subtle forms of discrimination. Consistent with predictions from theories of modern racism, Saucier et al.'s meta-analysis found that when the situation provides people with excuses or justifications for not helping, racial discrimination in helping is more likely.

■ Gender and Helping

Here's a quick, one-question quiz: Who helps more, men or women? Before you answer, consider the following situations:

A. Two strangers pass on the street. Suddenly, one of them needs help that might be dangerous to give. Other people are watching.

B. Two individuals have a close relationship. Every so often, one of them needs assistance that takes time and energy to provide but is not physically dangerous. No one else is around to notice whether help is given.

Is your answer different for these two situations? It's likely to be. Situation A is a classic male-helper scenario. Because much of the research on helping used to focus on emergency situations, such as in the bystander intervention studies, older reviews tended to find that, on average, men are more helpful than women and women receive more help than men (Eagly & Crowley, 1986). Men also may be more likely to help in dramatic ways when they feel in competition with another man. Frank McAndrew and Carin Perilloux (2012) found that if there is an opportunity to look more heroic than another man in the eyes of a woman observing, men may become especially likely to volunteer to endure pain to benefit the rest of their group. Situation B, in contrast, is the classic female-helper scenario.

Women seek help more often than men do.

TRUE

Every day, millions of people provide support for their friends and loved ones, and some reviews indicate that women are more likely to provide this kind of help than are men (Eagly, 2009; Hyde, 2014). Though it lacks the high drama of an emergency intervention, this type of helping, called "social support," plays a crucial role in the quality of our lives.

For types of helping that do not easily fit into either of these categories, the evidence for gender differences is not strong or reliable. Overall, then, there does not seem to be a general and consistent gender difference in who is most likely to help others. What about the other side of the coin, though: Is there a difference in who is likely to *seek* help? In this case, the stereotype is true: Men ask for help less frequently than do women—a difference replicated in several countries around the world (Chang, 2007; Mackenzie et al., 2006; Murray et al., 2008; Sherer, 2007). Help-seeking is less socially acceptable for men and is more threatening to their self-esteem and status (Rosette et al., 2015; Wills & DePaulo, 1991).

"Are you telling me you won't even ask the computerized navigational system for directions?"

Men are less likely to seek help than women, possibly because it is more threatening to their self-esteem.

Culture and Who Receives Help

Whom people feel obliged to help can vary as function of cultural norms and backgrounds. As we said earlier in the chapter, compared to individualists, collectivists may be more likely to help ingroup members but less likely to help outgroup members. Cultures also vary in their endorsement or applications of social norms. **Social norms** are general rules of conduct established by society. These norms embody standards of socially approved and disapproved behavior. The *norm of reciprocity*, for example, dictates that if someone has helped us, we should help him or her in return. We discussed reciprocal altruism earlier in this chapter; many animals, including humans, help those who have helped them. Although the norm of reciprocity is important across cultures, Joan Miller and others (2014) propose that reciprocal norms are emphasized more in friendships among European American populations than among Hindu Indian populations, where communal norms are more emphasized.

The *norm of equity* prescribes that when people are in a situation in which they feel overbenefited (receiving more benefits than earned), they should help those who are underbenefited (receiving fewer benefits than earned). Some people subscribe to the *norm of social responsibility*, which dictates that people should help those who need assistance. However, people may instead be motivated more by concerns about *justice or fairness*, which emphasizes that people should help those who *deserve* their assistance rather than simply because they need help (Lerner, 1998).

We discussed earlier in the chapter that people are less likely to help someone they think is responsible for his or her plight. This is consistent with the norms of justice or fairness we just described. Elizabeth Mullen and Linda Skitka (2009) proposed that this may be a stronger influence on helping in individualist cultures—where individuals may be expected to have more control over their own fates—than in a collectivist one. On the other hand, perceptions of how much the person in need contributes to society might affect the helping decisions of collectivists—who have stronger norms of interdependence—more than of individualists.

"To change the world we must be good to those who cannot repay us."

—Pope Francis

social norm   A general rule of conduct reflecting standards of social approval and disapproval.

To test these ideas, Mullen and Skitka (2009) had participants from the United States and the Ukraine (a more collectivistic society) read about 16 individuals who needed an organ transplant. Information about each individual suggested that some were more responsible for their illness than others (e.g., a person who continued to eat unhealthy foods and resist exercise despite warnings versus a person who had a genetically defective organ). The researchers also varied information about how much contribution the individuals seemed to make to society (e.g., a person who volunteers for multiple organizations versus a person who does not volunteer). After reading about all 16 people, participants were asked to indicate which of up to six of them should receive a transplant.

In both cultures, people were less likely to help patients who were more responsible for their organ failure or who contributed less to society. However, as can be seen in ● Figure 10.13, the issue of personal responsibility played a bigger role in the decisions made by the Americans, whereas the issue of contribution to society played a bigger role in the decisions by the Ukrainians.

There also may be cultural differences in seeking help. Heejung Kim and others (2012), for example, observed that Asians and Asian Americans report seeking social support less than European Americans do. This greater resistance

● **FIGURE 10.13**

Who Should Receive Help? A Cross-Cultural Difference

Americans and Ukrainians were asked to decide which 6 of up to 16 individuals should receive an organ transplant. Participants were given information about the individuals that varied in terms of how personally responsible they seemed to be for their illnesses and how much they seemed to contribute to their society. Although participants in both countries preferred helping individuals who were not responsible for their illness and who made contributions to society, Americans' decisions were affected more by how responsible the person seemed, whereas Ukrainians' decisions were affected more by whether the person made contributions to society. Based on Mullen & Skitka, 2009.

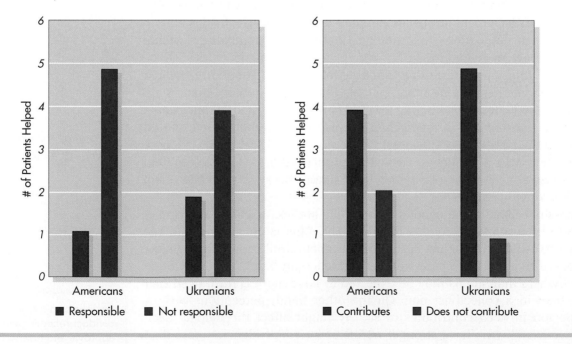

to seeking help among Asians and Asian Americans may be due to greater concerns about shame, receiving criticism, and hurting the relationship with the person or people whom they would ask for help. Indeed, Shelley Taylor and others (2007) found that seeking and receiving social support from close others are more stressful—both psychologically and physiologically—to Asian and Asian American students than to European American students. Asian students benefited more from what the researchers called *implicit social support*—support that comes from just thinking about close others but that does not involve actually seeking or receiving their help in coping with stressful events.

Years after the heroic altruism displayed by Ladder Company 6 firefighters on September 11, 2001, members of the company—and countless others like it—continue to risk their lives to save others. In this photo, Company 6 firefighter Jose Ortiz receives a medal for bravery from New York City Mayor Bill de Blasio in June 2014.

The Helping Connection

A consistent theme appears repeatedly in this chapter: a sense of connection fosters helping. Throughout the chapter, this connection has taken various forms—genetic relatedness, empathic concern, sense of responsibility for someone, perceived similarity, shared group membership, and so on. The relationship between helping and interpersonal connection runs like a bright red thread through much of the research on helping. For example:

- People are prone to help their kin, ingroup members, and people with whom they have a close or reciprocal relationship.

- Two kinds of connections lie at the heart of the empathy–altruism hypothesis: the cognitive connection of perspective taking and the emotional connection of empathic concern.

- In an emergency, bystanders who know the victim or know each other are more likely to intervene.

- People who respond empathically to another's suffering and consider the plight of others in their own moral reasoning are more likely to help than are others.

- Perceived similarity increases helping.

Taken as a whole, these points suggest that helping requires the recognition of individual human beings with whom we can have a meaningful connection. Which brings us back to Ladder Company 6 and the so many others who risked and even lost their lives that day trying to save others. Most of the people didn't know the others they were helping. But suddenly, horribly, fate had thrown them together, and suddenly their lives deeply mattered to each other. They felt responsible for each other. Many of those who helped in the face of grave danger may never have read the words that English poet John Donne wrote almost 400 years ago. But they would have understood them:

> No man is an island, entire of itself. Every man is a piece of the continent, a part of the main. If a clod be washed away by the sea, Europe is the less, as well as if a promontory were, as well as if a manor of thy friends or of thine own were. Any man's death diminishes me, because I am involved in mankind. And therefore never send to know for whom the bell tolls; it tolls for thee.

Review

Top 10 Key Points in Chapter 10

1. Among the factors that helped promote the evolution of altruism and empathy are kin selection (in which individuals protect their own genes by helping close relatives), reciprocal altruism (in which those who give also receive), and the survival advantages of intragroup cooperation and caring for offspring.

2. Helping others often makes the helper feel good, can relieve negative feelings such as guilt, and can improve mental and physical health. Long-term or high-risk helping, however, can be costly to the health and well-being of the helper.

3. According to the empathy–altruism hypothesis, taking the perspective of a person perceived to be in need creates the other-oriented emotion of empathic concern, which in turn produces the altruistic motive to reduce the other's distress.

4. Self-interested goals for longer-term acts of helping, such as volunteering, can promote a commitment to helping behavior to the extent that such goals are met.

5. The bystander effect, through which the presence of others inhibits helping, can occur because of obstacles on any of five steps on the path to helping. Diffusion of responsibility may be an especially important factor underlying this effect.

6. A good mood often increases helpfulness; a bad mood may increase or decrease helpfulness, depending on the context.

7. Prosocial role models and social influence have both been found to increase helping.

8. Individual differences that predict helping behaviors include agreeableness, humility, advanced moral reasoning, and, especially, empathy.

9. Attractive individuals and members of one's ingroups are more likely to receive help than are those who are less attractive or are members of an outgroup.

10. Cultural differences have been found in how much individuals differentiate between helping members of their ingroups versus outgroups, and in what roles various social norms play in determining whom to help.

Putting Common Sense to the Test

Evolutionary and Motivational Factors: Why Do People Help?

People are more likely to help someone in an emergency if the potential rewards seem high and the potential costs seem low.

Ⓣ **True.** *For both emergency situations and more long-term, well-planned helping, people's helping behaviors are determined in part by a cost–benefit analysis.*

Situational Influences: When Do People Help?

In an emergency, a person who needs help has a much better chance of getting it if three other people are present than if only one other person is present.

Ⓕ **False.** *In several ways, the presence of others inhibits helping.*

People are much more likely to help someone when they're in a good mood.

Ⓣ **True.** *Compared to neutral moods, good moods tend to elicit more helping and other prosocial behaviors.*

People are much less likely to help someone when they're in a bad mood.

Ⓕ **False.** *Compared to neutral moods, negative moods often elicit more helping and prosocial behaviors. This effect depends on a number of factors, including whether people take responsibility for their bad mood or blame it on others, but in many circumstances, feeling bad leads to doing good.*

Interpersonal Influences: Whom Do People Help?

Attractive people have a better chance than unattractive people of getting help when they need it.

Ⓣ **True.** *People are more likely to help those who are attractive.*

Women seek help more often than men do.

Ⓣ **True.** *At least for relatively minor problems, men ask for help less frequently than women do.*

Key Terms

altruistic (420)

audience inhibition (428)

bystander effect (426)

diffusion of responsibility (428)

egoistic (420)

empathy (416)

empathy–altruism hypothesis (421)

identity fusion (445)

indirect reciprocity (415)

kin selection (413)

negative state relief model (418)

pluralistic ignorance (427)

prosocial behaviors (412)

reciprocal altruism (414)

reluctant altruism (436)

social norm (447)

Aggression

In this chapter, we examine a disturbing aspect of human behavior: aggression. First, we ask, "What is aggression?" and consider its definition. After describing how aggression may vary by culture, gender, and individual differences, we examine various origins of aggression. We then explore a variety of situational factors that influence when people are likely to behave aggressively. Next, we focus on media effects on aggression, including the consequences of exposure to media violence and pornography. We conclude by discussing ways of reducing aggression and violence.

11

Guillem Valle/Corbis Wire/Corbis

453

It's a curious quirk of human nature

that so many of us love to go into a darkened room together and get scared. We pay good money to see violence displayed in vivid detail and bold colors in front of us and hear the eardrum-rattling sounds of destruction surrounding us. But when we go to the movies to watch superheroes battle supervillains, we do it with the understanding that we, in fact, are quite safe. It's a vicarious thrill we seek, an escape from our everyday lives into a fictional universe. So when that safe divide between the fictional universe on screen and the real world was shattered shortly after midnight on July 20, 2012, in Aurora, Colorado, the shock and horror would not be soon forgotten. It also would not be the last rampage of its kind.

About a half hour into the packed midnight premiere showing of the Batman movie, *The Dark Knight Rises,* a 24-year-old man James Holmes left the theater through a side exit door, propped the door to stay open, went to his car and changed into protective clothing, retrieved numerous firearms, and returned to the theater, where he proceeded to horrifically and seemingly randomly fire at the people in the theater, killing 12 and wounding 58 others. Details of the attack, and of some of the heroic attempts of several of the victims to shield friends and loved ones from the barrage of gunfire, are heartbreaking.

Almost exactly three years later, on July 23, 2015 (which itself was exactly one week after Holmes was convicted of multiple counts of murder, attempted murder, and other offenses), a 59-year-old man named John Houser stood up in a movie theater in Lafayette, Louisiana, early in the screening of the comedy, *Trainwreck,* and methodically fired his semiautomatic pistol at people in the theater, hitting 11 of them—some of them multiple times. Two young women died, nine people were wounded, and Houser then fatally shot himself in the head.

We expect to be safe at the movies. We expect this even more so in our schools and churches. And yet a month before the shootings in Lafayette, nine people were killed in a mass shooting in an historic African American church in Charleston, South Carolina. And five months after the shootings in the theater in Aurora, 26 people, along with the gunman, were killed at the Sandy Hook Elementary School in Newtown, Connecticut. With each of these tragedies people and government leaders vowed that "this time" we had to finally put an end to this. This cannot keep happening, we all would say, especially in a country that is not torn by war and economic chaos. And yet the memories of each case fade a bit with the news of the next one that would, inevitably, follow. The outcry after the massacre of little children at the Sandy Hook Elementary School was particularly strong. And yet about a year later a report revealed that since that tragedy there had been new school shootings in the United States at a rate of about one every 10 days (Straw, 2014)!

When the safety of a movie theater, a church, or a school is destroyed by violence, it raises profoundly important questions about the causes of aggression and violence and about how to reduce its prevalence. But while these high-profile incidents get most of the attention, every day there are numerous acts of aggression and violence that should also raise these questions and

Putting COMMON SENSE to the Test

Circle Your Answer

T F In virtually every culture, males are more violent than females.

T F For virtually any category of aggression, males are more aggressive than females.

T F Children who are spanked or otherwise physically disciplined (but not abused) for behaving aggressively tend to become less aggressive.

T F Blowing off steam by engaging in safe but aggressive activities (such as sports) makes people less likely to aggress later.

T F Exposure to TV violence in childhood is related to aggression later in life.

People leave messages of support on a board outside the church in Charleston, South Carolina, after a mass shooting there on June 17, 2015.

Travis Dove/The New York Times/Redux

promote their urgency. For example, there were well more than a *million* violent crimes and more than 13,000 murders in the United States alone in 2014. Multiply each of these crimes by the numbers of friends and loved ones who suffer along with the victims, and you can begin to get a sense of the massive toll that violence brings. And once you consider those numbers, think about this: These numbers are actually much lower than they were a couple of decades ago. The murder rate, for example, has been cut *in half* since the mid-1990s!

The suffering caused by aggression is not limited even to these millions of cases a year of violent crime, of course. Every day schoolchildren are bullied, sometimes relentlessly and with tragic outcomes. Every day people spread malicious gossip about others. Every day some parents wound their children with physical or verbal abuse. It is clear, then, that aggression and violence are not limited to a handful of crazed individuals who confuse fiction with reality or whose frustrations with life boil over into explosions of mass violence. It is all the more important, therefore, that we try to understand the root causes and situational triggers of aggression, and that is the goal of this chapter. It focuses primarily on aggression by individuals; aggression by groups, such as rampaging mobs, was discussed in Chapter 8. This chapter also discusses factors that reduce aggression.

What Is Aggression?

Although there are numerous ways one can define **aggression**, the definition that best represents the research today is that aggression is behavior that is intended to harm another individual. Aggressive behaviors come in many forms. Words as well as deeds can be aggressive. Quarreling couples who intend their spiteful remarks to hurt are behaving aggressively. Spreading a vicious rumor about someone is another form of aggression. Even failure to act can be aggressive, if that failure is intended to hurt someone, such as by not helping someone avoid what you know will be a humiliating outcome.

aggression Behavior intended to harm another individual.

A young woman gets blasted in the face with pepper spray by a police officer in Portland, Oregon, during a protest against the banking industry. Was the officer's use of pepper spray an instance of proactive aggression to restore order and prevent a more violent occurrence? Or was it reactive aggression, in which the officer's frustrations with the protestors boiled over and led to lashing out against some of them? The lines between these two categories of aggression can sometimes be quite blurry.

AP Images/Randy L. Rasmussen/File/The Oregonian

To distinguish them from less harmful behaviors, extreme acts of aggression are called *violence*. Some other terms in the language of aggression refer to emotions and attitudes. *Anger* consists of strong feelings of displeasure in response to a perceived injury; the exact nature of these feelings (for example, outrage, hate, or irritation) depends on the specific situation. *Hostility* is a negative, antagonistic attitude toward another person or group.

Aggression in which harm is inflicted as a means to a desired end is called **proactive aggression**. Aggression aimed at harming someone for personal gain, attention, or even self-defense fits this definition. If the aggressor believes that there is an easier way to obtain the goal, aggression will not occur. Some researchers call this type of aggression *instrumental aggression*. Harm that is inflicted for its own sake, in contrast, is **reactive aggression**. Some researchers call this type of aggression *emotional aggression*. Reactive aggression is often impulsive, carried out in the heat of the moment. The jealous lover strikes out in rage; fans of rival soccer teams go at each other with fists and clubs. Reactive aggression, however, can also be calm, cool, and calculating. Revenge, so the saying goes, is a dish best served cold.

Of course, sometimes it is hard to distinguish between proactive and reactive aggression. Why does a frustrated fighter illegally head butt his opponent—is it a deliberate, sneaky attempt to gain an advantage over a frustrating opponent, or does it simply reflect someone losing control and lashing out unthinkingly in frustration? It can be difficult to know where to draw the line between the two types of aggression and motives.

proactive aggression Aggressive behavior whereby harm is inflicted as a means to a desired end (also called instrumental aggression).

reactive aggression Aggressive behavior where the means and the end coincide; harm is inflicted for its own sake.

Culture, Gender, and Individual Differences

Just as not all types of aggression are alike, not all groups of people are alike in their attitudes and propensities toward aggression. To better understand the causes of aggression and what can be done about it, we need to consider how aggression is similar and different across cultures, gender, and individuals.

■ Culture and Aggression

Cultures vary dramatically in how—and how much—their members aggress against each other. We can see this variation across societies and across specific groups, or subcultures, within a society.

Comparisons Across Societies   The United States has enjoyed recent dramatic decreases in its rates of violent crimes, but it continues to be an exceptionally violent country (see Table 11.1). Its murder rate is one of the highest among politically stable, industrialized nations, far worse than the rates for Canada, Australia, New Zealand, and much of Western Europe. However, several countries in Eastern Europe, Africa, Asia, and the Americas have worse rates than the United States. ● Figure 11.1 illustrates some of the variation in homicide rates around the world.

Murder rates tend to be much higher in Central and South America, the Caribbean, and Southern and Middle Africa than in other regions in the world (United Nations Office on Drugs and Crime, 2011) (see ● Figure 11.2). A variety of factors contribute to this tendency, including poverty, drug trafficking, availability of guns, political and social unrest, and so on. Countries with wide disparities in income have murder rates almost four times greater than societies with more equal income distribution.

Another difference across countries concerns how individualistic or collectivistic cultures tend to be. As discussed throughout this book, individualist cultures place more emphasis on the values of independence, autonomy, and self-reliance, whereas collectivist cultures place greater emphasis on the values of interdependence, cooperation, and social harmony. Gordon Forbes and others (2009; 2011) hypothesized that individualist cultures, which are less concerned with social harmony and the avoidance of open conflict, are most likely to have a relatively high rate of aggression. To examine this idea, they asked college students in China (a highly collectivistic culture) and the United States (a highly individualistic culture) to answer questions about how they would likely respond in a particular conflict situation. The researchers found that men in the United States tended to be significantly more likely to advocate overt aggressive responses compared to men in China; the women tended not to differ in their responses across culture. A more recent study involving 15 countries found that countries high in individualism were associated with greater frequency of school violence (Menzer & Torney-Purta, 2012). In addition, Yan Li and others (2010) found that within a sample of Chinese adolescents, those who were more likely to endorse values associated with individualism tended to be more aggressive than were adolescents who more strongly endorsed collectivism values. Similarly, in both the United States and Thailand, the more participants saw themselves as independent from others, the more likely they were to report being aggressive in consumer interactions, such as by "being nasty" or "telling off" a salesperson (Polyorat et al., 2013). It is important to note, however, that collectivist cultures are not immune from aggression and violence. For example, murder rates in India and Korea (relatively collectivistic cultures) tend to be much higher than in the United Kingdom or France (relatively individualistic cultures).

The forms violence typically takes, and people's attitudes toward various kinds of aggression,

▲ **TABLE 11.1**

The Violent Crime Clock

Although the rates of violent crimes in the United States have declined in recent years, they are still distressingly high, as these averaged statistics illustrate, and are much higher than they were several decades ago.

In the United States in 2014, there was, on average:

One MURDER	every 36.9 minutes
One RAPE	every 4.5 minutes
One AGGRAVATED ASSAULT	every 42.5 seconds
One VIOLENT CRIME	every 26.3 seconds

Based on Federal Bureau of Investigation statistics. © Cengage Learning

● FIGURE 11.1

Murder Around the World

These figures indicate the reported number of recorded intentional homicides per 100,000 people in each of several countries in 2012, or the most recent year for which statistics are available, according to United Nations statistics published in 2014. Interpret the numbers with great caution, however, because there are large differences in reporting and recording practices in the various countries, but the basic point is clear: There is wide variation in the frequency of murder around the world.

© Cengage Learning®

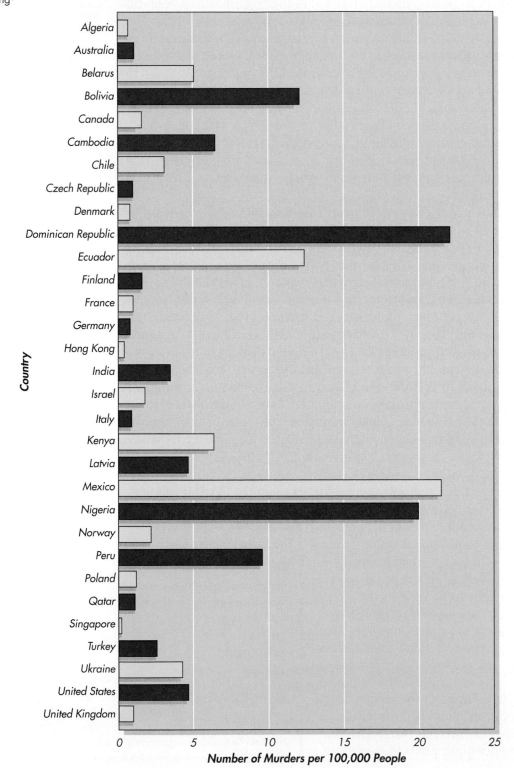

also differ internationally. The frequency of incidents in which an individual enters a public place like a school and shoots large numbers of people for no apparent reason seems to be especially high in the United States and, according to various reports, has been either growing or holding steady in recent years, even as the overall murder and violent crime rates have been declining. The violence in the United States also tends to involve individuals rather than groups of people. Group attacks against other groups in political, ethnic, tribal, or other institutionalized conflict are seen throughout the world but are particularly associated with parts of the Middle East, Africa, Eastern Europe, and South America. Violence related to drug gangs and battles is especially high in South America. And violent mobs of European football (what Americans call soccer) fans are not uncommon in England and other parts of Europe—behavior rarely seen at American sports events.

Relative to most of the world, the United States has a tremendous amount of gun-related violence (see ● Figure 11.3). The prevalence of handguns in the United States is exceptionally high. Even when compared to countries with which it shares much culturally, such as England and Australia, attitudes about guns tend to be much more permissive and positive in the United States, especially among males (Cooke, 2004). Indeed, although the rate of violent crime is actually *lower* in the United States than in the United Kingdom or Canada, the murder rate is *much* higher in the United States. Researchers believe that the higher murder rate in the United States is due to the prevalence of guns. According to one report, the firearm homicide rate was about 20 times higher in the United States than in other high-income countries; for 15- to 24-year-olds, the rate was almost 43 times higher (Richardson & Hemenway, 2011)!

Cultures also differ in their attitudes about aggression. In a study involving students at 36 universities in 19 different countries around the world, there was considerable variation in how acceptable the students found different actions, such as a husband slapping a wife or vice versa (Douglas & Straus, 2006). For example, almost 80% of the respondents from a university in India did not strongly disapprove of a husband slapping a wife, compared to only about 24% at a university in the United States. According to a UNICEF (2012) report, a majority of adolescent girls and boys in India and in Nepal believe that it is acceptable for a man to beat his wife (Sinha, 2012). In general, respondents from Europe were more approving of a husband slapping a wife than were respondents from Australia and New Zealand, who in turn tended to be somewhat more approving than respondents from North America. In contrast, these trends were reversed for the question of whether respondents had ever injured a dating partner—on this issue, North American rates tended to be highest. Even within the same region, cultural differences can lead to very different attitudes and behaviors regarding aggression between men and women. A study of Israeli youths revealed that rates of dating violence were much higher among Israeli Arabs than Israeli Jews, apparently reflecting the very different norms between the two cultures (Sherer, 2009).

What is considered to be aggression and unacceptable in relation to children also can differ across cultures. For example, in Japan, it is not highly unusual for Japanese adult businessmen to grope schoolgirls on public transportation (Ryall, 2015), a practice that would be considered aggressive and unacceptable in many other cultures, including the far more violent United States. In recent years this

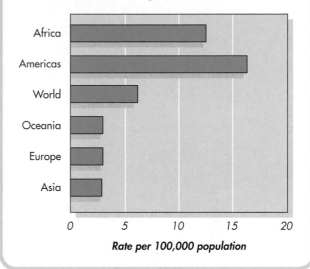

● FIGURE 11.2

Murder by World Region

Rates of recorded intentional homicides per 100,000 people in the population, in each region of the populated world.
United Nations Office of Drugs and Culture, 2013.

Rate per 100,000 population

"We have a pattern now of mass shootings in this country that has no parallel anywhere else in the world."
—Barack Obama, after a mass shooting in California, December 2, 2015

● **FIGURE 11.3**

Gun-Related Murder Rates

This chart indicates the gun-related murders per 100,000 people in each of several countries in the Organization for Economic Cooperation and Development (OECD). The United States stands out as extremely high on this measure. The one OECD country from the West that surpasses the United States is Mexico, which has about triple the U.S. rate.
Based on Fisher, 2012.

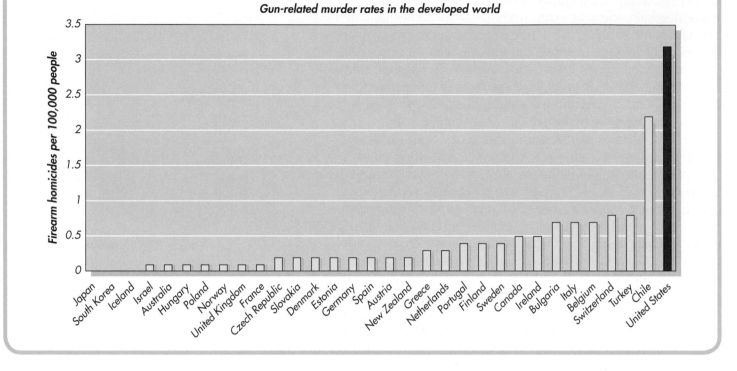

Gun-related murder rates in the developed world

practice, often called *chikan*, has become more widely criticized in Japan and a number of steps have been taken to curtail it, but the problem persists. Indeed, the head of a special police unit set up to combat this problem of groping was himself arrested in 2014 for allegedly groping a schoolgirl in front of a train station (Ryall, 2014). Some train companies in Tokyo introduced female-only cars to protect women and girls against groping. For similar reasons a program was announced to reserve some subway cars for women in Seoul, South Korea, to protect them from groping, but the plan was scrapped due to an outpouring of criticism (Jung-Yoon, 2011; Kiong, 2011). A Japanese 3-D video game called *Rape-Lay* has players simulate raping a woman and her two "virgin schoolgirl" daughters in a subway. This game caused an international uproar in February 2009 when it was discovered to be on sale (temporarily) at Amazon.com (Fennelly, 2009). Numerous websites, DVDs, and even fetish clubs in Japan are available for men to watch or act out their fantasies of groping schoolgirls and young women in train cars.

Another example of cultural variation in attitudes and definitions of aggression concerns female genital mutilation—any of several procedures in which, according to some estimates, the genitals of approximately 6,000 girls a day are cut in many countries around the world, particularly in parts of Africa and Asia. It is estimated that about 140 *million* females worldwide have undergone this procedure, mostly in childhood and often without anesthesia or sterile techniques (World Health Organization, 2012). The cultures that practice this consider it an important, sacred ritual, but the cultures that condemn it consider it an inhumane and dangerous act of violence and have vigorously called for a worldwide ban (Addison, 2014; Allam, 2012; Corbett, 2008).

Bullying Around the World   One form of aggression that is prevalent across virtually all cultures is bullying (Chester et al., 2015; Volk et al., 2015). Children and adolescents around the world are physically, sexually, or emotionally bullied by their peers. Bullying involves intentional harm (physically or psychologically), repetition (the victim is targeted a number of times), and a power imbalance (the bully abuses his or her power over the victim). The reported prevalence of bullying varies widely across research studies, with estimates on the low end suggesting that 5% or 10% of schoolchildren are involved in bullying, and estimates on the high end suggesting numbers as high as 70% to 90%. When Wendy Craig and her colleagues (2000; Pepler et al., 2004) set up hidden video cameras and microphones to get an unfiltered peek into aggression in schoolyards in Canada, they saw bullying in mid-size schools at a rate of 4.5 episodes per hour. Cyberbullying—bullying through electronic devices and social media—is a twenty-first-century version of an age-old problem.

Some cultural differences have been reported in how and where bullying occurs. Bullying in the classroom and involving a large group (such as an entire class) bullying a single target may be more characteristic of East Asian than Western countries, whereas bullying in the playground and involving students who don't know each other well may be more typical in Western cultures (Sittichai & Smith, 2015).

These seemingly ordinary rites of childhood can lead to extraordinary suffering, including feelings of panic, nervousness, and distraction in school; recurring memories of abuse; depression and anxiety that can endure through adulthood; and even suicide (Landoll et al., 2015; Reed et al., 2015). It is worth noting that the shooters in many and perhaps most of the instances of school shootings during the past couple of decades reportedly felt that they had been bullied or picked on by peers.

Nonviolent Cultures   Although violence seems to be just about everywhere, a handful of societies stand out as nonviolent exceptions. Bruce Bonta, Douglas Fry, and their colleagues have identified a number of societies around the world that are almost completely without violence (Bonta, 2013; Fry, 2012). For example, the Chewong, who live in the mountains of the Malay Peninsula, do not even have words in their language for quarreling, fighting, aggression, or warfare. The most serious act of aggression noted during a year among the Ifaluk, who live on a small atoll in the Federated States of Micronesia, involved a man who "touched another on the shoulder in anger, an offense which resulted in a stiff fine." The Amish, the Hutterites, and the Mennonites are all societies that reside in the relatively violent United States (as well as in Canada) but remain remarkably nonviolent. Table 11.2 lists some of the other societies that these researchers identified as nonviolent. What makes all of these societies so nonviolent? Bonta (2013) emphasizes that these cultures cherish peacefulness, which has become a core part of their identity. Many of these societies have religious or mythological reasons for remaining peaceful, which seems to have helped them stay nonviolent even in the face of violent contact from others.

The peace of one of these nonviolent communities was shattered on the morning of October 2, 2006. A 32-year-old milk truck driver named Charles Roberts, a father of three, burst into a one-room Amish schoolhouse in Pennsylvania, carrying three firearms, two knives, and up to 600 rounds of ammunition, along with other materials to carry out a horrific attack. He let the boys and a few adults leave, and then lined up the girls—ages 6 to 13—against the blackboard,

▲ **TABLE 11.2**

Nonviolent Societies

In addition to those discussed in the text, this table lists a few of the other societies that researchers identified as nonviolent.

Society	Comments
Balinese (Indonesian island of Bali)	A researcher who was there for four years never even witnessed two boys fighting.
Paliyan (South India)	A man said, "If struck on one side of the face, you turn the other side toward the attacker."
Batek (Peninsular Malaysia)	They believe that one of their diseases is caused when someone is angry with another.
Glwi (Central Kalahari Desert of southern Africa)	They abhor violence and take pleasure from fortunate events only if they are in the company of group members.
Ladakhis (Northern India)	Villagers indicate that they have no memory of any fighting in the village.
Zapotec (Southern Mexico)	They have very strong values that oppose violence, in contrast to other communities nearby where fighting and machismo are prevalent.

Based on Bonta, 1997, 2013; Miklikowska & Fry, 2010.

tied them up, and shot them one by one. After police burst in, Roberts shot and killed himself. Five of the girls were killed, and five more were critically injured.

The details of the massacre were truly nightmarish. At least two of the girls who were shot had asked the killer to shoot them first, in the hope of sparing some of the younger girls. And yet, in a remarkable display of this community's commitment to its principles of peace and forgiveness, families of the slain and injured children offered prayers for the killer and his family. According to some reports, the very night of the killings some Amish "stood in the kitchen of the murderer's family, their arms around his sobbing father, and said, 'We will forgive Charlie.'" One member of the community suggested that the forgiveness displayed by the Amish in this incident could be "a gift to the world. . . . Maybe there's something to learn about how nations might treat other nations" (Dueck, 2006, p. A25).

Subcultures Within a Country   There are important variations in aggression within particular societies as a function of age, class, race, and region. For example, teenagers and young adults have a much greater rate of involvement in violent crime—as both offenders and victims—than any other age group. What about race? Despite the stories that get the most attention on the news, the large majority of murders are intraracial rather than interracial. Among incidents when the killer's race was identified in the United States in 2013, almost 92% of black murder victims were killed by black offenders, and almost 85% of white murder victims were slain by white offenders. Nevertheless, African Americans live in a much more violent America than do whites. The proportion of African Americans—particularly African American males—who are the perpetrators or victims of homicide is consistently much higher than that of other racial groups. For example, according to a 2014 report from the U.S. Department of Justice, although African Americans represented about 13% of the U.S. population in 2010, they were victims of about half of all murders. Reliable data about homicide rates among other racial or ethnic groups are much more limited. Some evidence suggests having an ethnic minority background can be tied to higher instances of aggression in other parts of the world (Lahlah et al., 2013).

Regional differences are also striking. In the United States, the murder rate is consistently highest in the South, followed by the West. Some scholars have attributed the greater violence in the South and West to a *culture of honor* that is prevalent among white males in these regions. The culture of honor encourages violent responses to perceived threats against one's status as an honorable, powerful man (Barnes et al., 2012; Cohen et al., 1998; Hayes & Lee, 2005; Vandello et al., 2013). Other scholars believe that the consistently high rates of murder and violent crime in the South are due to hot weather (Anderson & Anderson, 1996; Anderson & DeLisi, 2011). We will focus more on both the culture of honor and the relationship between heat and aggression later in the chapter.

■ Gender and Aggression

Despite all the variation across cultures, one thing is universal: Men are more violent than women. This has been found in virtually all cultures studied around the world. Almost 90% of identified murderers in the United States in 2013 were male, and about 78% of murder victims were male. Despite the significant variation in total violence from one country to another, the gender difference remains remarkably stable over time and place: Men commit the very large majority of homicides, and men constitute the very large majority of murder victims (Buss, 2012; United Nations Office of Drugs and Crime, 2011). In the spate of school shootings discussed at various points in this chapter, all of the perpetrators were males. On the other hand, around the world the vast majority of people killed by an intimate partner—such as a family member or current or former romantic partner—are women.

In virtually every culture, males are more violent than females.
TRUE

What about aggression in general, as opposed to violence? In meta-analyses involving hundreds of samples from numerous countries, John Archer (2004) and Noel Card and his colleagues (2008) found that males are consistently more physically aggressive than females. This was true across all ages and cultures sampled. Females were as likely to feel anger as males, but they were much less likely to act on their anger in aggressive ways. Even among children between 1 and 6 years old, boys show higher rates of physical aggression than girls.

So does all this mean that the stereotype that males are more aggressive than females is correct? Not necessarily. Most of the earlier research on this issue focused on the form of aggression that is typical of males: physical aggression. But think back to our definition of aggression: It concerns intent to harm. There are many ways to harm someone other than through physical means. More recent research has recognized this, and the results challenge the notion that males are more aggressive than females. The findings that emerged can be summarized by a child's remark noted by researchers Britt Galen and Marion Underwood (1997): "Boys may use their fists to fight, but at least it's over with quickly; girls use their tongues, and it goes on forever" (p. 589).

For virtually any category of aggression, males are more aggressive than females.
FALSE

This research reveals that although boys tend to be more *overtly* aggressive than girls, boys do not tend to be more aggressive than girls when it comes to *indirect* or *relational* aggression. Indeed, for these types of aggression, girls sometimes are more aggressive than boys. Indirect forms of aggression include acts such as telling lies to get someone in trouble or shutting a person out of desired activities. Relational aggression is one kind of indirect aggression that particularly targets a person's relationships and social status, such as by threatening to end a friendship, engaging in gossip and backbiting, and trying to get others to dislike the target. The results of meta-analyses (Archer, 2004; Card et al., 2008) that have reviewed the very large research literature on the topic from around the world have found a very small but statistically significant gender difference, with girls exhibiting somewhat more indirect aggression than boys (see ● Figure 11.4).

Why are girls at least as aggressive as boys on relational (but not physical) forms of aggression? Researchers believe that one reason is because females typically care more about relationships and intimacy than males do and so may see injuring someone socially as particularly effective. Another reason may be that strong norms encourage boys to aggress physically, but these same norms discourage girls from doing so (Busching & Krahé, 2015; Crick et al., 1999; McEachern & Snyder, 2012; Spieker et al., 2012).

In addition to gender differences, there may be differences in the types of aggression people exhibit as a function of sexual orientation. Mark Sergeant and

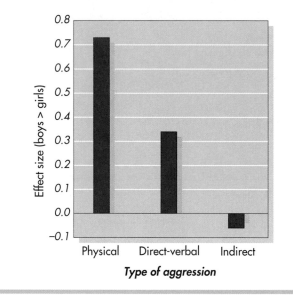

● FIGURE 11.4

Gender and Types of Aggression

The results of a meta-analysis of 148 studies involving children and adolescents across several countries indicate that the magnitude and direction of gender differences in aggression depend on the type of aggression. The height of the bars in this graph indicates the degree to which boys show more aggression than girls; the higher the bar, the more aggression is shown by boys relative to girls. Boys tended to be much more physically aggressive than girls, as well as to be more verbally aggressive (although this difference was smaller). Regarding indirect aggression, however, girls tended to be more aggressive than boys. This difference was small but statistically reliable across the set of studies.
Based on Card et al., 2008.

others (2006), for example, found that gay men reported significantly lower levels of physical aggression than straight men did, but there was no difference between the two groups on self-reported rates of indirect aggression.

A research finding that is often met with a great deal of surprise and skepticism is that there is no reliable gender difference in the percentage of women and men who physically assault their intimate partners. That is, women are at least as likely to aggress against their intimate partners as men are. This has by now been reported in more than 300 studies over the past few decades (Straus, 2011; Straus & Gozjolko, 2014). These results not only defy most people's expectations and stereotypes, they also do not match up with statistics from the police or agencies involved in helping people suffering from intimate partner violence. Researchers in this area explain that the reason for this difference is that men are far less likely than women to report to the police or various agencies that their partners physically assaulted them. Norms play a role in this, of course, as it is seen by many as far more acceptable for a woman to hit her male partner than it is for a man to hit his female partner. Another, and somewhat related, important reason is that the consequences of aggression and violence are far from equal. Women are more often killed, seriously injured, or sexually assaulted during domestic disputes than are men (Straus, 2011; Straus & Gozjolko, 2014). As Barbara Morse (1995) put it, "Women were more often the victims of severe partner assault and injury not because men strike more often, but because men strike harder" (p. 251). Rates of aggression and violence in the form of sexual assault differ greatly by gender, with males being overwhelmingly more likely to be perpetrators and females to be targets.

Individual Differences

Although it is clear that aggression can vary across culture and gender, a different question is whether aggressiveness varies reliably between individuals. In other words, are some people simply more aggressive than others, across time and contexts, and, if so, what personality traits are associated with it? The evidence related to the first part of the question, about stability, is fairly clear: Although situational variables (as we will see later in this chapter) certainly do influence whether and how someone will aggress, there are some stable individual differences in aggressiveness. Aggression in childhood does predict aggression in adolescence and adulthood (along with adult criminality, alcohol abuse, and other antisocial behaviors), although the strength of this relationship can vary as a function of the child's upbringing (Ehrenreich et al., 2014; Kokko et al., 2014; Warburton & Anderson, 2015).

What types of personalities tend to be associated with aggressiveness? Researchers often identify individuals' personalities based on what are called the "Big Five" factors—five dimensions that account for a great deal of variability in people's personalities across gender and culture. These five dimensions are (1) agreeableness (good-natured, trustful, cooperative), (2) conscientiousness (responsible, orderly, dependable), (3) openness to experience (intellectual, independent-minded, prefer novelty), (4) extraversion (outgoing, energetic, assertive), and (5) neuroticism (easily upset, emotionally unstable). Of these five factors, being low in agreeableness is a particularly strong predictor of aggression. Being low on the dimension of openness, and high on the dimension of neuroticism, are also associated with aggression (Barlett & Anderson, 2012).

Some traits associated with aggression tend to predict aggression reliably only under conditions of provocation—that is, situations in which the individual feels threatened, insulted, or stressed (Bettencourt, Talley et al., 2006). Among these traits are *emotional susceptibility* (the tendency to feel distressed, inadequate, and vulnerable to perceived threats), *Type A personality* (the tendency to be driven by feelings of inadequacy to try to prove oneself through personal accomplishments), and *impulsivity* (being relatively unable to control one's thoughts and behaviors). When not provoked, individuals with these traits are not much more likely than others to behave aggressively. Provocation, however, can light the relatively short fuses of these individuals, leading to the potential explosion of aggression.

Many people assume that individuals with low self-esteem are more likely to aggress than people with average or high self-esteem. The evidence on this is mixed at best (Bushman et al., 2009; Donnellan et al., 2005; Locke, 2009). The relationship between self-esteem and aggression may also be quite different across cultures; the results of a recent meta-analysis of studies conducted in China found that *higher* self-esteem was moderately associated with greater aggression (Teng et al., 2015). Although self-esteem is not a great predictor of aggression, *narcissism* clearly is. Narcissism involves having an inflated sense of self-worth and self-love, having low empathy for others, tending to focus on the self rather than others, and being especially sensitive to perceived insults. Narcissism is consistently and positively correlated with aggression in response to provocation, particularly if the provocation is public rather than private (Chester & DeWall, 2015; DeWall et al., 2013; Krizan & Johar, 2015). Narcissism is one of the three traits some researchers call the **Dark Triad** (which we admit sounds like what should be the name of the villains in the next *Star Wars* movie) for their role in aggressiveness and violence. The other two traits in the Dark Triad are Machiavellianism (characterized by manipulativeness) and psychopathy (characterized by impulsivity, poor self-control, and a lack of empathy) (Goodboy & Martin, 2015; Pabian et al., 2015).

One factor that has a very clear and consistent relationship with aggression is self-control (DeWall et al., 2013; Denson, DeWall, & Finkel, 2012). Poor self-control is part of the trait psychopathy in the Dark Triad. Individuals with strong self-control can resist impulses and are able to act in ways that are consistent with their personal and societal standards for appropriate behavior. Children low in self-control tend to be more aggressive as young adults, and poor self-control is one of the strongest predictors of crime, cyberbullying, and aggression toward strangers and romantic partners (DeWall, Finkel, & Denson, 2011; Li et al., 2014; Moffitt et al., 2011; Pratt & Cullen, 2000; Vazsonyi et al., 2012).

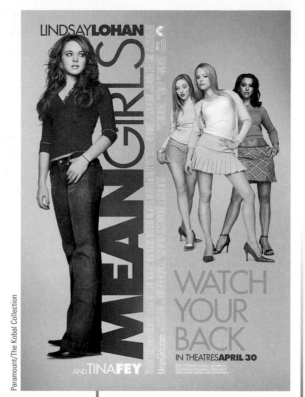

Paramount/The Kobal Collection

The movie *Mean Girls,* starring Lindsay Lohan and Rachel McAdams, depicted high school girls engaged in an escalating battle of indirect, relational aggression.

"I was thinking I'd like to write a movie about what they call 'relational aggression' among girls."
—Tina Fey, on the origins of the movie, *Mean Girls* (Stack, 2014)

Dark Triad   A set of three traits that are associated with higher levels of aggressiveness: Machiavellianism, psychopathy, and narcissism.

Origins of Aggression

Aggression has been a prevalent part of human interaction throughout human history and around the world. It is not surprising that many have speculated about the origins of aggression. Where does it come from? Are we *born* aggressive, or are we *taught* to be aggressive? Many have argued for one side or the other of the "nature-nurture" debate—the "nature" side holding that aggression is an innate characteristic of human beings and the "nurture" side holding that aggression is learned through experience. The reality is, however, that both nature and nurture play their respective roles. The effects of learning are not disputed; aggression is, at least to some extent, "made" by experience. Nor is there any doubt that in aggression, as in all human behavior, biology and environment interact. Indeed, contemporary research on aggression is paying increasing attention to the interactions of genes and environment (Rhee et al., 2015; R. L. Simons et al., 2013; Tuvbald & Beaver, 2013; Vitaro et al., 2015). Although others may continue to argue the nature–nurture debate, social psychological research makes clear that the origins of human aggression represent a profound interaction of evolved mechanisms and environmental and social factors.

In this section, we look at the theory and research most relevant to tracing the origins of human aggression. In reviewing each perspective, we examine how well it can account for the overall prevalence of aggression as well as for the cultural and gender differences that we have discussed.

■ Evolutionary Psychology

Evolutionary psychological accounts of aggression use principles of evolution to understand both the roots and the contemporary patterns of human aggression. For example, in his book *The Most Dangerous Animal: Human Nature and the Origins of War,* David Livingstone Smith (2007) emphasizes that human warfare originated not only to obtain valuable resources but also to attract mates and forge intragroup bonds. Smith argues that although our long-ago ancestors put themselves at risk when they engaged in fighting and warfare, they also increased their chances of attracting mates and achieving status in a group. Therefore, the individuals who could and would fight had greater chances for reproductive success, and they would pass down these tendencies to their offspring, who would tend to do the same, and so on. The greater reproductive success of warriors over pacifists would result in the tendencies toward aggression and war to evolve to become part of human nature.

"The most persistent sound which reverberates through men's history is the beating of war drums."
—Arthur Koestler

Evolution should have favored the inhibition of aggression against those who are genetically related to us. Consistent with that hypothesis, Martin Daly and Margo Wilson (1996; 2005) report that birth parents are much less likely to abuse or murder their own offspring than stepparents are to harm stepchildren. In two samples studied, preschool children living with a stepparent or foster parent were 70 to 100 times more likely to be fatally abused than were children living with both biological parents.

What can account for the gender differences in overt aggression? According to an evolutionary perspective, males are competitive with each other because females select high-status males for mating, and aggression is a means by which males were able to achieve and maintain status. As researcher Vladas Griskevicius said in an interview about his work on this topic, "For men, . . . not caring about status, which can be implied by backing away from a fight, can be evolutionary suicide" (*Science Daily*, 2008, December 8). Similarly, Joseph Vandello and Jennifer

Bosson (2013) argue that for many men, *manhood* is a status that is precarious. In other words, it must be earned and maintained repeatedly through action. Situations that threaten this status increase the likelihood and acceptability of aggressive behavior (Kroeper et al., 2014; Mescher & Rudman, 2014; Reidy et al., 2014). Also consistent with evolutionary accounts are crime statistics that indicate that male-to-male violence is most likely to occur when one male is perceived as challenging the other's status or social power, and male-to-female violence is predominantly triggered by sexual jealousy (Buss & Duntley, 2014; Wilson & Daly, 1996).

Sarah Ainsworth and Jon Maner (2014) hypothesized that when heterosexual men's motivations about mating are activated, they should become more aggressive toward other men whom they consider to be a potential threat to their ability to attract women. To test this idea in one of their experiments, they had heterosexual male participants see photos of 10 female faces. For the men in the *mating-prime* condition, these photos were very attractive. For the men in the *control* condition, the photos were less attractive. Next the participants saw a photo and read a description of a male confederate who they thought would be their opponent in an upcoming competitive game. For the participants in the *average-partner* condition, the confederate seemed rather nerdy and nonthreatening, and he did not say anything about dating in his self-description. For the participants in the *dominant-partner* condition, the confederate seemed athletic and high-status, and he described himself as liking to date whenever he can.

The participants then played a reaction-time game over the computer against their alleged opponent (in fact, the game was programmed by the experimenters). The winner of each round would get to blast the loser with some aversive noise in their headphones. Aggressiveness was measured by how loud the participants set the noise blasts that their opponent apparently would receive. As can be seen in ● Figure 11.5, the results supported the hypothesis that mating-related motivations would trigger heightened aggression toward a male who poses a potential threat to this motivation. Participants were especially aggressive only if this motivation had been primed and the male confederate seemed relatively socially dominant.

Of course, as noted earlier, women also aggress. From an evolutionary perspective, reproductive success is dependent on the survival of one's offspring. Because women are much more limited than men in terms of the number of children they can have, evolution presumably favored those women who were committed to protecting their children. Indeed, much research on aggression by females has focused on maternal aggression, whereby females aggress to defend their offspring against threats by others. For example, females in a variety of species attack male strangers who come too close to their offspring (Ferreira et al., 2000; Gammie et al., 2000). In a similar vein, Anne Campbell (1999) proposed that females tend to place a higher value on protecting their own lives—again, in order to protect their offspring. This hypothesis may explain not only why human males engage more often in risky, potentially self-destructive behaviors but also why human females, when they do aggress, are more likely to use less obvious, and thus less dangerous, means—such as

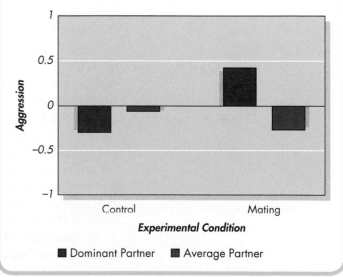

● **FIGURE 11.5**

Blasting the Competition

Male participants were given opportunities to aggress against another man by blasting him with aversive noise as part of a competitive game. Participants were especially aggressive if they had first been primed with mating-related motivations (by looking at photos of attractive women) and if they thought their opponent was a socially dominant man.
Based on Ainsworth & Maner, 2014.

"It's a guy thing."

indirect or relational aggression rather than overt physical aggression. Relational aggression also may be particularly effective for women because it can harm the reputations of rival females—which can make men less interested in them (Griskevicius et al., 2009; Vaillancourt, 2005).

■ Genes, Hormones, and the Brain

Whatever the evolutionary roots, it is clear that biological factors play very important roles in contemporary human aggression. We look at several of these factors in this section.

Genes We discussed earlier that aggressiveness is a relatively stable personality characteristic; children relatively high in aggressiveness are more likely to be aggressive later in life. Can this aggressive personality type be due to genes? To answer this question, researchers often compare monozygotic twins (who are identical in their genetic makeup) with dizygotic twins (who share only part of their genes). On any heritable trait, monozygotic twins will be more similar than dizygotic twins. Researchers also conduct studies of children who are adopted—to the extent a trait is heritable, adopted children will resemble their biological parents more than they resemble their adoptive parents. Analyses from these kinds of studies suggest that heritability explains between about a third and a half of the variation in aggression in children. The strength of this relationship can vary, however, depending on the type of aggression studied, such as physical or relational aggression (Ball et al., 2008; Bezdjian et al., 2011; Niv et al., 2013; Yeh et al., 2010).

Researchers are also focusing on identifying which particular genes or patterns of genes may be especially involved in human aggression. Variations in the monoamine oxidase A (MAOA) gene, for instance, have been linked to aggressive behavior in a growing number of studies (Gorodetsky et al., 2014; Stetler et al., 2014).

The Role of Testosterone In addition to the question of heritability, researchers have long been interested in determining what specific biological factors influence aggression. Because of the persistent sex differences in physical aggression among humans and other animals, many researchers have wondered if testosterone plays a role. Although men and women both have this "male sex hormone," men usually have much higher levels than women. Research conducted on a variety of animals has found a strong relation between testosterone levels and aggression. Some research with humans similarly found a strong link. For example, one study found that college fraternities whose members tended to have higher testosterone levels were more rambunctious and exhibited more crude behavior than other fraternities; fraternities whose members had lower testosterone levels tended to be more academically successful and socially responsible, and their members smiled more (Dabbs et al., 1996). Some studies have also shown a positive relationship between testosterone and aggression or aggression-related behaviors (such as competitiveness) in women (Cashdan, 2003; Dabbs & Dabbs, 2000).

Another line of research that supported the idea that testosterone predicts aggressiveness may strike you as somewhat odd. Look at your index and ring fingers. Which is longer, from tip to where they connect with the hand? Believe it or not, a number of studies have shown some intriguing correlations among finger-length ratio, testosterone, and aggression. Men tend to have relatively shorter index fingers relative to ring fingers; shorter ratios (especially on the right hand) are considered more "masculine." Lower ratios (called low *2D:4D* in the literature, with 2-D and 4-D meaning the second and fourth digits, respectively) are thought to be associated with exposure to higher prenatal testosterone levels. Studies have shown that for men, lower 2D:4D ratios (that is, more "masculine" ratios) are associated with higher scores for the trait of physical aggression, reports of being more threatening and physically aggressive toward their dating partners, personalities higher in aggressive dominance, and mental toughness and aptitude in sports (Bailey & Hurd, 2005; Cousins et al., 2009; Golby & Meggs, 2011).

However, a meta-analysis of dozens of studies was able to assess how reliable and strong these kinds of findings are, and the results were underwhelming, reporting only a small relationship between 2D:4D ratios and aggression in men (and no reliable relationship in women) (Hönekopp & Watson, 2011). More generally, the initial confidence that many had in the link between testosterone and human aggression has met with a harsh reality: The association between testosterone and human aggression is weaker and less reliable than expected. Other factors seem to play critical roles in determining when and whether this association is likely to emerge.

Recent research has pointed to one such factor that may be very important: the hormone cortisol. The combination of high testosterone and low cortisol is what predicts aggression, perhaps particularly aggression in the context of status-seeking or dominance behaviors. When cortisol levels are high, in contrast, the effects of testosterone on aggression are more likely to be blocked or inhibited (Denson, Ronay, et al., 2013; Mehta & Prasad, 2015).

The Role of Serotonin   Another biological factor linked to human aggression is the neurotransmitter serotonin (de Almeida et al., 2015; Ficks & Waldman, 2014; Helmbold et al., 2015). Serotonin appears to work like a braking mechanism to restrain impulsive, reactive acts of aggression. Low levels of serotonin in the nervous systems of humans and many animals are associated with high levels of aggression. Drugs that boost serotonin's activity can dampen aggressiveness, along with a range of other impulsive and socially deviant behaviors.

Brain and Executive Functioning   In addition to hormones and neurotransmitters, the frontal lobe of the brain is another hot topic in research on the biological underpinnings of human aggression. Researchers using a variety of techniques have found evidence linking abnormalities in frontal lobe structures with tendencies toward aggressive and violent behavior (de Almeida et al., 2015; Raine, 2013; Reznikova et al., 2015). The prefrontal cortex in particular has been implicated. Impaired prefrontal processing can disrupt what is called **executive functioning**, the cognitive abilities and processes that allow humans to plan or inhibit their actions. Executive functioning enables people to respond to situations in a reasoned, flexible manner, as opposed to being driven purely by external stimuli (Hoaken et al., 2007). A growing body of research finds a link between poor executive functioning and high aggression (Buckholtz, 2015; Perkins et al., 2014; Raaijmakers et al., 2008; Sorge et al., 2015; Verlinden et al., 2014).

executive functioning   The cognitive abilities and processes that allow humans to plan or inhibit their actions.

Concussions, Brain Functioning, and Aggression

This fMRI image from a study by Ruma Goswami and others (2015) of former professional football players with a history of concussions highlights the uncinate fasciculus, which connects the orbitofrontal cortex with the anterior temporal lobe. The areas in red and blue signal differences in functioning between the football players and control participants, and these differences were associated with more aggression and impulsivity and compromised executive functioning

From Goswami et al., 2015.

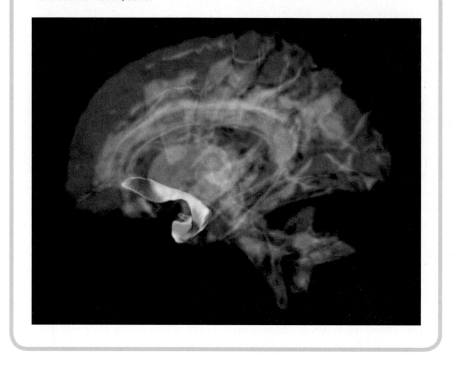

One noteworthy recent finding is that very aggressive teenagers showed different patterns of brain activity in response to witnessing someone else in pain than did less aggressive youth (Decety et al., 2009). In particular, when watching situations in which someone intentionally inflicted pain on another person, healthy teenagers showed brain activity associated with empathy. The highly aggressive teens, however, exhibited a pattern of brain activity associated with experiencing rewards, suggesting that they enjoyed watching others experience pain that someone intentionally inflicted on them. In addition, the aggressive teenagers showed less activation in areas associated with self-regulation and moral reasoning when seeing someone inflict pain on another than did the nonaggressive teenagers.

Recently a great deal of attention has been dedicated to the issue of concussions, especially in sports, and the link between concussions and aggression, along with other impulsive behaviors. Ruma Goswami and others (2015), for example, examined the brains (through fMRI scans) and the aggressive and impulsive tendencies of a group of retired Canadian Football League players with a history of multiple concussions. The researchers found that damage to the uncinate fasciculus, which connects the orbitofrontal cortex with the anterior temporal lobe, was associated with more aggression and impulsivity and compromised executive functioning. ● Figure 11.6 illustrates this brain region.

■ How Is Aggression Learned?

Regardless of the precise contribution of genetic and biological factors, it is clear that aggressive behavior is strongly affected by learning (Bandura, 1973). Rewards obtained by aggression today will increase its use tomorrow. Such rewards come in two flavors: *positive reinforcement,* when aggression produces desired outcomes, and *negative reinforcement,* when aggression prevents or stops undesirable outcomes. The child who gets a toy by hitting the toy's owner is likely to hit again. So, too, the child who can stop other children from teasing by shoving them away has learned the fateful lesson that aggression pays. Children who see aggression producing more good outcomes, and fewer bad outcomes, are more aggressive than other children (Guerra, 2012; Krahé & Busching, 2014).

Rewards are one part of the learning equation, but what about punishment? Punishment is often promoted as a way to reduce aggressive behavior. Research suggests that punishment is most likely to decrease aggression when it

"No society that feeds its children on tales of successful violence can expect them not to believe that violence in the end is rewarded."

— Margaret Mead

(1) immediately follows the aggressive behavior, (2) is strong enough to deter the aggressor, and (3) is consistently applied and perceived as fair and legitimate by the aggressor. However, such stringent conditions are seldom met, and when they are not met, punishment can backfire. When courts are overburdened and prisons are overcrowded, which is often the case, the relationship between crime and punishment can seem more like a lottery than a rational system in which the punishment fits the crime. In short, the *certainty* of punishment is more important than its *severity* (Berkowitz, 1998). Some politicians and police officials in New York City believe that the dramatic reduction in crime in the city in recent decades (from 2,245 murders in 1990 to only 328 in 2014—an 85% drop!) is due in large part to a policy change in the 1990s in which the police began to swiftly and consistently punish all kinds of crimes, even relatively minor crimes such as vandalism, to send the message that crime will lead to punishment. (Other factors that likely contributed to the steep decline in crime include the reduction in guns and drugs—particularly crack cocaine—and the increase in the age of the population.)

Corporal Punishment   On November 4, 2014, Adrian Peterson, star running back for the National Football League's Minnesota Vikings, pleaded "no contest" to the charge of assaulting his 4-year-old son with a tree branch (known as a "switch"), which caused injuries to several parts of the boy's body. Peterson, a religious Christian who often tweets Bible verses and is known to be unusually patient and accessible to fans, initially was shocked by the charges and the widespread outrage that people around the country had to his actions toward his son. Peterson claimed he simply was being a responsible father in disciplining his son, and he had done it in a way that was common in his culture and upbringing. Certainly the severity of the beating Peterson gave his son was extreme, but the Peterson case raises some more general questions about the ethics and effectiveness of using physical force to discipline children.

Corporal punishment remains a widely endorsed and frequently used way to punish children for bad behavior. **Corporal punishment** can be defined as physical force (such as spanking or hitting) intended to cause a child pain, but not injury, for the purpose of controlling or correcting the child's behavior. Although it is less prevalent than it used to be, the majority of children in the United States today experience spanking and other forms of corporal punishment (Lansford et al., 2014; Lapré & Marsee, 2015; S. J. Lee et al., 2015). Elizabeth Gershoff and others (2015) report that more than 200,000 students in public schools in the United States received corporal punishment in school during the 2009–2010 school year. There is a good deal of variability across cultures and countries in how frequently corporal punishment is used, but it remains quite common around the world. In a study of almost 31,000 families in 24 developing countries, for example, almost two-thirds of parents reported that their child had been corporally punished in the last month (Lansford & Deater-Deckard, 2012).

So corporal punishment is rather common. Does it work, though? More specifically, does being spanked or receiving other forms of corporal punishment reduce subsequent acts of aggression and antisocial behavior by a child? Spanking a child may result in immediate obedience to the adult and a quick reduction in aggression or other bad behavior, but in the long run, according to numerous studies, not only doesn't it work, it tends to backfire: More corporal punishment now is associated with more aggression later. Elizabeth Gershoff (2002) conducted

"I object to violence because when it appears to do good, the good is only temporary; the evil it does is permanent."
—Mahatma Ghandi

corporal punishment   Physical force (such as spanking or hitting) intended to cause a child pain, but not injury, for the purpose of controlling or correcting the child's behavior.

a meta-analysis of 88 studies conducted over six decades and involving more than 36,000 people. Her analysis revealed strong evidence for a positive correlation between corporal punishment and several categories of subsequent antisocial behaviors, such as aggression later as a child, aggression as an adult, and adult criminal behavior. More recent studies and reviews continue to find evidence for the relationship between corporal punishment and later problems of aggression, violence, criminality, drug abuse, dating violence, and mental health problems (Afifi et al., 2012; Hipwell et al., 2014; MacKenzie et al., 2015; Straus, 2010). The American Academy of Pediatrics (2015) publicizes to parents that it "strongly opposes striking a child for any reason."

Corporal punishment seems to teach the child that physical force is an effective and appropriate way to deal with problems. The relationship between parental corporal punishment and children's subsequent aggression is influenced by a number of factors, however, including the overall family environment, the emotions displayed by the parents during the punishment, and cultural and ethnic differences (Benjet & Kazdin, 2003; Pagani et al., 2009; L. G. Simons et al., 2013). For example, corporal punishment may be less likely to increase aggressiveness when it is administered in the context of an overall warm and supportive parent-child relationship (Baumrind, 1997; Deater-Deckard et al., 1998), although some recent research suggests the negative effects of corporal punishment may emerge even then (S. J. Lee et al., 2013). Genevieve Lapré and Monica Marsee (2015) found that the association between corporal punishment and later aggressiveness was weaker in African American than European American families.

Social Learning Theory   One of the authors of this book remembers many a late, cold afternoon as a teenager playing informal but competitive games of football and hockey with friends. The way he and his friends played them, both games were played without protective equipment and were quite rough, but football was the more physically brutal of the two. Yet despite the fact that virtually every play culminated in a pile of boys jumping on the flattened body of an opponent, it was very rare that an actual fight would break out. When this same group of friends played hockey, on the other hand, virtually every single game they played featured at least one fight. Why? Although he was years away from his first social psychology class, this future social psychologist was quite sure that he and his friends were basing their behavior on role models. Rarely had they seen professional football players stop and fight on the field. But rarely had they seen a professional hockey game in which that *didn't* happen.

The power of models to modify behavior is a crucial tenet of Albert Bandura's (1977) **social learning theory**. Social learning theory emphasizes that we learn from the example of others as well as from direct experience with rewards and punishments. Models influence the prosocial, helpful behavior described in Chapter 10. They also affect antisocial, aggressive behavior. In a classic study, Bandura and his associates (1961) observed the behavior of mildly frustrated children. Those who had previously watched an adult throw around, punch, and kick an inflatable doll (known as a Bobo doll, named after the character depicted on it) were more aggressive when they later played with the Bobo doll than were those who had watched a quiet, subdued adult. These children followed the adult model's lead not only in degree of aggression but also in the kinds of aggression they exhibited. Subsequent research has amply demonstrated that a wide range of aggressive models can elicit a wide range of aggressive imitations. Furthermore, these models do not have to be present; people on TV—even cartoon

> Children who are spanked or otherwise physically disciplined (but not abused) for behaving aggressively tend to become less aggressive.
>
> **FALSE**

social learning theory   The theory that behavior is learned through the observation of others as well as through the direct experience of rewards and punishments.

characters—can serve as powerful models of aggression (Bandura, 1983; Baron & Richardson, 1994; Berkowitz, 1993). This latter point—that children could learn aggression by seeing it modeled by cartoon characters—proved to foreshadow what eventually would become a tremendous amount of research on the effects of observing violence in the media. We discuss this large body of research a bit later, but its roots can be traced to Bandura's pioneering Bobo doll research.

People learn more than specific aggressive behaviors from aggressive models. They also develop more positive attitudes and beliefs about aggression in general, and they construct aggressive "scripts" that serve as guides for how to behave and solve social problems. These scripts can be activated automatically in various situations, leading to quick, often unthinking aggressive responses that follow the scripts they have learned (Bennett et al., 2005; Huesmann, 1998). Learning these scripts from their parents is one of the reasons that there are positive correlations between witnessing parents behaving aggressively or violently with each other during conflicts and individuals' subsequent aggressiveness as adolescents and adults (O'Leary et al., 2014; Perkins et al., 2014; Zarling et al., 2013). When parents use physical force to discipline their children, they also may be teaching the children a script of how to deal with conflict.

Consider the boys described just above who fought during hockey but not football games. Could their fighting during hockey be due to something about the sport of hockey itself, or did these boys learn aggressive scripts from watching how professional hockey players used their fists to deal with frustrations and provocations? An interesting study by Chris Gee and Larry Leith (2007) supports the social learning hypothesis. Gee and Leith analyzed the penalty records from 200 games of the National Hockey League (NHL). The NHL is the major professional hockey league in North America, and in recent years it has come to include top players from numerous countries around the world. When they were young and developing into hockey players, players born in North America were much more likely to have been exposed to models of aggression and fighting, and to have been rewarded (and not punished severely) for fighting and aggressive play, than were players born in Europe. Subsequently, even though these athletes all were playing the same sport on the same teams in the NHL, Gee and Leith found that the players born in North America were much more likely to be called for aggressive penalties than were players born in Europe (see ● Figure 11.7). Also, of all the infractions that the North Americans committed, more than 32% were for fighting or "roughing," whereas only 16% of the penalties for European players were for these particularly aggressive infractions.

Aggression or violence scripts play important roles in the lives of many young men and women who have committed violent crimes. In a thorough analysis of 416 young violent offenders from two New York City neighborhoods, Deanna Wilkinson and Patrick Carr (2008) found that 93% had seen someone get beaten badly, 75% had seen someone get knifed, 92% had seen someone get shot, and 77% had seen someone get killed. More than three-quarters of these

Mario Tama/Getty Images News/Getty Images

Boys in Baghdad play with toy guns, imitating the adult behavior they have observed in their war-torn country. When U.S. troops patrolled the area regularly, they traded the toy guns for pens to get them off the streets.

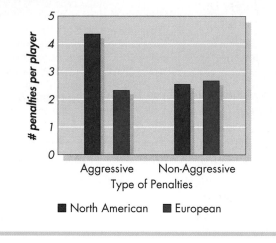

● FIGURE 11.7

Social Learning of Aggression in Hockey: North America Versus Europe

Researchers examined all the penalties called against National Hockey League players born in North America or Europe during 200 games. North American players were likely to have been exposed to more aggressive role models and positive reinforcement for fighting and aggression in hockey than their European counterparts. Consistent with this point, the results depicted here show that the North Americans were much more likely to be called for aggressive (but not for nonaggressive) penalties than the Europeans were.

Based on Gee & Leith, 2007.

 # penalties per player / *Type of Penalties* (Aggressive, Non-Aggressive)

■ North American   ■ European

violent offenders reported that a close friend had been killed through violence. Wilkinson and Carr collected chilling interviews with these individuals, many of which illustrated how so much early exposure to violence taught these individuals the unfortunate lesson that violence is the appropriate way to deal with conflicts and to attain high status in the neighborhood.

This kind of influence of aggressive modeling is consistent with a particularly tragic outcome known as the **cycle of violence**. Children who witness parental violence or who are themselves abused are more likely as adults to inflict abuse on intimate partners or their children, or, perhaps, to be victims of intimate violence (Cochran et al., 2011; Gómez, 2011; Smith et al., 2011; Sunday et al., 2011). Fortunately, just as aggressive models can increase aggressive behavior, nonaggressive models can decrease it. Observing a nonaggressive response to a provoking situation teaches a peaceful alternative and strengthens existing restraints against aggression. In addition, observing someone who is calm and reasonable may help an angry person settle down rather than strike out. Nonviolence and prosocial behavior can, like aggression, be contagious (Donnerstein & Donnerstein, 1976; Gibbons & Ebbeck, 1997).

To account for gender differences in aggression, social learning approaches emphasize that males and females are taught different lessons about aggression. Boys may be more likely than girls to be taught that physical aggression is an appropriate and rewarding way to handle conflict or manipulate other people, whereas relational aggression may be rewarded for girls at least as much or perhaps more than it is for boys (Bosson & Vandello, 2011; Bowker & Etkin, 2014; Crick & Rose, 2000; Werner & Grant, 2009). For example, in a study of third- and fourth-graders in an urban elementary school in Philadelphia, Tracy Evian Waasdorp and others (2013) found that overt aggression was associated with more popularity for boys and less popularity for girls, whereas relational aggression was more strongly associated with popularity for girls than boys.

Bandura's social learning theory has been one of the most important social psychological approaches to the study of human aggression since his classic early experiments in the early 1960s. Its simplicity should not obscure the fact that it can help explain a great amount of human behavior. Daniel Batson and Adam Powell (2003) wrote that social learning theory "has probably come closer to [the goal of accounting for the most facts with the fewest principles] than has any other theory in the history of social psychology" (p. 466).

Culture and Honor

Socialization of aggression also varies from culture to culture. For example, Giovanna Tomada and Barry Schneider (1997) reported that adolescent boys in traditional villages in Italy are encouraged to aggress as an indication of their sexual prowess and in preparation for their dominant role in the household.

cycle of violence The transmission of domestic violence across generations.

These authors believe that this is why schoolyard bullying among elementary school boys is significantly higher in central and southern Italy than it is in Norway, England, Spain, or Japan. Similarly, some researchers believe that *machismo*—which in its most stereotyped characterization prescribes that challenges, abuse, and even differences of opinion "must be met with fists or other weapons" (Ingoldsby, 1991, p. 57)—contributes to the fact that rates of violence are higher among Latin American men than among European American men (Harris, 1995).

Machismo may represent one form of what anthropologists call a **culture of honor**, which emphasizes honor and social status, particularly for males, and the role of aggression in protecting that honor. Even minor conflicts or disputes are often seen as challenges to social status and reputation and can therefore trigger aggressive responses. Several such subcultures exist around the world (and *Star Trek* fans might recognize the Klingon empire as an intergalactic example of a culture of honor). In an extensive series of studies, Dov Cohen, Richard Nisbett, Joseph Vandello, and their colleagues have examined various cultures of honor. Their original focus was on white men in the American South (Nisbett & Cohen, 1996). Rates of violence are consistently higher in the South than in all other regions of the country—the consistency of this difference is remarkable. Southerners are more likely than Northerners to agree that "a man has the right to kill" in order to defend his family and house, and they are more accepting of using violence to protect one's honor than are people from other parts of the country. (Note, however, that Southerners are *not* more likely than other Americans to accept violence unrelated to the protection of honor.)

Data from surveys, field experiments, and laboratory experiments suggest that this culture of honor promotes aggressive and violent behavior. In one series of experiments, Cohen and others (1996) investigated how white male American students who had grown up either in the North or in the South responded to insults. The experiments, conducted on a large Midwestern campus, involved an encounter between the participant and the confederate as they got in each other's way in a narrow hallway (see ● Figure 11.8). The confederate did not give way to the participant, bumped into him, and hurled an insult. Compared with Northerners, Southerners were more likely to think that their masculine reputations had been threatened, exhibited greater physiological signs of being upset, appeared more physiologically primed for aggression (their testosterone levels rose), and engaged in more aggressive and dominant subsequent behavior—such as giving firmer handshakes and being more unwilling to yield to a subsequent confederate as they walked toward each other in a very narrow hallway.

More recently Ryan Brown and others (2009) found that cultures of honor are associated with school violence. For example, states in the United States associated with cultures of honor had more than twice as many school shootings per capita as other states, and high-school students from culture-of-honor states were significantly more likely to bring a weapon to school. Lindsey Osterman and Ryan Brown (2011) also found that suicide rates are higher in culture-of-honor states, which the authors speculate may be due in part to greater concern and focus on interpersonal threat and loss of status, and a greater feeling of personal responsibility for failure to protect one's honor. Irshad Altheimer (2013) assessed the degree to which a very diverse set of 51 nations adhered to the culture of honor and found that countries with higher degrees

culture of honor   A culture that emphasizes honor and social status, particularly for males, and the role of aggression in protecting that honor.

Insult, Aggression, and the Southern Culture of Honor

The confederate (dressed in blue) seen here is annoyed that he has to move in order to let the participant (in the red shirt) pass by him down the narrow hallway. This setup replicates the situation used in a series of studies by Dov Cohen and colleagues (1996). When the confederate had to yield a second time to let the participant pass, he bumped and insulted him. White male participants from the South were more affected and reacted more aggressively in response to this insult than did those from the North.

A. Fein

of culture of honor had the highest homicide rates. (We should note that in these studies comparing various regions or countries, the researchers statistically control for other factors that might be related to these variables, such as differences in economic conditions, so that the results they report are not due to these other factors.)

Institutions support norms about the acceptability of honor-based violence. Cohen and Nisbett (1997) illustrated this in a clever experiment in which they sent letters to employers all over the United States from a fictitious job applicant who admitted that he had been convicted of a felony. To half the employers, the applicant reported that he had impulsively killed a man who had been having an affair with his fiancée and then taunted him about it in a crowded bar. To the other half, the applicant reported that he had stolen a car because he needed the money to pay off debts. Employers from the South and the West (which has a culture of honor similar to that of the South) were more likely than their Northern counterparts to respond in an understanding and cooperative way to the letter from the convicted killer—but not to the letter from the auto thief.

Joseph Vandello and Dov Cohen (2003) examined the culture of honor in Brazil in other research. Vandello and Cohen found that a wife's infidelity harmed a man's reputation more in the eyes of Brazilian students than in the eyes of students from the northern United States. In a related study, Vandello, Cohen, and others (2009) had participants from Chile (a culture that emphasizes honor) or Canada (a culture that is neutral concerning honor) listen to a tape of a man describing how he behaved violently toward his wife during a conflict. In one condition, the conflict was triggered when the husband thought she was flirting with another man at a party. In a different condition, the conflict was triggered by something having nothing to do with jealousy or threats to the man's honor. The Chilean participants rated the violence as more acceptable and rated the husband more positively across several dimensions than the Canadian participants did when the conflict was related to jealousy, but there was no cultural difference when the conflict was not related to jealousy or honor (see ● Figure 11.9).

Cultures of honor exist in individualist and collectivist cultures, but they may emphasize different types of threats. Ayse Uskul and others make the case that people in the collectivist culture of Turkey focus more on protecting the honor of one's family and close others, whereas people in more individualistic cultures emphasize honor focused on the individual (Uskul et al., 2012, 2014, 2015). Patricia Rodriguez Mosquera and others (2014) found a similar difference in emphasis on family-based honor between Pakistanis (a more collectivistic culture) and European Americans.

● FIGURE 11.9

Culture of Honor and Attitudes About Domestic Violence

Participants from Chile (a culture that emphasizes honor) or Canada (a neutral culture regarding honor) listened to a tape of a man describing his violent behavior toward his wife during a conflict. When the conflict was not triggered by an honor-related issue, Chileans and Canadians did not differ in how acceptable they thought the violence was. When the conflict was triggered by the husband perceiving his wife flirting with another man at a party, however, the Chileans were significantly more accepting of the violence than the Canadians were.

Based on Vandello et al., 2009.

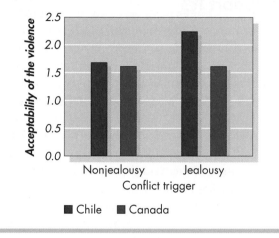

Situational Influences on Aggression

Whatever the fundamental origins of aggression, it is clear that specific, immediate situational factors can promote or inhibit it. In this section, we take a close look at several of these factors, ranging from frustration and heat to higher-order thinking.

▣ The Frustration–Aggression Hypothesis

In 1939, the year that World War II began, John Dollard and his colleagues published *Frustration and Aggression*, which quickly had enormous influence on theory and research on aggression. This book set forth two major propositions that taken together were called the **frustration–aggression hypothesis**: (1) frustration—which is produced by interrupting a person's progress toward an expected goal—will always elicit the motive to aggress; and (2) all aggression is caused by frustration.

Dollard and his colleagues claimed that the motive to aggress is a psychological drive that resembles physiological drives like hunger. According to this theory, just as food deprivation elicits a hunger drive, so frustration elicits an aggressive drive. Just as the hunger drive prompts the search for food, so the aggressive drive prompts the attempt to inflict injury. But what if we're unable to aggress against the source of our frustration? After all, we can't hit the boss, nor can we strike out against abstractions such as health problems or financial setbacks. Dollard and his colleagues believed that in such instances the aggressive drive can seep out in the form of **displacement**. Here, the inclination to aggress is deflected from the real

frustration–aggression hypothesis The idea that (1) frustration always elicits the motive to aggress and (2) all aggression is caused by frustration.

displacement Aggressing against a substitute target because aggressive acts against the source of the frustration are inhibited by fear or lack of access.

target to a substitute. After a bad day at work or school, do you sometimes come home and yell at the first available target—be it friend, lover, or pet?

Drawing from the ancient idea of **catharsis**, Dollard and his colleagues believed that displacing aggression in these ways can be effective at reducing the drive to aggress further. Since the Dollard group defined aggression quite broadly—to include making hostile jokes, telling violent stories, cursing, and observing the aggression of others, real or fictional—they held out the hope that engaging in some relatively harmless pursuit could drain away energy from more violent tendencies.

■ The Frustration–Aggression Hypothesis: Does the Evidence Support It?

Obviously, there is a connection between frustration and aggression. Break into a line of shoppers at the supermarket or interrupt a student cramming for an exam, and you can see it for yourself. James Holmes, the shooter in *The Dark Knight Rises* movie theater tragedy described in the introduction to the chapter, reportedly bought a high-powered rifle hours after he failed an important exam at the University of Colorado (Harris, 2012).

Soon after the frustration–aggression theory was proposed, however, critics pointed out that the Dollard group had overstated their case. Early on, Neal Miller (1941), one of the originators of the hypothesis, acknowledged that frustration does not always produce aggressive inclinations. The other absolute, that all aggression is caused by frustration, was soon overturned as well. The concepts of displacement and catharsis were also subjected to close scrutiny. Although there were some inconsistent findings concerning displacement over the years, a meta-analysis of 49 published articles found significant evidence for displaced aggression in response to provocation (Marcus-Newhall et al., 2000). Provoked individuals are especially likely to displace aggression toward others they dislike or others who are outgroup members (Pedersen et al., 2008). But what about catharsis? Dollard and his colleagues described catharsis as a two-step sequence. First, aggression reduces the level of physiological arousal. Second, because arousal is reduced, people are less angry and less likely to aggress further. It sounds logical, and many people believe it. But when put to the test, catharsis has not lived up to its advertisement. Most researchers have concluded that the catharsis idea is a myth. Aggressive behavior may sometimes reduce the likelihood of further immediate aggression, but so can just letting the frustration simply dissipate over time. For that matter, a response incompatible with aggression, such as sympathy or humor, can be more effective. In the long run, successful aggression sets the stage for more aggression later. In sum, relying on catharsis is dangerous medicine—more likely to inflame aggression than to put it out (Bushman, 2002; Geen & Quanty, 1977).

■ Negative Affect

By now it is clear that the original frustration–aggression hypothesis has a lot of flaws. But Leonard Berkowitz (1989) offered a different way to think about frustration as a trigger of aggression that has more merit. Berkowitz proposed that frustration is but one of many unpleasant experiences that can lead to aggression by creating negative, uncomfortable feelings. It is these negative feelings, and not the frustration itself, that can trigger aggression.

A wide variety of noxious stimuli and bad feelings can create negative feelings and increase aggression: noise, crowding, physical pain, threatened self-esteem, feelings of jealousy, social rejection, bad odors, and your favorite team losing a big

---

Blowing off steam by engaging in safe but aggressive activities (such as sports) makes people less likely to aggress later.

FALSE

catharsis A reduction of the motive to aggress that is said to result from any imagined, observed, or actual act of aggression.

game (Berkowitz, 1998; De Steno et al., 2006; Leary et al., 2006). Reactions to a very common unpleasant condition, hot weather, are especially intriguing. Many people assume that temperature and tempers rise together, while others think it's just a myth. Who is right?

Heat and Aggression: Losing Your Cool   Craig Anderson and others conducted extensive research on the question of whether heat leads to aggression, and data across time, cultures, and methodologies strongly support the notion that people lose their cool in hot temperatures and behave more aggressively (Anderson, 2001, 2012; Anderson et al., 2000). More violent crimes occur in the summer than in the winter, in hot years than in cooler years, and in hot cities than in cooler cities at any given time of year. Every year the numbers of political uprisings, riots, homicides, assaults, rapes, and reports of violence peak in the summer months. Alan Reifman and others (1991) found that as the temperature rises, Major League Baseball pitchers are more likely to hit batters with a pitch. The pitchers aren't wilder in general (such as in the number of walks they give up or wild pitches they throw)—they are just more likely to hit batters (see ● Figure 11.10).

With climate change having the potential to make hotter temperatures much more common in years to come, some scholars have speculated about the effects this may have on aggression and violence. Matthew Ranson (2014), for example, conducted a sophisticated analysis of 30 years of monthly data on temperature and crime rates in nearly 3,000 counties in the United States. Based on these analyses he estimates that global warming will cause an additional 22,000 murders, 1.2 million aggravated assaults, and a host of other criminal behaviors over the remainder of the century, at a financial cost of over $100 billion.

Given the earlier discussion of the culture of honor and the high incidence of violence in the American South, you may wonder whether it is culture or heat that contributes to the violence. At this point, evidence points to both influences as important. Each probably has independent effects on aggression. In addition, they may interact with each other. For example, the relatively high temperatures of the region may support aggressive norms (Anderson et al., 2000; Nisbett & Cohen, 1996).

Provocation and Social Rejection   Most aggressive incidents can be directly linked to some type of provocation, such as an insult or social rejection. The negative affect it causes plays an important role in triggering aggression. Many experiments have demonstrated this point. For example, a participant in an experiment might find himself or herself insulted, or suddenly ignored by the other participants who engage in pleasant interactions only with each other during the experiment. These studies have shown that these kinds of insults or rejections increase the likelihood of aggressive responses (Bettencourt, Talley, et al., 2006; DeWall et al., 2010; Williams & Wesselmann, 2011). The effect of social rejection may be particularly strong when the person feels disrespected, rather than simply disliked, by the rejection (DeBono & Muraven, 2014). In an interesting correlational study, Richard Larrick and others

"By far, the worst thing about the firehouse was the heat. It got really, really hot inside there the last few weeks of shooting. We had no air conditioning and the hotter it got, the angrier we got."
—Jason, one of the people living in the firehouse on MTV's *The Real World: Boston*

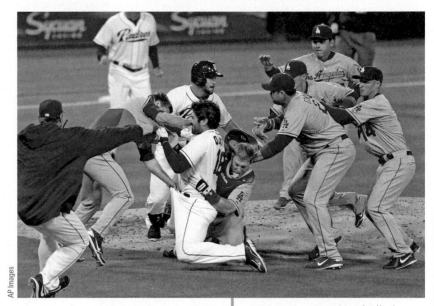

AP Images

A Major League Baseball player charges into a pitcher after getting hit by a pitch, sparking a brawl. Research indicates that negative affect caused by heat and frustration can increase aggression like this.

● **FIGURE 11.10**

Temper and Temperature in Baseball

This figure shows the average number of players hit by pitches (HBPs) per game during the 1986 through 1988 Major League Baseball seasons. As the temperature increased, so did the likelihood that pitchers would hit batters (with balls often thrown more than 90 miles per hour and often thrown at a batter's head). Players' general wildness or fatigue, as measured by walks, wild pitches, passed balls, and errors, did not increase with temperature, suggesting that the heat–HBP correlation perhaps was due to hotter temperatures that led to hotter tempers.

From Reifman, A. S., Larrick, R. P., and Fein, S., "Temper and temperature on the diamond: The heat-aggression relationship in major league baseball," *Personality and Social Psychology Bulletin* vol 17 (p. 6). Copyright © 1991 Sage Publications, Inc. Reprinted by permission.

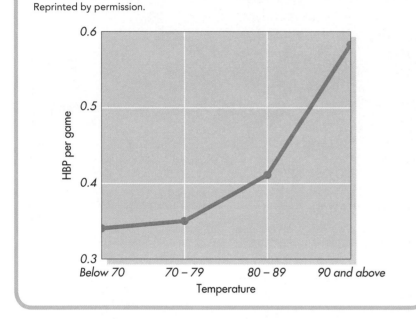

(2011) replicated the finding we reported earlier of baseball pitchers being more likely to hit opposing batters when it was hot outside, but they found additionally that pitchers were especially likely to hit batters in the heat if their teammates had been hit first—suggesting that provocation strengthened the effect of heat on their likelihood to aggress.

On a more extreme level, social rejection has been cited as the most significant risk factor for adolescent violence (Leary et al., 2006). Indeed, in 13 of the 15 school shootings between 1995 and 2001 that Mark Leary and others (2003) examined, the shooters had apparently been frustrated by social rejection.

Culture and Negative Affect The types of negative affect experienced by people can vary according to culture, as can their reactions to it. For example, Michael Boiger and others (2013) found that American participants in their study were relatively more likely to experience anger than their Japanese participants, and the reverse was true for the experience of shame. Shinobu Kitayama and others (2015) propose that for people in collectivist cultures, such as Japan, anger in reaction to frustration might violate cultural values of social harmony. Instead, collectivist cultures show greater support for hierarchy and social rankings, and anger in these settings is more likely to reflect a display of dominance from those occupying a high social status. Consistent with this hypothesis, Jiyoung Park and others (2013) found that Japanese individuals of relatively low status expressed anger less often than those of higher status did. For Americans, in contrast, those who felt they had relatively low status expressed anger more frequently than did those who felt they had relatively high status.

■ Arousal

In Chapter 9 we described the process of *excitation transfer*, in which the arousal created by one stimulus can intensify an individual's emotional response to another stimulus. For example, men who engaged in vigorous exercise were later more attracted to an attractive female than were those who had barely moved (White et al., 1981). Physical exercise is a highly arousing but emotionally neutral experience. Can it increase aggression as well as attraction? The research of Dolf Zillmann (1983; 2003) suggests that it can. The scope of excitation transfer is not limited to physical exercise. Noise, violent movies, arousing music—all have been shown to increase aggression. Heat has an interesting effect on arousal: Although people believe that heat lowers arousal, it actually increases it. This misperception makes heat a prime candidate for excitation transfer, as people are likely to misattribute arousal caused by heat to something else, such as anger, which can then lead to aggression (Anderson et al., 1996). Later in this chapter, we describe the effects of another arousing stimulus—pornography—on the inclination to aggress.

■ Thought: Automatic and Deliberate

Step by step, we have been making our way toward a comprehensive theory of social and situational influences on aggression, particularly reactive aggression. We've examined several kinds of unpleasant experiences (frustration, heat, provocation, and social rejection) that create negative affect. We've considered how arousal can contribute to aggression. The next step is to add cognition. People don't just feel; they also think. These thoughts may be as primitive as automatic, unconscious associations, or they may be higher-order, conscious deliberations.

Aggressive Cues   As we have already stated, no other stable, relatively wealthy country in the world comes even close to the United States in terms of the prevalence of guns used in violent crime. Guns of course are only an instrument—it's the people who are pulling the trigger. But social psychologist Leonard Berkowitz wondered whether guns were in fact entirely neutral. He hypothesized that the presence of a weapon can act as a situational cue that automatically triggers aggressive thoughts and feelings, thereby increasing the likelihood of aggression. In a classic study designed to test this idea, he and Anthony LePage (1967) had a confederate provoke male participants who could later respond by giving the confederate electric shocks (although in reality the confederate was not shocked). On a table near the shock apparatus just happened to be some objects scattered about, allegedly left there from a previous experiment.

For half of the participants, these objects were a revolver and rifle, and for the other half, they were badminton racquets and shuttlecocks. Berkowitz and LePage found that participants delivered more shocks to the confederate when a revolver and rifle were present than when badminton racquets and shuttlecocks were. In other words, although they didn't use these weapons, their mere presence seemed to make the participants more aggressive. This tendency for the presence of guns to increase aggression came to be known as the **weapons effect**. As Berkowitz put it: "The finger pulls the trigger, but the trigger may also be pulling the finger" (1968, p. 22).

Individuals may differ in what associations they have with various weapons. Bruce Bartholow and others (2005) found that hunters were less likely than nonhunters to associate hunting guns with aggression. Hunters had more positive associations with hunting guns; for example, they linked guns with sport and the pleasurable experiences they had had hunting with friends and family. Nonhunters not only had more negative, aggressive thoughts after exposure to hunting guns than did hunters, but they also behaved more aggressively while doing a subsequent task. However, exposure to assault guns had a very different effect: Hunters had more negative, aggressive associations with assault guns than did nonhunters, and they behaved more aggressively than nonhunters after exposure to them. In other words, hunters cognitively differentiated hunting guns from assault guns more than nonhunters did, and so these two types of weapons triggered very different effects for them.

Jennifer Klinesmith and others (2006) found that weapons had an effect on men's testosterone levels as well as on their aggression. Male college students in this experiment handled either a handgun or a children's game for 15 minutes. Relative to the students who interacted with the game, the students who interacted with the gun showed increased testosterone levels and exhibited greater aggression against another person (by adding a lot of "Frank's Red Hot Sauce" to a cup of

> **weapons effect**   The tendency that the likelihood of aggression will increase by the mere presence of weapons.

water they thought another subject would have to drink!). The greater the increase in testosterone in response to the gun, the more hot sauce the students added to the other person's drink.

More generally, any object or external characteristic that is associated with successful aggression, or with pain or unpleasantness, can serve as an aggression-enhancing situational cue (Berkowitz, 1993; 1998; 2008). Even brief exposure to words associated with hot temperatures can trigger aggressive thoughts (DeWall & Bushman, 2009).

Higher-Order Cognition Automatic associations can influence aggression, but more thoughtful, higher-order processing of information also plays a very important role in determining whether and how people will aggress. For example, an angry person might refrain from acting aggressively if he or she realizes that the potential costs of fighting seem too high. People who believe that aggression is inappropriate in a particular situation or whose moral values and principles mandate nonviolent behavior may realize that better alternatives to aggression exist (Huesmann & Guerra, 1997). Considering the behavior of other people in the immediate situation can also influence an individual's considerations. If others are reacting aggressively to the situation, aggression can be contagious (Freeman et al., 2011; Levy & Nail, 1993).

People's thoughts about the intentions of other people can determine whether they are likely to respond aggressively. Some individuals exhibit a **hostile attribution bias** in that they tend to perceive hostile intent in others. Research has found hostile attribution bias to be associated with both physical and relational aggression (Bailey & Ostrov, 2008; Orobio de Castro et al., 2002; Werner, 2012). For example, children who are chronically aggressive and have been rejected by their peers see hostile intent where others don't (Crick & Dodge, 1994; Helfritz-Sinville & Stanford, 2014; Helseth et al., 2015). Such perceptions then increase their aggression, and their peers respond by rejecting them further, locking these children into an ever-escalating vicious circle. Chronically aggressive adults, too, tend to expect and perceive hostility in others' motives and behaviors (Dill et al., 1997). Michael Schönenberg and Aiste Jusyte (2014) had a group of male violent offenders in a correctional facility in Germany view photos of faces and judged what emotion the person depicted was experiencing. Some of the photos were ambiguous—they were a mix of fear and anger, or of happiness and anger (see ● Figure 11.11). Compared to a control group of participants (of the same age and educational status), the violent prisoners were much more likely to interpret the ambiguous faces as angry. This result illustrates the violent men's bias of perceiving relatively more hostility in others, which is likely to trigger more aggressive responses in turn.

■ The Struggle for Self-Control: Rumination, Alcohol, and Other Factors

Not all insults, frustrations, or other situational triggers lead to aggressive behaviors, of course. More often than not we control our aggressive impulses and restrict our desire for revenge to our fantasies. It is quite clear that the ability to practice self-control is vital to the inhibition of aggression. It is also quite clear that behind a majority of aggressive and violent acts lies the failure of self-control (Denson, DeWall, & Finkel, 2012; DeWall, Finkel, & Denson, 2011).

We have discussed already in this chapter the role of executive functioning and the prefrontal cortex in enabling people to exhibit self-control and resist aggression. But various situational factors can impair our self-control. One such factor is **rumination**. In the context of anger and aggression, rumination involves

hostile attribution bias The tendency to perceive hostile intent in others.

rumination In the context of aggression, rumination involves repeatedly thinking about and reliving an anger-inducing event, focusing on angry thoughts and feelings, and perhaps even planning or imagining revenge.

● FIGURE 11.11

Biased Toward Hostility

The face in the middle is perfectly ambiguous in terms of the emotion expressed—it is a combination of the angry face on the left with the happy face on the right. Michael Schönenberg and Aiste Jusyte (2014) found that men with a history of violence were much more likely to perceive faces like the ambiguous one in the middle here as angry than were control participants.
Images sent to authors from Michael Schönenberg, 2015. Originals from Langner et al., 2010 .

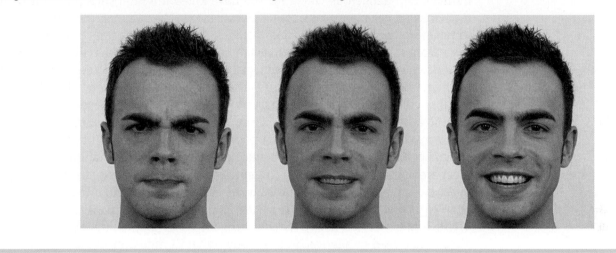

repeatedly thinking about and reliving an anger-inducing event, focusing on angry thoughts and feelings, and perhaps even planning or imagining revenge. Angry rumination can take a minor situational factor that otherwise might have faded away after a few minutes and enable it to retain its force to cause anger and aggression over a long period of time. A growing set of studies have demonstrated that this kind of rumination contributes to direct and displaced aggression, arousal and raised blood pressure, negative affect, and aggressive cognitions (Denson, Moulds, & Grisham, 2012; DeWall, Finkel, & Denson, 2011; Pedersen et al., 2011). Rumination also reduces people's self-control abilities. Therefore this is another way that rumination contributes to aggression—by impairing people's ability to inhibit aggression (see ● Figure 11.12) (Denson et al., 2011; Denson, DeWall, & Finkel, 2012).

● FIGURE 11.12

The Path from Provocation to Aggression: The Roles of Rumination and Self-Control

Research by Thomas Denson and others (2011; Denson, DeWall, & Finkel, 2012) has shown that an anger-inducing provocation, such as an insult or social rejection, can trigger angry rumination, which in turn reduces self-control, which in turn increases the likelihood and severity of aggression.
Denson et al., 2011.

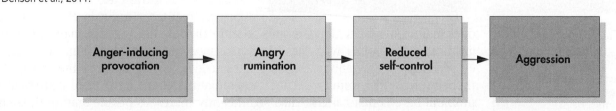

Some other conditions make it more difficult to engage in the higher-order cognition and self-control mechanisms that can inhibit aggressive impulses. High arousal, for example, impairs the cognitive control of aggression (Zillmann et al., 1975). When you are very emotional and angry, it is hard to focus on anything else or to be as reasonable as you might ordinarily like to be. One unusual example of this might be the story of a man in Nepal who was bitten by a cobra in August 2012. He chased the cobra and bit it back! Why did he kill the cobra in this rather intimate and dangerous way? "I could have killed it with a stick but bit it with my teeth instead because I was angry," he explained ("Nepali man bites snake to death in revenge attack," 2012).

Alcohol is a notorious obstacle to self-control. Alcohol is implicated in the majority of violent crimes, suicides, automobile fatalities, and sexually aggressive incidents between college students. The evidence is quite clear about this point: Alcohol consumption often increases aggressive behavior (Bushman et al., 2012; Carr & VanDeusen, 2004; Exum, 2006; Graham et al., 2006). But *how* does alcohol increase aggression? As many people who drink alcohol know, alcohol can lower people's inhibitions, and reducing inhibitions against aggression certainly facilitates aggressive behaviors (Ito et al., 1996). Alcohol impairs people's executive functioning, which as we discussed earlier involves cognitive processes that enable people to plan or inhibit actions (Giancola et al., 2012; Watkins et al., 2014; Weiss & Marksteiner, 2007). This in turn increases aggression. Another way that alcohol can lead to aggression is through what Claude Steele and Robert Josephs (1990) called *alcohol myopia.* That is, alcohol narrows people's focus of attention. Intoxicated people respond to initial, salient information about the situation but often miss later, more subtle indicators. They may therefore focus on a perceived provocation, such as an insult or threat to one's status, and fail to see or think about information that would explain away this provocation or to consider the long-term problems of retaliation, such as injury, guilt, or arrest. This narrowed focus can therefore make aggression much more likely to occur, unless the intoxicated person's narrow focus can be distracted toward something safer (Eckhardt et al., 2015; Hicks et al., 2015; Giancola, 2013).

Whereas alcohol reduces people's executive functioning and self-control, nonalcoholic sugar-rich drinks can boost them, especially when people's cognitive resources are already depleted through fatigue or other factors, and this in turn can reduce aggression (Denson, von Hippel, Kemp, & Teo, 2010; DeWall, Deckman, et al., 2011). Have you seen those commercials (for the candy bar, Snickers) in which people are nasty and aggressive because they're hungry? According to some researchers, being "hangry" (hungry + angry) really does lead to heightened aggression because the low glucose associated with hunger leaves our brains with less of the energy required for self-control (Bushman et al., 2014). What about caffeine? Does it give people a boost that might help them control their impulses if their cognitive resources have been depleted? The problem here is that caffeine also significantly increases people's arousal, such as by raising blood pressure and adrenaline—and this in turn can *increase* aggression

> "I could have killed it with a stick but bit it with my teeth instead because I was angry."
> —A Nepali man explains why he bit to death a cobra that had bitten him in August 2012.

Behind most aggressive acts lies the failure of self-control. Alcohol is one key factor in impairing people's executive functioning and self-control, leading to fights like this one outside a pub in Bristol, England.

Matt Cardy/Getty Images News/Getty Images

(James et al., 2015). Indeed, Thomas Denson, Mandi Jacobson, and others (2012) found that participants who *thought* they had consumed caffeine (but actually did not) showed reduced aggression after they had been cognitively depleted by a long and boring mental task, but those who actually consumed caffeine did not.

Situational Influences: Putting It All Together

Some researchers have attempted to take all these factors we've been discussing that influence reactive aggression and put them together into one overarching model. Craig Anderson and others produced the especially influential General Aggression Model (GAM) (Anderson et al., 1996; DeWall, Anderson, & Bushman, 2011). The basics of this model propose:

1. Various aversive experiences (such as frustration or heat), situational cues (such as weapons), and individual differences (such as a hostile attribution bias) can create negative affect, high arousal, and/or aggressive thoughts, each of which can lead to aggressive behavior
2. Whether aggressive behavior is then likely to result depends in part on the outcome of higher-order thinking, which can either inhibit aggression (such as by recognizing the danger of the situation or recognizing that what seemed like a provocation was really just an accident) or facilitate it (such as by perceiving that aggression is encouraged by one's peers in this situation or that a provocation was intentional).

Eli Finkel (2014) and colleagues (Denson, DeWall, & Finkel, 2012; Finkel, DeWall et al., 2012) recently introduced the I^3 theory (pronounced "I-cubed theory"). This theory emphasizes the role of self-control in aggression, which we just discussed in the previous section. The three *I*s in this theory stand for:

1. *Instigation*—social factors that often trigger aggressive impulses, such as provocation or social rejection
2. *Impellance*—personality and situational factors that promote the urge to aggress when encountering instigating factors, such as angry rumination or trait aggressiveness
3. *Inhibition*—the various factors of self-control we described in the previous section

This theory pits the forces of instigation and impellance on the one hand against the power of inhibition on the other to determine the likelihood of aggression. For example, strong provocation coupled with angry rumination can overpower a person's self-control abilities that have been compromised by alcohol, resulting in an elevated likelihood of aggression.

● Figure 11.13 presents a diagram that includes aspects of both the General Aggression and the I^3 models, along with a few

"Violence is the last refuge of the incompetent."

—Isaac Asimov

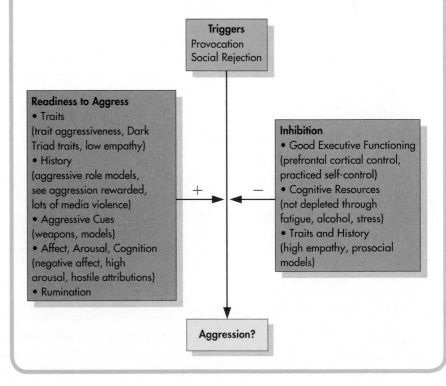

● **FIGURE 11.13**

Factors Promoting and Inhibiting Reactive Aggression

This graph attempts to pull together a variety of the situational and individual-difference factors that we've discussed in this chapter to illustrate the path from a trigger of potential aggression to actual aggression. It is based in part on the General Aggression Model (e.g., DeWall & Anderson, 2011) and I^3 theory (Denson, DeWall, & Finkel, 2012). The factors on the left ("Readiness to Aggress") are among those that make aggression more likely. The factors on the right ("Inhibition") make aggression less likely.

Triggers
Provocation
Social Rejection

Readiness to Aggress
● Traits
(trait aggressiveness, Dark Triad traits, low empathy)
● History
(aggressive role models, see aggression rewarded, lots of media violence)
● Aggressive Cues
(weapons, models)
● Affect, Arousal, Cognition
(negative affect, high arousal, hostile attributions)
● Rumination

Inhibition
● Good Executive Functioning
(prefrontal cortical control, practiced self-control)
● Cognitive Resources
(not depleted through fatigue, alcohol, stress)
● Traits and History
(high empathy, prosocial models)

Aggression?

other factors we've discussed in this chapter. The likelihood that a trigger of potential aggression toward someone will result in actual aggression is heightened by the kinds of factors listed on the left side of the figure and reduced by the factors listed on the right side.

Media Effects

Violence depicted in the media has been a target of attack and counterattack for decades. But the amount, intensity, and graphic nature of the violence have continued to escalate. According to a 2009 report by the American Academy of Pediatrics, by the age of 18 the average American young person will have on average viewed about 200,000 acts of violence on television alone. About 97% of 12- to 17-year-olds in the United States play video games, and the majority report playing violent video games (Willoughby et al., 2012). And all this exposure is not limited to the United States—it is a global phenomenon. Violent imagery in the lyrics and videos of popular music also run rampant. If consumers didn't enjoy violence in TV, film, music, videos, and video games, these media would not be featuring it. So can it really be harmful? We explore this question in the sections that follow.

■ Violence in Popular Media: Does Life Imitate Art?

Are people inspired to be violent from what they see in popular media? It often seems that way. Consider the following 5 reports, which is just a sample of the many similar incidents that have been reported.

(1) On May 31, 2014, two 12-year-old girls stabbed their friend 19 times, allegedly because they were inspired by a fan-fiction supernatural character named Slender Man, which was popular on some Internet forums. (2) The night James Holmes opened fire in the Colorado theater showing the Batman movie in July 2012, he reportedly referred to himself as "The Joker"—the villain who brought random violence to innocent masses in the previous Batman movie. (3) Dylan Klebold and Eric Harris were big fans of the violent video game *Doom* when they went on their 1999 shooting spree at Columbine High School, and reports indicate that they based their plans for their massacre on the game. (4) Anders Behring Breivik, who killed 77 people in bombing and shooting attacks in Norway in 2011, said that he played violent video games such as *Call of Duty: Modern Warfare 2* and *World of Warcraft* for training purposes before the attacks. He claimed that he played these games for about 16 hours a day in 2006, doing little else but playing and sleeping for the entire year (Gibbs & Koranyi, 2012; Pancevski, 2012; Paterson, 2012). (5) Tim Kretschmer, the shooter in a March 2009 rampage at a high school in Winnenden, Germany, had numerous brutally violent video games and videos. This led one of Germany's largest retail chains to stop selling films or games with very violent material (Roxborough, 2009).

Let's look at one such incident in some more detail. On September 13, 2006, Kimveer Gill, a 25-year-old man, drove up to Dawson College in Montreal, pulled three guns from his car, and started shooting students. In total, Gill shot 20 people. Gill had no apparent connection or dispute with Dawson College or its students. Rather, it seemed, he had a tremendous amount of hostility toward the world in general. He had written numerous postings on the Internet about his loathing for humanity and about his fascination with guns, death, and violent video games. "Life is a video game. You've got to die sometime," he wrote in one blog

(Struck, 2006, p. A12). These are the same words another young killer had used after killing police officers in Alabama in 2003, in a scene similar to one depicted in the killer's favorite violent video game (Kampis, 2005).

According to one report, when Danny Ledonne heard about the shootings at Dawson College in Montreal, he threw up. Ledonne, living in Colorado, had no connection to Kimveer Gill or his victims, but Ledonne had heard that the killer was a big fan of the extremely violent video game he had posted on the Internet, called *Super Columbine Massacre.* The game was based on the massacre at Columbine High School, in which two seniors shot and killed 12 students and a teacher and injured many others. Gill was fascinated by the shootings, both the real event and the video game version. "When I heard about the Dawson shootings," Ledonne said, "people asked me, 'Gosh. How do you feel to have blood on your hands?'" (Gerson, 2006, p. A12).

David Pearson/Alamy

Can playing violent video games cause children and young adults to become more aggressive and violent? A growing body of research suggests that it can.

Indeed, many of the boys and young men involved in the waves of school shootings had consumed a steady diet of violent video games, including the shooter behind the mass killings at the elementary school in Newtown, Connecticut. Each shooting, moreover, was soon followed by additional threats and violent acts. According to one analysis, there were 400 copycat incidents in the United States and Canada in the month after the Columbine shooting (Tobin, 2006). Table 11.3 lists just a few of the many other violent incidents that may have been inspired by exposure to violence depicted in popular media. Yet no one can ever prove that a specific fictional depiction was the primary cause of a specific act of violence. There are always other possibilities.

If you ask people whether exposure to media violence causes real aggression, most would probably say that they doubt that it does or that there has never been clear evidence one way or another on this question. When this issue is discussed on the news or in the media in general, the reports tend to conclude that the relevant scientific evidence is weak and mixed, at best. Defenders of the entertainment industry consistently argue that there is no evidence that viewing media violence causes real-world aggression. Social psychologists and others who study this issue are often confronted by people who assert, "I've played lots of violent video games and I never killed anyone."

"People asked me, 'Gosh. How do you feel to have blood on your hands?'"
—Danny Ledonne, after learning that the school shooter at Dawson College in 2006 was a fan of the video game he had posted on the Internet

"According to a national survey of 12- to 17-year-olds in the United States, 99% of boys and 94% of girls play video games."
—Lenhart et al., 2008

The Research Findings   But what does the social psychological research *really* say on this matter? There has been a tremendous amount of research on this issue in the past several decades, and it has produced enough evidence that six major professional societies in the United States—the American Psychological Association, the American Academy of Pediatrics, the American Academy of Child and Adolescent Psychiatry, the American Medical Association, the American Academy of Family Physicians, and the American Psychiatric Association—together concluded that the research "reveals unequivocal evidence that media violence increases the likelihood of aggressive and violent behavior in both immediate and long-term contexts" (Anderson et al., 2003, p. 81). More recently, the American Academy of Pediatrics

▲ TABLE 11.3

Copycat Violence?

Although it's impossible to prove that any specific media depiction caused a specific violent action, there have been some close connections. We've discussed several recent cases in the text. In addition to those, here are some others.

Violent Fiction	Subsequent Violent Fact
The Matrix (a trilogy of films starring Keanu Reeves)	Numerous killers have cited the influence of these movies in their violent outbursts. Many of them believed they were in a real-life version of the matrix.
Dexter (TV series about a serial killer)	A teenager strangled his 10-year-old brother to death, later explaining that he was inspired by the serial killer character Dexter.
Twilight (series of romance books and movies featuring vampires)	A boy bit at least 11 girls because he was inspired by his love of the movie.
Money Train (movie starring Wesley Snipes and Woody Harrelson)	In several incidents in New York City, people doused subway token collectors with flammable liquids and burned them, just as had been depicted in the movie.
Natural Born Killers (movie starring Woody Harrelson and Juliette Lewis)	At least eight murders have been cited as having been inspired by this violent film, including the case of a student who decapitated a classmate because he "wanted to be famous, like the natural born killers" (Brooks, 2002, p. 10).
"F*** tha Police" (song by gangsta rap group N.W.A.)	Rifles used in the shooting of a police officer in North Carolina were emblazoned with the letters N.W.A.
Scream (movie starring Neve Campbell, Courteney Cox, and Drew Barrymore)	Several brutal attacks apparently copied elements of the movie, including the costume worn and the scare tactics used by the fictional killer. For example, a Belgian man put on a *Scream* costume before killing a 15-year-old girl with two kitchen knives.
Fight Club (movie starring Brad Pitt)	A teen obsessed with *Fight Club* set off a bomb at a Manhattan Starbucks in an act that was similar to an event in the movie. A friend said, "He thought he was Tyler Durden," the lead character from the movie (Gendar et al., 2009, p. 7).
Professional wrestling	Mimicking a dangerous wrestling move he had seen on TV, a 7-year-old boy accidentally killed his 3-year-old brother in Dallas.
The Life and Death of Lord Erroll (a controversial book)	The author's son was killed in an act very similar to the murder that had been described in her book. The author later said, "In some terrible way, I think I pressed the trigger" (Alderson, 2001, p. 6).
Grand Theft Auto (video game)	Two teenagers in Tennessee fired shotgun blasts at passing cars on a highway, leaving one dead and another wounded. They claimed they didn't mean to kill anyone but simply wanted to emulate *Grand Theft Auto*, their favorite video game.

© Cengage learning®

> *"There's an audience of people who love this genre who are not violent. In fact, they sort of use it to vent their violent nature so they don't have to act it out in real life."*
> —Actress Jamie Lee Curtis, star of *Halloween* and some of its sequels, defending horror movie blood and gore

(2009), which represents 60,000 child specialists, stated, "Exposure to violence in media, including television, movies, music, and video games, represents a significant risk to the health of children and adolescents. Extensive research indicates that media violence can contribute to aggressive behavior, desensitization to violence, nightmares, and fear of being harmed" (p. 1495). The general public may not be aware of this, but the majority of the scientific community is more convinced than ever.

What is the evidence behind these conclusions? The best way to investigate the issue of media violence is to use multiple methods, each of which has different sets of strengths and weaknesses. This is exactly what researchers in this area have done. What is particularly impressive about this research is that the results have been strikingly consistent across methods. In longitudinal studies researchers examine individuals' exposure to violent media early in life and then their real-world aggression years later. In one classic longitudinal study, for example, the extent to which 8-year-olds watched violent TV predicted their aggressiveness and criminality as adults, even when statistically controlling for other factors such as socioeconomic status and parenting practices (Huesmann et al., 2003) (● Figure 11.14).

In addition to longitudinal studies, researchers have conducted cross-sectional research, which looks at the relation between individuals' exposure to violent media and their aggressive behavior at a single point in time, and experimental research, in which they randomly assign individuals to watch or play violent or nonviolent media and then measure their subsequent aggressive thoughts, feelings, and behaviors. Several meta-analyses that review and combine the results of dozens or even hundreds of studies have found across all these types of research a significant link between violent media and actual aggressive thoughts and behaviors. One review, for example, examined the relationship between exposure to media violence and real aggression in 46 longitudinal studies, 86 cross-sectional surveys, 28 field experiments, and 124 laboratory experiments—totaling more than 50,000 participants. The positive relationship between exposure to media violence and real aggressive behavior was present across all four types of studies (Anderson & Bushman, 2002a; Anderson et al., 2004). More recently, Tobias Greitemeyer and Dirk Mügge (2014) reviewed about 100 different studies specifically on playing violent or prosocial video games, involving nearly 40,000 participants. As can be seen in ● Figure 11.15, playing violent video games was associated with increased aggressive behavior, cognition, and affect, and decreased prosocial behavior and affect, whereas playing prosocial games had the opposite pattern.

Gari Wyn Williams/Alamy

Teenage cosplayers dress up as violent characters while on their way to a comic book and gaming convention in Italy. Although most gamers do no harm outside their fictional worlds, there are disturbingly frequent acts of copycat violence apparently inspired by violent examples from popular culture.

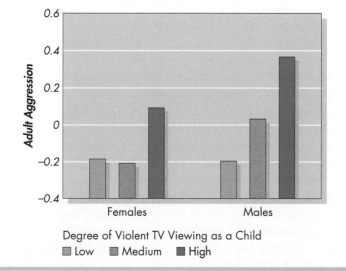

● **FIGURE 11.14**

Violent TV Viewing and Aggression 15 Years Later

A longitudinal study tracked individuals over a 15-year period. Based on how much TV violence they viewed as 8-year-olds, individuals were categorized as having viewed low (lower 20%), medium (middle 60%), or high (upper 20%) levels of TV violence. Their aggressiveness as adults was measured 15 years later. For both females and males, those who tended to watch the greatest amount of violent TV as children tended to be the most aggressive as adults.
Based on Huesmann et al., 2003.

Degree of Violent TV Viewing as a Child
■ Low ■ Medium ■ High

● **FIGURE 11.15**

Playing Violent and Prosocial Video Games: Links with Thoughts, Feelings, and Actions

A recent meta-analysis of 98 studies involving about 37,000 participants in multiple countries found significant relationships between playing violent or prosocial video games and a number of outcomes. The sizes of the bars in this graph represent the magnitude of the relationships between video-game playing and these other variables; bars in a positive direction indicate a positive relationship; bars in a negative direction indicate a negative relationship. Playing violent video games (blue bars) was associated with increased aggressive behavior, cognition, and affect, and decreased prosocial behavior and affect. Playing prosocial games (red bars) had the opposite pattern. Based on Greitemeyer & Mügge, 2014.

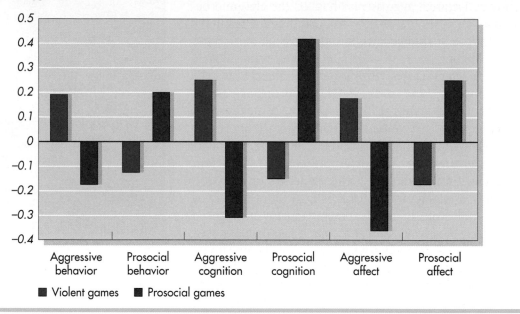

Physical violence is not the only kind of aggression portrayed in the media. Sarah Coyne and John Archer (2004) found examples of indirect or relational aggression in 92% of programs on British television shows that were popular with adolescents, a rate much higher than physical aggression. Compared to physical aggressors, the indirect aggressors in these shows tended to be more rewarded for their aggression, and they were more likely to be female and attractive. The results of an experiment Coyne and her colleagues (2004) conducted suggested that television exposure to indirect aggression had immediate effects on adolescents' own behavior, such as decreasing helping behavior, evaluating others more negatively, and advocating indirect aggression in response to an ambiguous situation.

In a series of subsequent studies Coyne and others (2008, 2012) randomly assigned female college students to watch film clips involving physical aggression (from the movie *Kill Bill)*, relational aggression (from the movie *Mean Girls)*, or no aggression (from the movie *What Lies Beneath)*. Although the different clips produced equal degrees of excitement and arousal, the clips showing either physical or relational aggression led the students to become more aggressive (blasting a confederate with painful noise) and primed more relational aggression cognitions than did the nonaggressive clip. Elizabeth Behm-Morawitz and others (2015) note as well that relational aggression (or what these researchers call "social aggression") is very common in popular reality TV shows. They found that female college students who perceive the lifestyle on these shows (such as *Keeping Up With the Kardashians* and *The Bachelor)* to be desirable were especially favorable in their attitudes toward relational aggression.

It is important to note that media violence is neither a necessary nor a sufficient cause of real-world aggression and violence. In other words, not everyone exposed to media violence will necessarily become more aggressive, and not all acts of aggression are fueled by media violence. Similarly, not everyone who smokes gets lung cancer, and not everyone who gets lung cancer smoked. Rather, frequent exposure to media violence should be seen as an important risk factor for real-world aggression, just as frequent consumption of alcohol is a risk factor for various health problems. It is important to note as well that although the majority of published work supports the link between media violence and real-world aggression, some researchers are more skeptical. Chris Ferguson in particular has led the charge criticizing much of the research that has been published on this issue, and he has published a series of studies finding no effects of watching violent media or playing violent video games on children's and adolescents' aggression (Elson & Ferguson, 2014; Ferguson, 2015; Ferguson et al., 2015). Several of the most prominent researchers on aggression have countered these criticisms and challenged these null findings, and these counterarguments have in turn been rebutted by Ferguson and others, and so on. More work will surely be conducted in the coming years to clarify some of these issues.

> Exposure to TV violence in childhood is related to aggression later in life.
> **TRUE**

How Does Media Violence Cause These Effects?   Even if not every study or review agrees, clearly there have been dozens and dozens of studies that report that media violence can have both immediate and long-term effects. Another question, though, is *how* can it have these effects? Social psychologists have found several paths through which media violence produces real-world aggression. For instance, exposure to media violence can trigger aggressive and hostile thoughts, which in turn can lead individuals to interpret others' actions in hostile ways and promote aggression (Krahé, 2014). Combine these aggressive cognitions with the high arousal caused by these games, and the recipe for aggression becomes more potent.

Media violence influences aggression also by desensitizing individuals to violence. **Desensitization** to violence refers to a reduction in emotion-related physiological reactivity to real violence. Desensitization is one form of *habituation*. A novel stimulus gets our attention, and if it's sufficiently interesting or exciting, it elicits physiological arousal. But when we get used to something, our reactions diminish. Familiarity with violence reduces physiological arousal and corresponding brain activity to new incidents of violence (Brockmyer, 2015; Geen, 1981; Gentile et al., 2015; Montag et al., 2012). Desensitized to violence, we may become more accepting of it. Douglas Gentile and others (2015) demonstrated this point in an experiment that examined participants' brain activity using fMRI technology while they played violent and nonviolent versions of a video game. All the participants were young adult men who frequently played video games, but some of these gamers mostly played violent games and the others mostly played nonviolent games. The fMRI results revealed that the participants who had played a lot of violent video games showed suppression in neural responses in regions of the brain that typically are associated with emotions such as fear and disgust.

Media violence can also produce long-term effects by influencing people's values and attitudes toward aggression, making it seem more legitimate and even necessary for social interaction and the resolution of social conflicts. Consistent with social learning theory, children may learn that aggression and violence are common, normal ways of dealing with threats or problems and are often rewarded. Frequent exposure to such imagery fuels the aggressive scripts that children and adolescents develop, which they subsequently use to guide their behavior (Anderson & Huesmann, 2007).

The effects of exposure to violence in the media also operate through what George Gerbner and his colleagues (1986) called **cultivation**. Cultivation refers to

desensitization   Reduction in emotion-related physiological reactivity in response to a stimulus.

cultivation   The process by which the mass media (particularly television) construct a version of social reality for the public.

the capacity of the mass media to construct a social reality that people perceive as true, even if it isn't. The media tend to depict the world as much more violent than it actually is. This can make people become more fearful, more distrustful, more likely to arm themselves, and more likely to behave aggressively in what they perceive as a threatening situation (Morgan & Shanahan, 2010; Riddle & De Simone, 2013).

Can Media Cause Positive, Prosocial Effects? The vast amount of attention and research has focused on the negative effects of popular media, but can positive media images and messages produce prosocial rather than antisocial effects? The evidence thus far is encouraging. Chapter 10, on Helping Others, discusses some of this work, including a meta-analysis of 34 studies that found a reliable positive effect of prosocial television on children's prosocial behavior (Mares & Woodard, 2005). Also, if you go back to ● Figure 11.15 in this chapter, you can see that the graph there illustrates that playing prosocial video games is associated with increases in prosocial behavior and decreases in aggressive behavior (Greitemeyer & Mügge, 2014).

■ Pornography

Just as the effects of violence in popular media have been discussed and debated for decades, so too have the effects of media displays of sexual material. Defenders and opponents of pornography argue their positions passionately. So what does the social psychological research say?

It is important to recognize the challenges of conducting research on such a controversial and sensitive issue, such as the ethical challenges involved in conducting experiments using pornography. Even defining what is meant by pornography or obscenity is rarely straightforward. Because of the subjectivity involved in such definitions, the term **pornography** is used here to refer to explicit sexual material, regardless of its moral or aesthetic qualities. It is crucial, however, to distinguish between nonviolent and violent pornography in discussing the relationship between pornographic displays and aggression.

Nonviolent and Violent Pornography Earlier in this chapter, we described how both arousal and affect can influence aggression. The results of research on nonviolent pornography confirm the importance of these factors (Donnerstein et al., 1987). For many people, viewing attractive bodies elicits a pleasant emotional response and moderate levels of sexual arousal. This combination of positive affect and only moderate arousal is unlikely to trigger much aggression. Indeed, according to Michael Seto and colleagues (2001), there is little support for a direct causal link between the use of nonviolent pornography and sexual aggression. However, there is more evidence for an association between pornography use and attitudes supporting violence against women (Hald et al., 2010; Malamuth et al., 2012).

Adding violence to pornography greatly increases the possibility of harmful effects. Violent pornography is a triple threat: It brings together high arousal; negative emotional reactions such as shock, alarm, and disgust; and aggressive thoughts. Numerous online sites—including many that are free and can be viewed easily by minors—focus specifically on images of sexual violence against women and use depictions of women's pain as a selling point (Gossett & Byrne, 2002). Research suggests that the effects of violent pornography are gender-specific. Male-to-male aggression is no greater after exposure to violent pornography than it is after exposure to highly arousing but nonviolent pornography, but male-to-female aggression is markedly increased (Donnerstein & Malamuth, 1997; Linz et al., 1987; Malamuth & Donnerstein, 1982).

pornography Explicit sexual material.

Chris Ryan/Corbis Sports/Corbis

The combination of violence, arousal, and sexual imagery is part of the appeal to many fans of professional wrestling (as in this WWE event). Research on aggression suggests that this combination can also be particularly potent in contributing to real-world aggression among viewers.

Individual Differences   Not everyone is affected by pornography in the same way. According to a number of studies by Neil Malamuth and colleagues, the negative effects of pornography are especially likely to be evident among men who have relatively high levels of sexual arousal in response to violent pornography and also express attitudes and opinions indicating acceptance of violence toward women (see Table 11.4). These individuals report more sexually coercive behavior in the past and more sexually aggressive intentions for the future. Men who score relatively high on scales such as these are more predisposed to sexual aggression than other men. The effects of pornography on aggression or negative attitudes toward women are stronger for these men than they are for other men (Hald et al., 2010; Malamuth et al., 2012). Another risk factor concerns men's family histories. Leslie Gordon Simons and others (2012) reported that men who regularly use pornography and whose parents frequently used harsh corporal punishment were most likely to report engaging in sexually coercive behaviors.

Malamuth synthesized much of this research into the *confluence model of sexual aggression*. This model proposes that for the subset of individuals who already score high on multiple known risk factors of sexual aggression, consuming pornography (even nonviolent pornography, especially if it is highly arousing) adds "fuel to the fire" and increases the risk of sexually aggressive attitudes and behaviors (Hald & Malamuth, 2015, p. 100). According to this model, the presence of multiple risk factors at once—such as hostile, distrustful attitudes

---

▲ **TABLE 11.4**

Attitudes About Violence Toward Women and Rape Myths

Widely used in research on pornography, these two scales assess attitudes about violence toward women and beliefs about the nature of rape. A few items from each scale are shown here.

Acceptance of Interpersonal Violence (Toward Women): AIV Scale

1. Being roughed up is sexually stimulating to many women.

2. Many times a woman will pretend she doesn't want to have intercourse because she doesn't want to seem loose, but she's really hoping the man will force her.

3. A man is never justified in hitting his wife.

   Scoring: Persons scoring high in acceptance of violence toward women agree with items 1 and 2 but disagree with item 3.

Rape Myth Acceptance: RMA Scale

1. If a woman engages in necking or petting and she lets things get out of hand, it is her own fault if her partner forces sex on her.

2. Any female can get raped.

3. Many women have an unconscious wish to be raped, and may then unconsciously set up a situation in which they are likely to be attacked.

4. In the majority of rapes, the victim is promiscuous or has a bad reputation.

   Scoring: Persons scoring high in acceptance of rape myths agree with items 1, 3, and 4 but disagree with item 2.

Based on Burt, 1980.

toward women, acceptance of rape myths, sexual gratification from controlling women, a family history of abuse, and an impersonal attitude toward sexual relations—is particularly dangerous. For these individuals especially, pornography becomes a greater risk factor for aggression.

■ Objectification and Dehumanization

One characteristic of much pornography, and especially violent pornography, is the objectification of people, particularly of women. Beyond pornography, the media in general, such as through movies, video games, TV commercials, and music videos and lyrics, all too often portray various groups of people in relatively objectified or dehumanizing ways, relying on narrow, stereotypic depictions. And the media aren't the only causes of this problem. Stereotypes, jokes, and a host of ways in which some people are devalued may be transmitted widely in a culture through many channels. Whatever the source, the consequences are significant. As we discussed in Chapter 5, people often perceive and think about outgroup members more like objects and lower-order animals than like fellow humans. These tendencies have been found to make prejudice and aggression toward outgroups more likely to result (Goff et al., 2014; Kteily et al., 2015; Lee & Harris, 2014). For example, Laurie Rudman and Kris Mescher (2012) found that men who automatically associated women with animals or objects showed stronger inclination to sexually harass or rape women.

Dehumanization is an extremely common by-product of conflict and war between groups. Not only does the fighting between groups foster a biased perspective of the other group, but dehumanization in turn makes engaging in violence more tolerable and seemingly necessary. Although this may be a necessary tool of war, it also lowers the restraints against stepping over the ethical line into abuse and torture. In addition, it makes finding peace more difficult as the two sides may have so demonized the enemy that they cannot imagine trusting them enough to broker an end to the conflict.

As novelist George Orwell (1942) discovered during the Spanish Civil War, the cure for dehumanization is to restore the human connection. Sighting an enemy soldier holding up his pants with both hands while running beside a nearby trench, Orwell was unable to take the easy shot: "I had come here to shoot at 'Fascists'; but a man who is holding up his trousers isn't a 'Fascist,' he is visibly a fellow creature, similar to yourself, and you don't feel like shooting at him" (p. 254).

Reducing Aggression and Violence

In this final major section of the chapter, one key question remains: How can we reduce all this aggression we've been discussing? Do we have any reason to hope that rates of aggression and violence can be reduced? Are we simply aggressive animals who are destined to go on hurting and killing each other? Fortunately, there is reason for optimism. Why do we think that rates of aggression and violence can decline? Because they already have.

An intriguing and comprehensive book by psychologist Steven Pinker (2011), called *The Better Angels of Our Nature: Why Violence Has Declined,* is among the recent analyses that makes the case that we are living in a time that is less violent and more peaceful than at any period in human history. He calls this reduction in violence perhaps "the most important thing that has happened in human history" and that "no aspect of life is untouched by the retreat from violence" (p. xxi). This claim flies in the face of how people tend to perceive their contemporary world as extraordinarily violent. Reasons for this tendency include people's tendency to focus on recent events, the bias to publicize the most shocking and disturbing news stories, and so on. But in his book Pinker presents chart after chart illustrating a dramatic reduction of violence over the centuries. For example, see ● Figure 11.16 for the rates of homicide in Western Europe from 1300 to 2000, and in England and New England over several centuries.

So how have we moved away from our inner demons and toward "the better angels of our nature"? (This phrase, by the way, is from the closing of Abraham Lincoln's first inaugural address.) There are numerous causes, as there must be, for such huge changes. Among these are better education and enhanced power of reason, including moral reasoning, that allows us to better see beyond our immediate needs and circumstances and think in more abstract and universal terms. Norms have changed dramatically to discourage aggression. It's no longer acceptable in most modern societies, as it once was, to answer a perceived insult with the challenge of a duel to the death, for example, or to treat fellow humans as property. Pinker and others also argue that people's motivations and abilities to practice self-control of aggressive impulses are stronger today, and as we have seen in this chapter, self-control plays a crucially important role in moderating aggression.

The historical trends, therefore, are encouraging, as are more recent huge drops in the rates of homicide and violent crime in the United States since the early 1990s. But the better angels of our nature still have strong competition from our inner demons, as the numerous studies and stories reported throughout this chapter make clear. So what can we do to reduce aggression and violence in our lives today? We turn to examine this question for the remainder of this chapter.

◼ Thoughts, Feelings, and Self-Control

Let's start with the enhanced education, intelligence, and reasoning that Pinker proposed helped cause the decline in violence over the past several centuries. Continued improvements in these areas clearly can pave the way for more prosocial and less antisocial behaviors. Along with education and reason—particularly moral reasoning—comes empathy. As discussed in Chapter 10, empathy plays a vital role in promoting helpful, cooperative behavior. The lack of empathy similarly contributes greatly to numerous forms of aggression and violence, including bullying, sexual assault, and abuse of animals (Bussey et al., 2015; Day et al., 2010; Mancke et al., 2015; Schwartz et al., 2012). Improving education and moral reasoning is likely to improve empathy. In addition, numerous programs and interventions are designed specifically to teach individuals to be more empathic, such as by training them to see things from others' perspectives through various exercises, assignments, and role-play. Several of these programs have been very successful at reducing aggression (Feddes et al., 2015; McGuire, 2008; Sahin, 2012). A meta-analysis of 19 studies found reliable support for the effectiveness of empathy training programs (van Berkhout & Malouff, 2015). We will return to this issue at the end of this chapter in a discussion of bullying prevention.

Improved moral reasoning is one part of the formula behind what is known as *aggression replacement training*. The other two components are social competence training and aggression control. These themes are taught with guided instructions and role-playing, typically over the course of twice-weekly sessions for 10 weeks. For example, adolescents in the program go through exercises designed

● FIGURE 11.16

The Decline of Violence: Homicide Rates Over Several Centuries

The homicide rates per 100,000 people per year in five regions of Western Europe from the year 1300 to 2000 are depicted in the graph on the top. These rates for England (from 1300 to 1925) and New England (from 1630 to 1914) are presented in the graph on the bottom.

From Pinker, S., *The better angels of our nature: Why violence has declined.* Copyright © 2011 by Steven Pinker. Used by permission of Viking Penguin, a division of Penguin Group (USA) Inc. and Brockman Inc.

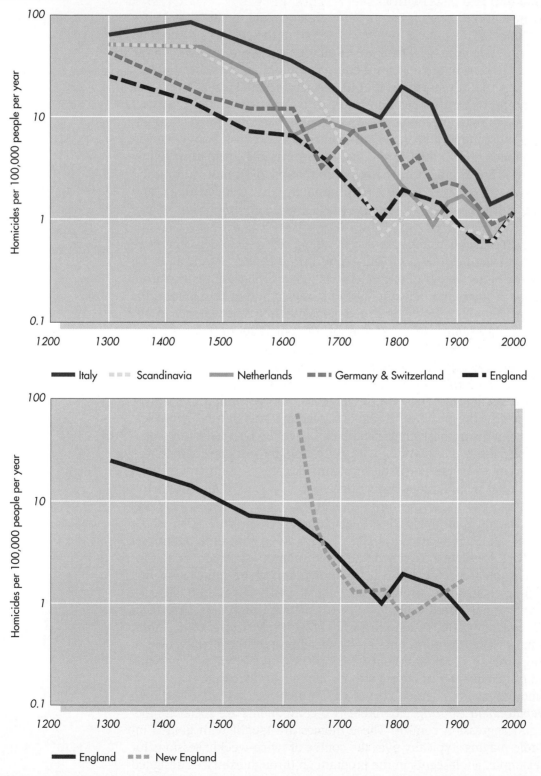

to help them detect when they are on the verge of becoming angry, and they are taught how to think and behave in response to those feelings in ways that steer them away from aggression. They are also taught social skills, such as making eye contact and developing interpersonal trust. Several studies of the effectiveness of aggression replacement training have reported very promising results (Glick & Gibbs, 2011; Holmqvist et al., 2009; Koposov et al., 2014).

As we have discussed multiple times in this chapter, failure at self-control plays a very important role in aggression and violence. In light of its importance researchers are beginning to study the effectiveness of methods designed to improve people's self-control abilities. Thomas Denson, Miriam Capper, and others (2011) found that participants high in trait aggressiveness were less aggressive after a provocation if they had completed a two-week self-control training task (requiring them to resist the impulse to use their dominant hand and instead use their nondominant hand between 8 a.m. and 6 p.m. every day!).

Improving self-control is the goal of one of the four types of interventions that Thomas Denson (2015) argues are the most promising for reducing reactive aggression. The other three successful interventions emphasize cognitive reappraisal, cognitive control, and mindfulness (● see Figure 11.17). Cognitive reappraisal programs train individuals to interpret provocations in more neutral, less emotional terms by thinking about the events from an objective, nonpersonal perspective. Cognitive control is related to self-control, but interventions targeting cognitive control more specifically focus on training the regulation of emotion, such as anger, in response to emotionally relevant stimuli. Finally mindfulness training involves getting people to be in a nonjudgmental, nonreactive state in which they more easily just accept their physical and mental experiences. Denson reviews evidence in support of each of these approaches (although the evidence for the effectiveness of mindfulness is the least developed at this point) in reducing aggression. Their effectiveness no doubt stems from the fact that each targets some aspects of executive functioning, which we have said earlier in this chapter plays a critically important role in moderating reactive aggression.

Individuals who have unusually severe problems with self-control, aggressive impulses, social skills, lack of empathy, and the other factors we've been discussing are likely to need more than these programs of education and training but

"Since war begins in the minds of men, it is in the minds of men that the defenses of peace must be constructed."
—Constitution of UNESCO

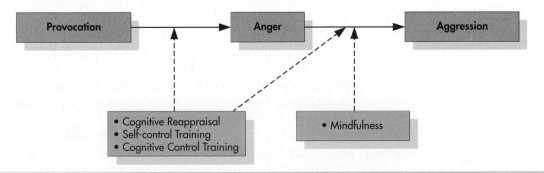

● **FIGURE 11.17**

Reducing Aggression: Four Interventions

The orange boxes illustrate a typical path toward reactive aggression. The blue boxes indicate the points at which each of four interventions can block this path and thereby reduce aggression, according to Thomas Denson (2015).
Based on Denson, 2015.

Students portray bullying during a skit as part of a bullying prevention program. Many school-wide programs to counter bullying, such as the ones described in the text, have produced very promising results.

Andy Holzman/La Daily News/ZUMA Press/Corbis

instead require more extensive therapy and treatment. Treatments using *behavior modification,* for example, are often used to try to alter individuals' behavior through learning principles that reinforce nonaggressive actions. Medications may also be used, such as to balance serotonin levels to help impulse control.

■ Sociocultural Approaches

In addition to educating, training, and treating individuals, what can be done at a broader level? Toward this end, an improved economy, healthier living conditions, and social support would each reduce the frustration, negative affect and thinking, and provocations that fuel much aggression. Improvements on these fronts would likely have a cascade of positive effects. For example, as Peter Sidebotham and Jon Heron (2006) observed, "The association between poverty and child maltreatment is one of the most consistent observations in the published research" (p. 499). Thus, protecting families from violence also means providing family members with educational and employment opportunities. Furthermore, because abuse of alcohol and other drugs so often leads to family violence, better education about the effects of such substances, as well as support for individuals who need help dealing with them, would be a worthy investment not only for these individuals but also for the people around them.

Because research has shown how the presence of weapons can promote aggressive thoughts, emotions, and actions, reducing the prevalence of guns in society—particularly guns associated strongly with violence rather than sport—may have a number of calming effects. At the same time, teaching and modeling nonviolent responses to frustrations and social problems—and encouraging responses that are incompatible with anger, such as humor and relaxation—are among the most effective things we can do for our society's children, and for each other.

A long history of social psychological research has established that fostering cooperation and shared goals across groups is an effective method for reducing intergroup hostilities and aggression. Changing the cost–reward payoffs associated with aggression within a culture should also reap benefits. Socialization practices that reward prosocial rather than antisocial behavior have the potential to greatly reduce the tendency to engage in bullying, fighting, and other aggressive behaviors. Conversely, when overt or indirect aggression is legitimized, the risks become greater.

The media, of course, play an important role in legitimizing—even glorifying—violence. What, then, can we do about it? If parents can help children select shows and games that provide compelling, vivid prosocial models for their children, the effects may be strong. Research on the effects of prosocial television and video games are quite encouraging in this regard, as discussed earlier in the chapter. Parents also are advised to watch television with their children, monitor their video game usage, teach them how the violence depicted in TV and video games differs from real life, and explain how imitating the fictional characters can produce undesirable outcomes. This kind of ongoing parental tutorial takes significant time and effort. But given the extent of media depictions of violence in our society, strengthening children's critical viewing skills is a wise investment.

Barbara Krahé and Robert Busching (2015) conducted a media intervention study along these lines. Students from several schools in Berlin, Germany, were made to monitor their use of electronic media and to reduce their usage, such as with a "media free weekend," and were encouraged to substitute that time for other activities. In five weekly sessions during school the researchers educated the students about the kinds of issues discussed in this chapter, including how violence is often rewarded in the media or how exposure to violence can lead to desensitization. The students' parents were also given guidelines for sensible media usage and about the harmful effects of exposure to media violence. The results of the program were impressive. The intervention significantly reduced students' use of violent media according to measures taken two years after the intervention. In addition, for students whose rates of aggression before the study were relatively high, the intervention significantly reduced their rates of both physical and relational aggression.

Daniel Linz and others (1992) also advocated using educational efforts to increase viewers' critical skills in evaluating media depictions that link violence and sex. A model for such efforts can be found in the debriefing provided to research participants exposed to violent pornography in experiments (Donnerstein et al., 1987). This debriefing emphasizes that rape myths are inaccurate and that violent pornography is unrealistic. Some research has shown long-term reductions in acceptance of rape myths and increases in sympathy for victims and survivors of rape for individuals presented with this information (Hong, 2000; Proto-Campise et al., 1998).

> *"Wars are poor chisels for carving out peaceful tomorrows."*
> —Martin Luther King, Jr.

■ Multiple-Level Approaches: Programs to Prevent Violence and Bullying

A variety of factors contribute to aggression and violence—and, as we have seen, the impact of any one factor often involves other factors simultaneously. The link between hot temperatures and aggression, for instance, involves factors such as arousal, aggressive thoughts, and negative affect. How harmful corporal punishment is can depend on other family dynamics. The most effective strategies for reducing aggression recognize this complexity and work on multiple levels.

Multisystemic Therapy   One of the most successful treatment programs for violent juvenile delinquents is called *multisystemic therapy (MST)*. This approach addresses individuals' problems at several different levels, including the needs of the adolescents and the many contexts in which they are embedded, such as family, peer group, school, and neighborhood (Borduin et al., 2009; Curtis et al., 2009; Henggeler et al., 2009; Letourneau et al., 2009; Timmons-Mitchell & Bender, 2006).

A case study of a 14-year-old boy named Luke illustrates this approach (Wells et al., 2012). Luke was engaging in some serious antisocial behaviors. Rather than just treat Luke with individual therapy, the therapist applying MST wanted to understand the family dynamics in which Luke lived. This enabled the therapist to learn that there was a lack of household routine or rules and that bad behavior was often rewarded (with attention and money) and good behavior was ignored. The therapist therefore worked with Luke's grandmother (his caregiver) and some other nearby family members to help set rules, establish routines, determine better and more consistent ways of handing sources of conflict, and to reward positive rather than negative behavior. This approach of learning about and working with his family and environment along with individualized treatment of Luke produced dramatic improvement in Luke's behavior and life.

Multiple studies evaluating the effectiveness of MST have reported positive results, especially for juveniles under 15 (van der Stouwe et al., 2014). For example, in one study violent juvenile offenders with an average of almost four felony arrests per person were assigned randomly to either MST or individual therapy during adolescence, and they were assessed more than two decades later. The adolescents were four times less likely to be arrested for a violent felony during the follow-up period if they were treated with MST than with individual therapy (Sawyer & Borduin, 2011). Even the *siblings* of juveniles who are treated with MST have been found to be three times less likely to be convicted of a felony 25 years later than siblings of offenders who were treated with individual therapy (Wagner et al., 2014). This illustrates the important point that one benefit of MST is that in treating the offender's entire family, the benefits can spread beyond the individual.

Although this type of multiple-level approach takes a lot of time and resources, the money saved by significantly reducing the rates of violent crimes and in keeping these individuals out of prison far outweighs the costs. For instance, in one study of 176 serious juvenile offenders, MST was estimated to have saved taxpayers and crime victims between $75,000 and $200,000 per MST participant (Klietz et al., 2010).

Bullying Prevention Comprehensive programs that operate on multiple levels have also proven to be effective in reducing the incidence of bullying in many schools around the world. Interest in preventing bullying has skyrocketed in recent years. A generation or so ago bullying was seen by many parents, teachers, school systems, and students as just rites of passage that kids have to go through. Particularly as a consequence of some high-profile cases of young people driven to suicide through bullying, attitudes about bullying have changed dramatically, especially among school administrators.

Anti-bullying programs are being implemented in countless schools around the world. The results of a meta-analysis of studies that have examined the effectiveness of 30 school-based bullying programs indicated that these programs reduced bullying by an average of more than 20% (Ttofi & Farrington, 2011). This review suggests that the most successful bullying prevention programs are the more intensive and long-lasting ones that—like multisystemic therapy—involve multiple levels, include parent meetings and training, firm disciplinary methods, better playground supervision, school conferences, classroom management, and individualized work with the students involved in bullying (Hymel et al., 2015; Ttofi & Farrington, 2009; Ttofi et al., 2015).

Perhaps the most influential such program is the *Olweus Bullying Prevention Program*. Dan Olweus, a professor of psychology in Norway, is a pioneer in research on bullying and is considered to be one of the world's true experts on the topic. His research on how to reduce and prevent bullying was first implemented in schools in Norway and was a resounding success. The Olweus Bullying Prevention Program has now spread to numerous schools throughout the United States and several other countries, and it has inspired or helped shape other programs as well. Bullying rates in these various schools typically drop by anywhere from 30% to 50% (Olweus & Limber, 2010). Table 11.5 lists some of the important components of the Olweus Bullying Prevention Program.

Whether or not intensive, multiple-level school bullying prevention programs are put in place in a particular school, other more modest strategies can help reduce bullying as well. For example, Mustafa Sahin (2012) found that having bullies in several primary schools in Turkey go through an empathy-training program over the course of 11 weeks significantly reduced their bullying behavior compared to a control group. Another approach that many schools are taking is to specifically target bystanders—students who witness acts of bullying but may not do anything to intervene. Inspired in part by the bystander intervention research on helping behavior discussed in Chapter 10, these programs highlight the important role that peers can play in either allowing or discouraging bullying (Nickerson et al., 2014; Pfetsch et al., 2011; Polanin et al., 2012).

An interesting line of research by Elizabeth Levy Paluck and Hana Shepherd (2012) targeted *particular* peers. These researchers hypothesized that they could use peer social influence to make students at a high school in Connecticut less accepting of harassment and bullying behavior. To do this the researchers used surveys of the students to identify a set of students who were the most socially connected in the school, and who therefore had the most potential for social influence to spread throughout the student body. A randomly selected subset of them were then recruited to participate in an intervention program. During two training sessions a professional facilitator led these students in discussions of harassment and bullying in school and what roles various students can play in these behaviors (such as an ally to targeted students or a bystander to the events). These students also prepared to help lead a school-wide assembly on the topic. They performed a skit at the assembly and led a call for tolerance. The researchers found that the socially connected students did in fact change their peers' perceptions of the acceptability of harassment and bullying and led a reduction in many of these behaviors.

Putting It All Together   Table 11.6 lists some of the possible steps to reduce aggression and violence that the research we've reviewed in this chapter suggests. You may not agree that all of these actions are desirable or practical, and you may prefer others that are not mentioned. What's important to realize is that there are many things that can be done to reduce aggression. And because aggression is caused by multiple factors, it is only through multiple paths that we can reach this goal.

▲ **TABLE 11.5**

The Olweus Bullying Prevention Program

Some of the components of the very successful bullying prevention program developed by psychologist Dan Olweus are listed here.

School-Level Components

- Form a bullying prevention coordinating committee.
- Train committee members and staff.
- Adopt school-wide rules against bullying.
- Develop appropriate positive and negative consequences for students' behavior.
- Hold a school-wide kick-off event to launch the program.
- Involve parents.

Classroom-Level Components

- Post and enforce school-wide rules against bullying.
- Hold regular classroom meetings to discuss bullying and related topics.

Individual-Level Components

- Ensure that all staff intervene on the spot when bullying is observed.
- Meet with students involved in bullying, and meet with their parents.
- Develop individual intervention plans for involved students.

Community-Level Components

- Involve community members on the bullying prevention coordinating committee.
- Adults (in and out of school) should use consistent nonphysical, nonhostile negative consequences when rules are broken and should function as positive role models.

Based on Olweus & Limber, 2010.

▲ **TABLE 11.6**

Some Steps to Reduce Aggression and Violence

Although there may be other reasons to endorse or reject the ideas below, social psychological research on aggression suggests that each has the potential to reduce aggression.

- Reward nonaggressive behavior.

- Provide attractive models of peaceful behavior.

- Reduce all forms of aggression in our society, including physical punishment of children, fighting in sports, violence in the media, and war.

- Reduce frustration by improving the quality of life in housing, health care, employment, and child care.

- Provide fans and air-conditioned shelters when it's hot.

- Reduce access to and display of weapons.

- Apologize when you've angered someone, and regard apologies as a sign of strength—not weakness. Encourage others to do likewise.

- Stop and think when you feel your temper rising. Control it instead of letting it control you.

- Discourage excessive drinking of alcohol and support efforts to provide treatment for alcohol abuse.

- Develop good communication skills in families and relationships, thereby helping to avoid misperceptions, jealousy, and distrust.

- Pay attention and respond to warning signs of trouble in adolescents, including social isolation, talk of violence, and consumption of violence-filled literature and other media.

- Increase education to promote development of skills involving empathy, self-control, and how to solve interpersonal problems with reason rather than emotion.

© Cengage Learning®

Review

Top 10 Key Points in Chapter 11

1. Males tend to be more physically aggressive than females, but females tend to be at least as—and perhaps somewhat more—indirectly or relationally aggressive compared to males.

2. Individuals tend to be more aggressive if they are low in agreeableness and high on the Dark Triad traits of Machiavellianism, psychopathy, and narcissism.

3. Impairments in several areas of the brain, especially to regions associated with executive functioning, are associated with aggressiveness, as is the combination of high testosterone and low cortisol.

4. Corporal punishment of children is associated with long-term increases in their aggressive behavior.

5. Social learning theory emphasizes that we learn from the example of others as well as from direct experience with rewards and punishments; aggressive models teach not only specific behaviors but also more general attitudes and ideas about aggression and aggressive "scripts" that guide behavior.

6. Cultures of honor promote status-protecting aggression among men in several parts of the world.

7. A wide variety of aversive experiences and stimuli can create negative feelings and increase aggression, including frustration, heat, pain, and social rejection.

8. Self-control failure is behind most acts of aggression and violence; poor executive functioning, angry rumination, high arousal, and low glucose are among the factors that can impair self-control.

9. A large number of studies, using a variety of different methods, have shown a significant positive relationship between exposure to media violence and real-world aggressive cognitions and behaviors.

10. Comprehensive programs that operate on multiple levels tend to be most effective in reducing aggression and preventing bullying in schools.

Putting Common Sense to the Test

Culture, Gender, and Individual Differences

In virtually every culture, males are more violent than females.

(T) **True.** *In almost all cultures and time periods that have been studied, men commit the large majority of violent crimes.*

For virtually any category of aggression, males are more aggressive than females.

(F) **False.** *Girls tend to be somewhat more indirectly, or relationally, aggressive than boys.*

Origins of Aggression

Children who are spanked or otherwise physically disciplined (but not abused) for behaving aggressively tend to become less aggressive.

(F) **False.** *Evidence indicates that the use of even a little physical punishment to discipline children is associated with increases in subsequent aggressive and antisocial behavior by the children, even years later, although this relationship may depend on a variety of other factors.*

Situational Influences on Aggression

Blowing off steam by engaging in safe but aggressive activities (such as sports) makes people less likely to aggress later.

(F) **False.** *Although people may be less likely to aggress immediately after such activities, initial aggression makes future aggression more—not less—likely.*

Media Effects

Exposure to TV violence in childhood is related to aggression later in life.

(T) **True.** *Laboratory experiments, field experiments, and correlational research all suggest a link between exposure to violence on TV and subsequent aggressive behavior.*

Key Terms

aggression (455)
catharsis (478)
corporal punishment (471)
cultivation (491)
culture of honor (475)
cycle of violence (474)
Dark Triad (465)

desensitization (491)
displacement (477)
executive functioning (469)
frustration–aggression hypothesis (477)
hostile attribution bias (482)
pornography (492)

proactive aggression (456)
reactive aggression (456)
rumination (482)
social learning theory (472)
weapons effect (481)

Law

This chapter examines applications of social psychology to the law. First, we consider the social psychology of such evidence as eyewitness testimony and alibis, lie-detector tests and confessions, and the forensic sciences. Next we examine three stages of a jury trial: jury selection, an often controversial process; the courtroom drama in which jurors are exposed to a combination of evidence and other, possibly biasing, information; and jury deliberation, where the jury reaches a group decision. We also consider the process by which a vast majority of defendants plead guilty, thereby avoiding trial. Next, we consider posttrial factors such as sentencing and prison, the possible result of a conviction or guilty plea. Finally, we discuss people's perceptions of justice both inside and outside the courtroom.

12

It seems that there is always a high-profile case in the news that spotlights a crime of sex, violence, money, passion, or celebrity and that captures the public's interest. The twenty-first century is still young, and yet we have already witnessed the public trials of corrupt Wall Street executives, celebrities, and terrorists. The high-profile cases against Olympic sprinter Oscar Pistorius in South Africa and Boston Marathon bomber Dzhokhar Tsarnaev are but two examples. There will be others to come, of course. But few will fascinate and confuse the world quite like the three trials and appeals in Italy of Amanda Knox.

On November 2, 2007, British exchange student Meredith Kercher was found raped and murdered in Perugia, Italy. Almost immediately, police suspected 20-year-old Amanda Knox, an American student and one of Kercher's roommates—the only one who stayed in Perugia. Knox had no history of crime or violence and no motive. But something about her demeanor led police to believe she was lying when she said she was with Raffaele Sollecito, her new Italian boyfriend, that night.

On and off for the next four days, several police officials interrogated Knox. Her final interrogation started on November 5 a few minutes after 10 p.m. and lasted until November 6 at 6 a.m. In many ways, Knox was a vulnerable suspect—young, far from home, without family, and speaking in a foreign language in which she was not fluent. Knox says she was repeatedly threatened and called a liar. She was told that Sollecito, her boyfriend, had disavowed her alibi, which he did under pressure but immediately retracted, and that physical evidence placed her at the scene, which was not true. She was then encouraged to imagine how the gruesome crime had occurred, a trauma, she was told, that she had obviously repressed. Eventually, in the wee hours of the morning, Knox broke down and confessed in a "dreamlike vision." Despite a law that requires the recording of suspect interrogations, police and prosecutors said the sessions were not recorded. That morning, the chief of police announced: *Caso chiuso* (case closed).

A few weeks after Knox's confession was taken, DNA found on the victim and throughout the crime scene unequivocally identified a man who had fled to Germany. When he was first arrested he said Knox was not involved. Months later, he changed his story, said that Knox and Sollecito were involved, and received a substantially reduced sentence. Over the ensuing months, police forensic experts said that physical evidence put Knox at the crime scene, and eyewitnesses, previously silent, came forward with varying claims to have seen Knox in the vicinity that night. One witness said he saw Knox outdoors brandishing a knife.

What followed in a sequence of events in the courts of Italy was astonishing. In December of 2009, an eight-person jury convicted Knox and Sollecito of murder. The two were sentenced to 26 and 25 years in prison, respectively. Two years later, in October of 2011, having been granted a new trial, they were acquitted and released. The Italian appeals court released a strongly worded 143-page opinion in which it criticized the prosecution and concluded that there was no credible evidence, motive, or plausible theory of guilt. Both defendants returned home—Knox to Seattle; Sollecito to his home in Italy. But this was not to be the end

---

Putting COMMON SENSE to the Test

Circle Your Answer

T   F   Eyewitnesses find it relatively difficult to recognize members of a race other than their own.

T   F   The more confident an eyewitness is about an identification, the more accurate he or she is likely to be.

T   F   It is not possible to knowingly fool a lie-detector test.

T   F   Without being beaten or threatened, innocent people sometimes confess to crimes they did not commit.

T   F   Contrary to popular opinion, women are harsher as trial jurors than men are.

T   F   One can usually predict a jury's final verdict by knowing where the individual jurors stand the first time they vote.

In a tragedy that captivated the world's attention in 2007, British student Meredith Kircher was brutally murdered while studying in Perugia, Italy (left). Within four days, American student Amanda Knox and her new boyfriend, Raphaelle Solecito, were arrested for the murder (center) after Knox had "confessed." Shortly afterward, physical evidence revealed the guilt of Rudy Guede (right). After four years in jail for a crime they did not commit, Knox and Solecito were acquitted. Guede remains in prison.

of the story. In Italy, the prosecution is permitted to appeal an acquittal. This prosecutor did just that and the two were retried. In January of 2014, Knox and Sollecito were convicted a second time and re-sentenced. Once again, they appealed. In what would prove to be the final act of an eight-year drama, on March 27, 2015, the news from Rome was announced: Italy's highest court annulled the convictions and declared both defendants innocent (Burleigh, 2015; Povoledo, 2015).

Although this case occurred in Italy, it illustrates the profound relevance of social psychology at work in all legal systems and raises many questions: How reliable are confessions, eyewitnesses, alibis, forensic science experts, and other types of evidence presented in court? What kinds of people serve as jurors, and when they do can they set aside their biases? Are jurors influenced by pretrial publicity and other outside information not in evidence? Then, how do they reach a verdict after days, weeks, or months of presentations, often followed by exhausting deliberation? In this chapter, we take social psychology into the courtroom to answer these questions. But first, let's place the trial process in a broader context.

In the U.S. criminal justice system, the trial is just the tip of an iceberg. Once a crime is committed, it must be detected and then reported if it is to receive further attention. Through investigation, the police find a suspect and decide whether to make an arrest. If they do, the suspect is jailed or bail is set and a judge or grand jury decides if there is sufficient evidence for a formal accusation. If there is sufficient evidence, the prosecuting and defense lawyers begin a lengthy process known as "discovery," during which time they gather evidence. At this point, in the United States, 96% of defendants plead guilty as part of a plea deal negotiated by the lawyers. In the relatively few cases that do go to trial, the ordeal does not then end with a verdict. After conviction, the trial judge imposes punishment in the form of a sentence and the defendant decides whether to appeal to a higher court. For those in prison, decisions concerning their release are made by parole boards. As ● Figure 12.1 illustrates, the criminal justice apparatus is complex and the actors behind the scenes are numerous. Social psychologists have a lot to say about various aspects of the legal system (Bartol & Bartol, 2015; Costanzo & Krauss, 2015; Greene & Heilbrun, 2014; Kovera & Borgida, 2010).

The issues that social psychologists study are varied and important. At present, researchers are looking at a wide range of issues—such as whether police can tell when someone is lying and how they can make these judgments more accurately (Granhag et al., 2015; Vrij, 2008); how cognitive biases interfere with the processes of investigation (Simon, 2012); how juries make decisions in civil lawsuits that involve large sums of money (Bornstein et al., 2008; Reyna et al., 2015); why people cooperate with authorities and obey the law (Tyler, 2011); how information can best be gathered in the wake of 9/11 (Loftus, 2011); how the U.S. Supreme Court receives oral arguments and makes decisions (Wrightsman, 2006, 2008); and how social psychology can be used to improve the prison experience (Haney, 2006) and prevent the wrongful convictions of innocent people (Cutler, 2011). Importantly, much of what social psychologists have discovered with regard to law and justice is not known to judges, lawyers, and laypeople as a matter of common sense (Borgida & Fiske, 2007). In the coming pages, we look at the social psychology of evidence, jury decision making, sentencing and prison, and perceptions of justice.

Eyewitness Testimony

Once the commission of a crime is discovered, police investigate in an effort to identify the perpetrator. Eyewitnesses are interviewed, suspects are interrogated, and all sorts of physical evidence in the form of fingerprints, shoe prints, hair samples, DNA-rich biological materials, ballistics, and autopsy results are collected and analyzed. Solving crimes is not easy. In this all-too-human enterprise, as we'll see, some of the most critical types of evidence that police gather are subject to social influences and the potential for bias and error.

"I'll never forget that face!" When these words are uttered, police officers, judges, and juries all take notice. Too often, however, eyewitnesses make mistakes. On March 8, 2009, the CBS show *60 Minutes* aired the story of Jennifer Thompson and Ronald Cotton. One night in 1984, in North Carolina, a young man broke into Thompson's apartment, cut the phone wires, and raped her. She described him to the police, helped construct a composite sketch, and then positively identified Ronald Cotton as her assailant. Cotton had alibis for his whereabouts that night, but based on Thompson's eyewitness identification, he was found guilty and sentenced to life in prison. Ten years later, DNA tests of semen stains revealed that Cotton was innocent and that Bobby Poole, a known offender, was the real assailant. In 1995, after 10 years in prison, Cotton was released and

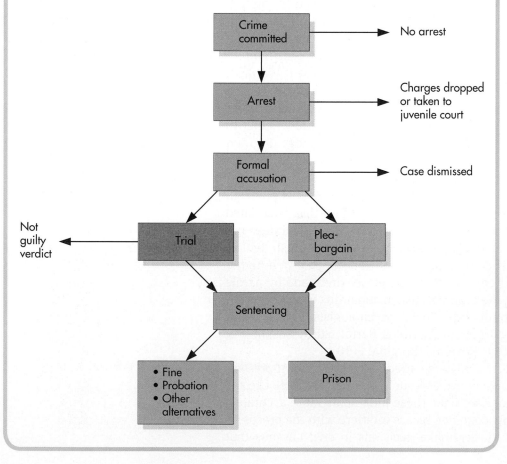

● **FIGURE 12.1**

Overview of the American Criminal Justice System

This flowchart presents the movement of cases through different branches of the criminal justice system. As illustrated here, the trial is just one aspect of the criminal justice system. Adapted from the President's Commission on Law Enforcement and Administration of Justice, 1967.

offered $5,000 in compensation. He has since put the pieces of his life back together. Thompson, upon realizing that she had identified an innocent man, said, "I remember feeling sick, but also I remember feeling just an overwhelming sense of just guilt. . . . I cried and cried and I wept and I was angry at me and I beat myself up for it for a long time." Thompson-Cannino and Cotton (2009) went on to write a book together entitled, *Picking Cotton: Our Memoir of Injustice and Redemption.*

Every year, thousands of people are charged with crimes solely on the basis of eyewitness evidence. Many of these eyewitness accounts are accurate, but many are not—which is why psychologists have been interested in the topic for more than 100 years (Doyle, 2005). About 20 years ago, the National Institute of Justice reported on 28 wrongful convictions in which convicted felons were proved innocent by new tests of old DNA evidence after varying numbers of years in prison. Remarkably, as in Ronald Cotton's case, every one of these convictions involved a mistaken identification (Connors et al., 1996). Now, more than 300 DNA exonerations later, it is clear: Eyewitness error is the most common cause of wrongful convictions (Brewer & Wells, 2011; Cutler, 2013; Lindsay et al., 2007; Wells, Memon, & Penrod, 2006).

In 1999, the U.S. Department of Justice took a bold step in response to this discovery: It assembled a group of police, prosecutors, defense attorneys, and research psychologists to devise a set of "how-to" guidelines. Led by social psychologist Gary Wells, this Technical Working Group went on to publish *Eyewitness Evidence: A Guide for Law Enforcement* (Technical Working Group, 1999; Wells et al., 2000).

As eyewitnesses, people can be called upon to remember just about anything— a face, a weapon, an accident, or a conversation. To date, hundreds of tightly controlled studies of eyewitness testimony have been conducted. Based on this research, three conclusions can be drawn: (1) eyewitnesses are imperfect; (2) certain personal and situational factors can systematically influence their performance, and (3) judges, juries, and lawyers are not adequately informed about these factors. It appears that even the U.S. Supreme Court harbors outdated misconceptions about the nature of eyewitness memory (Wells & Quinlivan, 2009).

People tend to think that human memory works like a video camera—that if you turn on the power and focus the lens, all events will be recorded for subsequent playback. Unfortunately, it's not that simple. Over the years, researchers have found it useful to view memory as a three-stage process involving the

Jennifer Thompson was traumatized twice: the first time when she was raped, the second when she learned that she had identified a man proved to be innocent by DNA tests 10 years later. Here you can see Thompson talking to Ronald Cotton, the man she picked from a lineup. Notice the resemblance between Cotton and Bobby Poole, her actual assailant.

Poole

Cotton

encoding, storage, and *retrieval* of information. The first of these stages, encoding, refers to a witness's perceptions at the time of the event in question. Second, the witness rehearses and stores the information in memory to avoid forgetting. Third, the witness retrieves the information from storage when needed. This model suggests that errors can occur at three different points.

◼ Perceiving the Crime

Some kinds of persons and events are more difficult to perceive than others. Common sense tells us that a quick glimpse, bad lighting, long distance, physical disguise, and distraction can all limit a witness's perceptions. In one study, for example, Rod Lindsay and others (2008) had approximately 1,300 participants observe a target person, outdoors, at one of various distances ranging from 5 meters (16 feet) to 50 meters (164 feet). They found, first, that the witnesses were not accurate at estimating distance and, second, that the further witnesses were from the target, the less accurate they were at identifying the target in a lineup shortly afterward.

Research has uncovered other aspects of the witnessing situation that can impair accuracy. Consider the effects of a witness's emotional state. Often people are asked to recall a bloody shooting, a car wreck, or an assault—emotional events that trigger high levels of *stress.* In a study that illustrates the debilitating effects of stress, Charles Morgan and others (2004) randomly assigned trainees in a military survival school to undergo a realistic high-stress or low-stress mock interrogation. Twenty-four hours later, he found that those in the high-stress condition had difficulty identifying their interrogators in a lineup. In another study, Tim Valentine and Jan Mesout (2009) fitted adult visitors to the London Dungeon—a house of horrors—with a wireless heart monitor and asked them afterward to describe and identify a scary person they had encountered inside. The more anxious visitors were in the Dungeon, the less accurate they were later at describing and identifying the scary person in a lineup.

Alcoholic intoxication, often common in the commission of crimes, can also cause problems. Surprisingly, it is not uncommon for eyewitnesses in the real world to have been under the influence of alcohol. In one study, 75% of police officers who were surveyed reported that while investigating crimes they routinely encounter witnesses who are drunk or under the influence of other drugs during the crime or the interview with police (Evans et al., 2009). In a second study, an analysis of criminal case files from a district attorney's office—involving rape, assault, and robbery—revealed that 13% of eyewitnesses and 28% of suspects were under the influence of alcohol or other drugs. What's more, these witnesses were just as likely as those who were sober to play a role in the police investigation (Palmer et al., 2013).

It is clear that alcohol can impair eyewitness perception and memory. When participants in one study witnessed a live staged crime, those who had earlier consumed fruit juice were more accurate in their recollections than were those who had been served an alcoholic beverage (Yuille & Tollestrup, 1990). Other research shows that although people can recognize a perpetrator presented to them when they are intoxicated, they often make false identifications when the actual perpetrator is absent (Dysart et al., 2002). Still other research shows that alcohol can reduce other aspects of memory. In one study, participants were approached in bars—some who were drinking, others who were not—and asked to watch and recall a mock crime. Three to five days later, their memory was tested. Compared with witnesses who were sober, those who had been intoxicated produced fewer and less accurate memories of the event as a whole (van Oorsouw & Merckelbach, 2012).

The **weapon-focus effect** is also an important factor. Across a wide range of settings, research shows that when a criminal pulls out a gun, a razor blade, or a knife, witnesses are less able to identify that culprit than if no weapon is present (Fawcett et al., 2011; Steblay 1992). There are two possible reasons for this effect. First, people are agitated by the sight of a menacing stimulus, as when participants in one study were approached by an experimenter who was holding a syringe or threatening to administer an injection (Maass & Kohnken, 1989). Second, even in a harmless situation, a witness's eyes lock in on a weapon like magnets, drawing attention away from the face (Hope & Wright, 2007). To demonstrate, Elizabeth Loftus and others (1987) showed people slides of a customer who walked up to a bank teller and pulled out either a pistol or a checkbook. By tracking eye movements, these researchers found that people spent more time looking at the gun than at the checkbook. The net result: An impairment in the ability to identify the criminal in a lineup.

Additional research has confirmed that the weapon-focus effect is caused by the capture of a witness's attention. One study showed that the effect is eliminated when the witnessed event occurs at a shooting range, where guns are expected to be seen (Pickel, 1999). A second study showed that the presence of a non-threatening novel object—not just a weapon—has the same effect, pulling a mock witness's attention away from the culprit and reducing identification accuracy (Erickson et al., 2014). A third study showed that although mock witnesses were less accurate at identifying a videotaped assailant who used a shotgun rather than his fists or a beer bottle, this effect was reversed by placing a large sports sticker on the assailant's cheek, which redirected the witnesses' attention to the face (Carlson & Carlson, 2012).

Race is another important consideration. By varying the racial makeup of participants and target persons in laboratory and real-life interactions, researchers discovered that people are more accurate at recognizing members of their own racial group than of a race other than their own—an effect known as the **cross-race identification bias** (Malpass & Kravitz, 1969). In one field study, for example, 86 convenience store clerks in El Paso, Texas, were asked to identify three customers—one white, one African American, and one Mexican American—all experimental confederates who had stopped in and made a purchase earlier that day. It turned out that the white, black, and Mexican American clerks were all most likely to accurately identify customers belonging to their own racial or ethnic group (Platz & Hosch, 1988).

The finding that "they all look alike" (referring to members of other groups) is found reliably and in many different racial and ethnic groups. Christian Meissner and John Brigham (2001) statistically combined the results of 39 studies involving a total of 5,000 mock witnesses. They found that the witnesses were consistently less accurate and more prone to making false identifications when they tried to recognize target persons from racial and ethnic groups other than their own. Sadly, the cross-race bias is not a mere laboratory phenomenon. Numerous real-world cases have been discovered in which eyewitnesses misidentified innocent

Universal Images Group/Getty Images

After the tragic assassination of President John F. Kennedy, dozens of eyewitnesses came forward to describe what they saw. Some reported one gunman in the sixth-floor window of a nearby building, others reported two or three gunmen in the building, and still others thought the shots were fired from the ground. Such are the pitfalls of eyewitness testimony.

weapon-focus effect The tendency for the presence of a weapon to draw attention and impair a witness's ability to identify the culprit.

cross-race identification bias The tendency for people to be more accurate at recognizing members of their own racial group than of other groups.

suspects who were of a race other than their own (Wilson et al., 2013). Paralleling this research, studies also show that children, young adults, and the elderly have more difficulty recognizing others of an *age* group other than their own (Rhodes & Anastasi, 2012).

■ Storing the Memory

Can remembrances of the remote past be trusted? As you might expect, memory for faces and events tends to decline with the passage of time. Longer intervals between an event and its retrieval are generally associated with increased forgetting. But not all recollections fade, and time alone does not cause memory slippage. Consider the plight of bystanders who witness firsthand such incidents as terrorist bombings, shootings, plane crashes, or fatal car accidents. Afterward, they may talk about what they saw, read about it, hear what other bystanders have to say, and answer questions from investigators and reporters. By the time witnesses to these events are officially questioned, they are likely to have been exposed to so much postevent information that one wonders if their original memory is still "pure."

According to Elizabeth Loftus (1996), it probably is not. Many years ago, based on her own studies of eyewitness testimony, Loftus proposed a now classic theory of reconstructive memory. After people observe an event, she theorized, information they receive later about that event—whether the information is true or not—becomes integrated into the fabric of their memory. An initial experiment by Loftus and Palmer (1974) illustrated the point. Participants viewed a film of a traffic accident and then answered questions, including: "About how fast were the cars going when they *hit* each other?" Other participants answered the same question, except that the verb *hit* was replaced by *smashed, collided, bumped,* or *contacted.* All participants saw the same accident, yet the wording of the question affected their reports. ● Figure 12.2 shows that participants given the "smashed" question estimated the highest average speed and those responding to the "contacted" question estimated the lowest. But there's more. One week later, participants were called back for more probing. Had the wording of the questions caused them to reconstruct their memories of the accident? Yes. When asked whether they had seen broken glass at the accident (none was actually present), 32% of the "smashed" participants said they had. As Loftus had predicted, what these

● **FIGURE 12.2**

Biasing Eyewitness Reports With Loaded Questions

Participants viewed a film of a traffic accident and then answered this question: "About how fast were these cars going when they (hit, smashed, or contacted) each other?" As shown, the wording of the question influenced speed estimates (top). One week later, it also caused participants to reconstruct their memory of other aspects of the accident (bottom).

From Loftus, G. R., and Loftus, E. F., *Human memory: The processing of information.* Copyright © 1976.

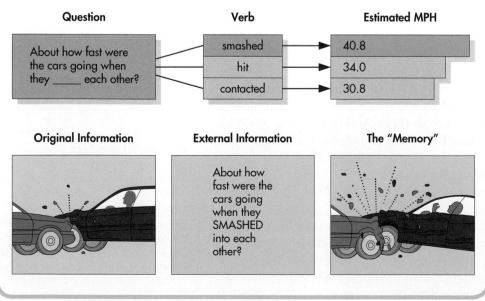

Question	Verb	Estimated MPH
About how fast were the cars going when they ____ each other?	smashed	40.8
	hit	34.0
	contacted	30.8

Original Information	External Information	The "Memory"
	About how fast were the cars going when they SMASHED into each other?	

participants remembered of the accident was based on two sources: the event itself and postevent information.

This **misinformation effect** has aroused a great deal of controversy. It's clear that eyewitnesses can be compromised when exposed to postevent information—as when they are told, for example, that either the person they identified or someone else had confessed during an interrogation (Hasel & Kassin, 2009). It's also now clear that witnesses who are under intense stress (Morgan et al., 2013) or who are not alert—for example, because they have been sleep-deprived (Frenda et al., 2014)—are especially vulnerable. But does this information actually alter a witness's real memory, making it impossible to ever retrieve it? Or do participants merely follow the experimenter's suggestion, leaving their true memory intact for retrieval under other, yet-to-be-identified conditions? Either way, whether memory is truly and fully altered or not, it is clear that eyewitness *reports* are hopelessly biased by postevent information and that this effect can be dramatic (Frenda et al., 2011).

In one laboratory study, Craig Stark and others (2010) showed participants a series of slides showing a man stealing a woman's wallet and tucking it into his jacket pocket. These same participants then heard a recorded account of the event that was accurate or misinformed them that the man hid the wallet in his pants pocket. All were later tested about the details of the event while lying in an MRI scanner. Sure enough, a substantial number of misinformation participants incorrectly recalled that the thief put the wallet in his pants, not his jacket—and said that they remembered that detail from the photographs. Interestingly, the neuro-imaging data from the MRI scans showed that the true memories—those based on the slides—were accompanied by more activation of the visual cortex of the brain, while false memories—those based on the audio recording—were accompanied by more activation in the auditory cortex.

This phenomenon raises an additional and troubling question. If adults can be misled by postevent information, what about young children? In 1988, Margaret Kelly Michaels, a 26-year-old preschool teacher, was found guilty of 115 counts of sex abuse at the Wee Care Nursery School in New Jersey. The charges against her were shocking. For a period of more than seven months, the jury was told, she danced nude in the classroom, stripped the children, and raped them with kitchen utensils and Lego blocks.

Were the children's stories accurate? On the one hand, there were some striking consistencies in the testimonies of 19 child witnesses. On the other hand, the social workers and investigators who conducted the interviews often prompted the children with suggestive leading questions, told them that Michaels was a bad person, urged them to describe acts they had initially denied, offered bribes for disclosures, and pressured those who claimed ignorance. There was no physical evidence of abuse and no other witnesses even though the acts were supposed to have occurred in an open classroom. Michaels was found guilty and sentenced to 47 years in prison. After serving five of those years, she was released when the state appeals court overturned the conviction on the ground that the children's testimony could not be trusted. "One day you're getting ready for work and making coffee, minding your business," said Michaels, "and the next minute you are an accused child molester."

Can suggestive interview procedures cause young children to confuse appearance and reality? Over the years, research has shown that numerous children are maltreated at home and elsewhere and yet they are reluctant for various reasons to report these experiences to authorities. At the same time, thousands of sex abuse charges have been filed against babysitters, preschool teachers, and family

misinformation effect The tendency for false postevent misinformation to become integrated into people's memory of an event.

members. In light of these events, judges and juries struggle to decide: Are preschoolers competent to take the witness stand, or are they suggestible, too prone to confuse reality and fantasy? To provide guidance to the courts, researchers have studied the factors that influence children's eyewitness memory (Bottoms et al., 2009; Bruck & Ceci, 1999; Lamb et al., 2008).

This research has evolved through several stages. At first, simple laboratory experiments showed that preschoolers were more likely than older children and adults to incorporate misleading "trick" questions into their memories for simple stories (Ceci et al., 1987). Other studies showed that interviewers could get young children to change their memories (or at least their answers) simply by repeating a question over and over—a behavior that implies that the answer given is not good enough (Poole & White, 1991). But are young children similarly suggestible about stressful real-life experiences?

In one study, Leichtman and Ceci (1995) told nursery-school children about a clumsy man named Sam Stone who always broke things. A month later, a man visited the school, spent time in the classroom, and left. The next day, the children were shown a ripped book and a soiled teddy bear and asked what had happened. Reasonably, no one said that they saw Stone cause the damage. But then, over the next 10 weeks, they were asked suggestive questions ("I wonder if Sam Stone was wearing long pants or short pants when he ripped the book?"). The result: When a new interviewer asked the children in the class to tell what happened, 72% of the 3- and 4-year-olds blamed Stone for the damage, and 45% said they saw him do it. One child "recalled" that Stone took a paintbrush and painted melted chocolate on the bear. Others "saw" him spill coffee, throw toys in the air, rip the book in anger, and soak the book in warm water until it fell apart. It's important to realize that false memories in children are not necessarily a by-product of bad questioning procedures. Even when interviews are neutral, false reports can stem from children's exposure to misinformation from such outside sources such as television (Principe et al., 2000), parents (Poole & Lindsay, 2001), and classmates (Principe & Ceci, 2002), and the use of anatomical dolls and diagrams as props that interviewers sometimes use to get children to demonstrate how they were touched (Poole et al., 2011).

To summarize, research shows that repetition, misinformation, and leading questions can bias a child's memory report and that preschoolers are particularly vulnerable in this regard. Somehow, the courts must distinguish between true and false claims on a case-by-case basis. To assist in this endeavor, both to motivate child victims of maltreatment who are reluctant to come forward and to minimize the effects of suggestibility, researchers have proposed that clear interviewing guidelines be set so that future child witnesses will be questioned in a manner that is supportive but objective and nonbiasing (Hershkowitz et al., 2014; Lamb et al., 2008).

■ Identifying the Culprit

For eyewitnesses, testifying is only the last in a series of efforts to retrieve what they saw from memory. Before witnesses reach the courtroom, they are questioned by police and lawyers, view a lineup or mug shots, and possibly even assist in creating a facial composite or an artist's sketch of the perpetrator. Yet each of these experiences can increase the risk of error and distortion.

Imagine trying to reconstruct a culprit's face by selecting a set of eyes, a nose, a mouth, a hairstyle, and so on, from vast collections of features and then combining

"Do you swear to tell your version of the truth as you perceive it, clouded perhaps by the passage of time and preconceived notions?"

© 1989 Sidney Harris/ScienceCartoonsPlus.com

them into a composite of the face. Research shows that this process seldom produces a face that resembles the actual culprit (Kovera et al., 1997). To further complicate matters, the face-construction process itself may confuse witnesses, making it more difficult for them later to identify the culprit. In one study, for example, participants were asked to select from six pictures a person's face they had seen two days earlier. Sixty percent accurately identified the target. When they first tried to reconstruct the face using a computerized facial composite program, however, their identification accuracy dropped to 18% (Wells et al., 2005).

An eyewitness's greatest impact on a case occurs when he or she makes a positive identification from a photographic or live lineup. Once police have made an arrest, they often call on their witnesses to view a lineup that includes the suspect and five to seven other individuals. This procedure may take place within hours or days of a crime or months later. Either way, the lineup often results in tragic cases of mistaken identity. Through the application of eyewitness research findings, this risk can be reduced (Cutler, 2013; Wells et al., 1998; Wells et al., 2007).

Basically, five factors can affect identification performance at this stage. The first is the lineup *construction*. To be fair, a lineup should contain four to eight innocent persons, called "fillers" or "foils," who match the witness's general description of the culprit. If the witness describes seeing a white male in his 20s with curly hair, for example, foils should not be included that are old, nonwhite, and bald. Also, anything that makes a suspect distinctive compared to the others in the lineup increases his or her chance of being selected (Buckhout, 1974). This is what happened to Steve Titus, who was mistakenly accused of rape when the police showed the victim his picture alongside those of five other men. Although the foils resembled Titus in appearance, his picture stood out like a sore thumb. It was the smallest and the only one without a border (Loftus & Ketcham, 1991). Eyewitness choices from a lineup can also be influenced by the emotional expression on a suspect's face relative to fillers. In one experiment, for example, "innocent" suspects were more likely to get identified from a photographic lineup when their picture depicted an angry expression, which made them look more like a criminal, *and* when the fillers in the lineup did not also depict angry expressions (Flowe et al., 2014).

Second, lineup *instructions* to the witness are very important. In a study by Roy Malpass and Patricia Devine (1981), students saw a staged act of vandalism, after which they attended a lineup. Half of the students received "biased" instructions: They were led to believe that the culprit was in the lineup. The others were told that he might or might not be present. Lineups were then presented either with or without the culprit. When the students received biased instructions, they felt compelled to identify *someone* and often picked an innocent person (see Table 12.1). Additional studies have both confirmed and qualified this basic result: When the criminal is present in the lineup, biased instructions are not problematic. When the criminal is not in the lineup, however—which occurs whenever the police suspect is truly innocent— biased instructions substantially increase the rate of mistaken identifications (Clark, 2005; Steblay, 1997). Again, the story of Steve Titus is a case in point. The police told the victim to pick her assailant from a group of six. After studying the pictures for several minutes and shaking

▲ **TABLE 12.1**

Effects of Lineup and Instructions on False Identifications

After witnessing a crime, participants were told either that the culprit was in the lineup (biased instruction) or that he might or might not be present (unbiased instruction). Participants then viewed a lineup in which the real culprit was present or absent. Notice the percentage of participants in each group who identified an innocent person. Those who received the biased instruction were more likely to make a false identification, picking an innocent person rather than no one at all, especially when the real culprit was not in the lineup.

Percentage of False Identifications

	Unbiased Instructions	Biased Instructions
Culprit present	0	25
Culprit absent	33	78

Based on Malpass, R., and Devine, P., "Eyewitness identification: Lineup instructions and the absence of the offender," *Journal of Applied Psychology* vol 66 (pp. 482–489). Copyright © 1981 by the American Psychological Association.

her head in confusion, she was urged to concentrate and make a choice. "This one is the closest," she said. "It has to be this one" (Loftus & Ketcham, 1991, p. 38).

Third, the *format* of a lineup also influences whether a witness feels compelled to make a selection. When witnesses are presented with a *simultaneous* spread of all photographs, they tend to make relative, multiple-choice-like judgments, comparing the different alternatives and picking the one who looks most like the criminal. This strategy increases the tendency to make a false identification. The solution: To show the same photos in a *sequential lineup,* one picture at a time, and ask the witness for each photo – is this him, yes or no? In this procedure, witnesses tend to make absolute judgments by comparing each target person with their memory of the criminal. This situation diminishes the risk of a forced and often false identification of a filler and possibly innocent suspect—not only in the laboratory (Lindsay et al., 1991; Lindsay & Wells, 1985) but in a massive field experiment, involving nearly 500 real lineups in the police departments of Charlotte, North Carolina; Tucson, Arizona; San Diego, California; and Austin, Texas (Wells et al., 2015).

The problem with the simultaneous photo spread is that it leads witnesses to make "relative judgments"—in other words, to compare the lineup members to each other and pick the one that comes closest to their memory. Making a relative judgment may work well if the actual criminal is in the lineup. But if the actual criminal is not in the lineup (which happens whenever the police have a suspect who is actually innocent), witnesses may make a selection anyway, putting the innocent suspect at risk. Some researchers expressed the concern that this procedure might reduce the number of correct identifications when the actual perpetrator is in the lineup. This is a strictly testable question, and the results are clear: In a meta-analysis of 72 comparisons of simultaneous and sequential lineups involving more than 13,000 mock witnesses, identifications were more accurate when the photos were presented in a sequential format (Steblay, Dysart, & Wells, 2011).

The fourth factor is perhaps the most subtle, as it pertains to *familiarity-induced* biases. Research shows that people often remember a face but not the circumstances in which they saw that face. In one study, for example, participants witnessed a staged crime and then looked through mug shots. A few days later, they were asked to view a lineup. The result was startling: Participants were just as likely to identify an innocent person whose picture was in the mug shots as they were to pick the actual criminal (Brown et al., 1977)! Many different studies have shown that witnesses will often identify from a lineup someone they had seen in another context, including innocent bystanders who also happened to be at the crime scene (Deffenbacher et al., 2006).

A fifth factor concerns whether a *double-blind procedure* is used. There always exists the risk that a police officer who administers a lineup—typically containing a suspect and some innocent foils—will inadvertently steer a witness's identification decision, most likely to the suspect (who may or may not be the culprit). For that reason, social psychologists have argued for a procedure in which not only the witness is "blind" as to who the suspect is but so is the officer who administers the lineup.

In a study that specifically addressed this question, Sarah Greathouse and Margaret Bull Kovera (2009) paired student "witnesses" to a staged theft with student "police" who were trained how to administer a simultaneous or sequential photo lineup using either biased or unbiased instructions. In these lineups, a picture of the actual culprit was either present or absent. Half the administrators were *informed* of who the police suspect was in the lineup; the other half were *blind* as to the suspect's identity. The results showed that under relatively biasing conditions (simultaneous photo spreads and biased instructions), witnesses made more suspect identifications—even when the suspect was truly innocent—when the administrator was informed rather than blind. Videotapes of the sessions showed that the informed administrators unwittingly increased identification rates by telling witnesses to look carefully, by asking them to look again when they failed to make a selection, and in some cases by letting on that they knew who the suspect was. Other studies too have shown that comments made by a lineup administrator can influence eyewitness identification decisions (Clark et al., 2009). This research strongly supports a point of reform, recently adopted in several states, which eyewitness researchers have long advocated: A double-blind procedure in which neither the suspect nor the police administrator know who the suspect is within the lineup.

■ Testifying in Court

Eyewitnesses can be inaccurate, but that's only part of the problem. The other part is that their testimony is not easy to evaluate. To examine how juries view eyewitness testimony, Gary Wells, Rod Lindsay, and others conducted a series of early studies in which they staged the theft of a calculator in the presence of unsuspecting research participants, who were later cross-examined after trying to pick the culprit from a photo spread. Other participants, who served as mock jurors, observed the questioning and judged the witnesses. Overall, the jurors overestimated how accurate the eyewitnesses were and could not distinguish between witnesses whose identifications were correct and those whose identifications were incorrect (Lindsay et al., 1981; Wells et al., 1979).

There appear to be two problems. First, people do not know about many aspects of human perception and memory through common sense. Brian Cutler and others (1988) found that mock jurors were not particularly sensitive to the effects of lineup instructions, weapon focus, and certain other aspects of an eyewitnessing situation, such as the cross-race bias, in evaluating the testimony of an eyewitness. People are knowledgeable about some factors but not others (Desmarais & Read, 2011). The second problem is that people tend to base their judgments of an eyewitness largely on how *confident* that witness is, a factor that is only modestly predictive of accuracy. This statement may seem surprising, but studies have shown that the witness who declares "I am absolutely certain" is not necessarily more likely to be right than the one who appears less certain (Penrod & Cutler, 1995; Sporer et al., 1995).

Why are eyewitness confidence and accuracy not more highly related? The reason is that confidence levels can be raised and lowered by factors that do not have an impact on identification accuracy. To demonstrate, Elizabeth Luus and Wells (1994) staged a theft in front of pairs of participants and then had each separately identify the culprit from a photographic lineup. After the participants made their identifications, the experimenters led them to believe that their partner, a co-witness, either had picked the same person, a similar-looking different person, or a dissimilar-looking different person or had said that the thief was not in the lineup. Participants were then questioned by a police officer who asked, "On a scale from 1 to 10, how confident are you in your identification?" The result: Participants became more confident when told that a co-witness picked the same person or a dissimilar

Courtesy of Gary L. Wells

In 2009, social psychologist Gary Wells appeared on the CBS news show *60 Minutes*, where he explained how various aspects of a lineup, how photographs are presented, and how witnesses are instructed can influence the tendency for people to make correct or incorrect identifications.

alternative and less confident when told that the co-witness picked a similar alternative or none at all. Other studies too have shown that eyewitnesses can be influenced by the reports of co-witnesses (Gabbert et al., 2003; Skagerberg, 2007).

Other studies show that a witness's confidence can be influenced by other types of extraneous information. John Shaw (1996) found that mock witnesses who are repeatedly questioned about their observations become more and more confident over time—even though they did not become more accurate. Demonstrating what they called "the dud effect," Steve Charman and his colleagues (2011) found that an eyewitness's confidence in a mistaken identification is inflated by the presence of fillers in the lineup that bear no resemblance to the criminal. By contrast to these duds, the witness's lineup choice seems closer and more correct.

Particularly problematic when it comes to a witness's stated level of confidence is the *post-identification feedback effect,* first demonstrated by Gary Wells and Amy Bradfield (1998), which has shown that eyewitnesses who made incorrect identifications and then received positive feedback from the experimenter about those identifications went on not only to become more confident but to reconstruct their entire memory of the eyewitnessing experience. In a series of studies, they showed participants a security camera videotape of a man who shot a guard followed by a set of pictures that did not contain the actual gunman (in other words, all identifications made were false). The experimenter then said to some witnesses, but not to others, "Oh good. You identified the actual murder suspect." When witnesses were later asked about the whole experience, those given the confirming feedback "recalled" that they had paid more attention to the event, had a better view of the culprit, and found it easier to make the identification (see ● Figure 12.3). After some 20 studies involving 20,000 mock witnesses, it is now clear: Positive feedback can alter an eyewitness's account of the eyewitnessing experience and inflate his or her level of confidence (Steblay, Wells, & Douglass, 2014).

This post-identification feedback effect raises an important question: Does the inflation of witnesses' confidence make it even harder for juries to discriminate between accurate and mistaken eyewitnesses? To answer this question, Laura Smalarz and Gary Wells (2014) conducted a two-phased laboratory experiment. In the first phase, participants watched a 90-second video of a simulated crime in which a man at an airport switched his bag with that belonging to another passenger. Afterward, they were told that the bag left behind contained a bomb and that the purpose of the study was to see if they could identify the

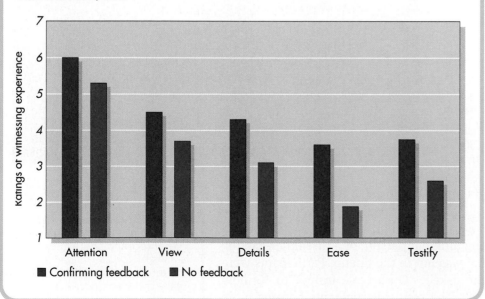

● **FIGURE 12.3**

The Biasing Effects of Post-Identification Feedback

Participants saw a gunman on videotape and then tried to make an identification from a set of photographs in which he was absent. Afterward, the experimenter gave some witnesses but not others confirming feedback about their selection. As shown, those given the confirming feedback later recalled that they had paid more attention to the event, had a better view of it, could make out details of the culprit's face, and found it easier to make the identification. They were also more willing to testify in court.
Wells & Bradfield, 1998.

■ Confirming feedback ■ No feedback

culprit from a photo lineup. At that point, they made an identification that was either correct or mistaken after which half were randomly assigned to receive positive feedback. All witnesses were then interviewed on camera—as if giving testimony.

In Phase 2 of this study, a second group of participants watched a set of witness interviews from Phase 1 and then indicated whether they thought each witness had made a correct or incorrect identification. The result was sobering. When watching witnesses who did not receive feedback, Phase 2 participants believed 70% of those who were accurate and only 36% of those who were mistaken—they could tell the difference. When watching witnesses who received positive feedback before their interviews, however, Phase 2 participants believed 64% of those who were accurate and 63% of those who were mistaken. ● Figure 12.4 shows that by bolstering witnesses who made mistaken identifications, positive feedback made it impossible for outside observers to make accurate distinctions. These findings, and other similar results (Douglass et al., 2010), led Smalarz and Wells (2015) to reason that in the real world—where witnesses routinely get positive feedback—it is especially difficult for judges and juries to evaluate the accuracy of their identifications.

Improving Eyewitness Justice

Having described the problems with information obtained from eyewitnesses, social psychologists are in a position to put their knowledge to use in two important ways: (1) By educating judges and juries about the science so they can better evaluate eyewitnesses who testify in court, and (2) by making eyewitness identification evidence itself more accurate.

To educate juries, psychologists sometimes testify as eyewitness experts at trial. Just like medical doctors who testify about a patient's physical condition, economists who testify on monopolies and other antitrust matters, and architectural engineers who testify on the structural integrity of buildings, psychologists are often called by one party or the other to inform the trial jury about relevant aspects of human perception, memory, and behavior (Cutler, 2009).

What, specifically, do these experts say to the jury? What findings do they present in court? Several years ago, researchers surveyed 64 eyewitness experts, many of whose studies are described in this chapter. The principles listed in Table 12.2 were seen by the vast majority of respondents as highly reliable and worthy of expert testimony (Kassin et al., 2001). Does the jury need to be informed? On some matters, yes. Research shows that there are certain aspects of the psychology of eyewitness testimony (for example, the fact that lineup instructions and presentation format can affect whether eyewitnesses will identify an innocent person) that the average person does not already know as a matter of common sense (Desmarais & Read, 2011).

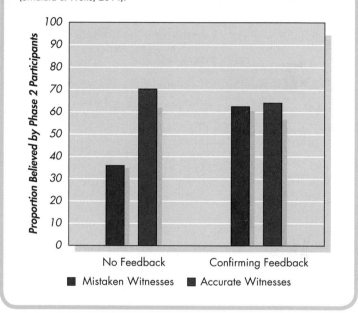

● **FIGURE 12.4**

How Post-Identification Feedback to Witnesses Impairs Juries

Phase 1 participants watched a crime video and then made a correct or incorrect identification. Randomly, half of these witnesses then received positive feedback before giving "testimony" on camera that was later viewed by a second set of participants. When watching witnesses who did not receive feedback, Phase 2 participants were able to distinguish between those who were accurate vs. inaccurate (left). When watching witnesses who had received positive feedback, however, Phase 2 participants could no longer tell the difference (right). After receiving positive feedback, as often happens in the real world, inaccurate witnesses became more confident—and, therefore, more believable.
(Smalarz & Wells, 2014).

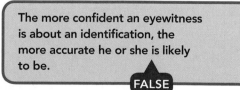

The more confident an eyewitness is about an identification, the more accurate he or she is likely to be.

FALSE

▲ **TABLE 12.2**

What Eyewitness Experts Say in Court

Presented with a list of eyewitness factors, 64 experts were asked what research findings were strong enough to present in court. In order of how much support they elicited, the following are among the most highly regarded topics of expert testimony.

Eyewitness Factor	Statement
Wording of questions	An eyewitness's testimony about an event can be affected by how the questions put to the witness are worded.
Lineup instructions	Police instructions can affect an eyewitness's willingness to make an identification.
Mug shot–induced bias	Exposure to mug shots of a suspect increases the likelihood that the witness will later choose that suspect in a lineup.
Confidence malleability	An eyewitness's confidence can be influenced by factors that are unrelated to the accuracy of an identification.
Postevent information	Eyewitness testimony about an event often reflects not only what the witness actually saw but also information he or she obtained later on.
Child suggestibility	Young children are more vulnerable than adults to interviewer suggestion, peer pressures, and other social influences.
Alcoholic intoxication	Alcoholic intoxication impairs an eyewitness's later ability to recall persons and events.
Cross-race bias	Eyewitnesses are more accurate at identifying members of their own race than they are at identifying members of other races.
Weapon focus	The presence of a weapon impairs an eyewitness's ability to accurately identify the perpetrator's face.
Accuracy confidence	An eyewitness's confidence is not a good predictor of the accuracy of his or her identification.

From Kassin, S. M., Tubb, V. A., Hosch, H. M., and Memon, A., "On the 'general acceptance' of eyewitness testimony research: A new survey of the experts," *American Psychologist*, May 2001. Copyright © 2001 by the American Psychological Association. Reprinted by permission.

In recent years, psychologists have also helped to improve upon the accuracy of eyewitness identifications. They have done so by replicating their laboratory experiments in police departments; by testifying not only in trials but before state legislatures and criminal justice commissions; by appearing on national news shows; by submitting briefs to courts; and by inspiring a wave of reforms—all designed to improve the procedures used in getting lineup identifications from eyewitnesses. At present, for example, a growing number of police departments have started to require the use of double-blind lineups, unbiased instructions, sequential presentation formats, and the immediate assessment of a witness's confidence—without feedback.

■ The Alibi: Eyewitness to Innocence

Suppose you discovered, much to your surprise, that you were considered a suspect in a criminal investigation. You are innocent, so you simply have to account for your whereabouts for the time of the crime. If you remember where you were at the time of the crime, you have an alibi—an alibi is simply a claim that you were elsewhere. However, having an alibi is the easy part; proving an alibi is another matter altogether (Olson & Wells, 2004, p. 157).

Just as police and prosecutors seek out eyewitnesses to identify suspects and build a case against them, defendants often call upon their own witnesses, or *alibis*, to help vouch for their whereabouts at the time of the crime. There are several ways that someone under suspicion can offer proof of innocence. Sometimes physical evidence can be used—such as ATM receipts, cell phone or GPS records, or surveillance video. At other times, other people are cited—such as a spouse, friend, neighbor, cashier, or waitress. Intuitively, people see some alibis as more credible than others. In one study, participants endorsed the belief that that 62% of biologically related alibis would lie for a defendant, compared to 50% of alibis related by marriage and 32% of witnesses whose relation is merely social (Hosch et al., 2011). In a second study, experienced police officers reported that the most believable alibi stories are those that include physical evidence, which is rare, or a statement from an unrelated stranger, which is also rare (Dysart & Strange, 2012).

How accurate and honest are alibi witnesses? Are they willing to lie for someone they know and like? Are their memories subject to influence from outside sources? To answer these questions, Stephanie Marion and Tara Burke (2013) devised an ingenious experiment in which they brought student participants into the lab with student confederates hired to act as co-participants on several tasks. At the start of each session, determined by random assignment, some student pairs were led to believe that personality tests they had earlier taken showed them to be very similar, at which point they worked together on the first task and had a friendly conversation. Other student pairs were led to believe that they were dissimilar, at which point they were separated to work on the first task in different rooms. Several minutes into every session, the confederate left to use the restroom. She then returned to the lab with cash in her pocket, which she then placed in her wallet, or without any sign of money.

At one point, the experimenter reentered the room, announced that money was missing from an adjacent lab room, and asked the students if they had seen anything. The confederate immediately said, "No, we were both here the whole time." At a later time, when the students were working in separate rooms, the experimenter turned to the participant and asked the alibi question—was the confederate in the room during the entire experiment? Would the participant vouch for the suspicious confederate? Overall, only 23% corroborated the confederate's false alibi. In fact, even though participants liked the similar-friendly confederate more than the dissimilar-neutral confederate, they were not more likely to corroborate her alibi. What did matter was whether participants had seen physical evidence of guilt. Compared to 36% in the no-cash condition, only 10% corroborated her alibi in the cash condition. At least among new acquaintances, it appears that witnesses are not willing to lie even for someone they like.

Confessions

Every now and then, an extraordinary event comes along that shakes the way you think. The Central Park jogger case was one of these events. In 1989, five boys who were 14 to 16 years old were found guilty of a monstrous assault and rape of a female jogger in New York's Central Park after they confessed (four of them did so on videotape) in vivid detail. Thirteen years later, a serial rapist named Matias Reyes stepped forward from prison to admit that he alone, not the boys, had committed the crime. To fully investigate Reyes's claim, the district attorney DNA-tested the semen from the crime scene and found that it was a match: Reyes was the rapist. The five boys, now men, were innocent. All their confessions were false, and the convictions were vacated (Burns, 2011).

■ Suspect Interviews: The Psychology of Lie Detection

Sometimes police identify a suspect for interrogation by talking to witnesses and informants, obtaining physical evidence from the crime scene, and other methods of investigation. Often, however, police decide to interrogate a particular person based solely on a personal judgment they make by conducting a special pre-interrogation interview that exposes deception. In *Criminal Interrogation and Confessions,* an influential manual on interrogation first published in 1962 and now in its fifth edition, Inbau and others (2013) have proposed a process by which police can distinguish truths from lies. In this approach, police are advised to ask nonaccusatory questions and then to observe changes in the suspect's verbal and nonverbal behavior—looking, for example, at eye contact, pauses, posture, fidgety movements—to determine if he or she is telling the truth.

For a person under suspicion, a police officer's judgment at this stage is crucial because it can determine whether a suspect is judged deceptive and interrogated or presumed innocent and sent home. In theory, this approach makes sense. As described in Chapter 4 on social perception, however, research has consistently shown that most verbal and nonverbal demeanor cues that are suggested do not discriminate at high levels of accuracy between truth-telling and deception (DePaulo et al., 2003; Hartwig & Bond, 2011). In fact, research shows that people on average are only 54% accurate; that training produces little if any improvement; and that police officers, psychiatrists, customs inspectors, judges, and other "professionals" tend to perform only slightly better, if at all (Meissner & Kassin, 2002; Vrij, 2008).

That people are notoriously inept at making accurate judgments of truth and deception can be seen every day—which is why Ponzi scheme perpetrators like Bernie Madoff and other con artists can fool even an affluent and intelligent clientele. Are there more accurate means of lie detection? To improve performance, police over the years have used a **polygraph**, or what most of us would call a lie-detector test. A polygraph is an electronic instrument that simultaneously records multiple channels of physiological arousal. The signals are picked up by sensors attached to different parts of the body. For example, rubber tubes are strapped around a suspect's torso to measure breathing, blood-pressure cuffs are wrapped around the upper arm to measure pulse rate, and electrodes are placed on the fingertips to record sweat-gland activity, or perspiration. These signals are then boosted by amplifiers and converted into a visual display.

The polygraph is used to detect deception on the assumption that when people lie, they become anxious and physiologically aroused in ways that can be measured. Here's how the test is conducted. After convincing a suspect that the polygraph works and establishing his or her baseline level of arousal, the examiner asks a series of yes-no questions and compares how the suspect reacts to emotionally arousing *crime-relevant questions* ("Did you steal the money?") and *control questions* that are arousing but not relevant to the crime ("Did you take anything that did not belong to you when you were younger?"). In theory, suspects who are innocent, whose denials are truthful, should be more aroused by the control questions; guilty suspects, whose denials are false, should be more aroused by the crime-relevant questions.

Does the lie-detector test really work? Many laypeople think of it as foolproof, but scientific opinion is split. Some researchers report accuracy rates of up to 80% to 90%. Others believe that such claims are exaggerated. One well-documented problem is that truthful persons too often fail the test. A second problem is that people who understand the test can fake the results. Studies show that you can beat the polygraph by tensing your muscles, squeezing your toes, or using other "countermeasures" while answering the *control* questions. By artificially inflating the responses to "innocent" questions that are used as a basis of comparison, one can mask the stress that is aroused by lying on the crime-relevant questions (Honts et al., 2002).

What, then, are we to conclude? The National Research Council (2003) concluded that there is no simple answer. Under certain conditions—for example, when the suspect is naive and the examiner is competent—it is possible for the polygraph to detect truth and deception at fairly high levels of accuracy. In fact, handheld "pocket" polygraphs have been used for rapid screening of terrorism suspects in the field. Still, the problems identified by research are hard to overcome, which is why the U.S. Supreme Court ruled, in the context of a military court martial, that judges may refuse to admit polygraph test results into evidence (*United States v. Scheffer*, 1998).

polygraph   A mechanical instrument that records physiological arousal from multiple channels; it is often used as a lie-detector test.

Seeking alternatives, researchers are trying to develop tests that distinguish truth and deception through the use of a modified polygraph test that asks different types of questions (Ben-Shakhar & Elaad, 2003); the measurement of involuntary electrical activity in the brain (Meixner & Rosenfeld, 2014); pupil dilation when the person being tested is asked to lie, which requires more cognitive effort than telling the truth (Dionisio et al., 2001); the Implicit Association Test, or IAT, which shows that people are quicker to respond to true statements than to false statements (Sartori et al., 2008); the use of fMRI to measure blood oxygen levels in areas of the brain that are linked to deception (Bhatt et al., 2009; Kozel et al., 2005); and thermal imaging cameras in airports to detect lying through rises in skin temperature (Warmelink et al., 2011). Especially in light of the post–9/11 need for intelligence gathering from terrorism suspects, prisoners of war, witnesses, and informants, researchers are also working to improve the quality of the interviewing methods used in the field (Loftus, 2011).

> **It is not possible to knowingly fool a lie-detector test.**
>
> **FALSE**

Police Interrogations: Social Influence Under Pressure

As the events of the Central Park jogger case unfolded, questions mounted: Why would five boys—or anyone else, for that matter—confess to a crime they did not commit? What social influences are brought to bear on suspects interrogated by police? Many years ago, police detectives would use brute force to get confessions. Among the commonly used coercive methods were prolonged confinement and isolation; explicit threats; deprivations of sleep, food, and other needs; extreme sensory discomfort (for example, by shining a bright, blinding strobe light on a suspect's face); and assorted forms of physical violence (for example, forcing suspects to stand for hours at a time or beating them with a rubber hose, which seldom left visible marks).

Today, the police are required to warn suspects of their Miranda rights to silence and an attorney, and the tactics they use are more psychological in nature. In *Criminal Interrogation and Confessions,* Inbau et al. (2013) advise police, once they have identified a suspect they believe to be lying, to conduct a process of interrogation. This process begins when police put a suspect alone—with no friends or family present—into a small, bare, soundproof room, a physical environment that is designed to arouse feelings of social isolation and discomfort. Next, they present a vivid nine-step procedure designed to get suspects to confess (see Table 12.3).

Once a suspect is isolated, this method of interrogation offers two approaches. One approach is to pressure the suspect into submission by expressing certainty in his or her guilt and even, at times, claiming falsely to have damaging evidence such as fingerprints or an eyewitness. In this way, the accused is led to believe that it is futile to continue in his or her denials. A second approach is to befriend the suspect, offer sympathy and friendly advice, and "minimize" the offense by offering face-saving excuses or blaming the victim. Under stress, feeling trapped, lulled into a false sense of security, and led to expect leniency, many suspects agree to give a confession. This approach is carefully designed to increase the anxiety associated with denial and reduce the anxiety associated with confession. It may sound like interrogation process springs from a *Law &*

▲ **TABLE 12.3**

The Nine Steps of Interrogation

1. Confront the suspect with assertions of his or her guilt.

2. Develop "themes" that appear to justify or excuse the crime.

3. Interrupt all statements of innocence and denial.

4. Overcome all of the suspect's objections to the charges.

5. Keep the increasingly passive suspect from tuning out.

6. Show sympathy and understanding and urge the suspect to tell all.

7. Offer the suspect a face-saving explanation for his or her guilty action.

8. Get the suspect to recount the details of the crime.

9. Convert that statement into a full written confession.

Inbau et al., 2001. © Cengage Learning

"I'm neither a good cop nor a bad cop, Jerome. Like yourself, I'm a complex amalgam of positive and negative personality traits that emerge or not, depending on circumstances."

Order TV script, but in real life these tactics are routinely used (for a firsthand account of the training, see Starr, 2013; for a social-psychological perspective, see Davis & O'Donahue, 2004; Kassin, 2015).

In an observational study of 182 live and videotaped interrogations, Richard Leo (1996) found that detectives used an average of five to six tactics per suspect. In a survey of 631 police investigators, Kassin and others (2007) found that the most common reported tactics were to physically isolate suspects, identify contradictions in their accounts, establish rapport, and confront them with evidence of their guilt, appeals to self-interests, and offer sympathy and moral justification. Whatever specific methods are used, it is clear that being accused and pointedly questioned about a crime is a very stressful experience. In one study, participants who were accused of cheating on a laboratory task—compared to those who were not accused—were less able to process the rights they were given to remain silent and to have a lawyer present (Scherr & Madon, 2013). It is also now clear that physically painful methods of persuasion, often referred to as "enhanced interrogation" techniques, were used after 9/11 to interrogate suspected terrorists (McKelvey, 2007; O'Mara, 2009).

■ False Confessions: Why Innocent People Confess

It could be argued that trickery and deception does not pose a serious problem during interrogation because only perpetrators confess; innocent people never confess to crimes they did not commit. This assumption, however, is incorrect. As hard as it is to believe, a number of chilling cases of false confessions are on record. Illustrating the point is the story of Amanda Knox, the American college student accused but ultimately absolved of the tragic murder of her roommate in Italy. Also illustrating the point is the Central Park jogger case in which five false confessions to a rape were taken. In fact, research shows that false confessions were present in more than 25% of all cases involving prisoners who were convicted and later proved innocent by DNA evidence (Garrett, 2011). It's important to realize that this sample represents just the tip of an iceberg. Although most case studies arise from the United States and England, proven false confessions have been documented in countries all over the world (Kassin et al., 2010).

In 1989, 16-year-old Kharey Wise (left) and four other teenagers confessed to raping a jogger in New York's Central Park. Based solely on his confession, Wise was convicted and sent to prison. Thirteen years later, Matias Reyes (right) admitted that he alone, not the boys, had committed the crime. DNA tests confirmed that Reyes was the rapist. The boys, despite their confessions, were innocent. In 2014, the city of New York compensated them for their wrongful convictions.

It seems unimaginable. Why would an innocent person ever confess to police to a crime he or she did not commit? There are two reasons—and two types of false confession. Sometimes innocent people under police interrogation agree to confess as an act of mere *compliance*—to escape a very stressful situation. Applying basic decision-making psychology, Stephanie Madon and her colleagues note that human beings in general are influenced more by rewards and punishments that are immediate than by those that are delayed (Madon et al., 2012; Yang et al., 2015). People are particularly shortsighted when they are hungry, tired, stressed, or otherwise fatigued and unable to maintain their self-control (Davis & Leo, 2012)—for example, late at night or early in the morning (Scherr et al., 2014). For a suspect who is under intense interrogation, stopping the process through confession may feel so urgent that he or she does not fully consider the future consequence of doing so. Madon et al. (2012) demonstrated this type of shortsightedness in a series of experiments in which participants were more likely to admit to various transgressions (such as buying alcohol before they were 21, driving without a license, illegally downloading music, shoplifting, or taking credit for someone else's idea) when doing so was in their immediate interest and the negative consequence would come later.

In real life, the process of interrogation can be so stressful that the short-term benefit of confession outweighs the long-term benefit of denial. The experiences of Amanda Knox and the Central Park jogger boys illustrate the point. All had been in custody and interrogated overnight, relentlessly, for several hours, before giving their confessions. Such long periods of time bring fatigue, despair, and a deprivation of sleep and other need states. In both cases, the police and suspects disagree about what happened during these unrecorded hours so it is not possible to know for sure. In both cases, however, the defendants claimed that they felt threatened and uncertain as to what would happen if they refused to confess. In both cases, the defendants then tried to withdraw their confessions as soon as the pressure of interrogation had passed.

In contrast to instances in which innocent people confess as an act of compliance, or obedience to authority, sometimes the process of interrogation can cause innocent people to confess because they come to believe that they are guilty of the crime. In these instances, the false confession illustrates a strong form of social influence known as *internalization.* This process was evident in the story of three men and three women in Beatrice, Nebraska. In 1989, they were convicted of the murder of a 68-year-old woman. Five pled guilty; four gave vividly detailed confessions to police as a result of intense interrogations. Twenty years later, all six defendants were pardoned after DNA testing cleared them and identified the actual culprit. After reinvestigation, the Nebraska Attorney General's Office concluded that despite all the confessions, these individuals were innocent "beyond all doubt." Yet remarkably, all of them had come to internalize the erroneous belief in their own guilt. One woman stood by her statement until just before she was pardoned, at which point she said, "I guess I was brainwashed" (Hammel, 2008).

Is it really possible to get people to confess to an act they did not commit? Based on the events of actual cases, Kassin and Kiechel (1996) theorized that two factors can increase this risk: (1) a suspect who lacks a clear memory of the event in question and (2) the presentation of false evidence. To test this hypothesis, they recruited pairs of college students to work on a fast- or slow-paced computer task. At one point, the computer crashed and students were accused of having caused the damage by pressing a key they had been specifically instructed to

▲ TABLE 12.4

Factors That Produce False Confessions

As participants worked on a fast- or slow-paced task, the computer crashed, and they were accused of causing the damage. A confederate then said that she had or had not seen the participants hit the forbidden key. As shown, many participants signed a confession (compliance), and some even "admitted" their guilt in private to another confederate (internalization). Despite their innocence, many participants in the fast-false witness condition confessed on both measures.

	Control		False Witness	
	Slow	Fast	Slow	Fast
Compliance	35%	65%	89%	100%
Internalization	0%	12%	44%	65%

Based on Kassin, S. M., and Kiechel, K. L., "The social psychology of false confessions: compliance, internalization, and confabulation," *Psychological Science* vol 7, no 3 (Table 1, p. 127).

avoid. All students were truly innocent and denied the charge. In half the sessions, however, the second student (who was really a confederate) said that she had seen the student hit the forbidden key.

Demonstrating the process of compliance, many students confronted by this false witness agreed to sign a confession handwritten by the experimenter. Further demonstrating the process of internalization, some students later "admitted" guilt to a stranger (also a confederate) after the study was supposedly over and the two were alone. In short, innocent people who are vulnerable to suggestion can be induced to confess and to internalize guilt by the presentation of false evidence (see Table 12.4). This finding, that people can be induced into making internalized false confessions, has been replicated in many different types of experiments (Horselenberg et al., 2003; Nash & Wade, 2009; Perillo & Kassin, 2011; Shaw & Porter, 2015).

False evidence is one tactic that can cause innocent people to confess. An offer of leniency can have the same effect. Melissa Russano and others (2005) asked participants to solve a series of problems, sometimes alone and sometimes with a fellow participant (who was actually a confederate). In the alone trials, participants were instructed not to seek or give assistance. In a guilty condition, the confederate asked for help, inducing most participants to break the rule. In an innocent condition, no such request was made. Moments later, the experimenter returned, accused the pair of participants of cheating—a possible violation of their university honor code—and then interrogated everyone as to whether they had cheated. As part of this interrogation, the experimenter offered leniency for cooperation to some participants, minimized the seriousness of the violation to others, used both tactics, or used no tactics at all. Would students sign a confession to cheating? Yes. Both promises and minimization increased the number of true confessions among students who broke the rule. But these same tactics also increased the rate of false confessions among students who did nothing wrong.

Everyone agrees that the objective of an interrogation is to draw confessions from people who are guilty, not from those who are innocent. In that vein, interrogation tactics that put innocent people at risk should be avoided if possible. There is, however, a basic problem with interrogation: It is a process of social influence that police employ on suspects that they believe to be guilty. Can this expectation of guilt lead police to use tactics that draw false confessions? To test this hypothesis, Fadia Narchet and others (2011) trained eight young men, over five weeks, on how to conduct interrogations using various techniques. In a study like the one just described, these trainees were asked to interrogate guilty and innocent participants to determine if they had cheated on the alone task. In some cases, the interrogators were led to believe the participant was probably guilty; in other cases, that he or she was probably innocent. Did expectations influence outcomes? Yes. ● Figure 12.5 shows that interrogators elicited confessions from most participants who had actually cheated regardless of expectations. But when they interrogated participants who did not cheat, interrogators with guilty expectations used more coercive tactics and produced a high rate of false confessions.

Confessions in the Courtroom

How does the legal system treat confessions produced by police interrogations? The process is straightforward. Whenever a suspect confesses but then recants the statement, pleads not guilty, and goes to trial, the judge must determine whether the statement was voluntary or coerced. If the confession was clearly coerced—as when a suspect is isolated for long periods of time, deprived of food or sleep, threatened, or abused—it is excluded. If the confession is not coerced, it is admitted into evidence for the jury to evaluate.

In these cases, juries are confronted with a classic attribution dilemma: A suspect's statement may indicate guilt (personal attribution) or it may simply provide the suspect with a way to avoid the unpleasant consequences of silence (situational attribution). According to attribution theory, jurors should reject all confessions made in response to external pressure. But wait. Remember the fundamental attribution error? In Chapter 4, we saw that people tend to overattribute behavior to persons and overlook the influence of situational forces. Is it similarly possible, as in the Amanda Knox and Central Park jogger cases, that jurors view suspects who confess as guilty even if their confessions were coerced during interrogation?

To examine this question, Kassin and Sukel (1997) had mock jurors read one of three versions of a double murder trial. In a control version that did not contain a confession, only 19% voted guilty. In a low-pressure version in which the defendant was said to have confessed immediately upon questioning, the conviction rate rose considerably, to 62%. But there was a third, high-pressure condition in which participants were told that the defendant had confessed out of fear while his hands were cuffed behind his back, causing him pain. How did jurors in this situation react? Reasonably, they judged the confession to be coerced and said it did not influence their verdicts. Yet the conviction rate in this situation increased sharply, this time from 19% to 50%. Apparently, people are powerfully influenced by evidence of a confession, even when they concede that it was coerced. Confessions are powerfully incriminating not only to laypeople. The same pattern of result was found in a study involving judges (Wallace & Kassin, 2012).

Why are juries so strongly influenced by a confession, even when the defendant recants it and proclaims his or her innocence? There are three reasons. The

---

● **FIGURE 12.5**

Interrogation as a Self-Fulfilling Prophecy: Do Guilty Expectations Produce False Confessions?

Participants were asked to solve a series of problems, sometimes alone and sometimes with a confederate. Half were induced to cheat on the alone task, making them guilty of violating the rule; the other half were not induced to cheat, making them innocent. Eight young men then interrogated participants to determine if they had cheated. In some cases, the interrogators were led to believe the participant was probably guilty; in other cases, that he or she was probably innocent. As shown, interrogators produced confessions from most participants who had cheated. Armed with guilty expectations, however, they also produced a high rate of false confessions from participants who were innocent.

Narchet et al., 2011. © Cengage Learning

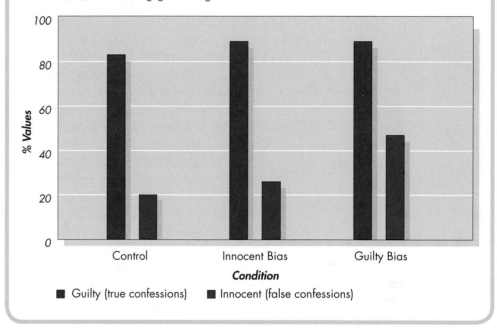

first is that common sense leads us to trust people who make statements against self-interest. Most people believe that they would never confess to a crime they did not commit—and they evaluate others accordingly (Blandón-Gitlin et al., 2010; Henkel et al., 2008; Leo & Liu, 2009). The second reason for the impact of confessions, even when they are false, is that typically confessions contain a great deal of detail. Analyzing 38 proven false confessions, Garrett (2010) found that 95% contained accurate details about the crime that the confessor may have picked up through secondhand sources. In fact, when Sara Appleby and her colleagues (2013) analyzed 20 confessions later proved to be false, they found that many of them contained not only details about the crime but a full narrative story of who, what, when, where, and why—sometimes even including apologies and expressions of remorse. The third reason for the strong effect of confessions is that confessions are so persuasive they can corrupt other evidence. Led to believe that a defendant had confessed, for example, people are more likely to identify him in a lineup (Hasel & Kassin, 2009) and more likely to perceive his handwriting as a match to that found on a bank robbery note (Kukucka & Kassin, 2014). These added items of evidence serve to "corroborate" the confession.

What if confessions are video recorded? Today, many police departments tape confessions for presentation in court. But could you tell the difference between a true confession and a false confession? Maybe not. Inside prison walls, Kassin, Meissner, and Norwick (2005) videotaped male inmates giving full confessions to the crimes for which they were incarcerated and concocting false confessions to offenses suggested by the researchers that they did not commit. College students and police investigators then watched and judged 10 different inmates, each of whom gave a true or false confession to one of five crimes. The results showed that neither group exhibited high levels of accuracy.

In light of recently discovered false confessions, a number of states are beginning to require that the full interrogations be video recorded. This is an important reform to current practice, in part because the presence of a camera inhibits police from using extreme interrogation tactics and in part because it enables judges and juries to see for themselves how a confession came about and the extent to which the suspect was coerced (Kassin et al., 2010). In a world in which police interrogations are sometimes video recorded, how should these events be staged? In a series of experiments, Daniel Lassiter and his colleagues (2001) taped mock confessions from three different camera angles so that either the suspect or the interrogator or both were visible. All participants heard the same exchanges of words, but those who watched the suspects saw the situations as less coercive overall than did those who were focused only on the interrogators. Follow-up research has shown that even the perceptions of experienced trial judges are influenced by these variations in camera perspective (Lassiter et al., 2007). The practical policy implications are clear: When the camera directs all eyes at the accused, jurors are likely to underestimate the amount of pressure exerted by the "hidden" interrogator.

■ Pleading Guilty in the Shadow of Trial

Defendants often make a special form of confession outside the police station with the prosecutor and often the defense lawyer present. That confession involves pleading guilty, typically in exchange for lesser charges and a more lenient sentence.

Every day, thousands of defendants decide to plead guilty. In fact, an estimated 97% of convicted defendants in the U.S. federal criminal justice system now resolve their cases in this way. This is the highest number ever recorded. For legal systems all over the world, this process represents a "shortcut" alternative to trial that results in enormous savings of time, money, and other resources (Rauxloh, 2012).

It is clear that people are far more likely to plead guilty if they had committed the crime for which they are charged than if they had not. However, with so many cases getting resolved outside of court, as part of an agreement between a prosecutor and defendant, the courts have wondered if there is an "innocence problem"—whether innocent people who fear ultimate conviction and a harsh sentence, sometimes plead guilty "in the shadow of trial" (Bibas, 2004; Bushway & Redlich, 2012).

In an article entitled "Why Innocent People Plead Guilty," Federal Judge Jed Rakoff (2014) described how an innocent person might make a rational decision to plead guilty, in the same way that an innocent person might confess to police, after considering the crime that is charged, the strength of the evidence, the punishment alternatives, and the pressures that are brought to bear on the process: "If the defendant wants to plead guilty, the prosecutor will offer him a considerably reduced charge, but only if the plea is agreed to promptly." To the extent that these decisions are further "informed" by pressure from the prosecutor—a figure of authority in a position to command a high of obedience (Milgram, 1974)—the decision to plead guilty is often made in the presence of powerful social influences (Bordens & Bassett, 1985).

The incidence of false guilty pleas in the United States is not known (Tor et al., 2010). Laboratory experiments that have involved role-playing in hypothetical scenarios or in which participants make decisions that they believe will have a real consequence have shown that many innocent people will accept a false guilty plea—at rates as high as 33% (Gregory et al., 1978), 43% (Russano et al., 2005), and 56% (Dervan & Edkins, 2012). The problem is not found just in the laboratory. Approximately 10% of innocent people who were wrongfully convicted in the United States had pled guilty rather than risk conviction on more serious charges. As you might also expect, not all defendants are equally at risk. Research shows that the rate of self-reported false guilty pleas is particularly high among juveniles —18% (Malloy et al., 2014) and defendants with mental illness—37% (Redlich et al., 2010).

Certain types of cases can also create problems. In studies that have sought hypothetical decisions from practicing attorneys, researchers have found that their plea recommendations were predictably influenced by how strong the evidence was against the defendant (Kramer et al., 2007; Pezdek & O'Brien, 2014). It appears that a defendant's race may also play a role. In one simulation study, practicing defense attorneys recommended harsher plea agreements for black defendants than for white defendants—even when the crime and the evidence were the same (Edkins, 2011).

> **Without being beaten or threatened, innocent people sometimes confess to crimes they did not commit.**
> **TRUE**

Jury Decision Making

The criminal justice system is multilayered and complex. Yet through it all, the trial—a relatively infrequent but highly dramatic event—is the heart and soul of the system. The threat of trial is what motivates parties to gather evidence and, later, to negotiate a plea agreement. And when it is over, the trial by judge or jury forms the basis for sentencing and appeals decisions. In this section, we examine the three stages of an American trial: (1) jury selection; (2) the presentation of evidence, arguments, and instructions; and (3) the processes by which juries deliberate to reach a verdict.

■ Jury Selection

If you're ever accused of a crime in the United States or involved in a lawsuit, you have a constitutional right to a trial by an impartial jury from your community. This right is considered essential to doing justice within a democracy. Yet whenever a controversial verdict is reached in a high-profile case, people, right or wrong, blame the 12 individuals who constituted the jury. That's why it is important to know how juries are selected.

Jury selection is a three-stage process. First, the court uses voter registration lists, telephone directories, and other sources to compile a master list of eligible citizens who live in the community. Second, so that a representative sample can be obtained, a certain number of people from the list are randomly drawn and summoned for duty. If you've ever been called, you know what happens next. Before people who appear in court are placed on a jury, they are subject to what is known as **voir dire**, a pretrial interview in which the judge and lawyers question the prospective jurors for signs of bias. If someone knows one of the parties, has an interest in the outcome of the case, or has already formed an opinion, the judge will excuse that person "for cause." In fact, if it can be proven that an entire community is biased, perhaps because of pretrial publicity, then the trial might be postponed or moved to another location.

Although the procedure seems straightforward, there is more to the story. In addition to deselecting individuals who are clearly biased, the lawyers are permitted to exercise **peremptory challenges**. That is, they can reject a certain limited number of prospective jurors even if they seem fair and open-minded, and they can do so without having to state reasons or win the judge's approval. Why would a lawyer challenge someone who appears to be impartial? What guides lawyers' decisions to accept some jurors and reject others? These questions make the process of voir dire particularly interesting to social psychologists (Vidmar & Hans, 2007).

"I see jury selection has begun."

Tom Cheney/The New Yorker Collection 1999/Cartoonbank.com

Trial Lawyers as Intuitive Psychologists Rumor has it that trial lawyers have used some unconventional methods to select juries. Under pressure to make choices quickly and without much information, lawyers rely on implicit personality theories and stereotypes. An implicit personality theory is a set of assumptions that people make about how certain attributes are related to each other and to behavior. When we believe that all members of a group share the same attributes, these implicit theories are called stereotypes.

As far as trial practice is concerned, how-to books claim that the astute lawyer can predict a juror's verdict by his or her gender, race, age, ethnic background, and other simple demographics. It has been suggested, for example, that athletes lack sympathy for fragile and injured victims, that engineers are unemotional, that men with beards resist authority, and that cabinetmakers are so meticulous in their work that they will never be completely satisfied with the evidence. Clarence Darrow, one of the most prominent trial attorneys of the twentieth century, suggested that jurors of southern European descent favored the defense whereas those from Scandinavia favored the prosecution. Other lawyers have theorized that women are more skeptical as jurors than men, particularly in response to attractive female witnesses. Still others offer selection advice based on faces, facial expressions, body language, and clothing. Perhaps the most interesting rule of thumb is also the simplest: "If you don't like a juror's face, chances are he doesn't like yours either!" (Wishman, 1986, pp. 72–73).

voir dire The pretrial examination of prospective jurors by the judge or opposing lawyers to uncover signs of bias.

peremptory challenge A means by which lawyers can exclude a limited number of prospective jurors without the judge's approval.

The intuitive approach to jury selection may provide for colorful stories from inside the courtroom, but the consequences of this kind of stereotyping for justice can be troubling for two reasons. First, if lawyers approach a prospective juror with a set of expectations, say based on stereotypes, they are likely to ask questions designed to confirm their beliefs and increase the likelihood of doing so. As we saw in Chapter 4, several social psychology studies have demonstrated that this type of confirmation bias can produce a self-fulfilling prophecy. In the venue of jury selection, the same process is at work. In a mock trial study, practicing attorneys were asked to prepare a voir dire strategy on the basis of juror profiles. The results showed that they formulated theories, asked questions to test those theories, and ultimately formed conclusions that were biased by the questions they asked (Otis et al., 2014).

A second problem with relying on stereotypes for jury selection is this: What if a prosecutor were to use peremptory challenges to exclude from the jury all whites, blacks, Latinos, or Asians; or all men or all women, possibly stripping the jury of the defendant's peers? In recent years, the U.S. Supreme Court has for the first time limited the use of peremptory challenges to prevent lawyers from systematically excluding prospective jurors on the basis of race. According to the Court, judges can now require lawyers suspected of discriminating in this way to explain the basis of their challenges (*Batson v. Kentucky,* 1986; *Miller-El v. Dretke,* 2005).

Citing social psychological research on stereotyping and prejudice, Samuel Sommers and Michael Norton (2008) point to two problems: (1) The influence of conscious and unconscious racial stereotypes on social perceptions is prevalent and likely to influence lawyers in the courtroom; and (2) these racial biases are difficult to identify in specific instances because lawyers, like everyone else, typically do not acknowledge having been influenced by their stereotypes. In a study that illustrated both points, Sommers and Norton (2007) presented college students, law students, and attorneys with a summary of a criminal trial involving a black defendant and asked them to choose between two prospective jurors with various characteristics—one white, the other black. As predicted, all groups were far more likely to challenge the juror who was black rather than the one who was white, yet very few subjects cited race as a factor in their decisions. It is sad, today, but true: Peremptory challenges are still being used in some parts of the country, without serious oversight, to exclude disproportionate numbers of African Americans (Liptak, 2015).

The intuitive approach to jury selection sometimes leads to discrimination on the basis of race and other characteristics. This approach is also not very effective. Thus, although some experienced trial attorneys take pride in their jury-selection skills, researchers have found that most lawyers cannot effectively predict how jurors will vote, either on the basis of their intuitive rules of thumb (Olczak et al., 1991) or by relying on how prospective jurors answer questions during the voir dire (Kerr et al., 1991; Zeisel & Diamond, 1978). Apparently, whether a juror characteristic predicts verdicts depends on the specifics of each and every case. Hence a new service industry was born: scientific jury selection.

> Contrary to popular opinion, women are harsher as trial jurors than men are.
>
> **FALSE**

Scientific Jury Selection   In a movie based on John Grisham's *Runaway Jury,* a ruthless jury consultant named Rankin Fitch, played by actor Gene Hackman, helps lawyers select jurors through the use of intrusive high-tech surveillance work. Burrowing deep into the lives of prospective jurors, Fitch trails them, investigates them, and even resorts at times to bribery, blackmail, and intimidation. Determined to stack the jury in order to defend gun company defendants against a multimillion-dollar wrongful death lawsuit, Fitch declares, "A trial is too important to be left up to juries."

Grisham's depiction of jury consulting is a work of fiction, not fact. But it is based on a kernel of truth. Instead of relying on hunches, successful stock market investors, baseball managers, and poker players play the odds whenever they can. Now many trial lawyers do too. In recent years, the "art" of jury selection has been transformed into something of a "science" (Lieberman & Sales, 2007).

This use of jury consultants began during the Vietnam War era, when the federal government prosecuted a group of antiwar activists known as the Harrisburg Seven. The case against the defendants was strong, and the trial was to be held in the conservative city of Harrisburg, Pennsylvania. To help the defendants select a jury, sociologist Jay Schulman and his colleagues (1973) surveyed the local community by interviewing 840 residents. Two kinds of information were taken from each resident: demographic (for example, sex, race, age, and education) and attitudes relevant to the trial (for example, attitudes toward the government, the war, and political dissent). By correlating these variables, Schulman's team came up with a profile of the ideal defense juror: "a female Democrat with no religious preference and a white-collar job or a skilled blue-collar job" (p. 40). Guided by this result, the defense selected its jury. The rest is history: Against all odds, the trial ended in a hung jury, split 10 to 2 in favor of acquittal.

In *Runaway Jury,* a film based on John Grisham's novel, actor Gene Hackman played feared jury consultant Rankin Fitch. In a film that blurred fact and fiction, Fitch not only researched prospective jurors for jury selection purposes but also engaged in jury tampering, blackmail, and other illegal tactics in a desperate but failed effort to win the verdict.

Today, the technique known as **scientific jury selection** is used often, especially in high-profile criminal trials and civil trials in which large sums of money are at stake. Research shows, for example, that jurors are differently predisposed when confronted with cases that pit lone individuals against large corporations, with some people favoring big business and others harboring an anti-business prejudice (Hans, 2000). How is scientific jury selection carried out? What are the methods used? The procedure is simple. Because lawyers are often not allowed to ask jurors intrusive and personal questions, they try to determine jurors' attitudes and verdict tendencies from information that is known about their backgrounds. The relevance of this information can be determined through focus groups, mock juries, or community-wide surveys, in which statistical relationships are sought between broad demographic factors and attitudes relevant to a particular case. Then, during the voir dire, lawyers ask prospective jurors about their backgrounds and use peremptory challenges to exclude those whose profiles are associated with unfavorable attitudes.

As you might expect, scientific jury selection is a controversial enterprise. By law, consultants are not permitted to communicate with or approach the prospective jurors themselves, despite the tactics portrayed in *Runaway Jury*. But how effective are the techniques that are employed? It's hard to say. On the one hand, trial lawyers who have used scientific jury selection boast an impressive winning percentage. On the other hand, it is impossible to know the extent to which these victories are attributable to the jury-selection surveys (Strier, 1999). So does scientific jury selection work? Although more data are needed to evaluate the claims made, it appears that attitudes can influence verdicts in some cases and that pretrial research can help lawyers identify these attitudes (Lieberman, 2011; Seltzer, 2006). As we'll soon see, the link between attitudes and verdicts is particularly strong in cases that involve capital punishment.

Before concluding our review of scientific jury selection, let's stop to consider an ethical question: Is justice enhanced or impaired by the intervention of

scientific jury selection A method of selecting juries through surveys that yield correlations between demographics and trial-relevant attitudes.

professional jury consultants? Is the real goal for lawyers to eliminate jurors who are biased or to create juries slanted in their favor? Those who practice scientific jury selection argue that picking juries according to survey results is simply a more refined version of what lawyers are permitted to do by intuition. If there's a problem, they say, it is not in the *science* but in the *law* that permits trial attorneys to use peremptory challenges to exclude jurors who are not obviously biased. In response, critics argue that scientific jury selection tips the scales of justice in favor of wealthy clients who can afford the service, an outcome that further widens the socioeconomic gap that exists within the courts. Hence, Neil and Dorit Kressel (2002), authors of *Stack and Sway: The New Science of Jury Consulting,* argue that peremptory challenges, which enable lawyers and their consultants to strike jurors who are not overtly biased, should be abolished.

Juries in Black and White: Does Race Matter?   To what extent does a juror's race color his or her decision making in court? Research suggests that there is no simple answer. In one study, Norbert Kerr and others (1995) tested the most intuitive hypothesis of all, that jurors favor defendants who are similar to themselves. They presented mixed-race groups with a strong or weak case involving a black or white defendant. They found that when the evidence was weak, the participants were more lenient in their verdicts toward the defendant of the same race. Yet when the evidence was strong, they were harsher against that similar defendant, as if distancing themselves from his or her wrongdoing.

In a second study, Sommers and Ellsworth (2001) tested the popular notion that jurors will show preference for others of their racial group when a crime involves race, as when it is a motivated hate crime or when attorneys "play the race card" in arguments to the jury. Yet they found the opposite pattern. When race was not an issue that is "on the radar," white jurors predictably treated the defendant more favorably when he was white than when he was black. Yet when race was made a prominent issue at trial, white jurors bent over backward *not* to appear prejudiced and did not discriminate. Other research has shown that jurors may at times be motivated to watch for racist tendencies in themselves, leading them to process trial information even more carefully when a defendant is black than when he or she is white (Sargent & Bradfield, 2004). Even jurors with measurable racist tendencies exhibit less bias in the verdicts when race is brought out into the open (Cohn et al., 2009).

The potential for individual jurors to exhibit racial bias may also depend on the composition of the jury with whom they expect to deliberate. In a courthouse located in Ann Arbor, Michigan, Sommers (2006) showed a *Court TV* summary of a sexual assault trial in which the defendant was African American. A total of 200 locals participated in 29 six-person mock juries after a voir dire that either did or did not make race an issue. Ultimately, the juries that were formed were either all white or heterogeneous, consisting of four whites and two blacks. After the videotaped trial summary but before the groups deliberated, each juror was asked to indicate his or her verdict preference. Look at ● Figure 12.6, and you'll see that jurors were influenced

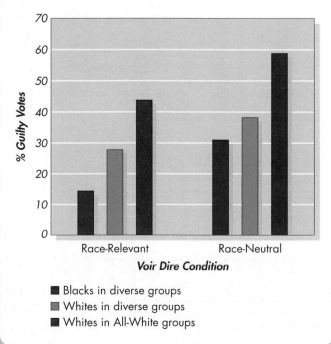

● **FIGURE 12.6**

Effects of Racial Diversity on the Jury

Six-person mock juries watched the trial of an African American defendant in groups that were homogeneous (all white) or diverse (four white, two black). In some cases, the issue of race was raised during the voir dire; in others, it was not. Either way, the white jurors in homogeneous groups were more likely to vote guilty than white jurors in diverse groups who, in turn, were more likely to vote guilty than black jurors in diverse groups. It seems that individual jurors are influenced in their decisions by the racial composition of their groups.
Sommers, 2006.

■ Blacks in diverse groups
■ Whites in diverse groups
■ Whites in All-White groups

by the racial composition of their groups as a whole. In diverse groups, 34% of white jurors voted guilty compared to 23% of black jurors—a small difference. In the all-white groups, however, 51% of jurors voted guilty, which represented a significant jump compared to both blacks and whites in the more diverse groups.

Death Qualification   On September 21, 2011, 43-year-old Troy Davis was executed by lethal injection for the 1989 murder of off-duty police officer Mark MacPhail in Savannah, Georgia. Davis had been convicted at trial on the basis of several eyewitnesses and informants who said they heard him confess. Over the years, however, many witnesses recanted their testimony, saying they were pressured to give it. New evidence seemed to implicate someone else. The courts were unconvinced. Whatever the truth may have been, the Davis execution was highly controversial, drawing protest and criticism from around the world. In his final dying words, Davis maintained his innocence: "Well, first of all I'd like to address the MacPhail family. I'd like to let you all know, despite the situation—I know all of you are still convinced that I'm the person that killed your father, your son and your brother, but I am innocent."

Over the years, the death penalty has stimulated a heated public debate throughout America (Bedau & Cassell, 2004)—and in the U.S. Supreme Court (Mandery, 2013). Think about it: If you had to sentence someone to die, could you do it? Not everyone answers this question in the same way. Yet your answer could mean the difference between life and death for a defendant convicted of murder.

AP Images/Hyosub Shin/AJC

On September 21, 2011, Troy Davis was executed for the 1989 murder of a Georgia police officer. Davis had been convicted on the basis of eyewitnesses and informants who said they heard him confess. New evidence later cast doubt on his guilt, leading supporters of Davis and opponents of the death penalty to protest his execution. In the United States, the death penalty is both permissible and a recurring source of controversy.

Today, a majority of American states permit capital punishment. Among those that do, the jury tends to decide not only the verdict but the sentence as well. The use of juries in this way may be the more "cautious" way to proceed. In a recent analysis of capital case in Delaware, which recently shifted from the use of juries to judges, a comparison suggested that juries are more reluctant than judges are to vote for death (Hans et al., 2015).

In these cases, it is not surprising that sentencing decisions are influenced not only by the facts of a specific case but also by jurors' general attitudes toward the death penalty. Kevin O'Neil and his colleagues (2004) found that these attitudes are composed of various beliefs, such as beliefs in the legitimacy of retribution and revenge ("There are some murderers whose death would give me a sense of personal satisfaction"), deterrence ("The death penalty makes criminals think twice before committing murder"), and cost ("Executing a murderer is less expensive than keeping him in jail for the rest of his life"). Monica Miller and David Hayward (2008) found that people who favor the death penalty are more likely to hold fundamentalist religious views and a belief in the literal interpretation of the Bible. Brooke Butler and Gary Moran (2007) found that people who favor the death penalty also tend to harbor authoritarian beliefs and the belief that the world is a just place in which people get what they deserve and deserve what they get.

In cases involving crimes punishable by death and in which the jury makes both decisions, a special jury-selection practice known as **death qualification** is typically used. Through death qualification, judges may exclude all prospective jurors who say that they would refuse to vote for the death penalty. These jurors are excluded for the entire trial. To ensure that *sentencing* decisions are unbiased, it makes sense to exclude those who admit they are close-minded. But does this same selection practice tip the balance toward the prosecution when it comes to the *verdict*? In other words, are death-qualified juries prone to convict?

In a series of studies, Phoebe Ellsworth, Craig Haney, and others have examined this question. Their results have shown that compared to people who oppose the death penalty, those who support it are more prosecution-minded on a host of issues. For example, they are more concerned about crime, more trustful of police, more cynical about defense lawyers, and less tolerant of procedures that are designed to protect the accused (Fitzgerald & Ellsworth, 1984; Haney et al., 1994). When it comes to trial verdicts, the difference can be substantial. In one study, 288 people watched a videotaped murder trial and then participated in mock juries. The results showed that jurors who said they were willing to impose the death penalty were more likely to vote guilty both before and after deliberating than were those who would have been excluded for their refusal to impose a death sentence (Cowan et al., 1984).

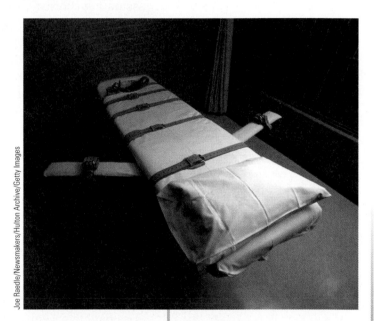

Similar results have been found in studies of real jurors (Moran & Comfort, 1986). In fact, Haney (1984) found that hearing death-qualification voir dire questions themselves is biasing because these questions presume the defendant's guilt and communicate to prospective jurors that the courts consider death a desirable form of punishment. In his studies, even randomly selected mock jurors were more likely to vote for conviction—and for the death penalty—when exposed to such questions during the voir dire than when they were not.

As the research evidence mounted, American courts had to face a sobering prospect. Were hundreds of prisoners on death row tried by juries that were biased against them? In the case of *Lockhart v. McCree* (1986), the U.S. Supreme Court considered the issue. To help to inform the Court, the American Psychological Association submitted an exhaustive review of the literature (Bersoff & Ogden, 1987)—but to no avail. In an opinion that disappointed many social psychologists, the Court rejected the research and ruled that death qualification does not violate a defendant's right to a fair trial.

Should the Supreme Court have been persuaded by the research findings of social psychologists? Some say yes (Ellsworth, 1991); others say no (Elliott, 1991). Either way, it is important to devise alternative, nonprejudicial methods that can be used to select capital juries. For example, research shows that many people who would be excluded because of a *general* opposition to capital punishment also admit that they would consider the death penalty for *specific* defendants found guilty of committing atrocious acts of violence—suggesting that perhaps these individuals should not be removed from the jury (Cox & Tanford, 1989). This issue continues to spark interest and concern among social psychologists (Costanzo, 1997). It is especially relevant now, in light of sobering revelations brought about by DNA tests showing that many prisoners, including many on death row, did not commit the crimes for which they were convicted (Baumgartner et al., 2008).

Joe Raedle/Newsmakers/Hulton Archive/Getty Images

Worldwide, the most common methods of execution are by hanging, shooting, and beheading. In the United States, the most commonly used methods are electrocution, poisonous gas, and lethal injection—as administered in this death chamber in Huntsville, Texas. For more information on the death penalty, such as up-to-date lists of death-row inmates, visit http://www.deathpenaltyinfo.org/home.

death qualification A jury-selection procedure used in capital cases that permits judges to exclude prospective jurors who say they would not vote for the death penalty.

The Courtroom Trial

Once a jury is selected, the trial officially begins and the evidence previously gathered comes to life. The evidence produced in the courtroom can range far and wide, from eyewitness testimony, informants, alibis, and confessions to DNA and other types of physical "CSI" evidence, medical tests, handwriting samples, diaries, fingerprints, photographs, and business documents. The trial is a well-orchestrated event. Lawyers for both sides make opening statements. Witnesses then answer questions under oath. Lawyers make closing arguments. The judge instructs the jury. Yet there are many problems in this all-too-human enterprise: The evidence may not be accurate or reliable, jurors may harbor misconceptions or bias from extraneous factors, judges' instructions may fall on deaf ears, and the process of deliberation may cause some jurors to vote for a verdict that contradicts their beliefs. The social psychology of jury decision making is involved and fascinating (Bornstein & Greene, 2011; Lieberman & Krauss, 2009; Vidmar & Hans, 2007). In this section, we identify some of the problems and possible solutions.

Over the years, psychologists and other social scientists have sought to evaluate the competence of trial juries to reach accurate verdicts. In *The American Jury,* Henry Kalven and Hans Zeisel (1966) surveyed 550 judges who had presided over 3,576 criminal jury trials nationwide. While each jury was deliberating, judges were asked to indicate what their verdict would be. A comparison of their responses to the actual jury verdicts revealed that judges and juries agreed on a verdict in 78% of all cases (in a separate study of civil cases, typically involving disputes over money, a 78% agreement rate was also observed). Among the 22% of cases in which there was a disagreement, it was because the jury voted to acquit a defendant that judges perceived to be guilty. This last result suggests that juries are more lenient than judges.

Are juries competent, objective, and accurate in their verdicts? There is no simple way to answer this question. As a general rule, research has shown that juries are sound decision makers, even in cases containing complex evidence, and that jury verdicts are based largely on the strength of the evidence presented at trial (Diamond & Rose, 2005; Eisenberg et al., 2005; Hans et al., 2011). Still, as we saw earlier, juries tend to accept eyewitness identifications and confessions—often without sufficient scrutiny or concern about the situations and ways in which these types of evidence were taken. To help inform juries in these cases, psychologists sometimes testify as expert witnesses (Cutler & Kovera, 2011).

Nonevidentiary Influences   A trial is a well-orchestrated event that follows strict rules of evidence and procedure. The goal is to ensure that juries base their verdicts solely on the evidence and testimony presented in court—not on rumors, newspaper stories, a defendant's physical appearance, and other information. The question is: "To what extent is this goal achieved, and to what extent are jury verdicts tainted by nonevidentiary influences?" Before Amanda Knox was tried for murder in Perugia, Italy, in 2007, newspapers and social media—not only in Italy, but in the United States, Great Britain, and elsewhere in the world—were saturated with stories about Knox, her past, her Italian boyfriend, her alleged confession, and witnesses who claimed to have seen her near the crime scene. By the time Knox went to trial, her jury had already been exposed to a good deal of information that was not in evidence.

Many high-profile cases find their way into newspapers and other mass media long before they appear in court. In these instances, the legal system struggles with this dilemma: Does exposure to pretrial news stories

"Ask the judge whether we can find the defendant not guilty and still execute him."

After the Boston Marathon bombing in 2013, defendant Dzhokhar Tsarnaev sought to move his trial out of the city on the ground that local news media coverage made it impossible for him to get a fair trial there. A federal appeals court denied this request, however, and ruled that a jury drawn from the Boston area, even though knowledgeable about the case, could still be fair and impartial. On April 8, 2015, Tsarnaev was found guilty on all counts. Two months later, he was sentenced to death. This case illustrates a common concern about the effects of pretrial publicity on juries.

corrupt the pool of prospective jurors? Public opinion surveys consistently show that the more people know about a case, the more likely they are to presume the defendant guilty, even when they claim to be impartial (Kovera, 2002; Moran & Cutler, 1991). There is nothing mysterious about this result. The information in news reports usually comes from the police or district attorney's office, so it often reveals facts unfavorable to the defense. The question is whether these reports have an impact on juries that go on to hear evidence in court and deliberate to a verdict.

To examine the effects of pretrial publicity, Geoffrey Kramer and his colleagues (1990) played a videotaped re-enactment of an armed robbery trial to hundreds of people participating in 108 mock juries. Before watching the tape, participants were exposed to news clippings about the case. Some read news material that was neutral. Others read information that was incriminating—for example, revealing that the defendant had a prior record or implicating the defendant in a hit-and-run accident in which a child was killed. Even though participants were instructed to base their decisions solely on the evidence, pretrial publicity had a marked effect. Among those exposed to neutral material, 33% voted guilty after deliberating in a jury. Among those exposed to the prejudicial material, that figure increased to 48%. What's worse, neither judges nor defense lawyers could identify in a simulated voir dire which jurors had been biased by the publicity. As shown in ● Figure 12.7, 48% of jurors who were questioned and perceived to be impartial—those who said they were unaffected—went on to vote guilty (Kerr et al., 1991).

In light of our constant access to news over the Internet, the problem of juries' exposure to pretrial publicity has never been more pressing. More recent studies

● **FIGURE 12.7**

Contaminating Effects of Pretrial Publicity

In this study, participants were exposed to prejudicial or neutral news reports about a defendant, watched a videotaped trial, and voted before and after participating in a mock jury deliberation. As shown, pretrial publicity increased the conviction rate both before and after deliberation, even among participants perceived to be impartial by judges and lawyers. From Kerr, M. I., Kramer, G. P., Carroll, J. S., and Alfini, J. J., "On the effectiveness of voir dire in criminal cases with prejudicial pretrial publicity: An empirical study," *American University Law Review* vol 40 (pp. 665–701). Copyright © 1991 American University Law Review. Reprinted with permission.

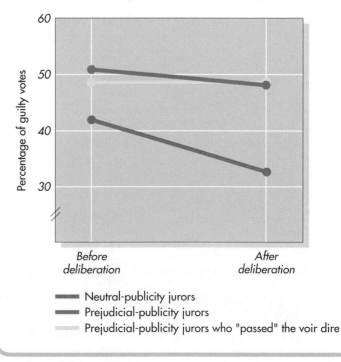

━━━ Neutral-publicity jurors
━━━ Prejudicial-publicity jurors
━━━ Prejudicial-publicity jurors who "passed" the voir dire

have served only to reinforce the conclusion that this problem can have consequences at trial. In one study, Tarika Daftary-Kapur and her colleagues (2014) recruited mock jurors in New York City during and before a prominent murder trial that was in the local news. The trial involved three police officers who had shot an unarmed African American man by the name of Sean Bell. As the trial progressed, these participants were sent periodic trial updates from the courtroom and answered questions as if they were on the jury. Based on their natural exposure to local newspapers articles, which they divulged over the course of their several weeks of participation, and the contents of those articles, analyses showed that the more natural exposure participants had to pro-prosecution news stories versus pro-defense stories, the more likely they were to see the defendants guilty—from the start of the trial to the finish, regardless of the judge's instruction they were given to disregard outside information. Tracking the same case, the same results were replicated in a controlled mock jury experiment conducted in Boston.

Pretrial publicity is potentially dangerous in two respects. First, it often divulges information that is not later allowed into the trial record. Second is the matter of timing. Because many news stories precede the actual trial, jurors learn certain facts even before they enter the courtroom. From what is known about the power of first impressions, the implications are clear. If jurors receive prejudicial news information about a defendant before trial, that information will distort the way they interpret the facts of the case (Hope et al., 2004). In fact, an analysis of secretly recorded mock jury deliberations showed that exposure to pretrial publicity was openly discussed and completely tainted their discussions of the defendant and evidence—despite the judge's warning to disregard that information (Ruva & LeVasseur, 2012; Ruva & Guenther, 2015). So, is there a solution? Since the biasing effects persist despite the practices of jury selection, the presentation of hard evidence, cautionary words from the judge, and open jury deliberations, justice may demand that highly publicized cases be postponed or their trials moved to less-informed communities (Steblay et al., 1999; Studebaker & Penrod, 1997).

Is it possible that juries are influenced by pretrial publicity of a more general nature that is unrelated to their specific case? Perhaps you have watched the popular television drama *CSI* (which stands for "crime scene investigation"), which focuses on the process by which police investigators collect and analyze fingerprints, bodily fluids, and other types of forensic evidence (the original is set in Las Vegas; spin-offs were later set in Miami and New York). Many legal commentators are speculating that the public's exposure to this show is tilting jury verdicts; they call it the "CSI effect." The fear is that the television programs lead jurors to have unrealistically high expectations that cause them to vote cautiously for acquittal because they find the actual evidence insufficient to support a guilty verdict.

If it is a real phenomenon, then the CSI effect would represent a special type of pretrial publicity potentially influencing an entire population of juries. Tom Tyler (2006a) is quick to note, however, that although the hypothesis is plausible, there is at present no hard evidence to support it. Just as jurors are biased by news stories, they occasionally receive extralegal information within the body of the trial itself. If a witness discloses hearsay that is not considered reliable, or blurts out something about the defendant's past that the courts consider prejudicial—in either case, information the jury is not supposed to hear—then what? What happens next, typically, is that the opposing lawyer will object, and the judge will sustain the objection and instruct the jury to disregard the disclosure.

If something seems wrong with this series of events, you should know that it is a script often replayed in the courtroom. But can people really strike information from their minds the way court reporters can strike it from the record? Can people on a jury resist the forbidden fruit of inadmissible testimony? Although common sense suggests they cannot, the research is mixed. In one study, a group of mock jurors read about a murder case based on evidence so weak that not a single juror voted guilty. A second group read the same case, except that the prosecution introduced an illegally obtained tape recording of a phone call made by the defendant: "I finally got the money to pay you off. . . . When you read the papers tomorrow, you'll know what I mean." The defense argued that the illegal tape should not be admissible, but the judge disagreed. At this point, the conviction rate increased to 26%. In a third group, as in the second, the tape was brought in and the defense objected. Yet this time, the judge sustained the objection and told jurors to disregard the tape. The result: 35% voted for conviction (Sue et al., 1973). Other studies as well have revealed that jurors are often not deterred by "limiting instructions" (Steblay et al., 2006).

Why do people not follow a judge's order to disregard inadmissible evidence? There are several possible explanations (Lieberman & Arndt, 2000). Imagine yourself in the jury box, and three reasons will become apparent. First, the added instruction draws attention to the information in controversy. It's like being told not to think about white bears. As we saw in Chapter 3, trying to suppress a specific thought increases its tendency to intrude upon our consciousness (Wegner, 1994). A second reason is that a judge's instruction to disregard, much like censorship, restricts a juror's decision-making freedom. As a result, it can backfire by arousing reactance. So, when a judge emphasizes the ruling by *forbidding* jurors from using the information ("You have no choice but to disregard it"), they become even *more* likely to use it (Wolf & Montgomery, 1977). The third reason is the easiest to understand. Jurors want to reach the right decision. If they stumble onto relevant information, they want to use that information whether it satisfies the law's technical rules or not.

To test this third hypothesis, Kassin and Sommers (1997) had mock jurors read a transcript of a double murder trial that was based on weak evidence, leading only 24% to vote guilty. Three other groups read the same case except that the state's evidence included a wiretapped phone conversation in which the defendant confessed to a friend. In all cases, the defense lawyer objected to the disclosure. When the judge ruled to admit the tape into evidence, the conviction rate increased considerably, to 79%. But when the judge excluded the tape and instructed jurors to disregard it, their reaction depended on the reason the tape was excluded. When told to disregard the tape because it was barely audible and could not be trusted, participants mentally erased the information, as they should, and delivered the same 24% conviction rate as in the no-tape control group. But when told to disregard the item because it had been illegally obtained, 55% voted guilty. Despite the judge's warning, these latter participants were unwilling to ignore testimony they saw as highly relevant merely because of a legal technicality.

The Judge's Instructions   One of the most important rituals in any trial is the judge's instructions to the jury. It is through these instructions that juries are educated about relevant legal concepts, informed of the verdict options, admonished to disregard extralegal factors, and advised on how to conduct their deliberations. To make verdicts adhere to the law, juries are supposed to comply with these instructions. The task seems simple enough, but there are problems.

To begin with, the jury's intellectual competence has been called into question. For years, the courts have doubted whether jurors understood their instructions. One skeptical judge put it bluntly when he said that "these words may as well be spoken in a foreign language" (Frank, 1949, p. 181). He may have been right. When actual instructions are tested with community mock jurors, the results reveal high levels of misunderstanding—a serious problem in light of the fact that jurors seem to have many preconceptions about crimes and the requirements of the law. There is, however, reason for hope. Research has shown that when conventional instructions—which are poorly structured, esoteric, and filled with complex legal terms—are rewritten in plain English, comprehension rates increase markedly (Elwork et al., 1982). Supplementing a judge's instructions with flowcharts, computer animations, and other audiovisual aids is also effective (Brewer et al., 2004).

A lack of comprehension is one reason that a judge's instruction may have little impact. But there's a second reason: Sometimes juries disagree with the law, thus raising the controversial issue of **jury nullification**. Because juries deliberate in private, they can choose to disregard, or "nullify," the judge's instructions. The pages of history are filled with poignant examples. Consider the case of someone tried for euthanasia, or "mercy killing." By law, it is murder. But to the defendant, it might be a noble act on behalf of a loved one. Faced with this kind of conflict—an explosive moral issue on which public opinion is sharply divided—juries often evaluate the issue in human terms, use personal notions of commonsense justice, and vote despite the law for acquittal (Finkel, 1995; Niedermeier et al., 1999). This nullification tendency is particularly likely to occur when jurors who disagree with the law are told of their right to nullify it (Meissner et al., 2003). In these instances, research suggests the possibility that a nullification instruction may unleash a form of "chaos," liberating jurors to follow their emotions in an emotionally charged case (Horowitz et al., 2006).

Jury nullification is what happened in cases pertaining to physician-assisted suicide, as was practiced by the late Jack Kevorkian, a pathologist. During the 1990s, Kevorkian presided over 130 deaths. For three of these incidents, he was tried for murder, and the juries, sympathetic to his plight, practiced nullification and acquitted him. Then he injected a terminally ill man with a lethal dose of drugs, videotaped the death, gave the tape to CBS News, and again challenged authorities to take him to court. They did, and in 1999, after having defied the law in the boldest of ways, Kevorkian was found guilty. He was Prisoner #284797 in a Michigan state prison until he was released on parole in June 2007. He died four years later at the age of 83.

In this Detroit courtroom, Dr. Jack Kevorkian was tried for an assisted suicide. Although physician-assisted suicide is illegal in Michigan, the jury in this case "nullified" the law in favor of its own conceptions of justice and voted not guilty. However, Kevorkian was eventually convicted and sent to prison. He died at the age of 83, four years after he was released.

Brian Bohannon–Booth News Service/Corbis

jury nullification The jury's power to disregard, or "nullify," the law when it conflicts with personal conceptions of justice.

■ Jury Deliberation

Anyone who has seen the original 1957 movie *Twelve Angry Men* can appreciate how colorful and passionate a jury's deliberation can be. This film classic opens with a jury eager to convict a young man of murder—no ifs, ands, or buts. The group selects a foreperson and takes a show-of-hands vote. The result is an 11-to-1 majority, with actor Henry Fonda the lone dissenter. After many tense moments, Fonda manages to convert his peers, and the jury votes unanimously for acquittal.

It is often said that the unique power of the jury stems from the wisdom that emerges when individuals come together privately as one *group*. Is this assumption justified? *Twelve Angry Men* is a work of fiction, but does it realistically portray what transpires in the jury room? And in what ways does the legal system influence the group dynamics? By interviewing jurors after trials and by recruiting people to participate on mock juries and then recording their deliberations, researchers have learned a great deal about how juries make their decisions.

Leadership in the Jury Room

In theory, all jurors are created equal. In practice, however, dominance hierarchies tend to develop. As in other decision-making groups, a handful of individuals lead the discussion while others join in at a lower rate or watch from the sidelines, speaking only to cast their votes (Hastie et al., 1983). It's almost as if there is a jury within the jury. The question is, what kinds of people emerge as leaders?

It is often assumed that the foreperson is the leader. The foreperson, after all, calls for votes, acts as a liaison between the judge and jury, and announces the verdict in court. It seems like a position of importance, yet the selection process is very quick and casual. It's interesting that foreperson selection outcomes do follow a predictable pattern (Stasser et al., 1982). People of higher occupational status or with prior experience on a jury are frequently chosen. Interestingly too, the first person who speaks is often chosen to be the foreperson (Strodtbeck et al., 1957). And when jurors deliberate around a rectangular table, those who sit at the heads of the table are more likely to be chosen than are those seated in the middle (Bray et al., 1978; Strodtbeck & Hook, 1961).

If you find such inequalities bothersome, fear not: Forepersons may act as nominal leaders, but they do not exert more than their fair share of influence over the group. In fact, although they spend more time than other jurors talking about procedural matters, they spend less time expressing opinions about the verdict (Hastie et al., 1983). Thus, it may be most accurate to think of the foreperson not as the jury's leader but as its moderator. In *Twelve Angry Men*, actor Martin Balsam—not Henry Fonda—was the foreperson. He was also among the least influential members of the jury.

The Dynamics of Deliberation

If the walls of the jury room could talk, they would tell us that the decision-making process typically passes through three stages (Hastie et al., 1983; Stasser et al., 1982). Like other problem-solving groups, juries begin in a relaxed *orientation* period during which they set an agenda, talk in open-ended terms, raise questions, and explore the facts. Then, once differences of opinion are revealed (usually after the first vote is taken), factions develop and the group shifts

In the classic movie *Twelve Angry Men*, Henry Fonda plays a lone juror who single-handedly converts his 11 guilty-voting peers to vote for acquittal. Sometimes life imitates art; in this case, it does not. Research shows that majorities on the first jury vote usually prevail in the final verdict.

Everett Collection

● FIGURE 12.8

Jury Deliberations: The Process

Juries move through various tasks en route to a verdict. They begin by setting and reviewing the case. If all jurors agree, they return a verdict. If not, they continue to discuss the case until they reach a consensus. If the holdouts refuse to vote with the majority, the jury becomes deadlocked. Cengage Learning®

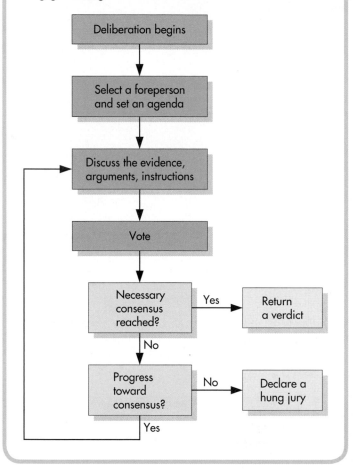

abruptly into a period of *open conflict*. With the battle lines sharply drawn, discussion takes on a more focused, argumentative tone. Together, jurors scrutinize the evidence, construct stories to account for that evidence, and discuss the judge's instructions (Pennington & Hastie, 1992). If all jurors agree, they return a verdict. If not, the majority tries to achieve a consensus by converting the holdouts through information and social pressure. If unanimity is achieved, the group enters a period of *reconciliation*, during which it smoothes over the conflicts and affirms its satisfaction with the outcome. If the holdouts continue to disagree, the jury declares itself hung. This process is diagrammed in ● Figure 12.8.

When it comes to decision-making *outcomes*, deliberations follow a predictable course first discovered by Kalven and Zeisel (1966). By interviewing the members of 225 juries, they were able to reconstruct how these juries split on their very first vote. Out of 215 juries that opened with an initial majority, 209 reached a final verdict consistent with that first vote. This finding—which was later bolstered by the results of mock jury studies (Kerr, 1981; Stasser & Davis, 1981; see Table 12.5)—led Kalven and Zeisel (1966) to conclude that "the deliberation process might well be likened to what the developer does for an exposed film; it brings out the picture, but the outcome is predetermined" (p. 489). Setting aside Henry Fonda's *Twelve Angry Men* heroics, one can usually predict the final verdict by knowing where the individual jurors stand the first time they vote. Juries are not generally more or less subject to bias than the individuals who constitute the groups (Kerr et al., 1999). Hence, "majority rules" seems to describe what happens not only in juries but in most other small decision-making groups (Hastie & Kameda, 2005).

There is one exception to this majority-wins rule in the jury room. In criminal trials, deliberation tends to produce a **leniency bias** that favors the defendant. All other factors being equal, individual jurors are more likely to vote guilty on their own than they are in a group; they are also more prone to convict before deliberations than they are afterward (Kerr & MacCoun, 2012; MacCoun & Kerr, 1988). Look again at Table 12.5, and you'll see that juries that are equally divided in their initial vote are ultimately likely to return not-guilty verdicts. Perhaps it is easier for individual jurors to raise a "reasonable doubt" in other people's mind than it is to erase all doubt. In this regard, it is interesting to note that in their classic study, as described earlier, Kalven and Zeisel found that juries are more lenient than their judges would have been. Perhaps this disagreement is due, in part, to the fact that juries decide as groups and judges decide as individuals.

Knowing that the majority tends to prevail doesn't tell us how juries manage to resolve disagreements en route to a verdict. From the conformity studies discussed in Chapter 7, we know that there are two possibilities. Sometimes people conform because through a process of *informational influence* they are genuinely persuaded by what others say. At other times, people yield to the pressures of *normative influence* by changing their overt behavior in the majority's direction

leniency bias The tendency for jury deliberation to produce a tilt toward acquittal.

even though they disagree in private. Justice demands that juries reach a consensus through a vigorous exchange of views and information, not as the result of heavy-handed social pressure. But is that how it works? Research shows that juries achieve unanimity not by one process or the other but by a combination of both (Kaplan & Schersching, 1981). Research also shows that certain factors can upset the delicate balance between informational and normative influences. Social pressure is increased, for example, in juries that vote by a public roll call or show of hands (Davis et al., 1989) and in deadlocked juries that are called back into the courtroom and urged by the judge to resolve their differences (Smith & Kassin, 1993).

Several years ago, the U.S. Supreme Court addressed questions pertaining to the decision-making dynamics of the jury in two ways. In the following pages, we look at these important issues and what they mean.

Jury Size: How Small Is Too Small?

How many people does it take to form a jury? In keeping with British tradition, twelve has been the magic number. Then, in the case of *Williams v. Florida* (1970), the defendant was convicted of armed robbery by a six-person jury. He appealed the verdict to the U.S. Supreme Court but lost. As a result of this precedent, American courts are now permitted to cut trial costs by using six-person juries in cases that do not involve the death penalty. Juries consisting of fewer than six are not permitted (*Ballew v. Georgia,* 1978).

What is the impact of moving from twelve to six? The Supreme Court approached this question as a social psychologist would. It sought to determine whether the change would affect the decision-making process. Unfortunately, the Court misinterpreted the available research so badly that Michael Saks (1974) concluded that it "would not win a passing grade in a high school psychology class" (p. 18). Consider whether a reduction in size affects the ability of those in the voting minority to resist normative pressures. The Supreme Court did not think it would. Citing Asch's (1956) conformity studies, the Court argued that an individual juror's resistance depends on the *proportional* size of the majority. But is that true? Is the lone dissenter caught in a 5-to-1 bind as well insulated from the group norm as the minority in a 10-to-2 split? The Court argued that these 83%-to-17% divisions are psychologically identical. But wait. Asch's research showed exactly the opposite—that the mere presence of a single ally enables dissenters to keep their independence better than anything else.

Research has shown that the size of a jury has other effects too. Michael Saks and Molli Marti (1997) conducted a meta-analysis of studies involving 15,000 mock jurors who deliberated in over 2,000 6-person or 12-person juries. Overall, they found that the smaller juries were less likely to represent minority segments of the population. They were also more likely to reach a unanimous verdict and to do so while deliberating for shorter periods of time. Even in civil trials, in which juries have to make complex decisions on how much money to award the plaintiff, six-person groups spend less time discussing the case (Davis et al., 1997).

Less-Than-Unanimous Verdicts

The jury's size is not all that has changed. In 1972, the Supreme Court considered whether states may accept jury verdicts that are

---

▲ TABLE 12.5

The Road to Agreement: From Individual Votes to a Group Verdict

Research has shown how verdicts are reached by mock juries that begin with different combinations of initial votes. You can see that the results support the majority-wins rule. But also note the evidence for a leniency bias: When the initial vote is split, juries gravitate toward acquittal (Kerr, 1981, as cited in Stasser et al., 1982).

Initial Votes (Guilty–Not Guilty)	Final Jury Verdicts (%)		
	Conviction	Acquittal	Hung
6–0	100	0	0
5–1	78	7	16
4–2	44	26	30
3–3	9	51	40
2–4	4	79	17
1–5	0	93	7
0–6	0	100	0

© Cengage Learning®

One can usually predict a jury's final verdict by knowing where the individual jurors stand the first time they vote. ▲ **TRUE**

▲ **TABLE 12.6**

Johnson v. Louisiana (1972): Contrasting Views

"Notice the contrasting views in the U.S. Supreme Court's decision to permit jury verdicts that are not unanimous. Justice White wrote the majority opinion and Justice Douglas wrote the dissent. The decision was reached by a vote of 5 to 4."

Mr. Justice White, for the Majority

"We have no grounds for believing that majority jurors, aware of their responsibility and power over the liberty of the defendant, would simply refuse to listen to arguments presented to them in favor of acquittal, terminate discussion, and render a verdict. On the contrary, it is far more likely that a juror presenting reasoned argument in favor of acquittal could either have his arguments answered or would carry enough other jurors with him to prevent conviction. A majority will cease discussion and outvote a minority only after reasoned discussion has ceased to have persuasive effect or to serve any other purpose—when a minority, that is, continues to insist upon acquittal without having persuasive reasons in support of its position."

Mr. Justice Douglas, for the Minority

"Non-unanimous juries need not debate and deliberate as fully as most unanimous juries. As soon as the requisite majority is attained, further consideration is not required either by Oregon or by Louisiana even though the dissident jurors might, if given the chance, be able to convince the majority. . . . The collective effort to piece together the puzzle of historical truth . . . is cut short as soon as the requisite majority is reached in Oregon and Louisiana. . . . It is said that there is no evidence that majority jurors will refuse to listen to dissenters whose votes are unneeded for conviction. Yet human experience teaches us that polite and academic conversation is no substitute for the earnest and robust argument necessary to reach unanimity."

© Cengage Learning®

not unanimous. In one opinion, two defendants had been convicted by jury verdicts that were not unanimous—one by a vote of 11 to 1, the other by 10 to 2 (*Apodaca v. Oregon*, 1972). In a second opinion, a guilty verdict was determined by a 9-to-3 margin (*Johnson v. Louisiana*, 1972). In both decisions, the Supreme Court upheld the convictions.

The Court was divided in its view of these cases. Five justices argued that a rule allowing verdicts that are not unanimous would not adversely affect the jury; four justices believed that it would reduce the intensity of deliberations and undermine the potential for minority influence. Table 12.6 presents these dueling points of view. Which do you find more convincing? Imagine yourself on a jury that needs only a 9-to-3 majority to return a verdict. You begin by polling the group and find that you already have the 9 votes needed. What next? According to one script, the group continues to argue vigorously and with open minds. According to the alternative scenario, the group begins to deliberate, but the dissenters are quickly cast aside because their votes are not needed. Again, which scenario seems more realistic?

To answer that question, Reid Hastie and others (1983) recruited more than 800 people from the Boston area to take part in 69 mock juries. After watching a reenactment of a murder trial, the groups were instructed to reach a verdict by a 12-to-0, a 10-to-2, or an 8-to-4 margin. The differences were striking. Compared with juries that needed unanimous decisions, the others spent less time discussing the case and more time voting. After reaching the required number of votes, they often rejected the holdouts, terminated discussion, and returned a verdict. Afterward, participants in the non-unanimous juries rated their peers as more close-minded and themselves as less informed and less confident about the verdict. What's worse, Hastie's team saw in tapes of the deliberations that majority-rule juries often adopted "a more forceful, bullying, persuasive style" (1983, p. 112). After being permitted to videotape 50 non-unanimous civil juries in Arizona, Shari Diamond and colleagues (2006) similarly observed that thoughtful minorities were sometimes "marginalized" by majorities that had the power to ignore them.

Today, only two states permit less-than-unanimous verdicts in criminal trials. A substantially higher number do so for civil cases. Research has shown that this procedure weakens jurors who are in the voting minority, breeds close-mindedness, short-circuits the discussion, and leaves many jurors uncertain about the decision. Yet in April of 2014, faced with an appeal of a non-unanimous verdict in Louisiana, the US. Supreme Court declined to revisit the question. *Henry Fonda, step aside. The jury has reached its verdict.*

Posttrial Sentencing and Prison

In Italy, Amanda Knox and Raffaele Sollecito were sentenced to 26 and 25 years, respectively, in prison after they were convicted of the murder for which they were ultimately found innocent. In contrast, Rudy Guede—the perpetrator who fled Italy and whose fingerprints, shoe prints, and DNA littered the crime scene, leading him to plead guilty—was sentenced to 30 years, but that sentence was reduced to 16 years after he implicated Knox and apologized for his role in the crime. As this case illustrates, sentencing decisions are human judgments of great consequence. The question is: "What influences these judgments?"

■ The Sentencing Process

Defendants who are found not guilty are free to go home. For those convicted of crimes, however, the jury's verdict is followed by a second decision to determine the nature and extent of their punishment. Sentencing decisions are usually made by judges, not juries, and they are often controversial. One reason for the controversy is that many people see judges as being too lenient (Stalans & Diamond, 1990). Another is that people disagree on the goals served by imprisonment. For many judges, the goal of a prison sentence is practical: to incapacitate offenders and deter them from committing future crimes. For many citizens, however, there is a more powerful motive at work: to exact retribution, or revenge, against the offender for his or her misdeeds. Research shows that people are driven by this "just deserts" motive, recommending sentences of increasing harshness for crimes of increasing severity, regardless of whether the offender is seen as likely to strike again and regardless of whether such sentences deter crime or serve other useful purposes (Carlsmith et al., 2002; Carlsmith, 2006; Darley et al., 2000; Darley & Pittman, 2003). Interestingly, research also shows that although people think that "sweet revenge" against someone who exploited them will make them feel better, sometimes it has the opposite effect (Carlsmith et al., 2008).

Judges also disagree about issues related to sentencing. Thus, a recurring public complaint is that there is too much **sentencing disparity**—that punishments for crime are inconsistent from one judge to the next. To document the problem, Anthony Partridge and William Eldridge (1974) compiled identical sets of files from 20 actual cases and sent them to 50 federal judges for sentencing recommendations. They found major disparities in the sentences the judges said they would impose. In one case, for example, judges had read about a man who was convicted of extortion and tax evasion. One judge recommended a three-year prison sentence, while another recommended 20 years in prison and a fine of $65,000. It's hard to believe these two judges read the same case. But other studies have uncovered similar differences.

Some judges are unusually creative in their sentencing of convicted felons. For example, a judge in Houston ordered a piano teacher who molested two students to donate his piano to a local school, a South Dakota judge sentenced cattle rustlers to shovel manure for a week, and a Florida judge ordered drunk drivers to display a bumper sticker on their cars that said "Convicted DUI" (Greene et al., 2007). In recent years, the federal government and many state governments have created sentencing guidelines to minimize the disparities and bring greater consistency into the process (Ruback & Wroblewski, 2001).

Still, sentencing decisions can be influenced by irrelevant factors. For example, Birte Englich and others (2006) theorized that judges would be influenced

sentencing disparity Inconsistency of sentences for the same offense from one judge to another.

by the well-known "anchoring effect"—the tendency to use one stimulus as an "anchor," or reference point, in judging a second stimulus. In a series of studies conducted in Germany, these researchers presented legal professionals—mostly judges—with materials about a criminal case. All participants received the same file except that some files suggested a low sentencing number (one year) and others suggested a high number (three years). Regardless of whether the number was presented as a prosecutor's recommendation, a question from a journalist, or a random roll of the dice, those first exposed to the high anchor point assigned harsher sentences than those exposed to the lower anchor point.

Some influences on this all-too-human decision-making process are even more disturbing. By combing through U.S. death penalty statistics, researchers long ago discovered that sentencing decisions are consistently biased by race: All else being equal, convicted murderers are more likely to be sentenced to death if they are black or if the victim is white (Baldus et al., 1990). Informed by the racial stereotyping studies we saw in Chapter 5, Jennifer Eberhardt and her colleagues (2006) revisited a number of capital cases involving black defendants, this time looking for an even more subtle effect. For each case, they obtained a photograph of the defendant and had college students rate the degree to which he had a stereotypically black appearance—for example, a broad nose, thick lips, and dark skin. Using these ratings, they found that when the victim was black, the defendant's appearance was unrelated to sentencing. When the victim was white, however, the death penalty odds were predictable by the blackness of the defendant's appearance (24% among the least stereotypical; 58% among the most stereotypical). It seems that there are shades of black that influence whether judges and juries see defendants to be "deathworthy."

Taking the problem one step further, Rebecca Hetey and Eberhardt (2014) wondered if people's perceptions of the racial makeup of a prison system had an effect on their belief in the need for reform. In a study conducted in California, white registered voters waiting at a train station were shown a brief video on an iPad about the state prison system. Some participants were shown a sample of mug shots in which very few of the inmates depicted were black; others saw a sample in which nearly half of were black. Afterward, participants were told about a state sentencing law that was highly and often unjustly punitive and then were asked to sign a petition to reform that law. As predicted, the decision to sign the petition was biased by perceptions of the racial makeup of the prison population: While 52% signed the petition in the less-black condition, only 27% agreed to do so in the more-black condition. These researchers concluded: "Just as the Blackness of a specific defendant can increase people's desire to punish, so too could the Blackness of the penal institution increase people's acceptance of punitive policies" (p. 1950).

■ The Prison Experience

It is no secret that the prison population in the United States has grown over the years, that many prisons are overcrowded, and that the situation has worsened as a result of recently toughened sentencing guidelines. It is also no secret that prison life can be cruel, violent, and degrading. The setting is highly oppressive and regimented, many prison guards are abusive, and many inmates fall into a state of despair (Paulus, 1988). Indeed, many are psychologically disturbed and in need of treatment they do not receive (Kupers, 1999). Clearly, prisoners are not representative of the population as a whole. Still it is natural for social psychologists to wonder: Is there something about the prison *situation* that leads guards and prisoners to behave as they do? Would the rest of us react in the same way?

For ethical reasons, one obviously cannot place research participants inside a real prison. So, many years ago, a team of researchers from Stanford University did the next best thing: They constructed a simulated prison in the basement of the psychology department building (Haney et al., 1973; Haney & Zimbardo, 1998; Zimbardo et al., 1973). Complete with iron-barred cells, a solitary-confinement closet, and a recreation area for guards, the facility housed 21 participants—all healthy and stable men between the ages of 17 and 30 who had answered a newspaper ad promising $15 a day for a two-week study of prison life. By the flip of a coin, half the participants were designated as guards and the other half became prisoners. Neither group was told specifically how to fulfill its role.

On the first day, each of the participant prisoners was unexpectedly "arrested" at his home, booked, fingerprinted, and driven to the simulated prison by officers of the local police department. These prisoners were then stripped, searched, and dressed in loose-fitting smocks with an identification number, a nylon stocking to cover their hair, and rubber sandals. A chain was bolted to the ankle of each prisoner. The guards were dressed in khaki uniforms and supplied with night-sticks, handcuffs, reflector sunglasses, keys, and whistles. The rules specified that prisoners were to be called by number, routinely lined up to be counted, fed three bland meals, and permitted three supervised toilet visits per day. The stage was set. It remained to be seen just how seriously the participants would take their roles and react to one another in this novel setting.

The events of the next few days were startling. Filled with a sense of power and authority, a few guards became progressively more abusive. They harassed the inmates, forced them into crowded cells, woke them during the night, and subjected them to hard labor and solitary confinement. These guards were particularly cruel when they thought they were alone with a prisoner. The prisoners themselves were rebellious at first, but their efforts were met with retaliation. Soon they all became passive and demoralized. After 36 hours, the experimenters had to release their first prisoner, who was suffering from acute depression. On subsequent days, other prisoners had to be released. By the sixth day, those who remained were so shaken by the experience that the study was terminated. It is reassuring, if not remarkable, that after a series of debriefing sessions, participants seemed to show no signs of lasting distress.

This study was instantly criticized on both methodological and ethical grounds (Banuazizi & Movahedi, 1975; Savin, 1973). Still, the results are fascinating. Within a brief period of time, under relatively mild conditions, and with a group of men not prone to violence, the Stanford study recreated some of the prisoner and guard behaviors actually found behind prison walls. But would this occur today, in the twenty-first century? To find out, social psychologists Steve Reicher and Alex Haslam (2006) worked in 2002 with the British Broadcasting Corporation (BBC) to create a survivorlike reality TV special called *The Experiment*, modeled after Zimbardo's study. Shown in four episodes, the television special brought together 15 men, all of whom were carefully screened, were warned that they would be exposed to hardships, and were randomly assigned to prisoner and guard roles. Determined to set limits, monitor events closely, and adhere to ethical guidelines for research with human subjects, Haslam and Reicher did not fully recreate the conditions of the original study and did not observe the same kinds of brutality from the guards. In their view, these findings challenge the conclusion that normal people can be dehumanized by the mere assignment to institutional roles. They also note that while the Stanford prison study demonstrated oppression and

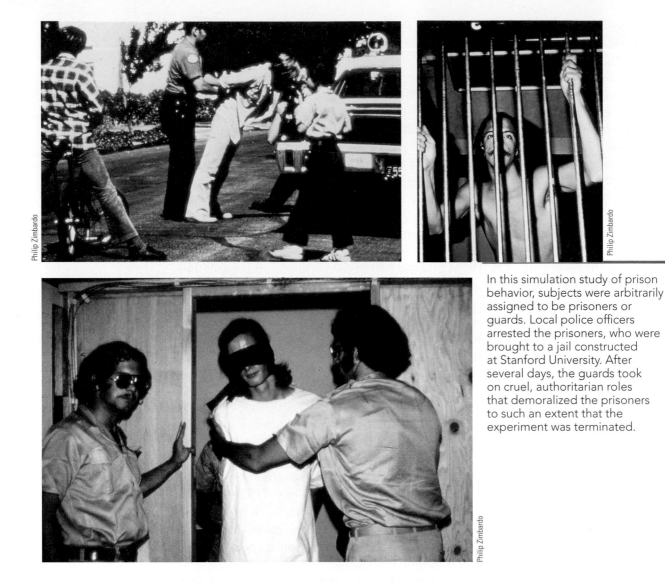

Philip Zimbardo

In this simulation study of prison behavior, subjects were arbitrarily assigned to be prisoners or guards. Local police officers arrested the prisoners, who were brought to a jail constructed at Stanford University. After several days, the guards took on cruel, authoritarian roles that demoralized the prisoners to such an extent that the experiment was terminated.

abuse of power, it also provided a glimpse into how members of low-status groups can form a shared identity—which provides a basis for the social psychology of resistance (Haslam & Reicher, 2012).

One other profound question has arisen concerning the Stanford prison study, the same question that is often raised about Milgram's obedience experiments: Did the behavior of guards reflect on the power of the situation they were in or were the men who took part in the study uniquely prone to violence? Seeking an answer to this question, Thomas Carnahan and Sam McFarland (2007) posted two newspaper ads—one, like Zimbardo's, for a study on prison life; the other, identical in every way except that it omitted the words "prison life." Those who volunteered for the prison study scored higher on tests that measure aggressiveness, authoritarianism, and narcissism and lower on tests that measure empathy and altruism. Reflecting on the differences, these researchers suggested that perhaps the Stanford prison study had attracted individuals who were prone to antisocial behavior. In response, Haney and Zimbardo (2009) note that volunteers in the original study were also tested and that no personality differences were found between them and the general population. More important, they note, no differences were found between those assigned to prisoner and guard roles within the experiment.

Reiterating his belief in the power of the situation, Zimbardo (2007) points to the striking parallels between the behaviors observed in his simulated prison and the sadistic abuses of real prisoners in 2004, more than 30 years later, by military guards at the Abu Ghraib Prison in Iraq. Noting that various social psychological factors create a "perfect storm" that leads good people to behave in evil ways, Zimbardo refers to this unfortunate transformation as the "Lucifer Effect," named after God's favorite angel, Lucifer, who fell from grace and ultimately became Satan.

Perceptions of Justice

People tend to measure the success of a legal system by its ability to produce fair and accurate results. But is that all there is to justice? Let's step back for a moment from the specifics and ask if it is possible to define justice in a way that is unrelated to outcomes.

Justice as a Matter of Procedure

In a book entitled *Procedural Justice* (1975), John Thibaut and Laurens Walker proposed that our satisfaction with the way legal and other disputes are resolved depends not only on outcomes but also on the procedures used to achieve those outcomes. Two aspects of procedure are important in this regard: One is *decision control*—whether a procedure affords the involved parties the power to accept, reject, or otherwise influence the final decision. The other is *process control*—whether it offers the parties an opportunity to present their case to a third-party decision maker. In the courtroom, of course, the disputants are limited in their decision control. Thus, their satisfaction must depend on whether they feel that they had a chance to express their views.

There are two ways to look at the effects of process control on perceptions of justice. Originally, it was thought that people want an opportunity to express their opinions only because having a voice in the process improves the odds of achieving a favorable ruling. In this view, process control is satisfying only because it increases decision control (Thibaut & Walker, 1978). However, research suggests that people value the chance to present their side of a story to an impartial decision maker even when they do not prevail in the ultimate outcome. In other words, process control is more than just an instrumental means to an end. When people believe that they have a voice in the proceedings, are treated with respect, and are judged by an impartial decision maker, process control can be an end in itself (Lind et al., 1990).

This aspect of the legal system is important because it makes the system appear fair and legitimate and helps to foster cooperation—which is why many social psychologists study people's perceptions of justice (Tornblom & Vermunt, 2007; Tyler, 2011). It means, for example, that regardless of whether people agree or disagree with how a case turns out, they can find solace in the fact that both sides had their "day in court," at least when the decision maker is seen as impartial. Yet certain members of the legal community are openly critical of that so-called day in court. As law professor Alan Dershowitz once put it, "Nobody really wants justice. Winning is the only thing to most participants in the criminal justice system, just as it is to professional athletes" (1982, p. xvi).

Dershowitz's skepticism is centered on something many of us take for granted: the **adversarial model** of justice. In the adversarial system (practiced in North America, Great Britain, and a handful of other countries), the prosecution and defense oppose each other, each presenting one side of the story in order to win a favorable verdict. In contrast, other countries use an **inquisitorial model**, in which a neutral investigator gathers the evidence from both sides and presents the findings in court. With two such different methods of doing justice, social psychologists could not resist the temptation to make comparisons (van Koppen & Penrod, 2003).

Interested in which approach people prefer, Laurens Walker and others (1974) constructed a business simulation in which two companies competed for a cash prize. Participants who were assigned to the role of president of a company learned that someone on their staff was accused of spying on the competition. To resolve the dispute, a "trial" was held. In some cases, the trial followed an adversarial procedure in which the two sides were presented by law students who were chosen by participants and whose payment was contingent on winning. Other cases followed an inquisitorial model in which a single law student who was appointed by the experimenter and paid regardless of the outcome presented both sides. Regardless of whether they had won or lost the verdict, participants who took part in an adversarial trial were more satisfied than those involved in an inquisitorial trial. Even impartial observers preferred the adversarial proceedings.

Other researchers found similar results, not only in the United States and Great Britain, where citizens are accustomed to the adversarial system, but in France and Germany as well (Lind et al., 1978). This perception of procedural justice is not limited to adversarial methods of resolving legal disputes. Rather, it seems that any method that offers participants a *voice* in the proceedings, including methods that are nonadversarial, is seen as most fair and just—not only in law, but also in business, politics, school settings, and intimate relationships. It is also important in this regard for people to perceive that they were granted as much "voice" as others were (Van Prooijen et al., 2006) and that the decision maker was open-minded, not acting purely out of self-interest (De Cremer, 2004). In matters of justice, people all over the world are motivated not only by the desire for personal gain but by a need to be recognized, respected, and treated fairly by others who are impartial. Research thus shows that for people to accept the rule of law and comply with outcomes they do not like, they must see the decision-making procedures as fair (Mazerolle et al., 2014; Tyler, 2006b).

■ Culture, Law, and Justice

When it comes to the basics of human behavior, much of the research in this chapter can be universally applied. In eyewitness testimony, the problems and limitations of human memory—as seen in our ability to accurately encode, store, and retrieve certain types of information—are universal. In police interviews and interrogations, suspects all over the world, including some who are innocent, are more likely to confess when they are isolated and intensely pressured than when they are not. In courtrooms wherever juries are used, their decision making will invariably reflect the joint influences of their personal dispositions, the information they receive in court, and the conformity dynamics that seize hold of small groups. Finally, recurring stories of prison abuses have shown that prison is a social setting that tends to bring out the worst in guards and their prisoners—wherever they are.

Although the similarities are clear, they should not mask important cross-cultural differences. Because cultures have different norms, customs, and values, they also

adversarial model A dispute-resolution system in which the prosecution and defense present opposing sides of the story.

inquisitorial model A dispute-resolution system in which a neutral investigator gathers evidence from both sides and presents the findings in court.

create different laws to regulate their citizens' behavior. To be sure, certain universal values have evolved among humans and are passed from one generation to the next, such as prohibitions against physical violence, taking someone's property without consent, and deception in important transactions. In other ways, however, the world's cultural and religious groups differ markedly in the behaviors they scorn and seek to regulate. In some countries but not in others, it is against the law to have sex outside of marriage, take more than one husband or wife, assist in a suicide, gamble, eat meat, or drink alcohol. Based on the belief in an afterlife, some religions prohibit autopsies. Others impose strict dress codes, particularly for women.

In diverse populations such as the United States, these cultural practices can put governments and cultures into conflict with one another. In one highly publicized case, a Japanese woman living in California was prosecuted for drowning her two children in the Pacific Ocean before being rescued while she was trying to drown herself. At trial, she testified that she had tried to commit *oyaku-shinju*, a Japanese custom of parent–child suicide, after learning that her husband was having an affair. Her motive, she said, was to save her children from the shame that their father had brought to the family. In a second case, a Navajo defendant was prosecuted for using the hallucinogen peyote, an illegal substance in the United States. He argued that the substance is used to achieve spiritual exaltation and should be protected by the freedom of religion. (Immigrants from Yemen, Kenya, and Somalia have similarly been arrested for chewing khat leaves in social gatherings, the way Americans chew tobacco, even though the effect is comparable to drinking three espressos.) In a third case, two Cambodian immigrants were prosecuted for trying to eat a 4-month-old puppy, an acceptable practice in their homeland but not in the United States. As these examples illustrate, judges and juries are sometimes asked to consider *cultural defenses* in their decision making (Renteln, 2004).

Just as nations differ in the crime laws that are set, the study of *comparative law* shows that they also differ in the processes used to enforce these laws. Importantly, for example, nations differ in their use of juries (Kaplan & Martin, 2006). In Great Britain, the United States, Canada, and Australia, the accused has a right to be tried by a jury composed of fellow citizens. In France, Russia, and Brazil, that right is reserved for only the most serious crimes. In India and throughout Asia, all defendants are tried by professional judges, not juries. Yet China recently introduced mixed panels consisting of one judge and two lay jurors. Beginning in 2009, Japan also started to use a quasijury system, called *saiban-in*, in which three law-trained judges and six lay citizens chosen by lottery come together to render verdicts and sentencing decisions by a majority vote. Ever since juries were abolished in Japan during World War II, all Japanese defendants have been tried by three-judge panels; almost all have been convicted, typically after confessing to save face and minimize embarrassment to the family.

For people judged guilty of serious crimes, the consequences may also vary from one country to another. As noted earlier, "doing justice" often means punishing those who violate rules as a means of seeking retribution. But whether people are offended enough to seek revenge depends in part on the power of individualist and collectivist norms within the culture. For example, research shows that American college students are offended more when their personal rights are violated—for example, when a co-worker steals the credit for their idea, while Korean students are offended more when their sense of duty and obligation is violated—for example, when a co-worker fails to contribute his or her promised share in a cooperative effort (Shteynberg et al., 2009).

When it comes to punishment, the most notable cultural difference concerns the death penalty. When Iraq's former president Saddam Hussein was executed by hanging in December of 2006, many world leaders, including many of Hussein's enemies, took the opportunity to condemn the execution and, more generally, capital punishment. According to Amnesty International (2012), there are strong differences of opinion and practice across the world regarding the death penalty. Currently, 97 countries prohibit the death penalty for all crimes (Australia, Austria, Belgium, Canada, Colombia, Denmark, England, France, Germany, Greece, Ireland, Italy, Mexico, the Netherlands, Norway, Portugal, Spain, Sweden, Switzerland, Turkey, and Venezuela are prominent examples); 8 ban the death penalty in general but permit it for exceptional crimes, such as espionage, or crimes committed in exceptional circumstances (Brazil, Chile, Israel, and Peru are some examples); 36 countries allow for the death penalty in law but do not execute people as a matter of practice (Algeria, Kenya, Morocco, and Russia are some examples); and 57 countries permit and use the death penalty (in addition to the United States, the others include China, Cuba, Egypt, Iran, Iraq, India, Japan, Pakistan, Saudi Arabia, and Thailand). On matters of crime and punishment, it is clear that cultural influences are substantial.

Closing Statement

This chapter focuses on criminal justice, from the gathering of evidence from witnesses and suspects to the various stages of a jury trial, sentencing, and prison. Yet we've only scratched the surface. In recent years, more and more judges, lawyers, and policy makers have come to recognize that social psychology can make important contributions to the legal system. Thus, social psychologists are called on with increasing frequency for expert advice in and out of court and are cited in the opinions written by judges. Clearly, the collection, presentation, and evaluation of evidence are imperfect human enterprises and subject to bias. Through an understanding of social psychology, however, we can now identify the problems—and even some solutions.

Review

Top 10 Key Points in Chapter 12

1. For what it illustrates about flaws in human evidence and in the trial process, the conviction and ultimate acquittal of Amanda Knox in Italy illustrate some of the ways in which social psychology is relevant to the legal system.

2. Eyewitness errors—a common contributor to wrongful convictions—are caused by limitations in perception and memory that arise when people are stressed, distracted, misled by extraneous information, and try to recognize members of a race other than their own.

3. Through research, social psychologists have found ways to minimize eyewitness error in lineups—for example, by making sure that the suspect does not stand out, that witnesses be told that the actual offender may not be in the lineup, and that police who administer the lineup are "blind" as to who the suspect is.

4. Although police often identify suspects during an interview designed to determine if the person is lying, research shows that, like everyone else, their judgments of truth and deception are not accurate.

5. Police use various methods of interrogation to get suspects to confess, but many wrongful conviction cases and laboratory research have shown that innocent people can be induced by certain tactics into false confessions to crimes they did not commit.

6. Although jury selection is supposed to ensure that juries be representative and impartial, lawyers can strike a certain number of prospective jurors based on personal theories and stereotypes—or advice from hired consultants who conduct "scientific jury selection" research.

7. Juries are conscientious in their decision-making, but research shows that they can be influenced by pretrial publicity, inadmissible testimony, and their own personal conceptions of justice, often in disregard of the judge's instructions.

8. In jury deliberations, members of a voting majority convince others to join in a 12-person unanimous verdict through informational and social influences—though in some states, six person juries or non-unanimous verdicts are permitted.

9. In the Stanford prison study, researchers built a simulated prison and recruited young men to act as guards and prisoners. Illustrating the power of situational roles, they found that some guards were abusive, prisoners became passive, and the study had to be terminated.

10. Our sense of justice is not just about winning and losing but about the fairness of procedures—hence, people of all cultures prefer models of justice that offer them a voice in the proceedings and an impartial decision maker.

Putting Common Sense to the Test

Eyewitness Testimony

Eyewitnesses find it relatively difficult to recognize members of a race other than their own.

(T) **True.** *Researchers have observed this cross-race identification bias in both laboratory and field settings.*

The more confident an eyewitness is about an identification, the more accurate he or she is likely to be.

(F) **False.** *Studies have shown that the confidence of an eyewitness does not reliably predict accuracy, in part because confidence is influenced by post-identification factors.*

Confessions

It is not possible to knowingly fool a lie-detector test.

(F) **False.** *It is possible to beat a lie-detector test by elevating arousal when "innocent" questions are asked but not by trying to suppress arousal in response to "guilty" questions.*

Without being beaten or threatened, innocent people sometimes confess to crimes they did not commit.

(T) **True.** *Innocent suspects sometimes confess, either to escape an unpleasant situation or because they are led to believe they committed a crime they cannot recall.*

Jury Decision Making

Contrary to popular opinion, women are harsher as trial jurors than men are.

(F) **False.** *Demographic factors such as gender do not consistently predict juror verdicts; men may be harsher in some cases, women in others.*

One can usually predict a jury's final verdict by knowing where the individual jurors stand the first time they vote.

(T) **True.** *As a result of both informational and normative group influences, the preference of the initial voting majority usually prevails.*

Key Terms

adversarial model (550)
cross-race identification bias (511)
death qualification (535)
inquisitorial model (550)

jury nullification (540)
leniency bias (542)
misinformation effect (513)
peremptory challenge (530)
polygraph (522)

scientific jury selection (532)
sentencing disparity (545)
voir dire (530)
weapon-focus effect (511)

Business

This chapter examines the social side of business—specifically, the role of social factors in the workplace and their influence on economic decisions. First, we look at social influences on personnel selection and performance appraisals made within organizations. Then, we examine leadership and worker motivation. Finally, we explore economic decision making, the stock market, and other business settings.

13

ullstein bild/Getty Images

Whenever two adults meet for the first time,

the opening line of their conversation is predictable: "So, what do you do?" "Oh, I'm a (social psychologist). And you?" For many people, work is an integral part of their personal identity. Of course, most of us would rather spend next Monday morning lying on a warm and breezy beach, reading a paperback novel, and sipping a tropical fruit drink, but most people spend more time working than playing. In large part, we work to make money. But jobs also provide us with activity, a sense of purpose, and a social community. Imagine that you had just won $10 million in a lottery. Would you continue to work? When Gallup pollsters asked this question in 2013, 68% of Americans said they would continue, either at their current jobs or elsewhere. This is the highest number Gallup has ever recorded since they first asked the question in 1997. Thus, it is important to identify the social influences on this significant human experience.

There is a flip side to the importance of work: *un*employment. The financial crisis that struck in the United States and elsewhere in 2007 caused the worst job market since the Great Depression. Worldwide, an estimated 210 million people were listed as out of work, with the largest increases found in the United States, New Zealand, Spain, and Taiwan. According to the U.S. Bureau of Labor Statistics, the unemployment rate in the United States, which hit a high of 10% in 2009, was down to a bit over 5% by 2015. Sadly, behind these numbers are real people—men and women who had lost jobs and are unable to find new jobs, plunging them into a bad situation, often through no fault of their own. If you have a job, it is an important part of your life; if you don't have a job and want one, that fact too becomes an important part of your life (to learn about the individual experience of unemployment, see Wanberg, 2012).

industrial/organizational (I/O) psychology The study of human behavior in business and other organizational settings.

This chapter considers applications of social psychology to business. First, we'll look at **industrial/organizational (I/O) psychology**, the study of human behavior in the workplace. This subdiscipline of psychology is broad and includes in its ranks both social and nonsocial psychologists who do research, teach in business schools or universities, and work in government and private industry. Whatever the setting, I/O psychology raises important practical questions about job interviews, evaluations, promotions, leadership, motivation, and other aspects of life in the workplace. Next, we'll examine some social influences on economic decision making in the stock market and elsewhere in the business world.

The impact of social psychological factors in the workplace was first recognized many years ago—thanks, oddly enough, to a study of industrial lighting. The year was 1927. Calvin Coolidge was president, baseball legend Babe Ruth hit 60 home runs, Charles Lindbergh flew across the Atlantic for the first time, and the U.S. economy seemed sound, though the stock market would soon crash, triggering the Great Depression. Just outside Chicago, the Hawthorne plant of the Western Electric Company employed 30,000 men and women who manufactured telephones and central office equipment. As in other companies, management wanted to boost productivity. The bottom line was important.

Putting COMMON SENSE to the Test

Circle Your Answer

T F Although flawed, job interviews consistently make for better hiring decisions.

T F A problem with having workers evaluate their own job performance is that self-ratings are overly positive.

T F The most effective type of leader is one who knows how to win support through the use of reward.

T F People who feel overpaid work harder on the job than those who see their pay as appropriate.

T F People losing money on an investment tend to cut their losses rather than hang tough

Courtesy of AT&T Archives

These women were among the assembly plant workers who took part in the classic Hawthorne studies of productivity in the workplace.

At first, managers thought that they could make workers at the plant more productive by altering the illumination levels in the factory. Proceeding logically, they increased the lighting for one group of workers in a special test room, kept the same lighting in a control room, and compared the effects. To their surprise, productivity rates increased in both rooms. At that point, a team of psychologists was brought in to vary other conditions in the factory. Over the next five years, groups of employees from various departments were selected to do their work in a test room where, at different times, they were given more rest periods, coffee breaks, a free mid-morning lunch, shorter work days, shorter weeks, a new location, overtime, financial incentives, dimmer lights, or just a different method of payment. At one point, the researchers even went back and reinstated the original pre-study conditions inside the test room. Yet no matter what changes were made, productivity levels always increased.

The Hawthorne project, described in a classic book entitled *Management and the Worker* (Roethlisberger & Dickson, 1939), has had a great impact on the study of behavior in the workplace. At first, the researchers were puzzled and discouraged. With positive effects observed among all test-room workers (even when the original pretest conditions were in place), it seemed that the project had failed. Ponder the results, however, and you'll see why these studies are so important. With striking consistency, workers became more productive—not because of any of the specific changes made but because they had been singled out for special assignment. Many researchers have criticized the methods used in this study and the ways the results have been interpreted (Adair, 1984; Chiesa & Hobbs, 2008; Parsons, 1974). Still, the phenomenon that has become known as the **Hawthorne effect** laid a foundation for I/O psychology.

The Hawthorne plant no longer exists, but the study that was conducted there helped psychologists understand the profound impact of social influences

Hawthorne effect The finding that workers who were given special attention increased their productivity regardless of what actual changes were made in the work setting.

"And the dim fluorescent lighting is meant to emphasize the general absence of hope."

in the workplace. Interested in the conditions that affect worker satisfaction, motivation, and performance, today's researchers study all aspects of life in the workplace, including the effects of monitoring workers' activity on the computer (Alge, 2001); the benefits of sabbatical (Davidson et al., 2010); how to get the most out of workday breaks during the day (Hunter & Wu, in press); perceptions and realities of sexual harassment (O'Leary-Kelly et al., 2009); the relationship between daylight saving time, sleep, and workplace injuries (Barnes & Wagner, 2009); the perpetrators and targets of bullying in the workplace (Glaso et al., 2009); and the effects of sabotage, revenge, sexist humor, and other forms of insidious behavior in the workplace (Greenberg, 2010).

The three of us who write this textbook all work on college campuses amid students, professors, and administrators. We spend most of our time in classrooms, offices, and research laboratories. For women and men in other occupations—store clerks, factory workers, Uber drivers, carpenters, doctors, web designers, farmers, teachers, accountants, firefighters, and airline pilots—the workplace is very different. Yet despite the diversity of roles and settings, certain common concerns arise: How are applicants selected for jobs? How is performance then evaluated? What makes for an effective leader? What motivates people to work hard and feel satisfied with this aspect of their lives? And what factors influence the kinds of economic decisions that people make? Let's enter the workplace and address these important questions.

These days, people have flexibility to make a living away from the traditional workplace. *Shark Tank* is a reality TV show in which aspiring entrepreneur-contestants seek funds from the above panel of "shark" investors for a new business. If they are interested, sharks will negotiate a deal and invest their own money. In lieu of a traditional job, forming one's own business offers an alternative, though risky, way to make a living.

Another way to make a living is by participating in the new technology-driven "sharing economy" in which people rent, trade, or share their homes, cars, and other assets through peer-to-peer transactions. As seen above, Uber is an American-based company that operates a mobile app that people with smartphones can use when they need a ride. Using the app, you submit a GPS-enabled request for a car that is routed to freelance Uber drivers in the vicinity who use their own vehicles. By 2015, this alternative form of taxi service was available in 58 countries and 300 cities worldwide.

Personnel Selection

For all kinds of organizations, the secret to success in our increasingly competitive world begins with the recruitment and development of a competent work staff. For that reason, personnel selection is the first important step (Guion, 2011; Schmitt, 2012).

■ The Typical Job Interview

If you've ever applied for a job you wanted, you know that sometimes you have to climb hurdles and jump through hoops to land the position. The routine is a familiar one: You submit a résumé or post one online, fill out an application, and, if you're lucky, perhaps bring in samples of your work or take a standardized test that measures various abilities, personality traits, or honesty. You may even be placed on the "hot seat" in a face-to-face interview. In a typical interview, an agent of the company and an applicant meet in person, providing a two-way opportunity for the applicant and employer to evaluate each other. What a social perception dilemma this opportunity presents! As an applicant, you have only a half hour or so to make a favorable impression. As an interviewer, you have the same brief period of time to penetrate the applicant's self-presentation while presenting the company in a favorable light.

Very few employers would consider hiring a complete stranger for a responsible position without an interview. Would *you*? Like most of us, you probably trust your own ability to size people up. But should you? Do interviews promote sound hiring, or do they produce decisions that are biased by job-irrelevant personal characteristics? Civil rights laws explicitly forbid employers to discriminate on the basis of sex, race, age, religion, national origin, or disability. Does the interview process itself intensify or diminish these possible sources of bias? And are interviews valid and predictive of performance?

Focusing on the possibility of race and ethnic background biases in an interview setting, some researchers have reported good news. By statistically combining the results of 31 studies involving more than 11,000 job applicants, Allen Huffcutt and Philip Roth (1998) found that black and Hispanic applicants receive interview ratings only slightly lower on average than those obtained by their white counterparts. Perhaps the face-to-face interactions provided by interviews humanize applicants, bringing to life their interest in the job, their social skills, and other relevant attributes that do not show up on paper. This relative lack of bias also seems to characterize subjective evaluations of job performance—where supervisor (and peer) ratings of black, white, and Hispanic workers are more similar to one another, not less so, than "objective" measures of performance (Roth et al., 2003).

Although most employers have learned to guard against discriminatory hiring practices, there is one possible source of bias that is difficult to regulate: physical appearance. Except for certain types of work (such as modeling), beauty is not relevant to job performance. Yet people in general tend to favor others who are attractive. Does this bias operate in hiring situations? To answer this question, Cynthia Marlowe and others (1996) presented a set of job application folders—including résumés and photographs—to 112 male and female managers of a financial institution. Believing they were evaluating prospective employees, each

Today, many job seekers and companies meet online through websites like LinkedIn.

Chris Ratcliffe/Bloomberg/Getty Images

manager rank-ordered four equivalent and qualified applicants: two men and two women, one of each of whom was highly attractive. The result: Physical appearance had a large impact, with 62% of managers selecting an attractive applicant as their top choice. Other research has confirmed that human resource professionals show a preference for applicants who are attractive. In fact, an applicant may be adversely affected merely by a scar or stain on the face—which steals attention, distracts the interviewer, and results in less positive outcomes (Madera & Hebl, 2012).

Another potential source of bias concerns the extent to which an interviewer shares similarities with the interviewee. After interviewing 120 hiring managers, Lauren Rivera (2012) concluded that cultural similarity plays a role in the hiring process—similarities in outside interests, experiences, and self-presentation styles. As one consultant put it, "You want someone that makes you feel comfortable, that you enjoy hanging out with" (p. 1007). In a laboratory test of this effect, Jøri Gytre Horverak and her colleagues (2012) presented managers in Norway with a hiring candidate who was either native to their country or an immigrant who was depicted as completely adapted, interested in exploring, or uninterested in the native culture. Reflecting the fact that all candidates' qualifications were identical, the managers rated them all as equally fit for the job. Yet the immigrant who was not interested in the manager's culture was rated as the least hirable.

Although interviews often result in the right selection of new employees, they sometimes lack predictive validity (Eder & Harris, 1999). Part of the problem is that most job applicants use impression management tactics to present themselves in a positive light, as you'd expect, and that some engage in more self-promotion than others—often with positive results (Barrick et al., 2010). Some college seniors who enter the job market are also more confident in their interviewing skills than others, and confidence predicts success months later (Tay et al., 2006). Even the quality of an applicant's handshake (as determined by its strength, firmness of grip, duration, and whether it is accompanied by eye contact) predicts how highly he or she will be rated by an interviewer after an hour-long mock interview (Stewart et al., 2008).

"Faking" in an employment interview—which occurs whenever a job applicant consciously presents himself or herself in distorted ways in order to create a favorable impression—may well compromise the predictive validity of the process. For that reason, researchers have recently sought to develop a questionnaire that measures faking. In a series of studies, Julia Levashina and Michael Campion (2007) asked hundreds of college seniors who were active on the job market to anonymously rate the degree to which they engaged in various faking behaviors during their most recent interviews. Some of the behaviors involved outright lying ("I claimed that I have skills I do not have"); others involved forms of exaggeration ("I exaggerated my responsibilities on previous jobs"), ingratiation ("I laughed at the interviewer's jokes even when they were not funny"), and image protection ("When asked directly, I did not mention some problems that I had in past jobs"). It will be interesting in future research to see whether applicants' responses on this questionnaire can be used to predict their success or failure—not only during the interview process but also later on the job.

Even if applicants are completely honest in their self-presentations, another potential problem with interviews is that employers often have preconceptions that can distort the process. In a field study that illustrated the problem, Amanda Phillips and Robert Dipboye (1989) surveyed 34 managers from different branch offices of a large corporation and 164 job applicants that these managers had interviewed. They found that the managers' pre-interview expectations—which were based on written application materials—influenced the kinds of interviews they conducted as well as the outcomes: The higher their expectations, the more time they spent "recruiting" rather than "evaluating" and the more likely they were to make a favorable

Although flawed, job interviews consistently make for better hiring decisions.

FALSE

hiring decision. Similarly, Thomas Dougherty and others (1994) found that interviewers with positive rather than negative expectations sounded warmer, more outgoing, and more cheerful. They also gave more information and spent more time promoting the company. It seems that job interviews can become part of a cycle, or self-fulfilling prophecy. Without realizing it, employers use the opportunity to create realities that bolster their preexisting beliefs (see ● Figure 13.1).

Cybervetting People tend to think that when they apply for a job, the information they submit through applications, résumés, transcripts, letters of recommendation, and other work-related credentials will largely determine if they are interviewed and hired. Not so anymore. If you have a Facebook page, a Twitter page, or a Pinterest account, if you've posted pictures of yourself on Instagram or videos on YouTube, or if you've expressed opinions on blogs, you should know that these personal traces of you may well be examined when you apply for a job.

In recent years, a new wrinkle has worked its way into the personnel selection process. In part because employers are wary that applicants present themselves in less-than-fully-honest ways for impression management purposes, and in light of the fact that over 3 billion people now inhabit the Internet, most employers now engage in **cybervetting**—using the Internet to get informal, noninstitutional data about applicants that they did not choose to share (Berkelaar & Buzzanell, 2015). Cybervetting is now a common but controversial selection practice. Despite concerns about whether it is ethical to "spy" on applicants in this way, employers would say that they merely seek *honest signals* about an applicant's ability, character, and "fit" —information that is hard for applicants to fake (Bangerter et al., 2012; Roulin & Bangerter, 2013). To add to concerns about ethics, some companies have been asking applicants for their social networking site passwords so they could access even more private information (Levinson, 2011).

Two questions can be raised about cybervetting: (1) What kinds of information do employers seek and get in their Internet searches of applicants? (2) What effects does this new approach to personnel selection have on who gets hired? In an effort to answer the first question, Brenda Berkelaar and Patrice Buzzanell (2015) interviewed 45 employers from companies in the financial services, education, law, information technology, media, manufacturing, and other industries, about their selection practices. Most employers reported cybervetting good applicants after receiving their résumés. Specifically, more than 90% said they used visual information (avatars, site designs, and "definitely pictures"—so, yes, applicants who had posted "naughty" or lewd pictures were disqualified), 75% used textual information (focusing on content, communication skills, spelling, typos, and grammar), over 50% used technological information (such as the professional look of a Facebook page or time spent playing games on social media sites), and 50% used relational information (number and quality of friends and contacts within the industry). Ironically, half of the employers said that the complete absence of an online presence has caused them to lower their evaluations of an applicant.

What are the effects of cybervetting on the quality of hiring decisions? Does an individual's online persona accurately portray the person to be hired, and are

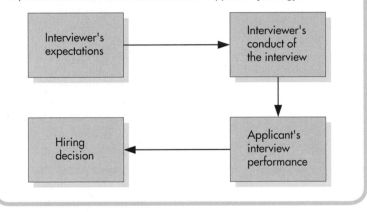

● **FIGURE 13.1**

Job Interviews: A Self-Fulfilling Prophecy?

One study indicates that interviewers' expectations influence the kinds of interviews conducted and applicants' performance. The higher the expectations, the more the interviewer tries to impress rather than evaluate the applicant and make a favorable hiring decision. Without realizing it, employers may use job interviews to create a reality that supports their prior beliefs.

Phillips, A. P., & Dipboye, R. L. (1989). Correlational tests of predictions from a process model of the interview. *Journal of Applied Psychology, 74,* 41–52

cybervetting A controversial new practice by which employers use the internet to get informal, non-institutional data about applicants that they did not choose to share.

the social perceptions of employers predictive of job performance, or subject to bias and error? Despite the prevalence of the practice, there is no research on these ultimate questions. But what about the controversial practice, banned in some U.S. states, of demanding that applicants disclose their social networking passwords? Has this ever happened to you? If it does, how would you respond? In one recent study, Travis Schneider and others (2015) posed this hypothetical situation to 892 Canadian participants by asking them to imagine that they have applied for a highly desirable job but that the hiring manager required passwords. At that point, they were asked what they would do. It's a tough call. How would *you* respond? Overall, 58% of men and women said they would refuse. Importantly, so did 72% of Asians, 79% of gays, and 77% of those without a formal religion. Based on these results, it appears that these groups would be disproportionately harmed by this requirement.

■ "Scientific" Alternatives to Traditional Interviews

Face-to-face interviews bring to life both job-relevant and not-so-relevant personal characteristics. Given that the process is so variable, should interviews be eliminated? Should they, perhaps, be computerized, leaving applicants to interact with companies through a programmed sequence of questions and answers administered by computer? Online interviews may offer a forum for an initial screening of applicants. Chances are, however, not too many people would feel comfortable making important life decisions in such an impersonal manner. Is it possible, then, to preserve the human touch of an interview while eliminating the bias and error?

Standardized Tests Today, many companies use standardized written tests in the personnel selection process. Three general types of test are used for this purpose.

Tests of intelligence are designed to measure intellectual and cognitive abilities, job-specific knowledge and skills, or "street smarts" and common sense, which all may contribute to success on the job. With regard to measures of general intelligence, the use of cognitive ability tests in the workplace is a matter of some debate. On the basis of extensive research, some psychologists believe that cognitive ability tests are useful because they are predictive of job success in high-stakes work settings (Gottfredson, 2002; Schmidt, 2002)—importantly, without discriminating against minorities and others who lack the resources to pay for test preparation courses (Kuncel & Hezlett, 2010; Sackett et al., 2008).

The predictive benefits of cognitive ability testing in the workplace have been amply demonstrated. Still, some researchers caution that although general intelligence is a relevant factor, it is not fully captured by standardized tests and that other factors should be considered as well in personnel selection. When Kevin Murphy and others (2003) surveyed more than 700 professionals in the field, therefore, they found that most agreed that intelligence is not fully captured by standardized tests, that different jobs require different cognitive abilities, and that both cognitive and noncognitive selection measures should be used.

Recently it was estimated that 2,500 U.S. companies also use *personality testing* to measure traits that predict such work-related outcomes as leadership, productivity, helpfulness, absenteeism, and theft (Cha, 2005). For example, research shows that people who score high rather than low in the trait of conscientiousness—which tends to make them more achievement oriented, dependable, orderly, and cautious—are more likely in general to perform well on the job (Dudley et al., 2006). Another example: People who score as extroverted rather than introverted are especially likely to succeed as business managers and salespersons (Hurtz & Donovan, 2000; Salgado, 1997). Research shows that young adults who have high self-esteem, self-confidence, and a sense of control tend to seek out more challenging lines of work and, as a result, are more satisfied with their jobs later in life (Judge et al., 2000). Research also shows that people who have a certain cluster of traits that include emotional stability, conscientiousness, and agreeableness are more likely to exhibit good organizational citizenship behaviors (Chiaburu et al., 2011).

These research findings are clear. But does that mean that companies should test all job applicants and hire those with favorable personalities? Reflecting this trend, one *U.S. News & World Report* writer explains "why a psychologist might be at your next interview" (Wolgemuth, 2009). But is this a sound development in the practical world of personnel selection? Not according to five editors of the research journals that have published much of this personality research. In an article they collectively wrote, these editors concluded that although certain personality factors may well relate to job performance, researchers would need to devise tests that are more predictive—tests that do not rely on the motivated applicant's self-report and therefore cannot easily be faked (Morgeson et al., 2007).

Third, a number of companies have recently begun to administer **integrity tests**—questionnaires designed specifically to assess an applicant's honesty and character by asking direct questions concerning illicit drug use, shoplifting, petty theft, and other transgressions. The tests are easy to administer, and the responses are scored by computer. Narrative profiles are provided, and arbitrary cutoff scores are often used to determine if an applicant has passed or failed (Camara & Schneider, 1994).

Are integrity tests useful for predicting job performance? A major concern about integrity tests—and personality tests too, for that matter—is that applicants may be able to fake the tests on their own or with the help of coaching. Specifically, the concern is that applicants will use the tests to present themselves in overly positive ways—for example, as highly stable, conscientious, agreeable, or extroverted (Schmitt & Oswald, 2006). But is this the case with integrity tests? Can they be faked?

Let's consider the two different types of integrity tests that are used: (1) *overt tests,* in which the purpose is obvious to the test-taker, and (2) *covert tests,* in which items measure broad personality characteristics that are not clearly related to the workplace. To examine the susceptibility of these tests to faking, George Alliger and others (1996) gave both overt and covert tests to college students. Some were told to just take the tests, others were instructed to "fake good," and still others were coached and given specific strategies for how to beat the tests. ● Figure 13.2 shows how well the students did. On the overt test, the scores increased for those instructed to fake good and then increased again among those who were specifically coached. Yet on the covert personality test, scores were unaffected by these interventions. Other studies, too, reinforce the point: When it comes to faking, the covert tests, quite literally, pass the test (Alliger & Dwight, 2000).

But are such instruments sufficiently valid to be used for personnel selection? This is a source of much debate. Although there is reason for skepticism, controlled experiments suggest that both types of tests do predict various work-related behaviors (Berry et al., 2007). How useful are integrity tests in practice? Deniz Ones and others (1993) conducted a meta-analysis of tests taken by thousands of workers and found that test scores were highly predictive of job performance and of counterproductive behaviors such as theft, absenteeism, lateness, and other disciplinary problems. When Chad Van Iddekinge and others (2012) revisited the issue in a more recent meta-analysis of 104 separate studies, they also found that integrity test scores were predictive of job performance and counterproductive behaviors but to a lesser

integrity tests Questionnaires designed to test a job applicant's honesty and character.

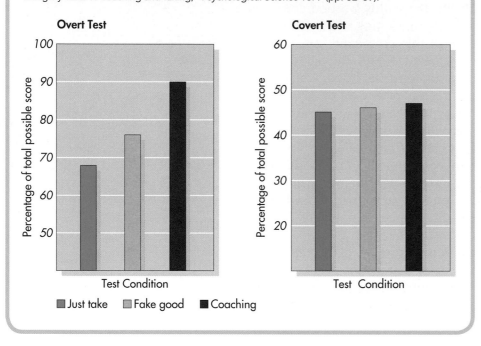

● **FIGURE 13.2**

Can Integrity Tests Be Faked?

Alliger and others (1996) gave college students overt and covert integrity tests. Some just took the test; others were told to "fake good"; others were coached. On the overt test, scores increased for subjects who faked good or were coached (left). On the covert test, scores were unaffected by these interventions (right).

From Alliger, G. M., Lilienfield, S. O., and Mitchell, K. E., "The susceptibility of overt and covert integrity tests to coaching and faking," *Psychological Science* vol 7 (pp. 32–39).

Overt Test

Covert Test

■ Just take   ■ Fake good   ■ Coaching

degree. At this point, it seems clear that integrity tests have value for use in personnel selection; how much value is not yet clear (Sackett & Schmitt, 2012).

Structured Interviews Another way to improve personnel selection decisions is through the use of **structured interviews**. A structured interview is much like a standardized test in that the same information is obtained in the same situation from all applicants, who are then compared on a common, relevant set of dimensions (Campion et al., 1997; Pettersen & Durivage, 2008). By asking exactly the same set of questions or using the same set of tasks, employers can stop themselves from unwittingly conducting biased interviews that merely confirm their pre-existing conceptions.

Studies have shown that structured interviews are more informative than conventional interviews in the selection of insurance agents, sales clerks, and other workers (Wiesner & Cronshaw, 1988). They are also more predictive than paper-and-pencil personality tests (Huffcutt et al., 2001)—perhaps because they are more difficult to fake (Van Iddekinge et al., 2005). In fact, structured interviews can be conducted by phone and later scored from a taped transcript, providing information received that can be used to predict a future worker's attendance rate, productivity, and tenure on the job (Schmidt & Rader, 1999).

Does the structured interview completely eliminate the human element that comes with conventional interviews? It appears that the answer is no. Structured interviews typically are preceded by a meet-and-greet session in which the interviewer and applicant engage in small talk to get acquainted before the serious questioning begins. In light of social psychology research showing that people form first impressions quickly on the basis of appearances and a thin slice of behavior, Murray Barrick and his colleagues (2010) examined whether this "pre-interview" predicts the outcomes that follow. In a mock interview study of college-level accounting students, they found that the impressions interviewers formed in the initial meeting—including their sense of the applicants' competence—were highly predictive of post-interview evaluations and of whether the applicants later received internship offers from actual accounting firms.

To create a more structured, multidimensional setting for selection and evaluation purposes, many organizations use **assessment centers**, in which several applicants take part in a group of activities such as written tests, situational tests, and role-playing exercises that are monitored by a group of evaluators. Instead of one method (an interview) and one evaluator (an interviewer), multiple methods and evaluators are used. Assessment centers are widely assumed to be more effective

structured interview An interview in which each job applicant is asked a standard set of questions and evaluated on the same criteria.

assessment center A structured setting in which job applicants are exhaustively tested and judged by multiple evaluators.

than traditional interviews at identifying applicants who will succeed in a particular position (Thornton & Rupp, 2006). When companies struggle to cut hiring costs, assessments are sometimes streamlined to involve fewer evaluators, fewer exercises, briefer exercises, and other types of shortcuts (Borman et al., 1997). Still, research shows that this multidimensional approach is a good way to make hiring decisions that ultimately are quite predictive of job performance (Arthur et al., 2003; Hoffman et al., 2015; Meriac et al., 2008).

In recent years, the business world has become more increasingly global, more competitive, and more reliant on technology to hire the best talent and to cut costs. Hundreds of multinational corporations—such as Google, Nestle, Toyota, Ericsson, Nike, Apple, Audi, Samsung, Barclays, and Heineken, to name just a few—with facilities in countries outside their home are a case in point. In light of these changes, the classic assessment center must extend its reach. To this end, Alex Howland and his colleagues (2015), looking forward, have proposed the coming of a Virtual Assessment Center (VAC). Driven by emerging technologies, a VAC would rely on LinkedIn and other social networking sites for recruitment; use e-learning classrooms for training and professional development; facilitate company-wide sharing of documents, say for testing purposes, using Dropbox and other Cloud-based services; conduct meetings and assessments via Skype and other videoconference platforms; and use immersive virtual reality, once available, to simulate actual work situations. At present, there is no research on these various aspects of a VAC and whether they will provide a comparable substitute for existing practices. Stay tuned. The work on this front is likely to come at a rapid pace.

More and more companies today are using Skype and other videoconferencing platforms to interview job candidates who are in a remote location.

Personnel Selection as a Two-Way Street For many years, researchers focused on the ways in which different personnel selection procedures serve employers. As we noted earlier, however, the hiring process is a two-way street in which organizations and applicants size each other up. How do job seekers feel about the methods just described? What is *your* reaction to these methods? In general, people see concrete, job-specific tests and interview situations as the most fair, and they dislike impersonal standardized tests of intelligence, personality, and honesty (Rosse et al., 1994; Rynes & Connerly, 1993). For employers on the lookout for strong recruits, the perceived fairness of the selection process that is used may well influence whether top applicants accept the offers that are made (Bauer et al., 1998).

Even the format of an interview can leave a lasting impression. Flawed as it may be, how does the face-to-face interview compare with computer-mediated sessions? These days, as just noted, interviewers and job applicants are often geographically separated, which necessitates either costly travel or use of computer-mediated interviews, phone interviews, and videoconferencing. If you've ever communicated in these ways, you know how different the interaction can be. But how effective are these media? At the campus recruitment center of a large Canadian university, 970 students who submitted résumés to jobs that were posted on the Internet interviewed with 346 organizations. These were actual interviews. Most were held in person, but some were conducted by telephone or videoconferencing. When questioned about the experience afterward, the students in the in-person interviews saw the process as more fair, saw the outcome as more favorable, and were more likely to accept the job if offered (Chapman et al., 2003; also see Sears et al., 2013). Apparently, it may be difficult to replace the connection and caring that are signaled by in-person contact.

■ Affirmative Action

Affirmative action is a policy that gives special consideration to women and members of underrepresented minority groups in recruitment, hiring, admissions, and promotion decisions. This policy is among the most emotional social issues of our time. On one side of the debate is the argument that preferential treatment is necessary both to overcome historical inequities and to bring the benefits of diversity to the workplace. On the other side is the claim that the policy results in unfair reverse discrimination. Surveys show that Americans are divided on the issue: Women are more supportive than men, and African Americans and Hispanic Americans are more supportive than whites (Crosby et al., 2006; Shteynberg et al., 2011). To some extent, the result depends on how the question is posed: When phrasing includes the word "help," 60% of Americans favor affirmative action. When the word "preference" is used instead, support drops to 46% (Kopicki, 2014).

Proponents of affirmative action often accuse opponents of harboring conscious or unconscious prejudice. In contrast, opponents argue that they support a meritocracy, a form of justice in which everyone receives an equal opportunity and then rewards are matched to contributions. In support of this reasoning, Ramona Bobocel and others (1998) studied affirmative action attitudes and found that opposition was associated with a strong belief in the principle of merit, not with measures of racial prejudice. So, would these opponents favor preferential selection procedures to rectify the injustice of a workplace contaminated by discrimination? It appears that many would. When opponents of affirmative action were led to see women and minorities as targets of discrimination in a particular workplace, which itself undermines the principle of merit, they became more favorable toward a system of preferential treatment (Son Hing et al., 2002).

Further complicating the question of deservingness is whether all minorities are seen as full-fledged members of their group and equally entitled. In an article titled "Are You Minority Enough?" Diana Sanchez and George Chavez (2010) describe a study in which they presented research participants with a Latino candidate for a highly selective minority internship. The candidate's résumé was strong and included backgrounds in research and business, computer skills, volunteer experience, and a 3.6 college GPA. For some participants, the candidate's résumé indicated a fluency in Spanish and English; for others, he was fluent only in English (according to the U.S. Census Bureau, 78% of Latino Americans speak Spanish). In their ratings, participants saw the Spanish-speaking candidate as more of a Latino minority than the English-only candidate, as more suitable for affirmative action, and as more deserving of the internship. Interestingly, Latino participants in a second study shared these perceptions. And in a follow-up study, Jessica Good and her colleagues (2013) found that people do not perceive others of black/white biracial descent—because of their white ancestry—as "minorities" worthy of affirmative action.

Amidst political debate, many questions are raised. According to Rupert Nacoste (1996), affirmative action affects those the policy is designed to help, those who feel excluded by it, the organizations that implement it, and the interactions among these three interested groups. In addition, Nacoste argues that people react not to the abstract concept of affirmative action but to the procedures that are used to implement the concept and that these reactions can set off "procedural reverberations" within the system. For example, people will be dissatisfied and the system will reverberate to the extent that policy is set secretly rather than in the open, that interested parties have no opportunity to express their views, and that group membership considerations are seen as more important than the individual contributions of each applicant. Nacoste's notion of procedural interdependence is diagrammed in ● Figure 13.3.

After years of research on attitudes toward affirmative action, it is now clear that although there are sharp differences of opinion, people's reactions depend—and can be changed by—how the policy is implemented. There is no single approach. Faye Crosby and her colleagues (2006) note that policies have ranged from "soft" forms of affirmative action, such as outreach programs designed to identify, recruit, or specially train applicants from underrepresented groups, to "hard" forms of affirmative action that give preference in hiring to applicants from targeted groups who are equally or less qualified than others. Based on a meta-analysis of 126 studies involving 29,000 respondents, David Harrison and others (2006) found that people are most

● **FIGURE 13.3**

Affirmative Action: Effects on Individuals, Groups, and Organizations

Affirmative action affects target group members the policy is designed to help, nontarget group members who feel excluded by it, organizations that implement it, and the interactions among these groups. According to Nacoste, people's reactions to affirmative action procedures can set off procedural reverberations (P) within the system.

From Nacoste, R. W., "Social psychology and the affirmative action debate," *Journal of Social and Clinical Psychology* vol 15 (pp. 261–282). Copyright © 1996 by The Guilford Press. Reprinted with permission.

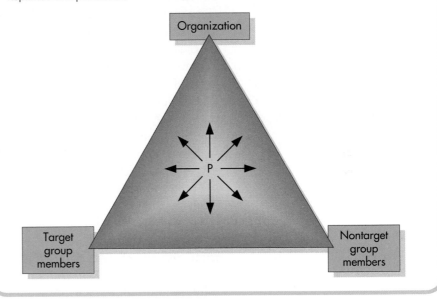

favorable toward softer forms of affirmative action and least favorable toward quotas and other hard policies that favor some applicants over others regardless of their qualifications. By describing different affirmative action programs to business school students, Ariel Levi and Yitzhak Fried (2008) found not only that people prefer a soft affirmative action policy but that they are most supportive of a policy that influenced the hiring and training of new employees and least supportive of a policy that affected promotions and layoffs for existing employees.

As you might expect, many people who do not personally benefit from affirmative action react negatively to the policy and to those who benefit from it (Heilman et al., 1996). What about the *recipients* of affirmative action? Does the policy bolster or psychologically undermine those it is intended to help? In an early series of studies, Madeline Heilman and others (1987) selected male and female college students to serve as leaders of a two-person task. These students were then led to think that they had been chosen for the leadership role either by a preferential selection process that was based on gender or by a merit selection process based solely on qualifications. The result: The women (but not the men) who believed they were chosen because of their gender later devalued their own performance, even after receiving positive feedback.

There are three explanations for why preferential selection policies may have negative effects. First, people perceive a procedure as unjust if it excludes those who are qualified simply because of their nonmembership in a group (Barnes Nacoste, 1994; Heilman et al., 1996). Second, the recipients become less able to attribute success on the job to their own abilities and efforts, leading them and co-workers to harbor doubts about their competence (Heilman et al., 1992; Major et al., 1994). Third, preferential selection is seen as a form of assistance, a situation that can lead recipients to feel stigmatized by what they assume to be the negative perceptions of others (Heilman & Alcott, 2001). As a result of a meta-analysis of research on these issues, Lisa Leslie and her colleagues (2014) have concluded that when individuals are hired in a preferential selection process, an unfortunate chain of events is set into motion: Drawing on existing stereotypes, others assume that these individuals lack competence or social warmth; this stigma leads these individuals to question their own qualifications; and these self-doubts increase the risk of failure.

Are the recipients of affirmative action doomed to feel stigmatized, like second-class citizens? Not necessarily. We saw earlier that the way people tend to react to a preferential selection procedure depends on how it is structured and for what purpose it is implemented. Research shows that people draw negative inferences about themselves and others when employment selections are made *solely* on the basis of sex, skin color, or ethnic background. But would they react more favorably to a preferential selection process if it is clear that merit-based factors also play a role and that the person chosen is competent and qualified for the position?

To find out, Heilman and her colleagues (1998) again brought together male and female participants to take part in a joint two-person task that required a leader and a follower. As in prior experiments, the researchers administered a bogus qualifications test and then assigned each female to the leadership role. Some participants were told that the appointment was based strictly on *merit* (that the person with the higher test score had been selected as the leader). Others were told that the process favored the woman in a way that was *preferential equivalent* (that she was chosen only when her score was similar to that of her male counterpart), *preferential minimum standard* (that she was chosen only if she was minimally qualified), or *preferential absolute* (that she was chosen regardless of merit). The result: Appointed female leaders later rated their own performance and leadership abilities most favorably and saw the process as most fair when their appointment was based on merit, not gender (see ● Figure 13.4). Also important is that they did not devalue their performance or see the selection process as unfair in the preferential equivalent condition, where merit was clearly taken into account. Similarly, neither male co-participants nor observers were troubled by this type of preferential selection process. The key, clearly, is that people need to know that they were selected on the basis of merit (Unzueta et al., 2010). In light of these findings, Table 13.1 offers guidelines for managing affirmative action programs in a way that feels just to all concerned.

■ Culture and Organizational Diversity

For many years, the study of organizational behavior was "culture blind and culture bound" (Gelfand et al., 2007). As a result of two dramatic historical changes, researchers now look at the workplace through a broader lens. The first change has resulted from affirmative action programs, which increase the number of women and minorities who populate most organizations. The second is the worldwide trend toward globalization, which has brought people from disparate cultures into daily contact with each other as co-workers.

Georgia Chao and Henry Moon (2005) note that every individual worker has a multidimensional identity that can be placed within a *cultural mosaic* consisting of the various "tiles" of his or her demographic groups (such as age, gender, race, and ethnic heritage), geographical background (such as country of origin, region,

● **FIGURE 13.4**

Varying Effects of Affirmative Action on Women

College women appointed as task leaders were told that they were selected by merit or by gender. Those in the gender condition were further told that preference was given (1) only if they were *equivalent* to their male partner, (2) only if they met a *minimum standard,* or (3) *absolutely* regardless of merit. These participants later rated their performance and leadership highest and saw the process as most fair when their appointment was based on merit rather than on preference. But the score was not much lower in the equivalent condition where merit was taken into account.

Heilman, M. E., Battle, W. S., Keller, C. E., & Lee, R. A. (1998). Type of affirmative action policy: A determinant of reactions to sex-based preferential selection? *Journal of Applied Psychology*, 83, 190–205.

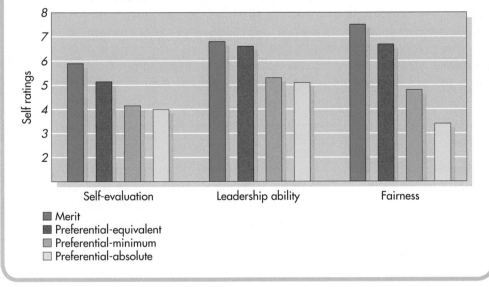

climate, and population density), and personal associations (such as with religion, profession, and political affiliation). In some ways, everyone is similar; in other ways, no two people are alike. For researchers who study organizational behavior, the challenge is to fully represent the complexity that comes with a diverse workplace in order to identify possible problems and solutions (Bond & Haynes, 2014).

As diversity has become a fact of life, researchers have sought to understand what effect this change is having on motivation, morale, and performance in the workplace. A pessimist would predict that diversity would breed division and conflict, making worker teams less effective. In contrast, an optimist would predict that diversity increases the range of perspectives and skills that are brought to bear on a problem, enhancing productivity and creative problem solving by providing a group with a larger pool of resources to draw from.

What is the net impact of diversity on a group's performance? There is evidence for both effects. One meta-analysis suggests the diversity can cause increased conflict and less social integration in a group, but can also lead to greater creativity and overall satisfaction (Stahl et al., 2010). As to the bottom line, some studies suggest that it can literally pay for organizations to have a diverse workforce. In an analysis of over 500 businesses in the United States, Cedric Herring (2009) found that businesses with greater racial and gender diversity earned greater revenue and had higher profits than those with less diversity. These findings are merely correlational, however, and cannot be used to infer cause and effect. So other researchers went on to conduct an experimental test of this hypothesis. They

▲ **TABLE 13.1**

Managing Affirmative Action

Preferential selection practices are often seen as unjust, and they often lead recipients to doubt their own competence. Pratkanis and Turner (1996) recommend that the steps listed here be taken to minimize these negative effects.

1. Set and communicate clear and explicit qualifications criteria (background, knowledge, skills, etc.) to be used in selection decisions.

2. Be certain that selection procedures are perceived as fair by targeted applicants and their co-workers.

3. Provide the target applicant and co-workers with specific feedback about the target's job qualifications.

4. Develop socialization strategies that keep target applicants from making negative self-attributions.

5. Emphasize the target applicant's unique contributions to the organization.

6. Point out that affirmative action does not imply hiring by quotas, since other job-relevant attributes are considered as well.

7. Recognize that affirmative action is not a panacea and that it cannot be expected to solve all the problems faced by the targeted groups.

© Cengage Learning®

randomly assigned students in an entrepreneurship program to work groups of varying gender diversity. Each group's task was to run a fake business in which they had to produce, market, and sell products, sell stocks, and divide tasks and duties. Groups performed best, had the highest number of sales, and most profit, when there were equal numbers of men and women on a team than when the gender breakdown was more one-sided (Hoogendoorn et al., 2013).

At present, there is no single or conclusive answer to the questions that have been raised about diversity effects in business. The effect is likely to depend on the nature of the diversity, whether similarities or differences are accentuated, the proportion of majority to minority members, whether there is a culture of smooth integration within the organization, the type of work to be completed, the group's ability and motivation, and other factors (Mannix & Neale, 2005; van Knippenberg & Schippers, 2007).

A workplace may strive for diversity, but its success may well depend on its philosophy and approach. Reflecting a society-wide debate, many companies struggle with this question: Is it better to acknowledge group differences in the workplace by celebrating multiculturalism, or ignore these differences in an effort to encourage a uniform, color-blind environment? To see if there is a relationship between the beliefs held within a company and how engaged its minority workers feel, Victoria Plaut and others (2009) conducted an online "diversity climate survey" of 5,000 white and minority employees from 18 departments of a large health care organization. By comparing departments, they found that the more multicultural the dominant white employees were in their diversity beliefs (endorsing "employees should recognize and celebrate racial and ethnic differences" rather than "employees should downplay their racial and ethnic differences"), the more engaged their minority workers felt (for example, "I am proud to tell others that I work at this organization").

The real-world correlation is intriguing, but it does not prove that the multicultural beliefs within the organization *caused* minority employees to feel more engaged. To test that hypothesis directly, Valerie Purdie-Vaughns and others

(2008) presented African American corporate professionals with a brochure for a fictitious management consulting firm. For participants assigned to a value-diversity condition, the brochure stated: "While other consulting firms mistakenly try to shape their staff into a single mold, we believe that embracing our diversity enriches our culture." For others in a color-blind condition, the brochure stated: "While other firms mistakenly focus on their staff's diversity, we train our diverse workforce to embrace their similarities." Did the African American participants, experienced in the corporate world, feel comfortable with this company? If the brochure photographs depicted a high level of minority representation, they were fine. If the photos depicted a low level of minority representation, however, their comfort level depended on the company's diversity beliefs. In this case, they trusted the multicultural firm that celebrated diversity and difference more than the color-blind firm that sought to minimize it.

Performance Appraisals

Even after a person is hired, the evaluation process continues. Nobody enjoys being scrutinized by a boss or anyone else, for that matter. Still, **performance appraisal**—the process of evaluating an employee's work and communicating the results to that person—is an inevitable fact of life in the workplace (Murphy & Cleveland, 1995). Performance appraisals provide a basis for placement decisions, transfers, promotions, raises and salary cuts, bonuses, and layoffs. They also give feedback to employees about the quality of their work and their status within the organization. Performance appraisal is also at times the subject of policy debates as well—as in questions recently raised over how teachers should be evaluated and rewarded (Gollan, 2011).

It would be easy if a worker's performance could be measured by purely *objective* and quantifiable criteria—as when researchers are judged by the number of articles they publish, baseball pitchers by their won–loss percentage and earned run average, hedge fund managers by the amount of money they make, car dealers by the number of cars they sell, and college professors by their student enrollments. These kinds of quantitative measures are often not available, however, and they do not take into account the quality of work. By necessity, then, performance appraisals are often based on *subjective* measures such as the perceptions of employees by supervisors, co-workers, and sometimes even the employees themselves.

■ Supervisor Ratings

Based on the assumption that supervisors stay informed about the performance of their subordinates, they are often called on to make evaluations. Such evaluations are important. But are the ratings accurate? And is the process fair? The process has both benefits and drawbacks. On the one hand, research shows that supervisors are influenced more by a worker's on-the-job knowledge, ability, and dependability than by less relevant factors such as friendliness (Borman et al., 1995). On the other hand, as we'll see, evaluators predictably fall prey to the social perception biases described elsewhere in this book.

Over the years, a number of appraisal-related problems have been identified. A good deal of research has identified various types of rating errors. One prominent example is the *halo effect*—a failure to discriminate among different and distinct

performance appraisal The process of evaluating an employee's work within the organization.

aspects of a single worker's performance (Cooper, 1981). In Chapter 4, we saw that people's impressions of one another are guided by implicit personality theories—by the preconceptions they have about the relationships among different traits. Believing that someone is warm, we assume that he or she is also generous and good-natured. In a similar manner, supervisors who believe that a worker is unproductive may also rate that worker negatively on teamwork, independence, creativity, and other distinct dimensions. Halo effects are most pronounced when evaluators rate someone they do not know well or when a time delay has caused their memory of performance to fade (Koslowski et al., 1986; Murphy & Balzer, 1986).

One illustration of the halo effect pertains to the stereotypes people have about workers who start their day early or late. In recent years, inspired in part by the increased numbers of women with children in the workplace, flexible work practices have become more common—including some measure of flexibility in work times relative to the more traditional 9-to-5 day. Flexible work practices increase employee satisfaction and productivity. But do supervisors hold stereotypes about workers who arrive late to the start of the day? Kai Chi Yam and others (2014) questioned 149 pairs of full-time employees and their supervisors from different industries. Within their sample, employees reported starting times that ranged from 5 a.m. to 9:45 a.m. Even though the employees put in the same total number of hours, supervisors saw the early starters as more conscientious and gave higher ratings to their job performance. In a follow-up study, college students read about a fictitious worker whose eight-hour work day was said to start early or late, and they too exhibited this morning bias.

A second problem is that evaluators differ in the average numerical ratings they give to others. Because of what is known as the *restriction of range problem*, some people provide uniformly high, lenient ratings; others are inclined to give stingy, low ratings; and still others gravitate toward the center of the numerical scale. In all cases, people who use a restricted range fail to make adequate distinctions. Sometimes the differences among raters are considerable, as was seen in a study of managers employed in numerous organizations (Scullen et al., 2000)—in part, because of differences in their personality. Individuals who have agreeable personalities tend to be lenient in their ratings of others, while those who are highly conscientious tend to be harsher (Bernardin et al., 2000). In a meta-analysis of 25 studies, John Georgesen and Monica Harris (1998) also found that people who are in power, compared to those who are not in power, consistently give lower performance ratings to others who are in subordinate positions.

In addition to problems with rating error and bias, supervisors may intentionally distort their evaluations, depending on their objectives within the organization (Murphy et al., 2004). In a study of students in a human management resources course, for example, raters gave higher ratings overall when their goal was to encourage group harmony, to ensure fairness and accuracy, or to motivate those they were rating, than when the purpose was merely to help members to identify strengths and weaknesses (Wang et al., 2010). An obvious but often overlooked fact of life in the workplace is that performance evaluation is not just a measurement process but one that serves social and communication purposes as well.

Self-Evaluations

Although performance appraisals are typically made by supervisors, input is often sought from co-workers, subordinates, clients, customers, and others whose opinions are relevant. You may not realize it, but by filling out course-evaluation surveys in college, you may have had an influence on tenure and promotion decisions involving your own professors. As when workers are asked to evaluate their managers, these evaluations provide valuable "upward feedback."

One particularly interesting source of information comes from self-evaluations. If you've ever had to describe yourself in a personal statement for a job application, you know that a self-evaluation is not a lesson in modesty. Most people see themselves in overly flattering terms, taking credit for success, denying the blame for failure, having an inflated sense of control, and exhibiting unrealistic optimism about the future. Add the fact that people want to present themselves favorably to others and it comes as no surprise that self-evaluations in the workplace are consistently more positive than the ratings made by supervisors (Campbell & Lee, 1988)—and less predictive of job success (Shore et al., 1992). In a simple illustration of this point, studies have shown that workers tend to underestimate the number of times they'd been absent compared with co-workers (Harrison & Shaffer, 1994; Johns, 1994).

Another reason why self-evaluations should be taken with a grain of salt is that individuals differ in the extent to which they tend to present themselves in a positive light. Research shows that the more power people have in an organization, the higher their self-evaluations are (Georgesen & Harris, 1998). Similarly, men in general are more boastful than women and more likely to overestimate their own performance (Beyer, 1990). Insofar as work appraisals are based on self-evaluations, then, these differences put both subordinates and female employees at a disadvantage.

> A problem with having workers evaluate their own job performance is that self-ratings are overly positive. **TRUE**

New and Improved Methods of Appraisal

Performance appraisals cannot always be trusted. When more objective measures of work output are not available, however, organizations have no choice but to rely on imperfect and sometimes prejudiced human judges. For researchers, the challenge is to find ways to boost the accuracy of the evaluations that are made.

One solution concerns the timing of evaluations in relation to the observation of performance. Evaluations are less prone to error when made right after performance than when there's a delay of days, weeks, or months. Alternatively, evaluators should take notes and keep clear records of their observations, perhaps using behavioral checklists. Part of the problem is that once memory for details begins to fade, evaluators fall back on stereotypes and other biases (Murphy & Balzer, 1986; Sanchez & De La Torre, 1996).

A second possible solution is to teach raters some of the skills necessary for making accurate appraisals. Over the years, various training programs have been developed, and research suggests that accuracy can be boosted by alerting evaluators to the biases of social perception, focusing their attention on job-relevant behaviors, sharpening their memory skills, informing them of performance norms that serve as a frame of reference within the organization, and providing them with practice and feedback in the use of rating scales (Day & Sulsky 1995; Hedge & Kavanagh, 1988). No system will ever be perfect, but much improvement is possible, particularly when people are motivated to be accurate (Salvemini et al., 1993).

Third, it is now common in most organizations to collect and combine a full circle of ratings from multiple evaluators in a process that is referred to as a 360-degree performance appraisal. As in assessment centers, a multiple-rater system in which a final evaluation represents the average of ratings made by independent sources with different perspectives is more complete than the conventional single-rater approach (Conway & Huffcutt, 1997; Lepsinger & Lucia, 2009). In a typical 360-degree assessment, an employee's performance is rated by superiors, peers, subordinates, the employees themselves, and sometimes even outside stakeholders such as customers, clients, students, and patients. In this way, whatever idiosyncratic bias a single individual brings to his or her ratings can be offset by others. Although there is debate over how to combine, compare, and contrast different sources, research shows that this approach is an improvement over single-rater methods (Craig & Hannum, 2006; Morgeson et al., 2005). In light of globalization trends in the twenty-first century, the presence of multinational corporations, and the reality that every organization is nested within a broader culture, researchers have also become interested in cultural aspects of performance appraisal (Atwater et al., 2009; Peretz & Fried, 2012).

Due-Process Considerations

In the all-too-human enterprise of performance appraisal, accuracy is not the only concern. There's also another problem: *perceptions of fairness*. Is it fair that one professor is tenured while another is not, or that one worker is laid off while another is retained and a third is promoted? Precisely because the stakes are high in decisions that are made about personnel, performance ratings may be biased and sometimes deliberately distorted by those motivated by political and self-serving agendas in the workplace. Particularly at the executive level, office politics are an organizational fact of life (Gioia & Longnecker, 1994).

To enhance perceptions of fairness, Robert Folger and his colleagues (1992) proposed a "due-process" model of performance appraisal. In general, this model is designed to guard the rights of employees in the same way that the criminal justice system seeks to protect the accused. The model consists of three principles. The first is that there should be *adequate notice*—that is, clear performance standards that employees can understand and ask questions about. The second is that employees should receive a *fair hearing* in which they are evaluated by a supervisor who knows their work and in which they receive timely feedback as well as an opportunity to present their own case. The third principle is that appraisals should be based on *evidence* of job performance, not on prejudice, corruption, or external considerations. As indicated by research on how people react to pay raises, pay cuts, promotions, layoffs, and the implementation of affirmative action policies, procedural fairness (*how* decisions are made) can be just as important to people as a favorable outcome (*what* decisions are made). Thus, workers who are dissatisfied with their pay are more likely to retaliate (for example, by calling in sick, stealing or wasting the company's supplies, or damaging equipment) when they believe the procedures used to determine pay are unfair and were not consulted about the decision (Skarlicki & Folger, 1997).

Recent research has shown that people judge organizational justice according to a large number of criteria—such as the transparency and fairness of the procedures that are used; the extent to which the procedures used and the outcomes they produce are explained; the extent to which affected workers are treated with dignity, politeness, and respect; and the decision-making outcomes by which salaries, promotions, and other resources are allocated. Together, the combination of these specific types of justice influences people's satisfaction, commitment, and on-the-job performance within the workplace (Ambrose & Schminke, 2009). In fact, a recent meta-analysis of 83 studies revealed that employees' perceptions of unfairness in the workplace were associated with increases in negative emotional states, stress, burnout, and physical and mental health problems (Robbins et al., 2012).

Leadership

Regardless of where you're employed, the work experience depends in large part on the quality of the leadership in the organization. A leader is someone who can move a group of people toward a common goal. He or she may be a head of state, the president of a college or university, the principal investigator of a research team, the executive officer of a corporation, a scientist or engineer with a vision for the future, or the manager or head coach of a sports team.

Across a wide range of life settings, researchers have long wondered: What personal and situational factors make for effective leadership? There is no single formula. Some leaders succeed by winning supporters; others lead by mending fences, uniting rivals, negotiating deals, building coalitions, solving problems, or stirring emotions (see Table 13.2). Whatever the strategy, there is one common denominator: Good leadership is about social influence (Avolio, 2011; Avolio et al., 2014; Bass & Bass, 2008; Goethals et al., 2004; Northouse, 2013).

■ The Classic Trait Approach

One approach to the study of leadership is to identify traits that characterize "natural-born" leaders, those who have the "right stuff." According to the Great Person Theory of history, exceptional individuals rise up to determine the course of human events. This approach has had some support over the years, since certain traits—such as ambition, intelligence, a need for power, self-confidence, a high energy level, and an ability to be flexible and adapt to change—are characteristic of people who go on to become leaders (Hogan et al., 1994; Kenny & Zaccaro, 1983). Even physical height may play a role. In this regard, it is striking that across the entire twentieth century, the tallest candidate for U.S. president won an astonishing 23 out of 25 elections—that's 92% of the time (1972 and 1976 were the only exceptions).

On the basis of past research, Shelley Kirkpatrick and Edwin Locke (1991) argued that certain stable characteristics are associated with successful leadership among business executives. In particular, they pointed to the importance of *cognitive ability* (intelligence and an ability to quickly process large amounts of information), *inner drive* (a need for achievement, ambition, and a high energy level), *leadership motivation* (a desire to influence others in order to reach a common goal), *expertise* (specific knowledge of technical issues relevant to the organization), *creativity* (an ability to generate original ideas), *self-confidence* (faith in one's own abilities and ideas), *integrity* (reliability, honesty, and an open communication style),

▲ **TABLE 13.2**

Quotable Conceptions of Leadership

"The purpose of all rulers is the well-being of those they rule."
—Saint Augustine

"The most important quality in a leader is that of being acknowledged as such."
—Andre Maurois

"I am a leader by default, only because nature does not allow a vacuum."
—Bishop Desmond Tutu

"If one is lucky, a solitary fantasy can totally transform one million realities."
—Maya Angelou

"When the effective leader is finished with his work, the people say it happened naturally."
—Lao Tse

"Never tell people how to do things. Tell them what to do and they will surprise you with their ingenuity."
—General George Patton

"We must become the change we want to see."
—Mahatma Gandhi

"The final test of a leader is that he leaves behind him in other men the conviction and will to carry on."
—Walter J. Lippmann

"Leadership should be born out of the understanding of the needs of those who would be affected by it."
—Marian Anderson

"No man will make a great leader who wants to do it all himself, or to get all the credit for doing it."
—Andrew Carnegie

"The task of the leader is to get his people from where they are to where they have not been."
—Henry Kissinger

© Cengage Learning®

In June 2012, James Dimon, CEO of JPMorgan Chase, testified to Congress about the bank's multibillion dollar trading losses. Coming a few short years after the near collapse and bailout of Wall Street banks, regulators were concerned about risks that were taken. This incident and others like it have stimulated a good deal of discussion of "ethical leadership" in business—a new and previously unexplored aspect of leadership (see Ng & Feldman, 2015; Stouten et al., 2012).

and *flexibility* (ability to adapt to the needs of followers and changes in the situation). "Regardless of whether leaders are born or made," they say, "it is unequivocally clear that leaders are not like other people" (p. 58). Locke (2000) picked up on this theme in *The Prime Movers,* a book in which he describes the traits that "great wealth creators"—self-made multimillionaires and billionaires—seem to have in common. Zaccaro (2007) adds that various aspects of leadership can best be predicted by unique combinations of attributes rather than by single traits. Still others have noted that leaders who exhibit more positive emotions than negative are more effective, suggesting that "a happy leader is a good leader" (Joseph et al., 2015).

In contrast to this trait approach, situationally oriented theories were introduced based on the notion that the emergence of a given leader depends on time, place, and circumstances—that different situations call for different types of leaders (Vroom & Jago, 2007). As the needs, expectations, and resources of a group change, so too will the person best suited to lead it. Studies of presidential leadership in particular can be used to illustrate the point about situations and leadership (Goethals, 2005). For example, David Winter (1987) found that presidential candidates are more likely to be elected and reelected when their primary motive in life—whether it is achievement, power, or affiliation—matches what Americans want most at that time. An alternative to the classic trait perspective, then, is a view that leadership is the product of a unique interaction between the person and the surrounding situation.

Situations may well dictate the success of a particular leadership style. During the emergence of the dot-com era, for example, the traditional image of a leader who presides from the top down over a hierarchical command structure gave way to a corporate culture in which a leader should be accessible, fluid, lateral, and relationship oriented. But is this situational doctrine necessarily incompatible with the classic trait approach? Maybe not. In *Primal Leadership,* Daniel Goleman, Richard Boyatzis, and Annie McKee (2002) argue that the primary job of leadership is emotional and that great leaders are endowed with *emotional intelligence,* an ability to know how people are feeling and how to use that information to guide their own actions. Great leaders are men and women who exude interest, enthusiasm, and other positive emotions and whose energy is contagious. Precisely because demands change from one time, situation, and organization to the next, however, leaders with emotional intelligence are by nature flexible in their style, serving as visionaries, coaches, pacesetters, and so on as needed.

■ Contingency Models of Leadership

contingency model of leadership The theory that leadership effectiveness is determined both by the personal characteristics of leaders and by the control afforded by the situation.

Illustrative of an interactional perspective is Fred Fiedler's (1967) **contingency model of leadership**. Fiedler argues that a key difference among leaders is whether they are *primarily task oriented* (single-mindedly focused on the job) or *relations oriented* (concerned about the feelings of employees). The amount of control that a leader has determines which type of leadership is more effective. Leaders enjoy *high situational control* when they have good relations with their staff, a position of power, and a clearly structured task. In contrast, leaders exhibit *low situational control* when they have poor relations with their staff, limited power, and a task that is not clearly defined.

Combining these personal and situational components, studies of various work groups suggest that task-oriented leaders are the most effective in clear-cut situations that are either low or high in control and that relations-oriented leaders perform better in situations that afford a moderate degree of control. In low-control situations, groups need guidance, which task-oriented leaders provide by staying focused on the job. In high-control situations, where conditions are already favorable, these same leaders maintain a relaxed, low profile. Relations-oriented leaders are different. They offer too little guidance in low-control situations, and they meddle too much in high-control situations. In ambiguous situations, however, relations-oriented leaders—precisely because of their open, participative, social style—motivate workers to solve problems in creative ways.

Studies of military units, sports teams, schools, hospitals, and other organizations generally support Fiedler's model. While this support is far from unanimous, the main point is well taken: Good leadership requires a match between an individual's personal style and the demands of a specific situation (Fiedler & Chemers, 1984). A mismatch—that is, the wrong type of person for the situation—can have negative consequences for both the leader and his or her organization. For example, Martin Chemers and others (1985) surveyed college administrators to determine both their leadership style and their situational control. They found that mismatches were associated with increased job stress, stress-related illness, and absence from work, symptoms that diminish a leader's productivity and competence (Fiedler & Garcia, 1987; Fiedler et al., 1992).

Making decisions is one of the most important tasks for any leader. In the two-way street between leaders and followers, however, it is often important to solicit the opinions of others. How much participation should leaders invite? According to the **normative model of leadership** proposed by Victor Vroom and Philip Yetton (1973), leaders vary in this regard. Some are highly autocratic and directive (they invite no feedback from workers), while others are highly participative (they frequently seek and use suggestions from workers). For effective long-term leadership, the key is to invite just the right amount of worker participation—not too much (which is often not efficient) and not too little (which can lower morale). As to what constitutes the right amount, Vroom and Yetton argued that it depends on various factors such as the clarity of the problem, the information available to the leader and followers, and whether it's more important that the decision be right or that one have support.

Although the ideal leader is one who adjusts his or her style to meet the situation, people generally prefer leaders who involve them in important decisions. Research shows that participative decision making boosts worker morale, motivation, and productivity and reduces turnover and absenteeism rates. Benefits such as these have been found especially in situations where employees want to have input (Vroom & Jago, 1988) and when they are involved in decision making directly rather than through elected representatives (Rubenowitz et al., 1983).

◼ Transactional Leadership

Although contingency models take both the person and situation into account, Edwin Hollander (1985) criticized these "top-down" views of leadership in which

normative model of leadership
The theory that leadership effectiveness is determined by the amount of feedback and participation that leaders invite from workers.

A pioneer of the technology revolution, Steve Jobs (1955-2011), co-founder of Apple, was one of the most visionary and transformational business leaders of our time (left). Elon Musk—engineer, inventor, founder and CEO Tesla Motors—is also considered one of the most forward-looking leaders of our time. Many experts believe that his developing line of fully electric sports cars and supercharger stations will revolutionize the automobile industry (right).

workers are portrayed as inert, passive, faceless creatures to be mobilized at the management's discretion. Instead, he sees leadership as a two-way social exchange in which there is mutual and reciprocal influence between a leader and followers. According to Hollander, a good **transactional leader** is one who gains compliance and support from followers by setting clear goals for them, by offering tangible rewards, by providing assistance, and by fulfilling psychological needs in exchange for an expected level of job performance. Transactional leadership thus rests on the leader's willingness and ability to reward subordinates who keep up their end of the bargain and to correct those who do not.

■ Transformational Leadership

Think about some of the greatest leaders of the past century, those who were able to transform the status quo by making supporters believe that anything was possible. Martin Luther King, Jr., epitomized that kind of leader. So did Franklin D. Roosevelt, Mahatma Gandhi, John F. Kennedy, Ronald Reagan, and Nelson Mandela. In their classic book *In Search of Excellence,* Thomas Peters and Robert Waterman (1982) studied 62 of America's best businesses and found that their success was due largely to the ability of the leaders to elicit extraordinary efforts from ordinary human beings.

Leading the technological revolution of the past 50 years, which has completely transformed modern living, the two most prominent models of such leadership were Bill Gates of Microsoft and the late Steve Jobs of Apple—co-founders of the two most important technology companies in the world. In 1975, Gates dropped out of Harvard and co-founded what was then a small company by the name of Microsoft. Long before it seemed possible, he envisioned a day when there would be a PC in every home and office. Then as it was becoming clear that the future would reside in cyberspace, he shocked the business world by refocusing Microsoft around the Internet. Retired from Microsoft, he is now one of the richest and most philanthropic people in the world. In 1973, Steve Jobs, like Gates, also dropped out of college. He soon co-founded Apple and helped popularize and innovate the "Mac," bringing to it the mouse, a sleek design, and other creative elements. Until

transactional leader A leader who gains compliance and support from followers primarily through goal setting and the use of rewards.

Jobs died in October of 2011, his most recent innovations were the iPod, iPad, and iPhone—the all-in-one gadget. In an industry that demands an ability to anticipate the future, adapt quickly to change, take great risks, and enlist support from others, both Gates and Jobs were world leaders.

What's special about successful leaders? Based on the work of political scientist James MacGregor Burns (1978, 2003), Bernard Bass (1998; Bass & Riggio, 2006) calls them **transformational leaders**. Transformational leaders motivate others to transcend their personal needs in the interest of a common cause, particularly in times of growth, change, and crisis. Through consciousness raising and raw emotional inspiration, they articulate a clear vision for the future and then mobilize others to join in that vision. Over the years, Bass and his colleagues asked people who work for various business managers and executives, military officers, school principals, fire chiefs, government bureaucrats, and store owners to describe the most outstanding leaders they know (Bass & Avolio, 1990). As shown in Table 13.3, the descriptions they gave revealed four attributes: charisma, inspirational motivation, intellectual stimulation, and an individualized consideration of others. Other studies have shown that transformational leaders are also more extroverted than the average person (Bono & Judge, 2004)—and more likely to exhibit positive emotions (Joseph et al., 2015).

To measure the extent to which individuals possess the attributes of transactional and transformational leadership styles, Bass (1985) devised the Multifactor Leader Questionnaire, or MLQ. Using this instrument, researchers have studied leadership in different cultures and in different types of organizations, including automobile manufacturers, express-mail companies, multinational corporations, banks, government agencies, and military groups. Others have varied the use of the different leadership styles in controlled laboratory settings. Indicating that inspiration is universally a more powerful motivator than reward, the results have shown that transformational leaders are more effective than transactional leaders (Bass, 1998; Lowe et al., 1996) and exert influence by getting others to identify with them and the group they represent (Kark et al., 2003). In light of their ability to exert influence, it is not surprising that in a study of 39 managers and 130 employees in six companies, those who emerged as transformational leaders on the MLQ were also more socially networked within their organizations (Bono & Anderson, 2005).

People are drawn like magnets to transformational leaders who have what it takes. But wait. Does this mean that Adolf Hitler and other authoritarian heads of state were leaders of the same stripe as Mahatma Gandhi, Franklin D. Roosevelt, and Nelson Mandela? Is there a "dark side of transformational leadership" (Tourish, 2013)? One would hope not. To separate human evil from virtue, Bass and Steidlmeier (1999) sought to distinguish between what they call pseudo-transformational leaders, who appeal to emotions rather than to reason and manipulate ignorant followers to further their own personal interests, and *authentic* transformational leaders, who morally uplift followers and help them transform their collective visions into realities.

Topham/The Image Works, Inc

Shown at his famous "I have a dream" speech in Washington, D.C., in August 1963, Martin Luther King, Jr., was a transformational leader who inspired massive change by making supporters believe that anything was possible.

The most effective type of leader is one who knows how to win support through the use of reward.

FALSE

transformational leader   A leader who inspires followers to transcend their own needs in the interest of a common cause.

Characteristics of Transformational Leaders

When people are asked to describe the best leaders they know, four characteristics are most often cited: charisma, an ability to inspire others, intellectual stimulation, and individualized consideration. These attributes are evident in the self-descriptions given here.

Characteristic	Description	Sample Items
Charisma	Has a vision; gains respect, trust, and confidence; promotes a strong identification of followers.	I have a sense of mission that I communicate to them. They are proud to be associated with me.
Inspiration	Gives pep talks, increases optimism and enthusiasm, and arouses emotion in communications.	I present a vision to spur them on. I use symbols and images to focus their efforts.
Intellectual stimulation	Actively encourages a reexamination of existing values and assumptions; fosters creativity and the use of intelligence.	I enable them to think about old problems in new ways. I place strong emphasis on careful problem solving before taking action.
Individualized consideration	Gives personal attention to all members, acts as adviser and gives feedback in ways that are easy to accept, understand, and use for personal development.	I coach individuals who need it. I express my appreciation when they do a good job.

Based on Bass & Avolio, 1990.

■ Leadership Among Women and Minorities

The fact that Americans elected Barack Obama the first African American president of the United States was remarkable in both historical and current contexts. Look at the leaders of America's Fortune 500 companies at the start of 2015, and you'll find that a mere 4.8% of the CEOs are women—a percentage that is somewhat higher in the health care industry, government, or educational institutions. Look at the percentage of African Americans, Latinos, and Asians in the top ranks of the same organizations, and you'll see that they don't fare any better (at the start of 2015, there were only five African American CEOs, or 1%).

Despite progress that has been made in entry- and middle-level positions, working women and minorities who seek positions of leadership have still not fully broken through the "glass ceiling"—a barrier so subtle that it is transparent, yet so strong that it keeps them from reaching the top of the hierarchy (Morrison & Von Glinow, 1990). Indeed, women may also encounter "glass walls" that keep them from moving laterally within an organization—for example, from positions in public relations to those in core areas such as production, marketing, and sales (Lopez, 1992).

Many women are highly qualified for positions of power. Research shows that male and female managers have very similar aspirations, abilities, values, and job-related skills. Reviewing what is now a massive amount of research literature on sex differences in leadership, Alice Eagly and Linda Carli (2007) found that female leaders in the workplace are as task oriented as their male counterparts and that male and female leaders in general are equally effective. The only difference seems to be that men are more controlling and women more democratic in their approaches. As a result, men may be more effective as leaders in positions that require a more directive style (for example, in the military), whereas women may be more effective in managerial settings that require openness and cooperation. When college students in one study were assigned to participate in long-term work groups, centralized leadership structures emerged over time in all-male groups, while more balanced decentralized leadership structures emerged in all-female groups (Berdahl & Anderson, 2005).

This portrayal of women as leaders is consistent with Judy Rosener's (1995) observation that today's leading women draw effectively on qualities traditionally seen as feminine. It is also consistent with Sally Helgesen's (1995) observation that female managers interact more with subordinates, invite them to participate in the decision-making process, share information and power, and spin more extensive networks, or "webs of inclusion"—a leadership style she sees as a feminine advantage. Research shows that men and women differ in their style, not in the capacity for leadership. A meta-analysis of 45 comparative studies suggests that female leaders may even be slightly more transactional and transformational than men (Eagly et al., 2003). Other researchers are quick to caution that all claims of a gender advantage in favor of men or women are based on stereotypes and are overstated (Vecchio, 2002).

If women are competent to serve as leaders, why have so relatively few managed to reach the top in executive positions? For women, the path to power—from their entry into the labor market, to recruitment, hiring, and up the promotion ladder—is something of an obstacle course (Ragins & Sundstrom, 1989)—or, as Eagly & Carli (2007) put it, a labyrinth. Three sets of impediments have been identified. One is that many women are deeply conflicted about having to juggle a career and family and often feel as though they have to pick one or the other (Halpern & Cheung, 2008). A second impediment is that some women shy away from highly competitive, hierarchical positions that offer the potential for leadership in favor of professions that involve helping people (Pratto et al., 1997). The third impediment is societal. Lingering stereotypes portray women as followers, not as having the leadership traits commonly associated with masculinity. As a result, some people are uneasy about women in leadership roles—particularly women who have a task-oriented or who occupy "masculine" positions, as in business (Eagly & Karau, 2002; Koenig et al., 2011). Suggesting a possible means of overcoming this problem, Shaki Asgari and others (2012) conducted a series of experiments showing that exposing women to female leaders with whom they can identify enhances their self-concept for leadership.

In a survey of 100 male and female corporate executives, Karen Lyness and Donna Thompson (2000) found that although the men and women were equally successful, the women had to overcome more barriers to get where they were going—such as being excluded from informal social networks, being passed over for jobs that required relocating, and not fitting into the corporate culture. To further complicate matters, research shows that people in general exhibit a bias against motherhood when it comes to recommending women with children for promotion (Heilman & Okimoto, 2008).

Statistics show that minorities also fight an uphill battle for leadership positions. President Barack Obama is a most extraordinary exception. In the world of business, at the start of 2015, only five U.S. companies in the Fortune 500 group had an African American CEO: Kenneth Chenault of American Express, Delphi's Rodney O'Neal, Merck's Kenneth Frazier, Carnival's Arnold Donald, and Ursula Burns of Xerox. What seems to be the barrier to entry?

"'If you were taking a new job and had your choice of boss, would you prefer to work for a man or woman?' According to a 2006 Gallup poll that asked this question, 34 percent of men preferred a male boss and 10 percent preferred a female boss, and 56 percent had no preference. Among women, 40 percent preferred a male boss, 26 percent preferred a female boss, and 32 percent had no preference."

—Carroll, 2006

Research is mixed on the question of whether employee evaluations are biased by race (Roth et al., 2003; Sackett & DuBois, 1991; Stauffer & Buckley, 2005; Waldman & Avolio, 1991). Still, in light of what social psychologists have discovered about the subtleties of modern racism, described in Chapter 5, business leaders should beware of the indirect ways in which minorities are handicapped in the pursuit of leadership. Many years ago, in a study of African Americans in the banking industry, many said that they had felt excluded socially from informal work groups, were not "networked," and lacked the sponsors, role models, and mentors needed for advancing in an organization (Irons & Moore, 1985). Similarly, a study of business school graduates revealed that African American and Hispanic men were less likely than others to have mentoring relationships with the influential white men in their respective companies (Dreher & Cox, 1996).

Overcoming the obstacles, some minorities do manage to break through the racial divide into positions of leadership. How did these individuals, and others who have risen to executive ranks, do it? In *Breaking Through,* David Thomas and John Gabarro (1999) studied the career trajectories and experiences of 54 managers and executives in three large companies. Referring to the corporate career ladder as a tournament, they discovered that the successful African American, Asian American, and Hispanic American executives they studied climbed slowly at first to positions of middle management but were then fast-tracked relative to their white peers into the executive suite. Minority managers have to build a solid foundation early, they suggested, "because they are promoted only after proving themselves again and again." At every step of this developmental process, they found that mentors played a key role—opening doors, offering challenging assignments, and sponsoring them for recruitment into important, high-profile positions. In *Leading in Black and White,* Ancella Livers and Keith Caver (2003) further suggested, based on the self-reports of black professionals, that success involved some common ingredients such as having a distinct identity and a heightened focus on race, office politics, networking, and, again, the need for mentors. People need other people, and the corporate world is no exception.

■ Cultural Influences on Leadership

Virtually all the research on leadership we have discussed was focused on Western cultures. But does the meaning of leadership take the same shape across the world? Does a good leader look the same in the United States as he or she does in China, Brazil, or Greece?

In an overview of leadership and culture research, Marcus Dickson and his colleagues (2012) note that while there are universal aspects of leadership, there are also aspects that are culture-specific. For example, Mansour Javidan and Dale Carl (2005) asked Taiwanese and Canadian employees to describe their superiors. They found that the Canadian managers were seen as visionaries—they had realistic visions of the future, conveyed a clear sense of direction, and set realistic goals. In contrast, Taiwanese managers were seen more as mobilizers—they helped make the work challenging and gave constructive feedback and praise. These researchers speculate that in the more individualistic culture of Canada, where employees set their sights on personal advancement, a visionary leader can facilitate their goals by creating a strong sense of direction. Yet in the more collectivistic culture of Taiwan, where a premium is placed on cooperation, belonging, and interpersonal harmony, employees prefer a mobilizing leader who creates a positive work environment.

Bor-Shiuan Cheng and his colleagues (2004) suggested that paternalistic leadership styles are dominant in East Asian contexts. Paternalistic leadership styles stem from Confucian ideals characterized by authoritarianism, benevolence, and moral character. Authoritarianism is a form of leadership in which superiors have control, power, and authority to command obedience, compliance, and respect from subordinates. In return, good leaders show benevolence—a gentle and nurturing concern for those in their care. The East Asian leader should also serve as an ethical role model, demonstrating the virtue others are expected to follow. Interviews of employees in China, Japan, South Korea, and Taiwan, indicate that a paternalistic leadership style was prevalent across all four countries (Cheng et al., 2014).

After a crash landing of an aircraft that killed two passengers and wounded several others, Asiana Airlines CEO Yoon Young-doo, fourth from right, and other board members, bow in apology during a news conference in Seoul, South Korea. This reaction illustrates that the paternalistic leaders seen in collectivistic cultures feel the brunt of responsibility for the group.

Leaders from collectivistic cultures also bear the brunt of responsibility for the group. Consider two recent tragedies—the 2013 Asiana Airlines plane crash and the nuclear crisis at a Tokyo Electric Power Company's (TEPCO) plant following the 2011 earthquake and tsunami. Although neither leader of these companies was directly responsible for their incidents, both publicly apologized. The president of TEPCO also resigned, saying, "I take responsibility for this accident, which has undermined trust in nuclear safety and brought much grief and fear to society" (Tabuchi, 2011).

Is this type of response universal, or a cultural phenomenon? As we've seen elsewhere, East Asian cultures emphasize the group over individuals, so one would expect groups to be held responsible for both good and bad outcomes. Since a group's leader serves as proxy for the group as a whole, Yuriko Zemba and others theorized that people in East Asian cultures would assign more blame to a company's leader for mishaps in the workplace and assign more credit to a leader for an act of heroism in the workplace. In one study, Japanese and American participants read a brief vignette involving a pupil who suffered from food poisoning at school. Although the principal had no direct involvement in the incident, Japanese participants assigned more blame to him than Americans did (Zemba et al., 2006). In a second study, participants read about an incident in which an employee of a company helped to save someone's life. Once again, even though the company president was not directly involved, Japanese participants gave him more credit than American participants did (Zemba & Young, 2012). These studies support the notion that people in collectivist cultures perceive leaders as proxies for the group they hold responsible—for both good and bad outcomes.

Motivation at Work

During the summer of 2015, the *New York Times* published an exposé titled "Inside Amazon: Wrestling Big Ideas in a Bruising Workplace" (Kantor & Streitfeld, 2015). The article describes a highly charged, competitive culture at Amazon.com, where employees, called Amazonians, are monitored every minute of the day using various metrics of productivity; and where they are encouraged to work late hours, criticize each other's ideas, and send feedback to each other's bosses. This workplace is a strict and unforgiving meritocracy in which large numbers of employees leave and are released, producing a "burn and churn" pattern in human resources terms. Amazon founder and CEO Jeff Bezos responded to defend the

Erin Lubin/Bloomberg via Getty Images

In 2015, based on surveys of thousands of employees from hundreds of companies, *Fortune* identified Google as the best company to work for in America—for the sixth year in a row. Headquartered in Mountain View, California, in the heart of Silicon Valley, Google provides its staff with gourmet meals, onsite doctors, child care, a spa, laundry service, twelve weeks of parental leave, and time to spend on independent projects. It's no wonder that Google's employees are so motivated and that the company receives hundreds of resumes a day.

work environment as intense but friendly. In an open letter to workers, he said, "I don't recognize this Amazon and I very much hope you don't, either."

This story sparked a debate about workplace culture and how to strike a balance. At about the same time as the Amazon story broke, a book was published by the American Psychological Association entitled *The Psychologically Healthy Workplace* (Grawitch & Ballard, 2015). With chapters written by different experts, this book asks, how can an organization create and maintain a psychologically healthy workplace without sacrificing the bottom line, optimizing the well-being of employees and shareholders alike? To strike a balance, questions are raised about employees' involvement in the company and its decision making; work-life balance, which often means providing employees with a flexible work schedule; and employee development and recognition, which involves both money and nonmonetary awards for significant achievements.

What motivates individuals to work hard, and to work well? What determines your on-the-job satisfaction, attendance, loyalty, and commitment? People's attitudes about their job can positively and negatively affect their productivity and performance (Judge & Kammeyer-Mueller, 2012). Are you driven strictly by economics, or do you have other personal needs to fulfill? There is no single answer. At work, as in the rest of life, our behavior often stems from the convergence of many different motives. Hence, I/O psychologists have found that people's satisfaction at work depends on a host of factors, economic and otherwise—such as leadership quality, a sense of justice, social relationships and comparisons, and the opportunity for advancement. Even the mere newness of a job can prove invigorating. In a longitudinal one-year study of new workers, Wendy Boswell and others (2009) found that satisfaction peaks during an initial honeymoon period before trending downward and settling in.

■ Economic Reward Models

Out of necessity, people work to make a living. Yet in strictly economic terms, the issue of payment is complicated. To begin with, someone's overall satisfaction with his or her compensation depends not only on salary (gross income, take-home pay) but also on raises (upward changes in pay, how these changes are determined), how income is distributed (the number of checks received or salary differences within the company), and what benefits an employer offers (stock options, tuition credits, on-site gym facilities, vacation time, sick leave, health insurance, pensions, and other services). Each of these factors constitutes part of a formula for satisfaction (Heneman & Schwab, 1985; Judge & Welbourne, 1994). In fact, many rewards are not monetary but symbolic—such as titles, office size, location, carpeting, furnishings, windows, and the ability to regulate access by others (Sundstrom, 1986).

Perhaps the most basic theory of worker motivation is Victor Vroom's (1964) **expectancy theory**. According to Vroom, people are rational decision makers who analyze the benefits and costs of the possible courses of action. Accordingly,

expectancy theory The theory that workers become motivated when they believe that their efforts will produce valued outcomes.

he said, workers become motivated and exert effort when they believe that (1) their effort will result in an improved performance, (2) their performance will be recognized and rewarded, and (3) the monetary and symbolic rewards that are offered are valuable and desirable. Over the years, this theory has been used with some success to predict worker attendance, productivity, and other job-related behaviors (Mitchell, 1974; Van Eerde & Thierry, 1996).

Goal setting is particularly important for motivation. Research shows that people perform better at work and are more productive when they are given specific goals and clear standards for success and failure than when they're simply told to "do your best" (Locke & Latham, 1990). Financial incentives, in particular, can effectively boost worker productivity without compromising the quality of the work (Jenkins et al., 1998). Based on past research, Edwin Locke and Gary Latham (2002) offer a practically useful theory of goal setting. The key, they maintain, is for people to set *specific* and *difficult* goals for themselves or others. This practice increases goal-related choice, effort, and persistence, increases productivity and other aspects of performance, brings reward and satisfaction, and triggers a willingness to take on new challenges and set new goals, thus setting into motion a self-perpetuating cycle of high performance (see ● Figure 13.5).

The value of goal setting in the workplace cannot be overstated. In recent years, many organizations have moved from a focus on the individual to work teams. Reflecting this shift in practice, researchers have wondered whether goal setting functions at the group level in the same way that it does for individuals. A recent meta-analysis of this research indicates that it does: For groups as well as for individuals, it is best to set goals that are specific and difficult (Kleingeld et al., 2011).

Starbucks is the largest coffeehouse company in the world, with 22,766 stores in 65 countries—including this one in Ho Chi Minh City, Vietnam. Starbucks is known for providing workers with customizable "Special Blend" benefits packages, in addition to salary, that may include bonuses, stock options, product discounts, adoption assistance, college assistance, sabbaticals, and health coverage.

Bonuses, Bribes, and Intrinsic Motivation

People may strive for reward, but there's more to money than just economics and more to motivation than the size of a paycheck. Social psychological factors must also be considered. Under certain conditions, reward systems that increase *extrinsic motivation* may undermine *intrinsic motivation*. As we saw in Chapter 3, people are thought to be extrinsically motivated when they engage in an activity

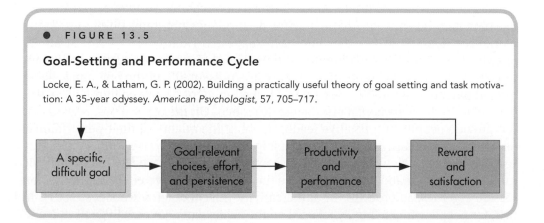

● FIGURE 13.5

Goal-Setting and Performance Cycle

Locke, E. A., & Latham, G. P. (2002). Building a practically useful theory of goal setting and task motivation: A 35-year odyssey. *American Psychologist, 57,* 705–717.

A specific, difficult goal → Goal-relevant choices, effort, and persistence → Productivity and performance → Reward and satisfaction

● **FIGURE 13.6**

The Effect of Payment on Intrinsic Motivation: Turning Play Into Work

In this study, participants worked three times on puzzles they found interesting. After each session, the amount of free time participants spent on the puzzles served as a record of their intrinsic motivation. During the second session, half of the participants were paid for puzzles they completed and half were not. Those paid in the second session later showed less interest in the puzzles when the money was no longer available.

From Deci, E. L., "Effects of externally mediated rewards on intrinsic motivation," *Journal of Personality and Social Psychology* vol 18 (pp. 105–115). Copyright © 1971 by the American Psychological Association. Reprinted by permission.

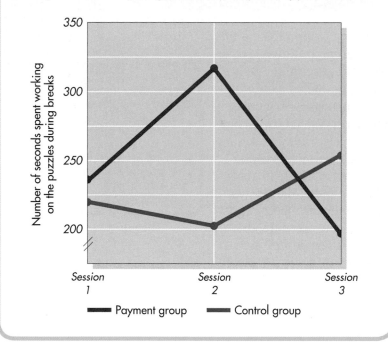

for money, recognition, or other tangible rewards. In contrast, people are said to be intrinsically motivated when they perform for the sake of interest, challenge, or sheer enjoyment. Business leaders want employees to feel intrinsically motivated and committed to their work. So where do expectancy theory and incentive programs fit in? Is tangible reward the bottom line or not?

Research shows that when people start getting paid for a task they already enjoy, they sometimes lose interest in it. In the first demonstration of this effect, Edward Deci (1971) recruited college students to work for three one-hour sessions on block-building puzzles they found interesting. During the first and third sessions, all participants were treated in the same manner. In the second session, however, half were paid one dollar for each puzzle they completed. To measure intrinsic motivation, Deci left participants alone during a break in the first and third sessions and recorded the amount of time they spent on the puzzles rather than on other available activities. Compared with participants in the unrewarded group, those who had been paid in the second session later showed less interest in the puzzles when the money was no longer available (see ● Figure 13.6).

This paradoxical finding that rewards undermine intrinsic motivation has been observed for many years in laboratory and field studies (Deci & Ryan, 1985; Lepper & Greene, 1978; Tang & Hall, 1995). By making people feel controlled rather than autonomous, various extrinsic factors commonly found in the workplace—deadlines, punishment, close supervision, evaluation, and competition—also have adverse effects on motivation and performance. Thus, Teresa Amabile (1996) found that people who were paid for artistic activities, compared with others who were not paid, produced work that was later judged to be less creative by independent raters. To be maximally productive, people should feel internally driven, not compelled by outside forces.

But wait. If money undermines intrinsic motivation, should employers *not* use monetary incentives? Are the pay-for-performance programs often used in the workplace doomed to fail, as some have suggested (Kohn, 1993)? Not at all. To answer these questions, it's important to realize that any given reward can be interpreted in two ways, depending on how it is presented. On the one hand, being offered payment can make a person feel bribed, bought off, and controlled, which can result in the detrimental effects just described. On the other hand, rewards often provide people with positive feedback about the quality of their performance, as when people earn bonuses, scholarships, and verbal praise from others they respect. Research shows that although controlling rewards tend to lower intrinsic motivation, informational rewards have the opposite positive effect on motivation (Eisenberger & Cameron, 1996) and creativity (Eisenberger & Rhoades, 2001). In fact, for people who are highly focused on the achievement of certain goals at work, or elsewhere, tangible inducements tend to boost intrinsic motivation (Durik & Harackiewicz, 2007; Harackiewicz & Elliot, 1993).

◾ Equity Considerations

A second aspect of payment that influences motivation is the perception that it is fair. According to *equity theory*, presented in Chapter 9, people want rewards to be equitable. In other words, the ratio between inputs and outcomes should be the same for the self as it is for others. Relative to co-workers, then, the more effort you exert, and the more you contribute, the more money you should earn. If you feel overpaid or underpaid, however, you will experience distress and try to relieve it by (1) restoring actual equity, say, by working less or getting a raise, or (2) convincing yourself that equity already exists (Cropanzano, 1993).

"Your interest in the salary makes me wonder how 'self-motivated' you really are."

Equity theory has some fascinating implications for behavior in the workplace. Consider Jerald Greenberg's (1988) study of employees in a large insurance firm. To allow for refurbishing, nearly 200 workers had to be moved temporarily from one office to another. The workers were randomly assigned to offices that usually belonged to others who were higher, lower, or equal in rank. Predictably, the usual occupants with the higher rank had a more spacious office, fewer occupants, and a larger desk. Would the random assignments influence job performance? By keeping track of the number of insurance cases processed and by rating the complexity of the cases and the quality of the decisions made, Greenberg was able to derive a measure of job performance for each worker before, during, and after the office switch. To restore equity, he reasoned, workers assigned to higher-status offices would feel overcompensated and improve their job performance and those sent to lower-status offices would feel undercompensated and slow their performance down. That is exactly what happened. ● Figure 13.7 shows that the results offered sound support for equity theory.

Satisfaction depends not only on equity outcomes but also on the belief that the means used to determine those outcomes were fair and clearly communicated (Brockner & Wiesenfeld, 1996; Folger, 1986). For example, Greenberg (1990) studied workers in three manufacturing plants owned by the same parent company. Business was slow, so the company reduced its payroll through temporary pay cuts. Would the cuts make workers feel underpaid? If so, how would the workers restore equity? Concerned that the policy might trigger employee theft, Greenberg randomly varied the conditions in the three plants. In one, the employees were told, without an explanation, that they would receive a 15% pay cut for 10 weeks. In the second plant, the same pay cut was accompanied by an explanation and expressions of regret. In the third plant, salaries were not cut. By keeping track of inventories for the 10 weeks before, during, and after the pay cuts, Greenberg was able to estimate the employee theft rate. The result: Workers whose pay had been cut stole more from the company, presumably to restore equity, but only when they were not provided with an adequate explanation for their loss. When it comes to getting paid, praised, and treated with respect, people are most dedicated to their jobs when they believe they are being treated fairly (Folger & Cropanzano, 1998).

People are so sensitive to unfairness, underpayment, and maltreatment that these feelings can cause stress and compromise their health. In a survey of more than 3,500 workers, Bennett Tepper (2001) discovered that those who felt

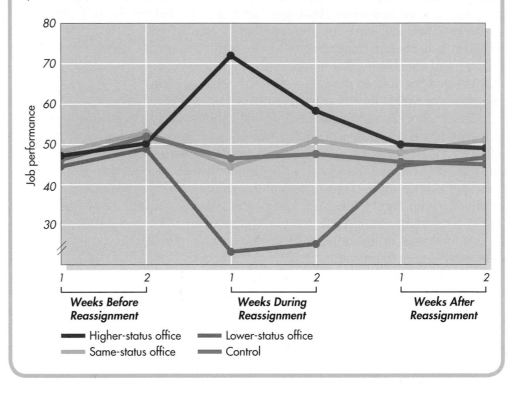

● FIGURE 13.7

Equity in the Workplace

Insurance company workers were moved temporarily to offices that were the workplaces of those who were higher, lower, or equal in status to their own rank. Supporting equity theory, those assigned to the offices of higher-status individuals increased their job performance, and those sent to offices of lower-status individuals showed a decrease. When workers were reassigned to their original offices, productivity levels returned to normal.

From Greenberg, J., "Equity and workplace status: A field experiment," *Journal of Applied Psychology* vol 73 (pp. 606–613). Copyright © 1988 by the American Psychological Association. Reprinted by permission.

victimized by injustice in the workplace also reported the most fatigue, anxiety, and depression. Particularly stressful is the combination of feeling underpaid and unfairly treated. Theorizing that people will lose sleep over these concerns, Greenberg (2006) studied 467 nurses at four private hospitals, two of which cut nurses' salaries by 10% and two of which did not. In one hospital from each group, he taught nursing supervisors how to help promote feelings of organizational justice. Across a six-month period, participants periodically reported on their nighttime sleep patterns. The results showed two interesting patterns: (1) Underpaid nurses reported more symptoms of insomnia than those whose salaries were unchanged; and (2) this problem was reduced among underpaid nurses whose supervisors had been trained to treat them fairly (see ● Figure 13.8).

Equity in the workplace is important, perhaps more so for men than for women. In studies of reward allocation, people are led to believe that they and a partner are working at a task for which they will be paid. They work separately, receive false feedback on their performance, and then are told that they must decide how to divide a joint reward. In this situation, women typically pay themselves less than men do and react less strongly when they are underpaid by others (Major &

Deaux, 1982). Studies of outcomes outside the laboratory reinforced the point. An old study of male and female graduates of an Ivy League business school showed that men were more likely than women to negotiate starting salaries that were higher than the salaries the companies initially offered (Gerhart & Rynes, 1991). Other studies have since confirmed the point: Men negotiate more aggressively than women do—or, to put it another way, "Women don't ask" (Babcock & Laschever, 2003).

The gender wage gap has been narrowing in recent years, but it has not been fully closed. According to the U.S. Bureau of Labor Statistics, American women in 1980 earned only 60 cents for every dollar that men were paid. By 1990, the figure was up slightly, to 72 cents. By 2006, it had climbed to 81 cents. In 2012, it was at 82 cents.

There are many possible explanations for this gender wage gap. One is that women expect less pay than men do, even when they are equally qualified—an expectation that may stem from a long history of discrimination (Major & Konar, 1984). Second, women sometimes care less about money and more about interpersonal relationships (Crosby, 1982). Third, women may be satisfied with less money because they compare themselves with other women instead of with their more highly paid male counterparts (Bylsma et al., 1995; Chesler & Goodman, 1976). Fourth, women on average tend to rate themselves less favorably than do men, so even when they work harder and perform better, they feel less entitled (Major et al., 1984). Whatever the explanation, it is clear that the gender gap in wages is deeply rooted in history (Goldin, 1990). It appears equally clear, however, that working women are not content to remain underpaid relative to men. Perhaps the gender wage gap will vanish as successive generations of women become more established in high-paying careers.

The Progress Principle

A great deal of research has centered on the effects of money and other intrinsic or extrinsic rewards. There is no question that people work primarily to make a living and that money is a powerful motivating force. But is one's compensation the key to job satisfaction? Through a meta-analysis of 92 studies that reported correlations between pay and various aspects of job satisfaction, Timothy Judge and his colleagues (2010) found that although the correlation is greater than zero, people's level of satisfaction at work was only weakly correlated with how much they were paid. With regard to the implications, they concluded, "Given a choice, individuals would be better off weighing other job attributes more heavily than pay" (p. 163).

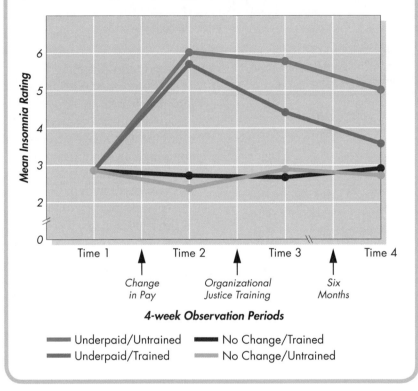

● **FIGURE 13.8**

Losing Sleep Over Underpayment and Organizational Injustice

Nurses were studied at four hospitals—two that cut their salaries, two that did not. In one hospital of each group, supervisors were trained to promote feelings of organizational justice. For six months, participating nurses reported on their nighttime sleep patterns. As shown, those whose salaries had been cut reported more sleep loss than the others, but the problem was reduced among nurses whose supervisors had been trained to treat them fairly.

Greenberg, J. (2006). Losing sleep over organizational injustice: Attenuating insomniac reactions to underpayment inequity with supervisory training in interactional justice. *Journal of Applied Psychology*, 91, 58–69.

> People who feel overpaid work harder on the job than those who see their pay as appropriate.
>
> **TRUE**

"Productivity is up nine percent since I made everyone a vice-president."

Ed Fisher The New Yorker Collection/The Cartoon Bank

Clearly, there is more to motivation in the workplace than money—at least for some people. But what is it? In a *Harvard Business Review* article entitled "What Really Motivates Workers," Teresa Amabile and Steven Kramer (2010) surveyed more than 600 managers from dozens of companies to rank the impact of various factors on employee motivation. They ranked "recognition for good work" as number one—even ahead of financial incentives. "Unfortunately," note Amabile and Kramer, "those managers are wrong."

In a massive multiyear study described in their book *The Progress Principle,* Amabile and Kramer (2011) tracked 238 "knowledge workers" from a variety of settings through entries in a structured diary that they e-mailed to researchers at the end of every work day (a knowledge worker is someone who thinks for a living—such as software engineers, architects, scientists, writers, and lawyers). Each day, the workers reported on their activities, emotions, and motivation levels. Through nearly 12,000 entries, the results showed that people's sense that they had made meaningful progress in their work was the aspect of their day most frequently associated with a positive mood; feelings of joy, warmth, and pride; a perception of support; a sense of accomplishment; and a high level of motivation. As one computer programmer put it, "I smashed that bug that's been frustrating me for almost a calendar week. That may not be an event to you, but I live a very drab life, so I'm all hyped."

Overall, participants noted progress on 76% of their best days and only 25% of their worst days. The association between making progress and feeling good is a correlation that can be interpreted in different ways. On the basis of this association, however, Amabile and Kramer offer advice on how to set this positive process in motion. Managers, they note, can motivate workers, not only through financial incentives—seldom mentioned in diary entries—but by facilitating progress. They can do this by providing more time, resources, encouragement, and personal assistance; by removing unnecessary obstacles, distractions, and demands; by keeping a daily progress checklist; and then by celebrating the incremental advances or "small wins" that are made along the way. More research is needed, but thus far the Progress Principle shows great promise (Fink, 2013).

Economic Decision Making

"Money is power, freedom, a cushion, the root of all evil, the sum of blessings."

—Carl Sandburg

People are intensely focused on money—anxious to have more of it and afraid to be without it. In powerful and symbolic ways, money arouses emotion, activates thought, and motivates action. We ran a Google search on the word *money* in the summer of 2012 and found that there were 2.6 billion entries, exceeding the 357 million entries generated by the word *happiness.* (Being social psychologists, we were interested to find that *love* conquered all at 4.97 billion entries.)

■ The Symbolic Power of Money

Although actor and comedian W. C. Fields once said that a rich man is nothing but a poor man with money, common sense and recent research suggest that money can change people in interesting ways.

Think about it. If you had a fortune, you would be financially independent. How would that make you feel? In a series of laboratory experiments, Kathleen Vohs and her colleagues (2006) found that when college students were merely primed to think about money, they became more self-sufficient, more autonomous, and less social in relation to others. In each study, the researchers primed money in some participants but not others in subtle ways—for example, by having them read an essay that mentioned money, by presenting them with scrambled sentences that relate to money, by having them count a large stack of Monopoly money, or by seating them at a computer with a screensaver that featured images of floating bills. Across the board, those who were exposed to money cues later became more independent. Put into a social situation, they preferred working alone rather than on a team, they put more distance between themselves and a fellow participant, they sought less help on a puzzle they could not solve, and they gave less help to someone who needed it. Reflecting on these findings, Vohs speculates that "money changes people at a core, basic level," that "having money makes people feel less connected and more independent, whereas having little money makes you feel more interdependent with others" (Carpenter, 2005, p. 27).

Let's take this speculation one step further. If money leads us to feel more self-sufficient, does it lessen our need for approval and blunt the pain of social rejection? And following rejection, do we attach greater value to money? Through research conducted in China, Xinyue Zhou and others (2009) sought to answer these questions. In one study, they brought a handful of university students together for a getting-acquainted conversation. The students were then separated and asked to pick someone from the group they'd like to work with. At that point, by random assignment, all students were told that they had to be dismissed—either because everyone selected them (social acceptance) or because no one selected them (social rejection). Afterward, they completed a set of money-related tasks. Here's the interesting part: When asked to draw a Chinese coin from memory, students in the rejection condition drew larger coins. They also said they were more willing to permanently give up such pleasures as chocolate, sunshine, and the beach in exchange for the equivalent of $1.4 million. Rejection had increased the subjective value of money.

In a second study, students engaged in what they thought to be a "finger dexterity" task: They counted out either 80 pieces of paper or 80 $100 bills. Next they played a computerized online ball-tossing game, presumably with three live students. In the normal condition, the game proceeded uneventfully. In a rejection condition, however, the others soon started to exclude the participant from the ball toss. When later asked how they felt about the game, those who had been rejected and who had counted paper were more distressed than those who had counted money. Somehow, the money served to buffer students from the distress normally caused by social rejection (see ● Figure 13.9).

There is now a wealth of research (pun intended) on the symbolic power of money to "prime" people's thoughts, feelings, and motivations. At last count, 165 studies in 18 countries studies

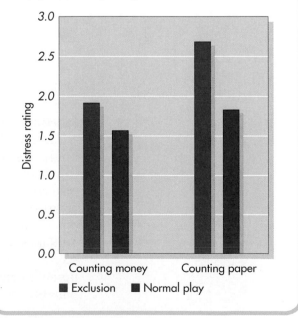

● **FIGURE 13.9**

Links Between Money and Social Rejection

After counting either blank pieces of paper or money, some research participants but not others were told other players had excluded them from an online ball-tossing game. As seen in terms of how they felt about the game, excluded participants who had counted paper were more distressed than before (right), yet those who had counted money were not (left). It appears that money and the self-sufficiency that it symbolizes can mute the adverse effects of social rejection.

Zhou, X., Vohs, K. D., & Baumeister, R. F. (2009). The symbolic power of money: Reminders after money alter social distress and physical pain. *Psychological Science*, 20, 700–706.

have suggested that priming money has two effects on us. First, people become less interpersonally attuned, less prosocial toward others, less caring, and less interdependent. Second, people primed with money start to focus on matters of price, trade, economics, and the virtues of a free market; they exhibit a heightened work ethic, putting more effort into challenging tasks; and they become more likely to succeed (Caruso et al., 2013; Vohs, 2015).

Social Influences in the Stock Market

For all its tangible and symbolic benefits, and although human motivation is complex, money plays a prominent role. For that reason, social psychologists have become interested in how people make economic decisions, for example, when they invest in the stock market. The stock market can be remarkably volatile, as it has been over the past decade—surging up, plummeting down, and inching its way back up in ways that resemble a roller-coaster ride. Why is the market sometimes so volatile? Today, some of the movement is caused by high-frequency trading, an automated system used by large investment banks and hedge funds in which computers are preprogrammed to transact very large orders, at high speeds, based on various price movements. This aspect of the market is captured in Michael Lewis's (2015) bestseller, *Flash Boys*.

Moving from computers to people who make stock market decisions, we ask: Are the companies we invest in so unpredictable from day-to-day fundamental news or are social psychological factors at work? To what extent are day-to-day price movements determined by rational economic indicators such as the gross domestic product, interest rates, inflation, consumer confidence, employment statistics, industry trends, company-specific earnings, political uncertainty, and stock prices that are too high or too low and need correction? In contrast, to what extent is the stock market influenced by fear, greed, false beliefs, financial analysts who appear on TV, rumors that spread over the Internet, conformity pressures, and other social influences, all compounded by the speed and volume with which traders can buy and sell stocks online?

The odds of making money are better in the stock market than in the slot machines found in gambling casinos. Historically, most investors have come out ahead. In many ways, however, choosing stocks is a form of gambling. In *A Random Walk Down Wall Street*, first published in 1981, economist Burton Malkiel (2007) reported that over the long haul, mutual fund portfolios compiled by experts perform no better than randomly selected groups of stocks. Thus, when *Consumer Reports* several years ago evaluated the advice given by professional brokers, it concluded that "a monkey throwing darts at the stock pages . . . could probably do as well in overall investment performance, perhaps even better" (Shefrin & Statman, 1986, p. 52).

But don't some professionals turn a greater profit than others? And if stock prices rise and fall in reaction to market conditions and the success of a company in relation to its competitors, can't the astute investor or short-term day trader take advantage of these relationships? The answer to both questions is "not necessarily." It is certainly true that some analysts and brokers perform better than others do for a period of time, perhaps even for a few years. This can be seen in TipRanks, a company that tracks analysts' predictions over time and then assigns scores to them based on the proven accuracy of their predictions (https://www.tipranks.com). Short-term stock market predictions are fraught with error. The only way to guarantee profit is to have and use confidential inside information, which is illegal. Yet studies show that the average person has a measure of faith in professional investors, overestimating their rate of success relative to their actual performance (Törngren & Montgomery, 2004).

If stock market decisions are not made on strictly economic grounds, then on what are they based? As described in *Greed and Fear*, Hersh Shefrin's (2006) book on the behavioral finance and the psychology of investing, predictions of the future on Wall Street are heavily influenced by social psychological factors. In October 1987, for example, the U.S. stock market crashed, resulting in an estimated loss of $500 billion. Shortly afterward, Nobel Prize–winning economist Robert Shiller sent questionnaires to a large group of active traders to try to determine what caused the crisis. For the 1,000 or so investors who responded, the key event was news about the market itself, including a sharp decline that occurred on the morning of the crash. In other words, price movements in the stock market were triggered not by objective economic information but by other price movements in the market. Shiller describes this work in *Animal Spirits: How Human Psychology Drives the Economy, and Why It Matters for Global Capitalism* (Akerloff & Shiller, 2009). Does this phenomenon ring a bell? Studies on the processes of social comparison and conformity have shown that when people feel they cannot clearly and concretely measure their own opinion, they turn to others for guidance. Perhaps that is why investors are more influenced by news and stock market tips during periods of rising or falling prices than they are during periods of relative stability (Schachter et al., 1985).

With respect to coin flips and other chance events, gamblers too often assume that hot streaks are due to turn cold and vice versa. Yet when it comes to games of skill, such as basketball, people often make the opposite assumptions that a hot streak forecasts continued success and a cold spell predicts failure. Both assumptions are incorrect. One event does not imply another. But what about the ups and downs of a stock market? Do either of these beliefs color the decisions investors make?

To explore this question, Stanley Schachter and others (1987) presented college students with recent price histories of stocks that had increased, decreased, or remained stable over a three-week period. The conventional wisdom on Wall Street, of course, is that investors should buy low and sell high. Yet most participants indicated they would buy stocks that had risen and sell stocks that had fallen. In a follow-up study, very similar decisions

The floor of a stock exchange is a setting fraught with social influence (left). Today's investors are also bombarded by social influences from business shows such as CNBC's *Mad Money*, starring Jim Cramer (right).

were made by more sophisticated students attending the business school at Columbia University.

Do people always go with the flow of the marketplace, or do they sometimes buck the trend to buy low and sell high? Paul Andreasson (1987) argued that the answer depends on attributions. According to Andreasson, investors may follow conventional wisdom. But, he asked, what about price changes for which they have a ready explanation? What if a rise in a stock's price is attributed to certain company or world events? As far as the stock market is concerned, attributions such as these can produce self-fulfilling prophecies by leading investors to believe that the changes will persist—that rising prices will continue to climb or that declining prices will continue to fall. To test his hypothesis, Andreasson simulated a stock market on the computer and found that without news stories to explain the fluctuations, research participants assumed that prices would gravitate to previous levels. The result: They bought stocks when the price was low and sold when the price was high. However, those who also received *Wall Street Journal* explanations for the changes pursued the less profitable strategy, buying stocks that were climbing (based on the assumption that they would continue to do so) and selling those that were on the decline (based on the same assumption of continuity).

Even unpublished rumors can have this effect. Nicholas DiFonzo and Prashant Bordia (1997) conducted a stock market simulation in which unconfirmed company rumors were leaked to some participants but not others. Interestingly, the participants said that they felt that the rumors were not credible and thus did not sway their decisions. Yet they traded on these rumors as if they were hard facts. It doesn't stretch the imagination to see how all these findings might relate to actual behavior in the stock market. Faced with upward and downward movements, the financial news media often seize upon current events for a quick explanation. In some cases, the rumors spread like wildfire through the business community. Whether the news is true or false is irrelevant. Either way, it can turn an initial rise into a bull rally and an initial dip into a steep dive. For this reason, researchers are using laboratory simulations to mimic the decision making that causes stock market bubbles, crashes, and other phenomena (Porter & Smith, 2003). Researchers have also focused how social influences in stock market trading can be influenced by such extraneous factors as the presentation of price fluctuations in the form of visual graphs (Duclos, 2015).

Sometimes emotional factors can lead us astray. Contradicting rational theories of economic decision making, research shows that people fall prey to the **endowment effect**, a tendency to inflate the value of objects they already own (Thaler, 1980). In a study that demonstrates this point, people demanded a higher price for a coffee mug that had been given to them than they did for a comparable mug that they did not yet own (Kahneman et al., 1990). In a second study, researchers observed the orders placed by Australian stock market investors and found that sellers valued their own shares higher than buyers did, regardless of the current market price (Furche & Johnstone, 2006).

As investors, it has long seemed that people also fall prey to the *disposition effect,* a tendency for people to sell stocks that have risen too early and to hold stocks that have declined too long (Shefrin & Statman, 1985). Experiments have confirmed this pattern and have shown that people value gains and losses relative to the price they paid for their shares. Using purchase price as a reference point, we are more likely to take risks in order to avert possible losses than to maximize our gains (Barberis & Xiong, 2009; Weber & Camerer, 1998).

endowment effect The tendency for people to inflate the value of objects, goods, or services they already own.

■ Commitment, Entrapment, and Escalation

Stock market behavior, like other business decisions that individuals, small groups, and organizations make, is complicated by another social factor. Shefrin and Meir Statman (1985) argued that many investors lack the self-control necessary for sound investment decisions. As we just noted, people who own shares of a stock that is climbing often sell too early so they can enjoy the quick pleasure of making a profit. This tendency is easy to understand. But when people own stock that is falling, they often wait too long before selling in the hope that they might avoid a financial loss. Why do people continue to hang on in a failing situation—a decision-making disease that Shefrin (2006) calls "Get-Evenitis"? When the handwriting is on the wall, why compound the problem by throwing good money after bad?

In *Too Much Invested to Quit,* Alan Teger (1980) described a dollar-auction game that illustrates part of the dilemma. Imagine yourself in this situation: The auctioneer tells you and other participants that a $1 bill is about to be sold. As in a typical auction, the highest bidder will receive the dollar in exchange for the amount bid. Yet contrary to convention, the second-highest bidder must also pay the amount bid and will receive nothing in return. You and the other participants are asked not to communicate, and the minimum opening bid is set at five cents. Then, before you know it, the bidding begins. In laboratory experiments, two participants compete in the auction. They are supplied with a small amount of money that is theirs to keep, and they are free to quit the experiment at any time. What happens next might seem startling. Some pairs reasonably choose to take the money and run without making a single bid. Other pairs, however, get involved in escalating bidding wars. According to Teger, bidding for the dollar frequently climbs into the $5 range—more than the amount allocated for play by the experimenter. On one occasion, the auctioneer had to terminate the game after the two participants had bid $24.95 and $25!

The dollar auction helps us to grasp how we can become financially overcommitted in real life. In Chapter 8, we saw that individuals and groups can become *entrapped* by their own initial commitments as they try to justify or salvage investments they have already made. In business, the economic conditions in which an investment is made sometimes justify continued commitment. When there is a reasonable likelihood of success and when potential earnings are high relative to the additional necessary costs, it may pay to persist. With certain long-term investments, sizable up-front costs have to be endured before the delayed benefits are likely to materialize. As in the dollar auction, however, entrapment may occur when economic conditions do not provide a basis for optimism.

Why do investors, business executives, and others losing money on a failing investment so often "hang tough," only to sink deeper and deeper? Why do supervisors who recommend that a worker be hired later overrate that worker's job performance compared with others in the company who were not involved in the hiring (Schoorman, 1988)? Why do NBA teams continue to start players who were selected as top draft picks even though they have not performed well (Staw & Hoang, 1995)? One explanation for these **escalation effects** is that while people ordinarily avoid taking large financial risks to gain money, they are often willing to take risks to keep from losing money. When offered a hypothetical choice between a certain gain of $1,000 and a 50–50 shot at a gain of $2,500, most people choose the smaller guaranteed alternative. Yet when offered a choice between a

escalation effect The tendency for people to persist in failing investments to avert loss, which causes losses to mount.

certain loss of $1,000 and a 50–50 shot at a loss of $2,500, most people roll the dice (Kahneman & Tversky, 1979).

Our aversion to loss accounts for part of the problem, but it's clear that social psychological factors also contribute heavily to the escalation effect. Research has shown that individuals who make the decisions that lead to loss are more likely than others to persist or even to invest further when they feel personally responsible. Why? There are two reasons, both of which make sense (Moon, 2001). One is that people are trained to finish what they have started—a desire for completion that can lead people to throw good money or time after bad (Garland & Conlon, 1998). The second, according to Barry Staw, Joel Brockner, and others, is that sometimes people remain committed to a failing course of action in order to justify their prior decisions, protect their self-esteem, or save face in front of others. Thus, Staw and his colleagues (1997) found that banks were less likely to cut their losses on bad business and real estate loans when the executives who had funded those loans were still with the bank than when they were not. Zhang and Baumeister (2006) found that participants whose self-esteem was threatened were more likely to become entrapped in a failing laboratory game, losing more money as a result. Especially in groups, people don't want to admit that they wasted money in something that will not pay off, so they double down on the failed investment in the hopes of turning it around (Sleesman et al., 2012; Wieber et al., 2015)

In organizations, escalation effects can be minimized by removing the individuals who made the initial investment from the decision making later on. Fortunately, individual investors can also learn to use various de-escalation strategies designed to make them more responsive to available evidence and keep them from throwing good money after bad (Simonson & Staw, 1992). In one study, for example, Richard Larrick and others (1990) found that people often violate the **sunk cost principle** of economics, which states that only future costs and benefits, not past commitments, or "sunk costs" should be considered in making a decision.

To appreciate the practical implications, imagine that you've bought a $40 ticket to a basketball game weeks in advance. Now, on the day of the game, you don't feel well, it's snowing, and your favorite player is injured. Do you still go to the game to make sure you use the ticket? Not wanting to "waste" the money, many of us would go even though the money is already sunk, and even though we would have to bear the added costs of getting sick, driving in bad weather, and sitting through a boring game. To see if there is a more rational economic choice, ask yourself this question: Would you go to the game if someone called on game day and offered you a free ticket? If you said that you would go if you'd paid for the ticket but not if it were free, then—like investors who don't know when to cut their losses—you fell into the sunk cost trap and should have stayed home.

Over and over again, studies have shown that human adults fall prey to the sunk cost bias, allowing their economic decisions to be infected by past investments of time, money, and effort, a maladaptive tendency that, curiously, is *not* exhibited by children or laboratory animals (Arkes & Ayton, 1999). Thankfully, we are trainable. In a study of University of Michigan professors, Larrick and others (1990) found that the economists in the sample were more likely than their counterparts in other disciplines to use the sunk cost principle—not only in hypothetical problems but also in personal decisions. More important, they found that others can be taught to apply the rule as well. Indeed, a full month after exposure

sunk cost principle The economic rule of thumb that only future costs and benefits, not past commitments, should be considered in making a decision.

to a brief training session, college students were more likely to report that they were using the rule in their own lives.

Is it possible to promote a de-escalation of commitment to sunk costs without professional training? Mercifully, yes, it appears that people can learn from life experiences. In one study, researchers tested and compared people of different ages and found that older adults were less likely to fall into the sunk cost trap than were younger adults (Strough et al., 2008). In a second study, researchers compared U.S. Americans and Indians in various sunk cost situations and found that the Indian participants were less likely to commit the sunk cost error, perhaps because their collectivist orientation increased their need to justify their original decisions (Yoder et al., 2014). In a third series of studies, researchers sought to de-bias the mind through mindfulness meditation, a means of focusing awareness on the present moment and clearing the mind of other thoughts, including those of the past. Consistently, they found that participants trained in mindfulness meditation were nearly twice as likely to resist the sunk cost bias relative to participants in a "think whatever comes to mind" control group (Hafenbrack et al., 2014). Other research too has shown that people can resist the sunk cost trap when they are encouraged to think about the present and future, not the past (Molden & Hui, 2011).

People losing money on an investment tend to cut their losses rather than hang tough.

FALSE

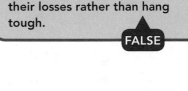

Review

Top 10 Key Points in Chapter 13

1. Classic studies from the 1920's and 1930's revealed the Hawthorne Effect, the finding that workers singled out for special attention, knowing they were being observed, increased their productivity.

2. Traditional job interviews often give rise to poor selection decisions because interviewers are tainted by pre-interview expectations and applicants present themselves less-than-candid ways.

3. To improve personnel selection, employers use standardized tests, structured interviews, assessment centers, and even "cybervetting"—the practice using the internet to get information about applicants that they did not choose to share.

4. Affirmative action, immigration, and globalization of business have combined to increase diversity in the workplace—a state that can enhance team performance by increasing the range of perspectives brought to bear on a problem.

5. Although employee performance can sometimes be evaluated by objective measures (e.g., sales figures), subjectivity poses a common problem—as when a supervisor's ratings are biased by expectations and other personal tendencies, and when self-ratings are inflated by self-serving motives.

6. Research supports different approaches to leadership—including the classic trait approach to identify the personal characteristics of great leaders; contingency models, in which that different types of leadership is needed to suit situational demands; transactional leaders who derive influence by the use of reward; and transformational leaders, who motivate and inspire followers to work for a common cause.

7. Despite gains made in recent years, working women and minorities are still, for various societal reasons, underrepresented in positions of leadership.

8. In addition to being influenced by economic rewards, motivation in the workplace is also influenced by social factors—as when workers become more productive when they feel overcompensated and less productive when they feel undercompensated.

9. The effect of reward on behavior depends on how it is presented—when presented as a bribe to engage in a task, intrinsic motivation in the rewarded activity is reduced; when presented as a bonus for quality performance, intrinsic motivation is enhanced.

10. Research on economic decision-making shows that people often become entrapped by their initial commitments, leading them to stick to a failing course of action and throw good money after bad.

Putting Common Sense to the Test

Personnel Selection

Although flawed, job interviews consistently make for better hiring decisions.

Ⓕ **False.** *Although interviews may lessen the tendency among employers to make simple stereotyped judgments, they often lack predictive validity.*

Performance Appraisals

A problem with having workers evaluate their own job performance is that self-ratings are overly positive.

Ⓣ **True.** *Self-evaluations of job performance are not only more positive than ratings made by others but also less predictive of success.*

Leadership

The most effective type of leader is one who knows how to win support through the use of reward.

Ⓕ **False.** *Great leaders articulate a vision and then inspire others to join in that vision and work for a common cause.*

Motivation at Work

People who feel overpaid work harder on the job than those who see their pay as appropriate.

Ⓣ **True.** *People who feel overpaid work harder to restore their sense of equity.*

Economic Decision Making

People losing money on an investment tend to cut their losses rather than hang tough.

Ⓕ **False.** *People often remain committed to a failing course of action in order to justify the initial decision to themselves and others.*

Key Terms

assessment center (564)

contingency model of
  leadership (576)

cybervetting (561)

endowment effect (594)

escalation effect (595)

expectancy theory (584)

Hawthorne effect (557)

industrial/organizational (I/O)
  psychology (556)

integrity tests (563)

normative model of
  leadership (577)

performance appraisal (571)

structured interview (564)

sunk cost principle (596)

transactional leader (578)

transformational leader (579)

Health and Well-Being

This chapter explores the social psychology of physical and mental health. We focus first on the links between stress and health. Four questions are asked in this regard: What causes stress, how does it affect the body, how do we appraise potentially stressful situations, and what are some ways of coping with stress? Next we discuss some of the social influences on treatment and prevention. We then conclude on a positive note, looking at the roots of happiness.

Richard Price/Getty Images

14

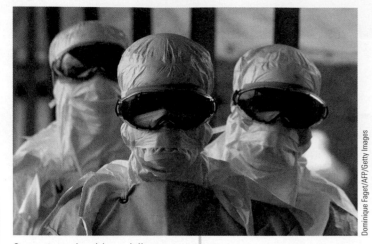

Sometimes health and illness are inherently social in nature. The highly contagious Ebola virus, which broke out in 2014, rapidly became the largest Ebola epidemic in history, affecting all of West Africa. To prevent person-to-person transmission, health care workers at this hospital in Liberia, and elsewhere, had to wear protective suits. In total, 28 thousand cases were identified, 15 thousand confirmed, and 11,314 resulting in deaths.

Dominique Faget/AFP/Getty Images

When Laurence Sterne, an eighteenth-century English novelist, weighed the value of good health, he concluded that it was "above all gold and treasure." Most would agree—which is why health care is so important to everyone and why political, moral, economic, and legal debates over health care in the United States have been such a contentious topic. This long and complex debate clearly illustrates the intensity of feelings on this issue. In matters of life and death, everyone cares deeply, including social psychologists.

The reasons that social psychologists study *mental health* and such disorders as anxiety and depression are obvious. Human beings are inherently social creatures, and our psychological well-being can be both damaged and repaired by our relationships with other people. But social psychologists are also interested in *physical health*, a domain normally associated with medicine. Working in universities, medical schools, hospitals, and government agencies, many social psychologists are involved in the relatively new area of **health psychology**—the application of psychology to the promotion of physical health and the prevention and treatment of illness (Straub, 2015; Taylor, 2015).

You may wonder: What does social psychology have to do with catching a cold, or a contagious virus, having a heart attack, or being afflicted by cancer? If you could turn the clock back a few years and ask your family doctor, his or her reply would be "nothing." In the past, physical illness was considered a purely biological event. But this narrow medical perspective has given way to a broader model, which holds that health is a joint product of biological, psychological, and social factors.

Part of the reason for this expanded view is that illness patterns over the years have changed in significant ways. In the year 1900, the principal causes of death in the United States were contagious diseases such as polio, smallpox, tuberculosis, typhoid fever, malaria, influenza, and pneumonia. Today, none of these infectious illnesses are leading killers. And when there is an outbreak of highly contagious disease, as in the Ebola virus in West Africa, in 2014, the social isolation of those infected becomes a necessary means of containment. Indeed, Americans today are most likely to die (in order of risk) from heart disease, cancers, strokes, accidents, and chronic lower respiratory diseases (AIDS is not in the top ten in the United States but sixth worldwide). Interestingly, these diseases can sometimes be prevented through changes in lifestyle, outlook, and behavior. In light of useful research that has been conducted in recent years, this chapter focuses first on stress: what causes it, what it does to the body, and how we appraise stressful situations in

---

Putting COMMON SENSE to the Test

Circle Your Answer

T F The accumulation of daily hassles does more to make people sick than catastrophes or major life changes.

T F Like humans, zebras get ulcers.

T F Stress can weaken the heart, but it cannot affect the immune system.

T F When it comes to physical health, research does not support popular beliefs about the power of positive thinking.

T F People who have lots of friends are healthier and live longer than those who live more isolated lives.

T F In all countries and at all levels of wealth, the more money people have, the happier they are.

order to cope with them. Next, we look at some social influences on the treatment and prevention of illness. Finally, we consider the pursuit of happiness and life satisfaction.

Stress and Health

Stress is an unpleasant state of arousal that arises when we perceive that the demands of a situation threaten our ability to cope effectively. Nobody knows the precise extent of the problem, but stress is a potent killer. Regardless of who you are, when you were born, or where you live, you have no doubt experienced stress. Sitting in rush-hour traffic, packing your belongings to move, losing your job and looking for work, getting married or divorced, arguing with a close friend, worrying about the health of a parent or your child, paying off loans, and struggling to make financial ends meet are examples of stresses and strains we all must live with.

Clearly, what stresses an entire generation or population can be influenced by world events. In a nationwide survey of over 3,000 men and women, as reported in *Stress in America*, the American Psychological Association (2015) asked respondents to indicate the sources of stress in their lives. Overall, on a 10-point scale (where 1 = little or none, 10 = a great deal), Americans reported an average of 4.9, which was less than the 6.2 reported in 2007, the first year that this annual survey was started. But not everyone is okay. Seventy-two percent of Americans cited money as a source of stress in their lives—22% say it is an extreme. In fact, when people were asked about the most significant sources of stress in their lives, money emerged at the top of the list (see Table 14.1). The effects on health and well-being are clear. Among the symptoms most commonly reported: irritability and anger, nervousness, lack of energy and motivation, fatigue, feeling overwhelmed, and sadness and depression.

From the standpoint of population demographics, it appears that some types of people are more likely to report feeling stressed than others. Analyzing national surveys that were conducted from 1983 to 2009, Sheldon Cohen and Denise Janicki-Deverts (2012) found that more stress is consistently reported by women than men, minority respondents than whites, people who are unemployed than employed, those who are employed rather than retired, and people in general who are younger, less educated, and have lower incomes.

Whether the stress is short term or long term, serious or mild, and despite these group differences, no one is immune from stress and there is no escape. But there are ways to cope. According to Richard Lazarus and Susan Folkman (1984), the stress-and-coping process is an ongoing transaction between a person and his or her environment. Faced with an event that may prove threatening, our subjective **appraisal** of the situation determines how we will experience the stress and what **coping** strategies we will use—in other words, what thoughts, feelings, and behaviors we will employ to try to reduce the stress. At times, people also take proactive steps to keep a potentially stressful event from occurring in the first place. As we'll see, effective coping helps to maintain good health; ineffective coping can cause harm (Monat et al., 2007; Harrington, 2013).

In the next two sections, we examine two questions that are relevant to health and well-being: (1) What causes stress, and (2) how does stress "get into" the

According to the World Health Organization, the average life expectancy from birth ranges widely from a low of 47 years in Malawi to a high of 83 in Japan and San Marino. (The average life expectancy is 79 in the United States and 81 in Canada.) For up-to-date health statistics, you can visit online the World Health Organization (www.who.org) and the National Center for Health Statistics (www.cdc.gov/nchs).

health psychology The study of physical health and illness by psychologists from various areas of specialization.

stress An unpleasant state of arousal in which people perceive the demands of an event as taxing or exceeding their ability to satisfy or alter those demands.

appraisal The process by which people make judgments about the demands of potentially stressful events and their ability to meet those demands.

coping Efforts to reduce stress.

▲ TABLE 14.1

What Americans Cite as Top Stressors

	Very Significant	Some what Significant	Not very Significant	Not At All Significant
Money	31%	33%	20%	16%
Work	22%	38%	23%	17%
Relationships (e.g., spouse, kids, girl/boyfriend)	17%	27%	26%	30%
Health problems affecting my family	17%	26%	26%	31%
Family responsibilities	17%	30%	27%	26%
Housing costs (e.g., mortgage or rent)	16%	24%	25%	35%
The economy	16%	34%	29%	22%
Job stability	16%	19%	19%	46%
Personal health concerns	15%	30%	29%	25%
Personal safety	6%	18%	33%	44%

American Psychological Association, 2015.

Anthony Robbins offers a simple two-step formula for handling stress: (1) Don't sweat the small stuff, and (2) remember that it's all small stuff.

body? Then we look at appraisal and coping, processes that account for why an event that flattens one person can prove harmless to another. As all the pieces come together, we'll see that the answers to these questions provide a broad and useful model of the stress-and-coping process (see ● Figure 14.1).

What Causes Stress?

Make a list of the stressors in your own life and you'll probably find that the items on your list can be sorted into three major categories: catastrophes, major life events, and daily hassles. Before we consider these causes of psychological stress, however, let's step back and ask a more basic research question: How can a psychologist know how much stress a person is under? How can it be measured? There are many different sources of stress, or **stressors**, and their effects can be defined in different ways (Cohen et al., 2007).

Over years, two different types of approaches have been taken. Using *self-report,* many researchers have asked people to check off life events that have happened to them from a list of known stressors; others have asked people to keep daily diaries in which they report on stressful experiences as they occur; still others conducted live interviews to get more detailed information about the source and extent of the stress. Looking at stress as a bodily response to perceived threat, other researchers use *physiological measures* by analyzing stress hormone levels in blood, urine, or saliva samples; or by recording autonomic arousal through heart rate, respiration rate, blood pressure, or sweat gland activity. It may even be possible to assess the effects

stressor Anything that causes stress.

of stress on the body over time. In recent years, researchers have observed that accumulated levels of cortisol (a stress hormone) found in hair samples are associated with exposure to stress—suggesting that hair cortisol may provide a "biomarker" for life stress (Russell et al., 2012). In one study, for example, hair cortisol levels were higher in a sample of men and women who were out of work than in a comparison sample of others who were employed (Dettenborn et al., 2010).

Crises and Catastrophes

We are running from the wave, and we can see the water right behind us. We run toward the other side of the island. When we get about halfway across, we meet people running and screaming from the other direction. Then we see the water in front of us too. The waves meet, and we are under water. (Dittmann, 2005, p. 36)

On December 26, 2004, one of the worst natural disasters in history spread over Southeast Asia, India, Indonesia, and Africa. It started when a powerful earthquake struck deep under the Indian Ocean, triggering massive tsunamis that obliterated cities, seaside communities, and holiday resorts. Approximately 320,000 people in a dozen countries were killed; thousands of survivors were injured and traumatized in the process.

Eight months later, Hurricane Katrina stampeded through the Gulf Coast of the United States with winds of up to 175 miles per hour, devastating areas in Florida, Mississippi, Alabama, and Louisiana and killing nearly 2,000 people. In New Orleans, the surge breached the levees, flooding 80% of the city and neighboring parishes. Causing an estimated $81 billion in damage, Hurricane Katrina became the costliest natural disaster in U.S. history. It was not, of course, the last. Floods, fires, tornadoes, and earthquakes are part of life in many regions of the world. The largest natural disaster area ever was declared in the summer of 2012 because of the droughts that afflicted 26 states. Then Hurricane Sandy pounded the Northeast, devastating beach towns along the coast.

The intense stress that natural catastrophes impose on a population can also be caused by human beings. Sometimes the disaster that strikes is accidental—as in the massive BP oil spill of 2010 that gushed millions of gallons of oil into the Gulf of Mexico, killing wildlife and causing billions of dollars in damage. At other times, human-caused disasters result from malicious motives. The terrorist assault on the World Trade Center and the Pentagon on September 11, 2001, was a different kind of tragedy that no one who was old enough to witness it will ever forget. Americans all over the world took the attack personally and were touched by it, whether they were present or not. In a nationwide telephone survey of 560 adults conducted later that week, 90% said they were experiencing some symptoms of stress and 44% reported "substantial" symptoms such as recurring thoughts, dreams, and memories; difficulty falling or staying asleep; difficulty concentrating on work; and unprovoked outbursts of anger (Schuster et al., 2001). These problems were far more common among New Yorkers than in people living in other areas (Schlenger et al., 2002). Even within Manhattan, researchers found that the

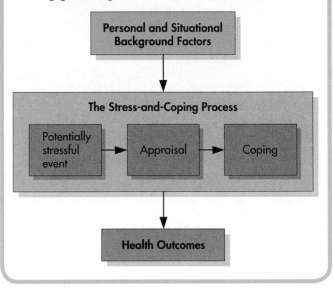

● **FIGURE 14.1**

The Stress-and-Coping Process

This process involves a potentially stressful event, the appraisal of that event, and attempts to cope. Played out against a variety of background factors unique to each individual, the stress-and-coping process influences health outcomes.

© Cengage Learning®

U.S. Air Force photo by Master Sgt. Mark C. Olsen

In the fall of 2012, from Florida up through New England and Canada, Hurricane Sandy was the deadliest hurricane to ever strike the Atlantic coast and the second-costliest hurricane in United States history. As seen here, the peninsula town of Mantoloking, New Jersey was especially hard hit.

closer residents lived to Ground Zero, the more traumatized and depressed they were by the experience. The most profoundly affected were those who worked in the towers or nearby, those who had friends and family in the vicinity, and rescue workers who were called to the scene (Galea et al., 2002).

The harmful effects of catastrophic stressors on health have long been documented. Paul and Gerald Adams (1984) examined the public records in Othello, Washington, before and after the 1980 eruption of the Mount St. Helens volcano, which spewed thick layers of ash all over the area. After the eruption, they observed increases in calls made to a mental health crisis line, police reports of domestic violence, referrals to a local alcohol treatment center, and visits to the emergency room. Then there was an earthquake that shook San Francisco in 1989. Houses collapsed, highways buckled, overpasses fell apart, water mains burst, and fires raged out of control, leaving thousands of people homeless. By coincidence, Susan Nolen-Hoeksema and Jannay Morrow (1991) had administered some trauma-relevant measures to a group of Stanford University students two weeks before the earthquake. Follow-up assessments 10 days later and again after six weeks provided these investigators with a before and after examination of coping. They found that people who had initially been more distressed and those who had encountered more danger during the quake experienced the most psychological distress afterward.

The scarring effects of large-scale disasters are without dispute. Based on their review of 52 studies, Anthony Rubonis and Leonard Bickman (1991) found that high rates of psychological disorders are common among residents of areas that have been hit by these catastrophic events. In a study of disasters involving 377 counties, a team of researchers found that compared with the years preceding each disaster, the suicide rate increased by 14% after floods, 31% after hurricanes, and 63% after earthquakes (Krug et al., 1998). Other events that can have similarly traumatic effects include war, car accidents, plane crashes, violent crimes, physical or sexual abuse, and the death of a loved one (Kubany et al., 2000).

War in particular leaves deep, permanent psychological scars. Soldiers in combat are trained by experience to believe that they have to kill or be killed. They suffer intense anxiety and see horrifying injuries, death, and destruction, all of which leaves them with images and emotions that do not fade. Given this level of stress, it's not surprising that when a war is over, some veterans suffer greatly. In World War I, the problem was called "shell shock." In World War II, it was called "combat fatigue." Now the problem is seen as a specific form of **posttraumatic stress disorder (PTSD)** and is identified by such enduring symptoms as recurring anxiety, sleeplessness, nightmares, intrusive bad thoughts, flashbacks, attention problems, and social withdrawal. What's worse, families

posttraumatic stress disorder (PTSD) A condition in which a person experiences enduring physical and psychological symptoms after an extremely stressful event.

are often shattered when a loved one returns from war and seems different, as if still trapped in combat (McCarty-Gould, 2000). Time alone does not heal the wounds of war-induced PTSD. In a longitudinal study of 88,000 American soldiers who had returned from the war in Iraq, researchers found that soldiers had more mental health problems three to six months after their return than immediately afterward, with the number of reported PTSD cases rising from 49% to 59% (Milliken et al., 2007). Research has shown that certain soldiers are more vulnerable than others—especially those who were exposed to high levels of combat, had discharged a weapon, and had witnessed someone being wounded or killed (Xue et al., 2015).

These soldiers, like thousands of other troops and civilians, have experienced the recent wars in Iraq and Afghanistan firsthand. It has long been recognized that combat leaves psychological scars and increases the risk of posttraumatic stress disorder.

War can traumatize civilian populations as well. In Israel, 16% of adults had personally been exposed to a terrorist attack, and 37% had a close friend or family member who had been exposed (Bleich et al., 2003). With regard to the mental health consequences, a study of 905 Jewish and Palestinian citizens revealed that exposure to terrorism was associated with PTSD symptoms in both groups—more so among the Palestinian citizens, members of an ethnic minority who have fewer coping resources to turn to when in distress (Hobfoll et al., 2006).

Over the years, clinical psychologists have studied PTSD and the life experiences that precipitate its onset (Friedman et al., 2014). Based on a nationwide survey of 6,000 Americans aged 15 to 54 years, Ronald Kessler and others (1995) estimated that 8% of the population (5% of men, 10% of women) suffer posttraumatic stress disorder in the course of a lifetime and that the symptoms often persist for many years. Among the experiences that produced these traumas were witnessing a murder or injury, the death of a loved one, life-threatening accidents, serious illness, war, fires and natural disasters, physical and sexual assaults, and prison. From a meta-analysis of 290 studies involving thousands of participants, it is clear that PTSD is more prevalent among women than among men, even though men are more likely to experience potentially traumatic events (Tolin & Foa, 2006).

◼ Major Life Events

Some people are lucky enough to avoid major catastrophes. But nobody can completely avoid stress. Indeed, change itself may cause stress by forcing us to adapt to new circumstances. This hypothesis was first proposed by Thomas Holmes and Richard Rahe (1967), who interviewed hospital patients and found that their illnesses had often been preceded by major changes in some aspect of their lives. Some of the changes were negative (getting hurt, divorced, or fired), but others were positive (getting married or promoted or having a baby). To measure life stress, Holmes and Rahe devised the Social Readjustment Rating Scale (SRRS), a checklist of 43 major life events each assigned a numerical value based on the amount of readjustment it requires. Among the events sampled (and the numerical values they were assigned) were the death of a spouse (100), divorce (73), imprisonment (63), marriage (50), job loss (47), pregnancy (40), school transfer (20), and even vacations (13).

The simple notion that change is inherently stressful has an intuitive ring about it. But is change per se, whether positive or negative, necessarily harmful? There are two problems with this idea. First, although there is a statistical link between negative events and illness, research does not similarly support the claim that positive "stressors" such as taking a vacation, graduating, winning a lottery, starting a new career, or getting married are similarly harmful (Stewart et al., 1986). Happiness is not the absence of distress, nor is distress the absence of happiness. A person can simultaneously experience both emotions (Carver & Scheier, 1990), and the health consequences are different (Taylor, 1991).

The second complicating factor is that the impact of any change depends on who the person is and how the change is interpreted. Moving to a new country, for example, is less stressful to immigrants who can speak the new language than to those who cannot (Berry et al., 1992); victims of physical assault who wonder "what if?" take longer to recover emotionally than those who do not (El Leithy et al., 2006). And workers who have stressful jobs cope better when they disengage during nonwork times than when they do not (Sonnentag & Fritz, 2015). To sum up: Change in a person's life may provide a crude estimate of stress and future health, but the predictive equation is often complicated by other factors.

■ Microstressors: The Hassles of Everyday Life

Think again about the stress in your life, and catastrophes and other exceptional events will spring to mind. Yet the most common source of stress arises from the hassles that irritate us every day. Environmental factors such as crowding, loud noise, extreme heat or cold, and cigarette smoke are all sources of stress. Car problems, gas prices, waiting in lines, traffic, losing keys, bad workdays, money troubles, airport delays, disrupted Wi-Fi connections, and other "microstressors" also place a constant strain on us. Unfortunately, there is nothing "micro" about the impact of these stressors on health and well-being. Studies suggest that the accumulation of daily hassles contributes more to illness than do major life events (Kohn et al., 1991). Interpersonal conflicts are the most upsetting of our daily stressors and have a particularly long-lasting impact (Bolger et al., 1989).

One problem that plagues many people in the workplace is occupational stress (Barling et al., 2005). One type of reaction is *burnout*—a prolonged response to job stress that is characterized by emotional exhaustion, cynicism, disengagement, and a lack of personal accomplishment. Teachers, doctors, nurses, police officers, social workers, and others in human-service professions are especially at risk. Faced with relentless job pressures, those who are burned out describe themselves as feeling drained, frustrated, hardened, apathetic, and lacking in energy and motivation (Leiter et al., 2014; Maslach, 1982). In many ways, burnout is hard to distinguish from depression (Bianchi et al., 2015). People are most likely to have this experience when they do not have enough resources at work—such as support from supervisors and friendly relations with co-workers—to meet the demands of the job (Lee & Ashforth, 1996).

Over the years, research had suggested that burnout is an experience that afflicts women more than men. It now appears that the role of gender is more complex. An analysis of 183 studies has shown both men and women are potentially susceptible to burnout under bad circumstances—but the symptoms are different. Female employees are 8% more likely than men to become *emotionally exhausted* in the workplace, feeling overwhelmed and physically drained. However, men are 14% more likely to become *depersonalized* at work, withdrawing and distancing themselves from clients and co-workers (Purvanova & Muros, 2010).

Another form of daily stress comes from commuting to and from work. At present, more than 120 million Americans commute to work each weekday—by car or by public transportation, for an average of 25 minutes (Rampell, 2011). Research has shown that driving to work often proves stressful (Koslowsky et al., 1995). Commuting long distances by train can have the same effect. Studying railroad commuters who traveled regularly from their homes in suburban New Jersey to work in Manhattan, Gary Evans and Richard Wener (2006) found that the longer their commute was, the more stress they reported feeling, the sloppier they were at a simple proofreading task, and the higher was their level of cortisol—a stress hormone that was measured by taking saliva samples after the morning trips.

On the home front, financial pressure is a particularly common and dramatic source of stress (American Psychological Association, 2015). Several years ago, a three-year study of more than 400 married American couples showed that those who are strained by a tight budget and have difficulty paying the bills experience more distress and conflict in their marriages (Conger et al., 1999). A follow-up study of African American families showed that economic hardship spells emotional distress for parents and adjustment problems for their children (Conger et al., 2002).

In recent years, health psychologists have come to realize that *socioeconomic status* (SES) is a powerful proxy for the hassles of everyday living. Across a range of health outcomes, individuals who are less educated, have lower status jobs, and earn less or no income are more likely to suffer from health problems relative to others who are better off (Adler et al., 1994). There are two reasons for this association. First, people who live in low-income neighborhoods are invariably subject to more exposure to noise, crowding, crime, poor diet, and other stressors. Second, people of low socioeconomic status have fewer tangible, medical, social, and psychological resources to help them meet these daily challenges. For children who grow up in low SES families, the influences can accumulate over time and endure (Matthews & Gallo, 2011).

Tim Boyle/Getty Images

Randy Olson/National Geographic Image Collection/Alamy

Waiting in line at Chicago's O'Hare Airport, a common occurrence in these days of heightened security, is the kind of microstressor that plagues air travelers on a daily basis (top). The streets of Kolkata, India—a city with 4.8 million people—are crowded with vendors, pedestrians, and taxis. Today there are 35 "mega cities" in the world with populations over 10 million, many in developing countries, where urban areas absorb the rising population—and stress (bottom).

The accumulation of daily hassles does more to make people sick than catastrophes or major life changes.

TRUE

How Does Stress Affect the Body?

The term *stress* was first popularized by endocrinologist Hans Selye (1936). As a young medical student, Selye noticed that patients who were hospitalized for many different illnesses often had similar symptoms, such as muscle weakness, a loss of weight and appetite, and a lack of ambition. Maybe these symptoms were part of a generalized response to an attack on the body, he thought. In the 1930s, Selye tested this hypothesis by exposing laboratory rats to various stressors, including heat, cold, heavy exercise, toxic substances, food deprivation, and electric shock. As anticipated, the different stressors all produced a similar physiological response: enlarged adrenal glands, shrunken lymph nodes, and bleeding stomach ulcers. Borrowing a term from engineering, Selye called the reaction *stress*—a word that quickly became part of everyday language.

■ The General Adaptation Syndrome

According to Selye, the body naturally responds to stress in a three-stage process that he called the **general adaptation syndrome** (see ● Figure 14.2). Sparked by the recognition of a threat—such as a predator, an enemy soldier, a speeding car, or a virus—the body has an initial *alarm* reaction. To meet the challenge, adrenaline and other hormones are poured into the bloodstream, creating physiological arousal. Heart rate, blood pressure, and breathing rates increase, while slower, long-term functions such as growth, digestion, and the operation of the immune system are inhibited. At this stage, the body mobilizes all of its resources to ward off the threat. Next comes a *resistance* stage, during which the body remains aroused and on the alert. There is continued release of stress hormones, and local defenses are activated. But if the stress persists for a prolonged period of time, the body will fall into an *exhaustion* stage. According to Selye, our antistress resources are limited. In

general adaptation syndrome   A three-stage process (alarm, resistance, and exhaustion) by which the body responds to stress.

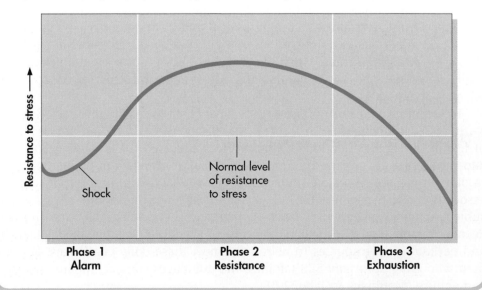

● **FIGURE 14.2**

The General Adaptation Syndrome

According to Selye (1936), the human body responds to threat in three phases: alarm, resistance, and exhaustion.

Selye, H. (1936). A syndrome produced by diverse nocuous agents. *Nature*, 138, 32 .

Resistance to stress →

Shock

Normal level of resistance to stress

Phase 1
Alarm

Phase 2
Resistance

Phase 3
Exhaustion

fact, however, research has shown that exhaustion occurs not because our stress-fighting resources are limited but because their overuse causes other systems in the body to break down, which puts us at risk for illness and even death. Selye's basic model thus makes an important point: Stress may be an adaptive short-term reaction to threat, but over time it compromises our health and well-being (for the latest scientific research on the biology and psychology of stress, see Contrada & Baum, 2011).

A stress response is found in all mammals. So why, asks neuroscientist Robert Sapolsky (2004), don't zebras get ulcers? Sapolsky notes that the physiological stress response is superbly designed through evolution to help animals mobilize to fight or escape in acute emergencies. For the zebra, this occurs when a hungry lion leaps out from a bush and sprints at top speed across the savanna. For humans, it occurs during combat or competitive sports and perhaps even on first dates and in job interviews. But think about the list of situations you find stressful, and you'll see that people become anxious over things that would make no sense to a zebra. "We humans live well enough and long enough, and are smart enough, to generate all sorts of stressful events purely in our heads," says Sapolsky. From the perspective of the evolution of the animal kingdom, he notes, psychological stress is a "recent invention" (p. 5). The reason stress causes ulcers and other illnesses, then, is that the response is designed for acute physical emergencies, yet we turn it on often and for prolonged periods of time as we worry about taxes, mortgages, oral presentations, the job market, marital problems, and the inevitability of death.

All humans respond bodily to stress, which is what enables us to mount a defense. Physiologically, the sympathetic nervous system is activated and more adrenaline is secreted, which increases the heart rate and heightens arousal. Then all at once the liver pours extra sugar into the bloodstream for energy, the pupils dilate to let in more light, breathing speeds up for more oxygen, perspiration increases to cool down the body, blood clots faster to heal wounds, saliva flow is inhibited, and digestion slows down to divert blood to the brain and skeletal muscles. Faced with threat, the body readies itself for action. But what, behaviorally, is the nature of the defense?

Many years ago, Walter Cannon (1932) described the body as prepared for "fight or flight." To be sure, men often lash out aggressively when under siege. But do women respond similarly? In her book *The Tending Instinct,* Shelley Taylor (2002) argues that while men frequently exhibit the classic fight-or-flight reaction to stress, women are more likely to exhibit a "tend-and-befriend" response. Prepared by evolution, in order to enhance the survival of their offspring, she argues, women adapt to hardship by caring for their children and seeking out others who might help. Consistent with this argument, studies have shown that, under stress, women become more nurturing than men—and more affiliative. Interestingly, animal and human studies show that when females are isolated, unsupported, and in social distress, they exhibit elevated levels of the hormone oxytocin, which, in turn, increases their tendency to seek out social contact (Taylor, 2012).

Like humans, zebras get ulcers.

FALSE

What Stress Does to the Heart

Coronary heart disease (CHD) is a narrowing of the blood vessels that carry oxygen and nutrients to the heart muscle. It is by far the leading cause of death in the United States among both men and women. According to the American Heart Association, an estimated 80 million American adults (one in three) suffer from CHD. For many, the result is a heart attack, which occurs when the precious blood supply to the heart is blocked. This causes an uncomfortable feeling of pressure, fullness, squeezing, or pain in the center of the chest—and sometimes sweating, dizziness, nausea, fainting, and shortness of breath. Every year, 735,000 Americans have a heart attack—525,000 for the first time. One-third do not survive (for more information, you can visit http://www.americanheart.org).

Several factors are known to increase the risk of CHD. The three most important are hypertension, or high blood pressure; cigarette smoking; and high cholesterol. (Other risk factors include a family history of CHD, a high-fat diet, obesity, and a lack of exercise.) People with one of the three major risk factors are twice as likely to develop CHD, those with two risk factors are three and a half times as likely, and those with all three are six times as likely. These statistics are compelling and should not be taken lightly. Combined, however, these variables account for fewer than half the known cases of CHD. What's missing from the equation is the fourth major risk factor: psychological stress—from work, from marital troubles, and from the kinds of negative life events that plague people who lack resources because they are poor (Gallo & Matthews, 2003; Hjemdahl et al., 2012; Matthews, 2005).

In 1956, cardiologists Meyer Friedman and Ray Rosenman were studying the relationship between cholesterol and coronary heart disease. After noticing that husbands were more likely than their wives to have CHD, they speculated that work-related stress might be the reason (at the time, most women did not work outside the home). To test this hypothesis, Friedman and Rosenman interviewed 3,000 healthy middle-aged men. Those who seemed the most hard-driving, competitive, impatient, time-conscious, and quick to anger were classified as having a **Type A personality** (also called coronary-prone behavior pattern—a more optimistic label since it is easier to change a behavior pattern than a personality). Roughly an equal number of men who were easygoing, relaxed, and laid back were classified as having a Type B personality. Interestingly, out of 258 men who went on to have heart attacks over the following nine years, 69% had been classified as Type A and only 31% as Type B (Rosenman et al., 1975).

The Type A, or coronary-prone, behavior pattern is made up of a cluster of traits, including competitive drive, a sense of time urgency, and a dangerous mix of anger, cynicism, and hostility (Friedman & Booth-Kewley 1987; Matthews, 1988). In interviews and written questionnaires, Type As report that they walk fast, talk fast, work late, interrupt speakers in mid-sentence, detest waiting in lines, race through yellow lights when they drive, lash out at others in frustration, strive to win at all costs, and save time by multitasking. In contrast, "there are those who breeze through the day as pleased as park rangers—despite having deadlines and kids and a broken down car and charity work and scowling Aunt Agnes living in the spare bedroom" (Carey, 1997, p. 75).

By the early 1980s, the influence of the Type A behavior pattern on CHD was widely accepted. A panel of distinguished scientists convened by the National Heart, Lung, and Blood Institute concluded that the Type A pattern was a risk factor for CHD, comparable to more traditional risks such as high blood pressure, smoking, high blood cholesterol, and obesity. But science, like time, moves on. Later studies of Type A and CHD obtained weaker results that varied depending on how Type A was measured and the kind of population that was studied (Matthews, 1988). Certainty about the bad effects of "hurry sickness" and "workaholism" began to crumble.

One issue that arose concerned measurement. Specifically, it turns out that the strength of the link between Type A behavior and coronary heart disease depends on how people are diagnosed. In the original study, Friedman and Rosenman classified men by means of a structured interview in which they could observe the men's verbal and nonverbal behavior. Afterward, however, many psychologists—in their haste to pursue this vital line of research—tried to identify Type A people using quick, easy-to-take questionnaires instead of time-consuming interviews. The questionnaires were not nearly as predictive. Apparently, the Type A pattern is more evident from a

Type A personality   A pattern of behavior characterized by extremes of competitive striving for achievement, a sense of time urgency, hostility, and aggression.

person's interview *behavior* (whether he or she constantly checks the time, speaks quickly, interrupts the interviewer, and makes restless fidgety movements) than from *self-reports*. When interviews are used to make the diagnosis, 70% of men who have CHD also have a Type A behavior pattern—compared with only 46% of those who are healthy (Miller et al., 1991).

The Type A behavior pattern was also refined conceptually, and a new line of inquiry sprang up. This research showed the primary toxic ingredient in CHD is *hostility*—as seen in people who are constantly angry, resentful, cynical, suspicious, and mistrustful of others (see Table 14.2). Apparently, people who are always in a negative emotional state and are quick to explode are besieged by stress. Because the heart is just a dumb pump and the blood vessels mere hoses, the health result is predictable: "The cardiovascular stress-response basically consists of making them work harder for a while, and if you do that on a regular basis, they will wear out, just like any pump or hoses you could buy at Sears" (Sapolsky, 1994, p. 42). In the long run, chronic hostility and anger can be lethal (Miller et al., 1996; Siegman & Smith, 1994). In fact, people who have lots of anger and suppress it are as likely to develop high blood pressure as those with anger who express it. It's the emotion that is toxic, not whether you hold it in or let it out (Everson-Rose & Lewis, 2005).

What else explains the connection between hostility and coronary heart disease? One possibility is that hostile people are less health-conscious—that they tend to smoke more, consume more caffeine and alcohol, exercise less, sleep less, and eat less healthy foods. They are also less likely to comply with advice from doctors (Leiker & Hailey, 1988; Siegler, 1994). A second explanation is that hostile people are physiologically reactive, so in tense social situations they exhibit greater increases in blood pressure, pulse rate, and adrenaline, a hormone that accelerates the buildup of fatty plaques on the artery walls, causing hardening of the arteries (Krantz & McCeney, 2002). In fact, research shows that people who are hostile exhibit more intense cardiovascular reactions not only during the event that makes them angry—say, being involved in a heated argument (Davis et al., 2000)—but long afterward as well, when asked to relive the event (Frederickson et al., 2000).

As a result of all this research and its many offshoots, a whole new subfield has grown that is sure to produce more valuable and practical insights in years to come (Hjemdahl et al., 2012; Matthews, 2013). For example, developmental researchers have found that growing up poor during childhood and adolescence increases the risk of cardiovascular disease in adulthood—sometimes even among those who elevated their socioeconomic status as adults (Galobardes et al., 2006). Focused on the link between positive states of mind and cardiovascular health, other researchers have found that such states as optimism, happiness, and the Japanese concept of *ikigai*—which means "having a life worth living"—are associated with a more healthful lifestyle and a reduction in the risk of cardiovascular disease (Boehm & Kubzansky, 2012). Testing a biopsychosocial model of stress responses, still others have found that orienting people to think of their physiological arousal during a stressful public speaking task as adaptive can have beneficial effects on their cardiovascular stress responses—a demonstration of "mind over matter" (Jamieson et al., 2012).

Research demonstrating psychological influences on CHD has broadened quite a bit from the initial studies of the Type A personality. In light of scientific interest in these intersections between the heart and the mind, this new subfield,

---

▲ **TABLE 14.2**

How "Hostile" Is Your Pattern of Behavior?

- When in the express checkout line at the supermarket, do you often count the items in the baskets of the people ahead of you to be sure they aren't over the limit?

- When an elevator doesn't come as quickly as it should, do your thoughts quickly focus on the inconsiderate behavior of the person on another floor who's holding it up?

- When someone criticizes you, do you quickly begin to feel annoyed?

- Do you frequently find yourself muttering at the television during a news broadcast?

- When you are held up in a slow line in traffic, do you quickly sense your heart pounding and your breath quickening?

Williams, R. (1993). *Anger kills.* New York: Times Books.

appropriately enough, has been called *psychocardiology* (Jordan et al., 2007)—or the practice of *cardiac psychology* (Allan & Fisher, 2011).

What Stress Does to the Immune System

Increasingly, it has become clear that psychological stress produces a wide range of effects on the body, including increases in the risk of chronic back pain, diabetes, appendicitis, upper respiratory infections, arthritis, herpes, gum disease, common colds, and some forms of cancer. How can stress have so broad a range of disabling effects? Answer: By compromising the body's immune system, the first line of defense against illness (Ader, 2007).

The **immune system** is a complex surveillance system that fights bacteria, viruses, parasites, fungi, and other "nonself" substances that invade the body. The system contains more than a trillion specialized white blood cells called *lymphocytes* that circulate throughout the bloodstream and secrete chemical antibodies. These shark-like search-and-destroy cells protect us 24 hours a day by patrolling the body and attacking trespassers. The immune system is also equipped with large scavenger cells that zero in on viruses and cancerous tumors. Serving as a "sixth sense" for foreign invaders, the immune system continually renews itself. For example, during the few seconds it took to read this sentence, your body produced 10 million new lymphocytes.

Today, many health psychologists specializing in **psychoneuroimmunology,** or **PNI** (*psycho* for the mind, *neuro* for the nervous system, and *immunology* for the immune system) study the connections among the brain, behavior, the immune system, health, and illness. Before we get into some of the fascinating results, let's pause for a moment and consider three of the methods these researchers use to spy on the operations of the immune system. One method is to take blood samples from animal or human participants exposed to varying degrees of stress and count the number of lymphocytes and other white blood cells circulating in the bloodstream. A second is to extract blood, add cancerous tumor cells to the mix, and measure the extent to which the natural killer cells destroy the tumors. A third method is to "challenge" the living organism by injecting a foreign agent into the skin and measuring the amount of swelling that arises at the site of the injection. The more swelling there is, the more potent the immune reaction is assumed to be (Ader, 2007; Daruna, 2012; Segerstrom, 2012).

It is now clear that stress can affect the immune system, at least temporarily. The medical community used to reject the idea outright, but not anymore. What changed? First, animal experiments showed that rats exposed to noise, overcrowding, or inescapable shocks, and primates separated from their social companions, exhibit a drop in immune cell activity compared with nonexposed animals (Coe, 1993; Moynihan & Ader, 1996). A link was also observed in humans. Intrigued by the fact that people often become sick and die shortly after they are widowed, R. W. Barthrop and others (1977) took blood samples from 26 men and women whose spouses had recently died. Compared with nonwidowed controls, these grief-stricken spouses exhibited a weakened immune response. This demonstration was the first of its kind.

Additional studies soon revealed weakened immune responses in NASA astronauts after their reentry into the atmosphere and splashdown, in people deprived of sleep for a prolonged period of time, in students in the midst of final exams, in men and women recently divorced or separated, in people caring for a family member with Alzheimer's disease, in snake-phobic people who are exposed to a live snake, and in workers who have just lost their jobs. Even in the laboratory,

immune system A biological surveillance system that detects and destroys "nonself" substances that invade the body.

psychoneuroimmunology (PNI) A subfield of psychology that examines the links among psychological factors, the brain and nervous system, and the immune system.

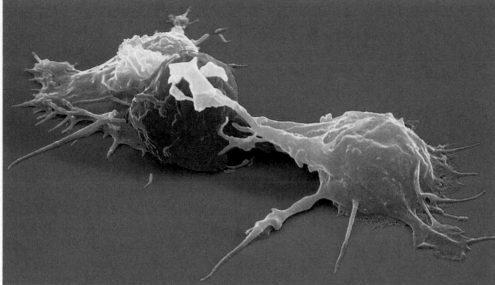

Eye of Science/Science Source

This color-enhanced microscopic image shows two "natural killer" immune cells (in yellow) engulfing and destroying a leukemia cell (in red). The human immune system contains more than a trillion specialized white blood cells.

people who are given complex arithmetic problems to solve or painful stimuli to tolerate exhibit changes in immune cell activity that last for one or more hours after the stress has subsided (Cohen & Herbert, 1996).

In an intriguing study, Arthur Stone and others (1994) paid 48 volunteers to take a harmless but novel protein pill every day for 12 weeks—a substance that would lead the immune system to respond by producing an antibody. Every day, the participants completed a diary in which they reported about their moods and experiences at work, at home, in financial matters, in leisure activities, and in social relationships with their friends, spouses, and children. The participants also gave daily saliva samples that were later used to measure the amount of antibody produced. The results were striking, as were their implications: The more positive events participants experienced in a given day, the more antibody was produced. The more negative events they experienced, the less antibody was produced.

In many ways, it is now clear that negative experiences and the emotions they elicit can weaken our immune system's ability to protect us from injuries, infections, and a wide range of illnesses (Kiecolt-Glaser et al., 2002). In an experiment that well illustrates this point in action, researchers brought healthy male and female volunteers into a clinical research laboratory, administered a battery of questionnaires, injected them with a needle in the arm, and then used a vacuum pump to raise a blister. In follow-up visits during the next eight days, the researchers measured the speed with which the wounds were healing. They found that participants whose questionnaires indicated that they had anger control problems—for example, losing their temper or boiling inside—secreted more of the stress hormone cortisol in response to the blistering procedure and the wound was slower to heal over time (Gouin et al., 2008).

Clearly, psychological states can "get into" the immune system. As illustrated in ● Figure 14.3, there are two possible ways this can happen. First, people who are under intense stress tend to smoke more, ingest more alcohol and drugs, sleep less, exercise less, and have poorer diets, behaviors that tend to compromise the immune system. For example, one study showed that when healthy male adults were kept awake from 3:00 to 7:00 a.m., immune cell activity diminished and returned to normal only after a full night of uninterrupted sleep (Irwin et al., 1994). Second, stress triggers the release of adrenaline and other stress hormones

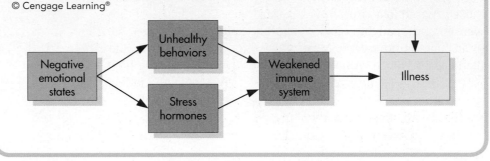

● **FIGURE 14.3**

Pathways from Stress to Illness

Hostility, stress, and other negative emotional states may cause illness in two ways: (1) by promoting unhealthful behaviors (more alcohol, less sleep, and so on) and (2) by triggering the release of hormones that weaken the immune system.
© Cengage Learning®

into the bloodstream, and these hormones tend to suppress immune cell activity. The result is a temporary lowering of the body's resistance (Cohen & Williamson, 1991). Whatever mechanism is at work, hundreds of studies show that the effects of stress on the immune system are complex. Brief stressors (such as a shark attack, a tough exam, or an injury) can enhance the immune response in ways that are adaptive in the short term, but chronic life stressors (such as a high-pressure job, a bad marriage, or a family illness) can suppress the immune response over time, putting the organism at risk (Segerstrom & Miller, 2004).

The adverse effect of chronic stress is particularly evident and alarming in women who experience high levels of stress during pregnancy. One research team found that pregnant women from diverse backgrounds deliver their infants sooner and at a lower birth weight when they had endured pregnancy-specific stress—say, because of health concerns, parenting concerns, relationship strains, and other related issues—than when they were not similarly stressed (Lobel et al., 2008). Other studies too are now contributing to a growing sense that a prospective mother's level of stress during pregnancy can have adverse effects on her health and increase the likelihood of a preterm birth and the risks associated with it (Christian, 2015; Dunkel Schetter, 2011).

The Links Between Stress and Illness

If chronic stress can weaken the immune system, are people who are stressed in life more likely to become sick? Might some people, for example, be psychologically more susceptible than others to catching the flu? Sheldon Cohen and his colleagues (1993) conducted a fascinating and elaborate study to help answer this question. They paid 420 volunteers to spend nine days in a medical experiment and risk exposure to a common cold virus. In the first two days, participants filled out several questionnaires, including one that measured recent stressful experiences in their lives. They also received a physical examination, including a blood test. Then, to simulate the person-to-person transmission of a virus, the researchers dropped a clear liquid solution into each participant's nose. Those randomly assigned to the control group received a placebo saline solution. Others, less fortunate, received a cold virus in doses that tend to produce illness rates of 20% to 60%.

For the next week, participants were quarantined in large apartments, where they were examined daily by a nurse who took their temperature, extracted mucus samples, and looked for signs of colds, such as sneezing, watery eyes, stuffy nose, and sore throat. (The participants did not realize it, but the nurse also kept track of the number of tissues they used.) All participants were healthy at the start of the project, and not a single one in the saline control group developed a cold. Yet among those exposed to a virus, 82% became infected, and 46% of those who were infected caught a cold, symptoms and all. A virus is a virus, so often there is no escape. Most interesting, however, is that life stress made a difference. Among those who became infected, high-stress participants were more likely to catch a cold than were the low-stress participants—53% compared with 40%. In short, people whose lives are filled with stress are particularly vulnerable to contagious illness.

In a follow-up of this experiment, Cohen and others (1998) interviewed 276 volunteers about recent life stressors, infected them with a cold virus, and then measured whether or not they developed a cold. They found that some types of stress were more toxic than others. Specifically, people who had endured *chronic* stressors that lasted for more than a month (like ongoing marital problems or unemployment) were more likely to catch a cold than those who had experienced *acute* short-term stress (such as a fight with a spouse or a reprimand at work). ● Figure 14.4 shows that the longer a stressor had lasted, the more likely a person was to catch a cold. Over time, stress breaks down the body's immune system.

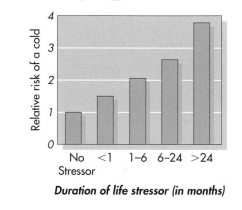

● **FIGURE 14.4**

Stress Duration and Illness

Two hundred seventy-six volunteers were interviewed about recent life stress, then infected with a cold virus. As shown above, the more months a stressor had lasted, the more likely a person was to catch the cold. Over time, stress breaks down the body's immune system.
Cohen, S., Frank, E., Doyle, W. J., Skoner, D. P., Rabin, B. S., & Gwaltney, J. M. (1998). Types of stressors that increase susceptibility to the common cold in healthy adults. *Health Psychology*, 17, 214–223.

Duration of life stressor (in months)

The effects of stress are clear. But it appears that certain personal characteristics and life circumstances can buffer people against the adverse health effects. In yet another viral challenge study, Cohen and his colleagues (2006) found that the more sociable people were in life, the more resistant they were to developing the lab-induced cold. Using the same method, they also found that the more social support people have in life—as measured, for example, by whether or not they said that someone had hugged them during the day—the less likely they were to become infected with the virus (Cohen et al., 2015).

These common-cold studies are important because they demonstrate not only that stress can weaken the immune system but also that it can leave us vulnerable to illness as a result. Does stress have similar effects on more serious illnesses? Can it, for example, hasten the spread of HIV/AIDS or cancer? In an early test of this hypothesis, Madeline Visintainer and others (1982) implanted tumorous cancer cells into laboratory rats, some of which were then exposed repeatedly to shocks they could not escape. After a month, 50% of the animals not shocked died of cancer. Yet relative to that baseline, the death rate climbed to 73% among those subjected to the inescapable shock. This study was among the first to show that psychological states such as a feeling of helplessness can influence the spread of cancer.

The growth of tumors in helpless white laboratory rats is interesting, but does the same principle apply to people? For obvious ethical reasons, researchers cannot fill humans with despair or inject lethal tumors into their bodies to test the cause-and-effect chain directly. But they can examine the medical records of people whose lives have been struck by tragedy. Investigations of this sort have revealed that cancer appears more often than normal in people who are prone to being in a negative emotional state (Sklar & Anisman, 1981). In one large-scale study, investigators looked up 2,000 male employees of the Western Electric Company in Chicago whose personalities had been assessed in 1958. At that time, test scores had shown that some of the men were low in self-esteem, unhappy, and depressed. The outcome: Some 20 years later, these men were more likely than their co-workers to have died of cancer (Persky et al., 1987).

Let's be clear about what these results mean. Nobody disputes that cancer is caused by genetic and other biological factors as well as exposure to toxic substances. But individuals who are clinically depressed or under great stress have weakened immune systems and a heightened susceptibility to infectious agents, which, in some cases, may result in a higher death rate from cancer and other diseases as well (Cohen et al., 2007; Kiecolt-Glaser, 2009; Miller et al., 2009).

For people who are married, divorce is a particularly gut-wrenching experience. In the United States, approximately 40% of first marriages end in divorce (Tejada-Vera & Sutton, 2009). The process is logistically, financially, socially, and emotionally disruptive. Most people manage the transition and adapt to the change (Amato, 2010). For some men and women, however, divorce is an acute stressor that can have long-lasting effects on their physical and mental health (Lucas, 2005; Sbarra & Nietert, 2009). Can divorce be fatal? In an ambitious meta-analysis, David Sbarra and his colleagues (2011) combined the results of 32 studies of 6.5 million men and women, 755,000 divorces, and 160,000 deaths in 11 countries (United States, Canada, Great Britain, Japan, Sweden, Germany, Finland, Norway, Russia, Israel, and the Netherlands). Consistent with prior research showing that divorce is associated with increased alcohol consumption, insomnia, and other negative health behaviors, the results were sobering. Relative to their married counterparts, people who were divorced at the start of the prospective studies were later 23% more likely to die early from all causes of death during follow-up assessments. This risk was most elevated for men and those younger than 65 years of age. On questions of cause and effect, and how to interpret these associations, more research is needed. What's clear, however, is that although most people are resilient, divorce is a stressful life event, frequently with adverse consequences for health, life, and well-being (Sbarra et al., 2015).

> Stress can weaken the heart, but it cannot affect the immune system.
>
> **FALSE**

Processes of Appraisal

Some 2,500 years ago, an anonymous author wrote an extraordinary poem about human suffering: the Book of Job. A pious and prosperous man when the poem opens, Job is soon beset by great calamities. He loses his property, his children, and his health. Job and his friends try to understand how these terrible things could happen. His friends argue that Job's plight must be a punishment sent by God and tell Job to repent. Because he believes that his sufferings far exceed any wrongdoing on his part, Job cannot accept this explanation. In despair, he doubts his capacity to withstand continued hardship and longs for death. But eventually Job finds strength and peace through trusting in God's will. From the perspective of the stress-and-coping model shown in Figure 14.1, Job and his friends were engaged in the process of appraisal. They considered possible explanations for Job's suffering and formed expectations about his ability to cope with his situation. These same themes are found in research on stress and coping.

■ Attributions and Explanatory Styles

Depression is a mood disorder characterized by feelings of sadness, pessimism, and apathy and slowed thought processes. Other symptoms include disturbances in sleeping and eating patterns and a reduced interest in sex. Every year, between

6% and 7% of the U.S. population experiences a major depression. Many more suffer from briefer, milder bouts with the blues. Sometimes called the "common cold" of psychological disorders, depression is universal and widespread (Gotlib & Hammen, 2009).

About twice as many women as men seek treatment for being depressed. During the course of a lifetime, an estimated 12% of American men and 21% of women will suffer from a major depression (Kessler et al., 1994). This sex difference first begins to appear in adolescence, although the disparity is a bit smaller in less developed nations (Culbertson, 1997). While depression has many causes, some researchers have focused on the attributions people make for the positive and negative events of their lives.

In 1975, Martin Seligman argued that depression results from a feeling of **learned helplessness**, the acquired expectation that one cannot control important outcomes. In a classic series of experiments, Seligman found that dogs strapped into a harness and exposed to painful electric shocks soon became passive and gave up trying to escape, even in new situations where escape was possible. In contrast, dogs that had not received uncontrollable shocks quickly learned the escape routine. As applied to humans, this finding suggested that prolonged exposure to uncontrollable events might similarly cause apathy, inactivity, a loss of motivation, and pessimism. In human research participants, those exposed to inescapable bursts of noise thus failed to protect themselves in a later situation where the noise could be easily avoided. Seligman was quick to note that people who are exposed to uncontrollable events become, in many ways, like depressed individuals: discouraged, pessimistic about the future, and lacking in initiative. Thus, he saw depression as a form of learned helplessness.

Lynn Abramson and her colleagues (1989) later proposed that depression is a state of *hopelessness* brought on by the negative self-attributions people make for failure. In fact, some people have a **depressive explanatory style**—a tendency to attribute bad events to factors that are internal rather than external ("It's my fault"), stable rather than unstable ("It will not change"), and global rather than specific ("It spreads to all parts of my life"). Research supports this proposition. Whether people are trying to explain social rejection, a sports defeat, low grades, or their inability to solve an experimenter's puzzle, those who are depressed are more likely than others to blame factors that are within the self, unlikely to change, and broad enough to impair other aspects of life. The result: hopelessness and despair (Abramson et al., 1989; Metalsky et al., 1993). This way of thinking may signal a vulnerability to future depression. Indeed, when Lauren Alloy and her colleagues (2006) measured the explanatory styles of nondepressed newly entered college students and then followed up on these students in their junior year, they found that those with a negative explanatory style in their first year—compared to classmates with a more positive style—were far more likely to have suffered from a major or minor depressive disorder (see ● Figure 14.5).

■ The Human Capacity for Resilience

Stress affects people differently, an observation that first led Suzanne Kobasa and her colleagues (1982) to wonder why some of us are more resilient than others in the face of stress. Kobasa studied some 200 business executives who were under

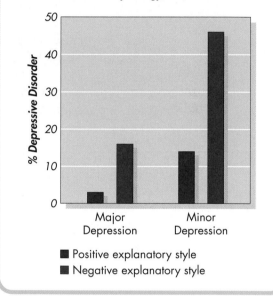

● **FIGURE 14.5**

Using Attributional Styles to Predict Depression

In this study, researchers measured the explanatory styles of first-year college students. As juniors two years later, those with a negative rather than positive style in their first year were more likely to suffer from a major or minor depressive disorder.
Alloy, L. B., Abramson, L. Y., Whitehouse, W. G., Hogan, M. E., Panzarella, C., & Rose, D. T. (2006). Prospective incidence of first onsets and recurrences of depression in individuals at high and low cognitive risk for depression. *Journal of Abnormal Psychology*, 115, 145–156.

■ Positive explanatory style
■ Negative explanatory style

learned helplessness   A phenomenon in which experience with an uncontrollable event creates passive behavior in the face of subsequent threats to well-being.

depressive explanatory style   A habitual tendency to attribute negative events to causes that are stable, global, and internal.

stress. Many said they were frequently sick, affirming the link between stress and illness; others had managed to stay healthy. The two groups were similar in terms of age, education, job status, income, and ethnic and religious background. But it was clear from various tests that they differed in their attitudes toward themselves, their jobs, and the people in their lives. Based on these differences, Kobasa identified a personality style that she called *hardiness* and concluded that hardy people have three characteristics: (1) commitment—a sense of purpose with regard to one's work, family, and other domains; (2) challenge—an openness to new experiences and a desire to embrace change; and (3) control—the belief that one has the power to influence important future outcomes.

Research supports the general point that resilience, or hardiness, serves as a buffer against stress (Funk, 1992). As you might expect, most people are exposed to at least one highly traumatic event during the course of a lifetime. Yet while many react with PTSD, others maintain their equilibrium and mental health: "Roughly 50 percent to 60 percent of the U.S. population is exposed to traumatic stress but only 5 percent to 10 percent develop PTSD" (Ozer et al., 2003, p. 54). Thus, Ann Masten (2001) and George Bonanno (2004) both argue that most human beings are highly resilient and exhibit a remarkable capacity to thrive in the wake of highly aversive events. In fact, Vicki Helgeson and her colleagues (2006) note that many people who confront heart attacks, cancer, divorce, war, family illness, and other traumas will often find ways to accept, benefit, and grow from the experience.

It's clear that people with different personalities cope with stress in different ways (Carver & Connor-Smith, 2010; Friedman & Kern, 2014). What are the specific characteristics of hardiness, resilience, and the ability to find benefit in loss? In two-part longitudinal interviews of Israeli Jews and Arabs during a period of intense terrorist and rocket attacks, Steven Hobfoll and others (2009) found that 64% of those interviewed experienced chronic or delayed distress, while 36% were mostly resistant to symptoms or completely resilient. Comparisons of the two groups showed that resilience in this population was more common among men than women; among Jews, who are in the majority of the population, than Arabs, an ethnic minority; and among people in general with more education, more money, and more social support from friends. These findings may be specific to the populations and events of Israel. More likely, however, they tell us something more generally about the characteristics of resilience. Let's see.

People often have feelings of self-efficacy in some life domains but not others.

MANKOFF

Robert Mankoff The New Yorker Collection/The Cartoon Bank

Self-Efficacy When Kobasa and others (1982) first identified hardiness as an adaptive trait, they—and other researchers—were quick to notice that the perception of control is an important ingredient (Florian et al., 1995). Early on, research showed that the harmful effects of crowding, noise, heat, and other stressors are reduced when people think they can exert control over these aspects of their environment (Glass & Singer, 1972). The perception of control is especially meaningful for people whose lives are regulated to a large extent by others. For example, elderly residents of nursing homes who were given more control over daily routines became happier and more active (Langer & Rodin, 1976; Schulz, 1976). Other studies showed that patients with heart disease, cancer, and AIDS were better adjusted emotionally when they felt that they could influence the course of their illness (Helgeson, 1992; Rodin, 1986; Thompson et al., 1993).

The perception of control refers to the expectation that our behaviors can produce satisfying outcomes. But people also differ in the extent to which they believe that they can perform these behaviors in the first place. These concepts seem related, but in fact they refer to different beliefs, both of which are necessary for us to feel that we control important outcomes in our lives (Skinner, 1996). According to Albert Bandura (1997), these latter expectations are based on feelings of competence, or **self-efficacy**. Some individuals may be generally more confident than others, says Bandura, but self-efficacy is a state of mind that varies from one specific task and situation to another. In other words, you may have high self-efficacy about meeting new people but not about raising your grades. Or you may have high self-efficacy about solving a math problem but not about writing a paper.

Research on self-efficacy has shown that the more of it you have at a particular task, the more likely you are to take on that task, try hard, persist in the face of failure, and succeed. The implications for mental and physical health are particularly striking. For example, individuals with high self-efficacy on health-related matters are more likely, if they want, to stay physically fit, abstain from alcohol, and tolerate the pain of arthritis, childbirth, and migraine headaches (Maddux, 1995)—and even to stop smoking (Baldwin et al., 2006) or lose weight (Linde et al., 2006).

At times, having a strong sense of self-efficacy may literally mean the difference between life and death. In one recent study, Urmimala Sarkar and colleagues (2009) recruited 1,024 heart disease patients and tracked their health over time. At the start of the study, all participants completed a Cardiac Self-Efficacy Scale in which they indicated how confident they were in their ability to maintain their usual activities, engage in sexual activity, and get aerobic exercise. Over the ensuing years, 124 of the patients were hospitalized and 235 died. When the patients were sorted into four categories of self-efficacy—from the highest scores to the lowest—the results showed that the higher their self-efficacy at the start of the study, the more likely they were to survive hospitalization years later (see ● Figure 14.6).

Dispositional Optimism The reason it's important to understand our attributions for past outcomes and our perceptions of control in present situations is

● **FIGURE 14.6**

Self-Efficacy: A Matter of Life and Death?

One thousand and twenty-four heart disease patients varying in "cardiac self-efficacy" were tracked over time. As shown, the higher their cardiac self-efficacy scores were at the start of the study, the more likely they were to survive hospitalization up to 78 months later.

From Sarkar, U., Ali, S., & Whooley, M. A., "Self-efficacy as a marker of cardiac function and predictor of heart failure hospitalization and mortality in patients with stable coronary heart disease: Findings from the Heart and Soul Study," *Health Psychology* vol 28 (pp. 166–173). Copyright © 2009 by the American Psychological Association. Reprinted by permission.

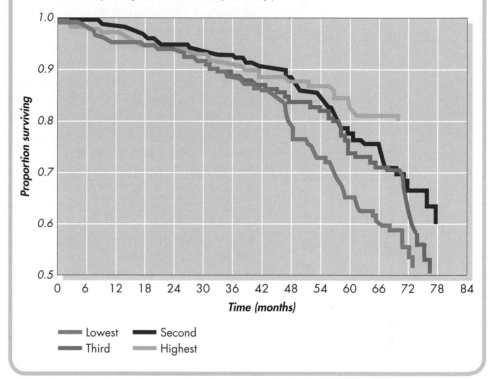

self-efficacy A person's belief that he or she is capable of the specific behavior required to produce a desired outcome in a given situation.

that both have implications for our outlook on the future. In *Learned Optimism,* Seligman (1991) argued that a generalized tendency to expect positive outcomes is characterized by a nondepressive explanatory style. According to Seligman, optimists tend to blame failure on factors that are external, temporary, and specific, and to credit success to factors that are internal, permanent, and global.

Research shows that although optimism is a personality characteristic that is partly inherited, it is powerfully shaped by personal experiences, social influences, and the course of development over the lifespan. Tracking nearly 10,000 adults over four years, for example, researchers found that optimism progressively increased from the age of 50 to 70, then declined (Chopik et al., 2015). Given our capacity for change, and in light of the advantages that optimism brings, Suzanne Segerstrom (2006a), like Seligman, thus notes that even pessimists can retrain themselves to think in optimistic ways.

Consider your own view of the future. Are you the eternal optimist who looks on the bright side and generally expects good things to happen, or do you tend to believe in Murphy's Law, that if something can go wrong it will? By asking questions such as these, Michael Scheier and Charles Carver (1985) categorized college students along this dimension and found that dispositional optimists reported fewer illness symptoms during the semester than did pessimists. Correlations between optimism and health are common and reliable. Studies have shown that optimists are more likely to take an active problem-focused approach in coping with stress (Nes & Segerstrom, 2006). As a result, they are more likely to complete a rehabilitation program for alcoholics; make a quicker, fuller recovery from coronary artery bypass surgery; and, among gay men concerned about AIDS, take a more active approach to the threat (Scheier & Carver, 1992). In a study of 1,306 healthy adult men from the Boston area, those reporting high levels of optimism rather than pessimism were half as likely to have coronary heart disease 10 years later (Kubzansky et al., 2001). In a study of 5,000 municipal workers in Finland, those who were high rather than low in optimism were healthier and missed fewer days from work if they were struck by a death or serious illness in the family over the next five years (Kivimäki et al., 2005).

In the course of a lifetime, everyone has setbacks. But an optimistic disposition may help us weather the storms better. There may well be long-term social and health implications. In one study, researchers collected personal essays written in the 1940s by 99 men who had just graduated from Harvard and then analyzed these materials to determine what each man's explanatory style had been in his youth. Thirty-five years later, those who in their youth had an optimistic outlook were healthier than their more pessimistic peers (Peterson et al., 1988).

How can these results be explained? There are two possibilities: one biological, the other behavioral. In research that supports a biological explanation, investigators analyzing blood samples have found that optimists exhibit a stronger immune response to stress than pessimists do (Kamen-Siegel et al., 1991; Segerstrom et al., 1998). In research that supports a behavioral explanation, Christopher Peterson and others (1988) scored the explanatory styles of 1,528 healthy young adults from questionnaires they had filled out between 1936 and 1940. Astonishingly, after 50 years, the optimists (specifically, those who had made global rather than specific attributions for good events) were less likely to have died an accidental, reckless, or violent death. In light of volumes of research on the subject, it is now clear that both explanations are correct (Scheier & Carver, 2014).

There's an old saying: "Where there's life, there's hope." Perhaps the opposite is also true: "Where there's hope, there's life." In a stunning illustration of this possibility, Susan Everson and others (1996) studied 2,428 middle-aged men

"The optimist proclaims we live in the best of all possible worlds; and the pessimist fears this is true."
—James Cabell

"The most important thing in illness is never to lose heart."
—Nikolai Lenin

in Finland. Based on the extent to which they agreed with two simple statements ("I feel that it is impossible to reach the goals I would like to strive for" and "The future seems hopeless, and I can't believe that things are changing for the better"), the men were initially classified as having a high, medium, or low sense of hopelessness. When the investigators checked the death records roughly six years later, they found that the more hopeless the men were at the start, the more likely they were to have died of various causes—even when the men were otherwise equated for their age and prior health status. Compared with those who were low in hopelessness, the highs were more than twice as likely to die from cancer and four times more likely to die of cardiovascular disease (see ● Figure 14.7). These results bring to life what Norman Cousins (1989) described as "the biology of hope," reminding us that "positive expectations can be self-fulfilling" (Peterson, 2000).

■ Pollyanna's Health

Pollyanna is the upbeat heroine created by American writer Eleanor Porter. Although she used to get bad press for her boundless belief that even the most ominous cloud has a bright silver lining, the research in this section suggests that Pollyanna should be an extraordinarily healthy person.

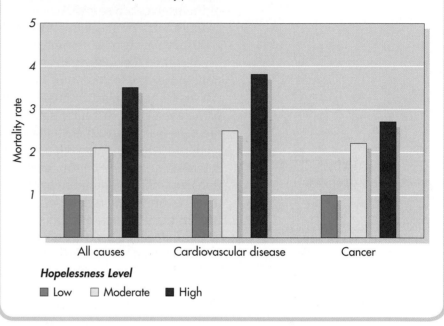

● FIGURE 14.7

Hopelessness and the Risk of Death

Among middle-aged men in Finland, those who were initially high rather than low in hopelessness were more likely to die within six years—overall, from cancer and from cardiovascular disease. Those who were moderate in hopelessness fell between the two extremes.

From Everson, S. A., et al., "Hopelessness and risk of mortality and incidence of myorcardial infarction and cancer," *Psychosomatic Medicine* vol 58 (pp. 113-121). Copyright © 1996 Wolters Kluwer Health. Reprinted by permission.

Let's be clear about what "positive psychology" research means. The mind is a powerful tool that can be used to hurt, heal, and protect the body (Ray, 2004). Still, no credible scientist believes that our attributions, perceptions of control, optimism, or other sources of resilience are the sole determinants of a long life. A positive outlook cannot guarantee future good health. So although we should appreciate the powers of the mind to influence the body, it would be a cruel mistake to blame victims of illness for having a bad outlook on life. In *The Self-Healing Personality*, Howard Friedman (1991) said, "We must walk a fine line between blaming patients on the one hand and absolving them of any role in their health on the other" (p. 96).

This sentiment animated a recent debate in the *Annals of Behavioral Medicine*. On one side, Lisa Aspinwall and Richard Tedeschi (2010a) advocated for the application of health psychology research to help in the fight against certain illnesses, notably coronary heart disease. James Coyne and Howard Tennen (2010) countered that no research supports exaggerated claims that positive thinking can prevent cancer and, indeed, that making such claims is irresponsible. In a rejoinder partially entitled "throwing the baby out with the bathwater," Aspinwall and Tedeschi (2010b) agreed that many dubious claims have found their way into the popular press. They were quick to point out, however, that the research evidence is strong when it comes to the psychological influences on coronary heart disease and certain other conditions and that even if positive thinking cannot cure cancer or extend life, the possible benefits to a patient's quality of life and emotional well-being should not be overlooked. In their words, "it is irresponsible to ignore, denigrate, or deny the reality of the experiences of people who report benefits and growth while enduring life-threatening illnesses and other traumas, and to forego the opportunity to find ways to facilitate and enhance these experiences."

It's also important to recognize that there may be drawbacks to positive thinking, especially if it leads us to see ourselves and the events around us in ways that are grossly unrealistic. As we saw in Chapter 3, people with overly positive views of themselves are sometimes disliked by their friends and seen as boastful, inconsiderate, and oversensitive to criticism (Colvin et al., 1995; Heatherton & Vohs, 2000). It may also be detrimental for people to believe that they have control over events when they do not. In a study of patients suffering from a loss of kidney function, those who felt that they had control over their health became more depressed, not less, after having a transplant that failed (Christensen et al., 1991). In a study of first-year law students, optimists exhibited a stronger immune response than did pessimists when their transition to law school was easy but a weaker immune response when the transition was difficult (Segerstrom, 2006b). Faced with some setbacks, a sense of control can help us bounce back. But setting control expectations too high can do more harm than good in the wake of negative outcomes.

This brings us back to Job. At the end of this biblical account, Job recovers his health, his property, and his family prosperity. He does not, however, regain the sense of personal control and optimism that he enjoyed prior to being struck by calamity. Instead, Job's hard-won serenity is based on his belief that life has meaning and purpose. Pollyanna has her charm, but Job is a hero of the human condition.

> When it comes to physical health, research does not support popular beliefs about the power of positive thinking.
>
> **FALSE**

Ways of Coping With Stress

Leaving home. Studying for final exams. Preparing for an athletic competition. Breaking up with a boyfriend or girlfriend. Working long nights—or not at all. Waiting on long security lines at the airport. Having children. Raising children. Struggling to meet the deadline to complete a textbook. Stress is inevitable. No one can prevent it. The best we can do is to minimize its harmful effects on our health. Depending on the person and the stressor, people can cope by trying to solve the problem, talking to friends, inviting distractions, sleeping or drinking too much to escape, praying, brooding, venting, lashing out, laughing it off, getting outside help, pretending that all is well—or freaking out. Combining all psychological theories and research, it appears that there are about 400 specific ways to cope with stress (Skinner et al., 2003). In a recent nationwide survey, men and women were asked about how they manage the stress in their lives. As you can see in ● Figure 14.8, people cope in a wide variety of ways—some healthy, others not so much (American Psychological Association, 2015).

By grouping specific strategies that are similar, researchers study different general types of coping. Based on the self-reports of large numbers of people, Charles Carver and others (1989) constructed a multidimensional questionnaire they called COPE that measures 12 distinct methods of coping (see Table 14.3).

Noting that people can use different coping strategies, Lazarus and Folkman (1984) distinguished two general types. The first is **problem-focused coping**, which refers to cognitive and behavioral efforts to reduce stress by overcoming

> **problem-focused coping** Cognitive and behavioral efforts to alter a stressful situation.

● **FIGURE 14.8**

How Americans Manage Stress

There is no single way to manage stress. When American men and women were asked to indicate how they do it, the list that emerged was quite varied. Here are the top ten most cited responses.

From American Psychological Association (February 4, 2015). *Stress in America.* Copyright © 2015 by the American Psychological Association. Reprinted by permission.

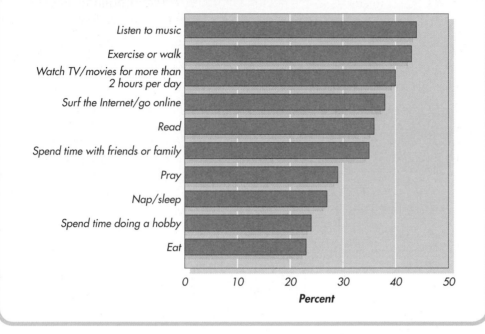

the source of the problem. Trouble in school? Study harder, hire a tutor, or reduce your workload. Marriage on the rocks? Talk it out or see a counselor. Problem finding work? Look for an internship, expand your search, or try a new location. As indicated in several of the items in Table 14.3, the goal is to attack the source of stress. A second approach is **emotion-focused coping**, which consists of efforts to manage our emotional reactions to stressors rather than trying to change the stressors themselves. If you struggle at school, at work, or in a relationship, you can keep a stiff upper lip, accept what is happening, tune out, or vent your emotions. According to Lazarus and Folkman, we tend to take an active, problem-focused approach when we think we can overcome a stressor but fall back on an emotion-focused approach when we perceive the problem to be out of our control. Lisa Aspinwall and Shelley Taylor (1997) note that there is a third alternative: **proactive coping**, which consists of up-front efforts to ward off or modify the onset of a stressful event. As we'll see, coping is an ongoing process by which we try to prevent—not just react to—life's bumps and bruises.

■ Problem-Focused Coping

Problem-focused coping seems like the prime candidate for a starring role in the war against stress. Surely our most active and assertive efforts are associated with better health (Aspinwall & Taylor, 1992). And clearly we often benefit from confronting a stressor head on rather than avoiding it. Consider something we all are guilty of on occasion: procrastination—a purposeful delay in beginning

emotion-focused coping
Cognitive and behavioral efforts to reduce the distress produced by a stressful situation.

proactive coping   Up-front efforts to ward off or modify the onset of a stressful event.

▲ **TABLE 14.3**

Ways of Coping with Stress

These statements describe some coping strategies that people say they use. The strategies are listed in order from those that are relatively common to those that are less common.

Planning/Active Coping

- I try to come up with a strategy about what to do.
- I take additional action to try to get rid of the problem.

Positive Reinterpretation

- I look for something good in what is happening.
- I try to make it seem more positive.

Acceptance

- I learn to live with it.
- I accept that this has happened and can't be changed.

Seeking Social Support

- I talk to someone about how I feel.
- I ask people who had similar experiences what they did.

Restraint Coping

- I force myself to wait for the right time to do something.
- I make sure not to make matters worse by acting too soon.

Focusing on/Venting Emotions

- I get upset and let my emotions out.
- I let my feelings out.

Suppression of Competing Activities

- I put aside other activities to concentrate on this.
- If necessary I let other things slide a little.

Mental Disengagement

- I turn to work . . . to take my mind off things.
- I go to the movies or watch TV, to think about it less.

Turning to Religion

- I seek God's help.
- I try to find comfort in my religion.

Behavioral Disengagement

- I give up the attempt to get what I want.
- I admit to myself that I can't deal with it.

Denial

- I refuse to believe that it has happened.
- I pretend that it hasn't really happened.

Alcohol and Drugs

- I drink alcohol or take drugs to think about it less.

Carver, C. S., Scheier, M. F., & Weintraub, J. K. (1989). Assessing coping strategies: A theoretically based approach. *Journal of Personality and Social Psychology, 56,* 267–283.

or completing a task, often accompanied by feelings of discomfort (Ferrari et al., 1995). In a longitudinal study of college students enrolled in a health psychology class, Dianne Tice and Roy Baumeister (1997) administered a questionnaire at the start of the semester that assesses the extent to which people tend to procrastinate. True to their word, those students who were classified from their test scores as procrastinators turned in their term papers later than did their classmates and received lower grades. More interesting was the relationship to daily reports of stress and physical health. Early on, while procrastinators were in the "putting it off" stage of their projects, they were relatively stress-free compared with others. Later in the semester, however, as the deadline neared and passed, procrastinators were under greater stress and reported having more symptoms of illness. In the end, the short-term benefits of avoidance were outweighed by the long-term costs.

In dealing with essential tasks, it is better to confront and control than to avoid. But is this always a beneficial approach? There are two reasons why sometimes it is not. First, to exert control a person must stay vigilant, alert, and actively engaged, which is physiologically taxing (Light & Obrist, 1980). Second, a controlling orientation can cause problems if it leads us to develop an overcontrolling, stress-inducing, Type A pattern of behavior—whether that means always having the last word in an argument, "driving" from the back seat of a car, or planning every last detail of a leisurely vacation. Not all events are within our control or important enough to worry about. There are times when it's better to just let go (Friedland et al., 1992; Wright et al., 1990).

When we use the word *control,* we usually have in mind active efforts to manage something: win an argument, work out a marital problem, or solve a problem at work. But control comes in many guises. Knowledge, for instance, is a form of control. Knowing why something happens increases your chance of making sure it goes your way—if not now, then the next time. Sometimes we can cope effectively with tragedies such as technological disasters, terrorist acts, and spousal abuse by blaming the perpetrators for their actions. In these situations, holding others responsible can force a helpful response, such as financial compensation or police protection.

But what about self-blame? Is it ever adaptive to cope with a bad situation by blaming oneself? According to Ronnie Janoff-Bulman (1979), it depends on whether you blame your behavior or yourself as a person. People can change their own behavior, she notes, so behavioral self-blame paves the way for control in an effort to reduce current stresses or avoid future ones. But it is not similarly adaptive, she warns, to blame your own enduring personal characteristics, which are harder to change. Janoff-Bulman (1992) later amended this hypothesis, noting that it may take time to realize the mental health benefits of behavioral self-blame. This prediction was tested in studies of how female rape victims adjust to the trauma. Consistently, both behavioral and characterological self-blame were associated with an increase in distress. Contrary to prediction, rape victims who blame their own behavior for what happened do *not* cope better than those who blame their character (Frazier & Schauben, 1994; Hall et al., 2003).

In light of past research, Patricia Frazier (2003) offers a somewhat more complex perspective on blame, control, and coping. Clearly, she notes, it can be adaptive for the victims of rape and other traumas to own a sense of future control (Carver et al., 2000; Frazier et al., 2004). But noting that behavioral self-blame for a past trauma does not guarantee the prevention of future trauma, she distinguishes past, present, and future control—and what each implies about the dreaded possibility of a future recurrence. In a longitudinal study of female rape victims appearing in an emergency room, she assessed attributions of blame and responsibility, perceptions of control, and feelings of distress periodically from two weeks up to a year later. Overall, women blamed the rapist more than they blamed themselves, a tendency that strengthened over time. As in other studies, however, those who assigned more blame either to the rapist or to themselves were more distressed. Apparently, the problem with behavioral self-blame, once thought to be adaptive, is that it did not engender feelings of future safety. In this regard, the most useful sense of control was over the *present:* Women who believed that they could help themselves get better and facilitate their own recovery were more optimistic about the future and the least distressed.

There is one more complicating factor when it comes to the attributions of blame that people make when bad things happen to them. In a study involving 5,991 middle-school boys and girls from 26 public schools, Hannah Schacter and Jaana Juvonen (2015) presented participants with vignettes in which they were asked to imagine that they were humiliated in front of peers at school. Afterward, they were asked a number of attribution questions concerning the extent to which they would blame themselves ("my fault and cannot change it") or their behavior in that situation ("I should have been more careful"). Interestingly, the attributions made depended on the broader context of their own school. In schools where bullying levels were high, participants blamed their behavior; in schools were bullying was not common, however, where they could not as easily blame the situation, they blamed themselves. These findings present this counterintuitive implication: "When schools manage to decrease bullying, the few who remain victimized need additional support to prevent more maladaptive forms of self-blame" (p. 841).

■ Emotion-Focused Coping

Stress is by definition an unpleasant and arousing experience that fills people with negative and unhealthy emotions. Do some coping mechanisms focus on this emotional aspect of adversity?

Positive Emotions: Building Blocks of Emotion-Focused Coping Following the terrorist attacks of 9/11, many Americans reported in public opinion polls that they cried and felt sad, angry, fearful, anxious, and disgusted. Under conditions so tragic, one would not also expect people to feel positive emotions. But it is possible for positive and negative feelings to coexist—as when we find consolation in loss or a silver lining in the dense gray clouds (Folkman & Moskowitz, 2000).

People who cope well and are resilient tend to experience positive emotions in the face of stress—a common capacity that Ann Masten (2001) termed "ordinary magic." How is it that positive emotions work like magic? On the basis of numerous studies, Barbara Frederickson (2009) offers a two-step theory of why our fleeting but pleasant positive emotions are so effective. First, she notes that positive emotions help people to *broaden* their outlook in times of stress so they can cope with adversity—in part by providing a welcome distraction from the anger, fear, and other negative states that increase blood pressure and arousal and narrow the focusing of attention.

To test the hypothesis that positive emotion is adaptive in this way, Frederickson and colleagues (2003) contacted 46 college students days after September 11, 2001, who had previously taken part in a study on stress and coping. Across the board, the students felt angry, sad, and fearful; they also felt scorn toward the attackers. But many also expressed positive feelings of gratitude (to be alive), love (a renewed appreciation for loved ones), and interest (in unfolding world events). In fact, those who scored as most resilient before the crisis were later the most likely to have these positive emotions and least likely to suffer depression after the crisis. By coping with positive emotions in one situation after another, Frederickson (2009) suggests, people over time *build* personal resources—learning, for example, how to stay calm, focused, in control, and capable of giving and receiving emotional support.

Positive emotions may serve the coping process better than negative emotions, but are all positive emotions equally adaptive? Maybe not. Sarah Pressman and Sheldon Cohen (2012) analyzed the language used by 88 influential deceased psychologists in their writings. Specifically, they categorized and counted the words used that were positive or negative and high or low in arousal. These distinctions resulted in four types of emotion words: positive-high arousal (*lively, enthusiastic, energetic*) positive-low arousal (*calm, peaceful, content*), negative-high arousal (*tense, afraid, angry*), and negative-low arousal (*lonely, drowsy, tired*). On average, the psychologists sampled had lived an average of 79 years. Even after controlling for the possible effects of sex, year of birth, and other factors, Pressman and Cohen found that the more positive-high arousal emotion words the psychologists had used in their writings, the longer they lived—by an average of five years. The use of positive-low arousal emotion words was not similarly associated with longevity.

Research on positive emotions reminds us not to overintellectualize the coping process and underestimate the value of emotion-focused coping. Look back at Table 14.3, and you will see many instances of emotion-focused coping, such as acceptance, denial, focusing on or venting of emotions, disengaging mentally and behaviorally, or turning to religion. By and large, we will see that there are two other general ways to cope with the emotional aspects of stress: shutting down and opening up. Let's examine the health effects of each of these strategies.

Shutting Down: Suppressing Unwanted Thoughts   Often we react to stress by shutting down and trying to deny or suppress the unpleasant thoughts and feelings. One specific form of avoidance coping is distraction. Consider what happens when terrorists take innocent victims hostage. Police surround the site and negotiations begin. Are certain ways of coping with this frightening situation particularly effective? To help answer this question, 57 airline employees voluntarily participated in a remarkable training exercise conducted by the Special Operations and Research Staff of the FBI Academy (Auerbach et al., 1994; Strentz & Auerbach, 1988). Some volunteers were trained in problem-focused coping techniques such as helping each other, interacting with their captors, and gathering intelligence. Others were trained in emotion-focused techniques designed to decrease anxiety—such as distraction, deep breathing, and muscle relaxation. Volunteers in a control condition did not receive any specific instruction.

After the training session, the volunteers were "abducted" by FBI agents acting as terrorists. Automatic weapons were fired (with blanks), and bloody injuries were simulated. The volunteers were then "held captive" in one room and isolated by having pillowcases placed over their heads. A few cooperative "hostages" were released. Four days later, other FBI agents "stormed" the building and "rescued" the remaining hostages. The exercise was conducted in a realistic manner, and the volunteers found it exceedingly stressful. Those who had been instructed in anxiety-management techniques coped better than those given problem-solving training or no training at all. In this kind of situation, where individuals have little actual control over events, distraction and other emotion-focused techniques were more effective in reducing distress than were problem-focused efforts to exert control.

Although potentially effective, suppression of unwanted thoughts from awareness can also have a peculiar, paradoxical effect. As described in Chapter 3, Daniel Wegner (1997) conducted a series of studies in which he told people not to think of a white bear and found that they could not then keep the image from popping to mind. What's more, he found that among participants who were permitted later to think about the bear, those who had earlier tried to suppress the image were unusually preoccupied with it, providing evidence of a rebound effect. Sometimes, the harder you try not to think about something, the less likely you are to succeed (Wegner et al., 1998). The solution: focused distraction. When participants were told to imagine a tiny red Volkswagen every time the forbidden bear intruded into consciousness, the rebound effect vanished (Wenzlaff & Wegner, 2000).

What do white bears and red cars have to do with coping? A lot. When people try to block stressful thoughts from awareness, the problem may worsen. That's where focused distraction comes in. In a study of pain tolerance, Delia Cioffi and James Holloway (1993) had people put a hand into a bucket of ice-cold water and keep it there until they could no longer bear the pain. One group was instructed to avoid thinking about the sensation. A second group was told to form a mental picture of their home. Afterward, those who had coped through suppression were slower to recover from the pain than were those who had used focused self-distraction. To manage stress—whether it's caused by physical pain, a strained romance, final exams, or problems at work—distraction ("think about lying on the beach") is a better coping strategy than mere suppression ("don't think about the pain").

Keeping secrets and holding in strong emotions may also be physically taxing. In the laboratory, James Gross and Robert Levenson (1997) showed female students funny, sad, and neutral films. Half the time, they told the students to not let their feelings show. From a hidden camera, videotapes confirmed that when they were asked to conceal their feelings, the students were less expressive. But physiological recordings revealed that as they watched the funny and sad films, the students exhibited a greater cardiovascular response when they tried to inhibit their feelings than when they did not. Physiologically, the effort to suppress the display of emotion backfired. Also in the laboratory, Michael Slepian and his colleagues (2012) found that people who harbored and recall important secrets (for example, concerning cheating or sexual orientation) perceived distances to be farther, hills to be steeper, and physical tasks to require more effort—all suggesting that "as with physical burdens, secrets weigh people down" (p. 619).

A real-life study by Steve Cole and his colleagues (1996) pushes this point a profound step further. These investigators identified 80 gay men in the Los Angeles area who were newly infected with the HIV virus but had no symptoms, administered various psychological tests, and monitored their progress every six months for nine years. They found that in men who were partly "in the closet"—compared with those who were open about their homosexuality—the infection spread more rapidly, causing them to die sooner. This provocative correlation does not prove that "coming out" is healthier than "staying in." In a controlled laboratory experiment, however, participants who were instructed to suppress rather than express turbulent emotional thoughts exhibited a temporary decrease in the activity of certain immune cells (Petrie et al., 1998). At least in Western cultures that encourage self-expression, actively concealing your innermost thoughts and feelings can be hazardous to your health.

Opening Up: Confronting One's Demons The research just described suggests that just as shutting down can sometimes have benefits, so too can the opposite form of coping: opening up. There are two aspects to this emotional means of coping with stress. The first is acknowledging and understanding our emotional reactions to important events; the second is expressing these inner feelings to ourselves and others (Stanton et al., 2000).

According to James Pennebaker (1997), psychotherapy, self-help groups, and various religious rituals have something in common: All offer a chance for people to confide in someone, spill their guts, confess, and talk freely about their troubles—maybe for the first time. To test for the healing power of opening up, Pennebaker conducted a series of controlled studies in which he brought college students into a laboratory and asked them to talk into a tape recorder or write for 20 minutes either about past traumas or trivial daily events. While speaking or writing, the students were upset and physiologically aroused. Many tearfully recounted accidents, failures, instances of physical or sexual abuse, loneliness, the death or divorce of their parents, shattered relationships, and their fears about the future. Soon these students felt better than ever. Pennebaker found that when they opened up, their systolic blood pressure levels rose during the disclosures but then later dipped below their preexperiment levels. The students even exhibited a decline in the number of times they visited the campus health center over the next six months. Other studies, too, have shown that keeping personal secrets can be stressful and that "letting it out" and "getting it off your chest" can have true therapeutic effects on mental and physical health. These effects are especially strong when participants are comfortable with disclosure, when the disclosures are made across multiple sessions, and when the events being described are recent and traumatic (Frattaroli, 2006; Lepore & Smyth, 2002).

It appears that confession may be good for the body as well as the soul. But why does it help to open up? Why do *you* sometimes feel the need to talk out your problems? One possibility, recognized a full century ago by Sigmund Freud, is that the experience provides a much-needed *catharsis,* a discharge of tension—like taking the lid off a boiling pot of water to slow the boiling. People who experience trauma—whether it's a bout with cancer, death, an accident, a natural disaster, or exposure to violence—are often haunted by intrusive images of their stressor that pop to mind and cannot be stopped. In these cases, disclosure may bring emotional closure. Another explanation for the benefits of opening up, one favored by Pennebaker, is that talking about a problem can help you to sort out your thoughts, understand the problem better, and gain *insight,* in cognitive terms. Whatever the reason, it's clear that opening up, perhaps to someone else, can be therapeutic—provided that the listener can be trusted. This last point is critical: Despite the potential for gain, opening up can also cause great distress when the people we confide in react with rejection or unwanted advice or, worse, betray what was said to others (Kelly & McKillop, 1996).

Indicating the importance of the "to whom" part of opening up, Stephen Lepore and colleagues (2000) exposed college students to disturbing Nazi Holocaust images. Afterward, the students were randomly divided into groups and asked to talk about their reactions to themselves while alone in a room, to a validating confederate who smiled and agreed, or to an invalidating confederate who avoided eye contact and disagreed. An additional group was given no opportunity to talk. As reported two days later, students who talked alone or to a validating confederate—compared to those who did not talk—said they had fewer intrusive Holocaust thoughts in the intervening period and were less stressed when reexposed to the original images. However, for students who talked to an invalidating confederate the benefits of opening up were muted. This finding supports our earlier conclusion: It is better to discuss one's demons than to conceal them—but the extent of the benefit depends on whether the people we talk to are supportive. It's no wonder, then, that people are more likely to join mutual support groups, both live and online, when they suffer from stigmatizing disorders such as AIDS, alcoholism, breast cancer, and prostate cancer than when they have less embarrassing but equally toxic illnesses such as heart disease and diabetes (Davison et al., 2000).

Self-Focus: Getting Trapped Versus Getting Out   In Chapter 3, we saw that people spend little time actually thinking about the self—and when they do, they wish they were doing something else (Csikszentmihalyi & Figurski, 1982). According to self-awareness theory, self-focus brings out our personal shortcomings the way staring in a mirror draws our attention to every blemish on the face. It comes as no surprise, then, that self-focus seems to intensify some of the most undesirable consequences of emotion-focused coping. Here's the script.

The state of self-awareness can be induced in us by external stimuli such as mirrors, cameras, and audiences. Mood, too, plays a role. Peter Salovey (1992) found that, compared with a neutral mood state, both positive and negative moods increase awareness of the self. Thus, when a stressful event occurs, the negative feelings that arise magnify self-focus. What happens next depends on a person's self-esteem, as people with a negative self-concept experience more negative moods when self-focused than do those with a positive self-concept

Stan Honda/AFP/Getty Images

Healthy distractions such as exercise are a good way to break out of the trap of self-focused depression.

(Sedikides, 1992). The end result is a self-perpetuating feedback loop: Being in a bad mood triggers self-focus, which in people with low self-esteem further worsens the mood. This vicious circle forms the basis for a self-focusing model of depression according to which coping with stress by attending to your own feelings only makes things worse (Mor & Winquist, 2002; Pyszczynski & Greenberg, 1992).

A great deal of research has shown that individuals who respond to distress by rumination and repetitive thought—by constantly fixating on themselves, their feelings, their symptoms, and the source of their distress—are more likely to become anxious and depressed than those who allow themselves to be distracted (Nolen-Hoeksema, 1991; Nolen-Hoeksema et al., 2008). Although some types of self-focus may be useful, as when people react to a stressful event by focusing on the positives or worrying in ways that lead them to plan, problem solve, and alter their expectations in adaptive ways, the adverse effects are clear (Watkins, 2008). Over the years, and across a range of different cultures, research has also shown that girls and women in particular have a tendency to ruminate, confront their negative feelings, and seek treatment for being depressed, while boys and men resort to alcohol and other drugs, physical activity, antisocial behavior, and other means of distraction. As a general rule, it appears that women who are upset tend to brood, while men who are upset are more likely to act out (Culbertson, 1997; Nolen-Hoeksema & Girgus, 1994).

Thankfully, there are healthier alternatives. To redirect attention away from the self, it helps to become absorbed in an activity such as aerobic exercise, gardening, writing, or reading a book. Whatever the activity, it should be difficult, demanding, and fully engaging. Ralph Erber and Abraham Tesser (1992) found that people who were in a bad mood felt better after performing a difficult task than a simple task or none at all. Difficult tasks, it appears, can "absorb" a bad mood. Meditation—which calls on you to focus your attention on a chosen non-self object—can have positive effects for the same reason (Lutz et al., 2008). Referring to techniques of focused relaxation that he had developed, Cardiologist Herbert Benson recommended that people sit comfortably, close their eyes, relax the muscles, breathe deeply, and silently utter some word over and over again. Says Benson (1993), "By practicing two basic steps—the repetition of a sound, word, phrase, prayer, or muscular activity; and a passive return to the repetition whenever distracting thoughts recur—you can trigger a series of physiological changes that offer protection against stress" (p. 256).

■ Proactive Coping

According to Lisa Aspinwall and Shelley Taylor (1997), people often benefit from *proactive coping*, which consists of up-front efforts to ward off or modify the onset of a stressful event. As illustrated in ● Figure 14.9, coping can be seen as an ongoing process by which we try to prevent as well as react to the bumps and bruises of daily life. Also as shown, the first line of defense involves the accumulation of resources—personal, financial, social, and otherwise—that can later, if needed, serve as a buffer against stress. In this section, we look at two possible resources: social support and religion.

Social Support   If the world is crashing down around you, what do you do? Do you try to stop it? Do you try to manage your emotions? Or do you try to get help from others? Throughout this book, we have seen that no man or woman is an island, that human beings are social animals, that people need people, and that to get by you need a little help from friends. But do our social nature and our connections to others have anything to do with health? Do close family ties, lovers, buddies, on-line support groups, and relationships at work serve as a buffer against stress? The answer is yes. The evidence is now overwhelming that **social support** has therapeutic effects on our physical and psychological well-being (Cohen, 2004; Uchino, 2009).

David Spiegel, of Stanford University's School of Medicine, came to appreciate the value of social connections many years ago when he organized support groups for women with advanced breast cancer. The groups met weekly in 90-minute sessions to laugh, cry, share stories, and discuss ways of coping. Spiegel had fully expected the women to benefit emotionally from the experience. But he found something else he did not expect: These women lived an average of 18 months longer than did similar others who did not attend the groups. According to Spiegel (1993), "The added survival time was longer than any medication or other known medical treatment could be expected to provide for women with breast cancer so far advanced" (pp. 331–332).

Similar discoveries were then made by other researchers. In one study, Lisa Berkman and Leonard Syme (1979) surveyed 7,000 residents of Alameda County, California, and conducted a 9-year follow-up of mortality rates. They found that the more social contacts people had, the longer they lived. This was true of both men and women, young and old, rich and poor, and people from all racial and ethnic backgrounds. James House and others (1988) studied 2,754 adults interviewed during visits to their doctors. He found that the most socially active men were two to three times less likely to die within 9 to 12 years than others of similar age who

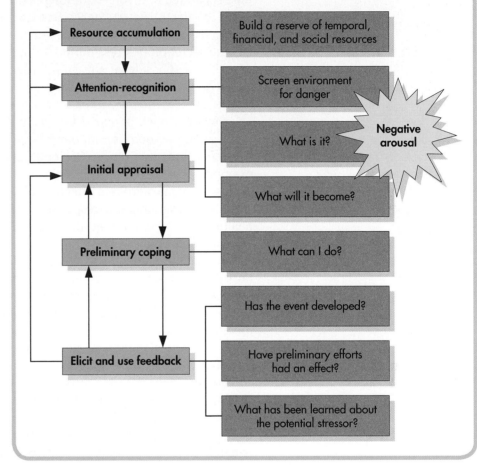

● **FIGURE 14.9**

Aspinwall and Taylor's Model of Proactive Coping

Coping can be seen as an ongoing, multistep process by which people try to prevent, not just react to, life's daily stressors.

From Aspinwall and Taylor, "A stitch in time: Self-regulation and proactive coping," *Psychological Bulletin* vol 121 (pp. 417–436). Copyright © 1997 by the American Psychological Association. Reprinted by permission.

social support   The helpful coping resources provided by friends and other people.

were more isolated. According to House, social isolation was statistically just as predictive of an early death as smoking or high cholesterol.

Research findings like these are common. For example, married people are more likely than those who are single, divorced, or widowed to survive cancer for five years (Taylor, 1990), gay men infected with HIV are less likely to contemplate suicide if they have close ties than if they do not (Schneider et al., 1991), people who have a heart attack are less likely to have a second one if they live with someone than if they live alone (Case et al., 1992), and people, once married, who are then separated or divorced for long periods of time, are at an increased risk of early death (Sbarra & Nietert, 2009). Based on this type of research, Bert Uchino (2006) concluded that in times of stress, having social support lowers blood pressure, lessens the secretion of stress hormones, and strengthens immune responses.

On the flip side of the coin, research shows that people who are socially isolated, as measured objectively, or feeling lonely, as measured by their own self-reports, are at risk to exhibit more behavioral problems (such as smoking, an inactive "couch potato" lifestyle, and poorer sleep) and biological risk factors (such as high blood pressure and weaker immune functions). The net effect is a shortened life expectancy (Cacioppo et al., 2015; Holt-Lunstad et al., 2015). For example, a study of first-year college students showed that feelings of loneliness during the semester were linked to elevated levels of the stress hormone cortisol and a weakened immune response to a flu shot they had received at the university health clinic (Pressman et al., 2005). There is no doubt about it: Being isolated from other people can be hazardous to your health.

The health value of social support has been amply demonstrated in the laboratory. In one experiment, female college students were instructed to immerse one hand into an ice-water container for up to three minutes. Every 20 seconds, they rated how much they felt; overall pain tolerance was measured by how long they lasted. Throughout the session, their blood pressure and heart rate were recorded. Levels of cortisol, a stress hormone, were taken from saliva samples after the session. Some participants were accompanied by a fellow student, actually a confederate, who was highly supportive. Others were accompanied by a neutral confederate or none at all. The benefits of social support—even in the form of a stranger—were clear: Participants accompanied by a supportive confederate, relative to the others, exhibited lower blood pressure, a lower hear rate, lower cortisol reactivity, lower pain ratings (Roberts et al., 2015).

Our social connections are therapeutic for many reasons. Friends may encourage us to get out, eat well, exercise, and take care of ourselves. They also give sympathy, reassurance, someone to talk to, advice, and a second opinion. There is, however, a striking exception to this rule. Of all the social networks that support us, romantic partnerships, as in marriage, are the most powerful. But while men and women who are happily married live longer than those who are single or divorced, marital conflict breeds stress, elevated blood pressure, ulcers, depression, alcohol and drug abuse, changes in immune function, and other unhealthy effects, especially for women (Kiecolt-Glaser & Newton, 2001).

The health benefits of social support show just how important it is to connect with others. Are there any drawbacks to an active social life? Is it possible, for example, that the more people we see in a day—such as family, friends, classmates, teammates, co-workers, and neighbors—the more exposed we are to colds or the flu? Natalie Hamrick and others (2002) asked 18- to 30-year-old adults about recent stressful events and about their social lives, then had them keep a health diary for three months. Based on past research, they expected that participants under high stress would get sick more than those under low stress. But what about people

People who have lots of friends are healthier and live longer than those who live more isolated lives.

TRUE

with high versus low levels of social contact? What do you think? Would their social connections make them vulnerable to illness or protect them? It depends. Look at ● Figure 14.10 and you'll see that for people under low stress, social connections did not matter. For people under high stress, however, those with high levels of social contact were *more* likely to catch a cold or flu. It's healthy to be popular except, perhaps, during flu season.

The Religious Connection Finally, it is clear that religion provides a deeply important source of social and emotional support for many people. There are more than 6 billion people on Earth who belong to hundreds of religions—the most populated, in order, being Christianity, Islam, Hinduism, and Buddhism (Judaism and others have many fewer adherents). Only about 15% to 20% of the world's population is unaffiliated with a religious group. In the United States, two-thirds of all adults describe religion as a very important part of their lives. Is there a link between religiosity and health?

This is an interesting but controversial question. On the one hand, population surveys suggest that people who regularly attend religious services live longer than those who do not (McCullough et al., 2000). When you think about it, this correlation makes some intuitive sense. Religious faith may fill people with hope and optimism rather than with despair, offer the physiological benefits of relaxation in prayer, provide a community lifeline of social support to prevent isolation, and promote a safe and healthy way of life by discouraging such toxic habits as drinking and smoking. After analyzing 30 years of health data from 2,600 California adults, for example, William Strawbridge and others (2001) found that men and women who regularly attend religious services drink less, smoke less, and exercise more. On the other hand, some researchers caution that the correlations between religiosity and longevity are modest and can be interpreted in other ways. It's possible, for example, that nonsmokers, teetotalers, and others who regularly abstain from unhealthful behaviors are more likely to adopt religion as part of their lives than smokers, drinkers, and risk-takers, and that their survival comes from who they are, not from their attendance at religious services (Sloan et al., 1999).

At this point, the research is suggestive but not conclusive: A religious way of life is associated with physiological benefits, health, and longevity, but the basis for these correlations—and the ultimate causal question of whether becoming religious will increase one's health—is a compelling question that remains to be determined (Miller & Thoresen, 2003; Plante & Thoresen, 2007; Powell et al., 2003; Seeman et al., 2003).

▧ Culture and Coping

Everyone in the world feels stress during the course of a lifetime. Whether the result of a natural disaster, the death of a loved one, the breakup of a relationship, war, serious illness, an accident, or the chronic microstressors of studying, working, and trying to make ends meet, stress is universal to the human experience. But do people in all cultures solve problems and cope in the same ways?

● FIGURE 14.10

Does Being Popular Always Promote Health?

Young adults were asked about recent stressful events and about their social lives—and then kept a health diary for three months. As you can see, social contact made no difference for people under low stress. For people under high stress, however, those with active social lives were more likely to get sick. Social contact increases exposure to infectious agents—and can bring illness for those whose resistance is compromised by stress.

From Hamrick, N., Cohen, S., and Rodriguez, M. S., "Being popular can be healthy or unhealthy: Stress, social network diversity, and incidence of upper respiratory infection," *Health Psychology* vol 21 (pp. 294–298). Copyright © 2002 by the American Psychological Association. Reprinted by permission.

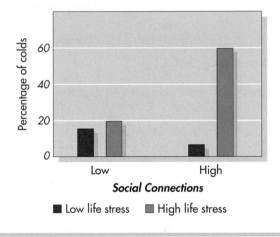

Percentage of colds

Social Connections

■ Low life stress   ■ High life stress

Most of the research on coping is conducted with people from Western cultures, in which individualism and independence are highly valued. Do people from collectivist cultures that value interdependence use the same coping mechanisms that are listed in Table 14.3? The answer may not be as obvious as it seems. In view of the differences between Eastern and Western cultures, for example, one might predict that Asians are more likely than European Americans to cope with stress by turning to others for support. Yet Shelley Taylor and her colleagues (2004) found that when they asked college students to describe what they do to relieve stress, only 39% of South Koreans (compared to 57% of Americans) said they sought social support. Additional research has confirmed this surprising cultural difference. Regardless of whether the source of stress is social, academic, financial, or health related; across age groups; and in diverse Asian samples that included Chinese, Japanese, Korean, and Vietnamese participants, the result is always the same: People from Asian cultures are less likely to seek out social support in times of stress.

Additional probing has shed light on this difference. In individualistic cultures, people often use others to service their personal goals. Yet in collectivist cultures, where social groups take precedence over the self, people are reluctant to strain relationships by calling on others for support. This being the case, Heejung Kim and her colleagues (2008) distinguished between *explicit social support* (disclosing one's distress to others and seeking their advice, aid, or comfort) and *implicit social support* (merely thinking about or being with close others without openly asking for help). In a study that asked participants to imagine themselves in one of these two situations, Asian Americans reacted with more stress to the explicit social support situation, while European Americans found the more contained implicit situation more stressful (Taylor et al., 2007).

There may be an important exception to this cultural difference. Other research suggests that East Asian Americans in times of need are more likely to seek out peers, whose support is "discretionary," than to rely on family members, whose support is "obligatory." In either case, they benefit more when they see the social support they receive as mutual as opposed to one-sided (Wang & Lau, 2015). It also appears that although East Asians and Asian Americans are less likely to seek people out in times of need, social support that comes without prompting is different. Comparing the effects of solicited and unsolicited social support, research has shown that for Asian Americans, support reduced stress and increased positive emotions—when it was unsolicited (Mojaverian & Kim, 2013).

To better understand the "collectivist coping style," Paul Heppner and others (2006) administered extensive questionnaires to more than 3,000 Asian college students in Taiwan, many of whom had endured the kinds of traumatic events described in this chapter (the three most frequent were breakups, academic pressure, and the death or illness of a loved one). Table 14.4 shows five ways of coping that were

---

▲ **TABLE 14.4**

Collectivist Coping Styles

The following sample statements describe five common types of coping styles, in order of frequency of usage, that have emerged from studies in Taiwan.

Acceptance, Reframing, and Striving	**91%**
● Tried to accept the trauma for what it offered me	
● Believed I would grow from surviving the traumatic event	
● Realized that the trauma served an important purpose in my life	

Avoidance and Detachment	**71%**
● Saved face by not telling anyone	
● Pretended to be okay	
● Kept my feelings within myself in order not to worry my parents	

Family Support	**66%**
● Shared my feelings with my family	
● Knew that I could ask assistance from my family	
● Followed the guidance of my elders	

Religion and Spirituality	**40%**
● Found comfort in my religion or spirituality	
● Found guidance from my religion	
● Found comfort through prayer or other religious rituals	

Private Emotional Outlets	**30%**
● Saved face by seeking advice from a professional I did not know	
● Chatted with people about the trauma on the Internet	
● Ate in excess	

Heppner, P. P., Heppner, M. J., Lee, D., Wang, Y., Park, H., & Wang, L. (2006). Development and validation of a collectivist coping styles inventory. *Journal of Counseling Psychology, 53,* 107–125.

identified. In order of how often they are used, the strategies are (1) acceptance, reframing, and striving; (2) avoidance and detachment; (3) family support; (4) religion and spirituality; and (5) private emotional outlets. Of the five strategies, participants rated acceptance as the most helpful. Do these results describe how Taiwanese adults cope with stress? What about Asians from Korea, Japan, China, and elsewhere? Interest is growing in these questions and, more generally, in the intersections of social psychology, culture, and health (Gurung, 2010).

Recent research by Jacqueline Chen and other (2012) sheds some light on these questions. These investigators note that social support can take a variety of forms—most notably, problem-solving support (providing insight, advice, money, and other tangible resources to help resolve the stressor) and emotion-focused support (providing comfort, reassurance, and a boost to self-esteem). In one study, college students from the United States and Japan were asked to describe their most recent social interaction with someone they were close to and then to indicate whether they did something to try to help that person. Overall American participants were twice as likely as the Japanese participants to spontaneously report giving social support in their interactions. But ● Figure 14.11 shows that the two groups also differed in terms of the types of social support they provided: Americans gave more emotion-focused support aimed at helping their close other feel better about himself or herself; Japanese gave more problem-focused support aimed at helping to resolve the stressor.

● **FIGURE 14.11**

Culture and Social Support

Cultural differences in giving social support are complicated. As seen here, Americans report giving more *emotion-focused support* aimed at helping their close other *feel better*; Japanese report giving more *problem-focused support* aimed at helping to *resolve the stressor*.
From Chen, J. M., Kim, H. S., Mojaverian, T., & Morling, B., "Culture and social support provision: Who gives what and why," *Personality and Social Psychology Bulletin* vol 38 (pp. 3–13). Copyright © 2012 Sage Publications, Inc. Reprinted with permission.

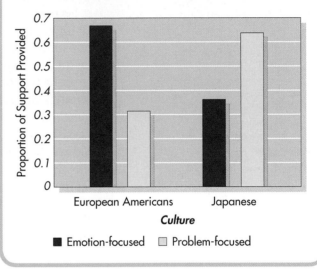

Treatment and Prevention

Understanding what social support is and how it works is important in the study of health because so many of our problems and prospects occur in a social context and so many of our efforts to cope involve other people. Indeed, as we'll see in this section, health psychologists try to find ways in which social influences can be used to improve the development of treatment and prevention programs.

■ Treatment: The "Social" Ingredients

Often what ails us can be treated through medical intervention. The treatments vary widely—from a simple change in diet to vitamin and mineral supplements, aspirin, antibiotics, surgery, and the like. Medicine is vital to health. In addition, however, treatment has a social component, what the family doctor used to call "bedside manner." What are the active social ingredients?

To begin to answer this question, let's consider research on the benefits of psychotherapy. Over the years, studies have shown that although there are vastly different schools of thought and techniques for doing psychotherapy, all approaches are somewhat effective and, surprisingly, all are generally equivalent (Smith et al., 1980; Wampold et al., 1997). Apparently, despite the surface differences, all psychotherapies have a great deal in common at a deeper level and these common factors—more than the specific techniques used—provide the active ingredients necessary for change. What are some of these factors?

First, all healers—regardless of whether they are medical doctors, psychologists, or others—provide *social support,* a close human relationship characterized by warmth, expressions of concern, a shoulder to cry on, and someone to talk to. Earlier, we discussed the benefits to health and longevity of having social contacts. In psychological therapy, studies have shown that the better the "working alliance" is between a therapist and client, the more favorable the outcome is likely to be (Horvath & Luborsky, 1993). As psychotherapist Hans Strupp (1996) put it, "The simple and incontrovertible truth is that if you are anxious or depressed, or if you are experiencing difficulties with significant people in your life, chances are that you feel better if you talk to someone you can trust" (p. 1017).

Second, all therapies offer a ray of *hope* to people who are sick, demoralized, unhappy, or in pain. In all aspects of life, people are motivated by upbeat, positive expectations. Although some of us are more optimistic than others, optimism is a specific expectation that can be increased or decreased in certain situations (Armor & Taylor, 1998). Indeed, a common aspect of all treatments is that they communicate and instill positive expectations. It has been suggested that high expectations can spark change even when they are not justified (Prioleau et al., 1983). This suggestion is consistent with the well-known placebo effect in medicine, whereby patients improve after being given an inactive drug or treatment. Believing can help make it so, which is how faith healers, shamans, and witch doctors all over the world have managed to perform "miracle cures" with elaborate rituals. Even modern medicine exploits the power of hope. As Walter Brown (1998) puts it, "The symbols and rituals of healing—the doctor's office, the stethoscope, the physical examination—offer reassurance" (p. 91).

A third important ingredient is *choice.* Allowing patients to make meaningful choices, such as deciding on a type of treatment, increases the effectiveness of treatments for alcoholism (Miller, 1985) and obesity (Mendonca & Brehm, 1983). Choosing to undergo an effortful or costly treatment is particularly beneficial in this regard. The person who voluntarily pays in time, money, or discomfort needs to self-justify that investment—a predicament sure to arouse cognitive dissonance. As seen in Chapter 6, one way to reduce dissonance is to become ultramotivated to succeed: "Why have I chosen to do this? Because I really want to get better." Perhaps because highly motivated individuals are more careful and conscientious about carrying out the prescribed treatment, they tend to improve more.

Danny Axsom (1989) tested this specific proposition in a study of snake phobias. Participants, all of whom were highly snake-phobic, were or were not given an explicit choice about undertaking a treatment that was described as either requiring "extreme exertion" or being "easy." Among the four experimental conditions, participants who were given an explicit choice about continuing an effortful treatment reported the greatest motivation to change their phobic behavior and came closest to the five-foot-long New Jersey corn snake used to measure approach behavior.

■ Prevention: Getting the Message Across

We live in what could aptly be described as the era of prevention in that many serious health threats are preventable. Just watch TV, leaf through a magazine, or surf the Internet: There are programs for AIDS prevention; campaigns to persuade smokers to break the habit; sunscreens that protect the skin from harmful rays; screening for various types of cancer; warnings about high-sugar foods, high-fat

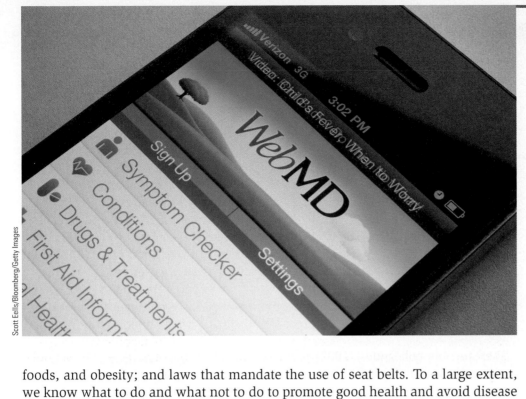

Scott Eells/Bloomberg/Getty Images

Today, people can find all sorts of information and advice on health-related issues on WebMD and other Internet sites. Providing information wherever you are, this app is displayed on a mobile device.

foods, and obesity; and laws that mandate the use of seat belts. To a large extent, we know what to do and what not to do to promote good health and avoid disease and injury. But just how do we convince ourselves and others to translate that knowledge into action?

Nowhere is this problem more acute than among people who suffer from AIDS. Earlier in the chapter, we noted that heart attacks, cancer, strokes, and accidents are now more common causes of death than infectious diseases. But AIDS, the first truly global epidemic, came along and spread at an alarming rate. Years ago, AIDS was described as a microbiological time bomb. In 1981, five homosexual men in North America were diagnosed with AIDS and were among only 189 cases reported that year. By 1996, the number of cases in North America had skyrocketed to three-quarters of a million and included heterosexual men, women, and children (Mann, 1992). In 2014, the World Health Organization estimated that 35 million people worldwide are currently infected with HIV; an estimated 1.5 million died in that year alone. Worldwide, both numbers are down from previous years. However, the number of new infections continues to climb in parts of Latin America, sub-Saharan Africa, North Africa, the Middle East, Eastern Europe, and parts of Asia.

The AIDS virus is transmitted from one person to another in infected blood, semen, and vaginal secretions. People who are HIV-positive may have no symptoms for several years and may not even realize they are infected. Eventually, however, the virus will ravage the immune system by destroying lymphocytes that help ward off disease. What's frightening about AIDS is that it appears fatal, that it is increasing at a rate of one new case every few seconds, and that, despite more than 25 years of testing, there is no vaccine that can prevent its occurrence (Stine, 2014).

The most effective way to slow the spread of AIDS is to alter people's beliefs, motivations, and risk-taking behaviors (Fisher & Fisher, 1992; Fisher et al., 1994; Gerrard et al., 1996; Kalichman, 2006)—and that's where social psychology comes in. Across a range of perspectives, several basic steps emerge (see ● Figure 14.12).

For social psychologists, the challenge in addressing the HIV crisis is to convert the science into a practice that works. In an excellent illustration, Jeffrey

● FIGURE 14.12

Aiming for Good Health

Several major factors help convince people to engage in healthy practices. Recognition that a threat to health exists is a necessary first step. Positive models and healthy subjective norms encourage people to adopt health-protective behaviors. A sense of self-efficacy about being able to carry out healthy behaviors and the belief that such behaviors will be effective increase the likelihood of active efforts.
© Cengage Learning®

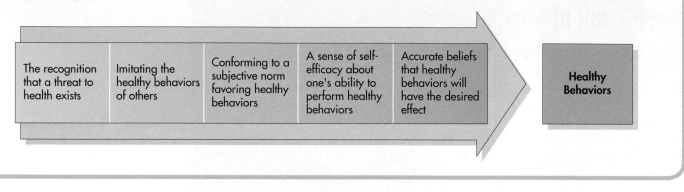

Fisher and his colleagues (2002) theorized that HIV prevention in city schools, which is essential for controlling the number of newly infected teens, requires a three-pronged attack. In their model, students must be provided with accurate *information* about HIV transmission and how to prevent it, with a personal and social *motivation* to engage in HIV-preventative behaviors, and with the *behavioral skills* necessary to follow through—notably, by using condoms. Armed with this model, these investigators set up HIV prevention programs in four urban high schools, devised a control group that lacked these "active ingredients," and found that the program, when administered by the classroom teachers, changed HIV-prevention behavior, increasing condom use up to a year later—all for an estimated cost of $2.22 per student. Other similarly oriented efforts have been developed as well, also with good success (Albarracín et al., 2005). The behavioral skills part of the program is complicated by the fact that the behavior in question requires the cooperation of two people. For that reason, studies show that the more adolescents communicate with their dating partners about sex, the more likely they are to use condoms (Widman et al., 2014).

Armed with a theory and various effective techniques, social psychologists are looking to make important strides in the fight against AIDS. There are two caveats, however. First, it is necessary (and not that easy) for prevention programs to attract the kinds of high-risk participants for whom they are designed. Yet this is exactly the group, ironically, that is least likely to attend. In a study of 350 inhabitants of a high-risk community, Allison Earl and her colleagues (2009) found that people who were the most informed, most motivated, and most skilled at using condoms to prevent the spread of HIV were also the most likely to accept an offer to participate in the program. Those who were less informed, less motivated, and less skilled were less receptive. Clearly, for any HIV prevention program to work, it must bring in those members of the community who need it most.

The second caveat is that a focus on educating "healthy" people in the use of condoms addresses the spread of HIV prevention from one perspective. A second approach is to focus prevention efforts on HIV positive individuals who can transmit the virus. To achieve this objective, it is necessary to increase the number of HIV positive individuals who are aware of their infections. It is also necessary to educate the few who know they are infected and yet still engage in behaviors that put sex partners at risk. With an eye on this objective, Ann O'Leary and Richard Wolitski (2009) describe a number of possible ways to encourage those who are knowingly infected to take responsibility, reject rationalization and excuse making, humanize and empathize with their sex partners, and bring their behavior in line with their own moral standards.

The Pursuit of Happiness

Long before the emergence of social psychology, philosophers regarded happiness as the ultimate state of being. In the U.S. Declaration of Independence, Thomas Jefferson thus cited life, liberty, and "the pursuit of happiness" as the most cherished of human rights. But what is happiness, and how is it achieved? Aristotle said it was the reward of an active life. Freud linked it with both work and love. Others have variously suggested that happiness requires money and power, health and fitness, religion, beauty, the satisfaction of basic needs, and an ability to derive pleasure from the events of everyday life. In recent years, social psychologists have applied their theories and methods to the study of this most basic human motive: the pursuit of happiness (Diener & Biswas-Diener, 2008; Gilbert, 2006; Haidt, 2006; Hanson, 2013; Lynn et al., 2015; Lyubomirsky, 2013).

To study happiness—or **subjective well-being (SWB)**, as social psychologists like to call it—one must be able to measure it. How do researchers know whether someone is happy? Simple: They ask. Better yet, they use questionnaires such as the Satisfaction with Life Scale, in which people respond to statements such as "If I could live my life over, I would change almost nothing" (Diener et al., 1984; Pavot & Diener, 1993). As Marcus Aurelius said, "No man is happy who does not think himself so."

Using self-reports, surveys show that 75% of American adults rate themselves as happy and that in 86% of all nations sampled, the ratings are, on average, more often positive than neutral (Diener, 2000). In general, people who are happy also tend to have cheerful moods, high self-esteem, a sense of personal control, more memories of positive as opposed to negative events, and optimism about the future (Myers & Diener, 1995). Even more than physical beauty or material wealth, happiness underlies people's belief that life is worth living (King & Napa, 1998). A meta-analysis of 225 studies revealed that happiness gives rise to many successful life outcomes in the domains of marriage, friendship, health, income, and work performance (Lyubomirsky et al., 2005).

It's no secret that our outlook on life becomes rosy right after you win a big game, fall in love, land a great job, or make money and that the world seems gloomy right after you lose, fall out of love, or suffer a personal tragedy or financial setback. Predictably, the events of everyday life trigger fluctuations in mood. For example, research shows that even after other factors are accounted for, city people are happier when they live near green spaces where there are parks, trees, and other greenery (White et al., 2013). People are most happy on Fridays and Saturdays and least happy on Mondays and Tuesdays (Larsen & Kasimatis, 1990). Even during the day, happiness levels fluctuate like clockwork. For example, David Watson and others (1999) asked college students to rate their mood states once a day for 45 days, always at a different hour. They found, on average, that the students felt best during the middle of the day (noon to 6 p.m.) and worst in the early morning and late evening hours.

subjective well-being (SWB)
One's happiness, or life satisfaction, as measured by self-report.

The most recent World Happiness Report (2015) revealed that Switzerland edged out Denmark as the happiest country in the world. This picturesque image shows Lucerne, in central Switzerland, with the mountain range of Mt Pilatus in the background.

But what determines our long-term satisfaction, and why are some of us happier than others? Seeking the roots of happiness, Ed Diener and his colleagues (1999) reviewed many years of research and found that subjective well-being is not meaningfully or consistently related to demographic factors such as age, sex, racial and ethnic background, IQ, education level, or physical attractiveness. Contrary to popular belief, people are not less happy during the so-called crisis years of midlife or in old age than during their youth and "peak" young-adult years. Men and women do not differ on this measure, and, in the United States, African and Hispanic Americans are as happy as white Americans. It's clear that people from all walks of life have ways to make themselves happy.

In a survey of "online happiness seekers," Acacia Parks and others (2012) found that most cited such activities as engaging in acts of kindness, pursuing important goals, expressing gratitude, staying optimistic, doing physical exercise, and nurturing social relationships.

Overall, there are three key predictors of happiness: *social relationships* (people with an active social life, close friends, and a happy marriage are more satisfied than those who lack these intimate connections), *employment status* (regardless of income, employed people are happier than those who are out of work), and *physical and mental health* (people who are healthy are happier than those who are not). Reflecting the impact of these factors, worldwide surveys of more than 100,000 respondents in 55 countries have shown that happiness levels vary from one culture to the next (Diener & Suh, 2000).

Although specific rankings fluctuate a bit from one survey to the next, national happiness ratings are consistently higher in some countries of the world than in others. In a massive poll commissioned by the United Nations General Assembly, the *World Happiness Report 2015*— first published in 2012, then twice revised and updated—revealed that the happiest countries in the world are clustered in Northern Europe with average life evaluation scores of 7+ on a 0–10 scale. The least happy countries tend to be found in sub-Saharan Africa with average life evaluation scores that range from 3 to 4. The Geography of Happiness is presented in ● Figure 14.13. The report notes that although relative wealth clearly distinguishes the nations on the list, "Political freedom, strong social networks and an absence of corruption are together more important than income in explaining well-being differences between the top and bottom countries" (Helliwell et al., 2015). It comes as no surprise, therefore, that in a poll of 132,516 people from 128 countries, the more satisfied people were with their country as a whole, the happier they were with the state of their own lives (Morrison et al., 2011).

■ Does Money Buy Happiness?

Over the years, the most interesting statistical relationship has been between income and subjective well-being. We all know the saying that "money can't buy happiness"—though some people (particularly those who are financially strapped) do not believe it. But is wealth truly a key to happiness? To some extent, yes, but the evidence is more complex than you'd think. Ed Diener and Martin Seligman (2004) note that multimillionaires from the Forbes list of the 400 richest

Singer Pharrell Williams performs his 2014 hit song "Happy." His lyrics tell the tale:

*"Here come bad news talking this and that
Yeah, give me all you got, don't hold back
Yeah, well I should probably warn you I'll be just fine
Yeah, no offense to you don't waste your time
Here's why - Because I'm happy."*

● **FIGURE 14.13**

Geography of Happiness

Based on surveys taken between 2012 and 2014, this map depicts the geographic distribution of national averages based on people's ratings of life satisfaction. On this map, countries are ranked into groups, with the darkest green for the highest averages and the darkest red for the lowest.

Helliwell et al., 2015 - *World Happiness Report 2015*

Americans report high levels of life satisfaction (5.8 on a 7-point scale), but so do the Masai, a herding people in East Africa with no electricity or running water who live in huts made with dung (5.7 on the same 7-point scale).

As seen in the huge disparity in wealth between the happiest countries of Northern Europe and the unhappiest countries of sub-Saharan Africa, cross-national studies reveal a strong positive association between a nation's wealth and the subjective well-being of its people. There are some exceptions. But as a general rule, the more money a country has, the happier its citizens are (Ng & Diener, 2014). Within any given country, however, the differences between wealthy and middle-income people are modest. In one survey, for example, a group of the wealthiest Americans said they were happy 77% of the time, which was only moderately higher than the 62% figure reported by those of average income. In addition, comparisons within a single culture over time show that there is no relationship between affluence and happiness. On average, Americans are two to three times richer now than 50 years ago—before we had computers, flat-screen TVs, GPS systems, iPhones, iPads, Facebook pages, and digital cameras that fit into the palm of your hand. Yet the number of respondents who said they were "very happy" was 35% in 1957 and only 32% in 1998 (see ● Figure 14.14).

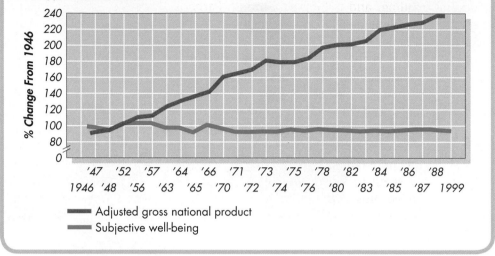

● **FIGURE 14.14**

Wealth and Subjective Well-Being

Over a period of more than 40 years, Americans became twice as wealthy, as measured by adjusted per person income—but they were no happier, as measured in public opinion polls. From Kassin, S., *Psychology*, 3rd ed. Copyright © 1997. Reprinted by permission of Pearson Education, Inc., Upper Saddle River, NJ.

Adjusted gross national product

Subjective well-being

So what are we to conclude? At this point, it appears that having shelter, food, safety, and security is essential for subjective well-being. But once these basic needs are met, particularly in an already prosperous society, additional increases in wealth do not appreciably raise levels of happiness. Why doesn't money contribute more to subjective well-being? One reason is that our perceptions of wealth are not absolute but, instead, are relative to certain personally set standards (Parducci, 1995). These standards are derived from two sources: other people and our own past.

According to *social comparison theory,* as described in Chapter 3, people tend to naturally compare themselves to others and feel contented or deprived depending on how they fare in this comparison. To demonstrate, Ladd Wheeler and Kunitate Miyake (1992) had college students for two weeks keep a written record of every time they mentally compared their own grades, appearance, abilities, possessions, or personality traits to someone else's. Consistently, these diaries revealed that making "upward comparisons" (to others who were better off) sparked negative feelings, while making "downward comparisons" (to others who were worse off) triggered positive feelings. That is why the middle-class worker whose neighbors can't pay their bills feels fortunate but the upper-class social climber who rubs elbows with the rich and famous feels deprived. This relativity may also help explain why there are only modest relationships between happiness and actual income and perceptions of financial status (Johnson & Krueger, 2006).

It is also natural for people to use their own recent past as a basis of comparison. According to *adaptation-level theory,* our satisfaction with the present depends on the level of success to which we are accustomed. Get married, buy a new house or car, get the job you were aiming for, or a promotion, and you will surely enjoy a wave of euphoria. Before long, however, the glitter will wear off and you'll adapt to your better situation and raise your standard of

"It matters little whether one is rich or poor, successful or unsuccessful, or beautiful or plain: Happiness is completely relative . . . the pleasantness of any particular experience depends on its relationship to a context of other experiences, real or imagined."

—Allen Parducci

comparison. This phenomenon is known as *hedonic adaptation.* Indeed, when Philip Brickman and others (1978) interviewed 22 people who had won between $50,000 and $1 million in a lottery, they found that these people did not rate themselves as happier than in the past. Compared to others from similar backgrounds, the winners said that they now derived less pleasure from routine activities such as shopping, reading, and talking to a friend. Perhaps the more money you have, the more you need to stay happy. The results of a Chicago public opinion poll suggest that this is the case: Whereas people who earned less than $30,000 a year said that $50,000 would fulfill their dreams, those who earned more than $100,000 said it would take $250,000 to make them happy (Csikszentmihalyi, 1999). Highlighting a dark side of the "American dream," research shows that the more materialistic people are, the less satisfied they seem to be (Nickerson et al., 2003). Economists have thus come to appreciate that our sense of well-being stems in part from the gap between our income and material aspirations (Stutzer, 2004).

It would be a mistake to assume that people "adapt" to gains and losses in money, or other positive and negative life events, in the same way and at the same rate. Recent longitudinal studies that track the same people over time have shown that the effects of some major life events are more persistent than others. For example, people tend to adapt quickly, typically within two years, to the initial boost in happiness that comes from marriage—and divorce is often followed by an increase in life satisfaction, as people adapt after the ordeal has ended. Yet the impact of disability, unemployment, and the grief that follows the death of a spouse tend to last longer—and childbirth is followed by a range of conflicting—positive and negative—patterns (Lucas, 2007; Luhmann et al., 2012).

There's one other possible and intriguing explanation for why money, per se, and other major life events, is not more predictive of happiness over time: Perhaps each of us, as a result of both biological and environmental factors, has a set baseline level of happiness, a "set point" toward which we gravitate. This notion is supported by three recent findings. One is that ratings of happiness are higher among pairs of identical twins than among fraternal twins—leading David Lykken (2000) to suggest that there may be a genetic basis for having a certain set level of contentment. A second finding is that the fluctuations in mood that accompany positive and negative life events tend to wear off over time. For example, in a study that spanned two years, Eunkook Suh and others (1996) studied participants for two years and found that only experiences occurring in the last three months correlated with reports of subjective well-being. Getting engaged or married, breaking up, starting a new job, and being hospitalized are the kinds of high-impact experiences that people assume have lasting if not permanent effects on happiness levels (Gilbert et al., 1998)—but in fact, the impacts are often temporary. A third finding is that happiness levels, like personality traits, are relatively stable over time and place, which leads to the conclusion that some people are, in general, happier than others (DeNeve & Cooper, 1998).

Leo Cullum The New Yorker Collection/The Cartoon Bank

"Remember how I said I was happiest when we had nothing?"

In all countries and at all levels of wealth, the more money people have, the happier they are.

 FALSE

■ Emerging Science on How to Increase Happiness

The pursuit of happiness is a powerful human motive that is not fully understood. Each of us may well be predisposed by nature toward a particular set point, but it is clear that our happiness is not completely set in stone. In a 17-year longitudinal study of individuals in Germany, researchers found that 24% of the respondents had significantly higher or lower levels of life satisfaction in the last five years of the study than they did in the first five years (Fujita & Diener, 2005). In national surveys that spanned from 1981 to 2007, other researchers found that average happiness ratings increased in 45 out of 52 countries in which multiple surveys were administered over time—an increase that was linked to increasing democratization in these countries (Inglehart et al., 2008).

Realizing that happiness is malleable, both for individuals and large populations, social psychologists are now trying to figure out how people can produce sustainable increases in subjective well-being (Lyubomirsky et al., 2005). Consider this question: If you had money to spend, would you rather use it to purchase an experience or a material object? Would one type of purchase make you happier? Leaf Van Boven and Thomas Gilovich (2003) conducted a national telephone survey in which they asked people of varying income levels about a time they purchased an experience (they most often named tickets to a concert, theater, travel, dinner, or spa) or a material object (they most often named clothing, jewelry, a computer, or electronic equipment) to make themselves happy. Respondents were then asked to indicate which purchase, if any, made them happier. ● Figure 14.15 shows that except at the lowest income levels, where people have to satisfy basic material needs, the experiences they purchased—thanks, in part, to the memories that lingered—made them happier than the material objects (see Van Boven, 2005).

● **FIGURE 14.15**

What Yields More Happiness: Experiences or Material Objects?

After recalling a time when they spent money on an experience or a material object, people in general said that the experiences they purchased made them happier than the material objects.

From Van Boven, L., "Experientialism, materialism, and the pursuit of happiness," *Review of General Psychology* vol 9 (pp. 132–142). Copyright © 2005 by the American Psychological Association. Reprinted by permission.

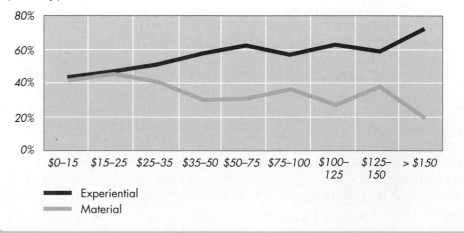

As to what other uses of money we find particularly satisfying, there is this happy commentary on human nature: In a study of 136 countries all over the world, researchers found that spending money on other people—*prosocial spending*—is associated with greater happiness than spending money on one's self (Aknin et al., 2013). Giving gifts and making others happy leaves us with a warm glow—not only among adults but in toddlers as well. When you stop to think about it, in the context of social psychology, this benefit makes sense. Humans are social creature; spending on others we care about satisfies our basic need to belong (Dunn et al., 2014).

Social psychological research has uncovered other ways to boost happiness levels as well. For example, people who are prompted by random assignment to write gratitude letters, savor a happy memory, or engage in acts of kindness exhibit increases in subjective well-being compared to others in a control group (Sin & Lyubomirsky, 2009). As for the fact that people tend to "adapt" to a positive change in fortune, get used to it, and revert to their own baseline levels, a collateral question comes into play: Once your level of happiness is raised, is there a way to ensure that you stay that way? In answer to this question, researchers are now looking for ways to prevent hedonic adaptation so that the benefits of positive changes will endure over time (Sheldon & Lyubomirsky, 2012).

Quite apart from developments in Western psychological science is the question of how, if at all, governments should try to foster happiness in their citizens. Consider the Kingdom of Bhutan—a small, secluded, landlocked Buddhist country nestled high in the Himalayan Mountains and bordering India and Tibet. In 1972, the King of Bhutan adopted "Gross National Happiness" (GNH) as its national goal instead of the Gross National Product—making a choice of happiness over wealth. Every year since that time, the government has systematically measured GNH and has shaped policies designed to sustain it. In contrast to the Western scientist's measurement focus on people's ratings of their own subjective well-being, happiness in the GNH is a multidimensional concept that measures many aspects of the quality of a person's material, physical, social, and spiritual life. By tracking these indicators over time and in various communities, the GNH is used to advance government policies in ways that increase happiness in people who are "not

Bhutan is a small Buddhist country nestled high in the Himalayan Mountains between India and Tibet. In the only program of its kind, designed to prioritize subjective well-being over material wealth, the government has set "Gross National Happiness" (GNH) as its national goal and seeks to increase the GNH of its population.

AP Images/Gurinder Osan

Felix Hug/Terra/Corbis

yet happy." The indicators that make up the GNH appear in ● Figure 14.16 (for a fascinating case study on the GNH in Bhutan, see Ura et al., 2012).

What is particularly fascinating about the Bhutan story is that it is part of a new cross-national trend. Several years ago, social psychologist Ed Diener (2000) proposed that all countries should collect SWB information from their citizens and then adopt what he called "National Accounts of Well-Being." The goal would be to assess how happy a population is and create national policies aimed at increasing that level of happiness. The research literature offers a good deal of guidance—showing, for example, the happiest nations are economically developed and have strong rules of law, human rights, efficient governments, high employment rates, environmental quality, income security programs, political freedom, and physical health. Today, Diener and his colleagues (2015) present an alphabetized list of

● **FIGURE 14.16**

Bhutan's Gross National Happiness (GNH) Indicators

From Ura, K., Alkire, S., & Zangmo, T. "Case study: Bhutan: Gross National Happiness and the GNH index," in J. Helliwell, R. Layard, & J. Sachs (Eds.) *World Happiness Report* (p. 115). Copyright © 2012 Columbia University (The Earth Institute). Reprinted with permission.

43 countries—from Australia through the United States—in which SWB statistics are being collected from its citizens.

The research described in this section offers some concrete advice on how people can maximize their levels of happiness. Should social psychologists and nations use this research to seek to maximize levels of happiness within a population? In light of the undisputed benefits of being happy, this hardly seems like a controversial question. But let's stop and ponder the question. Concerned that there is a possible dark side to the *pursuit* of happiness, Iris Mauss and her colleagues (2011) asked, "Can seeking happiness make people unhappy?" Echoing this concern, June Gruber and others (2011) suggested that sometimes being "too happy" is not adaptive because excessive positive emotions can lead people to engage in risky behaviors and not pay enough attention to possible threats (consuming alcohol, having sex with strangers, driving too fast). What's more, some situations call for fear, anger, or a more sober emotional state for coping purposes. They also note that although most people say they are reasonably happy, many report wanting to be even happier—a state of desire that can have paradoxical effects: "The more people strive for happiness, the more likely it is that they will become disappointed about how they feel" (p. 226). Since people who are happy tend to be content with what they have rather than focused on what they lack, this last point is particularly thought-provoking. Is it possible to be *too focused* on being happy? Is it possible to be *too happy?* Stay tuned for future research on these questions.

Review

Top 10 Key Points in Chapter 14

1. Stress is an unpleasant state that arises when people feel as if the demands of a situation exceed their ability to cope with it.

2. There are many causes of stress, or stressors—most notably, these include natural disasters and catastrophes such as war; major negative life events such as a death in the family; and everyday hassles or "microstressors" such as noise, traffic, and a life of poverty.

3. Although the body responds to the stress of acute emergencies (e.g., by releasing adrenaline into the bloodstream, creating physiological arousal), this "stress response" will reach a period of exhaustion and cause the body to break down because it is not built for chronic, long-term situations.

4. Research shows that stress increases the risk of coronary heart disease (CHD) and suppresses immune cell activity, so people under stress are more likely to catch a cold when exposed to a virus—and perhaps other illnesses as well.

5. Some people are more resilient than others in the face of stress—in particular, it is adaptive for people to believe they have control over their own fate and to have a generally optimistic outlook on the future.

6. There are three ways in general to cope with stress: *problem-focused coping* (trying to overcome the source), *emotion-focused coping* (trying to manage the emotional turmoil), *and proactive coping* (establishing a lifestyle that buffers stress before it strikes, e.g., by having a strong social support network, or religion).

7. Although stress is universal, the way we cope is influenced by culture—e.g., people from individualist cultures tend to lean on friends for social support; not wanting to strain "discretionary" relationships, those from collectivist cultures are more likely to turn to family, religion, and private emotional outlets.

8. Most people report being relatively happy, but there are individual and cross-national differences in happiness, or "subjective well-being," the key ingredients being social relationships, employment, and health.

9. On the question of whether money buys happiness, research is mixed, showing that while more affluent nations have happier on average citizens than poorer nations, the correlations between income and happiness within populations, and over time, are modest.

10. Recognizing the malleability of happiness, researchers—and nations—have begun to focus on how to increase happiness levels and have found, for example, that people become happier when they spend money on experiences rather than material objects and when they spend money on others rather than on themselves.

Putting Common Sense to the Test

What Causes Stress?

The accumulation of daily hassles does more to make people sick than catastrophes or major life changes.

Ⓣ **True.** *Car problems, arguments with friends, and other "microstressors" contribute more to our levels of stress than larger but less frequent stressors.*

How Does Stress Affect the Body?

Like humans, zebras get ulcers.

Ⓕ **False.** *Stress causes ulcers in humans, not zebras. That's because the stress response is designed for acute emergencies; but in people, it is activated often and for long periods of time.*

Stress can weaken the heart, but it cannot affect the immune system.

Ⓕ **False.** *Recent research has shown that stress and other psychological states can alter the activity of white blood cells in the immune system and affect our resistance to illness.*

Processes of Appraisal

When it comes to physical health, research does not support popular beliefs about the power of positive thinking.

Ⓕ **False.** *Consistently, people who are optimistic—and situations that promote optimism—are associated with better health outcomes.*

Ways of Coping With Stress

People who have lots of friends are healthier and live longer than those who live more isolated lives.

Ⓣ **True.** *Across a range of studies, researchers have found that social support is strongly associated with positive health outcomes.*

The Pursuit of Happiness

In all countries and at all levels of wealth, the more money people have, the happier they are.

Ⓕ **False.** *Research results are complex, but it is clear that once people have enough money to satisfy basic needs, additional wealth does not produce more happiness.*

Key Terms

appraisal (603)

coping (603)

depressive explanatory style (619)

emotion-focused coping (625)

general adaptation syndrome (610)

health psychology (603)

immune system (614)

learned helplessness (619)

posttraumatic stress disorder (PTSD) (606)

proactive coping (625)

problem-focused coping (624)

psychoneuroimmunology (PNI) (614)

self-efficacy (621)

social support (633)

stress (603)

stressor (604)

subjective well-being (SWB) (641)

Type A personality (612)

Glossary

adversarial model A dispute-resolution system in which the prosecution and defense present opposing sides of the story.

affective forecasting The process of predicting how one would feel in response to future emotional events.

aggression Behavior intended to harm another individual.

altruistic Motivated by the desire to improve another's welfare.

ambivalent sexism A form of sexism characterized by attitudes about women that reflect both negative, resentful beliefs and feelings and affectionate and chivalrous but potentially patronizing beliefs and feelings.

applied research Research whose goal is to make applications to the world and contribute to the solution of social problems.

appraisal The process by which people make judgments about the demands of potentially stressful events and their ability to meet those demands.

assessment center A structured setting in which job applicants are exhaustively tested and judged by multiple evaluators.

attachment style The way a person typically interacts with significant others.

attitude A positive, negative, or mixed reaction to a person, object, or idea.

attitude scale A multiple-item questionnaire designed to measure a person's attitude toward some object.

attribution theory A group of theories that describe how people explain the causes of behavior.

audience inhibition Reluctance to help for fear of making a bad impression on observers.

availability heuristic The tendency to estimate the likelihood that an event will occur by how easily instances of it come to mind.

aversive racism Racism that concerns the ambivalence between fair-minded attitudes and beliefs, on the one hand, and unconscious and unrecognized prejudicial feelings and beliefs, on the other hand.

base-rate fallacy The finding that people are relatively insensitive to consensus information presented in the form of numerical base rates.

basic research Research whose goal is to increase the understanding of human behavior, often by testing hypotheses based on a theory.

bask in reflected glory (BIRG) To increase self-esteem by associating with others who are successful.

behavioral economics An interdisciplinary subfield that focuses on how psychology—particularly social and cognitive psychology—relates to economic decision making.

behavioral genetics A subfield of psychology that examines the role of genetic factors in behavior.

belief in a just world The belief that individuals get what they deserve in life, an orientation that leads people to disparage victims.

belief perseverance The tendency to maintain beliefs even after they have been discredited.

biased sampling The tendency for groups to spend more time discussing shared information (information already known by all or most group members) than unshared information (information known by only one or a few group members).

bogus pipeline A phony lie-detector device that is sometimes used to get respondents to give truthful answers to sensitive questions.

bogus pipeline technique A procedure in which research participants are (falsely) led to believe that their responses will be verified by an infallible lie detector.

brainstorming A technique that attempts to increase the production of creative ideas by encouraging group members to speak freely without criticizing their own or others' contributions.

bystander effect The effect whereby the presence of others inhibits helping.

catharsis A reduction of the motive to aggress that is said to result from any imagined, observed, or actual act of aggression.

central route to persuasion The process by which a person thinks carefully about a communication and is influenced by the strength of its arguments.

central traits Traits that exert a powerful influence on overall impressions.

cognitive dissonance theory The theory holding that inconsistent cognitions arouse psychological tension that people become motivated to reduce.

collective effort model The theory that individuals will exert effort on a collective task to the degree that they think their individual efforts will be important, relevant, and meaningful for achieving outcomes that they value.

collectivism A cultural orientation in which interdependence, cooperation, and social harmony take priority over personal goals.

communal relationship A relationship in which the participants expect and desire mutual responsiveness to each other's needs.

companionate love A secure, trusting, stable partnership.

compliance Changes in behavior that are elicited by direct requests.

confederate Accomplice of an experimenter who, in dealing with the real participants in an experiment, acts as if he or she is also a participant.

confirmation bias The tendency to seek, interpret, and create information that verifies existing beliefs.

conformity The tendency to change our perceptions, opinions, or behavior in ways that are consistent with group norms.

confound A factor other than the independent variable that varies between the conditions of an experiment, thereby calling into question what caused any effects on the dependent variable.

construct validity The extent to which the measures used in a study measure the variables they were designed to measure and the manipulations in an experiment manipulate the variables they were designed to manipulate.

contact hypothesis The theory that direct contact between hostile groups will reduce intergroup prejudice under certain conditions.

contingency model of leadership The theory that leadership effectiveness is determined both by the personal characteristics of leaders and by the control afforded by the situation.

coping Efforts to reduce stress.

corporal punishment Physical force (such as spanking or hitting) intended to cause a child pain, but not injury, for the purpose of controlling or correcting the child's behavior.

correlation coefficient A statistical measure of the strength and direction of the association between two variables.

correlational research Research designed to measure the association between variables that are not manipulated by the researcher.

counterfactual thinking The tendency to imagine alternative events or outcomes that might have occurred but did not.

covariation principle A principle of attribution theory that holds that people attribute behavior to factors that are present when a behavior occurs and are absent when it does not.

cross-cultural research Research designed to compare and contrast people of different cultures.

cross-race identification bias The tendency for people to be more accurate at recognizing members of their own racial group than of other groups.

cultivation The process by which the mass media (particularly television) construct a version of social reality for the public.

culture A system of enduring meanings, beliefs, values, assumptions, institutions, and practices shared by a large group of people and transmitted from one generation to the next.

culture of honor A culture that emphasizes honor and social status, particularly for males, and the role of aggression in protecting that honor.

cybervetting A controversial new practice by which employers use the internet to get informal, non-institutional data about applicants that they did not choose to share.

cycle of violence The transmission of domestic violence across generations.

Dark Triad A set of three traits that is associated with higher levels of aggressiveness: Machiavellianism, psychopathy, and narcissism.

death qualification A jury-selection procedure used in capital cases that permits judges to exclude prospective jurors who say they would not vote for the death penalty.

debriefing A disclosure, made to participants after research procedures are completed, in which the researcher explains the purpose of the research, attempts to resolve any negative feelings, and emphasizes the scientific contribution made by the participants' involvement.

deception In the context of research, a method that provides false information to participants.

deindividuation The loss of a person's sense of individuality and the reduction of normal constraints against deviant behavior.

dependent variable In an experiment, a factor that experimenters measure to see if it is affected by the independent variable.

depressive explanatory style A habitual tendency to attribute negative events to causes that are stable, global, and internal.

desensitization Reduction in emotion-related physiological reactivity in response to a stimulus.

dialecticism An Eastern system of thought that accepts the coexistence of contradictory characteristics within a single person.

diffusion of responsibility The belief that others will or should take the responsibility for providing assistance to a person in need.

discrimination Behavior directed against persons because of their membership in a particular group.

displacement Aggressing against a substitute target because aggressive acts against the source of the frustration are inhibited by fear or lack of access.

distraction–conflict theory A theory that the presence of others will produce social facilitation effects only when those others distract from the task and create attentional conflict.

door-in-the-face technique A two-step compliance technique in which an influencer prefaces the real request with one that is so large that it is rejected.

downward social comparison The defensive tendency to compare ourselves with others who are worse off than we are.

dual-process model of persuasion The theory that people can be influenced by a persuasive communication either through a careful consideration of arguments or by responding to superficial cues.

egoistic Motivated by the desire to improve one's own welfare.

elaboration The process of thinking about and scrutinizing the arguments contained in a persuasive communication.

embodied cognition An interdisciplinary subfield that examines the close links between our minds and the positioning, experiences, and actions of our bodies.

emotion-focused coping Cognitive and behavioral efforts to reduce the distress produced by a stressful situation.

empathy Understanding or vicariously experiencing another individual's perspective and feeling sympathy and compassion for that individual.

empathy–altruism hypothesis The proposition that empathic concern for a person in need produces an altruistic motive for helping.

endowment effect The tendency for people to inflate the value of objects, goods, or services they already own.

equity theory The theory that people are most satisfied with a relationship when the ratio between benefits and contributions is similar for both partners.

escalation effect The tendency for people to persist in failing investments to avert loss, which causes losses to mount.

evaluation apprehension theory A theory that the presence of others will produce social facilitation effects only when those others are seen as potential evaluators.

evaluative conditioning The process by which we form an attitude toward a neutral stimulus because of its association with a positive or negative person, place, or thing.

evolutionary psychology A subfield of psychology that uses the principles of evolution to understand human social behavior.

exchange relationship A relationship in which the participants expect and desire strict reciprocity in their interactions.

excitation transfer The process whereby arousal caused by one stimulus is added to arousal from a second stimulus and the combined arousal is attributed to the second stimulus.

executive functioning The cognitive abilities and processes that allow humans to plan or inhibit their actions.

expectancy theory The theory that workers become motivated when they believe that their efforts will produce valued outcomes.

experiment A form of research that can demonstrate causal relationships because (1) the experimenter has control over the events that occur and (2) participants are randomly assigned to conditions.

experimental realism The degree to which experimental procedures are involving to participants and lead them to behave naturally and spontaneously.

experimenter expectancy effects The effects produced when an experimenter's expectations about the results of an experiment affect his or her behavior toward a participant and thereby influence the participant's responses.

external validity The degree to which there can be reasonable confidence that the results of a study would be obtained for other people and in other situations.

facial electromyograph (EMG) An electronic instrument that records facial muscle activity associated with emotions and attitudes.

facial feedback hypothesis The hypothesis that changes in facial expression can lead to corresponding changes in emotion.

false-consensus effect The tendency for people to overestimate the extent to which others share their opinions, attributes, and behaviors.

foot-in-the-door technique A two-step compliance technique in which an influencer sets the stage for the real request by first getting a person to comply with a much smaller request.

frustration–aggression hypothesis The idea that (1) frustration always elicits the motive to aggress and (2) all aggression is caused by frustration.

fundamental attribution error The tendency to focus on the role of personal causes and underestimate the impact of situations on other people's behavior.

general adaptation syndrome A three-stage process (alarm, resistance, and exhaustion) by which the body responds to stress.

group A set of individuals who interact over time and have shared fate, goals, or identity.

group cohesiveness The extent to which forces push group members closer together, such as through feelings of intimacy, unity, and commitment to group goals.

group polarization The exaggeration of initial tendencies in the thinking of group members through group discussion.

group support systems Specialized interactive computer programs that are used to guide group meetings, collaborative work, and decision-making processes.

groupthink A group decision-making style characterized by an excessive tendency among group members to seek concurrence.

hard-to-get effect The tendency to prefer people who are highly selective in their social choices over those who are more readily available.

Hawthorne effect The finding that workers who were given special attention increased their productivity regardless of what actual changes were made in the work setting.

health psychology The study of physical health and illness by psychologists from various areas of specialization.

hostile attribution bias The tendency to perceive hostile intent in others.

hypothesis A testable prediction about the conditions under which an event will occur.

identity fusion A strong sense of "oneness" and shared identity with a group and its individual members.

idiosyncrasy credits Interpersonal "credits" that a person earns by following group norms.

illusory correlation An overestimate of the association between variables that are only slightly or not at all correlated.

immune system A biological surveillance system that detects and destroys "nonself" substances that invade the body.

Implicit Association Test (IAT) A covert measure of unconscious attitudes derived from the speed at which people respond to pairings of concepts—such as black or white with good or bad.

implicit attitude An attitude, such as prejudice, that one is not aware of having.

implicit egotism A nonconscious form of self-enhancement.

implicit racism Racism that operates unconsciously and unintentionally.

impression formation The process of integrating information about a person to form a coherent impression.

independent variable In an experiment, a factor that experimenters manipulate to see if it affects the dependent variable.

indirect altruism A kind of reciprocal altruism in which an individual who helps someone becomes more likely to receive help from someone else

individualism A cultural orientation in which independence, autonomy, and self-reliance take priority over group allegiances.

industrial/organizational (I/O) psychology The study of human behavior in business and other organizational settings.

information integration theory The theory that impressions are based on (1) perceiver dispositions and (2) a weighted average of a target person's traits.

informational influence Influence that produces conformity when a person believes others are correct in their judgments.

informed consent An individual's deliberate, voluntary decision to participate in research, based on the researcher's description of what will be required during such participation.

ingroup favoritism The tendency to discriminate in favor of ingroups over outgroups.

ingroups Groups with which an individual feels a sense of membership, belonging, and identity.

inoculation hypothesis The idea that exposure to weak versions of a persuasive argument increases later resistance to that argument.

inquisitorial model A dispute-resolution system in which a neutral investigator gathers evidence from both sides and presents the findings in court.

insufficient deterrence A condition in which people refrain from engaging in a desirable activity, even when only mild punishment is threatened.

insufficient justification A condition in which people freely perform an attitude-discrepant behavior without receiving a large reward.

integrative agreement A negotiated resolution to a conflict in which all parties obtain outcomes that are superior to what they would have obtained from an equal division of the contested resources.

integrity tests Questionnaires designed to test a job applicant's honesty and character.

interactionist perspective An emphasis on how both an individual's personality and environmental characteristics influence behavior.

internal validity The degree to which there can be reasonable certainty that the independent variables in an experiment caused the effects obtained on the dependent variables.

interrater reliability The degree to which different observers agree on their observations.

intimate relationship A close relationship between two adults involving emotional attachment, fulfillment of psychological needs, or interdependence.

jigsaw classroom A cooperative learning method used to reduce racial prejudice through interaction in group efforts.

jury nullification The jury's power to disregard, or "nullify," the law when it conflicts with personal conceptions of justice.

kin selection Preferential helping of genetic relatives, which results in the greater likelihood that genes held in common will survive.

learned helplessness A phenomenon in which experience with an uncontrollable event creates passive behavior in the face of subsequent threats to well-being.

leniency bias The tendency for jury deliberation to produce a tilt toward acquittal.

loneliness A feeling of deprivation about existing social relations.

lowballing A two-step compliance technique in which the influencer secures agreement with a request but then increases the size of that request by revealing hidden costs.

matching hypothesis The proposition that people are attracted to others who are similar in physical attractiveness.

mere exposure effect The phenomenon whereby the more often people are exposed to a stimulus, the more positively they evaluate that stimulus.

mere presence theory The proposition that the mere presence of others is sufficient to produce social facilitation effects.

meta-analysis A set of statistical procedures used to review a body of evidence by combining the results of individual studies to measure the overall reliability and strength of particular effects.

mind perception The process by which people attribute humanlike mental states to various animate and inanimate objects, including other people.

minority influence The process by which dissenters produce change within a group.

misinformation effect The tendency for false postevent misinformation to become integrated into people's memory of an event.

modern racism A form of prejudice that surfaces in subtle ways when it is safe, socially acceptable, and easy to rationalize.

multicultural research Research designed to examine racial and ethnic groups within cultures.

mundane realism The degree to which the experimental situation resembles places and events in the real world.

need for affiliation The desire to establish and maintain many rewarding interpersonal relationships.

need for closure The desire to reduce cognitive uncertainty, which heightens the importance of first impressions.

need for cognition (NC) A personality variable that distinguishes people on the basis of how much they enjoy effortful cognitive activities.

negative state relief model The proposition that people help others in order to counteract their own feelings of sadness.

nonverbal behavior Behavior that reveals a person's feelings without words, through facial expressions, body language, and vocal cues.

normative influence Influence that produces conformity when a person fears the negative social consequences of appearing deviant.

normative model of leadership The theory that leadership effectiveness is determined by the amount of feedback and participation that leaders invite from workers.

obedience Behavior change produced by the commands of authority.

operational definition The specific procedures for manipulating or measuring a conceptual variable.

outgroup homogeneity effect The tendency to assume that there is greater similarity among members of outgroups than among members of ingroups.

outgroups Groups with which an individual does not feel a sense of membership, belonging, or identity.

overjustification effect The tendency for intrinsic motivation to diminish for activities that have become associated with reward or other extrinsic factors.

passionate love Romantic love characterized by high arousal, intense attraction, and fear of rejection.

peremptory challenge A means by which lawyers can exclude a limited number of prospective jurors without the judge's approval.

performance appraisal The process of evaluating an employee's work within the organization.

peripheral route to persuasion The process by which a person does not think carefully about a communication and is influenced instead by superficial cues.

personal attribution Attribution to internal characteristics of an actor, such as ability, personality, mood, or effort.

persuasion The process by which attitudes are changed.

pluralistic ignorance The state in which people in a group mistakenly think that their own individual thoughts, feelings, or behaviors are different from those of the others in the group.

polygraph A mechanical instrument that records physiological arousal from multiple channels; it is often used as a lie-detector test.

pornography Explicit sexual material.

posttraumatic stress disorder (PTSD) A condition in which a person experiences enduring physical and psychological symptoms after an extremely stressful event.

prejudice Negative feelings toward persons based on their membership in certain groups.

primacy effect The tendency for information presented early in a sequence to have more impact on impressions than information presented later.

priming The tendency for recently used or perceived words or ideas to come to mind easily and influence the interpretation of new information.

prisoner's dilemma A type of dilemma in which one party must make either cooperative or competitive moves in relation to another party. The dilemma is typically designed so that the competitive move appears to be in one's self-interest, but if both sides make this move, they both suffer more than if they had both cooperated.

private conformity The change of beliefs that occurs when a person privately accepts the position taken by others.

private self-consciousness A personality characteristic of individuals who are introspective, often attending to their own inner states.

proactive aggression Aggressive behavior whereby harm is inflicted as a means to a desired end (also called instrumental aggression).

proactive coping Up-front efforts to ward off or modify the onset of a stressful event.

problem-focused coping Cognitive and behavioral efforts to alter a stressful situation.

process gain The increase in group performance so that the group outperforms the individuals who make up the group.

process loss The reduction in group performance due to obstacles created by group processes, such as problems of coordination and motivation.

prosocial behaviors Actions intended to benefit others.

psychological reactance The theory that people react against threats to their freedom by asserting themselves and perceiving the threatened freedom as more attractive.

psychoneuroimmunology (PNI) A subfield of psychology that examines the links among psychological factors, the brain and nervous system, and the immune system.

public conformity A superficial change in overt behavior without a corresponding change of opinion that is produced by real or imagined group pressure.

public self-consciousness A personality characteristic of individuals who focus on themselves as social objects, as seen by others.

racism Prejudice and discrimination based on a person's racial background, or institutional and cultural practices that promote the domination of one racial group over another.

random assignment A method of assigning participants to the various conditions of an experiment so that each participant in the experiment has an equal chance of being in any of the conditions.

random sampling A method of selecting participants for a study so that everyone in a population has an equal chance of being in the study.

reactive aggression Aggressive behavior where the means and the end coincide; harm is inflicted for its own sake.

realistic conflict theory The theory that hostility between groups is caused by direct competition for limited resources.

reciprocal altruism Altruism that involves an individual helping another (despite some immediate risk or cost) and becoming more likely to receive help from the other in return

reciprocity A mutual exchange between what we give and receive—for example, liking those who like us.

relative deprivation Feelings of discontent aroused by the belief that one fares poorly compared with others.

reluctant altruism Altruistic kinds of behavior that result from pressure from peers or other sources of direct social influence

resource dilemmas Social dilemmas involving how two or more people will share a limited resource.

rumination In the context of aggression, rumination involves repeatedly thinking about and reliving an anger-inducing event, focusing on angry thoughts and feelings, and perhaps even planning or imagining revenge.

scientific jury selection A method of selecting juries through surveys that yield correlations between demographics and trial-relevant attitudes.

self-awareness theory The theory that self-focused attention leads people to notice self-discrepancies, thereby motivating either an escape from self-awareness or a change in behavior.

self-concept The sum total of an individual's beliefs about his or her own personal attributes.

self-disclosure Revelations about the self that a person makes to others.

self-efficacy A person's belief that he or she is capable of the specific behavior required to produce a desired outcome in a given situation.

self-esteem An affective component of the self, consisting of a person's positive and negative self-evaluations.

self-fulfilling prophecy The process by which one's expectations about a person eventually lead that person to behave in ways that confirm those expectations.

self-handicapping   Behaviors designed to sabotage one's own performance in order to provide a subsequent excuse for failure.

self-monitoring   The tendency to change behavior in response to the self-presentation concerns of the situation.

self-perception theory   The theory that when internal cues are difficult to interpret, people gain self-insight by observing their own behavior.

self-presentation   Strategies people use to shape what others think of them.

self-regulation   The process by which people control their thoughts, feelings, or behavior in order to achieve a personal or social goal.

self-schema   A belief people hold about themselves that guides the processing of self-relevant information.

sentencing disparity   Inconsistency of sentences for the same offense from one judge to another.

sexism   Prejudice and discrimination based on a person's gender, or institutional and cultural practices that promote the domination of one gender over another.

sexual orientation   A person's preference for members of the same sex (homosexuality), opposite sex (heterosexuality), or both sexes (bisexuality).

situational attribution   Attribution to factors external to an actor, such as the task, other people, or luck.

sleeper effect   A delayed increase in the persuasive impact of a noncredible source.

social categorization   The classification of persons into groups on the basis of common attributes.

social cognition   The study of how people perceive, remember, and interpret information about themselves and others.

social comparison theory   The theory that people evaluate their own abilities and opinions by comparing themselves to others.

social dilemma   A situation in which a self-interested choice by everyone will create the worst outcome for everyone.

social dominance orientation   A desire to see one's ingroup as dominant over other groups and a willingness to adopt cultural values that facilitate oppression over other groups.

social exchange theory   A perspective that views people as motivated to maximize benefits and minimize costs in their relationships with others.

social facilitation   A process whereby the presence of others enhances performance on easy tasks but impairs performance on difficult tasks.

social identity model of deindividuation effects (SIDE)   A model of group behavior that explains deindividuation effects as the result of a shift from personal identity to social identity.

social identity theory   The theory that people favor ingroups over outgroups in order to enhance their self-esteem.

social impact theory   The theory that social influence depends on the strength, immediacy, and number of source persons relative to target persons.

social learning theory   The theory that behavior is learned through the observation of others as well as through the direct experience of rewards and punishments.

social loafing   A group-produced reduction in individual output on tasks where contributions are pooled.

social neuroscience   The study of the relationship between neural and social processes.

social norm   A general rule of conduct reflecting standards of social approval and disapproval.

social perception   A general term for the processes by which people come to understand one another.

social psychology   The scientific study of how individuals think, feel, and behave in a social context.

social role theory   The theory that small gender differences are magnified in perception by the contrasting social roles occupied by men and women.

social support   The helpful coping resources provided by friends and other people.

Sociometer Theory   The theory that self-esteem is a gauge that monitors our social interactions and sends signals us as to whether our behavior is acceptable to others.

stereotype   A belief or association that links a whole group of people with certain traits or characteristics.

stereotype content model   A model proposing that the relative status and competition between groups influence group stereotypes along the dimensions of competence and warmth.

stereotype threat   The experience of concern about being evaluated based on negative stereotypes about one's group.

stigmatized   Being persistently stereotyped, perceived as deviant, and devalued in society because of membership in a particular social group or because of a particular characteristic.

stress   An unpleasant state of arousal in which people perceive the demands of an event as taxing or exceeding their ability to satisfy or alter those demands.

stressor   Anything that causes stress.

structured interview   An interview in which each job applicant is asked a standard set of questions and evaluated on the same criteria.

subject variable   A variable that characterizes preexisting differences among the participants in a study.

subjective well-being (SWB)   One's happiness, or life satisfaction, as measured by self-report.

subliminal presentation   A method of presenting stimuli so faintly or rapidly that people do not have any conscious awareness of having been exposed to them.

sunk cost principle   The economic rule of thumb that only future costs and benefits, not past commitments, should be considered in making a decision.

superordinate goal   A shared goal that can be achieved only through cooperation among individuals or groups.

system justification theory   A theory that proposes that people are motivated (at least in part) to defend and justify the existing social, political, and economic conditions.

Terror Management Theory   The theory that humans cope with the fear of their own death by constructing worldviews that help to preserve their self-esteem.

that's-not-all technique   A two-step compliance technique in which the influencer begins with an inflated request, then decreases its apparent size by offering a discount or bonus.

theory   An organized set of principles used to explain observed phenomena.

theory of planned behavior   The theory that attitudes toward a specific behavior combine with subjective norms and perceived control to influence a person's actions.

transactional leader   A leader who gains compliance and support from followers primarily through goal setting and the use of rewards.

transactive memory   A shared system for remembering information that enables multiple people to remember information together more efficiently than they could do so alone.

transformational leader   A leader who inspires followers to transcend their own needs in the interest of a common cause.

triangular theory of love   A theory proposing that love has three basic components—intimacy, passion, and commitment—that can be combined to produce eight subtypes.

two-factor theory of emotion   The theory that the experience of emotion is based on two factors: physiological arousal and a cognitive interpretation of that arousal.

Type A personality   A pattern of behavior characterized by extremes of competitive striving for achievement, a sense of time urgency, hostility, and aggression.

voir dire   The pretrial examination of prospective jurors by the judge or opposing lawyers to uncover signs of bias.

weapon-focus effect   The tendency for the presence of a weapon to draw attention and impair a witness's ability to identify the culprit.

weapons effect   The tendency that the likelihood of aggression will increase by the mere presence of weapons.

what-is-beautiful-is-good stereotype   The belief that physically attractive individuals also possess desirable personality characteristics.

References

Abelson, R. P. (1981). Psychological status of the script concept. *American Psychologist, 36,* 715–729.

Abelson, R. P., Aronson, E., McGuire, W. J., Newcomb, T. M., Rosenberg, M. J., & Tannenbaum, P. H. (1968). *Theories of cognitive consistency: A sourcebook.* Chicago: Rand McNally.

Abramson, L. Y., Metalsky, G. I., & Alloy, L. B. (1989). Hopelessness depression: A theory-based subtype of depression. *Psychological Review, 96,* 358–372.

Acevedo, B. P., & Aron, A. (2009). Does a long-term relationship kill romantic love? *Review of General Psychology, 13,* 59–65.

Acevedo, B. P., Aron, A., Fisher, H. E., & Brown, L. L. (2012) Neural correlates of long-term intense romantic love. *Social Cognitive and Affective Neuroscience, 7,* 145–159.

Acker, M., & Davis, M. H. (1992). Intimacy, passion, and commitment in adult romantic relationships: A test of the triangular theory of love. *Journal of Social and Personal Relationships, 9,* 21–50.

Ackerman, J. M., Griskevicius, V., & Li, N. P. (2011). Let's get serious: Communicating commitment in romantic relationships. *Journal of Personality and Social Psychology, 100,* 1079–1094.

Adair, J. G. (1984). The Hawthorne effect: A reconsideration of the methodological artifact. *Journal of Applied Psychology, 69,* 334–345.

Adair, W. L., & Brett, J. M. (2005). The negotiation dance: Time, culture, and behavioral sequences in negotiation. *Organization Science, 16,* 33–51.

Adams, J. S. (1965). Equity in social exchange. *Advances in Experimental Social Psychology, 2,* 267–299.

Adams, J., Parkinson, L., & Sanson-Fisher, R. W. (2008). Enhancing self-report of adolescent smoking: the effects of bogus pipeline and anonymity. *Addictive Behaviors, 33,* 1291–1296.

Adams, P. R., & Adams, G. R. (1984). Mount Saint Helens's ash-fall: Evidence for a disaster stress reaction. *American Psychologist, 39,* 252–260.

Addison, S. (2014, July 26). Britain arrests two in suspected female genital mutilation case. *Reuters.*

Ader, R. (Ed.). (2007). *Psychoneuroimmunology* (4th ed.). Burlington, MA: Elsevier.

Adherents.com. (2015). Major religions of the world ranked by number of adherents. Available at http://www.adherents.com/Religions_By_Adherents.html.

Adla, A. A., Zarate, P. P., & Soubie, J. L. (2011). A proposal of toolkit for GDSS facilitators. *Group Decision and Negotiation, 20,* 57–77.

Adler, N. E., Boyce, T., Chesney, M. A., Cohen, S., Folkman, S., Kahn, R. L., & Syme, S. L. (1994). Socioeconomic status and health: The challenge of the gradient. *American Psychologist, 49,* 15–24.

Adorno, T., Frenkel-Brunswik, E., Levinson, D., & Sanford, R. N. (1950). The authoritarian personality. New York: Harper.

Afifi, T. O., Mota, N. P., Dasiewicz, P., MacMillan, H. L., & Sareen, J. (2012). Physical punishment and mental disorders: Results from a nationally representative U.S. sample. *Pediatrics, 130,* 184–192.

Aggarwal, P., & O'Brien, C. L. (2008). Social loafing on group projects: Structural antecedents and effect on student satisfaction. *Journal of Marketing Education, 30,* 255–264.

Aguiar, P., Vala, J., Correia, I., & Pereira, C. (2008). Justice in our world and in that of others: Belief in a just world and reactions to victims. *Social Justice Research, 21,* 50–68.

Aharon, I., Etcoff, N., Ariely, D., Chabris, C. F., O'Connor, E., & Breiter, H. C. (2001). Beautiful faces have variable reward value: fMRI and behavioral evidence. *Neuron, 32,* 537–551.

Ahmed, A. (2015, July 3). *And now, what Mexico thinks of Donald Trump.* New York Times, p. A4.

Ainsworth, M., Blehar, M. C., Waters, E., & Wall, S. (1978). *Patterns of attachment: A psychological study of the strange situation.* Hillsdale, NJ: Erlbaum.

Ainsworth, S. E., & Maner, J. K. (2014). Assailing the competition: Sexual selection, proximate mating motives, and aggressive behavior in men. *Personality and Social Psychology Bulletin, 40,* 1648–1658.

Ajzen, I. (1991). The theory of planned behavior. *Organizational Behavior and Human Decision Processes, 50,* 179–211.

Ajzen, I., & Fishbein, M. (1977). Attitude-behavior relations: A theoretical analysis and review of empirical research. *Psychological Bulletin, 84,* 888–918.

Ajzen, I., & Fishbein, M. (2005). The influence of attitudes on behavior. In D. Albarracín, B. T. Johnson, & M. P. Zanna (Eds.), *The handbook of attitudes* (pp. 173–221). Hillsdale, NJ: Erlbaum.

Akerloff, G. A., & Shiller, R. J. (2009). *Animal spirits: How human psychology drives the economy, and why it matters for global capitalism.* Princeton, NJ: Princeton University Press.

Aknin, L. B., et al. (2013). Prosocial spending and well-being: Cross-cultural evidence for a psychological universal. *Journal of Personality and Social Psychology, 104,* 635–652.

Aknin, L. B., Broesch, T., Hamlin, J. K., Van de Vondervoort, J. W. (2015). Prosocial behavior leads to happiness in a small-scale rural society. *Journal of Experimental Psychology: General, 144*(4), 788–795.

Albarracín, D., Gillette, J. C., Earl, A. N., Glasman, L. R., Durantini, M. R., & Ho, M.-H. (2005). A test of major assumptions about behavior change: A comprehensive look at the effects of passive and active HIV-prevention interventions since the beginning of the epidemic. *Psychological Bulletin, 131,* 856–897.

Albarracín, D., Johnson, B. T., Fishbein, M., & Muellerleile, P. A. (2001). Theories of reasoned action and planned behavior as models of condom use: A meta-analysis. *Psychological Bulletin, 127,* 142–161.

Albert, T. (2015, March 14). Good Samaritan law shields California doctor from liability. *American Medical News,* amdemnews.com/article/20050314/profession/303149965/5/.

Alderson, A. (2001, Nov 11). Mother blames herself for the White Mischief copycat murder of her son. *The Telegraph,* http://www.telegraph.co.uk/news/worldnews/africaandindianocean/kenya/1362143/Mother-blames-herself-for-the-White-Mischief-copycat-murder-of-her-son.html.

Alessandri, G., Vecchione, M., Eisenberg, N., & Łaguna, M. (2015). On the factor structure of the Rosenberg (1965) General Self-Esteem Scale. *Psychological Assessment, 27,* 621–635.

Alexander, G. M. (2003). An evolutionary perspective of sex-typed toy preferences: Pink, blue, and the brain. *Archives of Sexual Behavior, 32,* 7–14.

Alexander, G. M., & Hines, M. (2002). Sex differences in response to children's toys in nonhuman primates (*Cercopithecus aethiops sabaeus*). *Evolution and Human Behavior, 23,* 467–479.

Alge, B. J. (2001). Effects of computer surveillance on perceptions of privacy and procedural justice. *Journal of Applied Psychology, 86,* 797–804.

Allam, A. (2012). A toxic mix of tradition and religion; Egypt. *Financial Times (London, England),* p. 3.

Allan, R., & Fisher, J. (Eds.). (2011). *Heart and mind: The practice of cardiac psychology* (2nd ed.). Washington, DC: American Psychological Association.

Allen, J., Weinrich, M., Hoppitt, W., & Rendell, L. (2013). Network-based diffusion analysis reveals cultural transmission of lobtail feeding in humpback whales. *Science, 340,* 485–488.

Allen, J. B., Kenrick, D. T., Linder, D. E., & McCall, M. A. (1989). Arousal and attribution: A response-facilitation alternative to misattribution and negative-reinforcement models. *Journal of Personality and Social Psychology, 57,* 261–270.

Allen, V. L. (1965). Situational factors in conformity. In L. Berkowitz (Ed.), *Advances in Experimental Social Psychology, 2,* 133–175.

Allen, V. L., & Levine, J. M. (1969). Consensus and conformity. *Journal of Experimental Social Psychology, 5,* 389–399.

Allen, V. L., & Levine, J. M. (1971). Social support and conformity: The role of independent assessment of reality. *Journal of Experimental Social Psychology, 7,* 48–58.

Alliger, G. M., & Dwight, S. A. (2000). A meta-analytic investigation of the susceptibility of integrity tests to faking and coaching. *Educational and Psychological Measurement, 60,* 59–72.

Alliger, G. M., Lilienfeld, S. O., & Mitchell, K. E. (1996). The susceptibility of overt and covert integrity tests to coaching and faking. *Psychological Science, 7,* 32–39.

Alloy, L. B., Abramson, L. Y., Whitehouse, W. G., Hogan, M. E., Panzarella, C., & Rose, D. T. (2006). Prospective incidence of first onsets and recurrences of depression in individuals at high and low cognitive risk for depression. *Journal of Abnormal Psychology, 115,* 145–156.

Allport, F. H. (1924). *Social psychology.* Boston: Houghton Mifflin.

Allport, F. H., et al. (1953). The effects of segregation and the consequences of desegregation: A social science statement. *Minneapolis Law Review, 37,* 429–440.

Allport, G. W. (1954). *The nature of prejudice.* Reading, MA: Addison-Wesley.

Allport, G. W., & Postman, L. J. (1947). *The psychology of rumor.* New York: Holt.

Alquist, J. L., Ainsworth, S. E., Baumeister, R. F., Daly, M., & Stillman, T. F. (2015). The making of might-have-beens: Effects of free will belief on counterfactual thinking. *Personality and Social Psychology Bulletin, 41,* 268–283.

Alterovitz, S. S.-R., & Mendelsohn, G. A. (2009). Partner preferences across the life span: Online dating by older adults. *Psychology and Aging, 24,* 513–517.

Altheimer, I. (2013). Cultural processes and homicide across nations. *International Journal of Offender Therapy and Comparative Criminology, 57,* 842–863.

Altman, I. (1973). Reciprocity of interpersonal exchange. *Journal for Theory of Social Behavior, 3,* 249–261.

Altman, I., & Taylor, D. A. (1973). *Social penetration: The development of interpersonal relationships.* New York: Holt, Rinehart and Winston.

Alvidrez, A., & Weinstein, R. S. (1999). Early teacher perceptions and later student academic achievement. *Journal of Educational Psychology, 91,* 731–746.

Alwin, D. F. (1990). Cohort replacement and changes in parental socialization values. *Journal of Marriage and the Family 52,* 347–360.

Amabile, T. M. (1996). *Creativity in context.* New York: Westview.

Amabile, T. M., & Kramer, S. J. (2010). What really motivates workers. *Harvard Business Review, 88* (1), 44–45.

Amabile, T. M., & Kramer, S. J. (2011). *The Progress Principle: Using small wins to ignite joy, engagement, and creativity at work.* Cambridge, MA: Harvard Business Press.

Amabile, T. M., Hill, K. G., Hennessey, B. A., & Tighe, E. M. (1994). The work preference inventory: Assessing intrinsic and extrinsic motivation orientations. *Journal of Personality and Social Psychology, 66,* 950–967.

Amato, P. R. (2010). Research on divorce: Continuing trends and new developments. *Journal of Marriage and Family, 72,* 650–666.

Ambady, N. (2010). The perils of pondering: Intuition and thin slice judgments. *Psychological Inquiry, 21,* 271–278.

Ambady, N., & Rosenthal, R. (1993). Half a minute: Predicting teacher evaluations from thin slices of nonverbal behavior and physical attractiveness. *Journal of Personality and Social Psychology, 64,* 431–441.

Ambrose, M. L., & Schminke, M. (2009). The role of overall justice judgments in organizational justice research: A test of mediation. *Journal of Applied Psychology, 94,* 491–500.

American Academy of Pediatrics (2009). Policy statement—media violence. *Pediatrics, 124,* 1495–1503.

American Academy of Pediatrics (2015, May 5). *Where we stand: Spanking.* http://www.healthychildren.org/English/family-life/family-dynamics/communication-discipline/Pages/Where-We-Stand-Spanking.aspx.

American Psychological Association. (2002). Ethical principles of psychologists and code of conduct. *American Psychologist, 57,* 1060–1073.

American Psychological Association. (2008, October 7). *Stress in America 2008 Survey: Executive summary.* Washington, DC: American Psychological Association. Available at http://apahelpcenter.mediaroom.com/index.php?s=pageC.

American Psychological Association (2010). Amendments to the 2002 "Ethical principles of psychologists and code of conduct." *American Psychologist, 65,* 493.

American Psychological Association. (2015, February 4). Stress in America: Paying with our health. Washington, DC: American Psychological Association. Available at: http://www.apa.org/news/press/releases/stress/2014/highlights.aspx.

Amnesty International. (2012). *Choice and prejudice: Discrimination against Muslims in Europe.* London: Amnesty International.

Amodio, D. M. (2014). The neuroscience of prejudice and stereotyping. *Nature Reviews Neuroscience, 15,* 670–682.

Amodio, D. M., Bartholow, B. D., & Ito, T. A. (2014). Tracking the dynamics of the social brain: ERP approaches for social cognitive and affective neuroscience. *Social Cognitive and Affective Neuroscience, 9,* 385–393.

Andersen, S. M., & Chen, S. (2002). The relational self: An interpersonal social-cognitive theory. *Psychological Review, 109,* 619–645.

Anderson, C. A. (2001). Heat and violence. *Current Directions in Psychological Science, 10,* 33–38.

Anderson, C. A. (2012). Climate change and violence. In D. Christie (Ed.), *The encyclopedia of peace psychology.* Hoboken, NJ: Wiley-Blackwell.

Anderson, C. A., & Anderson, K. B. (1996). Violent crime rate statistics in philosophical context: A destructive testing approach to heat and southern culture of violence effects. *Journal of Personality and Social Psychology, 70,* 740–756.

Anderson, C. A., & Bushman, B. J. (2002a). The effects of media violence on society. *Science, 295,* 2377–2379.

Anderson, C. A., & DeLisi, M. (2011). Implications of global climate change for violence in developed and developing countries. In J. P. Forgas, A. W. Kruglanski, & K. D. Williams (Eds.), *The psychology of social conflict and aggression* (pp. 249–265). New York: Psychology Press.

Anderson, C. A., & Huesmann, L. R. (2007). Human aggression: A social-cognitive review. In M. A. Hogg & J. Cooper (Eds.), *The Sage handbook of social psychology* (pp. 259–287). London: Sage.

Anderson, C. A., & Sechler, E. S. (1986). Effects of explanation and counter-explanation on the development and use of social theories. *Journal of Personality and Social Psychology, 50,* 24–34.

Anderson, C. A., Anderson, K. B., & Deuser, W. E. (1996). Examining an affective framework: Weapon and temperature effects on aggressive thoughts, affect, and attitudes. *Personality and Social Psychology Bulletin, 22,* 366–376.

Anderson, C. A., Anderson, K. B., Dorr, N., DeNeve, K. M., & Flanagan, M. (2000). Temperature and aggression. In M. P.

Zanna (Ed.), *Advances in experimental social psychology* (Vol. 32, pp. 63–133). San Diego, CA: Academic Press.

Anderson, C. A., Berkowitz, L., Donnerstein, E., Huesmann, L. R., Johnson, J. D., Linz, D., Malamuth, N. M., & Wartella, E. (2003). The influence of media violence on youth. *Psychological Science in the Public Interest, 4,* 81–110.

Anderson, C. A., Carnagey, N. L., Flanagan, M., Benjamin, A. J., Eubanks, J., & Valentine, J. C. (2004). Violent video games: Specific effects of violent content on aggressive thoughts and behavior. *Advances in Experimental Social Psychology, 36,* 199–249.

Anderson, C. A., Lepper, M. R., & Ross, L. (1980). Perseverance of social theories: The role of explanation in the persistence of discredited information. *Journal of Personality and Social Psychology, 39,* 1037–1049.

Anderson, J. L., Crawford, C. B., Nadeau, J., & Lindberg, T. (1992). Was the Duchess of Windsor right? A cross-cultural review of the socioecology of ideals of female body shape. *Ethology and Sociobiology, 13,* 197–227.

Anderson, J. R., Kuroshima, H., Takimoto, A., & Fujita, K. (2013). Third-party social evaluation of humans by monkeys. *Nature communications, 4,* 1561.

Anderson, N. H. (1965). Averaging versus adding as a stimulus combination rule in impression formation. *Journal of Experimental Social Psychology, 70,* 394–400.

Anderson, N. H. (1968). Likableness ratings of 555 personality-trait words. *Journal of Personality and Social Psychology, 9,* 272–279.

Anderson, N. H. (1981). *Foundations of Information Integration Theory.* New York: Academic Press.

Anderson, N. H., & Hubert, S. (1963). Effects of concomitant verbal recall on order effects in personality impression formation. *Journal of Verbal Learning and Verbal Behavior, 2,* 379–391.

Andreasson, P. B. (1987). On the social psychology of the stock market: Aggregate attributional effects and the regressiveness of prediction. *Journal of Personality and Social Psychology, 53,* 490–496.

Andreychik, M. R., & Gill, M. J. (2015). Do natural kind beliefs about social groups contribute to prejudice? Distinguishing bio-somatic essentialism from bio-behavioral essentialism, and both of these from entitativity. *Group Processes & Intergroup Relations, 18,* 454–474.

Andrighetto, L., Baldissarri, C., Lattanzio, S., Loughnan, S., & Volpato, C. (2014). Humanitarian aid? Two forms of dehumanization and willingness to help after natural disasters. *British Journal of Social Psychology, 53,* 573–584.

Ansari, A., & Klinenberg, E. (2015). How to make online dating work. *The New York Times,* June 13, 2015.

Antonio, A. L., Chang, M. J., Hakuta, K., Kenny, D. A., Levin, S., & Milem, J. F. (2004). Effects of racial diversity on complex thinking in college students. *Psychological Science, 15,* 507–510.

Apfelbaum, E. P., Pauker, K., Ambady, N., Sommers, S. R., & Norton, M. I. (2008). Learning (not) to talk about race: When older children underperform in social categorization. *Developmental Psychology, 44,* 1513–1518.

Apodaca v. Oregon, 406 U.S. 404 (1972).

Appleby, S. C., Hasel, L. E., & Kassin, S. M. (2013). Police-induced confessions: An empirical analysis of their content and impact. *Psychology, Crime and Law, 19,* 111–128.

Archer, J. (2004). Sex differences in aggression in real-world settings: A meta-analytic review. *Review of General Psychology, 8,* 291–322.

Arditi, L. (2015, July 10). Leaders to police: Honor Good Samaritan act. *The Providence Journal,* p. A6.

Arendt, H. (1963). *Eichmann in Jerusalem: A report on the banality of evil.* New York: Viking.

Arkes, H. R., & Ayton, P. (1999). The sunk cost and Concorde effects: Are humans less rational than lower animals? *Psychological Bulletin, 125,* 591–600.

Arkin, R. M. (1981). Self-presentation styles. In J. T. Tedeschi (Ed.), *Impression management theory and social psychological research* (pp. 311–333). New York: Academic Press.

Arluke, A. (2012). Interpersonal barriers to stopping animal abuse: Exploring the role of adolescent friendship norms and breeches. *Journal of Interpersonal Violence, 27,* 2939–2958.

Armor, D. A., & Taylor, S. E. (1998). Situated optimism: Specific outcome expectancies and self-regulation. *Advances in Experimental Social Psychology, 30,* 309–379.

Arnocky, S., Ribout, A., Mirza, R., & Knack, J. M. (2014). Perceived mate availability influences intrasexual competition, jealousy and mate guarding behavior. *Journal of Evolutionary Psychology, 12,* 45–64.

Aron, A., & Westbay L. (1996). Dimensions of the prototype of love. *Journal of Personality and Social Psychology, 70,* 535–551.

Aron, A., Dutton, D. G., Aron, E. N., & Iverson, A. (1989). Experiences of falling in love. *Journal of Social and Personal Relationships, 6,* 243–257.

Aron, A., Norman, C. C., Aron, E. N., McKenna, C., & Heyman, R. E. (2000). Couples' shared participation in novel and arousing activities and experienced relationship quality. *Journal of Personality and Social Psychology, 78,* 273–284.

Aronson, E. (1969). The theory of cognitive dissonance: A current perspective. *Advances in Experimental Social Psychology, 4,* 1–34.

Aronson, E. (1992). Stateways can change folkways. In R. M. Baird & S. E. Rosenbaum (Eds.), *Bigotry, prejudice, and hatred: Definitions, causes, and solutions* (pp. 185–201). Buffalo, NY: Prometheus.

Aronson, E. (1999). Dissonance, hypocrisy, and the self-concept. In E. Harmon-Jones & J. Mills (Eds.), *Cognitive dissonance: Progress on a pivotal theory in social psychology* (pp. 103–126). Washington, DC: American Psychological Association.

Aronson, E. (2004). Reducing hostility and building compassion: Lessons from the jigsaw classroom. In A. G. Miller (Ed.), *The social psychology of good and evil* (pp. 469–488). New York: Guilford.

Aronson, E. (2011). Reducing prejudice and building empathy in the classroom. In M. A. Gernsbacher et al. (Eds.), *Psychology and the real world: Essays illustrating fundamental contributions to society* (pp. 230–236). New York: Worth.

Aronson, E., & Carlsmith, J. M. (1963). Effect of severity of threat on the devaluation of forbidden behavior. *Journal of Abnormal and Social Psychology, 66,* 584–588.

Aronson, E., & Carlsmith, J. M. (1968). Experimentation in social psychology. In G. Lindzey & E. Aronson (Eds.), *Handbook of social psychology* (2nd ed., Vol. 2, pp. 1–79). Reading, MA: Addison-Wesley.

Aronson, E., & Cope, V (1968). My enemy's enemy is my friend. *Journal of Personality and Social Psychology, 8,* 8–12.

Aronson, E., & Linder, D. (1965). Gain and loss of esteem as determinants of interpersonal attractiveness. *Journal of Experimental Social Psychology, 1,* 156–172.

Aronson, E., & Mills, J. (1959). The effect of severity of initiation on liking for a group. *Journal of Abnormal and Social Psychology, 59,* 177–181.

Aronson, E., Blaney, N., Stephan, C., Sikes, J., & Snapp, M. (1978). *The jigsaw classroom.* Beverly Hills, CA: Sage.

Aronson, J., Lustina, M. J., Good, C., Keough, K., Steele, C. M., & Brown, J. (1999). When white men can't do math: Necessary and sufficient factors in stereotype threat. *Journal of Experimental Social Psychology, 35,* 29–46.

Arthur, W., Day, E. D., McNelly, T. L., & Edens, P. S. (2003). A meta-analysis of the criterion-related validity of assessment center dimensions. *Personnel Psychology, 56,* 125–154.

Asch, S. E. (1946). Forming impressions of personality. *Journal of Abnormal and Social Psychology, 41,* 258–290.

Asch, S. E. (1951). Effects of group pressure upon the modification and distortion of judgments. In H. Guetzkow (Ed.), *Groups, leadership, and men.* Pittsburgh: Carnegie Press.

Asch, S. E. (1955, November). Opinions and social pressure. *Scientific American*, pp. 31–35.

Asch, S. E. (1956). Studies of independence and conformity: A minority of one against a unanimous majority. *Psychological Monographs, 70*, 416.

Asch, S. E., & Zukier, H. (1984). Thinking about persons. *Journal of Personality and Social Psychology, 46*, 1230–1240.

Asgari, S., Dasgupta, N., & Stout, J.G. (2012). When do counter-stereotypic ingroup members inspire versus deflate? The effect of successful professional women on young women's leadership self-concept. *Personality and Social Psychology Bulletin, 38*, 370–383.

Askenasy, H. (1978). *Are we all Nazis?* Secaucus, NJ: Lyle Stuart.

Askew, K., Buckner, J. E., Taing, M. U., Ilie, A., Bauer, J. A., & Coovert, M. D. (2014). Explaining cyberloafing: The role of the theory of planned behavior. *Computers in Human Behavior, 36*, 510–519.

Aspinwall, L. G., & Taylor, S. E. (1992). Modeling cognitive adaptation: A longitudinal investigation of the impact of individual differences and coping on college adjustment and performance. *Journal of Personality and Social Psychology, 63*, 989–1003.

Aspinwall, L. G., & Taylor, S. E. (1993). The effects of social comparison direction, threat, and self-esteem on affect, self-evaluation, and expected success. *Journal of Personality and Social Psychology, 64*, 708–722.

Aspinwall, L. G., & Taylor, S. E. (1997). A stitch in time: Self-regulation and proactive coping. *Psychological Bulletin, 121*, 417–436.

Aspinwall, L. G., & Tedeschi, R. G. (2010a). The value of positive psychology for health psychology: Progress and pitfalls in examining the relation of positive phenomena to health. *Annals of Behavioral Medicine, 39*, 4–15.

Aspinwall, L. G., & Tedeschi, R. G. (2010b). Of babies and bathwater: a reply to Coyne and Tennen's views on positive psychology and health. *Annals of Behavioral Medicine, 39*, 27–34.

Atran, S., & Norenzayan, A. (2004). Religion's evolutionary landscape: Counterintuition, commitment, compassion, communion. *Behavioral and Brain Sciences, 27*, 713–770.

Attrill, A. (2015). *The manipulation of online self-presentation: Create, Edit, Re-edit and Present.* New York: Palgrave Macmillan.

Atwater, L., Wang, M., Smither, J. W., & Fleenor, J. W. (2009). Are cultural characteristics associated with the relationship between self and others' ratings of leadership? *Journal of Applied Psychology, 94*, 876–886.

Auerbach, S. M., Kiesler, D. J., Strentz, T., Schmidt, J. A., & Serio, C. D. (1994). Interpersonal impacts and adjustment to the stress of simulated captivity: An empirical test of the Stockholm Syndrome. *Journal of Social and Clinical Psychology, 13*, 207–221.

Aviezer, H., Hassin, R. R., Ryan, J., Grady, C., Susskind, J., Anderson, A., & Bentin, S. (2008). Angry, disgusted, or afraid? Studies on the malleability of emotion perception. *Psychological Science, 19*, 724–732.

Avolio, B. J. (2011). *Full range leadership development.* Thousand Oaks, CA: Sage.

Avolio, B. J., Walumbwa, F. O., & Day, D. V. (Eds.). (2014). *The Oxford handbook of leadership and organizations.* New York: Oxford University Press.

Axsom, D. (1989). Cognitive dissonance and behavior change in psychotherapy. *Journal of Experimental Social Psychology, 25*, 234–252.

Axsom, D., & Cooper, J. (1985). Cognitive dissonance and psychotherapy: The role of effort justification in inducing weight loss. *Journal of Experimental Social Psychology, 21*, 149–160.

Axtell, R. E. (1993). *Do's and taboos around the world* (3rd ed.). New York: John Wiley.

Babcock, L., & Laschever, S. (2003). *Women don't ask: Negotiation and the gender divide.* Princeton, NJ: Princeton University Press.

Back, M. D., Schmukle, S. C., & Egloff, B. (2008). Becoming friends by chance. *Psychological Science, 19*, 439–440.

Back, M. D., Stopfer, J. M., Vazire, S., Gaddis, S., Schmukle, S. C., Egloff, B., & Gosling, S. D. (2010). Facebook profiles reflect actual personality, not self-idealization. *Psychological Science, 21*, 372–374.

Badal, S., & Harter, J. K. (2014). Gender diversity, business-unit engagement, and performance. *Journal of Leadership & Organizational Studies, 21*, 354–365.

Bagemihl, B. (1999). *Biological exuberance: Animal homosexuality and natural diversity.* New York: St. Martin's Press.

Bahrick, H. P., Hall, L. K., & Berger, S. A. (1996). Accuracy and distortion in memory for high school grades. *Psychological Science, 7*, 265–271.

Bailenson, J. N., & Yee, N. (2005). Digital chameleons: Automatic assimilation of nonverbal gestures in immersive virtual environments. *Psychological Science, 16*, 814–819.

Bailey, A. A., & Hurd, P. L. (2005). Finger length ratio (2D:4D) correlates with physical aggression in men but not in women. *Biological Psychology, 68*, 215–222.

Bailey, C. A., & Ostrov, J. M. (2008). Differentiating forms and functions of aggression in emerging adults: Associations with hostile attribution biases and normative beliefs. *Journal of Youth and Adolescence, 37*, 713–722.

Bailey, J. M., & Pillard, R. C. (1991). A genetic study of male sexual orientation. *Archives of General Psychiatry, 48*, 1089–1096.

Bailey, J. M., & Zucker, K. J. (1995). Childhood sex-typed behavior and sexual orientation: A conceptual analysis and quantitative review. *Developmental Psychology, 31*, 43–55.

Bailey, J. M., Dunne, M. P., & Martin, N. G. (2000). Genetic and environmental influences on sexual orientation and its correlates in an Australian twin sample. *Journal of Personality and Social Psychology, 78*, 524–536.

Bailey, J. M., Pillard, R. C., Neale, M. C., & Agyei, Y. (1993). Heritable factors influence sexual orientation in women. *Archives of General Psychiatry, 50*, 217–223.

Bailey, J. O., & Bailenson, J. N. (2015). Virtual reality and collaboration. In R. A. Calvo et al. (Eds.), *The Oxford handbook of affective computing* (pp. 494–502). New York: Oxford University Press.

Balcetis, E., Cole, S., & Sherali, S. (2014). The motivated and mindful perceiver: Relationships among motivated perception, mindfulness, and self-regulation. In A. Ie, C. T. Ngnoumen, & E. J. Langer (Eds.), *The Wiley Blackwell handbook of mindfulness* (Vols. I and II) (pp. 200–215). West Sussex, UK: Wiley-Blackwell.

Balcetis, E., & Dunning, D. (2006). See what you want to see: Motivational influences on visual perception. *Journal of Personality and Social Psychology, 91*, 612–625.

Balcetis, E., & Dunning, D. (2007). Cognitive dissonance and the perception of natural environments. *Psychological Science, 18*, 917–921.

Balcetis, E., & Dunning, D. (2010). Wishful seeing: more desired objects are seen as closer. *Psychological Science, 21*, 147–152.

Baldus, D. C., Woodworth, G., & Pulaski, C. A. (1990). *Equal justice and the death penalty: A legal and empirical analysis.* Boston: Northeastern University Press.

Baldwin, M., & Landau, M. J. (2014). Exploring nostalgia's influence on psychological growth. *Self and Identity, 13*, 128–147.

Baldwin, M., Biernat, M., & Landau, M. J. (2015). Remembering the real me: Nostalgia offers a window to the intrinsic self. *Journal of Personality and Social Psychology, 108*, 128–147.

Baldwin, A. S., Rothman, A. J., Hertel, A. W., Linde, J. A., Jeffery, R. W., Finch, E. A., & Lando, H. A. (2006). Specifying the determinants of the initiation and maintenance of behavior change: An examination of self-efficacy, satisfaction, and smoking cessation. *Health Psychology, 25*, 626–634.

Bales, R. F. (1958). Task roles and social roles in problem-solving groups. In E. E. Maccoby, T. M. Newcomb, & E. L. Hartley (Eds.), *Readings in social psychology* (3rd ed., pp. 437–447). New York: Holt.

Ball, H. A., Arseneault, L., Taylor, A., Maughan, B., Caspi, A., & Moffitt, T. E. (2008). Genetic and environmental influences on victims, bullies and bully-victims in childhood. *Journal of Child Psychology and Psychiatry, 49*, 104–112.

Ballew v. Georgia, 435 U.S. 223 (1978).

Balliet, D., & Van Lange, P. M. (2013). Trust, conflict, and cooperation: A meta-analysis. *Psychological Bulletin, 139*, 1090–1112.

Balliet, D., Wu, J., & De Dreu, C. W. (2014). Ingroup favoritism in cooperation: A meta-analysis. *Psychological Bulletin, 140*, 1556–1581.

Banaji, M. R., & Steele, C. M. (1989). Alcohol and self-evaluation: Is a social cognition approach beneficial? *Social Cognition, 7*, 137–151.

Bandura, A. (1973). *Aggression: A social learning analysis.* Englewood Cliffs, NJ: Prentice-Hall.

Bandura, A. (1977). *Social learning theory.* Englewood Cliffs, NJ: Prentice-Hall.

Bandura, A. (1983). Psychological mechanisms of aggression. In R. G. Geen & E. I. Donnerstein (Eds.), *Aggression: Theoretical and empirical reviews: Vol. l. Theoretical and methodological issues* (pp. 1–40). New York: Academic Press.

Bandura, A. (1997). *Self-efficacy: The exercise of control.* New York: W. H. Freeman.

Bandura, A., Ross, R., & Ross, S. (1961). Transmission of aggression through imitation of aggressive models. *Journal of Abnormal and Social Psychology, 63*, 575–582.

Bangerter, A., Roulin, N., & König, C. J. (2012). Personnel selection as a signaling game. *Journal of Applied Psychology, 97*, 719–738.

Banuazizi, A., & Movahedi, S. (1975). Interpersonal dynamics in a simulated prison: A methodological analysis. *American Psychologist, 30*, 152–160.

Barberis, N., & Xiong, W. (2009). What drives the disposition effect? An analysis of a long-standing preference-based explanation. *Journal of Finance, 64*, 751–784.

Barbulescu, R., & Bidwell, M. (2013). Do women choose different jobs from men? Mechanisms of application segregation in the market for managerial workers. *Organization Science, 24*, 737–756.

Barden, J., & Petty, R. E. (2008). The mere perception of elaboration creates attitude certainty: Exploring the thoughtfulness heuristic. *Journal of Personality and Social Psychology, 95*, 489–509.

Bargh, J. A., & Chartrand, T. L. (1999). The unbearable automaticity of being. *American Psychologist, 54*, 462–479

Bargh, J. A., & McKenna, K. Y. A. (2004). The internet and social life. *Annual Review of Psychology, 55*, 1–20.

Bargh, J. A., & Pietromonaco, P. (1982). Automatic information processing and social perception: The influence of trait information presented outside of conscious awareness on impression formation. *Journal of Personality and Social Psychology, 43*, 437–449.

Bargh, J. A., Chaiken, S., Govender, R., & Pratto, F. (1992). The generality of the automatic attitude activation effect. *Journal of Personality and Social Psychology, 62*, 893–912.

Bargh, J. A., Chen, M., & Burrows, L. (1996). Automaticity of social behavior: Direct effects of trait construct and stereotype activation on action. *Journal of Personality and Social Psychology, 71*, 230–244.

Bargh, J. A., Lombardi, W. J., & Higgins, E. T. (1988). Automaticity of chronically accessible constructs in person x situation effects on person perception: It's just a matter of time. *Journal of Personality and Social Psychology, 55*, 599–605.

Bargh, J. A., Schwader, K. L., Hailey, S. E., Dyer, R. L., & Boothby, E. J. (2012). Automaticity in social-cognitive processes. *Trends in Cognitive Sciences, 16*, 593–605.

Barkan, R., Ayal, S., Gino, F., & Ariely, D. (2012). The pot calling the kettle black: Distancing response to ethical dissonance. *Journal of Experimental Psychology: General, 141*, 757–773.

Barling, J., Kelloway, K., & Frone, M. (2005). *Handbook of occupational stress.* Los Angeles: Sage.

Barnes, C. D., Brown, R. P., & Tamborski, M. (2012). Living dangerously: Culture of honor, risk-taking, and the nonrandomness of "accidental" deaths. *Social Psychological and Personality Science, 3*, 100–107.

Barnes, C. M., & Wagner, D. T. (2009). Changing to daylight saving time cuts into sleep and increases workplace injuries. *Journal of Applied Psychology, 94*, 1305–1317.

Barnes, R. D., Ickes, W., & Kidd, R. F. (1979). Effects of the perceived intentionality and stability of another's dependency on helping behavior. *Personality and Social Psychology Bulletin, 5*, 367–372.

Barnes, T. (2014, June 17). Racial incident involving fans strikes nerves during World Cup. *USA Today*, http://worldcup.usatoday.com/2014/06/17/racial-incident-involving-fans-strikes-nerve-during-world-cup.

Barnes Nacoste, R. (1994). If empowerment is the goal . . . : Affirmative action and social interaction. *Basic and Applied Social Psychology, 15*, 87–112.

Baron, A. S., & Banaji, M. R. (2006). The development of implicit attitudes: Evidence of race evaluations from ages 6 and 10 and adulthood. *Psychological Science, 17*, 53–58.

Baron, R. A. (1997). The sweet smell of helping: Effects of pleasant ambient fragrance on prosocial behavior in shopping malls. *Journal of Personality and Social Psychology, 23*(5), 498–503.

Baron, R. A., & Richardson, D. R. (1994). *Human aggression* (2nd ed.). New York: Plenum.

Baron, R. S. (1986). Distraction-conflict theory: Progress and problems. In L. Berkowitz (Ed.), *Advances in experimental social psychology* (Vol. 19, pp. 1–40). Orlando, FL: Academic Press.

Baron, R. S. (2005). So right it's wrong: Groupthink and the ubiquitous nature of polarized group decision making. In M. P. Zanna (Ed.), *Advances in experimental social psychology* (pp. 219–253). San Diego: Elsevier Academic Press.

Baron, R. S., Hoppe, S. I., Kao, C. F., Brunsman, B., Linneweh, B., & Rogers, D. (1996). Social corroboration and opinion extremity. *Journal of Experimental Social Psychology, 32*, 537–560.

Barrett, H. C., Todd, P. M., Miller, G. F., & Blythe, P. W. (2005). Accurate judgments of intention from motion cues alone: A cross-cultural study. *Evolution and Human Behavior, 26*, 313–331.

Barrett, L. F., & Mesquita, B., & Gendron, M. (2011). Emotion perception in context. *Current Directions in Psychological Science, 20*, 286–290.

Barrick, M. R., Swider, B. W., & Stewart, G. L. (2010). Initial evaluations in the interview: Relationships with subsequent interviewer evaluations and employment offers. *Journal of Applied Psychology, 95*, 1163–1172.

Barron, L. G., & Hebl, M. (2013). The force of law: The effects of sexual orientation antidiscrimination legislation on interpersonal discrimination in employment. *Psychology, Public Police, and Law, 19*, 191–205.

Bartholow, B. D., Anderson, C. A., Carnagey, N. L., & Benjamin, A. J., Jr. (2005). Interactive effects of life experience and situational cues on aggression: The weapons priming effect in hunters and nonhunters. *Journal of Experimental Social Psychology, 41*, 48–60.

Bartholow, B. D., Henry, E. A., Lust, S. A., Saults, J. S., & Wood, P. K. (2012). Alcohol effects on performance monitoring and adjustment: Affect modulation and impairment of evaluative cognitive control. *Journal of Abnormal Psychology, 121*, 173–186.

Barthrop, R. W., Lazarus, L., Luckhurst, E., Kiloh, L. G., & Penny, R. (1977). Depressed lymphocyte function after bereavement. *Lancet, 1*, 834–839.

Bartlett, T. (2011). The fraud who fooled (almost) everyone. *The Chronicle of Higher Education*, November 3.

Bartlett, T. (2015, June 2). The unraveling of Michael LaCour. *The Chronicle of Higher Education*. www.chronicle.com.

Bartol, C. R., & Bartol, A. M. (2015). *Psychology and Law: Research and Practice*. Thousand Oaks, CA: Sage Publications.

Baruah, J., & Paulus, P. B. (2011). Category assignment and relatedness in the group ideation process. *Journal of Experimental Social Psychology, 47,* 1070–1077.

Bass, B. M. (1985). *Leadership and performance beyond expectations*. New York: Free Press.

Bass, B. M. (1998). *Transformational leadership: Industry, military, and educational impact*. Mahwah, NJ: Erlbaum.

Bass, B. M., & Avolio, B. J. (1990). *Manual: The multifactor leadership questionnaire*. Palo Alto, CA: Consulting Psychologists Press.

Bass, B. M., & Bass, R. (2008). *The Bass handbook of leadership: Theory, research, and managerial applications* (4th ed.). New York: The Free Press.

Bass, B. M., & Riggio, R. E. (2006). *Transformational leadership* (2nd ed.). Mahwah, NJ: Erlbaum.

Bass, B. M., & Steidlmeier, P. (1999). Ethics, character, and the authentic transformational leadership behavior. *Leadership Quarterly, 10,* 181–217.

Bassili, J. N. (2003). The minority slowness effect: Subtle inhibitions in the expression of views not shared by others. *Journal of Personality and Social Psychology, 84,* 261–276.

Bassili, J. N., & Provencal, A. (1988). Perceiving minorities: A factor-analytic approach. *Personality and Social Psychology Bulletin, 14,* 5–15.

Bates, J. A., & Lanza, B. A. (2013). Conducting psychology student research via the Mechanical Turk crowdsourcing service. *North American Journal of Psychology, 15,* 385–394.

Bateson, M., Nettle, D., & Roberts, G. (2006). Cues of being watched enhance cooperation in a real-world setting. *Biology Letters, 2,* 412–414.

Batson v. Kentucky, 476 U.S. 79 (1986).

Batson, C. D. (1991). *The altruism question*. Hillsdale, NJ: Erlbaum.

Batson, C. D. (2009a). Empathy and altruism. In C. R. Snyder & S. J. Lopez (Eds.), *Oxford handbook of positive psychology* (2nd ed., pp. 417–426). New York: Oxford University Press.

Batson, C. D. (2009b). These things called empathy: Eight related but distinct phenomena. In J. Decety & W. Ickes (Eds.), *The social neuroscience of empathy* (pp. 3–15). Cambridge, MA: MIT.

Batson, C. D. (2011). *Empathy in humans*. New York: Oxford University Press.

Batson, C. D. (2012). A history of prosocial behavior research. In A. W. Kruglanski, & W. Stroebe (Eds.), *Handbook of the history of social psychology* (pp. 243–264). New York: Psychology Press.

Batson, C. D., & Powell, A. A. (2003). Altruism and prosocial behavior. In T. Millon & M. J. Lerner (Eds.), *Handbook of psychology: Personality and social psychology* (Vol. 5, pp. 463–484). New York: Wiley.

Batson, C. D., Lishner, D. A., Cook, J., & Sawyer, S. (2005). Similarity and nurturance: Two possible sources of empathy for strangers. *Basic and Applied Social Psychology, 27,* 15–25.

Bauer, I., Wrosch, C., & Jobin, J. (2008). I'm better off than most other people: The role of social comparisons for coping with regret in young adulthood and old age. *Psychology and Aging, 23,* 800–811.

Bauer, T. N., Maertz, C. P., Dolen, M. R., & Campion, M. A. (1998). Longitudinal assessment of applicant reactions to employment testing and test outcome feedback. *Journal of Applied Psychology, 83,* 892–903.

Baumeister, R. F. (1982). A self-presentational view of social phenomena. *Psychological Bulletin, 91,* 3–26.

Baumeister, R. F. (1984). Choking under pressure: Self-consciousness and paradoxical effects of incentives on skillful performance. *Journal of Personality and Social Psychology, 46,* 610–620.

Baumeister, R. F. (1991). *Escaping the self*. New York: Basic Books.

Baumeister, R. F. (2000). Gender differences in erotic plasticity: The female sex drive as socially flexible and responsive. *Psychological Bulletin, 126,* 347–374.

Baumeister, R. F., & Leary, M. R. (1995). The need to belong: Desire for interpersonal attachments as a fundamental human motivation. *Psychological Bulletin, 117,* 497–529.

Baumeister, R. F., & Scher, S. J. (1988). Self-defeating behavior patterns among normal individuals: Review and analysis of common self-destructive tendencies. *Psychological Bulletin, 104,* 3–22.

Baumeister, R. F., & Tice, D. M. (1984). Role of self-presentation and choice in cognitive dissonance under forced compliance: Necessary or sufficient causes? *Journal of Personality and Social Psychology, 46,* 5–13.

Baumeister, R. F., & Vohs, K. D. (Eds.). (2004). *Handbook of self-regulation: Research, theory, and applications*. New York: Guilford.

Baumeister, R. F., Bratslavsky, E., Finkenauer, C., & Vohs, K. D. (2001). Bad is stronger than good. *Review of General Psychology, 5,* 323–370.

Baumeister, R. F., Campbell, J. D., Krueger, J. I., & Vohs, K. D. (2003). Does high self-esteem cause better performance, interpersonal success, happiness, or healthier lifestyles? *Psychological Science in the Public Interest, 4,* 1–44.

Baumeister, R. F., Chesner, S. P., Sanders, P. S., & Tice, D. M. (1988). Who's in charge here? Group leaders do lend help in emergencies. *Personality and Social Psychology Bulletin, 14,* 17–22.

Baumgartner, F. R., De Bouf, S. L., & Boydstun, A. E. (2008). *The decline of the death penalty and the discovery of innocence*. New York: Cambridge University Press.

Baumrind, D. (1997). Necessary distinctions. *Psychological Inquiry, 8,* 176–229.

Bavishi et al., 2010.

Baxter, L. A. (1987). Self-disclosure and disengagement. In V. J. Derleg & J. H. Berg (Eds.), *Self-disclosure: Theory, research, and therapy* (pp. 155–174). New York: Plenum.

Bazerman, M. H., & Gino, F. (2012). Behavioral ethics: Toward a deeper understanding of moral judgment and dishonesty. *Annual Review of Law and Social Science, 8,* 85–104.

Bazerman, M. H., & Neale, M. A. (1992). *Negotiating rationally*. New York: Free Press.

Bazerman, M. H., & Tenbrunsel, A. E. (2011). *Blind spots: Why we fail to do what's right and what to do about it*. Princeton, NJ: Princeton University Press.

Bazzini, D., Curtin, L., Joslin, S., Regan, S., & Martz, D. (2010). Do animated Disney characters portray and promote the beauty-goodness stereotype? *Journal of Applied Social Psychology, 40,* 2687–2709.

Beaman, A., Barnes, P., Klentz, B., & McQuirk, B. (1978). Increasing helping rates through information dissemination: Teaching pays. *Personality and Social Psychology Bulletin, 4,* 406–411.

Beaman, A. L., Klentz, B., Diener, E., & Svanum, S. (1979). Objective self-awareness and transgression in children: A field study. *Journal of Personality and Social Psychology, 37,* 1835–1846.

Beaton, E. A., Schmidt, L. A., Schulkin, J., Antony, M. M., Swinson, R. P., & Hall, G. B. (2008). Different neural responses to stranger and personally familiar faces in shy and bold adults. *Behavioral Neuroscience, 122,* 704–709.

Becker, J. C., & Swim, J. K. (2011). Seeing the unseen: Attention to daily encounters with sexism as way to reduce sexist beliefs. *Psychology of Women Quarterly, 35,* 227–242.

Beckerman, S., & Valentine, P. (Eds.). (2002). *Cultures of multiple fathers: The theory and practice of partible paternity in lowland South America*. Gainesville: University Press of Florida.

Bedau, H., & Cassell, P. (Eds.). (2004). *Debating the death penalty: Should America have capital punishment?* New York: Oxford University Press.

Beer, J. S. (2015). Cognitive neuroscience of social behavior. In B. Gawronski & G. V. Bodenhausen (Eds.), *Theory and explanation in social psychology* (pp. 183–204). New York: Guilford Press.

Behm-Morawitz, E., Lewallen, J., & Miller, B. (2015). Real Mean Girls? Reality television viewing, social aggression, and gender-related beliefs among female emerging adults. *Psychology of Popular Media Culture*, in press.

Beidel, D. C., & Turner, S. M. (1998). *Shy children, phobic adults: Nature and treatment of social phobia*. Washington, DC: American Psychological Association.

Beilock, S. L., & Carr, T. H. (2001). On the fragility of skilled performance: What governs choking under pressure? *Journal of Experimental Psychology: General, 130*, 701–725.

Bell, A. P., Weinberg, M. S., & Hammersmith, S. K. (1981). *Sexual preference: Its development in men and women*. Bloomington: Indiana University Press.

Bell, E., & Kandler, C. (2015). The origins of party identification and its relationship to political orientations. *Personality and Individual Differences, 83*, 136–141.

Belmore, S. M. (1987). Determinants of attention during impression formation. *Journal of Experimental Psychology: Learning, Memory, and Cognition, 13*, 480–489.

Bem, D. J. (1965). An experimental analysis of self-persuasion. *Journal of Experimental Social Psychology, 1*, 199–218.

Bem, D. J. (1967). Self-perception: An alternative interpretation of cognitive dissonance phenomena. *Psychological Review, 74*, 183–200.

Bem, D. J. (1972). Self-perception theory. *Advances in Experimental Social Psychology, 6*, 1–62.

Bem, D. J. (1996). Exotic becomes erotic: A developmental theory of sexual orientation. *Psychological Review, 103*, 320–335.

Bem, D. J. (2000). Exotic becomes erotic: Interpreting the biological correlates of sexual orientation. *Archives of Sexual Behavior, 29*, 531–548.

Ben-Hur, S., Kinley, N., & Jonsen, K. (2012). Coaching executive teams to reach better decisions. *Journal of Management Development, 31*, 711–723.

Ben-Shakhar, G., & Elaad, E. (2003). The validity of psychophysiological detection of information with the Guilty Knowledge Test: a meta-analytic review. *Journal of Applied Psychology, 88*, 131–151.

Ben-Zeev, T., Fein, S., & Inzlicht, M. (2005). Arousal and stereotype threat. *Journal of Experimental Social Psychology, 41*, 174–181.

Benjamin, L. T., & Simpson, J. A. (2009). The power of the situation: The impact of Milgram's obedience studies on personality and social psychology. *American Psychologist, 64*, 12–19.

Benjet, C., & Kazdin, A. E. (2003). Spanking children: The controversies, findings and new directions. *Clinical Psychology Review, 23*, 197–224.

Bennett, S., Farrington, D. P., & Huesmann, L. R. (2005). Explaining gender differences in crime and violence: The importance of social cognitive skills. *Aggression and Violent Behavior, 10*, 263–288.

Bensley, D. A., Crowe, D. S., Bernhardt, P., Buckner, C., & Allman, A. L. (2010). Teaching and assessing critical thinking skills for argument analysis in psychology. *Teaching of Psychology, 37*, 91–96.

Benson, H. (1993). The relaxation response. In D. Goleman & J. Gurin (Eds.), *Mind body medicine: How to use your mind for better health* (pp. 233–257). Yonkers, NY: Consumer Reports Books.

Benson, P. L., Karabenick, S. A., & Lerner, R. M. (1976). Pretty pleases: The effects of physical attractiveness, race, and sex on receiving help. *Journal of Experimental Social Psychology, 12*, 409–415.

Berdahl, J. L., & Anderson, C. (2005). Men, women, and leadership centralization in groups over time. *Group Dynamics: Theory, Research, and Practice, 9*, 45–57.

Berg, J. H., & McQuinn, R. D. (1986). Attraction and exchange in continuing and noncontinuing dating relationships. *Journal of Personality and Social Psychology, 50*, 942–952.

Bergey, P., & King, M. (2014). Team machine: A decision support system for team formation. *Decision Sciences Journal of Innovative Education, 12*, 109–130.

Berglas, S., & Jones, E. E. (1978). Drug choice as a self-handicapping strategy in response to noncontingent success. *Journal of Personality and Social Psychology, 36*, 405–417.

Berkelaar, B. L., & Buzzanell, P. M. (2015). Online employment screening and digital career capital: Exploring employers' use of online information for personnel selection. *Management Communication Quarterly, 29*, 84–113.

Berkman, L., & Syme, S. L. (1979). Social networks, host resistance, and mortality: A nine-year follow-up study of Alameda County residents. *American Journal of Epidemiology, 109*, 186–204.

Berkowitz, L. (1993). *Aggression: Its causes, consequences, and control*. New York: McGraw-Hill.

Berkowitz, L. (1998). Affective aggression: The role of stress, pain, and negative affect. In R. G. Geen & E. Donnerstein (Eds.), *Human aggression: Theories, research, and implications for social policy* (pp. 49–72). San Diego: Academic Press.

Berkowitz, L. (2008). On the consideration of automatic as well as controlled psychological processes in aggression. *Aggressive Behavior, 34*, 117–129.

Berkowitz, L., & Donnerstein, E. (1982). External validity is more than skin deep: Some answers to criticisms of laboratory experiments. *American Psychologist, 37*, 245–257.

Berkowitz, L., & LePage, A. (1967). Weapons as aggression-eliciting stimuli. *Journal of Personality and Social Psychology, 7*, 202–207.

Bermeitinger, C., Goelz, R., Johr, N., Neumann, M., Ecker, U., & Doerr, R. (2009). The hidden persuaders break into the tired brain. *Journal of Experimental Social Psychology, 45*, 320–326.

Bernardin, H. J., Cooke, D. K., & Villanova, P. (2000). Conscientiousness and agreeableness as predictors of rating leniency. *Journal of Applied Psychology, 85*, 232–236.

Berns, G. S., Chappelow, J., Zink, C. F., Pagnoni, G., Martin-Skurski, M. E., & Richards, J. (2005). Neurobiological correlates of social conformity and independence during mental rotation. *Biological Psychiatry, 58*, 245–253.

Bernstein, M. J., & Claypool, H. M. (2012). Social exclusion and pain sensitivity: Why exclusion sometimes hurts and sometimes numbs. *Personality and Social Psychology Bulletin, 38*, 185–196.

Bernstein, M. J., Young, S. G., Brown, C. M., Sacco, D. F., & Claypool, H. M. (2008). Adaptive responses to social exclusion: Social rejection improves detection of real and fake smiles. *Psychological Science, 19*, 981–983.

Bernsten, D., & Rubin, D. C. (Eds.). (2012). *Understanding autobiographical memory: Theories and approaches*. New York: Cambridge University Press.

Berry, C. M., Sackett, P. R., & Wiemann, S. (2007). A review of recent developments in integrity test research. *Personnel Psychology, 60*, 271–301.

Berry, D. S., & Zebrowitz-McArthur, L. (1986). Perceiving character in faces: The impact of age-related craniofacial changes in social perception. *Psychological Bulletin, 100*, 3–18.

Berry, J. W. (1979). A cultural ecology of social behavior. *Advances in Experimental Social Psychology, 12*, 177–206.

Berry, J. W., Poortinga, Y. H., Segall, M. H., & Dasen, P. R. (1992). *Cross-cultural psychology: Research and application*. Cambridge: Cambridge University Press.

Berscheid, E. (1966). Opinion change and communicator-communicatee similarity and dissimilarity. *Journal of Personality and Social Psychology, 4*, 670–680.

Berscheid, E. (2010). Love in the fourth dimension. *Annual Review of Psychology, 61*, 1–25.

Berscheid, E., & Meyers, S. A. (1996). A social categorical approach to a question about love. *Personal Relationships, 3*, 19–43.

Berscheid, E., & Regan, P. (2004). *The psychology of interpersonal relationships*. Upper Saddle River, NJ: Prentice-Hall.

Berscheid, E., & Reis, H. T. (1998). Attraction and close relationships. In D. Gilbert, S. Fiske, & G. Lindzey (Eds.), *Handbook of social psychology* (4th ed.). New York: McGraw-Hill.

Berscheid, E., & Walster, E. (1974). A little bit about love. In T. Huston (Ed.), *Foundations of interpersonal attraction* (pp. 355–381). New York: Academic Press.

Berscheid, E., Dion, K., Walster, E., & Walster, G. W. (1971). Physical attractiveness and dating choice: A test of the matching hypothesis. *Journal of Experimental Social Psychology, 7,* 173–189.

Berscheid, E., Snyder, M., & Omoto, A. M. (1989). The relationship closeness inventory: Assessing the closeness of interpersonal relationships. *Journal of Personality and Social Psychology, 57,* 792–807.

Berscheid, E., Walster, E., & Campbell, R. (1972). *Grow old along with me.* Unpublished manuscript, Department of Psychology, University of Minnesota.

Bersoff, D. N., & Ogden, D. W. (1987). In the Supreme Court of the United States: Lockhart v. *McCree. American Psychologist, 42,* 59–68.

Bessenoff, G. R. (2006). Can the media affect us? Social comparison, self-discrepancy, and the thin ideal. *Psychology of Women Quarterly, 30,* 239–251

Bettencourt, B. A., Molix, L., Talley, A., & Eubanks, J. P. (2007). Numerical representation and cross-cut role assignments: Majority members' responses under cooperative interaction. *Journal of Experimental Social Psychology, 43,* 553–564.

Bettencourt, B. A., Molix, L., Talley, A. E., Sheldon, K. M. (2006). Psychological need satisfaction through social roles. In T. Postmes & J. Jetten (Eds.), *Individuality and the group: Advances in social identity* (pp. 196–214). Thousand Oaks, CA: Sage.

Bettencourt, B. A., Talley, A., Benjamin, A. J., & Valentine, J. (2006). Personality and aggressive behavior under provoking and neutral conditions: A meta-analytic review. *Psychological Bulletin, 132,* 751–777.

Betts, L., & Hartley, J. (2012). The effects of changes in the order of verbal labels and numerical values on children's scores on attitude and rating scales. *British Educational Research Journal, 38,* 319–331.

Beu, D. S., & Buckley, M. R. (2004). This is war: How the politically astute achieve crimes of obedience through the use of moral disengagement. *Leadership Quarterly, 15,* 551–568.

Beyer, S. (1990). Gender differences in the accuracy of self-evaluations of performance. *Journal of Personality and Social Psychology, 59,* 960–970.

Beyerlein, M., Prasad, A., Cordas, J., & Brunese, P. (2015). Virtual project teams. In F. Chiocchio, E. K. Kelloway, & B. Hobbs (Eds.), *The psychology and management of project teams* (pp. 393–422). New York: Oxford University Press.

Bezdjian, S., Tuvblad, C., Raine, A., & Baker, L. A. (2011). The genetic and environmental covariation among psychopathic personality traits, and reactive and proactive aggression in childhood. *Child Development, 82,* 1267–1281.

Bhatt, S., Mbwana, J., Adeyemo, A., Sawyer, A., Hailu, A., & VanMeter, J. (2009). Lying about facial recognition: An fMRI study. *Brain and Cognition, 69,* 382–390.

Bianchi, R., Schonfeld, I. S., & Laurent, E. (2015). Burnout–depression overlap: A review. *Clinical Psychology Review, 36,* 28–41.

Bibas, S. (2004). Plea bargaining outside the shadow of trial. *Harvard Law Review, 117,* 2463–2547.

Bickman, L. (1974). The social power of a uniform. *Journal of Applied Social Psychology, 4,* 47–61.

Biesanz, J. C., & Human, L. J. (2010). The cost of forming more accurate impressions: Accuracy motivated perceivers see the personality of others more distinctively but less normatively. *Psychological Science, 21,* 589–594.

Bilton, N. (2014). Tinder, the fast-growing dating app, taps an age-old truth. *The New York Times,* October 29, 2014.

Bisseling, D., & Sobral, F. (2011). A cross-cultural comparison of intragroup conflict in the Netherlands and Brazil. *International Journal of Conflict Management, 2,* 151–169.

Bizer, G., Krosnick, J., Holbrook, A., Wheeler, S., Rucker, D., & Petty, R. E. (2004). The impact of personality on cognitive, behavioral, and affective political processes: The effects of need to evaluate. *Journal of Personality, 72,* 995–1027.

Blair, I. V., Dasgupta, N., & Glaser, J. (2015). Implicit attitudes. In M. Mikulincer, P. R. Shaver, E. Borgida, & J. A. Bargh (Eds.), *APA handbook of personality and social psychology,* Volume 1: *Attitudes and social cognition* (pp. 665–691). Washington, DC: American Psychological Association.

Blair, I. V., Park, B., & Bachelor, J. (2003). Understanding intergroup anxiety: Are some people more anxious than others? *Group Processes and Intergroup Relations, 6,* 151–169.

Blanchard, B. (2011). Chinese girl dies in hit-and-run that sparked outrage. *Reuters,* October 21.

Blandón-Gitlin, I., Sperry, K., & Leo, R. A. (2010). Jurors believe interrogation tactics are not likely to elicit false confessions: Will expert witness testimony inform them otherwise? *Psychology, Crime, & Law, 17,* 239–260.

Blank, H., Ziegler, R., & de Bloom, J. (2012). Self-monitoring and linguistic adaptation. *Social Psychology, 43,* 67–80.

Blanken, I., van de Ven, N., & Zeelenberg, M. (2015). A meta-analytic review of moral licensing. *Personality and Social Psychology Bulletin, 41,* 540–558.

Blanton, H., Jaccard, J., Klick, J., Mellers, B., Mitchell, G., & Tetlock, P. E. (2009). Strong claims and weak evidence: Reassessing the predictive validity of the IAT. *Journal of Applied Psychology, 94,* 567–582.

Blascovich, J. (2014). Challenge, threat, and social influence in digital immersive virtual environments. In J. Gratch, S. Marsella, J. Gratch, & S. Marsella (Eds.), *Social emotions in nature and artifact* (pp. 44–54). New York: Oxford University Press.

Blass, T. (1991). Understanding behavior in the Milgram obedience experiment: The role of personality, situations, and their interactions. *Journal of Personality and Social Psychology, 60,* 398–413.

Blass, T. (1992). The social psychology of Stanley Milgram. *Advances in Experimental Social Psychology, 25,* 227–329.

Blass, T. (1999). The Milgram paradigm after 35 years: Some things we now know about obedience to authority. *Journal of Applied Social Psychology, 25,* 955–978.

Blass, T. (2004). *The man who shocked the world.* New York: Basic Books.

Blass, T. (2009). From New Haven to Santa Clara: A historical perspective on the Milgram obedience experiments. *American Psychologist, 64,* 37–45.

Blass, T. (2012). A cross-cultural comparison of studies of obedience using the Milgram paradigm: A review. *Social and Personality Psychology Compass, 6,* 196–205.

Bleich, A., Gelkopf, M., & Solomon, Z. (2003). Exposure to terrorism, stress-related mental health symptoms, and coping behaviors among a nationally representative sample in Israel. *Journal of the American Medical Association, 290,* 612–620.

Blogowska, J., Saroglou, V., & Lambert, C. (2013). Religious prosociality and aggression: It's real. *Journal for The Scientific Study of Religion, 52,* 524–536.

Bobocel, D. R., Son Hing, L. S., Davey, L. M., Stanley, D. J., & Zanna, M. P. (1998). Justice-based opposition to social policies: Is it genuine? *Journal of Personality and Social Psychology, 75,* 653–669.

Bochner, S., & Insko, C. A. (1966). Communicator discrepancy, source credibility, and opinion change. *Journal of Personality and Social Psychology, 4,* 614–621.

Bodenhausen, G. V. (1990). Stereotypes as judgmental heuristics: Evidence of circadian variations in discrimination. *Psychological Science, 1,* 319–322.

Boehm, J. K., & Kubzansky, L. D. (2012). The heart's content: The association between positive psychological well-being and cardiovascular health. *Psychological Bulletin, 138,* 655–691.

Bogart, L. M., & Helgeson, V. S. (2000). Social comparisons among women with breast cancer: A longitudinal investigation. *Journal of Applied Social Psychology, 30,* 547–575.

Bohner, G., & Dickel, N. (2011). Attitudes and attitude change. *Annual Review of Psychology, 62,* 391–417.

Boiger, M., Mesquita, B., Uchida, Y., & Barrett, L. F. (2013). Condoned or condemned: The situational affordance of anger and shame in the United States and Japan. *Personality and Social Psychology Bulletin, 39,* 540–553.

Boldero, J., & Francis, J. (2000). The relation between self-discrepancies and emotion: The moderating roles of self-guide importance, location relevance, and social self-domain centrality. *Journal of Personality and Social Psychology, 78,* 38–52.

Bolger, N., DeLongis, A., Kessler, R. C., & Schilling, E. A. (1989). Effects of daily stress and negative mood. *Journal of Personality and Social Psychology, 57,* 808–818.

Bollich, K. L., Rogers, K. H., & Vazire, S. (2015). Knowing more than we can tell: People are aware of their biased self-perceptions. *Personality and Social Psychology Bulletin.*

Bonanno, G. A. (2004). Loss, trauma, and human resilience: Have we underestimated the human capacity to thrive after extremely aversive events? *American Psychologist, 59,* 20–28.

Bond, M. A., & Haynes, M. C. (2014). Workplace diversity: A social-ecological framework and policy implications. *Social Issues & Policy Review, 8,* 167–201.

Bond, C. F., Jr., & Titus, L. T. (1983). Social facilitation: A metaanalysis of 241 studies. *Psychological Bulletin, 94,* 265–292.

Bond, C., & DePaulo, B. (2006). Accuracy of deception judgments. *Personality and Social Psychology Review, 10,* 214–234.

Bond, R., & Smith, P. B. (1996). Culture and conformity: A meta-analysis of studies using Asch's (1952b, 1956) line judgment task. *Psychological Bulletin, 119,* 111–137.

Boninger, D. S., Brock, T. C., Cook, T. D., Gruder, C. L., & Romer, D. (1990). Discovery of reliable attitude change persistence resulting from a transmitter tuning set. *Psychological Science, 1,* 268–271.

Boninger, D. S., Krosnick, J. A., & Berent, M. K. (1995). Origins of attitude importance: Self-interest, social identification, and value relevance. *Journal of Personality and Social Psychology, 68,* 61–80.

Bono, J. E., & Anderson, M. H. (2005). The advice and influence networks of transformational leaders. *Journal of Applied Psychology, 90,* 1306–1314.

Bono, J. E., & Judge, T. A. (2004). Personality and transformational and transactional leadership: A meta-analysis. *Journal of Applied Psychology, 89,* 901–910.

Bonta, B. D. (1997). Cooperation and competition in peaceful societies. *Psychological Bulletin, 121,* 299–320.

Bonta, B. (2013). Peaceful societies prohibit violence. *Journal of Aggression, Conflict, and Peace Research, 5,* 117–129.

Bordens, K. S., & Bassett, J. (1985). The plea bargaining process from the defendant's perspective: A field investigation. *Basic and Applied Social Psychology, 6,* 93–110.

Borduin, C. M., Schaeffer, C. M., & Heiblum, N. (2009). A randomized clinical trial of multisystemic therapy with juvenile sexual offenders: Effects on youth social ecology and criminal activity. *Journal of Consulting and Clinical Psychology, 77,* 26–37.

Borgida, E., & Fiske, S. T. (Eds.). (2007). *Psychological science in court: Beyond common knowledge.* Oxford, UK: Blackwell.

Borkenau, P., Mauer, N., Riemann, R., Spinath, F. M., & Angleitner, A. (2004). Thin slices of behavior as cues of personality and intelligence. *Journal of Personality and Social Psychology, 86,* 599–614.

Borman, W. C., Hanson, M. A., & Hedge, J. W. (1997). Personnel selection. *Annual Review of Psychology, 48,* 299–337.

Borman, W. C., White, L. A., & Dorsey, D. W. (1995). Effects of ratee task performance and interpersonal factors on supervisor and peer performance ratings. *Journal of Applied Psychology, 80,* 168–177.

Bornstein, B. H., & Greene, E. (2011). Jury decision making: Implications for and from psychology. *Current Directions in Psychological Science, 20,* 63–67.

Bornstein, B. H., Wiener, R. L., Schopp, R., & Willborn, S. L. (Eds.). (2008). *Civil juries and civil justice: Psychological and legal perspectives.* New York: Springer.

Bornstein, R. F. (1989). Exposure and affect: Overview and meta-analysis of research, 1968–1987. *Psychological Bulletin, 106,* 265–289.

Bornstein, R. F., & D'Agostino, P. R. (1992). Stimulus recognition and the mere exposure effect. *Journal of Personality and Social Psychology, 63,* 545–552.

Bose, U. (2015). Design and evaluation of a group support system supported process to resolve cognitive conflicts. *Computers in Human Behavior, 49,* 303–312.

Bosone, L., Martinez, F., & Kalampalikis, N. (2015). When the model fits the frame: The impact of regulatory fit on efficacy appraisal and persuasion in health communication. *Personality and Social Psychology Bulletin, 41,* 526–539.

Bossard, J. H. S. (1932). Residential propinquity as a factor in marriage selection. *American Journal of Sociology, 38,* 219–224.

Bosson, J. K., & Vandello, J. A. (2011). Precarious manhood and its links to action and aggression. *Current Directions in Psychological Science, 20,* 82–86.

Bosson, J. K., Johnson, A. B., Niederhoffer, K., & Swann, W. B., Jr. (2006). Interpersonal chemistry through negativity: Bonding by sharing negative attitudes about others. *Personal Relationships, 13,* 135–150.

Boswell, W. R., Shipp, A. J., Payne, S. C., & Culbertson, S. S. (2009). Changes in newcomer job satisfaction over time: Examining the pattern of honeymoons and hangovers. *Journal of Applied Psychology, 94,* 844–858.

Bottoms, B. L., Najdowski, C. J., & Goodman, G. S. (Eds.). (2009). *Children as victims, witnesses, and offenders: Psychological science and the law.* New York: Guilford Press.

Boucher, H. C., Peng, K., Shi, J., & Wang, L. (2009). Culture and implicit self-esteem: Chinese are "good" and "bad" at the same time. *Journal of Cross-Cultural Psychology, 40,* 24–45.

Bowker, J. C., & Etkin, R. G. (2014). Does humor explain why relationally aggressive adolescents are popular? *Journal of Youth and Adolescence, 43,* 1322–1332.

Bowlby, J. (1988). *A secure base.* New York: Basic Books.

Bowling, N. A., Alarcon, G. M., Bragg, C. B., & Hartman, M. J. (2015). A meta-analytic examination of the potential correlates and consequences of workload. *Work & Stress, 29,* 95–113.

Bradbury, T. N. (Ed.). (1998). *The developmental course of marital dysfunction.* New York: Cambridge University Press.

Bradbury, T. N., & Fincham, F. D. (1992). Attributions and behavior in marital interaction. *Journal of Personality and Social Psychology, 63,* 613–628.

Brader, T. (2006). *Campaigning for hearts and minds: How emotional appeals in political ads work.* Chicago: University of Chicago Press.

Brambilla, M., & Leach, C. W. (2014). On the importance of being moral: The distinctive role of morality in social judgment. *Social Cognition, 32,* 397–408.

Brannon, T. N., Markus, H. R., & Taylor, V. J. (2015). "Two souls, two thoughts," two self-schemas: Double consciousness can have positive academic consequences for African Americans. *Journal of Personality and Social Psychology, 108,* 586–609.

Brase, G. L., Adair, L., & Monk, K. (2014). Explaining sex differences in reactions to relationship infidelities: Comparisons of the roles of sex, gender, beliefs, attachment, and sociosexual orientation. *Evolutionary Psychology, 12,* 73–96.

Brauer, M., & Er-rafiy, A. (2011). Increasing perceived variability reduces prejudice and discrimination. *Journal of Experimental Social Psychology, 47,* 871–881.

Brauer, M., Er-rafiy, A., Kawakami, K., & Phills, C. E. (2012). Describing a group in positive terms reduces prejudice less effectively than describing it in positive and negative terms. *Journal of Experimental Social Psychology, 48,* 757–761.

Bray, R. M., Johnson, D., & Chilstrom, J. T., Jr. (1982). Social influence by group members with minority opinions: A comparison of Hollander & Moscovici. *Journal of Personality and Social Psychology, 43,* 78–88.

Bray, R. M., Struckman-Johnson, C., Osborne, M., McFarlane, J., & Scott, J. (1978). The effects of defendant status on decisions of student and community juries. *Social Psychology, 41,* 256–260.

Brean, H. (1958, March 31). What hidden sell is all about. *Life,* pp. 104–114.

Brehm, J. W. (1956). Post-decision changes in desirability of alternatives. *Journal of Abnormal and Social Psychology, 52,* 384–389.

Brehm, S. S., & Brehm, J. W. (1981). *Psychological reactance: A theory of freedom and control.* New York: Academic Press.

Brescoll, V. L., Dawson, E., & Uhlmann, E. (2010). Hard won and easily lost: The fragile status of leaders in gender-stereotype-incongruent occupations. *Psychological Science, 21,* 1640–1642.

Brescoll, V. L., Uhlmann, E. L., Moss-Racusin, C., & Sarnell, L. (2012). Masculinity, status, and subordination: Why working for a gender stereotype violator causes men to lose status. *Journal of Experimental Social Psychology, 48,* 354–357.

Bressan, P., & Martello, M. F. D. (2002). Talis Pater, Talis Filius: Perceived resemblance and the belief in genetic relatedness. *Psychological Science, 13,* 213–218.

Brewer, M. B. (2015). Motivated entitativity: When we'd rather see the forest than the trees. In S. J. Stroessner & J. W. Sherman (Eds.), *Social perception from individuals to groups* (pp. 161–176). New York: Psychology Press.

Brewer, N., & Wells, G. L. (2011). Eyewitness identification. *Current Directions in Psychological Science, 20,* 24–27.

Brewer, N., Harvey, S., & Semmler, C. (2004). Improving comprehension of jury instructions with audio-visual presentation. *Applied Cognitive Psychology, 18,* 765–776.

Brewster, Z. W., & Lynn, M. (2014). Black–white earnings gap among restaurant servers: A replication, extension, and exploration of consumer racial discrimination in tipping. *Sociological Inquiry, 84,* 545–569.

Brickman, P., Coates, D., & Janoff-Bulman, R. J. (1978). Lottery winners and accident victims: Is happiness relative? *Journal of Personality and Social Psychology, 36,* 917–927.

Bridgett, D. J., Burt, N. M., Edwards, E. S., & Deater-Deckard, K. (2015). Intergenerational transmission of self-regulation: A multidisciplinary review and integrative conceptual framework. *Psychological Bulletin, 141,* 602–654.

Briñol, P. & Petty, R. E. (2009). Persuasion: Insights from the self-validation hypothesis. *Advances in Experimental Social Psychology, 41,* 69–118.

Briñol, P., McCaslin, M. J., & Petty, R. E. (2012). Self-generated persuasion: Effects of the target and direction of arguments. *Journal of Personality and Social Psychology, 102,* 925–940.

Brochu, P. M., & Esses, V. M. (2011). What's in a name? The effects of the labels "fat" versus "overweight" on weight bias. *Journal of Applied Social Psychology, 41,* 1981–2008.

Brockmyer, J. F. (2015). Playing violent video games and desensitization to violence. *Child and Adolescent Psychiatric Clinics of North America, 24,* 65–77.

Brockner, J., & Wiesenfeld, B. M. (1996). An integrative framework for explaining reactions to decisions: Interactive effects of outcomes and procedures. *Psychological Bulletin, 120,* 189–208.

Broesch, T., Callaghan, T., Henrich, J., Murphy, C., & Rochat, P. (2011). Cultural variations in children's mirror self-recognition. *Journal of Cross-Cultural Psychology, 42,* 1018–1029.

Brooks, R., & Meltzoff, A. N. (2002). The importance of eyes: How infants interpret adult looking behavior. *Developmental Psychology, 38,* 958–966.

Brooks, X. (2002, December 19). Natural born copycats. *The Guardian,* www.theguardian.com/culture/2002/dec/20/artsfeatures1.

Brown v. Board of Education of Topeka.

Brown, E., Deffenbacher, K., & Sturgill, W. (1977). Memory for faces and the circumstances of encounter. *Journal of Applied Psychology, 62,* 311–318.

Brown, J. D. (2012). Understanding the better than average effect: Motives (still) matter. *Personality and Social Psychology Bulletin, 38,* 209–219.

Brown, M. A., & Brown, J. D. (2015). Self-enhancement biases, self-esteem, and ideal mate preferences. *Personality and Individual Differences, 74,* 61–65.

Brown, R. (1986). *Social psychology* (2nd ed.). New York: Free Press.

Brown, R. A. (2010). Perceptions of psychological adjustment, achievement outcomes, and self-esteem in Japan and America. *Journal of Cross-Cultural Psychology, 31,* 51–61.

Brown, R. P., Osterman, L. L., & Barnes, C. D. (2009). School violence and the culture of honor. *Psychological Science, 20,* 1400–1405.

Brown, R., & Kulik, J. (1977). Flashbulb memories. *Cognition, 5,* 73–99.

Brown, W. A. (1998, January). The placebo effect. *Scientific American,* pp. 90–95.

Brownstein, A., Read, S. J., & Simon, D. (2004). Bias at the race-track: Effects of individual expertise and task importance on predecision reevaluation of alternatives. *Personality and Social Psychology Bulletin, 30,* 891–904.

Bruck, M., & Ceci, S. J. (1999). The suggestibility of children's memory. *Annual Review of Psychology, 50,* 419–439.

Brunell, A. B., & Fisher, T. D. (2014). Using the bogus pipeline to investigate grandiose narcissism. *Journal of Experimental Social Psychology, 55,* 37–42.

Bruner, J. S., & Potter, M. C. (1964). Interference in visual recognition. *Science, 144,* 424–425.

Bruner, J. S., & Tagiuri, R. (1954). Person perception. In G. Lindzey (Ed.), *Handbook of social psychology* (Vol. 2, pp. 634–654). Reading, MA: Addison-Wesley.

Buckholtz, J. (2015). Social norms, self-control, and the value of antisocial behavior. *Current Behavior in Behavioral Sciences, 3,* 122–129.

Buckhout, R. (1974, December). Eyewitness testimony. *Scientific American,* pp. 23–31.

Bucolo, D.O., & Cohn, E.S. (2010). Playing the race card: Making race salient in defense opening and closing statements. *Legal and Criminological Psychology, 15,* 293–303.

Buhrmester, M. D., Fraser, W. T., Lanman, J. A., Whitehouse, H., & Swann, W. J. (2015). When terror hits home: Identity fused Americans who saw Boston bombing victims as "family" provided aid. *Self and Identity, 14,* 253–270.

Bui, N. H. (2012). False consensus in attitudes toward celebrities. *Psychology of Popular Media Culture, 1,* 236–243.

Burger, J. M. (1986). Increasing compliance by improving the deal: The that's-not-all technique. *Journal of Personality and Social Psychology, 51,* 277–283.

Burger, J. M. (1999). The foot-in-the-door compliance procedure: A multiple-process analysis and review. *Personality and Social Psychology Review, 3,* 303–325.

Burger, J. M. (2009). Replicating Milgram: Would people still obey today? *American Psychologist, 64,* 1–11.

Burger, J. M. (2014). Situational features in Milgram's experiment that kept his participants shocking. *Journal of Social Issues, 70,* 489–500.

Burger, J. M., & Caldwell, D. F. (2003). The effects of monetary incentives and labeling on the foot-in-the-door effect: Evidence for a self-perception process. *Basic and Applied Social Psychology, 25,* 235–241.

Burger, J. M., & Cornelius, T. (2003). Raising the price of agreement: Public commitment and the low-ball compliance procedure. *Journal of Applied Social Psychology, 33,* 923–934.

Burger, J. M., & Petty, R. E. (1981). The low-ball compliance technique: Task or person commitment? *Journal of Personality and Social Psychology, 40,* 492–500.

Burger, J. M., Horita, M., Kinoshita, L., Roberts, K., & Vera, C. (1997). Effects of time on the norm of reciprocity. *Basic and Applied Social Psychology, 19,* 91–100.

Burger, J. M., Messian, N., Patel, S., del Prado, A., & Anderson, C. (2004). What a coincidence! The effects of incidental similarity on compliance. *Personality and Social Psychology Bulletin, 30,* 35–43.

Burkart, J. M., et al. (2014). The evolutionary origin of human hyper-cooperation. *Nature Communications, 5,* Article 4747.

Burleigh, N. (2015). Will Amanda Knox be dragged back to Italy in murder case? *Newsweek,* March 19, 2015.

Burnette, J. L., Pollack, J. M., & Forsyth, D. R. (2011). Leadership in extreme contexts: A groupthink analysis of the May 1996 Mount Everest disaster. *Journal of Leadership Studies, 4,* 29–40.

Burns, J. M. (1978). *Leadership.* New York: Harper & Row.

Burns, J. M. (2003). *Transformational leadership.* New York: Atlantic Monthly Press.

Burns, S. (2011). *The Central Park Five: A Chronicle of a City Wilding.* New York: Knopf.

Burnstein, E., & Schul, Y. (1982). The informational basis of social judgments: The operations in forming an impression of another person. *Journal of Experimental Social Psychology, 18,* 217–234.

Burnstein, E., Crandall, C., & Kitayama, S. (1994). Some neo-Darwinian decision rules for altruism: Weighing cues for inclusive fitness as a function of the biological importance of the decision. *Journal of Personality and Social Psychology, 67,* 773–789.

Burri, A., Spector, T., & Rahman, Q. (2015). Common genetic factors among sexual orientation, gender nonconformity, and number of sex partners in female twins: Implications for the evolution of homosexuality. *Journal of Sexual Medicine, 12,* 1004–1011.

Burt, M. C. (1980). Cultural myths and supports for rape. *Journal of Personality and Social Psychology, 38,* 217–230.

Busching, R., & Krahé, B. (2015). The girls set the tone: Gendered classroom norms and the development of aggression in adolescence. *Personality and Social Psychology Bulletin, 41,* 659–676.

Bushman, B. J. (1988). The effects of apparel on compliance: A field experiment with a female authority figure. *Personality and Social Psychology Bulletin, 14,* 459–467.

Bushman, B. J. (2002). Does venting anger feed or extinguish the flame? Catharsis, rumination, distraction, anger, and aggressive responding. *Personality and Social Psychology Bulletin, 28,* 724–731.

Bushman, B. J., & Pollard-Sacks, D. (2014). Supreme Court decision on violent video games was based on the First Amendment, not scientific evidence. *American Psychologist, 69,* 306–307.

Bushman, B. J., DeWall, C. N., Pond, R. J., & Hanus, M. D. (2014). Low glucose relates to greater aggression in married couples. *PNAS Proceedings of The National Academy of Sciences of The United States of America, 111,* 6254–6257.

Bushman, B. J., Baumeister, R. F., Thomaes, S., Ryu, E., Begeer, S., & West, S. G. (2009). Looking again, and harder, for a link between low self-esteem and aggression. *Journal of Personality, 77,* 427–446.

Bushman, B. J., Giancola, P. R., Parrott, D. J., & Roth, R. M. (2012). Failure to consider future consequences increases the effects of alcohol on aggression. *Journal of Experimental Social Psychology, 48,* 591–595.

Buss, A. H. (1980). *Self-consciousness and social anxiety.* San Francisco: Freeman.

Buss, D. (2011). *Evolutionary psychology: The new science of the mind* (4th ed.). New York: Prentice-Hall.

Buss, D. M. (1989). Sex differences in human mate preferences: Evolutionary hypotheses tested in 37 cultures. *Behavioral and Brain Sciences, 12,* 1–14.

Buss, D. M. (2000). *The dangerous passion: Why jealousy is as necessary as love and sex.* New York: Free Press.

Buss, D. M. (2003). *The evolution of desire: Strategies of human mating* (rev. ed.). New York: Basic Books.

Buss, D. M. (2012). *Evolutionary psychology: The new science of the mind* (4th ed.). Boston: Allyn & Bacon.

Buss, D. M., & Duntley, J. D. (2014). Intimate partner violence in evolutionary perspective. In T. K. Shackelford & R. D. Hansen (Eds.), *The evolution of violence* (pp. 1–21). New York: Springer.

Buss, D. M., & Schmitt, D. P. (1993). Sexual strategies theory: An evolutionary perspective on human mating. *Psychological Review, 100,* 204–232.

Buss, D. M., & Shackelford, T. K. (1997). From vigilance to violence: Mate retention tactics in married couples. *Journal of Personality and Social Psychology, 72,* 346–361.

Buss, D. M., Larsen, R. J., Westen, D., & Semmelroth, J. (1992). Sex differences in jealousy: Evolution, physiology, and psychology. *Psychological Science, 3,* 251–255.

Bussey, K., Quinn, C., & Dobson, J. (2015). The moderating role of empathic concern and perspective taking on the relationship between moral disengagement and aggression. *Merrill-Palmer Quarterly, 61,* 10–29.

Butler, B., & Moran, G. (2007). The impact of death qualification, belief in a just world, legal authoritarianism, and locus of control on venirepersons' evaluations of aggravating and mitigating circumstances in capital trials. *Behavioral Sciences and the Law, 25,* 57–68.

Butz, D. A., & Yogeeswaran, K. (2011). A new threat in the air: Macroeconomic threat increases prejudice against Asian Americans. *Journal of Experimental Social Psychology, 47,* 22–27.

Bylsma, W. H., Major, B., & Cozzarelli, C. (1995). The influence of legitimacy appraisals on the determinants of entitlement beliefs. *Basic and Applied Social Psychology, 17,* 223–237.

Byrne, D. (1971). *The attraction paradigm.* New York: Academic Press.

Byrne, D. (1997). An overview (and underview) of research and theory within the attraction paradigm. *Journal of Social and Personal Relationships, 14,* 417–431.

Byrne, D., & Clore, G. L. (1970). A reinforcement model of evaluative processes. *Personality: An International Journal, 1,* 103–128.

Byrne, D., Clore, G. L., & Smeaton, G. (1986). The attraction hypothesis: Do similar attitudes affect anything? *Journal of Personality and Social Psychology, 51,* 1167–1170.

Byrne, R. M. J., & McEleney, A. (2000). Counterfactual thinking about actions and failures to act. *Journal of Experimental Psychology: Learning, Memory, and Cognition, 26,* 1318–1331.

Cacioppo, J. T., & Patrick, W. (2008). *Loneliness: Human nature and the need for social connection.* New York: Norton.

Cacioppo, J. T., & Petty, R. E. (1981). Electromyograms as measures of extent and affectivity of information processing. *American Psychologist, 36,* 441–456.

Cacioppo, J. T., & Petty, R. E. (1982). The need for cognition. *Journal of Personality and Social Psychology, 42,* 116–131.

Cacioppo, J. T., Cacioppo, S., Capitanio, J. P., & Cole, W. W. (2015). The neuroendocrinology of social isolation. *Annual Review of Psychology, 66,* 733–767.

Cacioppo, J. T., Crites, S. L., Berntson, G. G., & Coles, M. G. H. (1993). If attitudes affect how stimuli are processed, should they not affect the event-related brain potential? *Psychological Science, 4,* 108–112.

Cacioppo, J. T., Gardner, W. L., & Bernston, G. G. (1997). Beyond bipolar conceptualizations and measures: The case of attitudes and evaluative space. *Personality and Social Psychology Review, 1,* 3–25.

Cacioppo, J. T., Petty, R. E., & Morris, K. (1983). Effects of need for cognition on message evaluation, recall, and persuasion. *Journal of Personality and Social Psychology, 45,* 805–818.

Cacioppo, J. T., Petty, R. E., Feinstein, J. A., & Jarvis, W. B. G. (1996). Dispositional differences in cognitive motivation: The life and times of individuals varying in need for cognition. *Psychological Bulletin, 119,* 197–253.

Cacioppo, J. T., Petty, R. E., Losch, M. E., & Kim, H. S. (1986). Electromyographic activity over facial muscle regions can differentiate the valence and intensity of affective reactions. *Journal of Personality and Social Psychology, 50,* 260–268.

Cacioppo, S., Grippo, A. J., London, S., Goossens, L., & Cacioppo, J. T. (2015). Loneliness: Clinical import and interventions. *Perspectives on Psychological Science, 10,* 238–249.

Cai, D. A., Fink, E. L., & Xie, X. (2012). "Brother, can you spare some time, or a dime?": Time and money obligations in the United States and China. *Journal of Cross-Cultural Psychology, 43,* 592–613.

Caleo, S., & Heilman, M. E. (2014). Is this a man's world? Obstacles to women's success in male-typed domains. In R. J. Burke & D. A. Major (Eds.), *Gender in organizations: Are men allies or adversaries to women's career advancement?* (pp. 217–233). Northampton, MA: Edward Elgar.

Calogero, R. M., Tantleff-Dunn, S., & Thompson, J. (2011). *Self-objectification in women: Causes, consequences, and counteractions.* Washington, DC: American Psychological Association.

Calogero, R. M., Pina, A., & Sutton, R. M. (2014). Cutting words: Priming self-objectification increases women's intention to pursue cosmetic surgery. *Psychology of Women Quarterly, 38,* 197–207.

Camara, W. J., & Schneider, D. L. (1994). Integrity tests: Facts and unresolved issues. *American Psychologist, 49,* 112–119.

Cameron, J. J., Stinson, D. A., Gaetz, R., & Balchen, S. (2010). Acceptance is in the eye of the beholder: Self-esteem and motivated perceptions of acceptance from the opposite sex. *Journal of Personality and Social Psychology, 99,* 513–529.

Cameron, J., & Pierce, W. D. (1994). Reinforcement, reward, and intrinsic motivation: A meta-analysis. *Review of Educational Research, 64,* 363–423.

Cameron, J., Pierce, W. D., Banko, K. M., & Gear, A. (2005). Achievement-based rewards and intrinsic motivation: A test of cognitive mediators. *Journal of Educational Psychology, 97,* 641–655.

Cameron, L., Rutland, A., Hossain, R., & Petley, R. (2011). When and why does extended contact work? The role of high quality direct contact and group norms in the development of positive ethnic intergroup attitudes amongst children. *Group Processes & Intergroup Relations, 14,* 193–206.

Campbell, A. (1999). Staying alive: Evolution, culture, and women's intra-sexual aggression. *Behavioral and Brain Sciences, 22,* 203–252.

Campbell, D. J., & Lee, C. (1988). Self-appraisal in performance evaluation: Development versus evaluation. *Academy Management Review, 13,* 302–313.

Campion, M. A., Palmer, D. K., & Campion, J. E. (1997). A review of structure in the selection interview. *Personnel Psychology, 50,* 655–703.

Cannon, W. B. (1932). *The wisdom of the body.* New York: Norton.

Capozza, D., & Brown, R. (2000). *Social identity processes: Trends in theory and research.* London: Sage.

Caprara, G., Alessandri, G., & Eisenberg, N. (2012). Prosociality: The contribution of traits, values, and self-efficacy beliefs. *Journal of Personality and Social Psychology, 102,* 1289–1303.

Card, N. A., Stucky, B. D., Sawalani, G. M., & Little, T. D. (2008). Direct and indirect aggression during childhood and adolescence: A meta-analytic review of gender differences, intercorrelations, and relations to maladjustment. *Child Development, 79,* 1185–1229.

Cárdenas, R. A., & Harris, L. J. (2006). Symmetrical decorations enhance the attractiveness of faces and abstract designs. *Evolution and Human Behavior, 27,* 1–18.

Carey, B. (1997, April). Don't face stress alone. *Health,* pp. 74–76, 78.

Carey, H. R., & Laughlin, P. R. (2012). Groups perform better than the best individuals on letters-to-numbers problems: Effects of induced strategies. *Group Processes & Intergroup Relations, 15*(2), 231–242.

Carlo, G., Okun, M. A., Knight, G. P., & de Guzman, M. R. T. (2005). The interplay of traits and motives on volunteering: Agreeableness, extra-version and prosocial value motivation. *Personality and Individual Differences, 38,* 1293–1305.

Carlsmith, K. M. (2006). The roles of retribution and utility in determining punishment. *Journal of Experimental Social Psychology, 42,* 437–451.

Carlsmith, K. M., Darley, J. M., & Robinson, P. H. (2002). Why do we punish? Deterrence and just deserts as motives for punishment. *Journal of Personality and Social Psychology, 83,* 284–299.

Carlsmith, K. M., Wilson, T. D., & Gilbert, D. T. (2008). The paradoxical consequences of revenge. *Journal of Personality and Social Psychology, 95,* 1316–1324.

Carlson, C.A., & Carlson, M.A. (2012). A distinctiveness-driven reversal of the weapon-focus effect. *Applied Psychology in Criminal Justice, 8,* 36–53.

Carlson, E. N., & Furr, R. M. (2013). Resolution for meta-accuracy: Should people trust their beliefs about how others see them? *Social Psychological and Personality Science, 4,* 419–426.

Carlson, E. N., Vazire, S., & Furr, R. M. (2011). Meta-insight: Do people really know how others see them? *Journal of Personality and Social Psychology, 101,* 831–841.

Carlson, M. (2008). I'd rather go along and be considered a man: Masculinity and bystander intervention. *Journal of Men's Studies, 16,* 3–17.

Carnahan, T., & McFarland, S. (2007). Revisiting the Stanford Prison Experiment: Could participant self-selection have led to the cruelty? *Personality and Social Psychology Bulletin, 33,* 603–614.

Carnegie, D. (1936). *How to win friends and influence people.* New York: Simon & Schuster.

Carpenter, C. J. (2013). A meta-analysis of the effectiveness of the "but you are free" compliance gaining technique. *Communication Studies, 64,* 6–17.

Carpenter, S. (2005). The rich science of economic choice. *APS Observer, 18,* No. 4, 21–27.

Carr, J. L., & VanDeusen, K. M. (2004). Risk factors for male sexual aggression on college campuses. *Journal of Family Violence, 19,* 279–289.

Carr, P. B., Dweck, C. S., & Pauker, K. (2012). "Prejudiced" behavior without prejudice? Beliefs about the malleability of prejudice affect interracial interactions. *Journal of Personality and Social Psychology.*

Carroll, J. (2006, September 1). *Americans prefer male boss to a female boss. Gallup News Service* (http://www.gallup.com/poll/24346/americans-prefer-male-boss-female-boss.aspx#).

Carroll, J. M., & Russell, J. A. (1996). Do facial expressions signal specific emotions? Judging emotion from face in context. *Journal of Personality and Social Psychology, 70,* 205–218.

Cartwright, D., & Zander, A. (1960). Group cohesiveness: Introduction. In D. Cartwright & A. Zander (Eds.), *Group dynamics: Research and theory* (2nd ed., pp. 69–94). Evanston, IL: Row, Peterson.

Caruso, E. M., Vohs, K. D., Baxter, B., & Waytz, A. (2013). Mere exposure to money increases endorsement of free-market systems and social inequality. *Journal of Experimental Psychology: General, 142,* 301–306.

Carver, C. S., & Connor-Smith, J. (2010). Personality and coping. *Annual Review of Psychology, 61,* 679–704.

Carver, C. S., & Scheier, M. F. (1981). *Attention and self-regulation: A control-theory approach to human behavior.* New York: Springer-Verlag.

Carver, C. S., & Scheier, M. F. (1990). Origins and functions of positive and negative affect: A control-process view. *Psychological Review, 97,* 19–35.

Carver, C. S., & Scheier, M. F. (1998). *On the self-regulation of behavior.* New York: Cambridge University Press.

Carver, C. S., Harris, S. D., Lehman, J. M., Durel, L. A., Antoni, M. H., Spencer, S. M., & Pozo-Kaderman, C. (2000). How important is the perception of personal control? Studies of early stage breast cancer patients. *Personality and Social Psychology Bulletin, 26,* 139–149.

Carver, C. S., Scheier, M. F., & Weintraub, J. K. (1989). Assessing coping strategies: A theoretically based approach. *Journal of Personality and Social Psychology, 56,* 267–283.

Cascio, J., & Plant, E. A. (2015). Prospective moral licensing: Does anticipating doing good later allow you to be bad now? *Journal of Experimental Social Psychology, 56,* 110–116.

Case, C. R., Conlon, K. E., & Maner, J. K. (2015). Affiliation-seeking among the powerless: Lacking power increases social affiliative motivation. *European Journal of Social Psychology, 45,* 378–385.

Case, R. B., Moss, A. J., Case, N., McDermott, M., & Eberly, S. (1992). Living alone after myocardial infarction: Impact on prognosis. *Journal of the American Medical Association, 267,* 515–519.

Cashdan, E. (2003). Hormones and competitive aggression in women. *Aggressive Behavior, 29,* 107–115.

Caspi, A. (2000). The child is the father of man: Personality continuities from childhood to adulthood. *Journal of Personality and Social Psychology, 78,* 158–172.

Cassidy, J., & Shaver, P. R. (Eds.). (1999). *Handbook of attachment: Theory, research, and clinical applications.* New York: Guilford Press.

Cassidy, J., Kirsh, S. J., Scolton, K. L., & Parke, R. D. (1996). Attachment and representations of peer relationships. *Developmental Psychology, 32,* 892–904.

Castaño, N., Watts, T., & Tekleab, A. G. (2013). A reexamination of the cohesion–performance relationship meta-analyses: A comprehensive approach. *Group Dynamics: Theory, Research, and Practice, 17,* 207–231.

Castelli, L., Zogmaister, C., & Tomelleri, S. (2009). The transmission of racial attitudes within the family. *Developmental Psychology, 45,* 586–591.

Ceccarini, F., & Caudek, C. (2013). Anger superiority effect: The importance of dynamic emotional facial expressions. *Visual Cognition, 21,* 498–540.

Ceci, S. J., Ross, D. F., & Toglia, M. P. (1987). Suggestibility of children's memory: Psycholegal implications. *Journal of Experimental Psychology, 116,* 38–49.

Cesarani, D. (2004). *Eichmann: His life and crimes.* London: Heinemann. Cesario, J., & Higgins, E. T. (2008). Making message recipients "feel right": How nonverbal cues can increase persuasion. *Psychological Science, 19,* 415–420.

Cesario, J., & Higgins, E. T. (2008). Making message recipients "feel right": How nonverbal cues can increase persuasion. *Psychological Science, 19,* 415–420.

Cesario, J., Grant, H., & Higgins, E. T. (2004). Regulatory fit and persuasion: Transfer from "feeling right" *Journal of Personality and Social Psychology, 86,* 388–404.

Cesario, J., Plaks, J. E., & Higgins, E. T. (2006). Automatic social behavior as motivated preparation to interact. *Journal of Personality and Social Psychology, 90,* 893–910.

Cha, A. E. (2005, March 27). Employers relying on personality tests to screen applicants. *Washington Post,* p. A01.

Chaiken, S. (1979). Communicator physical attractiveness and persuasion. *Journal of Personality and Social Psychology, 37,* 1387–1397.

Chaiken, S. (1980). Heuristic versus systematic information processing and the use of source versus message cues in persuasion. *Journal of Personality and Social Psychology, 39,* 752–766.

Chaiken, S. (1987). The heuristic model of persuasion. In M. P. Zanna, J. M. Olson, & C. P. Herman (Eds.), *Social influence: The Ontario symposium* (Vol. 5, pp. 3–39). Hillsdale, NJ: Erlbaum.

Chaiken, S., & Baldwin, M. W. (1981). Affective-cognitive consistency and the effect of salient behavioral information on the self-perception of attitudes. *Journal of Personality and Social Psychology, 41,* 1–12.

Chakroff, A., & Young, L. (2015). Harmful situations, impure people: An attribution asymmetry across moral domains. *Cognition, 136,* 30–37.

Chambers, J. R., & De Dreu, C. W. (2014). Egocentrism drives misunderstanding in conflict and negotiation. *Journal of Experimental Social Psychology, 51,* 15–26.

Chambers, J. R., Swan, L. K., & Heesacker, M. (2015). Perceptions of U.S. social mobility are divided (and distorted) along ideological lines. *Psychological Science, 26,* 413–423.

Chandrashekaran, M., Walker, B. A., Ward, J. C., & Reingen, P. H. (1996). Modeling individual preference evolution and choice in a dynamic group setting. *Journal of Marketing Research, 33,* 211–223.

Chang, H. (2007). Psychological distress and help-seeking among Taiwanese college students: Role of gender and student status. *British Journal of Guidance & Counselling, 35,* 347–355.

Chao, G. T., & Moon, H. (2005). The cultural mosaic: A metatheory for understanding the complexity of culture. *Journal of Applied Psychology, 90,* 1128–1140.

Chapdelaine, A., Kenny, D. A., & LaFontana, K. M. (1994). Matchmaker, matchmaker, can you make me a match? Predicting liking between two unacquainted persons. *Journal of Personality and Social Psychology, 67,* 83–91.

Chapman, D. S., Uggerslev, K. L., & Webster, J. (2003). Applicant reactions to face-to-face and technology-mediated interviews: A field investigation. *Journal of Applied Psychology, 88,* 944–953.

Charities Aid Foundation (2014). World giving index 2014: A global view of giving trends. *Charities Aid Foundation report.*

Charman, S. D., Wells, G. L., & Joy, S. W. (2011). The dud effect: Adding highly dissimilar fillers increases confidence in lineup identifications. *Law and Human Behavior, 35,* 479–500.

Chartrand, T. L., & Bargh, J. A. (1999). The chameleon effect: The perception-behavior link and social interaction. *Journal of Personality and Social Psychology, 76,* 893–910.

Chartrand, T. L., & Lakin, J. L (2013). The antecedents and consequences of human behavioral mimicry. *Annual Review of Psychology, 64,* 285–308.

Chartrand, T. L., & van Baaren, R. (2009). Human mimicry. *Advances in Experimental Social Psychology, 41,* 219–274.

Chatard, A., & Selimbegovic, L. (2011). When self-destructive thoughts flash through the mind: Failure to meet standards affects the accessibility of suicide-related thoughts. *Journal of Personality and Social Psychology, 100,* 587–605.

Chemers, M. M., Hays, R. B., Rhodewalt, F., & Wysocki, J. (1985). A person-environment analysis of job stress: A contingency model explanation. *Journal of Personality and Social Psychology, 49,* 628–635.

Chen, F. F., & Kenrick, D. T. (2002). Repulsion or attraction: Group membership and assumed attitude similarity. *Journal of Personality and Social Psychology, 83,* 111–125.

Chen, J. M., Kim, H. S., Mojaverian, T., & Morling, B. (2012). Culture and social support provision: Who gives what and why. *Personality and Social Psychology Bulletin, 38,* 3–13.

Chen, R., Austin, J. P., Miller, J. K., & Piercy, F. P. (2014). Chinese and American individuals' mate selection criteria: Updates, modifications, and extensions. *Journal of Cross-Cultural Psychology, 46,* 101–118.

Chen, S., & Chaiken, S. (1999). The heuristic-systematic model in its broader context. In S. Chaiken & Y. Trope (Eds.), *Dual-process theories in social psychology* (pp. 73–96). New York: Guilford.

Chen, S., Langner, C. A., & Mendoza-Denton, R. (2009). When dispositional and role power fit: Implications for self-expression and self-other congruence. *Journal of Personality and Social Psychology, 96,* 710–727.

Chen, V. H., & Wu, Y. (2015). Group identification as a mediator of the effect of players' anonymity on cheating in online games. *Behaviour & Information Technology, 34,* 658–667.

Chen, Y.-R., Brockner, J., & Chen, X.-P. (2002). Individual-collective primacy and ingroup favoritism: Enhancement and protection effects. *Journal of Experimental Social Psychology, 38,* 482–491.

Cheng, B.-S., Chou, L.-F., Wu, T.-Y., Huang, M.-P., & Farh, J.-L. (2004). Paternalistic leadership and subordinate responses: Establishing a leadership model in Chinese organizations. *Asian Journal of Social Psychology, 7,* 89–117.

Cheng, B.-S., et al. (2014). Paternalistic leadership in Four East Asian societies: Generalizability and cultural differences of the triad model. *Journal of Cross-Cultural Psychology, 45,* 82–90.

Cheng, C. M., & Chartrand, T. L. (2003). Self-monitoring without awareness: Using mimicry as a nonconscious affiliation strategy. *Journal of Personality and Social Psychology, 85,* 1170–1179.

Cheng, F. K. (2015). A qualitative study of Buddhist altruistic behavior. *Journal of Human Behavior in the Social Environment, 25,* 204–213.

Cherry, E. C. (1953). Some experiments on the recognition of speech, with one and with two ears. *Journal of the Acoustical Society of America, 25,* 975–979.

Chesler, P., & Goodman, E. J. (1976). *Women, money, and power.* New York: Morrow.

Chester, D. S., & DeWall, C. N. (2015). Sound the alarm: The effect of narcissism on retaliatory aggression is moderated by dACC reactivity to rejection. *Journal of Personality,* in press.

Chester, K. L., Callaghan, M., Cosma, A., Donnelly, P., Craig, W., Walsh, S., & Molcho, M. (2015). Cross-national time trends in bullying victimization in 33 countries among children aged 11, 13 and 15 from 2002 to 2010. *European Journal of Public Health, 25*(Supp2), 61–64.

Cheung, E. O., Gardner, W. L., & Anderson, J. F. (2015). Emotionships: Examining people's emotion-regulation relationships and their consequences for well-being. *Social Psychological and Personality Science, 6,* 407–414.

Cheung, W. Y., Wildschut, T., Sedikides, C., Hepper, E. G., Arndt, J., & Vingerhoets, A. J. (2013). Back to the future: Nostalgia increases optimism. *Personality and Social Psychology Bulletin, 39,* 1484–1496.

Chiaburu, D. S., Oh, I.-S., Berry, C. M., Li, N., & Gardner, R. G. (2011). The five-factor model of personality traits and organizational citizenship behaviors: A meta analysis. *Journal of Applied Psychology, 96,* 1140–1166.

Chiao, J. Y. (2011). Towards a cultural neuroscience of empathy and prosociality. *Emotion Review, 3,* 111–112.

Chiesa, M., & Hobbs, S. (2008). Making sense of social research: How useful is the Hawthorne Effect? *European Journal of Social Psychology, 38,* 67–74.

Chivers, M. L., Rieger, G., Latty, E., & Bailey, J. M. (2004). A sex difference in the specificity of sexual arousal. *Psychological Science, 15,* 736–744.

Choi, S. M., Lee, W.-N., & Kim, H.-J. (2005). Lessons from the rich and famous: A cross-cultural comparison of celebrity endorsement in advertising. *Journal of Advertising, 34,* 85–98.

Chopik, W. J., & Edelstein, R. S. (2014). Age differences in romantic attachment around the world. *Social Psychological and Personality Science, 5,* 892–900.

Chopik, W. J., Kim, E. S., & Smith, J. (2015). Changes in optimism are associated with changes in health over time among older adults. *Social Psychological and Personality Science,* 1–9.

Christensen, A. J., Turner, C. W., Smith, T. W., Holman, J. M., Jr., & Gregory, M. C. (1991). Health locus of control and depression in end-stage renal disease. *Journal of Counseling and Clinical Psychology, 59,* 419–424.

Christensen, A., & Heavey, C. L. (1993). Gender differences in marital conflict: The demand/withdraw interaction pattern. In S. Oskamp & M. Costanzo (Eds.), *Gender issues in contemporary society* (pp. 113–141). Newbury Park, CA: Sage.

Christian, L. M. (2015). Stress and immune function during pregnancy: An emerging focus in mind-body medicine. *Current Directions in Psychological Science, 24,* 3–9.

Chua, R. J., Morris, M. W., & Mor, S. (2012). Collaborating across cultures: Cultural metacognition and affect-based trust in creative collaboration. *Organizational Behavior and Human Decision Processes, 118,* 116–131.

Chung, J. M., Robins, R. W., Trzesniewski, K. H., Noftle, E. E., Roberts, B. W., & Widaman, K. F. (2014). Continuity and change in self-esteem during emerging adulthood. *Journal of Personality and Social Psychology, 106,* 469–483.

Cialdini, R. B. (2003). Crafting normative messages to protect the environment. *Current Directions in Psychological Science, 12,* 105–109.

Cialdini, R. B. (2009). *Influence: Science and practice* (5th ed.). New York: Pearson.

Cialdini, R. B., & Ascani, K. (1976). Test of a concession procedure for inducing verbal, behavioral, and further compliance with a request to give blood. *Journal of Applied Psychology, 61,* 295–300.

Cialdini, R. B., & De Nicholas, M. E. (1989). Self-presentation by association. *Journal of Personality and Social Psychology, 57,* 626–631.

Cialdini, R. B., & Goldstein, N. J. (2004). Social influence: Compliance and conformity. *Annual Review of Psychology, 55,* 591–621.

Cialdini, R. B., Cacioppo, J. T., Bassett, R., & Miller, J. A. (1978). Low-ball procedure for producing compliance: Commitment then cost. *Journal of Personality and Social Psychology, 36,* 463–476.

Cialdini, R. B., Kallgren, C. A., & Reno, R. R. (1991). A focus theory of normative conduct: A theoretical refinement and reevaluation of the role of norms in human behavior. *Advances in Experimental Social Psychology, 24,* 201–234.

Cialdini, R. B., Reno, R. R., & Kallgren, C. A. (1990). A focus theory of normative conduct: Recycling the concept of norms to reduce littering in public places. *Journal of Personality and Social Psychology, 58,* 1015–1026.

Cialdini, R. B., Schaller, M., Houlihan, D., Arps, K., Fultz, J., & Beaman, A. L. (1987). Empathy-based helping: Is it selflessly or selfishly motivated? *Journal of Personality and Social Psychology, 52,* 749–758.

Cialdini, R. B., Trost, M. R., & Newsom, J. T. (1995). Preference for consistency: The development of a valid measure and the discovery of surprising behavioral implications. *Journal of Personality and Social Psychology, 69,* 318–328.

Cialdini, R. B., Vincent, J. E., Lewis, S. K., Catalan, J., Wheeler, D., & Darby, B. L. (1975). Reciprocal concessions procedure for inducing compliance: The door-in-the-face technique. *Journal of Personality and Social Psychology, 31,* 206–215.

Cikara, M. (2015). Intergroup Schadenfreude: Motivating participation in collective violence. *Current Opinion in Behavioral Science, 3,* 12–17.

Cikara, M., & Van Bavel, J. J. (2014). The neuroscience of intergroup relations: An integrative review. *Perspectives on Psychological Science, 9,* 245–274.

Cikara, M., Bruneau, E., Van Bavel, J. J., & Saxe, R. (2014). Their pain gives us pleasure: How intergroup dynamics shape empathic failures and counter-empathic responses. *Journal of Experimental Social Psychology, 55,* 110–125.

Cimpian, A., & Salomon, E. (2014). Refining and expanding the proposal of an inherence heuristic in 5human understanding. *Behavioral and Brain Sciences, 37,* 506–519.

Cioffi, D., & Holloway, J. (1993). Delayed costs of suppressed pain. *Journal of Personality and Social Psychology, 64,* 274–282.

Clark, D. M. T., Loxton, N. J., & Tobin, S. J. (2015). Declining loneliness over time: Evidence from American colleges and high schools. *Personality and Social Psychology Bulletin, 41,* 78–89.

Clark, J. K., & Evans, A. T. (2014). Source credibility and persuasion: The role of message position in self-validation. *Personality and Social Psychology Bulletin, 40,* 1024–1036.

Clark, J. K., & Wegener, D. T. (2013). Message position, information processing, and persuasion: The discrepancy motives model. *Advances in Experimental Social Psychology, 47,* 189–232.

Clark, J. K., Wegener, D. T., Habashi, M. M., & Evans, A. T. (2012). Source expertise and persuasion: The effects of perceived opposition or support on message scrutiny. *Personality and Social Psychology Bulletin, 38*(1), 90–100.

Clark, M. S. (1984). Record keeping in two types of relationships. *Journal of Personality and Social Psychology, 47,* 549–557.

Clark, M. S., & Mills, J. (1979). Interpersonal attraction in exchange and communal relationships. *Journal of Personality and Social Psychology, 37,* 12–24.

Clark, M. S., & Mills, J. (1993). The difference between communal and exchange relationships: What it is and is not. *Personality and Social Psychology Bulletin, 19,* 684–691.

Clark, M. S., & Mills, J. R. (2012). A theory of communal (and exchange) relationships. In P. M. Van Lange, A. W. Kruglanski, & E. T. Higgins (Eds.), *Handbook of theories of social psychology* (Vol. 2) (pp. 232–250). Thousand Oaks, CA: Sage.

Clark, R. D., III, & Maass, A. (1990). The effects of majority size on minority influence. *European Journal of Psychology, 20,* 99–117.

Clark, R. D., III. (2001). Effects of majority defection and multiple minority sources on minority influence. *Group Dynamics, 5,* 57–62.

Clark, S. E. (2005). A re-examination of the effects of biased lineup instructions in eyewitness identification. *Law and Human Behavior, 29,* 395–424.

Clark, S. E., Marshall, T. E., & Rosenthal, R. (2009). Lineup administrator influences on eyewitness identification decisions. *Journal of Experimental Psychology: Applied, 15,* 63–75.

Clifford, M. M., & Walster, E. H. (1973). The effect of physical attractiveness on teacher expectations. *Sociology of Education, 46,* 248–258.

Clobert, M., Saroglou, V., & Hwang, K. (2015). Buddhist concepts as implicitly reducing prejudice and increasing prosociality. *Personality and Social Psychology Bulletin, 41,* 513–525.

Cochran, J. K., Sellers, C. S., Wiesbrock, V., & Palacios, W. R. (2011). Repetitive intimate partner victimization: An exploratory application of social learning theory. *Deviant Behavior, 32,* 790–817.

Coe, C. L. (1993). Psychosocial factors and immunity in nonhuman primates: A review. *Psychosomatic Medicine, 55,* 298–308.

Coenders, M., Lubbers, M., Scheepers, P., & Verkuyten, M. (2008). More than two decades of changing ethnic attitudes in the Netherlands. *Journal of Social Issues, 64,* 269–285.

Cogsdill, E. J., Todorov, A. T., Spelke, E. S., & Banaji, M. R. (2014). Inferring character from faces: A developmental study. *Psychological Science, 25,* 1132–1139.

Cohen, D., & Nisbett, R. E. (1997). Field experiments examining the culture of honor: The role of institutions in perpetuating norms about violence. *Personality and Social Psychology Bulletin, 23,* 1188–1199.

Cohen, D., Nisbett, R. E., Bowdle, B. F., & Schwarz, N. (1996). Insult, aggression, and the southern culture of honor: An "experimental ethnography" *Journal of Personality and Social Psychology, 70,* 945–960.

Cohen, D., Vandello, J., & Rantilla, A. K. (1998). The sacred and the social: Cultures of honor and violence. In P. Gilbert & B. Andrews (Eds.), *Shame: Interpersonal behavior, psychopathology, and culture* (pp. 261–282). Cambridge: Oxford University Press.

Cohen, G. L. (2003). Party over policy: The dominating impact of group influence on political beliefs. *Journal of Personality and Social Psychology, 85,* 808–822.

Cohen, G. L., Steele, C. M., & Ross, L. D. (1999). The mentor's dilemma: Providing critical feedback across the racial divide. *Personality and Social Psychology Bulletin, 25,* 1302–1318.

Cohen, S. (2004). Social relationships and health. *American Psychologist, 59,* 676–684.

Cohen, S., & Herbert, T. (1996). Health psychology: Psychological factors and physical disease from the perspective of human psychoneuroimmunology. *Annual Review of Psychology, 47,* 113–142.

Cohen, S., & Janicki-Deverts, D. (2012). Who's stressed? Distributions of psychological stress in the United States in probability samples from 1983, 2006, and 2009. *Journal of Applied Social Psychology, 42,* 1320–1334.

Cohen, S., Janicki-Deverts, D., & Miller, G. E. (2007). Psychological stress and disease. *Journal of the American Medical Association, 298,* 1685–1687.

Cohen, S., & Williamson, G. (1991). Stress and infectious disease in humans. *Psychological Bulletin, 109,* 5–24.

Cohen, S., Doyle, W. J., Turner, R., Alper, C. M., & Skoner, D. P. (2006). Sociability and susceptibility to the common cold. *Psychological Science, 14,* 389–395.

Cohen, S., Frank, E., Doyle, W. J., Skoner, D. P., Rabin, B. S., & Gwaltney, J. M. (1998). Types of stressors that increase susceptibility to the common cold in healthy adults. *Health Psychology, 17,* 214–223.

Cohen, S., Janicki-Deverts, D., Turner, R. B., & Doyle, W. J. (2015). Does hugging provide stress-buffering social support? A study of susceptibility to upper respiratory infection and illness. *Psychological Science, 26,* 135–147.

Cohen, S., Tyrrell, D. A. J., & Smith, A. P. (1993). Negative life events, perceived stress, negative affect, and susceptibility to the common cold. *Journal of Personality and Social Psychology, 64,* 131–140.

Cole, S. W., Kemeny, M. E., Taylor, S. E., Visscher, B. R., & Fahey, J. L. (1996). Accelerated course of human immunodeficiency virus infection in gay men who conceal their homosexual identity. *Psychosomatic Medicine, 58,* 219–231.

Cohn, E. S., Bucolo, D., Pride, M., & Sommers S. R. (2009). Reducing White juror bias: The role of race salience and racial attitudes. *Journal of Applied Social Psychology. 39,* 1953–1973.

Collins, N. L., & Feeney, B. C. (2000). A safe haven: An attachment theory perspective on support seeking and caregiving in intimate relationships. *Journal of Personality and Social Psychology, 78,* 1053–1073.

Collins, N. L., & Miller, L. C. (1994). Self-disclosure and liking: A meta-analytic review. *Psychological Bulletin, 116,* 457–475.

Columb, C., & Plant, E. (2011). Revisiting the Obama Effect: Exposure to Obama reduces implicit prejudice. *Journal of Experimental Social Psychology, 47,* 499–501.

Colvin, C. R., Block, J., & Funder, D. C. (1995). Overly positive self-evaluations and personality: Negative implications for mental health. *Journal of Personality and Social Psychology, 68,* 1152–1162.

Cone, J., & Rand, D. G. (2014). Time pressure increases cooperation in competitively framed social dilemmas. *PLoS ONE, 10,* e115756.

Conger, R. D., Reuter, M. A., & Elder, G. H., Jr. (1999). Couple resilience to economic pressure. *Journal of Personality and Social Psychology, 76,* 54–71.

Conger, R. D., Wallace, L. E., Sun, Y., Simons, R. L., McLoyd, V. C., & Brody, G. H. (2002). Economic pressure in African American families: A replication and extension of the family stress model. *Developmental Psychology, 38,* 179–193.

Conner, M., Godin, G., Sheeran, P., & Germain, M. (2013). Some feelings are more important: Cognitive attitudes, affective attitudes, anticipated affect, and blood donation. *Health Psychology.*

Connors, E., Lundregan, T., Miller, N., & McEwen, T. (1996). *Convicted by juries, exonerated by science: Case studies in the use of DNA evidence to establish innocence after trial.* Washington, DC: U.S. Department of Justice.

Contrada, R. J., & Baum, A. (Eds.). (2011). *The Handbook of stress science: Biology, psychology, and health.* New York: Springer.

Conway, A. R., Cowan, N., & Bunting, M. F. (2001). The cocktail party phenomenon revisited: The importance of working memory capacity. *Psychonomic Bulletin & Review, 8,* 331–335.

Conway, J. M., & Huffcutt, A. I. (1997). Psychometric properties of multi-source performance ratings: A meta-analysis of subordinate, supervisor, peer, and self-ratings. *Human Performance, 10,* 331–360.

Conway, L. G., III, & Schaller, M. (2005). When authorities' commands backfire: Attributions about consensus and effects on deviant decision making. *Journal of Personality and Social Psychology, 89,* 311–326.

Conway, M. A. (1995). *Flashbulb memories.* Mahwah, NJ: Erlbaum.

Conway, M. A., & Pleydell-Pearce, C. W. (2000). The construction of autobiographical memories in the self-memory system. *Psychological Review, 107,* 261–288.

Conway, M. A., Wang, Q., Hanyu, K., & Haque, S. (2005). A cross-cultural investigation of autobiographical memory: On the universality and cultural variation of the "Reminiscence Bump" *Journal of Cross-Cultural Psychology, 36,* 739–749.

Cook, J. E., Purdie-Vaughns, V, Garcia, J., & Cohen, G. L. (2012). Chronic threat and contingent belonging: Protective benefits of values affirmation on identity development. *Journal of Personality and Social Psychology, 102,* 479–496.

Cook, T. D., & Campbell, D. T. (1979). *Quasi-experimentation: Design and analysis issues for field settings.* Chicago: Rand McNally.

Cooke, C. A. (2004). Young people's attitudes towards guns in America, Great Britain, and Western Australia. *Aggressive Behavior, 30,* 93–104.

Cooley, C. H. (1902). *Human nature and the social order.* New York: Schocken Books.

Cooper, J. (2007). *Cognitive dissonance: Fifty years of classic theory.* London: Sage.

Cooper, J., & Fazio, R. H. (1984). A new look at dissonance theory. In L. Berkowitz (Ed.), *Advances in experimental social psychology* (Vol. 17, pp. 229–267). New York: Academic Press.

Cooper, J., & Hogg, M. (2007). Feeling the anguish of others: A theory of vicarious dissonance. *Advances in Experimental Social Psychology, 39,* 359–403.

Cooper, J., & Neuhaus, I. M. (2000). The "hired gun" effect: Assessing the effect of pay, frequency of testifying, and credentials on the perception of expert testimony. *Law and Human Behavior, 24.*

Cooper, J., Zanna, M. P., & Goethals, G. R. (1974). Mistreatment of an esteemed other as a consequence affecting dissonance reduction. *Journal of Experimental Social Psychology, 10,* 224–233.

Cooper, M. L., Frone, M. R., Russell, M., & Mudar, P. (1995). Drinking to regulate positive and negative emotions: A motivational model of alcohol use. *Journal of Personality and Social Psychology, 69,* 990–1005.

Cooper, W. H. (1981). Ubiquitous halo. *Psychological Bulletin, 90,* 218–224.

Coopersmith, S. (1967). *The antecedents of self-esteem.* San Francisco: Freeman.

Copeland, J. T. (1994). Prophecies of power: Motivational implications of social power for behavioral confirmation. *Journal of Personality and Social Psychology, 67,* 264–277.

Corbett, S. (2008, January 20). *A cutting tradition. New York Times,* p. 44.

Correll, J., Hudson, S. M., Guillermo, S., & Ma, D. S. (2014). The police officer's dilemma: A decade of research on racial bias in the decision to shoot. *Social and Personality Psychology Compass, 8,* 201–213.

Correll, J., Park, B., Judd, C. M., & Wittenbrink, B. (2002). The police officer's dilemma: Using ethnicity to disambiguate potentially threatening individuals. *Journal of Personality and Social Psychology, 83,* 1314–1329.

Correll, J., Park, B., Judd, C. M., & Wittenbrink, B. (2007a). The influence of stereotypes on decisions to shoot. *European Journal of Social Psychology, 37,* 1102–1117.

Correll, J., Park, B., Judd, C. M., Wittenbrink, B., Sadler, M. S., & Keesee, T. (2007b). Across the Thin Blue Line: Police officers and racial bias in the decision to shoot. *Journal of Personality and Social Psychology, 92,* 1006–1023.

Corriveau, K. H., & Harris, P. L. (2010). Preschoolers (sometimes) defer to the majority in making simple perceptual judgments. *Developmental Psychology, 46,* 437–445.

Corriveau, K. H., Fusaro, M., & Harris, P. L. (2009). Going with the flow: Preschoolers prefer nondissenters as informants. *Psychological Science, 20,* 372–377.

Coscarelli, J. (2012). Jonah Lehrer's self-plagiarizing issues are snowballing. http://nymag.com/daily/intel/2012/06/jonah-lehrer-plagiarism-new-yorker-examples-pile-up.html.

Cose, E. (1997). *Color-blind: Seeing beyond race in a race-obsessed world.* New York: HarperCollins.

Costanzo, M. (1997). *Just revenge: Costs and consequences of the death penalty.* New York: St. Martin's Press.

Costanzo, M., & Krauss, D. (2015). *Forensic and Legal Psychology: Psychological Science Applied to Law* (2nd ed.). New York: Worth.

Costello, K., & Hodson, G. (2014). Explaining dehumanization among children: The interspecies model of prejudice. *British Journal of Social Psychology, 53,* 175–197.

Courbalay, A., Deroche, T., Prigent, E., Chalabaev, A., & Amorim, M. (2015). Big Five personality traits contribute to prosocial responses to others' pain. *Personality and Individual Differences, 78,* 94–99.

Cousins, A. J., Fugére, M. A., & Franklin, M. (2009). Digit ratio (2D:4D), mate guarding, and physical aggression in dating couples. *Personality and Individual Differences, 46,* 709–713.

Cousins, N. (1989). *Headfirst: The biology of hope.* New York: Dutton.

Cowan, C. L., Thompson, W. C., & Ellsworth, P. C. (1984). The effects of death qualification on jurors' predisposition to convict and on the quality of deliberation. *Law and Human Behavior, 8,* 53–80.

Cowley, G. (1996, June 3). The biology of beauty. *Newsweek,* pp. 61–69.

Cox, M., & Tanford, S. (1989). An alternative method of capital jury selection. *Law and Human Behavior, 13,* 167–183.

Coyne, J. C., & Tennen, H. (2010). Positive psychology in cancer care: Bad science, exaggerated claims, and unproven medicine. *Annals of Behavioral Medicine, 39,* 16–26.

Coyne, S. M., & Archer, J. (2004). Indirect aggression in the media: A content analysis of British television programs. *Aggressive Behavior, 30,* 254–271.

Coyne, S. M., Archer, J., & Eslea, M. (2004). Cruel intentions on television and in real life: Can viewing indirect aggression increase viewers' subsequent indirect aggression? *Journal of Experimental Child Psychology, 88,* 234–253.

Coyne, S. M., Linder, J. R., Nelson, D. A., & Gentile, D. A. (2012). "Frenemies, fraitors, and mean-em-aitors": Priming effects of viewing physical and relational aggression in the media on women. *Aggressive Behavior, 38,* 141–149.

Coyne, S. M., Nelson, D. A., Lawton, F., Haslam, S., Rooney, L., Titterington, L., et al. (2008). The effects of viewing physical and relational aggression in the media: Evidence for a cross-over effect. *Journal of Experimental Social Psychology, 44*, 1551–1554.

Craig, S. B., & Hannum, K. (2006). Research update: 360-degree performance assessment. *Consulting Psychology Journal: Practice and Research, 58*, 117–124.

Craig, W. M., Pepler, D., & Atlas, R. (2000). Observations of bullying in the playground and in the classroom. *School Psychology International, 21*, 22–36.

Cramer, R. E., McMaster, M. R., Bartell, P. A., & Dragna, M. (1988). Subject competence and the minimization of the bystander effect. *Journal of Applied Social Psychology, 18*, 1133–1148.

Crano, W. D. (2000). Milestones in the psychological analysis of social influence. *Group Dynamics: Theory, Research, and Practice, 4*, 68–80.

Crano, W. D., & Prislin, R. (Eds.). (2014). *Attitudes and attitude change*. New York: Psychology Press.

Crano, W. D., & Seyranian, V (2009). How minorities prevail: The context/comparison-leniency contract model. *Journal of Social Issues, 65*, 335–363.

Crawford, M. T., & Salaman, L. (2012). Entitativity, identity, and the fulfillment of psychological needs. *Journal of Experimental Social Psychology, 48*, 726–730.

Crick, N. R., & Dodge, K. A. (1994). A review and reformulation of social information-processing mechanisms in children's social adjustment. *Psychological Bulletin, 115*, 74–101.

Crick, N. R., & Rose, A. J. (2000). Toward a gender-balanced approach to the study of social-emotional development: A look at relational aggression. In R. G. Geen & E. Donnerstein (Eds.), *Human aggression: Theories, research, and implications for social policy* (pp. 153–168). San Diego: Academic Press.

Crick, N. R., Werner, N. E., Casas, J. F., O'Brien, K. M., Nelson, D. A., Grotpeter, J. K., & Markon, K. (1999). Childhood aggression and gender: A new look at an old problem. In D. Bernstein (Ed.), *Gender and motivation* (pp. 75–141). Lincoln, NE: University of Nebraska Press.

Crocker, J., & Park, L. E. (2004). The costly pursuit of self-esteem. *Psychological Bulletin, 130*, 392–414.

Crocker, J., Voelkl, K., Testa, M., & Major, B. (1991). Social stigma: The affective consequences of attributional ambiguity. *Journal of Personality and Social Psychology, 60*, 218–228.

Croizet, J. C., & Claire, T. (1998). Extending the concept of stereotype and threat to social class: The intellectual underperformance of students from low socioeconomic backgrounds. *Personality and Social Psychology Bulletin, 24*, 588–594.

Cronbach, L. J. (1955). Processes affecting scores on "understanding of others" and "assumed similarity." *Psychological Bulletin, 52*, 177–193.

Cropanzano, R. (Ed.). (1993). *Justice in the workplace: Approaching fairness in human resource management*. Hillsdale, NJ: Erlbaum.

Crosby, F. (1982). *Relative deprivation and working women*. New York: Oxford University Press.

Crosby, F. J., Iyer, A., & Sincharoen, S. (2006). Understanding affirmative action. *Annual Review of Psychology, 57*, 585–611.

Croyle, R., & Cooper, J. (1983). Dissonance arousal: Physiological evidence. *Journal of Personality and Social Psychology, 45*, 782–791.

Crozier, W. R. (Ed.). (2001). *Shyness: Development, consolidation, and change*. London: Routledge.

Crozier, W. R., & Alden, L. E. (Eds.). (2005). *The essential handbook of social anxiety for clinicians*. New York: John Wiley & Sons.

Crutchfield, R. S. (1955). Conformity and character. *American Psychologist, 10*, 195–198.

Cryder, C. E., Springer, S., & Morewedge, C. K. (2012). Guilty feelings, targeted actions. *Personality and Social Psychology Bulletin, 38*, 607–618.

Csikszentmihalyi, M. (1999). If we are so rich, why aren't we happy? *American Psychologist, 54*, 821–827.

Csikszentmihalyi, M., & Figurski, T. J. (1982). Self-awareness and aversive experience in everyday life. *Journal of Personality, 50*, 15–28.

Cue, M. (2012). Uefa probes claims banana thrown at Balotelli. *The Times (London)*, June 15, thetimes.co.uk.

Culbertson, F. M. (1997). Depression and gender: An international review. *American Psychologist, 52*, 25–31.

Cumming, G. (2014). The new statistics: Why and how. *Psychological Science, 25*, 7–29.

Cunningham, M. R. (1979). Weather, mood, and helping behavior: Quasi experiments with the sunshine Samaritan. *Journal of Personality and Social Psychology, 37*, 1947–1956.

Cunningham, M. R., Roberts, A. R., Wu, C., Barbee, A. P., & Druen, P. B. (1995). "Their ideas of beauty are, on the whole, the same as ours": Consistency and variability in the cross-cultural perception of female physical attractiveness. *Journal of Personality and Social Psychology, 68*, 261–279.

Cunningham, W. A., Johnson, M. K., Gatenby, J. C., Gore, J. C., & Banaji, M. R. (2003). Neural components of social evaluation. *Journal of Personality and Social Psychology, 85*, 639–649.

Curtis, N. M., Ronan, K. R., Heiblum, N., & Crellin, K. (2009). Dissemination and effectiveness of multisystemic treatment in New Zealand: A benchmarking study. *Journal of Family Psychology, 23*, 119–129.

Curtis, R. C., & Miller, K. (1986). Believing another likes or dislikes you: Behaviors making the beliefs come true. *Journal of Personality and Social Psychology, 51*, 284–290.

Cutler, B. L. (Ed.). (2009). *Expert testimony on the psychology of eyewitness identification*. New York: Oxford University Press.

Cutler, B. L. (Ed.). (2011). *Convictions of the innocent: Lessons from psychological research*. Washington, DC: American Psychological Association.

Cutler, B. L. (Ed.). (2013). *Reform of eyewitness identification procedures*. Washington, DC: American Psychological Association.

Cutler, B. L., & Kovera, M. B. (2011). Expert psychological testimony. *Current Directions in Psychological Science, 20*, 53–57.

Cutler, B. L., Penrod, S. D., & Stuve, T. E. (1988). Juror decision making in eyewitness identification cases. *Law and Human Behavior, 12*, 41–55.

Dabbs, J. M., & Dabbs, M. G. (2000). *Heroes, rogues, and lovers: Testosterone and behavior*. New York: McGraw-Hill.

Dabbs, J. M., Jr., Hargrove, M. F., & Heusel, C. (1996). Testosterone differences among college fraternities: Well-behaved vs. *rambunctious. Personality and Individual Differences, 20*, 157–161.

Dadvand, P., et al. (2015). Green spaces and cognitive development in primary schoolchildren. *Proceedings of the National Academy of Sciences, 112*, 7937–7942.

Daftary-Kapur, T., Penrod, S. D., O'Connor, M., & Wallace, B. (2014). Examining pretrial publicity in a shadow jury paradigm: Issues of slant, quantity, persistence and generalizability. *Law and Human Behavior, 38*, 462–477.

Daly, M., & Wilson, M. (1996). Violence against stepchildren. *Current Directions in Psychological Science, 5*, 77–81.

Daly, M., & Wilson, M. (2005). The "Cinderella effect" is no fairy tale: Comment. *Trends in Cognitive Sciences, 9*, 507–508.

Daniel, E., Bilgin, A. S., Brezina, I., Strohmeier, C. E., & Vainre, M. (2015). Values and helping behavior: A study in four cultures. *International Journal of Psychology, 50*, 186–192.

Daniel, F., & Braasch, J. G. (2013). Application exercises improve transfer of statistical knowledge in real-world situations. *Teaching of Psychology, 40*, 200–207.

Darke, P. R., & Chaiken, S. (2005). The pursuit of self-interest: Self-interest bias in attitude judgment and persuasion. *Journal of Personality and Social Psychology, 89*, 864–883.

Darley, J. M., & Batson, C. D. (1973). From Jerusalem to Jericho: A study of situational and dispositional variables in helping behavior. *Journal of Personality and Social Psychology, 27,* 100–108.

Darley, J. M., & Fazio, R. (1980). Expectancy confirmation processes arising in the social interaction sequence. *American Psychologist, 35,* 867–881.

Darley, J. M., & Gross, P. H. (1983). A hypothesis-confirming bias in labeling effects. *Journal of Personality and Social Psychology, 44,* 20–33.

Darley, J. M., & Latané, B. (1968). Bystander intervention in emergencies: Diffusion of responsibility. *Journal of Personality and Social Psychology, 8,* 377–383.

Darley, J. M., & Pittman, T. S. (2003). The psychology of compensatory and retributive justice. *Personality and Social Psychology Review, 7,* 324–336.

Darley, J. M., Carlsmith, K. M., & Robinson, P. H. (2000). Incapacitation and just deserts as motives for punishment. *Law and Human Behavior, 24,* 659–684.

Daruna, J. H. (2012). *Introduction to psychoneuroimmunology* (2nd ed.). San Diego: Academic Press.

Darwin, C. (1872). *The expression of the emotions in man and animals.* London: John Murray.

Dasgupta, N., Scircle, M. M., & Hunsinger, M. (2015). Female peers in small work groups enhance women's motivation, verbal participation, and career aspirations in engineering. *PNAS Proceedings of The National Academy of Sciences of The United States of America, 112,* 4988–4993.

David, N., Bewernick, B. H., Cohen, M. X., Newen, A., Lux, S., Fink, G. R., Shah, N. J., & Vogeley, K. (2006). Neural representations of self versus other: Visual-spatial perspective taking and agency in a virtual ball-tossing game. *Journal of Cognitive Neuroscience, 18,* 898–910.

Davidson, A. R., & Jaccard, J. J. (1979). Variables that moderate the attitude-behavior relation: Results of a longitudinal survey. *Journal of Personality and Social Psychology, 37,* 1364–1376.

Davidson, A. R., Yantis, S., Norwood, M., & Montano, D. E. (1985). Amount of information about the attitude object and attitude-behavior consistency. *Journal of Personality and Social Psychology, 49,* 1184–1198.

Davidson, O. B., Eden, D., Westman, M., Cohen-Charash, Y., Hammer, L. B., Kluger, A. N., & Spector, P. E. (2010). Sabbatical leave: Who gains and how much? *Journal of Applied Psychology, 95,* 953–964.

Davies, K., Tropp, L. R., Aron, A., Pettigrew, T. F., & Wright, S. C. (2011). Cross-group friendships and intergroup attitudes: A meta-analytic review. *Personality and Social Psychology Review, 15,* 332–351.

Davies, P. G., Spencer, S. J., Quinn, D. M., & Gerhardstein, R. (2002). Consuming images: How television commercials that elicit stereotype threat can restrain women academically and professionally. *Personality and Social Psychology Bulletin, 28,* 1615–1628.

Davis, B. P., & Knowles, E. S. (1999). A Disrupt-Then-Reframe technique of social influence. *Journal of Personality and Social Psychology, 76,* 192–199.

Davis, D., & Leo, R. A. (2012). Interrogation-related regulatory decline: Ego-depletion, failures of self-regulation and the decision to confess. *Psychology, Public Policy, and Law, 18,* 673–704.

Davis, D., & O'Donahue, W. (2004). The road to perdition: Extreme influence tactics in the interrogation room. In W. O'Donahue (Ed.), *Handbook of Forensic Psychology* (pp. 897–996). San Diego: Academic Press.

Davis, J. H., Au, W. T., Hulbert, L., Chen, X., & Zarnoth, P. (1997). Effects of group size and procedural influence on consensual judgments of quantity: The example of damage awards and mock civil juries. *Journal of Personality and Social Psychology, 73,* 703–718.

Davis, J. H., Kameda, T., Parks, C., Stasson, M., & Zimmerman, S. (1989). Some social mechanics of group decision-making: The distribution of opinion, polling sequence, and implications for consensus. *Journal of Personality and Social Psychology, 57,* 1000–1012.

Davis, J. L., & Rusbult, C. E. (2001). Attitude alignment in close relationships. *Journal of Personality and Social Psychology, 81,* 65–84.

Davis, M. C., Matthews, K. A., & McGrath, C. (2000). Hostile attitudes predict elevated vascular resistance during interpersonal stress in men and women. *Psychosomatic Medicine, 62,* 17–25.

Davis, S. (1990). Men as success objects and women as sex objects: A study of personal advertisements. *Sex Roles, 23,* 43–50.

Davison, K. P., Pennebaker, J. W., & Dickerson, S. S. (2000). Who talks? The social psychology of illness support groups. *American Psychologist, 55,* 205–217.

Dawes, R. M. (1980). Social dilemmas. *Annual Review of Psychology, 31,* 169–193.

Dawkins, R. (1976). *The selfish gene.* Oxford: Oxford University Press.

Dawkins, R. (2006). *The selfish gene* (30th anniversary edition). Oxford: Oxford University Press.

Day, A., Casey, S., & Gerace, A. (2010). Interventions to improve empathy awareness in sexual and violent offenders: Conceptual, empirical, and clinical issues. *Aggression and Violent Behavior, 15,* 201–208.

Day, D. D., & Sulsky, L. M. (1995). Effects of frame-of-reference training and information configuration on memory organization and rating accuracy. *Journal of Applied Psychology, 80,* 158–167.

Day, D. V., Schleicher, D. J., Unckless, A. L., & Hiller, N. J. (2002). Self-monitoring personality at work: A meta-analytic investigation of construct validity. *Journal of Applied Psychology, 87,* 390–401.

de Almeida, R. M., Cabral, J. C., & Narvaes, R. (2015). Behavioural, hormonal and neurobiological mechanisms of aggressive behaviour in human and nonhuman primates. *Physiology & Behavior, 143,* 121–135.

De Cremer, D. (2004). The influence of accuracy as a function of leader's bias: The role of trustworthiness in the psychology of procedural justice. *Personality and Social Psychology Bulletin, 30,* 293–304.

De Dreu, C. K. W., Beersma, B., Steinel, W., & Van Kleef, G. A. (2007). The psychology of negotiation: Principles and basic processes (pp. 608–629). In A. W. Kruglanski & E. T. Higgins (Eds.), *Social psychology: Handbook of basic principles* (2nd ed.). New York: Guilford.

De Dreu, C. W. (2012). Oxytocin modulates the link between adult attachment and cooperation through reduced betrayal aversion. *Psychoneuroendocrinology, 37,* 871–880.

De Dreu, C., & De Vries, N. (Eds.). (2001). *Group consensus and minority influence: Implications for innovation.* London: Blackwell.

de Hoog, N., Stroebe, W., & de Wit, J. B. F. (2007). The impact of vulnerability to and severity of a health risk on processing and acceptance of fear-arousing communications: A meta-analysis. *Review of General Psychology, 11,* 258–285.

De Houwer, J., Teige-Mocigemba, S., Spruyt, A., & Moors, A. (2009). Implicit measures: A normative analysis and review. *Psychological Bulletin, 135,* 347–368.

De Houwer, J. D. (2014). A propositional model of implicit evaluation. *Social and Personality Psychology Compass, 8,* 342–353.

De Raad, B. (2000). *The big five personality factors: Theory and applications.* Germany: Hogrefe & Huber.

DeSteno, D. (2015). Compassion and altruism: How our minds determine who is worthy of help. *Current Opinion in Behavioral Sciences, 3,* 80–83.

De Steno, D. A., & Salovey, P. (1996). Evolutionary origins of sex differences in jealousy? Questioning the "fitness" model. *Psychological Science, 7,* 367–372.

De Steno, D. M., Valdesolo, P., & Bartlett, M. Y. (2006). Jealousy and the threatened self: Getting to the heart of the green-eyed monster. *Journal of Personality and Social Psychology, 91,* 626–641.

De Veer, M. W., Gallup, G. G., Theall, L. A., van den Bos, R., & Povinelli, D. J. (2003). An 8-year longitudinal study of mirror self-recognition in chimpanzees *(Pan troglodytes)*. *Neuropsychologia, 41*, 229–234.

de Waal, F. (2013). *The bonobo and the atheist: In search of humanism among the primates.* New York: Norton.

de Waal, F. B. M. (1996). *Good natured: The origins of right and wrong in humans and other animals.* Cambridge, MA: Harvard University Press.

de Waal, F. B. M. (2008). Putting the altruism back into altruism: The evolution of empathy. *Annual Review of Psychology, 59*, 279–300.

de Waal, F. B., & Berger, M. L. (2000). Payment for labor in monkeys. *Nature, 404*, 563.

de Waal, F. M., Smith Churchland, P., Pievani, T., & Parmigiani, S. (2014). *Evolved morality: The biology and philosophy of human conscience.* Leiden, Netherlands: E J Brill.

Deater-Deckard, K., Dodge, K. A., Bates, J. E., & Pettit, G. S. (1998). Multiple-risk factors in the development of externalizing behavior problems: Group and individual differences. *Development and Psychopathology, 10*, 469–493.

Deaux, K., & Emswiller, T. (1974). Explanations for successful performance on sex-linked tasks: What is skill for the male is luck for the female. *Journal of Personality and Social Psychology, 29*, 80–85.

DeBono, A., & Muraven, M. (2014). Rejection perceptions: Feeling disrespected leads to greater aggression than feeling disliked. *Journal of Experimental Social Psychology, 55*, 43–52.

DeBono, K. G., Leavitt, A., & Backus, J. (2003). Product packaging and product evaluation: An individual difference approach. *Journal of Applied Social Psychology, 33*, 513–521.

Decety, J. (2011). Dissecting the neural mechanisms mediating empathy. *Emotion Review, 3*, 92–108.

Decety, J., & Cowell, J. M. (2015). The equivocal relationship between morality and empathy. In J. Decety & T. Wheatle (Eds.), *The moral brain: A multidisciplinary perspective* (pp. 279–302). Cambridge, MA: MIT Press.

Decety, J., Echols, S., & Correll, J. (2010). The blame game: The effect of responsibility and social stigma on empathy for pain. *Journal of Cognitive Neuroscience, 22*, 985–997.

Decety, J., Michalska, K. J., Akitsuki, Y., & Lahey, B. B. (2009). Atypical empathic responses in adolescents with aggressive conduct disorder: A functional MRI investigation. *Biological Psychology, 80*(2), 203–211.

Decety, J., & Svetlova, M. (2012). Putting together phylogenetic and ontogenetic perspectives on empathy. *Developmental Cognitive Neuroscience, 2*, 1–24.

Deci, E. L. (1971). Effects of externally mediated rewards on intrinsic motivation. *Journal of Personality and Social Psychology, 18*, 105–115.

Deci, E. L., & Ryan, R. M. (1985). *Intrinsic motivation and self-determination in human behavior.* New York: Plenum.

Deer, B. (2011). How the case against the MMR vaccine was fixed. *British Medical Journal, 342*, 77–82.

Deffenbacher, K. A., Bornstein, B. H., & Penrod, S. D. (2006). Mugshot exposure effects: Retroactive interference, mugshot commitment, source confusion, and unconscious transference. *Law and Human Behavior, 30*, 287–307.

Demiray, B., & Janssen, S.M.J. (2015). The self-enhancement function of autobiographical memory. *Applied Cognitive Psychology, 29*, 49–60.

DeNeve, K. M., & Cooper, H. (1998). The happy personality: A meta-analysis of 137 personality traits and subjective well-being. *Psychological Bulletin, 124*, 197–229.

Denissen, J. A., Penke, L., & Schmitt, D. P. (2008). Self-esteem reactions to social interactions: Evidence for sociometer mechanisms across days, people, and nations. *Journal of Personality and Social Psychology, 95*, 181–196.

Denrell, J. (2005). Why most people disapprove of me: Experience sampling in impression formation. *Psychological Review, 112*, 951–978.

Denson, T. F. (2015). Four promising interventions for reducing reactive aggression. *Current Opinion in Behavioral Science, 3*, 136–141.

Denson, T. F., Capper, M. M., Oaten, M., Friese, M., & Schofield, T. P. (2011). Self-control training decreases aggression in response to provocation in aggressive individuals. *Journal of Research in Personality, 45*, 252–256.

Denson, T. F., DeWall, C., & Finkel, E. J. (2012). Self-control and aggression. *Current Directions in Psychological Science, 21*, 20–25.

Denson, T. F., Jacobson, M., von Hippel, W., Kemp, R. I., & Mak, T. (2012). Caffeine expectancies but not caffeine reduce depletion-induced aggression. *Psychology of Addictive Behaviors, 26*, 140–144.

Denson, T. F., Moulds, M. L., & Grisham, J. R. (2012). The effects of analytical rumination, reappraisal, and distraction on anger experience. *Behavior Therapy, 43*, 355–364.

Denson, T. F., Ronay, R., von Hippel, W., & Schira, M. M. (2013). Endogenous testosterone and cortisol modulate neural responses during induced anger control. *Social Neuroscience, 8*, 165–177.

Denson, T. F., von Hippel, W., Kemp, R. I., & Teo, L. S. (2010). Glucose consumption decreases impulsive aggression in response to provocation in aggressive individuals. *Journal of Experimental Social Psychology, 46*, 1023–1028.

DePaulo, B. (2011). Living single: Lightening up those dark, dopey myths. In W. R. Cupach, & B. H. Spitzberg (Eds.), *The dark side of close relationships II* (pp. 409–439). New York: Routledge/Taylor & Francis Group.

DePaulo, B. M., & Morris, W. L. (2005). Singles in society and in science. *Psychological Inquiry, 16*, 57–83.

DePaulo, B. M., Lindsay, J. J., Malone, B. E., Muhlenbruck, L., Charlton, K., & Cooper, H. (2003). Cues to deception. *Psychological Bulletin, 129*, 74–112.

Derlega, V. J., Metts, S., Petronio, S., & Margulis, S. T. (1993). *Self-disclosure.* Newbury Park, CA: Sage.

Derlega, V. J., Wilson, M., & Chaikin, A. L. (1976). Friendship and disclosure reciprocity. *Journal of Personality and Social Psychology, 34*, 578–587.

DeRosa, D. M., Smith, C. L., & Hantula, D. A. (2007). The medium matters: Mining the long-promised merit of group interaction in creative idea generation tasks in a meta-analysis of the electronic group brainstorming literature. *Computers in Human Behavior, 23*, 1549–1581.

Dershowitz, A. M. (1982). *The best defense.* New York: Vintage Books.

Dervan, L. & Edkins, V. A. (2012). The innocent defendant's dilemma: An innovative empirical study of plea bargaining's innocence problem. *Journal of Criminal Law and Criminology, 103*, 1–48.

Desmarais, S. L., & Read, J. D. (2011). After 30 years, what do we know about what jurors know? A meta-analytic review of lay knowledge regarding eyewitness factors. *Law and Human Behavior, 35*, 200–210.

Deters, F. G., & Mehl, M. R. (2013). Does posting Facebook status updates increase or decrease loneliness? An online social networking experiment. *Social Psychological & Personality Science, 4*, 579–586.

Dettenborn, L., Tietze, A., Bruckner, F., & Kirschbaum, C. (2010). Higher cortisol content in hair among long-term unemployed individuals compared to controls. *Psychoneuroendocrinology, 35*, 1404–1409.

Deutsch, M., & Gerard, H. B. (1955). A study of normative and informational social influences upon individual judgment. *Journal of Abnormal and Social Psychology, 51*, 629–636.

Devine, P. G. (1989). Stereotypes and prejudice: Their automatic and controlled components. *Journal of Personality and Social Psychology, 56*, 5–18.

Devos, T., Gavin, K., & Quintana, F. J. (2010). Say "adios" to the American dream? The interplay between ethnic and national identity among Latino and Caucasian Americans. *Cultural Diversity and Ethnic Minority Psychology, 16*, 37–49.

DeWall, C. N., & Anderson, C. A. (2011). The general aggression model. In P. R. Shaver & M. Mikulincer (Eds.), *Human aggression and violence: Causes, manifestations, and consequences* (pp. 15–33). Washington, DC: American Psychological Association.

DeWall, C. N., & Bushman, B. J. (2009). Hot under the collar in a lukewarm environment: Words associated with hot temperature increase aggressive thoughts and hostile perceptions. *Journal of Experimental Social Psychology, 45*, 1045–1047.

DeWall, C. N., Anderson, C. A., & Bushman, B. J. (2013). Aggression and violence. In I. Weiner (Ed.), *Comprehensive handbook of psychology* (2nd ed.); H. Tenn & J. Suls (Eds.), Volume 5: *Personality and social psychology*. New York: Wiley.

DeWall, C. N., Maner, J. K., & Rouby, D. A. (2009). Social exclusion and early-stage interpersonal perception: Selective attention to signs of acceptance. *Journal of Personality and Social Psychology, 96*, 729–741.

DeWall, C., Anderson, C. A., & Bushman, B. J. (2011). The general aggression model: Theoretical extensions to violence. *Psychology of Violence, 1*, 245–258.

DeWall, C., Deckman, T., Gailliot, M. T., & Bushman, B. J. (2011). Sweetened blood cools hot tempers: Physiological self-control and aggression. *Aggressive Behavior, 37*, 73–80.

DeWall, C., Finkel, E. J., & Denson, T. F. (2011). Self-control inhibits aggression. *Social and Personality Psychology Compass, 5*, 458–472.

DeWall, C., Twenge, J. M., Bushman, B., Im, C., & Williams, K. (2010). A little acceptance goes a long way: Applying social impact theory to the rejection-aggression link. *Social Psychological and Personality Science, 1*, 168–174.

Diamond, L. M. (2003). Was it a phase? Young women's relinquishment of lesbian/bisexual identities over a 5-year period. *Journal of Personality and Social Psychology, 84*, 352–364.

Diamond, L. M. (2007). A dynamical systems approach to female same-sex sexuality. *Perspectives on Psychological Science, 2*, 142–161.

Diamond, M. (1993). Homosexuality and bisexuality in different populations. *Archives of Sexual Behavior, 22*, 291–310.

Diamond, S. S., & Rose, M. R. (2005). Real juries. *Annual Review of Law and Social Science, 1*, 255–284.

Diamond, S. S., Rose, M. R., & Murphy, B. (2006). Revisiting the unanimity requirement: The behavior of the non-unanimous civil jury. *Northwestern Law Review, 100*, 201–230.

Dickson, M. W., Castaño, N., Magomaeva, A., & Den Hartog, D. N. (2012). Conceptualizing leadership across cultures. *Journal of World Business, 47*, 483–492.

Dickter, C. L., & Newton, V. A. (2013). To confront or not to confront: Non-targets' evaluations of and responses to racist comments. *Journal of Applied Social Psychology, 43*, 262–275.

Diener, E. (1980). Deindividuation: The absence of self-awareness and self-regulation in group members. In P. B. Paulus (Ed.), *Psychology of group influence* (pp. 209–242). Hillsdale, NJ: Erlbaum.

Diener, E. (2000). Subjective well-being: The science of happiness, and a proposal for a national index. *American Psychologist, 55*, 34–43.

Diener, E., & Biswas-Diener, R. (2008). *Happiness: Unlocking the mysteries of psychological wealth*. Malden, MA: Blackwell.

Diener, E., & Seligman, M. E. P. (2004). Beyond money: Toward an economy of well-being. *Psychological Science in the Public Interest, 5*, whole No. 1.

Diener, E., & Suh, E. M. (Eds.). (2000). *Culture and subjective well-being*. Cambridge, MA: MIT Press.

Diener, E., Emmons, R. A., Larsen, R. J., & Griffin, S. (1984). The Satisfaction with Life Scale. *Journal of Personality Assessment, 49*, 71–75.

Diener, E., Fraser, S. C., Beaman, A. L., & Kelem, R. T. (1976). Effects of deindividuation variables on stealing among Halloween trick-or-treaters. *Journal of Personality and Social Psychology, 33*, 178–183.

Diener, E., Oishi, S., & Lucas, R. E. (2015). National accounts of subjective well-being. *American Psychologist, 70*, 234–242.

Diener, E., Suh, E. M., Lucas, R. E., & Smith, H. L. (1999). Subjective well-being: Three decades of progress. *Psychological Bulletin, 125*, 276–302.

Diener, E., Wolsic, B., & Fujita, F. (1995). Physical attractiveness and subjective well-being. *Journal of Personality and Social Psychology, 69*, 120–129.

DiFonzo, N., & Bordia, P. (1997). Rumor and prediction: Making sense (but losing dollars) in the stock market. *Organizational Behavior and Human Decision Processes, 71*, 329–353.

Dijksterhuis, A., & Aarts, H. (2003). Of wildebeests and humans: The preferential detection of negative stimuli. *Psychological Science, 14*, 14–18.

Dijksterhuis, A., & Bargh, J. A. (2001). The perception-behavior expressway: Automatic effects of social perception on social behavior. *Advances in Experimental Social Psychology, 33*, 1–40.

Dill, K. E., Anderson, C. A., Anderson, K. B., & Deuser, W. E. (1997). Effects of aggressive personality on social expectations and social perceptions. *Journal of Research in Personality, 31*, 272–292.

Dillard, A. J., Schiavone, A., & Brown, S. L. (2008). Helping behavior and positive emotions: Implications for health and well-being. In S. J. Lopez (Ed.), *Positive psychology: Exploring the best in people*: Vol. 2. *Capitalizing on emotional experiences* (pp. 101–114). Westport, CT: Praeger.

Dimberg, U., Thunberg, M., & Elmehed, K. (2000). Unconscious facial reactions to emotional facial expressions. *Psychological Science, 11*, 86–89.

Dindia, K., & Allen, M. (1992). Sex differences in self-disclosure: A metaanalysis. *Psychological Bulletin, 112*, 106–124.

Dinero, R. E., Conger, R. D., Shaver, P. R., Widaman, K. F., & Larsen-Rife, D. (2008). The influence of family of origin and adult romantic partners on romantic attachment security. *Journal of Family Psychology, 22*, 622–632.

Dion, K. K., & Dion, K. L. (1996). Cultural perspectives on romantic love. *Personal Relationships, 3*, 5–17.

Dion, K. K., Berscheid, E., & Walster, E. (1972). What is beautiful is good. *Journal of Personality and Social Psychology, 24*, 285–290.

Dion, K. L. (2000). Group cohesion: From "field of forces" to multidimensional construct. *Group Dynamics, 4*, 7–26.

Dion, K. L., & Dion, K. K. (1976). Love, liking and trust in heterosexual relationships. *Personality and Social Psychology Bulletin, 2*, 187–190.

Dionisio, D. P., Granholm, E., Hillix, W. A., & Perrine, W. F. (2001). Differentiation of deception using pupillary responses as an index of cognitive processing. *Psychophysiology 38*, 205–211.

Dishon-Berkovits, M. (2014). Burnout: Contributing and protecting factors within the work–family interface. *Journal of Career Development, 41*, 467–486.

Dittmann, M. (2005). After the wave. *APA Monitor on Psychology, 36*, No. 3, p. 36.

Dizikes, C., & Sobol, R. R. (2012). Pediatric surgeon raced to save boys in lake despite his kids' concerns. *Chicago Tribune*, August 6. http://articles.chicagotribune.com/2012–08–06/news/chi-pediatric-surgeon-dies-saving-two-children-from-drowning-in-lake-michigan-20120805_1_compassionate-surgeon-and-one-pediatric-surgeon-liu.

Doleac, J. L., & Stein, L. C. D. (2013). The visible hand: Race and online market outcomes. *The Economic Journal, 123*, F469–F492.

Dolinski, D. (2000). On inferring one's beliefs from one's attempt and consequences for subsequent compliance. *Journal of Personality and Social Psychology, 78*, 260–272.

Dolinski, D. (2016). *Techniques of social influence: The psychology of gaining compliance.* New York: Routledge.

Dollard, J., Doob, L. W., Miller, N. E., Mowrer, O. H., & Sears, R. R. (1939). *Frustration and aggression.* New Haven, CT: Yale University Press.

Dominus, S. (2012). *What happened to the girls in Le Roy. The New York Times Magazine* March 7, 2012, p. 28.

Dommeyer, C. J. (2012). A new strategy for dealing with social loafers on the group project: The segment manager method. *Journal of Marketing Education, 34,* 113–127.

Donnellan, M. B., Trzesniewski, K. H., Robins, R. W., Moffitt, T. E., & Caspi, A. (2005). Low self-esteem is related to aggression, antisocial behavior, and delinquency. *Psychological Science, 16,* 328–335.

Donnerstein, E., & Donnerstein, M. (1976). Research in the control of interracial aggression. In R. G. Geen & E. C. O'Neal (Eds.), *Perspectives on aggression* (pp. 133–168). New York: Academic Press.

Donnerstein, E., & Malamuth, N. (1997). Pornography: Its consequences on the observer. In L. B. Schlesinger & E. Revitch (Eds.), *Sexual dynamics of anti-social behavior* (2nd ed., pp. 30–49). Springfield, IL: Charles C Thomas.

Donnerstein, E., Linz, D., & Penrod, S. (1987). *The question of pornography.* New York: Free Press.

Dornburg, C. C., Stevens, S. M., Hendrickson, S. L., & Davidson, G. S. (2009). Improving extreme-scale problem solving: Assessing electronic brainstorming effectiveness in an industrial setting. *Human Factors, 51,* 519–527.

Dornbusch, S. M., Hastorf, A. H., Richardson, S. A., Muzzy, R. E., & Vreeland, R. S. (1965). The perceiver and the perceived: Their relative influence on categories of interpersonal perception. *Journal of Personality and Social Psychology, 1,* 434–440.

dos Santos, M., & Wedekind, C. (2015). Reputation based on punishment rather than generosity allows for evolution of cooperation in sizable groups. *Evolution and Human Behavior, 36,* 59–64.

Dougherty, T. W., Turban, D. B., & Callender, J. C. (1994). Confirming first impressions in the employment interview: A field study of interviewer behavior. *Journal of Applied Psychology, 79,* 659–665.

Douglas, E. M., & Straus, M. A. (2006). Assault and injury of dating partners by university students in 19 countries and its relation to corporal punishment experienced as a child. *European Journal of Criminology, 7,* 293–318.

Douglass, A. B., Neuschatz, J. S., Imrich, J., & Wilkinson, M. (2010). Does post—identification feedback affect evaluations of eyewitness testimony and identification procedures? *Law and Human Behavior, 34,* 282–294.

Dover, T. L., Major, B., Kunstman, J. W., & Sawyer, P. J. (2015). Does unfairness feel different if it can be linked to group membership? Cognitive, affective, behavioral and physiological implications of discrimination and unfairness. *Journal of Experimental Social Psychology, 56,* 96–103.

Dovidio, J. F. (1984). Helping behavior and altruism: An empirical and conceptual overview. In L. Berkowitz (Ed.), *Advances in experimental social psychology* (Vol. 17, pp. 361–427). New York: Academic Press.

Dovidio, J. F., Brigham, J. C., Johnson, B. T., & Gaertner, S. L. (1996). Stereotyping, prejudice, and discrimination: Another look. In C. N. Macrae, C. Stangor, & M. Hewstone (Eds.), *Stereotypes and stereotyping* (pp. 276–319). New York: Guilford.

Dovidio, J. F., Eller, A., & Hewstone, M. (2011). Improving intergroup relations through direct, extended and other forms of indirect contact. *Group Processes & Intergroup Relations, 14,* 147–160.

Dovidio, J. F., Gaertner, S. L., Shnabel, N., Saguy, T., & Johnson, J. (2010). Recategorization and prosocial behavior: Common in-group identity and a dual identity. In S. Stürmer & M. Snyder (Eds.), *The psychology of prosocial behavior: Group processes, intergroup relations, and helping* (pp. 191–207). Wiley-Blackwell.

Dovidio, J. F., Piliavin, J., Schroeder, D. A., & Penner, L. (2006). *The social psychology of prosocial behavior.* Mahwah, NJ: Erlbaum.

Dovidio, J. F., Saguy, T., Gaertner, S. L., & Thomas, E. L. (2012). From attitudes to (in)action: The darker side of "we". In J. Dixon & M. Levine (Eds.), *Beyond prejudice: Extending the social psychology of conflict, inequality and social change* (pp. 248–268). New York: Cambridge University Press.

Downs, A. C., & Lyons, P. M. (1991). Natural observations of the links between attractiveness and initial legal judgments. *Personality and Social Psychology Bulletin, 17,* 541–547.

Doyle, J. M. (2005). *True witness: Cops, courts, science, and the battle against misidentification.* New York: Palgrave MacMillan.

Dreher, G. F., & Cox, T. H., Jr. (1996). Race, gender, and opportunity: A study of compensation attainment and the establishment of mentoring relationships. *Journal of Applied Psychology, 81,* 297–308.

Drigotas, S. M., & Rusbult, C. E. (1992). Shall I stay or should I go? A dependence model of breakups. *Journal of Personality and Social Psychology, 62,* 62–87.

Drigotas, S. M., Rusbult, C. E., & Verette, J. (1999). Level of commitment, mutuality of commitment, and couple well-being. *Personal Relationships, 6,* 389–409.

Driskell, T., & Salas, E. (2014). Training teams to high performance: Efficacy and implications for practice. In A. R. Gomes, R. Resende, & A. Albuquerque (Eds.), *Positive human functioning from a multidimensional perspective, Vol. 3: Promoting high performance* (pp. 33–57). Hauppauge, NY: Nova Science.

Duck, S., & Wright, P. H. (1993). Reexamining gender differences in same-gender friendships: A close look at two kinds of data. *Sex Roles, 28,* 709–727.

Duckitt, J., & Mphuthing, T. (1998). Group identification and intergroup attitudes: A longitudinal analysis in South Africa. *Journal of Personality and Social Psychology, 74,* 80–85.

Duclos, R. (2015). The psychology of investment behavior: (De)biasing financial decision-making one graph at a time. *Journal of Consumer Psychology, 25,* 317–325.

Dudley, N. M., Orvis, K. A., Lebiecki, J. E., & Cortina, J. M. (2006). A meta-analytic investigation of conscientiousness in the prediction of job performance: Examining the intercorrelations and the incremental validity of narrow traits. *Journal of Applied Psychology, 91,* 40–57.

Dueck, L. (2006, November 3). There's a lot we can learn from the Amish. *The Globe and Mail* (Canada), p. A25.

Dunbar, R. M. (2014). The social brain: Psychological underpinnings and implications for the structure of organizations. *Current Directions in Psychological Science, 23,* 109–114.

Dunham, Y., Baron, A. S., & Banaji, M. R. (2008). The development of implicit intergroup cognition. *Trends in Cognitive Sciences, 12,* 248–253.

Dunham, Y., Chen, E. E., & Banaji, M. R. (2013). Two signatures of implicit intergroup attitudes: Developmental invariance and early enculturation. *Psychological Science, 24,* 860–868.

Dunham, Y., Stepanova, E. V., Dotsch, R., & Todorov, A. (2015). The development of race-based perceptual categorization: Skin color dominates early category judgments. *Developmental Science, 18,* 469–483.

Dunkel Schetter, C. (2011). Psychological science on pregnancy: Stress processes, biopsychosocial models, and emerging research issues. *Annual Review of Psychology, 62,* 531–558.

Dunn, E. W., Aknin, L. B., & Norton, M. I. (2008). Spending money on others promotes happiness. *Science, 319,* 1687–1688.

Dunn, E. W., Aknin L. B., & Norton, M. I. (2014). Prosocial spending and happiness: using money to benefit others pays off. *Current Directions in Psychological Science, 23,* 41–47.

Dunning, D. (2005). *Self-insight: Roadblocks and detours on the path to knowing thyself.* New York: Psychology Press.

Dunning, D. (2015). Motivated cognition in self and social thought. In M. Mikulincer, P. R. Shaver, et al. (Eds.), *APA handbook of personality and social psychology, Volume 1: Attitudes and social cognition* (pp. 777–803). Washington, DC: American Psychological Association.

Dunning D., & Balcetis, E. (2013). Wishful seeing: How preferences shape visual perception. *Current Directions in Psychological Science, 22,* 33–37.

Dunning, D., & Sherman, D. A. (1997). Stereotypes and tacit inference. *Journal of Personality and Social Psychology, 73,* 459–471.

Dunning, D., Griffin, D. W., Milojkovic, J. D., & Ross, L. (1990). The over-confidence effect in social prediction. *Journal of Personality and Social Psychology, 58,* 568–581.

Dunning, D., Heath, C., & Suls, J. M. (2004). Flawed self-assessment: Implications for health, education, and the workplace. *Psychological Science in the Public Interest, 5,* 69–106.

Dunning, D., Johnson, K., Ehrlinger, J., & Kruger, J. (2003). Why people fail to recognize their own incompetence. *Current Directions in Psychological Science, 12,* 83–87.

Dunton, B. C., & Fazio, R. H. (1997). An individual difference measure of motivation to control prejudiced reactions. *Personality and Social Psychology Bulletin, 23,* 316–326.

Durán, M., Moya, M., & Megías, J. L. (2011). It's his right, it's her duty: Benevolent sexism and the justification of traditional sexual roles. *Journal of Sex Research, 48,* 470–478.

Durik, A. M., & Harackiewicz, J. M. (2007). Different strokes for different folks: Individual interest as a moderator of the effects of situational factors on task interest. *Journal of Educational Psychology, 99,* 597–610.

Dutton, D. G., & Aron, A. P. (1974). Some evidence for heightened sexual attraction under conditions of high anxiety. *Journal of Personality and Social Psychology, 30,* 510–517.

Dutton, K. (2010). *Split-second persuasion: The ancient art and new science of changing minds.* New York: Houghton Mifflin Harcourt.

Duval, S., & Wicklund, R. A. (1972). *A theory of objective self-awareness.* New York: Academic Press.

Duval, S., Duval, V. H., & Mulilis, J. P. (1992). Effects of self-focus, discrepancy between self and standard, and outcome expectancy favorability on the tendency to match self to standard or to withdraw. *Journal of Personality and Social Psychology, 62,* 340–348.

Dweck, C. S. (2012). Implicit theories. In P. M. Van Lange, A. W. Kruglanski, & E. Higgins (Eds.), *Handbook of theories of social psychology* (Vol. 2, pp. 43–61). Thousand Oaks, CA: Sage.

Dysart, J. E., & Strange, D. (2012). Beliefs about alibis and alibi investigations: A survey of law enforcement. *Psychology, Crime & Law, 18,* 11–25.

Dysart, J. E., Lindsay, R. C. L., MacDonald, T. K., & Wicke, C. (2002). The intoxicated witness: Effects of alcohol on identification accuracy from showups. *Journal of Applied Psychology, 87,* 170–175.

Dzokoto, V., Wallace, D. S., Peters, L., & Bentsi-Enchill, E. (2014). Attention to emotion and non-western faces: Revisiting the facial feedback hypothesis. *Journal of General Psychology, 141,* 151–168.

Eagly, A. H. (1987). *Sex differences in social behavior: A social-role interpretation.* Hillsdale, NJ: Erlbaum.

Eagly, A. H. (2009). The his and hers of prosocial behavior: An examination of the social psychology of gender. *American Psychologist, 64,* 644–658.

Eagly, A. H., & Carli, L. L. (1981). Sex of researchers and sex-typed communications as determinants of sex differences in influenceability: A meta-analysis of social influence studies. *Psychological Bulletin, 90,* 1–20.

Eagly, A. H., & Carli, L. L. (2007). *Through the labyrinth: The truth about how women become leaders.* Boston: Harvard Business School Publishing.

Eagly, A. H., & Crowley, M. (1986). Gender and helping behavior: A meta-analytic review of the social psychological literature. *Psychological Bulletin, 100,* 283–308.

Eagly, A. H., & Karau, S. J. (2002). Role congruity theory of prejudice toward female leaders. *Psychological Review, 109,* 573–598.

Eagly, A. H., & Wood, W. (2012). Social role theory. In P. M. Van Lange, A. W. Kruglanski, & E. T. Higgins (Eds.), *Handbook of theories of social psychology* (Vol. 2, pp. 458–476). Thousand Oaks, CA: Sage.

Eagly, A. H., Ashmore, R. D., Makhijani, M. G., & Longo, L. C. (1991). What is beautiful is good, but . . . : A meta-analytic review of research on the physical attractiveness stereotype. *Psychology Bulletin, 110,* 107–128.

Eagly, A. H., Johannesen-Schmidt, M. C., & van Engen, M. L. (2003). Transformational, transactional, and laissez-faire leadership styles: A meta-analysis comparing women and men. *Psychological Bulletin, 129,* 569–591.

Eagly, A. H., Mladinic, A., & Otto, S. (1994). Are women evaluated more favorably than men? An analysis of attitudes, beliefs, and emotions. *Psychology of Women Quarterly, 15,* 203–216.

Eagly, A. H., Wood, W., & Chaiken, S. (1978). Causal inferences about communicators and their effect on opinion change. *Journal of Personality and Social Psychology, 36,* 424–435.

Earl, A., Albarracín, D., Durantini, M., Gunnoe, J., Leeper, J., & Levitt, J. (2009). Participation in counseling programs: High-risk participants are reluctant to accept HIV-prevention counseling. *Journal of Consulting and Clinical Psychology, 77,* 668–679.

Earle, A., & Heymann, J. (2012). The cost of caregiving: Wage loss among caregivers of elderly and disabled adults and children with special needs. *Community, Work & Family, 15,* 357–375.

Earnshaw, V. A., Rosenthal, L., Carroll-Scott, A., Santilli, A., Gilstad-Hayden, K., & Ickovics, J. R. (2015). Everyday discrimination and physical health: Exploring mental health processes. *Journal of Health Psychology,* in press.

Easton, J., Schipper, L., & Shackelford, T. (2007). Morbid jealousy from an evolutionary psychological perspective. *Evolution and Human Behavior, 28,* 399–402.

Eastvold, A. D., Belanger, H. G., & Vanderploeg, R. D. (2012). Does a third party observer affect neuropsychological test performance? It depends. *The Clinical Neuropsychologist, 26,* 520–541.

Eastwick, P. W., & Finkel, E. J. (2008). Sex differences in mate preferences revisited: Do people know what they initially desire in a romantic partner? *Journal of Personality and Social Psychology, 94,* 245–264.

Eastwick, P. W., Finkel, E. J., Mochon, D., & Ariely, D. (2007). Selective versus unselective romantic desire: Not all reciprocity is created equal. *Psychological Science, 18,* 317–319.

Eastwick, P. W., Luchies, L. B., Finkel, E. J., & Hunt, L. L. (2014). The many voices of Darwin's descendants: Reply to Schmitt (2014). *Psychological Bulletin, 140,* 673–681.

Eaton, A. A., & Rose, S. (2011). Has dating become more egalitarian? A 35 year review using Sex Roles. *Sex Roles, 64,* 843–862.

Eberhardt, J. L., Davies, P. G., Purdie-Vaughns, V. J., & Johnson, S. L. (2006). Looking deathworthy: Perceived stereotypicality of black defendants predicts capital-sentencing outcomes. *Psychological Science, 17,* 383–386.

Eberly-Lewis, M. B., & Coetzee, T. M. (2015). Dimensionality in adolescent prosocial tendencies: Individual differences in serving others versus serving the self. *Personality and Individual Differences, 82,* 1–6.

Ebstein, R. P., Israel, S., Chew, S. H., Zhong, S., & Knafo, A. (2010). Genetics of human social behavior. *Neuron, 65,* 831–844.

Eckhardt, C. I., Parrott, D. J., & Sprunger, J. G. (2015). Mechanisms of alcohol-facilitated intimate partner violence. *Violence Against Women, 21,* 939–957.

Eden, C., & Ackermann, F. (2014). "Joined-up" policy-making: Group decision and negotiation practice. *Group Decision and Negotiation, 23,* 1385–1401.

Eden, D. (1990). Pygmalion without interpersonal contrast effects: Whole groups gain from raising manager expectations. *Journal of Applied Psychology, 75,* 394–398.

Eder, R. W., & Harris, M. M. (Eds.). (1999). *The employment interview handbook* (2nd ed.). Thousand Oaks, CA: Sage.

Edkins, V. A. (2011). Defense attorney plea recommendations and client race: Does zealous representation apply equally to all? *Law and Human Behavior, 35,* 413–425.

Edwards, K., & Smith, E. E. (1996). A disconfirmation bias in the evaluation of arguments. *Journal of Personality and Social Psychology, 71,* 5–24.

Ehrlichman, H., & Eichenstein, R. (1992). Private wishes: Gender similarities and differences. *Sex Roles, 26,* 399–422.

Ehrlinger, J., Gilovich, T., & Ross, L. (2005). Peering into the bias blind spot: People's assessments of bias in themselves and others. *Personality and Social Psychology Bulletin, 31,* 680–692.

Ehrenreich, S. E., Beron, K. J., Brinkley, D. Y., & Underwood, M. K. (2014). Family predictors of continuity and change in social and physical aggression from ages 9 to 18. *Aggressive Behavior, 40,* 421–439.

Eichstaedt, J., & Silvia, P. J. (2003). Noticing the self: Implicit assessment of self-focused attention using word recognition latencies. *Social Cognition, 21,* 349–361.

Eichstaedt, J. C., Schwartz, H. A., Kern, M. L., Park, G., Labarthe, D. R., Merchant, R. M., & . . . Seligman, M. P. (2015). Psychological language on Twitter predicts county-level heart disease mortality. *Psychological Science, 26,* 159–169.

Eisenberg, N., Guthrie, I. K., Cumberland, A., Murphy, B. C., Shepard, S. A., Zhou, Q., & Carlo, G. (2002). Prosocial development in early adulthood: A longitudinal study. *Journal of Personality and Social Psychology, 82,* 993–1006.

Eisenberg, N., Hofer, C., Sulik, M. J., & Liew, J. (2014). The development of prosocial moral reasoning and a prosocial orientation in young adulthood: Concurrent and longitudinal correlates. *Developmental Psychology, 50,* 58–70.

Eisenberg, N., Spinrad, T. L., & Knafo-Noam, A. (2015). Prosocial development. In M. E. Lamb & R. M. Lerner (Eds.), *Handbook of child psychology and developmental science, Vol. 3: Socioemotional processes* (7th ed.) (pp. 610–656). Hoboken, NJ: Wiley.

Eisenberg, T., Hannaford-Agor, P. L., Hans, V. P., Mott, N. L., Munsterman, G. T., Schwab, S. J., & Wells, M. T. (2005). Judge-jury agreement in criminal cases: A partial replication of Kalven & Zeisel's The American Jury. *Journal of Empirical Legal Studies, 2,* 171–206.

Eisenberger, N. I. (2015). Social pain and the brain: Controversies, questions, and where to go from here. *Annual Review of Psychology, 66,* 601–629.

Eisenberger, N. I., Inagaki, T. K., Muscatell, K. A., Haltom, K. E. B., & Leary, M. R. (2011). The neural sociometer: brain mechanisms underlying state self-esteem. *Journal of Cognitive Neuroscience, 23,* 3448–3455.

Eisenberger, N. I., Lieberman, M. I., & Williams, K. D. (2003). Does rejection hurt? An fMRI study of social exclusion. *Science, 302,* 290–292.

Eisenberger, R., & Cameron, J. (1996). Detrimental effects of reward: Reality or myth? *American Psychologist, 51,* 1153–1166.

Eisenberger, R., & Rhoades, L. (2001). Incremental effects of reward on creativity. *Journal of Personality and Social Psychology, 81,* 728–741.

Eisenberger, R., Cotterell, N., & Marvel, J. (1987). Reciprocation ideology. *Journal of Personality and Social Psychology, 53,* 743–750.

Ekman, P., & Friesen, W. V (1974). Detecting deception from the body or face. *Journal of Personality and Social Psychology, 29,* 288–298.

Ekman, P., & O'Sullivan, M. (1991). Who can catch a liar? *American Psychologist, 46,* 913–920.

Ekman, P., Friesen, W. V., O'Sullivan, M., Chan, A., Diacoyanni-Tarlatzis, I., Heider, K., Krause, R., LeCompte, W. A., Pitcairn, T., Ricci-Bitti, P., Scherer, K., Tomita, M., & Tzavaras, A. (1987). Universals and cultural differences in the judgments of facial expressions of emotion. *Journal of Personality and Social Psychology, 53,* 712–717.

El Leithy, S., Brown, G. P., & Robbins, I. (2006). Counterfactual thinking and posttraumatic stress reactions. *Journal of Abnormal Psychology, 115,* 629–635.

Elfenbein, H. A., & Ambady N. (2002). On the universality and cultural specificity of emotion recognition: A meta-analysis. *Psychological Bulletin, 128,* 203–235.

Elfenbein, H. A., & Ambady, N. (2003). When familiarity breeds accuracy: Cultural exposure and facial emotion recognition. *Journal of Personality and Social Psychology, 85,* 276–290.

Elkin, R. A., & Leippe, M. R. (1986). Physiological arousal, dissonance, and attitude change: Evidence for a dissonance-arousal link and a "don't remind me" effect. *Journal of Personality and Social Psychology, 51,* 55–65.

Ellemers, N., & Haslam, S. (2012). Social identity theory. In P. M. Van Lange, A. W. Kruglanski, & E. T. Higgins (Eds.), *Handbook of theories of social psychology* (Vol. 2, pp. 379–398). Thousand Oaks, CA: Sage.

Eller, A., Abrams, D., & Zimmermann, A. (2011). Two degrees of separation: A longitudinal study of actual and perceived extended international contact. *Group Processes & Intergroup Relations, 14,* 175–191.

Elliot, A. J., & Devine, P. G. (1994). On the motivational nature of cognitive dissonance: Dissonance as psychological discomfort. *Journal of Personality and Social Psychology, 67,* 382–394.

Elliot, A. J., & Niesta, D. (2008). Romantic red: Red enhances men's attraction to women. *Journal of Personality and Social Psychology, 95,* 1150–1164.

Elliot, A. J., & Pazda, A. D. (2012). Dressed for sex: Red as a female sexual signal in humans. *PLoS ONE, 7,* e34607.

Elliot, A. J., Greitemeyer, T., & Pazda, A. D. (2013). Women's use of red clothing as sexual signal in intersexual interaction. *Journal of Experimental Social Psychology, 49,* 599–602.

Elliott, M. A., Armitage, C. J., & Baughan, C. J. (2003). Drivers' compliance with speed limits: An application of the theory of planned behavior. *Journal of Applied Psychology, 88,* 964–972.

Elliott, R. (1991). Social science data and the APA: The Lockhart brief as a case in point. *Law and Human Behavior, 15,* 59–76.

Ellsworth, P. C. (1991). To tell what we know or wait for Godot? *Law and Human Behavior, 15,* 77–90.

Elms, A. C. (2009). Obedience lite. *American Psychologist, 64,* 32–36.

Elms, A., & Milgram, S. (1966). Personality characteristics associated with obedience and defiance toward authoritative command. *Journal of Experimental Research in Personality, 1,* 282–289.

Elson, M., & Ferguson, C. J. (2014). Twenty-five years of research on violence in digital games and aggression: Empirical evidence, perspectives, and a debate gone astray. *European Psychologist, 19,* 33–46.

Elwork, A., Sales, B. D., & Alfini, J. J. (1982). *Making jury instructions understandable.* Charlottesville, VA: Miche.

Emerson, M. O., Kimbro, R., & Yancey, G. (2002). Contact theory extended: The effects of prior racial contact on current social ties. *Social Science Quarterly, 83,* 745–761.

Engelhardt, C. R., Bartholow, B. D., Kerr, G. T., & Bushman, B. J. (2011). This is your brain on violent video games: Neural desensitization to violence predicts increased aggression following violent video game exposure. *Journal of Experimental Social Psychology, 47,* 1033–1036.

Englich, B., Mussweiler, T., & Strack, F. (2006). Playing dice with criminal sentences: The influence of irrelevant anchors on experts' judicial decision making. *Personality and Social Psychology Bulletin, 32,* 188–200.

English, T., & Chen, S. (2007). Culture and self-concept stability: Consistency across and within contexts among Asian Americans and European Americans. *Journal of Personality and Social Psychology, 93,* 478–490.

Eply, N., & Whitchurch, E. (2008). Mirror, mirror on the wall: Enhancement in self—recognition. *Personality and Social Psychology Bulletin, 34,* 1159–1170.

Erber, R., & Tesser, A. (1992). Task effort and the regulation of mood: The absorption hypothesis. *Journal of Experimental Social Psychology, 28,* 339–359.

Eres, R., & Molenberghs, P. (2013). The influence of group membership on the neural correlates involved in empathy. *Frontiers in Human Neuroscience, 7,* Article 176.

Ericksen, J. A., & Steffen, S. A. (1999). *Kiss and tell: Surveying sex in the twentieth century.* Cambridge, MA: Harvard University Press.

Erickson, W. B., Lampinen, J. M., & Leding, J. K. (2014). The weapon focus effect in target-present and target-absent line-ups: the roles of threat, novelty, and timing. *Applied Cognitive Psychology, 28,* 349–350.

Erol, R. Y., & Orth, U. (2011). Self-esteem development from age 14 to 30 years: A longitudinal study. *Journal of Personality and Social Psychology, 101,* 607–619.

Eschleman, K. J., Bowling, N. A., & Judge, T. A. (2015). The dispositional basis of attitudes: A replication and extension of Hepler and Albarracín (2013). *Journal of Personality and Social Psychology, 108,* e1–e15.

Eskine, K. J., Kacinic, N. A., & Prinz, J. J. (2011). A bad taste in the mouth: Gustatory influences on moral judgment. *Psychological Science, 22,* 295–299.

Espinoza, P., da Luz Fontes, A. A., & Arms-Chavez, C. J. (2014). Attributional gender bias: Teachers' ability and effort explanations for students' math performance. *Social Psychology of Education, 17,* 105–126.

Espinoza, R. E., & Willis-Esqueda, C. (2015). The influence of mitigation evidence, ethnicity, and SES on death penalty decisions by European American and Latino venire persons. *Cultural Diversity and Ethnic Minority Psychology, 21,* 288–299.

Evans, G. W., & Wener, R. E. (2006). Rail commuting duration and passenger stress. *Health Psychology, 25,* 408–412.

Evans, H., & Bartholomew, R. (2009). *Outbreak! The Encyclopedia of Extraordinary Social Behavior.* San Antonio, TX: Anomalist Books.

Evans, J. R., Schreiber Compo, N., & Russano, M. B. (2009). Intoxicated witnesses and suspects: Procedures and prevalence according to law enforcement. *Psychology, Public Policy, and Law, 15,* 194–221.

Everly, B. A., Shih, M. J., & Ho, G. C. (2012). Don't ask, don't tell? Does disclosure of gay identity affect partner performance? *Journal of Experimental Social Psychology, 48,* 407–410.

Evers, A., & Sieverding, M. (2014). Why do highly qualified women (still) earn less? Gender differences in long-term predictors of career success. *Psychology of Women Quarterly, 38,* 93–106.

Everson-Rose, S. A., & Lewis, T. T. (2005). Psychosocial factors in cardiovascular diseases. *Annual Review of Public Health, 26,* 469–500.

Everson, S. A., Goldberg, D. E., Kaplan, G. A., Cohen, R. D., Pukkala, E., Tuomiletho, P., & Salonen, J. T. (1996). Hopelessness and risk of mortality and incidence of myocardial infarction and cancer. *Psychosomatic Medicine, 58,* 113–121.

Exum, M. L. (2006). Alcohol and aggression: An integration of findings from experimental studies. *Journal of Criminal Justice, 34,* 131–145.

Facebook's "news" page. (2015). http://newsroom.fb.com/company-info/.

Fagin-Jones, S., & Midlarsky, E. (2007). Courageous altruism: Personal and situational correlates of rescue during the Holocaust. *Journal of Positive Psychology, 2,* 136–147.

Fairburn, C. G., & Brownell, K. D. (Eds.). (2002). *Eating disorders and obesity: A comprehensive handbook.* New York: Guilford Press.

Falk, C. F., & Heine, S. J. (2015). What is implicit self-esteem, and does it vary across cultures? *Personality and Social Psychology Review, 19,* 177–198.

Farrelly, D., Lazarus, J., & Roberts, G. (2007). Altruists attract. *Evolutionary Psychology, 5,* 313–329.

Fawcett, J. M., Russe, E. J., Peace, K. A., & Christie, J. (2011). Of guns and geese: A meta-analytic review of the "weapon focus" literature. *Psychology, Crime & Law, 17,* 1–32.

Fay, R. E., Turner, C. F., Klassen, A. D., & Gagnon, J. H. (1989). Prevalence and patterns of same-gender sexual contact among men. *Science, 243,* 343–348.

Fazio, R. H. (1990). Multiple processes by which attitudes guide behavior: The MODE model as an integrative framework. In M. P. Zanna (Ed.), *Advances in experimental social psychology* (Vol. 23, pp. 75–109). New York: Academic Press.

Fazio, R. H., & Olson, M. A. (2003). Implicit measures in social cognition research: Their meaning and use. *Annual Review of Psychology, 54,* 297–327.

Fazio, R. H., & Towles-Schwen, T. (1999). The MODE model of attitude-behavior processes. In S. Chaiken & Y. Trope (Eds.), *Dual-process theories in social psychology* (pp. 97–116). New York: Guilford.

Fazio, R. H., & Zanna, M. P. (1981). Direct experience and attitude-behavior consistency. In L. Berkowitz (Ed.), *Advances in experimental social psychology* (Vol. 14, pp. 162–202). New York: Academic Press.

Fazio, R. H., Ledbetter, J. E., & Towles-Schwen, T. (2000). On the costs of accessible attitudes: Detecting that the attitude object has changed. *Journal of Personality and Social Psychology, 78,* 197–210.

Fazio, R. H., Zanna, M. P., & Cooper, J. (1977). Dissonance and self perception: An integrative view of each theory's proper domain of application. *Journal of Experimental Social Psychology, 13,* 464–479.

Feddes, A. R., Mann, L., & Doosje, B. (2015). Increasing self-esteem and empathy to prevent violent radicalization: A longitudinal quantitative evaluation of a resilience training focused on adolescents with a dual identity. *Journal of Applied Social Psychology, 45,* 400–411.

Fehr, B., & Russell, J. A. (1991). The concept of love viewed from a prototype perspective. *Journal of Personality and Social Psychology, 60,* 425–438.

Fein, E., & Schneider, S. (1996). *The rules: Time-tested secrets for capturing the heart of Mr. Right.* New York: Warner Books.

Fein, S., & Spencer, S. J. (1997). Prejudice as self-image maintenance: Affirming the self through derogating others. *Journal of Personality and Social Psychology, 73,* 31–44.

Fein, S., Goethals, G. R., & Kugler, M. B. (2007). Social influence on political judgments: The case of presidential debates. *Political Psychology, 28,* 165–192.

Fein, S., Hoshino-Browne, E., Davies, P. G., & Spencer, S. J. (2003). Self-image maintenance goals and sociocultural norms in motivated social perception. In S. J. Spencer, S. Fein, M. P. Zanna, & J. M. Olson (Eds.), *Motivated social perception: The Ontario symposium* (Vol. 9, pp. 21–44). Mahwah, NJ: Erlbaum.

Fein, S., Morgan, S. J., Norton, M. I., & Sommers, S. R. (1997). Hype and suspicion: The effects of pretrial publicity, race, and suspicion on jurors' verdicts. *Journal of Social Issues, 53,* 487–502.

Feinberg, T. E., & Keenan, J. P. (Eds.). (2005). *The lost self: Pathologies of the brain and identity.* New York: Oxford University Press.

Feingold, A. (1988). Matching for attractiveness in romantic partners and same-sex friends: A meta-analysis and theoretical critique. *Psychological Bulletin, 104,* 226–235.

Feingold, A. (1992a). Gender differences in mate selection preferences: A test of the parental investment model. *Psychological Bulletin, 112,* 125–139.

Feingold, A. (1992b). Good-looking people are not what we think. *Psychological Bulletin, 111,* 304–341.

Feinstein, B. A., Hershenberg, R., Bhatia, V., Latack, J. A., Meuwly, N., & Davila, J. (2013). Negative social comparison on Facebook and depressive symptoms: Rumination as a mechanism. *Psychology of Popular Media Culture, 2,* 161–170.

FeldmanHall, O., Dalgleish, T., Evans, D., & Mobbs, D. (2015). Empathic concern drives costly altruism. *Neuroimage, 105,* 347–356.

Fenigstein, A. (2009). Private and public self-consciousness. In M. R. Leary & R. H. Hoyle (Eds.), *Handbook of individual differences in social behavior* (pp. 495–511). NY: The Guilford Press.

Fenigstein, A., & Abrams, D. (1993). Self-attention and the egocentric assumption of shared perspectives. *Journal of Experimental Social Psychology, 29,* 287–303.

Fenigstein, A., Scheier, M. F., & Buss, A. H. (1975). Public and private self-consciousness: Assessment and theory. *Journal of Consulting and Clinical Psychology, 43,* 522–527.

Fennelly, G. (2009, February 12). Amazon selling rape simulation game. *Belfast Telegraph.*

Ferguson, C. J. (2015). Do Angry Birds make for angry children? A meta-analysis of video game influences on children's and adolescents' aggression, mental health, prosocial behavior, and academic performance. *Perspectives on Psychological Science,* in press.

Ferguson, C. J., et al. (2015). Digital poison? Three studies examining the influence of violent video games on youth. *Computers in Human Behavior, 50,* 399–410.

Ferguson, E., Farrell, K., & Lawrence, C. (2008). Blood donation is an act of benevolence rather than altruism. *Health Psychology, 27,* 327–336.

Ferguson, M. (2007). On the automatic evaluation of end-states. *Journal of Personality and Social Psychology, 92,* 596–611.

Ferrari, J. R. (1998). Procrastination. In H. S. Friedman (Ed.), *Encyclopedia of mental health* (pp. 5.1–5.7). San Diego: Academic Press.

Ferrari, J. R., Diaz-Morales, J. F., O'Callaghan, J., Diaz, K., & Argumedo, D. (2007). Frequent behavioral delay tendencies by adults: International prevalence rates of chronic procrastination. *Journal of Cross-Cultural Psychology, 38,* 458–464.

Ferrari, J. R., Johnson, J. A., & McCowan, W. G. (1995). *Procrastination and task avoidance: Theory, research, and treatment.* New York: Plenum.

Ferreira, A., Picazo, O., Uriarte, N., Pereira, M., & Fernandez-Guasti, A. (2000). Inhibitory effect of buspirone and diazepam, but not of 8-OH-DPAT, on maternal behavior and aggression. *Pharmacology, Biochemistry and Behavior, 66,* 389–396.

Festinger, L. (1950). Informal social communication. *Psychological Review, 57,* 271–282.

Festinger, L. (1954). A theory of social comparison processes. *Human Relations, 7,* 117–140.

Festinger, L. (1957). *A theory of cognitive dissonance.* Stanford, CA: Stanford University Press.

Festinger, L., & Carlsmith, J. M. (1959). Cognitive consequences of forced compliance. *Journal of Abnormal and Social Psychology, 58,* 203–210.

Festinger, L., Pepitone, A., & Newcomb, T. (1952). Some consequences of de-individuation in a group. *Journal of Abnormal and Social Psychology, 47,* 382–389.

Festinger, L., Schachter, S., & Back, K. W. (1950). *Social pressures in informal groups: A study of human factors in housing.* New York: Harper.

Ficks, C. A., & Waldman, I. D. (2014). Candidate genes for aggression and antisocial behavior: A meta-analysis of association studies of the 5HTTLPR and MAOA-uVNTR. *Behavior Genetics, 44,* 427–444.

Fiedler, F. E. (1967). *A theory of leadership effectiveness.* New York: McGraw-Hill.

Fiedler, F. E., & Chemers, M. M. (1984). *Improving leadership effectiveness: The leader match concept* (2nd ed.). New York: Wiley.

Fiedler, F. E., & Garcia, J. E. (1987). *Leadership: Cognitive resources and performance.* New York: Wiley.

Fiedler, F. E., Murphy, S. E., & Gibson, F. W. (1992). Inaccurate reporting and inappropriate variables: A reply to Vecchio's (1990) examination of cognitive resource theory. *Journal of Applied Psychology, 77,* 372–374.

Filindra, A., & Pearson, & Merkowitz, S. (2013). Together in good times and bad? How economic triggers condition the effects of intergroup threat. *Social Science Quarterly, 94,* 1328–1345.

Fincham, F. D. (2003). Marital conflict, correlates, structure, and context. *Current Directions in Psychological Science, 12,* 23–27.

Fincham, F. D., Harold, G. T., & Gano-Phillips, S. (2000). The longitudinal association between attributions and marital satisfaction: Direction of effects and role of efficacy expectations. *Journal of Family Psychology, 14,* 267–285.

Fincham, F., Beach, S., & Davila, J. (2007). Longitudinal relations between forgiveness and conflict resolution in marriage. *Journal of Family Psychology, 21,* 542–545.

Fine, M. A., & Harvey, J. H. (Eds.). (2006). *Handbook of divorce and relationship dissolution.* Hillsdale, NJ: Erlbaum.

Fine, M. A., & Sacher, J. A. (1997). Predictors of distress following relationship termination among dating couples. *Journal of Social and Clinical Psychology, 16,* 381–388.

Fink, A. A. (2013). Review of "The Progress Principle": Using small wins to ignite joy, engagement, and creativity at work. *Personnel Psychology, 66,* 292–294.

Finkel, E. J., & Eastwick, P. W. (2008). Speed-dating. *Current Directions in Psychological Science, 17,* 193–197.

Finkel, E. J. (2014). The I3 Model: Metatheory, theory, and evidence. *Advances in Experimental Social Psychology, 49,* 1–104.

Finkel, E. J., Eastwick, P. W., & Reis, H. T. (2015). Best research practices in psychology: Illustrating epistemological and pragmatic considerations with the case of relationship science. *Journal of Personality and Social Psychology, 108,* 275–297.

Finkel, E. J., Eastwick, P. W., Karney, B. R., Reis, H. T., & Sprecher, S. (2012). Online dating: A critical analysis from the perspective of psychological science. *Psychological Science in the Public Interest, 13,* 3–66.

Finkel, E. J., Rusbult, C. E., Kumashiro, M., & Hannon, P. A. (2002). Dealing with betrayal in close relationships: Does commitment promote forgiveness? *Journal of Personality and Social Psychology, 82,* 956–974.

Finkel, N. J. (1995). *Commonsense justice: Jurors' notions of the law.* Cambridge, MA: Harvard University Press.

Finkelstein, M. A. (2009). Intrinsic vs. extrinsic motivational orientations and the volunteer process. *Personality and Individual Differences, 46,* 653–658.

Fischer, P., & Greitemeyer, T. (2013). The positive bystander effect: Passive bystanders increase helping in situations with high expected negative consequences for the helper. *The Journal of Social Psychology, 153,* 1–5.

Fischer, P., Krueger, J. I., et al. (2011). The bystander-effect: A meta-analytic review on bystander intervention in dangerous and non-dangerous emergencies. *Psychological Bulletin, 137,* 517–537.

Fishbein, M. (1980). A theory of reasoned action: Some applications and implications. In H. E. Howe & M. M. Page (Eds.), *Nebraska Symposium on Motivation* (Vol. 27, pp. 65–116). Lincoln: University of Nebraska Press.

Fishbein, M., & Ajzen, I. (1972). Attitudes and opinions. In P. H. Mussen & M. R. Rosenzweig (Eds.), *Annual Review of Psychology, 23,* 487–544.

Fisher, H. E. (2004). *Why we love: The nature and chemistry of romantic love.* New York: Henry Holt.

Fisher, H. (2015). Casual sex may be improving America's marriages. *Nautilus,* May/June 2015.

Fisher, J. D., & Fisher, W. A. (1992). Changing AIDS-risk behavior. *Psychological Bulletin, 111,* 455–474.

Fisher, J. D., Fisher, W. A., Bryan, A. D., & Misovich, S. J. (2002). Information-motivation-behavioral skills model-based HIV risk behavior change intervention for inner-city high school youth. *Health Psychology, 21,* 177–186.

Fisher, J. D., Fisher, W. A., Williams, S. S., & Malloy, T. E. (1994). Empirical tests of an information-motivation-behavioral skills model of AIDS-preventive behavior with gay men and heterosexual university students. *Health Psychology, 13,* 238–250.

Fisher, M. (2012, December 14). Chart: The U.S. has far more gun-related killings than any other developed country. *The Washington Post,* https://www.washingtonpost.com/news/worldviews/wp/2012/12/14/chart-the-u-s-has-far-more-gun-related-killings-than-any-other-developed-country/.

Fiske, A. P. (1992). The four elementary forms of sociality: Framework for a unified theory of social relations. *Psychological Review, 99,* 689–723.

Fiske, S. T., & Markus, H. R. (Eds.). (2012). *Facing social class: How societal rank influences interaction.* New York, NY: Russell Sage Foundation.

Fiske, S. T., & Neuberg, S. L. (1990). A continuum model of impression formation: From category-based to individuating processes: Influence of information and motivation on attention and interpretation. In M. P. Zanna (Ed.), *Advances in experimental social psychology* (Vol. 23, pp. 1–74). San Diego, CA: Academic Press.

Fiske, S. T., & Tablante, C. B. (2015). Stereotyping: Processes and content. In M. Mikulincer, P. R. Shaver, E. Borgida, & J. A. Bargh (Eds.), *APA handbook of personality and social psychology,* Volume 1*: Attitudes and social cognition* (pp. 457–507). Washington, DC: American Psychological Association.

Fiske, S. T., Cuddy, A., & Glick, P. (2007). Universal dimensions of social cognition: Warmth and competence. *Trends in Cognitive Sciences, 11,* 77–83.

Fitzgerald, C. J. (2009). Altruism and reproductive limitations. *Evolutionary Psychology, 7,* 234–252.

Fitzgerald, C. J., Thompson, M. C., & Whitaker, M. B. (2010). Altruism between romantic partners: Biological offspring as a genetic bridge between altruist and recipient. *Evolutionary Psychology, 8,* 462–476.

Fitzgerald, J. M. (1988). Vivid memories and the reminiscence phenomenon: The role of self-narrative. *Human Development, 31,* 261–273.

Fitzgerald, R., & Ellsworth, P. C. (1984). Due process vs. crime control: Death qualification and jury attitudes. *Law and Human Behavior, 8,* 31–52.

Fivush, R., & Haden, C.A. (Eds.). (2003). *Autobiographical memory and the construction of a narrative self: Developmental and cultural perspectives.* Mahwah, NJ: Erlbaum.

Fletcher, J. (2014, Aug 20). Is there a "rising tide" of anti-Semitism in the West? *BBC News Magazine.* http://www.bbc.com/news/magazine-28853221.

Florian, V, Mikulincer, M., & Taubman, O. (1995). Does hardiness contribute to mental health during a stressful real-life situation? The roles of appraisal and coping. *Journal of Personality and Social Psychology, 68,* 687–695.

Flory, J. D., Raikkonen, K., Matthews, K. A., & Owens, J. F. (2000). Self-focused attention and mood during everyday social interactions. *Personality and Social Psychology Bulletin, 26,* 875–883.

Flowe, H. D., Klatt, T., & Colloff, M. F. (2014). Selecting fillers on emotional appearance improves lineup identification accuracy. *Law and Human Behavior, 38,* 509–519.

Foels, R., & Pratto, F. (2015). The hidden dynamics of discrimination: How ideologies organize power and influence intergroup relations. In M. Mikulincer et al. (Eds.), *APA handbook of personality and social psychology,* Volume 2*: Group processes* (pp. 341–369). Washington, DC: American Psychological Association.

Folger, R. (1986). Rethinking equity theory: A referent cognitions model. In H. W. Bierhoff, R. L. Cohen, & J. Greenberg (Eds.), *Justice in social relations* (pp. 145–162). New York: Plenum.

Folger, R., & Cropanzano, R. (1998). *Organizational justice and human resource management.* Thousand Oaks, CA: Sage.

Folger, R., Konovsky, M. A., & Cropanzano, R. (1992). A due process metaphor for performance appraisal. *Research in Organizational Behavior, 14,* 129–177.

Folkman, S., & Moskowitz, J. T. (2000). Positive affect and the other side of coping. *American Psychologist, 55,* 647–654.

Follett, M. P. (1942). Constructive conflict. In H. C. Metcalf & L. Urwick (Eds.), *Dynamic administration: The collected papers of Mary Parker Follett* (pp. 30–49). New York: Harper.

Fong, K., & Mar, R. A. (2015). What does my avatar say about me? Inferring personality from avatars. *Personality and Social Psychology Bulletin, 41,* 237–249.

Forbes, C. E., & Leitner, J. B. (2014). Stereotype threat engenders neural attentional bias toward negative feedback to undermine performance. *Biological Psychology, 102,* 98–107.

Forbes, G. B., Collinsworth, L. L., Zhao, P., Kohlman, S., & LeClaire, J. (2011). Relationships among individualism-collectivism, gender, and ingroup/outgroup status, and responses to conflict: A study in China and the United States. *Aggressive Behavior, 37,* 302–314.

Forbes, G., Zhang, X., Doroszewicz, K., & Haas, K. (2009). Relationships between individualism-collectivism, gender, and direct or indirect aggression: A study in China, Poland, and the US. *Aggressive Behavior, 35,* 24–30.

Forgas, J. P. (2011). Can negative affect eliminate the power of first impressions? Affective influences on primacy and recency effects in impression formation. *Journal of Experimental Social Psychology, 47,* 425–429.

Forgas, J. P. (Ed.). (2000). *Feeling and thinking: Affective influences on social cognition.* New York: Cambridge University Press.

Forgas, J. P., & Bower, G. H. (1987). Mood effects on person perception judgments. *Journal of Personality and Social Psychology, 53,* 53–60.

Forgas, J. P., & East, R. (2008a). How real is that smile? Mood effects on accepting or rejecting the veracity of emotional facial expressions. *Journal of Nonverbal Behavior, 32,* 157–170.

Forgas, J. P., & Locke, J. (2005). Affective influences on causal inferences: The effects of mood on attributions for positive and negative interpersonal episodes. *Cognition and Emotion, 19,* 1071–1081.

Forgas, J. P., Baumeister, R. F., & Tice, D. M. (Eds.). (2009). *Psychology of self-regulation: Cognitive, affective, and motivational processes.* New York: Psychology Press.

Forgas, J. P., Dunn, E., & Granland, S. (2008). Are you being served . . . ? An unobtrusive experiment of affective influences on helping in a department store. *European Journal of Social Psychology, 38,* 333–342.

Forgas, J. P., & Rebekah, E. (2008). On being happy and gullible: Mood effects on skepticism and the detection of deception. *Journal of Experimental Social Psychology, 44,* 1362–1367.

Forrest-Bank, S., Jenson, J. M., & Trecartin, S. (2015). The Revised 28-Item Racial and Ethnic Microaggressions Scale (R28REMS): Examining the factorial structure for Black, Latino/Hispanic, and Asian young adults. *Journal of Social Service Research, 41,* 326–344.

Fortuna, K., & Knafo, A. (2014). Parental and genetic contributions to prosocial behavior during childhood. In L. M. Padilla-Walker, & G. Carlo (Eds.), *Prosocial development: A multidimensional approach* (pp. 70–89). New York: Oxford University Press.

Foster, C. A., Witcher, B. S., Campbell, W. K., & Green, J. D. (1998). Arousal and attraction: Evidence for automatic and controlled processes. *Journal of Personality and Social Psychology, 74,* 86–101.

Fosterling, F. (1992). The Kelley model as an analysis of variance analogy: How far can it be taken? *Journal of Experimental Social Psychology, 28,* 475–490.

Fowler, F. J., Jr. (2014). *Survey research methods.* Thousand Oaks, CA: Sage Publications.

Fowler, K. A., Lilienfeld, S. O., & Patrick, C. J. (2009). Detecting psychopathy from thin slices of behavior. *Psychological Assessment, 21,* 68–78.

Fox, E., Russo, R., & Dutton, K. (2002). Attentional bias for threat: Evidence for delayed disengagement from emotional faces. *Cognition and Emotion, 16,* 355–379.

Frank, J. (1949). *Courts on trial.* Princeton, NJ: Princeton University Press.

Frantz, C. M., Cuddy, A. J. C., Burnett, M., Ray, H., & Hart, A. (2004). A threat in the computer: The race Implicit Association Test as a stereotype threat experience. *Personality and Social Psychology Bulletin, 30,* 1611–1624.

Frattaroli, J. (2006). Experimental disclosure and its moderators: A meta-analysis. *Psychological Bulletin, 132,* 823–865.

Frazier, P. A. (2003). Perceived control and distress following sexual assault: A longitudinal test of a new model. *Journal of Personality and Social Psychology, 84,* 1257–1269.

Frazier, P., & Schauben, L. (1994). Causal attributions and recovery from rape and other stressful events. *Journal of Social and Clinical Psychology, 13,* 1–14.

Frazier, P., Greer, C., Gabrielsen, S., Tennen, H., Park, C., & Tomich, P. (2013). The relation between trauma exposure and prosocial behavior. *Psychological Trauma: Theory, Research, Practice, and Policy, 5,* 286–294.

Frazier, P., Steward, J., & Mortensen, H. (2004). Perceived control and adjustment to trauma: A comparison across events. *Journal of Social and Clinical Psychology, 23,* 303–324.

Frederickson, B. L., Maynard, K. E., Helms, M. J., Haney, T. L., Siegler, I. C., & Barefoot, J. C. (2000). Hostility predicts magnitude and duration of blood pressure response to anger. *Journal of Behavioral Medicine, 23,* 229–243.

Fredrickson, B. L. (2009). *Positivity: Groundbreaking research reveals how to embrace the hidden strength of positive emotions, overcome negativity, and thrive.* New York: Crown Books.

Fredrickson, B. L., Roberts, T., Noll, S. M., Quinn, D. M., & Twenge, J. M. (1998). That swimsuit becomes you: Sex differences in self-objectification, restrained eating, and math performance. *Journal of Personality and Social Psychology, 75,* 269–284.

Fredrickson, B. L., Tugade, M. M., Waugh, C. E., & Larkin, G. R. (2003). What good are positive emotions in crisis? A prospective study of resilience and emotions following the terrorist attacks on the United States on September 11th, 2001. *Journal of Personality and Social Psychology, 84,* 365–376.

Freeberg, T. M., Krama, T., Vrublevska, J., Krams, I., & Kullberg, C. (2014). Tufted titmouse (Baeolophus bicolor) calling and risk-sensitive foraging in the face of threat. *Animal Cognition, 17,* 1341–1352.

Freedman, J. L., & Fraser, S. C. (1966). Compliance without pressure: The foot-in-the-door technique. *Journal of Personality and Social Psychology, 4,* 195–202.

Freedman, J. L., & Sears, D. O. (1965). Warning, distraction, and resistance to influence. *Journal of Personality and Social Psychology, 1,* 262–266.

Freeman, K., Hadwin, J. A., & Halligan, S. L. (2011). An experimental investigation of peer influences on adolescent hostile attributions. *Journal of Clinical Child and Adolescent Psychology, 40,* 897–903.

Frenda, S. J., Nichols, R. M., & Loftus, E. F. (2011). Current issues and advances in misinformation research. *Current Directions in Psychological Science, 20,* 20–23.

Frenda, S. J., Patihis, L., Loftus, E. F., Lewis, H. C., & Fenn, K. M. (2014). Sleep deprivation and false memories. *Psychological Science, 25,* 1674–1681.

Freud, S. (1905). *Fragments of an analysis of a case of hysteria. Collected papers* (Vol. 3). New York: Basic Books. (Reprinted in 1959).

Frey, K. S., Hirschstein, M. K., Edstrom, L. V., & Snell, J. L. (2009). Observed reductions in school bullying, nonbullying aggression, and destructive bystander behavior: A longitudinal evaluation. *Journal of Educational Psychology, 101,* 466–481.

Friedland, N., Keinan, G., & Regev, Y. (1992). Controlling the uncontrollable: Effects of stress on illusory perceptions of controllability. *Journal of Personality and Social Psychology, 63,* 923–931.

Friedman, H. S. (1991). *The self-healing personality.* New York: Henry Holt.

Friedman, H. S., & Booth-Kewley, S. (1987). The "disease-prone personality": A meta-analytic view of the construct. *American Psychologist, 42,* 539–555.

Friedman, H. S., & Kern, M. L. (2014). Personality, well-being, and health. *Annual Review of Psychology, 65,* 719–742.

Friedman, M. J., Keane, T. M., & Resick, P. A. (Eds.). (2014). *Handbook of PTSD: Science and practice* (2nd ed.). New York: Guilford Press.

Friedrich, J., Fethersonhaugh, D., Casey, S., & Gallagher, D. (1996). Argument integration and attitude change: Suppression effects in the integration of one-sided arguments that vary in persuasiveness. *Personality and Social Psychology Bulletin, 22,* 179–191.

Friend, R., Rafferty, Y., & Bramel, D. (1990). A puzzling misinterpretation of the Asch "conformity" study. *European Journal of Social Psychology, 20,* 29–44.

Fritzsche, B. A., Finkelstein, M. A., & Penner, L. A. (2000). To help or not to help: Capturing individuals' decision policies. *Social Behavior and Personality, 28,* 561–578.

Fry, D. P. (2012). Life without war. *Science, 336,* 879–884.

Fu, A. S., & Markus, H. R. (2014). My mother and me: Why tiger mothers motivate Asian Americans but not European Americans. *Personality and Social Psychology Bulletin, 40,* 739–749.

Fugère, M. A., Leszczynski, J. P., & Cousins, A. J. (2014). *The social psychology of attraction and romantic relationships.* New York: Palgrave Macmillan.

Fujino, N., & Okamura, H. (2009, April). Factors affecting the sense of burden felt by family members caring for patients with mental illness. *Archives of Psychiatric Nursing, 23*(2), 128–137.

Fujita, F., & Diener, E. (2005). Life satisfaction set point: Stability and change. *Journal of Personality and Social Psychology, 88,* 158–164.

Funk, S. C. (1992). Hardiness: A review of theory and research. *Health Psychology, 11,* 335–345.

Furche, A., & Johnstone, D. (2006). Evidence of the endowment effect in stock market order placement. *Journal of Behavioral Finance, 7,* 145–154.

Furnham, A. (2003). Belief in a just world: Research progress over the past decade. *Personality and Individual Differences, 34,* 795–817.

Furnham, A., Simmons, K., & McClelland, A. (2000). Decisions concerning the allocation of scarce medical resources. *Journal of Social Behavior and Personality, 15,* 185–200.

Gabbert, F., Memon, A., & Allan, K. (2003). Memory conformity: Can eyewitnesses influence each other's memories for an event? *Applied Cognitive Psychology, 17,* 533–543.

Gabel, M., & Brunner, H. (2003). *Global Inc.: An atlas of the multinational corporation.* New York: New Press.

Gabrielson, R., Jones, R. G., & Sagara, E. (2014, Oct 10). Deadly force, in black and white. *ProPublica,* http://www.problica.org/article/deadly-force-in-black-and-white.

Gaertner, S. L., & Dovidio, J. F. (1986). The aversive form of racism. In J. F. Dovidio & S. L. Gaernter (Eds.), *Prejudice, discrimination, and racism* (pp. 61–89). San Diego, CA: Academic Press.

Gaertner, S. L., & Dovidio, J. F. (2010). Common ingroup identity model. In J. M. Levine & M. A. Hogg (Eds.), *Encyclopedia of group processes and intergroup relations* (Vol. 1, pp. 119–122). Thousand Oaks, CA: Sage.

Gaertner, S. L., & Dovidio, J. F. (2012). The common ingroup identity model. In P. M. Van Lange, A. W. Kruglanski, & E. T. Higgins (Eds.), *Handbook of theories of social psychology* (Vol. 2, pp. 439–457). Thousand Oaks, CA: Sage.

Gailliot, M. T. (2013). Hunger and reduced self-control in the laboratory and across the world: Reducing hunger as a self-control panacea. *Psychology, 4,* 59–66.

Gailliot, M. T., Peruche, B. M., Plant, E. A., & Baumeister, R. F. (2009). Stereotypes and prejudice in the blood: Sucrose drinks reduce prejudice and stereotyping. *Journal of Experimental Social Psychology, 45,* 288–290.

Gailliot, M., Baumeister, R., DeWall, C., Maner, J., Plant, E., Tice, D., Brewer, L., & Schmeichel, B. (2007). Self-control relies on glucose as a limited energy source: Willpower is more than just a metaphor. *Journal of Personality and Social Psychology, 92,* 325–336.

Galanou, C., Galanakis, M., Alexopoulos, E., & Darviri, C. (2014). Rosenberg Self-Esteem Scale Greek validation on student sample. *Psychology, 5,* 819–827.

Galanter, M. (1999). *Cults: Faith, healing, and coercion* (2nd ed.). New York: Oxford University Press.

Galea, S., Ahern, J., Resnick, H., Kilpatrick, D., Bucuvalas, M., Gold, J., & Vlahov, D. (2002). Psychological sequelae of the September 11 terrorist attacks in New York City. *New England Journal of Medicine, 346,* 982–987.

Galen, B. R., & Underwood, M. K. (1997). A developmental investigation of social aggression among children. *Developmental Psychology, 33,* 589–600.

Galinsky, A. D., Stone, J., & Cooper, J. (2000). The reinstatement of dissonance and psychological discomfort following failed affirmations. *European Journal of Social Psychology, 30,* 123–147.

Galinsky, A. D., Wang, C. S., & Ku, G. (2008). Perspective-takers behave more stereotypically. *Journal of Personality and Social Psychology, 95,* 404–419.

Gallo, L. C., & Matthews, K. A. (2003). Understanding the association between socioeconomic status and physical health: Do negative emotions play a role? *Psychological Bulletin, 129,* 10–51.

Gallup, G. G., Jr. (1977). Self-recognition in primates: A comparative approach to the bidirectional properties of consciousness. *American Psychologist, 32,* 329–337.

Galobardes, B., Smith, G. D., & Lynch, J. W. (2006). Systematic review of the influence of childhood socioeconomic circumstances on risk for cardiovascular disease in adulthood. *Annals of Epidemiology, 16,* 91–104.

Game, F., Carchon, I., & Vital-Durand, F. (2003). The effect of stimulus attractiveness on visual tracking in 2- to 6-month-old infants. *Infant Behavior & Development, 26,* 135–150.

Gammie, S. C., Olaghere-da-Silva, U. B., & Nelson, R. J. (2000). 3-Bromo-7-nitroindazole, a neuronal nitric oxide synthase inhibitor, impairs maternal aggression and citrulline immunoreactivity in prairie voles. *Brain Research, 870,* 80–86.

Gamson, W. A., Fireman, B., & Rytina, S. (1982). *Encounters with unjust authority.* Homewood, IL: Dorsey.

Gangestad, S. W. (1993). Sexual selection and physical attractiveness: Implications for mating dynamics. *Human Nature, 4,* 205–235.

Gangestad, S. W., & Simpson, J. A. (2000). The evolution of human mating: Trade-offs and strategic pluralism. *Behavioral and Brain Sciences, 23,* 573–587.

Gangestad, S. W., & Snyder, M. (2000). Self-monitoring: Appraisal and reappraisal. *Psychological Bulletin, 126,* 530–555.

Garcia, S. M., Weaver, K., Moskowitz, G. B., & Darley, J. M. (2002). Crowded minds: The implicit bystander effect. *Journal of Personality and Social Psychology, 83,* 843–853.

Gardikiotis, A. (2011). Minority influence. *Social and Personality Psychology Compass, 5,* 679–693.

Gardner, W. L., & Knowles, M. L. (2008). Love makes you real: Favorite television characters are perceived as "real" in a social facilitation paradigm. *Social Cognition, 26,* 156–168.

Garland, H., & Conlon, D. E. (1998). Too close to quit: The role of project completion in maintaining commitment. *Journal of Applied Social Psychology, 28,* 2025–2048.

Garnero, A., Kampelmann, S., & Rycx, F. (2014). The heterogeneous effects of workforce diversity on productivity, wages, and profits. *Industrial Relations: A Journal of Economy & Society, 53,* 430–477.

Garrett, B. L. (2010). The substance of false confessions. *Stanford Law Review, 62,* 1051–1119.

Garrett, B. L. (2011). *Convicting the innocence: When criminal prosecutions go wrong.* Cambridge, MA: Harvard University Press.

Gaucher, D., Friesen, J., & Kay, A. C. (2011). Evidence that gendered wording in job advertisements exists and sustains gender inequality. *Journal of Personality and Social Psychology, 101,* 109–128.

Gawronski, B., & Bodenhausen, G. V. (2006). Associative and propositional processes in evaluation: An integrative review of implicit and explicit attitude change. *Psychological Bulletin, 132,* 692–731.

Gawronski, B., Brochu, P. M., Sritharan, R., & Strack, F. (2012). Cognitive consistency in prejudice-related belief systems: Integrating old-fashioned, modern, aversive, and implicit forms of prejudice. In B. Gawronski & F. Strack (Eds.), *Cognitive consistency: A fundamental principle in social cognition* (pp. 369–389). New York: Guilford.

Gawronski, B., Galdi, S., & Arcuri, L. (2015). What can political psychology learn from implicit measures? Empirical evidence and new directions. *Political Psychology, 36,* 1–17.

Geary, D. C. (2000). Evolution and proximate expression of human paternal investment. *Psychological Bulletin, 126,* 55–77.

Gee, C. J., & Leith, L. M. (2007). Aggressive behavior in professional ice hockey: A cross-cultural comparison of North American and European born NHL players. *Psychology of Sport and Exercise, 8,* 567–583.

Geen, R. G. (1981). Behavioral and physiological reactions to observed violence: Effects of prior exposure to aggressive stimuli. *Journal of Personality and Social Psychology, 40,* 868–875.

Geen, R. G. (1991). Social motivation. *Annual Review of Psychology, 42,* 377–399.

Geen, R. G., & Quanty, M. B. (1977). The catharsis of aggression: An evaluation of a hypothesis. In L. Berkowitz (Ed.), *Advances in experimental social psychology* (Vol. 10, pp. 1–37). New York: Academic Press.

Geis, F. L., Brown, V, Jennings (Walstedt), J., & Porter, N. (1984). TV commercials as achievement scripts for women. *Sex Roles, 10,* 513–525.

Geiselman, R. E., Haight, N. A., & Kimata, L. G. (1984). Context effects in the perceived physical attractiveness of faces. *Journal of Experimental Social Psychology, 20,* 409–424.

Gelfand, M. J. (2012). Culture's constraints: International differences in the strength of social norms. *Current Directions in Psychological Science, 21,* 420–424.

Gelfand, M. J., Raver, J. L., et al. (2011). Differences between tight and loose cultures: A 33-nation study. *Science, 332*(6033), 1100–1104.

Gelfand, M. J., Severance, L., et al. (2015). Culture and getting to yes: The linguistic signature of creative agreements in the United States and Egypt. *Journal of Organizational Behavior,* in press.

Gendar, A., Burke, K., & McShane, L. (2009, July 16). "Fight Club" bomber: Teen nabbed in Memorial Day blast at East Side Starbucks. *New York Daily News,* p. 7.

Gentile, B., Grabe, S., Dolan-Pascoe, B., Twenge, J. M., Wells, B. E., & Maitino, A. (2009). Gender differences in domain-specific self-esteem: A meta-analysis. *Review of General Psychology, 13,* 34–45.

Gentile, D. A., Anderson, C. A., Yukawa, S., Ihori, N., Saleem, M., & Ming, L. M., et al. (2009). The effects of prosocial video games on prosocial behaviors: International evidence from correlational, longitudinal, and experimental studies. *Personality and Social Psychology Bulletin, 35,* 752–763.

Gentile, D. A., Swing, E. L., Anderson, C. A., Rinker, D., & Thomas, K. M. (2015). Differential neural recruitment during violent video game play in violent- and nonviolent-game players. *Psychology of Popular Media Culture,* in press.

Georgesen, J. C., & Harris, M. J. (1998). Why's my boss always holding me down? A meta-analysis of power effects on performance evaluations. *Personality and Social Psychology Review, 2,* 184–195.

Gerard, H. B., Whilhelmy, R. A., & Connolley, R. S. (1968). Conformity and group size. *Journal of Personality and Social Psychology, 8,* 79–82.

Gerber, J., & Wheeler, L. (2009). On being rejected: A meta-analysis of experimental research on rejection. *Perspectives on Psychological Science, 4,* 468–488.

Gerbner, G., Gross, L., Morgan, M., & Signorielli, N. (1986). Living with television: The dynamics of the cultivation process. In J. Bryant & D. Zillmann (Eds.), *Perspectives on media effects* (pp. 17–40). Hillsdale, NJ: Erlbaum.

Gergen, K. J. (1973). Social psychology as history. *Journal of Personality and Social Psychology, 26,* 309–320.

Gerhart, B., & Rynes, S. (1991). Determinants and consequences of salary negotiations by male and female MBA graduates. *Journal of Applied Psychology, 76,* 256–262.

Gershoff, E. T. (2002). Corporal punishment by parents and associated child behaviors and experiences: A meta-analytic and theoretical review. *Psychological Bulletin, 128,* 539–579.

Gershoff, E. T., Purtell, K. M., & Holas, I. (2015). *Corporal punishment in U.S. public schools: Legal precedents, current practices, and future policy.* New York: Springer.

Gerson, J. (2006, September 21). Montreal shootings disturb Columbine game creator. *Toronto Star,* p. A12.

Gervais, W. M. (2013). In godlessness we distrust: Using social psychology to solve the puzzle of anti-atheist prejudice. *Social and Personality Psychology Compass, 7,* 366–377.

Gervais, W. M., & Norenzayan, A. (2012). Like a camera in the sky? Thinking about God increases public self-awareness and socially desirable responding. *Journal of Experimental Social Psychology, 48,* 298–302.

Ghumman, S., & Barnes, C. M. (2013). Sleep and prejudice: A resource recovery approach. *Journal of Applied Social Psychology, 43,* 166-178.

Giancola, P. R. (2013). Alcohol and aggression: Theories and mechanisms. In M. McMurran (Ed.), *Alcohol-related violence: Prevention and treatment* (pp. 37–59). Wiley-Blackwell.

Giancola, P. R., Godlaski, A. J., & Roth, R. M. (2012). Identifying component-processes of executive functioning that serve as risk factors for the alcohol-aggression relation. *Psychology of Addictive Behaviors, 26,* 201–211.

Giancola, P. R., Josephs, R. A., Parrott, D. J., & Duke, A. A. (2010). Alcohol myopia revisited: Clarifying aggression and other acts of disinhibition through a distorted lens. *Perspectives on Psychological Science, 5,* 265–278.

Gibbons, F. X., Kingsbury, J. H., Weng, C., Gerrard, M., Cutrona, C., Wills, T. A., & Stock, M. (2014). Effects of perceived racial discrimination on health status and health behavior: A differential mediation hypothesis. *Health Psychology, 33,* 11–19.

Gibbons, F. X., & McCoy, S. B. (1991). Self-esteem, similarity, and reactions to active versus passive downward comparison. *Journal of Personality and Social Psychology, 60,* 414–424.

Gibbons, F. X., Lane, D. J., Gerrard, M., Reis-Bergan, M., Lautrup, C., Pexa, N., & Blanton, H. (2002). Comparison level preferences after performance: Is downward comparison theory still useful? *Journal of Personality and Social Psychology, 83,* 865–880.

Gibbons, S. L., & Ebbeck, V. (1997). The effect of different teaching strategies on the moral development of physical education students. *Journal of Teaching in Physical Education, 17,* 85–98.

Gibbs, W., & Koranyi, B. (2012). Mass killer planned bigger attack; Tells court he prepared by playing World of Warcraft "a lot." *The Gazette* (Montreal), April 20, p. A17.

Gibson, B., & Sachau, D. (2000). Sandbagging as a self-presentational strategy: Claiming to be less than you are. *Personality and Social Psychology Bulletin, 26,* 56–70.

Giesler, R. B., Josephs, R. A., & Swann, W. B., Jr. (1996). Self-verification in clinical depression: The desire for negative evaluation. *Journal of Abnormal Psychology, 105,* 358–368.

Gigerenzer, G., Hertwig, R., & Pachur, T. (Eds.). (2011). *Heuristics: The Foundations of Adaptive Behavior.* New York: Oxford University Press.

Gilbert, D. (2006). *Stumbling on happiness.* New York: Alfred A. Knopf.

Gilbert, D. T., & Jones, E. E. (1986). Perceiver-induced constraint: Interpretations of self-generated reality. *Journal of Personality and Social Psychology, 50,* 269–280.

Gilbert, D. T., & Malone, P. S. (1995). The correspondence bias. *Psychological Bulletin, 117,* 21–38.

Gilbert, D. T., McNulty, S. E., Giuliano, T. A., & Benson, J. E. (1992). Blurry words and fuzzy deeds: The attribution of obscure behavior. *Journal of Personality and Social Psychology, 62,* 18–25.

Gilbert, D. T., Pinel, E. C., Wilson, T. D., Blumberg, S. J., & Wheatley, T. (1998). Immune neglect: A source of durability bias in affective forecasting. *Journal of Personality and Social Psychology, 75,* 617–638.

Gilbert, S. J. (1981). Another look at the Milgram obedience studies: The role of the gradated series of shocks. *Personality and Social Psychology Bulletin, 7,* 690–695.

Gillig, P. M., & Greenwald, A. G. (1974). Is it time to lay the sleeper effect to rest? *Journal of Personality and Social Psychology, 29,* 132–139.

Gilovich, T., Griffin, D., & Kahneman, D. (Eds.). (2002). *Heuristics and biases: The psychology of intuitive judgment.* New York: Cambridge University Press.

Gilovich, T., Medvec, V. H., & Savitsky, K. (2000). The spotlight effect in social judgment: An egocentric bias in estimates of the salience of one's own actions and appearance. *Journal of Personality and Social Psychology, 78,* 211–222.

Gilson, L. L., Maynard, M. T., Young, N. J., Vartiainen, M., & Hakonen, M. (2015). Virtual teams research: 10 years, 10 themes, and 10 opportunities. *Journal of Management, 41,* 1313–1337.

Giner-Sorolla, R., & Chaiken, S. (1997). Selective use of heuristic and systematic processing under defensive motivation. *Personality and Social Psychology Bulletin, 23,* 84–97.

Gino, F., Ayal, S., & Ariely, D. (2009). Contagion and differentiation in unethical behavior: The effect of one bad apple on the barrel. *Psychological Science, 20,* 393–398.

Gioia, D. A., & Longnecker, C. O. (1994). Delving into the dark side: The politics of executive appraisal. *Organizational Dynamics, 22,* 47–58.

Girvan, E. J., Deason, G., & Borgida, E. (2015). The generalizability of gender bias: Testing the effects of contextual, explicit, and implicit sexism on labor arbitration decisions. *Law and Human Behavior,* in press.

Gjelten, G. (2015, Feb 26). Pew study on religion finds increased harassment of Jews. *NPR.* http://www.npr.org/sections/thetwo-way/2015/02/26/389250366/pew-study-on-religion-finds-increased-harassment-of-jews.

Gladwell, M. (2005). *Blink: The power of thinking without thinking.* New York: Little, Brown, and Company.

Glanz, J., & Schwartz, J. (September 26, 2003). Dogged engineer's effort to assess shuttle damage. *New York Times,* p. A1.

Glaser, T., Dickel, N., Liersch, B., Rees, J., Süssenbach, P., & Bohner, G. (2015). Lateral attitude change. *Personality and Social Psychology Review, 19,* 257–276.

Glasman, L. R., & Albarracín, D. (2006). Forming attitudes that predict future behavior: A meta-analysis of the attitude-behavior relation. *Psychological Bulletin, 132,* 778–822.

Glaso, L., Nielsen, M. B., & Einarsen, S. (2009). Interpersonal problems among perpetrators and targets of workplace bullying. *Journal of Applied Social Psychology, 39,* 1316–1333.

Glass, D. C., & Singer, J. E. (1972). *Urban stress.* New York: Academic Press.

Glassman, J., Prosch, M., & Shao, B. M. (2015). To monitor or not to monitor: Effectiveness of a cyberloafing countermeasure. *Information & Management, 52,* 170–182.

Glick, B., & Gibbs, J. C. (2011). *Aggression replacement training: A comprehensive intervention for aggressive youth* (3rd ed. rev. and exp.). Champaign, IL: Research Press.

Glick, P., & Fiske, S. T. (2001). Ambivalent sexism. In M. P. Zanna (Ed.), *Advances in experimental social psychology* (*Vol. 33,* pp. 115–188). San Diego, CA: Academic Press.

Glick, P., & Fiske, S. T. (2012). An ambivalent alliance: Hostile and benevolent sexism as complementary justifications for gender inequality. In J. Dixon & M. Levine (Eds.), *Beyond prejudice: Extending the social psychology of conflict, inequality and social change* (pp. 70–88). New York: Cambridge University Press.

Glick, P. & Fiske, S. T., et al. (2000). Beyond prejudice as simple antipathy: Hostile and benevolent sexism across cultures. *Journal of Personality and Social Psychology, 79,* 763–775.

Global Deception Research Team. (2006). A world of lies. *Journal of Cross-Cultural Psychology, 37,* 60–74.

Godfrey, D. K., Jones, E. E., & Lord, C. G. (1986). Self-promotion is not ingratiating. *Journal of Personality and Social Psychology, 50,* 106–115.

Goel, V. (2014, June 30). Facebook tinkers with users' emotions in news feed experiment, stirring outcry. *New York Times,* p. B1.

Goethals, G. R. (2005). Presidential leadership. *Annual Review of Psychology, 56,* 545–570.

Goethals, G. R., & Darley, J. (1977). Social comparison theory: An attributional approach. In J. M. Suls & R. L. Miller (Eds.), *Social comparison processes: Theoretical and empirical perspectives* (pp. 259–278). Washington, DC: Hemisphere.

Goethals, G. R., Cooper, J., & Naficy, A. (1979). Role of foreseen, foreseeable, and unforeseeable behavioral consequences in the arousal of cognitive dissonance. *Journal of Personality and Social Psychology, 37,* 1179–1185.

Goethals, G. R., Sorensen, G., & Burns, J. M. (Eds.). (2004). *Encyclopedia of leadership.* Thousand Oaks, CA: Sage.

Goff, P. A., Eberhardt, J. L., Williams, M. J., & Jackson, M. C. (2008). Not yet human: Implicit knowledge, historical dehumanization, and contemporary consequences. *Journal of Personality and Social Psychology, 94,* 292–306.

Goff, P. A., Jackson, M. C., Di Leone, B. A. L., Culotta, C. M., & DiTomasso, N. A. (2014). The essence of innocence: Consequences of dehumanizing Black children. *Journal of Personality and Social Psychology, 106,* 526–545.

Goff, P. A., Steele, C. M., & Davies, P. G. (2008). The space between us: Stereotype threat and distance in interracial contexts. *Journal of Personality and Social Psychology, 94,* 91–107.

Goffman, E. (1955). On face-work: An analysis of ritual elements in social interaction. *Psychiatry, 18,* 213–231.

Goffman, E. (1959). *The presentation of self in everyday life.* Garden City: Doubleday.

Golby, J., & Meggs, J. (2011). Exploring the organizational effect of prenatal testosterone upon the sporting brain. *Journal of Sports Science and Medicine, 10,* 445–451.

Goldberg, P. (1968). Are women prejudiced against women? *Transaction, 5,* 28–30.

Goldhagen, D. J. (1996). *Hitler's willing executioners: Ordinary Germans and the Holocaust.* New York: Knopf.

Goldin, C. (1990). *Understanding the gender gap: An economic history of American women.* New York: Oxford University Press.

Goldstein, N. J., & Cialdini, R. B. (2007). The spyglass self: A model of vicarious self-perception. *Journal of Personality and Social Psychology, 92,* 402–417.

Goleman, D., Boyatzis, R., & McKee, A. (2002). *Primal leadership: Realizing the power of emotional intelligence.* Cambridge, MA: Harvard Business School Press.

Golgowski, N. (2015, April 10). Troy University students charged in Florida spring break gang rape filmed on cell phone. *New York Daily News,* http://www.nydailynews.com/news/national /troy-university-students-charged-spring-break-gang-rape-article-1.2181244.

Gollan, J. (2011, January 21). Rethinking evaluations when almost every teacher gets an "A" *The New York Times.* Available at http://www.nytimes.com.

Golombok, S., & Hines, M. (2002). Sex differences in social behavior. In P. K. Smith & C. H. Hart (Eds.), *Blackwell handbook of childhood social development* (pp. 117–136). Malden, MA: Blackwell.

Gómez, A. (2011). Testing the cycle of violence hypothesis: Child abuse and adolescent dating violence as predictors of intimate partner violence in young adulthood. *Youth & Society, 43,* 171–192.

Gonzaga, G., Campos, B., & Bradbury, T. (2007). Similarity, convergence, and relationship satisfaction in dating and married couples. *Journal of Personality and Social Psychology, 93,* 34–48.

Gonzalez, A. Q., & Koestner, R. (2006). What Valentine announcements reveal about the romantic emotions of men and women. *Sex Roles, 55,* 767–773.

Good, C., Aronson, J., & Inzlicht, M. (2003). Improving adolescents' standardized test performance: An intervention to reduce the effects of stereotype threat. *Journal of Applied Developmental Psychology, 24,* 645–662.

Good, C., Rattan, A., & Dweck, C. S. (2012). Why do women opt out? Sense of belonging and women's representation in mathematics. *Journal of Personality and Social Psychology, 102,* 700–717.

Good, J. J., Sanchez, D. T., & Chavez, G. F. (2013). White ancestry in perceptions of Black/White biracial individuals: Implications for affirmative action contexts. *Journal of Applied Social Psychology, 43,* E276–E286.

Goodboy, A. K., & Martin, M. M. (2015). The personality profile of a cyberbully: Examining the Dark Triad. *Computers in Human Behavior, 49,* 1–4.

Goodman, J. K., Cryder, C. E., & Cheema, A. (2013). Data collection in a flat world: The strengths and weaknesses of mechanical Turk samples. *Journal of Behavioral Decision Making, 26,* 213–224.

Goodwin, G. P. (2015). Moral character in person perception. *Current Directions in Psychological Science, 24,* 38–44.

Goodwin, G. P., Piazza, J., & Rozin, P. (2014). Moral character predominates in person perception and evaluation. *Journal of Personality and Social Psychology, 106,* 148–168.

Goodwin, S. A., Fiske, S. T., Rosen, L. D., & Rosenthal, A. M. (2002). The eye of the beholder: Romantic goals and impression biases. *Journal of Experimental Social Psychology, 38,* 232–241.

Gorchoff, S., John, O., & Helson, R. (2008). Contextualizing change in marital satisfaction during middle age: An 18-year longitudinal study. *Psychological Science, 19,* 1194–1200.

Gorman, E. H., & Kmec, J. A. (2009). Hierarchical rank and women's organizational mobility: Glass ceilings in corporate law firms. *American Journal of Sociology, 114,* 1428–1474.

Gorodetsky, E., Bevilacqua, L., Carli, V., Sarchiapone, M., Roy, A., Goldman, D., & Enoch, M. (2014). The interactive effect of MAOA-LPR genotype and childhood physical neglect on aggressive behaviors in Italian male prisoners. *Genes, Brain & Behavior, 13,* 543–549.

Gosling, P., Denizeau, M., & Oberlé, D. (2006). Denial of responsibility: A new mode of dissonance reduction. *Journal of Personality and Social Psychology, 90,* 722–733.

Gosling, S. (2008). *Snoop: What your stuff says about you.* New York: Basic Books.

Gosling, S. D., & Mason, W. (2015). Internet research in psychology. *Annual Review of Psychology, 66,* 877–902.

Gossett, J. L., & Byrne, S. (2002). "CLICK HERE": A content analysis of Internet rape sites. *Gender and Society, 16,* 689–709.

Goswami, R., Dufort, P., Tartaglia, M. C., Green, R. E., Crawley, A., Tator, C. H., & . . . Davis, K. D. (2015). Frontotemporal correlates of impulsivity and machine learning in retired professional athletes with a history of multiple concussions. *Brain Structure & Function,* in press.

Gotlib, I. H., & Hammen, C. L. (Eds.). (2009). *Handbook of depression* (2nd ed.). New York: Guilford.

Gottfredson, L. S. (2002). Where and why g matters: Not a mystery. *Human Performance, 15,* 25–46.

Gottfried, M. (2007, August 23). A rape witnessed, a rape ignored. *St. Paul Pioneer Press.*

Gottfried, M. (2008, July 18). Man gets 12 years for hallway rape captured on video. *St. Paul Pioneer Press.*

Gottman, J. M. (1994). *What predicts divorce?* Hillsdale, NJ: Erlbaum.

Gottman, J. M. (1998). Psychology and the study of marital processes. *Annual Review of Psychology, 49,* 169–197.

Gottman, J. M., & Levenson, R. W. (1992). Marital processes predictive of later dissolution: Behavior, physiology, and health. *Journal of Personality and Social Psychology, 63,* 221–233.

Gouin, J., Kiecolt-Glaser, J., Malarkey, W., & Glaser, R. (2008). The influence of anger expression on wound healing. *Brain, Behavior, and Immunity, 22,* 699–708.

Gouldner, A. W. (1960). The norm of reciprocity: A preliminary statement. *American Sociological Review, 25,* 161–178.

Gracia, E., García, F., & Lila, M. (2009). Public responses to intimate partner violence against women: The influence of perceived severity and personal responsibility. *The Spanish Journal of Psychology, 12,* 648–656.

Graham, K., Osgood, D. W., Wells, S., & Stockwell, T. (2006). To what extent is intoxication associated with aggression in bars? A multilevel analysis. *Journal of Studies on Alcohol, 67,* 382–390.

Grammer, K., & Thornhill, R. (1994). Human facial attractiveness and sexual selection: The role of averageness and symmetry. *Journal of Comparative Psychology, 108,* 233–242.

Granberg, D., & Bartels, B. (2005). On being a lone dissenter. *Journal of Applied Social Psychology, 35,* 1849–1858.

Granhag, P.A., Vrij, A., & Verschuere, B. (Eds.). (2015). *Deception detection: Current challenges and new approaches.* Chichester, England: Wiley.

Grawitch, M. J., & Ballard, D. W. (Eds.). (2015). *The psychologically healthy workplace: Building a win-win environment for organizations and employees.* Washington, DC: American Psychological Association.

Gray-Little, B., & Hafdahl, A. R. (2000). Factors influencing racial comparisons of self-esteem: A quantitative review. *Psychological Bulletin, 126,* 26–54.

Gray, H. M., Gray, K., & Wegner, D. M. (2007, February 2). Dimensions of mind perception. *Science, 315,* 619.

Gray, J. (1997). *Men are from Mars, women are from Venus.* New York: HarperCollins.

Gray, K., Ward, A. F., & Norton, M. I. (2014). Paying it forward: Generalized reciprocity and the limits of generosity. *Journal of Experimental Psychology: General, 143,* 247–254.

Gray, R. (2004). Attending to the execution of a complex sensorimotor skill: Expertise differences, choking, and slumps. *Journal of Experimental Psychology: Applied, 10,* 42–54.

Greathouse, S. M., & Kovera, M. B. (2009). Instruction bias and line-up presentation moderate the effects of administrator knowledge on eyewitness identification. *Law and Human Behavior, 33,* 70–82.

Green, J. D., Sedikides, C., & Gregg, A. P. (2008). Forgotten but not gone: The recall and recognition of self-threatening memories. *Journal of Experimental Social Psychology, 44,* 547–561.

Greenaway, K. H., Haslam, S. A., Cruwys, T., Branscombe, N. R., Ysseldyk, R., & Heldreth, C. (2015). From "we" to "me": Group identification enhances perceived personal control with consequences for health and well-being. *Journal of Personality and Social Psychology, 109,* 53–74.

Greenberg, J. (1988). Equity and workplace status: A field experiment. *Journal of Applied Psychology, 73,* 606–613.

Greenberg, J. (1990). Employee theft as a reaction to underpayment inequity: The hidden costs of pay cuts. *Journal of Applied Psychology, 75,* 561–568.

Greenberg, J. (2006). Losing sleep over organizational injustice: Attenuating insomniac reactions to underpayment inequity with supervisory training in interactional justice. *Journal of Applied Psychology, 91,* 58–69.

Greenberg, J. (Ed). (2010). *Insidious workplace behavior.* New York: Routledge/Taylor & Francis.

Greenberg, J., & Arndt, J. (2012). Terror management theory. In P. M. Van Lange, A. W. Kruglanski, & E. T. Higgins (Eds.), *Handbook of theories of social psychology* (Vol. 1, pp. 398–415). Thousand Oaks, CA: Sage.

Greenberg, J., Landau, M., Kosloff, S., & Solomon, S. (2009). How our dreams of death transcendence breed prejudice, stereotyping, and conflict: Terror Management Theory. In T. D. Nelson (Ed.), *Handbook of prejudice, stereotyping, and discrimination* (pp. 309–332). New York: Psychology Press.

Greenberg, J., Solomon, S., & Pyszczynski, T. (1997). Terror management theory of self-esteem and cultural worldviews: Empirical assessments and conceptual refinements. *Advances in Experimental Social Psychology, 29,* 61–139.

Greenberg, M. S., & Westcott, D. R. (1983). Indebtedness as a mediator of reactions to aid. In J. D. Fisher, A. Nadler, & B. M. DePaulo (Eds.), *New directions in helping: Vol. 1. Recipient reactions to aid* (pp. 85–112). New York: Academic Press.

Greene, E., & Heilbrun, K. (2014). *Wrightsman's Psychology and the Legal System* (8th ed.). Belmont, CA: Cengage.

Greene, E., Heilbrun, K., Fortune, W. H., & Nietzel, M. T. (2007). *Wrightsman's psychology and the legal system* (6th ed.). Belmont, CA: Wadsworth.

Greenfield, P. M. (2013). The changing psychology of culture from 1800 through 2000. *Psychological Science, 24,* 1722–1731.

Greenwald, A. G. (1968). Cognitive learning, cognitive responses to persuasion, and attitude change. In A. Greenwald, T. Brock, & T. Ostrom (Eds.), *Psychological Foundations of Attitudes* (pp. 147–170). New York: Academic Press.

Greenwald, A. G. (1980). The totalitarian ego: Fabrication and revision of personal history. *American Psychologist, 35,* 603–618.

Greenwald, A. G. (1992). New look 3: Unconscious cognition reclaimed. *American Psychologist, 47,* 766–779.

Greenwald, A. G., & Farnham, S. D. (2000). Using the Implicit Association Test to measure self-esteem and self-concept. *Journal of Personality and Social Psychology, 79,* 1022–1038.

Greenwald, A. G., Banaji, M. R., & Nosek, B. A. (2015). Statistically small effects of the Implicit Association Test can have societally large effects. *Journal of Personality and Social Psychology, 108,* 553–561.

Greenwald, A. G., McGhee, D. E., & Schwartz, J. L. K. (1998). Measuring individual differences in implicit cognition: The implicit association test. *Journal of Personality and Social Psychology, 74,* 1464–1480.

Greenwald, A. G., Oakes, M. A., & Hoffman, H. G. (2003). Targets of discrimination: Effects of race on responses to weapons holders. *Journal of Experimental Social Psychology, 39,* 399–405.

Greenwald, A. G., & Pettigrew, T. F. (2014). With malice toward none and charity for some: Ingroup favoritism enables discrimination. *American Psychologist, 69,* 669–684.

Greenwald, A. G., Poehlman, T. A., Uhlmann, E. L., & Banaji, M. R. (2009). Understanding and using the Implicit Association Test: III. Meta-analysis of predictive validity. *Journal of Personality and Social Psychology, 97,* 17–41.

Greenwald, A. G., Pratkanis, A. R., Leippe, M. R., & Baumgardner, M. H. (1986). Under what conditions does theory obstruct research progress? *Psychological Review, 93,* 216–229.

Greenwald, A. G., Spangenberg, E. R., Pratkanis, A. R., & Eskenazi, J. (1991). Double-blind tests of subliminal self-help audiotapes. *Psychological Science, 2,* 119–122.

Gregory, W. L., Mowen, J. C., & Linder, D. E. (1978). Social psychology and plea bargaining: Applications, methodology, and theory. *Journal of Personality and Social Psychology, 36,* 1521–1530.

Greitemeyer, T. (2009). Stereotypes of singles: Are singles what we think? *European Journal of Social Psychology, 39,* 368–383.

Greitemeyer, T. (2014). Article retracted, but the message lives on. *Psychonomic Bulletin & Review, 21,* 557–561.

Greitemeyer, T. (2014). Playing violent video games increases intergroup bias. *Personality and Social Psychology Bulletin, 40,* 70–78.

Greitemeyer, T., & Mügge, D. O. (2014). Video games do affect social outcomes: A meta-analytic review of the effects of violent and prosocial video game play. *Personality and Social Psychology Bulletin, 40,* 578–589.

Greitemeyer, T., & Mügge, D. O. (2015). When bystanders increase rather than decrease intentions to help. *Social Psychology, 46,* 116–119.

Griskevicius, V., Goldstein, N. J., Mortensen, C. R., Cialdini, R. B., & Kenrick, D. T. (2006). Going along versus going alone: When fundamental motives facilitate strategic nonconformity. *Journal of Personality and Social Psychology, 91,* 281–294.

Griskevicius, V., Tybur, J. M., Ackerman, J. M., Delton, A. W., Robertson, T. E., & White, A. E. (2012). The financial consequences of too many men: Sex ratio effects on saving, borrowing, and spending. *Journal of Personality and Social Psychology, 102,* 69–80.

Griskevicius, V., Tybur, J. M., Gangestad, S. W., Perea, E. F., Shapiro, J. R., & Kenrick, D. T. (2009). Aggress to impress: Hostility as an evolved context-dependent strategy. *Journal of Personality and Social Psychology, 96,* 980–994.

Gross, J. J., & Levenson, R. W. (1997). Hiding feelings: The acute effects of inhibiting negative and positive emotion. *Journal of Abnormal Psychology, 106,* 95–103.

Grossman, M., & Wood, W. (1993). Sex differences in intensity of emotional experience: A social role interpretation. *Journal of Personality and Social Psychology, 65,* 1010–1020.

Grote, N. K., & Clark, M. S. (2001). Perceiving unfairness in the family: Cause or consequence of marital distress? *Journal of Personality and Social Psychology, 80,* 281–293.

Grover, K. W., & Miller, C. T. (2012). Does expressed acceptance reflect genuine attitudes? A bogus pipeline study of the effects of mortality salience on acceptance of a person with AIDS. *The Journal of Social Psychology, 152,* 131–135.

Groves, K. S., Feyerherm, A., & Gu, M. (2015). Examining cultural intelligence and cross-cultural negotiation effectiveness. *Journal of Management Education, 39,* 209–243.

Gruber, J., Mauss, I. B., & Tamir, M. (2011). A dark side of happiness? How, when, and why happiness is not always good. *Perspectives on Psychological Science, 6,* 222–233.

Guan, Y., et al. (2015). Differences in career decision-making profiles between American and Chinese university students: The relative strength of mediating mechanisms across cultures. *Journal of Cross-Cultural Psychology, 46,* 1–17.

Gudykunst, W., & Bond, M. H. (1997). Intergroup relations across cultures. In J. W. Berry, M. H. Segall, & C. Kagitçibasi (Eds.), *Handbook of cross-cultural psychology: Social behavior and applications* (2nd ed., Vol. 3, pp. 119–161). Needham Heights, MA: Allyn & Bacon.

Guéguen, N. (2007). Bust size and hitchhiking: A field study. *Perceptual and Motor Skills, 105,* 1294–1298.

Guéguen, N. (2012). The sweet smell of . . . implicit helping: Effects of pleasant ambient fragrance on spontaneous help in shopping malls. *The Journal of Social Psychology, 152,* 397–400.

Guéguen, N., & Fischer-Lokou, J. (2004). Hitchhikers' smiles and receipt of help. *Psychological Reports, 94,* 756–760.

Guéguen, N., & Lamy, L. (2009). Hitchhiking women's hair color. *Perceptual and Motor Skills, 109,* 941–948.

Guéguen, N., & Stefan, J. (2013). Hitchhiking and the "Sunshine driver": Further effects of weather conditions on helping behavior. *Psychological Reports, 113,* 994–1000.

Guéguen, N., & Stefan, J. (2015). Men's judgment and behavior toward women wearing high heels. *Journal of Human Behavior in The Social Environment, 25,* 416–425.

Guéguen, N., Bougeard-Delfosse, C., & Jacob, C. (2015). The positive effect of the mere presence of a religious symbol on compliance with an organ donation request. *Social Marketing Quarterly, 21,* 92–99.

Guéguen, N., Dupré, M., Georget, P., & Sénémeaud, C. (2015). Commitment, crime, and the responsive bystander: Effect of the commitment form and conformism. *Psychology, Crime & Law, 21,* 1–8.

Guéguen, N., et al. (2013). I'm free but I'll comply with your request: Generalization and multidimensional effects of the evoking freedom technique. *Journal of Applied Social Psychology, 43,* 116–137.

Guerra, N. G. (2012). Can we make violent behavior less adaptive for youth? *Human Development, 55,* 105–106.

Guerrero, L. K., La Valley, A. G., & Farinelli, L. (2008). The experience and expression of anger, guilt, and sadness in marriage: An equity theory explanation. *Journal of Social and Personal Relationships, 25,* 699–724.

Guion, R. M. (2011). *Assessment, measurement, and prediction for personnel decisions* (2nd ed.). New York: Routledge.

Gulker, J. E., Mark, A. Y., & Monteith, M. J. (2013). Confronting prejudice: The who, what, and why of confrontation effectiveness. *Social Influence, 8,* 280–293.

Gump, B. B., & Kulik, J. A. (1997). Stress, affiliation, and emotional contagion. *Journal of Personality and Social Psychology, 72,* 305–319.

Günaydin, G., Zayas, Y, Selcuk, E., & Hazan, C. (2012). I like you but I don't know why: Objective facial resemblance to significant others influences snap judgments. *Journal of Experimental Social Psychology, 48,* 350–353.

Gurung, R. A. R. (2010). *Health psychology: A cultural approach* (2nd ed.). Belmont, CA: Wadsworth.

Gutsell, J. N., & Inzlicht, M. (2012). Intergroup differences in the sharing of emotive states: Neural evidence of an empathy gap. *Social Cognitive and Affective Neuroscience, 7,* 596–603.

Hackel, L. M., Looser, C. E., & Van Bavel, J. J. (2014). Group membership alters the threshold for mind perception: The role of social identity, collective identification, and intergroup threat. *Journal of Experimental Social Psychology, 52,* 15–23.

Hackman, J. R., & Katz, N. (2010). Group behavior and performance. In S. T. Fiske, D. T. Gilbert, & G. Lindzey (Eds.), *Handbook of social psychology, Vol. 2* (5th ed.) (pp. 1208–1251). Hoboken, NJ: Wiley.

Haddock, G., Maio, G., Arnold, K., & Huskinson, T. (2008). Should persuasion be affective or cognitive? The moderating effects of need for affect and need for cognition. *Personality and Social Psychology Bulletin, 34,* 769–778.

Hafenbrack, A. C., Kinias, Z., & Barsade, S. G. (2014). Debiasing the mind through meditation: Mindfulness and the sunk-cost bias. *Psychological Science, 25,* 369–376.

Hafer, C. L. (2000). Do innocent victims threaten the belief in a just world? Evidence from a modified Stroop task. *Journal of Personality and Social Psychology, 79,* 165–173.

Hafer, C. L., & Bègue, L. (2005). Experimental research on just-world theory: Problems, developments, and future challenges. *Psychological Bulletin, 131,* 128–167.

Hagger, M. S. Wood, C. Stiff, & C. Chatzisarantis, N. L. D. (2010). Ego depletion and the strength model of self-control: A meta-analysis. *Psychological Bulletin, 136,* 495–525.

Haidt, J. (2001). The emotional dog and its rational tail: A social intuitionist approach to moral judgment. *Psychological Review, 108,* 998–1002.

Haidt, J. (2006). *The happiness hypothesis: Finding modern truth in ancient wisdom.* New York: Basic Books.

Haidt, J. J. (2012). *The righteous mind: Why good people are divided by politics and religion.* New York: Pantheon.

Haidt, J. J. (2017, anticipated). *Three stories about capitalism: The moral psychology of everyday life.* New York: Pantheon.

Haines, H., & Vaughan, G. M. (1979). Was 1898 a "great date" in the history of experimental social psychology? *Journal of the History of the Behavioral Sciences, 15,* 323–332.

Halabi, S., Dovidio, J. F., & Nadler, A. (2012). Responses to intergroup helping: Effects of perceived stability and legitimacy of intergroup relations on Israeli Arabs' reactions to assistance by Israeli Jews. *International Journal of Intercultural Relations, 36,* 295–301.

Halberstadt, J., & Rhodes, G. (2003). It's not just average faces that are attractive: Computer-manipulated averageness makes birds, fish, and automobiles attractive. *Psychonomic Bulletin and Review, 10,* 149–156.

Hald, G., Malamuth, N. M., & Yuen, C. (2010). Pornography and attitudes supporting violence against women: Revisiting the relationship in non-experimental studies. *Aggressive Behavior, 36,* 14–20.

Hald, G. M., & Malamuth, N. N. (2015). Experimental effects of exposure to pornography: The moderating effect of personality and mediating effect of sexual arousal. *Archives of Sexual Behavior, 44,* 99–109.

Hall, E. V., Phillips, K. W., & Townsend, S. M. (2015). A rose by any other name?: The consequences of subtyping "African-Americans" from "Blacks." *Journal of Experimental Social Psychology, 56,* 183–190.

Hall, S., French, D. P., & Marteau, T. M. (2003). Causal attributions following serious unexpected negative events: A systematic review. *Journal of Social and Clinical Psychology, 22,* 515–536.

Halpern, D. F., & Cheung, F. M. (2008). *Women at the top: Powerful leaders tell us how to combine work and family.* New York: Wiley-Blackwell.

Hamamura, T., & Xu, Y. (2015). Changes in Chinese culture as examined through changes in personal pronoun usage. *Journal of Cross-Cultural Psychology, 46,* 930–941.

Hamer, D. H., Rice, G., Risch, N., & Ebers, G. (1999). Genetics and male sexual orientation. *Science, 285,* 803.

Hamermesh, D. S. (2013). *Beauty pays: Why attractive people are more successful.* Princeton, NJ: Princeton University Press.

Hamermesh, D. S., & Biddle, J. E. (1994). Beauty and the labor market. *American Economic Review, 84,* 1174–1195.

Hamilton, D. L., & Rose, T. L. (1980). Illusory correlation and the maintenance of stereotypic beliefs. *Journal of Personality and Social Psychology, 39,* 832–845.

Hamilton, D. L., Chen, J. M., & Way, N. (2011). Dynamic aspects of entitativity: From group perceptions to social interaction. In R. M. Kramer, G. J. Leonardelli, & R. W. Livingston (Eds.), *Social cognition, social identity, and intergroup relations: A Festschrift in honor of Marilynn B. Brewer* (pp. 27–52). New York: Psychology Press.

Hamilton, J. G. & Lobel, M. (2015). Psychosocial factors associated with risk perceptions for chronic diseases in younger and middle-aged women. *Women & Health,* in press.

Hamilton, W. D. (1964). The genetical evolution of social behavior: I and II. *Journal of Theoretical Biology, 7,* 1–52.

Hamlin, J. K. (2013). Moral judgment and action in preverbal infants and toddlers: Evidence for an innate moral core. *Current Directions in Psychological Science, 22,* 186–193.

Hamlin, J. K. (2015). The infantile origins of our moral brains. In J. Decety & T. Wheatley (Eds.), *The moral brain: A multidisciplinary perspective* (pp. 105–122). Cambridge, MA: MIT Press.

Hammel, P. (2008, November 29). Psychologist had dual role in confessions of Beatrice 6. *Omaha World-Herald.*

Hammersla, J. F., & Frease-McMahan, L. (1990). University students' priorities: Life goals vs. relationships. *Sex Roles, 23,* 1–14.

Hamrick, N., Cohen, S., & Rodriguez, M. S. (2002). Being popular can be healthy or unhealthy: Stress, social network diversity, and incidence of upper respiratory infection. *Health Psychology, 21,* 294–298.

Han, S., & Shavitt, S. (1994). Persuasion and culture: Advertising appeals in individualistic and collectivistic societies. *Journal of Experimental Social Psychology, 30,* 326–350.

Haney, C. (1984). On the selection of capital juries: The biasing effects of the death-qualification process. *Law and Human Behavior, 8,* 121–132.

Haney, C. (2006). *Reforming punishment: Psychological limits to the pains of imprisonment.* Washington, DC: American Psychological Association.

Haney, C., & Zimbardo, P. G. (1998). The past and future of U.S. prison policy: Twenty-five years after the Stanford Prison Experiment. *American Psychologist, 53,* 709–727.

Haney, C., & Zimbardo, P. G. (2009). Persistent dispositionalism in interactionist clothing: Fundamental attribution error in explaining prison abuse. *Personality and Social Psychology Bulletin, 35,* 807–814.

Haney, C., Banks, C., & Zimbardo, P. (1973). Interpersonal dynamics in a simulated prison. *International Journal of Criminology and Penology, 1,* 69–97.

Haney, C., Hurtado, A., & Vega, L. (1994). "Modern" death qualification: New data on its biasing effects. *Law and Human Behavior, 18,* 619–633.

Hans, V. P. (2000). *Business on trial: The civil jury and corporate responsibility.* New Haven, CT: Yale University Press.

Hans, V. P., et al. (2015). The death penalty: Should the judge or jury decide who dies? *Journal of Empirical Legal Studies, 12,* 70–99.

Hans, V. P., Kaye, D. H., Dann, B. M., Farley, E. J., & Albertson, S. (2011). Science in the jury box: Jurors' comprehension of mitochondrial DNA evidence. *Law and Human Behavior, 35,* 60–71.

Hansen, C. H., & Hansen, R. D. (1988). Finding the face in the crowd: An anger superiority effect. *Journal of Personality and Social Psychology, 54,* 917–924.

Hanson, R. (2013). *Hardwiring happiness: The new brain science of contentment, calm, and confidence.* New York: Random House.

Harackiewicz, J. M., & Elliot, A. J. (1993). Achievement goals and intrinsic motivation. *Journal of Personality and Social Psychology, 65,* 904–915.

Harackiewicz, J. M., Canning, E. A., Tibbetts, Y., Giffen, C. J., Blair, S. S., Rouse, D. I., & Hyde, J. S. (2014). Closing the social class achievement gap for first-generation students in undergraduate biology. *Journal of Educational Psychology, 106,* 375–389.

Haraldsson, H. (2014, Jan 23). Ted Nugent calls Obama a chimpanzee and subhuman mongrel. *PoliticusUSA,* http://www.politicususa.com/2014/01/23/ted-nugent-calls-obama-chimpanzee-subhuman-mongrel.html.

Hardin, E. E., & Larsen, J. T. (2014). Distinct sources of self-discrepancies: Effects of being who you want to be and wanting to be who you are on well-being. *Emotion, 14,* 214–226.

Hardin, G. (1968). The tragedy of the commons. *Science, 162,* 1243–1248.

Haritos-Fatouros, M. (2002). *Psychological origins of institutionalized torture.* London: Routledge.

Harkins, S. G., & Petty, R. E. (1981). Effects of source magnification of cognitive effort on attitudes: An information processing view. *Journal of Personality and Social Psychology, 40,* 401–413.

Harkins, S. G., & Petty, R. E. (1987). Information utility and the multiple source effect. *Journal of Personality and Social Psychology, 52,* 260–268.

Harmon-Jones, E., & Mills, J. (Eds.). (1999). *Cognitive dissonance: Progress on a pivotal theory in social psychology.* Washington, DC: American Psychological Association.

Harmon-Jones, E., Brehm, J. W., Greenberg, J., Simon, L., & Nelson, D. E. (1996). Evidence that the production of aversive consequences is not necessary to create cognitive dissonance. *Journal of Personality and Social Psychology, 70,* 5–16.

Harmon-Jones, E., Harmon-Jones, C., & Levy, N. (2015). An action-based model of cognitive-dissonance processes. *Current Directions in Psychological Science, 24,* 184–189.

Harrington, J. R., & Gelfand, M. J. (2014). Tightness–looseness across the 50 United States. *PNAS Proceedings of The National Academy of Sciences of The United States of America, 111,* 7990–7995.

Harrington, R. (2013). *Stress, health & well-being: Thriving in the 21st century.* Belmont, CA: Wadsworth, Cengage Learning.

Harris, C. R. (2002). Sexual and romantic jealousy in heterosexual and homosexual adults. *Psychological Science, 13,* 7–12.

Harris, C. R. (2003). A review of sex differences in sexual jealousy, including self-report data, psychophysiological responses, interpersonal violence, and morbid jealousy. *Personality and Social Psychology Review, 7,* 102–128.

Harris, C. R. (2005). Male and female jealousy: Still more similar than different: Reply to Sagarin. *Personality and Social Psychology Review, 9,* 76–86.

Harris, C. R., & Christenfeld, N. (1996). Gender, jealousy, and reason. *Psychological Science, 7,* 364–366.

Harris, D. (2012). James Holmes bought rifle after failing oral exam at University of Colorado. *ABC News,* July 25.

Harris, L. T., & Fiske, S. T. (2011). Dehumanized perception: A psychological means to facilitate atrocities, torture, and genocide?. *Zeitschrift Für Psychologie/Journal of Psychology, 219,* 175–181.

Harris, M. B. (1995). Ethnicity, gender, and evaluations of aggression. *Aggressive Behavior, 21,* 343–357.

Harris, M. J., & Perkins, R. (1995). Effects of distraction on interpersonal expectancy effects: A social interaction test of the cognitive busyness hypothesis. *Social Cognition, 13,* 163–182.

Harris, M. J., & Rosenthal, R. (1985). Mediation of interpersonal expectancy effects. *Psychological Bulletin, 97,* 363–386.

Harrison, D. A., & Shaffer, M. A. (1994). Comparative examinations of self-reports and perceived absenteeism norms: Wading through Lake Wobegon. *Journal of Applied Psychology, 79,* 240–251.

Harrison, D. A., Kravitz, D. A., Mayer, D. M., Leslie, L. M., & Lev-Arey, D. (2006). Understanding attitudes toward affirmative action programs in employment: Summary and meta-analysis of 35 years of research. *Journal of Applied Psychology, 91,* 1013–1036.

Hart, W., Albarracín, D., Eagly, A. H., Lindberg, M., Lee, K. H., & Brechan, I. (2009). Feeling validated vs. being correct: A meta-analysis of exposure to information. *Psychological Bulletin, 135,* 555–588.

Hartwig, M., & Bond, C. F. (2011). Why do lie-catchers fail? A lens model meta-analysis of human lie judgments. *Psychological Bulletin, 137,* 643–659.

Hartwig, M., & Bond, C. F. (2014). Lie detection from multiple cues: A meta-analysis. *Applied Cognitive Psychology, 28,* 661–667.

Harvey, J. H., & Manusov, V L. (Eds.). (2001). *Attribution, communication behavior, and close relationships.* New York: Cambridge University Press.

Harvey, J. H., & Omarzu, J. (2000). *Minding the close relationship: A theory of relationship enhancement.* New York: Cambridge University Press.

Hasel, L. E., & Kassin, S. M. (2009). On the presumption of evidentiary independence: Can confessions corrupt eyewitness identifications? *Psychological Science, 20,* 122–126.

Haslam, N. (2015). Dehumanization and intergroup relations. In M. Mikulincer, P. R. Shaver, E. Borgida, & J. A. Bargh (Eds.), *APA handbook of personality and social psychology,* Volume 2: Group processes (pp. 295–314). Washington, DC: American Psychological Association.

Haslam, S. A., & Reicher, S. (2007). Beyond the banality of evil: Three dynamics of an interactionist social psychology of tyranny. *Personality and Social Psychology Bulletin, 33,* 615–622.

Haslam, S. A., & Reicher, S. D. (2012). When prisoners take over the prison: A social psychology of resistance. *Personality and Social Psychology Review, 16,* 154–179.

Haslam, S. A., Reicher, S. D., & Birney, M. (2014). Nothing by mere authority: Evidence that in an experimental analogue of the Milgram paradigm participants are motivated not by orders but by appeals to science. *Journal of Social Issues, 70,* 473–488.

Haslam, S. A., Reicher, S. D., Millard, K., & McDonald, R. (2014). "Happy to have been of service": The Yale archive as a window into the engaged followership of participants in Milgram's "obedience" experiments. *British Journal of Social Psychology, 54,* 55–83.

Hass, R. G. (1981). Effects of source characteristics on the cognitive processing of persuasive messages and attitude change. In R. Petty, T. Ostrom, & T. Brock (Eds.), *Cognitive responses in persuasion* (pp. 141–172). Hillsdale, NJ: Erlbaum.

Hass, R. G. (1984). Perspective taking and self-awareness: Drawing an E on your forehead. *Journal of Personality and Social Psychology, 46,* 788–798.

Hass, R. G., & Eisenstadt, D. (1990). The effects of self-focused attention on perspective-taking and anxiety. *Anxiety Research, 2,* 165–176.

Hass, R. G., & Grady, K. (1975). Temporal delay, type of forewarning, and resistance to influence. *Journal of Experimental Social Psychology, 11,* 459–469.

Hass, R. G., Katz, I., Rizzo, N., Bailey, J., & Moore, L. (1992). When racial ambivalence evokes negative affect, using a disguised measure of mood. *Personality and Social Psychology Bulletin, 18,* 786–797.

Hassin, R., & Trope, Y. (2000). Facing faces: Studies on the cognitive aspects of physiognomy. *Journal of Personality and Social Psychology, 78,* 837–852.

Hastie, R., & Kameda, T. (2005). The robust beauty of majority rules in group decisions. *Psychological Review, 112,* 494–508.

Hastie, R., Penrod, S. D., & Pennington, N. (1983). *Inside the jury.* Cambridge, MA: Harvard University Press.

Hastings, P. D., Miller, J. G., Kahle, S., & Zahn-Waxler, C. (2014). The neurobiological bases of empathic concern for others. In M. Killen & J. G. Smetana (Eds.), *Handbook of moral development* (2nd ed.) (pp. 411–434). New York: Psychology Press.

Hatemi, P. K., Hibbing, J. R., Medland, S. E., Keller, M. C., Alford, J. R., Smith, K. B., Martin, N. G., & Eaves, L. J. (2010). Not by twins alone: Using the extended family design to investigate genetic influence on political beliefs. *American Journal of Political Science, 54,* 798–814.

Hatfield, E. (1988). Passionate and companionate love. In R. J. Sternberg & M. L. Barnes (Eds.), *The psychology of love* (pp. 191–217). New Haven, CT: Yale University Press.

Hatfield, E., & Rapson, R. L. (1993). *Love, sex, and intimacy: Their psychology, biology, and history.* New York: HarperCollins.

Hatfield, E., Greenberger, E., Traupmann, J., & Lambert, P. (1982). Equity and sexual satisfaction in recently married couples. *Journal of Sex Research, 18,* 18–32.

Hatfield, E., Rapson, R. L., & Aumer-Ryan, K. (2008). Social justice in love relationships: Recent developments. *Social Justice Research, 21*, 413–431.

Hatfield, E., Rapson, R. L., & Martel, L. D. (2007). Passionate love. In S. Kitayama & D. Cohen (Eds.), *Handbook of cultural psychology*. New York: Guilford.

Hauser, D. J., Preston, S. D., & Stansfield, R. B. (2014). Altruism in the wild: When affiliative motives to help positive people overtake empathic motives to help the distressed. *Journal of Experimental Psychology: General, 143*, 1295–1305.

Hawkins, D. L., Pepler, D. J., & Craig, W. M. (2001). Naturalistic observations of peer interventions in bullying. *Social Development, 10*, 512–527.

Hawkley, L. C., Thisted, R. A., & Cacioppo, J. T. (2009). Loneliness predicts reduced physical activity: Cross-sectional & longitudinal analyses. *Health Psychology, 28*, 354–363.

Hay, D. F., & Cook, K. V. (2007). The transformation of prosocial behavior from infancy to childhood. In C. A. Brownell & C. B. Kopp (Eds.), *Socio-emotional development in the toddler years: Transitions and transformations* (pp. 100–131). New York: Guilford.

Hayes, T. C., & Lee, M. R. (2005). The southern culture of honor and violent attitudes. *Sociological Spectrum, 25*, 593–617.

Haynes, G., & Gilovich, T. (2010). "The ball don't lie": How inequity aversion can undermine performance. *Journal of Experimental Social Psychology, 46*, 1148–1150.

Hays, G. (2008). Central Washington offers the ultimate act of sportsmanship. Available at http://sports.espn.go.com/ncaa/columns/story?columnist=hays_graham&id=3372631.

Hays, R. B. (1985). A longitudinal study of friendship development. *Journal of Personality and Social Psychology, 48*, 909–924.

Hazan, C., & Diamond, L. M. (2000). The place of attachment in human mating. *Review of General Psychology, 4*, 186–204.

Hazan, C., & Shaver, P. (1987). Romantic love conceptualized as an attachment process. *Journal of Personality and Social Psychology, 52*, 511–524.

Hearold, S. (1986). A synthesis of 1043 effects of television on social behavior. In G. Comstock (Ed.), *Public communication and behavior* (Vol. 1, pp. 65–133). Orlando, FL: Academic Press.

Hearst, P. C. (1982). *Every secret thing*. New York: Doubleday.

Heatherton, T. F. (2011). Neuroscience of self and self-regulation. *Annual Review of Psychology, 62*, 363–390.

Heatherton, T. F., & Polivy, J. (1991). Development and validation of a scale for measuring state self-esteem. *Journal of Personality and Social Psychology, 60*, 895–910.

Heatherton, T. F., & Vohs, K. D. (2000). Interpersonal evaluations following threats to self: Role of self-esteem. *Journal of Personality and Social Psychology, 78*, 725–736.

Heavey, C., & Simsek, Z. (2015). Transactive memory systems and firm performance: An upper echelons perspective. *Organization Science*, in press.

Hebl, M. R., & Avery, D. R. (2013). Diversity in organizations. In N. W. Schmitt, S. Highhouse, & I. B. Weiner (Eds.), *Handbook of psychology*, Vol. 12: *Industrial and organizational psychology* (2nd ed.) (pp. 677–697). Hoboken, NJ: Wiley.

Hebl, M. R., & Heatherton, T. F. (1998). The stigma of obesity in women: The difference is black and white. *Personality and Social Psychology Bulletin, 24*, 417–426.

Hebl, M. R., & Turchin, J. M. (2005). The stigma of obesity: What about men? *Basic and Applied Social Psychology, 27*, 267–275.

Hebl, M. R., King, E. B., & Perkins, A. (2009). Ethnic differences in the stigma of obesity: Identification and engagement with a thin ideal. *Journal of Experimental Social Psychology, 45*, 1165–1172.

Hedge, J. W., & Kavanagh, M. J. (1988). Improving the accuracy of performance evaluations: Comparison of three methods of performance appraiser training. *Journal of Applied Psychology, 73*, 68–73.

Hegtvedt, K. A. (2014). Ethics and experiments. In M. J. Webster, J. Sell, M. J. Webster, & J. Sell (Eds.), *Laboratory experiments in the social sciences* (2nd ed.) (pp. 23–51). San Diego, CA, US: Elsevier.

Heider, F. (1958). *The psychology of interpersonal relations*. New York: Wiley.

Heidrich, C., & Chiviacowsky, S. (2015). Stereotype threat affects the learning of sport motor skills. *Psychology of Sport and Exercise, 18*, 42–46.

Heilman, M. E., & Alcott, V. B. (2001). What I think you think of me: Women's reactions to being viewed as beneficiaries of preferential selection. *Journal of Applied Psychology, 86*, 574–582.

Heilman, M. E., & Okimoto, T. G. (2008). Motherhood: A potential source of bias in employment decisions. *Journal of Applied Psychology, 93*, 189–198.

Heilman, M. E., Battle, W. S., Keller, C. E., & Lee, R. A. (1998). Type of affirmative action policy: A determinant of reactions to sex-based preferential selection? *Journal of Applied Psychology, 83*, 190–205.

Heilman, M. E., Block, C. J., & Lucas, J. A. (1992). Presumed incompetent? Stigmatization and affirmative action efforts. *Journal of Applied Psychology, 77*, 536–544.

Heilman, M. E., McCullough, W. F., & Gilbert, D. (1996). The other side of affirmative action: Reactions of nonbeneficiaries to sex-based preferential selection. *Journal of Applied Psychology, 81*, 346–357.

Heilman, M. E., Simon, M. C., & Repper, D. P. (1987). Intentionally favored, unintentionally harmed? Impact of sex-based preferential selection on self-perceptions and self-evaluations. *Journal of Applied Psychology, 72*, 62–68.

Heine, S. J. (2005). Where is the evidence for pancultural self-enhancement? A reply to Sedikides, Gaertner, & Toguchi (2003). *Journal of Personality and Social Psychology, 89*, 531–538.

Heine, S. J., & Hamamura, T. (2007). In search of East Asian self-enhancement. *Personality and Social Psychology Review, 11*, 1–24.

Heine, S. J., Kitayama, S., Lehman, D. R., Takata, T., Ide, E., Lueng, C., & Matsumoto, H. (2001). Divergent consequences of success and failure in Japan and North America: An investigation of self-improving motivations and malleable selves. *Journal of Personality and Social Psychology, 81*, 599–615.

Heine, S. J., Lehman, D. R., Markus, H. R., & Kitayama, S. (1999). Is there a universal need for positive self-regard? *Psychological Review, 106*, 756–794.

Heine, S. J., Takata, T., & Lehman, D. R. (2000). Beyond self-presentation: Evidence for self-criticism among Japanese. *Personality and Social Psychology Bulletin, 26*, 71–78.

Heine, S. J., Takemoto, T., Moskalenko, S., Lasaleta, J., & Henrich, J. (2008). Mirrors in the head: Cultural variation in objective self-awareness. *Personality and Social Psychology Bulletin, 34*, 879–887.

Heinrich, L. M., & Gullone, E. (2006). The clinical significance of loneliness: A literature review. *Clinical Psychology Review, 26*, 695–718.

Helfritz-Sinville, L. E., & Stanford, M. S. (2014). Hostile attribution bias in impulsive and premeditated aggression. *Personality and Individual Differences, 56*, 45–50.

Helgesen, S. (1995). *Web of inclusion: A new architecture for building great organizations*. New York: Doubleday.

Helgeson, V. S. (1992). Moderators of the relation between perceived control and adjustment to chronic illness. *Journal of Personality and Social Psychology, 63*, 652–666.

Helgeson, V. S., Reynolds, K. A., & Tomich, P. L. (2006). A meta-analytic review of benefit finding and growth. *Journal of Consulting and Clinical Psychology, 74*, 797–816.

Heller, J. F., Pallak, M. S., & Picek, J. M. (1973). The interactive effects of intent and threat on boomerang attitude change. *Journal of Personality and Social Psychology, 26*, 273–279.

Helliwell, J., Layard, R., & Sachs, J. (Eds.). (2012). *World Happiness Report*. New York: Columbia University: The Earth Institute.

Helliwell, J., Layrd, R., & Sachs, J. (Eds.). (2015). *World Happiness Report 2015*. New York: Columbia University: The Earth Institute.

Helmbold, K., et al. (2015). Effects of serotonin depletion on punishment processing in the orbitofrontal and anterior cingulate cortices of healthy women. *European Neuropsychopharmacology, 25*, 846–856.

Helseth, S. A., Waschbusch, D. A., King, S., & Willoughby, M. T. (2015). Aggression in children with conduct problems and callous-unemotional traits: Social information processing and response to peer provocation. *Journal of Abnormal Child Psychology*, in press.

Helzer, E. G., Furr, R. M., Hawkins, A., Barranti, M., Blackie, L., & Fleeson, W. (2014). Agreement on the perception of moral character. *Personality and Social Psychology Bulletin, 40*, 1698–1710.

Henchy, T., & Glass, D. C. (1968). Evaluation apprehension and the social facilitation of dominant and subordinate responses. *Journal of Personality and Social Psychology, 10*, 446–454.

Henderlong, J., & Lepper, M. R. (2002). The effects of praise on children's intrinsic motivation: A review and synthesis. *Psychological Bulletin, 128*, 774–795.

Henderson-King, D., Henderson-King, E., & Hoffman, L. (2001). Media images and women's self-evaluations: Social context and importance of attractiveness as moderators. *Personality and Social Psychology Bulletin, 27*, 1407–1416.

Henderson-King, E., & Henderson-King, D. (1997). Media effects on women's body esteem: Social and individual differences factors. *Journal of Applied Social Psychology, 27*, 399–417.

Henderson, L., & Zimbardo, P. (1998). Shyness. In H. S. Friedman (Ed.), *Encyclopedia of mental health*. San Diego: Academic Press.

Hendrick, C., & Hendrick, S. S. (Eds.). (2000). *Close relationships: A sourcebook*. Thousand Oaks, CA: Sage.

Hendrick, S. S., & Hendrick, C. (1995). Gender differences and similarities in sex and love. *Personal Relationships, 2,* 55–65.

Heneman, H. G., & Schwab, D. P. (1985). Pay satisfaction: Its multidimensional nature and measurement. *International Journal of Psychology, 20*, 129–141.

Henggeler, S. W., Letourneau, E. J., Chapman, J. E., Borduin, C. M., Schewe, P. A., & McCart, M. R. (2009). Mediators of change for multisystemic therapy with juvenile sexual offenders. *Journal of Consulting and Clinical Psychology, 77*, 451–462.

Henkel, L. A., Coffman, K. A. J., & Dailey, E. M. (2008). A survey of people's attitudes and beliefs about false confessions. *Behavioral Sciences and the Law, 26*, 555–584.

Hennessey, B. A. (2015). If I were Secretary of Education: A focus on intrinsic motivation and creativity in the classroom. *Psychology of Aesthetics, Creativity, and the Arts, 9*, 187–192.

Henningsen, D. D., & Henningsen, M. M. (2013). Generating ideas about the uses of brainstorming: Reconsidering the losses and gains of brainstorming groups relative to nominal groups. *Southern Communication Journal, 78*, 42–55.

Henry, D. B., Kobus, K., & Schoeny, M. E. (2011). Accuracy and bias in adolescents' perceptions of friends' substance use. *Psychology of Addictive Behaviors, 25*, 80–89.

Hepler, J. Albarracín, D. (2013). Attitudes without objects: Evidence for a dispositional attitude, its measurement, and its consequences. *Journal of Personality and Social Psychology, 104*, 1060–1076.

Heppner, P. P., Heppner, M. J., Lee, D., Wang, Y., Park, H., & Wang, L. (2006). Development and validation of a collectivist coping styles inventory. *Journal of Counseling Psychology, 53*, 107–125.

Herdt, G. (1998). *Same sex, different cultures: Exploring gay and lesbian lives*. Boulder, CO: Westview Press.

Herek, G. M. (2006). Legal recognition of same-sex relationships in the United States: A social science perspective. *American Psychologist, 61*, 607–621.

Herring, C. (2009). Does diversity pay? Race, gender, and the business case for diversity. *American Sociological Review, 74*, 208–224.

Hershkowitz, I., Lamb, M. E., & Katz, C. (2014). Allegation rates in forensic child abuse investigations: Comparing the revised and standard NICHD protocols. *Psychology, Public Policy, and Law, 20*, 336–344.

Hetey, R. C., & Eberhardt, J. L. (2014). Racial disparities in incarceration increase acceptance of punitive policies. *Psychological Science, 25*, 1949–1954.

Hewitt, P. L., Flett, G. L., Sherry, S. B., Habke, M., Parkin, M., Lam, R., McMurtry, B., Ediger, E., Fairlie, P., & Stein, M. B. (2003). The interpersonal expression of perfection: Perfectionistic self-presentation and psychological distress. *Journal of Personality and Social Psychology, 84*, 1303–1325.

Heyes, C. (2011). Automatic imitation. *Psychological Bulletin, 137*, 463–483.

Hicks, J. A., Fields, S., Davis, W. E., & Gable, P. A. (2015). Heavy drinking, impulsivity and attentional narrowing following alcohol cue exposure. *Psychopharmacology*, in press.

Higgins, C. A., & Judge, T. A. (2004). The effect of applicant influence tactics on recruiter perceptions of fit and hiring recommendations: A field study. *Journal of Applied Psychology, 89*, 622–632.

Higgins, E. T. (1989). Self-discrepancy theory: What patterns of self-beliefs cause people to suffer? In L. Berkowitz (Ed.), *Advances in experimental social psychology* (Vol. 22, pp. 93–136). New York: Academic Press.

Higgins, E. T. (1999). Self-discrepancy: A theory relating self and affect. In R. F. Baumeister (Ed.), *The self in social psychology* (pp. 150–181). Philadelphia, PA: Psychology Press/Taylor & Francis.

Higgins, E. T., & Rholes, W. S. (1978). "Saying is believing": Effects of message modification on memory and liking for the person described. *Journal of Experimental Social Psychology, 14*, 363–378.

Higgins, E. T., & Scholer, A. A. (2015). Goal pursuit functions: Working together. In M. Mikulincer et al. (Eds.), *APA handbook of personality and social psychology, Volume 1: Attitudes and social cognition* (pp. 843–889). Washington, DC: American Psychological Association.

Higgins, E. T., King, G. A., & Mavin, G. H. (1982). Individual construct accessibility and subjective impressions and recall. *Journal of Personality and Social Psychology, 43*, 35–47.

Higgins, E. T., Rholes, C. R., & Jones, C. R. (1977). Category accessibility and impression formation. *Journal of Experimental Social Psychology, 13*, 141–154.

Higgins, L. T., Zheng, M., Liu, Y., & Sun, C. H. (2002). Attitudes to marriage and sexual behaviors: A survey of gender and culture differences in China and the United Kingdom. *Sex Roles, 46*, 75–89.

Higgins, R. L., & Harris, R. N. (1988). Strategic "alcohol" use: Drinking to self-handicap. *Journal of Social and Clinical Psychology, 6*, 191–202.

Hilbig, B.E., & Hessler, C.M. (2013). What lies beneath: How the distance between truth and lie drives dishonesty. *Journal of Experimental Social Psychology, 49*, 263–266.

Hilbig, B. E., Glöckner, A., & Zettler, I. (2014). Personality and prosocial behavior: Linking basic traits and social value orientations. *Journal of Personality and Social Psychology, 107*, 529–539.

Hill, C. A. (1987). Affiliation motivation: People who need people . . . but in different ways. *Journal of Personality and Social Psychology, 52*, 1008–1018.

Hills, T. T., & Pachur, T. (2012). Dynamic search and working memory in social recall. *Journal of Experimental Psychology: Learning, Memory, and Cognition, 38*, 218–228.

Hilmert, C. J., Kulik, J. A., & Christenfeld, N. J. S. (2006). Positive and negative outcome modeling: The influence of another's similarity and dissimilarity. *Journal of Personality and Social Psychology, 90*, 440–452.

Hilton, J. L., & Darley, J. M. (1985). Constructing other persons: A limit on the effect. *Journal of Experimental Social Psychology, 21,* 1–18.

Hilton, J. L., & Darley, J. M. (1991). The effects of interaction goals on person perception. *Advances in Experimental Social Psychology, 24,* 235–267.

Hinsz, V. B., Tindale, R. S., & Vollrath, D. A. (1997). The emerging conceptualization of groups as information processors. *Psychological Bulletin, 121,* 43–64.

Hinsz, V. B., Tindale, R. S., Nagao, D. H., Davis, J. H., & Robertson, B. A. (1988). The influence of the accuracy of individuating information on the use of base rate information in probability judgment. *Journal of Experimental Social Psychology, 24,* 127–145.

Hinsz, V. B., Tindale, R. S., & Nagao, D. H. (2008). Accentuation of information processes and biases in group judgments integrating base-rate and case-specific information. *Journal of Experimental Social Psychology, 44,* 116–126.

Hipwell, A. E., Stepp, S. D., Xiong, S., Keenan, K., Blokland, A., & Loeber, R. (2014). Parental punishment and peer victimization as developmental precursors to physical dating violence involvement among girls. *Journal of Research on Adolescence, 24,* 65–79.

Hirsch, A. (2012) Moroccan legal system under fire over women's rights after teenager's suicide: Court ordered marriage of girl, 16, to alleged rapist. *The Guardian (London),* April 4, p. 18.

Hirt, E. R., Deppe, R. K., & Gordon, L. J. (1991). Self-reported versus behavioral self-handicapping: Empirical evidence for a theoretical distinction. *Journal of Personality and Social Psychology, 61,* 981–991.

Hitler, A. (1933). *Mein Kampf* (E. T. S. Dugdale, Trans.). Cambridge, MA: Riverside.

Hjemdahl, P., Rosengren, A., & Steptoe, A. (Eds.). (2012). *Stress and cardiovascular disease.* London: Springer-Verlag.

Hoaken, P. N. S., Allaby, D. B., & Earle, J. (2007). Executive cognitive functioning and the recognition of facial expressions of emotion in incarcerated violent offenders, non-violent offenders, and controls. *Aggressive Behavior, 33,* 412–421.

Hobfoll, S. E., Canetti-Nisim, D., & Johnson, R. J. (2006). Exposure to terrorism, stress-related mental health symptoms, and defensive coping among Jews and Arabs in Israel. *Journal of Consulting and Clinical Psychology, 74,* 207–218.

Hobfoll, S. E., Palmieri, P. A., Johnson, R. J., Canetti-Nisim, D., Hall, B. J., & Galea, S. (2009). Trajectories of resilience, resistance, and distress during ongoing terrorism: The case of Jews and Arabs in Israel. *Journal of Consulting and Clinical Psychology, 77,* 138–148.

Hodges, B. H., & Geyer, A. L. (2006). A nonconformist account of the Asch experiments: Values, pragmatics, and moral dilemmas. *Personality and Social Psychology Review, 10,* 2–19.

Hodson, G., Dovidio, J. F., & Gaertner, S. L. (2010). The aversive form of racism. In J. Chin (Ed.), *The psychology of prejudice and discrimination: A revised and condensed edition* (pp. 1–13). Santa Barbara, CA: Praeger/ABC-CLIO.

Hoever, I. J., van Knippenberg, D., van Ginkel, W. P., & Barkema, H. G. (2012). Fostering team creativity: Perspective taking as key to unlocking diversity's potential. *Journal of Applied Psychology.*

Hofling, C. K., Brotzman, E., Dalrymple, S., Graves, N., & Pierce, C. (1966). An experimental study of nurse-physician relations. *Journal of Nervous and Mental Disease, 143,* 171–180.

Hoffman, B. J., Kennedy, C. L., LoPilato, A. C., Monahan, E. L., & Lance, C. E. (2015). A review of the content, criterion-related, and construct-related validity of assessment center exercises. *Journal of Applied Psychology, 100,* 1143–1168.

Hofmann, S. G., & DiBartolo, P. M. (Eds.). (2014). *Social anxiety: Clinical, developmental, and social perspectives* (3rd ed.). San Diego: Elsevier Academic Press.

Hofmann, W., Baumeister, R. F., Förster, G., & Vohs, K. D. (2012). Everyday temptations: An experience sampling study of desire, conflict, and self-control. *Journal of Personality and Social Psychology, 102,* 1318–1335.

Hofmann, W., De Houwer, J., Perugini, M., Baeyens, F., & Crombez, G. (2010). Evaluative conditioning in humans: A meta-analysis. *Psychological Bulletin, 136,* 390–421.

Hofmann, W., Vohs, K. D., & Baumeister, R. F. (2012). What people desire, feel conflicted about, and try to resist in everyday life. *Psychological Science, 23,* 582–588.

Hofstede, G. (1980). *Culture's consequences.* Beverly Hills, CA: Sage.

Hogan, R., Curphy, G. J., & Hogan, J. (1994). What we know about leadership: Effectiveness and personality. *American Psychologist, 49,* 493–504.

Hogg, M. A. (2014). From uncertainty to extremism: Social categorization and identity processes. *Current Directions in Psychological Science, 23,* 338–342.

Hoigaard, R., & Ommundsen, Y. (2007). Perceived social loafing and anticipated effort reduction among young football (soccer) players: An achievement goal perspective. *Psychological Reports, 100,* 857–875.

Hollander, E. P. (1958). Conformity, status, and idiosyncrasy credit. *Psychological Review, 65,* 117–127.

Hollander, E. P. (1985). Leadership and power. In G. Lindzey & E. Aronson (Eds.), *Handbook of social psychology* (3rd ed., Vol. 2, pp. 485–537). New York: Random House.

Hollén, L. I., & Radford, A. N. (2009). The development of alarm call behaviour in mammals and birds. *Animal Behaviour, 78,* 791–800.

Holloway, R. A., Waldrip, A. M., & Ickes, W. (2009). Evidence that a simpático self-schema accounts for differences in the self-concepts and social behavior of Latinos versus Whites (and Blacks). *Journal of Personality and Social Psychology, 96,* 1012–1028.

Holmes, T. H., & Rahe, R. H. (1967). The Social Readjustment Rating Scale. *Journal of Psychosomatic Research, 11,* 213–218.

Holmqvist, R., Hill, T., & Lang, A. (2009). Effects of aggression replacement training in young offender institutions. *International Journal of Offender Therapy and Comparative Criminology, 53,* 74–92.

Holt-Lunstad, J., Smith, T. B., Baker, M., Harris, T., & Stephenson, D. (2015). Loneliness and social isolation as risk factors for mortality: A meta-analytic review. *Perspectives on Psychological Science, 10,* 227–237.

Homans, G. C. (1961). *Social behavior.* New York: Harcourt, Brace & World.

Hönekopp, J. (2006). Once more: Is beauty in the eye of the beholder? Relative contributions of private and shared taste to judgments of facial attractiveness. *Journal of Experimental Psychology: Human Perception and Performance, 32,* 199–209.

Hönekopp, J., & Watson, S. (2011). Meta-analysis of the relationship between digit-ratio 2D:4D and aggression. *Personality and Individual Differences, 51,* 381–386.

Honeycutt, J. M., Woods, B. L., & Fontenot, K. (1993). The endorsement of communication conflict rules as a function of engagement, marriage and marital ideology. *Journal of Social and Personal Relationships, 10,* 285–304.

Hong, L. (2000). Toward a transformed approach to prevention: Breaking the link between masculinity and violence. *Journal of American College Health, 48,* 269–279.

Hong, Y.-y., Wyer, R. S., Jr., & Fong, C. P. S. (2008). Chinese working in groups: Effort dispensability versus normative influence. *Asian Journal of Social Psychology, 11,* 187–195.

Hong, Y., Morris, M. W., Chiu, C., & Benet-Martinez, V. (2000). Multicultural minds: A dynamic constructivist approach to culture and cognition. *American Psychologist, 55,* 709–720.

Honts, C. R., Raskin, D. C., & Kircher, J. C. (2002). The scientific status of research on polygraph techniques: The case for polygraph tests (pp. 446–483). In D. L. Faigman, D. Kaye, M. J. Saks, &

J. Sanders (Eds.), *Modern scientific evidence: The law and science of expert testimony*. St. Paul, MN: West.

Hood, B. (2012). *The self illusion: How the social brain creates identity*. New York: Oxford University Press.

Hoogendoorn, S., Oosterbeek, H., & Van Praag, M. (2013). The impact of gender diversity on the performance of business teams: Evidence from a field experiment. *Management Science, 59,* 1514–1528.

Hoorens, V., & Nuttin, J. M. (1993). Overvaluation of own attributes: Mere ownership or subjective frequency? *Social Cognition, 11,* 177–200.

Hope, L., & Wright, D. (2007). Beyond unusual? Examining the role of attention in the weapon focus effect. *Applied Cognitive Psychology, 21,* 951–962.

Hope, L., Memon, A., & McGeorge, P. (2004). Understanding pretrial publicity: Predecisional distortion of evidence by mock jurors. *Journal of Experimental Psychology: Applied, 10,* 111–119.

Hornsey, M. J., & Jetten, J. (2004). The individual within the group: Balancing the need to belong with the need to be different. *Personality and Social Psychology Review, 8,* 248–264.

Hornsey, M. J., Wellauer, R., McIntyre, J. C., & Barlow, F. K. (2015). A critical test of the assumption that men prefer conformist women and women prefer nonconformist men. *Personality and Social Psychology Bulletin, 41,* 755–768.

Horowitz, I. A., Kerr, N. L., Park, E. S., & Gockel, C. (2006). Chaos in the courtroom reconsidered: Emotional bias and juror nullification. *Law and Human Behavior, 30,* 163–181.

Horry, R., Cheong, W., & Brewer, N. (2015). The other-race effect in perception and recognition: Insights from the complete composite task. *Journal of Experimental Psychology: Human Perception and Performance, 41,* 508–524.

Horry, R., Palmer, M. A., Sexton, M. L., & Brewer, N. (2012). Memory conformity for confidently recognized items: The power of social influence on memory reports. *Journal of Experimental Social Psychology, 48,* 783–786.

Horselenberg, R., Merckelbach, H., & Josephs, S. (2003). Individual differences and false confessions: A conceptual replication of Kassin and Kiechel (1996). *Psychology, Crime and Law, 9,* 1–18.

Horvath, A. O., & Luborsky, L. (1993). The role of the therapeutic alliance in psychotherapy. *Journal of Consulting and Clinical Psychology, 61,* 561–573.

Horverak, J. G., Bye, H. H., Sandal, G. M., & Pallesen, S. (2012). Managers' evaluations of immigrant job applicants: The influence of acculturation strategy on perceived person-organization fit (P-O Fit) and hiring outcome. *Journal of Cross-Cultural Psychology, 44,* 46–60.

Horwitz, S. (2015, Feb 13). FBI director acknowledged "hard truths" about racial bias in policing. *The Washington Post,* washingtonpost.com.

Hosch, H. M., Culhane, S. E., Jolly, K. W., Chavez, R. M., & Shaw, L. H. (2011). Effects of an alibi witness's relationship to the defendant on mock jurors' judgments. *Law and Human Behavior, 35,* 127–142.

Hoshino-Browne, E., Zanna, A. S., Spencer, S. J.; Zanna, M. P., Kitayama, S., & Lackenbauer, S. (2005). On the cultural guises of cognitive dissonance: The case of Easterners and Westerners. *Journal of Personality and Social Psychology, 89,* 294–310.

Houghton, D. P. (2008). Invading and occupying Iraq: Some insights from political psychology. *Peace and Conflict: Journal of Peace Psychology, 14,* 169–192.

House, J. S., Landis, K. R., & Umberson, D. (1988). Social relationships and health. *Science, 241,* 540–545.

Hovland, C. I., & Weiss, W. (1951). The influence of source credibility on communication effectiveness. *Public Opinion Quarterly, 15,* 635–650.

Hovland, C. I., Janis, I. L., & Kelley, H. H. (1953). *Communication and persuasion: Psychological studies of opinion change*. New Haven, CT: Yale University Press.

Hovland, C. I., Lumsdaine, A. A., & Sheffield, F. D. (1949). *Experiments on mass communication*. Princeton, NJ: Princeton University Press.

Howard, D. J. (1990). The influence of verbal responses to common greetings on compliance behavior: The foot-in-the-mouth effect. *Journal of Applied Social Psychology, 20,* 1185–1196.

Howard, P. N., & Hussain, M. (2011). Digital media and the Arab Spring. *Journal of Democracy, 22,* 35–48.

Howland, A. C., Rembisz, R., Wang-Jones, T. S., Heise, S. R., & Brown, S. (2015). Developing a virtual assessment center. *Consulting Psychology Journal: Practice and Research, 67,* 110–126.

Hu, X., Antony, J. W., Creery, J. D., Vargas, I. M., Bodenhausen, G. V., & Paller, K. A. (2015). Unlearning implicit social biases during sleep. *Science, 348,* 1013–1015.

Huang, C.-M., & Park, D. (2013). Cultural influences on Facebook photographs. *International Journal of Psychology, 48,* 334–43.

Huang, Q., Liu, H., & Zhong, X. (2013). The impact of transactive memory systems on team performance. *Information Technology & People, 26,* 191–212.

Huang, Y., Kendrick, K. M., & Yu, R. (2014). Conformity to the opinions of other people lasts for no more than 3 days. *Psychological Science, 25,* 1388–1393.

Huesmann, L. R. (1998). The role of social information processing and cognitive schema in the acquisition and maintenance of habitual aggressive behavior. In R. G. Geen & E. Donnerstein (Eds.), *Human aggression: Theories, research, and implications for social policy* (pp. 73–109). San Diego: Academic Press.

Huesmann, L. R., & Guerra, N. G. (1997). Children's normative beliefs about aggression and aggressive behavior. *Journal of Personality and Social Psychology, 72,* 408–419.

Huesmann, L. R., Moise-Titus, J., Podolski, C. P., & Eron, L. D. (2003). Longitudinal relations between children's exposure to TV violence and their aggressive and violent behavior in young adulthood: 1977–1992. *Developmental Psychology, 39,* 201–229.

Huffcutt, A. I., & Roth, P. L. (1998). Racial group differences in employment interview evaluations. *Journal of Applied Psychology, 83,* 179–189.

Huffcutt, A. I., Conway, J. M., Roth, P. L., & Stone, N. J. (2001). Identification and meta-analytic assessment of psychological constructs measured in employment interviews. *Journal of Applied Psychology, 86,* 897–913.

Hugenberg, K., & Corneille, O. (2009). Holistic processing is tuned for in-group faces. *Cognitive Science, 33,* 1173–1181.

Hull, J. G., & Young, R. D. (1983). Self-consciousness, self-esteem, and success-failure as determinants of alcohol consumption in male social drinkers. *Journal of Personality and Social Psychology, 44,* 1097–1109.

Human, L. J., & Biesanz, J. C. (2011). Through the looking glass clearly: Accuracy and assumed similarity in well-adjusted individuals' first impressions. *Journal of Personality and Social Psychology, 100,* 349–364.

Hung, T., Chi, N., & Lu, W. (2009). Exploring the relationships between perceived coworker loafing and counterproductive work behaviors: The mediating role of a revenge motive. *Journal of Business and Psychology, 24,* 257–270.

Hunsaker, S., Chen, H., Maughan, D., & Heaston, S. (2015). Factors that influence the development of compassion fatigue, burnout, and compassion satisfaction in emergency department nurses. *Journal of Nursing Scholarship, 47,* 186–194.

Hunter, E. M., & Wu, C. (in press). Give me a better break: Choosing workday break activities to maximize resource recovery. *Journal of Applied Psychology,* Aug 10, 2015.

Hur, M. H. (2006). Exploring the motivation factors of charitable giving and their value structure: A case study of Seoul, Korea. *Social Behavior and Personality, 34,* 661–680.

Hurtz, G. M., & Donovan, J. J. (2000). Personality and job performance: The Big Five revisited. *Journal of Applied Psychology, 85,* 869–879.

Huston, T. L., & Vangelisti, A. L. (1991). Socioemotional behavior and satisfaction in marital relationships: A longitudinal study. *Journal of Personality and Social Psychology, 61,* 721–733.

Huston, T. L., Caughlin, J. P., Houts, R. M., Smith, S. E., & George, L. J. (2001). The connubial crucible: Newlywed years as predictors of marital delight, distress, and divorce. *Journal of Personality and Social Psychology, 80,* 237–252

Hutchison, P., Abrams, D., & de Moura, G. R. (2013). Corralling the ingroup: Deviant derogation and perception of group variability. *The Journal of Social Psychology, 153,* 334–350.

Hutchison, P., Jetten, J., & Gutierrez, R. (2011). Deviant but desirable: Group variability and evaluation of atypical group members. *Journal of Experimental Social Psychology, 47,* 1155–1161.

Huynh, Q., Devos, T., & Smalarz, L. (2011). Perpetual foreigner in one's own land: Potential implications for identity and psychological adjustment. *Journal of Social and Clinical Psychology, 30,* 133–162.

Hyde, J. S. (2014). Gender similarities and differences. *Annual Review of Psychology, 65,* 373–398.

Hymel, S., McClure, R., Miller, M., Shumka, E., & Trach, J. (2015). Addressing school bullying: Insights from theories of group processes. *Journal of Applied Developmental Psychology, 37,* 16–24.

Igou, E. R. (2008). "How long will I suffer?" versus "How long will you suffer?" A self-other effect in affective forecasting. *Journal of Personality and Social Psychology, 95,* 899–917.

Ijzerman, H., & Semin, G. R. (2009). The thermometer of social relations: mapping social proximity on temperature. *Psychological Science, 20,* 1214–1220.

Imada, T. (2012). Cultural narratives of individualism and collectivism: A content analysis of textbook stories in the United States and Japan. *Journal of Cross-Cultural Psychology, 43,* 576–591.

Inagaki, T. K., & Eisenberger, N. L. (2013). Shared neural mechanisms underlying social warmth and physical warmth. *Psychological Science, 24,* 2272–2280.

Inbau, F. E., Reid, J. E., Buckley, J. P., & Jayne, B. C. (2001). *Criminal interrogation and confessions* (4th ed.). Gaithersburg, MD: Aspen.

Inbau, F. E., Reid, J. E., Buckley, J. P., & Jayne, B. C. (2013). *Criminal interrogation and confessions* (5th ed.). Burlington, MA: Jones & Bartlett.

Ingham, A. G., Levinger, G., Graves, J., & Peckham, V. (1974). The Ringelmann effect: Studies of group size and group performance. *Journal of Experimental Social Psychology, 10,* 371–384.

Inglehart, R., Foa, R., Peterson, C., & Welzel, C. (2008). Development, freedom, and rising happiness: A global perspective (1981–2007). *Current Perspectives on Psychological Science, 3,* 264–285.

Ingoldsby, B. B. (1991). The Latin American family: Familism vs. machismo. *Journal of Comparative Family Studies, 23,* 47–62.

Insko, C. A., Sedlak, A. J., & Lipsitz, A. (1982). A two-valued logic or two-valued balance resolution of the challenge of agreement and attraction effects in p-o-x triads, and a theoretical perspective on conformity and hedonism. *European Journal of Social Psychology, 12,* 143–167.

Insko, C. A., Wildschut, T., & Cohen, T. R. (2013). Interindividual-intergroup discontinuity in the prisoner's dilemma game: How common fate, proximity, and similarity affect intergroup competition. *Organizational Behavior and Human Decision Processes, 120,* 168–180.

Internet World Stats (2015). http://www.internetworldstats.com/stats.htm.

Inzlicht, M., & Schmader, T. (Eds.). (2012). *Stereotype threat: Theory, process, and application.* New York: Oxford University Press.

Ireland, M. E., & Pennebaker, J. W. (2010). Language style matching in writing: Synchrony in essays, correspondence, and poetry. *Journal of Personality and Social Psychology, 99,* 549–571.

Irons, E. D., & Moore, G. W. (1985). *Black managers: The case of the banking industry.* New York: Praeger.

Irwin, M., Mascovich, S., Gillin, J. C., Willoughby, R., Pike, J., & Smith, T. L. (1994). Partial sleep deprivation reduces natural killer cell activity in humans. *Psychosomatic Medicine, 56,* 493–498.

Isen, A. M. (1984). Toward understanding the role of affect in cognition. In R. S. Wyer & T. K. Srull (Eds.), *Handbook of social cognition* (Vol. 3, pp. 179–236). Hillsdale, NJ: Erlbaum.

Ito, T. A. (2011). Perceiving social category information from faces: Using ERPs to study person perception. In A. Todorov, S. T. Fiske, & D. A. Prentice (Eds.), *Social neuroscience: Toward understanding the underpinnings of the social mind* (pp. 85–100). New York: Oxford University Press.

Ito, T. A., Friedman, N. P., Bartholow, B. D., Correll, J., Loersch, C., Altamirano, L. J., & Miyake, A. (2015). Toward a comprehensive understanding of executive cognitive function in implicit racial bias. *Journal of Personality and Social Psychology, 108,* 187–218.

Ito, T. A., Larsen, J. T., Smith, N. K., & Cacioppo, J. T. (1998). Negative information weighs more heavily on the brain: The negativity bias in evaluative categorizations. *Journal of Personality and Social Psychology, 75,* 887–900.

Ito, T. A., Miller, N., & Pollock, V E. (1996). Alcohol and aggression: A metaanalysis on the moderating effects of inhibitory cues, triggering events, and self-focused attention. *Psychological Bulletin, 120,* 60–82.

Jacks, J. Z., & Cameron, K. A. (2003). Strategies for resisting persuasion. *Basic and Applied Social Psychology, 25,* 145–161.

Jackson, J. M. (1986). In defense of social impact theory: Comment on Mullin. *Journal of Personality and Social Psychology, 50,* 511–513.

Jackson, T., Chen, H., Guo, C., & Gao, X. (2006). Stories we love by: Conceptions of love among couples from People's Republic of China and the United States. *Journal of Cross-Cultural Psychology, 4,* 446–464.

James, J. E., Kristjansson, A. L., & Sigfusdottir, I. D. (2015). A gender-specific analysis of adolescent dietary caffeine, alcohol consumption, anger, and violent behavior. *Substance Use & Misuse, 50,* 257–267.

James, W. (1890). *Principles of psychology* (Vols. 1–2). New York: Holt.

Jamieson, J. P., Nock, M. K., & Mendes, W. B. (2012). Mind over matter: Reappraising arousal improves cardiovascular and cognitive responses to stress. *Journal of Experimental Psychology: General, 141,* 417–442.

Jamjoom, M. (2009, May 10). Saudi judge: It's OK to slap spendthrift wives. *CNN.com.*

Janis, I. L. (1968). Attitude change via role playing. In R. Abelson, E. Aronson, W. McGuire, T. Newcomb, M. Rosenberg, & P. Tennenbaum (Eds.), *Theories of cognitive consistency: A sourcebook* (pp. 810–818). Chicago: Rand McNally.

Janis, I. L. (1982). *Groupthink* (2nd ed.). Boston: Houghton Mifflin.

Janis, I. L., & Feshbach, S. (1953). Effects of fear arousing communications. *Journal of Abnormal and Social Psychology, 48,* 78–92.

Janis, I. L., & King, B. T. (1954). The influence of role playing on opinion change. *Journal of Abnormal and Social Psychology, 49,* 211–218.

Janis, I. L., Kaye, D., & Kirschner, P. (1965). Facilitating effects of "eating while reading" on responsiveness to persuasive communications. *Journal of Personality and Social Psychology, 1,* 181–186.

Jankowiak, W. R., & Fischer, E. F. (1992). A cross-cultural perspective on romantic love. *Ethnology, 31,* 149–155.

Janoff-Bulman, R. (1979). Characterological versus behavioral self-blame: Inquiries into depression and rape. *Journal of Personality and Social Psychology, 37*, 1798–1809.

Janoff-Bulman, R. (1992). *Shattered assumptions: Towards a new psychology of trauma*. New York: Free Press.

Jansari, A., & Parkin, A. J. (1996). Things that go bump in your life: Explaining the reminiscence bump in autobiographical memory. *Psychology and Aging, 11*, 85–91.

Janssen, L., Fennis, B. M., & Pruyn, A. (2010). Forewarned is fore-armed: Conserving self-control strength to resist social influence. *Journal of Experimental Social Psychology, 46*, 911–921.

Jarvis, W. B. G., & Petty, R. E. (1996). The need to evaluate. *Journal of Personality and Social Psychology, 70*, 172–194.

Javidan, M., & Carl, D. (2005). Leadership across cultures: A study of Canadian and Taiwanese executives. *MIR: Management International Review, 45*, 23–44.

Jenkins, G. D., Jr., Mitra, A., Gupta, N., & Shaw, J. D. (1998). Are financial incentives related to performance? A meta-analytic review of empirical research. *Journal of Applied Psychology, 83*, 777–787.

Jennings (Walstedt), J., Geis, F. L., & Brown, V (1980). Influence of television commercials on women's self-confidence and independent judgment. *Journal of Personality and Social Psychology, 38*, 203–210.

Jensen, K., Vaish, A., & Schmidt, M. H. (2014). The emergence of human prosociality: Aligning with others through feelings, concerns, and norms. *Frontiers in Psychology, 5*.

Jepson, C., & Chaiken, S. (1990). Chronic issue-specific fear inhibits systematic processing of persuasive communications. *Journal of Social Behavior and Personality, 5*, 61–84.

Jetten, J., & Hornsey, M. J. (Eds.). (2011). *Rebels in groups: Dissent, deviance, difference and defiance*. Chichester, UK: Wiley-Blackwell.

Jetten, J., & Hornsey, M. J. (2014). Deviance and dissent in groups. *Annual Review of Psychology, 65*, 461–485.

Jetten, J., & Mols, F. (2014). 50-50 hindsight: Appreciating anew the contributions of Milgram's obedience experiments. *Journal of Social Issues, 70*, 587–602.

Jetten, J., Branscombe, N. R., et al. (2015). Having a lot of a good thing: Multiple important group memberships as a source of self-esteem. *PloS ONE, 10*, e0131035.

Jetten, J., Hornsey, M. J., Spears, R., Haslam, S., & Cowell, E. (2010). Rule transgressions in groups: The conditional nature of newcomers' willingness to confront deviance. *European Journal of Social Psychology, 40*, 338–348.

Jiang, J., Zhang, Y., Ke, Y., Hawk, S. T., & Qiu, H. (2015). Can't buy me friendship? Peer rejection and adolescent materialism: Implicit self-esteem as a mediator. *Journal of Experimental Social Psychology, 58*, 48–55.

Job, V., Dweck, C. S., & Walton, G. M. (2010). Ego depletion—Is it all in your head? Implicit theories about willpower affect self-regulation. *Psychological Science, 21*, 1686–1693.

Job, V., Walton, G. M., Bernecker, K., & Dweck, C. S. (2015). Implicit theories about willpower predict self-regulation and grades in everyday life. *Journal of Personality and Social Psychology, 108*, 637–647.

Johansson, G., von Hofsten, C., & Jansson, G. (1980). Event perception. *Annual Review of Psychology, 31*, 27–53.

Johns, G. (1994). Absenteeism estimates by employees and managers: Divergent perspectives and self-serving perceptions. *Journal of Applied Psychology, 79*, 229–239.

Johnson v. Louisiana, 406 U.S. 356 (1972).

Johnson, D. J., & Rusbult, C. E. (1989). Resisting temptation: Devaluation of alternative partners as a means of maintaining commitment in close relationships. *Journal of Personality and Social Psychology, 57*, 967–980.

Johnson, J. T. (2009). The once and future self: Beliefs about temporal change in goal importance and goal achievement. *Self and Identity, 8*, 94–112.

Johnson, R. D., & Downing, L. L. (1979). Deindividuation and valance of cues: Effects on prosocial and antisocial behavior. *Journal of Personality and Social Psychology, 37*, 1532–1538.

Johnson, R. W., Kelly, R. J., & LeBlane, B. A. (1995). Motivational basis of dissonance: Aversive consequences or inconsistency. *Personality and Social Psychology Bulletin, 21*, 850–855.

Johnson, W., & Krueger, R. F. (2006). How money buys happiness: Genetic and environmental processes linking finances and life satisfaction. *Journal of Personality and Social Psychology, 90*, 680–691.

Jones, B. C., DeBruine, L. M., & Little, A. C. (2007). The role of symmetry in attraction to average faces. *Perception & Psychophysics, 69*, 1273–1277.

Jones, E. E. (1964). *Ingratiation: A social psychological analysis*. New York: Appleton-Century-Crofts.

Jones, E. E. (1990). *Interpersonal perception*. New York: Freeman.

Jones, E. E., & Davis, K. E. (1965). From acts to dispositions: The attribution process in person perception. *Advances in Experimental Psychology, 2*, 219–266.

Jones, E. E., & Harris, V. A. (1967). The attribution of attitudes. *Journal of Experimental Social Psychology, 3*, 1–24.

Jones, E. E., & Pittman, T. S. (1982). Toward a general theory of strategic self presentation. In J. Suls (Ed.), *Psychological perspectives on the self*. Hillsdale, NJ: Erlbaum.

Jones, E. E., & Sigall, H. (1971). The bogus pipeline: A new paradigm for measuring affect and attitude. *Psychological Bulletin, 76*, 349–364.

Jones, E. E., Davis, K. E., & Gergen, K. (1961). Role playing variations and their informational value for person perception. *Journal of Abnormal and Social Psychology, 63*, 302–310.

Jones, E. E., Rhodewalt, F., Berglas, S., & Skelton, J. A. (1981). Effects of strategic self-presentation on subsequent self-esteem. *Journal of Personality and Social Psychology, 41*, 407–421.

Jones, E. E., Rock, L., Shaver, K. G., Goethals, G. R., & Ward, L. M. (1968). Pattern of performance and ability attribution: An unexpected primary effect. *Journal of Personality and Social Psychology, 10*, 317–340.

Jones, E., & Sigall, H. (1971). "The Bogus Pipeline: A new paradigm for measuring affect and attitude." *Psychological Bulletin, 76*, 349–364.

Jones, J. H. (1997a). *Alfred C. Kinsey: A public/private life*. New York: Norton.

Jones, J. M. (1997b). *Prejudice and racism* (2nd ed.). New York: McGraw-Hill.

Jones, J. T., Pelham, B. W., Carvallo, M., & Mirenberg, M. C. (2004). How do I love thee? Let me count the Js: Implicit egotism and interpersonal attraction. *Journal of Personality and Social Psychology, 87*, 665–683.

Jones, R. G. (2015). Psychology of sustainability: An applied perspective. New York: Routledge/Taylor & Francis.

Jones, S. S. (2007). *Imitation in infancy: The development of mimicry. Psychological Science, 18*, 593–599.

Jones, T. F., Craig, A. S., Hoy, D., Gunter, E. W., Ashley, D. L., Barr, D. B., Brock, J. W., & Schaffner, W. (2000). Mass psychogenic illness attributed to toxic exposure at a high school. *New England Journal of Medicine, 342*, 96–100.

Jordan, J., Bardé, B., & Zeiher, A. M. (Eds.). (2007). *Contributions toward evidence-based psychocardiology: A systematic review of the literature*. Washington, DC: American Psychological Association.

Joseph, D. L., Dhanani, L. Y., Shen, W., McHugh, B. C., & McCord, M. A. (2015). Is a happy leader a good leader? A meta-analytic investigation of leader trait affect and leadership. *The Leadership Quarterly*.

Jost, J. T., Gaucher, D., & Stern, C. (2015). "The world isn't fair": A system justification perspective on social stratification and inequality. In M. Mikulincer et al. (Eds.), *APA handbook of personality and social psychology*, Volume 2: *Group processes* (pp. 317–340). Washington, DC: American Psychological Association.

Judge, T. A., & Kammeyer-Mueller, J. D. (2012). Job attitudes. *Annual Review of Psychology 63*, 341–367.

Judge, T. A., & Welbourne, T. M. (1994). A confirmatory investigation of the dimensionality of the Pay Satisfaction Questionnaire. *Journal of Applied Psychology, 79*, 461–466.

Judge, T. A., Bono, J. E., & Locke, E. A. (2000). Personality and job satisfaction: The mediating role of job characteristics. *Journal of Applied Psychology, 85*, 237–249.

Judge, T. A., Piccolo, R. F., Podsakoff, N. P., Shaw, J. C., & Rich, B. L. (2010). The relationship between pay and job satisfaction: A meta-analysis of the literature. *Journal of Vocational Behavior, 77*, 157–167.

Jung-Yoon, C. (2011). Seoul offers women-only subway cars; effort to reduce cases of abuse draws mixed reviews from potential users. *The Vancouver Sun*, August 24, p. B9.

Jussim, L. (2012). *Social perception and social reality: Why accuracy dominates bias and self-fulfilling prophecy*. New York: Oxford University Press.

Juvonen, J., Nishina, A., & Graham, S. (2006). Ethnic diversity and perceptions of safety in urban middle schools. *Psychological Science, 17*, 393–400.

Kagan, J. (1994). *Galen's prophecy: Temperament in human nature*. New York: Basic Books.

Kahneman, D. (2011). *Thinking, Fast and Slow*. New York: Farrar, Straus, & Giroux.

Kahneman, D., & Miller, D. T. (1986). Norm theory: Comparing reality to its alternatives. *Psychological Review, 93*, 136–153.

Kahneman, D., & Tversky A. (1979). Prospect theory: An analysis of decisions under risk. *Econometrika, 47*, 263–291.

Kahneman, D., Knetsch, J. L., & Thaler, R. H. (1990). Experimental tests of the endowment effect and the Coase theorem. *Journal of Political Economy, 98*, 1325–1348.

Kahneman, D., Slovic, P., & Tversky, A. (Eds.). (1982). *Judgment under uncertainty: Heuristics and biases*. New York: Cambridge University Press.

Kalichman, S. C. (Ed.). (2006). *Positive prevention: Reducing HIV transmission among people living with HIV/AIDS*. New York: Springer.

Kallgren, C. A., & Wood, W. (1986). Access to attitude-relevant information in memory as a determinant of attitude-behavior consistency. *Journal of Experimental Social Psychology, 22*, 328–338.

Kalpidou, M., Costin, D., & Morris, J. (2011). The relationship between Facebook and the well-being of undergraduate college students. *Cyberpsychology, Behavior, and Social Networking, 14*, 183–189.

Kalven, H., & Zeisel, H. (1966). *The American jury*. Boston: Little, Brown.

Kamen-Siegel, L., Rodin, J., Seligman, M. E. P., & Dwyer, J. (1991). Explanatory style and cell-mediated immunity in elderly men and women. *Health Psychology, 10*, 229–235.

Kampis, J. (2005, February 15). Lawsuit claims video violence precipitated Fayetteville shootings. *Tuscaloosa News* (Alabama).

Kane, A. A., & Rink, F. (2015). How newcomers influence group utilization of their knowledge: Integrating versus differentiating strategies. *Group Dynamics: Theory, Research, and Practice, 19*, 91–105.

Kantor, J., & Streitfeld, D. (2015). Inside Amazon: Wrestling Big Ideas in a Bruising Workplace. *The New York Times*, August 15, 2015. http://www.nytimes.com/2015/08/16/technology/inside-amazon-wrestling-big-ideas-in-a-bruising-workplace.html

Kaplan, M. F., & Martin, A. M. (Eds.). (2006) *Understanding world jury systems through social psychological research*. New York: Psychology Press.

Kaplan, M. F., & Schersching, C. (1981). Juror deliberation: An information integration analysis. In B. Sales (Ed.), *The trial process* (pp. 235–262). New York: Plenum.

Karaoğlan Yılmaz, F. G., Yılmaz, R., Öztürk, H. T., Sezer, B., & Karademir, T. (2015). Cyberloafing as a barrier to the successful integration of information and communication technologies into teaching and learning environments. *Computers in Human Behavior, 45*, 290–298.

Karau, S. J., & Williams, K. D. (1993). Social loafing: A meta-analytic review and theoretical integration. *Journal of Personality and Social Psychology, 65*, 681–706.

Karau, S. J., & Williams, K. D. (2001). Understanding individual motivation in groups: The collective effort model. In M. E. Turner (Ed.), *Groups at work: Theory and research. Applied social research* (pp. 113–141). Mahwah, NJ: Erlbaum.

Kark, R., Shamir, B., & Chen, G. (2003). The two faces of transformational leadership: Empowerment and dependency. *Journal of Applied Psychology, 88*, 246–255.

Karney, B. R., & Bradbury, T. N. (1995). The longitudinal course of marital quality and stability: A review of theory, method, and research. *Psychological Bulletin, 118*, 3–34.

Karney, B. R., & Bradbury, T. N. (2000). Attributions in marriage: State or trait? A growth curve analysis. *Journal of Personality and Social Psychology, 78*, 295–309.

Karremans, J. C., Stroebe, W., & Claus, J. (2006). Beyond Vicary's fantasies: The impact of subliminal priming and brand choice. *Journal of Experimental Social Psychology, 42*, 792–798.

Kashima, Y., & Kerekes, A. R. Z. (1994). A distributed memory model of averaging phenomena in person impression formation. *Journal of Experimental Social Psychology, 30*, 407–455.

Kashima, Y., Lyons, A., & Clark, A. (2013). The maintenance of cultural stereotypes in the conversational retelling of narratives. *Asian Journal of Social Psychology, 16*, 60–70.

Kassin, S. (1997). *Psychology* (3rd ed.). Upper Saddle River, NJ: Pearson Education.

Kassin, S. (2004). *Essentials of Psychology*. Upper Saddle River, NJ: Pearson Education.

Kassin, S. M. (2012). Why confessions trump innocence. *American Psychologist, 67*, 431–445.

Kassin, S. M. (2015). The social psychology of false confessions. *Social Issues and Policy Review, 9*, 24–49.

Kassin, S. M., & Kiechel, K. L. (1996). The social psychology of false confessions: Compliance, internalization, and confabulation. *Psychological Science, 7*, 125–128.

Kassin, S. M., & Sommers, S. R. (1997). Inadmissible testimony, instructions to disregard, and the jury: Substantive versus procedural considerations. *Personality and Social Psychology Bulletin, 23*, 1046–1054.

Kassin, S. M., & Sukel, H. (1997). Coerced confessions and the jury: An experimental test of the "harmless error" rule. *Law and Human Behavior, 21*, 27–46.

Kassin, S. M., Drizin, S. A., Grisso, T., Gudjonsson, G. H., Leo, R. A., & Redlich, A. D. (2010). Police-induced confessions: Risk factors and recommendations. *Law and Human Behavior, 34*, 3–38.

Kassin, S. M., Dror, I., & Kukucka, J. (2013). The forensic confirmation bias: Problems, perspectives, and proposed solutions. *Journal of Applied Research in Memory & Cognition, 2*, 42–52.

Kassin, S. M., Goldstein, C. J., & Savitsky, K. (2003). Behavioral confirmation in the interrogation room: On the dangers of presuming guilt. *Law and Human Behavior, 27*, 187–203.

Kassin, S. M., Kukucka, J., Lawson, V. Z., & DeCarlo, J. (2015). Does video recording alter the behavior of police during interrogation? A mock crime-and-investigation study. *Law and Human Behavior, 38*, 73–83.

Kassin, S. M., Leo, R. A., Meissner, C. A., Richman, K. D., Colwell, L. H., Leach, A.-M., & LaFon, D. (2007). Police interviewing and interrogation: A self-report survey of police practices and beliefs. *Law and Human Behavior, 31*, 381–400.

Kassin, S. M., Meissner, C. A., & Norwick, R. J. (2005). "I'd know a false confession if I saw one": A comparative study of college students and police investigators. *Law and Human Behavior, 29*, 211–227.

Kassin, S. M., Tubb, V. A., Hosch, H. M., & Memon, A. (2001). On the "general acceptance" of eyewitness testimony research: A new survey of the experts. *American Psychologist, 56*, 405–416.

Kassner, M. P., Wesselmann, E. D., Law, A. T., & Williams, K. D. (2012). Virtually ostracized: Studying ostracism in Immersive virtual environments. *Cyberpsychology, Behavior and Social Networking, 15*, 399–403.

Katz, D., & Braly, K. (1933). Racial stereotypes of one hundred college students. *The Journal of Abnormal and Social Psychology, 28*, 280–290.

Kaufman, D. Q., Stasson, M. F., & Hart, J. W. (1999). Are the tabloids always wrong or is that just what we think? Need for cognition and perceptions of articles in print media. *Journal of Applied Social Psychology, 29*, 1984–1997.

Kaul, C., Ratner, K. G., & Van Bavel, J. J. (2014). Dynamic representations of race: Processing goals shape race decoding in the fusiform gyri. *Social Cognitive and Affective Neuroscience, 9*, 326–332.

Kauppila, O. (2014). So, what am I supposed to do? A multilevel examination of role clarity. *Journal of Management Studies, 51*, 737–763.

Kay, A., & Furnham, A. (2013). Age and sex stereotypes in British television advertisements. *Psychology of Popular Media Culture, 2*, 171–186.

Kay, A. C., & Jost, J. T. (2003). Complementary justice: Effects of "poor but happy" and "poor but honest" stereotype exemplars on system justification and implicit activation of the justice motive. *Journal of Personality and Social Psychology, 85*, 823–837.

Kay, A. C., Jost, J. T., & Young, S. (2005). Victim derogation and victim enhancement as alternate routes to system justification. *Personality and Social Psychology Bulletin, 16*, 240–246.

Kayser, D. N., Greitemeyer, T., Fischer, P., & Frey, D. (2010). Why mood affects help giving, but not moral courage: Comparing two types of prosocial behaviour. *European Journal of Social Psychology, 40*, 1136–1157.

Keenan, J. P., Gallup, G. G., & Falk, D. (2003). *The face in the mirror: The search for the origins of consciousness.* New York: HarperCollins/Ecco.

Keillor, J. M., Barrett, A. M., Crucian, G. P., Kortenkamp, S., & Heilman, K. M. (2003). Emotional experience and perception in the absence of facial feedback. *Journal of the International Neurological Society, 8*, 130–135.

Keller, P. A. (1999). Converting the unconverted: The effect of inclination and opportunity to discount health-related fear appeals. *Journal of Applied Psychology, 84*, 403–415.

Kelley, H. H. (1950). The warm-cold variable in first impressions of persons. *Journal of Personality, 18*, 431–439.

Kelley, H. H. (1967). Attribution in social psychology. *Nebraska Symposium on Motivation, 15*, 192–238.

Kelly, A. E., & McKillop, K. J. (1996). Consequences of revealing personal secrets. *Psychological Bulletin, 120*, 450–465.

Kelman, H. C. (1961). Processes of opinion change. *Public Opinion Quarterly, 25*, 57–78.

Kelman, H. C. (1967). Human use of human subjects: The problem of deception in social psychology experiments. *Psychological Bulletin, 67*, 1–11.

Kelman, H. C., & Hamilton, V L. (1989). *Crimes of obedience: Toward a social psychology of authority and responsibility.* New Haven, CT: Yale University Press.

Kelman, H. C., & Hovland, C. I. (1953). "Reinstatement" of the communicator in delayed measurement of opinion change. *Journal of Abnormal and Social Psychology, 48*, 327–335.

Kemmelmeier, M., & Chavez, H. L. (2014). Biases in the perception of Barack Obama's skin tone. *Analyses of Social Issues and Public Policy (ASAP), 14*, 137–161.

Kemmelmeier, M., Jambor, E. E., & Letner, J. (2006). Individualism and good works: Cultural variation in giving and volunteering across the United States. *Journal of Cross-Cultural Psychology, 37*, 327–344.

Kenny, D. A. (1994). *Interpersonal perception: A social relations analysis.* New York: Guilford.

Kenny, D. A., & Acitelli, L. K. (2001). Accuracy and bias of perceptions of the partner in close relationships. *Journal of Personality and Social Psychology, 80*, 439–448.

Kenny, D. A., & Zaccaro, S. J. (1983). An estimate of variance due to traits in leadership. *Journal of Applied Psychology, 68*, 678–685.

Kenny, D. A., Albright, L., Malloy, T. E., & Kashy, D. A. (1994). Consensus in interpersonal perception: Acquaintance and the Big Five. *Psychological Bulletin, 116*, 245–258.

Kenrick, D. T., & Keefe, R. C. (1992). Age preferences in mates reflect sex differences in human reproductive strategies. *Behavioral and Brain Sciences, 15*, 75–133.

Kenrick, D. T., Gabrielidis, C., Keefe, R. C., & Cornelius, J. S. (1996). Adolescents' age preferences for dating partners: Support for an evolutionary model of life-history strategies. *Child Development, 67*, 1499–1511.

Kenrick, D. T., Goldstein, N. J., & Braver, S. L. (2012). *Six degrees of social influence: Science, application, and the psychology of Robert Cialdini.* New York: Oxford.

Kerr, N. L. (1981). Social transition schemes: Charting the group's road to agreement. *Journal of Personality and Social Psychology, 41*, 684–702.

Kerr, N. L., Hymes, R. W., Anderson, A. B., & Weathers, J. E. (1995). Defendant-juror similarity in mock juror judgments. *Law and Human Behavior, 19*, 545–567.

Kerr, N. L., Kramer, G. P., Carroll, J. S., & Alfini, J. J. (1991). On the effectiveness of voir dire in criminal cases with prejudicial pretrial publicity: An empirical study. *American University Law Review, 40*, 665–701.

Kerr, N. L., & MacCoun, R. (2012). Is the leniency asymmetry really dead?: Misinterpreting asymmetry effects in criminal jury deliberation. *Group Processes and Intergroup Behavior, 15*, 585–602.

Kerr, N. L., Niedermeier, K. E., & Kaplan, M. F. (1999). Bias in jurors vs. bias in juries: New evidence from the SDS perspective. *Organizational Behavior and Human Decision Processes, 80*, 70–86.

Kervyn, N. Bergsieker, H. B., & Fiske, S. T. (2012). The innuendo effect: Hearing the positive but inferring the negative. *Journal of Experimental Social Psychology, 48*, 77–85.

Kervyn, N., Fiske, S., & Yzerbyt, V. (2015). Forecasting the primary dimension of social perception: Symbolic and realistic threats together predict warmth in the Stereotype Content Model. *Social Psychology, 46*, 36–45.

Kessler, R. C., et al. (1994). Lifetime and 12-month prevalence of DSM-III-R psychiatric disorders in the United States. *Archives of General Psychiatry, 51*, 8–19.

Kessler, R. C., Sonnega, A., Bromet, E., Hughes, M., & Nelson, C. B. (1995). Posttraumatic stress disorder in the National Comorbidity Survey. *Archives of General Psychiatry, 52*, 1048–1060.

Key, W. B. (1973). *Subliminal seduction.* Englewood Cliffs, NJ: Signet.

Key, W. B. (1989). *The age of manipulation.* New York: Holt.

Keysar, B., & Henly, A. S. (2002). Speakers' overestimation of their effectiveness. *Psychological Science, 13*, 207–212.

Kiecolt-Glaser, J. K. (2009). Psychoneuroimmunology: Psychology's gateway to the biomedical future. *Perspectives on Psychological Science, 4*, 367–369.

Kiecolt-Glaser, J. K., & Newton, T. L. (2001). Marriage and health: His and hers. *Psychological Bulletin, 127*, 472–503.

Kiecolt-Glaser, J. K., McGuire, L., Robles, T., & Glaser, R. (2002). Psychoneuroimmunology: Psychological influences on immune function and health. *Journal of Consulting and Clinical Psychology, 70*, 537–547.

Kierein, N. M., & Gold, M. A. (2000). Pygmalion in work organizations: A meta-analysis. *Journal of Organizational Behavior, 21*, 913–928.

Kiesler, C. A. (1971). *The psychology of commitment*. New York: Academic Press.

Kiesler, C. A., & Kiesler, S. B. (1969). *Conformity*. Reading, MA: Addison-Wesley.

Kilbourne, J. (2003). Mass media: Shaping the self-concept: Beauty and the beast of advertising. In J. M. Henslin (Ed.), *Down to earth sociology: Introductory readings* (12th ed.) (pp. 421–424). New York: Free Press.

Kilham, W., & Mann, L. (1974). Level of destructive obedience as a function of transmitter and executant roles in the Milgram obedience paradigm. *Journal of Personality and Social Psychology, 29*, 696–702.

Kilianski, S. E. (2008). Who do you think I am? Accuracy in perceptions of others' self-esteem. *Journal of Research in Personality, 42*, 386–398.

Kim, H. S., Mojaverian, T., & Sherman, D. K. (2012). Culture and genes: Moderators of the use and effect of social support. In O. Gillath, G. Adams, & A. Kunkel (Eds.), *Relationship science: Integrating evolutionary, neuroscience, and sociocultural approaches* (pp. 73–90). Washington, DC: American Psychological Association.

Kim, H. S., Sherman, D. K., & Taylor, S. (2008). Culture and social support. *American Psychologist, 63*, 518–526.

Kim, H., & Markus, H. R. (1999). Deviance or uniqueness, harmony or conformity? A cultural analysis. *Journal of Personality and Social Psychology, 77*, 785–800.

Kimmel, A. J. (2012). Deception in research. In S. J. Knapp, M. C. Gottlieb, M. M. Handelsman, & L. D. VandeCreek (Eds.), *APA handbook of ethics in psychology*: Vol. 2. Practice, teaching, and research (pp. 401–421). Washington, DC: American Psychological Association.

King, E. B., Madera, J. M., Hebl, M. R., Knight, J. L., & Mendoza, S. A. (2006). What's in a name? A multiracial investigation of the role of occupational stereotypes in selection decisions. *Journal of Applied Social Psychology, 36*, 1145–1159.

King, L. A., & Napa, C. K. (1998). What makes a life good? *Journal of Personality and Social Psychology, 75*, 156–165.

Kinsey, A. C., Pomeroy, W. B., & Martin, C. E. (1948). *Sexual behavior in the human male*. Philadelphia: Saunders.

Kinsey, A. C., Pomeroy, W. B., Martin, C. E., & Gebhard, P. H. (1953). *Sexual behavior in the human female*. Philadelphia: Saunders.

Kiong, L. C. (2011). Moves to protect women rebuffed in some cities. *The Straits Times* (Singapore), December 17.

Kirkman, B. L., Rosen, B., Gibson, C. B., Tesluk, P., & McPherson, S. O. (2002). Five challenges to virtual team success: Lessons from Sabre, Inc. *Academy of Management Executive, 16*, 67–79.

Kirkpatrick, L. A., & Hazan, C. (1994). Attachment styles and close relationships: A four-year prospective study. *Personal Relationships, 1*, 123–142.

Kirkpatrick, S. A., & Locke, E. A. (1991). Leadership: Do traits matter? *Academy of Management Executive, 5*, 48–60.

Kirsch, A. C., & Murnen, S. K. (2015). "Hot" girls and "cool dudes": Examining the prevalence of the heterosexual script in American children's television media. *Psychology of Popular Media Culture, 4*, 18–30.

Kitayama, S., & Uchida, Y. (2003). Explicit self-criticism and implicit self-regard: Evaluating self and friend in two cultures. *Journal of Experimental Social Psychology, 39*, 476–482.

Kitayama, S., Duffy, S., Kawamura, T., & Larsen, J. T. (2003). Perceiving an object and its context in different cultures: A cultural look at New Look. *Psychological Science, 14*, 201–206.

Kitayama, S., Snibbe, A. C., Markus, H. R., & Suzuki, T. (2004). Is there any "free" choice? Self and dissonance in two cultures. *Psychological Science, 15*, 527–533.

Kitayama, S., et al. (2015). Expression of anger and ill health in two cultures: An examination of inflammation and cardiovascular risk. *Psychological Science, 26*, 211–220.

Kite, M. E. (1992). Age and the spontaneous self-concept. *Journal of Applied Social Psychology, 22*, 1828–1837.

Kivimäki, M., Vahtera, J., Elovainio, M., Helenius, H., Singh-Manoux, A., & Pentti, J. (2005). Optimism and pessimism as predictors of change in health after death or onset of severe illness in family. *Health Psychology, 24*, 413–421.

Klapwijk, A., & Van Lange, P. A. M. (2009). Promoting cooperation and trust in "noisy": situations: The power of generosity. *Journal of Personality and Social Psychology, 96*, 83–103.

Klein, N., & Epley, N. (2015). Group discussion improves lie detection. *Proceedings of the National Academy of Sciences, 112*, 7460–7465.

Klein, R. A., Ratliff, K. A., et al. (2014). Investigating variation in replicability: A "many labs" replication project. *Social Psychology, 45*, 142–152.

Klein, W. M. (1997). Objective standards are not enough: Affective, self-evaluative, and behavioral responses to social comparison information. *Journal of Personality and Social Psychology, 72*, 763–774.

Kleingeld, A., van Mierlo, H., & Arends, L. (2011). The effect of goal setting on group performance: A meta-analysis. *Journal of Applied Psychology, 96*, 1289–1304.

Kleinke, C. L. (1986). Gaze and eye contact: A research review. *Psychological Bulletin, 100*, 78–100.

Klietz, S. J., Borduin, C. M., & Schaeffer, C. M. (2010). Cost-benefit analysis of multisystemic therapy with serious and violent juvenile offenders. *Journal of Family Psychology, 24*, 657–666.

Klinesmith, J., Kasser, T., & McAndrew, F. T. (2006). Guns, testosterone, and aggression: An experimental test of a mediational hypothesis. *Psychological Science, 17*, 568–571.

Kling, K. C., Hyde, J. S., Showers, C. J., & Buswell, B. N. (1999). Gender differences in self-esteem: A meta-analysis. *Psychological Bulletin, 125*, 470–500.

Knafo, A., Schwartz, S. H., & Levine, R. V. (2009). Helping strangers is lower in embedded cultures. *Journal of Cross-Cultural Psychology, 40*, 875–879.

Knapton, H. M., Bäck, H., & Bäck, E. A. (2015). The social activist: Conformity to the ingroup following rejection as a predictor of political participation. *Social Influence, 10*, 97–108.

Kniffin, K., & Wilson, D. S. (2004). The effect of nonphysical traits on the perception of physical attractiveness: Three naturalistic studies. *Evolution and Human Behavior, 25*, 88–101.

Knobloch, S., Callison, C., Chen, L., Fritzsche, A., & Zillmann, D. (2005). Children's sex-stereotyped self-socialization through selective exposure to entertainment: Cross-cultural experiments in Germany, China, and the United States. *Journal of Communication, 55*, 122–138.

Knowles, E. S. (1983). Social physics and the effects of others: Tests of the effects of audience size and distance on social judgments and behavior. *Journal of Personality and Social Psychology, 45*, 1263–1279.

Knowles, M. L., Lucas, G. M., Baumeister, R. F., & Gardner, W. L. (2015). Choking under social pressure: Social monitoring among the lonely. *Personality and Social Psychology Bulletin, 41*, 805–821.

Knox, R. E., & Inskter, J. A. (1968). Postdecision dissonance at post-time. *Journal of Personality and Social Psychology, 8*, 319–323.

Ko, S. J., Judd, C. M., & Blair, I. V. (2006). What the voice reveals: Within- and between-category stereotyping on the basis of voice. *Personality and Social Psychology Bulletin, 32*, 806–819.

Kobasa, S. C., Maddi, S. R., & Kahn, S. (1982). Hardiness and health: A prospective study. *Journal of Personality and Social Psychology, 42*, 168–177.

Koch, A. J., D'Mello, S. D., & Sackett, P. R. (2015). A meta-analysis of gender stereotypes and bias in experimental simulations of employment decision making. *Journal of Applied Psychology, 100*, 128–161.

Koenig, A. M., & Eagly, A. H. (2014). Evidence for the social role theory of stereotype content: Observations of groups' roles shape stereotypes. *Journal of Personality and Social Psychology, 107*, 371–392.

Koenig, A. M., Eagly, A. H., Mitchell, A. A., & Ristikari, T. (2011). Are leader stereotypes masculine? A meta-analysis of three research paradigms. *Psychological Bulletin, 137*, 616–642.

Kohn, A. (1993). *Punished by rewards*. Boston: Houghton Mifflin.

Kohn, P. M., Lafreniere, K., & Gurevich, M. (1991). Hassles, health, and personality. *Journal of Personality and Social Psychology, 61*, 478–482.

Kokko, K., et al. (2014). Country, sex, and parent occupational status: Moderators of the continuity of aggression from childhood to adulthood. *Aggressive Behavior, 40*, 552–567.

Kolditz, T. A., & Arkin, R. M. (1982). An impression management interpretation of the self-handicapping strategy. *Journal of Personality and Social Psychology, 43*, 492–502.

Kong, D. T., Dirks, K. T., & Ferrin, D. L. (2014). Interpersonal trust within negotiations: Meta-analytic evidence, critical contingencies, and directions for future research. *Academy of Management Journal, 57*, 1235–1255.

Kopelman, S., & Rosette, A. S. (2008). Cultural variation in response to strategic emotions in negotiations. *Group Decision and Negotiation, 17*, 65–77.

Kopicki, A. (2014). *Answers to affirmative action depend on how you pose the question*. The New York Times, April 22, 2014 (http://nyti.ms/1f24CjL).

Koposov, R., Gundersen, K. K., & Svartdal, F. (2014). Efficacy of aggression replacement training among children from North-West Russia. *The International Journal of Emotional Education, 6*, 14–24.

Koslowski, S. W., Kirsch, M. P., & Chao, G. T. (1986). Job knowledge, ratee familiarity, conceptual similarity, and halo error: An exploration. *Journal of Applied Psychology, 71*, 45–49.

Koslowsky, M., Kluger, A., & Reich, M. (1995). *Commuting stress: Causes, effects, and methods of coping*. New York: Plenum Press.

Kouchaki, M., & Smith, I. H. (2014). The morning morality effect: The influence of time of day on unethical behavior. *Psychological Science, 25*, 95–102.

Kovacs, L. (1983). A conceptualization of marital development. *Family Therapy, 3*, 183–210.

Kovera, M. B. (2002). The effects of general pretrial publicity on juror decisions: An examination of moderators and mediating mechanisms. *Law and Human Behavior, 26*, 43–72.

Kovera, M. B., & Borgida, E. (2010). Social psychology and law. In S. T. Fiske, D. T. Gilbert, & G. Lindzey (Eds.), *Handbook of social psychology – Vol. 2* (5th ed., pp. 1343–1385). Hoboken, NJ: Wiley.

Kovera, M. B., Penrod, S. D., Pappas, C., & Thill, D. L. (1997). Identification of computer-generated facial composites. *Journal of Applied Psychology, 82*, 235–246.

Kowalski, R. M. (1993). Inferring sexual interest from behavioral cues: Effects of gender and sexually relevant attitudes. *Sex Roles, 29*, 13–36.

Kozak, M. N., Marsh, A. A., & Wegner, D. M. (2006). What do I think you're doing? Action identification and mind attribution. *Journal of Personality and Social Psychology, 90*, 543–555.

Kozel, F., Johnson, K., Mu, Q., Grenesko, E., Laken, S., & George, M. (2005). Detecting deception using functional magnetic resonance imaging. *Biological Psychiatry, 58*, 605–613.

Kraft-Todd, G., Yoeli, E., Bhanot, S., & Rand, D. (2015). Promoting cooperation in the field. *Current Opinion in Behavioral Sciences, 3*, 96–101.

Krahé, B. (2014). Media violence use as a risk factor for aggressive behavior in adolescence. *European Review of Social Psychology, 25*, 71–106.

Krahé, B., & Busching, R. (2014). Interplay of normative beliefs and behavior in developmental patterns of physical and relational aggression in adolescence: A four-wave longitudinal study. *Frontiers in Psychology, 5*, Article 1146.

Krahé, B., & Busching, R. (2015). Breaking the vicious cycle of media violence use and aggression: A test of intervention effects over 30 months. *Psychology of Violence, 5*, 217–226.

Kramer, G. M., Wolbransky, M., & Heilbrun, K. (2007). Plea bargaining recommendations by criminal defense attorneys: Evidence strength, potential sentence, and defendant preference. *Behavioral Sciences and the Law, 25*, 635–1664.

Kramer, G. P., Kerr, N. L., & Carroll, J. S. (1990). Pretrial publicity, judicial remedies, and jury bias. *Law and Human Behavior, 14*, 409–438.

Krantz, D. S., & McCeney, M. K. (2002). Effects of psychological and social factors on organic disease: A critical assessment of research on coronary heart disease. *Annual Review of Psychology, 53*, 341–369.

Kraus, M. W., Côté, S., & Keltner, D. (2010). Social class, contextualism, and empathic accuracy. *Psychological Science, 21*, 1716–23.

Kraus, M. W., Piff, P. K., Mendoza-Denton, R., Rheinschmidt, M. L., & Keltner, D. (2012). Social class, solipsism, and contextualism: How the rich are different from the poor. *Psychological Review, 119*, 546–572.

Kraus, S. J. (1995). Attitudes and the prediction of behavior: A meta-analysis of the empirical literature. *Personality and Social Psychology Bulletin, 21*, 58–75.

Kravitz, D. A., & Martin, B. (1986). Ringelmann rediscovered: The original article. *Journal of Personality and Social Psychology, 50*, 936–941.

Kray, L. J., George, L. G., Liljenquist, K. A., Galinsky, A. D., Tetlock, P. E., & Roese, N. J. (2010). From what might have been to what must have been: Counterfactual thinking creates meaning. *Journal of Personality and Social Psychology, 98*, 106–118.

Krebs, D. (1987). The challenge of altruism in biology and psychology. In C. Crawford, M. Smith, & D. Krebs (Eds.), *Sociobiology and psychology: Ideas, issues, and applications* (pp. 81–118). Hillsdale, NJ: Erlbaum.

Krendl, A. C., Ambady, N., & Kensinger, E. A. (2015). The dissociable effects of stereotype threat on older adults' memory encoding and retrieval. *Journal of Applied Research in Memory and Cognition, 4*, 103–109.

Krendl, A. C., Magoon, N. S., Hull, J. G., & Heatherton, T. F. (2011). Judging a book by its cover: The differential impact of attractiveness on predicting one's acceptance to high or low status social groups. *Journal of Applied Social Psychology, 41*, 2538–2550.

Kressel, N. J., & Kressel, D. F. (2002). *Stack and sway: The new science of jury consulting*. Boulder, CO: Westview Press.

Kressel, L. M., & Uleman, J. S (2015). The causality implicit in traits. *Journal of Experimental Social Psychology, 57*, 51–54.

Krieg, A., & Dickie, J. R. (2013). Attachment and hikikomori: A psychosocial developmental model. *The International Journal of Social Psychiatry, 59*, 61–72.

Kringelbach, M. L., et al. (2008). A specific and rapid neural signature for parental instinct. *PLoS ONE, 3(2)*: 1–7.

Krizan, Z., & Johar, O. (2015). Narcissistic rage revisited. *Journal of Personality and Social Psychology, 108*, 784–801.

Krizan, Z., & Windschitl, P. D. (2007). The influence of outcome desirability on optimism. *Psychological Bulletin, 133*, 95–121.

Kroeper, K. M., Sanchez, D. T., & Himmelstein, M. S. (2014). Heterosexual men's confrontation of sexual prejudice: The role of precarious manhood. *Sex Roles, 70*, 1–13.

Krueger, J. (1998). On the perception of social consensus. *Advances in Experimental Social Psychology, 30,* 163–240.

Krueger, J. (2000). The projective perception of the social world: A building block of social comparison processes. In J. Suls & L. Wheeler (Eds.), *Handbook of social comparison: Theory and research* (pp. 323–351). New York: Plenum/Kluwer.

Krueger, J. I., & DiDonato, T. E. (2008). Social categorization and the perception of groups and group differences. *Social and Personality Psychology Compass, 2,* 733–750.

Krug, E. G., Kresnow, M., Peddicord, J. P., Dahlberg, L. L., Powell, K. E., Crosby, A. E., & Annest, J. L. (1998). Suicide after natural disasters. *New England Journal of Medicine, 338,* 373–378.

Kruger, J., & Dunning, D. (1999). Unskilled and unaware of it: How difficulties in recognizing one's own incompetence lead to inflated self-assessments. *Journal of Personality and Social Psychology, 77,* 1121–1134.

Kruger, J., Wirtz, D., & Miller, D. T. (2005). Counterfactual thinking and the first instinct fallacy. *Journal of Personality and Social Psychology, 88,* 725–735.

Kruglanski, A. W., & Webster, D. M. (1996). Motivated closing of the mind: "Seizing" and "freezing." *Psychological Review, 103,* 263–283.

Krys, K., Hansen, K., Xing, C., Szarota, P., & Yang, M. (2014). Do only fools smile at strangers? Cultural differences in social perception of intelligence of smiling individuals. *Journal of Cross-Cultural Psychology, 45,* 314–321.

Kteily, N., Bruneau, E., Waytz, A., & Cotterill, S. (2015). The ascent of man: Theoretical and empirical evidence for blatant dehumanization. *Journal of Personality and Social Psychology, 109(5):* 901–931.

Kubany, E. S., Leisen, M. B., Kaplan, A. S., Watson, S. B., Haynes, S. N., Owens, J. A., & Burns, K. (2000). Development and preliminary validation of a brief broad-spectrum measure of trauma exposure: The Traumatic Life Events Questionnaire. *Psychological Assessment, 12,* 210–224.

Kubzansky, L. D., Sparrow, D., Vokonas, P., & Kawachi, I. (2001). Is the glass half empty or half full? A prospective study of optimism and coronary heart disease in the Normative Aging Study. *Psychosomatic Medicine, 63,* 910–916.

Kugler, T., & Bornstein, G. (2013). Social dilemmas between individuals and groups. *Organizational Behavior and Human Decision Processes, 120,* 191–205.

Kukucka, J., & Kassin, S. M. (2014). Do confessions taint perceptions of handwriting evidence? An empirical test of the forensic confirmation bias. *Law and Human Behavior, 38,* 256–270.

Kulik, J. A., Mahler, H. I. M., & Earnest, A. (1994). Social comparison and affiliation under threat: Going beyond the affiliate-choice paradigm. *Journal of Personality and Social Psychology, 66,* 301–309.

Kumkale, G. T., & Albarracín, D. (2004). The sleeper effect in persuasion: A meta-analytic review. *Psychological Bulletin, 130,* 143–172.

Kuncel, N. R., & Hezlett, S. A. (2010). Fact and fiction in cognitive ability testing for admissions and hiring decisions. *Current Directions in Psychological Science, 19,* 339–345.

Kunda, Z., Sinclair, L., & Griffin, D. (1997). Equal ratings but separate meanings: Stereotypes and the construal of traits. *Journal of Personality and Social Psychology, 72,* 720–734.

Kuntz-Wilson, W., & Zajonc, R. B. (1980). Affective discrimination of stimuli that cannot be recognized. *Science, 207,* 557–558.

Kupers, T. A. (1999). *Prison madness: The mental health crisis behind bars and what we must do about it.* New York: Jossey-Bass.

Kurbat, M. A., Shevell, S. K., & Rips, L. J. (1998). A year's memories: The calendar effect in autobiographical recall. *Memory and Cognition, 26,* 532–552.

Kurdek, L. (2008). Change in relationship quality for partners from lesbian, gay male, and heterosexual couples. *Journal of Family Psychology, 22,* 701–711.

Kurdek, L. A. (1991a). Correlates of relationship satisfaction in cohabiting gay and lesbian couples: Interpretation of contextual, investment, and problem-solving models. *Journal of Personality and Social Psychology, 61,* 910–922.

Kurdek, L. A. (1991b). The dissolution of gay and lesbian couples. *Journal of Social and Personal Relationships, 8,* 265–278.

Kurdek, L. A. (1999). The nature and predictors of the trajectory of change in marital quality for husbands and wives over the first 10 years of marriage. *Developmental Psychology, 35,* 1283–1296.

Kurdek, L. A. (2005). What do we know about gay and lesbian couples? *Current Directions in Psychological Science, 14,* 251–254.

Kurzban, R., Burton-Chellew, M. N., & West, S. A. (2015). The evolution of altruism in humans. *Annual Review of Psychology, 66,* 575–599.

Kutzner, F. L., & Fiedler, K. (2015). No correlation, no evidence for attention shift in category learning: Different mechanisms behind illusory correlations and the inverse base-rate effect. *Journal of Experimental Psychology: General, 144,* 58–75.

LaBouff, J., Rowatt, W. C., Johnson, M. K., Tsang, J., & Willerton, G. (2012). Humble persons are more helpful than less humble persons: Evidence from three studies. *The Journal of Positive Psychology, 7,* 16–29.

Lahlah, E., Van der Knaap, L. M., Bogaerts, S., & Lens, K. M. E. (2013). Making men out of boys? Ethnic differences in juvenile violent offending and the role of gender role orientations. *Journal of Cross-Cultural Psychology, 44,* 1321–1338.

Lai, J. M., Lam, L. W., & Lam, S. K. (2013). Organizational citizenship behavior in work groups: A team cultural perspective. *Journal of Organizational Behavior, 34,* 1039–1056.

Laible, D., Carlo, G., Murphy, T., Augustine, M., & Roesch, S. (2014). Predicting children's prosocial and co-operative behavior from their temperamental profiles: A person-centered approach. *Social Development, 23,* 734–752.

Laible, D. J., Murphy, T. P., & Augustine, M. (2014). Adolescents' aggressive and prosocial behaviors: Links with social information processing, negative emotionality, moral affect, and moral cognition. *The Journal of Genetic Psychology: Research and Theory on Human Development, 175,* 270–286.

Laird, J. D. (1974). Self-attribution of emotion: The effects of expressive behavior on the quality of emotional experience. *Journal of Personality and Social Psychology, 29,* 475–486.

Lakoff, G., & Johnson, M. (1999). *Philosophy in the flesh: The embodied mind and its challenge to western thought.* New York: Basic Books.

Laland, K. N., & Galef, B. G. (Eds.). (2009). *The question of animal culture.* Cambridge, MA: Harvard University Press.

Lalwani, A. K., Shavitt, S., & Johnson, T. (2006). What is the relation between cultural orientation and socially desirable responding? *Journal of Personality and Social Psychology, 90,* 165–178.

LaMarre, H. L., Knobloch-Westerwick, S., & Hoplamazian, G. J. (2012). Does the music matter? Examining differential effects of music genre on support for ethnic groups. *Journal of Broadcasting & Electronic Media, 56,* 150–167.

Lamb, M. E., Hershkowitz, I., Orbach, Y., & Esplin, P. W. (2008). *Tell me what happened: Structured investigative interviews of child victims and witnesses.* West Sussex, England: Wiley.

Lamm, C., Decety, J., & Singer, T. (2011). Meta-analytic evidence for common and distinct neural networks associated with direct experienced pain and empathy for pain. *Neuroimage, 54,* 2492–2502.

Lamm, H., & Myers, D. G. (1978). Group-induced polarization of attitudes and behavior. In L. Berkowitz (Ed.), Advances in experimental social psychology (Vol. 11, pp. 145–195). New York: Academic Press.

Lamont, R. A., Swift, H. J., & Abrams, D. (2015). A review and meta-analysis of age-based stereotype threat: Negative stereotypes, not facts, do the damage. *Psychology And Aging, 30*, 180–193.

Landau, M. J., Solomon, S., Greenberg, J., Cohen, F., Pyszczynski, T., Arndt, J., Miller, C. H., Ogilvie, D. M., & Cook, A. (2004). Deliver us from evil: The effects of mortality salience and reminders of 9/11 on support for President George W. Bush. *Personality and Social Psychology Bulletin, 30*, 1136–1150.

Landau, T. (1989). *About faces: The evolution of the human face.* New York: Anchor Books.

Landoll, R. R., La Greca, A. M., Lai, B. S., Chan, S. F., & Herge, W. M. (2015). Cyber victimization by peers: Prospective associations with adolescent social anxiety and depressive symptoms. *Journal of Adolescence, 42*, 77–86.

Lane, K. A., Kang, J., & Banaji, M. R. (2007). Implicit social cognition and law. *Annual Review of Law and Social Science, 3*, 427–451.

Lane, L. W., Groisman, M., & Ferreira, V. S. (2006). Don't talk about pink elephants! Speakers' control over leaking private information during language production. *Psychological Science, 17*, 273–277.

Lang, B. (2015, June 30). *Ellen DeGeneres influenced gay rights views more than any other celebrity. Variety*, http://variety.com/2015/tv/news/ellen-degeneres-gay-rights-gay-marriage-1201531462/.

Lange, F., & Eggert, F. (2014). Sweet delusion. Glucose drinks fail to counteract ego depletion. *Appetite, 75*, 54–63.

Lange, N. D., Thomas, R. P., Dana, J., & Dawes, R. M. (2011). Contextual biases in the interpretation of auditory evidence. *Law and Human Behavior, 35*, 178–187.

Langer, E. J. (1975). The illusion of control. *Journal of Personality and Social Psychology, 32*, 311–328.

Langer, E. J. (1989). *Mindfulness.* Reading, MA: Addison-Wesley.

Langer, E. J., & Rodin, J. (1976). The effects of choice and enhanced personal responsibility for the aged: A field experiment in an institutional setting. *Journal of Personality and Social Psychology, 34*, 191–198.

Langer, E. J., Blank, A., & Chanowitz, B. (1978). The mindlessness of ostensibly thoughtful action. *Journal of Personality and Social Psychology, 36*, 635–642.

Langer, G., Arnedt, C., & Sussman, D. (2004). Primetime Live poll: American sex survey: A peek beneath the sheets. Posted October 21, 2004. http://abcnews.go.com/Primetime/PollVault/story?id=156921

Langlois, J. H., & Roggman, L. A. (1990). Attractive faces are only average. *Psychological Science, 1*, 115–121.

Langlois, J. H., Kalakanis, L., Rubenstein, A. J., Larson, A., Hallam, M., & Smoot, M. (2000). Maxims or myths of beauty? A meta-analytic and theoretical review. *Psychological Bulletin, 126*, 390–423.

Langlois, J. H., Ritter, J. M., Roggman, L. A., & Vaughn, L. S. (1991). Facial diversity and infant preferences for attractive faces. *Developmental Psychology, 27*, 79–84.

Langlois, J. H., Roggman, L. A., & Musselman, L. (1994). What is average and what is not average about attractive faces? *Psychological Science, 5*, 214–220.

Langner, O., Dotsch, R., Bijlstra, G., Wigboldus, D. J., Hawk, S. T., & van Knippenberg, A. (2010). Presentation and validation of the Radboud Faces Database. *Cognition and Emotion, 24*, 1377–1388.

Langton, S. R. H., Watt, R. J., & Bruce, V. (2000). Do the eyes have it? Cues to the direction of social attention. *Trends in Cognitive Sciences, 4*, 50–59.

Lansford, J. E., & Deater-Deckard, K. (2012). Childrearing discipline and violence in developing countries. *Child Development, 83*, 62–75.

Lansford, J. E., Sharma, C., et al. (2014). Corporal punishment, maternal warmth, and child adjustment: A longitudinal study in eight countries. *Journal of Clinical Child and Adolescent Psychology, 43*(4), 670–685.

LaPiere, R. T. (1934). Attitudes vs. *action. Social Forces, 13*, 230–237.

Lapré, G. E., & Marsee, M. A. (2015). The role of race in the association between corporal punishment and externalizing problems: Does punishment severity matter? *Journal of Child and Family Studies*, in press.

Larrick, R. P., Morgan, J. N., & Nisbett, R. E. (1990). Teaching the use of cost-benefit reasoning in everyday life. *Psychological Science, 1*, 362–370.

Larrick, R. P., Timmerman, T. A., Carton, A. M., & Abrevaya, J. (2011). Temper, temperature, and temptation: Heat-related retaliation in baseball. *Psychological Science, 22*, 423–428.

Larsen, R. J., & Kasimatis, M. (1990). Individual differences in entrainment of mood to the weekly calendar. *Journal of Personality and Social Psychology, 58*, 164–171.

Larson, J. R., Jr., Foster-Fishman, P. G., & Franz, T. M. (1998). Leadership style and the discussion of shared and unshared information in decision-making groups. *Personality and Social Psychology Bulletin, 24*, 482–495.

Lassiter, G. D., Diamond, S. S., Schmidt, H. C., & Elek, J. K. (2007). Evaluating videotaped confessions: Expertise provides no defense against the camera-perspective effect. *Psychological Science, 18*, 224–226.

Lassiter, G. D., Geers, A. L., Munhall, P. J., Handley, I. M., & Beers, M. J. (2001). Videotaped confessions: Is guilt in the eye of the camera? *Advances in Experimental Social Psychology, 33*, 189–254.

Lassiter, G. D., Stone, J. I., & Rogers, S. L. (1988). Memorial consequences of variation in behavior perception. *Journal of Experimental Social Psychology, 24*, 222–239.

Latané, B. (1981). The psychology of social impact. *American Psychologist, 36*, 343–356.

Latané, B., & Darley, J. M. (1968). Group inhibition of bystander intervention. *Journal of Personality and Social Psychology, 10*, 215–221.

Latané, B., & Darley, J. M. (1970). *The unresponsive bystander: Why doesn't he help?* New York: Appleton-Century-Crofts.

Latané, B., & L'Herrou, T. (1996). Spatial clustering in the conformity game: Dynamic social impact in electronic groups. *Journal of Personality and Social Psychology, 70*, 1218–1230.

Latané, B., & Nida, S. (1981). Ten years of research on group size and helping. *Psychological Bulletin, 89*, 308–324.

Latané, B., & Werner, C. (1978). Regulation of social contact in laboratory rats: Time, not distance. *Journal of Personality and Social Psychology, 36*, 1128–1137.

Latané, B., & Wolf, S. (1981). The social impact of majorities and minorities. *Psychological Review, 88*, 438–453.

Latané, B., Liu, J. H., Nowak, A., Bonevento, M., & Zheng, L. (1995). Distance matters: Physical space and social impact. *Personality and Social Psychology Bulletin, 21*, 795–805.

Latané, B., Williams, K., & Harkins, S. (1979). Many hands make light the work: The causes and consequences of social loafing. *Journal of Personality and Social Psychology, 37*, 822–832.

Lau, R. L., & Rovner, I. B. (2009). Negative campaigning. *Annual Review of Political Science, 12*, 285–306.

Laurin, K., Kay, A. C., & Fitzsimons, G. M. (2012). Divergent effects of activating thoughts of God on self-regulation. *Journal of Personality and Social Psychology, 102*, 4–21.

Lavan, N., Lima, C. F., Harvey, H., Scott, S. K., & McGettigan, C. (2015). I thought that I heard you laughing: Contextual facial expressions modulate the perception of authentic laughter and crying. *Cognition and Emotion, 29*, 935–944.

Lavner, J. A., Karney, B. R., & Bradbury, T. N. (2014). Relationship problems over the early years of marriage: Stability or change? *Journal of Family Psychology, 28*, 979–985.

Lawrence, E., Rothman, A., Cobb, R., Bradbury, T., & Rothman, M. (2008). Marital satisfaction across the transition to parenthood. *Journal of Family Psychology, 22,* 41–50.

Lazarus, R. S., & Folkman, S. (1984). *Stress, appraisal, and coping.* New York: Springer.

Le, B., & Agnew, C. R. (2003). Commitment and its theorized determinants: A meta-analysis of the investment model. *Personal Relationships, 10,* 37–57.

Leary, M. R. (Ed.). (2001). *Interpersonal rejection.* New York: Oxford University Press.

Leary, M. R., & Baumeister, R. F. (2000). The nature and function of self-esteem: Sociometer theory. *Advances in Experimental Social Psychology, 32,* 1–62.

Leary, M. R., & Kowalski, R. M. (1995). *Social anxiety.* New York: Guilford Press.

Leary, M. R., & Tangney, J. P. (Eds.). (2003). *Handbook of self and identity.* New York: Guilford.

Leary, M. R., Kowalski, R. M., Smith, L., & Phillips, S. (2003). Teasing, rejection, and violence: Case studies of the school shootings. *Aggressive Behavior, 29,* 202–214.

Leary, M. R., Tchividjian, L. R., & Kraxberger, B. E. (1994). Self-presentation can be hazardous to your health: Impression management and health risk. *Health Psychology, 13,* 461–470.

Leary, M. R., Twenge, J. M., & Quinlivan, E. (2006). Interpersonal rejection as a determinant of anger and aggression. *Personality and Social Psychology Review, 10,* 111–132.

LeDoux, J. (2002). *The synaptic self: How our brains become who we are.* New York: Penguin Books.

LeDoux, J. E. (1996). *The emotional brain: The mysterious underpinnings of emotional life.* New York: Simon & Schuster.

Lee, J. A. (1988). Love-styles. In R. J. Sternberg & M. L. Barnes (Eds.), *The psychology of love* (pp. 38–67). New Haven, CT: Yale University Press.

Lee, L., Loewenstein, G., Ariely, D., Hong, J., & Young, J. (2008). If I'm not hot, are you hot or not? Physical-attractiveness evaluations and dating preferences as a function of one's own attractiveness. *Psychological Science, 19,* 669–677.

Lee, P., Gillespie, N., Mann, L., & Wearing, A. (2010). Leadership and trust: Their effect on knowledge sharing and team performance. *Management Learning, 41,* 473–491.

Lee, R. T., & Ashforth, B. E. (1996). A meta-analytic examination of the correlates of the three dimensions of job burnout. *Journal of Applied Psychology, 81,* 123–133.

Lee, S., Adair, W. L., & Seo, S. (2013). Cultural perspective taking in cross-cultural negotiation. *Group Decision and Negotiation, 22,* 389–405.

Lee, S. J., Altschul, I., & Gershoff, E. T. (2013). Does warmth moderate longitudinal associations between maternal spanking and child aggression in early childhood?. *Developmental Psychology, 49,* 2017–2028.

Lee, S. J., Altschul, I., & Gershoff, E. T. (2015). Wait until your father gets home? Mothers' and fathers' spanking and development of child aggression. *Children and Youth Services Review, 52,* 158–166.

Lee, V. K., & Harris, L. T. (2014). Dehumanized perception: Psychological and neural mechanisms underlying everyday dehumanization. In P. G. Bain, J. Vaes, & J. Leyens (Eds.), *Humanness and dehumanization* (pp. 68–85). New York: Psychology Press.

Legault, L., Gutsell, J. N., & Inzlicht, M. (2011). Ironic effects of antiprejudice messages: How motivational interventions can reduce (but also increase) prejudice. *Psychological Science, 22,* 1472–1477.

Legault, L., Gutsell, J. N., and Inzlicht, M. (2012). Ironic effects of antiprejudice messages: How motivational interventions can reduce (but also increase) prejudice. *Psychological Science, 22,* 1472–1477.

Lehman, D. R., Chiu, C.-Y., & Schaller, M. (2004). Psychology and culture. *Annual Review of Psychology, 55,* 689–714.

Lehman, D. R., Lempert, R. O., & Nisbett, R. E. (1988). The effects of graduate training on reasoning: Formal discipline and thinking about everyday-life events. *American Psychologist, 43,* 431–442.

Leichtman, M. D., & Ceci, S. J. (1995). The effects of stereotypes and suggestions on preschoolers' reports. *Developmental Psychology, 31,* 568–578.

Leigh, B. C., & Stacy, A. W. (1993). Alcohol outcome expectancies: Scale construction and predictive utility in higher-order confirmatory models. *Psychological Assessment, 5,* 216–229.

Leiker, M., & Hailey, B. J. (1988). A link between hostility and disease: Poor health habits? *Behavioral Medicine, 14,* 129–133.

Leippe, M. R., & Eisenstadt, D. (1994). Generalization of dissonance reduction: Decreasing prejudice through induced compliance. *Journal of Personality and Social Psychology, 67,* 395–413.

Leiter, M. P., Bakker, A. B., & Maslach, C. (Eds.). (2014). *Burnout at Work: A psychological perspective.* New York: Psychology Press.

Lenhart, A., Kahne, J., Middaugh, E., Macgill, A. R., Evans, C., & Vitak, J. (2008, September 16). *Teens, video games, and civics.* Washington, DC: Pew Internet and American Life Project.

Leo, R. A. (1996). Inside the interrogation room. *Journal of Criminal Law and Criminology, 86,* 266–303.

Leo, R. A., & Liu, B. (2009). What do potential jurors know about police interrogation techniques and false confessions? *Behavioral Sciences & the Law, 27,* 381–399.

Lepore, L., & Brown, R. (2002). The role of awareness: Divergent automatic stereotype activation and implicit judgment correction. *Social Cognition, 20,* 321–351.

Lepore, S. J., & Smyth, J. M. (2002). *The writing cure: How expressive writing promotes health and emotional well-being.* Washington, DC: American Psychological Association.

Lepore, S. J., Ragan, J. D., & Jones, S. (2000). Talking facilitates cognitive-emotional processes of adaptation to an acute stressor. *Journal of Personality and Social Psychology, 78,* 499–508.

Lepper, M. R., & Greene, D. (Eds.). (1978). *The hidden costs of reward.* Hillsdale, NJ: Erlbaum.

Lepper, M. R., Greene, D., & Nisbett, R. E. (1973). Undermining children's intrinsic interest with extrinsic reward: A test of the "overjustification" hypothesis. *Journal of Personality and Social Psychology, 28,* 129–137.

Lepsinger, R., & Lucia, A. D. (2009). *The art and science of360-degree feedback* (2nd ed.). New York: Wiley.

Lerner, M. J. (1980). *The belief in a just world: A fundamental delusion.* New York: Plenum.

Lerner, M. J. (1998). The two forms of belief in a just world: Some thoughts on why and how people care about justice. In L. Montada, & M. J. Lerner (Eds.), *Responses to victimization and belief in a just world: Critical issues in social justice* (pp. 247–269). New York: Plenum.

Lerner, M. J., & Simmons, C. H. (1966). Observers' reaction to the "innocent victim": Compassion or rejection? *Journal of Personality and Social Psychology, 4,* 203–210.

Leslie, L. M., Mayer, D. M., & Kravitz, D. A. (2014). The stigma of affirmative action: A stereotyping-based theory and meta-analytic test of the consequences for performance. *Academy of Management Journal, 57,* 964–989.

Letourneau, E. J., Henggeler, S. W., Borduin, C. M., Schewe, P. A., McCart, M. R., Chapman, J. E., & Saldana, L. (2009). Multisystemic therapy for juvenile sexual offenders: 1-year results from a randomized effectiveness trial. *Journal of Family Psychology, 23,* 89–102.

Leung, A. K.-Y., & Cohen, D. (2011). Within- and between-culture variation: Individual differences and the cultural logics of honor, face, and dignity cultures. *Journal of Personality and Social Psychology, 100,* 507–526.

Levashina, J., & Campion, M. A. (2007). Measuring faking in the employment interview: Development and validation of an interview faking behavior scale. *Journal of Applied Psychology, 92,* 1638–1656.

LeVay, S. (1991). A difference in hypothalamic structure between heterosexual and homosexual men. *Science, 253,* 1034–1037.

Leventhal, H. (1970). Findings and theory in the study of fear communications. In L. Berkowitz (Ed.), *Advances in experimental social psychology* (Vol. 5, pp. 119–186). New York: Academic Press.

Leventhal, H., Watts, J. C., & Pagano, F. (1967). Effects of fear and instructions on how to cope with danger. *Journal of Personality and Social Psychology, 6,* 313–321.

Levesque, M. J. (1997). Meta-accuracy among acquainted individuals: A social relations analysis of interpersonal perception and metaperception. *Journal of Personality and Social Psychology, 72,* 66–74.

Levesque, M. J., Nave, C. S., & Lowe, C. A. (2006). Toward an understanding of gender differences in inferring sexual interest. *Psychology of Women Quarterly, 30,* 150–158.

Levi, A. S., & Fried, Y. (2008). Differences between African Americans and Whites in reactions to affirmative action programs in hiring, promotion, training, and layoffs. *Journal of Applied Psychology, 93,* 1118–1129.

Levin, D. T., & Banaji, M. R. (2006). Distortions in the perceived lightness of faces: The role of race categories. *Journal of Experimental Psychology: General, 135,* 501–512.

Levin, S., Pratto, F., Matthews, M., Sidanius, J., & Kteily, N. (2013). A dual process approach to understanding prejudice toward Americans in Lebanon: An extension to intergroup threat perceptions and emotions. *Group Processes & Intergroup Relations, 16,* 139–158.

Levin, S., Taylor, P. L., & Caudle, E. (2007). Interethnic and interracial dating in college: A longitudinal study of social psychological predictors and outcomes. *Journal of Social and Personal Relationships, 24,* 323–341.

Levine, J. M. (1989). Reaction to opinion deviance in small groups. In P. B. Paulus (Ed.), *Psychology of group influence* (2nd ed., pp. 187–231). Hillsdale, NJ: Erlbaum.

Levine, J. M., & Choi, H.-S. (2010). Newcomers as change agents: Minority influence in task groups. In R. Martin & M. Hewstone (Eds.), *Minority influence and innovation: Antecedents, processes, and consequences.* New York: Psychology Press.

Levine, J. M., & Smith, E. R. (2013). Group cognition: Collective information search and distribution. In D. E. Carlston (Ed.), *The Oxford handbook of social cognition* (pp. 616–633). New York: Oxford University Press.

Levine, M., & Manning, R. (2013). Social identity, group processes, and helping in emergencies. *European Review of Social Psychology, 24,* 225–251.

Levine, M., Prosser, A., Evans, D., & Reicher, S. (2005, April). Identity and emergency intervention: How social group membership and inclusiveness of group boundaries shape helping behavior. *Personality and Social Psychology Bulletin, 31,* 443–453.

Levine, R. A., & Campbell, D. T. (1972). Ethnocentrism: Theories of conflict, ethnic attitudes, and group behavior. New York: Wiley.

Levine, R. V., Norenzayan, A., & Philbrick, K. (2001). Cross-cultural differences in helping strangers. *Journal of Cross-Cultural Psychology, 32,* 543–560.

Levine, R. V., Reysen, S., & Ganz, E. (2008). The kindness of strangers revisited: A comparison of 24 US cities. *Social Indicators Research, 85,* 461–481.

Levine, R., Sato, S., Hashimoto, T., & Verma, J. (1995). Love and marriage in eleven cultures. *Journal of Cross-Cultural Psychology, 26,* 554–571.

Levinson, M. (2011). Social networks: New hotbed for hiring discrimination claims. *Computer World.* Retrieved from http://www.cio.com/article/2409045/careers-staffing/social-networks—a-new-hotbed-for-hiring-discrimination-claims.html.

Levy, D. A., & Nail, P. R. (1993). Contagion: A theoretical and empirical review and reconceptualization. *Genetic, Social, and General Psychology Monographs, 119,* 233–284.

Levy, S. R., Ramírez, L., Rosenthal, L., & Karafantis, D. M. (2013). The study of lay theories: A piece of the puzzle for understanding prejudice. In M. R. Banaji & S. A. Gelman (Eds.), *Navigating the social world: What infants, children, and other species can teach us* (pp. 318–322). New York: Oxford University Press.

Lewin, K. (1935). *A dynamic theory of personality.* New York: McGraw-Hill.

Lewin, K. (1947). Group decision and social change. In T. M. Newcomb & E. L. Hartley (Eds.), *Readings in social psychology* (pp. 330–344). New York: Holt.

Lewin, K. (1951). Problems of research in social psychology. In D. Cartwright (Ed.), *Field theory in social science* (pp. 155–169). New York: Harper & Row.

Lewis, M. (2015). *Flash Boys.* New York: W. W. Norton.

Lewis, M., & Brooks-Gunn, J. (1979). *Social cognition and the acquisition of self.* New York: Plenum.

Li, J., Nie, Y., Boardley, I. D., Situ, Q., & Dou, K. (2014). Moral disengagement moderates the predicted effect of trait self-control on self-reported aggression. *Asian Journal of Social Psychology, 17,* 312–318.

Li, N. P., & Kenrick, D. T. (2006). Sex similarities and differences in preferences for short-term mates: What, whether, and why. *Journal of Personality and Social Psychology, 90,* 468–489.

Li, N. P., Bailey, J. M., Kenrick, D. T., & Linsenmeier, J. A. W. (2002). The necessities and luxuries of mate preferences: Testing the tradeoffs. *Journal of Personality and Social Psychology, 82,* 947–955.

Li, Y., Wang, M., Wang, C., & Shi, J. (2010). Individualism, collectivism, and Chinese adolescents' aggression: Intracultural variations. *Aggressive Behavior, 36,* 187–194.

Liao, J., O'Brien, A. T., Jimmieson, N. L., & Restubog, S. D. (2015). Predicting transactive memory system in multidisciplinary teams: The interplay between team and professional identities. *Journal of Business Research, 68,* 965–977.

Libby, L. K., & Eibach, R. P. (2002). Looking back in time: Self-concept change affects visual perspective in autobiographical memory. *Journal of Personality and Social Psychology, 82,* 167–179.

Libby, L. K., Valenti, G., Pfent, A., & Eibach, R. P. (2011). Seeing failure in your life: Imagery perspective determines whether self-esteem shapes reactions to recalled and imagined failure. *Journal of Personality and Social Psychology, 101,* 1157–1173.

Liden, R. C., Wayne, S. J., Jaworski, R. A., & Bennett, N. (2004). Social loafing: A field investigation. *Journal of Management, 30,* 285–304.

Lieberman J., & Krauss D. (2009). *Jury psychology: Social aspects of the trial process.* Burlington, VT: Ashgate.

Lieberman, J. D. (2011). The utility of scientific jury selection: Still murky after 30 years. *Current Directions in Psychological Science, 20,* 48–52.

Lieberman, J. D., & Arndt, J. (2000). Understanding the limits of limiting instructions. *Psychology, Public Policy, and Law, 6,* 677–711.

Lieberman, J., & Sales, B. (2007). *Scientific jury selection.* Washington, DC: American Psychological Association.

Lieberman, M. D. (2013). *Social: Why our brains are wired to connect.* New York: Crown.

Lifton, R. J. (1986). *The Nazi doctors: Medical killing and the psychology of genocide.* New York: Basic Books.

Light, K. C., & Obrist, P. A. (1980). Cardiovascular response to stress: Effects of opportunity to avoid shock experience, and performance feedback. *Psychophysiology, 17,* 243–252.

Likert, R. (1932). A technique for the measurement of attitudes. *Archives of Psychology, 140,* 1–55.

Lim, J., & Guo, X. (2008). A study of group support systems and the intergroup setting. *Decision Support Systems, 45,* 452–460.

Lind, E. A., Erickson, B. E., Friedland, N., & Dickenberger, M. (1978). Reactions to procedural models for adjudicative conflict resolution: A cross national study. *Journal of Conflict Resolution, 22,* 318–341.

Lind, E. A., Kanfer, R., & Farley, P. C. (1990). Voice, control, and procedural justice: Instrumental and noninstrumental concerns in fairness judgments. *Journal of Personality and Social Psychology, 59,* 952–959.

Linde, J. A., Rothman, A. J., Baldwin, A. S., & Jeffery, R. W. (2006). The impact of self-efficacy on behavior change and weight change among overweight participants in a weight loss trial. *Health Psychology, 25,* 282–291.

Lindell, A. K., & Lindell, K. L. (2014). Beauty captures the attention of the beholder. *Journal of Cognitive Psychology, 26,* 768–780.

Linder, D. E., Cooper, J., & Jones, E. E. (1967). Decision freedom as a determinant of the role of incentive magnitude in attitude change. *Journal of Personality and Social Psychology, 6,* 245–254.

Lindsay, R. C. L., & Wells, G. L. (1985). Improving eyewitness identifications from lineups: Simultaneous versus sequential lineup presentations. *Journal of Applied Psychology, 70,* 556–564.

Lindsay, R. C. L., Lea, J. A., & Fulford, J. A. (1991). Sequential lineup presentation: Technique matters. *Journal of Applied Psychology, 76,* 741–745.

Lindsay, R. C. L., Ross, D. F., Read, J. D., & Toglia, M. P. (Eds.). (2007). *The handbook of eyewitness psychology*: Vol. 2. Memory for people. Mahwah, NJ: Erlbaum.

Lindsay, R. C. L., Semmler, C., Weber, N., Brewer, N., & Lindsay, M. R. (2008). How variations in distance affect eyewitness reports and identification accuracy. *Law and Human Behavior, 32,* 526–535.

Lindsay, R. C. L., Wells, G. L., & Rumpel, C. M. (1981). Can people detect eyewitness-identification accuracy within and across situations? *Journal of Applied Psychology*, 66, 79–89.

Lindsey, A., King, E., Hebl, M., & Levine, N. (2015). The impact of method, motivation, and empathy on diversity training effectiveness. *Journal of Business and Psychology, 30,* 605–617.

Linville, P. W., & Jones, E. E. (1980). Polarized appraisals of outgroup members. *Journal of Personality and Social Psychology, 38,* 689–703.

Linville, P. W., Fischer, G. W., & Fischoff, B. (1992). Perceived risk and decision making involving AIDS. In J. B. Pryor & G. D. Reeder (Eds.), *The social psychology of HIV infection*. Hillsdale, NJ: Erlbaum.

Linz, D., Donnerstein, E., & Penrod, S. (1987). The findings and recommendations of the Attorney General's Commission on Pornography: Do the psychological "facts" fit the political fury? *American Psychologist*, 42, 946–953.

Linz, D., Wilson, B. J., & Donnerstein, E. (1992). Sexual violence in the mass media: Legal solutions, warnings, and mitigation through education. *Journal of Social Issues, 48,* 145–171.

Lippa, R. A. (2006). Is high sex drive associated with increased sexual attraction to both sexes? *Psychological Science,* 17, 46–52.

Liptak, A. (2015). *Exclusion of blacks from juries raises renewed scrutiny.* The New York Times, August 16, 2015.

Liu, C. H., & Chen, W. F. (2012). Beauty is better pursued: Effects of attractiveness in multiple-face tracking. *The Quarterly Journal of Experimental Psychology, 65,* 553–564.

Livers, A. B., & Caver, K. A. (2003). *Leading in black and white: Working across the racial divide in corporate America*. San Francisco: Jossey-Bass.

Lobchuk, M. M., McClement, S. E., McPherson, C., & Cheang, M. (2008). Does blaming the patient with lung cancer affect the helping behavior of primary caregivers? *Oncology Nursing Forum*, 35, 681–689.

Lobel, M., Cannella, D. L., Graham, J. E., DeVincent, C., Schneider, J., & Meyer, B. A. (2008). Pregnancy-specific stress, prenatal health behaviors, and birth outcomes. *Health Psychology, 27,* 604–615.

Locke, E. A. (2000). *The prime movers: Traits of the great wealth creators*. New York: AMACOM.

Locke, E. A., & Latham, G. P. (1990). *A theory of goal setting and task performance*. Englewood Cliffs, NJ: Prentice Hall.

Locke, E. A., & Latham, G. P. (2002). Building a practically useful theory of goal setting and task motivation: A 35-year odyssey. *American Psychologist, 57,* 705–717.

Locke, K. (2009). Aggression, narcissism, self-esteem, and the attribution of desirable and humanizing traits to self versus others. *Journal of Research in Personality, 43,* 99–102.

Löckenhoff, C. E., Chan, W., et al. (2014). Gender stereotypes of personality: Universal and accurate? *Journal of Cross-Cultural Psychology, 45,* 675–694.

Lockhart v. McCree, 54 U.S.L.W. 4449 (1986).

Loersch, C., Bartholow, B. D., Manning, M., Calanchini, J., & Sherman, J. W. (2015). Intoxicated prejudice: The impact of alcohol consumption on implicitly and explicitly measured racial attitudes. *Group Processes & Intergroup Relations, 18,* 256–268.

Loewenstein, G. F., Weber, E. U., Hsee, C. K., & Welch, N. (2001). Risk as feelings. *Psychological Bulletin, 127,* 267–286.

Loftus, E. F. (1996). *Eyewitness testimony* (reprint ed.). Cambridge, MA: Harvard University Press.

Loftus, E. F. (2011). Intelligence gathering post 9/11. *American Psychologist, 66,* 532–541.

Loftus, E. F., & Ketcham, K. (1991). *Witness for the defense: The accused, the eyewitness, and the expert who puts memory on trial.* New York: St. Martin's Press.

Loftus, E. F., & Palmer, J. C. (1974). Reconstruction of automobile destruction: An example of the interaction between language and memory. *Journal of Verbal Learning and Verbal Behavior, 13,* 585–589.

Loftus, E. F., Loftus, G. R., & Messo, J. (1987). Some facts about "weapon focus." *Law and Human Behavior, 11,* 55–62.

Loftus, G. R., & Loftus, E. F., *Human memory: The processing of information*. Copyright © 1976.

Long, E. C. J., & Andrews, D. W. (1990). Perspective taking as a predictor of marital adjustment. *Journal of Personality and Social Psychology, 59,* 126–131.

Lopez, J. A. (1992, March 3). Study says women face glass walls as well as ceilings. *Wall Street Journal*, pp. B1, B8.

Lortie-Lussier, M. (1987). Minority influence and idiosyncrasy credit: A new comparison of the Moscovici and Hollander theories of innovation. *European Journal of Social Psychology, 17,* 431–446.

Lo Sasso, A. T., Richards, M. R., Chou, C.-F., & Gerber, S. E. (2011). The $16,819 pay gap for newly trained physicians: The unexplained trend of men earning more than women. *Health Affairs, 30,* 193–201.

Losch, M. E., & Cacioppo, J. T. (1990). Cognitive dissonance may enhance sympathetic tonus, but attitudes are changed to reduce negative affect rather than arousal. *Journal of Experimental Social Psychology, 26,* 289–304.

Lott, A. J., & Lott, B. E. (1974). The role of reward in the formation of positive interpersonal attitudes. In T. L. Huston (Ed.), *Foundations of interpersonal attraction* (pp. 171–189). New York: Academic Press.

Lott, B. (1985). The devaluation of women's competence. *Journal of Social Issues, 41,* 43–60.

Loughnan, S., Haslam, N., Sutton, R. M., & Spencer, B. (2014). Dehumanization and social class: Animality in the stereotypes of "white trash," "chavs," and "bogans." *Social Psychology, 45,* 54–61.

Loula, F., Prasad, S., Harber, K., & Shiffrar, M. (2005). Recognizing people from their movement. *Journal of Experimental Psychology: Human Perception & Performance, 31,* 210–220.

Lowe, K., Kroeck, K., & Sivasubramaniam, N. (1996). Effectiveness correlates of transformational and transactional leadership: A meta-analytic review of the MLQ literature. *Leadership Quarterly, 7,* 385–425.

Lu, L., Yuan, Y. C., & McLeod, P. L. (2012). Twenty-five years of hidden profiles in group decision making: A meta-analysis. *Personality and Social Psychology Review, 16,* 54–75.

Lucas, R. E. (2005). Time does not heal all wounds: A longitudinal study of reaction and adaptation to divorce. *Psychological Science, 16*, 945–950.

Lucas, R. E. (2007). Adaptation and the set-point model of subjective well-being: Does happiness change after major life events? *Current Directions in Psychological Science, 16*, 945–950.

Luhmann, M., Hofmann, W., Eid, M., & Lucas, R. E. (2012). Subjective well-being and adaptation to life events: A meta-analysis. *Journal of Personality and Social Psychology, 102*, 592–615.

Lukachko, A., Hatzenbuehler, M. L., & Keyes, K. M. (2014). Structural racism and myocardial infarction in the United States. *Social Science & Medicine, 103*, 42–50.

Luke, A. (2015, June 21). Worldwide terror fuels hate crimes in Britain; North report probes anti-Muslim attack links. *Sunday Sun*, p. 18.

Luminet, O., & Curci, A. (Eds.). (2009). *Flashbulb memories: New issues and new perspectives*. New York: Psychology Press.

Luo, S., & Klohnen, E. C. (2005). Assortative mating and marital quality in newlyweds: A couple-centered approach. *Journal of Personality and Social Psychology, 88*, 304–326.

Lutz, A., Slagter, H. A., Dunne, J. D., & Davidson, R. J. (2008). Attention regulation and monitoring in meditation. *Trends in the Cognitive Sciences, 12*, 163–169.

Luus, C. A. E., & Wells, G. L. (1994). The malleability of eyewitness confidence: Co-witness and perseverance effects. *Journal of Applied Psychology, 79*, 714–723.

Lydon, J. E. (2010). How to forego forbidden fruit: The regulation of attractive alternatives as a commitment mechanism. *Social and Personality Psychology Compass, 4*, 635–644.

Lykes, V. A., & Kemmelmeier, M. (2014). What predicts loneliness? Cultural difference between individualistic and collectivistic societies in Europe. *Journal of Cross-Cultural Psychology, 45*, 468–490.

Lykken, D. T. (2000). *Happiness: The nature and nurture of joy and contentment*. New York: St. Martin's Press.

Lykken, D. T., & Tellegen, A. (1993). Is human mating adventitious or the result of lawful choice? A twin study of mate selection. *Journal of Personality and Social Psychology, 65*, 56–68.

Lyness, K. S., & Thompson, D. E. (2000). Climbing the corporate ladder: Do female and male executives follow the same route? *Journal of Applied Psychology, 85*, 86–101.

Lynn, S. J., O'Donohue, W. T., & Lilienfeld, S. O. (Eds.). (2015). *Health, happiness, and well-being: Better living through psychological science*. Thousand Oaks, CA: Sage Publications.

Lyubomirsky, S., King, L., & Diener, E. (2005). The benefits of frequent positive affect: Does happiness lead to success? *Psychological Bulletin, 131*, 803–855.

Lyubomirsky, S. (2013). *The myths of happiness: What should make you happy, but doesn't, what shouldn't make you happy, but does*. New York: Penguin.

Ma, D. S., & Correll, J. (2011). Target prototypicality moderates racial bias in the decision to shoot. *Journal of Experimental Social Psychology, 47*, 391–396.

Ma, X., Jin, Y., Luo, B, Zhang, G., Wei, R., & Liu, D. (2015). Giant pandas failed to show mirror self-recognition. *Animal Cognition, 18*, 713–721.

Maass, A., & Clark, R. D., III. (1984). Hidden impact of minorities: Fifteen years of minority influence research. *Psychological Bulletin, 95*, 428–450.

Maass, A., & Kohnken, G. (1989). Eyewitness identification: Simulating the "weapon effect." *Law and Human Behavior, 13*, 397–408.

Maass, A., D'Ettole, C., & Cadinu, M. (2008). Checkmate? The role of gender stereotypes in the ultimate intellectual sport. *European Journal of Social Psychology, 38*, 231–245.

Maass, A., Volpato, C., & Mucchi-Faina, A. (1996). Social influence and the verifiability of the issue under discussion: Attitudinal versus objective items. *British Journal of Social Psychology, 35*, 15–26.

MacCoun, R. J., & Kerr, N. L. (1988). Asymmetric influence in mock jury deliberation: Jurors' bias for leniency. *Journal of Personality and Social Psychology, 54*, 21–33.

MacDonald, G., & Leary, M. R. (2005). Why does social exclusion hurt? The relationship between social and physical pain. *Psychological Bulletin, 131*, 202–223.

Macionis, J. J. (2014). *Sociology* (15th ed.). New York: Pearson.

Mackay, N., & Barrowclough, C. (2005). Accident and emergency staff's perceptions of deliberate self-harm: Attributions, emotions, and willingness to help. *British Journal of Clinical Psychology, 44*, 255–267.

Mackenzie, C. S., Gekoski, W. L., & Knox, V. J. (2006). Age, gender, and the underutilization of mental health services: The influence of help-seeking attitudes. *Aging & Mental Health, 10*, 574–582.

MacKenzie, M. J., Nicklas, E., Brooks-Gunn, J., & Waldfogel, J. (2015). Spanking and children's externalizing behavior across the first decade of life: Evidence for transactional processes. *Journal of Youth and Adolescence, 44*, 658–669.

Mackie, D. M., & Smith, E. R. (2015). Intergroup emotions. In M. Mikulincer, P. R. Shaver, J. F. Dovidio, & J. A. Simpson (Eds.), *APA handbook of personality and social psychology, Volume 2: Group processes* (pp. 263–293). Washington, DC: American Psychological Association.

Mackie, D. M., & Worth, L. T. (1989). Processing deficits and the mediation of positive affect in persuasion. *Journal of Personality and Social Psychology, 57*, 27–40.

Mackie, D. M., Asuncion, A. G., & Rosselli, F. (1992). Impact of positive affect on persuasion processes. *Review of Personality and Social Psychology, 14*, 247–270.

Mackie, D. M., Worth, L. T., & Asuncion, A. G. (1990). Processing of persuasive in-group messages. *Journal of Personality and Social Psychology, 58*, 812–822.

MacLeod, C., & Campbell, L. (1992). Memory accessibility and probability judgments: An experimental evaluation of the availability heuristic. *Journal of Personality and Social Psychology, 63*, 890–902.

MacNeil, S., & Byers, E. S. (2009). Role of sexual self-disclosure in the sexual satisfaction of long-term heterosexual couples. *Journal of Sex Research, 46*, 3–14.

Maddux, J. E. (1995). *Self-efficacy, adaptation, and adjustment: Theory, research, and application*. New York: Perseus.

Maddux, W. W., Bivolaru, E., Hafenbrack, A. C., Tadmor, C. T., & Galinsky, A. D. (2014). Expanding opportunities by opening your mind: Multicultural engagement predicts job market success through longitudinal increases in integrative complexity. *Social Psychological and Personality Science, 5*, 608–615.

Madera, J. M., & Hebl, M. R. (2012). Discrimination against facially stigmatized applicants in interviews: An eye-tracking and face-to-face investigation. *Journal of Applied Psychology, 97*, 317–330.

Madera, J. M., & Hebl, M. (2013). Social exclusion of individuals through interpersonal discrimination. In C. N. DeWall (Ed.), *The Oxford handbook of social exclusion* (pp. 55–64). New York, NY, US: Oxford University Press.

Madera, J. M., Hebl, M., Dial, H., Martin, R., & Valian, V. (2015). Raising doubt in letters of recommendation for prospective faculty: Gender differences and their impact. *Journal of Applied Psychology*, in press.

Madey, S. F., Simo, M., Dillworth, D., Kemper, D., Toczynski, A., & Perella, A. (1996). They do get more attractive at closing time, but only when you are not in a relationship. *Basic and Applied Social Psychology, 18*, 387–393.

Madon, S., Guyll, M., Aboufadel, K., Montiel, E., Smith, A., Palumbo, P., & Jussim, L. (2001). Ethnic and national stereotypes: The Princeton trilogy revisited and revised. *Personality and Social Psychology Bulletin, 27*, 996–1010.

Madon, S., Guyll, M., Scherr, K., Greathouse, S., & Wells, G. L. (2012). Temporal discounting: The differential effect of proximal and distal consequences on confession decisions. *Law and Human Behavior, 36,* 13–20.

Madon, S., Guyll, M., Spoth, R., Cross, S. E., & Hilbert, S. J. (2003). The self-fulfilling influence of mother expectations on children's underage drinking. *Journal of Personality and Social Psychology, 84,* 1188–1205.

Madon, S., Jussim, L., Keiper, S., Eccles, J., Smith, A., & Palumbo, P. (1998). The accuracy and power of sex, social class, and ethnic stereotypes: A naturalistic study in person perception. *Personality and Social Psychology Bulletin, 24,* 1304–1318.

Madon, S., Willard, J., Guyll, M., & Scherr, K. C. (2011). Self-fulfilling prophecies: Mechanisms, power, and links to social problems. *Social and Personality Psychology Compass, 5,* 578–590.

Madon, S., Willard, J., Guyll, M., Trudeau, L., & Spoth, R. (2006). Self-fulfilling prophecy effects of mothers' beliefs on children's alcohol use: Accumulation, dissipation, and stability over time. *Journal of Personality and Social Psychology, 90,* 911–926.

Mahr, K. (2015, Jan 22). Modi launches campaign to tackle India's dwindling number of girls. *Yahoo News.* http://news.yahoo .com/modi-launches-campaign-tackle-indias-dwindling-number -girls-121115347.html.

Maio, G. R., & Haddock, G. (2015). *The psychology of attitudes and attitude change* (2nd ed.). Thousand Oaks, CA: Sage Publications.

Maio, G., & Olson, J. M. (Eds.). (2000). *Why we evaluate: Functions of attitudes.* Mahwah, NJ: Erlbaum.

Maio, G. R., & Thomas, G. (2007). The epistemic-teleological model of self-persuasion. *Personality and Social Psychology Review, 11,* 46–67.

Maister, L., Slater, M., Sanchez-Vives, M. V., & Tsakiris, M. (2015). Changing bodies changes minds: Owning another body affects social cognition. *Trends in Cognitive Sciences, 19,* 6–12.

Major, B., & Crocker, J. (1993). Social stigma: The affective consequences of attributional ambiguity. In D. M. Mackie & D. L. Hamilton (Eds.), *Affect, cognition, and stereotyping: Interactive processes in intergroup perception* (pp. 345–370). New York: Academic Press.

Major, B., & Deaux, K. (1982). Individual differences in justice behavior. In J. Greenberg & R. L. Cohen (Eds.), *Equity and justice in social behavior* (pp. 13–76). New York: Academic Press.

Major, B., & Konar, E. (1984). An investigation of sex differences in pay expectations and their possible causes. *Academy of Management Journal, 27,* 777–792.

Major, B., Carrington, P. I., & Carnevale, P. J. D. (1984). Physical attractiveness and self-esteem: Attributions for praise from an other-sex evaluator. *Personality and Social Psychology Bulletin, 10,* 43–50.

Major, B., Feinstein, J., & Crocker, J. (1994). Attributional ambiguity of affirmative action. *Basic and Applied Social Psychology, 15,* 113–142.

Major, B., Hunger, J. M., Bunyan, D. P., & Miller, C. T. (2014). The ironic effects of weight stigma. *Journal of Experimental Social Psychology, 51,* 74–80.

Makhanova, A., Miller, S. L., & Maner, J. K. (2015). Germs and the out-group: Chronic and situational disease concerns affect intergroup categorization. *Evolutionary Behavioral Sciences, 9,* 8–19.

Malamuth, N. M., & Donnerstein, E. I. (1982). The effects of aggressive-pornographic mass media stimuli. In L. Berkowitz (Ed.), *Advances in experimental social psychology* (Vol. 15, pp. 103–136). New York: Academic Press.

Malamuth, N. M., Hald, G., & Koss, M. (2012). Pornography, individual differences in risk and men's acceptance of violence against women in a representative sample. *Sex Roles, 66,* 427–439.

Malkiel, B. G. (2007). *A random walk down Wall Street: The time-tested strategy for successful investing* (9th ed.). New York: Norton.

Malle, B. F., & Holbrook, J. (2012). Is there a hierarchy of social inferences? The likelihood and speed of inferring intentionality, mind, and personality. *Journal of Personality and Social Psychology, 102,* 661–684.

Malle, B. F., & Knobe, J. (1997). Which behaviors do people explain? A basic actor-observer asymmetry. *Journal of Personality and Social Psychology, 72,* 288–304.

Malloy, L. C., Shulman, E. P., & Cauffman, E. (2014). Interrogations, confessions, and guilty pleas among serious adolescent offenders. *Law and Human Behavior, 38,* 181–193.

Malloy, T. E., & Albright, L. (1990). Interpersonal perception in a social context. *Journal of Personality and Social Psychology, 58,* 419–428.

Malpass, R. S., & Devine, P. G. (1981). Eyewitness identification: Lineup instructions and the absence of the offender. *Journal of Applied Psychology, 66,* 482–489.

Malpass, R. S., & Kravitz, J. (1969). Recognition for faces of own and other race. *Journal of Personality and Social Psychology, 13,* 330–334.

Manago, A. M., Taylor, T., & Greenfield, P. M. (2012). Me and my 400 friends: The anatomy of college students' Facebook networks, their communication patterns, and well-being. *Developmental Psychology, 48,* 369–380.

Mancke, F., Herpertz, S. C., & Bertsch, K. (2015). Aggression in borderline personality disorder: A multidimensional model. *Personality Disorders: Theory, Research, and Treatment, 6,* 278–291.

Mandery, E. J. (2013). *A Wild Justice: The death and resurrection of capital punishment in America.* New York: W.W. Norton.

Maner, J. K., Miller, S. L., Moss, J. H., Leo, J. L., & Plant, E. (2012). Motivated social categorization: Fundamental motives enhance people's sensitivity to basic social categories. *Journal of Personality and Social Psychology, 103,* 70–83.

Maner, J. K., Kenrick, D. T., Becker, D. V., Delton, A. W., Hofer, B., Wilbur, C. J., & Neuberg, S. L. (2003). Sexually selective cognition: Beauty captures the mind of the beholder. *Journal of Personality and Social Psychology, 85,* 1107–1120.

Mann, J. M. (1992). AIDS—The second decade: A global perspective. *Journal of Infectious Diseases, 165,* 245–250.

Manning, R., Levine, M., & Collins, A. (2008). The legacy of the 38 witnesses and the importance of getting history right. *American Psychologist, 63,* 562–563.

Marcus-Newhall, A., Pedersen, W. C., Carlson, M., & Miller, N. (2000). Displaced aggression is alive and well: A meta-analytic review. *Journal of Personality and Social Psychology, 78,* 670–689.

Mares, M.-L., & Woodard, E. (2005). Positive effects of television on children's social interactions: A meta-analysis. *Media Psychology, 7,* 301–322.

Margolin, G., & Wampold, B. E. (1981). A sequential analysis of conflict and accord in distressed and nondistressed marital partners. *Journal of Consulting and Clinical Psychology, 49,* 554–567.

Marion, S. B., & Burke, T. M. (2013). False alibi corroboration: Witnesses lie for suspects who seem innocent, whether they like them or not. *Law and Human Behavior, 37,* 136–143.

Markey, P. M. (2000). Bystander intervention in computer-mediated communication. *Computers in Human Behavior, 16,* 183–188.

Marks, J. (2011). *The alternative introduction to biological anthropology.* New York: Oxford.

Markus, H. (1977). Self-schemata and processing information about the self. *Journal of Personality and Social Psychology, 35,* 63–78.

Markus, H. R. (2008). Pride, prejudice, and ambivalence: Toward a unified theory of race and ethnicity. *American Psychologist, 63,* 651–670.

Markus, H. R., & Conner, A. (2013). *Clash!: 8 cultural conflicts that make us who we are.* New York, NY: Hudson Street Press.

Markus, H. R., & Kitayama, S. (1991). Culture and the self: Implications for cognition, emotion, and motivation. *Psychological Review, 98,* 224–253.

Markus, H. R., & Lin, L. R. (1999). Conflictways: Cultural diversity in the meanings and practices of conflict. In D. A. Prentice & D. T. Miller (Eds.), *Cultural divides: Understanding and overcoming group conflict* (pp. 302–333). New York: Russell Sage.

Markus, H. R., Uchida, Y., Omoregie, H., Townsend, S. M., & Kitayama, S. (2006). Going for the gold: Models of agency in Japanese and American contexts. *Psychological Science, 17,* 103–112.

Markus, H., Hamill, R., & Sentis, K. P. (1987). Thinking fat: Self-schemas for body weight and the processing of weight-relevant information. *Journal of Applied Social Psychology, 17,* 50–71.

Marlowe, C. M., Schneider, S. L., & Nelson, C. E. (1996). Gender and attractiveness biases in hiring decisions: Are more experienced managers less biased? *Journal of Applied Psychology, 81,* 11–21.

Marsh, A. A., Stoycos, S. A., Brethel-Haurwitz, K. M., Robinson, P., VanMeter, J. W., & Cardinale, E. M. (2015). Neural and cognitive characteristics of extraordinary altruists. *PNAS Proceedings of the National Academy of Sciences of the United States of America, 111,* 15036–15041.

Martin, C. L., & Ruble, D. N. (2010). Patterns of gender development. *Annual Review of Psychology, 61,* 353–381.

Martin, J., & Govender, K. (2011). "Making muscle junkies": Investigating traditional masculine ideology, body image discrepancy, and the pursuit of muscularity in adolescent males. *International Journal of Men's Health, 10,* 220–239.

Marzoli, D., Custodero, M., Pagliara, A., & Tommasi, L. (2013). Sun-induced frowning fosters aggressive feelings. *Cognition and Emotion, 27,* 1513–1521.

Maslach, C. (1979). Negative emotional biasing of unexplained arousal. *Journal of Personality and Social Psychology, 37,* 953–969. Maslach, C. (1982). *Burnout: The cost of caring.* Englewood Cliffs, NJ: Prentice-Hall.

Maslach, C. (1982). *Burnout: The cost of caring.* Englewood Cliffs, NJ: Prentice-Hall.

Mason, M. F., Tatkow, E. P., & Macrae, C. N. (2005). The look of love: Gaze shifts and person perception. *Psychological Science, 16,* 236–239.

Masser, B., Lee, K., & McKimmie, B. M. (2010). Bad woman, bad victim? Disentangling the effects of victim stereotypicality, gender stereotypicality and benevolent sexism on acquaintance rape victim blame. *Sex Roles, 62,* 494–504.

Masten, A. S. (2001). Ordinary magic: Resilience processes in development. *American Psychologist, 56,* 227–238.

Masuda, T., & Nisbett, R. E. (2006). Culture and change blindness. *Cognitive Science, 30,* 381–399.

Masuda, T., Gonzalez, R., Kwan, L., & Nisbett, R. E. (2008). Culture and aesthetic preference: Comparing the attention to context of East Asians and Americans. *Personality and Social Psychology Bulletin, 34,* 1260–1275.

Mathieu, J. E., Kukenberger, M. R., D'Innocenzo, L., & Reilly, G. (2015). Modeling reciprocal team cohesion–performance relationships, as impacted by shared leadership and members' competence. *Journal of Applied Psychology, 100,* 713–734.

Mathur, M., & Chattopadhyay, A. (1991). The impact of moods generated by TV programs on responses to advertising. *Psychology and Marketing, 8,* 59–77.

Matthews, K. A. (1988). Coronary heart disease and Type A behaviors: Update on and alternative to the Booth-Kewley and Friedman (1987) quantitative review. *Psychological Bulletin, 104,* 373–380.

Matthews, K. A. (2005). Psychological perspectives on the development of coronary heart disease. *American Psychologist, 60,* 783–796.

Matthews, K. A. (2013). Matters of the heart: Advancing psychological perspectives on cardiovascular diseases. *Perspectives on Psychological Science, 8,* 676–678.

Matthews, K. A., & Gallo, L. C. (2011). Psychological perspectives on pathways linking socioeconomic status and physical health. *Annual Review of Psychology, 62,* 501–530.

Matz, D. C., & Wood, W. (2005). Cognitive dissonance in groups: The consequences of disagreement. *Journal of Personality and Social Psychology, 88,* 22–37.

Mauss, I. B., Tamir, M., Anderson, C. L., & Savino, N. S. (2011). Can seeking happiness make people unhappy? Paradoxical effects of valuing happiness. *Emotion, 11,* 807–815.

Mazar, N., & Zhong, C. B. (2010). Do green products make us better people? *Psychological Science, 21,* 494–498.

Mazar, N., Amir, O., & Ariely, D. (2008). The dishonesty of honest people: a theory of self-concept maintenance. *Journal of Marketing Research,* 633–644.

Mazerolle, L., et al. (2014). *Procedural Justice and Legitimacy in Policing.* New York: Springer.

McAdams, D. P. (1989). *Intimacy: The need to be close.* New York: Doubleday.

McAndrew, F. T., & Perilloux, C. (2012). Is self-sacrificial competitive altruism primarily a male activity? *Evolutionary Psychology, 10,* 50–65.

McArthur, L. A. (1972). The how and what of why: Some determinants and consequences of causal attribution. *Journal of Personality and Social Psychology, 22,* 171–193.

McCabe, M. P., Ricciardelli, L. A., & Holt, K. (2010). Are there different sociocultural influences on body image and body change strategies for overweight adolescent boys and girls? *Eating Behaviors, 11,* 156–163.

McCarthy, E. (2009, April 24). On dating: Shared qualities for a successful relationship. *The Washington Post.*

McCarty-Gould, C. (2000). *Crisis and chaos: Life with the combat veteran.* New York: Nova Kroshka Books.

McCrae, R. R., & Costa, P. T., Jr. (2003). *Personality in adulthood: A five-factor theory perspective* (2nd ed.). New York: Guilford Press.

McCrae, R. R., Chan, W., Jussim, L., et al. (2013). The inaccuracy of national character stereotypes. *Journal of Research in Personality, 47,* 831–842.

McCreary, D. R. (2011). Body image and muscularity. In T. F. Cash & L. Smolak (Eds.), *Body image: A handbook of science, practice, and prevention* (2nd ed.) (pp. 198–205). New York: Guilford Press.

McCullough, M. E., Hoyt, W. T., Larson, D. B., Koenig, H. G., & Thoresen, C. (2000). Religious involvement and mortality: A meta-analytic review. *Health Psychology, 19,* 211–222.

McDonnell, G. P., Bornstein, B. H., Laub, C. E., Mills, M., & Dodd, M. D. (2014). Perceptual processes in the cross-race effect: Evidence from eyetracking. *Basic and Applied Social Psychology, 36,* 478–493.

McDougall, W. (1908). *An introduction to social psychology.* London: Methuen.

McEachern, A. D., & Snyder, J. (2012). Gender differences in predicting antisocial behaviors: Developmental consequences of physical and relational aggression. *Journal of Abnormal Child Psychology, 40,* 501–512.

McElwee, R. O., Dunning, D., Tan, P. L., & Hollmann, S. (2001). Evaluating others: The role of who we are versus what we think traits mean. *Basic and Applied Social Psychology, 23,* 123–136.

McGarty, C., Turner, J. C., Hogg, M. A., David, B., et al. (1992). Group polarization as conformity to the prototypical group member. *British Journal of Social Psychology, 31,* 1–19.

McGuire, J. (2008). A review of effective interventions for reducing aggression and violence. *Philosophical Transactions of the Royal Society B,* 1–21.

McGuire, W. J. (1964). Inducing resistance to persuasion. In L. Berkowitz (Ed.), *Advances in experimental social psychology* (Vol. 1, pp. 192–229). New York: Academic Press.

McGuire, W. J. (1967). Some impending reorientations in social psychology: Some thoughts provoked by Kenneth Ring. *Journal of Experimental Social Psychology, 3,* 124–139.

McGuire, W. J. (1968). Personality and susceptibility to social influence. In E. F. Borgatta & W. W. Lambert (Eds.), *Handbook of personality theory and research* (pp. 1130–1187). Chicago: Rand McNally.

McGuire, W. J. (1969). The nature of attitudes and attitude change. In G. Lindzey & E. Aronson (Eds.), *Handbook of social psychology* (2nd ed., Vol. 3, pp. 136–314). Reading, MA: Addison-Wesley.

McGuire, W. J., & McGuire, C. V (1988). Content and process in the experience of self. In L. Berkowitz (Ed.), *Advances in experimental social psychology* (Vol. 20, pp. 97–144). New York: Academic Press.

McGuire, W. J., McGuire, C. V., & Winton, W. (1979). Effects of household sex composition on the salience of one's gender in the spontaneous self-concept. *Journal of Experimental Social Psychology 15*, 77–90.

McKelvey, T. (2007). *Monstering: Inside America's policy of secret interrogations and torture in the terror war*. New York: Basic Books.

McKenna, K. Y. A., & Bargh, J. A. (1998). Coming out in the age of the Internet: "Demarginalization" through virtual group participation. *Journal of Personality and Social Psychology, 75*, 681–694.

McKimmie, B. M., Terry, D. J., & Hogg, M. A. (2009). Dissonance reduction in the context of group membership: The role of meta-consistency. *Group Dynamics: Theory, Research, and Practice, 13*, 103–119.

McLeish, K. N., & Oxoby, R. J. (2011). Social interactions and the salience of social identity. *Journal of Economic Psychology, 32*, 172–178.

McNatt, D. B. (2000). Ancient Pygmalion joins contemporary management: A meta-analysis of the result. *Journal of Applied Psychology, 85*, 314–322.

McPherson, M., Smith-Lovin, L., & Cook, J. M. (2001). Birds of a feather: Homophily in social networks. *Annual Review of Sociology, 27*, 415–444.

Mead, G. H. (1934). *Mind, self, and society*. Chicago: University of Chicago Press.

Mealey, L., Bridgstock, R., & Townsend, G. C. (1999). Symmetry and perceived facial attractiveness: A monozygotic co-twin comparison. *Journal of Personality and Social Psychology, 76*, 151–158.

Medvec, V. H., & Savitsky, K. (1997). When doing better means feeling worse: The effects of categorical cutoff points on counterfactual thinking and satisfaction. *Journal of Personality and Social Psychology, 72*, 1284–1296.

Medvec, V. H., Madey, S. F., & Gilovich, T. (1995). When less is more: Counterfactual thinking and satisfaction among Olympic medalists. *Journal of Personality and Social Psychology, 69*, 603–610.

Meeus, W. H. J., & Raaijmakers, Q. A. W. (1995). Obedience in modern society: The Utrecht studies. *Journal of Social Issues, 51*, 155–175.

Mehta, P. H., & Prasad, S. (2015). The dual-hormone hypothesis: A brief review and future research agenda. *Current Opinion in Behavioral Sciences, 3*, 163–168.

Meier, B. P., Schnall, S., Schwarz, N., & Bargh, J. A. (2012). Embodiment in social psychology. *Topics in Cognitive Science, 4*, 705–716.

Meineri, S., & Guéguen, N. (2011). "I hope I'm not disturbing you, am I?" Another operationalization of the foot-in-the-mouth paradigm. *Journal of Applied Social Psychology, 41*, 965–975.

Meissner, C. A., & Brigham, J. C. (2001). 30 years of investigating the own-race bias in memory for faces: A meta-analytic review. *Psychology, Public Policy, and Law, 7*, 3–35.

Meissner, C. A., & Kassin, S. M. (2002). "He's guilty!" Investigator bias in judgments of truth and deception. *Law and Human Behavior, 26*, 469–480.

Meissner, C. A., Brigham, J. C., & Pfeifer, J. E. (2003). Jury nullification: The influence of judicial instruction on the relationship between attitudes and juridic decision-making. *Basic and Applied Social Psychology, 25*, 243–254.

Meissner, C. A., Susa, K. J., & Ross, A. B. (2013). Can I see your passport please? Perceptual discrimination of own- and other-race faces. *Visual Cognition, 21*, 1287–1305.

Meixner, J. B., & Rosenfeld, J. P. (2014). Detecting knowledge of incidentally acquired, real-world memories using a P300-based concealed-information test. *Psychological Science, 25*, 1994–2005.

Melki, J. P., Hitti, E. A., Oghia, M. J., & Mufarrij, A. A. (2015). Media exposure, mediated social comparison to idealized images of muscularity, and anabolic steroid use. *Health Communication, 30*, 473–484.

Mell, J. N., Knippenberg, D. V., & Ginkel Van, W. P. (2014). The catalyst effect: The impact of transactive memory system structure on team performance. *Academy of Management Journal, 57*, 1154–1173.

Meltzoff, A. N., & Moore, M. K. (1977). Imitation of facial and manual gestures by human neonates. *Science, 198*, 75–78.

Mendel, R., Traut-Mattausch, E., Jonas, E., Leucht, S., Kane, J. M., Maino, K., Kissling, W., & Hamann, J. (2011). Confirmation bias: why psychiatrists stick to wrong preliminary diagnoses. *Psychological Medicine, 41*, 2651–2659.

Mendes, W. B., Blascovich, J., Lickel, B., & Hunter, S. (2002). Challenge and threat during social interaction with white and black men. *Personality and Social Psychology Bulletin, 28*, 939–952.

Mendonca, P. J., & Brehm, S. S. (1983). Effects of choice on behavioral treatment of overweight children. *Journal of Social and Clinical Psychology, 1*, 343–358.

Mendoza-Denton, R., & Page-Gould, E. (2008). Can cross-group friendships influence minority students' well-being at historically white universities? *Psychological Science, 19*, 933–939.

Menzer, M. M., & Torney-Purta, J. (2012). Individualism and socioeconomic diversity at school as related to perceptions of the frequency of peer aggression in fifteen countries. *Journal of Adolescence, 35*, 1285–1294.

Mercier, H., Trouche, E., Yama, H., Heintz, C., & Girotto, V. (2015). Experts and laymen grossly underestimate the benefits of argumentation for reasoning. *Thinking & Reasoning, 21*, 341–355.

Merikle, P., & Skanes, H. E. (1992). Subliminal self-help audiotapes: A search for placebo effects. *Journal of Applied Psychology, 77*, 772–776.

Merritt, A. C., Effron, D. A., & Monin, B. (2010). Moral self-licensing: When being good frees us to be bad. *Social and Personality Psychology Compass, 4*, 344–357.

Merritt, A. C., Effron, D. A., Fein, S., Savitsky, K. K., Tuller, D. M., & Monin, B. (2012). The strategic pursuit of moral credentials. *Journal of Experimental Social Psychology, 48*, 774–777.

Mescher, K., & Rudman, L. A. (2014). Men in the mirror: The role of men's body shame in sexual aggression. *Personality and Social Psychology Bulletin, 40*, 1063–1075.

Meslec, N., & Curşeu, P. L. (2013). Too close or too far hurts: Cognitive distance and group cognitive synergy. *Small Group Research, 44*, 471–497.

Mesmer-Magnus, J., & DeChurch, L. (2009). Information sharing and team performance: A meta-analysis. *Journal of Applied Psychology, 94*, 535–546.

Mesmer-Magnus, J. R., DeChurch, L. A., Jimenez-Rodriguez, M., Wildman, J., & Shuffler, M. (2011). A meta-analytic investigation of virtuality and information sharing in teams. *Organizational Behavior and Human Decision Processes, 115*, 214–225.

Messick, D. M., & Cook, K. S. (Eds.). (1983). *Equity theory: Psychological and sociological perspectives*. New York: Praeger.

Meston, C. M., & Frohlich, P. F. (2003). Love at first sight: Partner salience moderates roller-coaster-induced excitation transfer. *Archives of Sexual Behavior, 32*, 537–544.

Mesurado, B., et al. (2014). Parental expectations and prosocial behavior of adolescents from low-income backgrounds: A cross-cultural comparison between three countries—Argentina, Colombia, and Spain. *Journal of Cross-Cultural Psychology, 45,* 1471–1488.

Metalsky, G. I., Joiner, T. E., Hardin, T. S., & Abramson, L. Y. (1993). Depressive reactions to failure in a naturalistic setting: A test of the hopelessness and self-esteem theories of depression. *Journal of Abnormal Psychology, 102,* 101–109.

Meyers-Levy, J., Zhu, R., & Jiang, L. (2010). Context effects from bodily sensations: examining bodily sensations induced by flooring and the moderating role of product viewing distance. *Journal of Consumer Research, 37,* 1–14.

Mezulis, A. H., Abramson, L. Y., Hyde, J. S., & Hankin, B. L. (2004). Is there a universal positivity bias in attributions? A meta-analytic review of individual, developmental, and cultural differences in the self-serving attributional bias. *Psychological Bulletin, 130,* 711–747.

Mezzacappa, E. S., Katkin, E. S., & Palmer, S. N. (1999). Epinephrine, arousal, and emotion: A new look at two-factor theory. *Cognition and Emotion, 13,* 181–199.

Michelle, C. (2012). Co-constructions of gender and ethnicity in New Zealand television advertising. *Sex Roles, 66,* 21–37.

Mickelson, K. D., Kessler, R. C., & Shaver, P. R. (1997). Adult attachment in a nationally representative sample. *Journal of Personality and Social Psychology, 73,* 1092–1106.

Midlarsky, E., Fagan Jones, S., & Corley, R. P. (2005). Personality correlates of heroic rescue during the Holocaust. *Journal of Personality, 73,* 907–934.

Miklikowska, M., & Fry, D. P. (2010). Values for peace: Ethnographic lessons from the Mardu of Australia and the Semai of Malaysia. *Beliefs and Values, 2,* 124–137.

Mikolajewski, A. J., Chavarria, J., Moltisanti, A., Hart, S. A., & Taylor, J. (2014). Examining the factor structure and etiology of prosociality. *Psychological Assessment, 26,* 1259–1267.

Mikulincer, M., & Shaver, P. R. (2007). *Attachment patterns in adulthood: Structure, dynamics, and change.* New York: Guilford.

Miles, J. A., & Greenberg, J. (1993). Using punishment threats to attenuate social loafing effects among swimmers. *Organizational Behavior and Human Decision Processes, 56,* 246–265.

Milgram, S. (1963). Behavioral study of obedience. *Journal of Abnormal and Social Psychology, 67,* 371–378.

Milgram, S. (1970). The experience of living in cities. *Science, 167,* 1461–1468.

Milgram, S. (1974). *Obedience to authority: An experimental view.* New York: Harper & Row.

Milgram, S., & Toch, H. (1969). Collective behavior: Crowds and social movements. In G. Lindzey & E. Aronson (Eds.), *The handbook of social psychology* (2nd ed., Vol. 4, pp. 507–610). Reading, MA: Addison-Wesley.

Milgram, S., & Sabini, J. (1978). On maintaining urban norms: A field experiment in the subway. In A. Baum, J. E. Singer, & S. Valins (Eds.), *Advances in environmental psychology* (Vol. 1). Hillsdale, NJ: Erlbaum.

Milgram, S., Bickman, L., & Berkowitz, L. (1969). Note on the drawing power of crowds of different size. *Journal of Personality and Social Psychology, 13,* 79–82.

Milkman, K. L., Modupe, A., & Chugh, D. (2015). What happens before? A field experiment exploring how pay and representation differentially shape bias on the pathway into organizations.

Millar, M. (2002). Effects of guilt induction and guilt reduction on door in the face. *Communication Research, 29,* 666–680.

Miller-El v. Dretke, 545 U.S. 231 (2005).

Miller, A. G. (1986). *The obedience experiments: A case study of controversy in social science.* New York: Praeger.

Miller, A. G., Gordon, A. K., & Buddie, A. M. (1999). Accounting for evil and cruelty: Is to explain to condone? *Personality and Social Psychology Review, 3,* 254–268.

Miller, A. G., Jones, E. E., & Hinkle, S. (1981). A robust attribution error in the personality domain. *Journal of Experimental Social Psychology, 17,* 587–600.

Miller, D. T., & Prentice, D. A. (2016). Changing norms to change behavior. *Annual Review of Psychology, 67,* in press.

Miller, E. (2011). "There are no words that can possibly express how we feel": Toward an understanding of the social-psychological experiences of caregivers of the mentally ill. *Illness, Crisis, & Loss, 19,* 381–386.

Miller, G., Chen, E., & Cole, S. W. (2009). Health psychology: Developing biologically plausible models linking the social world and physical health. *Annual Review of Psychology, 60,* 501–524.

Miller, J. G. (1984). Culture and the development of everyday social explanation. *Journal of Personality and Social Psychology, 46,* 961–978.

Miller, J. G., Das, R., & Chakravarthy, S. (2011). Culture and the role of choice in agency. *Journal of Personality and Social Psychology, 101,* 46–61.

Miller, J. G., et al. (2014). Culture and the role of exchange vs. Communal norms in friendship. *Journal of Experimental Social Psychology, 53,* 79–93.

Miller, M. K., & Hayward, R. D. (2008). Religious characteristics and the death penalty. *Law and Human Behavior, 32,* 113–123.

Miller, N. E. (1941). The frustration-aggression hypothesis. *Psychological Review, 48,* 337–342.

Miller, N., & Campbell, D. T. (1959). Recency and primacy in persuasion as a function of the timing of speeches and measurements. *Journal of Abnormal and Social Psychology, 59,* 1–9.

Miller, R. S. (2012). *Intimate relationships* (6th ed.). New York: McGraw-Hill.

Miller, T. Q., Smith, T. W., Turner, C. W., Guijarro, M. L., & Hallet, A. J. (1996). A meta-analytic review of research on hostility and physical health. *Psychological Bulletin, 119,* 322–348.

Miller, T. Q., Turner, C. W., Tindale, R. S., Posavac, E. J., & Dugon, B. L. (1991). Reasons for the trend toward null findings in research on Type A behavior. *Psychological Bulletin, 110,* 469–485.

Miller, W. R. (1985). Motivation for treatment: A review with special emphasis on alcoholism. *Psychological Bulletin, 98,* 84–107.

Miller, W. R., & Thoresen, C. E. (2003). Spirituality, religion, and health: An emerging research field. *American Psychologist, 58,* 24–35.

Milliken, C. S., Auchterlonie, J. L., & Hoge, C. W. (2007). Longitudinal assessment of mental health problems among active and reserve component soldiers returning from the Iraq war. *JAMA: Journal of the American Medical Association, 298,* 2141–2148.

Milton, A. C., & Mullan, B. A. (2012). An application of the theory of planned behavior—A randomized controlled food safety pilot intervention for young adults. *Health Psychology, 31,* 250–259.

Mioshi, E., Bristow, M., Cook, R., & Hodges, J. R. (2009). Factors underlying caregiver stress in frontotemporal dementia and Alzheimer's disease. *Dementia and Geriatric Cognitive Disorders, 27,* 76–81.

Miranda, S. M. (1994). Avoidance of groupthink: Meeting management using group support systems. *Small Group Research, 25,* 105–136.

Mita, T. H., Dermer, M., & Knight, J. (1977). Reversed facial images and the mere exposure hypothesis. *Journal of Personality and Social Psychology, 35,* 597–601.

Mitchell, T. R. (1974). Expectancy models of job satisfaction, occupational preference, and effort: A theoretical, methodological, and empirical appraisal. *Psychological Bulletin, 81,* 1096–1112.

Miyamoto, Y., & Kitayama, S. (2002). Cultural variation in correspondence bias: The critical role of attitude diagnosticity of socially constrained behavior. *Journal of Personality and Social Psychology, 83,* 1239–1248.

Mobius, M. M., & Rosenblat, T. S. (2006). Why beauty matters. *American Economic Review, 96,* 222–235.

Moffitt, T. E., Arseneault, L., et al. (2011). A gradient of childhood self-control predicts health, wealth, and public safety. *PNAS Proceedings of The National Academy of Sciences of The United States of America, 108,* 2693–2698.

Mojaverian, T., & Kim, H. S. (2013). Interpreting a helping hand: Cultural variation in the effectiveness of solicited and unsolicited social support. *Personality and Social Psychology Bulletin, 39,* 88–99.

Mojza, E. J., Sonnentag, S., & Bornemann, C. (2011). Volunteer work as a valuable leisure-time activity: A day-level study on volunteer work, non-work experiences, and well-being at work. *Journal of Occupational and Organizational Psychology, 84,* 123–152.

Molden, D. C., & Hui, C. M. (2011). Promoting de-escalation of commitment: A regulatory-focus perspective on sunk costs. *Psychological Science, 22,* 8–12.

Molden, D. C., Hui, C. M., Scholer, A. A., Meier, B. P., Noreen, E. E., D'Agostino, P. R., & Martin, V. (2012). Motivational versus metabolic effects of carbohydrates on self-control. *Psychological Science, 23,* 1137–1144.

Moll, J., Krueger, F., Zahn, R., Pardini, M., de Oliveira-Souza, R., & Grafman, J. (2006). Human fronto-mesolimbic networks guide decisions about charitable donation. *PNAS Proceedings of The National Academy of Sciences of the United States of America, 103,* 15623–15628.

Monat, A., Lazarus, R. S., & Reevy, G. (Eds.). (2007). *The Praeger handbook on stress and coping.* New York: Praeger.

Mondschein, E. R., Adolph, K. E., & Tamis-LeMonda, C. S. (2000). Gender bias in mothers' expectations about infant crawling. *Journal of Experimental Child Psychology, 77,* 304–316.

Andrew Monroe and Glenn Reeder, 2014.

Montag, C., Weber, B., Trautner, P., Newport, B., Markett, S., Walter, N. T., & . . . Reuter, M. (2012). Does excessive play of violent first-person-shooter-video-games dampen brain activity in response to emotional stimuli? *Biological Psychology, 89,* 107–111.

Montañés, P., de Lemus, S., Bohner, G., Megías, J. L., Moya, M., & Garcia-Retamero, R. (2012). Intergenerational transmission of benevolent sexism from mothers to daughters and its relation to daughters' academic performance and goals. *Sex Roles, 66,* 468–478.

Monteith, M. J., & Mark, A. Y. (2009). The self-regulation of prejudice. In T. D. Nelson (Ed.), *Handbook of prejudice, stereotyping, and discrimination* (pp. 507–523). New York: Psychology Press.

Monteith, M. J., Ashburn-Nardo, L., Voils, C. I., & Czopp, A. M. (2002). Putting the brakes on prejudice: On the development and operation of cues for control. *Journal of Personality and Social Psychology, 83,* 1029–1050.

Monteith, M. J., Mark, A. Y., & Ashburn-Nardo, L. (2010). The self-regulation of prejudice: Toward understanding its lived character. *Group Processes & Intergroup Relations, 13,* 183–200.

Monteith, M. J., Woodcock, A., & Gulker, J. E. (2013). Automaticity and control in stereotyping and prejudice: The revolutionary role of social cognition across three decades of research. In D. E. Carlston (Ed.), *The Oxford handbook of social cognition* (pp. 74–94). New York: Oxford University Press.

Montoya, R.M., & Horton, R.S. (2013). A meta-analytic investigation into the processes underlying the similarity effect. *Journal of Social and Personal Relationships, 30,* 64–94.

Montoya, R. M., & Horton, R. S. (2014). A two-dimensional model for the study of interpersonal attraction. *Personality and Social Psychology Review, 18,* 59–86.

Montoya, R. M., Horton, R. S., & Kirchner, J. (2008). Is actual similarity necessary for attraction? A meta-analysis of actual and perceived similarity. *Journal of Social and Personal Relationships, 25,* 889–922.

Moon, H. (2001). Looking forward and looking back: Integrating completion and sunk-cost effects within an escalation-of-commitment progress decision. *Journal of Applied Psychology, 86,* 104–113.

Moon, T. (2013). The effects of cultural intelligence on performance in multicultural teams. *Journal of Applied Social Psychology, 43,* 2414–2425.

Moore, C., Detert, J. R., Treviño, L. K., Baker, V. L., & Mayer, D. M. (2012). Why employees do bad things: Moral disengagement and unethical organizational behavior. *Personnel Psychology, 65,* 1–48.

Moore, T. E. (1982). Subliminal advertising: What you see is what you get. *Journal of Marketing, 46,* 38–47.

Mor, N., & Winquist, J. (2002). Self-focused attention and negative affect: A meta-analysis. *Psychological Bulletin, 128,* 638–662.

Mor, S., Morris, M., & Joh, J. (2013). Identifying and training adaptive cross-cultural management skills: The crucial role of cultural metacognition. *Academy of Management Learning & Education, 12,* 453–475.

Moran, G., & Comfort, C. (1986). Neither "tentative" nor "fragmentary": Verdict preference of impaneled felony jurors as a function of attitude toward capital punishment. *Journal of Applied Psychology, 71,* 146–155.

Moran, G., & Cutler, B. L. (1991). The prejudicial impact of pretrial publicity. *Journal of Applied Social Psychology, 21,* 345–367.

Moran, J. M., Heatherton, T. F., & Kelley, W. M. (2009). Modulation of cortical midline structure by implicit and explicit self-relevance evaluation. *Social Neuroscience, 4,* 197–211.

Moreland, R. L., & Beach, S. R. (1992). Exposure effects in the classroom: The development of affinity among students. *Journal of Experimental Social Psychology, 28,* 255–276.

Moreland, R. L., & Levine, J. M. (2002). Socialization and trust in work groups. *Group Processes and Intergroup Relations, 5,* 185–201.

Morelli, S. A., Lieberman, M. D., & Zaki, J. (2015). The emerging study of positive empathy. *Social and Personality Psychology Compass, 9,* 57–68.

Morelli, S. A., Rameson, L. T., & Lieberman, M. D. (2014). The neural components of empathy: Predicting daily prosocial behavior. *Social Cognitive and Affective Neuroscience, 9,* 39–47.

Morewedge, C. K., Preston, J., & Wegner, D. M. (2007). Timescale bias in the attribution of mind. *Journal of Personality and Social Psychology, 93,* 1–11.

Morgan, C. A., Hazlett, G., Doran, A., Garrett, S., Hoyt, G., Thomas, P., et al. (2004). Accuracy of eyewitness memory for persons encountered during exposure to highly intense stress. *International Journal of Law and Psychiatry, 27,* 265–279.

Morgan, C. A., III, Southwick, S., Steffian, G., Hazlett, G. A., & Loftus, E. F. (2013). Misinformation can influence memory for recently experienced, highly stressful events. *International Journal of Law and Psychiatry, 36,* 11–17.

Morgan, W. B., Elder, K. B., & King, E. B. (2013). The emergence and reduction of bias in letters of recommendation. *Journal of Applied Social Psychology, 43,* 2297–2306.

Morgan, M., & Shanahan, J. (2010). The state of cultivation. *Journal of Broadcasting & Electronic Media, 54,* 337–355.

Morgeson, F. P., Campion, M. A., Dipboye, R. L., Hollenbeck, J. R., Murphy, K., & Schmitt, N. (2007). Reconsidering the use of personality tests in personnel contexts. *Personnel Psychology, 60,* 683–729.

Morgeson, F. P., Mumford, T. V., & Campion, M. A. (2005). Coming full circle: Using research and practice to address 27 questions about 360-degree feedback programs. *Consulting Psychology Journal: Practice and Research, 57,* 196–209.

Moriarty, T. (1975). Crime, commitment, and the responsive bystander: Two field experiments. *Journal of Personality and Social Psychology, 31,* 370–376.

Morr Serewicz, M. C., & Gale, E. (2008). First-date scripts: Gender roles, context, and relationship. *Sex Roles, 58,* 149–164.

Morrison, A. M., & Von Glinow, M. A. (1990). Women and minorities in management. *American Psychologist, 45,* 200–208.

Morrison, K., & Chung, A. H. (2011). "White" or "European American"? Self-identifying labels influence majority group members' interethnic attitudes. *Journal of Experimental Social Psychology, 47,* 165–170.

Morrison, M., Tay, L., & Diener, E. (2011). Subjective well-being and national satisfaction: Findings from a worldwide survey. *Psychological Science, 22,* 166–171.

Morrongiello, B. A., & Dawber, T. (2000). Mothers' responses to sons and daughters engaging in injury-risk behaviors on a playground: Implications for sex differences in injury rates. *Journal of Experimental Child Psychology, 76,* 89–103.

Morrongiello, B. A., Zdzieborski, D., & Normand, J. (2010). Understanding gender differences in children's risk taking and injury: A comparison of mothers' and fathers' reactions to sons and daughters misbehaving in ways that lead to injury. *Journal of Applied Developmental Psychology, 31,* 322–329.

Moscatelli, S., Albarello, F., Prati, F., & Rubini, M. (2014). Badly off or better off than them? The impact of relative deprivation and relative gratification on intergroup discrimination. *Journal of Personality and Social Psychology, 107,* 248–264.

Moscovici, S. (1980). Toward a theory of conversion behavior. In L. Berkowitz (Ed.), *Advances in Experimental Social Psychology, 6,* 149–202.

Moscovici, S., & Personnaz, B. (1991). Studies in social influence VI: Is Lenin orange or red? Imagery and social influence. *European Journal of Social Psychology, 21,* 101–118.

Moscovici, S., & Zavalloni, M. (1969). The group as a polarizer of attitudes. *Journal of Personality and Social Psychology, 12,* 125–135.

Moscovici, S., Lage, E., & Naffrechoux, M. (1969). Influence of a consistent minority on the responses of a majority in a color perception task. *Sociometry, 32,* 365–380.

Moscovici, S., Mugny, G., & Van Avermaet, E. (Eds.). (1985). *Perspectives on minority influence.* New York: Cambridge University Press.

Moskalenko, S., & Heine, S. J. (2003). Watching your troubles away: Television viewing as a stimulus for subjective self-awareness. *Personality and Social Psychology Bulletin, 29,* 76–85.

Moskowitz, G. B. (2014). The implicit volition model: The unconscious nature of goal pursuit. In J. W. Sherman, B. Gawronski, & Y. Trope (Eds.), *Dual-process theories of the social mind* (pp. 400–422). New York: Guilford Press.

Mosquera, P. R., Tan, L. X., & Saleem, F. (2014). Shared burdens, personal costs on the emotional and social consequences of family honor. *Journal of Cross-Cultural Psychology, 45,* 400–416.

Mostofsky, E., Maclure, M., Sherwood, J. B., Tofler, G. H., Muller, J. E., & Mittleman, M. A. (2012). Risk of acute myocardial infarction after the death of a significant person in one's life: The determinants of myocardial infarction onset study. *Circulation, 125,* 491–496.

Moss-Racusin, C. A., Dovidio, J. F., Brescoll, V. L., Graham, M. J., & Handelsman, J. (2012). Science faculty's subtle gender biases favor male students. *PNAS Proceedings of The National Academy of Sciences of the United States of America, 109,* 16474–16479.

Mouton, J., Blake, R., & Olmstead, J. (1956). The relationship between frequency of yielding and the disclosure of personal identity. *Journal of Personality, 24,* 339–347.

Moynihan, J. A., & Ader, R. (1996). Psychoneuroimmunology: Animal models of disease. *Psychosomatic Medicine, 58,* 546–558.

Mueller, J. H. (1982). Self-awareness and access to material rated as self-descriptive and nondescriptive. *Bulletin of the Psychonomic Society, 19,* 323–326.

Mugny, G., & Perez, J. A. (1991). *Social psychology of minority influence.* Cambridge: Cambridge University Press.

Mullen, B. (1983). Operationalizing the effect of the group on the individual: A self-attention perspective. *Journal of Experimental Social Psychology, 19,* 295–322.

Mullen, B. (1985). Strength and immediacy of sources: A meta-analytic evaluation of the forgotten elements of social impact theory. *Journal of Personality and Social Psychology, 48,* 1458–1466.

Mullen, B., Johnson, C., & Salas, E. (1991). Productivity loss in brainstorming groups: A meta-analytic integration. *Basic and Applied Social Psychology, 12,* 3–23.

Mullen, E., & Skitka, L. J. (2009). Comparing Americans' and Ukrainians' allocations of public assistance: The role of affective reactions in helping behavior. *Journal of Cross-Cultural Psychology, 40,* 301–318.

Muraven, M., & Baumeister, R. F. (1998). Self-control as a limited resource: Regulatory depletion patterns. *Journal of Personality and Social Psychology, 74,* 774–789.

Muraven, M., & Baumeister, R. F. (2000). Self-regulation and depletion of limited resources: Does self-control resemble a muscle? *Psychological Bulletin, 126,* 247–259.

Murphy, M. M., Slavich, G. M., Chen, E., & Miller, G. E. (2015). Targeted rejection predicts decreased anti-inflammatory gene expression and increased symptom severity in youth with asthma. *Psychological Science, 26,* 111–121.

Murphy, K. R., & Balzer, W. K. (1986). Systematic distortions in memory-based behavior ratings and performance evaluation: Consequences for rating accuracy. *Journal of Applied Psychology, 71,* 39–44.

Murphy, K. R., & Cleveland, J. N. (1995). *Understanding performance appraisal: Social, organizational, and goal-based perspectives.* Thousand Oaks, CA: Sage.

Murphy, K. R., Cronin, B. E., & Tam, A. P. (2003). Controversy and consensus regarding the use of cognitive ability testing in organizations. *Journal of Applied Psychology, 88,* 660–671.

Murphy, K., Cleveland, J., Skattebo, A., & Kinney, T. (2004). Raters who pursue different goals give different ratings. *Journal of Applied Psychology, 89,* 158–164.

Murphy, N. A., et al. (2015). Reliability and validity of nonverbal thin slices in social interactions. *Personality and Social Psychology Bulletin, 41,* 199–213.

Murphy, R. O., & Ackermann, K. A. (2014). Social value orientation: Theoretical and measurement issues in the study of social preferences. *Personality and Social Psychology Review, 18,* 13–41.

Murphy, V (2012). Woman dies during chat on Facebook. *The Mirror,* March 28, p. 14.

Murray, G., Judd, F., Jackson, H., Komiti, A., Wearing, A., Robins, G., et al. (2008). Big boys don't cry: An investigation of stoicism and its mental health outcomes. *Personality and Individual Differences, 44,* 1369–1381.

Murray, S. L., & Holmes, J. G. (1999). The (mental) ties that bind: Cognitive structures that predict relationship resilience. *Journal of Personality and Social Psychology, 77,* 1228–1244.

Murray, S. L., & Holmes, J. G. (2008). The commitment insurance system: Self-esteem and the regulation of connection in close relationships. *Advances in Experimental Social Psychology, 40,* 1–60.

Murray, S. L., & Holmes, J. G. (2011). *Interdependent minds: The dynamics of close relationships.* New York: Guilford Press.

Murray, S. L., Aloni, M., Holmes, J. G., Derrick, J. L., Stinson, D. A., & Leder, S. (2009). Fostering partner dependence as trust insurance: The implicit contingencies of the exchange script in close relationships. *Journal of Personality and Social Psychology, 96,* 324–348.

Murray, S. L., Holmes, J. G., & Collins, N. L. (2006). Optimizing assurance: The risk regulation system in relationships. *Psychological Bulletin, 132,* 641–666.

Murray, S. L., Holmes, J. G., & Griffin, D. W. (1996). The benefits of positive illusions: Idealization and the construction of satisfaction in close relationships. *Journal of Personality and Social Psychology, 70,* 79–98.

Murray, S. L., Holmes, J. G., Griffin, D. W., & Derrick, J. L. (2015). The equilibrium model of relationship maintenance. *Journal of Personality and Social Psychology, 108,* 93–113.

Murstein, B. I. (1986). *Paths to marriage.* Beverly Hills, CA: Sage.

Mussweiler, T., & Damisch, L. (2008). Going back to Donald: How comparisons shape judgmental priming effects. *Journal of Personality and Social Psychology, 95,* 1295–1315.

Mussweiler, T., & Rüter, K. (2003). What friends are for! The use of routine standards in social comparison. *Journal of Personality and Social Psychology, 85,* 467–481.

Mussweiler, T., & Strack, F. (2000). The "relative self": Informational and judgmental consequences of comparative self-evaluation. *Journal of Personality and Social Psychology, 79,* 23–38.

Myers, D. G., & Diener, E. (1995). Who is happy? *Psychological Science,* 6, 10–19.

Myers, D. G., & Lamm, H. (1976). The group polarization phenomenon. *Psychological Bulletin, 83,* 602–627.

Myllyneva, A., & Hietanen, J. K. (2015). There is more to eye contact than meets the eye. *Cognition, 134,* 100–109.

Na, J., & Kitayama, S. (2011). Spontaneous trait inference is culture-specific: Behavioral and neural evidence. *Psychological Science, 22,* 1025–1032.

Nacoste, R. W. (1996). Social psychology and the affirmative action debate. *Journal of Social and Clinical Psychology, 15,* 261–282.

Nadler, A., & Halabi, S. (2015). Helping relations and inequality between individuals and groups. In M. Mikulincer, P. R. Shaver, J. F. Dovidio, & J. A. Simpson (Eds.), *APA handbook of personality and social psychology, Volume 2: Group processes* (pp. 371–393). Washington, DC: American Psychological Association.

Nair, S., Sagar, M., Sollers, J. I., Consedine, N., & Broadbent, E. (2015). Do slumped and upright postures affect stress responses? A randomized trial. *Health Psychology, 34,* 632–641.

Narchet, F. M., Meissner, C. A., & Russano, M. B. (2011). Modeling the influence of investigator bias on the elicitation of true and false confessions. *Law and Human Behavior, 35,* 452–465.

Nash, R. A., & Wade, K. A. (2009). Innocent but proven guilty: Using false video evidence to elicit false confessions and create false beliefs. *Applied Cognitive Psychology, 23,* 624–637.

National Law Journal. (1990, September 10). *Rock group not liable for deaths.* p. 33.

National Research Council, Committee to Review the Scientific Evidence on the Polygraph, Division of Behavioral and Social Sciences and Education. (2003). *The polygraph and lie detection.* Washington, DC: National Academies Press.

Nazione, S., & Silk, K. J. (2013). Patient race and perceived illness responsibility: Effects on provider helping and bias. *Medical Education, 47,* 780–789.

Nederveen Pieterse, A., van Knippenberg, D., & van Dierendonck, D. (2013). Cultural diversity and team performance: The role of team member goal orientation. *Academy of Management Journal, 56,* 782–804.

Neel, R., & Shapiro, J. R. (2012). Is racial bias malleable? Whites' lay theories of racial bias predict divergent strategies for interracial interactions. *Journal of Personality and Social Psychology, 103,* 101–120.

Neil, C. J. Nguyen, T. H. . . . Horowitz, J. D. (2015). Relation of delayed recovery of myocardial function after Takotsubo cardiomyopathy to subsequent quality of life. *The American Journal of Cardiology, 115,* 1085–1089.

Nelson, T. D. (2011). Ageism: The strange case of prejudice against the older you. In R. L. Wiener & S. L. Willborn (Eds.), *Disability and aging discrimination: Perspectives in law and psychology* (pp 37–47). New York: Springer.

Nelson, T. D. (2015). *The handbook of prejudice, stereotyping, and discrimination* (2nd ed.). NY: Psychology Press.

Nemeth, C. (1986). Differential contributions of majority and minority influence. *Psychological Review, 93,* 23–32.

Nemeth, C., & Kwan, J. (1987). Minority influence, divergent thinking, and detection of correct solutions. *Journal of Applied Social Psychology, 17,* 788–799.

Nemeth, C., Mayseless, O., Sherman, J., & Brown, Y. (1990). Exposure to dissent and recall of information. *Journal of Personality and Social Psychology, 58,* 429–437.

Nemeth, C. J. (2016). *Rogues, rebels and dissent: Just because everyone agrees, doesn't mean they're right.* New York: Random House.

Nemeth, C. J., Connell, J. B., Rogers, J. D., & Brown, K. S. (2001). Improving decision making by means of dissent. *Journal of Applied Social Psychology, 31,* 48–58.

"Nepali man bites snake to death in revenge attack" (2012). *Reuters,* August 23.

Nes, L. S., & Segerstrom, S. C. (2006). Dispositional optimism and coping: A meta-analytic review. *Personality and Social Psychology Review, 10,* 235–251.

Neuman, W. R., Marcus, G. E., Crigler, A. N., & MacKuen, M. (Eds.). (2007). *The affect effect: Dynamics of emotion in political thinking and behavior.* Chicago: University of Chicago Press.

Neumann, R., & Strack, F. (2000). "Mood contagion": The automatic transfer of mood between persons. *Journal of Personality and Social Psychology, 79,* 211–223.

Newby-Clark, I. R., McGregor, I., & Zanna, M. P. (2002). Thinking and caring about cognitive inconsistency: When and from whom does attitudinal ambivalence feel uncomfortable? *Journal of Personality and Social Psychology, 82,* 157–166.

Newcomb, T. M. (1943). *Personality and social change: Attitude formation in a student community.* Ft. Worth, TX: Dryden Press.

Newcomb, T. M. (1961). *The acquaintance process.* New York: Holt, Rinehart and Winston.

Newheiser, A., & Barreto, M. (2014). Hidden costs of hiding stigma: Ironic interpersonal consequences of concealing a stigmatized identity in social interactions. *Journal of Experimental Social Psychology, 52,* 58–70.

Newheiser, A., & Olson, K. R. (2012). White and Black American children's implicit intergroup bias. *Journal of Experimental Social Psychology, 48,* 264–270.

Newheiser, A., Barreto, M., Ellemers, N., Derks, B., & Scheepers, D. (2015). Regulatory focus moderates the social performance of individuals who conceal a stigmatized identity. *British Journal of Social Psychology,* in press.

Newman, C. (2000, January). The enigma of beauty. *National Geographic,* pp. 94–121.

Newman, R. S. (2005). The cocktail party effect in infants revisited: Listening to one's name in noise. *Developmental Psychology, 41,* 352–362.

Newport, F. (2015). In U.S., 87% approve of black-white marriage, vs. 4% in 1958. *Gallup.* http://www.gallup.com/poll/163697/approve-marriage-blacks-whites.

Newton, E. K., Laible, D., Carlo, G., Steele, J. S., & McGinley, M. (2014). Do sensitive parents foster kind children, or vice versa? Bidirectional influences between children's prosocial behavior and parental sensitivity. *Developmental Psychology, 50,* 1808–1816.

Newtson, D. (1974). Dispositional inference from effects of actions: Effects chosen and effects foregone. *Journal of Experimental Social Psychology, 10,* 487–496.

Newtson, D., Hairfield, J., Bloomingdale, J., & Cutino, S. (1987). The structure of action and interaction. *Social Cognition, 5,* 191–237.

Ng, K. Y., & Van Dyne, L. (2005). Antecedents and performance consequences of helping behavior in work groups: A multilevel analysis. *Group and Organization Management, 30,* 514–540.

Ng, T. W. H., & Feldman, D. C. (2015). Ethical leadership: Meta-analytic evidence of criterion-related and incremental validity. *Journal of Applied Psychology, 100,* 948–965.

Ng, W., & Diener, E. (2014). What matters to the rich and the poor? Subjective well-being, financial satisfaction, and postmaterialist needs across the world. *Journal of Personality and Social Psychology, 107,* 326–338.

Nibler, R., & Harris, K. L. (2003). The effects of culture and cohesiveness in collectivistic and individualistic work groups: A cross-cultural analysis. *Journal of Organizational Behavior, 24,* 979–1001.

Nickerson, A. B., Aloe, A. M., Livingston, J. A., & Feeley, T. H. (2014). Measurement of the bystander intervention model for bullying and sexual harassment. *Journal of Adolescence, 37,* 391–400.

Nickerson, C., Schwarz, N., Diener, E., & Kahneman, D. (2003). Zeroing in on the dark side of the American dream: A closer look at the negative consequences of the goal for financial success. *Psychological Science, 14,* 531–536.

Niedenthal, P. M., Barsalou, L. W., Winkielman, P., Krauth-Gruber, S. & Ric, F. (2005). Embodiment in attitudes, social perception, and emotion. *Personality and Social Psychology Review, 9,* 184–211.

Niedermeier, K. E., Horowitz, I. A., & Kerr, N. L. (1999). Informing jurors of their nullification power: A route to a just verdict or judicial chaos? *Law and Human Behavior, 23,* 331–351.

Nier, J. A., & Gaertner, S. L. (2012). The challenge of detecting contemporary forms of discrimination. *Journal of Social Issues, 68,* 207–220.

Nieva, V F., & Gutek, B. A. (1981). *Women and work: A psychological perspective.* New York: Praeger.

Nisbett, R. E. (2003). *The geography of thought: How Asians and Westerners think differently . . . and why.* New York: Free Press.

Nisbett, R. E., & Cohen, D. (1996). *Culture of honor: The psychology of violence in the South.* Boulder, CO: Westview.

Nisbett, R. E., & Ross, L. (1980). *Human inference: Strategies and shortcomings of social judgment.* Englewood Cliffs, NJ: Prentice-Hall.

Nisbett, R. E., & Wilson, T. D. (1977). Telling more than we can know: Verbal reports on mental processes. *Psychological Review, 84,* 231–259.

Niv, S., Tuvblad, C., Raine, A., & Baker, L. A. (2013). Aggression and rule-breaking: Heritability and stability of antisocial behavior problems in childhood and adolescence. *Journal of Criminal Justice, 41,* 285–291.

Nock, M., Park, J., Finn, C., Deliberto, T., Dour, H., & Banaji, M. (2010). Measuring the suicidal mind: Implicit cognition predicts suicidal behavior. *Psychological Science, 21,* 511–517.

Nolen-Hoeksema, S. (1991). Responses to depression and their effects on the duration of depressive episodes. *Journal of Abnormal Psychology, 100,* 569–582.

Nolen-Hoeksema, S., & Girgus, J. S. (1994). The emergence of gender differences in depression during adolescence. *Psychological Bulletin, 115,* 424–443.

Nolen-Hoeksema, S., & Morrow, J. (1991). A prospective study of depression and posttraumatic stress symptoms after a natural disaster: The 1989 Loma Prieta earthquake. *Journal of Personality and Social Psychology, 61,* 115–121.

Nolen-Hoeksema, S., Wisco, B. E., & Lyubomirsky, S. (2008). Rethinking rumination. *Perspectives on Psychological Science, 3,* 400–424.

Norenzayan, A., & Nisbett, R. E. (2000). Culture and causal cognition. *Current Directions in Psychological Science, 9,* 132–135.

North, A. C., Hargreaves, D. J., & McKendrick, J. (1999). The influence of in-store music on wine selections. *Journal of Applied Psychology, 84,* 271–276.

North, M. S., & Fiske, S. T. (2014). Social categories create and reflect inequality: Psychological and sociological insights. In J. T. Cheng, J. L. Tracy, & C. Anderson (Eds.), *The psychology of social status* (pp. 243–265). New York: Springer.

North, M. S., & Fiske, S. T. (2015). Modern attitudes toward older adults in the aging world: A cross-cultural meta-analysis. *Psychological Bulletin, 141,* 993–1021.

Northouse, P. G. (2013). *Leadership: Theory and practice* (6th ed.). Thousand Oaks, CA: Sage.

Norton, K. I., Olds, T. S., Olive, S., & Dank, S. (1996). Ken and Barbie at life size. *Sex Roles, 34,* 287–294.

Norton, M. I., Sommers, S. R., Apfelbaum, E. P., Pura, N., & Ariely D. (2006). Color blindness and interracial interaction: Playing the political correctness game. *Psychological Science, 17,* 949–953.

Norton, M. I., Sommers, S. R., Vandello, J. A., & Darley, J. M. (2006). Mixed motives and racial bias: The impact of legitimate and illegitimate criteria on decision making. *Psychology, Public Policy, and Law, 12,* 36–55.

Nosek, B. A., Alter, G., et al. (2015). Promoting an open research culture. *Science, 348.*

Nosek, B. A., Banaji, M. R., & Greenwald, A. G. (2002). Harvesting implicit attitudes and stereotype data from the Implicit Association Test website. *Group Dynamics, 6,* 101–115.

Nosek, B. A., Hawkins, C. B., & Frazier, R. S. (2011). Implicit social cognition: From measures to mechanisms. *Trends in Cognitive Sciences, 15,* 152–159.

Nosenzo, D., Quercia, S., & Sefton, M. (2015). Cooperation in small groups: The effect of group size. *Experimental Economics, 18,* 4–14.

Nosko, A., Tieu, T.-T., Lawford, H., & Pratt, M. W. (2011). How do I love thee? Let me count the ways: Parenting during adolescence, attachment styles, and romantic narratives in emerging adulthood. *Developmental Psychology, 47,* 645–657.

O'Brien, B. (2009). Prime suspect: An examination of factors that aggravate and counteract confirmation bias in criminal investigations. *Psychology, Public Policy, and Law, 15,* 315–334.

O'Connor, S. C., & Rosenblood, L. K. (1996). Affiliation motivation in everyday experience: A theoretical comparison. *Journal of Personality and Social Psychology, 70,* 513–522.

O'Keefe, D. J., & Figge, M. (1997). A guilt-based explanation of the door-in-the-face influence strategy. *Human Communication Research, 42,* 64–81.

O'Keeffe, G. S., & Clarke-Pearson, K. (2011). The impact of social media on children, adolescents, and families. *Pediatrics, 127,* 800–804.

O'Leary-Kelly, A. M., Bowes-Sperry, L., Bates, C. A., & Lean, E. R. (2009). Sexual harassment at work: A decade (plus) of progress. *Journal of Management, 35,* 503–536.

O'Leary, A., & Wolitski, R. J. (2009). Moral agency and the sexual transmission of HIV *Psychological Bulletin, 135*(3): 478–494.

O'Leary, K. D., & Smith, D. A. (1991). Marital interaction. *Annual Review of Psychology, 42,* 191–212.

O'Leary, K. D., Tintle, N., & Bromet, E. (2014). Risk factors for physical violence against partners in the U.S. *Psychology of Violence, 4,* 65–77.

O'Mara, S. (2009). Torturing the brain. *Trends in the Cognitive Sciences, 13,* 497–500.

O'Neil, K. M., Patry, M. W., & Penrod, S. D. (2004). Exploring the effects of attitudes toward the death penalty on capital sentencing verdicts. *Psychology, Public Policy, and Law, 10,* 443–470.

O'Neill, A. M., Green, M., & Cuadros, P. (1996, September 2). *People,* 72.

Obergefell v. Hodges, 576 U.S. ___ (June 26, 2015).

Oceja, L., & Salgado, S. (2013). Why do we help? World change orientation as an antecedent of prosocial action. *European Journal of Social Psychology, 43,* 127–136.

Oda, R., et al. (2014). Personality and altruism in daily life. *Personality and Individual Differences, 56,* 206–209.

Oetzel, J., Garcia, A. J., & Ting-Toomey, S. (2008). An analysis of the relationships among face concerns and facework behaviors in perceived conflict situations: A four-culture investigation. *International Journal of Conflict Management, 19,* 382–403.

Ogilvy, D. (1985). *Ogilvy on advertising.* New York: Vintage Books.

Olczak, P. V, Kaplan, M. F., & Penrod, S. (1991). Attorneys' lay psychology and its effectiveness in selecting jurors: Three empirical studies. *Journal of Social Behavior and Personality, 6,* 431–452.

Oliver, M. G., & Hyde, J. S. (1993). Gender differences in sexuality: A meta-analysis. *Psychological Bulletin, 114,* 29–51.

Olson, E. A., & Wells, G. L. (2004). What Makes a Good Alibi? A Proposed Taxonomy. *Law and Human Behavior, 28,* 157–176.

Olson, J. M., Vernon, P. A., Harris, J. A., & Jang, K. L. (2001). The heritability of attitudes: A study of twins. *Journal of Personality and Social Psychology, 80,* 845–860.

Olson, M. A., & Fazio, R. H. (2001). Implicit attitude formation through classical conditioning. *Psychological Science, 12,* 413–417.

Olweus, D., & Limber, S. P. (2010). Bullying in school: Evaluation and dissemination of the Olweus Bullying Prevention Program. *American Journal of Orthopsychiatry, 80,* 124–134.

Omarzu, J. (2000). A disclosure decision model: Determining how and when individuals will self-disclose. *Personality and Social Psychology Review, 4,* 174–185.

Omoto, A. M., & Snyder, M. (1995). Sustained helping without obligation: Motivation, longevity of service, and perceived attitude change among AIDS volunteers. *Journal of Personality and Social Psychology, 68,* 671–686.

Omoto, A. M., Malsch, A. M., & Barraza, J. A. (2009). Compassionate acts: Motivations for and correlates of volunteerism among older adults. In B. Fehr, S. Sprecher, & L. G. Underwood (Eds.), *The science of compassionate love: Theory, research, and applications.* Malden, MA: Wiley-Blackwell.

Ones, D. S., Viswesvaran, C., & Schmidt, F. L. (1993). Comprehensive meta-analysis of integrity test validities: Findings and implications for personnel selection and theories of job performance. *Journal of Applied Psychology, 78,* 679–703.

Ong, D., & Wang, J. (2015). Income attraction: An online dating field experiment. *Journal of Economic Behavior & Organization, 111,* 13–22.

Ongley, S. F., Nola, M., & Malti, T. (2014). Children's giving: Moral reasoning and moral emotions in the development of donation behaviors. *Frontiers in Psychology, 5.*

Orenstein, P. (1994). *Schoolgirls: Young women, self-esteem, and the confidence gap.* New York: Anchor Books.

Orobio de Castro, B., Veerman, J. W., Koops, W., Bosch, J. D., & Monshouwer, H. J. (2002). Hostile attribution of intent and aggressive behavior: A meta-analysis. *Child Development, 73,* 916–934.

Orth, U., Robins, R. W., & Widaman, K. F. (2012). Life-span development of self-esteem and its effects on important life outcomes. *Journal of Personality and Social Psychology, 102,* 1271–1288.

Orth, U., Trzesniewski, K. H., & Robins, R. W. (2010). Self-esteem development from young adulthood to old age: A cohort-sequential longitudinal study. *Journal of Personality and Social Psychology, 98,* 645–658.

Orwell, G. (1942). Looking back on the Spanish War. In S. Orwell & I. Angus (Eds.), *The collected essays, journalism and letters of George Orwell: Vol. 2. My country right or left, 1940–1943* (pp. 249–267). New York: Harcourt, Brace & World.

Osborn, A. F. (1953). *Applied imagination.* New York: Scribner.

Osterman, L. L., & Brown, R. P. (2011). Culture of honor and violence against the self. *Personality and Social Psychology Bulletin, 37,* 1611–1623.

Oswald, F. L., Mitchell, G., Blanton, H., Jaccard, J., & Tetlock, P. E. (2015). Using the IAT to predict ethnic and racial discrimination: Small effect sizes of unknown societal significance. *Journal of Personality and Social Psychology, 108,* 562–571.

Otis, C. C., Greathouse, S. M., Kennard, J. B., & Kovera, M. B. (2014). Hypothesis testing in attorney-conducted voir dire. *Law and Human Behavior, 38,* 392–404.

Ottoni-Wilhelm, M., Estell, D. B., & Perdue, N. H. (2014). Role-modeling and conversations about giving in the socialization of adolescent charitable giving and volunteering. *Journal of Adolescence, 37,* 53–66.

Overbeek, G., Nelemans, S. A., Karremans, J., & Engels, R. C. (2013). The malleability of mate selection in speed-dating events. *Archives of Sexual Behavior, 42,* 1163–1171.

Owe, E., Vignoles, V. L., et al. (2013). Contextualism as an important facet of individualism-collectivism: Personhood beliefs across 37 national groups. *Journal of Cross-Cultural Psychology, 44,* 24–45.

Oxley, D. R., Smith, K., Alford, J., Hibbing, M., Miller, J., Scalora, M., Hatemi, P., & Hibbing, J. (2008). Political attitudes vary with physiological traits. *Science, 321,* 667–1670.

Oxley, N. L., Dzindolet, M. T., & Paulus, P. B. (1996). The effects of facilitators on the performance of brainstorming groups. *Journal of Social Behavior and Personality, 11,* 633–646.

Oyserman, D., & Lee, S. W. (2008). Does culture influence what and how we think? Effects of priming individualism and collectivism. *Psychological Bulletin, 134,* 311–342.

Oyserman, D., Coon, H. M., & Kemmelmeier, M. (2002). Rethinking individualism and collectivism: Evaluation of theoretical assumptions and meta-analyses. *Psychological Bulletin, 128,* 3–72.

Ozer, E. J., Best, S. R., Lipsey, T. L., & Weiss, D. S. (2003). Predictors of post-traumatic stress disorder and symptoms in adults: A meta-analysis. *Psychological Bulletin, 129,* 52–71.

Özgen, E. (2004). Language, learning, and color perception. *Current Directions in Psychological Science, 13,* 95–98.

Pabian, S., De Backer, C. S., & Vandebosch, H. (2015). Dark Triad personality traits and adolescent cyber-aggression. *Personality and Individual Differences, 75,* 41–46.

Pachur, T., Hertwig, R., & Steinmann, F. (2012). How do people judge risks: Availability heuristic, affect heuristic, or both? *Journal of Experimental Psychology: Applied, 18,* 314–330.

Packard, V. (1957). *The hidden persuaders.* New York: Pocket Books.

Packer, D. J. (2008). Identifying systematic disobedience in Milgram's obedience experiments. *Perspectives on Psychological Science, 3,* 301–304.

Packer, D. J. (2014). On not airing our dirty laundry: Intergroup contexts suppress ingroup criticism among strongly identified group members. *British Journal of Social Psychology, 53,* 93–111.

Packer, D. J., Fujita, K., & Chasteen, A. L. (2014). The motivational dynamics of dissent decisions: A goal-conflict approach. *Social Psychological and Personality Science, 5,* 27–34.

Páez, D., Rimé, B., Basabe, N., Wlodarczyk, A., & Zumeta, L. (2015). Psychosocial effects of perceived emotional synchrony in collective gatherings. *Journal of Personality and Social Psychology, 108,* 711–729.

Pagani, L., Tremblay, R. E., Nagin, D., Zoccolillo, M., Vitaro, F., & McDuff, P. (2009). Risk factor models for adolescent verbal and physical aggression toward fathers. *Journal of Family Violence, 24,* 173–182.

Page-Gould, E., Mendoza-Denton, R., & Tropp, L. R. (2008). With a little help from my cross-group friend: Reducing anxiety in intergroup contexts through cross-group friendship. *Journal of Personality and Social Psychology, 95,* 1080–1094.

Page-Gould, E., Mendoza-Denton, R., Alegre, J., & Siy, J. (2010). Understanding the impact of cross-group friendship on interactions with novel outgroup members. *Journal of Personality and Social Psychology, 98,* 775–793.

Pager, D., & Shepherd, H. (2008). The sociology of discrimination: Racial discrimination in employment, housing, credit, and consumer markets. *Annual Review of Sociology, 34,* 181–209.

Palet, L. S. (2015, June 18). 100 percent of French women are harassed on public transport. *Ozy,* http://www.ozy.com/acumen /100-percent-of-french-women-are-haraassed-on-public -transport/60636.

Palmer, F. T., Flowe, H. D., Takarangi, M. K. T., & Humphries, J. E. (2013). Intoxicated witnesses and suspects: An archival analysis of their involvement in criminal case processing. *Law and Human Behavior, 37,* 54–59.

Paluck, E. L. (2009). Reducing intergroup prejudice and conflict using the media: A field experiment in Rwanda. *Journal of Personality and Social Psychology, 96,* 574–587.

Paluck, E. L. (2011). Peer pressure against prejudice: A high school field experiment examining social network change. *Journal of Experimental Social Psychology, 47,* 350–358.

Paluck, E. L., & Shepherd, H. (2012). The salience of social referents: A field experiment on collective norms and harassment behavior in a school social network. *Journal of Personality and Social Psychology.*

Pancevski, B. (2012). Breivik trial exposes mass killer as a lonely loser addicted to tall tales and screen games. *The Australian,* April 24, p. 9.

Parducci, A. (1995). *Happiness, pleasure, and judgment: The contextual theory and its applications.* Mahwah, NJ: Erlbaum.

Park, B. (1986). A method for studying the development of impressions of real people. *Journal of Personality and Social Psychology, 51,* 907–917.

Park, B., Choi, J., Koo, M., Sul, S., & Choi, I. (2013). Culture, self, and preference structure: Transitivity and context independence are violated more by interdependent people. *Social Cognition, 31,* 106–118.

Park, J., Kitayama, S., et al. (2013). Social status and anger expression: The cultural moderation hypothesis. *Emotion, 13,* 1122–1131.

Park, S., & Catrambone, R. (2007). Social facilitation effects of virtual humans. *Human Factors, 49,* 1054–1060.

Parks, A. C., Della Porta, M. D., Pierce, R. S., Zilca, R., & Lyubomirsky, S. (2012). Pursuing happiness in everyday life: The characteristics and behaviors of online happiness seekers. *Emotion, 12,* 1222–1234.

Parrott, D. J., & Lisco, C. G. (2015). Effects of alcohol and sexual prejudice on aggression toward sexual minorities. *Psychology of Violence, 5,* 256–265.

Parsons, C. A., Sulaeman, J., Yates, M. C., & Hamermesh, D. S. (2009). *Strike three: Discrimination, incentives, and evaluation.* University of North Carolina.

Parsons, H. M. (1974). What happened at Hawthorne? *Science, 183,* 922–932.

Partridge, A., & Eldridge, W. B. (1974). *The second circuit sentencing study: A report to the judges of the second circuit.* Washington, DC: Federal Judicial Center.

Paterson, T. (2012). Psychotic or not? The experts are still divided; Tony Paterson explained what we've learnt about the man who killed 77 people. *The Independent (London),* June 23, p. 24.

Patzer, G. L. (2006). *The power and paradox of physical attractiveness.* Boca Raton, FL: Brown Walker Press.

Paulhus, D. L. (1998). Interpersonal and intrapsychic adaptiveness of trait self-enhancement: A mixed blessing? *Journal of Personality and Social Psychology, 74,* 1197–1208.

Paulus, P. B. (1988). *Prison crowding: A psychological perspective.* New York: Springer-Verlag.

Paulus, P. B., & van der Zee, K. (2015). Creative processes in culturally diverse teams. In S. Otten, K. van der Zee, & M. B. Brewer (Eds.), *Towards inclusive organizations: Determinants of successful diversity management at work* (pp. 108–131). New York: Psychology Press.

Paulus, P. B., Kohn, N. W., Arditti, L. E., & Korde, R. M. (2013). Understanding the group size effect in electronic brainstorming. *Small Group Research, 44,* 332–352.

Paulus, P. B., Korde, R. M., Dickson, J. J., Carmelli, A., & Cohen-Meitar, R. (2015). Asynchronous brainstorming in an industrial setting: Exploratory studies. *Human Factors, 57*(6), 1076–1094.

Paulus, P. B., Nakui, T., Putman, V. L., & Brown, V (2006). Effects of task instructions and brief breaks on brainstorming. *Group Dynamics: Theory, Research, and Practice, 10,* 206–219.

Paunesku, D., Walton, G. M., Romero, C., Smith, E. N., Yeager, D. S., & Dweck, C. S. (2015). Mind-set interventions are a scalable treatment for academic underachievement. *Psychological Science, 26,* 784–793.

Pavitt, C. (1994). Another view of group polarizing: The "reasons for" one-sided oral argumentation. *Communication Research, 21,* 625–642.

Pavlov, I. P. (1927). *Conditioned Reflexes: An investigation of the physiological activity of the cerebral cortex.* Translated and edited by G. V Anrep. London: Oxford University Press.

Pavot, W., & Diener, E. (1993). Review of the Satisfaction with Life Scale. *Psychological Assessment, 5,* 164–172.

Pawlowski, B., Dunbar, R. I. M., & Lipowicz, A. (2000). Evolutionary fitness: Tall men have more reproductive success. *Nature, 403,* 156.

Payne, B. (2001). Prejudice and perception: The role of automatic and controlled processes in misperceiving a weapon. *Journal of Personality and Social Psychology, 81,* 181–192.

Payne, K., & Lundberg, K. (2014). The affect misattribution procedure: Ten years of evidence on reliability, validity, and mechanisms. *Social and Personality Psychology Compass, 8,* 672–686.

Pazda, A. D., Elliot, A. J., & Greitemeyer, T. (2012). Sexy red: Perceived sexual receptivity mediates the red-attraction relation in men viewing woman. *Journal of Experimental Social Psychology, 48,* 787–790.

Pazda, A. D., Prokop, P., & Elliot, A. J. (2014). Red and romantic rivalry: Viewing another woman in red increases perceptions of sexual receptivity, derogation, and intentions to mate-guard. *Personality and Social Psychology Bulletin, 40,* 1260–1269.

Peck, T. C., Seinfeld, S., Aglioti, S. M., & Slater, M. (2013). Putting yourself in the skin of a black avatar reduces implicit racial bias. *Consciousness and Cognition: An International Journal, 22,* 779–787.

Pedersen, W. C., Bushman, B. J., Vasquez, E. A., & Miller, N. (2008). Kicking the (barking) dog effect: The moderating role of target attributes on triggered displaced aggression. *Personality and Social Psychology Bulletin, 34,* 1382–1395.

Pedersen, W. C., Denson, T. F., Goss, R., Vasquez, E. A., Kelley, N. J., & Miller, N. (2011). The impact of rumination on aggressive thoughts, feelings, arousal, and behaviour. *British Journal of Social Psychology, 50,* 281–301.

Pedersen, W. C., Miller, L. C., Putch-Bhagavatula, A. D., & Yang, Y. (2002). Evolved sex differences in the number of partners desired? The long and the short of it. *Psychological Science, 13,* 157–161.

Pelham, B., & Carvallo, M. (2011). The surprising potency of implicit egotism: A reply to Simonsohn. *Journal of Personality and Social Psychology, 101,* 25–30.

Pelham, B. W. (1995). Self-investment and self-esteem: Evidence for a Jamesian model of self-worth. *Journal of Personality and Social Psychology, 69,* 1141–1150.

Pelham, B. W., Carvallo, M., & Jones, J. T. (2005). Implicit egotism. *Current Directions in Psychological Science, 14,* 106–110.

Pelham, B. W., Mirenberg, M. C., & Jones, J. T. (2002). Why Susie sells sea-shells by the seashore: Implicit egotism and major life decisions. *Journal of Personality and Social Psychology, 82,* 469–487.

Pelto, P. J. (1968). The difference between "tight" and "loose" societies. *Transaction, 5,* 37–40.

Peng, K., & Nisbett, R. E. (1999). Culture, dialectics, and reasoning about contradiction. *American Psychologist, 54,* 741–754.

Pennebaker, J. W. (1997). Writing about emotional experiences as a therapeutic process. *Psychological Science, 8,* 162–166.

Pennebaker, J. W., Dyer, M. A., Caulkins, R. J., Litowitz, D. L., Ackreman, P. L., Anderson, D. B., & McGraw, K. M. (1979). Don't the girls get prettier at closing time: A country and western application to psychology. *Personality and Social Psychology Bulletin, 5,* 122–125.

Penner, L. A. (2004). Volunteerism and social problems: Making things better or worse? *Journal of Social Issues, 60,* 645–666.

Penner, L. A., Hagiwara, N., Eggly, S., Gaertner, S. L., Albrecht, T. L., & Dovidio, J. F. (2013). Racial healthcare disparities: A social psychological analysis. *European Review of Social Psychology, 24,* 70–122.

Pennington, N., & Hastie, R. (1992). Explaining the evidence: Tests of the story model for juror decision making. *Journal of Personality and Social Psychology, 62,* 189–206.

Penrod, S. D., & Cutler, B. (1995). Witness confidence and witness accuracy: Assessing their forensic relation. *Psychology, Public Policy, and Law, 1,* 817–845.

Peplau, L. A. (2003). Human sexuality: How do men and women differ? *Current Directions in Psychological Science, 12,* 37–40.

Peplau, L. A., & Fingerhut, A. W. (2007). The close relationships of lesbians and gay men. *Annual Review of Psychology, 58,* 405–424.

Peplau, L. A., & Perlman, D. (Eds.). (1982). *Loneliness: A sourcebook of current theory, research, and therapy.* New York: Wiley.

Peplau, L. A., Garnets, L. D., Spalding, L. R., Conley, T. D., & Veniegas, R. C. (1998). A critique of Bem's "Exotic becomes erotic" theory of sexual orientation. *Psychological Review, 105,* 387–394.

Pepler, D., Craig, W., Yuile, A., & Connolly, J. (2004). Girls who bully: A developmental and relational perspective. In M. Putallaz & K. L. Bierman (Eds.), *Aggression, antisocial behavior, and violence among girls: A developmental perspective* (pp. 90–109). New York: Guilford.

Peretz, H., & Fried, Y. (2012). National cultures, performance appraisal practices, and organizational absenteeism and turnover: A study across 21 countries. *Journal of Applied Psychology, 97,* 448–459.

Perillo, J. T., & Kassin, S. M. (2011). Inside interrogation: The lie, the bluff, and false confessions. *Law and Human Behavior, 35,* 327–337.

Perilloux, C., & Kurzban, R. (2015). Do men overperceive women's sexual interest? *Psychological Science, 26,* 70–77.

Perilloux, C., Easton, J. A., & Buss, D. M. (2012). The misperception of sexual interest. *Psychological Science, 23,* 146–151.

Perkins, S. C., Smith-Darden, J., Ametrano, R. M., & Graham-Bermann, S. (2014). Typologies of violence exposure and cognitive processing in incarcerated male adolescents. *Journal of Family Violence, 29,* 439–451.

Perloff, R. M. (2010). *The dynamics of persuasion: Communication and attitudes in the 21st century* (4th ed.). New York: Taylor & Francis.

Perrett, D. (2010). *In your face: The new science of human attraction.* UK: Palgrave Macmillan.

Persky, V. W., Kempthorne-Rawson, J., & Shekelle, R. B. (1987). Personality and risk of cancer: 20-year follow-up of the Western Electric Study. *Psychosomatic Medicine, 49,* 435–449.

Peruche, B. M., & Plant, E. A. (2006). The correlates of law enforcement officers' automatic and controlled race-based responses to criminal suspects. *Basic and Applied Social Psychology, 28,* 193–199.

Peters, T. J., & Waterman, R. H. (1982). *In search of excellence: Lessons from America's best-run companies.* New York: Warner.

Peterson, C. (2000). The future of optimism. *American Psychologist, 55,* 44–55.

Peterson, C., Seligman, M. E., & Vaillant, G. E. (1988). Pessimistic explanatory style is a risk factor for physical illness: A thirty-five-year longitudinal study. *Journal of Personality and Social Psychology, 55,* 23–27.

Petrie, K. J., Booth, R. J., & Pennebaker, J. W. (1998). The immunological effects of thought suppression. *Journal of Personality and Social Psychology, 75,* 1264–1272.

Pettersen, N., & Durivage, A. (2008). *The structured interview.* Quebec: Presses de l'Université du Québec.

Pettigrew, T. F., & Tropp, L. R. (2000). Does intergroup contact reduce prejudice: Recent meta-analytic findings. In S. Oskamp (Ed.), *Reducing prejudice and discrimination: The Claremont Symposium on Applied Social Psychology* (pp. 93–114). Mahwah, NJ: Erlbaum.

Pettigrew, T. F., & Tropp, L. R. (2006). A meta-analytic test of intergroup contact theory. *Journal of Personality and Social Psychology, 90,* 751–783.

Pettigrew, T. F., & Tropp, L. R. (2008). How does intergroup contact reduce prejudice? Meta-analytic tests of three mediators. *European Journal of Social Psychology, 38,* 922–934.

Pettigrew, T. F., Tropp, L. R., Wagner, U., & Christ, O. (2011). Recent advances in intergroup contact theory. *International Journal of Intercultural Relations, 35,* 271–280.

Petty, R. E., & Cacioppo, J. T. (1983). The role of bodily responses in attitude measurement and change. In J. Cacioppo & R. Petty (Eds.), *Social psychophysiology: A sourcebook* (pp. 51–101). New York: Guilford.

Petty, R. E., & Cacioppo, J. T. (1984). The effects of involvement on response to argument quantity and quality: Central and peripheral routes to persuasion. *Journal of Personality and Social Psychology, 46,* 69–81.

Petty, R. E., & Cacioppo, J. T. (1986). *Communication and persuasion: Central and peripheral routes to attitude change.* New York: Springer-Verlag.

Petty, R. E., & Fazio, R. H., & Brinol, P. (Eds.). (2009). *Attitudes: Insights from the new implicit measures.* New York: Psychology Press.

Petty, R. E., & Krosnick, J. A. (Eds.). (1995). *Attitude strength: Antecedents and consequences.* Mahwah, NJ: Erlbaum.

Petty, R. E., & Wegener, D. T. (1998). Attitude change: Multiple roles for persuasion variables. In D. Gilbert, S. Fiske, & G. Lindzey (Eds.), *The handbook of social psychology* (4th ed., pp. 323–390). New York: McGraw-Hill.

Petty, R. E., Briñol, P., & Tormala, Z. L. (2002). Thought confidence as a determinant of persuasion: The self-validation hypothesis. *Journal of Personality and Social Psychology, 82,* 722–741.

Petty, R. E., Cacioppo, J. T., & Goldman, R. (1981). Personal involvement as a determinant of argument-based persuasion. *Journal of Personality and Social Psychology, 41,* 847–855.

Petty, R. E., Schumann, D. W., Richman, S. A., & Strathman, A. J. (1993). Positive mood and persuasion: Different roles for affect under high- and low-elaboration conditions. *Journal of Personality and Social Psychology, 64,* 5–20.

Pew Research Center (2015a, Feb 26). Latest trends in religious restrictions and hostilities. *Pew Research Center.*

Pew Research Center (2015b, June 11). *Multiracial in America.* Pew Research Center.

Pezdek, K., & O'Brien, M. (2014). Plea bargaining and appraisals of eyewitness evidence by prosecutors and defense attorneys. *Psychology, Crime & Law, 20,* 222–241.

Pfau, M., Kenski, H. C., Nitz, M., & Sorenson, J. (1990). Efficacy of inoculation strategies in promoting resistance to political attack messages: Application to direct mail. *Communication Monographs, 57,* 25–43.

Pfetsch, J., Steffgen, G., Gollwitzer, M., & Ittel, A. (2011). Prevention of aggression in schools through a bystander intervention training. *International Journal of Developmental Science, 5,* 139–149.

Pham, M. N., Barbaro, N., Mogilski, J. K., & Shackelford, T. K. (2015). Coalitional mate retention is correlated positively with friendship quality involving women, but negatively with male–male friendship quality. *Personality and Individual Differences, 79,* 87–90.

Phelan, J. E., Moss-Racusin, C. A., & Rudman, L. A. (2008). Competent yet out in the cold: Shifting criteria for hiring reflect backlash toward agentic women. *Psychology of Women Quarterly, 32,* 406–413.

Phillips, A. G., & Silvia, P. J. (2005). Self-awareness and the emotional consequences of self-discrepancies. *Personality and Social Psychology Bulletin, 31,* 703–713.

Phillips, A. P., & Dipboye, R. L. (1989). Correlational tests of predictions from a process model of the interview. *Journal of Applied Psychology, 74,* 41–52.

Picazo, C., Gamero, N., Zornoza, A., & Peiró, J. M. (2015). Testing relations between group cohesion and satisfaction in project teams: A cross-level and cross-lagged approach. *European Journal of Work and Organizational Psychology, 24,* 297–307.

Pickel, K. L. (1999). The influence of context on the "weapon focus" effect. *Law and Human Behavior, 23,* 299–311.

Piferi, R. L., Jobe, R. L., Jones, W. H., & Gaines, S. O., Jr. (2006). Giving to others during national tragedy: The effects of altruistic and egoistic motivations on long-term giving. *Journal of Social and Personal Relationships, 23,* 171–184.

Piff, P. K. (2014). Wealth and the inflated self: Class, entitlement, and narcissism. *Personality and Social Psychology Bulletin, 40,* 34–43.

Piff, P. K., Kraus, M. W., Côté, S., Cheng, B. H., & Keltner, D. (2010). Having less, giving more: The influence of social class on prosocial behavior. *Journal of Personality and Social Psychology, 99,* 771–84.

Piliavin, J. A., & Siegl, E. (2008). Health benefits of volunteering in the Wisconsin Longitudinal Study. *Journal of Health and Social Behavior, 48,* 450–464.

Pillemer, D. B., Picariello, M. L., Law, A. B., & Reichman, J. S. (1996). Memories of college: The importance of educational episodes. In D. C. Rubin (Ed.), *Remembering our past Studies in autobiographical memory* (pp. 318–337). New York: Cambridge University Press.

Pinel, E. C., & Long, A. E. (2012). When I's meet: Sharing subjective experience with someone from the outgroup. *Personality and Social Psychology Bulletin, 38,* 296–307.

Pinel, E. C., Long, A. E., Landau, M. J., Alexander, K., & Pyszczynski, T. (2006). Seeing I to I: A pathway to interpersonal connectedness. *Journal of Personality and Social Psychology, 90,* 243–257.

Pinker, S. (2011). *The better angels of our nature: Why violence has declined.* New York: Viking.

Pinter, B., & Greenwald, A. G. (2011). A comparison of minimal group induction procedures. *Group Processes & Intergroup Relations, 14,* 81–98.

Pinter, B., & Wildschut, T. (2012). Self-interest masquerading as ingroup beneficence: Altruistic rationalization and interindividual-intergroup discontinuity. *Small Group Research, 43*(1), 105–123.

Pittarello, A., Leib, M., Gordon-Hecker, T., & Shalvi, S. (2015). Justifications shape ethical blind spots. *Psychological Science, 26,* 794–804.

Pittman, T. S. (1975). Attribution of arousal as a mediator of dissonance reduction. *Journal of Experimental Social Psychology, 11,* 53–63.

Plaks, J. E., & Higgins, E. T. (2000). Pragmatic use of stereotyping in teamwork: Social loafing and compensation as a function of inferred partner-situation fit. *Journal of Personality and Social Psychology, 79,* 962–974.

Plaks, J. E., Malahy, L., Sedlins, M., & Shoda, Y. (2012). Folk beliefs about human genetic variation predict discrete versus continuous racial categorization and evaluative bias. *Social Psychological and Personality Science, 3,* 31–39.

Plant, E. A., & Butz, D. A. (2006). The causes and consequences of an avoidance-focus for interracial interactions. *Personality and Social Psychology Bulletin, 32,* 833–846.

Plant, E. A., & Devine, P. G. (1998). Internal and external motivation to respond without prejudice. *Journal of Personality and Social Psychology, 75,* 811–832.

Plant, E. A., & Devine, P. G. (2009). The active control of prejudice: Unpacking the intentions guiding control efforts. *Journal of Personality and Social Psychology, 96,* 640–652.

Plante, T. G., & Thoresen, C. E. (Eds.). (2007). *Spirit, science, and health: How the spiritual mind fuels physical wellness.* Westport, CT: Praeger.

Platek, S. M., Wathne, K., Tierney, N. G., & Thomson, J. W. (2008). Neural correlates of self-face recognition: An effect-location meta-analysis. *Brain Research, 1232,* 173–184.

Platz, S. J., & Hosch, H. M. (1988). Cross-racial/ethnic eyewitness identification: A field study. *Journal of Applied Social Psychology, 18,* 972–984.

Plaut, V. C., Cheryan, S., & Stevens, F. G. (2015). New frontiers in diversity research: Conceptions of diversity and their theoretical and practical implications. In M. Mikulincer, P. R. Shaver, E. Borgida, & J. A. Bargh (Eds.), *APA handbook of personality and social psychology, Volume 1: Attitudes and social cognition* (pp. 593–619). Washington, DC: American Psychological Association.

Plaut, V. C., Garnett, F. G., Buffardi, L. E., & Sanchez-Burks, J. (2011). "What about me?" Perceptions of exclusion and Whites' reactions to multiculturalism. *Journal of Personality and Social Psychology, 101,* 337–353.

Plaut, V. C., Thomas, K. M., & Goren, M. J. (2009). Is multiculturalism or color blindness better for minorities? *Psychological Science, 20,* 444–446.

Plötner, M., Over, H., Carpenter, M., & Tomasello, M. (2015). Young children show the bystander effect in helping situations. *Psychological Science, 26,* 499–506.

Plotnik, J. M., de Waal, F. B. M., & Reiss, D. (2006). Self-recognition in an Asian elephant. *Proceedings of the National Academy of Sciences, 103,* 17053–17057.

Polanin, J. R., Espelage, D. L., & Pigott, T. D. (2012). A meta-analysis of school-based bulling prevention programs' effects on bystander intervention behavior. *School Psychology Review, 41,* 47–65.

Polivy, J., Garner, D. M., & Garfinkel, P. E. (1986). Causes and consequences of the current preference for thin female physiques. In C. P. Herman, M. P. Zanna, & E. T. Higgins (Eds.), *The Ontario symposium: Vol. 3. Physical appearance, stigma, and social behavior* (pp. 89–112). Hillsdale, NJ: Erlbaum.

Polyorat, K., Jung, J. M., & Hwang, Y. Y. (2013). Effects of self-construals on consumer assertiveness/aggressiveness: Evidence from Thai and U.S. samples. *Journal of Cross-Cultural Psychology, 44,* 738–747.

Pontari, B. A., & Schlenker, B. R. (2000). The influence of cognitive load on self-presentation: Can cognitive busyness help as well as harm social performance? *Journal of Personality and Social Psychology, 78,* 1092–1108.

Poole, D. A., & White, L. T. (1991). Effects of question repetition on the eyewitness testimony of children and adults. *Developmental Psychology, 27,* 975–986.

Poole, D. A., Bruck, M., & Pipe, M. E. (2011). Forensic interviewing aids: Do props help children answer questions about touching? *Current Directions in Psychological Science, 20,* 11–15.

Poole, D., & Lindsay, D. S. (2001). Children's eyewitness reports after exposure to misinformation from parents. *Journal of Experimental Psychology: Applied, 7,* 27–50.

Pornpitakpan, C. (2004). The persuasiveness of source credibility: A critical review of five decades' evidence. *Journal of Applied Social Psychology, 34,* 243–281.

Porter, D. P., & Smith, V. L. (2003). Stock market bubbles in the laboratory. *Journal of Behavioral Finance, 4,* 7–20.

Posavac, H. D., Posavac, S. S., & Posavac, E. J. (1998). Exposure to media images of female attractiveness and concern with body weight among young women. *Sex Roles, 38,* 187–201.

Post, J. M. (2011). Crimes of obedience: "Groupthink" at Abu Ghraib. *International Journal of Group Psychotherapy, 61,* 49–66.

Post, S. G. (2005). Altruism, happiness, and health: It's good to be good. *International Journal of Behavioral Medicine, 12,* 66–77.

Postmes, T., Spears, R., & Cihangir, S. (2001). Quality of decision making and group norms. *Journal of Personality and Social Psychology, 80,* 918–930.

Povinelli, D. J., Gallup, G. G., Jr., Eddy, T. J., Bierschwale, D. T., Engstrom, M. C., Perilloux, H. K., & Toxopeus, I. B. (1997). Chimpanzees recognize themselves in mirrors. *Animal Behaviour, 53,* 1083–1088.

Povoledo, E. (2015). *Amanda Knox acquitted of 2007 murder by Italy's highest court.* The New York Times, March 27, 2015.

Powell, L. H., Shahabi, L., & Thoresen, C. E. (2003). Religion and spirituality: Linkages to physical health. *American Psychologist, 58,* 36–52.

Powers, S. I., Pietromonaco, P. R., Gunlicks, M., & Sayer, A. (2006). Dating couples' attachment styles and patterns of cortisol reactivity and recovery in response to a relationship conflict. *Journal of Personality and Social Psychology, 90,* 613–628.

Pozzoli, T., Ang, R. P., & Gini G. (2012). Bystanders' reactions to bullying: a cross-cultural analysis of personal correlates among Italian and Singaporean students. *Social Development, 21,* 686–703.

Prati, F., Moscatelli, S., Pratto, F., & Rubini, M. (2015). Predicting support for Arabs' autonomy from social dominance: The role of identity complexity and dehumanization. *Political Psychology,* in press.

Pratkanis, A. R. (1992). The cargo-cult science of subliminal persuasion. *Skeptical Inquirer, 16,* 260–272.

Pratkanis, A. R. (2007). *The science of social influence.* New York: Psychological Press.

Pratkanis, A. R., & Turner, M. E. (1994). Nine principles of successful affirmative action: Mr. Branch Rickey, Mr. Jackie Robinson, and the integration of baseball. *Nine: A Journal of Baseball History and Social Policy Perspectives, 3,* 36–65.

Pratkanis, A. R., & Turner, M. E. (1996). The proactive removal of discriminatory barriers: Affirmative action as effective help. *Journal of Social Issues, 52,* 111–132.

Pratkanis, A. R., Greenwald, A. G., Leippe, M. R., & Baumgardner, M. H. (1988). In search of reliable persuasion effects: III. The sleeper effect is dead. Long live the sleeper effect. *Journal of Personality and Social Psychology, 54,* 203–218.

Pratt, T. C., & Cullen, F. T. (2000). The empirical status of Gottfredson and Hirschi's general theory of crime: A meta-analysis. *Criminology, 38,* 931–964.

Pratto, F., & John, O. P. (1991). Automatic vigilance: The attention-grabbing power of negative social information. *Journal of Personality and Social Psychology, 61,* 380–391.

Pratto, F., Çidam, A., et al. (2013). Social dominance in context and in individuals: Contextual moderation of robust effects of social dominance orientation in 15 languages and 20 countries. *Social Psychological and Personality Science, 4,* 587–599.

Pratto, F., Stallworth, L. M., Sidanius, J., & Sieres, B. (1997). The gender gap in occupational attainment: A social dominance approach. *Journal of Personality and Social Psychology, 72,* 37–53.

Prebble, S. C., Addis, D. R., & Tippett, L. J. (2013). Autobiographical memory and sense of self. *Psychological Bulletin, 139,* 815–840.

Prentice-Dunn, S., & Rogers, R. W. (1982). Effects of public and private self-awareness on deindividuation and aggression. *Journal of Personality and Social Psychology, 43,* 503–513.

Prentice-Dunn, S., & Rogers, R. W. (1983). Deindividuation in aggression. In R. G. Geen & E. I. Donnerstein (Eds.), *Aggression: Theoretical and empirical reviews: Vol. 2. Issues in research* (pp. 155–171). New York: Academic Press.

Prentice, D. A., & Carranza, E. (2002). What women should be, shouldn't be, are allowed to be, and don't have to be: The contents of prescriptive gender stereotypes. *Psychology of Women Quarterly, 26,* 269–281.

Prentice, D. A., & Miller, D. T. (1996). Pluralistic ignorance and the perpetuation of social norms by unwitting actors. *Advances in Experimental Social Psychology, 28,* 161–209.

President's Commission on Law Enforcement and Administration of Justice. (1967). *The challenge of crime in a free society.* Washington, DC: U.S. Government Printing Office.

Presidential Commission on the Space Shuttle Challenger Accident. (1986). *Report of the Presidential Commission on the Space Shuttle Challenger Accident.* Washington, DC: U.S. Government Printing Office.

Pressman, S. D., & Cohen, S. (2012). Positive emotion word use and longevity in famous deceased psychologists. *Health Psychology, 31,* 297–305.

Pressman, S. D., Cohen, S., Miller, G. E., Barkin, A., Rabin, B. S., & Treanor, J. J. (2005). Loneliness, social network size, and immune response to influenza vaccination in college freshmen. *Health Psychology, 24,* 297–306.

Prestwich, A., Conner, M. T., Lawton, R. J., Ward, J. K., Ayres, K., & McEachan, R. C. (2012). Randomized controlled trial of collaborative implementation intentions targeting working adults' physical activity. *Health Psychology, 31,* 486–495.

Priester, J. R., & Petty, R. E. (1995). Source attributions and persuasion: Perceived honesty as a determinant of message scrutiny. *Personality and Social Psychology Bulletin, 21,* 637–654.

Priester, J. R., Cacioppo, J. T., & Petty, R. E. (1996). The influence of motor processes on attitudes toward novel versus familiar semantic stimuli. *Personality and Social Psychology Bulletin, 22,* 442–447.

Principe, G. F., & Ceci, S. J. (2002). "I saw it with my own ears": The effects of peer conversations on preschoolers' reports of nonexperienced events. *Journal of Experimental Child Psychology, 83,* 1–25.

Principe, G. F., Ornstein, P. A., Baker-Ward, L., & Gordon, B. N. (2000). The effects of intervening experiences on children's memory for a physical examination. *Applied Cognitive Psychology 14,* 59–80.

Prioleau, L., Murdock, M., & Brody, N. (1983). An analysis of psychotherapy versus placebo studies. *Behavioral and Brain Sciences, 6,* 275–310.

Prokosch, M., Coss, R., Scheib, J., & Blozis, S. (2009). Intelligence and mate choice: Intelligent men are always appealing. *Evolution and Human Behavior, 30,* 11–20.

Pronin, E., Berger, J., & Molouki, S. (2007). Alone in a crowd of sheep: Asymmetric perceptions of conformity and their roots in an introspection illusion. *Journal of Personality and Social Psychology, 92,* 585–595.

Pronin, E., Gilovich, T., & Ross, L. (2004). Objectivity in the eye of the beholder: Divergent perceptions of bias in self versus others. *Psychological Review, 111,* 781–799.

Pronin, E., Wegner, D. M., McCarthy, K., & Rodriguez, S. (2006). Everyday magical powers: The role of apparent mental causation in the overestimation of personal influence. *Journal of Personality and Social Psychology, 91,* 218–231.

Prot, S., Gentile, D. A., et al. (2014). Long-term relations among prosocial-media use, empathy, and prosocial behavior. *Psychological Science, 25,* 358–368.

Proto-Campise, L., Belknap, J., & Wooldredge, J. (1998). High school students' adherence to rape myths and the effectiveness of high school rape-awareness programs. *Violence Against Women, 4,* 308–328.

Pruetz, J. D., & Lindshield, S. (2012). Plant-food and tool transfer among savanna chimpanzees at Fongoli, Senegal. *Primates, 53,* 133–145.

Pruitt, D. G. (2012). A history of social conflict and negotiation research. In A. W. Kruglanski & W. Stroebe (Eds.), *Handbook of the history of social psychology* (pp. 431–452). New York: Psychology Press.

Pryor, J. B., & Merluzzi, T. V. (1985). The role of expertise in processing social interaction scripts. *Journal of Experimental Social Psychology, 21,* 362–379.

Pryor, J. B., Reeder, G. D., & Monroe, A. E. (2012). The infection of bad company: Stigma by association. *Journal of Personality and Social Psychology, 102,* 224–241.

Pryor, J. B., Reeder, G. D., Wesselmann, E. D., Williams, K. D., & Wirth, J. H. (2013). The influence of social norms upon behavioral expressions of implicit and explicit weight-related stigma in an interactive game. *Yale Journal of Biology and Medicine, 86,* 189–201.

Purdie-Vaughns, V., Steele, C. M., Davies, P. G., Ditlmann, R., & Crosby, J. R. (2008). Social identity contingencies: How diversity cues signal threat or safety for African Americans in mainstream institutions. *Journal of Personality and Social Psychology, 94,* 615–630.

Purvanova, R. K. (2014). Face-to-face versus virtual teams: What have we really learned?. *The Psychologist-Manager Journal, 17,* 2–29.

Purvanova, R. K., & Muros, J. P. (2010). Gender differences in burnout: A meta-analysis. *Journal of Vocational Behavior, 77,* 168–185.

Pyszczynski, T. A., Solomon, S., & Greenberg, J. (2002). *In the wake of 9/11: The psychology of terror.* Washington, DC: American Psychological Association.

Pyszczynski, T., Solomon, S., & Greenberg, J. (2015). Thirty years of terror management theory: From genesis to revelation. *Advances in Experimental Social Psychology, 52,* 1–70.

Pyszczynski, T., & Greenberg, J. (1987). Self-regulatory preservation and the depressive self-focusing style: A self-awareness theory of reactive depression. *Psychological Bulletin, 201,* 122–138.

Pyszczynski, T., & Greenberg, J. (1992). *Hanging on and letting go.* New York: Springer-Verlag.

Pyszczynski, T., Greenberg, J., Solomon, S., Arndt, J., & Schimel, J. (2004). Why do people need self-esteem? A theoretical and empirical review. *Psychological Bulletin, 130,* 435–468.

Qin, P., Duncan, N., & Northoff, G. (2013). Why and how is the self-related to the brain midline regions? *Frontiers in Human Neuroscience, 7,* 909.

Qualter, P., et al. (2015). Loneliness across the life span. *Perspectives on Psychological Science, 10,* 250–264.

Qualter, T. H. (1962). *Propaganda and psychological warfare.* New York: Random House.

Quayle, M., & Naidoo, E. (2012). Social risk and attribution: How considering the social risk of attributions can improve the performance of Kelley's ANOVA model in applied research. *Journal of Applied Social Psychology, 42,* 1694–1715.

Quinn, D. M., Kahng, S. K., & Crocker, J. (2004). Discreditable: Stigma effects of revealing a mental illness history on test performance. *Personality and Social Psychology Bulletin, 30,* 803–815.

Quirk, R., & Campbell, M. (2015). On standby? A comparison of online and offline witnesses to bullying and their bystander behaviour. *Educational Psychology, 35,* 430–448.

Raaijmakers, M. A. J., Smidts, D. P., Sergeant, J. A., Maassen, G. H., Posthumus, J. A., van Engeland, H., et al. (2008). Executive functions in preschool children with aggressive behavior: Impairments in inhibitory control. *Journal of Abnormal Child Psychology, 36,* 1097–1107.

Radel, R., & Clement-Guillotin, C. (2012). Evidence of motivational influences in early visual perception: Hunger modulates conscious access. *Psychological Science, 23,* 232–234.

Ragins, B. R., & Sundstrom, E. (1989). Gender and power in organizations: A longitudinal perspective. *Psychological Bulletin, 105,* 51–88.

Raine, A. (2013). *The anatomy of violence: The biological roots of crime.* New York: Pantheon/Random House.

Rakoff, J. (2014). Why innocent people plead guilty. *The New York Review of Books,* Nov. 20, 2014.

Ramírez-Esparza, N., Chung, C. K., Sierra-Otero, G., & Pennebaker, J. W. (2012). Cross-cultural constructions of self-schemas: Americans and Mexicans. *Journal of Cross-Cultural Psychology, 43,* 233–250.

Ramírez-Esparza, N., Gosling, S. D., & Pennebaker, J. W. (2008). Paradox lost: Unraveling the puzzle of Simpatía. *Journal of Cross-Cultural Psychology, 39,* 703–715.

Rampell, C. (2011). Commuter Nation. *The New York Times,* September 11, 2011. http://economix.blogs.nytimes.com/2011/09/22/commuter-nation/.

Rand, D. G. & Epstein, Z. G. (2014). Risking your life without a second thought: Intuitive decision-making and extreme altruism. *PLoS ONE, 9,* e109687.

Rand, D. G., & Nowak, M. A. (2013). Human cooperation. *Trends in Cognitive Sciences, 17*(8), 413–425.

Rand, D. G., Newman, G. E., & Wurzbacher, O. M. (2015). Social context and the dynamics of cooperative choice. *Journal of Behavioral Decision Making, 28,* 159–166.

Ranson, M. (2014). Crime, weather, and climate change. *Journal of Environmental Economics and Management, 67,* 274–302.

Rattan, A., & Ambady, N. (2013). Diversity ideologies and intergroup relations: An examination of colorblindness and multiculturalism. *European Journal of Social Psychology, 43,* 12–21.

Rauxloh, R. (2012). *Plea bargaining in national and international law.* London: Routledge.

Ray, E., & Heyes, C. (2010). Imitation in infancy: The wealth of the stimulus. *Developmental Science,* 1–14.

Ray, O. (2004). How the mind hurts and heals the body. *American Psychologist, 59,* 29–40.

Rayner, R. (2010). Channeling Ike. *The New Yorker,* April 26.

Redlich, A. D., Summers, A., & Hoover, S. (2010). Self-reported false confessions and false guilty pleas among offenders with mental illness. *Law and Human Behavior, 34,* 70–90.

Reed, K. P., Nugent, W., & Cooper, R. L. (2015). Testing a path model of relationships between gender, age, and bullying victimization and violent behavior, substance abuse, depression, suicidal ideation, and suicide attempts in adolescents. *Children and Youth Services Review, 55,* 128–137.

Reeder, G. D. (1993). Trait-behavior relations and dispositional inference. *Personality and Social Psychology Bulletin, 19,* 586–593.

Reeder, G. D., & Brewer, M. B. (1979). A schematic model of dispositional attribution in interpersonal perception. *Psychological Review, 86,* 61–79.

Reeder, G. D., Davison, D. M., Gipson, K. L., & Hesson-McInnis, M. S. (2001). Identifying the motivations of African American volunteers working to prevent HIV/AIDS. *AIDS Education and Prevention, 13,* 343–354.

Regan, D. T. (1971). Effects of a favor and liking on compliance. *Journal of Experimental Social Psychology, 7,* 627–639.

Regan, D. T., & Kilduff, M. (1988). Optimism about elections: Dissonance reduction at the ballot box. *Political Psychology, 9,* 101–107.

Regan, P. (2011). *Close relationships.* New York: Routledge.

Regan, P. C., & Berscheid, E. (1997). Gender differences in characteristics desired in a potential sexual and marriage partner. *Journal of Psychology and Human Sexuality, 9,* 25–37.

Regan, P. C., & Berscheid, E. (1999). *Lust: What we know about human sexual desire.* Thousand Oaks, CA: Sage.

Regan, P. C., Kocan, E. R., & Whitlock, T. (1998). Ain't love grand! A prototype analysis of the concept of romantic love. *Journal of Social and Personal Relationships, 15,* 411–420.

Reicher, S. D., & Haslam, S. A. (2006). Rethinking the psychology of tyranny: The BBC prison study. *British Journal of Social Psychology, 45,* 1–40.

Reicher, S. D., Haslam, S. A., & Miller, A. G. (2014). What makes a person a perpetrator? The intellectual, moral, and methodological arguments for revisiting Milgram's research on the influence of authority. *Journal of Social Issues, 70,* 393–408.

Reicher, S. D., Haslam, S. A., & Smith, J. R. (2012). Working towards the experimenter: Reconceptualizing obedience within the Milgram paradigm as identification-based followership. *Perspectives on Psychological Science, 7,* 315–324.

Reidy, D. E., Berke, D. S., Gentile, B., & Zeichner, A. (2014). Man enough? Masculine discrepancy stress and intimate partner violence. *Personality and Individual Differences, 68,* 160–164.

Reifman, A. S., Larrick, R. P., & Fein, S. (1991). Temper and temperature on the diamond: The heat-aggression relationship in major-league baseball. *Personality and Social Psychology Bulletin, 17,* 580–585.

Reifman, A., Klein, J. G., & Murphy, S. T. (1989). Self-monitoring and age. *Psychology and Aging, 4,* 245–246.

Reinhard, M.-A., Greifeneder, R., & Scharmach, M. (2013). Unconscious processes improve lie detection. *Journal of Personality and Social Psychology, 105,* 721–739.

Reinhard, M.-A., Messner, M., & Sporer, S. L. (2006). Explicit persuasive intent and its impact on success at persuasion: The determining roles of attractiveness and likeableness. *Journal of Consumer Psychology, 16,* 249–259.

Reis, H. T., Maniaci, M. R., Caprariello, P. A., Eastwick, P. W., & Finkel, E. J. (2011). Familiarity does indeed promote attraction in live interaction. *Journal of Personality and Social Psychology, 101,* 557–570.

Reisenzein, R. (1983). The Schachter theory of emotion: Two decades later. *Psychological Bulletin, 94,* 239–264.

Reiss, D., & Marino, L. (2001). Mirror self-recognition in the bottlenose dolphin: A case of cognitive convergence. *Proceedings of the National Academy of the Sciences, 98,* 5937–5942.

Remley, A. (1988, October). The great parental value shift: From obedience to independence. *Psychology Today,* 56–59.

Rendell, L., & Whitehead, H. (2001). Culture in whales and dolphins. *Behavioral and Brain Sciences, 24,* 309–382.

Renteln, A. D. (2004). *The cultural defense.* New York: Oxford University Press.

Reskin, B. (2012). The race discrimination system. *Annual Review of Sociology, 38,* 17–35.

Reyna, V., Hans, V. P., Corbin, J. C., Yeh, R., Lin, K., & Royer, C. (2015). The gist of juries: Testing a model of damage award decision making. *Psychology, Public Policy, and Law.*

Reyniers, D., & Bhalla, R. (2013). Reluctant altruism and peer pressure in charitable giving. *Judgment and Decision Making, 8,* 7–15.

Reznikova, T. N., et al. (2015). Functional activity of brain structures and predisposition to aggression in patients with lingering diseases of the CNS. *Human Physiology, 41,* 27–33.

Rhatigan, D. L., & Axsom, D. K. (2006). Using the investment model to understand battered women's commitment to abusive relationships. *Journal of Family Violence, 21,* 153–162.

Rhee, E., Uleman, J. S., Lee, H. K., & Roman, R. J. (1995). Spontaneous self-descriptions and ethnic identities in individualistic and collectivistic cultures. *Journal of Personality and Social Psychology, 69,* 142–152.

Rhee, S. H., Lahey, B. B., & Waldman, I. D. (2015). Comorbidity among dimensions of childhood psychopathology: Converging evidence from behavior genetics. *Child Development Perspectives, 9,* 26–31.

Rhode, D. L. (2010). *The beauty bias: The injustice of appearance.* New York: Oxford University Press.

Rhodes, G. (2006). The evolutionary psychology of facial beauty. *Annual Review of Psychology, 57,* 199–226.

Rhodes, G., Simmons, L. W., & Peters, M. (2005). Attractiveness and sexual behavior: Does attractiveness enhance mating success? *Evolution and Human Behavior, 26,* 186–201.

Rhodes, G., Sumich, A., & Byatt, G. (1999). Are average facial configurations attractive only because of their symmetry? *Psychological Science, 10,* 52–58.

Rhodes, G., Zebrowitz, L. A., Clark, A., Kalick, S. M., Hightower, A., & McKay, R. (2001). Do facial averageness and symmetry signal health? *Evolution and Human Behavior, 22,* 31–46.

Rhodes, M. G., & Anastasi, J. S. (2012). The own-age bias in face recognition: A meta-analytic and theoretical review. *Psychological Bulletin, 138,* 146–174.

Rhodes, N., & Wood, W. (1992). Self-esteem and intelligence affect influenceability: The mediating role of message reception. *Psychological Bulletin, 111,* 156–171.

Rhodewalt, F. (1990). Self-handicappers: Individual differences in the preference for anticipatory, self-protective acts. In R. L. Higgins, C. R. Synder, & S. Berglas (Eds.), *Self-handicapping: The paradox that isn't* (pp. 69–106). New York: Plenum.

Rhodewalt, F., & Agustsdottir, S. (1986). Effects of self-presentation on the phenomenal self. *Journal of Personality and Social Psychology, 50,* 47–55.

Rholes, W. S., & Simpson, J. A. (Eds.). (2004). *Adult attachment: Theory, research, and clinical implications.* New York: Guilford.

Ricciardelli, L. A., & McCabe, M. P. (2011). Body image development in adolescent boys. In T. F. Cash & L. Smolak (Eds.), *Body image: A handbook of science, practice, and prevention* (2nd ed.) (pp. 85–92). New York: Guilford.

Rich, A., Brandes, K., Mullan, B., & Hagger, M. S. (2015). Theory of planned behavior and adherence in chronic illness: A meta-analysis. *Journal of Behavioral Medicine.*

Richardson, E. G., & Hemenway, D. (2011). Homicide, suicide, and unintentional firearm fatality: Comparing the United States with other high-income countries, 2003. *The Journal of Trauma, 70,* 238–243.

Richardson, M. J., Marsh, K. L., & Schmidt, R. C. (2005). Effects of visual and verbal interaction on unintentional interpersonal coordination. *Journal of Experimental Psychology: Human Perception and Performance, 31,* 62–79.

Richman, S. B., Slotter, E. B., Gardner, W. L., & DeWall, C. N. (2015). Reaching out by changing what's within: Social exclusion increases self-concept malleability. *Journal of Experimental Social Psychology, 57,* 64–77.

Riddle, K., & De Simone, J. J. (2013). A Snooki effect? An exploration of the surveillance subgenre of reality TV and viewers' beliefs about the "real" real world. *Psychology of Popular Media Culture, 2,* 237–250.

Rieger, G., Chivers, M. L., & Bailey, J. M. (2005). Sexual arousal patterns of bisexual men. *Psychological Science, 16,* 579–584.

Rieger, G., Linsenmeier, J. A. W., Gygax, L., & Bailey, J. M. (2008). Sexual orientation and childhood gender nonconformity: Evidence from home videos. *Developmental Psychology, 44,* 46–58.

Riek, B. M., Mania, E. W., & Gaertner, S. L. (2013). Reverse subtyping: The effects of prejudice level on the subtyping of counterstereotypic outgroup members. *Basic and Applied Social Psychology, 35,* 409–417.

Riek, B. M., Mania, E. W., Gaertner, S. L., McDonald, S. A., & Lamoreaux, M. J. (2010). Does a common ingroup identity reduce intergroup threat? *Group Processes & Intergroup Relations, 13,* 403–423.

Riemer, H., Shavitt, S., Koo, M., & Markus, H. (2014). Preferences don't have to be personal: Expanding attitude theorizing with a cross-cultural perspective. *Psychological Review, 121,* 619–648.

Rijnbout, J. S., & McKimmie, B. M. (2012). Deviance in group decision-making: Group-member centrality alleviates negative consequences for the group. *European Journal of Social Psychology, 42,* 915–923.

Rilling, J. K., & Sanfey, A. G. (2011). The neuroscience of social decision-making. *Annual Review of Psychology, 6,* 223–248.

Rimal, R. N., & Real, K. (2005). Assessing the perceived importance of skin cancer: How question-order effects are influenced by issue involvement. *Health Education & Behavior, 32,* 398–412.

Rind, B., & Strohmetz, D. B. (2001). Effect on restaurant tipping of a helpful message written on the back of customers' checks. *Journal of Applied Social Psychology, 31,* 1379–1384.

Ringelmann, M. (1913). Recherches sur les moteurs animés: Travail de l'homme. *Annales de l'Institut National Agronomique,* 2e série, tom XII, 1–40.

Riniolo, T. C., Johnson, K. C., Sherman, T. R., & Misso, J. A. (2006). Hot or not: Do professors perceived as physically attractive receive higher student evaluations? *Journal of General Psychology, 133,* 19–35.

Rivera, L. A. (2012). Hiring as cultural matching: The case of elite professional service firms. *American Sociological Review, 77,* 999–1022.

Roach, M. (2008). *Bonk: The curious coupling of science and sex.* New York: Norton.

Robbins, J. M., Ford, M. T., & Tetrick, L. E. (2012). Perceived unfairness and employee health: A meta-analytic integration. *Journal of Applied Psychology, 97,* 235–272.

Roberts, G. (2015). Partner Choice Drives the Evolution of Cooperation via Indirect Reciprocity. *PLOS ONE, 10*(6), e0129442.

Roberts, M. H., Klatzkin, R. R., & Mechlin, B. (2015). Social support attenuates physiological stress responses and experimental pain sensitivity to cold pressor pain. *Annals of Behavioral Medicine, 49,* 557–569.

Robins, R. W., Mendelsohn, G. A., Connell, J. B., & Kwan, V. S. Y. (2004). Do people agree about the causes of behavior? A social relations analysis of behavior ratings and causal attributions. *Journal of Personality and Social Psychology, 86,* 334–344.

Robinson, J. P., Shaver, P. R., & Wrightsman, L. S. (Eds.). (1991). *Measures of personality and social psychological attitudes.* New York: Academic Press.

Robinson, J. P., Shaver, P. R., & Wrightsman, L. S. (Eds.). (1998). *Measures of political attitudes.* New York: Academic Press.

Rochat, F., & Blass, T. (2014). Milgram's unpublished obedience variation and its historical relevance. *Journal of Social Issues, 70,* 456–472.

Rockloff, M. J., Greer, N., & Evans, L. G. (2012). The effect of mere presence on electronic gaming machine gambling. *Journal of Gambling Issues, 27,* 1–14.

Rodin, J. (1986). Aging and health: Effects of the sense of control. *Science, 233,* 1271–1276.

Rodriguez Mosquera, P. M., Fischer, A. H., & Manstead, A. S. R. (2004). Inside the heart of emotion. On culture and relational concerns. In L. Z. Tiedens & C. W. Leach (Eds.), *The social life of emotions* (pp. 187–202). Cambridge: Cambridge University Press.

Rodriguez Mosquera, P. M., Fischer, A. H., Manstead, A. S. R., & Zaalberg, R. (2008). Attack, disapproval, or withdrawal? The role of honour in anger and shame responses to being insulted. *Cognition & Emotion, 22,* 1471–1498.

Roese, N. J. (1997). Counterfactual thinking. *Psychological Bulletin, 121,* 133–148.

Roese, N. J., & Jamieson, D. W. (1993). Twenty years of bogus pipeline research: A critical review and meta-analysis. *Psychological Bulletin, 114,* 363–375.

Roese, N. J., & Olson, J. M. (Eds.). (1995). *What might have been: The social psychology of counterfactual thinking.* Hillsdale, NJ: Erlbaum.

Roese, N. J., & Summerville, A. (2005). What we regret most . . . and why. *Personality and Social Psychology Bulletin, 31,* 1273–1285.

Roethlisberger, F. J., & Dickson, W. J. (1939). *Management and the worker.* Cambridge, MA: Harvard University Press.

Rofé, Y. (1984). Stress and affiliation: A utility theory. *Psychological Review, 91,* 235–250.

Rogers, M., Miller, N., Mayer, F. S., & Duval, S. (1982). Personal responsibility and salience of the request for help: Determinants of the relation between negative affect and helping behavior. *Journal of Personality and Social Psychology, 43,* 956–970.

Rogers, R. W. (1983). Cognitive and psychological processes in fear appeals and attitude change: A revised theory of protection motivation. In J. Cacioppo & R. Petty (Eds.), *Social psychophysiology: A sourcebook* (pp. 153–176). New York: Guilford.

Rogers, R. W., & Mewborn, R. C. (1976). Fear appeals and attitude change: Effects of a threat's noxiousness, probability of occurrence, and the efficacy of coping responses. *Journal of Personality and Social Psychology, 34,* 54–61.

Rohrer, J. H., Baron, S. H., Hoffman, E. L., & Swander, D. V (1954). The stability of autokinetic judgments. *Journal of Abnormal and Social Psychology, 49,* 595–597.

Rook, K. S. (1987). Reciprocity of social exchange and social satisfaction among older women. *Journal of Personality and Social Psychology, 52,* 145–154.

Rook, K. S., & Peplau, L. A. (1982). Perspectives on helping the lonely. In L. A. Peplau & D. Perlman (Eds.), *Loneliness: A sourcebook of current theory, research and therapy* (pp. 351–378). New York: Wiley.

Rosenbaum, M. E. (1986). The repulsion hypothesis: On the non-development of relationships. *Journal of Personality and Social Psychology, 51,* 1156–1166.

Rosenberg, S., Nelson, C., & Vivekananthan, P. S. (1968). A multidimensional approach to the structure of personality impressions. *Journal of Personality and Social Psychology, 9,* 283–294.

Rosenbloom, T., Shahr, A., Perlman, A., Estreich, D., & Kirzner, E. (2007). Success on a practical driver's license test with and without the presence of another testee. *Accident Analysis and Prevention, 39,* 1296–1301.

Rosener, J. B. (1995). *America's competitive secret: Utilizing women as a management strategy.* New York: Oxford University Press.

Rosenfeld, M. J. (2014). Couple longevity in the era of same-sex marriage in the United States. *Journal of Marriage and Family, 76,* 905–918.

Rosenfeld, M. J., & Thomas, R. J. (2012). Searching for a mate: The rise of the Internet as a social intermediary. *American Sociological Review, 77,* 523–547.

Rosenman, R. H., Brand, R. J., Jenkins, C. D., Friedman, M., Strau, R., & Wurm, M. (1975). Coronary heart disease in the Western Collaborative Group Study: Final follow-up experience of 8 1/2 years. *Journal of the American Medical Association, 233,* 872–877.

Rosenthal, L., & Levy, S. R. (2013). Thinking about mutual influences and connections across cultures relates to more positive intergroup attitudes: An examination of polyculturalism. *Social and Personality Psychology Compass, 7,* 547–558.

Rosenthal, L., Earnshaw, V. A., Carroll-Scott, A., Henderson, K. E., Peters, S. M., McCaslin, C., & Ickovics, J. R. (2015). Weight- and race-based bullying: Health associations among urban adolescents. *Journal of Health Psychology, 20,* 401–412.

Rosenthal, A. M., Sylva, D., Safron, A., & Bailey, M. J. (2012). The male bisexuality debate revisited: Some bisexual men have bisexual arousal patterns. *Archives of Sexual Behavior, 41,* 135–147.

Rosenthal, L., & Starks, T. J. (2015). Relationship stigma and relationship outcomes in interracial and same-sex relationships: examination of sources and buffers. *Journal of Family Psychology,* in press.

Rosenthal, R. (1976). *Experimenter effects in behavioral research.* New York: Irvington.

Rosenthal, R. (1985). From unconscious experimenter bias to teacher expectancy effects. In J. B. Dusek, V. C. Hall, & W. J. Meyer (Eds.), *Teacher expectancies* (pp. 37–65). Hillsdale, NJ: Erlbaum.

Rosenthal, R. (2002). Covert communication in classrooms, clinics, courtrooms, and cubicles. *American Psychologist, 57,* 839–849.

Rosenthal, R., & Jacobson, L. (1968). *Pygmalion in the classroom: Teacher expectation and pupils' intellectual development.* New York: Holt, Rinehart and Winston.

Rosette, A. S., Mueller, J. S., & Lebel, R. D. (2015). Are male leaders penalized for seeking help? The influence of gender and asking behaviors on competence perceptions. *The Leadership Quarterly,* in press.

Rosh, L., Offermann, L. R., & Van Diest, R. (2012). Too close for comfort? Distinguishing between team intimacy and team cohesion. *Human Resource Management Review, 22,* 116–127.

Rosnow, R. L., & Rosenthal, R. (1993). *Beginning behavioral research: A conceptual primer.* New York: Macmillan.

Ross, E. A. (1908). *Social psychology: An outline and source book.* New York: Macmillan.

Ross, L. (1977). The intuitive psychologist and his shortcomings: Distortions in the attribution process. In L. Berkowitz (Ed.), *Advances in experimental social psychology* (Vol. 10, pp. 174–221). New York: Academic Press.

Ross, L., Amabile, T. M., & Steinmetz, J. L. (1977). Social roles, social control, and biases in social-perception processes. *Journal of Personality and Social Psychology, 35,* 485–494.

Ross, L., Bierbrauer, G., & Hoffman, S. (1976). The role of attribution processes in conformity and dissent. *American Psychologist, 31,* 148–157.

Ross, L., Greene, D., & House, P. (1977). The false consensus phenomenon: An attributional bias in self-perception and social-perception processes. *Journal of Experimental Social Psychology, 13,* 279–301.

Rosse, J. G., Miller, J. L., & Stecher, M. D. (1994). A field study of job applicants' reactions to personality and cognitive ability testing. *Journal of Applied Psychology, 79,* 987–992.

Roth, P. L., Huffcutt, A. I., & Bobko, P. (2003). Ethnic group differences in measures of job performance: A new metaanalysis. *Journal of Applied Psychology, 88,* 694–706.

Rothbaum, F., & Tsang, B. Y. (1998). Lovesongs in the United States and China: On the nature of romantic love. *Journal of Cross-Cultural Psychology, 29,* 306–319.

Roulin, N., & Bangerter, A. (2013). Social networking websites in personnel selection: A signaling perspective on recruiters' and applicants' perceptions. *Journal of Personnel Psychology, 12,* 143–151.

Routledge, C. Arndt, J., Wildschut, T., Sedikides, C., Hart, C. M., Juhl, J., & Schlotz, W. (2011). The past makes the present meaningful: Nostalgia as an existential resource. *Journal of Personality and Social Psychology, 101,* 638–652.

Rowatt, W. C., Cunningham, M. R., & Druen, P. B. (1999). Lying to get a date: The effect of facial physical attractiveness on the willingness to deceive prospective dating partners. *Journal of Social and Personal Relationships, 16,* 209–223.

Roxborough, S. (2009, March 19). German retailer pulls violent DVDs, games. *Reuters.* Available at http://www.reuters.com/article/filmNews/idUSTRE52I7WC20090319.

Rozin, P., & Fallon, A. E. (1987). A perspective on disgust. *Psychological Review, 94,* 23–41.

Rozin, P., & Royzman, E. B. (2001). Negativity bias, negativity dominance, and contagion. *Personality and Social Psychology Review, 5,* 296–320.

Ruback, R. B., & Wroblewski, J. (2001). The federal sentencing guidelines: Psychological and policy reasons for simplification. *Psychology, Public Policy, and Law, 7,* 739–775.

Rubenowitz, S., Norrgren, F., & Tannenbaum, A. S. (1983). Some social psychological effects of direct and indirect participation in ten Swedish companies. *Organization Studies, 4,* 243–259.

Rubin, D. C. (Ed.). (1996). *Remembering our past: Studies in autobiographical memory.* New York: Cambridge University Press.

Rubin, J. Z., Provenzano, F. J., & Luria, Z. (1974). The eye of the beholder: Parents' views on sex of newborns. *American Journal of Orthopsychiatry, 44,* 512–519.

Rubin, Z. (1973). *Liking and loving.* New York: Holt, Rinehart and Winston.

Rubonis, A. Y, & Bickman, L. (1991). Psychological impairment in the wake of disaster: The disaster-psychopathology relationship. *Psychological Bulletin, 109,* 384–399.

Rudman, L. A., & Fetterolf, J. C. (2014). How accurate are meta-perceptions of sexism? Evidence for the illusion of antagonism between hostile and benevolent sexism. *Group Processes & Intergroup Relations, 17,* 275–285.

Rudman, L. A., & Mescher, K. (2012). Of animals and objects: Men's implicit dehumanization of women and likelihood of sexual aggression. *Personality and Social Psychology Bulletin, 38,* 734–746.

Rudman, L. A., Fetterolf, J. C., & Sanchez, D. T. (2013). What motivates the sexual double standard? More support for male versus female control theory. *Personality and Social Psychology Bulletin, 39,* 250–263.

Rudman, L. A., Mescher, K., & Moss-Racusin, C. A. (2013). Reactions to gender egalitarian men: Perceived feminization due to stigma-by-association. *Group Processes & Intergroup Relations, 16,* 572–599.

Rudman, L. A., Moss-Racusin, C. A., Phelan, J. E., & Nauts, S. (2012). Status incongruity and backlash effects: Defending the gender hierarchy motivates prejudice against female leaders. *Journal of Experimental Social Psychology, 48,* 165–179.

Ruffle, B. J., & Sosis, R. (2006). Cooperation and the in-group-out-group bias: A field test on Israeli kibbutz members and city residents. *Journal of Economic Behavior and Organization, 60,* 147–163.

Ruggs, E. N., Hebl, M. R., & Williams, A. (2015). Weight isn't selling: The insidious effects of weight stigmatization in retail settings. *Journal of Applied Psychology, 100,* 1483–1496.

Rusbult, C. E., & Buunk, B. P. (1993). Commitment processes in close relationships: An interdependence analysis. *Journal of Social and Personal Relationships, 10,* 175–204.

Rusbult, C. E., Agnew, C. R., & Arriaga, X. B. (2012). The investment model of commitment processes. In P. Van Lange, A. Kruglanski, & E. T. Higgins (Eds.), *Handbook of theories of social psychology* (Vol. 2, pp. 218–231). Thousand Oaks, CA: Sage.

Rusbult, C. E., Martz, J. M., & Agnew, C. R. (1998). The investment model scale: Measuring commitment level, satisfaction level, quality of alternatives, and investment size. *Personal Relationships, 5,* 357–391.

Rushton, J. P. (1981). The altruistic personality. In J. P. Rushton & R. M. Sorrentino (Eds.), *Altruism and helping behavior: Social, personality, and developmental perspectives* (pp. 251–266). Hillsdale, NJ: Erlbaum.

Russano, M. B., Meissner, C. A., Narchet, F. M., & Kassin, S. M. (2005). Investigating true and false confessions within a novel experimental paradigm. *Psychological Science, 16,* 481–486.

Russell, E., Koren, G., Rieder, M., & Van Uum, S. (2012). Hair cortisol as a biological marker of chronic stress: Current status, future directions and unanswered questions. *Psychoneuroendocrinology, 37,* 589–601.

Ruva, C. L., & Guenther, C. C. (2015). From the shadows into the light: How pretrial publicity and deliberation affect mock jurors' decisions, impressions, and memory. *Law and Human Behavior, 39,* 294–310.

Ruva, C. L., & LeVasseur, M. A. (2012). Behind closed doors: The effect of pretrial publicity on jury deliberations. *Psychology, Crime & Law, 18,* 431–452.

Ryall, J. (2014, Nov 4). Head of Japanese police anti-groping unit arrested for allegedly molesting girl. *South China Morning Post [Hong Kong],* p. A10.

Ryall, J. (2015, Apr 21). Japanese police deploy stickers to combat gropers. *The Telegraph (U. K.)*, http://www.telegraph.co.uk/news/worldnews/asia/japan/11551598/Japanese-police-deploy-stickers-to-combat-gropers.html.

Rydell, R. J., Hamilton, D. L., & Devos, T. (2010). Now they are American, now they are not: Valence as a determinant of the inclusion of African Americans in the American identity. *Social Cognition, 28*, 161–179.

Rydell, R. J., Van Loo, K. J., & Boucher, K. L. (2014). Stereotype threat and executive functions: Which functions mediate different threat-related outcomes? *Personality and Social Psychology Bulletin, 40*, 377–390.

Rynes, S. L., & Connerly, M. L. (1993). Applicant reactions to alternative selection procedures. *Journal of Business and Psychology, 4*, 261–277.

Saad, G. (2007). *The evolutionary bases of consumption.* Mahwah, NJ: Erlbaum.

Sabin, J. A., & Greenwald, A. G. (2012). The influence of implicit bias on treatment recommendations for 4 common pediatric conditions: Pain, urinary tract infection, attention deficit hyperactivity disorder, and asthma. *American Journal of Public Health, 102*, 988–995.

Sachdeva, S., Iliev, R., & Medin, D. L. (2009). Sinning saints and saintly sinners. *Psychological Science, 20*, 523–528.

Sackett, P. R., & DuBois, C. L. Z. (1991). Rater-ratee race effects on performance evaluation: Challenging meta-analytic conclusions. *Journal of Applied Psychology, 76*, 873–877.

Sackett, P. R., & Schmitt, N. (2012). On reconciling conflicting meta-analytic findings regarding integrity test validity. *Journal of Applied Psychology, 97*, 550–556.

Sackett, P. R., Borneman, M. J., & Connelly, B. S. (2008). High-stakes testing in higher education and employment: Appraising the evidence for validity and fairness. *American Psychologist, 63*, 215–227.

Sacks, O. (1985). *The man who mistook his wife for a hat.* New York: Summit.

Sagar, H. A., & Schofield, J. W. (1980). Racial and behavioral cues in black and white children's perceptions of ambiguously aggressive acts. *Journal of Personality and Social Psychology, 39*, 590–598.

Sagarin, B. J. (2005). Reconsidering evolved sex differences in jealousy: Comment on Harris (2003). *Personality and Social Psychology Review, 9*, 62–75.

Saguy, T., Quinn, D. M., Dovidio, J. F., & Pratto, F. (2010). Interacting like a body: Objectification can lead women to narrow their presence in social interactions. *Psychological Science, 21*, 178–182.

Sahin, M. (2012). An investigation into the efficiency of empathy training program on preventing bullying in primary schools. *Children and Youth Services Review, 34*, 1325–1330.

Saks, M. J. (1974). Ignorance of science is no excuse. *Trial, 10*, 18–20.

Saks, M. J., & Marti, M. W. (1997). A meta-analysis of the effects of jury size. *Law and Human Behavior, 21*, 451–468.

Salas, E., Nichols, D. R., & Driskell, J. E. (2007). Testing three team training strategies in intact teams: A meta-analysis. *Small Group Research, 38*, 471–488.

Salas, E., Tannenbaum, S. I., Kraiger, K., & Smith-Jentsch, K. A. (2012). The science of training and development in organizations: What matters in practice. *Psychological Science in the Public Interest, 13*, 74–101.

Saleem, M., Anderson, C. A., & Gentile, D. A. (2012). Effects of prosocial, neutral, and violent video games on children's helpful and hurtful behaviors. *Aggressive Behavior, 38*, 281–287.

Salgado, J. F. (1997). The five factor model of personality and job performance in the European community. *Journal of Applied Psychology, 82*, 30–43.

Salomon, K., Burgess, K. D., & Bosson, J. K. (2015). Flash fire and slow burn: Women's cardiovascular reactivity and recovery following hostile and benevolent sexism. *Journal of Experimental Psychology: General, 144*, 469–479.

Salovey, P. (1992). Mood-induced focus of attention. *Journal of Personality and Social Psychology, 62*, 699–707.

Salovey, P., Mayer, J. D., & Rosenhan, D. L. (1991). Mood and helping: Mood as a motivator of helping and helping as a regulator of mood. In M. S. Clark (Ed.), *Prosocial behavior* (Vol. 12, pp. 215–237). Newbury Park, CA: Sage.

Salvemini, N. J., Reilly, R. R., & Smither, J. W. (1993). The influence of rater motivation on assimilation effects and accuracy in performance ratings. *Organizational Behavior and Human Decision Processes, 55*, 41–60.

Salvers, M. P., Flanagan, M. E., Firmin, R., & Rollins, A. L. (2015). Clinicians' perceptions of how burnout affects their work. *Psychiatric Services, 66*, 204–207.

Sampson, E. E. (2000). Reinterpreting individualism and collectivism: Their religious roots and monologic versus dialogic person-other relationship. *American Psychologist, 55*, 1425–1432.

Sanchez-Burks, J., Nisbett, R. E., & Ybarra, O. (2000). Relational schemas, cultural styles, and prejudice against outgroups. *Journal of Personality and Social Psychology, 79*, 174–189.

Sanchez, D. T., & Chavez, G. (2010). Are you minority enough? Language ability affects targets' and perceivers' assessments of a candidate's appropriateness for affirmative action. *Basic and Applied Social Psychology, 32*, 99–107.

Sanchez, D. T., & Garcia, J. A. (2009). When race matters: Racially stigmatized others and perceiving race as a biological construction affect biracial people's daily well-being. *Personality and Social Psychology Bulletin, 35*, 1154–1164.

Sanchez, D. T., & Garcia, J. A. (2012). Putting race in context: Socioeconomic status predicts racial fluidity. In S. T. Fiske & H. R. Markus (Eds.), *Facing social class: How societal rank influences interaction* (pp. 216–233). New York: Russell Sage Foundation.

Sanchez, D. T., Shih, M. J., & Wilton, L. S. (2014). Exploring the identity autonomy perspective (IAP): An integrative theoretical approach to multicultural and multiracial identity. In V. Benet-Martínez & Y. Hong (Eds.), *The Oxford handbook of multicultural identity* (pp. 139–159). New York: Oxford University Press.

Sanchez, D. T., Young, D. M., & Pauker, K. (2015). Exposure to racial ambiguity influences lay theories of race. *Social Psychological and Personality Science, 6*, 382–390.

Sanchez, J. I., & De La Torre, P. (1996). A second look at the relationship between rating and behavioral accuracy in performance appraisal. *Journal of Applied Psychology, 81*, 3–10.

Sandal, G. M., et al. (2014). Intended self-presentation tactics in job interviews: A 10-country study. *Journal of Cross-Cultural Psychology, 45*, 939–958.

Sanders, A. R., Martin, E. R., Beecham, G. W., Guo, S., Dawood, K., Rieger, G., & . . . Bailey, J. M. (2015). Genome-wide scan demonstrates significant linkage for male sexual orientation. *Psychological Medicine, 45*, 1379–1388.

Sanders, G. S. (1981). Driven by distraction: An integrative review of social facilitation theory and research. *Journal of Experimental Social Psychology, 17*, 227–251.

Sanderson, C. A., & Evans, S. M. (2001). Seeing one's partner through intimacy-colored glasses: An examination of the processes underlying the intimacy goals-relationship satisfaction link. *Personality and Social Psychology Bulletin, 27*, 463–473.

Sandstrom, K. L. Martin, D. D., & Fine, G. A. (2009). *Symbols, selves, and social reality.* New York: Oxford University Press.

Santos, M. D., Leve, C., & Pratkanis, A. R. (1994). Hey buddy, can you spare seventeen cents? Mindful persuasion and the pique technique. *Journal of Applied Social Psychology, 24*, 755–764.

Sapolsky, R. M. (1994). *Why zebras don't get ulcers: A guide to stress, diseases, and coping.* New York: Freeman.

Sapolsky, R. M. (2004). *Why zebras don't get ulcers* (3rd ed.). New York: Owl Books.

Sarat, A. (Ed.). (2005). *Dissent in dangerous times.* Ann Arbor: University of Michigan Press.

Sarento, S., Boulton, A. J., & Salmivalli, C. (2015). Reducing bullying and victimization: Student- and classroom-level mechanisms of change. *Journal of Abnormal Child Psychology, 43,* 61–76.

Sargent, M. J., & Bradfield, A. L. (2004). Race and information processing in criminal trials: Does the defendant's race affect how the facts are evaluated? *Personality and Social Psychology Bulletin, 30,* 995–1008.

Sarkar, U., Ali, S., & Whooley, M. A. (2009). Self-efficacy as a marker of cardiac function and predictor of heart failure hospitalization and mortality in patients with stable coronary heart disease: Findings from the Heart and Soul Study. *Health Psychology, 28,* 166–173.

Sarnoff, I., & Zimbardo, P. (1961). Anxiety, fear, and social affiliation. *Journal of Abnormal and Social Psychology, 62,* 356–363.

Saroglou, V. (2014). *Religion, personality, and social behavior.* New York: Psychology Press.

Sartori, G. Agosta, S. Zogmaister, C. Ferrara, S. D., & Castiello, U. (2008). How to accurately assess autobiographical events. *Psychological Science, 19,* 772–780.

Sasaki, T., & Uchida, S. (2013). The evolution of cooperation by social exclusion. *Proceedings of the Royal Society of London B: Biological Sciences, 280,* 2012–2498.

Saucier, D. A., Miller, C. T., & Doucet, N. (2005). Differences in helping whites and blacks: A meta-analysis. *Personality and Social Psychology Review, 9,* 2–16.

Savani, K., & Markus, H. R. (2012). A processing advantage associated with analytic perceptual tendencies: European Americans outperform Asians on multiple object tracking. *Journal of Experimental Social Psychology, 48,* 766–769.

Savani, K., Markus, H. R., & Conner, A. L. (2008). Let your preference be your guide? Preferences and choices are more tightly linked for North Americans than for Indians. *Journal of Personality and Social Psychology, 95,* 861–76.

Savin, H. B. (1973). Professors and psychological researchers: Conflicting values in conflicting roles. *Cognition, 2,* 147–149.

Savitsky, K., Epley, N., & Gilovich, T. (2001). Do others judge us as harshly as we think? Overestimating the impact of our failures, shortcomings, and mishaps. *Journal of Personality and Social Psychology, 81,* 44–56.

Savitsky, K., Gilovich, T., Berger, G., & Medvec, V. H. (2003). Is our absence as conspicuous as we think? Overestimating the salience and impact of one's absence from a group. *Journal of Experimental Social Psychology, 39,* 386–392.

Sawyer, A. M., & Borduin, C. M. (2011). Effects of multisystemic therapy through midlife: A 21.9-year follow-up to a randomized clinical trial with serious and violent juvenile offenders. *Journal of Consulting and Clinical Psychology, 79,* 643–652.

Sawyer, P. J., Major, B., Casad, B. J., Townsend, S. M., & Mendes, W. (2012). Discrimination and the stress response: Psychological and physiological consequences of anticipating prejudice in interethnic interactions. *American Journal of Public Health, 102*(5), 1020–1026.

Sbarra, D. A., & Nietert, P. J. (2009). Divorce and death: Forty years of the Charleston Heart Study. *Psychological Science, 20,* 107–113.

Sbarra, D. A., Hasselmo, K., & Bourassa, K. J. (2015). Divorce and health: Beyond individual differences. *Current Directions in Psychological Science, 24,* 109–113.

Sbarra, D. A., Law, R. W., & Portley, R. M. (2011). Divorce and death: A meta-analysis and research agenda for clinical, social, and health psychology. *Perspectives on Psychological Science, 6,* 454–474.

Schaa, K. L., Roter, D. L., Biesecker, B. B., Cooper, L. A., & Erby, L. H. (2015). Genetic counselors' implicit racial attitudes and their relationship to communication. *Health Psychology, 34,* 111–119.

Schachter, S. (1951). Deviation, rejection, and communication. *Journal of Abnormal and Social Psychology, 46,* 190–207.

Schachter, S. (1959). *The psychology of affiliation: Experimental studies of the sources of gregariousness.* Stanford, CA: Stanford University Press.

Schachter, S. (1964). The interaction of cognitive and physiological determinants of emotional state. In L. Berkowitz (Ed.), *Advances in experimental social psychology* (Vol. 1, pp. 49–80). New York: Academic Press.

Schachter, S., & Singer, J. (1962). Cognitive, social, and physiological determinants of the emotional state. *Psychological Review, 69,* 379–399.

Schachter, S., & Singer, J. (1979). Comments on the Maslach and Marshall-Zimbardo experiments. *Journal of Personality and Social Psychology, 37,* 989–995.

Schachter, S., Hood, D., Gerin, W., Andreasson, P. B., & Rennert, M. (1985). Some causes and consequences of dependence and independence in the stock market. *Journal of Economic Behavior and Organization, 6,* 339–357.

Schachter, S., Ouellette, R., Whittle, B., & Gerin, W. (1987). Effects of trends and of profit or loss on the tendency to sell stock. *Basic and Applied Social Psychology, 8,* 259–271.

Schacter, H. L., & Juvonen, J. (2015). The effects of school-level victimization on self-blame: Evidence for contextualized social cognitions. *Developmental Psychology, 51,* 841–847.

Schaefer, M., Denke, C., Heinze, H., & Rotte, M. (2014). Rough primes and rough conversations: Evidence for a modality-specific basis to mental metaphors. *Social Cognitive and Affective Neuroscience, 9,* 1653–1659.

Schafer, M. H., & Ferraro, K. F. (2011). The stigma of obesity: Does perceived weight discrimination affect identity and physical health? *Social Psychology Quarterly, 74*(1), 76–97.

Schafer, R. B., & Keith, P. M. (1981). Equity and marital roles across the family life cycle. *Journal of Marriage and the Family, 43,* 359–367.

Schaller, M., & Neuberg, S. L. (2012). Danger, disease, and the nature of prejudice(s). In J. M. Olson & M. P. Zanna (Eds.), *Advances in Experimental Social Psychology* (Vol. 46), pp. 1–54. San Diego: Academic Press.

Schaller, M., Simpson, J. A., & Kenrick, D. T. (Eds.). (2006). *Evolution and social psychology.* New York: Taylor & Francis.

Schapiro, R. (2015, July 25). Hero teacher who took a bullet for a friend in Lafayette theater shooting is resting up, "doing fine" at home. *New York Daily News,* nydailynews.com/news/national/hero-teacher-la-theater-shooting-fine-home-article-1.2304039.

Scheepers, D., Spears, R., Doosje, B., & Manstead, A. S. R. (2006). The social functions of ingroup bias: Creating, confirming, or changing social reality. *European Review of Social Psychology, 17,* 359–396.

Scheier, M. F., & Carver, C. S. (1983). Two sides of the self: One for you and one for me. In J. Suls & A. G. Greenwald (Eds.), *Psychological perspectives on the self* (Vol. 2, pp. 123–157). Hillsdale, NJ: Erlbaum.

Scheier, M. F., & Carver, C. S. (1985). Optimism, coping, and health: Assessment and implications of generalized outcome expectancies. *Health Psychology, 4,* 219–247.

Scheier, M. F., & Carver, C. S. (1992). Effects of optimism on psychological and physical well-being: Theoretical overview and empirical update. *Cognitive Therapy and Research, 16,* 201–228.

Scheier, M. F., & Carver, C. S. (2014). Dispositional optimism. *Trends in Cognitive Sciences, 18,* 293–299.

Schel, A. M., Tranquilli, S., & Zuberbühler, K. (2009). The alarm call system of two species of black-and-white colobus monkeys

(Colobus polykomos and Colobus guereza). *Journal of Comparative Psychology, 123,* 136–150.

Scher, S. J., & Cooper, J. (1989). Motivational basis of dissonance: The singular role of behavioral consequences. *Journal of Personality and Social Psychology, 56,* 899–906.

Scherer, A. M., Windschitl, P. D., & Graham, J. (2015). An ideological house of mirrors: Political stereotypes as exaggerations of motivated social cognition differences. *Social Psychological and Personality Science, 6,* 201–209.

Scherr, K. C., & Madon, S. (2013). "Go ahead and sign": An experimental examination of Miranda waivers and comprehension. *Law and Human Behavior, 37,* 208–218.

Scherr, K. C., Miller, J. C., Kassin, S. M. (2014). "Midnight Confession": The effect of chronotype asynchrony on admissions of wrongdoing. *Basic and Applied Social Psychology, 36,* 321–328.

Schimel, J., & Greenberg, J. (2013). The birth and death of belonging. In C. N. DeWall (Ed.), *The Oxford handbook of social exclusion* (pp. 286–300). New York: Oxford University Press.

Schimmack, U., Oishi, S., & Diener, E. (2005). Individualism: A valid and important dimension of cultural differences between nations. *Personality and Social Psychology Review, 9,* 17–31.

Schino, G. (2007). Grooming and agonistic support: A meta-analysis of primate reciprocal altruism. *Behavioral Ecology, 18,* 115–120.

Schlenger, W. E., et al. (2002). Psychological reactions to terrorist attacks: Findings from the National Study of Americans' Reactions to September 11. *Journal of the American Medical Association, 288,* 581–588.

Schlenker, B. R. (1982). Translating actions into attitudes: An identity-analytic approach to the explanation of social conduct. In L. Berkowitz (Ed.), *Advances in experimental social psychology* (Vol. 15, pp. 193–247). New York: Academic Press.

Schlenker, B. R. (2003). Self-presentation. In M. R. Leary & J. P. Tangney (Eds.), *Handbook of self and identity* (pp. 492–518). New York: Guilford.

Schlenker, B. R., Weigold, M. F., & Hallam, J. R. (1990). Self-serving attributions in social context: Effects of self-esteem and social pressure. *Journal of Personality and Social Psychology, 58,* 855–863.

Schmader, T., Hall, W., & Croft, A. (2015). Stereotype threat in intergroup relations. In M. Mikulincer, P. R. Shaver, E. Borgida, & J. A. Bargh (Eds.), *APA handbook of personality and social psychology,* Volume 2: *Group processes* (pp. 447–471). Washington, DC: American Psychological Association.

Schmeichel, B. J., & Vohs, K. (2009). Self-affirmation and self-control: Affirming core values counteracts ego depletion. *Journal of Personality and Social Psychology, 96,* 770–782.

Schmidt, F. L. (2002). The role of general cognitive ability and job performance: Why there cannot be a debate. *Human Performance, 15,* 187–210.

Schmidt, F. L., & Rader, M. (1999). Exploring the boundary conditions for interview validity: Meta-analytic validity findings for a new interview type. *Personnel Psychology, 52,* 445–464.

Schmitt, N. (Ed.) (2012). *The Oxford handbook of personnel assessment and selection.* New York: Oxford University Press.

Schmitt, M. T., Branscombe, N. R., Postmes, T., & Garcia, A. (2014). The consequences of perceived discrimination for psychological well-being: A meta-analytic review. *Psychological Bulletin, 140,* 921–948.

Schmitt, D. P. (2003). Universal sex differences in the desire for sexual variety: Tests from 52 nations, 6 continents, and 13 islands. *Journal of Personality and Social Psychology, 85,* 85–104.

Schmitt, N., & Oswald, F. L. (2006). The impact of corrections for faking on the validity of noncognitive measures in selection settings. *Journal of Applied Psychology, 91,* 613–621.

Schneider, D. J. (1973). Implicit personality theory: A review. *Psychological Bulletin, 79,* 294–309.

Schneider, M. C., & Bos, A. L. (2014). Measuring stereotypes of female politicians. *Political Psychology, 35,* 245–266.

Schneider, S. G., Taylor, S. E., Hammen, C., Kemeny, M. E., & Dudley, J. (1991). Factors influencing suicide intent in gay and bisexual suicide ideators: Differing models for men with and without human immunodeficiency virus. *Journal of Personality and Social Psychology, 61,* 776–778.

Schneider, T. J., Goffin, R. D., & Daljeet, K. N. (2015). "Give us your social networking site passwords": Implications for personnel selection and personality. *Personality and Individual Differences, 73,* 78–83.

Schneiderman, R. M. (2008, October 30). *Do Americans still hate welfare?* New York.

Schönenberg, M., & Jusyte, A. (2014). Investigation of the hostile attribution bias toward ambiguous facial cues in antisocial violent offenders. *European Archives of Psychiatry and Clinical Neuroscience, 264,* 61–69.

Schoorman, F. D. (1988). Escalation bias in performance appraisals: An unintended consequence of supervisor participation in hiring decisions. *Journal of Applied Psychology, 73,* 58–62.

Schuldt, J. P., Konrath, S. H., & Schwarz, N. (2011). "Global warming" or "climate change"? Whether the planet is warming depends on question wording. *Public Opinion Quarterly, 75,* 115–124.

Schuldt, J. P., Roh, S., & Schwarz, N. (2015). Questionnaire design effects in climate change surveys: Implications for the partisan divide. *Annals of the American Academy of Political and Social Science, 658,* 67–85.

Schulman, J., Shaver, P., Colman, R., Emrick, B., & Christie, R. (1973, May). Recipe for a jury. *Psychology Today,* pp. 37–44, 77, 79–84.

Schultz, B., Ketrow, S. M., & Urban, D. M. (1995). Improving decision quality in the small group: The role of the reminder. *Small Group Research, 26,* 521–541.

Schulz, R. (1976). Effects of control and predictability on the physical and psychological well-being of the institutionalized aged. *Journal of Personality and Social Psychology, 33,* 563–573.

Schulz-Hardt, S., & Mojzisch, A. (2012). How to achieve synergy in group decision making: Lessons to be learned from the hidden profile paradigm. *European Review of Social Psychology, 23,* 305–343.

Schumann, K., Zaki, J., & Dweck, C. S. (2014). Addressing the empathy deficit: Beliefs about the malleability of empathy predict effortful responses when empathy is challenging. *Journal of Personality and Social Psychology, 107,* 475–493.

Schuster, M. A., Stein, B. D., Jaycox, L. H., Collins, R. L., Marshall, G. N., Elliott, M. N., Zhou, A. J., Kanouse, D. E., Morrison, J. L., & Berry, S. H. (2001). A national survey of stress reactions after the September 11, 2001, terrorist attacks. *New England Journal of Medicine, 345,* 1507–1512.

Schützwohl, A. (2004). Which infidelity type makes you more jealous? Decision strategies in a forced-choice between sexual and emotional infidelity. *Evolutionary Psychology, 2,* 121–128.

Schwartz, C. E., Wright, C. I., Shin, L. M., Kagan, J., & Rauch, S. L. (2003). Inhibited and uninhibited infants "grow up": Adult amygdalar response to novelty. *Science, 300,* 1952–1953.

Schwartz, R. L., Fremouw, W., Schenk, A., & Ragatz, L. L. (2012). Psychological profile of male and female animal abusers. *Journal of Interpersonal Violence, 27,* 846–861.

Schwartz, S. H. (1990). Individualism-collectivism: Critique and proposed refinements. *Journal of Cross-Cultural Psychology, 21,* 139–157.

Schwartz, S. H., & Gottlieb, A. (1980). Bystander anonymity and reaction to emergencies. *Journal of Personality and Social Psychology, 39,* 418–430.

Schwarz, N. (1990). Feelings as information: Information and motivational functions as affective states. In E. T. Higgins et al. (Eds.), *Handbook of motivation and cognition: Foundations of social behavior* (Vol. 2, pp. 527–561). New York: Guilford.

Schwarz, N., & Oyserman, D. (2011). Asking questions about behavior: Self-reports in evaluation research. In M. M. Mark, S. I. Donaldson, & B. Campbell (Eds.), *Social psychology and evaluation* (pp. 243–264). New York: Guilford.

Schwarz, N., Bless, H., & Bohner, G. (1991). Mood and persuasion: Affective states influence the processing of persuasive communications. In M. P. Zanna (Ed.), *Advances in experimental social psychology* (Vol. 24, pp. 161–199). New York: Academic Press.

Schwarz, N., Oyserman, D., & Peytcheva, E. (2010). Cognition, communication, and culture: Implications for the survey response process. In J. Harkness et al. (Eds.), *Survey methods in multinational, multiregional and multicultural contexts* (pp. 177–190). New York: Wiley.

Schwarzwald, J., Raz, M., & Zvibel, M. (1979). The applicability of the door-in-the-face technique when established behavioral customs exist. *Journal of Applied Social Psychology, 9*, 576–586.

Schwinger, M., Wirthwein, L., Lemmer, G., & Steinmayr, R. (2014). Academic self-handicapping and achievement: A meta-analysis. *Journal of Educational Psychology, 106*, 744–761.

Science Daily. (2008, December 8). Why do people make "a mountain out of a molehill?" Aggression, status, and sex. Retrieved from http://www.sciencedaily.com/releases/2008/12/081208140156.htm.

Scopelliti, I., Morewedge, C. K., McCormick, E., Min, H. L., Lebrecht, S., & Kassam, K. S. (2015). Bias blind spot: Structure, measurement, and consequences. *Management Science, 61*, 2468–2486.

Scullen, S. E., Mount, M., & Goff, M. (2000). Understanding the latent structure of job performance ratings. *Journal of Applied Psychology, 85*, 956–970.

Seacat, J. D., & Mickelson, K. D. (2009). Stereotype threat and the exercise/dietary health intentions of overweight women. *Journal of Health Psychology, 14*, 556–567.

Sears, G. J., Zhang, H., Wiesner, W. H., Hackett, R. D., & Yuan, Y. (2013). A comparative assessment of videoconference and face-to-face employment interviews. *Management Decision, 51*, 1733–1752.

Sebag-Montefiore, C. (2015, June 15). Rise of the ripped: With bodies sculpted to look like comic-book heroes, today's muscle men create an impossible template for masculinity. *Aeon,* http://aeon.co/magazine/culture/why-has-buff-become-best-for-men/.

Sechrist, G. B., & Milford, L. R. (2007). The influence of social consensus information on intergroup helping behavior. *Basic and Applied Social Psychology, 29*, 365–374.

Sedikides, C. (1992). Attentional effects on mood are moderated by chronic self-conception valence. *Personality and Social Psychology Bulletin, 18*, 580–584.

Sedikides, C., & Anderson, C. A. (1994). Causal perceptions of intertrait relations: The glue that holds person types together. *Personality and Social Psychology Bulletin, 20*, 294–302.

Sedikides, C., & Gregg, A. P. (2008). Self-enhancement: Food for thought. *Perspectives on Psychological Science, 3*, 102–116.

Sedikides, C., & Jackson, J. M. (1990). Social impact theory: A field test of source strength, source immediacy and number of targets. *Basic and Applied Social Psychology, 11*, 273–281.

Sedikides, C., & Spencer, S. J. (Eds.). (2007). *The self.* New York: Psychology Press.

Sedikides, C., Gaertner, L., & Toguchi, Y. (2003). Pancultural self-enhancement. *Journal of Personality and Social Psychology, 84*, 60–79.

Sedikides, C., Gaertner, L., & Vevea, J. L. (2005). Pancultural self-enhancement reloaded: A meta-analytic reply to Heine (2005). *Journal of Personality and Social Psychology, 89*, 539–551.

Seeman, T. E., Dubin, L. F., & Seeman, M. (2003). Religiosity/spirituality and health: A critical review of the evidence for biological pathways. *American Psychologist, 58*, 53–63.

Segerstrom, S. C. (2006a). *Breaking Murphy's law: How optimists get what they want from life and pessimists can too.* New York: Guilford Press.

Segerstrom, S. C. (2006b). How does optimism suppress immunity? Evaluation of three affective pathways. *Health Psychology, 25*, 653–657.

Segerstrom, S. C. (Ed.). (2012). *The Oxford Handbook of Psychoneuroimmunology.* New York: Oxford University Press.

Segerstrom, S. C., & Miller, G. E. (2004). Psychological stress and the human immune system: A meta-analytic study of 30 years of inquiry. *Psychological Bulletin, 130*, 601–630.

Segerstrom, S. C., Taylor, S. E., Kemeny, M. E., & Fahey, J. L. (1998). Optimism is associated with mood, coping, and immune change in response to stress. *Journal of Personality and Social Psychology, 74*, 1646–1655.

Seidman, G., & Miller, O. S. (2013). Effects of gender and physical attractiveness on visual attention to Facebook profiles. *Cyberpsychology, Behavior, and Social Networking, 16*, 20–24.

Seih, Y., Buhrmester, M. D., Lin, Yi., Huang, C., & Swann Jr., W. B. (2013). Do people want to be flattered or understood? The cross-cultural universality of self-verification. *Journal of Experimental Social Psychology, 49*, 169–172.

Sekaquaptewa, D., & Thompson, M. (2003). Solo status, stereotype threat, and performance expectancies: Their effects on women's performance. *Journal of Experimental Social Psychology, 39*, 68–74.

Sekaquaptewa, D., Espinoza, P., Thompson, M., Vargas, P., & von Hippel, W. (2003). Stereotypic explanatory bias: Implicit stereotyping as a predictor of discrimination. *Journal of Experimental Social Psychology, 39*, 75–82.

Sela, Y., Shackelford, T. K., Pham, M. N., & Zeigler-Hill, V. (2015). Women's mate retention behaviors, personality traits, and fellatio. *Personality and Individual Differences, 85*, 187–191.

Seligman, M. E. P. (1975). *On depression, development, and death.* San Francisco: Freeman.

Seligman, M. E. P. (1991). *Learned optimism.* New York: Knopf.

Sellaro, R., Derks, B., Nitsche, M. A., Hommel, B., van den Wildenberg, W. P., van Dam, K., & Colzato, L. S. (2015). Reducing prejudice through brain stimulation. *Brain Stimulation, 8*, 891–897.

Selterman, D., Apetroaia, A., & Waters, E. (2012). Script-like attachment representations in dreams containing current romantic partners. *Attachment and Human Development, 14*, 501–515.

Selterman, D. F., Apetroaia, A. I., Riela, S., & Aron, A. (2014). Dreaming of you: Behavior and emotion in dreams of significant others predict subsequent relational behavior. *Social Psychological and Personality Science, 5*, 111–118.

Seltzer, R. (2006). Scientific jury selection: Does it work? *Journal of Applied Social Psychology, 36*, 2417–2435.

Selye, H. (1936). A syndrome produced by diverse nocuous agents. *Nature, 138*, 32.

Senju, A., & Johnson, M. (2009). The eye contact effect: Mechanisms and development. *Trends in Cognitive Sciences, 13*, 127–134.

Seong, J. Y., Kristof-Brown, A. L., Park, W., Hong, D., & Shin, Y. (2015). Person-group fit: Diversity antecedents, proximal outcomes, and performance at the group level. *Journal of Management, 41*, 1184–1213.

Sergeant, M. J. T., Dickins, T. E., Davies, M. N. O., & Griffiths, M. D. (2006). Aggression, empathy and sexual orientation in males. *Personality and Individual Differences, 40*, 475–486.

Serna, J. & Megerian, C. (2014, April 14). Bus crash victim spent last moments helping others escape. *Los Angeles Times,* latimes.com/local/la-me-0415-bus-crash-20140415-story.html.

Seto, M. C., Marc, A., & Barbaree, H. E. (2001). The role of pornography in the etiology of sexual aggression. *Aggression and Violent Behavior, 6*, 35–53.

Seyle, D. C., & Newman, M. L. (2006). A house divided? The psychology of red and blue America. *American Psychologist, 61*, 571–580.

Shackelford, T. K., & Hansen, R. D. (2015). *The evolution of sexuality.* Cham, Switzerland: Springer International.

Shackelford, T. K., & Larsen, R. J. (1999). Facial attractiveness and physical health. *Evolution and Human Behavior, 20*, 71–76.

Shackelford, T. K., Voracek, M., Schmitt, D. P., Buss, D. M., Weekes-Shackelford, V A., & Michalski, R. L. (2004). Romantic jealousy in early adulthood and later life. *Human Nature, 15*, 283–300.

Shackelford, T. K., Weekes-Shackelford, V. A., & Schmitt, D. P. (2005). An evolutionary perspective on why some men refuse or reduce their child support payments. *Basic and Applied Social Psychology, 27*, 297–306.

Shalvi, S., Gino, F., Barkan, R., & Ayal, S. (2015). Self-serving justifications: Doing wrong and feeling moral. *Current Directions in Psychological Science, 24*, 125–130.

Shariff, A. F., & Norenzayan, A. (2007). God is watching you: Priming God concepts increases prosocial behavior in an anonymous economic game. *Psychological Science, 18*, 803–809.

Shariff, A. F., Willard, A. K., Andersen, T., & Norenzayan, A. (2015). Religious priming: A meta-analysis with a focus on prosociality. *Personality and Social Psychology Review*, in press.

Sharp, E. A., & Ganong, L. (2011). "I'm a loser, I'm not married, let's just all look at me": Ever-single women's perceptions of their social environment. *Journal of Family Issues, 32*, 956–980.

Shaver, K. G. (1970). Defensive attribution: Effects of severity and relevance on the responsibility assigned for an accident. *Journal of Personality and Social Psychology, 14*, 101–113.

Shaw, J., & Porter, S. (2015). Constructing rich false memories of committing crime. *Psychological Science, 26*, 291–301.

Shaw, J. S., III. (1996). Increases in eyewitness confidence resulting from postevent questioning. *Journal of Experimental Psychology: Applied, 2*, 126–146.

Shefrin, H. (2006). *Greed and fear: Understanding behavioral finance and the psychology of investing.* New York: Oxford University Press.

Shefrin, H. M., & Statman, M. (1985). The disposition to sell winners too early and ride losers too long: theory and evidence. *Journal of Finance, 40*, 777–790.

Shefrin, H. M., & Statman, M. (1986, February). How not to make money in the stock market. *Psychology Today*, pp. 52–57.

Sheldon, K. M., & Lyubomirsky, S. (2012). The challenge of staying happier: Testing the hedonic adaptation prevention model. *Personality and Social Psychology Bulletin, 38*, 670–680.

Shelton, J. N., & Richeson, J. A. (2005). Intergroup contact and pluralistic ignorance. *Journal of Personality and Social Psychology, 88*, 91–107.

Shelton, J. N., & Richeson, J. A. (2015). Interacting across racial lines. In M. Mikulincer, P. R. Shaver, E. Borgida, & J. A. Bargh (Eds.), *APA handbook of personality and social psychology, Volume 2: Group processes* (pp. 395–422). Washington, DC: American Psychological Association.

Shen, H., Wan, F., & Wyer, R. S. (2011). Cross-cultural differences in the refusal to accept a small gift: The differential influence of reciprocity norms on Asians and North Americans. *Journal of Personality and Social Psychology, 100*, 271–281.

Shepela, S. T., Cook, J., Horlitz, E., Leal, R., Luciano, S., Lutfy, E., Miller, C., Mitchell, G., & Worden, E. (1999). Courageous resistance: A special case of altruism. *Theory and Psychology, 9*, 787–805.

Shepperd, J. A. (1993b). Student derogation of the Scholastic Aptitude Test: Biases in perceptions and presentations of college board scores. *Basic and Applied Social Psychology, 14*, 455–473.

Shepperd, J. A., Klein, W. M. P., Waters, E. A., & Weinstein, N. D. (2013). Taking stock of unrealistic optimism. *Perspectives on Psychological Science, 8*, 395–411.

Sherer, M. (2007). Advice and help-seeking intentions among youth in Israel: Ethnic and gender differences. *Journal of Sociology & Social Welfare, 34*, 53–76.

Sherer, M. (2009). The nature and correlates of dating violence among Jewish and Arab youths in Israel. *Journal of Family Violence, 24*, 11–26.

Sherif, M. (1936). *The psychology of social norms.* New York: Harper.

Sherif, M. (1966). *In common predicament: Social psychology of intergroup conflict and cooperation.* Boston: Houghton Mifflin.

Sherif, M., Harvey, L. J., White, B. J., Hood, W. R., & Sherif, C. W. (1961). *The Robbers Cave experiment: Intergroup conflict and cooperation.* Middletown, CT: Wesleyan University Press.

Sherman, J. W., Gawronski, B., & Trope, Y. (2014). *Dual-process theories of the social mind.* New York: Guilford.

Sherman, J. W., Kruschke, J. K., Sherman, S. J., Percy, E. J., Petrocelli, J. V., & Conrey, F. R. (2009). Attentional processes in stereotype formation: A common model for category accentuation and illusory correlation. *Journal of Personality and Social Psychology, 96*, 305–323.

Sherman, J. W., Stroessner, S. J., Conrey, F. R., & Azam, O. A. (2005). Prejudice and stereotype maintenance processes: Attention, attribution, and individuation. *Journal of Personality and Social Psychology, 89*, 607–622.

Shih, M. J., Pittinsky, T. L., & Ho, G. C. (2012). Stereotype boost: Positive outcomes from the activation of positive stereotypes. In M. Inzlicht & T. Schmader (Eds.), *Stereotype threat: Theory, process, and application* (pp. 141–156). New York: Oxford University Press.

Shih, M., Bonam, C., Sanchez, D., & Peck, C. (2007). The social construction of race: Biracial identity and vulnerability to stereotypes. *Cultural Diversity and Ethnic Minority Psychology, 13*, 125–133.

Shore, T. H., Shore, L. M., & Thornton, G. C., III. (1992). Construct validity of self- and peer evaluations of performance dimensions in an assessment center. *Journal of Applied Psychology, 77*, 42–54.

Shotland, R. L., & Stebbins, C. A. (1980). Bystander response to rape: Can a victim attract help? *Journal of Applied Social Psychology, 10*, 510–527.

Shteynberg, G., Gelfand, M. J., & Kim, K. (2009). Peering into the "magnum mysterium" of culture: The explanatory power of descriptive norms. *Journal of Cross-Cultural Psychology, 40*, 46–69.

Shteynberg, G., Leslie, L. M., Knight, A. P., & Mayer, D. M. (2011). But affirmative action hurts us! Racer elated beliefs shape perceptions of White disadvantage and policy unfairness. *Organizational Behavior and Human Decision Processes, 115*, 1–12.

Sidebotham, P., & Heron, J. (2006). Child maltreatment in the "children of the nineties": A cohort study of risk factors. *Child Abuse and Neglect, 30*, 497–522.

Siegler, I. C. (1994). Hostility and risk: Demographic and lifestyle variables. In A. W. Siegman & T. W. Smith (Eds.), *Anger, hostility, and the heart* (pp. 199–214). Hillsdale, NJ: Erlbaum.

Siegman, A. W., & Smith, T. W. (1994). *Anger, hostility, and the heart.* Hillsdale, NJ: Erlbaum.

Siem, B., Lotz-Schmitt, K., & Stürmer, S. (2014). To help or not to help an outgroup member: The role of the target's individual attributes in resolving potential helpers' motivational conflict. *European Journal of Social Psychology, 44*, 297–312.

Silverstein, B., Perdue, L., Peterson, B., & Kelly, E. (1986). The role of the mass media in promoting a thin standard of bodily attractiveness for women. *Sex Roles, 14*, 519–532.

Silvia, P. (2006). Reactance and the dynamics of disagreement: Multiple paths from threatened freedom to resistance to persuasion. *European Journal of Social Psychology, 36*, 673–685.

Silvia, P. J., & Duval, T. S. (2001). Objective self-awareness theory: Recent progress and enduring problems. *Personality and Social Psychology Review, 5*, 230–241.

Simon, D. (2012). *In doubt: The psychology of the criminal justice process.* Cambridge, MA: Harvard University Press.

Simons, L. G., Simons, R. L., & Su, X. (2013). Consequences of corporal punishment among African Americans: The importance of context and outcome. *Journal of Youth and Adolescence, 42*, 1273–1285.

Simons, R. L., Simons, L. G., Lei, M., Beach, S. H., Brody, G. H., Gibbons, F. X., & Philibert, R. A. (2013). Genetic moderation of the impact of parenting on hostility toward romantic partners. *Journal of Marriage and Family, 75,* 325–341.

Simons, L., Simons, R. L., Lei, M., & Sutton, T. E. (2012). Exposure to harsh parenting and pornography as explanations for males' sexual coercion and females' sexual victimization. *Violence and Victims, 27,* 378–395.

Simonsohn, U. (2011). Spurious? Name similarity effects (implicit egotism) in marriage, job, and moving decisions. *Journal of Personality and Social Psychology, 101,* 1–24.

Simonson, I., & Staw, B. W. (1992). Deescalation strategies: A comparison of techniques for reducing commitment to losing courses of action. *Journal of Applied Psychology, 77,* 419–426.

Simpson, J. A. (1987). The dissolution of romantic relationships: Factors involved in relationship stability and emotional distress. *Journal of Personality and Social Psychology, 53,* 683–692.

Simpson, J. A., & Campbell, L. (Eds.). (2013). *The Oxford handbook of close relationships.* New York: Oxford University Press.

Simpson, J. A., Campbell, B., & Berscheid, E. (1986). The association between romantic love and marriage: Kephart (1967) twice revisited. *Personality and Social Psychology Bulletin, 12,* 363–372.

Simpson, J. A., Gangestad, S. W., & Lerma, M. (1990). Perception of physical attractiveness: Mechanisms involved in the maintenance of romantic relationships. *Journal of Personality and Social Psychology, 59,* 1192–1201.

Simpson, J. A., Rholes, W. S., & Phillips, D. (1996). Conflicts in close relationships: An attachment perspective. *Journal of Personality and Social Psychology, 71,* 899–914.

Sin, N. L., & Lyubomirsky, S. (2009). Enhancing well-being and alleviating depressive symptoms with positive psychology interventions: A practice-friendly meta-analysis. *Journal of Clinical Psychology, 65,* 467–487.

Sinclair, R. C., Hoffman, C., Mark, M. M., Martin, L. M., & Pickering, T. L. (1994). Construct accessibility and the misattribution of arousal: Schachter and Singer revisited. *Psychological Science, 5,* 15–19.

Singh, D. (1995). Female judgment of male attractiveness and desirability for relationships: Role of waist-to-hip ratio and financial status. *Journal of Personality and Social Psychology, 69,* 1089–1101.

Singh, D., & Randall, P. K. (2007). Beauty is in the eye of the plastic surgeon: Waist-hip ratio (WHR) and women's attractiveness. *Personality and Individual Differences, 43,* 329–340.

Singh, D., Dixson, B. J., Jessop, T. S., Morgan, B., & Dixson, A. F. (2010). Cross-cultural consensus for waist-hip ratio and women's attractiveness. *Evolution and Human Behavior, 31,* 176–181.

Singh, E. (2009). *Caste system in India: A historical perspective.* New Delhi: Kalpaz Publications.

Sinha, K. (2012). 57% of boys, 53% of girls think wife beating is justified. *The Times of India,* April 25.

Sistrunk, F., & McDavid, J. W. (1971). Sex variable in conforming behavior. *Journal of Personality and Social Psychology, 17,* 200–207.

Sittichai, R., & Smith, P. K., (2015). Bullying in South-East Asian countries: A review. *Aggression and Violent Behavior,* http://dx.doi.org/10.1016/j.avb.2015.06.002

Siu, A. M. H., Cheng, H. C. H., & Leung, M. C. M. (2006). Pro-social norms as a positive youth development construct: Conceptual bases and implications for curriculum development. *International Journal of Adolescent Medicine and Health, 18,* 451–457.

Skagerberg, E. M. (2007). Co-witness feedback in line-ups. *Applied Cognitive Psychology, 21,* 489–497.

Skarlicki, D. P., & Folger, R. (1997). Retaliation in the workplace: The roles of distributive, procedural, and interactional justice. *Journal of Applied Psychology, 82,* 434–443.

Skinner, A. L., Stevenson, M. C., & Camillus, J. C. (2015). Ambivalent sexism in context: Hostile and benevolent sexism moderate bias against female drivers. *Basic and Applied Social Psychology, 37,* 56–67.

Skinner, E. A. (1996). A guide to constructs of control. *Journal of Personality and Social Psychology, 71,* 549–570.

Skinner, E. A., Edge, K., Altman, J., & Sherwood, H. (2003). Searching for the structure of coping: A review and critique of category systems for classifying ways of coping. *Psychological Bulletin, 129,* 216–269.

Skitka, L. J., Mullen, E., Griffin, T., Hutchinson, S., & Chamberlin, B. (2002). Dispositions, scripts, or motivated correction? Understanding ideological differences in explanations for social problems. *Journal of Personality and Social Psychology, 83,* 470–487.

Sklar, L. S., & Anisman, H. (1981). Stress and cancer. *Psychological Bulletin, 89,* 369–406.

Skowronski, J. J., & Carlston, D. E. (1989). Negativity and extremity biases in impression formation: A review of explanations. *Psychology Bulletin, 105,* 131–142.

Slamecka, N. J., & Graff, P. (1978). The generation effect: Delineation of a phenomenon. *Journal of Experimental Psychology: Human Learning and Memory, 4,* 592–604.

Slater, D. (2013). *Love in the time of algorithms: What technology does to meeting and mating.* New York: Current.

Sleesman, D. J., Conlon, D. E., McNamara, G., & Miles, J. E. (2012). Cleaning up the big muddy: A meta-analytic review of the determinants of escalation of commitment. *Academy of Management Journal, 55,* 541–562.

Slepian, M. L., Young, S. G., Rule, N. O., Weisbuch, M., & Ambady, N. (2012). Embodied impression formation: Social judgments and motor cues to approach and avoidance. *Social Cognition, 30,* 232–240.

Sloan, R., Bagiella, E., & Powell, T. (1999). Religion, spirituality, and medicine. *Lancet, 353,* 664–667.

Slovic, P. (2000). *The perception of risk.* London: Earthscan.

Smalarz, L., & Wells, G. L. (2014). Post-identification feedback to eyewitnesses impairs evaluators' abilities to discriminate between accurate and mistaken testimony. *Law and Human Behavior, 38,* 194–202.

Smalarz, L., & Wells, G. L. (2015). Contamination of eyewitness self-reports and the mistaken-identification problem. *Current Directions in Psychological Science, 24,* 120–124.

Smart Richman, L., & Leary, M. R. (2009). Reactions to discrimination, stigmatization, ostracism, and other forms of interpersonal rejection: A multimotive model. *Psychological Review, 116,* 365–383.

Smeaton, G., Byrne, D., & Murnen, S. K. (1989). The repulsion hypothesis revisited: Similarity irrelevance or dissimilarity bias? *Journal of Personality and Social Psychology, 56,* 54–59.

Smidt, K. E., & DeBono, K. G. (2011). On the effects of product name on product evaluation: An individual difference perspective. *Social Influence, 6,* 131–141.

Smith, A., & Williams, K. D. (2004). RU there? Ostracism by cell phone text messages. *Group Dynamics: Theory, Research, and Practice, 8,* 291–301.

Smith, A., Jussim, L., & Eccles, J. (1999). Do self-fulfilling prophecies accumulate, dissipate, or remain stable over time? *Journal of Personality and Social Psychology, 77,* 548–565.

Smith, C. (2012a). Pittsburgh basketball game marred by horrible racist banana suited monkey chants. http://sports.yahoo.com/blogs/highschool-prep-rally/pittsburgh-basketball-game-marred-horrible-racist-banana-suited-131740578.html.

Smith, C. (2012b). San Antonio prep hoops fans accused of racism over "USA, USA" chant. http://sports.yahoo.com/blogs/highschool-prep-rally/san-antonio-prep-hoops-fans-accused-racismabover-usa-123930890.html.

Smith, C. A., Ireland, T. O., Park, A., Elwyn, L., & Thornberry, T. P. (2011). Intergenerational continuities and discontinuities in intimate partner violence: A two-generational prospective study. *Journal of Interpersonal Violence, 26,* 3720–3752.

Smith, D. L. (2007). *The most dangerous animal: Human nature and the origins of war.* New York: St. Martin's.

Smith, E. E. (2013). Social connection makes a better brain. *The Atlantic.* Retrieved from http://www.theatlantic.com/health/archive/2013/10/social-connection-makes-a-better-brain/280934/.

Smith, H. J., & Pettigrew, T. F. (2015). Advances in relative deprivation theory and research. *Social Justice Research, 28,* 1–6.

Smith, M. L., Glass, G. V., & Miller, T. I. (1980). *The benefits of psychotherapy.* Baltimore: Johns Hopkins University Press.

Smith, N. K., Cacioppo, J. T., Larsen, J. T., & Chartrand, T. L. (2003). May I have your attention, please: Electrocortical responses to positive and negative stimuli. *Neuropsychologia, 41,* 171–183.

Smith, P. B., & Bond, M. H. (1993). *Social psychology across cultures: Analysis and perspective.* New York: Harvester/Wheatsheaf.

Smith, S., McIntosh, W., & Bazzini, D. (1999). Are the beautiful good in Hollywood? An investigation of the beauty-and-goodness stereotype on film. *Basic and Applied Social Psychology, 21,* 69–80.

Smith, S. S., & Richardson, D. (1983). Amelioration of deception and harm in psychological research: The important role of debriefing. *Journal of Personality and Social Psychology, 44,* 1075–1082.

Smith, T. W., Snyder, C. R., & Perkins, S. C. (1983). The self-serving function of hypochondriacal complaints: Physical symptoms as self-handicapping strategies. *Journal of Personality and Social Psychology, 44,* 787–797.

Smith, V. L., & Kassin, S. M. (1993). Effects of the dynamite charge on the deliberations of deadlocked mock juries. *Law and Human Behavior, 17,* 625–643.

Smith-Genthôs, K. R., Reich, D. A., Lakin, J. L., & Casa de Calvo, M. P. (2015). The tongue-tied chameleon: The role of nonconscious mimicry in the behavioral confirmation process. *Journal of Experimental Social Psychology, 56,* 179–182.

Smolak, L., & Thompson, J. K. (Eds.). (2009). *Body image, eating disorders, and obesity in youth: Assessment, prevention, and treatment* (2nd ed.). Washington, DC: American Psychological Association.

Snibbe, A. C., Kitayama, S., Markus, H. R., & Suzuki, T. (2003). They saw a game: A Japanese and American (football) field study. *Journal of Cross-Cultural Psychology, 34,* 581–595.

Snyder, C. R., & Higgins, R. L. (1988). Excuses: Their effective role in the negotiation of reality. *Psychological Bulletin, 104,* 23–35.

Snyder, C. R., Higgins, R. L., & Stucky, R. J. (1983). *Excuses: Masquerades in Search of Grace.* New York: Wiley.

Snyder, C. R., Lassegard, M. A., & Ford, C. E. (1986). Distancing after group success and failure: Basking in reflected glory and cutting off reflected failure. *Journal of Personality and Social Psychology, 51,* 382–388.

Snyder, M. (1974). The self-monitoring of expressive behavior. *Journal of Personality and Social Psychology, 30,* 526–537.

Snyder, M. (1987). *Public appearances/private realities: The psychology of self-monitoring.* New York: Freeman.

Snyder, M. (1993). Basic research and practical problems: The promise of a "functional" personality and social psychology. *Personality and Social Psychology Bulletin, 19,* 251–264.

Snyder, M. (2013). B = f (P, S): Perspectives on persons and situations, from Lewin to Bond and beyond. *Asian Journal of Social Psychology, 16,* 16–18.

Snyder, M., & DeBono, K. (1985). Appeals to image and claims about quality: Understanding the psychology of advertising. *Journal of Personality and Social Psychology, 49,* 586–597.

Snyder, M., & Gangestad, S. (1986). On the nature of self-monitoring: Matters of assessment, matters of validity. *Journal of Personality and Social Psychology, 51,* 125–139.

Snyder, M., & Monson, T. C. (1975). Persons, situations, and the control of social behavior. *Journal of Personality and Social Psychology, 32,* 637–644.

Snyder, M., & Omoto, A. (2008). Volunteerism: Social issues perspectives and social policy implications. *Social Issues and Policy Review, 2,* 1–36.

Snyder, M., & Stukas, A. A. (1999). Interpersonal processes: The interplay of cognitive, motivational, and behavioral activities in social interaction. *Annual Review of Psychology, 50,* 273–303.

Snyder, M., & Swann, W. B., Jr. (1978). Behavioral confirmation in social interaction: From social perception to social reality. *Journal of Personality and Social Psychology, 36,* 1202–1212.

Snyder, M., Tanke, E. D., & Berscheid, E. (1977). Social perception and interpersonal behavior: On the self-fulfilling nature of social stereotypes. *Journal of Personality and Social Psychology, 35,* 656–666.

Soll, J. B., & Larrick, R. P. (2009). Strategies for revising judgment: How (and how well) people use others' opinions. *Journal of Experimental Psychology: Learning, Memory, and Cognition, 35,* 780–805.

Solomon, B. C., & Vazire, S. (2014). You are so beautiful . . . to me: Seeing beyond biases and achieving accuracy in romantic relationships. *Journal of Personality and Social Psychology, 107,* 516–528.

Sommers, S. (2006). On racial diversity and group decision making: Identifying multiple effects of racial composition on jury deliberations. *Journal of Personality and Social Psychology, 90,* 597–612.

Sommers, S. (2011). *Situations matter: Understanding how context transforms your world.* New York: Riverhead Books.

Sommers, S. R., & Ellsworth, P. C. (2001). White juror bias: An investigation of racial prejudice against Black defendants in the American courtroom. *Psychology, Public Policy, and Law, 7,* 201–229.

Sommers, S. R., & Ellsworth, P. C. (2009). "Race salience" in juror decision-making: Misconceptions, clarifications, and unanswered questions. *Behavioral Sciences and The Law, 27,* 599–609.

Sommers, S. R., & Norton, M. I. (2007). Race-based judgments, race-neutral justifications: Experimental examination of peremptory use and the Batson challenge procedure. *Law and Human Behavior, 31,* 261–273.

Sommers, S. R., & Norton, M. I. (2008). Race and jury selection: Psychological perspectives on the peremptory challenge debate. *American Psychologist, 63,* 527–539.

Sommers, S. R., Warp, L. S., & Mahoney, C. C. (2008). Cognitive effects of racial diversity: White individuals' information processing in heterogeneous groups. *Journal of Experimental Social Psychology, 44,* 1129–1136.

Son Hing, L. S., Bobocel, D. R., & Zanna, M. P. (2002). Meritocracy and opposition to affirmative action: Making concessions in the face of discrimination. *Journal of Personality and Social Psychology, 83,* 493–509.

Song, H., & Schwarz, N. (2009). If it's difficult to pronounce, it must be risky: Fluency, familiarity, and risk perception. *Psychological Science, 20,* 135–138.

Song, H., Vonasch, A. J., Meier, B. P., & Bargh, J. A. (2012). Brighten up: Smiles facilitate perceptual judgment of facial lightness. *Journal of Experimental Social Psychology, 48,* 450–452.

Song, R., Over, H., & Carpenter, M. (2015). Children draw more affiliative pictures following priming with third-party ostracism. *Developmental Psychology, 51,* 831–840.

Sonnentag, S., & Fritz, C. (2015). Recovery from job stress: The stressor-detachment model as an integrative framework. *Journal of Organizational Behavior, 36,* S72–S103.

Sorge, G. B., Skilling, T. A., & Toplak, M. E. (2015). Intelligence, executive functions, and decision making as predictors of antisocial behavior in an adolescent sample of justice-involved youth and a community comparison group. *Journal of Behavioral Decision Making,* in press.

Sovacool, B. K. (2008). Exploring scientific misconduct: Isolated individuals, impure institutions, or an inevitable idiom of modern science? *Bioethical Inquiry, 5,* 271–282.

Spears, R., & Postmes, T. (2015). Group identity, social influence, and collective action online: Extensions and applications of the

SIDE model. In S. S. Sundar (Ed.), *The handbook of the psychology of communication technology* (pp. 23–46). Wiley-Blackwell.

Spencer-Rodgers, J., Boucher, H. C., Mori, S. C., Wang, L., & Peng, K. (2009). The dialectical self-concept: Contradiction, change, and holism in East Asian cultures. *Personality and Social Psychology Bulletin, 35*, 29–44.

Spencer-Rodgers, J., Williams, M. J., & Peng, K. (2012). Culturally based lay beliefs as a tool for understanding intergroup and intercultural relations. *International Journal of Intercultural Relations, 36*, 169–178.

Spencer, S. J., Fein, S., Strahan, E. J., & Zanna, M. P. (2005). The role of motivation in the unconscious: How our motives control the activation of our thoughts and shape our actions. In J. P. Forgas, K. D. Williams, & S. M. Laham (Eds.), *Social motivation: Conscious and unconscious processes* (pp. 113–129). New York: Cambridge University Press.

Spencer, S. J., Fein, S., Wolfe, C. T., Fong, C., & Dunn, M. A. (1998). Automatic activation of stereotypes: The role of self-image threat. *Personality and Social Psychology Bulletin, 24*, 1139–1152.

Spencer, S. J., Steele, C. M., & Quinn, D. M. (1999). Stereotype threat and women's math performance. *Journal of Experimental Social Psychology, 35*, 4–28.

Spiegel, D. (1993). Social support: How friends, family, and groups can help. In D. Goleman & J. Gurin (Eds.), *Mind body medicine: How to use your mind for better health* (pp. 331–350). Yonkers, NY: Consumer Reports Books.

Spieker, S. J., Campbell, S. B., Vandergrift, N., Pierce, K. M., Cauffman, E., Susman, E. J., & Roisman, G. I. (2012). Relational aggression in middle childhood: Predictors and adolescent outcomes. *Social Development, 21*, 354–375.

Spielmann, S. S., MacDonald, G., Maxwell, J. A., Joel, S., Peragine, D., Muise, A., & Impett, E. A. (2013). Settling for less out of fear of being single. *Journal of Personality and Social Psychology, 105*, 1049–1073.

Sporer, S. L., Penrod, S. D., Read, J. D., & Cutler, B. L. (1995). Choosing, confidence, and accuracy: A meta-analysis of the confidence-accuracy relation in eyewitness identification studies. *Psychological Bulletin, 118*, 315–327.

Spradley, J. W., McCurdy, D. W., & Shandy, D. (2015). *Conformity and conflict: Readings in cultural anthropology* (15th ed.). New York: Pearson.

Sprecher, S. (1994). Two sides to the breakup of dating relationships. *Personal Relationships, 1*, 199–222.

Sprecher, S. (1999). "I love you more today than yesterday": Romantic partners' perceptions of changes in love and related affect over time. *Journal of Personality and Social Psychology, 76*, 46–53.

Sprecher, S. (2001). Equity and social exchange in dating couples: Associations with satisfaction, commitment, and stability. *Journal of Marriage and the Family, 63*, 599–613.

Sprecher, S., & Hendrick, S. S. (2004). Self-disclosure in intimate relationships: Associations with individual and relationship characteristics over time. *Journal of Social and Clinical Psychology, 23*, 857–877.

Sprecher, S., & Regan, P. C. (1998). Passionate and companionate love in courting and young married couples. *Sociological Inquiry, 68*, 163–185.

Sprecher, S., Wenzel, A., & Harvey, J. (Eds.). (2008). *Handbook of relationship initiation*. New York: Psychology Press.

Spunt, R. P., Meyer, M. L., & Lieberman, M. D. (2015). The default mode of human brain function primes the intentional stance. *Journal of Cognitive Neuroscience, 27*, 1116–1124.

Staats, A. W., & Staats, C. K. (1958). Attitudes established by classical conditioning. *Journal of Abnormal and Social Psychology, 57*, 37–40.

Stack, T. (2014, Nov 5). EW's "Mean Girls" reunion: The cast looks back on the 2004 hit. *Entertainment Weekly*, insidemovies. ew.com/2014/11/05/mean-girls-reunion.

Stahl, G. K., Maznevski, M. L., Voigt, A., & Jonsen, K. (2010). Unraveling the effects of cultural diversity in teams: A meta-analysis of research on multicultural work groups. *Journal of International Business Studies, 4*, 690–709.

Stalans, L. J., & Diamond, S. S. (1990). Formation and change in lay evaluations of criminal sentencing: Misperception and discontent. *Law and Human Behavior, 14*, 199–214.

Stalder, D. R. (2008). Revisiting the issue of safety in numbers: The likelihood of receiving help from a group. *Social Influence, 3*, 24–33.

Stankiewicz, J. M., & Rosselli, F. (2008). Women as sex objects and victims in print advertisements. *Sex Roles, 58*, 579–589.

Stanton, A. L., Kirk, S. B., Cameron, C. L., & Danoff-Berg, S. (2000). Coping through emotional approach: Scale construction and validation. *Journal of Personality and Social Psychology, 78*, 1150–1169.

Stark, C. E. L., Okado, Y., & Loftus, E. F. (2010). Imaging the reconstruction of true and false memories using sensory reactivation and the misinformation paradigms. *Learning and Memory, 17*, 485–488.

Starr, D. (2013). The interview. *The New Yorker*, December 9, 2013, 42–49.

Starzyk, K., Fabrigar, L., Soryal, A., & Fanning, J. (2009). A painful reminder: The role of level and salience of attitude importance in cognitive dissonance. *Personality and Social Psychology Bulletin, 35*, 126–137.

Stasser, G. (1992). Pooling of unshared information during group discussions. In S. Worchel, W. Wood, & J. A. Simpson (Eds.), *Group process and productivity* (pp. 48–67). Newbury Park, CA: Sage.

Stasser, G., & Davis, J. H. (1981). Group decision making and social influence: A social interaction sequence model. *Psychological Review, 88*, 523–551.

Stasser, G., & Titus, W. (2003). Hidden profiles: A brief history. *Psychological Inquiry, 14*, 304–313.

Stasser, G., Kerr, N. L., & Bray, R. M. (1982). The social psychology of jury deliberations: Structure, process, and product. In N. Kerr & R. Bray (Eds.), *The psychology of the courtroom* (pp. 221–256). New York: Academic Press.

Stasser, G., Stewart, D. D., & Wittenbaum, G. M. (1995). Expert roles and information exchange during discussion: The importance of knowing who knows what. *Journal of Experimental Social Psychology, 31*, 244–265.

Statista 2015: http://www.statista.com/.

Stauffer, J. M., & Buckley, M. R. (2005). The existence and nature of racial bias in supervisory ratings. *Journal of Applied Psychology, 90*, 586–591.

Staw, B. M. (1997). The escalation of commitment: An update and appraisal. In Z. Shapira (Ed.), *Organizational decision making. Cambridge series on judgement and decision making* (pp. 191–215). New York: Cambridge University Press.

Staw, B. M., & Hoang, H. (1995). Sunk costs in the NBA: Why draft order affects playing time and survival in professional basketball. *Administrative Science Quarterly, 40*, 474–493.

Steblay, N. K. Dysart, J. E., & Wells, G. L. (2011). Seventy-two tests of the sequential lineup superiority effect: A meta-analysis and policy discussion. *Psychology, Public Policy, and Law, 17*, 99–139.

Steblay, N. M. (1992). A meta-analytic review of the weapon-focus effect. *Law and Human Behavior, 16*, 413–424.

Steblay, N. M. (1997). Social influence in eyewitness recall: A meta-analytic review of lineup instruction effects. *Law and Human Behavior, 21*, 283–297.

Steblay, N., Besirevic, J., Fulero, S., & Jiminez-Lorente, B. (1999). The effects of pretrial publicity on juror verdicts: A meta-analytic review. *Law and Human Behavior, 23*, 219–235.

Steblay, N., Hosch, H. M., Culhane, S. E., & McWethy, A. (2006). The impact on juror verdicts of judicial instruction to disregard inadmissible evidence: A meta-analysis. *Law and Human Behavior, 30,* 469–492.

Steblay, N. K., Wells, G. L., & Douglass, A. B. (2014). The eyewitness post identification feedback effect 15 years later: Theoretical and policy implications. *Psychology, Public Policy, and Law, 20,* 1–18.

Steele, C. M. (1988). The psychology of self-affirmation: Sustaining the integrity of the self. In L. Berkowitz (Ed.), *Advances in experimental social psychology* (Vol. 21, pp. 261–302). New York: Academic Press.

Steele, C. M. (1997). A threat in the air: How stereotypes shape intellectual identity and performance. *American Psychologist, 52,* 613–629.

Steele, C. M. (1999). Thin ice: "Stereotype threat" and black college students. *Atlantic Monthly, 284,* 44–47, 50–54.

Steele, C. M., & Aronson, J. (1995). Stereotype vulnerability and the intellectual test performance of African Americans. *Journal of Personality and Social Psychology, 69,* 797–811.

Steele, C. M., & Josephs, R. A. (1990). Alcohol myopia: Its prized and dangerous effects. *American Psychologist, 45,* 921–933.

Steele, C. M., Spencer, S. J., & Aronson, J. (2002). Contending with group image: The psychology of stereotype and social identity threat. In M. P. Zanna (Ed.), *Advances in experimental social psychology* (Vol. 34, pp. 379–440). San Diego, CA: Academic Press.

Steele, C. M., Spencer, S. J., & Lynch, M. (1993). Self-image resilience and dissonance: The role of affirmational resources. *Journal of Personality and Social Psychology, 64,* 885–896.

Stefan, S., & David, D. (2013) Recent developments in the experimental investigation of the illusion of control: a meta-analytic review. *Journal of Applied Social Psychology, 43,* 377–386.

Steidle, A., & Werth, L. (2014). In the spotlight: Brightness increases self-awareness and reflective self-regulation. *Journal of Environmental Psychology, 39,* 40–50.

Stein, M. B., Walker, J. R., & Forde, D. R. (1996). Public-speaking fears in a community sample. *Archives of General Psychiatry, 53,* 169–174.

Steiner, I. D. (1972). *Group process and productivity.* New York: Academic Press.

Stenico, C., & Greitemeyer, T. (2014). The others will help: The presence of multiple video game characters reduces helping after the game is over. *The Journal of Social Psychology, 154,* 101–104.

Stephan, W. G. (1986). The effects of school desegregation: An evaluation 30 years after Brown. In M. J. Saks & L. Saxe (Eds.), *Advances in applied social psychology* (Vol. 3, pp. 181–206). Hillsdale, NJ: Erlbaum.

Stephan, W. G. (2014). Intergroup anxiety: Theory, research, and practice. *Personality and Social Psychology Review, 18,* 239–255.

Stephan, W. G., Renfro, C. L., Esses, V. M., Stephan, C. W., & Martin, T. (2005). The effects of feeling threatened on attitudes toward immigrants. *International Journal of Intercultural Relations, 29,* 1–19.

Stephens, N. M., Markus, H. R., & Phillips, L. T. (2014). Social class culture cycles: How three gateway contexts shape selves and fuel inequality. *Annual Review of Psychology, 65,* 611–634.

Stepper, S., & Strack, F. (1993). Proprioceptive determinants of emotional and nonemotional feelings. *Journal of Personality and Social Psychology, 64,* 211–220.

Stern, C., West, T. V., & Schoenthaler, A. (2013). The dynamic relationship between accuracy and bias in social perception research. *Social and Personality Psychology Compass, 7,* 303–314.

Sternberg, R. J. (1986). A triangular theory of love. *Psychological Review, 93,* 119–135.

Sternberg, R. J. (1997). *Successful intelligence: How practical and creative intelligence determine success in life.* New York: Plume.

Sternberg, R., & Barnes, M. L. (Eds.). (1986). *The psychology of love.* Yale University Press.

Sternberg, R. J. (1999). *Cupid's arrow: The course of love through time.* New York: Cambridge University Press.

Sternberg, R. J., & Weis, K. (Eds.). (2006). *The new psychology of love.* New Haven, CT: Yale University Press.

Sternglanz, R. W., & DePaulo, B. M. (2004). Reading nonverbal cues to emotions: Advantages and liabilities of relationship closeness. *Journal of Nonverbal Behavior, 28,* 245–266.

Stetler, D. A., Davis, C., Leavitt, K., Schriger, I., Benson, K., Bhakta, S., & . . . Bortolato, M. (2014). Association of low-activity MAOA allelic variants with violent crime in incarcerated offenders. *Journal of Psychiatric Research, 58,* 69–75.

Stevens, C. K., & Kristof, A. L. (1995). Making the right impression: A field study of applicant impression management during job interviews. *Journal of Applied Psychology, 80,* 587–606.

Stewart-Williams, S. (2007). Altruism among kin vs. nonkin: Effects of cost of help and reciprocal exchange. *Evolution and Human Behavior, 28,* 193–198.

Stewart-Williams, S. (2008). Human beings as evolved nepotists: Exceptions to the rule and effects of cost of help. *Human Nature, 19,* 414–425.

Stewart, A. J., Sokol, M., Healy, J. M., Jr., & Chester, N. L. (1986). Longitudinal studies of psychological consequences of life changes in children and adults. *Journal of Personality and Social Psychology, 50,* 143–151.

Stewart, G. L., Dustin, S. L., Barrick, M. R., & Darnold, T. C. (2008). Exploring the handshake in employment interviews. *Journal of Applied Psychology, 93,* 1139–1146.

Stewart, L. H., Ajina, S., Getov, S., Bahrami, B., Todorov, A., & Rees, G. (2012). Unconscious evaluation of faces on social dimensions. *Journal of Experimental Psychology: General,* April 2, 2012.

Steyn, R., & Mynhardt, J. (2008) Factors that influence the forming of self-evaluation and self-efficacy perceptions. *South African Journal of Psychology, 38,* 563–573.

Stine, G. J. (2014). *AIDS Update 2014.* New York: McGraw-Hill.

Stinson, D. A., Cameron, J. J., Wood, J. V., Gaucher, G., & Holmes, J. G. (2009). Deconstructing the "reign of error": Interpersonal warmth explains the self-fulfilling prophecy of anticipated acceptance. *Personality and Social Psychology Bulletin, 35,* 1165–1168.

Stinson, D. A., Logel, C., Shepherd, S., & Zanna. M. P. (2011). Rewriting the self—fulfilling prophecy of social rejection: Self-affirmation improves relational security and social behavior up to 2 months later. *Psychological Science, 22,* 1145–1149.

Stocks, E. L., Lishner, D. A., & Decker, S. K. (2009). Altruism or psychological escape: Why does empathy promote prosocial behavior? *European Journal of Social Psychology, 39,* 649–665.

Stoltzfus, N. (1996). *Resistance of the heart: Intermarriage and the Rosen-strasse protest in Nazi Germany.* New York: Norton.

Stone, A. A., Neale, J. M., Cox, D. S., Napoli, A., Valdimarsdottir, H., & Kennedy-Moore, E. (1994). Daily events are associated with a secretory immune response to an oral antigen in men. *Health Psychology, 13,* 440–446.

Stone, J. (2003). Self-consistency for low self-esteem in dissonance processes: The role of self-standards. *Personality and Social Psychology Bulletin, 29,* 846–858.

Stone, J., Lynch, C. I., Sjomeling, M., & Darley, J. M. (1999). Stereotype threat effects on black and white athletic performance. *Journal of Personality and Social Psychology, 77,* 1213–1227.

Stone, J., Perry, Z. W., & Darley, J. M. (1997). "White men can't jump": Evidence for the perceptual confirmation of racial stereotypes following a basketball game. *Basic and Applied Social Psychology, 19,* 291–306.

Stone, J., Wiegand, A. W., Cooper, J., & Aronson, E. (1997). When exemplification fails: Hypocrisy and the motive for self-integrity. *Journal of Personality and Social Psychology, 72,* 54–65.

Stone, W. F., Lederer, G., & Christie, R. (Eds.). (1993). *Strength and weakness: The authoritarian personality today.* New York: Springer-Verlag.

Stout, J. G., Dasgupta, N., Hunsinger, M., & McManus, M. A. (2011). STEM-ing the tide: Using ingroup experts to inoculate women's self-concept in science, technology, engineering, and mathematics (STEM). *Journal of Personality and Social Psychology, 100,* 255–270.

Stouten, J., van Dijke, M., & De Cremer, D. (2012). Ethical leadership: An overview and future perspectives. *Journal of Personnel Psychology, 11,* 1–6.

Strahan, E. J., Spencer, S. J., & Zanna, M. P. (2002). Subliminal priming and persuasion: Striking while the iron is hot. *Journal of Experimental Social Psychology, 38,* 556–568.

Straub, R. O. (2015). *Health psychology* (4th ed.). New York: Worth.

Strauman, T. J. (1992). Self-guides, autobiographical memory, and anxiety and dysphoria: Toward a cognitive model of vulnerability to emotional distress. *Journal of Abnormal Psychology, 101,* 87–95.

Straus, M. A. (2010). Criminogenic effects of corporal punishment by parents. In M. Herzog-Evans & I. Dréan-Rivette (Eds.), *Transnational criminology manual* (Vol. 1, pp. 373–390). Amsterdam: Wolf Legal Publishing.

Straus, M. A. (2011). Gender symmetry and mutuality in perpetration of clinical-level partner violence: Empirical evidence and implications for prevention and treatment. *Aggression and Violent Behavior, 16,* 279–288.

Straus, M. A., & Gozjolko, K. L. (2014). "Intimate Terrorism" and gender differences in injury of dating partners by male and female university students. *Journal of Family Violence, 29,* 51–65.

Straus, S. G., Parker, A. M., Bruce, J. B., & Dembosky, J. W. (2009). *The group matters: A review of the effects of group interaction on processes and outcomes in analytic teams.* Report WR-580-USG. Arlington, VA: Rand Corporation.

Straw, J. (2014, Feb 12). School shootings happen every 10 days since Sandy Hook, gun control group finds. *New York Daily News,* nydn.us/Me1i7Y.

Strawbridge, W. J., Shema, S. J., Cohen, R. D., & Kaplan, G. A. (2001). Religious attendance increases survival by improving and maintaining good health behaviors, mental health, and social relationships. *Annals of Behavioral Medicine, 23,* 68–74.

Strentz, T., & Auerbach, S. M. (1988). Adjustment to the stress of simulated captivity: Effects of emotion-focused versus problem-focused preparation on hostages differing in locus of control. *Journal of Personality and Social Psychology, 55,* 652–660.

Strick, M., van Baaren, R. B., Holland, R. W., & van Knippenberg, A. (2009). Humor in advertisements enhances product liking by mere association. *Journal of Experimental Psychology: Applied, 15,* 35–45.

Strier, F. (1999). Wither trial consulting: Issues and projections. *Law and Human Behavior, 23,* 93–115.

Strodtbeck, F. L., & Hook, L. (1961). The social dimensions of a twelve-man jury table. *Sociometry, 24,* 397–415.

Strodtbeck, F. L., James, R., & Hawkins, C. (1957). Social status in jury deliberations. *American Sociological Review, 22,* 713–719.

Stroebe, W. (2012). The truth about Triplett (1898), but nobody seems to care. *Perspectives on Psychological Science, 7,* 54–57.

Stroebe et al., 2010.

Stroessner, S. J., & Dweck, C. S. (2015). Inferring group traits and group goals: A unified approach to social perception. In S. J. Stroessner & J. W. Sherman (Eds.), *Social perception from individuals to groups* (pp. 177–196). New York: Psychology Press.

Strohmetz, D. B., Rind, B., Fisher, R., & Lynn, M. (2002). Sweetening the till: The use of candy to increase restaurant tipping. *Journal of Applied Social Psychology, 32,* 300–309.

Strough, J., Mehta, C. M., McFall, J. P., & Schuller, K. L. (2008). Are older adults less subject to the sunk-cost fallacy than younger adults? *Psychological Science, 19,* 650–652.

Strube, M. J. (2005). What did Triplett really find? A contemporary analysis of the first experiment in social psychology. *American Journal of Psychology, 118,* 271–286.

Struck, D. (2006, September 15). Gunman's writings presaged rampage; blog described fascination with death, laid out events that would unfold in Montreal. *Washington Post,* p. A12.

Strupp, H. H. (1996). The tripartite model and the Consumer Reports study. *American Psychologist, 51,* 1017–1024.

Studebaker, C. A., & Penrod, S. D. (1997). Pretrial publicity: The media, the law, and common sense. *Psychology, Public Policy, and Law, 3,* 428–460.

Stürmer, S., Snyder, M., & Omoto, A. M. (2005). Prosocial emotions and helping: The moderating role of group membership. *Journal of Personality and Social Psychology, 88,* 532–546.

Stutzer, A. (2004). The role of income aspirations in individual happiness. *Journal of Economic Behavior and Organization, 54,* 89–109.

Sudman, S., Bradburn, N. M., & Schwarz, N. (2010). *Thinking about answers: The application of cognitive processes to survey methodology.* New York: Jossey-Bass.

Sue, S., Smith, R. E., & Caldwell, C. (1973). Effects of inadmissible evidence on the decisions of simulated jurors: A moral dilemma. *Journal of Applied Social Psychology, 3,* 345–353.

Suh, E., Diener, E., & Fujita, F. (1996). Events and subjective well-being: Only recent events matter. *Journal of Personality and Social Psychology, 70,* 1091–1102.

Suhay, E. (2015). Explaining group influence: The role of identity and emotion in political conformity and polarization. *Political Behavior, 37,* 221–251.

Sullivan, D., Landau, M. J., Young, I. F., & Stewart, S. A. (2014). The dramaturgical perspective in relation to self and culture. *Journal of Personality and Social Psychology, 107,* 767–790.

Suls, J. M., & Wheeler, L. (Eds.). (2000). *Handbook of social comparison: Theory and research.* New York: Plenum.

Sunday, S., Kline, M., Labruna, V., Pelcovitz, D., Salzinger, S., & Kaplan, S. (2011). The role of adolescent physical abuse in adult intimate partner violence. *Journal of Interpersonal Violence, 26,* 3773–3789.

Sundie, J. M., Kenrick, D. T., Griskevicius, V., Tybur, J. M., Vohs, K. D., & Beal, D. J. (2011). Peacocks, Porsches, and Thorstein Veblen: Conspicuous consumption as a sexual signaling system. *Journal of Personality and Social Psychology, 100,* 664–680.

Sundstrom, E. (1986). *Work places.* New York: Cambridge University Press.

Surowiecki, J. (2005). *The wisdom of crowds.* New York: Anchor Books.

Swaine, J., Laughland, O., & Lartey, J. (2015). Black Americans killed by police twice as likely to be unarmed as white people. *The Guardian,* http://www.theguardian.com/us-news/2015/jun/01/black-americans-killed-by-police-analysis.

Swami, V, & Furnham, A. (2008). *The psychology of physical attraction.* New York: Routledge/Taylor & Francis.

Swann, W. B. Jr., Jetten, J., Gómez, Á., Whitehouse, H., & Bastian, B. (2012). When group membership gets personal: A theory of identity fusion. *Psychological Review, 119,* 441–456.

Swann, W. B., Jr. (1984). Quest for accuracy in person perception: A matter of pragmatics. *Psychological Review, 91,* 457–477.

Swann, W. B., Jr. (1987). Identity negotiation: Where two roads meet. *Journal of Personality and Social Psychology, 53,* 1038–1051.

Swann, W. B., Jr., & Bosson, J. K. (2010). Self and identity. In S. T. Fiske, D. T. Gilbert, & G. Lindzey (Eds.), *Handbook of social psychology* (5th ed.). New York: McGraw-Hill.

Swann, W. B., Jr., & Ely, R. J. (1984). A battle of wills: Self-verification versus behavioral confirmation. *Journal of Personality and Social Psychology, 46,* 1287–1302.

Swann, W. B., Jr., & Hill, C. A. (1982). When our identities are mistaken: Reaffirming self-conceptions through social interaction. *Journal of Personality and Social Psychology, 43,* 59–66.

Swann, W. B., Jr., Chang-Schneider, C. S., & McClarty, K. L. (2007). Do our self-views matter? Self-concept and self-esteem in everyday life. *American Psychologist, 62,* 84–94.

Swann, W. B., Jr., Hixon, J. G., & De La Ronde, C. (1992). Embracing the bitter "truth": Negative self-concepts and marital commitment. *Psychological Science, 3,* 118–121.

Swann, W. J., & Buhrmester, M. D. (2015). Identity fusion. *Current Directions in Psychological Science, 24,* 52–57.

Sweldens, S. Corneille, & O. Yzerbyt, V. (2014). The role of awareness in attitude formation through evaluative conditioning. *Personality and Social Psychology Review, 18,* 187–209.

Swim, J. K., & Hyers, L. L. (2009). Sexism. In T. D. Nelson (Ed.), *Handbook of prejudice, stereotyping, and discrimination* (pp. 407–430). New York: Psychology Press.

Swim, J. K., & Sanna, L. J. (1996). He's skilled, she's lucky: A meta-analysis of observers' attributions for women's and men's successes and failures. *Personality and Social Psychology Bulletin, 22,* 507–519.

t'Hart, P. (1998). Preventing groupthink revisited: Evaluating and reforming groups in government. *Organizational Behavior and Human Decision Processes, 73,* 306–326.

Tabuchi, H. (2011, May 20). Head of Japanese utility steps down after nuclear crisis. Retrieved August 15, 2015 from http://www.nytimes.com/2011/05/21/business/global/21iht-tepco21.html.

Tackett, J. L., Herzhoff, K., Kushner, S. C., & Rule, N. (2015). Thin slices of child personality: Perceptual, situational, and behavioral contributions. *Journal of Personality and Social Psychology.*

Tadmor, C. T., Hong, Y., Chao, M. M., Wiruchnipawan, F., & Wang, W. (2012). Multicultural experiences reduce intergroup bias through epistemic unfreezing. *Journal of Personality and Social Psychology, 103,* 750–772.

Tadmor, C. T., Galinsky, A. D., & Maddux, W. W. (2012). Getting the most out of living abroad: Biculturalism and integrative complexity as key drivers of creative and professional success. *Journal of Personality and Social Psychology, 103,* 520–542.

Tajfel, H. (1982). Social psychology of intergroup relations. *Annual Review of Psychology, 33,* 1–39.

Tajfel, H., Billig, M. G., Bundy, R. P., & Flament, C. (1971). Social categorization and intergroup behavior. *European Journal of Social Psychology, 1,* 149–178.

Tan, H. H., & Tan, M.-L. (2008). Organizational citizenship behavior and social loafing: The role of personality, motives, and contextual factors. *Journal of Psychology: Interdisciplinary and Applied, 142,* 89–108.

Tanford, S., & Penrod, S. (1984). Social influence model: A formal integration of research on majority and minority influence processes. *Psychological Bulletin, 95,* 189–225.

Tang, J-H., & Wang, C-C. (2012). Self-disclosure among bloggers: Re-examination of Social Penetration theory. *Cyberpsychology, Behavior, and Social Networking, 15,* 245–250.

Tang, S., & Hall, V. C. (1995). The overjustification effect: A meta-analysis. *Applied Cognitive Psychology, 9,* 365–404.

Tassinary, L. G., & Cacioppo, J. T. (1992). Unobservable facial actions and emotion. *Psychological Science, 3,* 28–33.

Táuber, S., & van Zomeren, M. (2012). Refusing intergroup help from the morally superior: How one group's moral superiority leads to another group's reluctance to seek their help. *Journal of Experimental Social Psychology, 48,* 420–423.

Tay, C., Ang, S., & Linn, V. (2006). Personality, biographical characteristics, and job interview success: A longitudinal study of the mediating effects of interviewing self-efficacy and the moderating effects of internal locus of causality. *Journal of Applied Psychology, 91,* 446–454.

Taylor, L. S., Fiore, A. T., Mendelsohn, G. A., & Cheshire, C. (2011). "Out of my league": A real-world test of the matching hypothesis. *Personality and Social Psychology Bulletin, 37,* 942–954.

Taylor, S. E. (1989). *Positive illusions: Creative self-deceptions and the healthy mind.* New York: Basic Books.

Taylor, S. E. (1990). Health psychology: The science and the field. *American Psychologist, 45,* 40–50.

Taylor, S. E. (1991). Asymmetrical effects of positive and negative events: The mobilization-minimization hypothesis. *Psychological Bulletin, 110,* 67–85.

Taylor, S. E. (2002). *The tending instinct: Women, men, and the biology of nurturing.* New York: Times Books.

Taylor, S. E. (2012). Tend and befriend theory. In P. Van Lange, A. Kruglanski, & E. T. Higgins (Eds.), *Handbook of theories of social psychology* (Volume 1), pp. 32–49. Thousand Oaks, CA: Sage.

Taylor, S. E. (2015). *Health psychology* (9th ed.). New York: McGraw-Hill.

Taylor, S. E. (2015). Social cognition and health. In M. Mikulincer, P. R. Shaver, E. Borgida, & J. A. Bargh (Eds.), *APA handbook of personality and social psychology,* Volume 1*: Attitudes and social cognition* (pp. 339–361). Washington, DC: American Psychological Association.

Taylor, S. E., & Brown, J. D. (1988). Illusion and well-being: A social psychological perspective on mental health. *Psychological Bulletin, 103,* 193–210.

Taylor, S. E., & Fiske, S. T. (1975). Point of view and perceptions of causality. *Journal of Personality and Social Psychology, 32,* 439–445.

Taylor, S. E., & Lobel, M. (1989). Social comparison activity under threat: Downward evaluation and upward contacts. *Psychological Review, 96,* 569–575.

Taylor, S. E., Lerner, J. S., Sherman, D. K., Sage, R. M., & McDowell, N. K. (2003). Portrait of the self-enhancer: Well adjusted and well liked or maladjusted and friendless? *Journal of Personality and Social Psychology, 84,* 165–176.

Taylor, S. E., Sherman, D. K., Kim, H. S., Jarcho, J., Takgi, K., & Dunagan, M. S. (2004). Culture and social support: Who seeks it and why? *Journal of Personality and Social Psychology, 87,* 354–362.

Taylor, S. E., Welch, W. T., Kim, H. S., & Sherman, D. K. (2007). Cultural differences in the impact of social support on psychological and biological stress responses. *Psychological Science, 18,* 831–837.

Taylor, V., & Walton, G. M. (2011). Stereotype threat undermines academic learning. *Personality and Social Psychology Bulletin, 37,* 1055–1067.

Tedeschi, J. T., Schlenker, B. R., & Bonoma, T. V. (1971). Cognitive dissonance: Private ratiocination or public spectacle? *American Psychologist, 26,* 685–695.

Tegarden, D., Tegarden, L., Smith, W., & Sheetz, S. (2015). De-fusing organizational power using anonymity and cognitive factions in a participative strategic planning setting. *Group Decision and Negotiation,* in press.

Teger, A. (1980). *Too much invested to quit.* New York: Pergamon Press.

Tejada-Vera, B., & Sutton, P. (2009). *Births, marriages, divorces, and deaths: Provisional data for July 2008* (National Vital Statistics Reports No. 57). Hyattsville, MD: National Center for Health Statistics.

Tenenbaum, H. R., & Leaper, C. (2002). Are parents' gender schemas related to their children's gender-related cognitions? A meta-analysis. *Developmental Psychology, 38,* 615–630.

Teng, Z., Liu, Y., & Guo, C. (2015). A meta-analysis of the relationship between self-esteem and aggression among Chinese students. *Aggression and Violent Behavior, 21,* 45–54.

Teo, A. R. (2010). A new form of social withdrawal in Japan: A review of hikikomori. *The International Journal of Social Psychiatry, 56,* 178–85.

Tepper, B. J. (2001). Health consequences of organizational injustice: Tests of main and interactive effects. *Organizational Behavior and Human Decision Processes, 86,* 197–215.

Tesser, A. (1993). The importance of heritability in psychological research: The case of attitudes. *Psychological Review, 100,* 129–142.

Thaler, R. (1980). Toward a positive theory of consumer choice. *Journal of Economic Behavior and Organization, 1*, 39–60.

Thibaut, J. W., & Kelley, H. H. (1959). *The social psychology of groups.* New York: Wiley.

Thibaut, J., & Walker, L. (1975). *Procedural justice: A psychological analysis.* Hillsdale, NJ: Erlbaum.

Thibaut, J., & Walker, L. (1978). A theory of procedure. *California Law Review, 66*, 541–566.

Thomas, D. A., & Gabarro, J. J. (1999). *Breaking through: The making of minority executives in corporate America.* Cambridge, MA: Harvard Business School Press.

Thomas, K. D., & Levant, R. F. (2012). Does the endorsement of traditional masculinity ideology moderate the relationship between exposure to violent video games and aggression? *The Journal of Men's Studies, 20*, 47–56.

Thompson-Cannino, J., & Cotton, R. (2009). *Picking cotton: Our memoir of injustice and redemption.* New York: St. Martin's Press.

Thompson, L. (2015). *The mind and heart of the negotiator* (6th ed.). Upper Saddle River, NJ: Pearson.

Thompson, L. L., Wang, J., & Gunia, B. C. (2010). Negotiation. *Annual Review of Psychology, 61*, 491–515.

Thompson, S. C., Sobolew-Shubin, A., Galbraith, M. E., Schwankovsky, L., & Cruzen, D. (1993). Maintaining perceptions of control: Finding perceived control in low-control circumstances. *Journal of Personality and Social Psychology, 64*, 293–304.

Thornton, B. (1992). Repression and its mediating influence on the defensive attribution of responsibility. *Journal of Research in Personality, 26*, 44–57.

Thornton, G. C., & Rupp, D. E. (2006). *Assessment centers in human resource management: Strategies for prediction, diagnosis, and development.* Mahwah, NJ: Erlbaum.

Thürmer, J. L., Wieber, F., & Gollwitzer, P. M. (2015). A self-regulation perspective on hidden-profile problems: If–then planning to review information improves group decisions. *Journal of Behavioral Decision Making, 28*, 101–113.

Thurstone, L. L. (1928). Attitudes can be measured. *American Journal of Sociology, 33*, 529–544.

Tice, D. M. (1991). Esteem protection or enhancement? Self-handicapping motives and attributions differ by trait self-esteem. *Journal of Personality and Social Psychology, 60*, 711–725.

Tice, D. M., & Baumeister, R. F. (1997). Longitudinal study of procrastination, performance, stress, and health: The costs and benefits of dawdling. *Psychological Science, 8*, 454–458.

Tiddi, B., Aureli, F., & Schino, G. (2010). Grooming for infant handling in tufted capuchin monkeys: A reappraisal of the primate infant market. *Animal Behaviour, 79*, 1115–1123.

Tiddi, B., Aureli, F., di Sorrentino, E., Janson, C. H., & Schino, G. (2011). Grooming for tolerance? Two mechanisms of exchange in wild tufted capuchin monkeys. *Behavioral Ecology, 22*, 663–669.

Tidwell, N. D., Eastwick, P. W., & Finkel, E. J. (2013). Perceived, not actual, similarity predicts initial attraction in a live romantic context: Evidence from the speed-dating paradigm. *Personal Relationships, 20*, 199–215.

Tierney, J. (2011). Social scientist sees bias within. *New York Times*, February 8, D1.

Tiggemann, M., & Williams, E. (2012). The role of self-objectification in disordered eating, depressed mood, and sexual functioning among women: A comprehensive test of objectification theory. *Psychology of Women Quarterly, 36*, 66–75.

Tilcsik, A. (2011). Pride and prejudice: Employment discrimination against openly gay men in the United States. *American Journal of Sociology, 117*, 586–626.

Tilker, H. A. (1970). Socially responsible behavior as a function of observer responsibility and victim feedback. *Journal of Personality and Social Psychology, 14*, 95–100.

Timmons-Mitchell, J., Bender, M. B., Kishna, M. A., & Mitchell, C. C. (2006). An independent effectiveness trial of multisystemic therapy with juvenile justice youth. *Journal of Clinical Child and Adolescent Psychology, 35*, 227–236.

Tjosvold, D., Hui, C., & Sun, H. (2004). Can Chinese discuss conflicts openly? Field and experimental studies of face dynamics in China. *Group Decision and Negotiation, 13*, 351–373.

Tobin, A. M. (2006, October 3). "Copycat effect" may explain cluster. *Toronto Star*, p. A7.

Tobin, S. J., & Raymundo, M. M. (2009). Persuasion by causal arguments: The motivating role of perceived causal expertise. *Social Cognition, 27*, 105–127.

Todd, A. R., Galinsky, A. D., & Bodenhausen, G. V (2012). Perspective taking undermines stereotype maintenance processes: Evidence from social memory, behavior explanation, and information solicitation. *Social Cognition, 30*, 94–108.

Todorov, A., Olivola, C. Y., Dotsch, R., & Mende-Siedlecki, P. (2015). Social attributions from faces: Determinants, consequences, accuracy, and functional significance. *Annual Review of Psychology, 66*, 519–545.

Todorov, A., Said, C. P., Engell, A. D., & Oosterhof, N. A. (2008). Understanding evaluation of faces on social dimensions. *Trends in Cognitive Sciences, 12*, 455–460.

Tolin, D. F., & Foa, E. B. (2006). Sex differences in trauma and post-traumatic stress disorder: A quantitative review of 25 years of research. *Psychological Bulletin, 132*, 959–992.

Tolstedt, B. E., & Stokes, J. P. (1984). Self-disclosure, intimacy, and the depenetration process. *Journal of Personality and Social Psychology, 46*, 84–90.

Tomada, G., & Schneider, B. H. (1997). Relational aggression, gender, and peer acceptance: Invariance across culture, stability over time, and concordance among informants. *Developmental Psychology, 33*, 601–609.

Toosi, N. R., Babbitt, L. G., Ambady, N., & Sommers, S. R. (2012). Dyadic interracial interactions: A meta-analysis. *Psychological Bulletin, 138*, 1–27.

Toosi, N. R., Sommers, S. R., & Ambady, N. (2012). Getting a word in group-wise: Effects of racial diversity on gender dynamics. *Journal of Experimental Social Psychology, 48*, 1150–1155.

Top, T. J. (1991). Sex bias in the evaluation of performance in the scientific, artistic, and literary professions: A review. *Sex Roles, 24*, 73–106.

Tor, A., Gazal-Ayal, O., & Garcia, S. M. (2010). Fairness and willingness to accept plea bargain offers. *Journal of Empirical Legal Studies, 7*, 97–116.

Tormala, Z. L., & Petty, R. E. (2002). What doesn't kill me makes me stronger: The effects of resisting persuasion on attitude certainty. *Journal of Personality and Social Psychology, 83*, 1298–1313.

Tormala, Z. L., Brinol, P., & Petty, R. E. (2006). When credibility attacks: The reverse impact of source credibility on persuasion. *Journal of Experimental Social Psychology, 42*, 684–691.

Tornblom, K., & Vermunt, R. (Eds.). (2007). *Distributive and procedural justice: Research and social applications.* Burlington, VT: Ashgate.

Törngren, G., & Montgomery, H. (2004). Worse than chance? Performance and confidence among professionals and lay-people in the stock market. *Journal of Behavioral Finance, 5*, 148–153.

Tourangeau, R., Rips, L. J., & Rasinksi, K. (2000). *The psychology of survey response.* New York: Cambridge University Press.

Tourangeau, R., Smith, T. W., & Rasinski, K. A. (1997). Motivation to report sensitive behaviors on surveys: Evidence from a bogus pipeline experiment. *Journal of Applied Social Psychology, 27*, 209–222.

Tourish, D. (2013). *The dark side of transformational leadership: A critical perspective.* New York: Routledge.

Trafimow, D., & Marks, M. (2015). Editorial. *Basic and Applied Social Psychology, 37*, 1–2.

Trafimow, D., Silverman, E. S., Fan, R. M. T., & Law, J. S. F. (1997). The effects of language and priming on the relative accessibility of the private self and collective self. *Journal of Cross-Cultural Psychology, 28,* 107–123.

Trafimow, D., Triandis, H. C., & Goto, S. G. (1991). Some tests of the distinction between the private and collective self. *Journal of Personality and Social Psychology, 60,* 649–655.

Trawalter, S., Adam, E. K., Chase-Lansdale, P., & Richeson, J. A. (2012). Concerns about appearing prejudiced get under the skin: Stress responses to interracial contact in the moment and across time. *Journal of Experimental Social Psychology, 48,* 682–693.

Triandis, H. C. (1994). *Culture and social behavior.* New York: McGraw-Hill.

Triandis, H. C. (1995). *Individualism and collectivism.* Boulder, CO: Westview.

Triandis, H., Chen, X. P., & Chan, D. K. (1998). Scenarios for the measurement of collectivism and individualism. *Journal of Cross-Cultural Psychology, 29,* 275–289.

Triplett, N. (1897–1898). The dynamogenic factors in pacemaking and competition. *American Journal of Psychology, 9,* 507–533.

Tripp, C., Jensen, T. D., & Carlson, L. (1994). The effects of multiple product endorsements by celebrities on consumers' attitudes and intentions. *Journal of Consumer Research, 20,* 535–547.

Trivers, R. L. (1971). The evolution of reciprocal altruism. *Quarterly Review of Biology, 46,* 35–57.

Trivers, R. L. (1972). Parental investment and sexual selection. In B. Campbell (Ed.), *Sexual selection and the descent of man* (pp. 136–179). Chicago: Aldine-Atherton.

Trivers, R. L. (1985). *Social evolution.* Menlo Park, CA: Benjamin/Cummings.

Troll, L. E., & Skaff, M. M. (1997). Perceived continuity of self in very old age. *Psychology and Aging, 12,* 162–169.

Trope, Y. (1986). Identification and inferential processes in dispositional attribution. *Psychological Review, 93,* 239–257.

Trope, Y., & Alfieri, T. (1997). Effortfulness and flexibility of dispositional judgment processes. *Journal of Personality and Social Psychology, 73,* 662–674.

Tropp, L. R. (2013). *Handbook of intergroup conflict.* Oxford: Oxford University Press.

Tropp, L. R., & Page-Gould, E. (2015). Contact between groups. In M. Mikulincer, P. R. Shaver, E. Borgida, & J. A. Bargh (Eds.), *APA handbook of personality and social psychology,* Volume 2: *Group processes* (pp. 535–560). Washington, DC: American Psychological Association.

Trötschel, R., Hüffmeier, J., Loschelder, D. D., Schwartz, K., & Gollwitzer, P. M. (2011). Perspective taking as a means to overcome motivational barriers in negotiations: When putting oneself into the opponent's shoes helps to walk toward agreements. *Journal of Personality and Social Psychology, 101,* 771–790.

Trzesniewski, K. H., Donnellan, M. B., & Robins, R. W. (2003). Stability of self-esteem across the life span. *Journal of Personality and Social Psychology, 84,* 205–220.

Tsapelas, I., Aron, A., & Orbuch, T. (2009). Marital boredom now predicts less satisfaction 9 years later. *Psychological Science, 20,* 543–545.

Tsukiura, T., & Cabeza, R. (2011). Shared brain activity for aesthetic and moral judgments: implications for the beauty-is-good stereotype. *Social Cognitive and Affective Neuroscience. 6,* 138–148.

Ttofi, M. M., & Farrington, D. P. (2009). What works in preventing bullying: Effective elements of anti-bullying programmes. *Journal of Aggression, Conflict and Peace Research, 1,* 13–24.

Ttofi, M. M., & Farrington, D. P. (2011). Effectiveness of school-based programs to reduce bullying: A systematic and meta-analytic review. *Journal of Experimental Criminology, 7,* 27–56.

Ttofi, M. M., Farrington, D. P., Lösel, F., Crago, R. V., & Theodorakis, N. (2015). School bullying and drug use later in life: A meta-analytic investigation. *School Psychology Quarterly,* in press.

Tubre, T. C., & Collins, J. M. (2000). Jackson and Schuler (1985) revisited: A meta-analysis of the relationships between role ambiguity, role conflict, and job performance. *Journal of Management, 26,* 155–169.

Turner, J. C. (1987). *Rediscovering the social group: A self-categorization theory.* Oxford, UK: Basil Blackwell.

Turner, J. C. (1991). *Social influence.* Pacific Grove, CA: Brooks/Cole.

Turner, M. E., & Pratkanis, A. R. (1998). Twenty-five years of groupthink theory and research: Lessons from the evaluation of a theory. *Organizational Behavior and Human Decision Processes, 73,* 105–115.

Tuvblad, C., & Beaver, K. M. (2013). Genetic and environmental influences on antisocial behavior. *Journal of Criminal Justice, 41,* 273–276.

Tversky, A., & Kahneman, D. (1973). Availability: A heuristic for judging frequency and probability. *Cognitive Psychology, 5,* 207–232.

Twenge, J. M. (2006). *Generation me: Why today's young Americans are more confident, assertive, entitled—and more miserable than ever before.* New York: Free Press.

Twenge, J. M. (2009). Change over time in obedience: The jury's still out, but it might be decreasing. *American Psychologist, 64,* 28–31.

Twenge, J. M., & Crocker, J. (2002). Race and self-esteem: Metaanalyses comparing Whites, Blacks, Hispanics, Asians, and American Indians. *Psychological Bulletin, 128,* 371–408.

Twenge, J. M., Campbell, W. K., & Freeman, E. C. (2012). Generational differences in young adults' life goals, concern for others, and civic orientation, 1966–2009. *Journal of Personality and Social Psychology, 102,* 1045–1062.

Twenge, J. M., Campbell, W. K., & Gentile, B. (2013). Changes in pronoun use in American books and the rise of individualism, 1960–2008. *Journal of Cross-Cultural Psychology, 44,* 406–415.

Tyler, T. R. (2006a). Viewing CSI and the threshold of guilt: Managing truth and justice in reality and fiction. *Yale Law Journal, 115,* 1050–1085.

Tyler, T. R. (2006b). *Why people obey the law.* Princeton, NJ: Princeton University Press.

Tyler, T. R. (2011). *Why people cooperate: The role of social motivations.* Princeton, NJ: Princeton University Press.

Tyson, M., Covey, J., & Rosenthal, H. E. S. (2014). Theory of planned behavior interventions for reducing heterosexual risk behaviors: A meta-analysis. *Health Psychology, 33,* 1454–1467.

Uchino, B. N. (2006). Social support and health: A review of physiological processes potentially underlying links to disease outcomes. *Journal of Behavioral Medicine, 29,* 377–387.

Uchino, B. N. (2009). Understanding the links between social support and physical health: A life-span perspective with emphasis on the separability of perceived and received support. *Perspectives on Psychological Science, 4,* 236–255.

Uleman, J. S., Rim, S., Saribay, S. A., & Kressel, L. M. (2012). Controversies, questions, and prospects for spontaneous social inferences. *Social and Personality Psychology Compass, 6,* 657–673.

Underwood, J., & Pezdek, K. (1998). Memory suggestibility as an example of the sleeper effect. *Psychonomic Bulletin and Review, 5,* 449–453.

UNICEF. (2012). *Progress for children: A report card on adolescents.* New York: United Nations Children's Fund.

United Nations General Assembly, *World Happiness Report 2015—* first published in 2012.

United Nations Office on Drugs and Crime (2011). *Global study on homicide.* Vienna.

United Nations Office on Drugs and Crime (2014). *Global study on homicide, 2013.* Vienna, Austria: United Nations.

United States v. Scheffer, 523 U.S. 303 (1998).

Unkelbach, C., Forgas, J. P., & Denson, T. F. (2008). The turban effect: The influence of Muslim headgear and induced affect on aggressive responses in the shooter bias paradigm. *Journal of Experimental Social Psychology, 44,* 1409–1413.

Unzueta, M. M., Gutiérrez, A. S., & Ghavami, N. (2010). How believing in affirmative action quotas affects White women's self-image. *Journal of Experimental Social Psychology, 46,* 120–126.

Ura, K., Alkire, S., & Zangmo, T. (2012). Case study: Bhutan: Gross National Happiness and the GNH index. In J. Helliwell, R. Layard, & J. Sachs (Eds.), *World Happiness Report* (pp. 108–145). New York: Columbia University: The Earth Institute.

Urdan, T., & Midgley, C. (2001). Academic self-handicapping: What we know, what more there is to learn. *Educational Psychology Review, 13,* 115–138.

USA Today. (2003, June 23). Gallup Poll results. Available at http://www.usatoday.com/news/polls/tables/live/0623.htm.

Uskul, A. K., & Over, H. (2014). Responses to social exclusion in cultural context: Evidence from farming and herding communities. *Journal of Personality and Social Psychology, 106,* 752–771.

Uskul, A. K., Cross, S. E., Alözkan, C., Gerçek-Swing, B., Ataca, B., Günsoy, C., & Sunbay, Z. (2014). Emotional responses to honour situations in Turkey and the northern USA. *Cognition and Emotion, 28,* 1057–1075.

Uskul, A. K., Cross, S. E., Günsoy, C., Gercek-Swing, B., Alözkan, C., & Ataca, B. (2015). A price to pay: Turkish and Northern American retaliation for threats to personal and family honor. *Aggressive Behavior, 41(6),* 594–607.

Uskul, A. K., Cross, S. E., Sunbay, Z., Gercek-Swing, B., & Ataca, B. (2012). Honor bound: The cultural construction of honor in Turkey and the northern United States. *Journal of Cross-Cultural Psychology, 43,* 1131–1151.

Uskul, A. K., Oyserman, D., Schwarz, N., Lee, S. S., & Xu, A. J. (2013). How successful you have been in life depends on the response scale used: The role of cultural mindsets in pragmatic inferences drawn from question format. *Social Cognition, 31,* 222–236.

Uz, I. (2015). The index of cultural tightness and looseness among 68 countries. *Journal of Cross-Cultural Psychology, 46,* 319–335.

Uzefovsky, F., et al. (2015). Oxytocin receptor and vasopressin receptor 1a genes are respectively associated with emotional and cognitive empathy. *Hormones and Behavior, 67,* 60–65.

Uziel, L. (2007). Individual differences in the social facilitation effect: A review and meta-analysis. *Journal of Research in Personality, 41,* 579–601.

Vaillancourt, T. (2005). Indirect aggression among humans: Social construct or evolutionary adaptation? In R. E. Tremblay, W. W. Hartup, & J. Archer (Eds.), *Developmental origins of aggression* (pp. 158–177). New York: Guilford.

Vaish, A., Grossmann, T., & Woodward, A. (2008). Not all emotions are created equal: The negativity bias in social-emotional development. *Psychological Bulletin, 134,* 383–403.

Valdesolo, P., Ouyang, J., & DeSteno, D. (2010). The rhythm of joint action: Synchrony promotes cooperative activity. *Journal of Experimental Social Psychology, 46,* 693–695.

Valentine, T., & Mesout, J. (2009). Eyewitness identification under stress in the London Dungeon. *Applied Cognitive Psychology, 23,* 151–161.

Vallacher, R. R., Read, S. J., & Nowak, A. (2002). The dynamical perspective in personality and social psychology. *Personality and Social Psychology Review, 6,* 264–273.

Van Bavel, J. J., & Cunningham, W. A. (2009). Self-categorization with a novel mixed-race group moderates automatic social and racial biases. *Personality and Social Psychology Bulletin, 35,* 321–335.

Van Bavel, J. J., Packer, D. J., & Cunningham, W. A. (2011). Modulation of the fusiform face area following minimal exposure to motivationally relevant faces: Evidence of in-group enhancement (not out group disregard). *Journal of Cognitive Neuroscience, 23,* 3343–3354.

Van Bavel, J. J., Hackel, L. M., & Xiao, Y. J. (2014). The group mind: The pervasive influence of social identity on cognition. In J. Decety & Y. Christen (Eds.), *New frontiers in social neuroscience* (pp. 41–56). Cham, Switzerland: Springer International Publishing.

Van Bavel, J. J., Packer, D. J., & Cunningham, W. A. (2008). The neural substrates of in-group bias: A functional magnetic resonance imaging investigation. *Psychological Science, 19,* 1131–1139.

van Berkhout, E. T., & Malouff, J. M. (2015). The efficacy of empathy training: A meta-analysis of randomized controlled trials. *Journal of Counseling Psychology,* in press.

Van Berkum, J. J. A., Holleman, B., Nieuwland, M. S., Otten, M., & Murre, J. M. (2009). Right or wrong? The brain's fast response to morally objectionable statements. *Psychological Science, 20,* 1092–1099.

van Bommel, M., van Prooijen, J., Elffers, H., & van Lange, P. M. (2014). Intervene to be seen: The power of a camera in attenuating the bystander effect. *Social Psychological and Personality Science, 5,* 459–466.

Van Boven, L. (2005). Experientialism, materialism, and the pursuit of happiness. *Review of General Psychology, 9,* 132–142.

Van Boven, L., & Gilovich, T. (2003). To do or to have? That is the question. *Journal of Personality and Social Psychology, 85,* 1193–1202.

van der Stouwe, T., Asscher, J. J., Stams, G. J., Deković, M., & van der Laan, P. H. (2014). The effectiveness of multisystemic therapy (MST): A meta-analysis. *Clinical Psychology Review, 34,* 468–481.

van der Toorn, J., Feinberg, M., Jost, J. T., Kay, A. C., Tyler, T. R., Willer, R., & Wilmuth, C. (2015). A sense of powerlessness fosters system justification: Implications for the legitimation of authority, hierarchy, and government. *Political Psychology, 36,* 93–110.

Van Dyne, L., & Saavedra, R. (1996). A naturalistic minority influence experiment: Effects on divergent thinking, conflict, and originality in work-groups. *British Journal of Social Psychology, 35,* 151–167.

Van Eerde, W., & Thierry, H. (1996). Vroom's expectancy models and work-related criteria: A meta-analysis. *Journal of Applied Psychology, 81,* 575–586.

van Ginkel, W. P., & van Knippenberg, D. (2008). Group information elaboration and group decision making: The role of shared task representations. *Organizational Behavior and Human Decision Processes, 105,* 82–97.

van Ginkel, W. P., & van Knippenberg, D. (2012). Group leadership and shared task representations in decision making groups. *The Leadership Quarterly, 23,* 94–106.

van Hoorn, A. (2015). Individualist–collectivist culture and trust radius: A multilevel approach. *Journal of Cross-Cultural Psychology, 46,* 269–276.

Van Iddekinge, C. H., Raymark, P. H., & Roth, P. L. (2005). Assessing personality with a structured employment interview: Construct-related validity and susceptibility to response inflation. *Journal of Applied Psychology, 90,* 536–552.

Van Iddekinge, C. H., Roth, P. L., Raymark, P. H., & Odle-Dusseau, H. N. (2012). The criterion-related validity of integrity tests: An updated meta-analysis. *Journal of Applied Psychology, 97,* 499–530.

van Koppen, P. J., & Penrod, S. D. (Eds). (2003). *Adversarial versus inquisitorial justice: Psychological perspectives on criminal justice systems.* New York: Kluwer Academic/Plenum.

van Oorsouw, K., & Merckelbach, H. (2012). The effects of alcohol on crime-related memories: A field study. *Applied Cognitive Psychology, 26,* 82–90.

van Osch, Y., Blanken, I., Meijs, M. H. J., & van Wolferen, J. (2015). A group's physical attractiveness is greater than the average attractiveness of its members: The group attractiveness effect. *Personality and Social Psychology Bulletin, 41,* 559–574.

Van Prooijen, J.-W., Van den Bos, K., Lind, E. A., & Wilke, H. (2006). How do people react to negative procedures? On the moderating role of authority's biased attitudes. *Journal of Experimental Social Psychology, 42,* 632–645.

Van Rooy, D., Vanhoomissen, T., & Van Overwalle, F. (2013). Illusory correlation, group size and memory. *Journal of Experimental Social Psychology, 49,* 1159–1167.

van Straaten, I., Engels, R., Finkenauer, C., & Holland, R. W. (2009). Meeting your match: Attractiveness similarity affects approach behavior in mixed-sex dyads. *Personality and Social Psychology Bulletin, 35,* 685–697.

van Vugt, M., & Kameda, T. (2014). Evolution of the social brain: Psychological adaptations for group living. In M. Mikulincer & P. R. Shaver (Eds.), *Mechanisms of social connection: From brain to group* (pp. 335–355). Washington, DC: American Psychological Association.

Vandello, J. A., & Bosson, J. K. (2013). Hard won and easily lost: A review and synthesis of theory and research on precarious manhood. *Psychology of Men & Masculinity, 14,* 101–113.

Vandello, J. A., & Cohen, D. (2003). Male honor and female fidelity: Implicit cultural scripts that perpetuate domestic violence. *Journal of Personality and Social Psychology, 84,* 997–1010.

Vandello, J. A., Cohen, D., Grandon, R., & Franiuk, R. (2009). Stand by your man: Indirect prescriptions for honorable violence and feminine loyalty in Canada, Chile, and the United States. *Journal of Cross-Cultural Psychology, 40,* 81–104.

Vandello, J. A., Hettinger, V. E., & Michniewicz, K. (2013). Region as culture. In A. Cohen (Ed.), *New directions in the psychology of culture.* Washington, DC: American Psychological Association.

VanderStoep, S. W., & Shaughnessy, J. J. (1997). Taking a course in research methods improves reasoning about real-life events. *Teaching of Psychology, 24,* 122–124.

Varnum, M. E. W. (2012). Social class differences in N400 indicate differences in spontaneous trait inference. *Journal of Experimental Psychology, 141(3),* 518–526.

Vazire, S. (2010). Who knows what about a person? The self–other knowledge asymmetry (SOKA) model. *Journal of Personality and Social Psychology, 98,* 281–300.

Vazire, S., & Carlson, E. N. (2011). Others sometimes know us better than we know ourselves. *Current Directions in Psychological Science, 20,* 104–108.

Vazire, S., & Wilson, T. (Eds.). (2012). *Handbook of Self-Knowledge.* New York: Guilford.

Vazsonyi, A. T., Machackova, H., Sevcikova, A., Smahel, D., & Cerna, A. (2012). Cyberbullying in context: Direct and indirect effects by low self-control across 25 European countries. *European Journal of Developmental Psychology, 9,* 210–227.

Vecchio, R. P. (2002). Leadership and the gender advantage. *Leadership Quarterly, 13,* 643–671.

Verduyn, P., et al. (2015). Passive Facebook usage undermines affective well-being: Experimental and longitudinal evidence. *Journal of Experimental Psychology: General, 144,* 480–488.

Verlinden, M., et al. (2014). Executive functioning and non-verbal intelligence as predictors of bullying in early elementary school. *Journal of Abnormal Child Psychology, 42,* 953–966.

Vetlesen, A. J. (2005). *Evil and human agency.* Cambridge: Cambridge University Press.

Vezzali, L., Crisp, R. J., Stathi, S., & Giovannini, D. (2015). Imagined intergroup contact facilitates intercultural communication for college students on academic exchange programs. *Group Processes & Intergroup Relations, 18,* 66–75.

Victoroff, J., & Kruglanski, A.W. (Eds.). (2009). *Psychology of terrorism: Classic and contemporary insights.* New York: Psychology Press.

Vidmar, N., & Hans, V P. (2007). *American juries: The verdict.* Amherst, NY: Prometheus.

Viglione, J., Hannon, L., & DeFina, R. (2011). The impact of light skin on prison time for Black female offenders. *The Social Science Journal, 48,* 250–258.

Vinokur, A., & Burnstein, E. (1974). Effects of partially shared persuasive arguments on group-induced shifts: A group-problem-solving approach. *Journal of Personality and Social Psychology, 29,* 305–315.

Visintainer, M., Volpicelli, J., & Seligman, M. (1982). Tumor rejection in rats after inescapable or escapable shock. *Science, 216,* 437–439.

Visser, P. S., & Mirabile, R. R. (2004). Attitudes in the social context: The impact of social network composition on individual-level attitude strength. *Journal of Personality and Social Psychology, 87,* 779–795.

Vitaro, F., Brendgen, M., Girard, A., Boivin, M., Dionne, G., & Tremblay, R. E. (2015). The expression of genetic risk for aggressive and non-aggressive antisocial behavior is moderated by peer group norms. *Journal of Youth and Adolescence, 44,* 1379–1395.

Vittengl, J. R., & Holt, C. S. (2000). Getting acquainted: The relationship of self-disclosure and social attraction to positive affect. *Journal of Social and Personal Relationships, 17,* 53–66.

Vogel, D. L., Wester, S. R., & Heesacker, M. (1999). Dating relationships and the demand/withdraw pattern of communication. *Sex Roles, 41,* 297–306.

Vogel, E. A., Rose, J. P., Roberts, L. R., & Eckles, K. (2014). Social comparison, social media, and self-esteem. *Psychology of Popular Media Culture, 3,* 206–222.

Vohs, K. D. (2015). Money priming can change people's thoughts, feelings, motivations, and behaviors: An update on 10 years of experiments. *Journal of Experimental Psychology: General, 144,* e86–e93.

Vohs, K. D., & Finkel, E. J. (Eds.). (2006). *Self and relationships: Connecting intrapersonal and interpersonal processes.* New York: Guilford.

Vohs, K. D., & Heatherton, T. F. (2000). Self-regulatory failure: A resource-depletion approach. *Psychological Science, 11,* 249–252.

Vohs, K. D., Baumeister, R. F., & Ciarocco, N. J. (2005). Self-regulation and self-presentation: Regulatory resource depletion impairs impression management and effortful self-presentation depletes regulatory resources. *Journal of Personality and Social Psychology, 88,* 632–657.

Volk, A. A., Della Cioppa, V., Earle, M., & Farrell, A. H. (2015). Social competition and bullying: An adaptive socioecological perspective. In V. Zeigler-Hill, L. M. Welling, & T. K. Shackelford (Eds.), *Evolutionary perspectives on social psychology* (pp. 387–399). Cham, Switzerland: Springer.

Vollhardt, J. R., & Staub, E. (2011). Inclusive altruism born of suffering: The relationship between adversity and prosocial attitudes and behavior toward disadvantaged outgroups. *American Journal of Orthopsychiatry, 81,* 307–315.

von Hippel, C., Wiryakusuma, C., Bowden, J., & Shochet, M. (2011). Stereotype threat and female communication styles. *Personality and Social Psychology Bulletin, 37,* 1312–1324.

von Hippel, W., & Henry, J. D. (2011). Aging and self-regulation. In K. D. Vohs, & R. F. Baumeister (Eds.), *Handbook of self-regulation: Research, theory, and applications* (2nd ed., pp. 321–335). New York: Guilford.

von Hippel, W., & Trivers, R. (2011). The evolution and psychology of self-deception. *Behavioral and Brain Sciences, 34,* 1–16.

von Hippel, W., Lakin, J. L., & Shakarchi, R. J. (2005). Individual differences in motivated social cognition: The case of self-serving information processing. *Personality and Social Psychological Bulletin, 31,* 1347–1357.

Von Lang, J., & Sibyll, C. (Eds.). (1983). *Eichmann interrogated* (R. Manheim, Trans.). New York: Farrar, Straus & Giroux.

Vonk, R. (1998). The slime effect: Suspicion and dislike of likeable behavior toward superiors. *Journal of Personality and Social Psychology, 74,* 849–864.

Voracek, M., & Fisher, M. L. (2002). Shapely centrefolds? Temporal change in body measures: Trend analysis. *British Medical Journal, 325,* 1447–1448.

Vorauer, J. D. (2003). Dominant group members in intergroup interaction: Safety or vulnerability in numbers? *Personality and Social Psychology Bulletin, 29,* 498–511.

Vorauer, J. D., & Sasaki, S. J. (2012). The pitfalls of empathy as a default intergroup interaction strategy: Distinct effects of trying to empathize with a lower status outgroup member who does versus does not express distress. *Journal of Experimental Social Psychology, 48,* 519–524.

Vorauer, J. D., & Sasaki, S. J. (2014). Distinct effects of imagine-other versus imagine-self perspective-taking on prejudice reduction. *Social Cognition, 32,* 130–147.

Vorauer, J. D., Cameron, J. J., Holmes, J. G., & Pearce, D. G. (2003). Invisible overtures: Fears of rejection and the signal amplification bias. *Journal of Personality and Social Psychology, 84,* 793–812.

Vrij, A. (2008). *Detecting lies and deceit: Pitfalls and opportunities.* Chichester, UK: Wiley.

Vrij, A., & Granhag, P. A. (2012). Eliciting cues to deception and truth: What matters are the questions asked. *Journal of Research in Memory and Cognition, 1,* 110–117.

Vrij, A., Mann, S., Fisher, R., Leal, S., Milne, R., & Bull, R. (2008). Increasing cognitive load to facilitate lie detection: The benefit of recalling an event in reverse order. *Law and Human Behavior, 32,* 253–265.

Vrij, A., Mann, S., Leal, S., & Fisher, R. (2010). "Look into my eyes": Can instruction to maintain eye contact facilitate lie detection? *Psychology, Crime & Law, 16,* 327–348.

Vroom, V H. (1964). *Work and motivation.* New York: Wiley.

Vroom, V H., & Jago, A. G. (1988). *Managing participation in organizations.* Englewood Cliffs, NJ: Prentice-Hall.

Vroom, V H., & Jago, A. G. (2007). The role of the situation in leadership. *American Psychologist, 62,* 17–24.

Vroom, V H., & Yetton, P. W. (1973). *Leadership and decisionmaking.* Pittsburgh: University of Pittsburgh Press.

Waasdorp, T. E., Baker, C. N., Paskewich, B. S., & Leff, S. S. (2013). The association between forms of aggression, leadership, and social status among urban youth. *Journal of Youth and Adolescence, 42,* 263–274.

Wageman, R., Fisher, C. M., & Hackman, J. R. (2009). Leading teams when the time is right: Finding the best moments to act. *Organizational Dynamics, 38,* 192–203.

Wagner, D. V., Borduin, C. M., Sawyer, A. M., & Dopp, A. R. (2014). Long-term prevention of criminality in siblings of serious and violent juvenile offenders: A 25-year follow-up to a randomized clinical trial of multisystemic therapy. *Journal of Consulting and Clinical Psychology, 82,* 492–499.

Waldman, D. A., & Avolio, B. J. (1991). Race effects in performance evaluations: Controlling for ability, education, and experience. *Journal of Applied Psychology, 76,* 897–901.

Walker, L., LaTour, S., Lind, E. A., & Thibaut, J. (1974). Reactions of participants and observers to modes of adjudication. *Journal of Applied Social Psychology, 4,* 295–310.

Wallace, D. B., & Kassin S. M. (2012). Harmless error analysis: How do judges respond to confession errors? *Law and Human Behavior, 36,* 151–157.

Wallis, C. (2011). Performing gender: A content analysis of gender display in music videos. *Sex Roles, 64,* 160–172.

Walster, E. (1966). Assignment of responsibility for important events. *Journal of Personality and Social Psychology, 3,* 73–79.

Walster, E., & Festinger, L. (1962). The effectiveness of "overheard" persuasive communications. *Journal of Abnormal and Social Psychology, 65,* 395–402.

Walster, E., Aronson, V., Abrahams, D., & Rottman, L. (1966). The importance of physical attractiveness in dating behavior. *Journal of Personality and Social Psychology, 4,* 508–516.

Walster, E., Walster, G. W., & Berscheid, E. (1978). *Equity: Theory and research.* Boston: Allyn & Bacon.

Walster, E., Walster, G. W., Piliavin, J., & Schmidt, L. (1973). "Playing hard-to-get": Understanding an elusive phenomenon. *Journal of Personality and Social Psychology, 26,* 113–121.

Walther, E., Weil, R., & Düsing, J. (2011). The role of evaluative conditioning in attitude formation. *Current Directions in Psychological Science, 20,* 192–196.

Walton, G. M. (2014). The new science of wise psychological interventions. *Current Directions in Psychological Science, 23,* 73–82.

Walton, G. M., Logel, C., Peach, J. M., Spencer, S. J., & Zanna, M. P. (2015). Two brief interventions to mitigate a "chilly climate" transform women's experience, relationships, and achievement in engineering. *Journal of Educational Psychology, 107,* 468–485.

Walton, G. M., & Cohen, G. L. (2007). A question of belonging: Race, social fit, and achievement. *Journal of Personality and Social Psychology, 92,* 82–96.

Walton, G. M., & Cohen, G. L. (2011). A brief social-belonging intervention improves academic and health outcomes of minority students. *Science, 331,* 1447–1451.

Walton, G. M., Cohen, G. L., Cwir, D., & Spencer, S. J. (2012). Mere belonging: The power of social connections. *Journal of Personality and Social Psychology, 102,* 513–532.

Walton and Cohen, 2015.

Wampold, B. E., Mondin, G. W., Moody, M., Stich, F., Benson, K., & Ahn, H. (1997). A meta-analysis of outcome studies comparing bona fide psychotherapies: Empirically, "all must have prizes" *Psychological Bulletin, 122,* 203–215.

Wanberg, C. R. (2012). The individual experience of unemployment. *Annual Review of Psychology, 63,* 369–396.

Wang, H., Masuda, T., Ito, K., & Rashid, M. (2012). How much information? East Asian and North American cultural products and information search performance. *Personality and Social Psychology Bulletin, 38,* 1539–1551.

Wang, S., & Lau, A. S. (2015). Mutual and non-mutual social support: Cultural differences in the psychological, behavioral, and biological effects of support seeking. *Journal of Cross-Cultural Psychology, 46,* 916–929.

Wang, X. M., Wong, K. F. E., & Kwong, J. Y. Y. (2010). The roles of rater goals and ratee performance levels in the distortion of performance ratings. *Journal of Applied Psychology, 95,* 546–561.

Warburton, W. A., & Anderson, C. A. (2015). Aggression, social psychology of. *International Encyclopedia of the Social & Behavioral Sciences* (2nd ed.), *1,* 373–380.

Ward, A. (2014, April 8). UConn riots: 30 arrested after NCAA championship win. Newsmax, www.newsmax.com/TheWire/uconn-riots-arrest-ncaachampionship/2014/04/08/id/564335.

Ward, L. M., & Friedman, K. (2006). Using TV as a guide: Associations between television viewing and adolescents' sexual attitudes and behavior. *Journal of Research on Adolescence, 16,* 133–156.

Ware, A., & Kowalski, G. S. (2012). Sex identification and love of sports: BIRGing and CORFing among sport fans. *Journal of Sport Behavior, 35,* 223–237.

Warmelink, L., Vrij, A., Mann, S., Leal, S., Forrester, D., & Fisher, R. (2011). Thermal imaging as a lie detection tool at airports. *Law and Human Behavior, 35,* 40–48.

Warneken, F., & Tomasello, M. (2006). Altruistic helping in human infants and young chimpanzees. *Science, 311,* 1301–1303.

Warneken, F., & Tomasello, M. (2014). Extrinsic rewards undermine altruistic tendencies in 20-month-olds. *Motivation Science, 1,* 43–48.

Warren, B. L. (1966). A multiple variable approach to the assortive mating phenomenon. *Eugenics Quarterly, 13,* 285–298.

Watkins, L. E., Maldonado, R. C., & DiLillo, D. (2014). Hazardous alcohol use and intimate partner aggression among dating couples: The role of impulse control difficulties. *Aggressive Behavior, 40,* 369–381.

Watkins, E. R. (2008). Constructive and unconstructive repetitive thought. *Psychological Bulletin, 134,* 163–206.

Watson, D., Wiese, D., Vaidya, J., & Tellegen, A. (1999). The two general activation systems of affect: Structural findings, evolutionary considerations, and psychobiological evidence. *Journal of Personality and Social Psychology, 76,* 820–838.

Watson, N., Bryan, B. C., & Thrash, T. M. Self-discrepancy: Long-term test–retest reliability and test–criterion predictive validity. *Psychological Assessment.* (in press).

Waugh, W., Brownell, C., & Pollock, B. (2015). Early socialization of prosocial behavior: Patterns in parents' encouragement of toddlers' helping in an everyday household task. *Infant Behavior & Development, 39,* 1–10.

Wax, E. (2008, November 22). Can love conquer caste? *Washington Post.* Wayment, H. A. (2004). It could have been me: Vicarious victims and disaster-focused distress. *Personality and Social Psychology Bulletin, 30,* 515–528.

Wayment, H. A. (2004). It could have been me: Vicarious victims and disaster-focused distress. *Personality and Social Psychology Bulletin, 30,* 515–528.

Waytz, A., & Epley, N. (2012). Social connection enables dehumanization. *Journal of Experimental Social Psychology, 48,* 70–76.

Waytz, A., Gray, K., Epley, N., & Wegner, D. M. (2010). Causes and consequences of mind perception. *Trends in the Cognitive Sciences, 14,* 383–388.

Waytz, A., Heafner, J., & Epley, N. (2014). The mind in the machine: Anthropomorphism increases trust in an autonomous vehicle. *Journal of Experimental Social Psychology, 52,* 113–117.

Weary, G., & Edwards, J. A. (1994). Individual differences in causal uncertainty. *Journal of Personality and Social Psychology, 67,* 308–318.

Weaver, J. R., & Bosson, J. K. (2011). I feel like I know you: Sharing negative attitudes of others promotes feelings of familiarity. *Personality and Social Psychology Bulletin, 37,* 481–491.

Weber, M., & Camerer, C. (1998). The disposition effect in securities trading: An experimental analysis. *Journal of Economic Behavior and Organization, 33,* 167–184.

Webster, D. M., Richter, L., & Kruglanski, A. W. (1996). On leaping to conclusions when feeling tired: Mental fatigue effects on impressional primacy. *Journal of Experimental Social Psychology, 32,* 181–195.

Webster, R. J., & Saucier, D. A. (2011). The effects of death reminders on sex differences in prejudice toward gay men and lesbians. *Journal of Homosexuality, 58,* 402–426.

Weeden, J., & Sabini, J. (2005). Physical attractiveness and health in Western societies: A review. *Psychological Bulletin, 131,* 635–653.

Wegener, D. T., & Petty, R. E. (1994). Mood management across affective states: The hedonic contingency hypothesis. *Journal of Personality and Social Psychology, 66,* 1034–1048.

Wegener, D. T., Petty, R. E., & Smith, S. M. (1995). Positive mood can increase or decrease message scrutiny: The hedonic contingency view of mood and message processing. *Journal of Personality and Social Psychology, 69,* 5–15.

Wegner, D. M. (1994). Ironic processes of mental control. *Psychological Review, 101,* 34–52.

Wegner, D. M. (1997). When the antidote is the poison: Ironic mental control processes. *Psychological Science, 8,* 148–153.

Wegner, D. M., Ansfield, M., & Pilloff, D. (1998). The putt and the pendulum: Ironic effects of the mental control of action. *Psychological Science, 9,* 196–199.

Wegner, D. M., Erber, R., & Raymond, P. (1991). Transactive memory in close relationships. *Journal of Personality and Social Psychology, 61,* 923–929.

Weiner, B. (1985). "Spontaneous" causal thinking. *Psychological Bulletin, 97,* 74–84.

Weiner, B. (2008). Reflections on the history of attribution theory and research. *Social Psychology, 39,* 151–156.

Weinstein, N. D. (1980). Unrealistic optimism about future life events. *Journal of Personality and Social Psychology, 39,* 806–820.

Weisman, O., et al. (2015). The association between 2D:4D ratio and cognitive empathy is contingent on a common polymorphism in the oxytocin receptor gene (OXTR rs53576). *Psychoneuroendocrinology, 58,* 23–32.

Weiss, E., & Marksteiner, J. (2007). Alcohol-related cognitive disorders with a focus on neuropsychology. *International Journal on Disability and Human Development, 6,* 337–342.

Weldon, M. S., Blair, C., & Huebsch, D. (2000). Group remembering: Does social loafing underlie collaborative inhibition? *Journal of Experimental Psychology: Learning, Memory, and Cognition, 26,* 1568–1577.

Wells, C., Adhyaru, J., Cannon, J., Lamond, M., & Baruch, G. (2010). Multisystemic therapy (MST) for youth offending, psychiatric disorder and substance abuse: Case examples from a UK MST team. *Child and Adolescent Mental Health, 15,* 142–149.

Wells, G. L., & Bradfield, A. L. (1998). "Good, you identified the suspect": Feedback to eyewitnesses distorts their reports of the witnessing experience. *Journal of Applied Psychology, 83,* 360–376.

Wells, G. L., & Petty, R. E. (1980). The effects of overt head-movements on persuasion: Compatibility and incompatibility of responses. *Basic and Applied Social Psychology, 1,* 219–230.

Wells, G. L., & Quinlivan, D. S. (2009). Suggestive eyewitness identification procedures and the Supreme Court's reliability test in light of eyewitness science: 30 years later. *Law and Human Behavior, 33,* 1–24.

Wells, G. L., Charman, S. D., & Olson, E. A. (2005). Building face composites can harm lineup identification performance. *Journal of Experimental Psychology: Applied, 11,* 147–156.

Wells, G. L., Lindsay, R. C. L., & Ferguson, T. J. (1979). Accuracy, confidence, and juror perceptions in eyewitness identification. *Journal of Applied Psychology, 64,* 440–448.

Wells, G. L., Malpass, R. S., Lindsay, R. C. L., Fisher, R. P., Turtle, J. W., & Fulero, S. M. (2000). From the lab to the police station: A successful application of eyewitness research. *American Psychologist, 55,* 581–598.

Wells, G. L., Memon, A., & Penrod, S. (2007). Eyewitness evidence: Improving its probative value. *Psychological Science in the Public Interest, 7,* 45–75.

Wells, G. L., Small, M., Penrod, S., Malpass, R. S., Fulero, S. M., & Brimacombe, C. A. E. (1998). Eyewitness identification procedures: Recommendations for lineups and photospreads, *Law and Human Behavior, 22,* 603–648.

Wells, G. L., Steblay, N. K., & Dysart, J. E. (2015). Double-blind photo lineups using actual eyewitnesses: An experimental test of a sequential versus simultaneous lineup procedure. *Law and Human Behavior, 39,* 1–14.

Wells, R. (2011). Social network acts to reduce suicide. *The Age (Melbourne, Australia).* p. 5.

Wendt, H., Euwema, M. C., & van Emmerik, I. H. (2009). Leadership and team cohesiveness across cultures. *The Leadership Quarterly, 20,* 358–370.

Wenzlaff, R. M., & Wegner, D. M. (2000). Thought suppression. *Annual Review of Psychology, 51,* 59–91.

Werner, N. E. (2012). Do hostile attribution biases in children and parents predict relationally aggressive behavior?. *The Journal of Genetic Psychology: Research and Theory on Human Development, 173*, 221–245.

Werner, N. E., & Grant, S. (2009). Mothers' cognitions about relational aggression: Associations with discipline responses, children's normative beliefs, and peer competence. *Social Development, 18*, 77–98.

Wesselmann, E. D., Reeder, G. D., & Pryor, J. B. (2012). The effects of time pressure on controlling reactions to persons with mental illness. *Basic and Applied Social Psychology, 34*, 565–571.

West, K., Hewstone, M., & Lolliot, S. (2014). Intergroup contact and prejudice against people with schizophrenia. *The Journal of Social Psychology, 154*, 217–232.

West, S. G., & Brown, T. J. (1975). Physical attractiveness, the severity of the emergency and helping: A field experiment and interpersonal simulation. *Journal of Experimental Social Psychology, 11*, 531–538.

West, T. V., & Kenny, D. A. (2011). The truth and bias model of judgment. *Psychological Review, 118*, 357–378.

Westaway, M. S., Jordaan, E. R., & Tsai, J. (2015). Investigating the psychometric properties of the Rosenberg Self-Esteem Scale for South African residents of greater Pretoria. *Evaluation & the Health Professions, 38*, 181–199.

Westen, D. (2007). *The political brain: The role of emotion in deciding the fate of the nation.* New York: Public Affairs.

Westen, D., Kilts, C., Blagov, P., Harenski, K., & Hamann, S. (2006). The neural basis of motivated reasoning: An fMRI study of emotional constraints on political judgment during the U.S. presidential election of 2004. *Journal of Cognitive Neuroscience, 18*, 1947–1958.

Wheeler, L., & Kim, Y. (1997). What is beautiful is culturally good: The physical attractiveness stereotype has different content in collectivist cultures. *Personality and Social Psychology Bulletin, 23*, 795–800.

Wheeler, L., & Miyake, K. (1992). Social comparison in everyday life. *Journal of Personality and Social Psychology, 62*, 760–773.

Wheeler, L., Koestner, R., & Driver, R. E. (1982). Related attributes in the choice of comparison others. *Journal of Experimental Social Psychology, 18*, 489–500.

Whitbeck, L. B., & Hoyt, D. R. (1994). Social prestige and assortive mating: A comparison of students from 1956 and 1988. *Journal of Social and Personal Relationships, 11*, 137–145.

White, G. L., Fishbein, S., & Rutstein, J. (1981). Passionate love: The misattribution of arousal. *Journal of Personality and Social Psychology, 41*, 56–62.

White, M. P., Alcock, I., Wheeler, B. W., & Depledge, M. H. (2013). Would you be happier living in a greener urban area? A fixed-effects analysis of panel data. *Psychological Science, 24*, 920–928.

Whitehead, G. I. (2014). Correlates of volunteerism and charitable giving in the 50 United States. *North American Journal of Psychology, 16*, 531–536.

Whittaker, J. O., & Meade, R. D. (1967). Social pressure in the modification and distortion of judgment: A cross-cultural study. *International Journal of Psychology, 2*, 109–113.

Whorf, B. L. (1956). Science and linguistics. In J. B. Carroll (Ed.), *Language, thought, and reality: Selected writings of Benjamin Lee Whorf* (pp. 207–219). Cambridge, MA: MIT Press.

Wicker, B., Keysers, C., Plailly, J., Royet, J. P., Gallese, V., & Rizzolatti, G. (2003). Both of us disgusted in my insula: The common neural basis of seeing and feeling disgust. *Neuron, 40*, 655–664.

Wicklund, R. A. (1975). Objective self-awareness. In L. Berkowitz (Ed.), *Advances in experimental social psychology* (Vol. 8, pp. 233–275). New York: Academic Press.

Widman, L., Noar, S. M., Choukas-Bradley, S., & Francis, D. B. (2014). Adolescent sexual health communication and condom use: A meta-analysis. *Health Psychology, 33*, 1113–1124.

Widmeyer, W. N., & Loy, J. W. (1988). When you're hot, you're hot! Warm-cold effects in first impressions of persons and teaching effectiveness. *Journal of Educational Psychology, 80*, 118–121.

Wieber, F., Thürmer, J. L., & Gollwitzer, P. M. (2015). Attenuating the escalation of commitment to a faltering project in decision-making groups: An implementation intention approach. *Social Psychological and Personality Science, 6*, 587–595.

Wiesner, W. H., & Cronshaw, S. F. (1988). A meta-analytic investigation of the impact of interview format and degree of structure on the validity of the employment interview. *Journal of Occupational Psychology, 61*, 275–290.

Wiggins, J. S. (Ed.). (1996). *The five-factor model of personality: Theoretical perspectives.* New York: Guilford.

Wilde, V. K., Martin, K. D., & Goff, P. A. (2014). Dehumanization as a distinct form of prejudice. *TPM-Testing, Psychometrics, Methodology in Applied Psychology, 21*, 301–307.

Wilder, D. A. (1977). Perception of groups, size of opposition, and social influence. *Journal of Experimental Social Psychology, 13*, 253–268.

Wilder, D. A., Simon, A. F., & Myles, F. (1996). Enhancing the impact of counterstereotypic information: Dispositional attributions for deviance. *Journal of Personality and Social Psychology, 71*, 276–287.

Wildschut, T., Sedikides, C., Arndt, J., & Routledge, C. (2006). Nostalgia: Content, Triggers, Functions. *Journal of Personality and Social Psychology, 91*, 975–993.

Wilken, B., Miyamoto, Y., & Uchida, Y. (2011). Cultural influences on preference consistency: Consistency at the individual and collective levels. *Journal of Consumer Psychology, 21*, 346–353.

Wilkinson, D. L., & Carr, P. J. (2008). Violent youths' response to high levels of exposure to community violence: What violent events reveal about youth violence. *Journal of Community Psychology, 36*, 1026–1051.

Willadsen-Jensen, E., & Ito, T. A. (2015). The effect of context on responses to racially ambiguous faces: Changes in perception and evaluation. *SCAN, 10*, 885–892.

Willard, G. & Gramzow, R. H. (2008). Exaggeration in memory: Systematic distortion of self-evaluative information under reduced accessibility. *Journal of Experimental Social Psychology, 44*, 246–259.

Willard, G., Isaac, K. J., & Carney, D. R. (2015). Some evidence for the nonverbal contagion of racial bias. *Organizational Behavior and Human Decision Processes, 128*, 96–107.

Willer, R. (2004). The effects of government-issued terror warnings on presidential approval ratings. *Current Research in Social Psychology, 10*, 1–12.

Williams v. Florida, 399 U.S. 78 (1970).

Williams, E. F., Gilovich, T., & Dunning, D. (2012). Being all that you can be: How potential performances influence assessments of self and others. *Personality and Social Psychology Bulletin, 38*, 143–154.

Williams, K. D., & Wesselmann, E. D. (2011). The link between ostracism and aggression. In J. P. Forgas, A. W. Kruglanski, & K. D. Williams (Eds.), *The psychology of social conflict and aggression* (pp. 37–51). New York: Psychology Press.

Williams, K. D., Cheung, C., & Choi, W. (2000). Cyberostracism: Effects of being ignored over the internet. *Journal of Personality and Social Psychology, 79*, 748–762.

Williams, K. D., Govan, C. L., Croker, V., Tynan, D., Cruickshank, M., & Lam, A. (2002). Investigations into differences between social- and cyberostracism. *Group Dynamics: Theory, Research, and Practice, 6*, 65–77.

Williams, L. E., & Bargh, J. A. (2008). Experiencing physical warmth promotes interpersonal warmth. *Science, 322*, 606–607.

Williams, M. J., & Eberhardt, J. L. (2008). Biological conceptions of race and the motivation to cross racial boundaries. *Journal of Personality and Social Psychology, 94,* 1033–1047.

Williams, R. (1993). *Anger kills.* New York: Times Books.

Williams. K. D., & Nida, S. A. (2011). Ostracism: Consequences and coping. *Current Directions in Psychological Science, 20,* 71–75.

Williams, W. M., & Ceci, S. J. (2015). National hiring experiments reveal 2:1 faculty preference for women on STEM tenure track. *PNAS Proceedings of the National Academy of Sciences of the United States of America, 112,* 5360–5365.

Willis, J., & Todorov, A. (2006). First impressions: Making up your mind after a 100-ms exposure to a face. *Psychological Science, 17,* 592–598.

Willoughby, T., Adachi, P. C., & Good, M. (2012). A longitudinal study of the association between violent video game play and aggression among adolescents. *Developmental Psychology, 48,* 1044–1057.

Wills, T. A. (1981). Downward comparison principles in social psychology. *Psychological Bulletin, 90,* 245–271.

Wills, T. A., & DePaulo, B. M. (1991). Interpersonal analysis of the help-seeking process. In C. R. Snyder & D. R. Forsyth (Eds.), *Handbook of social and clinical psychology: The health perspective* (pp. 350–375). New York: Pergamon Press.

Wilmot, M. P. (2015). A contemporary taxometric analysis of the latent structure of self-monitoring. *Psychological Assessment, 27,* 353–364.

Wilson, A. E., & Ross, M. (2000). The frequency of temporal and social comparisons in people's personal appraisals. *Journal of Personality and Social Psychology, 78,* 928–942.

Wilson, D. W. (1978). Helping behavior and physical attractiveness. *Journal of Social Psychology, 104,* 313–314.

Wilson, E. R., & Thompson, L. L. (2014). Creativity and negotiation research: The integrative potential. *International Journal of Conflict Management, 25,* 359–386.

Wilson, J. P., Hugenberg, K., & Bernstein, M. J. (2013). The cross-race effect and eyewitness identification: How to improve recognition and reduce decision errors in eyewitness situations. *Social Issues and Policy Review, 7,* 83–113.

Wilson, K., & Albarracín, D. (2015). Barriers to accessing HIV-prevention in clinic settings: Higher alcohol use and more sex partners predict decreased exposure to HIV-prevention counseling. *Psychology, Health & Medicine, 20,* 87–96.

Wilson, K. S., & Baumann, H. M. (2015). Capturing a more complete view of employees' lives outside of work: The introduction and development of new interrole conflict constructs. *Personnel Psychology, 68,* 235–282.

Wilson, M. I., & Daly, M. (1996). Male sexual proprietariness and violence against wives. *Current Directions in Psychological Science, 5,* 2–7.

Wilson, T. D. (2002). *Strangers to ourselves: Discovering the adaptive unconscious.* Cambridge, MA: Belknap Press.

Wilson, T. D., & Gilbert, D. T. (2003). Affective forecasting. *Advances in Experimental Social Psychology, 35,* 345–411.

Wilson, T. D., & Gilbert, D. T. (2013). The impact bias is alive and well. *Journal of Personality and Social Psychology, 105,* 740–748.

Wilson, T. D., Wheatley, T., Meyers, J. M., Gilbert, D. T., & Axsom, D. (2000). Focalism: A source of durability bias in affective forecasting. *Journal of Personality and Social Psychology, 78,* 821–836.

Wiltermuth, S. S. (2012). Synchronous activity boosts compliance with requests to aggress. *Journal of Experimental Social Psychology, 48,* 453–456.

Wiltermuth, S. S., & Heath, C. (2010). Synchrony and cooperation. *Psychological Science, 20,* 1–5.

Winch, R. F., Ktsanes, I., & Ktsanes, V (1954). The theory of complementary needs in mate selection: An analytic and descriptive study. *American Sociological Review, 19,* 241–249.

Winter, D. G. (1987). Leader appeal, leader performance, and the motive profiles of leaders and followers: A study of American presidents and elections. *Journal of Personality and Social Psychology, 52,* 41–46.

Wishman, S. (1986). *Anatomy of a jury: The system on trial.* New York: Times Books.

Wittenbrink, B., Judd. C. M., & Park, B. (1997). Evidence for racial prejudice at the implicit level and its relationship with questionnaire measures. *Journal of Personality and Social Psychology, 72,* 262–274.

Wojcik, S. P., & Ditto, P. H. (2014). Motivated happiness: Self-enhancement inflates self-reported subjective well-being. *Social Psychological and Personality Science, 5,* 825–834.

Wolf, S., & Montgomery, D. A. (1977). Effects of inadmissible evidence and level of judicial admonishment to disregard on the judgments of mock jurors. *Journal of Applied Social Psychology, 7,* 205–219.

Wolgemuth, L. (2009, June 17). Why a psychologist might be at your next interview. *U.S. News & World Report.*

Wong, R. Y.-m., & Hong, Y.-y. (2005). Dynamic influences of culture on cooperation in the prisoner's dilemma. *Psychological Science, 16,* 429–434.

Wood, J. V (1989). Theory and research concerning social comparisons of personal attributes. *Psychological Bulletin, 106,* 231–248.

Wood, W., & Eagly, A. H. (2010). Gender. In S. T. Fiske, D. T. Gilbert, & G. Lindzey (Eds.), *Handbook of social psychology,* Vol. 1 (5th ed.) (pp. 629–667). Hoboken, NJ: Wiley.

Wood, W., & Quinn, J. M. (2003). Forewarned and forearmed? Two meta-analysis syntheses of forewarnings of influence appeals. *Psychological Bulletin, 129,* 119–138.

Wood, W., Kallgren, C. A., & Preisler, R. M. (1985). Access to attitude-relevant information in memory as a determinant of persuasion: The role of message attributes. *Journal of Experimental Social Psychology, 21,* 73–85.

Wood, W., Lundgren, S., Ouellette, J. A., Busceme, S., & Blackstone, T. (1994). Minority influence: A meta-analytic review of social influence processes. *Psychological Bulletin, 115,* 323–345.

Wood, W., Pool, G. J., Leck, K., & Purvis, D. (1996). Self-definition, defensive processing, and influence: The normative impact of majority and minority groups. *Journal of Personality and Social Psychology, 71,* 1181–1193.

Woolley, A. W., Chabris, C. F., Pentland, A., Hashmi, N., & Malone, T. W. (2010). Evidence for a collective intelligence factor in the performance of human groups. *Science, 330,* 686–688.

Woolley, A. W., Gerbasi, M. E., Chabris, C. F., Kosslyn, S. M., & Hackman, J. R. (2008). Bringing in the experts: How team composition and collaborative planning jointly shape analytic effectiveness. *Small Group Research, 39,* 352–371.

Woolley, A. W., Hackman, J. R., Jerde, T. E., Chabris, C. F., Bennett, S. L., & Kosslyn, S. M. (2007). Using brain-based measures to compose teams: How individual capabilities and team collaboration strategies jointly shape performance. *Social Neuroscience, 2,* 96–105.

Word, C. O., Zanna, M. P., & Cooper, J. (1974). The nonverbal mediation of self-fulfilling prophecies in interracial interaction. *Journal of Experimental Social Psychology, 10,* 109–120.

World Health Organization. (2012). *Female genital mutilation.* Retrieved from http://www.who.int/mediacentre/factsheets/fs241/en/.

Worth, L. T., & Mackie, D. M. (1987). Cognitive mediation of positive affect in persuasion. *Social Cognition, 5,* 76–94.

Wright, L., von Bussman, K., Friedman, A., Khoury, M., & Owens, F. (1990). Exaggerated social control and its relationship to the Type A behavior pattern. *Journal of Research in Personality, 24,* 258–269.

Wright, P. H. (1982). Men's friendships, women's friendships and the alleged inferiority of the latter. *Sex Roles, 8,* 1–20.

Wright, R. A., & Contrada, R. J. (1986). Dating selectivity and interpersonal attraction: Toward a better understanding of the "elusive phenomenon." *Journal of Social and Personal Relationships, 3*, 131–148.

Wright, S. C., Aron, A., & Brody, S. M. (2008). Extended contact and including others in the self: Building on the Allport/Pettigrew legacy. In U. Wagner, L. R. Tropp, G. Finchilescu, & C. Tredoux (Eds.), *Improving intergroup relations: Building on the legacy of Thomas F. Pettigrew* (pp. 143–159). Malden: Blackwell.

Wrightsman, L. S. (2006). *The psychology of the Supreme Court.* New York: Oxford University Press.

Wrightsman, L. S. (2008). *Oral arguments before the Supreme Court: An empirical approach.* New York: Oxford University Press.

Wyer, N. A., Sadler, M. S., & Judd, C. M. (2002). Contrast effects in stereotype formation and change: The role of comparative context. *Journal of Experimental Social Psychology, 38*, 443–458.

Xu, H., Bègue, L., & Shankland, R. (2011). Guilt and guiltlessness: An integrative review. *Social and Personality Psychology Compass, 5*, 440–457.

Xue, C., et al. (2015). A meta-analysis of risk factors for combat-related PTSD among military personnel and veterans. *PLoS ONE, 10*, March 20, 2015, Article e0120270.

Yablo, P. D., & Field, N. P. (2007). The role of culture in altruism: Thailand and the United States. *Psychologia: An International Journal of Psychology in the Orient, 50*, 236–251.

Yam, K. C., Fehr, R., & Barnes, C. M. (2014). Morning employees are perceived as better employees: Employees' start times influence supervisor performance ratings. *Journal of Applied Psychology, 99*, 1288–1299.

Yang, Y., Madon, S., & Guyll, M. (2015). Short-sighted confession decisions: The role of uncertain and delayed consequences. *Law and Human Behavior, 39*, 44–52.

Yeh, M. T., Coccaro, E. F., & Jacobson, K. C. (2010). Multivariate behavior genetic analyses of aggressive behavior subtypes. *Behavior Genetics, 40*, 603–617.

Yen, H. (2012). Many resist census race labels. *Associated Press,* January 31.

Yeung, N. C. J., & von Hippel, C. (2008). Stereotype threat increases the likelihood that female drivers in a simulator run over jaywalkers. *Accident Analysis and Prevention, 40*, 667–674.

Yoder, C. Y., Mancha, R., & Agrawal, N. (2014). Culture-related factors affect sunk cost bias. *Behavioral Development Bulletin, 19*, 105–118.

Yopyk, D. J. A., & Prentice, D. A. (2005). Am I an athlete or a student? Identity salience and stereotype threat in student-athletes. *Basic and Applied Social Psychology, 27*, 329–336.

Young-Jones, A., Fursa, S., Byrket, J. S., & Sly, J. S. (2015). Bullying affects more than feelings: The long-term implications of victimization on academic motivation in higher education. *Social Psychology of Education, 18*, 185–200.

Young, R. K., Kennedy, A. H., Newhouse, A., Browne, P., & Thiessen, D. (1993). The effects of names on perceptions of intelligence, popularity, and competence. *Journal of Applied Social Psychology, 23*, 1770–1788.

Yu, D. W., & Shepard, G. H. (1998). Is beauty in the eye of the beholder? *Nature, 296*, 321–322.

Yu, R., & Wu, X. (2015). Working alone or in the presence of others: Exploring social facilitation in baggage X-ray security screening tasks. *Ergonomics, 58*, 857–865.

Yuille, J. C., & Tollestrup, P. A. (1990). Some effects of alcohol on eyewitness memory. *Journal of Applied Psychology, 75*, 268–273.

Yuki, M. (2003). Intergroup comparison versus intragroup relationships: A cross-cultural examination of social identity theory in North American and East Asian cultural contexts. *Social Psychology Quarterly, 66*, 166–183.

Zaccaro, S. J. (2007). Trait-based perspectives of leadership. *American Psychologist, 62*, 6–16.

Zajonc, R. B. (1965). Social facilitation. *Science, 149*, 269–274.

Zajonc, R. B. (1968). Attitudinal effects of mere exposure. *Journal of Personality and Social Psychology Monograph Supplement, 9*(2), 1–27.

Zajonc, R. B. (1980). Compresence. In P. B. Paulus (Ed.), *Psychology of group influence* (pp. 35–60). Hillsdale, NJ: Erlbaum.

Zajonc, R. B. (1993). Brain temperature and subjective emotional experience. In M. Lewis & J. M. Haviland (Eds.), *Handbook of emotions* (pp. 209–220). New York: Guilford.

Zajonc, R. B. (2001). Mere exposure: A gateway to the subliminal. *Current Directions in Psychological Science, 10*, 224–228.

Zajonc, R. B., Heingartner, A., & Herman, E. M. (1969). Social enhancement and impairment of performance in the cockroach. *Journal of Personality and Social Psychology, 13*, 82–92.

Zajonc, R. B., Murphy, S. T., & Inglehart, M. (1989). Feeling and facial efference: Implications of the vascular theory of emotion. *Psychological Review, 96*, 395–416.

Zanna, M. P., & Cooper, J. (1974). Dissonance and the pill: An attribution approach to studying the arousal properties of dissonance. *Journal of Personality and Social Psychology, 29*, 703–709.

Zanon, M., Novembre, G., Zangrando, N., Chittaro, L., & Silani, G. (2014). Brain activity and prosocial behavior in a simulated life-threatening situation. *Neuroimage, 98*, 134–146.

Zárate, M. A., Garcia, B., Garza, A. A., & Hitlan, R. T. (2004). Cultural threat and perceived realistic group conflict as dual predictors of prejudice. *Journal of Experimental Social Psychology, 40*, 99–105.

Zarling, A. L., et al. (2013). Internalizing and externalizing symptoms in young children exposed to intimate partner violence: Examining intervening processes. *Journal of Family Psychology, 27*, 945–955.

Zebrowitz, L. A., & Montepare, J. M. (2005). Appearance DOES Matter. *Science, 308*, 1565–1566.

Zebrowitz, L. A., Luevano, V. X., Bronstad, P. M., & Aharon, I. (2009). Neural activation to babyfaced men matches activation to babies. *Social Neuroscience, 4*, 1–10.

Zebrowitz, L. A., Wang, R., Bronstad, P. M., Eisenberg, D., Undurraga, E., Reyes-García, V., & Godoy, R. (2012). First impressions from faces among U.S. and culturally isolated Tsimane' people in the Bolivian rainforest. *Journal of Cross-Cultural Psychology, 43*, 119–134.

Zeisel, H., & Diamond, S. (1978). The effect of peremptory challenges on jury and verdict: An experiment in a federal district court. *Stanford Law Review, 30*, 491–531.

Zell, E., & Alicke, M. D. (2009). Self-evaluative effects of temporal and social comparison. *Journal of Experimental Social Psychology, 45*, 223–227.

Zell, E., Alicke, M. D., & Strickhouser, J. E. (2015). Referent status neglect: Winners evaluate themselves favorably even when the competitor is incompetent. *Journal of Experimental Social Psychology, 56*, 18–23.

Zemack-Rugar, Y., Bettman, J. R., & Fitzsimons, G. J. (2007). The effects of nonconsciously priming emotion concepts on behavior. *Journal of Personality and Social Psychology, 93*, 927–939.

Zemba, Y., & Young, M. J. (2012). Assigning credit to organizational leaders: How Japanese and Americans differ. *Journal of Cross-Cultural Psychology, 43*, 899–914.

Zemba, Y., Young, M. J., & Morris, M. W. (2006). Blaming leaders for organizational accidents: Proxy logic in collective- versus individual-agency cultures. *Organizational Behavior and Human Decision Processes, 101*, 36–51.

Zentall, T. R. (2012). Perspectives on observational learning in animals. *Journal of Comparative Psychology.*

Zentner, M., & Mitura, K. (2012). Stepping out of the caveman's shadow: Nations' gender gap predicts degree of sex differentiation in mate preferences. *Psychological Science, 23,* 1176–85.

Zerres, A., Hüffmeier, J., Freund, P. A., Backhaus, K., & Hertel, G. (2013). Does it take two to tango? Longitudinal effects of unilateral and bilateral integrative negotiation training. *Journal of Applied Psychology, 98,* 478–491.

Zhang, J., & Shavitt, S. (2003). Cultural values in advertisements to the Chinese X-generation. *Journal of Advertising, 32,* 23–33.

Zhang, L., & Baumeister, R. F. (2006). Your money or your self-esteem: Threatened egotism promotes costly entrapment in losing endeavors. *Personality and Social Psychology Bulletin, 32,* 881–893.

Zhang, S., & Kline, S. L. (2009). Can I make my own decision? A cross-cultural study of perceived social network influence in mate selection. *Journal of Cross-Cultural Psychology, 40,* 3–23.

Zhong, C. B., Bohns, V. K., & Gino, F. (2010). Good lamps are the best police: Darkness increases dishonesty and self-interested behavior. *Psychological Science, 21,* 311–314.

Zhou, X., Vohs, K. D., & Baumeister, R. F. (2009). The symbolic power of money: Reminders after money alter social distress and physical pain. *Psychological Science, 20,* 700–706.

Zhu, D. H. (2014). Group polarization in board decisions about CEO compensation. *Organization Science, 25,* 552–571.

Zhu, Y., McKenna, B., & Sun, Z. (2007a). Negotiating with Chinese: Success of initial meetings is key. *Cross Cultural Management: An International Journal, 14,* 354–364.

Zhu, Y., Zhang, L., Fan, J., & Han, S. (2007b). Neural basis of cultural influence on self-representation. *Neuroimage, 34,* 1310–1316.

Zillmann, D. (1983). Arousal and aggression. In R. G. Geen & E. I. Donnerstein (Eds.), *Aggression: Theoretical and empirical reviews: Vol. l. Theoretical and methodological issues* (pp. 75–101). New York: Academic Press.

Zillmann, D. (1984). Connections between sex and aggression. Hillsdale, NJ: Erlbaum.

Zillmann, D. (2003). Theory of affective dynamics: Emotions and moods. In J. Bryant, D. Roskos-Ewoldsen, & J. Cantor (Eds.), *Communication and emotion: Essays in honor of Dolf Zillmann* (pp. 533–567). Mahwah, NJ: Erlbaum.

Zillmann, D., Bryant, J., Cantor, J. R., & Day, K. D. (1975). Irrelevance of mitigating circumstances in retaliatory behavior at high levels of excitation. *Journal of Research in Personality, 9,* 282–293.

Zimbardo, P. G. (1969). The human choice: Individuation, reason, and order versus deindividuation, impulse, and chaos. *Nebraska Symposium on Motivation, 17,* 237–307.

Zimbardo, P. G. (1985, June). Laugh where we must, be candid where we can. *Psychology Today,* pp. 43–47.

Zimbardo, P. G. (2007). *The Lucifer effect: How good people turn evil.* New York: Random House.

Zimbardo, P. G., Banks, W. C., Haney, C., & Jaffe, D. (1973, April 8). The mind is a formidable jailer: A Pirandellian prison. *New York Times Magazine,* pp. 38–60.

Zuckerman, M., DePaulo, B. M., & Rosenthal, R. (1981). Verbal and nonverbal communication of deception. In L. Berkowitz (Ed.), *Advances in experimental social psychology* (Vol. 14, pp. 1–59). New York: Academic Press.

Zuckerman, M., Knee, C. R., Hodgins, H. S., & Miyake, K. (1995). Hypothesis confirmation: The joint effect of positive test strategy and acquiescence response set. *Journal of Personality and Social Psychology, 68,* 52–60.

Zuwerink, J. R., & Devine, P. G. (1996). Attitude importance and resistance to persuasion: It's not just the thought that counts. *Journal of Personality and Social Psychology, 70,* 931–944.

Name Index

Subject Index

Page numbers followed by *c* indicate captions; page numbers followed by *f* indicate figures; page numbers followed by *t* indicate tables.